The Complete Results & Line-ups of the European Football Championships 1958-2012

Romeo Ionescu

British Library Cataloguing in Publication Data
A catalogue record for this book is available from the British Library

ISBN 978-1-86223-249-5

72 St. Peter's Avenue, Cleethorpes, N.E. Lincolnshire, DN35 8HU, England

Printed by 4edge Limited

AN INTRODUCTION TO THE EUROPEAN FOOTBALL CHAMPIONSHIPS

ALTHOUGH the European Championship itself did not get underway until 5th April 1958, organised regional international tournaments were already well established throughout Europe.

Way back in 1883 England, Northern Ireland (then just Ireland), Scotland and Wales kicked-off the British Championship (known as the Home International Championship) followed, in 1924, by Denmark, Finland, Norway and Sweden with the Scandinavian Championship (the Nordic Cup). In 1927 Hugo Meisl, that great Austrian champion of the game, originated the Central European Championship between Austria, Czechoslovakia, Hungary, Italy and Switzerland. Indeed, although known as the Dr. Gero Cup from 1955, this tournament was variously called *The Nations Cup*, *The International Cup* and *The Europe Cup*!

Just as we have to thank a Frenchman, Jules Rimet, for the conception of the FIFA World Cup in 1930, we are indebted to another Frenchman, Henri Delaunay, for the European Championship. Monsieur Delaunay, the secretary of the French Football Federation, proposed the tournament in the mid-1950s but, sadly, died before the competition got under way, although the trophy still bears his name.

Originally known as *The European Nations' Cup*, the first tournament struggled to get off the ground and was poorly supported by the major footballing countries of Europe with only 17 entrants taking part.

However, following the success of the first series which ran from 1958-1960, most eligible countries entered the second series from 1962-1964 and now it would be unthinkable for any of the members of UEFA to boycott such an important event.

The name of the competition was changed to *The European Football Championship* in 1966 and is now considered to rank second only to the FIFA World Cup in order of importance.

THE EUROPEAN NATIONS' CUP 1958-60

PRELIMINARY ROUND

REPUBLIC OF IRELAND v CZECHOSLOVAKIA 2-0 (2-0)

Dalymount Park, Dublin 05.04.1959

Referee: Lucien Van Nuffel (BEL) Attendance: 42,000

REPUBLIC OF IRELAND: James O'Neill; Brendan McNally, Noel Cantwell (Cap), Mick McGrath, Charlie Hurley, Patrick Saward, Alfred Ringstead, Tommy Hamilton, Christy Doyle, George Cummins, Liam Tuohy.

CZECHOSLOVAKIA: Imrich Stacho; Jiri Tichy, Ján Popluhár, Gustav Mráz (23 Jiri Hildebrandt), Svatoplik Pluskal, Titus Buberník, Jan Brumovsky, Anton Moravcik, Ladislav Kacani, Pavol Molnar, Tadeas Kraus. Trainer: Rudolf Vytlacil

Goals: Tuohy (22), Cantwell (42 pen)

CZECHOSLOVAKIA v REPUBLIC OF IRELAND 4-0 (1-0)

Tehelne Pole, Bratislava 10.05.1959

Referee: Joseph Barberan (FRA) Attendance: 60,000

CZECHOSLOVAKIA: Imrich Stacho; Jiri Tichy, Ján Popluhár, Ladislav Novak, Stefan Matlak, Titus Bubernik, Ladislav Pavlovic, Adolf Scherer, Vlastimil Bubník, Ladislav Kacani, Milan Dolinsky. Trainer: Rudolf Vytlacil

REPUBLIC OF IRELAND: James O'Neill; Richard Whittaker, Noel Cantwell (Cap), Frank O'Farrell, Charlie Hurley, Mick McGrath, Alfred Ringstead, Tommy Hamilton, Arthur Fitzsimons, George Cummins, Liam Tuohy.

Goals: Stacho (4 pen), Bubernik (52), Pavlovic (66), Dolinsky (75)

FIRST ROUND

USSR v HUNGARY 3-1 (3-0)

Central V.I. Lenin, Moskva 28.09.1958

Referee: Alfred Grill (AUS) Attendance: 100,572

USSR: Vladimir Beliaev; Vladimir Kesarev, Anatoliy Maslionkin, Boris Kuznetsov, Iuriy Voinov, Viktor Tsarev, Slava Metreveli, Valentin Ivanov, Nikita Simonian (Cap), Alekper Mamedov, Anatoliy Ilyin. Trainer: Gavril Kachalin

HUNGARY: Bela Bakó; Bela Kárpáti, Ferenc Sípos, László Sárosi; Deszö Bundzsák, Pal Berendi; László Budai II, Janos Göröcs, Lajos Csordás, Lajos Tichy, József Bencsics. Trainer: Lajos Baróti

Goals: Ilyin (4), Metreveli (20), Ivanov (32), Göröcs (84)

HUNGARY v USSR 0-1 (0-0)

Népstadion, Budapest 27.09.1959

Referee: Józef Kowal (POL) Attendance: 90,000

HUNGARY: Gyula Grosics; Sandor Mátrai, Ferenc Sípos, László Sárosi; József Bozsik, Antal Kotász; Karoly Sándor, Janos Göröcs, Florian Albert, Lajos Tichy, Maté Fenyvesi. Trainer: Lajos Baróti

USSR: Lev Iashin; Vladimir Kesarev, Anatoliy Maslionkin, Boris Kuznetsov, Iuriy Voinov, Igor Netto (Cap), Slava Metreveli, Anatoliy Isaev, Valentin Ivanov, Valentin Bubukin, Mihail Meskhi. Trainer: Mihail Iakushin

Goal: Voinov (58)

FRANCE v GREECE 7-1 (3-0)

Parc des Princes, Paris 01.10.1958

Referee: Gottfried Dienst (SWI) Attendance: 37,590

FRANCE: Dominique Colonna; Raymond Kaelbel, André Lerond, Armand Penverne (Cap), Jean-Jacques Marcel, Yvon Douis, Raymond Kopa, Just Fontaine, Thadéd Cisowski, Maurice Lafont, Jean Vincent.
Trainers: Albert Batteux & Paul Nicholas

GREECE: Savvas Theodoridis; Takis Papoulidis, Kostas Linoxilakis (Cap), Mimis Stefanakos, Takis Loukanidis, Kostas Polihroniou, Lakis Emmanouilidis, Dimitrios Theofanis, Ilias Ifantis, Kostas Nestoridis, Giannis Holevas. Linoxilakis injured leave the field (70). Trainer: Rino Martini

Goals: Kopa (23), Fontaine (25, 85), Cisowski (29, 68), Ifantis (47), Vincent (61, 87)

GREECE v FRANCE 1-1 (0-0)

Panathinaikos, Athina 03.12.1958

Referee: Vincenzo Orlandini (ITA) Attendance: 26,000

GREECE: Savvas Theodoridis; Takis Papoulidis, Kostas Linoxilakis (Cap), Sotiris Aggelopoulos, Kostas Polihroniou, Giannis Nempidis, Giorgos Sideris, Andreas Papaemmanouil, Ilias Ifantis, Kostas Nestoridis, Stilianos Psihos.
Trainer: Andonis Miyakis

FRANCE: Claude Abbes; Raymond Kaelbel, Roger Marche (Cap), René Ferrier, Bruno Bollini, André Lerond, Maryan Wisnieski, Roland Guillas, Stéphane Bruey, Stanislas Dombeck, Léon Deladerriere.
Trainers: Albert Batteux & Paul Nicholas

Goals: Bruey (71), Marche (85 og)

ROMANIA v TURKEY 3-0 (0-0)

"23 August", Bucureşti 02.11.1958

Referee: Gottfried Dienst (SWI) Attendance: 70,000

ROMANIA: Costică Toma (Cap); Corneliu Popa, Alexandru Karikas, Dumitru Macri; Vasile Alexandru, Ion Nunweiller; Nicolae Oaidă, Gheorghe Constantin, Constantin Dinulescu, Haralambie Eftimie, Nicolae Tătaru.
Trainer: Augustin Botescu

TURKEY: Turgay Şeren (Cap); Ismail Kurt, Basri Dirimlili; Mustafa Ertan, Naçi Erdem, Ahmet Berman; Hilmi Kiremitçi, Can Bartu, Metin Oktay, Kadri Aytaç, Lefter Küçükandonyadis.
Trainer: Leonardo Remondini
Turgay was injured and replaced by Can Bartu (77)

Goals: Oaidă (62), Constantin (77), Dinulescu (81)

AUSTRIA v NORWAY 5-2 (3-2)

Wien 23.09.1959

Referee: Demostene Stathatos (GRE) Attendance: 37,000

AUSTRIA: Kurt Schmied; Rudolf Oslansky, Karl Stotz, Erich Hasenkopf; Gerhard Hanappi, Karl Koller; Paul Halla, Erich Hof, Horst Nemec, Wilhelm Huberts, Karl Skerlan.
Trainer: Karl Decker

NORWAY: Sverre Andersen; Arne Bakker, Åge Spydevold, Arne Natland, Thorbjorn Svenssen, Arnold Johannessen, Rolf Bjørn Backe, Åge Sørensen, Harald Hennum, Ove Odergaard, Finn Gundersen. Trainer: Kristian Henriksen

Goals: Nemec (2, 21), Odergaard (19, 55), Hof (25 pen, 75), Skerlan (59)

TURKEY v ROMANIA 2-0 (1-0)

Mithat Paşa, Istanbul 26.04.1959

Referee: Borce Nedelkovski (YUG) Attendance: 35,000

TURKEY: Özcan Arkoç; Ismail Kurt, Basri Dirimlili; Mustafa Ertan, Naçi Erdem, Ahmet Berman; Hilmi Kiremitçi, Can Bartu, Suat Mamat, Lefter Küçükandonyadis, Kadri Aytaç.
Trainer: Leonardo Remondini

ROMANIA: Costică Toma; Corneliu Popa, Alexandru Karikas, Valeriu Soare; Emeric Jenei, Ion Nunweiller; Nicolae Oaidă, Vasile Alexandru, Ion Alexandrescu, Francisc Zavoda, Vasile Anghel. Trainer: Augustin Botescu

Goals: Lefter (14 pen, 54)

YUGOSLAVIA v BULGARIA 2-0 (1-0)

JNA, Beograd 31.05.1959

Referee: Mihai Popa (ROM) Attendance: 40,000

YUGOSLAVIA: Vladimir Beara; Bruno Belin, Tomislav Crnković, Vasilije Sijaković, Dobrosav Krstić, Lazar Tasić, Dragoslav Sekularac, Aleksandar Petaković, Branko Zebec, Milan Galić, Branislav Mihajlović. Trainers: Dragomir Nikolić, Aleksandar Tirnanić, Ljubomir Lovrić

BULGARIA: Georgi Naidenov; Ilia Kirchev, Ivan Dimitrov, Christo Lazarov, Kiril Rakarov, Stoian Kitov, Ivan Kolev, Stefan Abadjiev, Panaiot Panaiotov, Bojidar Mitkov, Aleksander Vasilev. Trainers: Stoian Ormandjiev & Krum Milev

Goals: Galic (1), Tasic (87)

NORWAY v AUSTRIA 0-1 (0-1)

Oslo 20.05.1959

Referee: Werner Bergmann (E. GER) Att: 27,566

NORWAY: Asbjørn Hansen; Arne Natland, Hans Jacob Mathisen, Roar Johansen, Thorbjørn Svenssen, Tore Halvorsen, Bjørn Borgen, Per Kristoffersen, Harald Hennum, Kjell Kristiansen, Rolf Birger Pedersen.
Trainer: Kristian Henriksen

AUSTRIA: Kurt Schmied; Heinrich Büllwatsch, Karl Stotz, Erich Hasenkopf; Gerhard Hanappi, Karl Koller; Walter Horak, Adolf Knoll, Erich Hof, Josef Hamerl, Karl Skerlan.
Trainer: Karl Decker

Goal: Hof (32)

BULGARIA v YUGOSLAVIA 1-1 (0-0)

Vasil Levski, Sofia 25.10.1959

Referee: Kurt Tschenscher (W. GER) Attendance: 45,000

BULGARIA: Georgi Naidenov; Kiril Rakarov, Manol Manolov, Ivan Dimitrov, Dimitar Largov, Nikola Kovachev, Todor Diev, Georgi Sokolov, Panaiot Panaiotov, Dimitar Iakimov, Ivan Kolev. Kovachev sent off (81).
Trainers: Stoian Ormandjiev & Krum Milev

YUGOSLAVIA: Blagoje Vidinić; Vladimir Durković, Fahrudin Jusufi, Stevan Bena, Tomislav Crnković, Lazar Tasić, Luka Liposinović, Muhamed Mujić, Borivoje Kostić, Branislav Mihajlović, Dragoslav Sekularac. Trainers: Dragomir Nikolić, Aleksandar Tirnanić, Ljubomir Lovrić

Goals: Diev (54), Mujic (57)

EAST GERMANY v PORTUGAL 0-2 (0-1)

Walter-Ulbricht-Stadion, Berlin 21.06.1959

Referee: Alois Obtulovic (CZE) Attendance: 25,000

EAST GERMANY: Karl Heinz Spickenagel; Bringfried Müller, Werner Heine, Konrad Wagner; Waldemar Mühlbächer, Manfred Kaiser; Horst Assmy, Günter Schröter, Gerhard Vogt, Lothar Meyer, Günther Wirth.
Trainer: Fritz Gödicke

PORTUGAL: Acurcio Carrelo; Virgilio Mendes, Angelo Martins, Fernando Mendes, Raul Figueiredo, Vicente Lucas, Carlos Duarte, Antonio Teixeira, Lucas da Fonseca Matateu, Mario Coluna, Domiciano Gomes Cavem.
Trainer: José Maria Antunes

Goals: Matateu (12), Coluna (67)

PORTUGAL v EAST GERMANY 3-2 (1-0)

Das Antas, Porto 28.06.1959

Referee: Juan Gardeazabal-Garay (SPA) Att: 35,000

PORTUGAL: Acurcio Carrelo; Virgilio Mendes, Angelo Martins, Fernando Mendes, Raul Figueiredo, Alfredo Abrantes, Carlos Duarte, Antonio Teixeira, Lucas da Fonseca Matateu, Mario Coluna, Domiciano Gomes Cavem.
Trainer: José Maria Antunes

EAST GERMANY: Klaus Thiele; Bringfried Müller, Werner Heine, Konrad Wagner, Werner Unger, Siegfried Wolf, Roland Ducke, Günter Schröter, Gerhard Vogt, Dieter Erler, Horst Kohle. Trainer: Fritz Gödicke

Goals: Coluna (45, 62), Vogt (47), Cavem (68), Kohle (72)

POLAND v SPAIN 2-4 (1-2)

Slaski, Chorzów 28.06.1959

Referee: Arthur Edward Ellis (ENG) Attendance: 71,000

POLAND: Tomasz Stefaniszyn; Henryk Szczepanski, Roman Korynt, Jerzy Wozniak; Marceli Strzykalski, Edmund Zientara (Cap); Ernest Pol, Lucjan Brychczy, Stanislaw Hachorek, Jan Liberda, Krzysztof Baszkiewicz.
Trainers: Czeslaw Krug, Tadeusz Forys

SPAIN: Antonio RAMALLETS Simon; Fernando OLIVELLA Pons, Jesús GARAY Vecino, Sigfrido GRACIA Royo; Juan SEGARRA Iraceta (Cap), Enrique GENSANA Merola; Juan TEJADA Martinez, Enrique MATEOS Mancebo, Alfredo di STÉFANO Lauthé, Luis SUÁREZ Miramontes, Francisco GENTO López. Trainers: José Luis Costa, Ramón Gabilondo, José Luis Lasplazas

Goals: Pol (34), Suarez (40, 52), Di Stefano (42, 56), Brychczy (62)

SPAIN v POLAND 3-0 (1-0)

Chamartin, Madrid 14.10.1959

Referee: Gyula Balla (HUN) Attendance: 62,000

SPAIN: Antonio RAMALLETS Simon; Fernando OLIVELLA Pons, Jesús GARAY Vecino, Sigfrido GRACIA Royo; Juan SEGARRA Iraceta (Cap), Enrique GENSANA Merola; Juan TEJADA Martinez, Ladislao KUBALA Stecz, Alfredo di STÉFANO Lauthé, Luis SUÁREZ Miramontes, Francisco GENTO López. Trainers: José Luis Costa, Ramón Gabilondo, José Luis Lasplazas

POLAND: Tomasz Stefaniszyn; Henryk Szczepanski, Roman Korynt, Fryderyk Monica; Witold Majewski, Henryk Grzybowski, Edmund Zientara (Cap); Ernest Pol, Stanislaw Hachorek, Zbigniew Szarynski, Krzysztof Baszkiewicz.
Trainers: Czeslaw Krug, Tadeusz Forys

Goals: Di Stefano (31), Gensana (70), Gento (86)

DENMARK v CZECHOSLOVAKIA 2-2 (2-2)

Idraetsparken, København 23.09.1959

Referee: Johan Bronkhorst (HOL) Attendance: 32,000

DENMARK: Per Funch Jensen; Erling Linde Larsen, Poul Jensen, Bent Hansen, Hans Christian Nielsen, Erik Jensen, Poul Pedersen, John Danielsen, Harald Nielsen, Henning Enoksen, Jørn Sørensen. Trainer: Arne Sørensen

CZECHOSLOVAKIA: Imrich Stacho; Jiri Tichy, Ján Popluhár, Ladislav Novák, Stefan Matlak, Titus Buberník, Ladislav Pavlovic, Adolf Scherer, Vlastimil Bubník, Ladislav Kacani, Milan Dolinsky. Trainer: Rudolf Vytlacil

Goals: P. Pedersen (15), B. Hansen (19), Kacani (30), Dolinsky (43)

CZECHOSLOVAKIA v DENMARK 5-1 (1-1)

Brno 18.10.1959

Referee: Helmut Kohler (E. GER) Att: 30,000

CZECHOSLOVAKIA: Viliam Schrojf; Jiri Tichy, Ján Popluhár, Ladislav Novák, Svatopil Pluskal, Titus Buberník, Ladislav Pavlovic, Pavol Molnar, Anton Moravcik, Adolf Scherer, Milan Dolinsky. Trainer: Rudolf Vytlacil

DENMARK: Erling Sørensen; Richard Møller Nielsen, Poul Jensen, Bent Hansen, Hans Christian Nielsen, Flemming Nielsen, Poul Pedersen, John Kramer, Henning Enoksen, John Danielsen, Jørn Sørensen. Trainer: Arne Sørensen

Goals: Kramer (35), Bubernik (38, 56), Scherer (48, 87), Dolinsky (63)

QUARTER-FINALS

FRANCE v AUSTRIA 5-2 (3-1)

Stade Olympique Colombes, Paris 13.12.1959

Referee: Manuel Asensi (SPA) Attendance: 43,775

FRANCE: Georges Lamia; Jean Wendling, Roger Marche (Cap), Armand Penverne, Robert Jonquet, René Ferrier, François Heutte, Raymond Kopa, Just Fontaine, Lucien Muller, Jean Vincent. Trainers: Albert Batteux, Paul Nicholas, Jean Gauteroux, Alex Thépot, Georges Verriest, Henri Guérin

AUSTRIA: Kurt Schmied; Paul Halla, Karl Stotz, Karl Nickerl; Gerhard Hanappi, Karl Koller; Walter Horak, Helmut Senekowitsch, Horst Nemec, Rudolf Pichler, Karl Höfer. Trainer: Karl Decker

Goals: Fontaine (6, 18, 70), Vincent (38, 80), Horak (40), Pichler (65)

AUSTRIA v FRANCE 2-4 (1-0)

Prater, Wien 27.03.1960

Referee: Helge Andersen (DEN) Attendance: 38,000

AUSTRIA: Rudolf Szanwald; Johann Windisch, Giuseppe Koschier, Erich Hasenkopf; Gerhard Hanappi, Karl Koller; Walter Horak, Paul Kozlicek, Horst Nemec, Wilhelm Huberts, Erich Probst. Trainer: Karl Decker

FRANCE: Georges Lamia; Jean Wendling, Bruno Rodzik, Jean-Jacques Marcel, Raymond Kaelbel, René Ferrier, Pierre Grillet, Lucien Muller, François Heutte, Raymond Kopa (Cap), Bernard Rahis. Trainers: Albert Batteux, Jean Gauteroux, Alex Thépot, Georges Verriest, Henri Guérin.

Goals: Nemec (26), Marcel (46), Rahis (59), Probst (64), Heutte (77), Kopa (84 pen)

PORTUGAL v YUGOSLAVIA 2-1 (1-0)

Lisboa 08.05.1960

Referee: Joseph Barberan (FRA) Attendance: 50,000

PORTUGAL: Acurcio Carrelo; Virgilio Mendes, Angelo Martins, Fernando Mendes, Germano Figueiredo, David Julio, Hernani Silva, Joaquim Santana, Lucas da Fonseca Matateu, Mario Coluna, Domiciano Gomes "Cavem".
Trainer: José Maria Antunes

YUGOSLAVIA: Milutin Soskić; Vladimir Durković, Fahrudin Jusufi, Ante Zanetić, Tomislav Crnković, Zeljko Perusić, Dragoslav Sekularac, Muhamed Mujić, Branko Zebec, Milan Galić, Borivoje Kostić. Trainers: Dragomir Nikolić, Aleksandar Tirnanić, Ljubomir Lovrić

Goals: Santana (30), Matateu (70), Kostić (81)

YUGOSLAVIA v PORTUGAL 5-1 (2-1)

JNA, Beograd 22.05.1960

Referee: Josef Stoll (AUS) Attendance: 55,000

YUGOSLAVIA: Milutin Soskić; Vladimir Durković, Fahrudin Jusufi, Ante Zanetić, Zarko Nikolić, Zeljko Perusić, Zvezdan Cebinac, Tomislav Knez, Milan Galić, Dragoslav Sekularac, Borivoje Kostić. Trainers: Dragomir Nikolić, Aleksandar Tirnanić, Ljubomir Lovrić

PORTUGAL: Acurcio Carrelo; Virgilio Mendes, Mario João, Fernando Mendes, Germano Figueiredo, David Julio, Hernani Silva, Joaquim Santana, Lucas da Fonseca Matateu, Mario Coluna, Domiciano Gomes "Cavem".
Trainer: José Maria Antunes

Goals: Sekularac (8), Cavem (29), Cebinac (45), Kostic (50, 88), Galic (79)

ROMANIA v CZECHOSLOVAKIA 0-2 (0-2)

"23 August", Bucureşti 22.05.1960

Referee: Andor Dorogi (HUN) Attendance: 80,000

ROMANIA: Petre Mîndru; Corneliu Popa; Alexandru Apolzan (Cap), Valeriu Soare; Emerich Jenei, Ion Nunweiller; Emanoil Haşoti, Gavril Raksi, Viorel Mateianu, Haralambie Eftimie, Nicolae Tătaru. Trainer: Augustin Botescu

CZECHOSLOVAKIA: Imrich Stacho; Jozef Bomba, Ján Popluhár, Ladislav Novák; Titus Bubernik, Josef Masopust; Ladislav Pavlovic, Josef Vojta, Andrej Kvasnák, Vlastimil Bubník, Milan Dolínsky. Trainer: Rudolf Vytlacil

Goals: Masopust (8), Bubnik (45)

CZECHOSLOVAKIA v ROMANIA 3-0 (3-0)

Slovan, Bratislava 29.05.1960

Referee: Leif Gulliksen (NOR) Attendance: 50,000

CZECHOSLOVAKIA: Viliam Schrojf; Jozef Bomba, Ján Popluhár, Ladislav Novák; Titus Bubernik, Josef Masopust; Ladislav Pavlovic, Josef Vojta, Andrej Kvasnák, Vlastimil Bubník, Milan Dolínsky. Trainer: Rudolf Vytlacil

ROMANIA: Petre Mîndru; Corneliu Popa, Alexandru Fronea, Valeriu Soare; Vasile Alexandru, Ion Nunweiller; Gheorghe Cacoveanu, Gheorghe Constantin, Constantin Dinulescu, Viorel Mateianu, Nicolae Tătaru. Trainer: Augustin Botescu

Goals: Buberník (1, 15), Bubník (17)

SEMI-FINALS

FRANCE v YUGOSLAVIA 4-5 (2-1)

Parc des Princes, Paris 06.07.1960

Referee: Gaston Grandain (BEL) Attendance: 26,370

FRANCE: Georges Lamia; Jean Wendling, Bruno Rodzik; Jean-Jacques Marcel, Robert Herbin, René Ferrier; François Heutte, Lucien Muller, Maryan Wisnieski, Michel Stievenard, Jean Vincent (Cap). Trainers: Albert Batteux, Jean Gauteroux, Alex Thépot, Georges Verriest, Henri Guérin

YUGOSLAVIA: Milutin Soskić; Vladimir Durković, Fahrudin Jusufi, Ante Zanetić, Branko Zebec; Zeljko Perusić, Tomislav Knez; Dragoslav Sekularac, Milan Galić, Borivoje Kostić (Cap), Drazen Jerković. Trainers: Dragomir Nikolić, Aleksandar Tirnanić, Ljubomir Lovrić

Goals: Galić (11), Vincent (12), Heutte (43, 62), Wisnieski (52), Zanetić (55), Knez (75), Jerkovic (77, 78)

USSR v CZECHOSLOVAKIA 3-0 (1-0)

Vélodrome, Marseille Hour 21,30 6.07.1960

Referee: Cesare Jonni (ITA) Attendance: 25,184

USSR: Lev Iashin; Givi Chokheli, Anatoliy Maslionkin, Anatoliy Krutikov; Iuriy Voinov, Igor Netto (Cap); Slava Metreveli, Valentin Ivanov, Viktor Ponedelnik, Valentin Bubukin, Mikhail Meskhi. Trainer: Gavril Kachalin

CZECHOSLOVAKIA: Viliam Schrojf; Frantisek Safranek, Ján Popluhár, Ladislav Novák (Cap); Titus Bubernik, Josef Masopust; Josef Vojta, Anton Moravcik, Andrej Kvasnák, Vlastimil Bubník, Milan Dolínsky. Trainer: Rudolf Vytlacil

Goals: Ivanov (35, 58), Ponedelnik (64)

THIRD PLACE MATCH

FRANCE v CZECHOSLOVAKIA 0-2 (0-0)

Vélodrome, Marseille Hour 21,30 9.07.1960

Referee: Cesare Jonni (ITA) Attendance: 9,438

FRANCE: Jean Taillandier; Bruno Rodzik, André Chorda, Jean-Jacques Marcel, Robert Jonquet (Cap), Robert Siatka, François Heutte, Yvon Douis, Maryan Wisnieski, Michel Stievenard, Jean Vincent. Trainers: Albert Batteux, Jean Gauteroux, Alex Thépot, Georges Verriest, Henri Guérin

CZECHOSLOVAKIA: Viliam Schrojf; Frantisek Safranek, Ján Popluhár, Ladislav Novák (Cap); Titus Bubernik, Josef Masopust; Ladislav Pavlovic, Josef Vojta, Pavol Molnar, Vlastimil Bubník, Milan Dolínsky. Trainer: Rudolf Vytlacil

Goals: Bubnik (58), Pavlovic (88)

FINAL

USSR v YUGOSLAVIA 2-1 (0-1, 1-1) (AET)

Parc des Princes, Paris 10.07.1960

Referee: Arthur Edward Ellis (ENG) Attendance: 17,966

USSR: Lev Iashin; Givi Chokheli, Anatoliy Maslionkin, Anatoliy Krutikov; Iuri Voinov, Igor Netto (Cap); Slava Metreveli, Valentin Ivanov, Viktor Ponedelnik, Valentin Bubukin, Mikhail Meskhi. Trainer: Gavril Kachalin

YUGOSLAVIA: Blagoje Vidinić; Vladimir Durković, Fahrudin Jusufi, Ante Zanetić, Jovan Miladinović; Zeljko Perusić, Dragoslav Sekularac, Drazen Jerković, Milan Galić, Zeljko Matus, Borivoje Kostić (Cap). Trainers: Dragomir Nikolić, Aleksandar Tirnanić, Ljubomir Lovrić

Goals: Galić (43), Metreveli (49), Ponedelnik (113)

Goalscorers European Nations' Cup 1958-60

5 goals: Titus Buberník (Czechoslovakia), Just Fontaine, Jean Vincent (France)

4 goals: Milan Galić (Yugoslavia)

3 goals: Alfredo Di Stefano (Spain), Vlastimil Bubník, Milan Dolinsky (Czechoslovakia), Valentin Ivanov (USSR), Horst Nemec, Erich Hof (Austria), François Heutte (France), Borivoje Kostić (Yugoslavia), Mario Coluna (Portugal)

2 goals: Lefter (Turkey), Odergård (Norway), Suarez (Spain), Cavem, Matateu (Portugal), Metreveli, Ponedelnik (USSR), Cisowski, Kopa (France), Jerkovic (Yugoslavia), Pavlovic, Scherer (Czechoslovakia)

1 goal: Tuohy, Cantwell (Republic of Ireland), Göröcs (Hungary), Papaemanouil, Ifanidis (Greece), Diev (Bulgaria), Vogt, Kohle (East Germany), B. Hansen, P. Pedersen, Kramer (Denmark), Pol, Brychczy (Poland), Gensana, Gento (Spain), Probst, Horak, Pichler, Skerlan (Austria), Santana (Portugal), Oaidă, Constantin, Dinulescu (Romania), Voinov, Ilyin (USSR), Wisnieski, Marcel, Rahis, Bruey (France), Zanetic, Knez, Cebinac, Sekularac, Tasic, Mujic (Yugoslavia), Masopust, Kacani, Stacho (Czechoslovakia)

THE EUROPEAN NATIONS' CUP 1962-64

FIRST ROUND

NORWAY v SWEDEN 0-2 (0-2)

Oslo 21.06.1962

Referee: George Bowman (SCO) Attendance: 28,249

NORWAY: Sverre Andersen; Anders Svela, Ragnar Larsen, Roar Johansen, Trygve Andersen, Olav Nilsen, Roald Jensen, Arne Pedersen, John Krogh, Erik Johansen, Hakon Olav Blengsli. Trainer: Wilhelm Kment

SWEDEN: Bengt Nyholm; Orvar Bergmark, Lennart Wing, Gosta Lundell, Ake Johansson, Prawitz Oberg, Bengt Berndtsson, Owe Olsson, Orjan Martinsson, Harry Bild, Lennart Backman. Trainer: Lennart Nyman

Goals: Martinsson (10, 40)

SWEDEN v NORWAY 1-1 (0-0)

Malmö stadium 04.11.1962

Referee: Werner Bergmann (E. GER) Attendance: 8,726

SWEDEN: Arve Arvidsson; Hans Mild, Lennart Wing, Yngve Brodd, Ake Johansson, Prawitz Oberg, Leif Eriksson, Leif Skiold, Orjan Martinsson, Owe Olsson, Orjan Persson. Trainer: Lennart Nyman

NORWAY: Sverre Andersen; Ragnar Larsen, Edgar Stakset, Roar Johansen, Finn Thorsen, Trygve Andersen, Roald Jensen, Arne Pedersen, John Krogh, Olav Nilsen, Oddvar Richardson. Trainer: Ragnar Nikolay Larsen

Goals: Eriksson (49), Krogh (60)

DENMARK v MALTA 6-1 (3-0)

Idraetsparken, København 28.06.1962

Referee: Pieter Paulus Roomer (HOL) Attendance: 11,200

DENMARK: Erik Gaardhøje; Kai Johansen, Poul Jensen, Bent Hansen, John Madsen, Jørgen Olesen, Carl Bertelsen, Helge Jørgensen, Ole Madsen, Henning Enoksen, Eyvind Clausen. Trainer: Poul Petersen

MALTA: Alfred Mizzi; John Privitera, Lolly Debattista, Frank Zammit, Joseph Cilia, Lino Falzon, Eddie Theobald, Joseph Urpani, Tony Cauchi, Lolly Borg, Publius Demanuelle. Trainer: Joseph Griffiths

Goals: O.Madsen (9, 14, 49), Clausen (22), Enoksen (71), Bertelsen (80), Theobald (..)

MALTA v DENMARK 1-3 (1-2)

Gzira 08.12.1962

Referee: Raoul Righi (ITA) Attendance: 4,500

MALTA: Alfred Mizzi; John Privitera, Joseph Cilia, Joseph Cini, Emmanuel Attard, Louis Theobald, Lolly Borg, Eddie Theobald, Joseph Urpani, Frank Zammit, Sammy Nicholl. Trainer: Joseph Griffiths

DENMARK: Erik Gaardhoje; Kai Johansen, Preben Jensen, Egon Jensen, John Madsen, Carl Bertelsen, Jens Petersen, Carl Emil Christiansen, Ole Madsen, Tommy Troelsen, Eyvind Clausen. Trainer: Poul Petersen

Goals: O. Madsen (13), Urpani (39), Christiansen (42), Bertelsen (48)

REPUBLIC OF IRELAND v ICELAND 4-2 (2-1)

Dublin 12.08.1962

Referee: Robert Smith (WAL) Attendance: 20,246

IRELAND: Alan Kelly; Anthony Dunne, Tommy Traynor, Pat Saward, Charlie Hurley, Mick Meagan, Alfred Hale, Johnny Giles, Noel Cantwell, Ambrose Fogarty, Liam Tuohy.

ICELAND: Helgi Daníelsson; Arni Njálsson, Bjarni Felixson, Gardar Arnason, Hördur Felixson, Sveinn Jónsson, Skúli Agústsson, Thórólfur Beck, Ríkhardur Jónsson, Ellert Schram, Thórdur Jónsson. Trainer: Ríkhardur Jónsson

Goals: Cantwell (.., ..), Fogarty (..), Tuohy (..), R.Jónsson (.., ..)

ICELAND v REPUBLIC OF IRELAND 1-1 (0-1)

Laugardalsvöllur, Reykjavik 02.09.1962

Referee: Arnold Nilsen (NOR) Attendance: 9,100

ICELAND: Helgi Daníelsson; Arni Njálsson, Bjarni Felixson, Gardar Arnason, Jón Stefánsson, Sveinn Jónsson, Skúli Agústsson, Thórólfur Beck, Rikhardur Jónsson, Ellert Schram, Sigurdúr Jakobsson. Trainer: Ríkhardur Jónsson

IRELAND: Alan Kelly; Brendan McNally, Tommy Traynor, Ronnie Nolan, Charlie Hurley, Pat Saward, Dermot Curtis, Ambrose Fogarty, Noel Cantwell, Noel Peyton, Liam Tuohy.

Goals: Tuohy (..), Arnason (..)

ENGLAND v FRANCE 1-1 (0-1)

Hillsborough, Sheffield 03.10.1962

Referee: Hansen (DEN) Attendance: 35,380

ENGLAND: Ron Springett; James Armfield, Bobby Moore, Maurice Norman, Ramon Wilson, Ronald Flowers, Christopher Crowe, Alan Hinton, Michael Hellawell, James Greaves, Raymond Charnley. Manager: Walter Winterbottom

FRANCE: Pierre Bernard; Jean Wendling, Synakowski Maryan, André Lerond (Cap), André Chorda, Joseph Bonnel, Yvon Goujon, René Ferrier, Laurent Robuschi, Raymond Kopa, Paul Sauvage. Trainer: Henri Guérin

Goals: Goujon (8), Flowers (57 pen)

FRANCE v ENGLAND 5-2 (3-0)

Parc des Princes, Paris 27.02.1963

Referee: Joseph Kandlbinder (W. GER) Attendance: 23,986

FRANCE: Pierre Bernard; Jean Wendling, Synakowski Maryan, André Lerond (Cap), Bruno Rodzik, Joseph Bonnel, Yvon Goujon, Robert Herbin, Maryan Wisnieski, Yvon Douis, Lucien Cossou. Trainer: Henri Guérin

ENGLAND: Ron Springett; James Armfield, Bobby Moore, Brian Labone, Ronald Henry, Ronald Flowers, Robert Tambling, Robert Charlton, John Connely, James Greaves, Robert Smith. Manager: Alfred Ramsey

Goals: Wisnieski (3, 75), Douis (32), Cossou (43, 82), Smith (57), Tambling (74)

SPAIN v ROMANIA 6-0 (4-0)

Santiago Bernabeu, Madrid 01.11.1962

Referee: Kevin Howley (ENG) Attendance: 51,700

SPAIN: José VICENTE Train; Enrique Perez Diaz PACHIN, Francisco Rodriguez RODRI, Isacio Garcia CALLEJA; Francisco Garcia PAQUITO, Jesús Jordán GLARIA; Enrique Monterrubio COLLAR, ADELARDO Rodriguez Sánchez, José Fidalgo VELOSO, Fabian Vicente GUILLOT, Francisco López GENTO. Trainer: José Villalonga

ROMANIA: Vasile Sfetcu; Mircea Georgescu, Ion Nunweiller III, Dumitru Macri; Emil Petru, Constantin Koszka; Zoltan Ivansuc, Titus Ozon, Marin Voinea, Dumitru Popescu, Vasile Gergely. Trainer: Constantin Teaşcă

Goals: Guillot (7, 20, 70), Veloso (9), Collar (17), Macri (81 og)

POLAND v NORTHERN IRELAND 0-2 (0-1)

Slaski, Chorzów 10.10.1962

Referee: Bertil Wilhelm Lööw (SWE) Att: 31,500 (50,000)

POLAND: Edward Józef Szymkowiak; Henryk Szczepanski (Cap), Stanislaw Oslizlo, Ryszard Budka; Bernard Blaut, Wladyslaw Kawula; Eugeniusz Faber, Jan Liberda, Norbert Gajda, Lucjan Brychczy, Roman Lentner.
Trainers: Czeslaw Krug, Ryszard Koncewicz

N. IRELAND: Robert Irvine; Edward James Magill, Samuel Hatton, Alexander Elder, Robert Blanchflower (Cap), James Nicholson, William Humphries, Hubert Barr, Alexander Derek Dougan, James McIlroy, William Bingham. Manager: Robert Peacock. Trainer: William McCready

Goals: Dougan (17), Humphries (54)

ROMANIA v SPAIN 3-1 (2-0)

23 August, Bucureşti 25.11.1962

Referee: G. Pelomis (GRE) Attendance: 80,000

ROMANIA: Ion Voinescu; Corneliu Popa, Ion Nunweiller, Dumitru Ivan; Emil Petru, Constantin Koszka; Ion Pîrcălab, Gheorghe Constantin, Cicerone Manolache, Vasile Gergely, Nicolae Tătaru. Trainer: Gheorghe Popescu

SPAIN: José VICENTE Train; Feliciano Muñoz RIVILLA, Francisco Rodriguez RODRI, Isacio Garcia CALLEJA; Francisco Garcia PAQUITO, Jesús Jordán GLARIA; Enrique Monterrubio COLLAR, AMANCIO Amaro Varela, José Fidalgo VELOSO, Fabian Vicente GUILLOT, Francisco López GENTO.
Trainer: José Villalonga

Goals: Tătaru (2), Manolache (8), Constantin (61), Veloso (65)

NORTHERN IRELAND v POLAND 2-0 (1-0)

Windsor Park, Belfast 28.11.1962

Referee: Dittmar Huber (SWI) Attendance: 28,900

N. IRELAND: Robert Irvine; Edward James Magill, Alexander Elder; Robert D.Blanchflower (Cap), Terence Neill, James Nicholson; William Bingham, John Crossan, Alexander Derek Dougan, James McIlroy, Robert Braithwaite.
Manager: Robert Peacock

POLAND: Edward Józef Szymkowiak; Henryk Szczepanski (Cap), Stanislaw Oslizlo, Wlodzimierz Spiewak, Antoni Nieroba, Ryszard Grzegorczyk; Józef Galeczka, Lucjan Brychczy, Erwin Wilczek, Roman Lentner, Eugeniusz Faber.
Trainers: Czeslaw Krug, Ryszard Koncewicz

Goals: Crossan (9), Bingham (64)

YUGOSLAVIA v BELGIUM 3-2 (2-1)

JNA, Beograd 04.11.1962

Referee: Alois Obtulovic (CZE) Attendance: 35,000

YUGOSLAVIA: Milutin Soskić; Slavko Svinjarević, Fahrudin Jusufi, Petar Radaković, Velibor Vasović, Zeljko Perusić, Spasoje Samardzić, Vojislav Melić, Slaven Zambata, Milan Galić, Josip Skoblar. Trainers: Ljubomir Lovrić, Prvoslav Mihajlović, Hugo Rusevljanin

BELGIUM: Jean Nicolay; Yves Baré, Laurent Verbiest, Lucien Spronck, Georges Heylens, Pierre Hanon, Paul Van den Berg, Jef Jurion (Cap), Paul Van Himst, Jacky Stockman, Wilfried Puis. Trainer: Constant Vandenstock, Arthur Ceuleers

Goals: Skoblar (12, 32 pen), Stockman (26), Jurion (58), Vasović (88)

BELGIUM v YUGOSLAVIA 0-1 (0-1)

Heizel, Brussel 31.03.1963

Referee: Vicente Caballero (SPA) Attendance: 24,583

BELGIUM: Jean Nicolay; Georges Heylens, Laurent Verbiest, Martin Lippens, Jean Cornelis, Pierre Hanon, Jef Jurion (Cap), Jacky Stockman, Paul Van Himst, Paul Van den Berg, Wilfried Puis. Trainers: Constant Vandenstock, Arthur Ceuleers

YUGOSLAVIA: Milutin Soskić; Novak Tomić, Mirsad Fazlagić, Vladimir Popović, Velibor Vasović, Zeljko Perusić, Spasoje Samardzić, Djordje Pavlić, Milan Galić, Vojislav Melić, Josip Skoblar. Trainers: Ljubomir Lovrić, Prvoslav Mihajlović, Hugo Rusevljanin

Goal: Galić (20)

BULGARIA v PORTUGAL 3-1 (0-0)

Vasil Levski, Sofia 07.11.1962

Referee: Semih Zoroglu (TUR) Attendance: 50,000

BULGARIA: Georgi Naidenov (Cap); Vasil Metodiev, Dobromir Jechev, Dimo Dimov, Ivan Dimitrov, Nikola Kovachev, Todor Diev, Dimitar Iakimov, Georgi Asparuhov, Hristo Iliev, Ivan Kolev. Trainer: Georgi Pachedjiev

PORTUGAL: Alberto COSTA PEREIRA; ANGELO Martins, Fernando CRUZ, Domiciano Gomes "CAVEM", Raul MACHADO, JOSÉ CARLOS, Antonio SIMOES, EUSEBIO da Silva Ferreira, HERNANI Silva, Mario COLUNA, Manuel SERAFIM Pereira. Trainer: José Maria Antunes

Goals: Eusebio (49), Asparuhov (65, 77), Diev (82)

HUNGARY v WALES 3-1 (2-1)

Népstadion, Budapest 07.11.1962

Referee: Józef Kowal (POL) Attendance: 40,000

HUNGARY: Antal Szentmihályi; Sandor Mátrai, Kálmán Mészöly, Kálmán Sóvári; Ernö Solymosi, Ferenc Sípos; Karoly Sándor, Janos Göröcs, Flórián Albert, Lajos Tichy, Maté Fenyvesi. Trainer: Lajos Baroti

WALES: Anthony Millington; Stuart Williams, Melvyn Hopkins, Terence Hennessey, Melvyn Nurse, Victor Crowe, Terence Medwin, Ivor Allchurch, Melfyn Charles, Thomas Vernon, Barrie Jones.

Goals: Albert (5), Medwin (18), Tichy (33), Sándor (47)

PORTUGAL v BULGARIA 3-1 (2-0)

Ristelo, Lisboa 16.12.1962

Referee: Henri Faucheux (FRA) Attendance: 25,900

PORTUGAL: Alberto COSTA PEREIRA; ANGELO Martins, Fernando CRUZ, Mario COLUNA, Raul MACHADO, JOSÉ CARLOS, José AUGUSTO, EUSEBIO da Silva Ferreira, Augusto ROCHA, HERNANI Silva, Antonio SIMOES.
Trainer: José Maria Antunes

BULGARIA: Georgi Naidenov (Cap); Vasil Metodiev, Ivan Vutsov, Dimo Dimov, Ivan Dimitrov, Nikola Kovachev, Todor Diev, Stefan Abadjiev, Georgi Asparuhov, Hristo Iliev, Ivan Kolev. Trainer: Georgi Pachedjiev

Goals: Hernani (4, 27), Coluna (57), Iliev (83)

WALES v HUNGARY 1-1 (1-0)

Ninian Park, Cardiff 20.03.1963

Referee: John Spillane (IRE) Attendance: 30.413

WALES: David Hollins; Stuart Williams, Graham Williams, Terence Hennessey, Mike England, Alwyn Burton, Barrie Jones, Philip Woosnam, Graham Moore, Ivor Allchurch, Cliff Jones.

HUNGARY: Antal Szentmihályi; Sándor Mátrai, Kálmán Mészöly, László Sárosi; Ernö Solymosi, Ferenc Sípos; Karoly Sándor, János Göröcs, Flórián Albert, Lajos Tichy, Maté Fenyvesi. Trainer: Lajos Baroti

Goals: C. Jones (25 pen), Tichy (73 pen)

BULGARIA v PORTUGAL 1-0 (0-0)

Stadio Olimpico, Roma 23.01.1963

Referee: Giuseppe Adami (ITA) Attendance: 15,000

BULGARIA: Iordan Iosifov; Vasil Metodiev, Ivan Vutsov, Petar Velichkov, Ivan Dimitrov, Nikola Kovachev (Cap), Todor Diev, Stefan Abadjiev, Georgi Asparuhov, Hristo Iliev, Spiro Debarski. Trainers: Bela Volentin (Ung) & Georgi Pachedjiev

PORTUGAL: Alberto COSTA PEREIRA; Alberto FESTA, Fernando CRUZ, Mario COLUNA, Raul MACHADO, Antonio PAULA, Antonio SIMOES, Joaquim SANTANA, José TORRES, Augusto ROCHA, Manuel SERAFIM Pereira.
Trainer: José Maria Antunes

Goal: Asparuhov (87)

HOLLAND v SWITZERLAND 3-1 (1-1)

Amsterdam 11.11.1962

Referee: Joaquim Fernandes de Campos (POR) Att: 60,000

HOLLAND: Peter Van de Merwe; Guus Haak, Piet Ouderland, Fons van Wissen, Tonny Pronk, Bennie Muller, Sjaak Swart, Henk Groot, Tonny Van der Linden, Co Prins, Mick Clavan. Trainer: Elek Schwartz

SWITZERLAND: Felix Ansermet; Paul Stehrenberger, Jakob Kuhn, Heinz Schneiter, André Grobéty, Ely Tacchella, Roger Vonlanthen, Charles Hertig, Norbert Eschmann, Philippe Pottier, Anton Allemann. Trainer: Karl Rappan (Öst)

Goals: Van der Linden (21), Hertig (43), Swart (75), Groot (82)

CZECHOSLOVAKIA v EAST GERMANY 1-1 (0-0)

Strahov, Praha 31.03.1963

Referee: Gyula Balla (HUN) Attendance: 35,000

CZECHOSLOVAKIA: Vladimir Mokrohajsky; Jan Lala, Svatopluk Pluskal, Jan Popluhar, Ladislav Novak, Andrej Kvasnak, Josef Masopust, Tomas Pospichal, Adolf Scherer, Rudolf Kucera, Vaclav Masek. Trainer: Rudolf Vytlacil

EAST GERMANY: Harald Fritsche; Klaus Urbanczyk, Werner Heine (Cap), Dieter Krampe; Manfred Kaiser, Kurt Liebrecht; Henning Frenzel, Dieter Erler, Peter Ducke, Jürgen Nöldner, Roland Ducke.
Trainers: Karoly Soos (HUN) & Johannes Studener

Goals: Masek (66), P. Ducke (85)

SWITZERLAND v HOLLAND 1-1 (0-1)

Wankdorf, Bern 31.03.1963

Referee: Joseph Kandlbinder (W. GER) Attendance: 31,800

SWITZERLAND: Karl Elsener; André Grobéty, Heinz Schneiter, Werner Leimbruger, Hans Weber, Ely Tacchella, Rolf Wüthrich, Bruno Brizzi, Walter Heuri, Jakob Kuhn, Anton Allemann. Trainer: Karl Rappan

HOLLAND: Eddy Pieters Graafland; Guus Haak, Piet Ouderland, Fons van Wissen, Tonny Pronk, Jan Klaassens, Sjaak Swart, Henk Groot, Piet Kruiver, Rinus Bennaars, Coen Moulijn. Trainer: Elek Schwartz

Goals: Kruiver (6), Allemann (85)

ITALY v TURKEY 6-0 (4-0)

Stadio Comunale, Bologna 02.12.1962

Referee: Lucien van Nuffel (BEL) Attendance: 28,000

ITALY: William Negri; Cesare Maldini (Cap), Enzo Robotti; Paride Tumburus, Francesco Janich, Romano Fogli; Alberto Orlando, Giacomo Bulgarelli, Angelo Sormani, Gianni Rivera, Ezio Pascutti. Trainer: Edmondo Fabbri

TURKEY: Ozcan Arkoç; Candemir Berkman, Ahmet Berman; Suat Mamat, Naci Erdem (Cap), Mustafa Yürür; Tarik Kutver, Seref Has, Şenol Birol, Metin Oktay, Kadri Aytac. Trainer: Lubija Spajic

Goals: Rivera (15, 47), Orlando (22, 29, 35, 85)

EAST GERMANY v CZECHOSLOVAKIA 2-1 (0-0)

Walter-Ulbricht-Stadion, Berlin 21.11.1962

Referee: Sergei Alimov (USSR) Attendance: 50,000

EAST GERMANY: Horst Weigang; Klaus Urbanczyk, Werner Heine, Dieter Krampe; Manfred Kaiser, Kurt Liebrecht; Henning Frenzel, Dieter Erler, Peter Ducke, Gunter Schröter (Cap), Roland Ducke. Trainers: Karoly Soos & Johannes Studener

CZECHOSLOVAKIA: Viliam Schrojf; Jan Lala, Svatopluk Pluskal, Jiri Tichy, Ladislav Novak, Andrej Kvasnak, Josef Masopust, Tomas Pospichal, Josef Kadraba, Rudolf Kucera, Frantisek Valosek. Trainer: Rudolf Vytlacil

Goals: Erler (60), Liebrecht (80 pen), Kucera (90)

TURKEY v ITALY 0-1 (0-0)

Mithat Paşa, Istanbul 27.03.1963

Referee: Dimitar Rumenchev (BUL) Attendance: 30,000

TURKEY: Turgay Seren (Cap); Muzaffer Sipahi, Sürreya Özkefe; Özer Kanra, Güngör Tetik, Ismet Yurtsu; Ogün Altiparmak, Seref Has, Nedim Dogan, Suat Mamat, Ugur Köken. Trainer: Sabri Kiraz

ITALY: Lido Vieri; Cesare Maldini (Cap), Giacinto Facchetti; Paride Tumburus, Sandro Salvadore, Giovanni Trapattoni; Alberto Orlando, Giorgio Puia, Angelo Sormani, Mario Corso, Giampaolo Menichelli. Trainer: Edmondo Fabbri

Goal: Sormani (86)

SECOND ROUND

SPAIN v NORTHERN IRELAND 1-1 (0-0)

Bilbao 30.05.1963

Referee: Cesare Jonni (ITA) Attendance: 28,000

SPAIN: José VICENTE Train; Feliciano Muñoz RIVILLA, Luis María ECHEVERRIA, Severiano REIJA, Francisco Garcia PAQUITO, Enrique Perez PACHIN, AMANCIO Amaro, Felix RUIZ, Delio MOROLLON, ADELARDO Rodriguez, Enrique COLLAR. Trainer: José Villalonga

N. IRELAND: Robert Irvine; James Magill, Alex Elder, Martin Harvey, Terence Neill, William McCulough, William Bingham, William Humphries, John Crossan, William Irvine, Robert Braithwaite. Manager: Robert Peacock

Goals: Amancio (60), Irvine (76)

SWEDEN v YUGOSLAVIA 3-2 (1-1)

Malmö stadium 18.09.1963

Referee: John Keith Taylor (ENG) Attendance: 20,774

SWEDEN: Bengt Nyholm; Hans Rosander, Lennart Wing, Orvar Bergmark, Ake Johansson, Hans Mild, Lennart Backman, Prawitz Oberg, Agne Simonsson, Harry Bild, Orjan Persson. Trainer: Lennart Nyman

YUGOSLAVIA: Milutin Soskic; Fahrudin Jusufi, Mirko Braun, Zeljko Perusic, Velibor Vasovic, Vladimir Popovic, Spasoje Samardzic, Vojislav Melic, Slaven Zambata, Milan Galic, Josip Skoblar. Trainers: Ljubomir Lovric, Prvoslav Mihajlovic, Hugo Rusevljanin

Goals: Zambata (21), Persson (30, 60), Galic (64), Bild (72)

NORTHERN IRELAND v SPAIN 0-1 (0-0)

Belfast 30.10.1963

Referee: Andries Van Leeuwen (HOL) Attendance: 45,900

N.IRELAND: Victor Hunter; James Magill, Terence Neill, John Parke, Martin Harvey, William McCulough, William Bingham, William Humphries, Samuel Wilson, John Crossan, James Hill. Manager: Robert Peacock

SPAIN: Jose Casas PEPIN; Feliciano Muñoz RIVILLA, Fernando OLIVELLA, Severiano REIJA, Felix RUIZ, Ignacio ZOCO, Jesus María PEREDA, Luis DEL SOL, José Antonio ZALDUA, Luis SUÁREZ, Francisco GENTO. Trainer: José Villalonga

Goal: Gento (65)

DENMARK v ALBANIA 4-0 (3-0)

Idraetsparken, København 29.06.1963

Referee: Einar Boström (SWE) Attendance: 25,200

DENMARK: Erik Lykke Sørensen; Kai Johansen, Jens Jørgen Hansen, Bent Hansen, Birger Larsen, Jens Petersen, Eyvind Clausen, Ole Sørensen, Ole Madsen, Palle Bruun, Henning Enoksen. Trainer: Poul Petersen

ALBANIA: Sulejman Maliqati; Fatbardh Deliallisi, Skender Halili, Fatmir Frasheri, Gezim Kazmi, Lin Shllaku, Lorenc Vorfi, Mehdi Bushati, Pavllo Bukoviku, Panajot Pano, Thoma Duro. Trainer: Zyber Konçi

Goals: Petersen (16 pen), Madsen (25), Clausen (35), Enoksen (49)

YUGOSLAVIA v SWEDEN 0-0

JNA, Beograd 19.06.1963

Referee: Karl Kainer (AUS) Attendance: 45,000

YUGOSLAVIA: Milutin Soskic; Novak Tomic, Fahrudin Jusufi, Zeljko Perusic, Velibor Vasovic, Vladimir Popovic, Spasoje Samardzic, Drago Smailovic, Vladimir Kovacevic, Milan Galic, Josip Skoblar. Trainers: Ljubomir Lovric, Prvoslav Mihajlovic, Hugo Rusevljanin

SWEDEN: Bengt Nyholm; Orvar Bergmark, Lennart Wing, Bengt Gustavsson, Ake Johansson, Hans Mild, Kurt Hamrin, Torbjorn Jonsson, Prawitz Oberg, Lennart Backman, Orjan Persson. Trainer: Lennart Nyman

ALBANIA v DENMARK 1-0 (1-0)

Qemal Stafa, Tiranë 30.10.1963

Referee: Joseph Cassar Naudi (MAL) Attendance: 20,000

ALBANIA: Shefqet Topi; Fatbardh Deliallisi, Skender Halili, Fatmir Frashëri, Ali Mema, Lin Shllaku, Andon Zaho, Mehdi Bushati, Panajot Pano, Pavllo Bukoviku, Enver Ibershimi. Trainer: Loro Boriçi

DENMARK: Erik Lykke Sørensen; Kai Johansen, Jens Jørgen Hansen, Bent Hansen, John Madsen, Jens Petersen, Carl Bertelsen, Kjeld Thorst, Ole Madsen, Ole Sørensen, John Danielsen. Trainer: Poul Petersen

Goal: Pano (3)

HOLLAND v LUXEMBOURG 1-1 (1-1)

Amsterdam 11.09.1963

Referee: Arthur Blavier (BEL) Attendance: 48,000

HOLLAND: Eddy Pieter Graafland; Guus Haak, Piet Ouderland, Daan Schrijvers, Tonny Pronk, Jan Klaassens, Sjaak Swart, Henk Groot, Klaas Nuninga, Tonny Van der Linden, Coen Moulijn. Trainer: Elek Schwartz

LUXEMBOURG: Nico Schmitt; Ernest Brenner (Cap), Jean-Pierre Hoffstetter, Jean-Pierre Fiedler, Fernand Brosius, François Konter, Jean Klein, Ady Schmit, Louis Pilot, Paul May, Nicolas Hoffmann. Trainer: Robert Heinz

Goals: Nuninga (5), May (29)

LUXEMBOURG v HOLLAND 2-1 (1-1)

Rotterdam 30.10.1963

Referee: Marcel du Bois (FRA) Attendance: 35,000

HOLLAND: Eddy Pieter Graafland; Guus Haak, Cor Veldhoen, Fons Van Wissen, Tonny Pronk, Rinus Bennaars, Piet Giesen, Henk Groot, Piet Kruiver, Piet Keizer, Peter Petersen. Trainer: Elek Schwartz

LUXEMBOURG: Nico Schmitt; Ernest Brenner, Jean-Pierre Hoffstetter, Jean-Pierre Fiedler, Fernand Brosius, François Konter, Jean Klein, Ady Schmit (Cap), Camille Dimmer, Louis Pilot, Henri Klein. Trainer: Robert Heinz

Goals: Dimmer (20, 70), Kruiver (35)

AUSTRIA v REPUBLIC OF IRELAND 0-0

Wien 25.09.1963

Referee: Gere (HUN) Attendance: 26,000

AUSTRIA: Gernot Fraydl; Peter Vargo, Walter Glechner, Erich Hasenkopf; Rudolf Oslansky, Karl Koller; Rudolf Flögel, Erich Hof, Horst Nemec, Ernst Fiala, Johann Hörmayer. Trainer: Karl Decker

IRELAND: Alan Kelly; William Browne, Tommy Traynor, Raymond Brady, Charlie Hurley, Mick McGrath, Johnny Giles, Ronnie Whelan, Dermot Curtis, Ambrose Fogarty, Liam Tuohy.

REPUBLIC OF IRELAND v AUSTRIA 3-2 (1-1)

Dublin 13.10.1963

Referee: Aage Poulsen (DEN) Attendance: 40,000

IRELAND: Alan Kelly; Anthony Dunne, Tommy Traynor, Raymond Brady, Charlie Hurley, Mick McGrath, Johnny Giles, Andy McEvoy, Noel Cantwell, Ambrose Fogarty, Joseph Haverty.

AUSTRIA: Gernot Fraydl; Peter Vargo, Walter Glechner; Erich Hasenkopf, Johann Frank; Karl Koller, Walter Koleznik, Johannes Jank, Hans Buzek, Horst Nemec, Rudolf Flögel. Trainer: Karl Decker

Goals: Koleznik (38), Cantwell (45, 88 pen), Fogarty (66), Flögel (85)

BULGARIA v FRANCE 1-0 (1-0)

Vasil Levski, Sofia 29.09.1963

Referee: Faruk Talu (TUR) Attendance: 50,000

BULGARIA: Georgi Ivan Naidenov; Aleksandar Shalamanov, Ivan Dimitrov, Dobromir Jechev, Ivan Vutsov, Petar Velichkov, Stoian Kitov, Dimitar Iakimov, Todor Diev, Georgi Asparuhov, Ivan Kolev (Cap). Trainer: Bela Volentin

FRANCE: Pierre Bernard; Marcel Adamczyk, Pierre Michelin, Marcel Artelesa, André Chorda, Joseph Bonnel, Yvon Douis (Cap), Szkudlapski Theo, Laurent Robuschi, Lucien Cossou, Louis Buron. Trainer: Henri Guérin

Goal: Diev (24)

FRANCE v BULGARIA 3-1 (1-0)

Parc des Princes, Paris 26.10.1963

Referee: José María Ortiz de Mendibil (SPA) Att: 32,223

FRANCE: Pierre Bernard; Bruno Rodzik, Pierre Michelin, Marcel Artelesa, André Chorda, Robert Herbin, Yvon Douis (Cap), René Ferrier, Georges Lech, Yvon Goujon, Jean-Louis Buron. Trainer: Henri Guérin

BULGARIA: Georgi Ivan Naidenov; Vasil Metodiev, Ivan Dimitrov, Dobromir Jechev, Ivan Vutsov, Stefan Abadjiev, Petar Velichkov, Stoian Kitov, Dimitar Iakimov, Georgi Asparuhov, Ivan Kolev (Cap). Trainer: Bela Volentin

Goals: Goujon (44, 81), Iakimov (75), Herbin (78)

USSR v ITALY 2-0 (2-0)

Central V.I. Lenin, Moskva 13.10.1963

Referee: Ryszard Banasiuk (POL) Attendance: 102,000

USSR: Ramaz Urushadze; Eduard Dubinski, Albert Shesternev, Anatoliy Krutikov; Valeriy Voronin, Valeriy Korolenkov; Slava Metreveli, Igor Chislenko, Viktor Ponedelnik, Valentin Ivanov (Cap), Galimzian Khusainov. Trainer: Konstantin Beskov

ITALY: William Negri; Cesare Maldini (Cap), Giacinto Facchetti; Aristide Guarneri, Sandro Salvadore, Giovanni Trapattoni; Giacomo Bulgarelli, Mario Corso, Angelo Sormani, Gianni Rivera, Ezio Pascutti. Trainer: Edmondo Fabbri

Sent off: Pascutti (23)

Goals: Ponedelnik (22), Chislenko (42)

QUARTER-FINALS

ITALY v USSR 1-1 (0-1)

Stadio Olimpico, Roma 10.11.1963

Referee: Daniel Mellet (SWI) Attendance: 82,100

ITALY: Giuliano Sarti; Tarcisio Burgnich, Giacinto Facchetti; Aristide Guarneri, Sandro Salvadore (Cap), Giovanni Trapattoni; Angelo Domenghini, Giacomo Bulgarelli, Alessandro Mazzola, Gianni Rivera, Giampaolo Menichelli. Trainer: Edmondo Fabbri

USSR: Lev Iashin; Eduard Mudrik, Albert Shesternev, Anatoli Krutikov; Valeriy Voronin, Viktor Shustikov; Igor Chislenko, Valentin Ivanov (Cap), Gennadi Gusarov, Valeriy Korolenkov, Galimzian Khusainov. Trainer: Konstantin Beskov

Goals: Gusarov (33), Rivera (89)

EAST GERMANY v HUNGARY 1-2 (0-1)

Walter-Ulbricht-Stadion, Berlin 19.10.1963

Referee: Belov (USSR) Attendance: 33,400

EAST GERMANY: Jürgen Heinsch; Martin Skaba, Werner Heine (Cap), Dieter Krampe; Manfred Kaiser, Kurt Liebrecht; Rainer Nachtigall, Dieter Erler, Peter Ducke, Jürgen Nöldner, Hermann Stöcker.
Trainers: Karoly Soos & Johannes Studener

HUNGARY: Antal Szentmihályi; Sándor Mátrai, Kálmán Mészöly, László Sárosi; Istvan Nagy, Ernö Solymosi, Karoly Sándor; Gyula Rákosi, Flórián Albert, Ferenc Bene, Maté Fenyvesi. Trainer: Lajos Baroti

Goals: Bene (18), Nöldner (51), Rákosi (88)

HUNGARY v EAST GERMANY 3-3 (2-2)

Népstadion, Budapest 03.11.1963

Referee: Borce Nedelkovski (YUG) Attendance: 40,000

HUNGARY: Antal Szentmihályi; Sándor Mátrai, Kálmán Mészöly, Kálmán Ihász; Istvan Nagy, Ernö Solymosi; Karoly Sándor, Gyula Rákosi, Flórián Albert, Ferenc Bene, Maté Fenyvesi. Trainer: Lajos Baroti

EAST GERMANY: Jürgen Heinsch; Klaus Urbanczyk, Werner Heine (Cap), Dieter Krampe; Manfred Kaiser, Kurt Liebrecht; Rainer Nachtigall, Jürgen Nöldner, Peter Ducke, Dieter Erler, Roland Ducke. Trainers: Karoly Soos & Johannes Studener

Goals: Bene (7), Heine (12), Sándor (17), R. Ducke (26), Solymosi (51 pen), Erler (81)

LUXEMBOURG v DENMARK 3-3 (2-2)

Stade Municipal, Luxembourg 04.12.1963

Referee: Pierre Schwinté (FRA) Attendance: 6,921

LUXEMBOURG: Nico Schmitt; Ernest Brenner, Jean-Pierre Hoffstetter, François Konter, Fernand Brosius, Ady Schmit, Jean Klein, Paul May, Johny Leonard, Louis Pilot (Cap), Henri Klein. Trainer: Robert Heinz

DENMARK: Erik Lykke Sørensen; Kai Johansen, Jens Jørgen Hansen, Bent Hansen, John Madsen, Jens Petersen, Carl Bertelsen, Kjeld Thorst, Ole Madsen, Ole Sørensen, John Danielsen. Trainer: Poul Petersen

Goals: Pilot (1), Klein (23, 51), O. Madsen (9, 30, 46)

DENMARK v LUXEMBOURG 2-2 (1-1)

Idraetsparken, København 10.12.1963

Referee: Joseph Barbéran (FRA) Attendance: 39,400

DENMARK: Erik Lykke Sørensen; Kai Johansen, Jens Jørgen Hansen, Bent Hansen, John Madsen, Jens Petersen, John Danielsen, Ole Madsen, Carl Bertelsen, Ole Sørensen, Henning Enoksen. Trainer: Poul Petersen

LUXEMBOURG: Nico Schmitt; Ernest Brenner, Jean-Pierre Hoffstetter, François Konter (Cap), Fernand Brosius, Ady Schmit, Jean Klein, Paul May, Johny Leonard, Henri Klein, Louis Pilot. Trainer: Robert Heinz

Goals: Leonard (13), O. Madsen (16, 70), Schmit (84)

DENMARK v LUXEMBOURG 1-0 (1-0)

Amsterdam 18.12.1963

Referee: Pieter Paulus Roomer (HOL) Attendance: 5,700

DENMARK: Erik Lykke Sørensen; Kai Johansen, Jens Jørgen Hansen, Bent Hansen, John Madsen, Jens Petersen, Carl Bertelsen, Kjeld Thorst, Ole Madsen, Henning Enoksen, John Danielsen. Trainer: Poul Petersen

LUXEMBOURG: Nico Schmitt; Ernest Brenner, Jean-Pierre Hoffstetter, François Konter, Fernand Brosius, Ady Schmit (Cap), Jean Klein, Paul May, Johny Leonard, Louis Pilot, Henri Klein. Trainer: Robert Heinz

Goal: O. Madsen (42)

SPAIN v REPUBLIC OF IRELAND 5-1 (4-1)

Sevilla 11.03.1964

Referee: Lucien Van Nuffel (BEL) Attendance: 27,200

SPAIN: Jose Angel IRIBAR; Feliciano Muñoz RIVILLA, Fernando OLIVELLA, Isacio CALLEJA; Ignacio ZOCO, José María FUSTÉ; AMANCIO Amaro, Jesús María PEREDA, MARCELINO Martinez, Juan Manuel VILLA, Carlos LAPETRA. Trainer: José Villalonga

IRELAND: Alan Kelly; Theodore Foley, Tommy Traynor, Raymond Brady, Charlie Hurley, Mick Meagan, Johnny Giles, Andy McEvoy, Alfred Hale, Ambrose Fogarty, Joseph Haverty.

Goals: Amancio (5, 29), Fusté (12), McEvoy (18), Marcelino (33, 89)

REPUBLIC OF IRELAND v SPAIN 0-2 (0-1)

Dublin 08.04.1964

Referee: Gérard Versyp (BEL) Attendance: 38,100

IRELAND: Alan Kelly; Anthony Dunne, William Browne, Raymond Brady, Charlie Hurley, Johnny Fulham, Johnny Giles, Andy McEvoy, Noel Cantwell, Paddy Turner, Alfred Hale.

SPAIN: Jose Angel IRIBAR; Feliciano Muñoz RIVILLA, Fernando OLIVELLA, Isacio CALLEJA; Ignacio ZOCO, José María FUSTÉ; Pedro ZABALLA, Jesús María PEREDA, MARCELINO Martinez, Juan Manuel VILLA, Carlos LAPETRA. Trainer: José Villalonga

Goals: Zaballa (25, 88)

FRANCE v HUNGARY 1-3 (0-2)

Stade Olympique, Colombes Paris 25.04.1964

Referee: Cesare Jonni (ITA) Attendance: 35,274

FRANCE: Pierre Bernard (Cap); Georges Casolari, Pierre Michelin, Marcel Artelesa, André Chorda, Joseph Bonnel, Robert Herbin, Lucien Muller, Georges Lech, Nestor Combin, Lucien Cossou. Trainer: Henri Guérin

HUNGARY: Antal Szentmihályi; Sándor Mátrai, Kálmán Mészöly, Ferenc Sípos, Laszlo Sárosi; Janos Göröcs, István Nagy, Gyula Rákosi, Flórián Albert, Lajos Tichy, Maté Fenyvesi. Trainer: Lajos Baroti

Goals: Albert (15), Tichy (16, 70), Cossou (73)

HUNGARY v FRANCE 2-1 (1-1)

Népstadion, Budapest 23.05.1964

Referee: Concetto Lo Bello (ITA) Attendance: 80,000

HUNGARY: Antal Szentmihályi; Sándor Mátrai, Kálmán Meszöly, Ferenc Sípos, Laszlo Sárosi; Istvan Nagy, Gyula Rákosi; Maté Fenyvesi, Karoly Sándor, Lajos Tichy, Ferenc Bene. Trainer: Lajos Baroti

FRANCE: Pierre Bernard (Cap); Georges Casolari, Marcel Artelesa, Daniel Charles-Alfred, André Chorda, Joseph Bonnel, Edouard Stako, Angel Rambert, Georges Lech, Nestor Combin, Fleury Di Nallo. Trainer: Henri Guérin

Goals: Combin (2), Sípos (24), Bene (55)

SWEDEN v USSR 1-1 (0-0)

Rasunda, Stockholm 13.05.1964

Referee: James Finney (ENG) Attendance: 37,525

SWEDEN: Arne Arvidsson; Hans Rosander, Lennart Wing, Orvar Bergmark, Ake Johansson, Hans Mild, Kurt Hamrin, Harry Bild, Agne Simonsson, Orjan Martinsson, Orjan Persson. Trainer: Lennart Nyman

USSR: Lev Iashin; Eduard Mudrik, Albert Shesternev, Vladimir Glotov, Valeriy Voronin, Aleksey Korneev, Igor Chislenko, Valentin Ivanov (Cap), Gennadi Gusarov, Eduard Malofeev, Valeriy Korolenkov. Trainer: Konstantin Beskov

Goals: Ivanov (62), Hamrin (87)

USSR v SWEDEN 3-1 (1-0)

Central V.I.Lenin, Moskva 27.05.1964

Referee: Arthur Holland (ENG) Attendance: 102,000

USSR: Lev Iashin; Eduard Mudrik, Albert Shesternev, Vladimir Glotov, Valeriy Voronin, Aleksey Korneev, Igor Chislenko, Valentin Ivanov (Cap), Viktor Ponedelnik, Gennadi Gusarov, Galimzian Khusainov. Trainer: Konstantin Beskov

SWEDEN: Arne Arvidsson; Hans Rosander, Lennart Wing, Orvar Bergmark, Hans Mild, Anders Svensson, Kurt Hamrin, Harry Bild, Agne Simonsson, Orjan Martinsson, Orjan Persson. Trainer: Lennart Nyman

Goals: Ponedelnik (32, 56), Hamrin (78), Voronin (83)

SEMI-FINALS

SPAIN v HUNGARY 2-1 (1-0, 1-1) (AET)

Estadio Santiago Bernabeu, Madrid 17.06.1964

Referee: Arthur Blavier (BEL) Attendance: 34,713

SPAIN: Jose Angel IRIBAR; Feliciano Muñoz RIVILLA, Fernando OLIVELLA (Cap), Isacio CALLEJA; Ignacio ZOCO, José María FUSTÉ; AMANCIO Amaro, Jesús María PEREDA, MARCELINO Martinez, Luis SUÁREZ, Carlos LAPETRA. Trainer: José Villalonga

HUNGARY: Antal Szentmihályi; Sándor Mátrai, Kálmán Mészöly, Laszlo Sárosi; Istvan Nagy, Ferenc Sípos; Ferenc Bene, Imre Komora, Flórián Albert, Lajos Tichy, Maté Fenyvesi. Trainer: Lajos Baroti

Goals: Amancio (35), Bene (87), Pereda (115)

USSR v DENMARK 3-0 (2-0)

Nou Camp, Barcelona 17.06.1964

Referee: Concetto Lo Bello (ITA) Attendance: 38,556

USSR: Lev Iashin; Viktor Shustikov, Albert Shesternev, Eduard Mudrik, Valeri Voronin, Viktor Anichkin, Igor Chislenko, Valentin Ivanov (Cap), Viktor Ponedelnik, Gennadi Gusarov, Galimzian Khusainov. Trainer: Konstantin Boskov

DENMARK: Leif Nielsen; Jens Jørgen Hansen, Kaj Hansen, Bent Hansen; Birger Larsen, Erling Nielsen; Carl Bertelsen, Ole Sørensen, Ole Madsen, Kjeld Thorst, John Danielsen. Trainer: Poul Petersen

Goals: Voronin (19), Ponedelnik (40), Val. Ivanov (88)

THIRD PLACE MATCH

HUNGARY v DENMARK 3-1 (1-0, 1-1) (AET)

Camp Nou, Barcelona 20.06.1964

Referee: Daniel Mellet (SWI) Attendance: 3,869

HUNGARY: Antal Szentmihályi; Dezsö Novák, Kálmán Mészöly, Kálmán Ihász; Ernö Solymosi, Ferenc Sípos; Janos Farkas, Zoltan Varga, Flórián Albert, Ferenc Bene, Maté Fenyvesi. Trainer: Lajos Baroti

DENMARK: Leif Nielsen; Bent Wolmar, Kaj Hansen, Bent Hansen; Birger Larsen, Erling Nielsen; Carl Bertelsen, Ole Sørensen, Ole Madsen, Kjeld Thorst, John Danielsen. Trainer: Poul Petersen

Goals: Bene (11), Bertelsen (82), Novák (107 pen, 110)

FINAL

SPAIN v USSR 2-1 (1-1)

Estadio Santiago Bernabéu, Madrid 21.06.1964

Referee: Arthur Holland (ENG) Attendance: 79,115

SPAIN: José Angel IRIBAR; Feliciano Muñoz RIVILLA, Fernando OLIVELLA Pons (Cap), Isacio CALLEJA Garcia; Ignacio ZOCO Esparza, José María FUSTÉ Blanch; AMANCIO Amaro, Jesús María PEREDA Ruiz de Temino, MARCELINO Martinez Cao, Luis SUÁREZ, Carlos LAPETRA Coarasa. Trainer: José Villalonga

USSR: Lev Iashin; Viktor Shustikov, Albert Shesternev, Eduard Mudrik; Valeri Voronin, Viktor Anichkin; Igor Chislenko, Valentin Ivanov (Cap), Viktor Ponedelnik, Aleksei Korneev, Galimzyan Khusainov. Trainer: Konstantin Beskov

Goals: Pereda (6), Khusainov (8), Marcelino (84)

Goalscorers European Nations' Cup 1962-1964

11 goals: Ole Madsen (Denmark)

5 goals: Ferenc Bene (Hungary)

4 goals: AMANCIO Amaro (Spain), Viktor Ponedelnik (USSR), Lajos Tichy (Hungary), Alberto Orlando (Italy), Noel Cantwell (Republic of Ireland)

3 goals: MARCELINO Martinez, Vicente Guillot, José Fidalgo Veloso (Spain), Carl Bertelsen (Denmark), Gianni Rivera (Italy), Lucien Cossou, Yvon Goujon (France), Georgi Asparuhov (Bulgaria)

2 goals: R. Jonsson (Iceland), Hernani (Portugal), Skoblar, Galic (Yugoslavia), Kruiver (Holland), Diev (Bulgaria), Erler (East Germany), Dimmer, Klein (Luxembourg), Hamrin, Persson, Martinsson (Sweden), Clausen, Enoksen (Denmark), Wisnieski (France), Zaballa, Pereda (Spain), Albert, Novak, Sandor (Hungary), Voronin, Val. Ivanov (USSR), Fogarty, Tuohy (Republic of Ireland)

1 goal: Krogh (Norway), Theobald, Urpani (Malta), Flowers, Tambling, Smith (England), Tătaru, Manolache, Constantin (Romania), Jurion, Stockman (Belgium), Medwin, C. Jones (Wales), Eusebio, Coluna (Portugal), Allemann, Hertig (Switzerland), Kucera, Masek (Czechoslovakia), Irvine, Humphries, Dougan, Bingham, Crossan (N. Ireland), Zambata, Vasovic (Yugoslavia), Pano (Albania), Nuninga, Swart, Groot, Van der Linden (Holland), Koleznik, Flögel (Austria), Iakimov, Iliev (Bulgaria), Sormani (Italy), Heine, R. Ducke, Noldner, Liebrecht, P. Ducke (East Germany), Pilot, Schmit, Leonard, May (Luxembourg), Bild, Eriksson (Sweden), Petersen, Christiansen (Denmark), Combin, Herbin, Douis (France), Sípos, Solymosi, Rakosi (Hungary), Gusarov, Chislenko, Khusainov (USSR), McEvoy, Arnason (Republic of Ireland), Fuste, Gento, Collar (Spain)

THE EUROPEAN FOOTBALL CHAMPIONSHIP 1968

GROUP 1

REPUBLIC OF IRELAND v SPAIN 0-0

Dalymount Park, Dublin 23.10.1966

Referee: Hans Carlsson (SWE) Attendance: 38,000

IRELAND: Alan Kelly; Anthony Dunne, Noel Cantwell (Cap), Shay Brennan; Jimmy Conway, Mick Meagan, Frank O'Neill, Andy McEvoy, Ray Treacy, Johnny Giles, Anthony O'Connel.

SPAIN: José Angel IRIBAR Cortajarena; Manuel Martinez SANCHIS, Francisco SANTAMARÍA Briones, Severino REIJA Vazquez, Jesús Jordán GLARÍA, José Luis VIOLETA Lajusticia; Luciano Sánchez Rodriguez VAVÁ, LUIS Aragonés Suarez, Fernando ANSOLA San Martin, MARCIAL Pina Morales, Francisco García Gómez PAQUITO.
Trainer: Domingo Balmanyá

REPUBLIC OF IRELAND v TURKEY 2-1 (0-0)

Dalymount Park, Dublin 16.11.1966

Referee: Tage Sørensen (DEN) Attendance: 20,000

IRELAND: Patrick Dunne; Shay Brennan, Charles Hurley (Cap), Mick Meagan, Anthony Dunne, Jimmy Conway, Eamonn Dunphy, Frank O'Neill, Johnny Giles, Andy McEvoy, Joseph Haverty.

TURKEY: Ali Artuner; Talat Özkarsli, Ercan Aktuna, Yilmaz Şen, Fehmi Saginoglu, Ayhan Elmastaşoglu, Şeref Has, Nevzat Güzelirmak, Ogün Altiparmak, Fevzi Zemzem, Faruk Karadogan. Trainer: Adnan Süvari

Goals: O'Neill (60), McEvoy (74), Ogün (88)

SPAIN v REPUBLIC OF IRELAND 2-0 (2-0)

Estadio Mestalla, Valencia 07.12.1966

Referee: Pieter Paulus Roomer (HOL) Attendance: 25,000

SPAIN: José Angel IRIBAR Cortajarena; Manuel Martinez SANCHIS, Francisco Fernandez GALLEGO, Severino REIJA Vazquez; Francisco García Gómez PAQUITO, José Luis VIOLETA Lajusticia; Anastasio JARA Segovia, José Martinez Sánchez PIRRI, Fernando ANSOLA San Martin, LUIS Aragonés Suarez, JOSÉ MARÍA García Lavilla.
Trainer: Domingo Balmanyá

IRELAND: Alan Kelly; Shay Brennan, John Dempsey, Anthony Dunne; Charles Hurley (Cap), Mick Meagan; Frank O'Neill, Jimmy Conway, Alfred Hale, Eamonn Dunphy, Joseph Haverty.

Goals: José María (20), Pirri (35)

TURKEY v SPAIN 0-0

Mithat Paşa, Istambul 01.02.1967

Referee: Gyula Gere (HUN) Attendance: 35,000

TURKEY: Ali Artuner; Talat Özkarsli, Yilmaz Şen; Ercan Aktuna, Fehmi Saginoglu, Yusuf Tunalioglu; Şeref Has, Nevzat Güzelirmak, Ogün Altiparmak, Fevzi Zemzem, Faruk Karadogan. Trainer: Adnan Süvari

SPAIN: José Angel IRIBAR Cortajarena; Manuel Martinez SANCHIS, Francisco Fernandez GALLEGO, Severino REIJA Vazquez, Francisco García Gómez PAQUITO, José Luis VIOLETA Lajusticia; AMANCIO Amaro Varela, José Martinez Sánchez PIRRI, Ramón Moreno GROSSO, Manuel VELAZQUEZ Villaverde, JOSÉ MARÍA García Lavilla.
Trainer: Domingo Balmanyá

TURKEY v REPUBLIC OF IRELAND 2-1 (1-0)

19 Mayis, Ankara 22.02.1967

Referee: Dimitar Rumenchev (BUL) Attendance: 35,000

TURKEY: Ali Artuner; Şükrü Birand, Talat Özkarsli, Ercan Aktuna, Fehmi Elmastaşoglu, Şeref Has, Ergün Acuner, Ogün Altiparmak, Abdullah Çevrim, Faruk Karadogan.
Trainer: Adnan Süvari

IRELAND: Alan Kelly; Joe Kinnear, Charles Hurley (Cap), Alfred Finucane, Mick McGrath, Mick Meagan, Johnny Giles, Frank O'Neill, Charles Gallagher, Noel Cantwell, Eamonn Dunphy.

Goals: Ayhan (35), Ogün (78), Cantwell (89)

REPUBLIC OF IRELAND v CZECHOSLOVAKIA 0-2 (0-2)

Dalymount Park, Dublin 21.05.1967

Referee: Robert Schaut (BEL) Attendance: 9,000

IRELAND: Alan Kelly; Theodore Foley, John Dempsey, Alfred Finucane, Charles Hurley (Cap), Mick Meagan, Charles Gallagher, Andy McEvoy, Ray Treacy, Eamonn Dunphy, Ollie Conmy.

CZECHOSLOVAKIA: Ivo Viktor; Jan Lála, Kamil Majerník, Ján Popluhár, Vladimír Táborsky; Ján Geleta, Andrej Kvasnák; Juraj Szikora, Vojtech Masny, Jozef Adamec, Dusan Kabát.
Trainers: Jozef Marko, Jaciansky

Goals: Szikora (15), Masny (47)

SPAIN v TURKEY 2-0 (0-0)

Estadio San Mamés, Bilbao 31.05.1967

Referee: Dittmar Huber (SWI) Attendance: 40,000

SPAIN: José Angel IRIBAR Cortajarena; Manuel Martinez SANCHIS, Francisco Fernandez GALLEGO, Severino REIJA Vazquez; Francisco García Gómez PAQUITO, Jesús Jordán GLARÍA; José Armando UFARTE Ventosa, ADELARDO Rodriguez Sánchez, Ramón Moreno GROSSO, JOSÉ MARÍA García Lavilla, Francisco GENTO López. Trainer: Domingo Balmanyá

TURKEY: Ali Artuner; Şükrü Birand, Talat Özkarsli, Yilmaz Şen; Fehmi Saginoglu, Ayhan Elmastaşoglu; Şeref Has, Ergün Acuner, Ogün Altiparmak, Fevzi Zemzem, Faruk Karadogan. Trainer: Adnan Süvari

Goals: Grosso (63), Gento (80)

CZECHOSLOVAKIA v TURKEY 3-0 (1-0)

Bratislava 18.06.1967

Referee: Paul Schiller (AUS) Attendance: 20,000

CZECHOSLOVAKIA: Ivo Viktor; Jan Lála, Kamil Majerník, Ján Popluhár, Vladimir Táborsky; Ján Geleta, Andrej Kvasnák; Bohumil Vesely, Josef Jurkanin, Jozef Adamec, Dusan Kabát. Trainers: Jozef Marko, Jaciansky

TURKEY: Ali Artuner; Şükrü Birand, Hüseyin Yazici, Talat Özkarsli, Fehmi Saginoglu, Abdullah Çevrim, Şeref Has, Nevzat Güzelirmak, Ogün Altiparmak, Fevzi Zemzem, Ergün Acuner. Trainer: Adnan Süvari

Goals: Adamec (25, 70), Jurkanin (73)

CZECHOSLOVAKIA v SPAIN 1-0 (0-0)

Slavia, Praha 01.10.1967

Referee: Gerhard Schulemberg (W. GER) Att: 40,000

CZECHOSLOVAKIA: Ivo Viktor; Jan Lála, Alexander Horváth, Ján Popluhár, Vladimir Táborsky; Ján Geleta, Ladislav Kuna; Bohumil Vesely, Juraj Szikora, Jozef Adamec, Dusan Kabát. Trainers: Jozef Marko, Jaciansky

SPAIN: José Angel IRIBAR Cortajarena; Manuel Martinez SANCHIS, Antonio Alfonso Moreno TONONO, Francisco Fernandez GALLEGO, Severino REIJA Vazquez, José Martinez Sánchez PIRRI, Ramón Moreno GROSSO, ADELARDO Rodriguez Sánchez, AMANCIO Amaro Varela, MARCELINO Martinez Cao, JOSÉ MARÍA García Lavilla. Trainer: Domingo Balmanyá

Goal: Horváth (49)

SPAIN v CZECHOSLOVAKIA 2-1 (1-0)

Estadio Santiago Bernabeu, Madrid 22.10.1967

Referee: Antonio Sbardella (ITA) Attendance: 40,000

SPAIN: José Angel IRIBAR Cortajarena; Manuel Fernandez OSORIO, Francisco Fernandez GALLEGO, Antonio Alfonso Moreno TONONO, Severino REIJA Vazquez; José Martinez Sánchez PIRRI, MARCIAL Pina Morales, LUIS Aragonés Suarez; AMANCIO Amaro Varela, José Eulogio GáRATE Hormaechea, JOSÉ MARÍA García Lavilla. Trainer: Domingo Balmanyá

CZECHOSLOVAKIA: Ivo Viktor; Jan Lála, Alexander Horváth, Ján Popluhár, Vladimir Táborsky; Ján Geleta, Ladislav Kuna, Bohumil Vesely, Juraj Szikora, Vojtech Masny, Jaroslav Boros. Trainer: Jozef Marko, Jaciansky

Goals: Pirri (32), Gárate (61), Kuna (75)

TURKEY v CZECHOSLOVAKIA 0-0

Ankara 15.11.1967

Referee: Nicolae Mihăilescu (ROM) Attendance: 52,000

TURKEY: Ali Artuner; Talat Özkarsli, Yilmaz Şen; Ercan Aktuna, Fehmi Saginoglu, Nevzat Güzelirmak, Sanli Sarialioglu, Ayhan Elmastaşoglu, Ogün Altiparmak, Fevzi Zemzem, Faruk Karadogan. Trainer: Adnan Süvari

CZECHOSLOVAKIA: Ivo Viktor; Jan Lála, Ján Geleta, Ján Popluhár, Vladimir Táborsky; Andrej Kvasnák (.. Ivan Hrdlicka), Ladislav Kuna; Juraj Szikora, Josef Jurkanin, Vojtech Masny, Dusan Kabát. Trainer: Jozef Marko, Jaciansky

CZECHOSLOVAKIA v REPUBLIC OF IRELAND 1-2 (0-0)

Slavia, Praha 22.11.1967

Referee: Erwin Vetter (E. GER) Attendance: 8,000

CZECHOSLOVAKIA: Antonín Kramerius; Jan Lála, Alexander Horváth, Ján Popluhár, Vladimir Táborsky; Ján Geleta, Ladislav Kuna, Jozef Levicky, Juraj Szikora, Josef Jurkanin, Václav Vrána. Trainer: Jozef Marko, Jaciansky

IRELAND: Alan Kelly; Joe Kinnear, John Dempsey, Charles Hurley (Cap), Mick Meagan, Jimmy Conway, Eamonn Dunphy, Eamonn Rogers, Ollie Conmy, Ray Treacy, Turlough O'Connor.

Goals: Dempsey (58 og), Treacy (65), O'Connor (86)

	P	W	D	L	F	A	Pts
Spain	6	3	2	1	6	2	8
Czechoslovakia	6	3	1	2	8	4	7
Rep. of Ireland	6	2	1	3	5	8	5
Turkey	6	1	2	3	3	8	4

GROUP 2

PORTUGAL v SWEDEN 1-2 (1-1)

Nacional, Lisboa 13.11.1966

Referee: Jacques Colling (LUX) Attendance: 35,000

PORTUGAL: José Pereira; João Morais, Alexandre Baptista, HILÁRIO Rosário da Conceiçao, Jaime da Silva GRAÇA, Jacinto Santos, José Augusto, EUSÉBIO da Silva Ferreira, António MENDES, Mário COLUNA (Cap), Oliveira Duarte.
Trainer: Manuel da Luz Afonso

SWEDEN: Ronney Pettersson; Hans Selander, Kurt Axelsson, Björn Nordqvist, Rolf Björklund, Jim Nildén, Ingvar Svensson, Ulf Jansson, Inge Danielsson, Agne Simonsson, Tom Turesson.
Trainer: Orvar Bergmark

Goals: Graça (21), Danielsson (29, 86)

NORWAY v PORTUGAL 1-2 (1-1)

Oslo 08.06.1967

Referee: William McGillivray Syme (SCO) Att: 31,000

NORWAY: Kjell Kaspersen; Arild Mathisen, Roar Johansen, Finn Thorsen, Nils Arne Eggen, Trygve Bornø, Olav Nilsen, Harald Sunde, Harald Berg, Odd Iversen, Leif Eriksen.

PORTUGAL: Américo Lopes; João Morais, HILÁRIO Rosário da Conceiçao, Jaime da Silva GRAÇA, RAÚL Machado, José Carlos, José Augusto (Cap), EUSÉBIO da Silva Ferreira, José Maria, Custódio Pinto, Mansidao Estevao.
Trainer: José Gomes de Silva

Goals: Eusébio (15, 61), Iversen (34)

BULGARIA v NORWAY 4-2 (3-0)

Vasil Levski, Sofia 13.11.1966

Referee: Muzaffer Sarvan (TUR) Attendance: 30,000

BULGARIA: Simeon Simeonov; Aleksandar Shalamanov, Boris Gaganelov (Cap), Stoian Aleksiev, Dobromir Jechev, Ivan Davidov, Dinko Dermendjiev, Dimitar Penev, Petar Jekov, Nikola Tsanev, Aleksandar Vasilev.
Trainer: Dobromir Tashkov

NORWAY: Kjell Kaspersen; Roar Johansen, Finn Thorsen, Trygve Bornø, Arild Mathisen, Arne Pedersen, Olav Nilsen, Bjørn Borgen, Harald Berg, Per Kristoffersen, Kjetil Hasund.

Goals: Tsanev (18, 43), Jekov (42, 85), K. Hasund (59, 86)

SWEDEN v BULGARIA 0-2 (0-1)

Fotbollstadion, Solna 11.06.1967

Referee: Leo Callaghan (WAL) Attendance: 24,271

SWEDEN: Ronney Pettersson; Hans Selander, Kurt Axelsson, Björn Nordqvist, Rolf Björklund, Jim Nildén, Ingvar Svensson, Inge Danielsson, Tom Turesson, Agne Simonsson, Örjan Persson. Trainer: Orvar Bergmark

BULGARIA: Simeon Simeonov; Aleksandar Shalamanov, Ivan Dimitrov, Boris Gaganelov (Cap), Dobromir Jechev, Dimitar Penev, Georgi Popov, Hristo Bonev, Petar Jekov, Dimitar Iakimov, Dinko Dermendjiev. Trainer: Stefan Bojkov

Goals: Jekov (23), Dermendjiev (82)

SWEDEN v PORTUGAL 1-1 (0-1)

Fotbollstadion, Solna 01.06.1967

Referee: Kevin Howley (ENG) Attendance: 49,689

SWEDEN: Ronney Pettersson; Hans Selander, Kurt Axelsson, Bjørn Nordqvist, Rolf Bjørklund, Jim Nildın, Ingvar Svensson, Roger Magnusson, Tom Turesson, Agne Simonsson, Ørjan Persson. Trainer: Orvar Bergmark

PORTUGAL: Amırico Lopes; João Morais, HILARIO Rosαrio da Conceiηao, Jaime da Silva GRAHA, Raïl Machado, Josι Carlos, Josι Augusto (Cap), EUSIBIO da Silva Ferreira, Serafim Pereira, Custσdio Pinto, Fernando Peres.
Trainer: José Gomes de Silva

Goal: Pinto (19), Svensson (90)

NORWAY v BULGARIA 0-0

Ulleval, Oslo 29.06.1967

Referee: John Adair (NIR) Attendance: 20,000

NORWAY: Kjell Kaspersen; Arild Mathisen, Roar Johansen, Finn Thorsen, Nils Arne Eggen, Trygve Bornø, Olav Nilsen, Harald Sunde, Odd Iversen, Harald Berg, Kjetil Hasund.

BULGARIA: Simeon Simeonov; Aleksandar Shalamanov, Ivan Dimitrov, Boris Gaganelov (Cap), Dobromir Jechev, Dimitar Penev, Vasil Mitkov, Hristo Bonev, Petar Jekov, Dimitar Iakimov, Dinko Dermendjiev. Trainer: Stefan Bojkov

NORWAY v SWEDEN 3-1 (1-1)

Ullevål, Oslo 03.09.1967

Referee: Pawlik (POL) Attendance: 31,287

NORWAY: Kjell Kaspersen; Tore Børrehaug, Roar Johansen, Finn Thorsen, Nils Arne Eggen, Trygve Bornø, Olav Nilsen, Harald Sunde, Harald Berg, Odd Iversen, Sven Otto Birkeland.

SWEDEN: Ronney Pettersson; Hans Selander, Krister Kristensson, Bertil Elmstedt, Rolf Björklund, Tommy Svensson, Sven Lindman, Inge Danielsson, Thomas Nordahl, Leif Eriksson, Harry Bild. Trainer: Orvar Bergmark

Sent off: Selander (1)

Goals: Nordahl (19), Berg (24), Birkeland (46), Sunde (79)

SWEDEN v NORWAY 5-2 (2-0)

Fotbollstadion, Solna 05.11.1967

Referee: Rudolf Glöckner (E. GER) Attendance: 14,078

SWEDEN: Sven Gunnar Larsson; Sven Andersson, Björn Nordqvist, Bertil Elmstedt, Stig Johansson, Sven Lindman, Ulf Jansson, Inge Danielsson, Tom Turesson, Leif Eriksson, Ingvar Svahn. Trainer: Orvar Bergmark

NORWAY: Kjell Kaspersen; Arild Mathisen, Per Pettersen, Frank Olafsen, Nils Arne Eggen, Trygve Bornø, Olav Nilsen, Harald Sunde, Odd Iversen, Harald Berg, Kjetil Hasund.

Goals: Turesson (15, 89), Danielsson (39), Eriksson (48, 85), Iversen (57 pen), Nilsen (90)

BULGARIA v SWEDEN 3-0 (2-0)

Vasil Levski, Sofia 12.11.1967

Referee: Josip Dragomir Horvath (YUG) Att: 28,000

BULGARIA: Simeon Simeonov; Aleksandar Shalamanov, Dimitar Penev, Boris Gaganelov, Dobromir Jechev, Todor Kolev, Dinko Dermendjiev, Hristo Bonev, Georgi Asparuhov, Nikola Kotkov, Vasil Mitkov. Trainer: Stefan Bojkov

SWEDEN: Sven Gunnar Larsson; Sven Andersson, Bertil Elmstedt, Björn Nordqvist, Rolf Björklund, Sven Lindman, Ulf Jansson, Inge Danielsson, Tom Turesson, Leif Eriksson, Ingvar Svahn. Trainer: Orvar Bergmark

Goals: Kotkov (43), Mitkov (44), Asparuhov (75)

PORTUGAL v NORWAY 2-1 (1-1)

Porto 12.11.1967

Referee: Michel Kitabdjian (FRA) Attendance: 40,000

PORTUGAL: Américo Lopes; Manuel Rodrigues, HILÁRIO Rosário da Conceiçao, Jaime da Silva GRAÇA, RAÚL Machado, José Carlos, José Augusto, EUSÉBIO da Silva Ferreira, José TORRES, Mário COLUNA (Cap), Francisco NÓBREGA. Trainer: José Gomes de Silva

NORWAY: Kjell Kaspersen; Arild Mathisen, Per Pettersen, Tor Alsaker-Nøstdahl, Nils Arne Eggen, Trygve Bornø, Olav Nilsen, Harald Sunde, Kai Sjøberg, Harald Berg, Odd Iversen.

Goals: Torres (30), Nilsen (40), Graça (64)

BULGARIA v PORTUGAL 1-0 (0-0)

Vasil Levski 26.11.1967

Referee: Anvar Zverev (USSR) Attendance: 55,000

BULGARIA: Simeon Simeonov; Aleksandar Shalamanov, Dimitar Penev, Boris Gaganelov (Cap), Dobromir Jechev, Ivan Davidov, Dinko Dermendjiev, Hristo Bonev, Georgi Asparuhov, Nikola Kotkov, Vasil Mitkov.
Trainer: Stefan Bojkov

PORTUGAL: Américo Lopes; Manuel Rodrigues, HILÁRIO Rosário da Conceiçao, Jaime da Silva GRAÇA, Rui Rodrigues, José Carlos, José Augusto (Cap), EUSÉBIO da Silva Ferreira, José TORRES, José Pereira Pedras, António Simoes.
Trainer: José Gomes de Silva

Goal: Dermendjiev (63)

PORTUGAL v BULGARIA 0-0

Nacional, Lisboa 17.12.1967

Referee: Antonio Sbardella (ITA) Attendance: 20,000

PORTUGAL: Américo Lopes; Manuel Rodrigues, HILÁRIO Rosário da Conceiçao, Jaime da Silva GRAÇA, Rui Rodrigues, José Carlos, José Augusto (Cap), EUSÉBIO da Silva Ferreira, José TORRES, José Pereira Pedras, António Simoes.
Trainer: José Gomes de Silva

BULGARIA: Simeon Simeonov; Milko Gaidarski, Ivan Dimitrov, Boris Gaganelov (Cap), Dimitar Penev, Dobromir Jechev, Georgi Popov, Hristo Bonev, Nikola Kotkov, Dimitar Iakimov, Dinko Dermendjiev. Trainer: Stefan Bojkov

	P	W	D	L	F	A	Pts
Bulgaria	6	4	2	0	10	2	10
Portugal	6	2	2	2	6	6	6
Sweden	6	2	1	3	9	12	5
Norway	6	1	1	4	9	14	3

GROUP 3

FINLAND v AUSTRIA 0-0

Helsinki 02.10.1966

Referee: Peter Coates (IRE) Attendance: 10,070

FINLAND: Lars Näsman; Pertti Mäkipää, Reima Nummila, Timo Kautonen, Reijo Kanerva, Simo Syrjävaara, Juhani Peltonen, Matti Mäkelä, Tommy Lindholm, Markku Hyvärinen, Aulis Laine. Trainer: Olavi Laaksonen

AUSTRIA: Roman Pichler; Walter Gebhardt, Walter Glechner, Heinz Binder, Franz Viehböck, Horst Hirnschrodt, Robert Sara, Rudolf Flögel, Anton Fritsch, Thomas Parits, Johann Hörmayer. Trainer: Eduard Frühwirth

USSR v AUSTRIA 4-3 (3-1)

Central V.I. Lenin, Moskva 11.06.1967

Referee: Einar Boström (SWE) Attendance: 100,000

USSR: Lev Iashin; Valentin Afonin, Albert Shesternev (Cap), Murtaz Hurtsilava, Aleksandr Lenev, Valeri Voronin, Igor Chislenko, Jozsef Sabo, Anatolyi Bîshovets, Eduard Streltsov, Eduard Malofeev. Trainer: Mihail Iakushin

AUSTRIA: Roman Pichler; Helmut Wartusch, Walter Glechner, Gerhard Sturmberger, Erich Fak, Roland Eschelmüller, Erich Hof, Rudolf Flögel, Franz Wolny, Helmut Siber, Johann Hörmayer. Trainers: Erwin Alge & Hans Pesser

Goals: Malofeev (25), Bîshovets (36), Hof (38), Chislenko (43), Wolny (54), Siber (71), Streltsov (80)

GREECE v FINLAND 2-1 (1-0)

Kantatzogleio, Thessaloniki 16.10.1966

Referee: Zdenek Vales (CZE) Attendance: 30,000

GREECE: Takis Oikonomopoulos; Tasos Vasileiou, Giorgos Skrekis, Fotis Balopoulos, Frankiskos Sourpis, Stelios Skeiofilax, Stathis Haitas, Mimis Domazos, Alekos Alexiadis, Dimitris Papaioannou, Giorgos Dedes.
Trainer: Panayotis Markovits

FINLAND: Lars Näsman; Pertti Mäkipää, Reima Nummila, Timo Kautonen, Reijo Kanerva, Simo Syrjävaara, Juhani Peltonen, Matti Mäkelä, Arto Tolsa, Markku Hyvärinen, Aulis Laine. Trainer: Olavi Laaksonen

Goals: Alexiadis (39, 86), Mäkipää (57)

USSR v GREECE 4-0 (0-0)

Dinamo, Tbilisi 16.07.1967

Referee: Birger Nilsen (NOR) Attendance: 40,000

USSR: Lev Iashin; Viktor Anichkin, Albert Shesternev (Cap), Murtaz Hurtsilava, Aleksandr Lenev, Valeri Voronin, Igor Chislenko, Jozsef Sabo, Anatoliy Banishevski, Eduard Streltsov, Anatoliy Bîshovets. Trainer: Mihail Iakushin

GREECE: Takis Oikonomopoulos; Mimis Plessas, Takis Loukanidis, Mihalis Bellis, Aristeidis Kamaras, Mimis Domazos, Kostas Polihroniou (Cap), Stathis Haitas, Giorgos Sideris, Dimitris Papaioannou, Vasilis Botinos.
Trainer: Vasilis Petropoulos

Goals: Banishevski (50, 77), Sabo (72 pen), Chislenko (83)

FINLAND v GREECE 1-1 (1-1)

Olimpic, Helsinki 10.05.1967

Referee: Pieter Paulus Roomer (HOL) Attendance: 14,056

FINLAND: Martti Halme; Rainer Aho, Timo Kautonen, Reijo Kanerva, Reima Nummila, Matti Mäkela, Pertti Mäkipää, Semi Nuoranen, Arto Tolsa, Tommy Lindholm, Juhani Peltonen.
Trainer: Olavi Laaksonen

GREECE: Takis Oikonomopoulos; Mihalis Bellis, Hristos Zanteroglou, Alekos Sofianidis, Takis Loukanidis, Kostas Polihroniou (Cap), Stathis Haitas, Nikos Gioutsos, Mimis Domazos, Dimitris Papaioannou, Vasilis Botinos.
Trainer: Panayotis Markovits & Vasilis Petropoulos

Goals: Peltonen (18), Haitas (39)

USSR v FINLAND 2-0 (1-0)

Central V.I. Lenin, Moskva 30.08.1967

Referee: Muzaffer Sarvan (TUR) Attendance: 80,000

USSR: Anzor Kavazashvili; Valentin Afonin, Albert Shesternev (Cap), Murtaz Hurtsilava, Guram Tskhovrebov, Valeriy Maslov, Igor Chislenko, Jozsef Sabo, Anatoliy Banishevski, Anatoliy Bîshovets, Eduard Malofeev.
Trainer: Mihail Iakushin

FINLAND: Lars Näsman; Pertti Mäkipää, Seppo Kilponen, Timo Kautonen, Reima Nummila, Juhani Peltonen, Simo Syrjävaara, Kai Pahlman, Matti Mäkelä, Arto Tolsa, Aulis Laine. Trainer: Olavi Laaksonen

Goals: Hurtsilava (14), Chislenko (80)

FINLAND v USSR 2-5 (2-3)

Kuupitaa, Turun 06.09.1967

Referee: Pavel Spotak (CZE) Attendance: 7793

FINLAND: Lars Näsman; Matti Pitko, Seppo Kilponen, Pertti Mäkipää, Reima Nummila, Matti Mäkelä, Simo Syrjävaara, Aulis Laine, Arto Tolsa, Juhani Peltonen, Semi Nuoranen. Trainer: Olavi Laaksonen

USSR: Iuriy Pshenichnikov (80 Anzor Kavazashvili); Valentin Afonin, Viktor Anichkin, Murtaz Hurtsilava, Gennadi Logofet, Valeriy Maslov, Igor Chislenko, Jozsef Sabo, Anatoliy Banishevski, Anatoliy Bîshovets, Eduard Malofeev. Trainer: Mihail Iakushin

Goals: Sabo (2, 56 pen), Maslov (14), Peltonen (18 pen), Syrjävaara (25), Banishevski (35), Malofeev (63)

AUSTRIA v FINLAND 2-1 (1-0)

Wien 24.09.1967

Referee: Milivoje Gugulovic (YUG) Attendance: 28,000

AUSTRIA: Gerald Fuchsbichler; Walter Gebhardt, Walter Glechner, Johann Eigenstiller, Karl Fröhlich, Gerhard Sturmberger, Rudolf Flögel, Helmut Mätzler, Franz Wolny, Leopold Grausam, Helmut Redl. Trainers: Erwin Alge & Hans Pesser

FINLAND: Lars Näsman; Matti Pitko, Seppo Kilponen, Timo Kautonen, Reima Nummila, Matti Mäkelä, Simo Syrjävaara, Semi Nuoranen, Tommy Lindholm, Arto Tolsa, Juhani Peltonen. Trainer: Olavi Laaksonen

Goals: Flögel (17), Peltonen (57), Grausam (81)

GREECE v AUSTRIA 4-1 (2-0)

Karaiskaki, Peiraias 04.10.1967

Referee: Vasile Dumitrescu (ROM) Attendance: 40,000

GREECE: Takis Oikonomopoulos; Fotis Balopoulos, Hristos Zanteroglou, Kostas Polihroniou (Cap), Giannis Gkaitatzis, Takis Loukanidis, Mimis Domazos, Giorgos Sideris, Nikos Gioutsos, Dimitris Papaioannou, Vasilis Botinos. Trainer: Vasilis Petropoulos

AUSTRIA: Gerald Fuchsbichler; Walter Gebhardt, Walter Glechner, Johann Eigenstiller, Karl Fröhlich, Johann Frank, Rudolf Flögel, Anton Fritsch, Helmut Siber, Leopold Grausam, Helmut Redl. Trainers: Erwin Alge & Hans Pesser

Goals: Sideris (27, 34 pen, 63), Grausam (62), Papaioannou (75)

AUSTRIA v USSR 1-0 (0-0)

Prater, Wien 15.10.1967

Referee: Todor Bechirov (BUL) Attendance: 37,400

AUSTRIA: Wilhelm Harreither; Walter Gebhardt, Walter Glechner, Walter Stamm, Karl Fröhlich, Gerhard Sturmberger, Johann Eigenstiller, Walter Koleznik, Leopold Grausam, Rudolf Flögel, Helmut Siber. Trainers: Erwin Alge & Hans Pesser

USSR: Anzor Kavazashvili; Valentin Afonin, Albert Shesternev (Cap), Murtaz Hurtsilava, Guram Tskhovrebov, Valeriy Maslov, Viktor Anichkin, Jozsef Sabo, Anatoliy Banishevski, Eduard Streltsov, Anatoliy Bîshovets. Trainer: Mihail Iakushin

Goal: Grausam (50)

GREECE v USSR 0-1 (0-0)

Karaiskaki, Peiraias 31.10.1967

Referee: Gottfried Dienst (SWI) Attendance: 38,000

GREECE: Nikos Hristidis; Fotis Balopoulos, Hristos Zanteroglou, Kostas Polihroniou (Cap), Giannis Gkaitatzis, Takis Loukanidis, Mimis Domazos, Stathis Haitas, Nikos Gioutsos, Giorgos Sideris, Dimitris Papaioannou. Trainer: Vasilis Petropoulos

USSR: Anzor Kavazashvili; Valentin Afonin, Albert Shesternev (Cap), Murtaz Hurtsilava, Viktor Anichkin, Valeri Voronin, Igor Chislenko, Jozsef Sabo, Anatoliy Banishevski, Eduard Streltsov, Eduard Malofeev. Trainer: Mihail Iakushin

Goal: Malofeev (50)

AUSTRIA v GREECE 1-1 (1-0)

Prater, Wien 05.11.1967

Referee: Gere (HUN) Attendance: 25,000

AUSTRIA: Wilhelm Harreither; Walter Gebhardt, Walter Glechner, Walter Stamm, Karl Fröhlich, Walter Skocik, Johann Eigenstiller, Walter Koleznik, Helmut Siber, Leopold Grausam, Helmut Redl. Trainers: Erwin Alge & Hans Pesser

GREECE: Nikos Hristidis; Aristeidis Kamaras, Hristos Zanteroglou, Kostas Polihroniou (Cap), Giannis Gkaitatzis, Takis Loukanidis, Fotis Balopoulos, Giorgos Koudas, Mimis Domazos, Giorgos Sideris, Dimitris Papaioannou. Trainer: Vasilis Petropoulos

Goals: Siber (31), Sideris (71)

The match was abandoned in the 83rd minute

	P	W	D	L	F	A	Pts
USSR	6	5	0	1	16	6	10
Greece	6	2	2	2	8	9	6
Austria	6	2	2	2	8	10	6
Finland	6	0	2	4	5	12	2

GROUP 4

WEST GERMANY v ALBANIA 6-0 (2-0)

Westfalenstadion, Dortmund 08.04.1967

Referee: Martti Hirviniemi (FIN) Attendance: 30,000

WEST GERMANY: Hans Tilkowski; Bernd Patzke, Willi Schulz (Cap), Wolfgang Weber, Horst-Dieter Höttges; Franz Beckenbauer, Wolfgang Overath; Bernd Dörfel, Lothar Ulsaß, Gerhard Müller, Johannes Löhr. Trainer: Helmut Schön

ALBANIA: Mikel Janku; Fatmir Frashëri, Ali Mema, Thodor Vaso, Ramazan Ragami, Iosif Kazanxhi, Niko Xhaçka, Skender Hyka, Panayot Pano, Sabah Bizi, Bahri Ishka.
Trainer: Loro Boriçi

Goals: Müller (5, 23, 73, 80 pen), Löhr (77, 78)

YUGOSLAVIA v WEST GERMANY 1-0 (0-0)

Crvena Zvezda, Beograd 03.05.1967

Referee: José María Ortiz de Mendibil (SPA) Att: 50,000

YUGOSLAVIA: Ilija Pantelic; Mirsad Fazlagic, Fahrudin Jusufi, Marijan Brncic, Branko Rasovic, Dragan Holcer, Vojislav Melic, Radoslav Becejac, Mustafa Hasanagic, Josip Skoblar, Dragan Dzajic. Trainer: Rajko Mitic

WEST GERMANY: Josef Maier; Bernd Patzke, Hans-Hubert Vogts; Franz Beckenbauer, Willi Schulz (Cap), Klaus Fichtel; Siegfried Held, Hans Küppers, Gerhard Müller, Wolfgang Overath, Johannes Löhr. Trainer: Helmut Schön

Goal: Skoblar (69)

ALBANIA v YUGOSLAVIA 0-2 (0-1)

Qemal Stafa, Tiranë 14.05.1967

Referee: Xanthoulis (CYP) Attendance: 20,000

ALBANIA: Mikel Janku; Fatmir Frashëri, Iosif Kazanxhi, Thodor Vaso, Ali Mema, Lin Shllaku, Lorenc Vorfi, Medin Zhega, Panayot Pano (Cap), Ramazan Ragami, Niko Xhaçka.
Trainer: Loro Boriçi

YUGOSLAVIA: Miodrag Knezeviç; Mirsad Fazlagic, Marijan Brncic, Radoslav Becejac, Branko Rasovic, Dragan Holcer, Vojislav Melic, Petar Nadoveza, Slaven Zambata, Stjepan Lamza, Dragan Dzajic. Trainer: Rajko Mitic

Goals: Zambata (22, 56)

WEST GERMANY v YUGOSLAVIA 3-1 (1-0)

Volkspark, Hamburg 07.10.1967

Referee: Concetto Lo Bello (ITA) Attendance: 72,000

W. GERMANY: Josef Maier; Bernd Patzke, Horst-Dieter Höttges; Hans Siemensmeyer, Willi Schulz, Wolfgang Weber; Franz Roth, Uwe Seeler (Cap), Gerhard Müller, Wolfgang Overath, Johannes Löhr. Trainer: Helmut Schön

YUGOSLAVIA: Ilija Pantelic; Mirsad Fazlagic, Marijan Brncic, Stevan Nesticki, Branko Rasovic, Dragan Holcer, Slaven Zambata, Radoslav Becejac, Josip Skoblar, Ivan Osim, Dragan Dzajic. Trainer: Rajko Mitic

Goals: Löhr (11), Zambata (46), Müller (72), Seeler (87)

YUGOSLAVIA v ALBANIA 4-0 (1-0)

JNA, Beograd 02.11.1967

Referee: Andrei Rădulescu (ROM) Attendance: 35,000

YUGOSLAVIA: Radomir Vukcevic; Mirsad Fazlagic, Milan Damjanovic, Borivoje Djordjevic, Blagoje Paunovic, Dragan Holcer, Dragan Dzajic, Ivan Osim, Vojin Lazarevic, Edin Spreco, Krasnodar Rora. Trainer: Rajko Mitic

ALBANIA: Jani Rama; Frederik Jorgaqi, Gani Xhafa, Thodor Vaso, Ramazan Ragami, Lin Shllaku, Panayot Pano (Cap), Ali Mema, Medin Zhega, Sabah Bizi, Foto Andoni.
Trainer: Loro Boriçi

Goals: Spreco (44), Osim (52, 82), Lazarevic (70)

ALBANIA v WEST GERMANY 0-0

Qemal Stafa, Tiranë 17.12.1967

Referee: Ferdinand Marshall (AUS) Attendance: 20,000

ALBANIA: Koco Dinella; Frederik Gjinali, Frederik Jorgaqi, Lin Shllaku, Thodor Vaso, Ramazan Ragami, Ali Mema, Iosif Kazanxhi, Sabah Bizi, Panayot Pano, Medin Zhega.
Trainer: Loro Boriçi

W. GERMANY: Horst Wolter; Bernd Patzke, Horst-Dieter Höttges; Günter Netzer, Willi Schulz (Cap), Wolfgang Weber; Siegfried Held, Hans Küppers, Peter Meyer, Wolfgang Overath, Johannes Löhr. Trainer: Helmut Schön

	P	W	D	L	F	A	Pts
Yugoslavia	4	3	0	1	8	3	6
West Germany	4	2	1	1	9	2	5
Albania	4	0	1	3	0	12	1

GROUP 5

HOLLAND v HUNGARY 2-2 (2-0)

Feyenoord, Rotterdam 07.09.1966

Referee: Birger Nilsen (NOR) Attendance: 65,000

HOLLAND: Eddy Pieters Graafland; Frits Flinkevleugel, Rinus Israël, Daan Schrijvers, Cor Veldhoen, Miel Pijs, Bennie Muller, Sjaak Swart, Johan Cruijff, Klaas Nuninga, Piet Keizer. Trainer: Georg Kessler

HUNGARY: Antal Szentmihályi; Benö Káposzta, Kálmán Mészöly, Ferenc Sípos, Kálmán Ihász; Zoltán Varga, Gyula Rákosi; Dezsö Molnár, Ferenc Bene, Flórián Albert, János Farkas. Trainer: Rudolf Illovszky

Goals: Pijs (35), Cruijff (42), Molnar (70), Mészöly (86)

EAST GERMANY v HOLLAND 4-3 (0-2)

Zentralstadion, Leipzig 05.04.1967

Referee: Hannes Sigurdsson (ICE) Attendance: 40,000

EAST GERMANY: Horst Weigang; Otto Fräßdorf, Manfred Walter, Manfred Geisler; Herbert Pankau, Gerhard Körner, Dieter Erler (Cap); Roland Ducke, Henning Frenzel, Jürgen Nöldner, Eberhard Vogel.
Trainers: Karoly Soos & Werner Wolf

HOLLAND: Tonny Van Leeuwen; Wim Suurbier, Miel Pijs, Daan Schrijvers, Peter Kemper, Henk Groot, Piet De Zoete, Sjaak Swart, Klaas Nuninga, Jan Mulder, Piet Keizer. Trainer: Georg Kessler

Goals: Mulder (10, 68), Keizer (12), Vogel (50), Frenzel (62, 78, 85)

HUNGARY v DENMARK 6-0 (5-0)

Népstadion, Budapest 21.09.1966

Referee: Petros Tsouvaras (GRE) Attendance: 30,000

HUNGARY: Antal Szentmihályi; Benö Káposzta, Sándor Mátrai, Kálmán Ihász, Imre Mathesz; Kálmán Mészöly, Dezsö Molnár; Ferenc Bene, Flórián Albert, Zoltán Varga, János Farkas. Trainer: Rudolf Illovszky

DENMARK: Leif Nielsen; Johnny Hansen, John Worbye, Niels Erik Andersen, Henning Boel, Niels Møller, Bent Schmidt Hansen, René Møller, Henning Enoksen, Jens Jørgen Hansen, Ulrik Le Févre. Trainer: Poul Petersen

Goals: Albert (1, 30), Mészöly (9 pen), Bene (14), Farkas (36), Varga (83)

HUNGARY v HOLLAND 2-1 (2-0)

Népstadion, Budapest 10.05.1967

Referee: Franz Mayer (AUS) Attendance: 30,000

HUNGARY: Gyula Tamás; Sándor Mátrai, Kálmán Mészöly, Lajos Szücs, Kálmán Ihász; János Göröcs, Gyula Rákosi; Dezsö Molnár, Ferenc Bene, Flórián Albert, János Farkas. Trainer: Rudolf Illovszky

HOLLAND: Tonny Van Leeuwen (46 Pim Doesburg); Wim Suurbier, Rinus Israël, Hans Eijkenbroek, Cor Veldhoen; Henk Groot, Bennie Muller, Gerard Bergholtz, Jan Mulder, Klaas Nuninga, Piet Keizer. Trainer: Georg Kessler

Goals: Mészöly (18 pen), Farkas (30), Suurbier (63)

HOLLAND v DENMARK 2-0 (0-0)

Feyenoord, Rotterdam 30.11.1966

Referee: Anibal Da Silva Oliveira (POR) Attendance: 32,000

HOLLAND: Eddy Pieters Graafland; Wim Suurbier, Rinus Israël, Daan Schrijvers, Cor Veldhoen, Willy Dullens, Bennie Muller, Sjaak Swart, Klaas Nuninga, Willy Van der Kuylen, Piet Keizer. Trainer: Georg Kessler

DENMARK: Leif Nielsen; Johnny Hansen, John Worbye, Leif Hartwig, Henning Boel, Henning Munk Jensen, John Steen Olsen, Finn Wiberg, Keld Bak, Kjeld Thorst, Ulrik Le Févre. Trainer: Poul Petersen

Goals: Swart (58), Van der Kuylen (73)

DENMARK v HUNGARY 0-2 (0-1)

Idraetspark, København 24.05.1967

Referee: William John Gow (WAl) Attendance: 35,000

DENMARK: Leif Nielsen; Johnny Hansen, John Worbye, Kresten Bjerre, Jens Jørgen Hansen, Erik Sandvad, Finn Laudrup, Bent Schmidt Hansen, René Møller, Tom Søndergaard, Ulrik Le Févre.
Trainers: Erik Hansen & Ernst Netuka

HUNGARY: Gyula Tamás; Sándor Mátrai, Kálmán Mészöly, Kálmán Ihász, János Nagy; Lajos Szücs, Gyula Rákosi; Dezsö Molnár, Ferenc Bene, Flórián Albert, János Farkas. Trainer: Rudolf Illovszky

Goals: Albert (30), Bene (70)

DENMARK v EAST GERMANY 1-1 (0-1)

Idraetspark, København 04.06.1967

Referee: Joseph Hannet (BEL) Attendance: 30,000

DENMARK: Leif Nielsen; Johnny Hansen, John Worbye, Kresten Bjerre, Henning Boel, Erik Sandvad, Bent Schmidt Hansen, Finn Laudrup, René Møller, Tom Søndergaard, Ulrik Le Févre. Trainers: Erik Hansen & Ernst Netuka

EAST GERMANY: Jürgen Croy; Otto Fräßdorf, Manfred Walter, Manfred Geisler, Bernd Bransch; Harald Irmscher, Gerhard Körner; Roland Ducke, Henning Frenzel, Jürgen Nöldner, Wolfram Löwe.
Trainers: Karoly Soos & Werner Wolf

Goals: Löwe (5), Bjerre (64)

HOLLAND v EAST GERMANY 1-0 (1-0)

Olympiastadion, Amsterdam 13.09.1967

Referee: Thomas Wharton (SCO) Attendance: 42,000

HOLLAND: Eddy Pieters Graafland; Wim Suurbier, Rinus Israël, Hans Eijkenbroek, Cor Veldhoen, Henk Groot, Bennie Muller, Piet Keizer, Klaas Nuninga, Johan Cruijff, Jan Klijnjan.
Trainer: Georg Kessler

EAST GERMANY: Wolfgang Blochwitz; Otto Fräßdorf, Wolfgang Wruck, Manfred Geisler, Bernd Bransch; Herbert Pankau, Harald Irmscher; Roland Ducke (Cap), Henning Frenzel, Dieter Erler, Eberhard Vogel.
Trainers: Karoly Soos & Werner Wolf

Goal: Cruijff (2)

HUNGARY v EAST GERMANY 3-1 (1-0)

Népstadion, Budapest 27.09.1967

Referee: Tofik Bakhramov (USSR) Attendance: 70,000

HUNGARY: Gyula Tamás; Benö Káposzta, Sándor Mátrai, Lajos Szücs, Kálmán Ihász; János Göröcs, Gyula Rákosi; Ferenc Bene, Zoltán Varga, Flórián Albert, János Farkas.
Trainer: Rudolf Illovszky

EAST GERMANY: Jürgen Croy; Otto Fräßdorf, Herbert Pankau, Manfred Walter, Bernd Bransch; Gerhard Körner, Dieter Erler (Cap); Roland Ducke, Henning Frenzel, Peter Ducke, Eberhard Vogel.
Trainer: Karoly Soos & Werner Wolf

Goals: Farkas (9, 48, 50), Frenzel (58)

DENMARK v HOLLAND 3-2 (1-0)

Idraetsparken, København 04.10.1967

Referee: Malcolm Wright (NIR) Attendance: 34,000

DENMARK: Leif Nielsen; Johnny Hansen, John Worbye, Kresten Bjerre, Henning Boel, Erik Sandvad, John Steen Olsen, Finn Laudrup, Erik Dyreborg, Tom Søndergaard, Ulrik Le Févre. Trainers: Erik Hansen & Ernst Netuka

HOLLAND: Eddy Pieters Graafland; Wim Suurbier, Rinus Israël, Hans Eijkenbroek, Tonny Pronk, Henk Groot, Bennie Muller, Piet Keizer, Johan Cruijff, Wim Jansen, Klaas Nuninga.
Trainer: Georg Kessler

Goals: Bjerre (43 pen, 71), Søndergaard (54), Suurbier (83), Israël (85)

EAST GERMANY v DENMARK 3-2 (1-2)

Zentralstadion, Leipzig 11.10.1967

Referee: Ryszard Banasiuk (POL) Attendance: 25,000

EAST GERMANY: Wolfgang Blochwitz; Klaus Urbanczyk (Cap), Manfred Walter, Bernd Bransch; Herbert Pankau, Jürgen Nöldner, Gerhard Körner; Roland Ducke, Henning Frenzel, Peter Ducke, Eberhard Vogel.
Trainer: Karoly Soos & Werner Wolf

DENMARK: Leif Nielsen; Johnny Hansen, John Worbye, Kresten Bjerre, Henning Boel, Erik Sandvad, John Steen Olsen, Finn Laudrup, Erik Dyreborg, Tom Søndergaard, Ulrik Le Févre. Trainers: Erik Hansen & Ernst Netuka

Goals: Dyreborg (25), Körner (35 pen), Søndergaard (43), Pankau (59, 73)

EAST GERMANY v HUNGARY 1-0 (0-0)

Zentralstadion, Leipzig 29.10.1967

Referee: Robert Helies (FRA) Attendance: 55,000

EAST GERMANY: Wolfgang Blochwitz; Klaus Urbanczyk (Cap), Wolfgang Wruck, Bernd Bransch; Herbert Pankau, Harald Irmscher, Günter Hoge, Jürgen Nöldner, Henning Frenzel, Dieter Erler (Cap); Wolfram Löwe.
Trainers: Karoly Soos & Werner Wolf

HUNGARY: Gyula Tamás; Benö Káposzta, Miklós Páncsics, Lajos Szücs, Kálmán Ihász; Imre Mathesz, Gyula Rákosi; Ferenc Bene, Zoltán Varga, Flórián Albert, János Farkas.
Trainer: Rudolf Illovszky

Goal: Frenzel (51)

	P	W	D	L	F	A	Pts
Hungary	6	4	1	1	15	5	9
East Germany	6	3	1	2	10	10	7
Holland	6	2	1	3	11	11	5
Denmark	6	1	1	4	6	16	3

GROUP 6

ROMANIA v SWITZERLAND 4-2 (4-0)

Republicii, Bucureşti 02.11.1966

Referee: James Finney (ENG) Attendance: 15,000

ROMANIA: Mihai Ionescu; Corneliu Popa (Cap), Bujor Hălmăgeanu, Dan Coe, Mihai Mocanu; Simion Surdan, Dumitru Popescu; Ion Pîrcălab, Mircea Dridea, Constantin Frăţilă, Mircea Lucescu. Trainer: Ilie Oană

SWITZERLAND: Mario Prosperi; Alex Matter, Heinz Bäni, Georges Perroud, Hansruedi Fuhrer; Karl Odermatt, Richard Dürr; Vittore Gottardi, Fritz Künzli, René Pierre Quentin, Bruno Bernasconi. Trainer: Alfredo Foni

Goals: Dridea (8), Frăţilă (11, 25, 38), Künzli (54), Odermatt (70)

CYPRUS v ITALY 0-2 (0-0)

Gymnasion PS, Nicosia 22.03.1967

Referee: Atanas Kiriakov (BUL) Attendance: 11,105

CYPRUS: Varnavas Christofi; Panikos Iakovou, Costas Christou "Kattos"; Ploutis Pallas, Kostas Panagiotou (Cap), Christofis Christofi; George Kettenis, Drosos Kalotheou, Kostas Pierides, Panikos Krystallis, Andreas Stylianou.
Trainer: Gavalas

ITALY: Giuliano Sarti; Tarcisio Burgnich, Giacinto Facchetti (Cap); Giovanni Lodetti, Aristide Guarneri, Armando Picchi; Angelo Domenghini, Gianni Rivera, Renato Cappellini, Antonio Juliano, Mario Corso.
Trainers: Helenio Herrera & Ferruccio Valcareggi

Goals: Domenghini (76), Facchetti (88)

ITALY v ROMANIA 3-1 (2-1)

San Paolo, Napoli 26.11.1966

Referee: Gerhardt Schulenburg (W. GERM) Att: 75,000

ITALY: Giuliano Sarti; Spartaco Landini, Giacinto Facchetti (Cap); Ottavio Bianchi, Aristide Guarneri, Armando Picchi; Angelo Domenghini, Alessandro Mazzola, Virginio Depaoli, Antonio Juliano, Mario Corso.
Trainers: Helenio Herrera & Ferruccio Valcareggi

ROMANIA: Ilie Datcu; Corneliu Popa (Cap), Ion Barbu, Dan Coe, Augustin Pax Deleanu; Vasile Gergely, Nicolae Dobrin; Ion Pîrcălab, Constantin Frăţilă, Mircea Dridea, Mircea Lucescu. Trainer: Ilie Oană

Goals: Dobrin (7), Mazzola (30, 67), De Paoli (43)

ROMANIA v CYPRUS 7-0 (3-0)

23 August, Bucureşti 23.04.1967

Referee: Milivoje Gugulovic (YUG) Attendance: 10,000

ROMANIA: Mihai Ionescu; Corneliu Popa, Ion Nunweiller (Cap), Dumitru Nicolae, Mihai Mocanu; Vasile Gergely, Nicolae Dobrin; Florea Martinovici, Emil Dumitriu, Ion Ionescu, Mircea Lucescu. Trainer: Ilie Oană

CYPRUS: Varnavas Christofi; Panikos Iakovou, Costas Christou "Kattos", Christofis Christofi, Kostas Panagiotou (Cap), Ploutis Pallas; George Kettenis, Drosos Kalotheou, Kostas Pierides, Panikos Krystallis, Andreas Stylianou.
Trainer: Pambos Avramides

Goals: Lucescu (4), Martinovici (15), Dumitriu II (24, 52, 77), I. Ionescu (47, 86)

CYPRUS v ROMANIA 1-5 (1-0)

GPS, Nicosia 03.12.1966

Referee: Arthur Lentini (MAL) Attendance: 4,800

CYPRUS: Nikos Eleftheriades; Costas Christou "Kattos", Kyriakos Koureas, Christofis Christofi, Kostas Panagiotou, Ploutis Pallas, Nikos Kantzilieris, Kostas Pierides, Pambos Papadopoulos "Pamboulis", Panikos Krystallis, Andreas Stylianou. Trainer: Gavalas

ROMANIA: Mihai Ionescu; Corneliu Popa, Ion Nunweiller, Dan Coe, Augustin Pax Deleanu; Vasile Gergely, Nicolae Dobrin; Ion Pîrcălab, Constantin Frăţilă, Mircea Dridea, Mircea Lucescu. Trainer: Ilie Oană

Goals: C. Pierides (39), Dridea (49, 82), Lucescu (51), Frăţilă (65, 74)

SWITZERLAND v ROMANIA 7-1 (3-0)

Hardturn, Zürich 24.05.1967

Referee: Robert Lacoste (FRA) Attendance: 30,000

SWITZERLAND: Marcel Kunz; Markus Pfirter, Ely Tacchella, Bruno Michaud, Georges Perroud; Karl Odermatt, Heinz Bäni, Richard Dürr; Fritz Künzli, Rolf Blättler, René Pierre Quentin.
Trainer: Erwin Ballabio

ROMANIA: Mihai Ionescu (46 Ilie Datcu); Corneliu Popa, Ion Nunweiller, Dumitru Nicolae, Mihai Mocanu; Vasile Gergely, Nicolae Dobrin; Ion Pîrcălab, Mircea Dridea, Ion Ionescu, Mircea Lucescu. Trainer: Ilie Oană

Goals: Künzli (12, 67), Quentin (15, 32), Blättler (46, 59), Odermatt (63), Dobrin (70)

ROMANIA v ITALY 0-1 (0-0)

23 August, București 25.06.1967

Referee: Manuel Gomez Arribas (SPA) Attendance: 65,000

ROMANIA: Răducanu Necula; Nicolae Lupescu, Ion Nunweiller (Cap), Ion Barbu, Mihai Mocanu; Vasile Gergely, Iuliu Năftănăilă; Mircea Lucescu, Emil Dumitriu, Ion Ionescu, Radu Nunweiller. Trainer: Angelo Niculescu

ITALY: Enrico Albertosi; Armando Picchi, Adolfo Gori, Aristide Guarneri, Mario Bertini, Giacinto Facchetti (Cap); Gianni Rivera, Giacomo Bulgarelli, Antonio Juliano, Gianfranco Zigoni, Ezio Pascutti.
Trainer: Ferruccio Valcareggi

Goal: Bertini (81)

ITALY v CYPRUS 5-0 (2-0)

San Vito, Cosenza 01.11.1967

Referee: Antoine Queudeville (LUX) Attendance: 25,000

ITALY: Enrico Albertosi; Tarcisio Burgnich, Giacinto Facchetti (Cap); Romano Fogli, Giancarlo Bercellino, Armando Picchi; Angelo Domenghini, Antonio Juliano, Alessandro Mazzola, Giancarlo De Sisti, Luigi Riva.
Trainer: Ferruccio Valcareggi

CYPRUS: Varnavas Christofi; Costas Christou "Kattos", Kyriakos Koureas; Ploutis Pallas, Kostas Panagiotou (Cap), Christofis Christofi; Nikos Kantzilieris, Stavrinos Konstantinou, Sofoklis Sofokli "Kotrofos" (.. P. Papadopoulos "Pamboulis"), Panikos Krystallis, Andreas Stylianou.
Trainer: Pambos Avramides

Goals: Mazzola (12, 22), Riva (46, 55, 59)

SWITZERLAND v CYPRUS 5-0 (2-0)

Lugano 08.11.1967

Referee: Robert Schaut (BEL) Attendance: 4,000

SWITZERLAND: Marcel Kunz; Markus Pfirter, Bruno Michaud, Ely Tacchella, Georges Perroud; Karl Odermatt, Hansruedi Fuhrer, Richard Dürr; Fritz Künzli, Rolf Blättler, René Pierre Quentin. Trainer: Erwin Ballabio

CYPRUS: Varnavas Christofi; Costas Christou "Kattos", Kyriakos Koureas, Kostas Panagiotou (Cap), Ploutis Pallas, Christofis Christofi, Sofoklis Sofokli "Kotrofos", Panikos Krystallis, Nikos Kantzilieris, Stavrinos Konstantinou, Andreas Stylianou. Trainer: Pambos Avramides

Goals: Blättler (30, 55), Künzli (41), Dürr (56 pen), Odermatt (72)

SWITZERLAND v ITALY 2-2 (1-0)

Wankdorf, Bern 18.11.1967

Referee: Istvan Zsolt (HUN) Attendance: 55,000

SWITZERLAND: Marcel Kunz; Markus Pfirter, Ely Tacchella; Bruno Michaud, Georges Perroud, Karl Odermatt (Cap); Hansruedi Fuhrer, Richard Dürr, Fritz Künzli, Rolf Blättler, René Pierre Quentin. Trainer: Erwin Ballabio

ITALY: Enrico Albertosi; Tarcisio Burgnich, Giacinto Facchetti (Cap); Roberto Rosato, Giancarlo Bercellino, Armando Picchi; Angelo Domenghini, Antonio Juliano, Roberto Boninsegna, Giancarlo De Sisti, Luigi Riva.
Trainer: Ferruccio Valcareggi

Goals: Quentin (34), Riva (66, 85 pen), Künzli (68)

ITALY v SWITZERLAND 4-0 (3-0)

Amsicora, Cagliari 23.12.1967

Referee: Thomas Wharton (SCO) Attendance: 30,000

ITALY: Enrico Albertosi; Tarcisio Burgnich, Giacinto Facchetti (Cap); Giorgio Ferrini, Giancarlo Bercellino, Armando Picchi; Angelo Domenghini, Gianni Rivera, Alessandro Mazzola, Antonio Juliano, Luigi Riva.
Trainer: Ferruccio Valcareggi

SWITZERLAND: Marcel Kunz (82 Karl Grob); Markus Pfirter, Ely Tacchella; Bruno Michaud, Georges Perroud, Karl Odermatt (Cap); Hansruedi Fuhrer, Richard Dürr, Bruno Bernasconi, Fritz Künzli, René Pierre Quentin.
Trainer: Erwin Ballabio

Goals: A. Mazzola (3), Riva (13), Domenghini (45, 67)

CYPRUS v SWITZERLAND 2-1 (1-0)

Nicosia 17.02.1968

Referee: Pavol Spotak (CZE) Attendance: 8,000

CYPRUS: Andreas Filotas (.. Michalis Alkiviades); Costas Christou "Kattos", Panikos Iakovou, Ioannis Xypolitas, Kostas Panagiotou (Cap), Panikos Krystallis, Panikos Efthimiades, Andreas Christodoulou "Pakkos", Pambos Papadopoulos "Pamboulis", Menelaos Melis Asprou, Drosos Kalotheou.
Trainer: Pambos Avramides

SWITZERLAND: Marcel Kunz; Markus Pfirter, Bruno Michaud, Renzo Bionda, Paul Marti, Karl Odermatt (Cap), Hansruedi Fuhrer, Richard Dürr, Fritz Künzli, Rolf Blättler, René Pierre Quentin. Trainer: Erwin Ballabio

Goals: Panagiotou (9 og), Asprou (22), Papadopoulos (46)

	P	W	D	L	F	A	Pts
Italy	6	5	1	0	17	3	11
Romania	6	3	0	3	18	14	5
Switzerland	6	2	1	3	17	13	5
Cyprus	6	1	0	5	3	25	2

GROUP 7

POLAND v LUXEMBOURG 4-0 (0-0)

Pogon, Szczecin 02.10.1966

Referee: Erwin Vetter (E. GER) Attendance: 25,000

POLAND: Stanislaw Majcher; Roman Strzalkowski, Pawel Orzechowski, Henryk Brejza, Zygmunt Anczok; Ryszard Grzegorczyk, Zygmunt Schmidt; Jerzy Sadek, Jan Liberda (Cap), Andrzej Jarosik, Janusz Kowalik.
Trainer: Klemens Nowak

LUXEMBOURG: Théo Stendebach; Erwin Kuffer, François Konter (Cap), Fernand Jeitz, Jean-Pierre Hoffstetter, René Schneider, Jean Hardt, Jean Klein, Johny Leonard, Nicolas Hoffmann, Edouard Dublin. Trainer: Robert Heinz

Goals: Jarosik (49), Liberda (54), Grzegorczyk (73), Sadek (88)

LUXEMBOURG v FRANCE 0-3 (0-3)

Stade Municipal, Luxembourg 26.11.1966

Referee: Laurens van Ravens (HOL) Attendance: 3000

LUXEMBOURG: Théo Stendebach; Erwin Kuffer, Fernand Jeitz, Mathias Ewen, Jean-Pierre Hoffstetter; Nicolas Hoffmann, François Konter, Ady Schmit (Cap); Edouard Dublin, Johny Leonard, Joseph Kirchens.
Trainer: Robert Heinz

FRANCE: Georges Carnus; Jean Djorkaeff, Marcel Artelesa (Cap), Bernard Bosquier, André Chorda; Joseph Bonnel, Michel Watteau; Yves Herbet, Hervé Revelli, Georges Lech, Laurent Robuschi. Trainers: Jean Snella & José Arribas

Goals: Herbet (8), H. Revelli (40), Lech (41)

FRANCE v POLAND 2-1 (1-0)

Parc des Princes, Paris 22.10.1966

Referee: Gerhard Schulenburg (W. GER) Attendance: 25,000

FRANCE: Georges Carnus; Jean Djorkaeff, Claude Robin, Robert Budzinski, André Chorda; Jean-Claude Suaudeau, Jacques Simon; Yves Herbet, Georges Lech, Fleury di Nallo, Paul Courtin. Trainers: Jean Snella & José Arribas

POLAND: Jan Gomola; Jacek Gmoch, Roman Strzalkowski, Stanislaw Oslizlo (Cap), Zygmunt Anczok; Piotr Suski, Ryszard Grzegorczyk; Jerzy Sadek, Wlodzimierz Lubanski, Jan Liberda, Andrzej Jarosik. Trainer: Klemes Nowak

Goals: di Nallo (26), Grzegorczyk (61), Lech (85)

LUXEMBOURG v BELGIUM 0-5 (0-3)

Stade Municipal, Luxembourg 19.03.1967

Referee: Karl Göppel (SWI) Attendance: 10,000

LUXEMBOURG: Théo Stendebach; Erwin Kuffer, Fernand Jeitz, François Konter (Cap), Jean-Pierre Hoffstetter; Nicolas Hoffmann, Mathias Ewen, Louis Pilot, Edouard Dublin, Johny Leonard, Henri Klein. Trainer: Robert Heinz

BELGIUM: Jean Nicolay; Georges Heylens, Pierre Hanon, Jean Plaskie, Florent Bohez, Wilfried Van Moer, Jef Jurion (Cap), Johnny Thio, Jacky Stockman, Paul Van Himst, Wilfried Puis. Trainers: Constant Van den Stock, Raymond Goethals

Goals: Van Himst (20, 36), Stockman (29, 60, 73)

BELGIUM v FRANCE 2-1 (0-0)

Heisel, Brussel 11.11.1966

Referee: John Keith Taylor (ENG) Attendance: 43,404

BELGIUM: Jean Nicolay; Georges Heylens, Pierre Hanon, Jean Plaskie, Yves Baré, Wilfried Van Moer, Jef Jurion (Cap), Johnny Thio, Raoul Lambert, Paul Van Himst, Wilfried Puis.
Trainers: Constant Van den Stock, Raymond Goethals

FRANCE: Georges Carnus; Jean Djorkaeff, Claude Robin, Robert Budzinski, André Chorda; Jacques Simon, Jean-Claude Suaudeau; Bernard Blanchet, Hervé Revelli, Georges Lech, Gérard Hausser. Trainers: Jean Snella & José Arribas

Goals: Van Himst (51, 54), Lech (67)

LUXEMBOURG v POLAND 0-0

Stade Municipal, Luxembourg 16.04.1967

Referee: Einer Poulsen (DEN) Attendance: 7,000

LUXEMBOURG: René Hoffmann; Erwin Kuffer, Fernand Jeitz, Mathias Ewen, Jean-Pierre Hoffstetter (Cap), Ady Schmidt, François Konter; Jean Klein, Louis Pilot, Johny Leonard, Edouard Dublin. Trainer: Robert Heinz

POLAND: Konrad Kornek; Roman Strzalkowski, Jacek Gmoch, Stanislaw Oslizlo (Cap), Zygmunt Anczok; Zygfryd Szoltysik, Zygmunt Schmidt; Krzysztof Hausner, Wlodzimierz Lubanski, Jerzy Musialek, Andrzej Jarosik.
Trainer: Michal Matyas

POLAND v BELGIUM 3-1 (2-0)

Slaski, Chorzów 21.05.1967

Referee: Toimi Olkku (FIN) Attendance: 65,000

POLAND: Konrad Kornek; Pawel Kowalski, Roman Strzalkowski, Jacek Gmoch, Zygmunt Anczok; Zygmunt Schmidt, Piotr Suski; Jerzy Sadek, Zygfryd Szoltysik, Wlodzimierz Lubanski, Jan Liberda (Cap).
Trainer: Michal Matyas

BELGIUM: Jean Nicolay; Georges Heylens, Albert Sulon, Jean Plaskie, Florent Bohez; Prudent Bettens, Jozef Jurion (Cap); Wilfried van Moer; Jacques Stockman, Paul van Himst, Wilfried Puis.
Trainers: Constant van den Stock, Raymond Goethals

Goals: Lubanski (28, 41), Puis (52), Szoltysik (72)

POLAND v FRANCE 1-4 (1-2)

Dziesieciolecia, Warszawa 17.09.1967

Referee: Ferdinand Marschall (AUS) Attendance: 70,000

POLAND: Hubert Kostka; Pawel Kowalski, Jacek Gmoch, Stanislaw Oslizlo, Zygmunt Anczok; Lucjan Brychczy (Cap), Piotr Suski; Eugeniusz Faber, Zygfryd Szoltysik, Wlodzimierz Lubanski, Robert Gadocha. Trainer: Michal Matyas

FRANCE: Marcel Aubour; Jean Djorkaeff, Roland Mitoraj, Bernard Bosquier, Jean Baeza; Yves Herbet, Robert Herbin (Cap), Henri Michel; André Guy, Fleury di Nallo, Charly Loubet. Trainer: Louis Dugauguez

Goals: Herbin (13), Brychczy (26), di Nallo (34, 85), Guy (63)

BELGIUM v POLAND 2-4 (2-2)

Heysel, Brussel 08.10.1967

Referee: Juan Gardeazabal Garay (SPA) Attendance: 45,000

BELGIUM: Jean Nicolay; Georges Heylens, Pierre Hanon (Cap), Jean Plaskie, Yves Baré; Paul Vandenberg, Johnny Thio, Alfons Haagdoren; Johan Devrindt, Paul van Himst, Wilfried Puis. Trainers: Constant van den Stock, Raymond Goethals

POLAND: Hubert Kostka; Antoni Piechniczek, Jacek Gmoch, Stanislaw Oslizlo, Stefan Szefer; Henryk Brejza, Lucjan Brychczy (Cap), Zygmunt Schmidt; Janusz Zmijewski, Wlodzimierz Lubanski, Eugeniusz Faber.
Trainer: Michal Matyas

Goals: Devrindt (15, 35), Zmijewski (26, 52, 70), Brychczy (45)

FRANCE v BELGIUM 1-1 (0-1)

Stade Marcel Saupin, Nantes 28.10.1967

Referee: Francesco Francescon (ITA) Attendance: 14,591

FRANCE: Marcel Aubour; Jean Djorkaeff, Bernard Bosquier, Claude Quittet, Jean Baeza; Yves Herbet, Henri Michel, Robert Herbin (Cap); Fleury Di Nallo, Hervé Revelli, Charly Loubet.
Trainer: Louis Dugauguez

BELGIUM: Fernand Boone; Georges Heylens, Jean Plaskie, André Stassart, Jean Cornelis; Pierre Hanon, Nicolas Dewalque; Johan Devrindt, Roger Claessen, Raoul Lambert, Wilfried Puis.
Trainers: Constant Van den Stock, Raymond Goethals

Goals: Claessen (37), Herbin (85)

BELGIUM v LUXEMBOURG 3-0 (0-0)

Klokke, Bruges 22.11.1967

Referee: William O'Neill (IRE) Attendance: 8,000

BELGIUM: Fernand Boone; Georges Heylens, Jean Plaskie, Alfons Peeters, Jean Cornelis, Pierre Hanon, Jean Docks, Johnny Thio, Roger Claessen, Johan Devrindt, Wilfried Puis.
Trainers: Constant Vandenstock, Raymond Goethals

LUXEMBOURG: René Hoffmann; Erwin Kuffer, Fernand Jeitz, Mathias Ewen, Jean-Pierre Hoffstetter (Cap); Nicolas Hoffmann, Louis Pilot, Jean Klein, Edouard Dublin, Johny Leonard, Ady Schmit. Trainer: Robert Heinz

Goals: Thio (62, 77), Claessen (65)

FRANCE v LUXEMBOURG 3-1 (1-0)

Parc des Princes, Paris 23.12.1967

Referee: Anibal da Silva Oliveira (POR) Attendance: 7320

FRANCE: Marcel Aubour; Jean Djorkaeff, Claude Quittet, Bernard Bosquier (Cap), Jean Baeza; Richard Krawczyk, Henri Michel, Robert Szczepaniak; Charly Loubet, Didier Couecou, Georges Bereta. Trainer: Louis Dugauguez

LUXEMBOURG: René Hoffmann; Erwin Kuffer, Fernand Jeitz, Mathias Ewen, Jean-Pierre Hoffstetter (Cap), François Konter, Louis Pilot; Jean Klein, Edouard Dublin, Johny Leonard, Ady Schmit. Trainer: Robert Heinz

Goal: Loubet (42, 47, 53), Klein (85)

	P	W	D	L	F	A	Pts
France	6	4	1	1	14	6	9
Belgium	6	3	1	2	14	9	7
Poland	6	3	1	2	13	9	7
Luxembourg	6	0	1	5	1	18	1

GROUP 8

NORTHERN IRELAND v ENGLAND 0-2 (0-1)

Belfast 22.10.1966

Referee: Robert Holley Davidson (SCO) Att: 48,600

N.IRELAND: Patrick Jennings (46 William McFaul); John Parke, Alexander Elder, Samuel Todd, Martin Harvey, William McCullough, William Ferguson, John Crossan, William Irvine, Derek Dougan, George Best. Manager: Robert Peacock

ENGLAND: Gordon Banks; George Reginald Cohen, Ramon Wilson, Norbert Stiles, Jack Charlton, Robert Frederick Moore, Alan James Ball, Geoffrey Charles Hurst, Robert Charlton, Roger Hunt, Martin Stanford Peters.
Manager: Alfred Ramsey

Sent off: Ferguson (89)

Goals: Hunt (40), Peters (59)

SCOTLAND v NORTHERN IRELAND 2-1 (2-1)

Hampden Park, Glasgow 16.11.1966

Referee: John Keith Taylor (ENG) Attendance: 45,281

SCOTLAND: Robert Ferguson; John Greig, Thomas Gemmell, William John Bremner, Ronald McKinnon, John Clark, William Henderson, Robert Murdoch, Joseph McBride, Stephen Chalmers, Robert Lennox.
Manager: Malcolm MacDonald

N. IRELAND: Patrick Jennings; John Parke, Alexander Elder, Martin Harvey, Terence Neill, James Nicholson, Samuel J.Wilson, John Crossan, William Irvine, Derek Dougan, David Clements. Manager: Robert Peacock

Goals: Nicholson (9), Lennox (35), Murdoch (40)

WALES v SCOTLAND 1-1 (0-0)

Ninian Park, Cardiff 22.10.1966

Referee: Kenneth Dagnall (ENG) Attendance: 32,500

WALES: Gary Sprake; Peter J.Rodrigues, Graham Williams, William T.Hennessey, Harold Michael England, Barrington Gerard Hole, Gilbert Ivor Reece, Ronald Wyn Davies, Ronald Tudor Davies, Clifford William Jones, Alan Leslie Jarvis.
Manager: David Bowen

SCOTLAND: Robert Ferguson; John Greig, Thomas Gemmell, William John Bremner, Ronald McKinnon, John Clark, James Johnstone, Denis Law, Joseph McBride, James Curran Baxter, William Henderson.
Manager: Malcolm MacDonald

Goals: R.T. Davies (77), Law (86)

NORTHERN IRELAND v WALES 0-0

Belfast 12.04.1967

Referee: Kevin Howley (ENG) Attendance: 17,000

N. IRELAND: Roderick Mc Kenzie; David Craig, Alexander Elder, Arthur Stewart, Terence Neill, James Nicholson, Eric Welsh, D. Trainor, Derek Dougan, Walter Bruce, David Clements. Manager: Robert Peacock

WALES: Anthony Horace Millington; Rodney John Thomas, Graham Williams, Alan Leslie Jarvis, Edward Glyn James, Barrington Gerard Hole, Ronald Raymond Rees, William Alan Durban, Ronald Tudor Davies, Thomas Royston Vernon, Keith David Pring. Manager: David Bowen

ENGLAND v WALES 5-1 (3-1)

Wembley, London 16.11.1966

Referee: Thomas Wharton (SCO) Attendance: 76,000

ENGLAND: Gordon Banks; George Reginald Cohen, Ramon Wilson, Norbert Stiles, Jack Charlton, Robert Frederick Moore, Alan James Ball, Geoffrey Charles Hurst, Robert Charlton, Roger Hunt, Martin Stanford Peters.
Manager: Alfred Ramsey

WALES: Anthony Horace Millington; Robert Colin Green, Graham Williams, William Terrence Hennessey, Harold Michael England, Barrington Gerard Hole, Ronald Raymond Rees, Ronald Wyn Davies, Ronald Tudor Davies, Clifford William Jones, Alan Leslie Jarvis. Manager: David Bowen

Goals: Hurst (30, 34), R.W. Davies (36), R. Charlton (43), Hennessy (65 og), J. Charlton (84)

ENGLAND v SCOTLAND 2-3 (0-1)

Wembley, London 15.04.1967

Referee: Gerhard Schulenburg (W. GER) Att: 100,000

ENGLAND: Gordon Banks; George Reginald Cohen, Ramon Wilson, Norbert Stiles, Jack Charlton, Robert Frederick Moore, Alan James Ball, James Peter Greaves, Robert Charlton, Geoffrey Charles Hurst, Martin Stanford Peters.
Manager: Alfred Ramsey

SCOTLAND: Ronald Campbell Simpson; Thomas Gemmell, Edward Graham McCreadie, John Greig, Ronald McKinnon, William John Bremner, James McCalliog, Denis Law, William Semple Wallace, James Curran Baxter, Robert Lennox.
Manager: Robert Brown

Goals: Law (27), Lennox (78), J. Charlton (84), McCalliog (87), Hurst (88)

NORTHERN IRELAND v SCOTLAND 1-0 (0-0)

Windsor Park, Belfast 21.10.1967

Referee: James Finney (ENG) Attendance: 55,000

N. IRELAND: Patrick Jennings; William McKeag, John Parke, Arthur Stewart, Terence Neill, David Clements, William Campbell, John Crossan, Derek Dougan, James Nicholson, George Best. Manager: William Bingham

SCOTLAND: Ronald Campbell Simpson; Thomas Gemmell, Edward Graham McCreadie, John Greig, Ronald McKinnon, John Francombe Ure, William Semple Wallace, Robert Murdoch, James McCalliog, Denis Law, William Morgan. Manager: Robert Brown

Goal: Clements (69)

WALES v ENGLAND 0-3 (0-1)

Ninian Park, Cardiff 21.10.1967

Referee: John Robertson Gordon (SCO) Att: 45,000

WALES: Gary Sprake; Peter J. Rodrigues, Robert Colin Green, William Terrence Hennessey, Harold Michael England, Barrington Gerard Hole, Ronald Raymond Rees, William Alan Durban, John Francis Mahoney, Thomas Royston Vernon, Clifford William Jones. Manager: David Bowen

ENGLAND: Gordon Banks; George Reginald Cohen, Keith Robert Newton, Alan Patrick Mullery, Jack Charlton, Robert Frederick Moore, Alan James Ball, Roger Hunt, Robert Charlton, Geoffrey Charles Hurst, Martin Stanford Peters. Manager: Alfred Ramsey

Goals: Peters (34), R. Charlton (87), Ball (90 pen)

ENGLAND v NORTHERN IRELAND 2-0 (1-0)

Wembley, London 22.11.1967

Referee: Leo Callaghan (WAL) Attendance: 85,000

ENGLAND: Gordon Banks; George Reginald Cohen, Ramon Wilson, Alan Patrick Mullery, David Sadler, Robert Frederick Moore, Peter Thompson, Roger Hunt, Robert Charlton, Geoffrey Charles Hurst, Martin Stanford Peters. Manager: Alfred Ramsey

N. IRELAND: Patrick Jennings; John Parke, Alexander Elder, Arthur Stewart, Terence Neill, Martin Harvey, William Campbell, William Irvine, Samuel J. Wilson, James Nicholson, David Clements. Manager: William Bingham

Goals: Hurst (43), R. Charlton (62)

SCOTLAND v WALES 3-2 (1-1)

Hampden Park, Glasgow 22.11.1967

Referee: James Finney (ENG) Attendance: 57,000

SCOTLAND: Robert Brown Clark; James Philip Craig, Edward Graham McCreadie, John Greig, Ronald McKinnon, James Curran Baxter, James Johnstone, William John Bremner, Alan John Gilzean, William Johnston, Robert Lennox. Manager: Robert Brown

WALES: Gary Sprake; Peter J. Rodrigues, Robert Colin Green, William Terrence Hennessey, Edward Glyn James, Barrington Gerard Hole, Ronald Raymond Rees, Ronald Wyn Davies, Ronald Tudor Davies, William Alan Durban, Clifford William Jones. Manager: David Bowen

Goals: Gilzean (16, 65), R.T. Davies (18), Durban (57), McKinnon (78)

SCOTLAND v ENGLAND 1-1 (1-1)

Hampden Park, Glasgow 24.02.1968

Referee: Laurens van Ravens (HOL) Attendance: 134,000

SCOTLAND: Ronald Campbell Simpson; Thomas Gemmell, Edward Graham McCreadie, William McNeill, Ronald McKinnon, John Greig, Charles Cooke, William John Bremner, John Hughes, William Johnston, Robert Lennox. Manager: Robert Brown

ENGLAND: Gordon Banks; Keith Robert Newton, Ramon Wilson, Alan Patrick Mullery, Brian Leslie Labone, Robert Frederick Moore, Alan James Ball, Geoffrey Charles Hurst, Michael George Summerbee, Robert Charlton, Martin Stanford Peters. Manager: Alfred Ramsey

Goals: Peters (19), Hughes (39)

WALES v NORTHERN IRELAND 2-0 (0-0)

Wrexham 28.02.1968

Referee: Robert Holley Davidson (SCO) Att: 17,500

WALES: Anthony Horace Millington; Peter J. Rodrigues, Robert Colin Green, William Terrence Hennessey, Harold Michael England, Barrington Gerard Hole, Ronald Raymond Rees, Ronald Wyn Davies, Ronald Tudor Davies, William Alan Durban, Graham Williams. Manager: David Bowen

N. IRELAND: Patrick Jennings; David Craig, Alexander Elder, Martin Harvey, Samuel Todd, William McKeag, William Irvine, Arthur Stewart, Derek Dougan, James Nicholson, Terence Harkin. Manager: William Bingham

Goals: Rees (75), R.W. Davies (84)

	P	W	D	L	F	A	Pts
England	6	4	1	1	15	5	9
Scotland	6	3	2	1	10	8	8
Wales	6	1	2	3	6	12	4
Northern Ireland	6	1	1	4	2	8	3

QUARTER-FINALS

ENGLAND v SPAIN 1-0 (0-0)

Wembley, London 03.04.1968

Referee: Gilbert Droz (SWI) Attendance: 100,000

ENGLAND: Gordon Banks; Cyril Barry Knowles, Ramon Wilson, Alan Patrick Mullery, Jack Charlton, Robert Frederick Moore, Alan James Ball, Roger Hunt, Michael George Summerbee, Robert Charlton, Martin Stanford Peters. Manager: Alfred Ramsey

SPAIN: Salvador SADURNÍ Urpi; José Ignacio SAEZ Ruiz, Francisco Fernandez GALLEGO, Ignacio ZOCO Esparza, Juan Manuel CANÓS Ferrer; José Martinez Sánchez PIRRI, Manuel Polinario Muñoz "POLI", José CLARAMUNT Torres; AMANCIO Amaro Varela, Fernando ANSOLA San Martin, Ramón Moreno GROSSO. Trainer: Domingo Balmanya

Goal: R. Charlton (84)

YUGOSLAVIA v FRANCE 5-1 (4-1)

Crvena Zvezda, Beograd 24.04.1968

Referee: Paul Schiller (AUS) Attendance: 70,900

YUGOSLAVIA: Ilija Pantelić; Mirsad Fazlagić, Dragan Holcer; Rudolf Belin, Mladen Ramljak, Ljubomir Mihajlović; Ilija Petković, Dobrivoje Trivić, Vahidin Musemić, Ivan Osim, Dragan Dzajić. Trainer: Rajko Mitić

FRANCE: Marcel Aubour; Vincent Esteve, Claude Quittet, Bernard Bosquier (Cap), Jean Baeza; Yves Herbet, Jean Djorkaeff, Robert Szczepaniak; André Guy, Fleury di Nallo, Charly Loubet. Trainer: Louis Dugauguez

Goals: I. Petkovic (4, 20), V. Musemic (12 pen, 65), Dzajic (14), Di Nallo (21)

SPAIN v ENGLAND 1-2 (0-0)

Estadio Santiago Bernabeu, Madrid 08.05.1968

Referee: Josef Krnavek (CZE) Attendance: 120,000

SPAIN: Salvador SADURNÍ Urpi; José Ignacio SAEZ Ruiz, Francisco Fernandez GALLEGO, Ignacio ZOCO Esparza, Juan Manuel CANÓS Ferrer; José Martinez Sánchez PIRRI, Ramón Moreno GROSSO, Manuel VELAZQUEZ Villaverde, Joaquín RIFE Climent, AMANCIO Amaro Varela, Francisco GENTO López. Trainer: Domingo Balmanya

ENGLAND: Peter Phillip Bonetti; Keith Robert Newton, Ramon Wilson, Alan Patrick Mullery, Brian Leslie Labone, Robert Frederick Moore, Alan James Ball, Martin Stanford Peters, Robert Charlton, Roger Hunt, Norman Hunter. Manager: Alfred Ramsey

Goals: Amancio (48), Peters (55), Hunter (82)

BULGARIA v ITALY 3-2 (1-0)

Vasil Levski, Sofia 06.04.1968

Referee: Gerhard Schulenburg (W. GER) Attendance: 70,000

BULGARIA: Stancho Bonchev; Aleksandar Shalamanov, Dimitar Penev, Boris Gaganelov (Cap), Dobromir Jechev, Dimitar Iakimov, Georgi Popov, Petar Jekov, Georgi Asparuhov, Nikola Kotkov, Dinko Dermendjiev. Trainer: Stefan Bojkov

ITALY: Enrico Albertosi (66 Lido Vieri); Tarcisio Burgnich, Giacinto Facchetti (Cap); Mario Bertini, Giancarlo Bercellino, Armando Picchi; Angelo Domenghini, Antonio Juliano, Alessandro Mazzola, Gianni Rivera, Pierino Prati. Trainer: Ferruccio Valcareggi

Goals: Kotkov (11 pen), Penev (60 og), Dermendjiev (66), Jekov (73), Prati (83)

FRANCE v YUGOSLAVIA 1-1 (0-0)

Vélodrome, Marseille 06.04.1968

Referee: Erwin Vetter (E. GER) Attendance: 35,423

FRANCE: Marcel Aubour; Jean Djorkaeff, Claude Quittet, Bernard Bosquier (Cap), Jean Baeza; Robert Herbin, Jacques Simon; Charly Loubet, Nestor Combin, Fleury di Nallo, Georges Bereta. Trainer: Louis Dugauguez

YUGOSLAVIA: Ilija Pantelić; Mirsad Fazlagić, Dragan Holcer; Borivoje Djordjević, Blagoje Paunović, Ljubomir Mihajlović; Dzemaludin Musović, Ivan Osim, Vahidin Musemić, Dobrivoje Trivić, Dragan Dzajić. Trainer: Rajko Mitić

Goals: Musemic (66), Di Nallo (78)

ITALY v BULGARIA 2-0 (1-0)

San Paolo, Napoli 20.04.1968

Referee: Gottfried Dienst (SWI) Attendance: 95,000

ITALY: Dino Zoff; Tarcisio Burgnich, Giacinto Facchetti (Cap); Giorgio Ferrini, Aristide Guarneri, Ernesto Castano; Angelo Domenghini, Antonio Juliano, Alessandro Mazzola, Gianni Rivera, Pierino Prati. Trainer: Ferruccio Valcareggi

BULGARIA: Simeon Simeonov; Aleksandar Shalamanov, Ivan Dimitrov, Boris Gaganelov (Cap), Dobromir Jechev, Dimitar Penev, Georgi Popov, Hristo Bonev, Georgi Asparuhov, Dimitar Iakimov, Dinko Dermendjiev. Trainer: Stefan Bojkov

Goals: Prati (14), Domenghini (55)

HUNGARY v USSR 2-0 (1-0)

Népstadion, Budapest 04.05.1968

Referee: Laurens van Ravens (HOL) Attendance: 80,000

HUNGARY: Károly Fatér; Dezsö Novák, Ernö Solymosi, Kálmán Ihász, Kálmán Mészöly; Lajos Szücs, László Fazekas; János Göröcs, Zoltán Varga, János Farkas, Gyula Rákosi. Trainer: Károly Sós

USSR: Anzor Kavazashvili; Iuriy Istomin, Albert Shesternev (Cap), Murtaz Hurtsilava, Viktor Anichkin, Valeri Voronin, Igor Chislenko, Vladimir Kaplichnîi, Anatoliy Banishevski, Eduard Streltsov, Eduard Malofeev. Trainer: Mihail Iakushin

Goals: Farkas (21), Göröcs (85)

USSR v HUNGARY 3-0 (1-0)

Central V.I. Lenin 11.05.1968

Referee: Kurt Tschentscher (W. GER) Attendance: 102,000

USSR: Iuriy Pshenichnikov; Valentin Afonin, Albert Shesternev (Cap), Murtaz Hurtsilava, Viktor Anichkin, Valeri Voronin, Igor Chislenko, Vladimir Kaplichnîi, Anatoliy Banishevski, Anatoliy Bîshovets, Gennadiy Evriujihin. Trainer: Mihail Iakushin

HUNGARY: Gyula Tamás; Dezsö Novák, Ernö Solymosi, Kálmán Ihász, Kálmán Mészöly; Lajos Szücs, Zoltán Varga; Imre Komora, Flórián Albert, János Farkas, Gyula Rákosi. Trainer: Károly Sós

Goals: Solymosy (22 og), Hurtsilava (59), Bîshovets (73)

SEMI-FINALS

ITALY v USSR 0-0 (AET)

San Paolo, Napoli 05.06.1968

Referee: Kurt Tschenscher (W. GER) Attendance: 75,000

ITALY: Dino Zoff; Tarcisio Burgnich, Giacinto Facchetti (Cap); Giancarlo Bercellino, Ernesto Castano, Giorgio Ferrini; Angelo Domenghini, Antonio Juliano, Alessandro Mazzola, Gianni Rivera, Pierino Prati. Trainer: Ferruccio Valcareggi

USSR: Iuriy Pshenichnikov; Iuriy Istomin, Albert Shesternev (Cap), Vladimir Kaplichnîi, Valentin Afonin; Aleksandr Lenev, Eduard Malofeev, Gennadi Logofet; Anatoliy Banishevski, Anatoliy Bîshovets, Gennadiy Evriujihin. Trainer: Mihail Iakushin

ITALY won on the toss of a coin

YUGOSLAVIA v ENGLAND 1-0 (0-0)

Comunale, Firenze 05.06.1968

Referee: José María Ortiz de Mendibil (SPA) Att: 21,834

YUGOSLAVIA: Ilija Pantelic; Mirsad Fazlagic (Cap), Milan Damjanovic, Miroslav Pavlovic, Blagoje Paunovic; Dragan Holcer, Ilija Petkovic, Dobrivoje Trivic; Vahidin Musemic, Ivan Osim, Dragan Dzajic. Trainer: Rajko Mitic

ENGLAND: Gordon Banks; Keith Robert Newton, Ramon Wilson; Alan Patrick Mullery, Brian Leslie Labone, Robert Frederick Moore (Cap); Alan James Ball, Martin Stanford Peters, Robert Charlton, Roger Hunt, Norman Hunter. Manager: Alfred Ramsey

Sent off: Mullery (86)

Goal: Dzajic (86)

THIRD PLACE MATCH

ENGLAND v USSR 2-0 (1-0)

Stadio Olimpico, Roma 08.06.1968

Referee: Istvan Zsolt (HUN) Attendance: 50,000

ENGLAND: Gordon Banks; Thomas James Wright, Ramon Wilson; Norbert Stiles, Brian Leslie Labone, Robert Frederick Moore (Cap), Norman Hunter, Roger Hunt, Robert Charlton, Geoffrey Charles Hurst, Martin Stanford Peters. Manager: Alfred Ramsey

USSR: Iuriy Pshenichnikov; Iuriy Istomin, Albert Shesternev (Cap), Vladimir Kaplichnîi, Valentin Afonin; Aleksandr Lenev, Eduard Malofeev, Gennadi Logofet; Anatoliy Banishevski, Anatoliy Bîshovets, Gennadiy Evriujihin. Trainer: Mihail Iakushin

Goals: R. Charlton (39), Hurst (63)

FINAL

ITALY v YUGOSLAVIA 1-1 (0-1, 1-1) (AET)

Stadio Olimpico, Roma 08.06.1968

Referee: Gottfried Dienst (SWI) Attendance: 68,817

ITALY: Dino Zoff; Tarcisio Burgnich, Giacinto Facchetti (Cap); Giorgio Ferrini, Aristide Guarneri, Ernesto Castano; Angelo Domenghini, Antonio Juliano, Pietro Anastasi, Giovanni Lodetti, Pierino Prati. Trainer: Ferruccio Valcareggi

YUGOSLAVIA: Ilija Pantelic; Mirsad Fazlagic (Cap), Milan Damjanovic; Miroslav Pavlovic, Blagoje Paunovic, Dragan Holcer; Ilija Petkovic, Dobrivoje Trivic; Vahidin Musemic, Jovan Acimovic, Dragan Dzajic (Cap). Trainer: Rajko Mitić

Goals: Dzajic (39), Domenghini (80)

FINAL REPLAY

ITALY v YUGOSLAVIA 2-0 (2-0)

Stadio Olimpico, Roma 10.06.1968

Referee: José María Ortiz de Mendibil (SPA) Att: 32,886

ITALY: Dino Zoff; Tarcisio Burgnich, Giacinto Facchetti (Cap); Roberto Rosato, Aristide Guarneri, Sandro Salvadore; Angelo Domenghini, Alessandro Mazzola, Pietro Anastasi, Giancarlo De Sisti, Luigi Riva. Trainer: Ferruccio Valcareggi

YUGOSLAVIA: Ilija Pantelic; Mirsad Fazlagic (Cap), Milan Damjanovic; Miroslav Pavlovic, Blagoje Paunovic, Dragan Holcer; Jovan Acimovic, Dobrivoje Trivic, Vahidin Musemic, Idriz Hosic, Dragan Dzajic (Cap). Trainer: Rajko Mitic

Goals: Riva (12), Anastasi (31)

Goalscorers European Football Championship 1968

7 goals: Luigi Riva (Italy)

6 goals: János Farkas (Hungary)

5 goals: Gerhard Müller (Germany), Henning Frenzel (East Germany), Constantin Frățilă (Romania), Fritz Künzli (Switzerland), Angelo Domenghini, Alessandro Mazzola (Italy), Fleury Di Nallo (France), Robert Charlton, Geoffrey Hurst (England)

4 goals: Giorgos Sideris (Greece), Rolf Blättler (Switzerland), Paul Van Himst (Belgium), Martin Peters (England), Petar Jekov (Bulgaria)

3 goals: Inge Danielsson (Sweden), Dinko Dermendjiev (Bulgaria), Juhani Peltonen (Finland), Leopold Grausam (Austria), Anatoliy Banishevski, Igor Chislenko, Eduard Malofeev, Jozsef Sabo (USSR), Johannes Löhr (Germany), Dragan Dzajic, Vahidin Musemic, Slaven Zambata (Yugoslavia), Flórián Albert, Kálmán Mészöly (Hungary), Kresten Bjerre (Denmark), René Pierre Quentin, Karl Odermatt (Switzerland), Emil Dumitriu, Mircea Dridea (Romania), Janusz Zmijewski (Poland), Georges Lech, Charly Loubet (France), Jacques Stockman (Belgium)

2 goals: Ogün (Turkey), Pirri (Spain), Adamec (Czechoslovakia), Eriksson, Turesson (Sweden), Eusebio, Graça (Portugal), Kotkov, Tsanev (Bulgaria), K. Hasund, Iversen, Nilsen (Norway), Alexiadis (Greece), Siber (Austria), Petkovic, Osim (Yugoslavia), Bene (Hungary), Cruijff, Mulder, Suurbier (Holland), Pankau (East Germany), Søndergaard (Denmark), Dobrin, Lucescu, I. Ionescu (Romania), Brychczy, Lubanski, Grzegorczyk (Poland), Herbin (France), Claessen, Devrindt, Thio (Belgium), J. Charlton (England), R.T. Davies, R.W. Davies (Wales), Gilzean, Law, Lennox (Scotland), Bîshovets, Hurtsilava (USSR), Prati (Italy)

1 goal: Treacy, O'Connor, Cantwell, O'Neill, McEvoy (Republic of Ireland), Ayhan (Turkey), Amancio, Gárate, Grosso, Gento, José María (Spain), Kuna, Horváth, Jurkanin, Szikora, Masny (Czechoslovakia), Svensson, Nordahl (Sweden), Torres, Pinto (Portugal), Mitkov, Asparuhov (Bulgaria), Berg, Birkeland, Sunde (Norway), Papaioannou, Haitas (Greece), Syrjävaara, Makempar (Finland), Flögel, Hof, Wolny (Austria), Maslov, Streltsov (USSR), Seeler (Germany), Spreco, Lazarevic, Skoblar (Yugoslavia), Israël, Keizer, Swart, Van Der Kuylen, Pijs (Holland), Körner, Löwe, Vogel (East Germany), Dyreborg (Denmark), Martinovici (Romania), Dürr (Switzerland), Bertini, Facchetti, De Paoli, Anastasi (Italy), Asprou, Pamboulis, Kostakis (Cyprus), Szoltysik, Jarosik, Liberda, Sadek (Poland), Guy, Herbet, H. Revelli (France), Puis (Belgium), Klein (Luxembourg), Ball, Hunt, Hunter (England), Rees, Durban (Wales), Hughes, Mckinnon, Mccalliog, Murdoch (Scotland), Clements, Nicholson (N. Ireland), Varga, Molnar, Göröcs (Hungary)

Own goals: Dempsey (Republic of Ireland) for Czechoslovakia, Kostas (Cyprus) for Switzerland, Hennessy (Wales) for England, Solymosy (Hungary) for USSR, Penev (Bulgaria) for Italy

THE EUROPEAN FOOTBALL CHAMPIONSHIP 1972

GROUP 1

CZECHOSLOVAKIA v FINLAND 1-1 (1-1)

Praha 07.10.1970

Referee: William O'Neill (IRE) Attendance: 12,000

FINLAND: Paavo Heinonen; Pertti Mäkipää, Seppo Kilponen, Vilho Rajantie, Timo Kautonen, Jouko Suomalainen, Pekka Heikkilä, Raimo Toivanen, Pentti Toivola, Olavi Litmanen, Matti Paatelainen (73 Seppo Mäkelä).
Trainer: Olavi Laaksonen

CZECHOSLOVAKIA: Frantisek Schmucker; Jiri Vecerek, Jozef Bomba, Jozef Desiatnik (75 Oldrich Urban), Peter Mutkovic; Vladímir Mojzis, Dusan Bartovic; Stanislav Strunc, Alexander Nagy (69 Frantisek Hoholko), Pavel Stratil, Milan Albrecht. Trainers: Antonín Rygr, Vejvoda, Michael Vican

Goal: Albrecht (31), Paatelainen (44)

ROMANIA v FINLAND 3-0 (2-0)

"23 August", București 11.10.1970

Referee: Leonidas Vamvakopoulos (GRE) Att: 50,000

ROMANIA: Răducanu Necula; Lajos Sătmăreanu, Nicolae Lupescu, Cornel Dinu (Cap), Iosif Vigu; Ion Dumitru, Radu Nunweiller; Alexandru Neagu (46 Gheorghe Tătaru), Nicolae Dobrin, Florea Dumitrache, Florian Dumitrescu.
Trainer: Angelo Niculescu

FINLAND: Paavo Heinonen; Pertti Mäkipää (Cap), Seppo Kilponen, Vilho Rajantie, Timo Kautonen; Jouko Suomalainen (55 Seppo Mäkelä), Pekka Heikkila (67 Olavi Litmanen), Raimo Saviomaa, Pentti Toivola, Raimo Toivanen, Matti Paatelainen. Trainer: Olavi Laaksonen

Goals: Dumitrache (28, 42), R. Nunweiller (77)

WALES v ROMANIA 0-0

Ninian Park, Cardiff 11.11.1970

Referee: Arie van Gemert (HOL) Attendance: 50,000

WALES: Gareth Sprake; Peter Joseph Rodrigues, Harold Michael England, David Powell, Rodney John Thomas; William Alan Durban, Graham Moore; Barrington Gerard Hole, Richard Leslie Krzywicki, Ronald Wyn Davies, Ronald Raymond Rees. Trainer: David Bowen

ROMANIA: Răducanu Necula; Lajos Sătmăreanu, Nicolae Lupescu, Cornel Dinu (46 Bujor Hălmăgeanu), Mihai Mocanu; Ion Dumitru, Radu Nunweiller; Alexandru Neagu, Nicolae Dobrin (76 Flavius Domide), Florea Dumitrache, Florian Dumitrescu. Trainer: Angelo Niculescu

WALES v CZECHOSLOVAKIA 1-3 (0-0)

Swansea 21.04.1971

Referee: Einar Boström (SWE) Attendance: 20,000

WALES: Anthony Horace Millington; Peter Joseph Rodrigues, Rodney John Thomas; Leighton Phillips, Edward Glyn James, Thomas John Walley, Ronald Raymond Rees, William Alan Durban, Ronald Tudor Davies, Ronald Wyn Davies, John Francis Mahoney (.. Arfon Trevor Griffiths).
Manager: David Bowen

CZECHOSLOVAKIA: Ivo Viktor; Karol Dobias, Vladimír Hrivnák, Jozef Desiatnik, Vladimír Táborsky; Jaroslav Pollák, Ladislav Kuna, Jozef Adamec; Frantisek Vesely, Pavel Stratil, Ján Capkovic. Trainers: Ladislav Novák, Ladislav Kacáni

Goals: R.T. Davies (59 pen), Capkovic (78, 83), Táborsky (79)

CZECHOSLOVAKIA v ROMANIA 1-0 (0-0)

Slovan, Bratislava 16.05.1971

Referee: Fernando dos Santos Leite (POR) Att: 60,000

CSSR: Ivo Viktor; Karol Dobias, Vladimír Hrivnác, Jozef Desiatnik, Vladimír Táborski; Jaroslav Pollák, Ladislav Kuna; Jozef Adamec, Frantisek Vesely, Pavel Stratil (72 Karol Jokl), Ján Capkovic (76 Dusan Kabát).
Trainers: Ladislav Novák & Ladislav Kacáni

ROMANIA: Răducanu Necula; Lajos Sătmăreanu, Cornel Dinu, Dan Coe, Mihai Mocanu; Dan Sabin Anca, Ion Dumitru; Alexandru Neagu (61 Radu Nunweiller), Emerich Dembrovschi, Florea Dumitrache, Mircea Lucescu.
Trainer: Angelo Niculescu

Goal: Fr. Vesely (88)

FINLAND v WALES 0-1 (0-0)

Helsinki 26.05.1971

Referee: Günter Männig (E. GER) Attendance: 5,410

FINLAND: Lars Näsman; Timo Kautonen, Raimo Saviomaa, Vilho Rajantie, Jouko Suomalainen, Timo Nummelin, Pekka Heikkilä, Raimo Toivanen (.. Jarmo Flink), Matti Paatelainen, Arto Tolsa, Tommy Lindholm. Trainer: Olavi Laaksonen

WALES: Anthony Horace Millington; Malcolm Edward Page, Stephen Clifford Derrett, William Alan Durban, John Griffith Roberts, Raymond Mielczarek, Richard Leslie Krzywicki, Philip Wayne Jones, Ronald Raymond Rees, John Benjamin Toshack, Gilbert Ivor Reece. Manager: David Bowen

Goal: Toshack (54)

FINLAND v CZECHOSLOVAKIA 0-4 (0-2)

Helsinki 16.06.1971

Referee: Marian Srodecki (POL) Attendance: 4,658

FINLAND: Lars Näsman; Timo Kautonen, Vilho Rajantie, Seppo Kilponen, Jouko Suomalainen, Timo Nummelin, Pekka Heikkilä (.. Matti Paatelainen), Raimo Toivanen (.. Tommy Lindholm), Arto Tolsa, Jarmo Flink, Olavi Rissanen. Trainer: Olavi Laaksonen

CZECHOSLOVAKIA: Ivo Viktor; Karol Dobias, Vladimír Hrivnác, Jozef Desiatnik, Vladimír Táborski; Jaroslav Pollák, Ladislav Kuna; Jozef Adamec (76 Ivan Hrdlicka), Frantisek Vesely (76 Frantisek Karkó), Pavel Stratil, Ján Capkovic. Trainers: Ladislav Novák & Ladislav Kacáni

Goals: Capkovic (10), Pollák (16), Karkó (83, 90)

FINLAND v ROMANIA 0-4 (0-2)

Olimpic, Helsinki 22.09.1971

Referee: Pius Kamber (SWI) Attendance: 2,084

FINLAND: Lars Näsman (46 Paavo Heinonen); Jouko Suomalainen, Raimo Saviomaa, Ari Mäkynen, Esko Ranta; Raimo Toivanen (58 Timo Nummelin), Pekka Heikkila; Miika Toivola, Timo Rahja, Antero Nikkanen, Tommy Lindholm. Trainer: Olavi Laaksonen

ROMANIA: Răducanu Necula; Lajos Sătmăreanu, Nicolae Lupescu, Cornel Dinu, Mihai Mocanu; Ion Dumitru, Radu Nunweiller; Mircea Lucescu (Cap), Emerich Dembrovschi, Alexandru Neagu, Anghel Iordănescu (46 Gheorghe Tătaru). Trainer: Angelo Niculescu

Goals: Iordănescu (25), Lupescu (37), Dembrovschi (55), Lucescu (64 pen)

WALES v FINLAND 3-0 (1-0)

Swansea 13.10.1971

Referee: Kaj Rasmussen (DEN) Attendance: 10,301

WALES: Gareth Sprake (.. Anthony Horace Millington); Peter Joseph Rodrigues, Rodney John Thomas; John Griffith Roberts, Harold Michael England, William Terrence Hennessey, Brian Clifford Evans, Gilbert Ivor Reece, John Benjamin Toshack, William Alan Durban, Trevor Hockey. Manager: David Bowen

FINLAND: Lars Näsman; Seppo Kilponen, Raimo Saviomaa, Ari Mäkynen, Pekka Kosonen, Raimo Elo, Jarmo Flink, Miika Toivola, Heikki Suhonen (30 Henry Bergström), Pekka Heikkilä, Tommy Lindholm. Trainer: Olavi Laaksonen

Goals: Durban (10), Toshack (53), Reece (89)

CZECHOSLOVAKIA v WALES 1-0 (0-0)

Praha 27.10.1971

Referee: Mariano Medina Iglesias (SPA) Att: 32,000

CZECHOSLOVAKIA: Ivo Viktor; Karol Dobias, Vladimír Hrivnák, L'udevít Zlocha, Vladimír Táborsky; Jaroslav Pollák, Ladislav Kuna, Karol Jokl (65 Ondrej Danko), Bohumil Vesely (78 Zdenek Nehoda), Pavel Stratil, Dusan Kabat. Trainers: Ladislav Novák, Ladislav Kacáni

WALES: Anthony Horace Millington; Peter Joseph Rodrigues, Leighton Phillips, Alwyn Derek Burton, Rodney John Thomas; Terence Charles Yorath, William Terrence Hennessey (66 Ronald Raymond Rees); William Alan Durban, Brian Clifford Evans (78 Richard Leslie Krzywicki), Michael Richard Hill, Leighton James. Manager: David Bowen

Goal: Kuna (60)

ROMANIA v CZECHOSLOVAKIA 2-1 (1-0)

"23 August", Bucureşti 14.11.1971

Referee: Milivoje Gugulovic (YUG) Attendance: 70,000

ROMANIA: Răducanu Necula; Lajos Sătmăreanu, Nicolae Lupescu, Cornel Dinu, Augustin Deleanu; Dan Sabin Anca, Radu Nunweiller; Mircea Lucescu (Cap), Emerich Dembrovschi (72 Flavius Domide), Nicolae Dobrin, Anghel Iordănescu. Trainer: Angelo Niculescu

CZECHOSLOVAKIA: Ivo Viktor; Karol Dobias, Vladimír Hrivnác, Vladimír Hagara, Vladimír Táborski; Jaroslav Pollák, Ladislav Kuna, Ivan Hrdlicka; Bohumil Vesely (71 Zdenek Nehoda), Pavel Stratil, Ján Capkovic. Trainers: Ladislav Novák & Ladislav Kacáni

Goals: Dembrovschi (26), Capkovic (51), Dobrin (52)

ROMANIA v WALES 2-0 (1-0)

"23 August", Bucureşti 24.11.1971

Referee: Alfred Delcourt (BEL) Attendance: 50,000

ROMANIA: Răducanu Necula; Lajos Sătmăreanu, Nicolae Lupescu, Cornel Dinu, Augustin Deleanu; Ion Dumitru, Radu Nunweiller, Mircea Lucescu (Cap), Emerich Dembrovschi, Nicolae Dobrin, Anghel Iordănescu. Trainer: Angelo Niculescu

WALES: Anthony Horace Millington; Peter Joseph Rodrigues, Leighton Phillips, Herbert John Williams, Rodney John Thomas; Trevor Hockey, Leighton James, Michael Richard Hill (46 Cyril Davies), Ronald Tudor Davies, Gilbert Ivor Reece, Ronald Raymond Rees. Manager: David Bowen

Goals: Lupescu (9), Lucescu (74)

	P	W	D	L	F	A	Pts
Romania	6	4	1	1	11	2	9
Czechoslovakia	6	4	1	1	11	4	9
Wales	6	2	1	3	5	6	5
Finland	6	0	1	5	1	16	1

GROUP 2

NORWAY v HUNGARY 1-3 (0-2)

Ullevåll, Oslo 07.10.1970

Referee: Adrianus Boogaerts (HOL) Attendance: 15,000

NORWAY: Geir Karlsen; Per Pettersen, Finn Thorsen, Thor Spydevold, Sigbjørn Slinning; Trygve Bornø, Olav Nilsen, Svein Kvia, Egil Roger Olsen, Odd Iversen (86 Kjetil Hasund), Tor Fuglset (46 Finn Seemann). Trainer: Oivind Johannesen

HUNGARY: Adám Rothermel; Ernö Noskó, Kálmán Mészöly, Csaba Vidáts, Miklós Páncsics, Zoltán Halmosi, Sándor Müller; László Fazekas, Lajos Kocsis, Ferenc Bene, László Nagy. Trainer: József Hoffer

Goals: Bene (6), L. Nagy (23), Iversen (50), Karlsen (69 og)

FRANCE v NORWAY 3-1 (1-0)

Gerland, Lyon 11.11.1970

Referee: Antonio Saldanha Ribeiro (POR) Att: 10,357

FRANCE: Georges Carnus; Jean Djorkaeff (Cap), Jacques Novi, Bernard Bosquier, Jean-Paul Rostagni; Georges Lech, Henri Michel, Jean-Noël Huck, Michel Mézy; Louis Floch, Charly Loubet. Trainer: Georges Boulogne

NORWAY: Per Haftorsen; Per Pettersen, Arild Hetløen, Finn Thorsen, Thor Spydevold, Sigbjørn Slinning; Trygve Bornø, Olav Nilsen, Finn Seemann, Harry Hestad, Egil Roger Olsen. Trainer: Oivind Johannesen

Goals: Floch (30), G. Lech (55), Mézy (63), O. Nilsen (79)

BULGARIA v NORWAY 1-1 (1-0)

Vasil Levski, Sofia 15.11.1970

Referee: Mihael Kirakidis (CYP) Attendance: 28,000

BULGARIA: Iordan Filipov; Ivan Zafirov, Dobromir Jechev (Cap), Stefan Aladjov, Bojil Kolev, Georgi Denev, Tzvetan Atanasov (82 Kiril Raikov), Hristo Bonev, Atanas Mihailov (46 Dinko Dermendjiev), Asparuh Nikodimov, Vasil Mitkov. Trainer: Vasil Spasov

NORWAY: Per Haftorsen; Per Pettersen, Finn Thorsen, Arild Hetløen, Sigbjørn Slinning, Trygve Bornø, Thor Spydevold, Olav Nilsen, Egil Roger Olsen (83 Arnfinn Espeseth), Tor Fuglset, Kjetil Hasund. Trainer: Oivind Johannesen

Goals: Atanasov (29), Fuglset (83)

HUNGARY v FRANCE 1-1 (0-0)

Népstadion, Budapest 24.04.1971

Referee: Joaquim Fernandes de Campos (POR) Att: 45,867

HUNGARY: Adám Rothermel; Ernö Noskó, Lajos Szücs, Miklós Páncsics, Péter Juhász; László Fazekas, Sándor Zámbó, Flórián Albert, Lajos Kocsis; Ferenc Bene, Mihály Kozma (53 László Karsai). Trainer: József Hoffer

FRANCE: Georges Carnus; Roger Lemerre, Francis Camerini, Bernard Bosquier, Jean Djorkaeff (Cap), Georges Lech, Henri Michel, Jacques Novi, Georges Bereta; Hervé Revelli, Fleury Di Nallo, Charly Loubet. Trainer: Georges Boulogne

Goals: H. Revelli (64), Kocsis (70 pen)

BULGARIA v HUNGARY 3-0 (1-0)

Vasil Levski, Sofia 19.05.1971

Referee: Tofik Bahramov (USSR) Attendance: 40,000

BULGARIA: Stoian Iordanov; Milko Gaidarski, Dimitar Penev (Cap), Stefan Velitchkov, Dobromir Jechev, Bojil Kolev, Georgi Vasilev, Hristo Bonev, Petar Jekov, Atanas Mihailov (46 Petko Petkov), Mladen Vasilev. Trainer: Vasil Spasov

HUNGARY: Adám Rothermel; Tibor Fábián, Miklós Páncsics, Csaba Vidáts, Péter Juhász; Ede Dunai III, Sándor Zámbó, László Fazekas (46 László Karsai), Lajos Kocsis; Flórián Albert, Mihály Kozma (73 János Nagy II). Trainer: József Hoffer

Goals: Kolev (38), Petkov (48), Velitchkov (72)

NORWAY v BULGARIA 1-4 (0-4)

Ulleval, Oslo 09.06.1971

Referee: William John Gow (WAL) Attendance: 22,000

NORWAY: Kjell Kaspersen; Robert Nilsson, Finn Thorsen, Frank Olafsen (82 Arild Hetløen), Sigbjørn Slinning, Tor Egil Johansen (80 Harald Sunde), Per Pettersen, Olav Nilsen, Jan Fuglset, Odd Iversen, Tom Lund.
Trainer: Oivind Johannesen

BULGARIA: Stoian Iordanov (59 Biser Mihailov); Milko Gaidarski, Dimitar Penev, Stefan Velitchkov, Dobromir Jechev, Bojil Kolev, Georgi Vasilev (68 Georgi I.Georgiev), Hristo Bonev, Petar Jekov, Petko Petkov, Mladen Vasilev.
Trainer: Vasil Spasov

Goals: Bonev (26, 42 pen), Jekov (29), Ml. Vasilev (37), Iversen (79)

NORWAY v FRANCE 1-3 (0-2)

Ulleval, Oslo 08.09.1971

Referee: John Wright Paterson (SCO) Attendance: 16,544

NORWAY: Geir Karlsen (51 Svein Bjørn Olsen); Anbjørn Ekeland, Thor Spydevold, Tore Børrehaug, Sigbjörn Slinning; Tom Jacobsen, Jan Christiansen, Egil Olsen; Jan Fuglset, Tom Lund (51 Ola Dybwad Olsen), Kjetil Hasund.
Trainer: Oivind Johannesen

FRANCE: Georges Carnus; Jean Djorkaeff (Cap), Jacques Novi, Bernard Bosquier, Jean-Paul Rostagni, Henri Michel, Michel Mézy, Georges Bereta; Bernard Blanchet (75 Georges Lech), Jacques Vergnes, Charly Loubet.
Trainer: Georges Boulogne

Goals: Vergnes (33), Loubet (34), Blanchet (49), Dybwad Olsen (80)

HUNGARY v BULGARIA 2-0 (0-0)

Népstadion, Budapest 25.09.1971

Referee: Robert Davidson (SCO) Attendance: 75,000

HUNGARY: István Géczi; Tibor Fábián, Miklós Páncsics, Csaba Vidáts, Péter Juhász (79 Ernö Noskó); László Fazekas, Lajos Szücs, Sándor Zámbó (76 István Juhász), István Szöke, Ferenc Bene, Antal Dunai II. Trainer: Rudolf Illovszky

BULGARIA: Biser Mihailov; Milko Gaidarski, Dimitar Penev (Cap), Stefan Velitchkov, Dobromir Jechev, Bojil Kolev, Mladen Vasilev, Hristo Bonev, Petar Jekov (59 Georgi Vasilev), Petko Petkov, Dinko Dermendjiev. Trainer: Vasil Spasov

Goals: P. Juhász (49), Vidáts (51)

FRANCE v HUNGARY 0-2 (0-2)

Stade Olympique, Colombes Paris 09.10.1971

Referee: Gaspar Pintado Viu (SPA) Attendance: 21,756

FRANCE: Georges Carnus; Jean Djorkaeff (Cap), Jacques Novi, Bernard Bosquier, Jean-Paul Rostagni; Georges Lech, Henri Michel, Michel Mézy, Georges Bereta; Hervé Revelli, Charly Loubet (46 Gilbert Gress). Trainer: Georges Boulogne

HUNGARY: István Geczi; Ernö Noskó, Miklós Páncsics, Csaba Vidáts, Péter Juhász; László Fazekas, István Juhász, Lajos Szücs, Sándor Zámbó; Ferenc Bene, Antal Dunai II.
Trainer: Rudolf Illovszky

Goals: Bene (35), Zámbó (43)

HUNGARY v NORWAY 4-0 (3-0)

Népstadion, Budapest 27.10.1971

Referee: Dogan Babacan (TUR) Attendance: 30,000

HUNGARY: István Géczi; Ernö Noskó, Miklós Páncsics, Csaba Vidáts, Péter Juhász; István Juhász, Lajos Szücs; László Fazekas, Ferenc Bene, Antal Dunai II, Sándor Zámbó.
Trainer: Rudolf Illovszky

NORWAY: Geir Karlsen; Tore Børrehaug, Frank Olafsen, Tor Alsaker-Nøstdahl, Sigbjørn Slinning, Tom Jacobsen, Thor Spydevold, Per Pettersen, Kjetil Hasund, Jan Fuglset (79 Egil Roger Olsen), Roald Jensen. Trainer: Oivind Johannesen

Goals: Bene (22, 43), Dunai II (24), Szücs (63)

FRANCE v BULGARIA 2-1 (0-0)

Marcel Saupin, Nantes 10.11.1971

Referee: John Keith Taylor (ENG) Attendance: 9,405

FRANCE: Georges Carnus; Francis Camerini, Jacques Novi, Claude Quittet, Jean Djorkaeff (Cap); Georges Lech, Henri Michel, Michel Mézy; Bernard Blanchet, Hervé Revelli (82 Louis Floch), Charly Loubet. Trainer: Georges Boulogne

BULGARIA: Iordan Filipov; Ivan Zafirov, Dobromir Jechev, Dimitar Penev (Cap), Stefan Velitchkov; Hristo Bonev, Bojil Kolev, Georgi Denev, Dinko Dermendjiev; Mladen Vasilev, Petko Petkov (85 Georgi Tzvetkov). Trainer: Vasil Spasov

Goals: Bonev (54 pen), Lech (64), Loubet (87)

BULGARIA v FRANCE 2-1 (0-0)

Vasil Levski, Sofia 04.12.1971

Referee: Kurt Tschentscher (W. GER) Attendance: 18,000

BULGARIA: Rumen Goranov (65 Iordan Filipov); Milko Gaidarski, Dobromir Jechev, Dimitar Penev (Cap), Stefan Velitchkov (46 Viktor Ionov); Hristo Bonev, Bojil Kolev; Dinko Dermendjiev, Mladen Vasilev, Petar Jekov, Atanas Mihailov.
Trainer: Vasil Spasov

FRANCE: Georges Carnus; Jean Djorkaeff (Cap), Henri Michel, Bernard Bosquier, Jacques Novi, Marius Trésor; Georges Lech, Michel Mézy; Bernard Blanchet, Hervé Revelli (60 Louis Floch), Charly Loubet (76 Georges Bereta).
Trainer: Georges Boulogne

Goals: Jekov (47), Mihailov (82), Blanchet (84)

	P	W	D	L	F	A	Pts
Hungary	6	4	1	1	12	5	9
Bulgaria	6	3	1	2	11	7	7
France	6	3	1	2	10	8	7
Norway	6	0	1	5	5	18	1

GROUP 3

MALTA v GREECE 1-1 (0-0)

Empire Stadium, Gzira 11.10.1970

Referee: Concetto Lo Bello (ITA) Attendance: 15,000

MALTA: Alfred Mizzi; Joseph Grima, Alfred Mallia (78 John Privitera), Edward Vella, Emmanuel Micaleff, Anton Camilleri, Ronald Cocks, William Vassallo, John Bonnett (70 Charles Micaleff), Louis Arpa, Eddie Theobald. Trainer: Karm Borg

GREECE: Takis Oikonomopoulos; Giorgos Skrekis, Aristeidis Kamaras, Apostolos Toskas, Nikos Stathopoulos, Stathis Haitas, Kostas Eleutherakis, Mimis Domazos (Cap), Giorgos Koudas (68 Mihalis Kritikopoulos), Nikos Gioutsos (68 Antonis Antoniadis), Dimitris Papaioannou.
Trainer: Vasilis Petropoulos

Goals: Vassallo (66), Kritikopoulos (80)

GREECE v SWITZERLAND 0-1 (0-0)

Karaiskaki, Peiraias 16.12.1970

Referee: Milivoje Gugulovic (YUG) Attendance: 38,000

GREECE: Nikos Hristidis; Giorgos Skrekis, Aristeidis Kamaras, Aggelos Spiridon, Nikos Stathopoulos, Kostas Eleutherakis (75 Mihalis Kritikopoulos), Mimis Domazos (Cap), Stathis Haitas, Giorgos Koudas, Nikos Gioutsos, Dimitris Papaioannou. Trainer: Vasilis Petropoulos

SWITZERLAND: Mario Prosperi; Peter Ramseier, Anton Weibel, Georges Perroud, Marc Berset, Karl Odermatt, Rolf Blättler, Jakob Kuhn, Kurt Müller, Fritz Künzli (75 Walter Balmer), Peter Wenger (46 René Pierre Quentin).
Trainer: Louis Maurer

Goal: Müller (85)

MALTA v SWITZERLAND 1-2 (0-0)

Gzira 20.12.1970

Referee: Gocho Rusev (BUL) Attendance: 8,000

MALTA: Alfred Mizzi; John Privitera, Joseph Grima, Alfred Delia, Anton Camilleri, Emmanuel Micaleff, Ronald Cocks, William Vassallo, Charles Micaleff, Eddie Theobald (46 Edward Vella), John Bonnett. Trainer: Karm Borg

SWITZERLAND: Marcel Kunz; Peter Ramseier, Anton Weibel, Georges Perroud, Marc Berset, Karl Odermatt, Rolf Blättler, Jakob Kuhn, Kurt Müller, Fritz Künzli (64 Walter Balmer), Peter Wenger (49 René Pierre Quentin).
Trainer: Louis Maurer

Goals: Quentin (48), E. Theobald (56 pen), Künzli (59)

MALTA v ENGLAND 0-1 (0-1)

Empire Stadium, Gzira 03.02.1971

Referee: Ferdinand Marschall (AUS) Attendance: 29,751

MALTA: Alfred Mizzi; Joseph Grima, Alfred Mallia, Emmanuel Micaleff, Anton Camilleri, Edward Darmanin, Ronald Cocks, William Vassallo, Joseph Cini, Eddie Theobald, Louis Arpa. Trainer: Karm Borg

ENGLAND: Gordon Banks; Paul Reaney, Emlyn Walter Hughes, Alan Mullery, Roy Leslie McFarland, Norman Hunter, Alan James Ball, Martin Harcourt Chivers, Joseph Royle, James Colin Harvey, Martin Stanford Peters.
Manager: Alfred Ramsey

Goal: Peters (34)

ENGLAND v GREECE 3-0 (1-0)

Wembley, London 21.04.1971

Referee: Martti Hirviniemi (FIN) Attendance: 55,000

ENGLAND: Gordon Banks; Peter Edwin Storey, Emlyn Walter Hughes, Alan Mullery, Roy Leslie McFarland, Bobby Moore, Francis Henry Lee, Alan James Ball (78 Ralph Coates), Martin Harcourt Chivers, Geoffrey Charles Hurst, Martin Stanford Peters. Manager: Alfred Ramsey

GREECE: Nikos Hristidis; Giannis Gkaitatzis, Aggelos Spiridon, Apostolos Toskas, Dinos Kampas (75 Stathis Haitas), Nikos Stathopoulos, Takis Sunetopoulos, Giorgos Koudas, Giorgos Dedes (88 Giorgos Delikaris), Dimitris Papaioannou (Cap), Mihalis Kritikopoulos. Trainer: Vasilis Petropoulos

Goals: Chivers (23), Hurst (70), Lee (80)

SWITZERLAND v MALTA 5-0 (5-0)

Allemand, Luzern 21.04.1971

Referee: Gunnar Michaelsen (DEN) Attendance: 18,000

SWITZERLAND: Mario Prosperi; Jean Pierre Boffi, Peter Ramseier (46 Anton Weibel), Roland Citherlet, Pierre Chapuisat, Karl Odermatt, Rolf Blättler, Jakob Kuhn, Kurt Müller, Fritz Künzli, René Pierre Quentin.
Trainer: Louis Maurer

MALTA: Alfred Mizzi (46 Vincent Borg Bonaci); Joseph Grima, Alfred Mallia, Anton Camilleri, Emmanuel Micaleff, Edward Darmanin, Ronald Cocks, William Vassallo, Joseph Cini, John Bonnet, Louis Arpa (46 Alfred Delia).
Trainer: Karm Borg

Goals: Blättler (14), Künzli (18), Quentin (19), Citherlet (27), Müller (29)

ENGLAND v MALTA 5-0 (2-0)

Wembley, London 12.05.1971

Referee: Prelja Roed (NOR) Attendance: 35,000

ENGLAND: Gordon Banks; Christopher Lawler, Terence Cooper, Bobby Moore, Roy Leslie McFarland, Emlyn Walter Hughes, Francis Henry Lee, Ralph Coates, Martin Harcourt Chivers, Allan John Clarke, Martin Stanford Peters (75 Alan James Ball). Manager: Alfred Ramsey

MALTA: Vincent Borg Bonaci (46 Alfred Mizzi); Louis Pace, Joseph Grima, Anton Camilleri, Edward Darmanin, Alfred Delia, Ronald Cocks, Eddie Theobald, John Bonnet, William Vassallo, Louis Arpa. Trainer: Karm Borg

Goals: Chivers (30, 47), Lee (42), Clarke (46 pen), Lawler (75)

SWITZERLAND v ENGLAND 2-3 (2-2)

Basel 13.10.1971

Referee: Vital Loraux (BEL) Attendance: 55,000

SWITZERLAND: Marcel Kunz; Pierre Chapuisat (81 Georges Perroud), Peter Ramseier, Anton Weibel, Pirmin Stierli, Karl Odermatt, Jakob Kuhn, Rolf Blättler (75 Kurt Müller), Walter Balmer, Fritz Künzli, Daniel Jeandupeux. Trainer: Louis Maurer

ENGLAND: Gordon Banks; Christopher Lawler, Terence Cooper, Alan Mullery, Roy Leslie McFarland, Bobby Moore, Francis Henry Lee, Paul Edward Madeley, Martin Harcourt Chivers, Geoffrey Charles Hurst (85 John Radford), Martin Stanford Peters. Manager: Alfred Ramsey

Goals: Hurst (1), Jeandupeux (10), Chivers (12), Künzli (44), Weibel (77 og)

SWITZERLAND v GREECE 1-0 (0-0)

Wankdorf, Bern 12.05.1971

Referee: Ronald J.P. Jones (WAL) Attendance: 37,000

SWITZERLAND: Mario Prosperi; Peter Ramseier, Pierre Chapuisat, Anton Weibel, Georges Perroud, Karl Odermatt, Jakob Kuhn, Rolf Blättler, Walter Balmer, Fritz Künzli, Daniel Jeandupeux. Trainer: Louis Maurer

GREECE: Nikos Hristidis; Giannis Gkaitatzis, Apostolos Toskas, Dinos Kampas, Lakis Gklezos, Nikos Stathopoulos, Takis Sunetopoulos, Takis Hatziioannoglou (74 Mihalis Kritikopoulos), Thanasis Intzoglou (77 Giorgos Karafeskos), Dimitris Papaioannou (Cap), Giorgos Dedes.
Trainer: Vasilis Petropoulos

Goal: Odermatt (73)

ENGLAND v SWITZERLAND 1-1 (1-1)

Wembley, London 10.11.1971

Referee: Constantin Bărbulescu (ROM) Att: 100,000

ENGLAND: Peter Leslie Shilton; Paul Edward Madeley, Terence Cooper, Peter Edwin Storey, Laurence Valentine Lloyd, Bobby Moore, Michael George Summerbee (60 Martin Chivers), Alan James Ball, Geoffrey Charles Hurst, Francis Henry Lee (83 Rodney Marsh). Manager: Alfred Ramsey

SWITZERLAND: Mario Prosperi; Peter Ramseier, Pierre Chapuisat, Georges Perroud, Pirmin Stierli, Karl Odermatt, Rolf Blättler, Jakob Kuhn, Walter Balmer, Fritz Künzli, Daniel Jeandupeux (69 Petar Meier). Trainer: Louis Maurer

Goals: Summerbee (8), Odermatt (26)

GREECE v MALTA 2-0 (0-0)

Karaiskaki, Peiraias 18.06.1971

Referee: István Zsolt (HUNG) Attendance: 15,000

GREECE: Eleftherios Poupakis; Giannis Gounaris, Vasilis Siokos (85 Apostolos Toskas), Lakis Gklezos, Takis Eleutheriadis, Anastasios Papas (48 Giorgos Karafeskos), Stavros Sarafis (Cap), Mihalis Kritikopoulos, Kostas Davourlis, Kostas Aidiniou, Babis Stauropoulos.
Trainer: Vasilis Petropoulos

MALTA: Vincent Borg Bonaci; Louis Pace, Joseph Grima, Anton Camilleri, Edward Darmanin (68 Charles Micallef), Eddie Theobald, Ronald Cocks, John Bonnet, William Vassallo, Joseph Cini, Joseph Farrugia (46 Louis Arpa).
Trainer: Anthony Formosa

Goals: Davourlis (59), Aidiniou (80)

GREECE v ENGLAND 0-2 (0-0)

Karaiskaki, Peiraias 01.12.1971

Referee: José Maria Ortiz de Mendibil (SPA) Att: 45,000

GREECE: Nikos Hristidis; Theodoros Pallas, Apostolos Toskas, Anthimos Kapsis, Thanasis Aggelis, Kostas Eleutherakis, Mimis Domazos (Cap), Kostas Nikolaidis (73 Kostas Davourlis), Giorgos Koudas (61 Mihalis Kritikopoulos), Antonis Antoniadis, Dimitris Papaioannou.
Trainer: William Bingham

ENGLAND: Gordon Banks; Paul Edward Madeley, Emlyn Walter Hughes, Colin Bell, Roy Leslie McFarland, Bobby Moore (Cap), Francis Henry Lee, Alan James Ball, Martin Harcourt Chivers, Geoffrey Charles Hurst, Martin Stanford Peters. Manager: Alfred Ramsey

Goals: Hurst (57), Chivers (90)

	P	W	D	L	F	A	Pts
England	6	5	1	0	15	3	11
Switzerland	6	4	1	1	12	5	9
Greece	6	1	1	4	3	8	3
Malta	6	0	1	5	2	16	1

GROUP 4

SPAIN v NORTHERN IRELAND 3-0 (1-0)

Estadio Sánchez Pizjuan, Sevilla 11.11.1970

Referee: Gyula Emsberger (HUNG) Attendance: 48,000

SPAIN: José Angel IRIBAR Cortajarena; Joaquín RIFÉ II Climent, Francisco Fernandez GALLEGO, Juan Cruz SOL Oria (46 Juan López HITA); Enrique Álvarez COSTAS, José Luis VIOLETA Lajusticia; Antonio ARIETA II Araumbareña, LUIS Aragonés Suarez, Enrique Castro Gonzalez QUINI (46 Enrique LORA Millán), José Martinez Sánchez "PIRRI", Carlos REXACH Cerdá. Trainer: Ladislao Kubala

N. IRELAND: William McFaul; David Craig, Samuel Nelson, Thomas Jackson, W.J. Terence Neill; William J. O'Kane, David Sloan; George Best, Derek Dougan (23 Samuel J. Todd), Terence Harkin, David Clements.
Manager: William Bingham

Goals: Rexach (39), Pirri (59), Luis (76)

CYPRUS v USSR 1-3 (1-2)

GSP, Nicosia 15.11.1970

Referee: Petar Kostovski (YUG) Attendance: 13,000

CYPRUS: Michalis Alkiviades; Costas Christou "Kattos", Dimos Kavazis, Paschalis Fokkis, Kyriakos Koureas, Nikos Charalambous, Tasos Constantinou (83 Marios Kythreotis), Lakis Theodorou (75 Markos Markou), Pambos Papadopoulos "Pamboulis", Pavlos Vasiliou, Andreas Stylianou.
Trainer: Raymond Wood

USSR: Viktor Bannikov; Iuriy Istomin, Albert Shesternev (Cap), Evgeniy Lovchev, Vladimir Kaplichniy, Viktor Kolotov, Vladimir Muntian, Boris Kopeikin (70 Givi Nodia), Vladimir Fedotov, Vitaliy Shevchenko, Gennadiy Evriuzhikhin.
Trainer: Valentin Nikolaev

Goals: Kolotov (10), Evriuzhikhin (16), Charalambous (42), Shevchenko (50)

CYPRUS v NORTHERN IRELAND 0-3 (0-0)

Nicosia 03.02.1971

Referee: Francesco Francescon (ITA) Attendance: 9119

CYPRUS: Herodotos Herodotou "Koupanos"; Costas Christou "Kattos" (.. Lakis Theodorou), Dimos Kavazis, Stefanis Michael, Kallis Constantinou, Kyriakos Koureas, Nikos Charalambous, Pavlos Vasiliou, Pambos Papadopoulos "Pamboulis", Paschalis Fokkis, Andreas Stylianou.
Trainer: Raymond Wood

N. IRELAND: Patrick A. Jennings; David J. Craig, Samuel Nelson, Alan Hunter, W.J. Terence Neill, Samuel J. Todd, Bryan Hamilton, Alexander McMordie, A. Derek Dougan, James J. Nicholson, George Best. Manager: William Bingham

Goals: Nicholson (53), Dougan (55), Best (86 pen)

NORTHERN IRELAND v CYPRUS 5-0 (2-0)

Belfast 21.04.1971

Referee: Jacques Colling (LUX) Attendance: 19,153

N. IRELAND: Patrick A. Jennings; David J. Craig, David Clements, Martin Harvey, Alan Hunter, Samuel J. Todd (87 Peter Watson), Bryan Hamilton, Alexander McMordie, A.Derek Dougan, James J. Nicholson, George Best.
Manager: William Bingham

CYPRUS: Herodotos Herodotou "Koupanos"; Kokos Michael (.. Lakis Theodorou), Dimos Kavazis, Stefanis Michael (.. Christos Papettas), Kyriakos Koureas, Kallis Constantinou, Tasos Constantinou, Pavlos Vasiliou, Pambos Papadopoulos "Pamboulis", Paschalis Fokkis, Andreas Stylianou.
Trainer: Raymond Wood

Goals: Dougan (2), Best (44, 47, 56), Nicholson (85)

CYPRUS v SPAIN 0-2 (0-1)

Nicosia 09.05.1971

Referee: Constantin Bărbulescu (ROM) Attendance: 5,818

CYPRUS: Nikos Eleftheriades; Haris Kantzilieris, Kostas Alexandrou, Stefanis Michael, Dimos Kavazis, Kokos Antoniou, Christos Papettas, Pavlos Vasiliou (.. Lakis Theodorou), Pambos Papadopoulos "Pamboulis", Paschalis Fokkis, Andreas Stylianou. Trainer: Raymond Wood

SPAIN: Miguel REINA Santos; José Luis VIOLETA Lajusticia, Gregorio BENITO Rubio, Antonio Alfonso Moreno "TONONO", ANTONio Martinez Morales; José CLARAMUNT I Torres, José Martinez Sánchez "PIRRI", Fidel URIARTE Macho (46 Enrique LORA Millán); AMANCIO Amaro Varela, Enrique Castro Gonzalez QUINI, Ignacio CHURRUCA (.. Carlos REXACH Cerdá). Trainer: Ladislao Kubala

Goals: Pirri (3), Violeta (86)

USSR v SPAIN 2-1 (0-0)

V.I. Lenin, Moskva 30.05.1971

Referee: Ferdinand Biwersi (W. GER) Attendance: 102,000

USSR: Evgeniy Rudakov; Revaz Dzodzuashvili, Albert Shesternev (Cap), Valeriy Zîkov, Vladimir Kaplichniy, Viktor Kolotov, Vladimir Muntian (57 Vladimir Fedotov), Jozsef Sabo, Anatoliy Banishevski (76 Givi Nodia), Vitaliy Shevchenko, Gennadiy Evriuzhikhin. Trainer: Valentin Nikolaev

SPAIN: José Angel IRIBAR Cortajarena; Juan Cruz SOL Oria (65 Antonio Martinez Morales "ANTÓN"), Antonio Alfonso Moreno "TONONO", Gregorio BENITO Rubio, Francisco Fernandez GALLEGO; José Luis VIOLETA Lajusticia (62 Enrique LORA Millán), José CLARAMUNT I Torres, Fidel URIARTE Macho; Carlos REXACH Cerdá, AMANCIO Amaro Varela, Ignacio CHURRUCA Sistiaga.
Trainer: Ladislao Kubala

Goals: Kolotov (79), Shevchenko (83), Rexach (88)

USSR v CYPRUS 6-1 (3-0)

V.I.Lenin, Moskva 07.06.1971

Referee: Erik Beijar (FIN) Attendance: 35,000

USSR: Viktor Bannikov (46 Evgeniy Rudakov); Iuriy Istomin, Albert Shesternev (Cap), Valeriy Zîkov, Vladimir Kaplichniy, Viktor Kolotov, Vladimir Muntian, Anatoliy Banishevski, Vladimir Fedotov, Vitaliy Shevchenko, Gennadiy Evriuzhikhin (64 Vitaliy Hmelnitski). Trainer: Valentin Nikolaev

CYPRUS: Varnavas Christofi; Kokos Michael, Haris Kantzilieris (46 Lakis Theodorou), Stefanis Michael, Dimos Kavazis, Kallis Constantinou, Pavlos Vasiliou, Andreas Constantinou, Markos Markou, Paschalis Fokkis, Andreas Stylianou (74 Christos Papettas). Trainer: Raymond Wood

Goals: Fedotov (4, 86), Evriuzhikhin (23, 38), Kolotov (59), Michael (75), Banishevski (85)

USSR v NORTHERN IRELAND 1-0 (1-0)

V.I.Lenin, Moskva 22.09.1971

Referee: Ove Dahlberg (SWE) Attendance: 100,000

USSR: Evgeniy Rudakov; Revaz Dzodzuashvili, Albert Shesternev (Cap), Valeriy Zîkov, Murtaz Hurtsilava, Viktor Kolotov, Vladimir Muntian, Oleg Dolmatov, Vladimir Fedotov, Vitaliy Shevchenko (74 Levon Ishtoian), Gennadiy Evriuzhikhin. Trainer: Valentin Nikolaev

N. IRELAND: William S. McFaul; David J. Craig (60 Brian Hamilton), W.J. Terence Neill, Alan Hunter, Samuel Nelson, Daniel Hegan, David Clements, James J. Nicholson, William J. O'Kane, A. Derek Dougan, George Best.
Manager: Terence Neill

Goal: Muntian (43 pen)

NORTHERN IRELAND v USSR 1-1 (1-1)

Windsor Park, Belfast 13.10.1971

Referee: Rolf Nyhus (NOR) Attendance: 20,000

N. IRELAND: Patrick A. Jennings; Patrick J. Rice, Samuel Nelson, James J. Nicholson, Alan Hunter, William J. O'Kane, Alexander McMordie, Brian Hamilton (65 Martin H. O'Neill), W.J. Terence Neill, A. Derek Dougan (46 Thomas Cassidy), David Clements. Manager: Terence Neill

USSR: Evgeniy Rudakov; Revaz Dzodzuashvili, Albert Shesternev (Cap), Evgeniy Lovchev, Murtaz Hurtsilava, Viktor Kolotov, Nikolai Kiselev, Oleg Dolmatov, Anatoliy Konkov, Anatoliy Bîshovets, Vitaliy Shevchenko (60 Levon Ishtoian).
Trainer: Valentin Nikolaev

Goals: Nicholson (13), Bîshovets (32)

SPAIN v USSR 0-0

Estadio Ramon Sánchez Pizjuan, Sevilla 27.10.1971

Referee: Norman Burtenshaw (ENG) Attendance: 58,000

SPAIN: Miguel REINA Santos; Juan Cruz SOL Oria, Francisco Fernandez GALLEGO, Antonio Alfonso Moreno "TONONO", Antonio Martinez Morales "ANTÓN" (76 MARCIAL Pina Morales); Enrique LORA Millán, José CLARAMUNT I Torres; AMANCIO Amaro Varela, Enrique Castro Gonzalez QUINI, Joaquín Sierra Vallejo QUINO, Ignacio CHURRUCA Sistiaga.
Trainer: Ladislao Kubala

USSR: Evgeniy Rudakov; Revaz Dzodzuashvili, Albert Shesternev (Cap), Iuriy Istomin, Murtaz Hurtsilava, Viktor Kolotov, Vladimir Muntian, Oleg Dolmatov, Vladimir Fedotov (83 Nikolai Kiselev), Anatoliy Bîshovets, Levon Ishtoian (62 Vitaliy Shevchenko). Trainer: Valentin Nikolaev

SPAIN v CYPRUS 7-0 (3-0)

Estadio Los Cármenes, Granada 24.11.1971

Referee: Joseph M. Cassar Naudi (MAL) Attendance: 19,176

SPAIN: José Angel IRIBAR Cortajarena; Juan Cruz SOL Oria, Francisco Fernandez GALLEGO, Antonio Alfonso Moreno "TONONO", Juan López Hita; Enrique LORA Millán (80 José Agustin Aranzabal GAZTELU), José Martinez Sánchez "PIRRI", José CLARAMUNT I Torres; AMANCIO Amaro Varela (46 Francisco AGUILAR García), Joaquín Sierra Vallejo QUINO, José Francisco ROJO I Arroitia.
Trainer: Ladislao Kubala

CYPRUS: Herodotos Herodotou "Koupanos"; Ioannis Mertakkas, Dimos Kavazis, Charalambos Partasides, Kallis Constantinou, Stefanis Michael, Tasos Constantinou, Michalis Athinodorou "Tartaros", Kokos Antoniou (.. Lakis Theodorou), Pavlos Vasiliou, Andreas Stylianou (46 Michalakis Michael).
Trainer: Raymond Wood

Goals: Pirri (9, 47 pen), Quino (13, 22), Aguilar (63), Lora (66), Rojo (75)

NORTHERN IRELAND v SPAIN 1-1 (0-1)

Hull 16.02.1972

Referee: Jack K.Taylor (ENG) Attendance: 19,925

N. IRELAND: Patrick A. Jennings; Patrick J. Rice, Samuel Nelson, W.J. Terence Neill, Alan Hunter; David Clements, Brian Hamilton (.. Martin H. O'Neill); Alexander McMordie, Samuel J. Morgan, Samuel B. McIlroy, George Best.
Manager: Terence Neill

SPAIN: José Angel IRIBAR Cortajarena; Juan Cruz SOL Oria, Francisco Fernandez GALLEGO, Antonio Alfonso Moreno "TONONO", Enrique Álvarez COSTAS; Gregorio BENITO Rubio, Enrique LORA Millán (67 Miguel Ramos Vargas "MIGUELI"); Francisco AGUILAR García, Joaquín Sierra Vallejo QUINO, Enrique Castro Gonzalez QUINI (28 Manuel Ríos Quintanilla MANOLETE), José Francisco ROJO I Arroitia. Trainer: Ladislao Kubala

Goals: Rojo (41), Morgan (71)

	P	W	D	L	F	A	Pts
USSR	6	4	2	0	13	4	10
Spain	6	3	2	1	14	3	8
Northern Ireland	6	2	2	2	10	6	6
Cyprus	6	0	0	6	2	26	0

GROUP 5

DENMARK v PORTUGAL 0-1 (0-1)

Idraetsparken, København 14.10.1970

Referee: Leo Callaghan (WAL) Attendance: 18,000

DENMARK: Kaj Poulsen; Torben Nielsen, Poul H.Frederiksen, Erik Sandvad, Flemming Pedersen, Jens Jørgen Hansen, Bent Outzen, Jan Andersen (85 Per Madsen), Kurt Præst, Jørgen Markussen (90 Poul Erik Thygesen), Keld Pedersen. Trainer: Rudolf Strittich

PORTUGAL: Vitor Damas; Manuel PEDRO GOMES, HUMBERTO COELHO, JOSÉ CARLOS, HILARIO da Conceiçao, Fernando PERES da Silva, JOSÉ MARIA Junior (72 Augusto MATINE), Antonio SIMOES Costa (52 JAIME da Silva GRAÇA), ARTUR JORGE Braga Melo, EUSÉBIO da Silva Ferreira, JACINTO JOÃO. Trainer: José Gomes de Silva

Goal: João Jacinto (40)

SCOTLAND v DENMARK 1-0 (1-0)

Hampden Park, Glasgow 11.11.1970

Referee: Erich Linemayr (AUS) Attendance: 24,000

SCOTLAND: James Fergus Cruickshank; David Hay (.. William Pullar Jardine), John Greig, Patrick Gordon Stanton, Ronald McKinnon, Robert Moncur, James Johnstone, William McInanny Carr, Colin Stein, John O'Hare (75 Peter Barr Cormack), William Johnston. Manager: Robert Brown

DENMARK: Kaj Poulsen; Torben Nielsen, Poul H.Frederiksen, Erik Sandvad, Flemming Pedersen, Jens Jørgen Hansen, Bent Outzen, Kristen Nygaard, Morten Olsen (25 Poul Erik Thygesen), Keld Pedersen, Benny Nielsen.
Trainer: Rudolf Strittich

Goal: O'Hare (13)

BELGIUM v DENMARK 2-0 (2-0)

Klokke, Brugge 25.11.1970

Referee: John Carpenter (IRE) Attendance: 9,697

BELGIUM: Christian Piot; Léon Jeck, Georges Heylens (Cap), Nicolas Dewalque, Jean Thissen, Wilfried Van Moer (70 Jan Verheyen), Pierre Carteus, Erwin Van den Daele, Johnny Thio, Johan Devrindt, Raoul Lambert. Trainer: Raymond Goethals

DENMARK: Kaj Poulsen; Torben Nielsen, Poul H.Frederiksen, Erik Sandvad, Flemming Pedersen, Jens Jørgen Hansen, Bent Outzen, Kristen Nygaard (60 Poul Erik Thygesen), Keld Pedersen, Benny Nielsen (70 Mogens Haastrup), Morten Olsen. Trainer: Rudolf Strittich

Goals: Devrindt (18, 36)

BELGIUM v SCOTLAND 3-0 (1-0)

Stade Sclessin, Liège 03.02.1971

Referee: Antonio Sbardella (ITA) Attendance: 25,000

BELGIUM: Christian Piot; Jean Plaskie, Georges Heylens, Nicolas Dewalque, Jean Thissen, Wilfried Van Moer, Erwin Van den Daele, Léon Semmeling, Henri Depireux, Paul Van Himst (Cap), André Denul. Trainer: Raymond Goethals

SCOTLAND: James Fergus Cruickshank; David Hay, Thomas Gemmell, Patrick Gordon Stanton (46 Anthony Green), Ronald McKinnon, Robert Moncur, Archibald Gemmill, John Greig, Colin Stein (46 James Forrest), John O'Hare, Charles Cooke. Manager: Robert Brown

Goals: McKinnon (34 og), Van Himst (55, 83 pen)

BELGIUM v PORTUGAL 3-0 (2-0)

Park Astrid, Brussel 17.02.1971

Referee: Gaspar Pintado Viu (SPA) Attendance: 26,921

BELGIUM: Christian Piot; Jean Plaskie, Georges Heylens, Nicolas Dewalque, Jean Thissen, Wilfried Van Moer, Erwin Van den Daele, Léon Semmeling (46 Johnny Thio), Raoul Lambert, Paul Van Himst (Cap), André Denul.
Trainer: Raymond Goethals

PORTUGAL: Vitor Damas; MALTA da SILVA (46 Francisco REBELO), HUMBERTO COELHO, José ROLANDO, HILARIO da Conceiçao, Fernando Pascoal PAVAO, Fernando PERES da Silva, RUI Gouveia Pinto RODRIGUES (73 Félix Marques GUERREIRO), VITOR Manuel BATISTA, EUSÉBIO da Silva Ferreira, António SIMOES Costa.
Trainer: José Gomes de Silva

Goals: Lambert (15, 63 pen), Denul (80)

PORTUGAL v SCOTLAND 2-0 (1-0)

Estádio da Luz, Lisboa 21.04.1971

Referee: Michel Kitabdjian (FRA) Attendance: 35,000

PORTUGAL: Vitor Damas; MALTA da SILVA, HUMBERTO COELHO, JOSÉ CARLOS, ADOLFO António da Cruz, RUI Gouveia Pinto RODRIGUES, Fernando PERES da Silva, António SIMOES Costa, Tamagnini NENÉ (86 Fernando Pascoal PAVAO), VITOR Manuel BATISTA (75 ARTUR JORGE Braga Melo), EUSÉBIO da Silva Ferreira.
Trainer: José Gomes de Silva

SCOTLAND: Robert Brown Clark; David Hay, James Brogan, Patrick Gordon Stanton (74 Anthony Green), Ronald McKinnon, Robert Moncur, William Henderson, James McCalliog (62 Andrew Jarvie), David Thomson Robb, Peter Barr Cormack, Alan John Gilzean. Manager: Robert Brown

Goals: Stanton (22 og), Eusebio (82)

PORTUGAL v DENMARK 5-0 (2-0)

Estádio das Antas, Porto 12.05.1971

Referee: Malcolm Wright (NIR) Attendance: 20,000

PORTUGAL: Vitor Damas; MALTA da SILVA (75 Francisco REBELO), HUMBERTO COELHO, JOSÉ CARLOS (Cap), ADOLFO António da Cruz, RUI Gouveia Pinto RODRIGUES, Fernando PERES da Silva, Tamagnini NENÉ, EUSÉBIO da Silva Ferreira, VITOR Manuel BATISTA (83 ARTUR JORGE Braga), António SIMOES Costa. Trainer: José Gomes de Silva

DENMARK: Erik Lykke Sørensen; Henning Boel, Mogens Berg (46 Erik Nielsen), Erik Sandvad, Jørgen Rasmussen, Finn Laudrup, Preben Arentoft, Kresten Bjerre, Morten Olsen, Ole Bjørnmose, Benny Nielsen. Trainer: Rudolf Strittich

Goals: Rodrigues (18), Eusébio (42), Batista (48, 52), Sandvad (88 og)

DENMARK v BELGIUM 1-2 (0-0)

Idraetspark, København 26.05.1971

Referee: Kare Sirevaag (NOR) Attendance: 30,000

DENMARK: Erik Lykke Sørensen; Henning Boel, Mogens Berg, Erik Sandvad, Torben Nielsen, Finn Laudrup, Preben Arentoft, Kresten Bjerre, John Steen Olsen (75 Keld Pedersen), Ole Bjørnmose, Benny Nielsen (83 Birger Pedersen).
Trainer: Rudolf Strittich

BELGIUM: Christian Piot; Jean Plaskie, Georges Heylens, Erwin Van den Daele, Jean Thissen, Jan Verheyen, Jean Dockx, Léon Semmeling, Johan Devrindt, Paul Van Himst (Cap), Wilfried Puis. Trainer: Raymond Goethals

Goals: Devrindt (65, 75), Bjerre (76)

DENMARK v SCOTLAND 1-0 (1-0)

Idraetsparken, København 09.06.1971

Referee: Wolfgang Riedel (E. GER) Attendance: 38,600

DENMARK: Erik Lykke Sørensen; Torben Nielsen, Mogens Berg, Preben Arentoft, Jørgen Rasmussen, Kresten Bjerre, Finn Laudrup (75 Bent Outzen), Ole Bjørnmose, Ulrik Le Févre, Benny Nielsen (85 Keld Pedersen), Jørgen Kristensen.
Trainer: Rudolf Strittich

SCOTLAND: Robert Brown Clark; Francis Michael Munro, William Dickson, Patrick Gordon Stanton, Ronald McKinnon, Robert Moncur, Thomas McLean, Thomas Forsyth (60 David Thomson Robb), Colin Stein, Hugh Patrick Curran, James Forrest (55 John Scott). Manager: Robert Brown

Goals: Laudrup (42)

SCOTLAND v PORTUGAL 2-1 (1-0)

Hampden Park, Glasgow 13.10.1971

Referee: Brunon Piotrowicz (POL) Attendance: 50,000

SCOTLAND: Robert Wilson; William Pullar Jardine, Edmond Peter Colquhoun (81 Martin McLean Buchan), Patrick Gordon Stanton, David Hay, William John Bremner, Alexander James Cropley, George Graham, James Johnstone, John O'Hare, Archibald Gemmill.
Manager: Thomas Docherty

PORTUGAL: Vitor Manuel DAMAS; MALTA da SILVA, Francisco António CALO (66 Fernando PERES da Silva), RUI Gouveia Pinto RODRIGUES, ADOLFO António da Luz Calixto, JAIME da Silva GRAÇA, José ROLANDO Andrade Gonçalves, António SIMOES Costa, Tamagnini Manuel Gomes NENÉ, VITOR Manuel BATISTA, EUSÉBIO da Silva Ferreira (Cap) (46 ARTUR JORGE Braga Melo).
Trainer: José Gomes de Silva

Goals: O'Hare (23), Rodrigues (56), Gemmill (58)

SCOTLAND v BELGIUM 1-0 (1-0)

Pittodrie Park, Aberdeen 10.11.1971

Referee: Einar Boström (SWE) Attendance: 36,000

SCOTLAND: Robert Brown Clark; William Pullar Jardine, David Hay, William John Bremner, Martin McLean Buchan, Patrick Gordon Stanton, James Johnstone (79 John Angus Hansen), Stephen Murray, John O'Hare, Edwin Gray, Alexander James Cropley (48 Kenneth Dalglish). Manager: Thomas Docherty

BELGIUM: Christian Piot; André Stassart, Georges Heylens, Nicolas Dewalque, Léon Dolmans, Wilfried Van Moer (57 Maurice Martens), Erwin Van den Daele, Paul Van Himst (Cap), Léon Semmeling, Johan Devrindt, Wilfried Puis (69 Raoul Lambert). Trainer: Raymond Goethals

Goal: O'Hare (5)

PORTUGAL v BELGIUM 1-1 (0-0)

Estádio da Luz, Lisboa 21.11.1971

Referee: Kenneth Burns (ENG) Attendance: 53,600

PORTUGAL: Vitor Manuel DAMAS; MALTA da SILVA (46 OCTAVIO Joaquim Coelho), HUMBERTO COELHO, RUI Gouveia Pinto RODRIGUES, JOSÉ de Jesus MENDES, JAIME da Silva GRAÇA, Fernando PERES da Silva, António SIMOES Costa, Tamagnini Manuel Gomes NENÉ (62 ARTUR JORGE Braga Melo), José Augusto TORRES, EUSÉBIO da Silva Ferreira (Cap). Trainer: José Gomes de Silva

BELGIUM: Christian Piot; André Stassart, Georges Heylens, Nicolas Dewalque, Léon Dolmans, Jean Dockx, Erwin Van den Daele, Maurice Martens (69 Wilfried Puis), Léon Semmeling, Raoul Lambert, Paul Van Himst (Cap). Trainer: Raymond Goethals

Goals: Lambert (60), Peres (90 pen)

	P	W	D	L	F	A	Pts
Belgium	6	4	1	1	11	3	9
Portugal	6	3	1	2	10	6	7
Scotland	6	3	0	3	4	7	6
Denmark	6	1	0	5	2	11	2

GROUP 6

REPUBLIC OF IRELAND v SWEDEN 1-1 (1-0)

Dalymount Park, Dublin 14.10.1970

Referee: Robert Helies (FRA) Attendance: 30,000

IRELAND: Alan Kelly; Tommy Carroll (70 Joe Kinnear), John Dempsey, Tony Byrne, Anthony Dunne (Cap), Eamonn Dunphy, Paddy Mulligan, Mick Lawlor, Steve Heighway, Don Givens (83 Ray Treacy), Terry Conroy. Manager: Michael Meagan

SWEDEN: Sven Gunnar Larsson; Hans Selander, Krister Kristensson, Björn Nordqvist, Roland Grip, Tommy Svensson, Leif Eriksson, Jan Olsson, Inge Danielsson (46 Dan Brzokoupil), Ove Grahn, Bo Larsson. Trainer: Orvar Bergmark

Goals: Carroll (44 pen), Brzokoupil (61)

SWEDEN v REPUBLIC OF IRELAND 1-0 (0-0)

Fotbollstadion, Solna 28.10.1970

Referee: Pavel Kazakov (USSR) Attendance: 11,922

SWEDEN: Ronnie Hellström; Hans Selander, Krister Kristensson, Björn Nordqvist, Roland Grip (65 Claes Cronqvist), Tommy Svensson, Bo Larsson, Jan Olsson, Leif Eriksson, Ove Grahn, Dan Brzokoupil (61 Tom Turesson). Trainer: Orvar Bergmark

IRELAND: Alan Kelly; Shay Brennan (Cap), John Dempsey, Tony Byrne, Paddy Dunning, Eamonn Dunphy, Alfred Finucane, Mick Lawlor, Steve Heighway, Ray Treacy, Terry Conroy. Manager: Michael Meagan

Goal: Turesson (74)

AUSTRIA v ITALY 1-2 (1-2)

Prater, Wien 31.10.1970

Referee: Laurens van Ravens (HOL) Attendance: 54,953

AUSTRIA: Friedrich Koncilia (46 Herbert Rettensteiner); Johann Schmidradner, Gerhard Sturmberger (Cap), Norbert Hof, Peter Pumm; August Starek, Johann Ettmayer; Thomas Parits, Josef Hickersberger, Wilhelm Kreuz, Helmut Redl. Trainer: Leopold Stastny

ITALY: Enrico Albertosi; Tarcisio Burgnich, Giacinto Facchetti (Cap); Mario Bertini, Roberto Rosato, Pierluigi Cera; Angelo Domenghini, Gianni Rivera, Alessandro Mazzola, Giancarlo De Sisti, Luigi Riva (76 Sergio Gori). Trainer: Ferruccio Valcareggi

Goals: De Sisti (27), Parits (29), Mazzola (34)

ITALY v REPUBLIC OF IRELAND 3-0 (2-0)

Stadio Comunale, Firenze 08.12.1970

Referee: Robert Schaut (BEL) Attendance: 45,000

ITALY: Enrico Albertosi; Tarcisio Burgnich, Giacinto Facchetti (Cap); Mario Bertini, Roberto Rosato, Pierluigi Cera; Angelo Domenghini, Alessandro Mazzola, Roberto Boninsegna, Giancarlo De Sisti, Pierino Prati. Trainer: Ferruccio Valcareggi

IRELAND: Alan Kelly; Shay Brennan (Cap), John Dempsey, Tony Byrne, Paddy Dunning; Eamonn Dunphy (36 Mick Lawlor), Alfred Finucane; Eamonn Rogers, Terry Conroy, Don Givens, Ray Treacy. Manager: Michael Meagan Trainer: G. Martina

Goals: De Sisti (22 pen), Boninsegna (42), Prati (84)

REPUBLIC OF IRELAND v ITALY 1-2 (1-1)

Lansdowne Road, Dublin 10.05.1971

Referee: Gerhard Schulenburg (E. GER) Attendance: 25,000

IRELAND: Alan Kelly; Joe Kinnear, Paddy Mulligan, Tony Byrne, Anthony Dunne; Eamonn Dunphy, Johnny Giles (Cap); Eamonn Rogers (46 Alfred Finucane), Steve Heighway, Don Givens, Jimmy Conway. Manager: Michael Meagan Trainer: G. Martina

ITALY: Dino Zoff; Tarcisio Burgnich, Giacinto Facchetti (Cap); Mario Bertini, Roberto Rosato, Pierluigi Cera; Pierino Prati, Alessandro Mazzola, Roberto Boninsegna, Giancarlo De Sisti, Mario Corso. Trainer: Ferruccio Valcareggi

Goals: Boninsegna (15), Conway (23), Prati (59)

SWEDEN v AUSTRIA 1-0 (0-0)

Fotbollstadion, Solna 26.05.1971

Referee: Stanislaw Eksztajn (POL) Attendance: 5,416

SWEDEN: Ronnie Hellström; Hans Selander, Kurt Axelsson (46 Krister Kristensson), Björn Nordqvist, Roland Grip, Tommy Svensson, Jan Olsson, Bo Larsson, Sten Pålsson, Bengt Johansson, Örjan Persson.

AUSTRIA: Herbert Rettensteiner; Johann Schmidradner, Gerhard Sturmberger, Johann Eigenstiller, Peter Pumm, Josef Hickersberger, August Starek, Johann Ettmayer (81 Johann Geyer), Karl Kodat, Wilhelm Kreuz, Alfred Gassner (73 Geza Gallos). Trainer: Leopold Stastny

Goal: Olsson (60)

REPUBLIC OF IRELAND v AUSTRIA 1-4 (0-3)

Dalymount Park, Dublin 30.05.1971

Referee: Henry Öberg (NOR) Attendance: 16,000

IRELAND: Alan Kelly; Tony Byrne, Anthony Dunne (Cap), Eoin Hand, James Dunne, Eamonn Dunphy (46 Noel Campbell), Eamonn Rogers, Jimmy Conway, Don Givens (74 Jimmy Holmes), Ray Treacy, Steve Heighway. Manager: Michael Meagan

AUSTRIA: Herbert Rettensteiner; Johann Schmidradner, Gerhard Sturmberger, Johann Eigenstiller, Werner Kriess (78 Rainer Schlagbauer), August Starek, Norbert Hof, Johann Ettmayer, Josef Hickersberger, Wilhelm Kreuz, Karl Kodat. Trainer: Leopold Stastny

Goals: Schmidradner (4 pen), Kodat (11), Dunne (31 og), Rogers (46 pen), Starek (71)

SWEDEN v ITALY 0-0

Råsunda, Solna 09.06.1971

Referee: Rudolf Scheurer (SWI) Attendance: 36,528

SWEDEN: Ronnie Hellström; Christer Hult, Krister Kristensson, Björn Nordqvist (Cap), Roland Grip; Tommy Svensson, Bo Larsson; Leif Eriksson, Ove Kindvall (61 Jan Olsson), Bengt Johansson (74 Claes Cronqvist), Örjan Persson. Trainer: Georg Ericsson

ITALY: Dino Zoff; Tarcisio Burgnich, Giacinto Facchetti (Cap), Mario Bertini, Roberto Rosato (54 Luciano Spinosi), Pierluigi Cera; Angelo Domenghini, Alessandro Mazzola, Roberto Boninsegna, Giancarlo De Sisti, Pierino Prati. Trainer: Ferruccio Valcareggi

AUSTRIA v SWEDEN 1-0 (1-0)

Wien 04.09.1971

Referee: Rudolf Glöckner (E. GER) Attendance: 42,000

AUSTRIA: Herbert Rettensteiner; Johann Schmidradner, Gerhard Sturmberger, Johann Eigenstiller, Peter Pumm, August Starek, Norbert Hof, Johann Ettmayer (65 Alois Jagodic), Karl Kodat, Josef Stering (62 Josef Hickersberger), Johann Pirkner. Trainer: Leopold Stastny

SWEDEN: Ronnie Hellström; Christer Hult, Krister Kristensson, Kurt Axelsson, Roland Grip, Björn Nordqvist, Bo Larsson, Jan Olsson, Sten Pålsson (60 Hans Selander), Roland Sandberg (70 Dan Brzokoupil), Sven Lindman.

Goal: Stering (23)

ITALY v SWEDEN **3-0** (2-0)

San Siro, Milano 09.10.1971

Referee: Roger Machin (FRA) Attendance: 65,582

ITALY: Dino Zoff (46 Enrico Albertosi); Tarcisio Burgnich, Giacinto Facchetti (Cap); Mario Bertini, Roberto Rosato, Pierluigi Cera; Alessandro Mazzola (23 Mario Corso), Romeo Benetti II, Roberto Boninsegna, Gianni Rivera, Luigi Riva. Trainer: Ferruccio Valcareggi

SWEDEN: Ronnie Hellström; Christer Hult (52 Claes Cronqvist), Björn Nordqvist, Krister Kristensson (59 Hans Nilsson), Roland Grip, Thomas Nordahl; Curt Olsberg, Bo Larsson, Inge Danielsson, Ove Grahn, Roland Sandberg. Trainer: Georg Ericsson

Goals: Riva (3, 83), Boninsegna (41)

AUSTRIA v REPUBLIC OF IRELAND **6-0** (3-0)

Linz 10.10.1971

Referee: Karl Göppel (SWI) Attendance: 25,000

AUSTRIA: Adolf Antrich; Johann Schmidradner, Gerhard Sturmberger, Johann Eigenstiller, Peter Pumm, Rudolf Horvath, Norbert Hof, Johann Ettmayer, Johann Pirkner, Thomas Parits, Kurt Jara. Trainer: Leopold Stastny

IRELAND: Paddy Roche; Mick Gannon, Alfred Finucane (Cap), Tommy McConville, John Herrick, Mick Kearin (53 Damien Richardson), Paddy Mulligan, Mick Martin (69 Alfred Hale), Frank O'Neill, Mick Leech, Turlough O'Connor. Manager: William Tuohy

Goals: Parits (45, 51, 89), Jara (12, 85), Pirkner (41)

ITALY v AUSTRIA **2-2** (1-2)

Stadio Olimpico, Roma 20.11.1971

Referee: Gyula Emsberger (HUNG) Attendance: 58,752

ITALY: Dino Zoff; Tazio Roversi, Giacinto Facchetti (Cap); Mario Bertini (46 Gianfranco Bedin), Aldo Bet, Sergio Santarini; Pierino Prati, Romeo Benetti II (65 Claudio Sala), Roberto Boninsegna, Giancarlo De Sisti, Luigi Riva. Trainer: Ferruccio Valcareggi

AUSTRIA: Adolf Antrich; Johann Schmidradner, Rudolf Horvath, Johann Eigenstiller, Peter Pumm; Robert Sara, Norbert Hof; Johann Ettmayer (Cap), Helmut Köglberger, Johann Pirkner, Kurt Jara. Trainer: Leopold Stastny

Goals: Prati (10), Jara (36), Santarini (59 og), De Sisti (75)

	P	W	D	L	F	A	Pts
Italy	6	4	2	0	12	4	10
Austria	6	3	1	2	14	6	7
Sweden	6	2	2	2	3	5	6
Rep. of Ireland	6	0	1	5	3	17	1

GROUP 7

HOLLAND v YUGOSLAVIA **1-1** (0-1)

De Kuip, Rotterdam 11.10.1970

Referee: William Mullan (SCO) Attendance: 60,000

HOLLAND: Jan Van Beveren; Pleun Strik, Theo Laseroms, Rinus Israël, Theo Van Duivenbode, Wim Jansen, Wim Van Hanegem, Nico Rijnders, Jan Klijnjan, Willy Van der Kuylen (.. Henk Wery), Wietze Veenstra (50 Wytze Couperus). Trainer: Frantisek Fadrhonc

YUGOSLAVIA: Ivan Curkovic; Andelko Tesan, Dragoslav Stepanovic, Miroslav Pavlovic (25 Jovan Acimovic, .. Branko Oblak), Blagoje Paunovic, Dragan Holcer, Ilija Petkovic, Dusan Bajevic, Vahidin Musemic, Jure Jerkovic, Dragan Dzajic. Trainer: Rajko Mitic

Goals: Dzajic (22), Israël (49 pen)

LUXEMBOURG v YUGOSLAVIA **0-2** (0-1)

Stade Municipal, Luxembourg 14.10.1970

Referee: Vital Loraux (BEL) Attendance: 9,000

LUXEMBOURG: René Hoffmann; Erwin Kuffer (46 René Flenghi), Louis Pilot, Fernand Jeitz, Johny Hoffmann (Cap), Norbert Leszczynski, Ady Schmit, Paul Philipp, Nico Braun, Johny Leonard, Joseph Kirchens. Trainer: Ernst Melchior

YUGOSLAVIA: Dragomir Mutibaric; Andelko Tesan, Dragoslav Stepanovic, Borivoje Djordjevic, Blagoje Paunovic, Dragan Holcer, Ilija Petkovic, Dusan Bajevic, Josip Bukal, Jure Jerkovic, Dragan Dzajic. Trainer: Rajko Mitic

Goals: Bukal (41, 63)

EAST GERMANY v HOLLAND **1-0** (0-0)

Rudolf-Harbig-Stadion, Dresden 11.11.1970

Referee: Gösta Liedberg (SWE) Attendance: 35,000

EAST GERMANY: Jürgen Croy; Peter Rock, Michael Strempel, Klaus Sammer, Lothar Kurbjuweit; Frank Ganzera, Otto Fräßdorf (Cap), Henning Frenzel (54 Harald Irmscher), Hans-Jürgen Kreische; Peter Ducke, Eberhard Vogel. Trainer: Georg Buschner

HOLLAND: Jan Van Beveren; Wim Suurbier, Rinus Israël, Pleun Strik, Epi Drost, Wim Jansen, Johan Neeskens, Nico Rijnders, Wim Van Hanegem (.. Henk Wery), Jan Klijnjan, Piet Keizer. Trainer: Frantisek Fadrhonc

Goal: P. Ducke (56)

LUXEMBOURG v EAST GERMANY 0-5 (0-4)

Stade Municipal, Luxembourg 15.11.1970

Referee: Anton Bucheli (SWI) Attendance: 3,000

LUXEMBOURG: René Hoffmann (32 Jeannot Moes); Erwin Kuffer, René Flenghi, Fernand Jeitz, Johny Hoffmann (Cap), Jeannot Krecke, Louis Pilot, Ady Schmit (46 Nico Braun), Johny Leonard, Louis Trierweiler, Joseph Kirchens. Trainer: Ernst Melchior

EAST GERMANY: Jürgen Croy; Peter Rock, Lothar Kurbjuweit, Michael Strempel, Frank Ganzera; Harald Irmscher, Henning Frenzel (Cap) (63 Jürgen Sparwasser), Klaus Sammer, Hans-Jürgen Kreische; Peter Ducke (77 Rainer Schlutter), Eberhard Vogel. Trainer: Georg Buschner

Goals: Vogel (21), Kreische (29, 36, 39, 78)

EAST GERMANY v LUXEMBOURG 2-1 (1-0)

Freundschaft, Gera 24.04.1971

Referee: Hugh Wilson (NIR) Attendance: 15,000

EAST GERMANY: Jürgen Croy; Klaus Sammer, Frank Ganzera, Michael Strempel, Bernd Bransch; Konrad Weise, Helmut Stein (Cap), Rainer Schlutter; Jürgen Sparwasser (85 Frank Richter), Henning Frenzel, Hans-Jürgen Kreische. Trainer: Georg Buschner

LUXEMBOURG: René Hoffmann; Jean-Pierre Hoffmann, Fernand Jeitz, René Flenghi, Johny Hoffmann, Louis Trierweiler, Nicolas Hoffmann (Cap), Gilbert Dussier, Dominique Di Genova, Nico Braun, Joseph Kirchens. Trainer: Ernst Melchior

Goals: Kreische (31), Frenzel (88), Dussier (90)

HOLLAND v LUXEMBOURG 6-0 (4-0)

De Kuip, Rotterdam 24.02.1971

Referee: Faik Bajrami (ALB) Attendance: 34,000

HOLLAND: Jan Van Beveren; Wim Suurbier, Rinus Israël, Johan Neeskens, Epi Drost, Wim Jansen, Wim Van Hanegem, Theo Pahlplatz, Willy Lippens, Johan Cruijff, Piet Keizer. Trainer: Frantisek Fadrhonc

LUXEMBOURG: René Hoffmann; Léon Schmit, Louis Pilot, René Flenghi, Johny Hoffmann, Fernand Jeitz, Nicolas Hoffmann (Cap), Gilbert Dussier, Nico Braun, Paul Philipp, Joseph Kirchens. Trainer: Ernst Melchior

Goals: Lippens (26), Keizer (53, 80), Cruijff (59, 69), Suurbier (83)

EAST GERMANY v YUGOSLAVIA 1-2 (0-2)

Zentralstadion, Leipzig 09.05.1971

Referee: Paul Schiller (AUS) Attendance: 100,000

EAST GERMANY: Jürgen Croy; Konrad Weise, Klaus Sammer, Michael Strempel, Bernd Bransch; Rainer Schlutter, Helmut Stein (Cap), Hans-Jürgen Kreische; Henning Frenzel (77 Harald Irmscher), Peter Ducke, Eberhard Vogel (66 Wolfram Löwe). Trainer: Georg Buschner

YUGOSLAVIA: Radomir Vukcevic; Miroslav Pavlovic, Mladen Ramljak, Zoran Antonijevic, Blagoje Paunovic, Dragan Holcer, Ilija Petkovic (71 Nenad Bjekovic), Branko Oblak (63 Vladislav Bogicevic), Zoran Filipovic, Jovan Acimovic, Dragan Dzajic. Trainer: Vujadin Boskov

Goals: Filipovic (11), Dzajic (19), Löwe (70)

YUGOSLAVIA v HOLLAND 2-0 (1-0)

Hajduk, Split 04.04.1971

Referee: Kurt Tschenscher (W. GER) Attendance: 25,000

YUGOSLAVIA: Radomir Vukcevic; Miroslav Pavlovic, Dragoslav Stepanovic, Zoran Antonijevic (62 Ljubisa Rajkovic), Blagoje Paunovic, Dragan Holcer, Ilija Petkovic, Jure Jerkovic, Josip Bukal (58 Nenad Bjekovic), Jovan Acimovic, Dragan Dzajic. Trainer: Vujadin Boskov

HOLLAND: Jan Van Beveren; Wim Suurbier, Johan Neeskens, Pleun Strik, Epi Drost (80 Jan Klijnjan), Wim Jansen, Gerrie Mühren, Wim Van Hanegem, Henk Wery, Eef Mulders, Piet Keizer. Trainer: Frantisek Fadrhonc

Goals: Jerkovic (8), Dzajic (85)

HOLLAND v EAST GERMANY 3-2 (1-1)

De Kuip, Rotterdam 10.10.1971

Referee: Concetto Lo Bello (ITA) Attendance: 55,000

EAST GERMANY: Jürgen Croy; Bernd Bransch (Cap), Michael Strempel, Konrad Weise, Gerd Kische; Hans-Jürgen Kreische, Jürgen Sparwasser (68 Harald Irmscher), Klaus Sammer; Joachim Streich, Peter Ducke (80 Wolfram Löwe), Eberhard Vogel. Trainer: Georg Buschner

HOLLAND: Jan Van Beveren; Hans Venneker, Rinus Israël, Barry Hulshoff, Pleun Strik, Wim Jansen, Wim Van Hanegem, Henk Wery, Dick Van Dijk (78 Jan Jeuring), Johan Cruijff, Piet Keizer. Trainer: Frantisek Fadrhonc

Goals: Vogel (10, 82), Hulshoff (25), Keizer (52, 63)

YUGOSLAVIA v EAST GERMANY 0-0

JNA, Beograd 16.10.1971

Referee: Jack Taylor (ENG) Attendance: 3,000

YUGOSLAVIA: Ratomir Dujkovic; Ljubisa Rajkovic, Dragoslav Stepanovic, Miroslav Pavlovic, Dragan Holcer, Blagoje Paunovic, Ilija Petkovic, Branko Oblak (61 Petar Nikezic), Josip Bukal (.. Zoran Filipovic), Jovan Acimovic, Dragan Dzajic. Trainer: Vujadin Boskov

EAST GERMANY: Jürgen Croy; Bernd Bransch, Michael Strempel, Klaus Sammer, Konrad Weise, Gerd Kische; Helmut Stein (Cap) (80 Wolfram Löwe), Hans-Jürgen Kreische (71 Harald Irmscher), Joachim Streich, Peter Ducke, Eberhard Vogel. Trainer: Georg Buschner

YUGOSLAVIA v LUXEMBOURG 0-0

Buducnosti, Titograd 27.10.1971

Referee: Muzafer Sarvan (TUR) Attendance: 15,000

YUGOSLAVIA: Ratomir Dujkovic; Ljubisa Rajkovic (.. Zoran Filipovic), Dragoslav Stepanovic, Miroslav Pavlovic, Blagoje Paunovic, Dragan Holcer, Ilija Petkovic, Branko Oblak (.. Jure Jerkovic), Josip Bukal, Jovan Acimovic, Nenad Bjekovic. Trainer: Vujadin Boskov

LUXEMBOURG: Jeannot Moes; Jean-Pierre Hoffmann, René Kollwelter, René Flenghi, Johny Hoffmann, Jeannot Krecke, Nicolas Hoffmann (Cap), Gilbert Dussier, Nico Braun, Paul Philipp, Joseph Kirchens. Trainer: Ernst Melchior

LUXEMBOURG v HOLLAND 0-8 (0-5)

Philips, Eindhoven 17.11.1971

Referee: Michal Jursa (CZE) Attendance: 17,500

HOLLAND: Jan Van Beveren; Hans Venneker, Rinus Israël, Barry Hulshoff, Ruud Krol, Gerrie Mühren, Wim Jansen, Theo Pahlplatz, Oeki Hoekma, Johan Cruijff, Piet Keizer. Trainer: Frantisek Fadrhonc

LUXEMBOURG: Jeannot Moes (46 Théo Stendebach); Jean-Pierre Hoffmann, René Kollwelter, René Flenghi, Johny Hoffmann, Jeannot Krecke, Nicolas Hoffmann (Cap), Gilbert Dussier, Nico Braun, Paul Philipp, Joseph Kirchens. Trainer: Ernst Melchior

Goals: Cruijff (4, 14, 60), Keizer (7), Pahlplatz (12), Hulshoff (37), Hoekma (54), Israël (82)

	P	W	D	L	F	A	Pts
Yugoslavia	6	3	3	0	7	2	9
Holland	6	3	1	2	18	6	7
East Germany	6	3	1	2	11	6	7
Luxembourg	6	0	1	5	1	23	1

GROUP 8

POLAND v ALBANIA 3-0 (1-0)

Slaski, Chorzów 14.10.1970

Referee: Andreas Kouniaides (CYP) Attendance: 10,000

POLAND: Piotr Maksymilian Czaja; Wladyslaw Stachurski, Jerzy Jan Wyrobek, Jerzy Pawel Gorgon, Adam Marian Musial; Zygfryd Szoltysik, Kazimierz Deyna, Bronislaw Ryszard Bula; Joachim Jerzy Marx, Wlodzimierz Lubanski (Cap), Robert Gadocha. Trainer: Ryszard Koncewicz

ALBANIA: Koco Dinella; Fatmir Frashëri, Gëzim Kazmi, Bujar Cani, Perikli Dhalles; Lin Shllaku (Cap), Iljuz Ceço, Ramazan Ragami; Sabah Bizi, Panayot Pano, Medin Zhega. Trainer: Loro Boriçi

Goals: Gadocha (19), Lubanski (83), Szoltysik (90)

WEST GERMANY v TURKEY 1-1 (1-1)

Köln 17.10.1970

Referee: Paul Bonnet (MAL) Attendance: 53,000

WEST GERMANY: Josef Maier; Hans-Hubert Vogts, Horst-Dieter Höttges; Franz Beckenbauer, Klaus-Dieter Sieloff (66 Josef Heynckes), Wolfgang Weber; Reinhard Libuda, Klaus Fichtel, Gerhard Müller, Wolfgang Overath (Cap), Jürgen Grabowski. Trainer: Helmut Schön

TURKEY: Ali Artuner; Ergün Acuner, Muzaffer Sipahi, Ercan Aktuna, Alparslan Eratli, Kamuran Yavuz, Ziya Şengül, Sanli Sarialioglu, Metin Kurt, Cemil Turan, Ender Konca.

Goals: Kamuran (15), Müller (37 pen)

TURKEY v ALBANIA 2-1 (2-1)

Mithat Paşa, Istanbul 13.12.1970

Referee: János Biroczky (HUNG) Attendance: 40,000

TURKEY: Ali Artuner; Ergün Acuner, Ercan Aktuna, Muzaffer Sipahi, Alparslan Eratli, Kamuran Yavuz, Sanli Sarialioglu, Ziya Şengül, Metin Kurt, Cemil Turan, Ender Konca (.. Yaşar Mumcuoglu).

ALBANIA: Koco Dinella (46 Jani Rama); Perikli Dhalles, Safet Berisha, Bujar Cani, Astrit Ziu, Ramazan Ragami, Thodor Vaso, Sabah Bizi, Iljuz Ceço, Panayot Pano, Medin Zhega. Trainer: Loro Boriçi

Goals: Metin (4), Ziu (22), Cemil (43)

ALBANIA v WEST GERMANY 0-1 (0-1)

Qemal Stafa, Tiranë 17.02.1971

Referee: Todor Betchkirov (BUL) Attendance: 25,000

ALBANIA: Koco Dinella; Mihal Gjika, Perikli Dhalles, Bujar Cani, Gëzim Kazmi, Ramazan Ragami, Thodor Vaso, Sabah Bizi, Astrit Ziu, Iljuz Ceço, Panayot Pano. Trainer: Loro Boriçi

WEST GERMANY: Josef Maier; Hans-Hubert Vogts, Bernd Patzke (67 Michael Bella); Franz Beckenbauer, Karl-Heinz Schnellinger, Wolfgang Weber; Jürgen Grabowski, Günter Netzer, Gerhard Müller, Wolfgang Overath (Cap), Josef Heynckes. Trainer: Helmut Schön

Goal: Müller (34)

WEST GERMANY v ALBANIA 2-0 (2-0)

Villa Park, Karlsruhe 12.06.1971

Referee: Timoleon Latsios (GRE) Attendance: 46,000

WEST GERMANY: Josef Maier; Georg Schwarzenbeck, Hans-Hubert Vogts (89 Hartwig Bleidick); Klaus-Dieter Sieloff, Franz Beckenbauer, Herbert Wimmer; Jürgen Grabowski, Günter Netzer, Horst Köppel, Wolfgang Overath (Cap) (73 Siegfried Held), Josef Heynckes.
Trainer: Helmut Schön

ALBANIA: Baskim Muhedini; Mihal Gjika, Safet Berisha, Bujar Cani, Astrit Ziu, Faruk Sejdini, Ramazan Ragami, Sabah Bizi, Thodor Vaso, Panayot Pano (Cap), Medin Zhega.
Trainer: Loro Boriçi

Goals: Netzer (17), Grabowski (45)

TURKEY v WEST GERMANY 0-3 (0-1)

Mithat Paşa, Istanbul 25.04.1971

Referee: Karlo Kruashvili (USSR) Attendance: 45,000

TURKEY: Ali Artuner; K.Mehmet Işikal (.. Zekeriya Alp), Muzaffer Sipahi, Ercan Aktuna, Alparslan Eratli, Kamuran Yavuz, Sanli Sarialioglu (.. Fethi Heper), Ziya Şengül, B.Mehmet Oguz, Cemil Turan, Ender Konca.
Trainer: Cihat Arman

WEST GERMANY: Josef Maier; Hans-Hubert Vogts, Bernd Patzke; Herbert Wimmer, Franz Beckenbauer (Cap), Wolfgang Weber; Jürgen Grabowski, Horst Köppel (.. Heinz Flohe), Gerhard Müller, Günter Netzer, Josef Heynckes.
Trainer: Helmut Schön

Goals: Müller (43, 47), Köppel (73)

POLAND v TURKEY 5-1 (1-0)

Wisla, Kraków 22.09.1971

Referee: Antoine Queudeville (LUX) Attendance: 30,000

POLAND: Jan Gomola; Zygmunt Anczok, Andrzej Zygmunt, Jerzy Pawel Gorgon, Adam Marian Musial; Zygfryd Szoltysik, Kazimierz Deyna (46 Andrzej Jarosik), Bronislaw Ryszard Bula; Jan Banas, Wlodzimierz Lubanski (Cap), Robert Gadocha. Trainer: Kazimierz Górski

TURKEY: Ali Artuner (Cap), Abdurrahman Temeller, Ercan Aktuna, Muzaffer Sipahi, Zekeriya Alp, Yusuf Tunalioglu (78 Sanli Sarialioglu), Kamuran Yavuz, Vahap Özbayar; Metin Kurt, Fethi Heper, Cemil Turan (46 Nihat Yayöz).
Trainer: Arman Cihat

Goals: Bula (33), Lubanski (62, 73, 90), Gadocha (69), Nihat (83)

ALBANIA v POLAND 1-1 (1-1)

Qemal Stafa, Tiranë 12.05.1971

Referee: Robert Helies (FRA) Attendance: 20,000

ALBANIA: Koco Dinella; Mihal Gjika, Gëzim Kazmi, Bujar Cani, Perikli Dhalles; Thodor Vaso (46 Safet Berisha), Iljuz Ceço, Ramazan Ragami; Sabah Bizi, Panayot Pano (Cap), Medin Zhega. Trainer: Loro Boriçi

POLAND: Wladyslaw Jan Grotynski; Jan Aleksander Wrazy, Jerzy Jan Wyrobek, Walter Jerzy Winkler, Zygmunt Anczok; Zygfryd Szoltysik, Kazimierz Deyna (69 Leslaw Cmikiewicz), Bernard Adolf Blaut (Cap); Jan Banas, Wlodzimierz Lubanski, Robert Gadocha (46 Marian Kozerski).
Trainer: Kazimierz Górski

Goals: Banas (7), Zhega (32)

POLAND v WEST GERMANY 1-3 (1-1)

Dziesieciolecia, Warszawa 10.10.1971

Referee: Ferdinand Marschall (AUS) Attendance: 90,000

POLAND: Jan Tomaszewski; Adam Marian Musial, Stanislaw Oslizlo (Cap), Jerzy Pawel Gorgon, Zygmunt Anczok; Zygfryd Szoltysik, Bronislaw Ryszard Bula (46 Antoni Stefan Kot), Zygmunt Pawel Maszczyk; Jan Banas (60 Jerzy Miroslaw Sadek), Wlodzimierz Lubanski, Robert Gadocha.
Trainer: Kazimierz Górski

WEST GERMANY: Josef Dieter Maier; Paul Breitner, Franz Beckenbauer (Cap), Klaus Fichtel, Georg Schwarzenbeck; Herbert Wimmer, Horst Köppel, Günter Netzer; Jürgen Grabowski, Gerhard Müller, Josef Heynckes.
Trainer: Helmut Schön

Goals: Gadocha (28), Müller (29, 64), Grabowski (70)

ALBANIA v TURKEY 3-0 (1-0)

Qemal Stafa, Tiranë 14.11.1971

Referee: Ivan Placek (CZE) Attendance: 15,000

ALBANIA: Baskim Muhedini; Mihal Gjika, Safet Berisha, Bujar Cani, Astrit Ziu, Faruk Sejdini, Iljuz Ceço, Sabah Bizi, Ilir Pernaska, Panayot Pano (Cap), Maksut Leshteni (70 Nevruz Deçka). Trainer: Loro Boriçi

TURKEY: Ali Artuner; Vahit Kolukisa (.. Alparslan Eratli), Muzaffer Sipahi, Ercan Aktuna, Zekeriya Alp, B.Mehmet Oguz, Kamuran Yavuz, Vedat Okyar, Metin Kurt, Osman Arpacioglu, Necati Göçmen. Trainer: Cihat Arman

Goals: Pernaska (22, 53), Pano (50)

WEST GERMANY v POLAND 0-0

Volksparkstadion, Hamburg 17.11.1971

Referee: William Joseph Mullan (SCO) Attendance: 62,000

WEST GERMANY: Josef Dieter Maier; Horst-Dieter Höttges, Franz Beckenbauer, Wolfgang Weber (83 Ulrich Hoeneß), Georg Schwarzenbeck; Herbert Wimmer (70 Horst Köppel), Klaus Fichtel, Wolfgang Overath (Cap); Reinhard Libuda, Gerhard Müller, Jürgen Grabowski. Trainer: Helmut Schön

POLAND: Marian Henryk Szeja; Antoni Jan Szymanowski, Marian Wieslaw Ostafinski, Jerzy Pawel Gorgon, Zygmunt Anczok (64 Jerzy Jan Wyrobek), Zygfryd Szoltysik, Kazimierz Deyna, Bernard Adolf Blaut (Cap), Joachim Jerzy Marx, Wlodzimierz Lubanski, Grzegorz Boleslaw Lato (85 Bronislaw Ryszard Bula). Trainer: Kazimierz Górski

TURKEY v POLAND 1-0 (0-0)

Atatürk Izmir 5.12.1971

Referee: Petar Nikolov (BUL) Attendance: 65,000

TURKEY: Yasin Özdenak; Ekrem Günalp, Muzaffer Sipahi, Özer Yurteri, Zekeriya Alp (83 Vahit Kolukisa); Ayfer Elmastaşoglu, Vedat Okyar, B.Mehmet Oguz; Metin Kurt, Cemil Turan, Ender Konca (30 Çetin Erdogan). Trainer: Nicolae Petrescu (Rom)

POLAND: Marian Henryk Szeja; Antoni Jan Szymanowski, Marian Wieslaw Ostafinski, Jerzy Pawel Gorgon, Adam Marian Musial; Zygfryd Szoltysik, Kazimierz Deyna (70 Bronislaw Ryszard Bula), Bernard Adolf Blaut (Cap), Grzegorz Boleslaw Lato, Joachim Jerzy Marx, Robert Gadocha (63 Andrzej Jarosik). Trainer: Kazimierz Górski

Goal: Cemil (52)

	P	W	D	L	F	A	Pts
West Germany	6	4	2	0	10	2	10
Poland	6	2	2	2	10	6	6
Turkey	6	2	1	3	5	13	5
Albania	6	1	1	4	5	9	3

QUARTER-FINALS

ITALY v BELGIUM 0-0

San Siro, Milano 29.04.1972

Referee: Petar Nikolov (BUL) Attendance: 63,549

ITALY: Enrico Albertosi; Tarcisio Burgnich, Giacinto Facchetti (Cap); Gianfranco Bedin, Roberto Rosato, Pierluigi Cera; Angelo Domenghini (46 Franco Causio), Alessandro Mazzola, Pietro Anastasi, Giancarlo De Sisti, Luigi Riva. Trainer: Ferruccio Valcareggi

BELGIUM: Christian Piot; Erwin Van den Daele, Georges Heylens, Jean Thissen, Maurice Martens (49 Léon Dolmans), Wilfried Van Moer, Jan Verheyen, Jean Dockx; Léon Semmeling, Paul Van Himst (Cap), Raoul Lambert. Trainer: Raymond Goethals

BELGIUM v ITALY 2-1 (1-0)

Park Astrid, Brussel 13.05.1972

Referee: Paul Schiller (AUS) Attendance: 26,561

BELGIUM: Christian Piot; Erwin Van den Daele, Georges Heylens, Jean Thissen, Léon Dolmans; Wilfried Van Moer (46 Odilon Polleunis), Jean Dockx; Léon Semmeling, Paul Van Himst (Cap), Raoul Lambert, Jan Verheyen. Trainer: Raymond Goethals

ITALY: Enrico Albertosi; Tarcisio Burgnich, Giacinto Facchetti (Cap); Mario Bertini (46 Fabio Capello), Luciano Spinosi, Pierluigi Cera; Alessandro Mazzola, Romeo Benetti II, Roberto Boninsegna, Giancarlo De Sisti, Luigi Riva. Trainer: Ferruccio Valcareggi

Goals: Van Moer (24), Van Himst (71), Riva (86 pen)

ENGLAND v WEST GERMANY 1-3 (0-1)

Wembley, London 29.04.1972

Referee: Robert Helies (FRA) Attendance: 100,000

ENGLAND: Gordon Banks; Paul Edward Madeley, Emlyn Walter Hughes, Colin Bell, Bobby Moore, Norman Hunter, Francis Henry Lee, Alan James Ball, Martin Harcourt Chivers, Geoffrey Charles Hurst (62 Rodney Marsh), Martin Stanford Peters. Manager: Alfred Ramsey

WEST GERMANY: Josef Dieter Maier; Horst-Dieter Höttges, Paul Breitner; Georg Schwarzenbeck, Franz Beckenbauer (Cap), Herbert Wimmer; Jürgen Grabowski, Ulrich Hoeneß, Gerhard Müller, Günter Netzer, Siegfried Held. Trainer: Helmut Schön

Goals: Hoeneß (25), Lee (77), Netzer (85 pen), Müller (88)

WEST GERMANY v ENGLAND 0-0

Olimpic, Berlin 13.05.1972

Referee: Milivoje Gugulovic (YUG) Attendance: 72,000

WEST GERMANY: Josef Dieter Maier; Horst-Dieter Höttges, Paul Breitner; Georg Schwarzenbeck, Franz Beckenbauer (Cap), Herbert Wimmer; Ulrich Hoeneß (.. Josef Heynckes), Heinz Flohe, Gerhard Müller, Günter Netzer, Siegfried Held. Trainer: Helmut Schön

ENGLAND: Gordon Banks; Paul Edward Madeley, Emlyn Walter Hughes, Peter Edwin Storey, Roy Leslie McFarland, Bobby Moore, Alan James Ball, Colin Bell, Martin Harcourt Chivers, Rodney Marsh, Norman Hunter, Martin Peters (60 Michael Summerbee). Manager: Alfred Ramsey

HUNGARY v ROMANIA 1-1 (1-0)

Népstadion, Budapest 29.04.1972

Referee: David W. Smith (ENG) Attendance: 75,000

HUNGARY: István Géczi; Tibor Fábián, Miklós Páncsics, László Bálint, Péter Vépi; Lajos Kocsis (59 Ferenc Bene), Lajos Szücs; László Fazekas, László Branikovits, Antal Dunai, Sándor Zámbó. Trainer: Rudolf Illovszky

ROMANIA: Răducanu Necula; Lajos Sătmăreanu, Nicolae Lupescu, Cornel Dinu, Augustin Deleanu; Ion Dumitru, Radu Nunweiller; Mircea Lucescu (Cap), Emerich Dembrovschi, Flavius Domide, Anghel Iordănescu.
Trainer: Angelo Niculescu

Goals: Branikovits (11), Sătmăreanu (56)

ROMANIA v HUNGARY 2-2 (1-2)

"23 August", București 14.05.1972

Referee: Kurt Tschenscher (W. GER) Attendance: 80,000

ROMANIA: Răducanu Necula; Lajos Sătmăreanu, Nicolae Lupescu, Cornel Dinu, Augustin Deleanu; Ion Dumitru, Radu Nunweiller; Flavius Domide, Emerich Dembrovschi (74 Mircea Lucescu), Nicolae Dobrin, Anghel Iordănescu (66 Alexandru Neagu). Trainer: Angelo Niculescu

HUNGARY: István Géczi; Tibor Fábián, Miklós Páncsics, László Bálint, Péter Juhász; István Juhász, Lajos Kocsis (66 Lajos Kü), Lajos Szücs; István Szöke (66 Antal Dunai), Ferenc Bene, Sándor Zámbó. Trainer: Rudolf Illovszky

Goals: Szöke (4), Dobrin (14), Kocsis (36), Neagu (81)

HUNGARY v ROMANIA 2-1 (1-1)

JNA, Beograd 17.05.1972

Referee: Hristos Mihas (GRE) Attendance: 50,000

HUNGARY: Adám Rothermel; Tibor Fábián, Miklós Páncsics, László Bálint, Péter Juhász; István Juhász, Lajos Kocsis, Sándor Zámbó; István Szöke, Ferenc Bene, Lajos Kü. Trainer: Rudolf Illovszky

ROMANIA: Răducanu Necula; Lajos Sătmăreanu, Nicolae Lupescu, Cornel Dinu, Augustin Deleanu (52 Bujor Hălmăgeanu); Ion Dumitru, Radu Nunweiller; Mircea Lucescu, Nicolae Dobrin, Alexandru Neagu, Flavius Domide. Trainer: Angelo Niculescu

Goals: Kocsis (26), Neagu (32), Szöke (88)

YUGOSLAVIA v USSR 0-0

Crvena Zvezda, Beograd 30.04.1972

Referee: Rudolf Scheurer (SWI) Attendance: 99,000

YUGOSLAVIA: Enver Maric; Mladen Ramljak, Dragoslav Stepanovic, Miroslav Pavlovic, Blagoje Paunovic, Dragan Holcer, Bozidar Jankovic, Branko Oblak, Josip Bukal (85 Dusan Bajevic), Jovan Acimovic, Dragan Dzajic.
Trainer: Vujadin Boskov

USSR: Evgeniy Rudakov; Revaz Dzodzuashvili, Murtaz Hurtsilava (Cap), Vladimir Kaplichniy, Iuriy Istomin, Aleksandr Mahovikov (62 Vladimir Troshkin), Oleg Dolmatov, Anatoliy Baidachniy, Anatoliy Banishevski, Anatoliy Konkov, Eduard Kozinkevich (75 Gennadiy Evriuzhikhin).
Trainer: Nikolai Guliaev

USSR v YUGOSLAVIA 3-0 (0-0)

V.I.Lenin, Moskva 13.05.1972

Referee: Aurelio Angonese (ITA) Attendance: 103,000

USSR: Evgeniy Rudakov; Revaz Dzodzuashvili, Murtaz Hurtsilava (Cap), Nikolai Abramov, Iuriy Istomin, Viktor Kolotov, Vladimir Troshkin, Anatoliy Baidachniy (66 Boris Kopeikin), Anatoliy Banishevski, Anatoliy Konkov, Gennadiy Evriuzhikhin (46 Eduard Kozinkevich).
Trainer: Nikolai Guliaev

YUGOSLAVIA: Enver Maric; Mladen Ramljak, Dragoslav Stepanovic, Miroslav Pavlovic, Blagoje Paunovic, Dragan Holcer (56 Ilija Petkovic), Zoran Antonijevic, Branko Oblak (73 Jure Jerkovic), Bozidar Jankovic, Jovan Acimovic, Dragan Dzajic. Trainer: Vujadin Boskov

Goals: Kolotov (53), Banishevski (74), Kozinkevich (90)

SEMI-FINALS

WEST GERMANY v BELGIUM 2-1 (1-0)

Bosuil, Antwerpen 14.06.1972

Referee: William Joseph Mullan (SCO) Attendance: 60,000

WEST GERMANY: Josef Dieter Maier; Horst-Dieter Höttges, Paul Breitner; Georg Schwarzenbeck, Franz Beckenbauer (Cap), Herbert Wimmer; Josef Heynckes, Ulrich Hoeneß (59 Jürgen Grabowski), Gerhard Müller, Günter Netzer, Erwin Kremers. Trainer: Helmut Schön

BELGIUM: Christian Piot; Erwin Van den Daele, Georges Heylens, Jean Thissen, Léon Dolmans, Jean Dockx, Jan Verheyen, Maurice Martens (70 Odilon Polleunis), Léon Semmeling, Raoul Lambert, Paul Van Himst (Cap). Trainer: Raymond Goethals

Goals: Müller (23, 71), Pollenius (83)

USSR v HUNGARY 1-0 (0-0)

Astrid Park, Brussel 14.06.1972

Referee: Rudolf Glöckner (E. GER) Attendance: 5,000

USSR: Evgeniy Rudakov; Revaz Dzodzuashvili, Murtaz Hurtsilava (Cap), Vladimir Kaplichniy, Iuriy Istomin; Viktor Kolotov, Vladimir Troshkin, Anatoliy Baidachniy; Anatoliy Banishevski (65 Givi Nodia), Anatoliy Konkov, Vladimir Onishchenko. Trainer: Aleksandr Ponomariev

HUNGARY: István Geczi; Tibor Fábián, Miklós Páncsics, László Bálint, Péter Juhász; István Juhász, Lajos Kocsis (60 Flórián Albert), Lajos Kü; István Szöke, Ferenc Bene (60 Antal Dunai II), Sándor Zámbó. Trainer: Rudolf Illovszky

Goal: Konkov (53). Zambo missed penalty (84)

THIRD PLACE MATCH

BELGIUM v HUNGARY 2-1 (2-0)

Sclessin, Luik 17.06.1972

Referee: Einar Johan Boström (SWE) Attendance: 6,184

BELGIUM: Christian Piot; Erwin Van den Daele, Georges Heylens, Jean Thissen, Léon Dolmans; Jean Dockx, Jan Verheyen, Odilon Polleunis, Léon Semmeling, Raoul Lambert, Paul Van Himst (Cap). Trainer: Raymond Goethals

HUNGARY: István Geczi; Tibor Fábián, Miklós Páncsics, László Bálint, Péter Juhász; István Juhász, Florián Albert, Lajos Kü, Mihály Kozma, Antal Dunai II, Sándor Zámbó (46 Lajos Szűcs). Trainer: Rudolf Illovszky

Goals: Lambert (24), Van Himst (29), Kü (50 pen)

FINAL

WEST GERMANY v USSR 3-0 (1-0)

Heissel, Brussel 18.06.1972

Referee: Ferdinand Marshall (AUS) Attendance: 43,437

WEST GERMANY: Josef Dieter Maier; Horst-Dieter Höttges, Paul Breitner; Georg Schwarzenbeck, Franz Beckenbauer (Cap), Herbert Wimmer; Josef Heynckes, Ulrich Hoeneß, Gerhard Müller, Günter Netzer, Erwin Kremers. Trainer: Helmut Schön

USSR: Evgeniy Rudakov; Revaz Dzodzuashvili, Murtaz Hurtsilava (Cap), Vladimir Kaplichniy, Iuriy Istomin; Viktor Kolotov, Vladimir Troshkin, Anatoliy Baidachniy; Anatoliy Banishevski (63 Eduard Kozinkevich), Anatoliy Konkov (46 Oleg Dolmatov), Vladimir Onishchenko. Trainer: Aleksandr Ponomariev

Goals: Müller (27, 58), Wimmer (51)

Goalscorers European Football Championship 1972

11 goals: Gerhard Müller (West Germany)

5 goals: Martin Chivers (England), Johan Cruijff, Piet Keizer (Holland), Hans-Jürgen Kreische (East Germany)

4 goals: Jan Capkovic (Czechoslovakia), Ferenc Bene (Hungary), George Best (N. Ireland), José Martinez Sánchez Pirri (Spain), Viktor Kolotov (USSR), Johan Devrindt, Raoul Lambert, Paul Van Himst (Belgium), Thomas Parits (Austria), Wlodzimierz Lubanski (Poland)

3 goals: Hristo Bonev (Bulgaria), Lajos Kocsis (Hungary), Fritz Künzli (Switzerland), Geoffrey Hurst, Francis Lee (England), James Nicholson (N. Ireland), Gennadiy Evriuzhikhin (USSR), John O'Hare (Scotland), Kurt Jara (Austria), Roberto Boninsegna, Giancarlo De Sisti, Pierino Prati, Luigi Riva (Italy), Eberhard Vogel (East Germany), Robert Gadocha (Poland), Dragan Dzajic (Yugoslavia)

2 goals: Dembrovschi, Dobrin, Dumitrache, Lucescu, Lupescu, Neagu (Romania), Karkó (Czechoslovakia), Toshack (Wales), Jekov (Bulgaria), Blanchet, Lech, Loubet (France), Iversen (Norway), Szöke (Hungary), Müller, Odermatt, Quentin (Switzerland), Dougan (N. Ireland), Rexach, Rojo, Quino (Spain), Fedotov, Banishevski, Shevchenko (USSR), Batista, Eusébio, Rodrigues (Portugal), Israël, Hulshoff (Holland), Pernaska (Albania), Cemil (Turkey), Bukal (Yugoslavia), Netzer, Grabowski (West Germany)

1 goal: Paatelainen (Finland), Kuna, Pollák, Fr. Vesely, Táborsky, Albrecht (Czechoslovakia), Iordănescu, Sătmăreanu, R. Nunweiller (Romania), Durban, Reece, R.T. Davies (Wales), Dunai II, Szücs, Zámbó, P. Juhász, Vidáts, Branikovits, L. Nagy, Kü (Hungary), Mihailov, Ml. Vasilev, Kolev, Petkov, Velitchkov, Atanasov (Bulgaria), Vergnes, H. Revelli, Floch, Mézy (France), Dybwad Olsen, O. Nilsen, Fuglset (Norway), E. Theobald, Vassallo (Malta), Davourlis, Aidiniou, Kritikopoulos (Greece), Jeandupeux, Blättler, Citherlet (Switzerland), Summerbee, Clarke, Lawler, Peters (England), Michael, Charalambous (Cyprus), Morgan (N. Ireland), Aguilar, Lora, Violeta, Luis (Spain), Bîshovets, Muntian, Konkov, Kozinkevich (USSR), Laudrup, Bjerre (Denmark), Gemmill (Scotland), Peres, João Jacinto (Portugal), Denul, Pollenius, Van Moer (Belgium), Rogers, Conway, Carroll (Republic of Ireland), Olsson, Turesson, Brzokoupil (Sweden), Pirkner, Stering, Schmidradner, Kodat, Starek (Austria), Mazzola (Italy), Pahlplatz, Hoekma, Lippens, Suurbier (Holland), Löwe, Frenzel, P. Ducke (East Germany), Dussier (Luxembourg), Pano, Zhega, Ziu (Albania), Metin, Nihat, Kamuran (Turkey), Bula, Banas, Szoltysik (Poland), Filipovic, Jerkovic (Yugoslavia), Hoeneß, Köppel, Wimmer (West Germany)

Own goals: Karlsen (Norway) for Hungary, Weibel (Switzerland) for England, McKinnon (Scotland) for Belgium, Stanton (Scotland) for Portugal, Sandvad (Denmark) for Portugal, Dunne (Republic of Ireland) for Austria, Santarini (Italy) for Austria

THE EUROPEAN FOOTBALL CHAMPIONSHIP 1976

GROUP 1

ENGLAND v CZECHOSLOVAKIA 3-0 (0-0)

Wembley, London 30.10.1974

Referee: Michel Kitabdjian (FRA) Attendance: 86,000

ENGLAND: Raymond Clemence; Paul Madeley, Emlyn Hughes, Martin Dobson (65 Trevor Brooking), David Watson, Norman Hunter, Colin Bell, Gerald Francis, Frank Worthington (66 David Thomas), Michael Channon, Kevin Keegan. Manager: Donald Revie

CZECHOSLOVAKIA: Ivo Viktor; Ján Pivarník, Anton Ondrus, Jozef Capkovic (.. Rostislav Vojacek), Vojtech Varadín; Premysl Bicovsky (.. Ladislav Kuna), Ivan Pekárik, Miroslav Gajdusek; Marián Masny, Ján Svehlík, Pavel Stratil. Trainer: Václav Jezek

Goals: Channon (72), Bell (79, 82)

ENGLAND v PORTUGAL 0-0

Wembley, London 20.11.1974

Referee: Anton Bucheli (SWI) Attendance: 85,700

ENGLAND: Raymond Clemence; Paul Madeley, David Watson, Emlyn Hughes, Terence Cooper (24 Colin Todd), Trevor Brooking, Gerald Francis, Colin Bell, David Thomas, Michael Channon, Allan Clarke (71 Frank Worthington). Manager: Donald Revie

PORTUGAL: Vitor Manuel Afonso DAMAS de Oliveira; ARTUR Manuel Soares Correia, HUMBERTO Manuel Jesus COELHO (Cap), Carlos Alexandre Fortes ALHINHO, Firmino Baleizao da Graça Sardinha OSVALDINHO, Adelino de Jesus TEIXEIRA, OCTÁVIO Joaquim Coelho Machado, João António Ferreira Resende ALVES, VITOR Manuel Rosa MARTINS, Francisco Delfim Dias Faria CHICO (85 ROMEU Fernando Fernandes Silva), Tamagnini Gomes Baptista NÉNÉ (85 António Luis Alves Ribeiro OLIVEIRA).

ENGLAND v CYPRUS 5-0 (2-0)

Wembley, London 16.04.1975

Referee: Martti Hirviniemi (FIN) Attendance: 68,245

ENGLAND: Peter Shilton; Paul Madeley, David Watson, Colin Todd, Kevin Beattie, Colin Bell, Alan Ball, Alan Hudson, Michael Channon (.. David Thomas), Malcolm Macdonald, Kevin Keegan. Manager: Donald Revie

CYPRUS: Michalis Alkiviades (.. Andreas Constantinou); Christos Kovis, Demetrios Kizas, Kyriakos Koureas, Nikos Pantziaras, Stefanis Michael, Gregory Savva, Lakis Theodorou, Andreas Stylianou, Nikos Charalambous (.. A.Constantinou), Markos Markou.

Goals: MacDonald (3, 32, 52, 56, 87)

CYPRUS v ENGLAND 0-1 (0-1)

Limassol 11.05.1975

Referee: Tzvetan Stanev (BUL) Attendance: 21,000

CYPRUS: Andreas Constantinou; Christos Kovis, Demetrios Kizas, Stavros Stylianou, Nikos Pantziaras, Stefanis Michael, Tasos Constantinou, Andreas Miamiliotis (.. Christos Papettas), Gregory Savva, Nikos Charalambous, Dimitrakis Panagiotou (.. Kokos Antoniou).

ENGLAND: Raymond Clemence; Steven Whitworth, Kevin Beattie (41 Emlyn Hughes), David Watson, Colin Todd, Colin Bell, David Thomas, Alan Ball, Michael Channon, Malcolm Macdonald, Kevin Keegan (73 Dennis Tueart). Manager: Donald Revie

Goal: Keegan (6)

CZECHOSLOVAKIA v CYPRUS 4-0 (2-0)

Praha 20.04.1975

Referee: Heinz Einbeck (E. GER) Attendance: 5,000

CZECHOSLOVAKIA: Ivo Viktor; Ján Pivarník, Anton Ondrus, Jozef Capkovic (76 Ladislav Petrás), Zdenek Koubek; Premysl Bicovsky, Antonín Panenka, Miroslav Gajdusek; Marián Masny, Ján Svehlík, Zdenek Nehoda.
Trainer: Václav Jezek

CYPRUS: Fanos Stylianou; Christos Kovis, Demetrios Kizas, Stavros Stylianou, Nikos Pantziaras, Gregory Savva, Menelaos Asprou (.. Panikos Efthimiades), Stefanis Michael (.. Christos Yiolitis), Markos Markou, Nikos Charalambous, Andreas Stylianou.

Goals: Panenka (10, 35, 57 pen), Masny (78)

CYPRUS v PORTUGAL 0-2 (0-1)

Limassol 08.06.1975

Referee: Gheorghe Limona (ROM) Attendance: 9,000

CYPRUS: Fanos Stylianou; Christos Kovis, Demetrios Kizas, Stavros Stylianou, Nikos Pantziaras, Stefanis Michael, Christos Papettas (.. Andreas Kanaris), Markos Markou, Gregory Savva, Nikos Charalambous (.. Demetrios Economou "Koudas", Andreas Savva.

PORTUGAL: Vitor DAMAS; ARTUR Manuel, HUMBERTO COELHO, Fernando José António FREITAS Alexandrino, António BARROS, OCTÁVIO Machado, António Oliveira "TONI", João ALVES, Vitor Manuel da Cruz GODINHO, Tamagnini NÉNÉ (60 Mário Jorge MOINHOS de Matos), Mário da Silva "MARINHO" (75 FRANCISCO MARIO Pinto da Silva).

Goals: Néné (25), Moinhos (89)

CZECHOSLOVAKIA v PORTUGAL 5-0 (3-0)

Sparta, Praha 30.04.1975

Referee: Ferdinand Biwersi (W. GER) Attendance: 25,000

CZECHOSLOVAKIA: Ivo Viktor; Ján Pivarník, Anton Ondrus, Jozef Capkovic, Zdenek Koubek (76 Jindrich Svoboda); Premysl Bicovsky, Lubomír Knapp (81 Ján Medvid), Miroslav Gajdusek; Marián Masny, Ladislav Petrás, Zdenek Nehoda. Trainer: Václav Jezek

PORTUGAL: Vitor DAMAS; Francisco Moreira da Silva REBELO, HUMBERTO COELHO, Carlos ALHINHO, António Monteiro Teixeira de BARROS, OCTÁVIO Machado, António José da Conceiçao Oliveira "TONI" (50 Minervino José Lopes PIETRA), João ALVES, Samuel Ferreira FRAGUITO, Mário da Silva Mateus "MARINHO", Tamagnini NÉNÉ (64 Fernando Mendes Soares GOMES).

Goals: Bicovsky (11, 22), Nehoda (25, 46), Petrás (52)

CZECHOSLOVAKIA v ENGLAND 2-1 (1-1)

Bratislava 30.10.1975

Referee: Alberto Michelotti (ITA) Attendance: 45,000

CZECHOSLOVAKIA: Ivo Viktor; Ján Pivarník, Anton Ondrus, Ladislav Jurkemik, Koloman Gögh (.. Karol Dobias); Jaroslav Pollák, Premysl Bicovsky, Lubomír Knapp; Marián Masny, Peter Gallis, Zdenek Nehoda. Trainer: Václav Jezek

ENGLAND: Raymond Clemence; Paul Madeley, Ian Gillard, Gerald Francis, Roy McFarland (46 David Watson), Colin Todd, Kevin Keegan, Michael Channon (.. David Thomas), Malcolm Macdonald, Allan Clarke, Colin Bell. Manager: Donald Revie

This match was stopped in the 17th minute on 29.10.1975 because of fog and was fully replayed the following day.

Goals: Channon (27), Nehoda (45), Gallis (70)

PORTUGAL v CZECHOSLOVAKIA 1-1 (1-1)

Estádio das Antas, Porto 12.11.1975

Referee: Charles G. Corver (HOL) Attendance: 45,000

PORTUGAL: Vitor DAMAS; Francisco REBELO, HUMBERTO COELHO, Fernando FREITAS, ARTUR Correia, OCTÁVIO Machado, João ALVES, António Oliveira "TONI", Tamagnini NÉNÉ (46 António OLIVEIRA, 66 Mário Silva Mateus "MARINHO"), VITOR Manuel Ferreira BATISTA, Mário MOINHOS.

CZECHOSLOVAKIA: Ivo Viktor; Ján Pivarník, Anton Ondrus, Ladislav Jurkemik, Koloman Gögh; Premysl Bicovsky, Jaroslav Pollák, Jozef Móder; Marián Masny (.. Karol Dobias), Peter Gallis (41 Frantisek Vesely), Zdenek Nehoda. Trainer: Václav Jezek

Goals: Ondrus (5), Néné (6)

PORTUGAL v ENGLAND 1-1 (1-1)

Estádio José Alvalade, Lisboa 19.11.1975

Referee: Erich Linemayr (AUS) Attendance: 40,000

PORTUGAL: Vitor DAMAS; Francisco REBELO (49 António Carlos Sousa Laranjeira Lima "TAI"), RUI Gouveia Pinto RODRIGUES (49 Alvaro CAROLINO Nascimento), ARTUR Correia, Fernando FREITAS, OCTÁVIO Machado, João ALVES, António Oliveira "TONI", Tamagnini NÉNÉ, VITOR BATISTA, Mário MOINHOS.

ENGLAND: Raymond Clemence; Steven Whitworth, Kevin Beattie, Gerald Francis, David Watson, Colin Todd, Kevin Keegan, Michael Channon, Malcolm Macdonald (74 David Thomas), Trevor Brooking, Paul Madeley (75 Allan Clarke). Manager: Donald Revie

Goals: Rui Rodrigues (16), Channon (42)

CYPRUS v CZECHOSLOVAKIA 0-3 (0-3)

Limassol 23.11.1975

Referee: Sándor Petri (HUN) Attendance: 9,000

CYPRUS: Michalis Alkiviades; Ioannis Mertakkas, Paschalis Fokkis (.. Kallis Constantinou), Stavros Stylianou, Nikos Pantziaras, Stefanis Michael, Christos Papettas, Gregory Savva, Sotiris Kaiafas (.. Andreas Miamiliotis), Markos Markou, Andreas Kanaris.

CZECHOSLOVAKIA: Ivo Viktor; Ján Pivarník, Anton Ondrus, Ladislav Jurkemik, Koloman Gögh; Premysl Bicovsky, Jaroslav Pollák (.. Ján Medvid), Jozef Móder; Marián Masny, Ján Svehlík (.. Frantisek Vesely), Zdenek Nehoda. Trainer: Václav Jezek

Goals: Nehoda (9), Bicovsky (27), Masny (33)

PORTUGAL v CYPRUS 1-0 (1-0)

Estádio do Bonfim, Setúbal 03.12.1975

Referee: Richard Casha (MAL) Attendance: 4,000

PORTUGAL: António José Silva BOTELHO; ARTUR Correia, JOSÉ JESUS MENDES, Fernando FREITAS, António Lima "TAI", OCTÁVIO Machado, João ALVES, António Oliveira "TONI", António OLIVEIRA, VITOR BATISTA, Mário MOINHOS (46 MANUEL José Tavares FERNANDES).

CYPRUS: Fanos Stylianou; Ioannis Mertakkas, Stavros Stylianou, Kallis Constantinou, Nikos Pantziaras, Stefanis Michael, Christos Papettas (.. Panikos Efthymiades), Gregory Savva, Andreas Miamiliotis, Markos Markou, Andreas Kanaris (.. Dimitrakis Panagiotou).

Goal: Alves (20)

	P	W	D	L	F	A	Pts
Czechoslovakia	6	4	1	1	15	5	9
England	6	3	2	1	11	3	8
Portugal	6	2	3	1	5	7	7
Cyprus	6	0	0	6	0	16	0

GROUP 2

AUSTRIA v WALES 2-1 (0-1)

Prater, Wien 04.09.1974

Referee: Dogan Babacan (TUR) Attendance: 35,000

AUSTRIA: Herbert Rettensteiner; Johann Eigenstiller (Cap), Johannes Winklbauer, Eduard Krieger, Werner Kriess; Werner Walzer, August Starek, Rainer Schlagbauer (67 Helmut Köglberger), Wilhelm Kreuz, Johann Krankl, Josef Stering. Trainer: Leopold Stastny

WALES: Gary Sprake; Philip Roberts, David Roberts (Cap), John Roberts, Leighton Phillips; John Mahoney, Terence Yorath, Arfon Trevor Griffiths; Leighton James, John Toshack, Gilbert Ivor Reece. Manager: Michael Smith

Goals: Griffiths (34), Kreuz (63), Krankl (75)

LUXEMBOURG v HUNGARY 2-4 (2-2)

Stade Municipal, Luxembourg 13.10.1974

Referee: Magnus Petursson (ICE) Attendance: 3,000

LUXEMBOURG: Jeannot Moes; Roger Fandel, Joé Hansen, René Flenghi, Robert Da Grava, Jean Zuang, Louis Trierweiller, Paul Philipp (Cap), Gilbert Dussier, Nico Braun, Pierrot Langers. Trainer: Gilbert Legrand

HUNGARY: Ferenc Mészáros; Péter Török, László Harsányi, József Horváth, Mihály Kántor; László Bálint, László Fazekas, András Tóth; Mihály Pénzes, Tibor Kiss, László Nagy.

Goals: Dussier (14, 44 pen), Horváth (18), Nagy (30, 55), Bálint (70)

WALES v HUNGARY 2-0 (0-0)

Ninian Park, Cardiff 30.10.1974

Referee: Antonio da Silva Garrido (POR) Att: 15,000

WALES: Gary Sprake (84 Thomas John J. Phillips); Rodney John Thomas, Philip Roberts, John Mahoney, Harold Michael England, Leighton Phillips, Arfon Trevor Griffiths, Terence Yorath, Gilbert Ivor Reece, John Toshack, Leighton James.
Manager: Michael Smith

HUNGARY: Ferenc Mészáros; Péter Török, László Bálint, József Mucha, Mihály Kántor; Zoltán Halmosi, László Fazekas, András Tóth (63 József Póczik); László Fekete, Tibor Kiss, László Nagy.

Goals: Griffiths (57), Toshack (87)

AUSTRIA v HUNGARY 0-0

Prater, Wien 02.04.1975

Referee: Jack Taylor (ENG) Attendance: 80,000

AUSTRIA: Friedrich Koncilia; Johann Eigenstiller (Cap), Johannes Winklbauer, Erich Obermayer, Heinrich Strasser; Roland Hattenberger, Herbert Prohaska, Wilhelm Kreuz; Helmut Köglberger (69 Johann Pirkner), Johann Krankl, Alfred Riedl. Trainer: Leopold Stastny

HUNGARY: Ferenc Mészáros; Péter Török, László Bálint, János Nagy, József Tóth; Károly Csapó, Lajos Kocsis, József Horváth, András Tóth (68 Sándor Pinter); Ferenc Bene (Cap), László Branikovits (68 László Fekete).

WALES v LUXEMBOURG 5-0 (1-0)

Swansea 20.11.1974

Referee: Preben Christophersen (DEN) Attendance: 10,530

WALES: Gary Sprake; Rodney John Thomas, Harold Michael England, Philip Roberts, Leighton Phillips, John Mahoney (.. Brian Flynn), Terence Yorath, Arfon Trevor Griffiths, Leighton James, Gilbert Ivor Reece, John Toshack.
Manager: Michael Smith

LUXEMBOURG: Lucien Thill; Roger Fandel, René Flenghi, Joé Hansen, Robert Da Grava (73 Henri Roemer), Jean Zuang, Louis Pilot (Cap), Louis Trierweiler, Pierrot Langers (64 Jean-Paul Martin), Gilbert Dussier, Paul Philipp.
Trainer: Gilbert Legrand

Goals: Toshack (34), England (53), P. Roberts (70), Griffiths (73), Yorath (75)

HUNGARY v WALES 1-2 (0-1)

Népstadion, Budapest 16.04.1975

Referee: Pablo Augusto Sánchez Ibanez (SPA) Att: 25,000

HUNGARY: Ferenc Mészáros; Péter Török, János Nagy, László Bálint, József Tóth; Károly Csapó (56 Ferenc Bene), Lajos Kocsis, József Horváth (46 Sándor Pintér); Mihály Kozma, László Branikovits, János Máté.

WALES: William David Davies; Rodney John Thomas, Malcolm Edward Page, Leighton Phillips, John Roberts, Terence Yorath, John Mahoney, Arfon Trevor Griffiths, Gilbert Ivor Reece (83 David Smallman), John Toshack, Leighton James (59 Brian Flynn). Toshack missed penalty (14).
Manager: Michael Smith

Goals: Toshack (45), Mahoney (70), Branikovits (77)

LUXEMBOURG v AUSTRIA 1-2 (1-0)

Stade Municipal, Luxembourg 16.03.1975

Referee: Leonardus van der Kroft (HOL) Attendance: 4,000

LUXEMBOURG: Jeannot Moes; Roger Fandel, Joé Hansen, Louis Pilot (Cap), Jean-Louis Margue, Louis Trierweiler, Paul Philipp, Jean Zuang, Gilbert Zender (77 Jean-Paul Goerres), Gilbert Dussier, Nico Braun. Trainer: Gilbert Legrand

AUSTRIA: Friedrich Koncilia; Roland Hattenberger, Norbert Hof, Egon Pajenk, Johann Eigenstiller (Cap); Josef Hickersberger, Herbert Prohaska, Manfred Gombasch; Josef Stering, Kurt Welzl (39 Helmut Köglberger), Johann Krankl.
Trainer: Leopold Stastny

Goals: Braun (11), Köglberger (58), Krankl (75)

LUXEMBOURG v WALES 1-3 (1-2)

Stade Municipal, Luxembourg 01.05.1975

Referee: Jan Peeters (BEL) Attendance: 5,000

LUXEMBOURG: Jeannot Moes; Roger Fandel, Joé Hansen, Louis Pilot (Cap), Jean-Louis Margue, Louis Trierweiler, Jean Zuang, Paul Philipp, Jean-Paul Martin (50 Jeannot Krecke, 80 Henri Roemer), Nico Braun, Gilbert Zender.
Trainer: Gilbert Legrand

WALES: William David Davies; Malcolm Edward Page, Terence Yorath, Rodney John Thomas, David Roberts, John Mahoney, Leighton Phillips, Arfon Trevor Griffiths (.. Brian Flynn), Gilbert Ivor Reece, John Toshack, Leighton James.
Manager: Michael Smith

Goals: Reece (24), James (32, 83 pen), Philipp (39 pen)

HUNGARY v AUSTRIA 2-1 (2-1)

Népstadion, Budapest 24.09.1975

Referee: René Vigliani (FRA) Attendance: 35,000

HUNGARY: László Kovács; János Nagy, László Bálint, Tibor Rab, Sándor Lukács; Tibor Nyilasi, Lajos Kocsis, András Tóth (76 Sándor Pintér); László Pusztai, László Fazekas (Cap), László Nagy (46 Béla Váradi).

AUSTRIA: Friedrich Koncilia; Robert Sara, Erich Obermayer (46 Johannes Winklbauer), Bruno Pezzey, Werner Kriess (Cap); Peter Koncilia, Herbert Prohaska (46 Manfred Steiner), Kurt Jara; Günter Rinker, Kurt Welzl, Johann Krankl. Trainer: Leopold Stastny

Goals: Nyilasi (4), Krankl (17 pen), Pusztai (35)

AUSTRIA v LUXEMBOURG 6-2 (3-2)

Prater, Wien 15.10.1975

Referee: Miroslav Kopal (CZE) Attendance: 20,000

AUSTRIA: Friedrich Koncilia; Werner Kriess (Cap), Johannes Winklbauer, Bruno Pezzey, Heinrich Strasser; Herbert Prohaska, Peter Koncilia, Johann Ettmayer; Kurt Welzl, Johann Krankl, Kurt Jara. Trainer: Branko Elsner

LUXEMBOURG: René Hoffmann, Emile Lahure, Joé Hansen, Louis Pilot (Cap), Jean-Louis Margue, Jean Zuang, Louis Trierweiler, Paul Philipp, Pierrot Langers (75 Jeannot Krecke), Gilbert Dussier (65 François Hauer), Nico Braun. Trainer: Gilbert Legrand

Goals: Welzl (1, 46), Braun (5), Philipp (32 pen), Krankl (38 pen, 76), Jara (41), Prohaska (80)

HUNGARY v LUXEMBOURG 8-1 (4-0)

Haladás, Szombathely 19.10.1975

Referee: Nikola Dudin (BUL) Attendance: 10,000

HUNGARY: Adám Rothermel; János Nagy, László Bálint, Tibor Rab, Sándor Lukács; Tibor Nyilasi, József Kovács, Sándor Pintér; László Fazekas, Béla Váradi, László Nagy (40 Tibor Wollek).

LUXEMBOURG: Raymond Zender, Léon Schmit, Joé Hansen, Louis Pilot (Cap), Emile Lahure, Jean Zuang, Louis Trierweiler (50 René Flenghi), Paul Philipp, Pierrot Langers (70 Jeannot Krecke), Gilbert Dussier, Nico Braun. Trainer: Gilbert Legrand

Goal: Pinter (13), Nyilasi (21, 22, 44, 57, 67), Váradi (84), Wollek (78), Dussier (83)

WALES v AUSTRIA 1-0 (0-0)

Racecourt Ground, Wrexham 19.11.1975

Referee: Sergio Gonella (ITA) Attendance: 30,000

WALES: Brian William Lloyd; Rodney John Thomas, Ian Peter Evans, Leighton Phillips, Joseph Jones; John Mahoney, Terence Yorath (Cap), Arfon Trevor Griffiths; Brian Flynn, David Smallman, Leighton James. Manager: Michael Smith

AUSTRIA: Friedrich Koncilia; Robert Sara (Cap), Johannes Winklbauer, Bruno Pezzey, Werner Kriess (29 Heinrich Strasser); Manfred Steiner, Herbert Prohaska, Johann Ettmayer; Kurt Welzl (70 Josef Stering), Johann Krankl, Kurt Jara. Trainer: Branko Elsner

Goal: Griffiths (69)

	P	W	D	L	F	A	Pts
Wales	6	5	0	1	14	4	10
Hungary	6	3	1	2	15	8	7
Austria	6	3	1	2	11	7	7
Luxembourg	6	0	0	6	7	28	0

GROUP 3

NORWAY v NORTHERN IRELAND 2-1 (0-1)

Oslo 04.09.1974

Referee: Alfred Delcourt (BEL) Attendance: 7,200

NORWAY: Geir Karlsen; Reidar Goa, Jan Birkelund, Torkild Brakstad, Svein Grøndalen, Egil Austbø, Tor Egil Johansen, Svein Kvia, Jan Fuglset, Tom Lund, Harry Hestad. Trainer: Kjell Schou Andreassen

N. IRELAND: Patrick Jennings; Patrick Rice, David Craig (.. Hugh Dowd), William O'Kane, Alan Hunter, David Clements, Bryan Hamilton, Thomas Cassidy, Thomas Finney, Samuel McIlroy, Cristopher McGrath (.. Thomas Jackson). Manager: Terence Neill

Goals: Finney (3), T. Lund (59, 72)

SWEDEN v NORTHERN IRELAND 0-2 (0-2)

Fotbollstadion, Solna 30.10.1974

Referee: Theo Boosten (HOL) Attendance: 18,131

SWEDEN: Ronnie Hellström; Roland Andersson, Kent Karlsson, Björn Nordqvist, Björn Andersson, Staffan Tapper, Ove Kindvall (73 Thomas Nordahl), Bo Larsson, Conny Torstensson (46 Jan Mattson), Ralf Edström, Roland Sandberg.

N. IRELAND: Patrick Jennings; William O'Kane, Samuel Nelson (46 Ronald Blair), Hugh Dowd, Alan Hunter, Christopher Nicholl, Thomas Jackson, Martin O'Neill, Samuel Morgan, Samuel McIlroy, Bryan Hamilton.
Manager: Terence Neill

Goals: Nicholl (7), O'Neill (23)

YUGOSLAVIA v NORWAY 3-1 (1-1)

JNA, Beograd 30.10.1974

Referee: Antoine Queudeville (LUX) Attendance: 15,000

YUGOSLAVIA: Ognjen Petrovic; Vilson Dzoni, Dzemal Hadziabdic, Jure Jerkovic, Josip Katalinski, Ivan Buljan, Slavisa Zungul, Momcilo Vukotic, Ivan Surjak, Franjo Vladic (.. Ljubisa Rajkovic), Dragan Dzajic. Trainer: Ante Mladinic

NORWAY: Geir Karlsen; Öystein Wormdahl, Jan Birkelund, Torkild Brakstad, Svein Grøndalen, Egil Austbø, Tor Egil Johansen (72 Jan Fuglset), Svein Kvia, Terje Olsen, Tom Lund, Harry Hestad. Trainer: Kjell Schou Andreassen

Goals: T. Lund (36), M.Vukotic (43), Katalinski (58, 72)

NORWAY v YUGOSLAVIA 1-3 (0-3)

Ulleval, Oslo 09.06.1975

Referee: Edgar Pedersen (DEN) Attendance: 21,700

NORWAY: Erik Johannesen (77 Geir Karlsen); Erling Meirik, Reidar Goa (40 Trond Pedersen), Jan Birkelund, Svein Grøndalen, Tor Egil Johansen, Svein Kvia, Harry Hestad, Stein Thunberg, Tom Lund, Gabriel Høyland.
Trainer: Kjell Schou Andreassen

YUGOSLAVIA: Ognjen Petrović; Ivan Buljan, Dzemal Hadziabdic, Drazen Muzinić, Josip Katalinski, Vladislav Bogicevic, Danilo Popivoda, Branko Oblak, Ivan Surjak, Franjo Vladic (77 Vladimir Petrovic), Zvonko Ivezic.
Trainer: Ante Mladinic

Goals: Buljan (12), Bogicevic (13), Surjak (25), Thunberg (65)

NORTHERN IRELAND v YUGOSLAVIA 1-0 (1-0)

Windsor Park, Belfast 16.04.1975

Referee: Robert Wurtz (FRA) Attendance: 30,000

N. IRELAND: Patrick Jennings; Patrick Rice, Samuel Nelson, Christopher Nicholl, Alan Hunter, David Clements, Bryan Hamilton, Martin O'Neill, Derek Spence, Samuel McIlroy, Thomas Jackson. Manager: Terence Neill

YUGOSLAVIA: Ognjen Petrović; Drazen Muzinić, Dzemal Hadziabdić, Luka Peruzović, Josip Katalinski, Ivan Buljan, Slobodan Janković, Branko Oblak, Momcilo Vukotić (.. Franjo Vladić), Jure Jerković (77 Ivica Miljković), Ivan Surjak.
Trainer: Ante Mladinić

Goal: Hamilton (22)

SWEDEN v NORWAY 3-1 (1-0)

Solna, 30.06.1975

Referee: Rudolf Glöckner (E. GER) Attendance: 9,580

SWEDEN: Ronnie Hellström; Roland Andersson, Roy Andersson, Kent Karlsson, Jörgen Augustsson, Anders Linderoth, Ove Grahn, Eine Fredriksson (61 Curt Olsberg), Roland Sandberg, Thomas Nordahl, Benny Wendt (.. Jan Mattsson).

NORWAY: Erik Johannesen (80 Tore Antonsen); Erling Meirik, Helge Karlsen, Svein Grøndalen, Trond Pedersen, Tor Egil Johansen, Svein Kvia, Frode Larsen (69 Stein Thunberg), Erik Just Olsen, Helge Skuseth, Gabriel Høyland.
Trainer: Kjell Schou Andreassen

Goals: Nordahl (33, 56), E.J. Olsen (54), Grahn (65 pen)

SWEDEN v YUGOSLAVIA 1-2 (1-1)

Rasunda, Solna 04.06.1975

Referee: Vital Loraux (BEL) Attendance: 27,250

SWEDEN: Ronnie Hellström; Roland Andersson, Kent Karlsson, Björn Nordqvist, Jörgen Augustsson, Ove Grahn, Eine Fredriksson, Ralf Edström, Roland Sandberg, Thomas Sjöberg, Benny Wendt (46 Göran Hagberg), (66 Thomas Nordahl).

YUGOSLAVIA: Ognjen Petrovic; Ivan Buljan, Dzemal Hadziabdic, Drazen Muzinic, Josip Katalinski, Vladislav Bogicevic, Danilo Popivoda, Branko Oblak, Dusan Savic (53 Zvonko Ivezic), Franjo Vladic, Ivan Surjak.
Trainer: Ante Mladinic

Goals: Edström (16), Katalinski (41), Ivezic (78)

NORWAY v SWEDEN 0-2 (0-1)

Oslo 13.08.1975

Referee: Anders Mattsson (FIN) Attendance: 18,011

NORWAY: Tore Antonsen; Trond Pedersen, Helge Karlsen, Svein Grøndalen, Sigbjørn Slinning, Jan Hansen, Svein Kvia, Stein Thunberg (.. Tor Egil Johansen), Frode Larsen, Helge Skuseth, Gabriel Høyland (62 Svein Mathisen).
Trainer: Kjell Schou Andreassen

SWEDEN: Ronnie Hellström; Roland Andersson, Kent Karlsson, Björn Nordqvist, Jörgen Augustsson, Anders Linderoth, Ove Grahn, Ralf Edström, Roland Sandberg, Thomas Sjöberg, Benny Wendt (.. Jan Mattsson).

Goals: Sandberg (29), Sjöberg (53)

NORTHERN IRELAND v SWEDEN 1-2 (1-1)

Belfast 03.09.1975

Referee: Hans Joachim Weyland (W. GER) Att: 15,000

N. IRELAND: Patrick Jennings; Patrick Rice, Samuel Nelson, David Clements, Alan Hunter, Christopher Nicholl, Ronald Blair, Bryan Hamilton (.. Samuel Morgan), Derek Spence, Samuel McIlroy, Thomas Jackson. Manager: David Clements

SWEDEN: Ronnie Hellström; Roland Sandberg, Kent Karlsson, Björn Nordqvist, Jörgen Augustsson, Eine Fredriksson, Conny Torstensson, Anders Linderoth, Curt Olsberg (46 Staffan Tapper), Thomas Sjöberg, Jan Mattsson.

Goals: Hunter (32), Sjöberg (45), Torstensson (54)

YUGOSLAVIA v SWEDEN 3-0 (1-0)

Maksimir, Zagreb 15.10.1975

Referee: Walter Hungerbühler (SWI) Attendance: 45,000

YUGOSLAVIA: Ognjen Petrovic; Ivan Buljan, Dzemal Hadziabdic, Branko Oblak, Josip Katalinski, Drazen Muzinic, Drago Vabec, Jure Jerkovic, Ivan Surjak, Franjo Vladic, Dragan Dzajic. Trainer: Ante Mladinic

SWEDEN: Ronnie Hellström; Roland Andersson, Kent Karlsson, Björn Nordqvist, Jörgen Augustsson, Anders Linderoth, Staffan Tapper, Conny Torstensson, Roland Sandberg, Thomas Sjöberg (32 Jan Mattsson), Ralf Edström.

Goals: Oblak (17), Vladic (50), Vabec (83)

NORTHERN IRELAND v NORWAY 3-0 (2-0)

Belfast 29.10.1975

Referee: Gujón Finnbogasseon (ICE) Attendance: 8,000

N. IRELAND: Patrick Jennings; Patrick Rice, Samuel Nelson, Christopher Nicholl, Alan Hunter, Thomas Jackson, Bryan Hamilton, Samuel McIlroy, Samuel Morgan (.. Terence Cochrane), John Jamison, Thomas Finney.
Manager: David Clements

NORWAY: Geir Karlsen (68 Tom Risz Jacobsen); Trond Pedersen, Helge Karlsen, Svein Grøndalen (50 Børge Josefsen), Sigbjørn Slinning, Jan Hansen, Svein Kvia, Helge Skuseth, Gabriel Høyland, Pål Jacobsen, Harry Hestad.
Trainer: Kjell Schou Andreassen

Goals: Morgan (2), McIlroy (5), Hamilton (53)

YUGOSLAVIA v NORTHERN IRELAND 1-0 (1-0)

JNA, Beograd 19.11.1975

Referee: Antonio Camacho Jimenez (SPA) Att: 40,000

YUGOSLAVIA: Ognjen Petrovic; Ivan Buljan, Dzemal Hadziabdic, Branko Oblak, Josip Katalinski, Drazen Muzinic, Jure Jerkovic, Momcilo Vukotic, Ivan Surjak, Franjo Vladic, Dragan Dzajic. Trainer: Ante Mladinic

N. IRELAND: Patrick Jennings; Patrick Rice, Peter Scott, Christopher Nicholl, Alan Hunter, David Clements, Bryan Hamilton, Samuel McIlroy, Samuel Morgan, Thomas Jackson (.. Martin O'Neill), Thomas Finney.
Manager: David Clements

Goal: Oblak (23)

	P	W	D	L	F	A	Pts
Yugoslavia	6	5	0	1	12	4	10
Northern Ireland	6	3	0	3	8	5	6
Sweden	6	3	0	3	8	9	6
Norway	6	1	0	5	5	15	2

GROUP 4

DENMARK v SPAIN 1-2 (0-2)

Idraetsparken, København 25.09.1974

Referee: John Carpenter (IRE) Attendance: 27,300

DENMARK: Benno Larsen; Flemming Mortensen, Henning Munk Jensen, Jørgen Rasmussen, Kjeld Seneca; Niels Sørensen (70 Jørgen Jørgensen), Morten Olsen, Kristen Nygaard; Allan Simonsen, Henning Jensen, Niels Christian Holmstrøm (46 Ove Flindt Bjerg). Trainer: Rudolf Strittich

SPAIN: José Angel IRIBAR Cortajarena; Juan Cruz SOL Oria, Gregorio BENITO Rubio, Francisco CASTELLANOS Rodriguez, José Luis CAPON Gonzalez; Jesús MARTINEZ Rivadeneyra, José CLARAMUNT Torres, Juan Manuel ASENSI Ripoll; ROBERTO MARTINEZ Martinez (65 Juan Antonio GARCÍA SORIANO), Enrique Castro Gonzalez QUINI, MARCIAL Pina Morales. Claramunt sent off (89).
Trainer: Ladislao Kubala

Goals: Claramunt I (28 pen), R. Martinez (41), Nygaard (48 pen)

DENMARK v ROMANIA 0-0

Idraetsparken, Köbenhavn 13.10.1974

Referee: Ferdinand Biwersi (W. GER) Attendance: 15,700

DENMARK: Benno Larsen; Flemming Mortensen, Henning Munk Jensen, Steen Danielsen, Jørgen Rasmussen; Morten Olsen, Ulrik le Févre, Jørgen Jørgensen; Benny Nielsen, Flemming Lund, Niels-Christian Holmstrøm.
Trainer: Rudolf Strittich

ROMANIA: Răducanu Necula; Florin Cheran, Dumitru Antonescu, Alexandru Sătmăreanu, Teodor Anghelini; Ion Dumitru, Cornel Dinu (Cap), Anghel Iordănescu; Radu Nunweiller, Mircea Lucescu (80 Radu Troi), Attila Kun.
Trainer: Valentin Stănescu

SCOTLAND v SPAIN 1-2 (1-1)

Hampden Park, Glasgow 20.11.1974

Referee: Eric Linemayr (AUS) Attendance: 92,000

SCOTLAND: David Harvey; William Jardine, Kenneth Burns, Alexander Forsyth; Gordon McQueen, William John Bremner; Graeme James Souness, Thomas Hutchison (66 Kenneth Dalglish), James Johnstone, John Kelly Deans (60 Peter Lorimer), Joseph Jordan. Manager: William Ormond

SPAIN: José Angel IRIBAR Cortajarena; Francisco CASTELLANOS Rodriguez, Gregorio BENITO Rubio, Bernardo Blanquetti MIGUELI (67 Juan Cruz SOL Oria), José Luis CAPON Gonzalez; Enrique Álvarez COSTAS, Angel Maria VILLAR Llona, Javier PLANAS Abad; ROBERTO MARTINEZ Martinez, Enrique Castro Gonzalez QUINI, Carlos REXACH Cerdá. Trainer: Ladislao Kubala

Goals: Bremner (10), Quini (36, 60)

SPAIN v SCOTLAND 1-1 (0-1)

Estadio Luis Casanova, Valencia 05.02.1975

Referee: Alfred Delcourt (BEL) Attendance: 60,000

SPAIN: José Angel IRIBAR Cortajarena; Juan Cruz SOL Oria, Gregorio BENITO Rubio, Enrique Álvarez COSTAS (67 Bernardo Blanquetti MIGUELI), José Antonio CAMACHO Alfaro, José CLARAMUNT Torres, Angel Maria VILLAR Llona, Juan Manuel ASENSI Ripoll; Enrique Castro Gonzalez QUINI, José Eulogio GARATE Hormaechea (62 Alfredo MEGIDO), Carlos REXACH Cerdá. Trainer: Ladislao Kubala

SCOTLAND: David Harvey; William Jardine, Daniel McGrain, Gordon McQueen, Martin Buchan, Kenneth Dalglish, William John Bremner, Thomas Hutchison, Charles Cooke, Joseph Jordan (46 Derek James Parlane), Kenneth Burns (60 Paul Wilson). Manager: William Ormond

Goals: Jordan (1), Megido (66 pen)

SPAIN v ROMANIA 1-1 (1-0)

Estadio Santiago Bernabeu, Madrid 17.04.1975

Referee: Charles Corver (HOL) Attendance: 100,000

SPAIN: José Angel IRIBAR Cortajarena; José Antonio CAMACHO Alfaro, Gregorio BENITO Rubio, José Martinez Sánchez PIRRI, José Luis CAPON Gonzalez; Vicente Gonzalez DEL BOSQUE, Manuel VELAZQUEZ Villaverde (46 Javier IRURETAgoyena Amiano); Carlos REXACH Cerdá, Carlos Alonso Gonzalez SANTILLANA, José Eulogio GARATE Hormaechea, José Francisco ROJO I Arroitia.
Trainer: Ladislao Kubala

ROMANIA: Răducanu Necula; Florin Cheran, Gabriel Sandu, Alexandru Sătmăreanu, Teodor Anghelini; Dudu Georgescu, Ilie Balaci, Ion Dumitru; Radu Nunweiller (43 Zoltan Crişan), Attila Kun (43 Anghel Iordănescu), Mircea Lucescu (Cap).
Trainer: Valentin Stănescu

Goals: Velazquez (6), Crişan (70)

ROMANIA v DENMARK 6-1 (2-0)

"23 August", Bucureşti 11.05.1975

Referee: Nikolaos Zlatanos (GRE) Attendance: 60,000

ROMANIA: Răducanu Necula; Florin Cheran, Alexandru Sătmăreanu, Gabriel Sandu, Teodor Anghelini; Cornel Dinu (Cap), Ion Dumitru (80 Ilie Balaci), Nicolae Dobrin (80 Attila Kun); Zoltan Crişan, Dudu Georgescu, Mircea Lucescu.
Trainer: Valentin Stănescu

DENMARK: Benno Larsen (22 Per Poulsen); Flemming Mortensen, Henning Munk Jensen, Lars Larsen, Jørgen Rasmussen; Morten Olsen, Niels Sørensen (37 Frank Nielsen), Jørgen Jørgensen; Birger Mauritzen, Peter Dahl, Eigil Nielsen.
Trainer: Rudolf Strittich

Goals: Georgescu (28, 76), Crişan (40, 59), Lucescu (83), Dinu (85), Dahl (86)

ROMANIA v SCOTLAND 1-1 (1-0)

"23 August", Bucureşti 01.06.1975

Referee: Ertugrul Dilek (TUR) Attendance: 80,000

ROMANIA: Răducanu Necula; Florin Cheran, Alexandru Sătmăreanu, Gabriel Sandu, Teodor Anghelini; Ion Dumitru, Cornel Dinu (Cap), Dudu Georgescu (38 Ilie Balaci; Zoltan Crişan, Nicolae Dobrin (82 Attila Kun).
Trainer: Valentin Stănescu

SCOTLAND: James Grady Brown; Daniel Fergus McGrain, Francis Michael Munro, Gordon McQueen, Alexander Forsyth; William Ferguson Miller, Kenneth Dalglish, Bruce David Rioch (66 Robert Sharp Robinson), Derek James Parlane, Luigi Macari (66 Thomas Hutchison), Arthur Duncan.
Manager: William Ormond

Goals: D. Georgescu (21), McQueen (89)

DENMARK v SCOTLAND 0-1 (0-0)

Idraetsparken, København 03.09.1975

Referee: Robert Schaut (BEL) Attendance: 40,300

DENMARK: Birger Jensen; Flemming Mortensen, Henning Munk Jensen, Lars Larsen, Niels Tune, Ole Bjørnmose, Ove Flindt Bjerg, Benny Nielsen, Allan Simonsen, Henning Jensen, Ulrik Le Févre. Trainer: Rudolf Strittich

SCOTLAND: David Harvey; Daniel Fergus McGrain, Alexander Forsyth, William John Bremner, Gordon McQueen, Martin Buchan, Peter Lorimer, Kenneth Dalglish, Joseph Harper, Bruce David Rioch, Thomas Hutchison (60 Arthur Duncan). Manager: William Ormond

Goal: Harper (51)

SPAIN v DENMARK 2-0 (1-0)

Nou Camp, Barcelona 12.10.1975

Referee: Paul Bonnet (MAL) Attendance: 20,000

SPAIN: MIGUEL ANGEL Gonzalez Suarez; José Antonio RAMOS, Gregorio BENITO Rubio, Bernardo Blanquetti MIGUELI, José Luis CAPON Gonzalez; MARCIAL Pina Morales, Daniel SOLSONA Puig, José Martinez Sánchez PIRRI, Vicente Gonzalez DEL BOSQUE (46 Juan Manuel ASENSI Ripoll); Carlos Alonso Gonzalez SANTILLANA, Carlos REXACH Cerdá (.. Ignacio CHURRUCA Sistiaga). Trainer: Ladislao Kubala

DENMARK: Benno Larsen; John Andersen, Henning Munk Jensen, Lars Larsen, Johnny Hansen, Ole Rasmussen, Niels Sørensen (60 Carsten Nielsen), Heino Hansen, Peter Dahl, Lars Bastrup, Ove Flindt Bjerg. Trainer: Rudolf Strittich

Goals: Pirri (40), Capón (67)

SCOTLAND v DENMARK 3-1 (0-1)

Hampden Park, Glasgow 29.10.1975

Referee: Rolf Nyhus (NOR) Attendance: 50,000

SCOTLAND: David Harvey; Daniel Fergus McGrain, Stewart Houston, John Greig, Colin Jackson, Bruce David Rioch, Peter Lorimer, Kenneth Dalglish, Edward MacDougall (73 Derek Parlane), Richard Hartford, Archibald Gemmill. Manager: William Ormond

DENMARK: Benno Larsen; John Andersen, Henning Munk Jensen, Lars Larsen, Johnny Hansen, Niels Sørensen, Heino Hansen, Niels Tune (68 Frank Nielsen), Kristen Nygaard, Lars Bastrup, Jens Kolding. Trainer: Rudolf Strittich

Goals: Bastrup (20), Dalglish (48), Rioch (53), MacDougall (62)

ROMANIA v SPAIN 2-2 (0-1)

23 August, București 16.11.1975

Referee: Hans Joachim Weyland (W. GER) Att: 50,000

ROMANIA: Răducanu Necula; Teodor Anghelini, Gabriel Sandu, Alexandru Sătmăreanu, Teodor Lucuţă; Cornel Dinu (Cap), Dudu Georgescu; Mircea Lucescu, Mircea Sandu (46 Anghel Iordănescu), Nicolae Dobrin, Constantin Zamfir (61 Zoltan Crişan). Trainer: Valentin Stănescu

SPAIN: MIGUEL ANGEL Gonzalez Suarez; Juan Cruz SOL Oria, Gregorio BENITO Rubio, Bernardo Blanquetti MIGUELI, José Antonio CAMACHO Alfaro; José Martinez Sánchez PIRRI (Cap), Angel Maria VILLAR Llona, Vicente Gonzalez DEL BOSQUE; Enrique Castro Gonzalez QUINI (88 Jesus SATRÚSTEGUI), Carlos Alonso Gonzalez SANTILLANA, José Francisco ROJO I Arroitia (56 Francisco FORTES Calvo). Trainer: Ladislao Kubala

Goals: Villar (29), Santillana (57), Georgescu (72 pen), Iordănescu (80)

SCOTLAND v ROMANIA 1-1 (1-0)

Hampden Park, Glasgow 17.12.1975

Referee: Adolf Prokop (E. GER) Attendance: 11,375

ROMANIA: Răducanu Necula; Florin Cheran, Alexandru Sătmăreanu, Gabriel Sandu, Teodor Anghelini; Cornel Dinu, Ladislau Bölöni, Mihai Romilă; Mircea Lucescu (60 Zoltan Crişan), Dudu Georgescu, Anghel Iordănescu. Trainer: Cornel Drăguşin

SCOTLAND: James Fergus Cruickshank; John Brownlie, Colin Mac Donald Jackson, Martin McLean Buchan, William Donachie; Bruce David Rioch, Richard Asa Hartford, Kenneth Dalglish (73 Edward John Mac Dougall); John Doyle (73 Peter Patrick Lorimer), Andrew Mullen Gray, Archibald Gemmill. Manager: William Ormond

Goals: Rioch (42), Crişan (73)

	P	W	D	L	F	A	Pts
Spain	6	3	3	0	10	6	9
Romania	6	1	5	0	11	6	7
Scotland	6	2	3	1	8	6	7
Denmark	6	0	1	5	3	14	1

GROUP 5

FINLAND v POLAND **1-2** (1-1)

Olympiastadion, Helsinki 01.09.1974

Referee: John Wright Paterson (SCO) Attendance: 18,759

FINLAND: Pertti Alaja; Henry Forssell, Arto Tolsa, Erkki Vihtilä, Esko Ranta; Jouko Suomalainen (Cap), Timo Rahja (81 Antero Nikkanen), Aki Heiskanen; Miikka Toivola, Matti Paatelainen (64 Jarmo Manninen), Juha-Pekka Laine. Trainer: Olavi Laaksonen

POLAND: Jan Tomaszewski; Antoni Szymanowski, Jerzy Gorgon, Miroslaw Bulzacki, Adam Musial; Henryk Kasperczak (77 Marek Kusto), Leslaw Cmikiewicz (Cap), Zygmunt Maszczyk; Grzegorz Lato, Andrzej Szarmach, Robert Gadocha. Trainer: Kazimierz Górski.

Goals: Rahja (3), Szarmach (23), Lato (51)

HOLLAND v ITALY **3-1** (1-1)

Feyenoord, Rotterdam 20.11.1974

Referee: Pavel Kazakov (USSR) Attendance: 65,000

HOLLAND: Jan Jongbloed; Wim Suurbier, Arie Haan, Wim Rijsbergen, Ruud Krol; Willy Van der Kuylen, Johan Neeskens, Wim Van Hanegem, Johnny Rep (46 Willy van de Kerkhof), Johan Cruijff (Cap), Robert Rensenbrink. Trainer: Gregorius Knobel

ITALY: Dino Zoff (Cap); Francesco Rocca, Andrea Orlandini, Francesco Morini, Moreno Roggi; Giancarlo Antognoni, Antonio Juliano, Franco Causio, Roberto Boninsegna, Pietro Anastasi, Luciano Zecchini. Trainer: Fulvio Bernardini

Goals: Boninsegna (4), Rensenbrink (25), Cruijff (65, 79)

FINLAND v HOLLAND **1-3** (1-2)

Helsinki 25.09.1974

Referee: Wolfgang Riedel (E. GER) Attendance: 20,449

FINLAND: Harri Holli; Raimo Saari, Arto Tolsa, Erkki Vihtilä, Esko Ranta, Jouko Suomalainen, Aki Heiskanen (60 Olavi Rissanen), Raimo Hukka (54 Miikka Toivola), Timo Rahja, Rutger Petterson, Juha-Pekka Laine. Trainer: Olavi Laaksonen

HOLLAND: Jan Jongbloed; Kees Van Ierssel, Arie Haan, Theo De Jong, Ruud Krol, Wim Jansen, Johan Neeskens, Wim Van Hanegem (48 Rene Notten), Peter Ressel, Johan Cruijff (Cap), Johnny Rep (.. Ruud Geels). Trainer: Gregorius Knobel

Goals: Rahja (16), Cruijff (28, 40), Neeskens (51 pen)

ITALY v POLAND **0-0**

Stadio Olimpico, Roma 19.04.1975

Referee: Robert Hélies (FRA) Attendance: 80,000

ITALY: Dino Zoff; Claudio Gentile, Francesco Rocca, Mauro Bellugi, Giacinto Facchetti (Cap); Franco Cordova, Francesco Graziani, Giorgio Morini; Giancarlo Antognoni, Giorgio Chinaglia, Paolino Pulici. Trainer: Fulvio Bernardini

POLAND: Jan Tomaszewski; Antoni Szymanowski, Jerzy Gorgon, Wladyslaw Zmuda, Henryk Wawrowski; Zygmunt Maszczyk, Kazimierz Deyna (Cap), Henryk Kasperczak (46 Leslaw Cmikiewicz); Grzegorz Lato, Andrzej Szarmach, Robert Gadocha. Trainer: Kazimierz Górski

POLAND v FINLAND **3-0** (2-0)

Warty, Poznan 09.10.1974

Referee: Dusan Maksimovic (YUG) Attendance: 30,000

POLAND: Jan Tomaszewski; Antoni Szymanowski, Marian Ostafinski, Jerzy Wyrobek, Piotr Drzewiecki; Henryk Kasperczak (53 Roman Jakóbczak), Kazimierz Deyna (Cap), Bronislaw Bula; Grzegorz Lato, Andrzej Szarmach (74 Joachim Marx), Robert Gadocha. Trainer: Kazimierz Górski.

FINLAND: Harri Holli; Raimo Saari, Arto Tolsa, Erkki Vihtilä, Esko Ranta; Jouko Suomalainen (Cap), Aki Heiskanen (46 Rutger Petterson), Timo Rahja; Miikka Toivola, Matti Paatelainen (46 Juha-Pekka Laine), Olavi Rissanen. Trainer: Olavi Laaksonen

Goals: Kasperczak (12), Gadocha (14), Lato (53)

FINLAND v ITALY **0-1** (0-1)

Olympiastadion, Helsinki 05.06.1975

Referee: Walter Eschweiler (W. GER) Attendance: 17,732

FINLAND: Göran Enckelman; Erkki Vihtilä, Arto Tolsa, Matti Paatelainen (Cap), Esko Ranta, Jouko Suomalainen, Pauno Kymäläinen (46 Olavi Rissanen), Aki Heiskanen, Jarmo Manninen, Juha-Pekka Laine (77 Kalle Nieminen), Miikka Toivola. Trainer: Aulis Rytkönen

ITALY: Dino Zoff; Claudio Gentile, Francesco Rocca; Mauro Bellugi, Giacinto Facchetti (Cap), Franco Cordova (46 Andrea Orlandini); Francesco Graziani, Giancarlo Antognoni, Giorgio Chinaglia, Fabio Capello, Roberto Bettega. Trainer: Fulvio Bernardini

Goal: Chinaglia (26 pen)

HOLLAND v FINLAND 4-1 (2-1)

Nijmegen 03.09.1975

Referee: Eric Smyton (NIR) Attendance: 28,000

HOLLAND: Jan Van Beveren; Wim Suurbier, Adrianus Van Kraay, Niels Overweg, Ruud Krol (Cap), Wim Jansen, Jan Peters, Wim Van Hanegem, René van de Kerkhof, Harry Lubse, Willy Van der Kuylen. Trainer: Gregorius Knobel

FINLAND: Göran Enckelman; Erkki Vihtilä, Matti Paatelainen, Henry Forssell, Esko Ranta, Jouko Suomalainen, Aki Heiskanen, Hannu Hämäläinen, Olavi Rissanen, Ari Mäkynen, Eero Rissanen. Trainer: Aulis Rytkönen

Goals: Paatelainen (9), Van der Kuylen (29, 35, 55), Lubse (48)

POLAND v HOLLAND 4-1 (2-0)

Slaski, Chorzow 10.09.1975

Referee: Patrick Partridge (ENG) Attendance: 85,000

POLAND: Jan Tomaszewski; Antoni Szymanowski, Miroslaw Bulzacki, Wladyslaw Zmuda, Henryk Wawrowski; Henryk Kasperczak, Kazimierz Deyna (Cap), Zgmunt Maszczyk; Grzegorz Lato, Andrzej Szarmach, Robert Gadocha. Trainer: Kazimierz Górski

HOLLAND: Jan Van Beveren; Wim Suurbier, Adrianus van Kraay, Niels Overweg, Ruud Krol; Wim Jansen, Johan Neeskens, Wim Van Hanegem (46 Ruud Geels); René van de Kerkhof, Johan Cruijff (Cap), Willy Van der Kuylen. Trainer: Gregorius Knobel

Goals: Lato (14), Gadocha (44), Szarmach (62, 77), René van de Kerkhof (80)

ITALY v FINLAND 0-0

Stadio Olimpico, Roma 27.09.1975

Referee: Xanthoulis (GRE) Attendance: 29,203

ITALY: Dino Zoff; Francesco Rocca, Moreno Roggi; Romeo Benetti II, Mauro Bellugi, Giacinto Facchetti (Cap); Francesco Graziani, Eraldo Pecci, Giuseppe Savoldi I, Giancarlo Antognoni, Giorgio Morini. Trainer: Fulvio Bernardini

FINLAND: Göran Enckelman; Erkki Vihtilä, Matti Paatelainen (Cap), Arto Tolsa, Esko Ranta, Jouko Suomalainen, Aki Heiskanen, Pertti Jantunen, Olavi Rissanen (1 Hannu Hämäläinen), Ari Mäkynen (28 Timo Kautonen), Miika Toivola. Trainer: Aulis Rytkönen

HOLLAND v POLAND 3-0 (1-0)

Olympisch, Amsterdam 15.10.1975

Referee: Károly Palotai (HUNG) Attendance: 60,000

HOLLAND: Piet Schrijvers; Wim Suurbier, Adrianus van Kraay, Kees Krijgh, Ruud Krol, Wim Jansen, Johan Neeskens, Frans Thijssen, Ruud Geels, Johan Cruijff (Cap), René van de Kerkhof. Trainer: Gregorius Knobel

POLAND: Jan Tomaszewski; Antoni Szymanowski, Wladyslaw Zmuda, Miroslaw Bulzacki, Henryk Wawrowski; Zygmunt Maszczyk (67 Bronislaw Bula), Kazimierz Deyna, Henryk Kasperczak; Grzegorz Lato, Andrzej Szarmach, Robert Gadocha. Trainer: Kazimierz Górski

Goals: Neeskens (16), Geels (47), Thijsen (59)

POLAND v ITALY 0-0

Dziesieciolecia, Warszawa 26.10.1975

Referee: Paul Schiller (AUS) Attendance: 70,000

POLAND: Jan Tomaszewski; Antoni Szymanowski (Cap), Marian Ostafinski, Wladyslaw Zmuda, Henryk Wawrowski; Henryk Kasperczak, Kazimierz Deyna, Bronislaw Bula (59 Joachim Marx); Grzegorz Lato, Andrzej Szarmach, Robert Gadocha (78 Kazimierz Kmiecik). Trainer: Kazimierz Górski

ITALY: Dino Zoff; Claudio Gentile, Mauro Bellugi, Francesco Rocca, Giacinto Facchetti (Cap); Antonello Cuccureddu, Romeo Benetti II, Giancarlo Antognoni (85 Renato Zaccarelli); Franco Causio, Pietro Anastasi (66 Roberto Bettega), Paolino Pulici. Trainer: Fulvio Bernardini

ITALY v HOLLAND 1-0 (1-0)

Stadio Olimpico, Roma 22.11.1975

Referee: Robert Schaut (BEL) Attendance: 33,307

ITALY: Dino Zoff; Claudio Gentile, Giacinto Facchetti (Cap), Mauro Bellugi, Francesco Rocca; Franco Causio, Romeo Benetti II, Fabio Capello, Giancarlo Antognoni, Giuseppe Savoldi I, Paolino Pulici. Trainer: Fulvio Bernardini

HOLLAND: Piet Schrijvers; Wim Suurbier, Adrianus van Kraay, Kees Krijgh, Ruud Krol (Cap), Wim Jansen, Jan Peters, Frans Thijssen, Willy van de Kerkhof (70 Rene Notten), Ruud Geels, René van de Kerkhof. Trainer: Gregorius Knobel

Goal: Capello (20)

	P	W	D	L	F	A	Pts
Holland	6	4	0	2	14	8	8
Poland	6	3	2	1	9	5	8
Italy	6	2	3	1	3	3	7
Finland	6	0	1	5	3	13	1

GROUP 6

REPUBLIC OF IRELAND v USSR 3-0 (2-0)

Dalymount Park, Dublin 30.10.1974

Referee: Erik Axelryd (SWE) Attendance: 35,000

IRELAND: Paddy Roche; Joe Kinnear, Paddy Mulligan, Terence Mancini, Jimmy Holmes, Mick Martin, Johnny Giles (Cap), William Brady, Steve Heighway, Ray Treacy, Don Givens. Trainer: John Giles

USSR: Vladimir Pilgui; Sergei Nikulin, Sergei Olshanskiy (Cap), Viktor Matvienko, Vladimir Kaplichniy, Evgeni Lovchev, Vladimir Fedotov (59 Vladimir Fiodorov), Vladimir Onischenko, Viktor Kolotov, Vladimir Veremeev, Oleg Blohin. Trainer: Konstantin Beskov

Sent off: Mancini (32), Kaplichniy (32)

Goals: Givens (22, 30, 70)

USSR v TURKEY 3-0 (1-0)

Central, Kiev 02.04.1975

Referee: Robert Holley Davidson (SCO) Att: 100,000

USSR: Evgeni Rudakov; Anatoliy Konkov (65 Leonid Buriak), Viktor Matvienko, Mihail Fomenko, Stefan Reshko, Vladimir Troshkin, Vladimir Muntian, Vladimir Onischenko (80 Vladimir Fiodorov), Viktor Kolotov (Cap), Vladimir Veremeev, Oleg Blohin. Trainer: Valeriy Lobanovski

TURKEY: Sabri Dino; Kemal Batmaz, Ismail Arca, Ziya Şengül, Alpaslan Eratli, Zafer Göncüler, Engin Verel, Raşit Karasu, Ali Kemal Denizci, Cemil Turan, Metin Kurt (69 Tuncay Temeller). Trainer: Sabri Kiraz

Goals: Kolotov (25 pen, 56 pen), Blohin (75)

TURKEY v REPUBLIC OF IRELAND 1-1 (0-0)

Kemal Atatürk, Izmir 20.11.1974

Referee: Marian Srodecki (POL) Attendance: 67,000

TURKEY: Yasin Özdenak; Alpaslan Eratli, Ismail Arca, Ziya Şengül, Zekeriya Alp, Selçuk Yalçintaş, Engin Verel, Mehmet Türkan (80 Osman Arpacioglu), B. Mehmet Oguz, Cemil Turan, Metin Kurt. Trainer: Sabri Kiraz

IRELAND: Paddy Roche; Joe Kinnear, Paddy Mulligan, Eoin Hand, Tony Dunne, Mick Martin, Johnny Giles (Cap), William Brady, Steve Heighway, Don Givens, Terry Conroy (86 Jeremiah Dennehy). Trainer: John Giles

Goals: Dunne (54 og), Givens (60)

SWITZERLAND v TURKEY 1-1 (1-0)

Zürich 30.04.1975

Referee: Riccardo Lattanzi (ITA) Attendance: 23,000

SWITZERLAND: Hans Küng; Gilbert Guyot, Max Heer, Lucio Bizzini, Pius Fischbach, Ernst Rutschmann (.. Hans-Jörg Pfister), René Hasler (70 Hanspeter Schild), René Botteron, Kurt Müller, Daniel Jeandupeux, Rudolf Elsener. Trainer: René Hüssy

TURKEY: Yasin Özdenak; Alpaslan Eratli, Ismail Arca, Ziya Şengül, Zekeriya Alp, Fatih Terim, Niko Kovi, Engin Verel, Ali Kemal Denizci (.. Aydin Çelik), Gökmen Özdenak, Cemil Turan. Trainer: Sabri Kiraz

Goals: Ismail (43 og), Alpaslan (54)

TURKEY v SWITZERLAND 2-1 (1-1)

Izmir 01.12.1974

Referee: Milivoje Gugulovic (YUG) Attendance: 51,410

TURKEY: Yasin Özdenak; Alpaslan Eratli, Ismail Arca, Ziya Şengül, Zekeriya Alp, Engin Verel, K.Mehmet Özgül, Selçuk Yalçintaş (.. Raşit Karasu), Osman Arpacioglu (.. B. Mehmet Oguz), Cemil Turan, Metin Kurt. Trainer: Sabri Kiraz

SWITZERLAND: Erich Burgener; Gilbert Guyot, René Hasler, Lucio Bizzini, René Botteron, Hanspeter Schild, Jakob Kuhn, Rudolf Schneeberger, Hans-Jörg Pfister (.. Ernst Rutschmann), Daniel Jeandupeux, Kurt Müller. Trainer: René Hüssy

Goals: Schild (18), Ismail (28), B. Mehmet (85)

REPUBLIC OF IRELAND v SWITZERLAND 2-1 (2-0)

Lansdowne Road, Dublin 10.05.1975

Referee: Paul Schiller (AUS) Attendance: 50,000

IRELAND: Paddy Roche; Joe Kinnear, Paddy Mulligan, Eoin Hand, Tony Dunne, Mick Martin, Johnny Giles (Cap), William Brady, Terry Conroy, Ray Treacy, Don Givens. Trainer: John Giles

SWITZERLAND: Erich Burgener; Gilbert Guyot, René Hasler, Lucio Bizzini, Max Heer, René Botteron, Jakob Kuhn, Ernst Rutschmann, Hanspeter Schild, Daniel Jeandupeux, Kurt Müller. Trainer: René Hüssy

Goals: Martin (2), Treacy (28), Müller (74)

USSR v REPUBLIC OF IRELAND 2-1 (2-0)

Central, Kiev 18.05.1975

Referee: René Vigliani (FRA) Attendance: 100,000

USSR: Evgeni Rudakov; Anatoliy Konkov, Viktor Matvienko, Mihail Fomenko, Leonid Buriak, Vladimir Troshkin, Vladimir Muntian (46 Stefan Reshko), Vladimir Onischenko, Viktor Kolotov (Cap), Vladimir Veremeev (84 Vladimir Fiodorov), Oleg Blohin. Trainer: Valeriy Lobanovski

IRELAND: Paddy Roche; Joe Kinnear, Paddy Mulligan, Eoin Hand, Tony Dunne, Mick Martin, Johnny Giles (Cap), William Brady, Steve Heighway, Don Givens, Terry Conroy. Trainer: John Giles

Goals: Blohin (13), Kolotov (29), Hand (79)

SWITZERLAND v REPUBLIC OF IRELAND 1-0 (1-0)

Wankdorf, Bern 21.05.1975

Referee: Cesar da Luz Dias Correia (POR) Att: 15,000

SWITZERLAND: Erich Burgener; Gilbert Guyot, Lucio Bizzini, Serge Trinchero, Pius Fischbach, Jakob Kuhn, René Hasler, René Botteron, Ernst Rutschmann (.. Hans-Jörg Pfister), Kurt Müller (70 Rudolf Elsener), Daniel Jeandupeux. Trainer: René Hüssy

IRELAND: Paddy Roche; Tony Dunne, Paddy Mulligan, Eoin Hand, Jimmy Holmes, Mick Martin, Johnny Giles (Cap) (79 Gerard Daly), William Brady, Terry Conroy, Ray Treacy, Don Givens. Trainer: John Giles

Goal: Elsener (75)

SWITZERLAND v USSR 0-1 (0-0)

Hardturm, Zürich 12.10.1975

Referee: Leonardus van der Kroft (HOL) Att: 18,000

SWITZERLAND: Erich Burgener; Gilbert Guyot, Lucio Bizzini, Serge Trinchero (75 Rudolf Schneeberger), Pius Fischbach, Kurt Müller, Jakob Kuhn, René Botteron (75 Alfred Scheiwiler), Hans-Jörg Pfister, Peter Risi, Daniel Jeandupeux. Trainer: René Hüssy

USSR: Evgeni Rudakov; Anatoliy Konkov, Evgeni Lovchev, Mihail Fomenko (Cap), Viktor Zviagintzev, Vladimir Troshkin (31 Stefan Reshko), Vladimir Muntian, Vladimir Onischenko, Leonid Buriak (68 Vladimir Saharov), Vladimir Veremeev, Oleg Blohin. Trainer: Valeriy Lobanovski

Goal: Muntian (78)

REPUBLIC OF IRELAND v TURKEY 4-0 (3-0)

Dalymount Park, Dublin 29.10.1975

Referee: Angel Franco Martinez (SPA) Attendance: 25,000

IRELAND: Paddy Roche; Tony Dunne (83 Joe Kinnear), Paddy Mulligan, Eoin Hand, Jimmy Holmes, Mick Martin, Johnny Giles (Cap), William Brady, Steve Heighway (46 Terry Conroy), Ray Treacy, Don Givens. Trainer: John Giles

TURKEY: Yasin Özdenak (39 Rasim Kara); Sabahattin Erboga, Fatih Terim, Ismail Arca (33 Zafer Göncüler), Alpaslan Eratli, Kadir Özcan, Engin Verel, Necati Özçaglayan, Ali Kemal Denizci, Gökmen Özdenak, Cemil Turan. Trainer: Sabri Kiraz

Goals: Givens (25, 28, 34, 88)

USSR v SWITZERLAND 4-1 (2-1)

Central, Kiev 12.11.1975

Referee: Klaus Ohmsen (W. GER) Attendance: 30,000

USSR: Evgeni Rudakov; Anatoliy Konkov (75 Vladimir Saharov), Evgeni Lovchev, Mihail Fomenko (Cap), Viktor Zviagintzev, Vladimir Troshkin, Vladimir Muntian (65 Viktor Kolotov), Vladimir Onischenko, Leonid Buriak, Vladimir Veremeev, Oleg Blohin. Trainer: Valeriy Lobanovski

SWITZERLAND: Erich Burgener; Gilbert Guyot, Lucio Bizzini, Serge Trinchero, Pius Fischbach, René Botteron, Jakob Kuhn, Rudolf Schneeberger, Kurt Müller, Peter Risi, Daniel Jeandupeux. Trainer: René Hüssy

Goals: Konkov (13), Onischenko (14, 68), Risi (45), Veremeev (81)

TURKEY v USSR 1-0 (0-0)

Atatürk, Izmir 23.11.1975

Referee: Petar Hristov Nikolov (BUL) Attendance: 45,000

TURKEY: Rasim Kara; Turgay Semercioglu, Sabahattin Erboga, Ismail Arca, Kadir Özcan, Ali Kemal Denizci, Mehmet Türkan (90 Orhan Özselek), Fatih Terim, Gökmen Özdenak (89 Hüseyin Nuri), Cemil Turan, A. Kemal Denizci. Trainer: Sabri Kiraz

USSR: Evgeni Rudakov; Anatoliy Konkov, Valeri Zuev, Mihail Fomenko, Stefan Reshko, Viktor Zviagintzev, Vladimir Muntian (61 Leonid Buriak), Vladimir Onischenko, Viktor Kolotov (Cap), Vladimir Veremeev, Oleg Blohin. Trainer: Valriy Lobanovski

Goal: Reshko (17 og)

	P	W	D	L	F	A	Pts
USSR	6	4	0	2	10	6	8
Rep. of Ireland	6	3	1	2	11	5	7
Turkey	6	2	2	2	5	10	6
Switzerland	6	1	1	4	5	10	3

GROUP 7

ICELAND v BELGIUM 0-2 (0-1)

Laugardalsvöllur, Reykjavik 08.09.1974

Referee: Thomas Reynolds (WAL) Attendance: 7,600

ICELAND: Thorsteinn Olafsson; Eirikur Thorsteinsson, Jón Pétursson, Marteinn Geirsson, Jóhannes Edvaldsson, Karl Hermannsson, Grétar Magnússon, Gudgeir Leifsson, Teitur Thórdarson, Asgeir Eliasson (50 Matthias Hallgrimsson), Asgeir Sigurvinsson. Trainer: Anthony Knapp

BELGIUM: Christian Piot; Erwin Van den Daele, Gilbert Van Binst, Hugo Broos, Ludo Coeck (46 Julien Cools), Wilfried Van Moer, Jan Verheyen, Paul Van Himst (Cap), François Van der Elst, Jean Janssens (84 Jacques Teugels), Roger Henrotay. Trainer: Raymond Goethals

Goals: Van Moer (38), Teugels (87 pen)

FRANCE v EAST GERMANY 2-2 (0-1)

Parc des Princes, Paris 16.11.1974

Referee: Pablo Augusto Sánchez Ibanez (SPA) Att: 45,381

FRANCE: Jean-Paul Bertrand-Demanes; Jean François Jodar, Jean-Pierre Adams, Marius Trésor, François Bracci; Jean-Noël Huck, Henri Michel (65 Christian Synaeghel), Jean-Marc Guillou; Gérard Soler, Christian Coste (46 Jean Gallice), Georges Bereta (Cap). Trainer: Ştefan Kovacs

EAST GERMANY: Jürgen Croy; Gerd Kische, Konrad Weise, Hans-Jürgen Dörner, Siegmar Wätzlich; Lothar Kurbjuweit, Reinhard Häfner, Hans-Jürgen Kreische (83 Wolfgang Seguin), Reinhard Lauck; Jürgen Sparwasser (Cap), Martin Hoffmann. Trainer: Georg Buschner

Goals: Sparwasser (25), Kreische (57), Guillou (79, 89)

EAST GERMANY v ICELAND 1-1 (1-1)

Ernst-Grube-Stadion, Magdeburg 12.10.1974

Referee: Svein Inge Thime (NOR) Attendance: 15,800

EAST GERMANY: Ulrich Schulze; Manfred Zapf, Konrad Weise, Bernd Bransch (Cap), Siegmar Wätzlich (55 Hans-Jürgen Dörner); Lothar Kurbjuweit, Jürgen Pommerenke (71 Eberhard Vogel), Klaus Decker; Joachim Streich, Peter Ducke, Martin Hoffmann. Trainer: Georg Buschner

ICELAND: Thorsteinn Olafsson; Gisli Torfason (65 Eirikur Thorsteinsson), Jón Pétursson, Asgeir Sigurvinsson, Jóhannes Edvaldsson, Marteinn Geirsson, Gudgeir Leifsson, Grétar Magnússon, Teitur Thórdarson (85 Atli Thór Hédinsson), Matthias Hallgrimsson, Asgeir Eliasson. Trainer: Anthony Knapp

Goal: Hoffmann (7), Hallgrimsson (25)

EAST GERMANY v BELGIUM 0-0

Zentralstadion, Leipzig 07.12.1974

Referee: Sergio Gonella (ITA) Attendance: 35,000

EAST GERMANY: Jürgen Croy; Hans-Jürgen Dörner, Gerd Kische, Konrad Weise, Siegmar Wätzlich (70 Hans-Jürgen Kreische); Reinhard Lauck, Reinhard Häfner, Lothar Kurbjuweit; Martin Hoffmann, Joachim Streich, Eberhard Vogel (Cap). Trainer: Georg Buschner

BELGIUM: Christian Piot; Gilbert Van Binst, Erwin Van den Daele, Nicolas Dewalque, Hugo Broos, Maurice Martens, Julien Cools, Jan Verheyen, Paul Van Himst (Cap) (15 François Van der Elst), Raoul Lambert, Jacques Teugels. Trainer: Raymond Goethals

BELGIUM v FRANCE 2-1 (1-1)

Heizel, Brussel 12.10.1974

Referee: Kenneth Howard Burns (ENG) Att: 32,108

BELGIUM: Christian Piot; Gilbert Van Binst, Hugo Broos, Erwin Van den Daele, Maurice Martens; Wilfried Van Moer, Jan Verheyen, Paul Van Himst (Cap) (71 Jean Dockx); François Van der Elst, Raoul Lambert, Jacques Teugels. Trainer: Raymond Goethals

FRANCE: Dominique Baratelli; Jean François Jodar, Jean-Pierre Adams, Marius Trésor, François Bracci; Jean-Noël Huck, Henri Michel, Jean-Marc Guillou; Christian Coste, Bernard Lacombe (83 Jean Gallice), Georges Bereta (Cap). Trainer: Ştefan Kovacs

Goals: Martens (12), Coste (16), F. Van der Elst (75)

ICELAND v FRANCE 0-0

Laugardalsvöllur, Reykjavik 25.05.1975

Referee: Malcolm Wright (NIR) Attendance: 10,000

ICELAND: Sigurdur Dagsson; Gisli Torfason, Jón Pétursson, Marteinn Geirsson, Jóhannes Edvaldsson; Karl Hermannsson (77 Grétar Magnússon), Gudgeir Leifsson, Olafur Júliusson, Teitur Thórdarson, Asgeir Sigurvinsson, Matthias Hallgrimsson (55 Elmar Geirsson). Trainer: Anthony Knapp

FRANCE: Dominique Baratelli; Christian Lopez, Jean-Pierre Adams, Marius Trésor, François Bracci; Jean Gallice (75 Patrick Parizon), Henri Michel, Jean-Michel Larqué, Jean-Marc Guillou; Marc Berdoll, Georges Bereta (Cap). Trainer: Ştefan Kovacs

ICELAND v EAST GERMANY 2-1 (2-0)

Laugardalsvöllur, Reykjavik 05.06.1975

Referee: Ian Foote (SCO) Attendance: 13,000

ICELAND: Sigurdur Dagsson; Gisli Torfason, Jón Pétursson, Marteinn Geirsson, Jóhannes Edvaldsson, Hördur Hilmarsson (72 Karl Hermansson), Gudgeir Leifsson, Asgeir Sigurvinsson, Teitur Thórdarson, Elmar Geirsson (17 Matthias Hallgrimsson), Olafur Júliusson. Trainer: Anthony Knapp

EAST GERMANY: Jürgen Croy; Manfred Zapf (83 Hans-Jürgen Riediger), Gerd Kische, Konrad Weise, Siegmar Wätzlich; Jürgen Pommerenke, Rüdiger Schnuphase (55 Hans-Jürgen Dörner), Lothar Kurbjuweit; Martin Hoffmann, Joachim Streich, Eberhard Vogel (Cap).
Trainer: Georg Buschner

Goals: Edvaldsson (10), Sigurvinsson (33), Pommerenke (48)

FRANCE v ICELAND 3-0 (1-0)

Marcel Saupin, Nantes 03.09.1975

Referee: Albert Victor (LUX) Attendance: 20,000

FRANCE: Dominique Baratelli; Raymond Domenech, Jean-Pierre Adams, Marius Trésor, François Bracci; Jean-Noël Huck, Henri Michel (Cap), Jean-Marc Guillou; Dominique Rocheteau, Marc Molitor (46 Marc Berdoll), Albert Emon.
Trainer: Ştefan Kovacs

ICELAND: Arni Stefánsson, Gisli Torfason, Olafur Sigurvinsson, Marteinn Geirsson, Jón Pétursson; Jóhannes Edvaldsson, Gudgeir Leifsson, Hördur Hilmarsson (61 Karl Thórdarsson), Teitur Thórdarson, Matthias Hallgrimson (75 Elmar Geirsson), Asgeir Sigurvinsson.
Trainer: Anthony Knapp

Goals: Guillou (20, 74), Berdoll (87)

BELGIUM v ICELAND 1-0 (1-0)

Sclessin, Liège 06.09.1975

Referee: Henning Lund-Sörensen (DEN) Att: 9,371

BELGIUM: Christian Piot; Nicolas Dewalque, Gilbert Van Binst, Hugo Broos, Maurice Martens, Julien Cools, Jan Verheyen (61 Ludo Coeck), Odilon Polleunis, Johan Devrindt, Raoul Lambert, Jacques Teugels. Trainer: Raymond Goethals

ICELAND: Arni Stefánsson, Olafur Sigurvinsson, Björn Lárusson, Marteinn Geirsson, Jón Pétursson, Gisli Torfason, Gudgeir Leifsson, Asgeir Sigurvinsson, Teitur Thórdarson (.. Arni Sveinsson), Matthias Hallgrimson, Elmar Geirsson.
Trainer: Anthony Knapp

Goal: Lambert (43)

BELGIUM v EAST GERMANY 1-2 (0-0)

Astrid Park, Brussel 27.09.1975

Referee: Nicolae Rainea (ROM) Attendance: 17,281

BELGIUM: Christian Piot; Erwin Van den Daele, Eric Gerets, Nicolas Dewalque, Maurice Martens; Julien Cools, Ludo Coeck, Odilon Polleunis (78 Jean Janssens), Wilfried Puis, Johan Devrindt, Jacques Teugels. Trainer: Raymond Goethals

EAST GERMANY: Jürgen Croy (88 Hans-Ulrich Grapenthin); Hans-Jürgen Dörner (Cap), Joachim Fritsche, Konrad Weise, Lothar Kurbjuweit; Reinhard Häfner, Reinhard Lauck, Gerd Weber; Hans-Jürgen Riediger, Peter Ducke, Martin Hoffmann. Trainer: Georg Buschner

Goals: P. Ducke (50), Puis (60), Häfner (71)

EAST GERMANY v FRANCE 2-1 (0-0)

Zentralstadion, Leipzig 12.10.1975

Referee: Erik Fredriksson (SWE) Attendance: 30,000

EAST GERMANY: Jürgen Croy; Gerd Weber, Konrad Weise, Hans-Jürgen Dörner (Cap), Joachim Fritsche; Reinhard Häfner, Hartmut Schade, Reinhard Lauck; Joachim Streich (75 Martin Hoffmann), Peter Ducke, Eberhard Vogel.
Trainer: Georg Buschner

FRANCE: Dominique Baratelli; Gérard Janvion, Jean-Pierre Adams, Marius Trésor, François Bracci; Henri Michel (Cap), Jean Gallice, Jean-Marc Guillou, Dominique Bathenay; Dominique Rocheteau, Albert Emon. Trainer: Ştefan Kovacs

Goals: Bathenay (50), Streich (55), Vogel (77 pen)

FRANCE v BELGIUM 0-0

Parc des Princes, Paris 15.11.1975

Referee: Robert Holley Davidson (SCO) Att: 35,547

FRANCE: Dominique Baratelli; Raymond Domenech, Charles Orlanducci, Marius Trésor, François Bracci; Jean-Noël Huck (46 Jean-Michel Larqué), Henri Michel (Cap), Jean-Marc Guillou; Dominique Rocheteau, Christian Coste (78 Jean Gallice), Albert Emon. Trainer: Ştefan Kovacs

BELGIUM: Christian Piot; Gilbert Van Binst, Georges Leekens, Erwin Van den Daele, Jean Dockx; Julien Cools, Jan Verheyen, Ludo Coeck, René Vandereycken; Roger Van Gool, Raoul Lambert (78 Jacques Teugels).
Trainer: Raymond Goethals

Sent off: Larqué (67).

	P	W	D	L	F	A	Pts
Belgium	6	3	2	1	6	3	8
East Germany	6	2	3	1	8	7	7
France	6	1	3	2	7	6	5
Iceland	6	1	2	3	3	8	4

GROUP 8

BULGARIA v GREECE 3-3 (3-1)

Vasil Levski, Sofia 13.10.1974

Referee: Alberto Michelotti (ITA) Attendance: 30,000

BULGARIA: Stoian Iordanov; Ivan Zafirov, Dimitar Penev (Cap), Borislav Dimitrov, Bojil Kolev, Krasimir Borisov, Voin Voinov, Hristo Bonev, Traiko Sokolov (74 Pavel Panov), Georgi Denev, Chavdar Tzvetkov (58 Todor Barzov).
Trainers: Ioncho Arsov, Dimitar Doichinov, Manol Manolov

GREECE: Takis Oikonomopoulos; Theodoros Pallas, Giorgos Foiros, Lakis Gklezos, Kostas Iosifidis, Kostas Eleutherakis, Hristos Terzanidis, Stauros Sarafis (58 Dimitris Dimitriou), Giorgos Delikaris, Antonis Antoniadis, Dimitris Papaioannou (Cap). Trainer: Alketas Panagoulias

Goals: Bonev (2), Denev (27, 29), Antoniadis (28), Papaioannou (86), Gklezos (88)

MALTA v WEST GERMANY 0-1 (0-1)

Empire Stadium, Gzira 22.12.1974

Referee: Gyula Emsberger (HUNG) Attendance: 12,528

MALTA: Alfred Debono; Joseph Borg, Edward Vella, Edward Darmanin, John Holland, William Vassallo, Vincent Magro, Raymond Xuereb, Anthony Camilleri, Edward Aquilina (.. Richard Aquilina), Carlo Seychell.
Trainer: Terenzio Polvertini

W. GERMANY: Norbert Nigbur; Hans-Hubert Vogts, Karl-Heinz Körbel, Franz Beckenbauer (Cap), Bernard Dietz, Rainer Bonhof, Bernhard Cullmann (74 Rudolf Seliger), Heinz Flohe, Josef Pirrung (46 Bernd Nickel), Erwin Kostedde, Bernd Hölzenbein. Trainer: Helmut Schön

Goal: Cullmann (44)

GREECE v WEST GERMANY 2-2 (1-0)

Karaiskaki, Peiraias 20.11.1974

Referee: Nicolae Rainea (ROM) Attendance: 30,000

GREECE: Takis Oikonomopoulos; Giannis Kyrastas, Lakis Gklezos (62 Giorgos Foiros), Vasilis Siokos, Kostas Iosifidis, Kostas Eleutherakis, Mimis Domazos (Cap), Stauros Sarafis, Hristos Terzanidis, Dimitris Papaioannou (68 Ahilleas Aslanidis), Giorgos Delikaris. Trainer: Alketas Panagoulias

W. GERMANY: Josef Maier; Hans-Hubert Vogts, Helmut Kremers; Georg Schwarzenbeck, Franz Beckenbauer (Cap), Bernhard Cullmann (78 Hans-Josef Kapellmann); Rainer Geye, Herbert Wimmer, Bernd Hölzenbein, Ulrich Hoeneß, Josef Heynckes (81 Josef Pirrung). Trainer: Helmut Schön

Goals: Delikaris (12), Cullmann (51), Eleutherakis (70), Wimmer (82)

MALTA v GREECE 2-0 (1-0)

Gzira Stadium, Valletta 23.02.1975

Referee: Robert Matthewson (ENG) Attendance: 8,621

MALTA: Robert Gatt; George Ciantar, Edward Vella, Edward Darmanin, John Holland, William Vassallo, Vincent Magro, David Azzopardi (46 Carlo Seychell), Raymond Xuereb, Richard Aquilina, Anthony Camilleri.
Trainer: Terenzio Polvertini

GREECE: Vasilis Konstantinou; Theodoros Pallas, Vasilis Siokos, Giorgos Foiros, Kostas Iosifidis, Stauros Sarafis, Dimitris Dimitriou (29 Dimitris Paridis, 75 Lakis Nikolaou), Mimis Domazos (Cap), Mihalis Kritikopoulos, Antonis Antoniadis, Dimitris Papaioannou.
Trainer: Alketas Panagoulias

Goals: R. Aquilina (32), V. Magro (88)

GREECE v BULGARIA 2-1 (2-0)

Karaiskaki, Peiraias 18.12.1974

Referee: Paul Schiller (AUS) Attendance: 22,328

GREECE: Vasilis Konstantinou; Takis Eleutheriadis, Lakis Gklezos, Vasilis Siokos, Theodoros Pallas, Kostas Eleutherakis (Cap), Stauros Sarafis, Hristos Terzanidis, Dimitris Papaioannou (71 Giannis Kyrastas), Antonis Antoniadis, Ahilleas Aslanidis. Trainer: Alketas Panagoulias

BULGARIA: Iordan Filipov; Tzono Vasilev, Kiril Ivkov (Cap), Stefan Aladjov, Bojil Kolev, Kiril Stankov, Voin Voinov (46 Boris Angelov), Hristo Bonev, Nikola Hristov (69 Chavdar Tzvetkov), Georgi Denev, Nikolai Kurbanov.
Trainer: Stoian Ormandjiev

Goals: Sarafis (4), Antoniadis (40), Kolev (89)

BULGARIA v WEST GERMANY 1-1 (0-0)

Vasil Levski, Sofia 27.04.1975

Referee: Jan Dubach (SWI) Attendance: 65,000

BULGARIA: Iordan Filipov; Ivan Zafirov (Cap), Todor Marev, Milcho Evtimov, Bojil Kolev, Angel Rangelov, Atanas Aleksandrov (60 Radoslav Zdravkov), Borislav Dimitrov, Andrei Jeliazkov, Pavel Panov, Georgi Denev.
Trainer: Stoian Ormandjiev

W. GERMANY: Josef Maier; Hans-Hubert Vogts, Paul Breitner; Georg Schwarzenbeck, Franz Beckenbauer (Cap), Rainer Bonhof; Manfred Ritschel, Ulrich Hoeneß (73 Karl-Heinz Körbel), Wolfgang Seel, Günter Netzer, Josef Heynckes (34 Bernd Hölzenbein). Trainer: Helmut Schön

Goals: Kolev (73 pen), Ritschel (76 pen)

GREECE v MALTA 4-0 (2-0)

Toumpas, Thessaloniki 04.06.1975

Referee: Marijan Raus (YUG) Attendance: 17,500

GREECE: Stelios Papafloratos; Theodoros Pallas, Filotas Pellios (72 Lakis Nikolaou), Giorgos Foiros, Kostas Iosifidis, Dimitrios Anastasidis, Koulis Apostolidis, Ahilleas Aslanidis, Antonis Antoniadis (67 Nikolaos Kalampakas), Thomas Mauros, Dimitris Papaioannou (Cap).
Trainer: Alketas Panagoulias

MALTA: Robert Gatt (55 Alfred Debono); Joseph Borg, Edwin Farrugia, William Vassallo, Edward Darmanin, John Holland, Vincent Magro, David Azzopardi, Raymond Xuereb, Richard Aquilina, Carlo Seychell (46 Anthony Camilleri).
Trainer: Terenzio Polvertini

Goals: Mauros (32), Antoniadis (34 pen), Iosifidis (47), Papaioannou (50)

BULGARIA v MALTA 5-0 (3-0)

Vasil Levski, Sofia 11.06.1975

Referee: Michal Jursa (CZE) Attendance: 35,000

BULGARIA: Iordan Filipov; Ivan Zafirov (Cap), Todor Marev, Milcho Evtimov, Kostas Isakidis (59 Kiril Milanov), Borislav Dimitrov, Nikolai Kurbanov (46 Atanas Aleksandrov), Hristo Bonev, Andrei Jeliazkov, Pavel Panov, Georgi Denev.
Trainer: Stoian Ormandjiev

MALTA: Alfred Debono; George Ciantar, Edwin Farrugia, Edward Vella, John Holland, Edward Darmanin, Joseph Borg, Edward Aquilina, Vincent Magro, William Vassallo, Richard Aquilina (54 Raymond Xuereb). Trainer: Terenzio Polvertini

Goals: Dimitrov (2), Denev (22), Panov (25), Bonev (69 pen), Milanov (71)

WEST GERMANY v GREECE 1-1 (0-0)

Rheinstadion, Düsseldorf 11.10.1975

Referee: Clive Thomas (WAL) Attendance: 70,000

W. GERMANY: Josef Maier; Manfred Kaltz, Hans-Hubert Vogts; Karl-Heinz Körbel, Franz Beckenbauer (Cap), Paul Breitner; Bernd Hölzenbein, Erich Beer, Erwin Kostedde, Günter Netzer, Josef Heynckes. Trainer: Helmut Schön

GREECE: Papagiotis Kelesidis; Giannis Kyrastas, Giorgos Foiros, Takis Sunetopoulos (46 Koulis Apostolidis), Theodoros Pallas, Stauros Sarafis, Giorgos Koudas, Hristos Terzanidis, Giorgos Delikaris, Mihalis Kritikopoulos, Dimitris Papaioannou (Cap). Trainer: Alketas Panagoulias

Goals: Heynckes (67), Delikaris (79)

WEST GERMANY v BULGARIA 1-0 (0-0)

Neckerstadion, Stuttgart 19.11.1975

Referee: Alastair McKenzie (SCO) Attendance: 71,000

W. GERMANY: Josef Maier; Hans-Hubert Vogts, Bernard Dietz; Georg Schwarzenbeck, Franz Beckenbauer (Cap), Dietmar Danner; Bernd Hölzenbein, Herbert Wimmer, Erich Beer, Ulrich Stielike, Josef Heynckes. Trainer: Helmut Schön

BULGARIA: Iordan Filipov; Ivan Zafirov, Kiril Ivkov, Tzono Vasilev, Bojil Kolev (75 Pavel Panov), Boris Angelov, Atanas Aleksandrov (76 Voin Voinov), Hristo Bonev (Cap), Kiril Milanov, Angel Rangelov, Chavdar Tzvetkov.
Trainer: Stoian Ormandjiev

Goal: Heynckes (65)

MALTA v BULGARIA 0-2 (0-0)

Gzira Stadium, Valletta 21.12.1975

Referee: Norbert Rolles (LUX) Attendance: 7,174

MALTA: Alfred Debono; Sunny Gouder (46 Edward Vella), Edwin Farrugia, Edward Darmanin, John Holland, William Vassallo, Vincent Magro (89 Christopher Vella), David Azzopardi, Richard Aquilina, Edward Aquilina, Carlo Seychell.
Trainer: Terenzio Polvertini

BULGARIA: Georgi Tihanov; Ivan Zafirov (46 Iordan Iordanov), Kiril Ivkov, Tzono Vasilev, Boris Angelov, Angel Rangelov, Voin Voinov, Hristo Bonev (Cap), Kiril Milanov, Pavel Panov, Chavdar Tzvetkov (68 Atanas Aleksandrov).
Trainer: Stoian Ormandjiev

Goals: Panov (69), Iordanov (83)

WEST GERMANY v MALTA 8-0 (4-0)

Westfalenstadion, Dortmund 28.02.1976

Referee: Marian Kuston (POL) Attendance: 35,000

W. GERMANY: Josef Maier; Hans-Hubert Vogts, Bernard Dietz; Georg Schwarzenbeck, Franz Beckenbauer (Cap), Erich Beer; Bernd Hölzenbein, Herbert Wimmer (27 Hans Bongartz), Ronald Worm, Ulrich Stielike (.. Bernhard Cullmann), Josef Heynckes. Trainer: Helmut Schön

MALTA: Charles Sciberras; Oliver Losco, Edwin Farrugia, Sunny Gouder, John Holland, William Vassallo, Dennis Fenech, Richard Aquilina, Vincent Magro (.. Carlo Seychell), Raymond Xuereb, Mario Loporto (46 Edward Aquilina).
Trainer: Terenzio Polvertini

Goals: Worm (5, 27), Heynckes (34, 58), Beer (44 pen, 77), Vogts (82), Hölzenbein (88)

	P	W	D	L	F	A	Pts
West Germany	6	3	3	0	14	4	9
Greece	6	2	3	1	12	9	7
Bulgaria	6	2	2	2	12	7	6
Malta	6	1	0	5	2	20	2

QUARTER-FINALS

CZECHOSLOVAKIA v USSR 2-0 (1-0)

Slovan, Bratislava 24.04.1976

Referee: Hilmi Ok (TUR) Attendance: 50,000

CZECHOSLOVAKIA: Ivo Viktor; Karol Dobias, Jozef Capkovic, Anton Ondrus, Koloman Gögh; Jozef Móder (77 Lubomír Knapp), Jaroslav Pollák, Antonín Panenka; Marián Masny, Zdenek Nehoda, Ladislav Petrás (18 Karel Kroupa). Trainer: Václav Jezek

USSR: Aleksandr Prohorov; Anatoliy Konkov, Viktor Zviagintzev, Mihail Fomenko, Stefan Reshko, Viktor Matvienko, Evgeni Lovchev (57 Vladimir Veremeev), Vladimir Onischenko (68 Leonid Nazarenko), Viktor Kolotov (Cap), Vladimir Troshkin, Oleg Blohin. Trainer: Valeriy Lobanovski

Goals: Móder (34), Panenka (47)

USSR v CZECHOSLOVAKIA 2-2 (0-1)

Central, Kiev 22.05.1976

Referee: Alastair McKenzie (SCO) Attendance: 100,000

USSR: Evgeni Rudakov; Anatoliy Konkov (54 Aleksandr Minaev), Evgeni Lovchev, Mihail Fomenko (Cap), Viktor Zviagintzev, Vladimir Troshkin, Vladimir Muntian, Vladimir Onischenko, Leonid Buriak, Vladimir Veremeev, Oleg Blohin. Trainer: Valeriy Lobanovski

CZECHOSLOVAKIA: Ivo Viktor; Ján Pivarník, Jozef Capkovic (83 Ladislav Jurkemik), Anton Ondrus, Koloman Gögh; Karol Dobias, Jaroslav Pollák, Jozef Móder; Marián Masny, Zdenek Nehoda, Peter Gallis (88 Ján Svehlík). Trainer: Václav Jezek

Goals: Móder (45, 82), Buriak (53), Blohin (87)

SPAIN v WEST GERMANY 1-1 (1-0)

Estadio Santiago Bernabeu, Madrid 24.04.1976

Referee: Jack Taylor (ENG) Attendance: 63,000

SPAIN: José Angel IRIBAR Cortajarena; Juan Cruz SOL Oria, Gregorio BENITO Rubio, Bernardo Blanquetti MIGUELI (70 Sebastián ALABANDA), José Luis CAPON Gonzalez; José Antonio CAMACHO Alfaro, Angel Maria VILLAR Llona, Vicente Gonzalez DEL BOSQUE, Enrique Castro Gonzalez QUINI (.. Jesus SATRÚSTEGUI), Carlos Alonso Gonzalez SANTILLANA, Ignacio CHURRUCA Sistiaga. Trainer: Ladislao Kubala

W. GERMANY: Josef Maier; Hans-Hubert Vogts, Bernard Dietz (83 Peter Reichel); Georg Schwarzenbeck (.. Bernhard Cullmann), Franz Beckenbauer (Cap), Rainer Bonhof; Bernd Hölzenbein, Herbert Wimmer, Erich Beer, Dietmar Danner, Ronald Worm. Trainer: Helmut Schön

Goals: Santillana (22), Beer (60)

WEST GERMANY v SPAIN 2-0 (2-0)

Olimpyastadion, München 22.05.1976

Referee: Robert Wurtz (FRA) Attendance: 77,600

W. GERMANY: Josef Maier; Hans-Hubert Vogts, Bernard Dietz; Georg Schwarzenbeck, Franz Beckenbauer (Cap), Rainer Bonhof; Ulrich Hoeneß, Herbert Wimmer, Klaus Toppmöller, Erich Beer, Bernd Hölzenbein. Trainer: Helmut Schön

SPAIN: MIGUEL ANGEL Gonzalez Suarez; José Luis CAPON Gonzalez, Juan Cruz SOL Oria (18 Ignacio CORTABARRíA), José Martinez Sánchez PIRRI, José Antonio CAMACHO Alfaro; Angel Maria VILLAR Llona (46 José Antonio RAMOS), Vicente Gonzalez DEL BOSQUE, Juan Manuel ASENSI Ripoll; Enrique Castro Gonzalez QUINI, Carlos Alonso Gonzalez SANTILLANA, Ignacio CHURRUCA Sistiaga. Trainer: Ladislao Kubala

Goals: Hoeneß (17), Toppmöller (43)

YUGOSLAVIA v WALES 2-0 (1-0)

Maksimir, Zagreb 24.04.1976

Referee: Paul Schiller (AUS) Attendance: 50,000

YUGOSLAVIA: Ognjen Petrovic; Ivan Buljan, Dzemal Hadziabdic, Branko Oblak, Josip Katalinski, Drazen Muzinic, Danilo Popivoda, Jovan Acimovic, Ivan Surjak, Momcilo Vukotic (.. Jure Jerkovic), Drago Vabec. Trainer: Ante Mladinic

WALES: William David Davies; Rodney John Thomas, Malcolm Edward Page, John Mahoney, Leighton Phillips, Ian Peter Evans, Leighton James (.. Alan Curtis), Brian Flynn, Terence Yorath, John Toshack, Arfon Trevor Griffits. Manager: Michael Smith

Goals: Vukotic (1), D. Popivoda (55)

WALES v YUGOSLAVIA 1-1 (1-1)

Ninian Park, Cardiff 22.05.1976

Referee: Rudolf Glöckner (E. GER) Attendance: 50,000

WALES: William David Davies; Leighton Phillips, David Roberts, Ian Peter Evans, Malcolm Edward Page, Arfon Trevor Griffits (.. Alan Curtis), Terence Yorath, John Mahoney, Brian Flynn, John Toshack, Leighton James. Manager: Michael Smith

YUGOSLAVIA: Enver Maric; Drazen Muzinic, Dzemal Hadziabdic, Ivan Buljan, Josip Katalinski, Ivan Surjak, Slavisa Zungul (.. Franjo Vladic), Branko Oblak, Borislav Djordjevic, Jure Jerkovic, Danilo Popivoda. Trainer: Ante Mladinic

Goals: Katalinski (18 pen), Evans (38)

HOLLAND v BELGIUM 5-0 (2-0)

Feyenoord, Rotterdam 25.04.1976

Referee: Jean Dubach (SWI) Attendance: 38,000

HOLLAND: Piet Schrijvers; Wim Suurbier, Adrianus van Kraay, Wim Rijsbergen, Ruud Krol, Wim Jansen (82 Jan Peters), Johan Neeskens, Willy van de Kerkhof, Johnny Rep, Johan Cruijff (Cap), Robert Rensenbrink.
Trainer: Gregorius Knobel

BELGIUM: Christian Piot; Gilbert Van Binst, Eric Gerets, Georges Leekens, Maurice Martens, Julien Cools (46 François Van der Elst), Jan Verheyen, Ludo Coeck, René Vandereycken, Roger Van Gool, Raoul Lambert (81 Jacques Teugels).
Trainer: Raymond Goethals

Goals: Rensenbrink (17, 27, 58, 85), Neeskens (79 pen)

BELGIUM v HOLLAND 1-2 (1-0)

Heizel, Brussel 22.05.1976

Referee: Alberto Michelotti (ITA) Attendance: 19,050

BELGIUM: Jean-Marie Pfaff; Bob Dalving, Gilbert Van Binst, Michel Renquin, Maurice Martens (Cap), François Van der Elst, Julien Cools, René Verheyen, René Vandereycken, Willy Wellens, Roger Van Gool (66 Hervé Delesie).
Trainer: Guy Thys

HOLLAND: Piet Schrijvers; Wim Suurbier, Adrianus van Kraay, Wim Rijsbergen, Ruud Krol, Willy van de Kerkhof, Johan Neeskens, Wim Van Hanegem (87 Jan Peters), Johnny Rep, Johan Cruijff (Cap), Robert Rensenbrink.
Trainer: Gregorius Knobel

Goals: Van Gool (27), Rep (61), Cruijff (77)

SEMI-FINALS

CZECHOSLOVAKIA v HOLLAND 3-1 (1-0, 1-1) (AET)

Maksimir, Zagreb 16.06.1976

Referee: Clive Thomas (WAL) Attendance: 31,000

CZECHOSLOVAKIA: Ivo Viktor; Ján Pivarnik, Jozef Capkovic (106 Ladislav Jurkemik), Anton Ondrus (Cap), Koloman Gögh; Jaroslav Pollák, Antonín Panenka, Karol Dobias, Jozef Móder (96 Frantisek Vesely); Marián Masny, Zdenek Nehoda. Trainer: Václav Jezek

HOLLAND: Piet Schrijvers; Wim Suurbier, Adrianus van Kraay, Wim Rijsbergen (36 Wim Van Hanegem), Ruud Krol, Willy van de Kerkhof, Johan Neeskens, Wim Jansen (65 Ruud Geels), Johnny Rep, Johan Cruijff (Cap), Robert Rensenbrink.
Trainer: Gregorius Knobel

Sent off: Pollák (53), Neeskens (76), van Hanegem (115)

Goals: Ondrus (20, 74 og), Nehoda (114), Vesely (118)

YUGOSLAVIA v WEST GERMANY 2-4 (2-0, 2-2) (AET)

Crvena Zvezda, Beograd 17.06.1976

Referee: Alfred Delcourt (BEL) Attendance: 70,000

YUGOSLAVIA: Ognjen Petrovic; Ivan Buljan, Drazen Muzinic, Branko Oblak (106 Luka Peruzovic), Josip Katalinski, Ivan Surjak, Slavisa Zungul, Jure Jerkovic, Danilo Popivoda, Jovan Acimovic (106 Franjo Vladic), Dragan Dzajic (Cap).
Trainer: Ante Mladinic

W. GERMANY: Josef Maier; Hans-Hubert Vogts, Bernard Dietz; Georg Schwarzenbeck, Franz Beckenbauer (Cap), Rainer Bonhof; Ulrich Hoeneß, Herbert Wimmer (80 Dieter Müller), Erich Beer, Dietmar Danner (46 Heinz Flohe), Bernd Hölzenbein. Trainer: Helmut Schön

Goals: Popivoda (19), Dzajic (30), Flohe (65), D. Müller (82, 115, 119)

THIRD PLACE MATCH

YUGOSLAVIA v HOLLAND 2-3 (1-2, 2-2) (AET)

Maksimir, Zagreb 19.06.1976

Referee: Walter Hungerbühler (SWI) Attendance: 15,000

HOLLAND: Piet Schrijvers; Wim Suurbier, Adrianus van Kraay, Wim Jansen (46 Wim Meutstege), Ruud Krol (Cap); Peter Arntz (70 Kees Kist), Willy van de Kerkhof, Jan Peters, René van de Kerkhof, Ruud Geels, Robert Rensenbrink.
Trainers: Gregorius Knobel

YUGOSLAVIA: Ognjen Petrovic; Josip Katalinski, Ivan Buljan, Drazen Muzinic, Branko Oblak, Ivan Surjak, Slavisa Zungul (46 Vahid Halilhodzic), Jure Jerkovic, Danilo Popivoda, Jovan Acimovic (46 Franjo Vladic), Dragan Dzajic (Cap).
Trainer: Ante Mladinic

Goals: Geels (27, 107), Willy van de Kerkhoff (39), Katalinski (43), Dzajic (83)

FINAL

CZECHOSLOVAKIA v WEST GERMANY 2-2 (2-1, 2-2) (AET)

Crvena Zvezda, Beograd 20.06.1976

Referee: Sergio Gonella (ITA) Attendance: 30,790

CZECHOSLOVAKIA: Ivo Viktor; Ján Pivarník, Jozef Capkovic, Anton Ondrus (Cap), Koloman Gögh; Antonín Panenka, Jozef Móder, Karol Dobias (94 Frantisek Vesely); Marián Masny, Ján Svehlík (79 Ladislav Jurkemik), Zdenek Nehoda. Trainer: Václav Jezek

W. GERMANY: Josef Maier; Hans-Hubert Vogts, Bernard Dietz; Georg Schwarzenbeck, Franz Beckenbauer (Cap), Rainer Bonhof; Ulrich Hoeneß, Herbert Wimmer (46 Heinz Flohe), Dieter Müller, Erich Beer (79 Hans Bongartz), Bernd Hölzenbein. Trainer: Helmut Schön

Goals: Svehlík (8), Dobias (23), D.Müller (28), Hölzenbein (90)

Penalties: 1-0 Masny, 1-1 Bonhof, 2-1 Nehoda, 2-2 Flohe, 3-2 Ondrus, 3-3 Bongartz, 4-3 Jurkemik, Hoeneß, 5-3 Panenka

Goalscorers European Football Championship 1976

8 goals: Don Givens (Republic of Ireland)

6 goals: Tibor Nyilasi (Hungary)

5 goals: Malcolm Macdonald (England), Johann Krankl (Austria), Zdenek Nehoda (Czechoslovakia), Josip Katalinski (Yugoslavia), Johannes Cruijff, Robert Rensenbrink (Holland)

4 goals: Arfon Griffiths (Wales), Zoltan Crişan, Dudu Georgescu (Romania), Jean-Marc Guillou (France), Josef Heynckes, Dieter Müller (West Germany), Antonín Panenka (Czechoslovakia)

3 goals: Premysl Bicovsky, Jozef Móder (Czechoslovakia), Michael Channon (England), John Toshack (Wales), Gilbert Dussier (Luxembourg), Tom Lund (Norway), Ruud Geels, Johannes Neeskens, Willy van der Kuylen (Holland), Andrzej Szarmach, Grzegorz Lato (Poland), Oleg Blohin, Viktor Kolotov (USSR), Antonis Antoniadis (Greece), Georgi Denev (Bulgaria), Erich Beer (West Germany)

2 goals: Masny, Ondrus (Czechoslovakia), Bell (England), Néné (Portugal), James (Wales), Welzl (Austria), Braun, Philipp (Luxembourg), Nagy (Hungary), Dzajic, Oblak, Popivoda, M. Vukotic (Yugoslavia), Hamilton (Northern Ireland), Sjöberg, Nordahl (Sweden), Quini, Santillana (Spain), Rioch (Scotland), Gadocha (Poland), Rahja (Finland), Onischenko (USSR), Worm, Cullmann, Hölzenbein (West Germany), Delikaris, Papaioannou (Greece), Bonev, Kolev, Panov (Bulgaria)

1 goal: Dobias, Gallis, Petrás, Svehlík, Vesely (Czechoslovakia), Keegan (England), Alves, Moinhos, Rui Rodrigues (Portugal), Evans, Reece, Mahoney, England, P. Roberts, Yorath (Wales), Jara, Prohaska, Köglberger, Kreuz (Austria), Pinter, Váradi, Wollek, Pusztai, Horváth, Bálint, Branikovits (Hungary), Vladic, Vabec, Buljan, Bogicevic, Surjak, Ivezic (Yugoslavia), Morgan, Mcilroy, Hunter, O'Neill, Nicholl, Finney (N. Ireland), Torstensson, Sandberg, Grahn, Edström (Sweden), E.J. Olsen, Thunberg (Norway), Villar, Pirri, Capón, Velazquez, Megido, Claramunt I, R. Martinez (Spain), Iordănescu, Lucescu, Dinu (Romania), Dalglish, MacDougall, Harper, McQueen, Bremner, Jordan (Scotland), Bastrup, Dahl, Nygaard (Denmark), Thijsen, René van de Kerkhof, Willy van de Kerkhoff, Lubse, Rep (Holland), Capello, Chinaglia, Boninsegna (Italy), Kasperczak (Poland), Paatelainen (Finland), Buriak, Konkov, Veremeev, Muntian (USSR), Hand, Martin, Treacy (Republic of Ireland), Alpaslan, Ismail, B. Mehmet (Turkey), Risi, Elsener, Müller, Schild (Switzerland), Puis, Lambert, Martens, F. Van der Elst, Van Moer, Teugels, Van Gool (Belgium), Streich, Vogel, P. Ducke, Häfner, Pommerenke, Sparwasser, Kreische, Hoffmann (East Germany), Bathenay, Berdoll, Coste (France), Edvaldsson, Sigurvinsson, Hallgrimsson (Iceland), Flohe, Hoeneß, Ritschel, Toppmöller, Vogts, Wimmer (West Germany), Mauros, Iosifidis, Sarafis, Eleutherakis, Gklezos (Greece), Iordanov, Dimitrov, Milanov (Bulgaria), R. Aquilina, V. Magro (Malta)

Own goals: Reshko (USSR) & Dunne (Republic of Ireland) for Turkey, Ismail (Turkey) for Switzerland, Ondrus (Czechoslovakia) for Holland

THE EUROPEAN FOOTBALL CHAMPIONSHIP 1980

GROUP 1

DENMARK v REPUBLIC OF IRELAND 3-3 (1-2)

Idraetsparken, København 24.05.1978

Referee: Jan Beck (HOL) Attendance: 12,000

DENMARK: Birger Jensen; Johnny Hansen, Per Røntved, Henning Munk Jensen, Søren Lerby, Morten Olsen (76 Jan Højland), Benny Nielsen, Kristen Nygaard (66 Frank Arnesen), Jan Sørensen II, Henning Jensen, Jørgen Kristensen. Trainer: Kurt Nielsen

IRELAND: Mick Kearns; Paddy Mulligan, David O'Leary, Mark Lawrenson, Jimmy Holmes (51 Eamonn Gregg), Gerard Daly, Johnny Giles (Cap), Tony Grealish, Steve Heighway, Don Givens (46 Paul McGee), Frank Stapleton. Trainer: John Giles

Goals: Stapleton (11), Grealish (25), H. Jensen (31), Daly (65), B. Nielsen (79 pen), Lerby (80)

DENMARK v ENGLAND 3-4 (2-2)

Idraetsparken, København 20.09.1978

Referee: Adolf Prokop (E. GER) Attendance: 48,000

DENMARK: Birger Jensen; Flemming Nielsen, Henning Munk Jensen, Per Røntved, Søren Lerby, Frank Arnesen, Carsten Nielsen, Flemming Lund, Allan Simonsen, Benny Nielsen (46 Allan Hansen), Jørgen Kristensen. Trainer: Kurt Nielsen

ENGLAND: Raymond Clemence; Philip Neal, Michael Mills, Ray Wilkins, David Watson, Emlyn Hughes, Kevin Keegan, Steven Coppell, Robert Latchford, Trevor Brooking, Peter Barnes. Manager: Ronald Greenwood

Goals: Keegan (17, 23), Simonsen (27 pen), Arnesen (30), Latchford (52), Neal (83), Røntved (86)

REPUBLIC OF IRELAND v NORTHERN IRELAND 0-0

Lansdowne Road, Dublin 20.09.1978

Referee: Francis Rion (BEL) Attendance: 55,000

REPUBLIC OF IRELAND: Mick Kearns; Tony Grealish, Mark Lawrenson, Noel Synnot, Jimmy Holmes, Gerard Daly, Johnny Giles (Cap), William Brady, Steve Heighway (63 Don Givens), Paul McGee, Frank Stapleton (54 Mickey Walsh). Trainer: John Giles

NORTHERN IRELAND: Patrick Jennings; Patrick Rice, Samuel Nelson, Christopher Nicholl, Alan Hunter (72 Bryan Hamilton), James Nicholl, Martin O'Neill, David McCreery, Gerard Armstrong, Samuel McIlroy, Derek Spence (69 Terence Cochrane). Manager: Daniel Blanchflower

DENMARK v BULGARIA 2-2 (1-1)

Idraetsparken, København 11.10.1978

Referee: Angel Franco Martinez (SPA) Attendance: 30,000

DENMARK: Ole Kjær; Flemming Nielsen, Lars Larsen, Per Røntved, Søren Lerby, Morten Olsen, Heino Hansen, Frank Arnesen, Flemming Lund, Benny Nielsen, Jørgen Kristensen. Trainer: Kurt Nielsen

BULGARIA: Rumen Goranov; Plamen Nikolov, Petr Stankov, Georgi Bonev, Nikolai Grancharov (11 Ivan Iliev), Radoslav Zdravkov, Rusi Gochev, Georgi Slavkov (79 Aleksandar Ivanov), Stoicho Mladenov, Pavel Panov (Cap), Angel Stankov. Trainer: Zvetan Ilchev

Goals: B. Nielsen (17), Panov (32), Lerby (64), Iliev (85)

NORTHERN IRELAND v DENMARK 2-1 (0-0)

Belfast 25.10.1978

Referee: Rolf Haugen (NOR) Attendance: 30,000

N. IRELAND: Patrick Jennings; Patrick Rice, Samuel Nelson, James Nicholl, Alan Hunter, David McCreery, Martin O'Neill, Samuel McIlroy, Gerard Armstrong, Samuel Morgan (.. Derek Spence, 68 Trevor Anderson), Terence Cochrane. Manager: Daniel Blanchflower

DENMARK: Ole Kjær; Flemming Nielsen, Lars Larsen, Per Røntved, John Andersen, Ole Rasmussen, Carsten Nielsen, Ove Flindt Bjerg, Henrik Agerbeck (52 Jan Sørensen I), Henning Jensen, Jørgen Kristensen. Trainer: Kurt Nielsen

Goals: H. Jensen (51), Spence (63), Anderson (85)

REPUBLIC OF IRELAND v ENGLAND 1-1 (1-1)

Lansdowne Road, Dublin 25.10.1978

Referee: Heinz Aldinger (W. GER) Attendance: 50,000

IRELAND: Mick Kearns; Paddy Mulligan (Cap), David O'Leary (73 Eamonn Gregg), Mark Lawrenson, Jimmy Holmes, Gerard Daly, Tony Grealish, William Brady, Gerry Ryan, Don Givens, Paul McGee (65 Frank Stapleton). Trainer: John Giles

ENGLAND: Raymond Clemence; Philip Neal, Michael Mills, Ray Wilkins, David Watson (22 Philip Thompson), Emlyn Hughes, Kevin Keegan, Steven Coppell, Robert Latchford, Trevor Brooking, Peter Barnes (81 Anthony Woodcock). Manager: Ronald Greenwood

Goals: Latchford (8), Daly (27)

BULGARIA v NORTHERN IRELAND 0-2 (0-1)

Vasil Levski, Sofia 29.11.1978

Referee: Hilmi Ok (TUR) Attendance: 25,000

BULGARIA: Rumen Goranov; Nikolai Grancharov, Petr Stankov, Roman Karakolev, Georgi Dimitrov, Borislav Sredkov, Rusi Gochev, Georgi Slavkov, Stoicho Mladenov (67 Spas Djevizov), Pavel Panov (Cap), Angel Stankov (46 Chavdar Tzvetkov). Trainer: Zvetan Ilchev

N. IRELAND: Patrick Jennings; Bryan Hamilton, Samuel Nelson, Christopher Nicholl, James Nicholl, David McCreery, Martin O'Neill, Samuel McIlroy (69 Victor Moreland), Gerard Armstrong, William Caskey, Terence Cochrane (55 Cristopher McGrath). Manager: Daniel Blanchflower

Goals: Armstrong (17), Caskey (82)

NORTHERN IRELAND v BULGARIA 2-0 (2-0)

Windsor Park, Belfast 02.05.1979

Referee: Anders Mattsson (FIN) Attendance: 20,000

N. IRELAND: Patrick Jennings; Bryan Hamilton, Samuel Nelson, Christopher Nicholl (66 Victor Moreland), James Nicholl, David McCreery, Martin O'Neill, Samuel McIlroy, Gerard Armstrong, William Caskey (79 Derek Spence), Terence Cochrane. Manager: Daniel Blanchflower

BULGARIA: Stoian Stoianov; Tzono Vasilev, Kiril Ivkov (Cap), Georgi Bonev, Liuben Kolev, Aleksandar Rainov, Radoslav Zdravkov (65 Georgi Iliev), Borislav Sredkov, Spas Djevizov, Pavel Panov, Chavdar Tzvetkov.
Trainer: Ianko Dinkov

Goals: C. Nicholl (15), Armstrong (33)

ENGLAND v NORTHERN IRELAND 4-0 (1-0)

Wembley, London 07.02.1979

Referee: Ulf Eriksson (SWE) Attendance: 92,000

ENGLAND: Raymond Clemence; Philip Neal, Michael Mills, Anthony Currie, David Watson, Emlyn Hughes, Kevin Keegan, Steven Coppell, Robert Latchford, Trevor Brooking, Peter Barnes. Manager: Ronald Greenwood

N. IRELAND: Patrick Jennings; Patrick Rice, Samuel Nelson, Christopher Nicholl, James Nicholl, David McCreery, Martin O'Neill, Samuel McIlroy, Gerard Armstrong, William Caskey (74 Derek Spence), Terence Cochrane (.. Cristopher McGrath). Manager: Daniel Blanchflower

Goals: Keegan (25), Latchford (46, 64), Watson (50)

BULGARIA v REPUBLIC OF IRELAND 1-0 (0-0)

Vasil Levski, Sofia 19.05.1979

Referee: Josef Bucek (AUS) Attendance: 25,000

BULGARIA: Iordan Filipov; Nikolai Grancharov, Kiril Ivkov (Cap), Ivan Iliev, Tzono Vasilev, Radoslav Zdravkov, Krasimir Borisov, Pavel Panov, Voin Voinov, Andrei Jeliazkov, Chavdar Tzvetkov. Trainer: Zvetan Ilchev

IRELAND: Gerry Peyton; Eamonn Gregg, David O'Leary, Mick Martin, Jimmy Holmes (58 Paddy Mulligan), Gerard Daly, Johnny Giles (Cap), William Brady, Steve Heighway, Mickey Walsh (75 Paul McGee), Don Givens.
Trainer: John Giles

Goal: Tzvetkov (81)

REPUBLIC OF IRELAND v DENMARK 2-0 (1-0)

Lansdowne Road, Dublin 02.05.1979

Referee: Michel Vautrot (FRA) Attendance: 26,000

IRELAND: Gerry Peyton; Eamonn Gregg, Paddy Mulligan, Mick Martin, Jimmy Holmes, Gerard Daly, Johnny Giles (Cap), William Brady, Austin Hayes (61 Mickey Walsh), Frank Stapleton, Don Givens (71 Paul McGee). Trainer: John Giles

DENMARK: Ole Kjær; Flemming Nielsen, Per Røntved, Lars Larsen, Søren Lerby, Frank Arnesen, Morten Olsen, Flemming Lund, Allan Simonsen, Benny Nielsen (76 Henrik Agerbeck), Preben Elkjær. Trainer: Kurt Nielsen

Goals: Daly (44), Givens (66)

DENMARK v NORTHERN IRELAND 4-0 (2-0)

Idraetsparken, København 06.06.1979

Referee: Rudolf Frickel (W. GER) Attendance: 16,800

DENMARK: Ole Kjær; Ole Højgaard (75 Peter Poulsen), Søren Busk, Steen Ziegler, John Andersen, Frank Arnesen, Morten Olsen, Klaus Nørregård (59 Per Røntved), Søren Lerby, Allan Simonsen, Preben Elkjær. Trainer: Kurt Nielsen

N. IRELAND: Patrick Jennings; Patrick Rice, Samuel Nelson, James Nicholl, Alan Hunter, David McCreery, Martin O'Neill, Samuel McIlroy, Gerard Armstrong, Derek Spence, Bryan Hamilton. Manager: Daniel Blanchflower

Goals: Elkjær (31, 33, 82), Simonsen (63)

BULGARIA v ENGLAND 0-3 (0-1)

Vasil Levski, Sofia 06.06.1979

Referee: Ernst Dörflinger (SWI) Attendance: 50,000

BULGARIA: Iordan Filipov; Nikolai Grancharov, Kiril Ivkov (Cap), Georgi Bonev, Ivan Iliev, Radoslav Zdravkov (61 Todor Barzov), Voin Voinov (46 Rusi Gochev), Krasimir Borisov, Andrei Jeliazkov, Pavel Panov, Chavdar Tzvetkov. Trainer: Zvetan Ilchev

ENGLAND: Raymond Clemence; Philip Neal, Michael Mills, Philip Thompson, David Watson, Ray Wilkins, Kevin Keegan, Steven Coppell, Robert Latchford (66 Trevor Francis), Trevor Brooking, Peter Barnes (76 Anthony Woodcock). Manager: Ronald Greenwood

Goals: Keegan (33), Watson (54), Barnes (55)

ENGLAND v DENMARK 1-0 (1-0)

Wembley, London 12.09.1979

Referee: Cesar da Luz Dias Correia (POR) Att: 85,000

ENGLAND: Raymond Clemence; Philip Neal, Michael Mills, Philip Thompson, David Watson, Ray Wilkins, Steven Coppell, Terence McDermott, Kevin Keegan, Trevor Brooking, Peter Barnes. Manager: Ronald Greenwood

DENMARK: Birger Jensen; Ole Højgaard, Søren Busk, Steen Ziegler, Morten Olsen, Søren Lerby, Frank Arnesen, Benny Nielsen (31 Jens J.Bertelsen), Henning Jensen, Allan Simonsen, Preben Elkjær (80 Ove Flindt Bjerg). Trainer: Josef Piontek

Goal: Keegan (17)

NORTHERN IRELAND v ENGLAND 1-5 (0-2)

Belfast 17.10.1979

Referee: Alexis Ponnet (BEL) Attendance: 25,000

N. IRELAND: Patrick Jennings; Patrick Rice, Samuel Nelson, James Nicholl, Alan Hunter (46 Peter Rafferty), David McCreery, Thomas Cassidy, Samuel McIlroy, Gerard Armstrong, Thomas Finney (70 William Caskey), Victor Moreland. Manager: Daniel Blanchflower

ENGLAND: Peter Shilton; Philip Neal, Michael Mills, Philip Thompson, David Watson, Ray Wilkins, Kevin Keegan, Steven Coppell, Trevor Francis, Trevor Brooking (84 Terence McDermott), Anthony Woodcock. Manager: Ronald Greenwood

Goals: Francis (18, 62), Woodcock (34, 71), Moreland (49 pen), Nicholl (74 og)

REPUBLIC OF IRELAND v BULGARIA 3-0 (1-0)

Lansdowne Road, Dublin 17.10.1979

Referee: Heinz Einbeck (E. GER) Attendance: 22,000

IRELAND: Gerry Peyton; Paddy Mulligan (Cap), David O'Leary, Pierce O'Leary, Ashley Grimes, Mick Martin, William Brady, Tony Grealish, Steve Heighway, Paul McGee, Frank Stapleton. Trainer: John Giles

BULGARIA: Rumen Goranov (Cap); Tzono Vasilev, Georgi Dimitrov, Georgi Bonev, Ivan Iliev, Vanio Kostov (46 Kostadin Kostadinov), Todor Barzov, Plamen Markov, Andrei Jeliazkov, Boicho Velitchkov, Chavdar Tzvetkov. Trainer: Dobromir Tashkov

Goals: Martin (18), Grealish (46), Stapleton (83)

BULGARIA v DENMARK 3-0 (1-0)

Vasil Levski, Sofia 31.10.1979

Referee: Sotos Afxentiou (CYP) Attendance: 10,000

BULGARIA: Hristo Hristov; Tzono Vasilev, Borislav Dimitrov, Georgi Bonev, Ivan Iliev, Todor Barzov, Kostadin Kostadinov (70 Rusi Gochev), Plamen Markov, Boicho Velitchkov, Andrei Jeliazkov (Cap), Chavdar Tzvetkov. Trainer: Dobromir Tashkov

DENMARK: Ole Qvist; Jens Steffensen, Søren Busk, Steen Ziegler, Frank Olsen, Frank Arnesen, Søren Lerby, Jens J.Bertelsen, Kristen Nygaard (64 Carsten Nielsen), Henning Jensen, Allan Simonsen. Trainer: Josef Piontek

Goals: Jeliazkov (21), Tzvetkov (51, 88)

NORTHERN IRELAND v REPUBLIC OF IRELAND 1-0 (0-0)

Windsor Park, Belfast 21.11.1979

Referee: André Daina (SWI) Attendance: 15,000

NORTHERN IRELAND: Patrick Jennings; James Nicholl, Samuel Nelson, Christopher Nicholl, Alan Hunter, David McCreery, Martin O'Neill (66 Thomas Cassidy), Samuel McIlroy, Gerard Armstrong, Derek Spence, Victor Moreland. Manager: Daniel Blanchflower

REPUBLIC OF IRELAND: Mick Kearns; John Devine, David O'Leary, Pierce O'Leary, Ashley Grimes, Gerard Daly (53 Joe Waters), Mick Martin (Cap), Tony Grealish, Steve Heighway, Paul McGee (75 Don Givens), Frank Stapleton. Trainer: John Giles

Goal: Armstrong (54)

ENGLAND v BULGARIA 2-0 (1-0)

Wembley, London 22.11.1979

Referee: Erik Frederiksson (SWE) Attendance: 72,000

ENGLAND: Raymond Clemence; Vivian Anderson, Kenneth Sansom, Philip Thompson, David Watson, Ray Wilkins, Kevin Reeves, Glenn Hoddle, Trevor Francis, Raymond Kennedy, Anthony Woodcock. Manager: Ronald Greenwood

BULGARIA: Hristo Hristov; Roman Karakolev, Borislav Dimitrov, Georgi Bonev, Ivan Iliev, Georgi Dimitrov, Todor Barzov, Plamen Markov, Boicho Velitchkov (87 Krasimir Manolov), Andrei Jeliazkov (Cap), Chavdar Tzvetkov (29 Kostadin Kostadinov). Trainer: Dobromir Tashkov

Goals: Watson (9), Hoddle (69)

ENGLAND v REPUBLIC OF IRELAND 2-0 (1-0)

Wembley, London 06.02.1980

Referee: Klaus Scheurell (E. GER) Attendance: 90,299

ENGLAND: Raymond Clemence; Trevor Cherry, Kenneth Sansom, Philip Thompson, David Watson, Bryan Robson, Kevin Keegan, Terence McDermott, David Johnson (59 Steven Coppell), Anthony Woodcock, Laurence Cunningham. Manager: Ronald Greenwood

IRELAND: Gerry Peyton (60 Ron Healey); Christopher Hughton, David O'Leary (68 Pierce O'Leary), Mark Lawrenson, Ashley Grimes, Gerard Daly, Tony Grealish, William Brady (Cap), Fran O'Brien, Steve Heighway, Frank Stapleton. Trainer: John Giles

Goals: Keegan (34, 74)

	P	W	D	L	F	A	Pts
England	8	7	1	0	22	5	15
Northern Ireland	8	4	1	3	8	14	9
Rep. of Ireland	8	2	3	3	9	8	7
Bulgaria	8	2	1	5	6	14	5
Denmark	8	1	2	5	13	17	4

GROUP 2

NORWAY v AUSTRIA 0-2 (0-2)

Ulleval, Oslo 30.08.1978

Referee: Patrick Partridge (ENG) Attendance: 17,000

NORWAY: Tom R.Jacobsen; Helge Karlsen (14 Bjarne Berntsen), Jan Birkelund, Svein Grøndalen, Trond Pedersen, Einar Aas, Tor Egil Johansen (Cap), Stein Thunberg, Svein Mathisen, Odd Iversen (72 Arne Larsen-Økland), Hallvar Thoresen. Trainer: Tor Røste Fossen

AUSTRIA: Erwin Fuchsbichler; Robert Sara (Cap), Erich Obermayer, Bruno Pezzey, Heinrich Strasser; Heribert Weber, Herbert Prohaska, Kurt Jara (.. Reinhold Hintermaier); Walter Schachner, Johann Krankl, Wilhelm Kreuz.
Trainer: Karl Stotz

Goals: Pezzey (22), Krankl (43)

BELGIUM v NORWAY 1-1 (0-1)

Daknam, Lokeren 20.09.1978

Referee: Marijan Raus (YUG) Attendance: 5,272

BELGIUM: Jean-Marie Pfaff; Eric Gerets (46 François Van der Elst), Walter Meeuws, Georges Leekens, René Vandereycken, Julien Cools (Cap), Ludo Coeck, René Verheyen, Roger Van Gool, Paul Courant (59 Willy Geurts), Eddy Voordeckers. Trainer: Guy Thys

NORWAY: Tom R.Jacobsen; Trond Pedersen, Tore Kordahl, Einar Aas, Svein Grøndalen, Roger Albertsen, Bjarne Berntsen, Tor Egil Johansen, Hallvar Thoresen, Svein Mathisen (73 Stein Thunberg), Arne Larsen-Økland (87 Pål Jacobsen).
Trainer: Tor Røste Fossen

Goals: Larsen-Økland (7), Cools (64)

AUSTRIA v SCOTLAND 3-2 (1-0)

Prater, Wien 20.09.1978

Referee: Alberto Michelotti (ITA) Attendance: 73,000

AUSTRIA: Erwin Fuchsbichler; Robert Sara (Cap), Erich Obermayer, Bruno Pezzey, Heinrich Strasser; Heribert Weber, Herbert Prohaska (87 Franz Oberacher); Walter Schachner, Johann Krankl, Wilhelm Kreuz, Kurt Jara. Trainer: Karl Stotz

SCOTLAND: Allan Rough; Stuart Kennedy, Gordon McQueen, Martin Buchan, William Donachie; Graeme Souness, Asa Hartford, Archibald Gemmill (Cap); Kenneth Dalglish, Joseph Jordan (.. Arthur Graham), Andrew Gray.
Manager: Alistair MacLeod

Goals: Pezzey (25), Schachner (48), Kreuz (65), McQueen (66), A. Gray (78)

PORTUGAL v BELGIUM 1-1 (1-1)

Estádio José Alvalade, Lisboa 11.10.1978

Referee: Georges Konrath (FRA) Attendance: 20,000

PORTUGAL: Manuel Galrinho BENTO; GABRIEL Azevedo Mendes, EURICO Monteiro Gomes, HUMBERTO Manuel Jesus COELHO (Cap), Adelino Jesus TEIXEIRA, SHEU Han (46 ARTUR Manuel Soares Correia), António Luis Alves Ribeiro OLIVEIRA, João António Ferreira Resende ALVES, José Alberto COSTA, MANUEL José Tavares FERNANDES (71 Tamagnini Manuel Gomes Batista NÉNÉ), Fernando Mendes Soares GOMES.

BELGIUM: Jean-Marie Pfaff; Walter Meeuws, Eric Gerets, Hugo Broos, Michel Renquin, Julien Cools (Cap), Ludo Coeck, René Vandereycken, Frankie Vercauteren, Guy Dardenne (67 François Van der Elst), Eddy Voordeckers (60 Jan Ceulemans). Trainer: Guy Thys

Goals: Gomes (32), Vercauteren (37)

PORTUGAL v SCOTLAND 1-0 (1-0)

Estádio da Luz, Lisboa 29.11.1978

Referee: Ernst Dörflinger (SWI) Attendance: 60,000

PORTUGAL: Manuel BENTO; ARTUR Correia, HUMBERTO COELHO (Cap), Carlos ALHINHO, ALBERTO Gomes, Minervino PIETRA, António OLIVEIRA (82 EURICO Monteiro Gomes), João ALVES, José COSTA (46 SHÉU Han), Tamagnini NÉNÉ, Fernando GOMES.

SCOTLAND: Allan Rough; Stuart Kennedy, Francis Gray (65 William Donachie), David Narey, Gordon McQueen, Martin Buchan, Kenneth Dalglish, Asa Hartford, Joseph Jordan (78 Ian Wallace), Archibald Gemmill, John Robertson. Manager: John Stein

Goal: Alberto (20)

SCOTLAND v NORWAY 3-2 (1-1)

Hampden Park, Glasgow 25.10.1978

Referee: Vojtech Christov (CZE) Attendance: 60,000

SCOTLAND: James Stewart; William Donachie, Gordon McQueen, Martin Buchan, Francis Gray, Archibald Gemmill, Asa Hartford, Graeme Souness, Kenneth Dalglish, Andrew Gray, Arthur Graham. Manager: John Stein

NORWAY: Tom R.Jacobsen; Trond Pedersen (80 Helge Karlsen), Jan Birkelund, Tore Kordahl, Svein Grøndalen, Einar Aas, Tom Jacobsen (37 Jan Hansen), Tor Egil Johansen, Hallvar Thoresen, Svein Mathisen, Arne Larsen-Ökland. Trainer: Tor Røste Fossen

Goals: Aas (3), Dalglish (15, 82), Larsen-Ökland (64), Gemmill (88 pen)

BELGIUM v AUSTRIA 1-1 (1-0)

Astrid Park, Brussel 28.03.1979

Referee: Angel Franco Martinez (SPA) Attendance: 6,264

BELGIUM: Jean-Marie Pfaff; Walter Meeuws, Eric Gerets, Hugo Broos, Michel Renquin; Julien Cools (Cap) (70 Willy Geurts), René Vandereycken, Frankie Vercauteren; Albert Cluytens, François van der Elst, Jean Janssens. Trainer: Guy Thys

AUSTRIA: Friedrich Koncilia; Robert Sara (Cap), Erich Obermayer, Bruno Pezzey, Dietmar Mirnegg; Heribert Weber, Roland Hattenberger, Ernst Baumeister; Wilhelm Kreuz, Johann Krankl, Walter Schachner. Trainer: Karl Stotz

Goals: Vandereycken (20 pen), Krankl (60)

AUSTRIA v PORTUGAL 1-2 (0-1)

Prater, Wien 15.11.1978

Referee: Nicolae Rainea (ROM) Attendance: 75,000

AUSTRIA: Friedrich Koncilia; Robert Sara (Cap), Erich Obermayer, Bruno Pezzey, Heinrich Strasser; Roland Hattenberger, Herbert Prohaska, Kurt Jara (.. Ernst Baumeister); Walter Schachner, Wilhelm Kreuz (81 Felix Gasselich), Johann Krankl. Trainer: Karl Stotz

PORTUGAL: Manuel BENTO; ARTUR Correia, HUMBERTO COELHO (Cap), Carlos Alexandre Fortes ALHINHO, ALBERTO Gomes Fonseca Junior, Minervino José Lopes PIETRA, Adelino TEIXEIRA, João ALVES, José COSTA, Tamagnini NÉNÉ (88 Fernando Mendes Soares GOMES), António OLIVEIRA (87 SHÉU Han).

Goals: Néné (31), Schachner (73), Alberto (90)

AUSTRIA v BELGIUM 0-0

Prater, Wien 02.05.1979

Referee: Hilmi Ok (TUR) Attendance: 40,000

AUSTRIA: Friedrich Koncilia; Robert Sara (Cap), Erich Obermayer, Bruno Pezzey, Dietmar Mirnegg; Herbert Prohaska (75 Felix Gasselich), Roland Hattenberger, Ernst Baumeister; Wilhelm Kreuz (81 Reinhold Hintermaier), Johann Krankl, Walter Schachner. Trainer: Karl Stotz

BELGIUM: Michel Preud'homme; Walter Meeuws, Eric Gerets, Hugo Broos, Michel Renquin; Julien Cools (Cap), René Vandereycken, Frankie Vercauteren; Charles Jacobs (86 Guy Dardenne), François van der Elst, Jean Janssens. Trainer: Guy Thys

NORWAY v PORTUGAL 0-1 (0-1)

Oslo 09.05.1979

Referee: Siegfried Kirschen (E. GER) Attendance: 9,800

NORWAY: Roy Amundsen; Trond Pedersen, Einar Aas, Tore Kordahl, Svein Grøndalen; Jan Hansen, Tor Egil Johansen (70 Stein Thunberg), Roger Albertsen; Svein Mathisen (55 Isak Arne Refvik), Tom Lund, Arne Larsen-Økland.
Trainer: Tor Røste Fossen

PORTUGAL: Manuel BENTO; ARTUR Correia, HUMBERTO COELHO (Cap), Carlos ALHINHO, ALBERTO Gomes, EURICO Gomes, Tamagnini NÉNÉ (81 Fernando GOMES), Minervino PIETRA, João ALVES, António OLIVEIRA, José COSTA (90 António José BASTOS LOPES).

Goal: Alves (35)

NORWAY v BELGIUM 1-2 (1-1)

Ullevaal, Oslo 12.09.1979

Referee: Alojzy Jarguz (POL) Attendance: 11,255

NORWAY: Roy Amundsen; Trond Pedersen, Morten Vinje, Einar Aas, Svein Grøndalen; Roger Albertsen, Tor Egil Johansen, Jan Hansen (75 Rune Ottesen); Pål Jacobsen, Odd Iversen (83 Svein Mathisen), Hallvar Thoresen.
Trainer: Tor Røste Fossen

BELGIUM: Jean-Marie Pfaff; Walter Meeuws, Eric Gerets, Luc Millecamps, Michel Renquin; Julien Cools, René Vandereycken, Frankie Vercauteren (77 René Verheyen); Albert Cluytens, François Van der Elst, Jean Janssens (77 Jan Ceulemans). Trainer: Guy Thys

Goals: P. Jacobsen (7), Janssens (31), Van der Elst (65)

NORWAY v SCOTLAND 0-4 (0-3)

Ullevaal, Oslo 07.06.1979

Referee: Ib Nielsen (DEN) Attendance: 17,269

NORWAY: Tom R. Jacobsen; Helge Karlsen, Tore Kordahl, Svein Grøndalen, Trond Pedersen (67 Jan Hansen); Einar Aas, Roger Albertsen, Stein Thunberg (75 Torbjørn Svendsen); Hallvar Thoresen, Svein Mathisen, Arne Larsen-Ökland.
Trainer: Tor Røste Fossen

SCOTLAND: Allan Rough; George Burley (46 Paul Hegarty, 70 John Wark), Kenneth Burns, Gordon McQueen, Iain Munro; Asa Hartford, Kenneth Dalglish, Archibald Gemmill; Arthur Graham, Joseph Jordan, John Robertson.
Manager: John Stein

Goals: Jordan (32), Dalglish (39), Robertson (43), McQueen (55)

BELGIUM v PORTUGAL 2-0 (0-0)

Heizel, Brussel 17.10.1979

Referee: Ulf Eriksson (SWE) Attendance: 8,799

BELGIUM: Théo Custers; Walter Meeuws, Eric Gerets, Luc Millecamps, Michel Renquin (75 Philippe Garot), Julien Cools (Cap), Wilfried Van Moer (75 René Verheyen), René Vandereycken, François Van der Elst, Eddy Voordeckers, Jan Ceulemans. Trainer: Guy Thys

PORTUGAL: Manuel BENTO; ARTUR Correia, HUMBERTO COELHO (Cap), Carlos ALHINHO, ALBERTO Gomes, EURICO Gomes (51 António Manuel FRASCO Vieira), Minervino PIETRA (61 Rui Manuel Trindade JORDAO), António OLIVEIRA, ROMEU Fernando Fernandes Silva, Tamagnini NÉNÉ, Fernando GOMES.

Goals: Van Moer (46), Van der Elst (56)

AUSTRIA v NORWAY 4-0 (1-0)

Prater, Wien 29.08.1979

Referee: Jaromir Fausek (CZE) Attendance: 40,000

AUSTRIA: Friedrich Koncilia; Robert Sara (Cap), Erich Obermayer, Bruno Pezzey, Günter Pospisil; Roland Hattenberger, Herbert Prohaska (76 Heribert Weber), Wilhelm Kreuz, Walter Schachner, Hans Krankl, Kurt Jara.
Trainer: Karl Stotz

NORWAY: Roy Amundsen; Trond Pedersen, Morten Vinje, Einar Aas, Svein Grøndalen; Bjarne Berntsen, Tor Egil Johansen, Stein Thunberg (30 Rune Ottesen); Svein Mathisen (74 Thorbjørn Svendsen), Arne Larsen-Ökland, Pål Jacobsen.
Trainer: Tor Røste Fossen

Goals: Jara (42), Prohaska (46 pen), Kreuz (76), Krankl (86)

SCOTLAND v AUSTRIA 1-1 (0-1)

Hampden Park, Glasgow 17.10.1979

Referee: Károly Palotai (HUNG) Attendance: 80,000

SCOTLAND: Allan Rough; William Jardine, Gordon McQueen, Kenneth Burns, Iain Munro; Graeme Souness, Archibald Gemmill (Cap), John Wark; Arthur Graham (.. David Cooper), Kenneth Dalglish, John Robertson.
Manager: John Stein

AUSTRIA: Friedrich Koncilia; Robert Sara (Cap), Bruno Pezzey, Heribert Weber, Dietmar Mirnegg; Wilhelm Kreuz, Roland Hattenberger, Kurt Jara; Walter Schachner (81 Gerhard Steinkogler), Herbert Prohaska, Hans Krankl (.. Reinhold Hintermaier). Trainer: Karl Stotz

Goals: Krankl (41), Gemmill (75)

PORTUGAL v NORWAY 3-1 (1-1)

Estádio Nacional, Lisboa 01.11.1979

Referee: Riccardo Lattanzi (ITA) Attendance: 25,000

PORTUGAL: Manuel BENTO; ARTUR Correia, HUMBERTO COELHO (Cap), Carlos António Fonseca SIMOES, Alfredo Manuel Ferreira Silva MURÇA, António FRASCO, RODOLFO dos Reis Ferreira, José COSTA, Mauricio Zacarias REINALDO Rodrigues Gomes, Fernando GOMES, Tamagnini NÉNÉ.

NORWAY: Roy Amundsen; Georg Hammer, Morten Vinje, Einar Aas, Svein Grøndalen; Bjarne Berntsen (71 Jan Hansen), Tor Egil Johansen, Roger Albertsen; Hallvar Thoresen (81 Svein Mathisen), Arne Larsen-Ökland), Pål Jacobsen. Trainer: Tor Røste Fossen

Goals: Hammer (10), Artur (37), Néné (59, 71)

SCOTLAND v BELGIUM 1-3 (0-3)

Hampden Park, Glasgow 19.12.1979

Referee: Heinz Aldinger (W. GER) Attendance: 40,000

SCOTLAND: Allan Rough; William Jardine, Daniel McGrain, John Wark, Gordon McQueen, Kenneth Burns, Kenneth Dalglish, Robert Aitken, Derek Johnstone, Eamonn Bannon (46 David Provan), John Robertson. Manager: John Stein

BELGIUM: Théo Custers; Walter Meeuws, Eric Gerets, Luc Millecamps, Maurice Martens, Julien Cools (Cap), Wilfried Van Moer (49 Gérard Plessers), René Vandereycken, François Van der Elst, Erwin Vandenbergh (73 Guy Dardenne), Jan Ceulemans. Trainer: Guy Thys

Goals: Vandenbergh (18), Van der Elst (23, 30), Robertson (55)

PORTUGAL v AUSTRIA 1-2 (1-1)

Estádio da Luz, Lisboa 21.11.1979

Referee: Charles Corver (HOL) Attendance: 80,000

PORTUGAL: Manuel BENTO; ARTUR Correia (77 SHÉU Han), HUMBERTO COELHO (Cap), Carlos SIMOES, ALBERTO Gomes, António FRASCO (65 Rui Manuel JORDAO), RODOLFO dos Reis Ferreira, José COSTA, Tamagnini NÉNÉ, Mauricio REINALDO, Fernando GOMES.

AUSTRIA: Friedrich Koncilia; Robert Sara (Cap), Erich Obermayer, Bruno Pezzey, Dietmar Mirnegg; Wilhelm Kreuz, Kurt Jara, Roland Hattenberger; Walter Schachner, Herbert Prohaska, Kurt Welzl (.. Hans Krankl). Trainer: Karl Stotz

Goals: Welzl (36), Reinaldo (42), Schachner (51)

SCOTLAND v PORTUGAL 4-1 (2-0)

Hampden Park, Glasgow 26.03.1980

Referee: Robert Wurtz (FRA) Attendance: 20,233

SCOTLAND: Allan Rough; George Burley, Daniel McGrain, David Narey, Alexander McLeish, Alan Hansen, Kenneth Dalglish (.. Steven Archibald), Graeme Souness, Andrew Gray, Archibald Gemmill, John Robertson (76 David Provan). Manager: John Stein

PORTUGAL: Manuel BENTO; Adelino TEIXEIRA, HUMBERTO COELHO (Cap), Carlos SIMOES, ALBERTO Gomes, António FRASCO (76 CARLOS MANUEL Correia Santos), EURICO Gomes (35 SHÉU Han), José COSTA, Tamagnini NÉNÉ, Fernando GOMES, Rui JORDAO.

Goals: Dalglish (7), A. Gray (26), Archibald (67), Gomes (74), Gemmill (82 pen)

BELGIUM v SCOTLAND 2-0 (1-0)

Heizel, Brussel 21.11.1979

Referee: Eldar Azim Zade (USSR) Attendance: 14,289

BELGIUM: Théo Custers; Walter Meeuws, Eric Gerets, Luc Millecamps, Michel Renquin, Julien Cools (Cap), Wilfried Van Moer (66 René Verheyen), René Vandereycken, François Van der Elst, Jan Ceulemans, Eddy Voordeckers. Trainer: Guy Thys

SCOTLAND: Allan Rough; William Jardine, Iain Munro (61 Francis Gray), John Wark, Alan Hansen, William Miller, Kenneth Dalglish, Graeme Souness, Joseph Jordan (61 David Provan), Asa Hartford, John Robertson. Manager: John Stein

Goals: Van der Elst (6), Voordeckers (47)

	P	W	D	L	F	A	Pts
Belgium	8	4	4	0	12	5	12
Austria	8	4	3	1	14	7	11
Portugal	8	4	1	3	10	11	9
Scotland	8	3	1	4	15	13	7
Norway	8	0	1	7	5	20	1

GROUP 3

YUGOSLAVIA v SPAIN 1-2 (1-2)

Maksimir, Zagreb 04.10.1978

Referee: Erich Linemayr (AUS) Attendance: 50,000

YUGOSLAVIA: Zaljko Stincic; Vilson Dzoni, Vedran Rozic, Nenad Stojkovic, Drazen Muzinic; Velimir Zajec (66 Nikica Cukrov), Momcilo Vukotic, Ivan Surjak; Safet Susic, Vahid Halilhodzic, Slavisa Zungul (.. Dusan Savic). Trainer: Ante Mladinic

SPAIN: MIGUEL ANGEL Gonzalez Suarez; MARCELINO Pérez, Bernardo Blanquetti MIGUELI, Antonio OLMO, Secundino Suarez Vazquez "CUNDI"; Vicente Gonzalez DEL BOSQUE, Angel María VILLAR Llona, Juan Manuel ASENSI Ripoll; Juan Gómez Gonzalez "JUANITO" (85 José Vicente SÁNCHEZ Felip), Carlos Alonso Gonzalez SANTILLANA (88 RUBEN CANO Martinez), Javier Álvarez URÍA. Trainer: Ladislao Kubala

Goals: Juanito (20), Santillana (32), Halilhodzic (45)

ROMANIA v YUGOSLAVIA 3-2 (0-1)

Steaua, Bucureşti 25.10.1978

Referee: Riccardo Lattanzi (ITA) Attendance: 25,000

ROMANIA: Răducanu Necula; Teodor Anghelini, Costică Ştefănescu, Ştefan Sameş, Iosif Vigu; Mihai Romilă, Ladislau Bölöni, Anghel Iordănescu; Zoltan Crişan, Nicolae Dobrin, Doru Nicolae (46 Aurel Rădulescu). Trainer: Ştefan Kovacs

YUGOSLAVIA: Petar Borota; Drazen Muzinic, Dzemal Hadziabdic, Nenad Stojkovic, Ivan Surjak; Aleksandar Trifunovic (69 Vedran Rozic), Slavisa Zungul (69 Damir Desnica), Nikica Cukrov, Vahid Halilhodzic, Vladimir Petrovic, Safet Susic. Trainer: Ante Mladinic

Goals: Petrovic (21 pen), Sameş (62, 69), Iordănescu (75 pen), Desnica (90)

SPAIN v ROMANIA 1-0 (1-0)

Estadio Luis Casanova, Valencia 15.11.1978

Referee: Jan Keizer (HOL) Attendance: 50,000

SPAIN: MIGUEL ANGEL Gonzalez Suarez; MARCELINO Pérez, Bernardo Blanquetti MIGUELI, José Ramon ALESANCO Ventosa, José CARRETE; Angel María VILLAR Llona, Vicente Gonzalez DEL BOSQUE, Juan Manuel ASENSI Ripoll; Juan Carlos HEREDIA (75 Enrique SAURA Gil), Carlos Alonso Gonzalez SANTILLANA, José Francisco ROJO Arroitia (63 RUBEN CANO Martinez). Trainer: Ladislao Kubala

ROMANIA: Narcis Coman; Mihai Zamfir, Ştefan Sameş, Costică Ştefănescu, Iosif Vigu; Mihai Romilă, Anghel Iordănescu, Ladislau Bölöni; Zoltan Crişan, Dudu Georgescu, Aurel Rădulescu. Trainer: Ştefan Kovacs

Goal: Asensi (10)

SPAIN v CYPRUS 5-0 (1-0)

Estadio Helmántico, Salamanca 13.12.1978

Referee: Paul Bonnet (MAL) Attendance: 17,500

SPAIN: MIGUEL ANGEL Gonzalez Suarez; MARCELINO Pérez, José Ramon ALESANCO Ventosa, Bernardo Blanquetti MIGUELI, Secundino Suarez Vazquez "CUNDI"; Angel María VILLAR Llona (46 Eugenio LEAL), Vicente Gonzalez DEL BOSQUE, Juan Manuel ASENSI Ripoll; Juan Carlos HEREDIA (46 RUBEN CANO Martinez), Carlos Alonso Gonzalez SANTILLANA, Estanislao ARGOTE Salaberría. Trainer: Ladislao Kubala

CYPRUS: George Pantziaras; Filippos Kalotheou, Demetrios Kizas, Stefanos Lyssandrou, Nikos Pantziaras; Stavros Papadopoulos, Andreas Miamiliotis (.. Takis Antoniou), Demetrios Economou Koudas; Gregory Savva, Fivos Vrahimis, Andreas Kanaris.

Goals: Asensi (8), Del Bosque (10), Santillana (52, 77), R. Cano (63)

CYPRUS v YUGOSLAVIA 0-3 (0-1)

Makarios, Nicosia 01.04.1979

Referee: László Pádár (HUNG) Attendance: 4,500

CYPRUS: Fanos Stylianou; Filippos Kalotheou, Vasos Violaris, Stefanos Lyssandrou, Nikos Pantziaras (.. Andreas Papacostas), Andreas Kalimeras, Andreas Miamiliotis, Gregory Savva, Andreas Kissonergis, Demetrios Economou Koudas, Andreas Kanaris.

YUGOSLAVIA: Ratko Svilar; Ismet Hadzic, Nenad Starovlah, Nenad Stojkovic, Luka Peruzovic, Drazen Muzinic, Zlatko Vujovic, Nikica Cukrov, Dusan Savic (83 Miso Krsticevic), Ante Mirocevic (83 Nikola Jovanovic), Ivan Surjak. Trainer: Miljan Miljanic

Goals: Zl. Vujovic (40, 79), Surjak (87 pen)

ROMANIA v SPAIN 2-2 (0-0)

Central, Craiova 04.04.1979

Referee: Marcel van Langenhove (BEL) Attendance: 40,000

ROMANIA: Silviu Lung; Mihai Zamfir, Ştefan SameŞ, Cornel Dinu (Cap), Teodor Lucuţă; Ion Dumitru (80 Costică Ştefănescu), Mihai Romilă, Ladislau Bölöni; Mircea Lucescu (51 Zoltan Crişan), Dudu Georgescu, Dumitru Marcu. Trainer: Ştefan Kovács

SPAIN: Luis Miguel ARCONADA Echarre; Isidoro SAN JOSÉ Pozo, José Ramon ALESANCO Ventosa, Juan FELIPE Martín, MARCELINO Pérez; Juan Manuel ASENSI Ripoll, Vicente Gonzalez DEL BOSQUE (61 Secundino Suarez Vazquez "CUNDI"), Angel María VILLAR Llona; Enrique Castro Gonzalez QUINI (88 Francisco José CARRASCO Hidalgo), RUBEN CANO Martinez, Daniel Ruiz Bazan Justa "DANI". Trainer: Ladislao Kubala

Sent off: San José (58), Crişan (60)

Goals: Georgescu (56 pen, 64), Dani (58, 70)

CYPRUS v ROMANIA 1-1 (1-1)

Tsirion, Limassol 13.05.1979

Referee: Dimitar Parmakov (BUL) Attendance: 8,000

CYPRUS: George Pantziaras; Filippos Kalotheou, Stefanos Lyssandrou, Nikos Pantziaras, Nikos Patikkis; Stavros Papadopoulos, Loizos Mavroudis (79 George Aristidou), Gregory Savva; Sotiris Kaiafas, Marios Tsingis, Andreas Kissonergis (46 Fivos Vrahimis). Trainer: Kostas Talianos

ROMANIA: Andrei Speriatu; Mihai Zamfir, Constantin Cîrstea, Costică Ştefănescu, Petre Ivan; Ilie Bărbulescu, Ionel Augustin, Sevastian Iovănescu; Constantin Stan (65 Marcel Răducanu), Marin Radu (46 Rodion Cămătaru), Doru Nicolae. Trainer: Florin Halagian

Goals: Augustin (30), Kaiafas (33)

SPAIN v YUGOSLAVIA 0-1 (0-1)

Estadio Luis Casanova, Valencia 10.10.1979

Referee: Brian McGinley (SCO) Attendance: 40,000

SPAIN: Luis Miguel ARCONADA Echarre; Isidoro SAN JOSÉ Pozo, Bernardo Blanquetti MIGUELI, José Ramon ALESANCO Ventosa, Javier Álvarez URÍA; Angel María VILLAR Llona, Vicente Gonzalez DEL BOSQUE, Juan Manuel ASENSI Ripoll; Daniel Ruiz Bazan Justa "DANI", Enrique Castro Gonzalez QUINI (.. Carlos Alonso Gonzalez SANTILLANA), Juan Carlos HEREDIA. Trainer: Ladislao Kubala

YUGOSLAVIA: Dragan Pantelic; Zoran Vujovic, Velimir Zajec, Boro Primorac, Vedran Rozic; Milos Sestic (75 Drazen Muzinic), Miso Krsticevic, Safet Susic; Zlatko Vujovic, Blaz Sliskovic, Ivan Surjak. Trainer: Miljan Miljanic

Sent off: Migueli & Krsticevic (75)

Goal: Surjak (5)

YUGOSLAVIA v ROMANIA 2-1 (0-0)

Gradski, Titova Mitrovica 31.10.1979

Referee: Jan Redelfs (W. GER) Attendance: 35,000

YUGOSLAVIA: Dragan Pantelic; Ismet Hadzic, Nenad Starovlah, Velimir Zajec, Boro Primorac; Milos Sestic, Vladimir Petrovic, Zlatko Vujovic, Blaz Sliskovic (88 Nenad Stojkovic), Safet Susic, Ivan Surjak (84 Nikica Cukrov). Trainer: Miljan Miljanic

ROMANIA: Cristian Gheorghe; Nicolae Tilihoi, Costică Ştefănescu, Ştefan Sameş (72 Alexandru Nicolae), Ion Munteanu; Cornel Dinu, Ladislau Bölöni, Gheorghe Mulţescu; Zoltan Crişan, Marcel Răducanu, Ilie Balaci (77 Ionel Augustin). Trainer: Constantin Cernăianu

Goals: Zl. Vujovic (48), Sliskovic (50), Răducanu (79)

YUGOSLAVIA v CYPRUS 5-0 (1-0)

Vojvodina, Novi Sad 14.11.1979

Referee: Iordan Zhezhov (BUL) Attendance: 20,000

YUGOSLAVIA: Dragan Pantelic; Nikica Cukrov, Vedran Rozic, Velimir Zajec, Nenad Stojkovic, Milos Sestic, Vladimir Petrovic, Zlatko Vujovic (.. Dusan Savic), Blaz Sliskovic (13 Zlatko Kranjcar), Safet Susic, Ivan Surjak. Trainer: Miljan Miljanic

CYPRUS: George Pantziaras; Filippos Kalotheou, Neofytos Neofytou, Costas Constantinou, Stephanos Lyssandrou; Nikos Pantziaras, Loizos Mavroudis, Marios Tsingis, Andreas Kissonergis (.. Petros Theophanous); Sotiris Kaiafas, Andreas Kanaris.

Goals: Kranjcar (32, 50), Zl. Vujovic (60), V. Petrovic (75), D. Savic (87)

ROMANIA v CYPRUS 2-0 (1-0)

Dinamo, Bucureşti 18.11.1979

Referee: Dusan Krchnak (CZE) Attendance: 10,000

ROMANIA: Cristian Gheorghe; Nicolae Tilihoi, Alexandru Nicolae, Ştefan Sameş, Ion Munteanu; Ladislau Bölöni, Aurel Beldeanu (65 Ilie Balaci), Gheorghe Mulţescu; Zoltan Crişan (46 Sorin Cîrţu), Rodion Cămătaru, Marcel Răducanu. Trainer: Constantin Cernăianu

CYPRUS: Fanos Stylianou; Filippos Kalotheou, Neofytos Neofytou, Costas Constantinou, Stefanos Lyssandrou; Marios Tsingis (46 Demetrios Economou Koudas), Loizos Mavroudis (86 Fivos Vrahimis), Nikos Pantziaras; Sotiris Kaiafas, Pambos Papadopoulos, Andreas Kanaris. Trainer: Kostas Talianos

Goals: Mulţescu (42), Răducanu (75)

CYPRUS v SPAIN 1-3 (0-2)

Tsirion, Limassol 09.12.1979

Referee: Josef Bucek (AUS) Attendance: 15,000

CYPRUS: Herodotos Herodotou "Koupanos"; Nikos Pantziaras, Stefanos Lyssandrou, Demetrios Kizas, Filippos Kalotheou; Loizos Mavroudis, Stavros Papadopoulos, Marios Tsingis; Pambos Papadopoulos "Pamboulis" (.. Fivos Vrahimis), Petros Theofanous (.. Andreas Papacostas), Andreas Kanaris.

SPAIN: Luis Miguel ARCONADA Echarre; Javier Álvarez URÍA, Bernardo Blanquetti MIGUELI, Antonio OLMO, Secundino Suarez Vazquez "CUNDI"; Angel María VILLAR Llona (73 Jesús María ZAMORA Ansorena), Vicente Gonzalez DEL BOSQUE (71 Francisco José CARRASCO Hidalgo); Daniel Ruiz Bazan Justa "DANI", Enrique Castro Gonzalez QUINI, Carlos Alonso Gonzalez SANTILLANA, Enrique SAURA Gil. Trainer: Ladislao Kubala

Goals: Villar (5), Santillana (40), Vrahimis (69), Saura (87)

	P	W	D	L	F	A	Pts
Spain	6	4	1	1	13	5	9
Yugoslavia	6	4	0	2	14	6	8
Romania	6	2	2	2	9	8	6
Cyprus	6	0	1	5	2	19	1

GROUP 4

ICELAND v POLAND 0-2 (0-1)

Laugardalsvöllur 06.09.1978

Referee: Thomas Perry (NIR) Attendance: 6,594

ICELAND: Arni Stefánsson; Gísli Torfasson, Arni Sveinsson, Jón Pétursson, Jóhannes Edvaldsson (Cap); Hördur Hilmarsson (66 Ingi Björn Albertsson), Karl Thórdarson, Atli Edvaldsson; Pétur Pétursson, Janus Gudlaugsson, Gudmundur Thorbjörnsson. Trainer: Iuriy Ilichev

POLAND: Zygmunt Kukla; Antoni Szymanowski (Cap), Stefan Majewski, Henryk Maculewicz, Wojciech Rudy; Tadeusz Blachno, Leslaw Cmikiewicz, Bogdan Masztaler; Grzegorz Lato, Zbigniew Boniek, Marek Kusto. Trainer: Jacek Gmoch

Goals: Kusto (24), Lato (85)

HOLLAND v ICELAND 3-0 (1-0)

Nijmegen 20.09.1978

Referee: Anders Mattsson (FIN) Attendance: 15,000

HOLLAND: Piet Schrijvers; Jan Poortvliet, Ruud Krol (Cap), Ernie Brandts, Piet Wildschut, Wim Jansen, Arie Haan, Willy van de Kerkhof, Adri Koster (.. Jan Peters), Dick Nanninga, Robert Rensenbrink. Trainer: Johannes Zwartkruis

ICELAND: Thorsteinn Bjarnason; Janus Gudlaugsson, Arni Sveinsson, Jón Pétursson, Jóhannes Edvaldsson, Ingi Björn Albertsson (65 Dyri Gudmundsson), Karl Thórdarson, Atli Edvaldsson, Pétur Pétursson, Asgeir Sigurvinsson, Gudmundur Thorbjörnsson. Trainer: Iuriy Ilichev

Goals: Krol (31), Brandts (53), Rensenbrink (63 pen)

EAST GERMANY v ICELAND 3-1 (2-1)

Kurt-Wabbel-Stadion, Halle 04.10.1978

Referee: Thomas Reynolds (WAL) Attendance: 12,000

EAST GERMANY: Jürgen Croy; Hans-Jürgen Dörner (Cap), Konrad Weise, Lothar Hause, Gerd Weber; Reinhard Häfner (36 Lutz Lindemann), Jürgen Pommerenke, Lutz Eigendorf; Werner Peter, Hans-Jürgen Riediger, Martin Hoffmann. Trainer: Georg Buschner

ICELAND: Thorsteinn Bjarnason (46 Arni Stefánsson); Sigurdur Björgvinsson, Arni Sveinsson (60 Ingi Björn Albertsson), Jón Pétursson, Janus Gudlaugsson, Stefán Örn Sigurdsson, Karl Thórdarson, Atli Edvaldsson, Teitur Thórdarson, Pétur Pétursson, Gudmundur Thorbjörnsson. Trainer: Iuriy Ilichev

Goals: Peter (6), P. Pétursson (14 pen), Riediger (29), Hoffmann (72)

SWITZERLAND v HOLLAND 1-3 (1-1)

Wankdorf, Bern 11.10.1978

Referee: César da Luz Dias Correia (POR) Att: 23,000

SWITZERLAND: Erich Burgener; Pierre Chapuisat, Jakob Brechbühl, Yves Montandon, Lucio Bizzini, Markus Tanner (.. Roger Wehrli), Umberto Barberis, Marc Schnyder (.. Raimondo Ponte), Rudolf Elsener, Claudio Sulser, René Botteron. Trainer: Roger Vonlanthen

HOLLAND: Piet Schrijvers; Jan Poortvliet, Ruud Krol (Cap), Ernie Brandts, Hugo Hovenkamp (34 Johnny Dusbaba), Piet Wildschut, Arie Haan, Willy van de Kerkhof (.. Jan Peters), Ruud Geels, Dick Nanninga, Robert Rensenbrink. Trainer: Johannes Zwartkruis

Goals: Wildschut (19), Tanner (32), Brandts (67), Geels (90)

POLAND v SWITZERLAND 2-0 (1-0)

Olimpijski, Wroclaw 15.11.1978

Referee: Franz Wöhrer (AUS) Attendance: 45,000

POLAND: Zygmunt Kukla; Antoni Szymanowski (Cap), Wladyslaw Zmuda, Henryk Maculewicz, Stefan Majewski (84 Wojciech Rudy); Leslaw Cmikiewicz, Zbigniew Boniek, Adam Nawalka; Grzegorz Lato, Roman Ogaza, Stanislaw Terlecki. Trainer: Ryszard Kulesza

SWITZERLAND: Karl Engel; Pierre Chapuisat, Jakob Brechbühl, Yves Montandon, Lucio Bizzini (Cap); Umberto Barberis, René Botteron, André Meyer, Marc Schnyder, Claudio Sulser, Rudolf Elsener (46 Raimondo Ponte). Trainer: Roger Vonlanthen

Goals: Boniek (39), Ogaza (58)

HOLLAND v EAST GERMANY 3-0 (1-0)

Feyenoord, Rotterdam 15.11.1978

Referee: Ulf Eriksson (SWE) Attendance: 38,000

HOLLAND: Piet Schrijvers; Adrianus Van Kraay, Ruud Krol (Cap), Ernie Brandts, Hugo Hovenkamp, Piet Wildschut, Johan Neeskens (.. Johnny Metgod), Jan Peters, René van de Kerkhof (.. Adri Koster), Ruud Geels, Robert Rensenbrink. Trainer: Johannes Zwartkruis

EAST GERMANY: Jürgen Croy; Gerd Kische, Hans-Jürgen Dörner (Cap), Rüdiger Schnuphase, Gerd Weber, Lutz Eigendorf (70 Wolf-Rüdiger Netz), Reinhard Häfner, Lutz Lindemann; Hartmut Schade (47 Werner Peter), Hans-Jürgen Riediger, Martin Hoffmann. Trainer: Georg Buschner

Goals: Kische (17 og), Geels (72 pen, 89)

HOLLAND v SWITZERLAND 3-0 (0-0)

Philips, Eindhoven 28.03.1979

Referee: John Hunting (ENG) Attendance: 27,000

HOLLAND: Piet Schrijvers; Jan Poortvliet, Wim Jansen (Cap), Ernie Brandts, Piet Wildschut (85 Huub Stevens), Johan Neeskens, Jan Peters, Willy van de Kerkhof (.. Johnny Metgod), René van de Kerkhof, Kees Kist, Robert Rensenbrink. Trainer: Johannes Zwartkruis

SWITZERLAND: Erich Burgener; Jakob Brechbühl (67 Raimondo Ponte), Pierre Chapuisat, Yves Montandon, Lucio Bizzini (60 Roger Wehrli), René Botteron, Umberto Barberis, Heinz Hermann, Marc Schnyder, Claudio Sulser, Rudolf Elsener. Trainer: Roger Vonlanthen

Goals: Kist (55), Metgod (84), Peters (89)

EAST GERMANY v POLAND 2-1 (0-1)

Zentralstadion, Leipzig 18.04.1979

Referee: Eldar Azim-Zade (USSR) Attendance: 55,000

EAST GERMANY: Hans-Ulrich Grapenthin; Gerd Kische, Hans-Jürgen Dörner (Cap), Konrad Weise, Gerd Weber; Reinhard Häfner, Hartmut Schade (46 Jürgen Pommerenke), Lutz Lindemann; Hans-Jürgen Riediger, Joachim Streich, Martin Hoffmann. Trainer: Georg Buschner

POLAND: Zygmunt Kukla; Marek Dziuba (64 Wojciech Rudy), Pawel Janas, Wladyslaw Zmuda, Antoni Szymanowski (Cap); Stefan Majewski (76 Michal Wróbel), Leslaw Cmikiewicz, Zbigniew Boniek, Adam Nawalka; Grzegorz Lato, Roman Ogaza. Trainer: Ryszard Kulesza

Goals: Boniek (7), Streich (50), Lindemann (63)

POLAND v HOLLAND 2-0 (1-0)

Slaski, Chorzów 02.05.1979

Referee: Robert Charles Paul Wurtz (FRA) Att: 85,000

POLAND: Zygmunt Kukla; Marek Dziuba, Antoni Szymanowski (Cap), Wladyslaw Zmuda, Zbigniew Plaszewski; Leszek Lipka, Zbigniew Boniek, Adam Nawalka, Grzegorz Lato, Roman Ogaza, Stanislaw Terlecki (46 Wlodzimierz Mazur). Trainer: Ryszard Kulesza

HOLLAND: Piet Schrijvers; Huub Stevens, Ruud Krol (Cap), Ernie Brandts, Hugo Hovenkamp; Wim Jánsen, Jan Peters, Willy van de Kerkhof; René van de Kerkhof (46 Ruud Geels), Kees Kist, Robert Rensenbrink (73 Johnny Metgod). Trainer: Johannes Zwartkruis

Goals: Boniek (19), Mazur (63 pen)

SWITZERLAND v EAST GERMANY 0-2 (0-1)

Espenmoos, Saint Gallen 05.05.1979

Referee: Augusto Lamo Castillo (SPA) Attendance: 9,000

SWITZERLAND: Roger Berbig; Heinz Lüdi, Roger Wehrli, Lucio Bizzini, Heinz Hermann, Erni Maissen, Umberto Barberis, Markus Tanner, Thomas Zwahlen (73 Herbert Hermann), Jean-Paul Brigger (.. René Botteron), Raimondo Ponte. Trainer: Léon Walker

EAST GERMANY: Hans-Ulrich Grapenthin; Gerd Kische, Hans-Jürgen Dörner (Cap), Konrad Weise, Gerd Weber; Reinhard Häfner, Jürgen Pommerenke, Lutz Lindemann; Hans-Jürgen Riediger, Joachim Streich, Martin Hoffmann. Trainer: Georg Buschner

Goals: Lindemann (45), Streich (90)

SWITZERLAND v ICELAND 2-0 (1-0)

Wankdorf, Bern 22.05.1979

Referee: Albert Victor (LUX) Attendance: 28,000

SWITZERLAND: Walter Eichenberger; Heinz Lüdi, Jakob Brechbühl, Gian Pietro Zappa, Heinz Hermann, Erni Maissen, Umberto Barberis, Roger Wehrli (.. Markus Tanner), Raimondo Ponte (.. Marc Schnyder), René Botteron, Herbert Hermann. Trainer: Léon Walker

ICELAND: Thorsteinn Olafsson; Janus Gudlaugsson, Arni Sveinsson, Jón Pétursson, Jóhannes Edvaldsson (77 Ottó Gudmundsson), Marteinn Geirsson, Arnór Gudjohnsen, Atli Edvaldsson, Pétur Pétursson (.. Karl Thórdarson), Asgeir Sigurvinsson, Gudmundur Thorbjörnsson. Trainer: Iuriy Ilichev

Goals: Herbert Hermann (27), Zappa (53)

ICELAND v SWITZERLAND 1-2 (0-0)

Laugardalsvöllur, Reijkjavik 09.06.1979

Referee: Eamonn Farrell (IRE) Attendance: 10,469

ICELAND: Thorsteinn Olafsson; Janus Gudlaugsson, Trausti Haraldsson, Marteinn Geirsson, Jóhannes Edvaldsson, Arnór Gudjohnsen, Pétur Pétursson, Atli Edvaldsson, Teitur Thórdarson (.. Karl Thórdarson), Asgeir Sigurvinsson, Gudmundur Thorbjörnsson (67 Arni Sveinsson).
Trainer: Iuriy Ilichev

SWITZERLAND: Roger Berbig; Heinz Lüdi, Jakob Brechbühl, Gian Pietro Zappa, Roger Wehrli, Umberto Barberis, Heinz Hermann, Claude Andrey, Raimondo Ponte, Herbert Hermann (71 André Egli), René Botteron (.. Markus Tanner). Trainer: Léon Walker

Goal: Gudlaugsson (49), Ponte (59), Heinz Hermann (61)

SWITZERLAND v POLAND 0-2 (0-1)

Olimpique, Lausanne 12.09.1979

Referee: Otto Anderco (ROM) Attendance: 20,000

SWITZERLAND: Erich Burgener; Heinz Lüdi, Jakob Brechbühl, Gian Pietro Zappa, Lucio Bizzini (Cap); Umberto Barberis, Marc Schnyder, Claude Andrey; Hans-Jörg Pfister, Claudio Sulser (70 André Egli), Raimondo Ponte.
Trainer: Léon Walker

POLAND: Zygmunt Kukla; Marek Dziuba, Pawel Janas, Henryk Wieczorek, Wojciech Rudy; Stefan Majewski (85 Antoni Szymanowski), Zbigniew Boniek, Adam Nawalka; Grzegorz Lato (Cap), Kazimierz Kmiecik (85 Wlodzimierz Mazur), Stanislaw Terlecki. Trainer: Ryszard Kulesza.

Goals: Terlecki (34, 63)

ICELAND v HOLLAND 0-4 (0-0)

Laugardalsvöllur, Reijkjavik 05.09.1979

Referee: Clive Thomas (WAL) Attendance: 10,000

ICELAND: Thorsteinn Bjarnason; Arni Sveinsson, Trausti Haraldsson, Marteinn Geirsson, Johannes Edvaldsson, Dyri Gudmundsson, Pétur Pétursson, Atli Edvaldsson, Sigurlas Thorleifsson (75 Tómas Pálsson), Karl Thórdarson, Gudmundur Thorbjörnsson. Trainer: Iuriy Ilichev

HOLLAND: Piet Schrijvers; Ernie Brandts, Ruud Krol (Cap), Huub Stevens, Hugo Hovenkamp, Jan Poortvliet, Willy van de Kerkhof, Simon Tahamata, Tschen La Ling (.. Johnny Metgod), Dick Nanninga, René van de Kerkhof.
Trainer: Johannes Zwartkruis

Goals: Metgod (48), Willy van de Kerkhof (71), Nanninga (73, 87)

POLAND v EAST GERMANY 1-1 (0-0)

Slaski, Chorzów 26.09.1979

Referee: Patrick Partridge (ENG) Attendance: 70,000

POLAND: Zygmunt Kukla; Marek Dziuba (70 Wlodzimierz Mazur), Antoni Szymanowski (Cap), Pawel Janas, Wojciech Rudy; Leszek Lipka, Zbigniew Boniek, Adam Nawalka (74 Henryk Wieczorek); Grzegorz Lato, Roman Ogaza, Stanislaw Terlecki. Trainer: Ryszard Kulesza.

EAST GERMANY: Hans-Ulrich Grapenthin; Gerd Kische, Gert Brauer, Hans-Jürgen Dörner (Cap), Konrad Weise, Rüdiger Schnuphase; Reinhard Häfner, Lutz Lindemann, Gerd Weber; Hans-Jürgen Riediger, Martin Hoffmann.
Trainer: Georg Buschner

Goals: Häfner (62), Wieczorek (77)

ICELAND v EAST GERMANY 0-3 (0-0)

Laugardalsvöllur, Reykjavik 12.09.1979

Referee: Svein Inge Thime (NOR) Attendance: 9000

ICELAND: Thorsteinn Bjarnason; Örn Oskarsson, Arni Sveinsson, Marteinn Geirsson, Johannes Edvaldsson, Hördur Hilmarsson, Gudgeir Leifsson, Atli Edvaldsson, Sigurlas Thorleifsson, Asgeir Sigurvinsson, Gudmundur Thorbjörnsson
Trainer: Iuriy Ilichev

EAST GERMANY: Hans-Ulrich Grapenthin; Gerd Kische, Hans-Jürgen Dörner (Cap), Konrad Weise, Rüdiger Schnuphase, Gerd Weber, Reinhard Häfner, Lutz Lindemann; Hans-Jürgen Riediger, Joachim Streich, Martin Hoffmann.
Trainer: Georg Buschner

Goals: Weber (66 pen, 73), Streich (80)

POLAND v ICELAND 2-0 (0-0)

Wisla, Kraków 10.10.1979

Referee: Henning Lund-Sörensen (DEN) Att: 20,000

POLAND: Zygmunt Kukla; Pawel Janas, Antoni Szymanowski (Cap), Wojciech Rudy; Leszek Lipka, Henryk Wieczorek, Zbigniew Boniek, Adam Nawalka; Grzegorz Lato, Roman Ogaza, Stanislaw Terlecki (54 Janusz Sybis).
Trainer: Ryszard Kulesza

ICELAND: Thorsteinn Bjarnason; Örn Oskarsson, Trausti Haraldsson, Marteinn Geirsson, Johannes Edvaldsson (Cap), Dyri Gudmundsson, Pétur Pétursson, Atli Edvaldsson, Teitur Thórdarson, Asgeir Sigurvinsson, Arni Sveinsson.
Trainer: Iuriy Ilichev

Goals: Ogaza (55, 74 pen)

EAST GERMANY v SWITZERLAND 5-2 (3-1)

Weltjugend, Berlin 13.10.1979

Referee: Robert Wurtz (FRA) Attendance: 44,000

EAST GERMANY: Hans-Ulrich Grapenthin; Hans-Jürgen Dörner (Cap), Gert Brauer, Rüdiger Schnuphase, Gerd Kische; Reinhard Häfner, Lutz Lindemann, Gerd Weber; Hans-Jürgen Riediger, Joachim Streich (68 Peter Kotte), Martin Hoffmann. Trainer: Georg Buschner

SWITZERLAND: Erich Burgener; Heinz Lüdi, Jakob Brechbühl, Gian Pietro Zappa, Lucio Bizzini, Marc Schnyder, Umberto Barberis, Markus Tanner (.. Raimondo Ponte), Heinz Hermann, Claudio Sulser (.. André Egli), Hans-Jörg Pfister. Trainer: Léon Walker

Goals: Weber (1), Hoffmann (11, 75, 80), Barberis (19), Schnuphase (26), Pfister (72)

	P	W	D	L	F	A	Pts
Holland	8	6	1	1	20	6	13
Poland	8	5	2	1	13	4	12
East Germany	8	5	1	2	18	11	11
Switzerland	8	2	0	6	7	18	4
Iceland	8	0	0	8	2	21	0

HOLLAND v POLAND 1-1 (0-1)

Olympisch, Amsterdam 17.10.1979

Referee: Paolo Casarin (ITA) Attendance: 54,000

HOLLAND: Piet Schrijvers; Bennie Wijnstekers, Ruud Krol (Cap), Ernie Brandts (46 Tschen La Ling), Hugo Hovenkamp, Huub Stevens, Willy van de Kerkhof, Wim Jansen; Johnny Rep, Kees Kist, Simon Tahamata. Trainer: Johannes Zwartkruis

POLAND: Zygmunt Kukla; Marek Dziuba, Antoni Szymanowski (Cap), Pawel Janas, Wojciech Rudy; Leszek Lipka, Zbigniew Boniek, Adam Nawalka; Grzegorz Lato, Janusz Sybis (71 Wlodzimierz Mazur), Stanislaw Terlecki. Trainer: Ryszard Kulesza

Goals: Rudy (38), Stevens (64)

EAST GERMANY v HOLLAND 2-3 (2-1)

Zentralstadion, Leipzig 21.11.1979

Referee: Antonio José Silva Garrido (POR) Att: 90,000

EAST GERMANY: Hans-Ulrich Grapenthin; Gerd Kische, Hans-Jürgen Dörner (Cap), Konrad Weise, Gert Brauer; Reinhard Häfner, Gerd Weber (73 Jürgen Pommerenke), Rüdiger Schnuphase (60 Hartmut Schade); Peter Kotte, Joachim Streich, Martin Hoffmann. Trainer: Georg Buschner

HOLLAND: Piet Schrijvers; Bennie Wijnstekers, Ruud Krol (Cap), Michel Van de Korput, Hugo Hovenkamp (.. Kees Kist), Huub Stevens (.. Ernie Brandts), Dick Schoenaker, Frans Thijssen, Tschen La Ling, René van de Kerkhof, Simon Tahamata. Trainer: Johannes Zwartkruis

Sent off: Weise (40), La Ling (40)

Goals: Schnuphase (17), Streich (33 pen), Thijssen (45), Kist (50), René van de Kerkhof (67)

GROUP 5

FRANCE v SWEDEN 2-2 (0-0)

Parc des Princes, Paris 01.09.1978

Referee: Károly Palotai (HUNG) Attendance: 44,703

FRANCE: André Rey; Patrick Battiston, Patrice Rio, Christian Lopez, Maxime Bossis; Henri Michel (Cap) (77 Alain Giresse), Roger Jouve, Dominique Bathenay; Olivier Rouyer, Albert Gemmrich (65 Marc Berdoll), Didier Six. Trainer: Michel Hidalgo

SWEDEN: Ronnie Hellström; Hans Borg, Björn Nordqvist, Ronald Åhman, Håkan Arvidsson; Lennart Larsson, Anders Linderoth, Mats Nordgren; Anders Grönhagen, Thomas Sjöberg (75 Tommy Berggren), Benny Wendt. Trainer: Georg Ericsson

Goals: Nordgren (54), Berdoll (72), Six (85), Grönhagen (89)

SWEDEN v CZECHOSLOVAKIA 1-3 (1-1)

Fotbollstadion, Solna 04.10.1978

Referee: John Robertson Gordon (SCO) Att: 11,985

SWEDEN: Ronnie Hellström; Hans Borg, Björn Nordqvist, Ronald Åhman, Håkan Arvidsson, Lennart Larsson, Anders Linderoth, Mats Nordgren, Anders Grönhagen, Tommy Berggren (57 Billy Ohlsson), Benny Wendt. Trainer: Georg Ericsson

CZECHOSLOVAKIA: Pavol Michalík; Jozef Barmos, Anton Ondrus, Rostislav Vojácek, Koloman Gögh; Jaroslav Pollák, Frantisek Stambachr, Miloslav Gajdusek; Marián Masny, Karel Kroupa (.. Ján Kozák), Zdenek Nehoda. Trainer: Jozef Venglos

Goals: Borg (11 pen), Masny (15, 48), Nehoda (85)

LUXEMBOURG v FRANCE 1-3 (0-1)

Stade Municipal, Luxembourg 07.10.1978

Referee: Hendrik Weerink (HOL) Attendance: 12,000

LUXEMBOURG: Jeannot Moes; Hubert Meunier, Nico Rohmann, Jean-Louis Margue, Fernand Raths, Carlo Weis, Paul Philipp (Cap), Gilbert Dresch, Romain Michaux, Gilbert Dussier, Camille Neumann. Trainer: Gilbert Legrand

FRANCE: Dominique Dropsy; Patrick Battiston, Christian Lopez, Marius Trésor (Cap), Maxime Bossis; Jean-François Larios (64 Jean Petit), Roger Jouve, Francis Piasecki; Dominique Rocheteau (59 Albert Gemmrich), Bernard Lacombe, Didier Six. Trainer: Michel Hidalgo

Goal: Six (15), Trésor (63), Michaux (74), Gemmrich (80)

LUXEMBOURG v CZECHOSLOVAKIA 0-3 (0-1)

Stade Municipal, Luxembourg 01.05.1979

Referee: Bruno Galler (SWI) Attendance: 3,500

LUXEMBOURG: Jeannot Moes (Cap); Hubert Meunier, Léon Mond, Nico Rohmann, Jean-Louis Margue, Nico Wagner, Carlo Weis, Gilbert Dresch, Romain Michaux, Marcel Di Domenico, André Zwally. Trainer: Arthur Schoos

CZECHOSLOVAKIA: Jaroslav Netolicka; Jozef Barmos, Rotislav Vojácek, Anton Ondrus, Koloman Gögh; Antonín Panenka, Ján Kozák, Frantisek Stambachr (.. Karol Dobias); Marián Masny, Karel Kroupa (.. Ladislav Vízek), Miloslav Gajdusek. Trainer: Jozef Venglos

Goals: Masny (22), Gajdusek (67), Stambachr (68)

FRANCE v LUXEMBOURG 3-0 (1-0)

Parc des Princes, Paris 25.02.1979

Referee: Ronald Bridges (WAL) Attendance: 46,988

FRANCE: Dominique Dropsy; Patrick Battiston, Léonard Specht, Marius Trésor (Cap), Maxime Bossis; Jean Petit, Henri Michel, Francis Piasecki (61 Jean-François Larios); Dominique Rocheteau, Marc Berdoll (66 Eric Pécout), Albert Emon. Trainer: Michel Hidalgo

LUXEMBOURG: Jeannot Moes; Hubert Meunier, Jean-Louis Margue, Fernand Raths, Nico Rohmann; Carlo Weis (46 Jean Reiter), Paul Philipp (Cap), Gilbert Dresch, Romain Michaux, Nico Wagner, André Zwally (73 Camille Neumann). Trainer: Arthur Schoos

Goals: Petit (38), Emon (60), Larios (78)

SWEDEN v LUXEMBOURG 3-0 (2-0)

Malmö stadium 07.06.1979

Referee: Aleksander Suchanek (POL) Attendance: 7,298

SWEDEN: Ronnie Hellström; Stig Fredriksson, Håkan Arvidsson (70 Klas Johansson), Ronald Åhman, Hans Borg, Olle Nordin, Anders Linderoth, Mats Nordgren, Anders Grönhagen, Tore Cervin, Pär-Olof Ohlsson.
Trainer: Georg Ericsson

LUXEMBOURG: Jeannot Moes; Hubert Meunier, Francis Kremer, Nico Rohmann, Jean-Louis Margue, Carlo Weis, Paul Philipp (Cap), Gilbert Dresch (78 William Bianchini), Romain Michaux, Marcel Di Domenico, André Zwally.
Trainer: Arthur Schoos

Goals: Grönhagen (15), Cervin (29), Borg (53 pen)

CZECHOSLOVAKIA v FRANCE 2-0 (0-0)

Tehelné pole, Bratislava 04.04.1979

Referee: Heinz Aldinger (W. GER) Attendance: 48,138

CZECHOSLOVAKIA: Jaroslav Netolicka; Jozef Barmos, Rotislav Vojácek, Anton Ondrus, Koloman Gögh; Antonín Panenka, Ján Kozák, Frantisek Stambachr; Miloslav Gajdusek, Marián Masny, Zdenek Nehoda (59 Ladislav Vízek).
Trainer: Jozef Venglos

FRANCE: Dominique Dropsy; Raymond Domenech, Léonard Specht, Christian Lopez (Cap), Maxime Bossis; Jean Petit, Michel Platini, Jean-François Larios; Albert Emon, Marc Berdoll, Loic Amisse. Trainer: Michel Hidalgo

Goals: Panenka (68 pen), Stambachr (72)

SWEDEN v FRANCE 1-3 (1-1)

Fotbollstadion, Solna 05.09.1979

Referee: Angel Franco Martinez (SPA) Attendance: 14,395

SWEDEN: Ronnie Hellström; Mikael Rönnberg, Kent Jönsson, Hans Borg, Ingemar Erlandsson, Olle Nordin, Anders Linderoth, Mats Nordgren, Anders Grönhagen (75 Jan Svensson), Rutger Backe, Sigge Johansson.
Trainer: Georg Ericsson

FRANCE: Dominique Dropsy; Patrick Battiston, Léonard Specht, Christian Lopez, Maxime Bossis; Alain Moizan, Michel Platini (Cap), Dominique Bathenay; Dominique Rocheteau (55 Atre Jacques Zimako), Bernard Lacombe, Loic Amisse.
Trainer: Michel Hidalgo

Goals: Lacombe (14), Backe (24), Platini (54), Battiston (71)

CZECHOSLOVAKIA v SWEDEN 4-1 (3-0)

Praha 10.10.1979

Referee: Talat Tokat (TUR) Attendance: 40,000

CZECHOSLOVAKIA: Zdenek Hruska; Jozef Barmos, Rostislav Vojácek (.. Ladislav Jurkemik), Anton Ondrus, Koloman Gögh; Ján Kozák, Frantisek Stambachr, Antonín Panenka; Ladislav Vízek, Zdenek Nehoda (.. Karel Kroupa), Miloslav Gajdusek. Trainer: Jozef Venglos

SWEDEN: Jan Möller; Magnus Andersson, Kent Jönsson, Hans Borg, Ingemar Erlandsson, Mats Nordgren, Anders Linderoth, Peter Nilsson, Sigge Johansson (57 Eine Fredriksson), Pär-Olof Ohlsson (73 Anders Grönhagen), Jan Svensson. Trainer: Georg Ericsson

Goals: Nehoda (20), Kozák (34), Vízek (41, 78), Svensson (60)

LUXEMBOURG v SWEDEN 1-1 (1-0)

Stade de la Frontière, Esch sur Alzette 23.10.1979

Referee: Walter Horstmann (W. GER) Attendance: 2,123

LUXEMBOURG: Lucien Thill; Romain Michaux, Jean-Louis Margue, Jean Zuang, Nico Rohmann, Carlo Weis, Paul Philipp (Cap), Gilbert Dresch (72 Nico Wagner), Jeannot Reiter, Nico Braun, Marcel Di Domenico (60 Camille Neumann). Trainer: Louis Pilot

SWEDEN: Thomas Wernersson; Hans Borg, Thom Åhlund (70 Leif Lindén), Ulf Lundberg, Klas Johansson, Mats Nordgren, Eine Fredriksson, Peter Nilsson, Jan Svensson (41 Anders Grönhagen), Rutger Backe, Sigge Johansson. Trainer: Georg Ericsson

Goals: Braun (4 pen), Grönhagen (62)

FRANCE v CZECHOSLOVAKIA 2-1 (1-0)

Parc des Princes, Paris 17.11.1979

Referee: Horst Brummeier (AUS) Attendance: 39,973

FRANCE: Dominique Dropsy; Patrick Battiston, Léonard Specht, Christian Lopez (Cap), Maxime Bossis; Jean Petit, Alain Moizan, Gilles Rampillon; Atre Jacques Zimako, Bernard Lacombe (46 Eric Pécout), Loic Amisse. Trainer: Michel Hidalgo

CZECHOSLOVAKIA: Zdenek Hruska; Jozef Barmos, Ladislav Jurkemik, Anton Ondrus, Koloman Gögh; Antonín Panenka, Ján Kozák, Frantisek Stambachr; Ladislav Vízek, Karel Kroupa (72 Marián Masny), Miroslav Gajdusek. Trainer: Jozef Venglos

Goals: Pécout (67), Rampillon (76), Kozák (80)

CZECHOSLOVAKIA v LUXEMBOURG 4-0 (3-0)

Praha 24.11.1979

Referee: Marcel van Langenhove (BEL) Attendance: 15,000

CZECHOSLOVAKIA: Zdenek Hruska; Jozef Barmos, Ladislav Jurkemik (..Rostislav Vojácek), Anton Ondrus, Koloman Gögh; Ján Kozák, Antonín Panenka, Frantisek Stambachr; Marián Masny, Ladislav Vízek, Miloslav Gajdusek. Trainer: Jozef Venglos

LUXEMBOURG: Jeannot Moes, Romain Michaux, Jean Zuang, Nico Rohmann, Jean-Louis Margue, Carlo Weis, Nico Wagner, Paul Philipp (Cap), Jeannot Reiter, Marcel Di Domenico (70 Gilbert Dresch), Nico Braun. Trainer: Louis Pilot

Goals: Panenka (37), Masny (39, 45), Vízek (61)

	P	W	D	L	F	A	Pts
Czechoslovakia	6	5	0	1	17	4	10
France	6	4	1	1	13	7	9
Sweden	6	1	2	3	9	13	4
Luxembourg	6	0	1	5	2	17	1

GROUP 6

FINLAND v GREECE 3-0 (1-0)

Olympic, Helsinki 24.05.1978

Referee: Heinz Einbeck (E. GER) Attendance: 7,740

FINLAND: Pertti Alaja; Erkki Vihtilä, Arto Tolsa, Ari Mäkynen, Esko Ranta, Pertti Jantunen, Aki Heiskanen, Miika Toivola, Leo Houtsonen (60 Olavi Rissanen), Atik Ismail, Jyrki Nieminen. Trainer: Aulis Rytkönen

GREECE: Nikos Hristidis; Theodoros Pallas (78 Petros Karavitis), Kostas Iosifidis, Giorgos Foiros, Lakis Nikolaou, Hristos Terzanidis, Giannis Damanakis, Dimitris Papaioannou (Cap), Hristos Ardizoglou (46 Giorgos Semertzidis), Hlias Galakos, Thomas Mauros. Trainer: Alketas Panagoulias

Goals: Ismail (35, 85), Nieminen (82)

USSR v GREECE 2-0 (1-0)

Razdan, Erevan 20.09.1978

Referee: John Carpenter (IRE) Attendance: 55,000

USSR: Iuriy Degtiarev; Anatoliy Konkov (Cap), Vasiliy Zhupikov, Aleksandr Berezhnoi, Alexandr Bubnov, Sergei Prigoda, Leonid Buriak, Vladimir Bessonov, Iuriy Chesnokov, Vagiz Hidiatullin (71 Mihail An), Oleg Blohin. Trainer: Nikita Simonian

GREECE: Nikos Hristidis (Cap); Giannis Kyrastas, Petros Ravousis, Giorgos Foiros, Theodoros Pallas, Hristos Terzanidis, Dimitris Nikoloudis, Giannis Damanakis, Thomas Mauros, Giorgos Delikaris, Anastasios Mitropoulos. Trainer: Alketas Panagoulias

Goals: Chesnokov (20), Bessonov (53)

FINLAND v HUNGARY 2-1 (1-0)

Olimpiai, Helsinki 20.09.1978

Referee: Erik Fredriksson (SWE) Attendance: 4,797

FINLAND: Pertti Alaja; Erkki Vihtilä, Arto Tolsa, Risto Salonen, Esko Ranta, Pertti Jantunen, Jouko Suomalainen (57 Juha Helin), Miika Toivola, Seppo Pyykkö (76 Arto Uimonen), Atik Ismail, Jyrki Nieminen. Trainer: Aulis Rytkönen

HUNGARY: Sándor Gujdár; Sándor Paróczai, László Bálint, Zoltán Kereki, Sándor Lukács, József Kovács (58 László Szokolai), László Gyimesi, György Tatár, Sándor Pintér, József Kardos (.. Pécs), László Tieber.

Goals: Ismail (30), Pyykkö (53), Tieber (74)

GREECE v HUNGARY 4-1 (0-0)

Kautatzouleio, Thessaloniki 28.10.1978

Referee: Nikola Dudin (BUL) Attendance: 15,000

GREECE: Vasilis Konstantinou; Haralampos Xanthopoulos, Kostas Iosifidis, Petros Ravousis, Giorgos Foiros, Dimitris Nikoloudis, Hristos Ardizoglou (83 Anastasios Mitropoulos), Giorgos Delikaris (46 Giannis Damanakis), Hlias Galakos, Giorgos Koudas (Cap), Thomas Mauros.
Trainer: Alketas Panagoulias

HUNGARY: Béla Katzirz; Gyözö Martos, István Kocsis, Zoltán Kereki, Sándor Lukács, József Pál, György Tatár, Sándor Pintér, Sándor Zombori, László Szokolai (65 István Kovács), Béla Váradi.

Goals: Galakos (58, 67), Ardizoglou (71), Mauros (89), Váradi (90)

HUNGARY v USSR 2-0 (1-0)

Népstadion, Budapest 11.10.1978

Referee: Walter Eschweiler (W. GER) Attendance: 35,000

HUNGARY: Béla Katzirz; Gyözö Martos, István Kocsis, Zoltán Kereki, Sándor Lukács, József Pál, György Tatár, Sándor Pintér, László Szokolai (86 László Gyimesi), István Kovács (69 László Fekete), Béla Váradi.

USSR: Iuriy Degtiarev (42 Nikolai Gontar); Anatoliy Konkov (Cap), Vasiliy Zhupikov, Aleksandr Mahovikov, Aleksandr Bubnov, Aleksandr Berezhnoi, Leonid Buriak (65 Georgi Iartsev), Vladimir Bessonov, Vladimir Gutsaev, Vagiz Hidiatullin, Oleg Blohin. Trainer: Nikita Simonian

Goals: Váradi (26), Szokolai (60)

HUNGARY v GREECE 0-0

Népstadion, Budapest 02.05.1979

Referee: John Bartley Homewood (ENG) Att: 15,000

HUNGARY: Béla Katzirz; Péter Török, István Kocsis, László Bálint, László Kutasi, Béla Kovács, Károly Csapó (31 István Magyar), Sándor Zombori, László Fazekas, András Töröcsik, László Fekete (75 László Kuti).

GREECE: Papagiotis Kelesidis; Giannis Gounaris, Kostas Iosifidis, Giorgos Foiros, Anthimos Kapsis, Spiros Livathinos, Dimitris Nikoloudis (Cap), Giannis Damanakis (65 Vaggelis Kousoulakis), Hristos Ardizoglou (77 Kostas Orfanos), Giorgos Kostikos, Thomas Mauros.
Trainer: Alketas Panagoulias

GREECE v FINLAND 8-1 (5-0)

Panathinaikos, Athina 11.10.1978

Referee: Marcel van Langehove (BEL) Attendance: 8,000

GREECE: Vasilis Konstantinou; Giannis Kyrastas, Petros Ravousis, Giorgos Foiros, Theodoros Pallas, Dimitris Nikoloudis, Giorgos Delikaris, Hristos Ardizoglou, Anastasios Mitropoulos (67 Giorgos Semertzidis), Hlias Galakos (82 Hristos Ziakos), Thomas Mauros.
Trainer: Alketas Panagoulias

FINLAND: Göran Enckelman; Erkki Vihtilä, Arto Tolsa, Risto Salonen, Esko Ranta, Pertti Jantunen, Jouko Suomalainen (74 Kalle Nieminen), Aki Heiskanen, Seppo Pyykkö (29 Arto Uimonen), Atik Ismail, Jyrki Nieminen.
Trainer: Aulis Rytkönen

Goal: Nikoloudis (15, 25), Delikaris (23, 47), Mauros (38, 44, 75 pen), Heiskanen (61), Galakos (81)

USSR v HUNGARY 2-2 (1-1)

Dinamo, Tbilisi 19.05.1979

Referee: Brian McGinlay (SCO) Attendance: 75,000

USSR: Nikolai Gontar; Aleksandr Berezhnoi, Iuriy Adzhem, Aleksandr Mahovikov, Aleksandr Bubnov, Vitaliy Daraselia, Manuchur Machaidze, Vakhtang Koridze (70 David Kipiani), Iuriy Chesnokov (87 Vasiliy Zhupikov), Ramaz Shengelia, Oleg Blohin (Cap). Trainer: Nikita Simonian

HUNGARY: Zoltán Tóth; Péter Török (23 Gyözö Martos), István Kocsis, László Bálint, József Tóth, Béla Kovács (55 Tibor Rab), Tibor Nyilasi, György Tatár, László Pusztai, András Töröcsik, István Magyar.

Goals: Chesnokov (23), Tatár (33), Pusztai (63), Shengelia (75)

FINLAND v USSR 1-1 (0-1)

Olimpiastadion, Helsinki 04.07.1979

Referee: Ole Amundsen (DEN) Attendance: 13,119

FINLAND: Pertti Alaja; Mikko Lampi, Leo Houtsonen, Arto Tolsa, Esko Ranta, Seppo Pyykkö (77 Risto Salonen), Miika Toivola (77 Reima Kokko), Petteri Kupiainen, Jyrki Nieminen, Atik Ismail, Pasi Rautiainen. Trainer: Esko Malm

USSR: Sergei Romenskiy; Sergei Prigoda, Shota Khinchagashvili, Aleksandr Mahovikov (Cap), Aleksandr Bubnov, Vitaliy Daraselia, Vagiz Hidiatullin, Vladimir Bessonov, Iuriy Chesnokov, David Kipiani (70 Ramaz Shengelia), Aleksandr Hapsalis. Trainer: Nikita Simonian

Goals: Hapsalis (28), Ismail (55)

GREECE v USSR 1-0 (1-0)

Panathinaikos, Athina 12.09.1979

Referee: Antonio José Silva Garrido (POR) Att: 25,000

GREECE: Vasilis Konstantinou; Giannis Gounaris (74 Giannis Kyrastas), Kostas Iosifidis, Giorgos Foiros, Anthimos Kapsis, Giannis Damanakis, Spiros Livathinos, Hristos Ardizoglou (64 Kostas Orfanos), Dimitris Nikoloudis, Giorgos Delikaris (Cap), Hlias Galakos. Trainer: Alketas Panagoulias

USSR: Renat Dasaev; Sergei Prigoda (36 Sergei Shavlo), Aleksandr Bubnov, Aleksandr Mahovikov (Cap), Vagiz Hidiatullin, Sergei Nikulin, Fëdor Cherenkov, David Kipiani (46 Stepan Iurchishin), Iuriy Gavrilov, Aleksandr Maksimenkov, Ramaz Shengelia. Trainer: Konstantin Beskov

Goal: Nikoloudis (25)

HUNGARY v FINLAND 3-1 (2-0)

Nagyerdei, Debrecen 17.10.1979

Referee: Charles Corver (HOL) Attendance: 18,000

HUNGARY: Gábor Zsiborás; Gábor Szántó, József Salamon, László Kutasi (71 János Kiss), György Tatár, József Póczik, Mihály Borostyán (46 Béla Bodonyi), László Kiss, István Weimper, László Kuti, László Fekete.

FINLAND: Seppo Sairanen, Mikko Lampi, Arto Tolsa, Leo Houtsonen, Esko Ranta, Seppo Pyykkö, Miika Toivola, Pasi Rautiainen, Kai Haaskivi, Atik Ismail (68 Petteri Kupiainen), Heikki Suhonen (60 Juhani Himanka). Trainer: Esko Malm

Goals: Fekete (25, 44), M. Toivola (47), Tatár (49)

USSR v FINLAND 2-2 (0-0)

V.I.Lenin, Moskva 31.10.1979

Referee: A.Nikic (YUG) Attendance: 1500

USSR: Nikolai Gontar; Aleksandr Berezhnoi, Aleksandr Bubnov, Aleksandr Mahovikov (Cap), Vagiz Hidiatullin, Sergei Shavlo, Sergei Andreev, Vladimir Bessonov (65 Khoren Oganesian), Iuriy Gavrilov, Vladimir Veremeev, Stepan Iurchishin (72 Vladimir Kazachienok).
Trainer: Konstantin Beskov

FINLAND: Seppo Sairanen, Mikko Lampi, Arto Tolsa, Erkki Vihtilä, Esko Ranta, Leo Houtsonen, Seppo Pyykkö (46 Hannu Turunen), Kai Haaskivi, Juhani Himanka (72 Tuomo Hakala), Atik Ismail, Jyrki Nieminen. Trainer: Esko Malm

Goals: Andreev (50), Gavrilov (67), Haaskivi (76), Hakala (82)

	P	W	D	L	F	A	Pts
Greece	6	3	1	2	13	7	7
Hungary	6	2	2	2	9	9	6
Finland	6	2	2	2	10	15	6
USSR	6	1	3	2	7	8	5

GROUP 7

WALES v MALTA 7-0 (3-0)

Racecourse Ground, Wrexham 25.10.1978

Referee: Magnus Petursson (ICE) Attendance: 11,475

WALES: William David Davies; William Stevenson, Joseph Jones, Leighton Phillips, Malcolm Page, Michael Thomas, Carl Stephen Harris, Brian Flynn, Robert Ian Edwards, Robert James, Leslie Cartwright (16 Peter O'Sullivan).
Manager: Michael Smith

MALTA: Robert Gatt; George Ciantar, Edwin Farrugia (.. C.Consiglio), Simon Tortell, Mario Schembri, John Holland, Vincent Magro, Richard Aquilina (46 Ernest Spiteri Gonzi), George Xuereb, Raymond Xuereb, Carlo Seychell.
Trainer: Victor Scerri

Goals: Edwards (17, 45, 48, 50), P. O'Sullivan (20), M. Thomas (70), Flynn (73)

WALES v TURKEY 1-0 (0-0)

Wrexham 29.11.1978

Referee: Alojzy Jarguz (POL) Attendance: 11,794

WALES: William David Davies; William Stevenson, Joseph Jones, Leighton Phillips, Terence Yorath, Michael Thomas, Carl Stephen Harris, Brian Flynn, Nicholas Deacy, Phillip Dwyer, Leighton James. Manager: Michael Smith

TURKEY: Şenol Güneş; Turgay Semercioglu, Cem Pamiroglu, Necati Özçaglayan, Erdogan Arica, Fatih Terim, Mehmet Ekşi, Önder Mustafaoglu, Necdet Ergun, Sedat III Özen, Ahmet Ceylan (.. Isa Ertürk). Trainer: Coşkun Özari

Goal: Deacy (70)

TURKEY v WEST GERMANY 0-0

Izmir 01.04.1979

Referee: Miroslav Stupar (USSR) Attendance: 50,000

TURKEY: Şenol Güneş; Turgay Semercioglu, Cem Pamiroglu, Necati Özçaglayan, Fatih Terim, Engin Verel, Necdet Ergun, Tuna Güneysu, Erhan Önal, Sedat III Özen, Cemil Turan, B. Mustafa Denizli. Trainer: Coşkun Özari

W. GERMANY: Dieter Burdenski; Manfred Kaltz, Bernard Dietz (Cap); Rainer Bonhof, Ulrich Stielike, Herbert Zimmermann (.. Karlheinz Förster); Karl-Heinz Rummenigge (.. Walter Kelsch), Bernhard Cullmann, Klaus Toppmöller, Hans Müller, Ronald Borchers. Trainer: Josef Derwall

MALTA v WEST GERMANY 0-0

Empire Stadium, Gzira 25.02.1979

Referee: Vojtech Christov (CZE) Attendance: 8,450

MALTA: Charles Sciberras; David Buckingham, Edwin Farrugia, John Holland, Norman Buttigieg, Emmanuel Farrugia, Vincent Magro, Joseph Xuereb, Ernest Spiteri Gonzi (.. Carlo Seychell), Raymond Xuereb, George Xuereb. Trainer: Victor Scerri

W. GERMANY: Josef Maier (Cap); Manfred Kaltz, Bernard Dietz; Rainer Bonhof, Gerd Zewe (68 Klaus Toppmöller), Karlheinz Förster; Rüdiger Abramczik, Bernhard Cullmann, Klaus Fischer, Hans Müller, Karl-Heinz Rummenigge (68 Klaus Allofs). Trainer: Josef Derwall

WALES v WEST GERMANY 0-2 (0-1)

Wrexham 02.05.1979

Referee: Alberto Michelotti (ITA) Attendance: 30,000

WALES: William David Davies; Malcolm Page, Joseph Jones, Leighton Phillips, George Berry, John Francis Mahoney, Terence Yorath (.. Robert James), Carl Stephen Harris, Robert Ian Edwards (.. John Toshack), Alan Thomas Curtis, Michael Thomas. Manager: Michael Smith

W. GERMANY: Josef Maier (Cap); Manfred Kaltz, Bernard Dietz; Rainer Bonhof, Ulrich Stielike (88 Bernd Martin), Karlheinz Förster; Karl-Heinz Rummenigge, Bernhard Cullmann, Klaus Fischer, Herbert Zimmermann, Klaus Allofs. Trainer: Josef Derwall

Goals: Zimmermann (30), Fischer (52)

TURKEY v MALTA 2-1 (1-0)

Atatürk, Izmir 18.03.1979

Referee: Toma Manojlovski (YUG) Attendance: 45,000

TURKEY: Şenol Güneş; Turgay Semercioglu, Cem Pamiroglu, Necati Özçaglayan, Fatih Terim, Erhan Önal, Necdet Ergun, Tuna Güneysu, Bahtiyar Yorulmaz, Sedat III Özen, B.Mustafa Denizli. Trainer: Coşkun Özari

MALTA: Charles Sciberras; George Ciantar, Edwin Farrugia (65 David Buckingham), John Holland, Norman Buttigieg, Emmanuel Farrugia, Vincent Magro, Joseph Xuereb, Ernest Spiteri Gonzi, Raymond Xuereb, George Xuereb. Trainer: Victor Scerri

Goals: Sedat (43), Spiteri Gonzi (51), Fatih (57)

MALTA v WALES 0-2 (0-1)

Empire Stadium, Gzira 02.06.1979

Referee: Nikolaos Lagoyannis (GRE) Attendance: 8,358

MALTA: Charles Sciberras; David Buckingham, Edwin Farrugia, John Holland, Norman Buttigieg, Emmanuel Farrugia, Vincent Magro, Joseph Xuereb, Ernest Spiteri Gonzi (.. Emmanuel Fabri), Raymond Xuereb, George Xuereb. Trainer: Victor Scerri

WALES: William David Davies; William Stevenson, Joseph Jones, John Francis Mahoney, Peter Nicholas, Leighton Phillips, Carl Stephen Harris (.. Michael Thomas), Brian Flynn (.. Phillip Dwyer), Robert James, John Toshack, Alan Thomas Curtis. Manager: Michael Smith

Goals: Nicholas (15), Flynn (51)

WEST GERMANY v WALES 5-1 (4-0)

Müngersdorferstadion, Köln 17.10.1979

Referee: Jan Keizer (HOL) Attendance: 60,000

W. GERMANY: Dieter Burdenski; Manfred Kaltz, Bernard Dietz (Cap); Karlheinz Förster, Bernhard Cullmann, Bernd Schuster (64 Herbert Zimmermann); Karl-Heinz Rummenigge (.. Hans-Peter Briegel), Rainer Bonhof, Klaus Fischer, Hans Müller, Klaus Allofs. Trainer: Josef Derwall

WALES: William David Davies; William Stevenson, Joseph Jones (.. George Berry), John Francis Mahoney, Leighton Phillips, Phillip Dwyer, Peter Nicholas, Brian Flynn, Alan Thomas Curtis, John Toshack (.. Michael Thomas), Robert James. Manager: Michael Smith

Goals: Fischer (22, 38), Kaltz (32), Rummenigge (41), Förster (83), Curtis (85)

WEST GERMANY v TURKEY 2-0 (1-0)

Gelsenkirchen 22.12.1979

Referee: Rudolf Renggli (SWI) Attendance: 73,000

W. GERMANY: Norbert Nigbur; Manfred Kaltz, Bernard Dietz (Cap); Rainer Bonhof, Bernhard Cullmann, Bernd Förster; Karl-Heinz Rummenigge, Ulrich Stielike (.. Herbert Zimmermann), Klaus Fischer, Hans Müller, Harald Nickel. Trainer: Josef Derwall

TURKEY: Şenol Güneş; Turgay Semercioglu, Cem Pamiroglu, Güngör Tekin, Fatih Terim, Erhan Önal, Raşit Çetiner, Arif Güney (17 K.Mustafa Turgat), Mehmet Ekşi, Sedat III Özen, Sadullah Acele, Engin Verel. Trainer: Coşkun Özari

Goals: Fischer (15), Zimmermann (89)

MALTA v TURKEY 1-2 (0-2)

Empire Stadium, Gzira 28.10.1979

Referee: Gianfranco Menegalli (ITA) Attendance: 1,976

MALTA: John Bonello; David Buckingham, Edwin Farrugia, John Holland, Norman Buttigieg, Emmanuel Farrugia, Vincent Magro, Joseph Xuereb, George Xuereb, Raymond Xuereb (.. Emmanuel Fabri), Dennis Fenech. Trainer: Victor Scerri

TURKEY: Şenol Güneş; Turgay Semercioglu, Cem Pamiroglu, Erol Togay, Fatih Terim, Mehmet Ekşi, Necdet Ergun, Serdar Bali, Sedat III Özen, Isa Ertürk, B. Mustafa Denizli. Trainer: Coşkun Özari

Goals: Sedat (20), B. Mustafa (25), Em. Farrugia (70)

WEST GERMANY v MALTA 8-0 (3-0)

Wesser, Bremen 27.02.1980

Referee: Norbert Rolles (LUX) Attendance: 38,000

W. GERMANY: Dieter Burdenski; Manfred Kaltz, Bernhard Cullmann, Karlheinz Forster, Bernard Dietz (Cap); Rainer Bonhof, Bernd Förster (.. Walter Kelsch), Hans Müller; Karl-Heinz Rummenigge, Klaus Fischer, Klaus Allofs (60 Harald Nickel). Trainer: Josef Derwall

MALTA: John Bonello; Edwin Farrugia, Gennaro Camilleri (46 David Buckingham), John Holland, Norman Buttigieg, Emmanuel Farrugia, Joseph Xuereb, Emmanuel Fabri, Eric Schembri, Dennis Fenech, George Xuereb. Trainer: Victor Scerri

Goal: Allofs (12, 56), Bonhof (17 pen), Fischer (40, 90), J. Holland (62 og), Kelsch (70), Rummenigge (74)

TURKEY v WALES 1-0 (0-0)

Izmir 21.11.1979

Referee: Constantin Ghiță (ROM) Attendance: 50,000

TURKEY: Şenol Güneş; Turgay Semercioglu, Cem Pamiroglu, Erol Togay, Fatih Terim, Mehmet Ekşi, Arif Güney, Erhan Önal, Sedat III Özen, Isa Ertürk (.. K. Mustafa Turgat), B. Mustafa Denizli (.. Sadullah Acele). Trainer: Coşkun Özari

WALES: William David Davies; William Stevenson, Joseph Jones, Terence Yorath, George Berry, Leighton Phillips, Gordon John Davies (.. John Francis Mahoney), Peter Nicholas, Alan Thomas Curtis, Ian Patrick Walsh (65 Robert Ian Edwards), Michael Thomas. Manager: Michael Smith

Sent off: Stevenson (69)

Goal: Erhan Önal (80)

	P	W	D	L	F	A	Pts
West Germany	6	4	2	0	17	1	10
Turkey	6	3	1	2	5	5	7
Wales	6	3	0	3	11	8	5
Malta	6	0	1	5	2	21	1

FINAL ROUND

GROUP I

CZECHOSLOVAKIA v WEST GERMANY **0-1** (0-0)

Stadio Olimpico, Roma 11.06.1980

Referee: Alberto Michelotti (ITA) Attendance: 20,000

CZECHOSLOVAKIA: Jaroslav Netolicka; Jozef Barmos, Anton Ondrus (Cap), Ladislav Jurkemik, Koloman Gögh; Ján Kozák, Antonín Panenka, Frantisek Stambachr; Ladislav Vízek, Zdenek Nehoda, Miloslav Gajdusek (68 Marián Masny). Trainer: Jozef Venglos

W. GERMANY: Harald Schumacher; Manfred Kaltz, Bernhard Cullmann, Karlheinz Förster, Bernard Dietz (Cap); Bernd Förster (60 Felix Magath), Ulrich Stielike, Hans-Peter Briegel, Hans Müller; Karl-Heinz Rummenigge, Klaus Allofs. Trainer: Josef Derwall

Goal: Rummenigge (55)

HOLLAND v GREECE **1-0** (0-0)

San Paolo, Napoli 11.06.1980

Referee: Adolf Prokop (E. GER) Attendance: 15,000

HOLLAND: Piet Schrijvers (14 Pim Doesburg); Bennie Wijnstekers, Ruud Krol (Cap), Michel Van de Korput, Hugo Hovenkamp; Huub Stevens, Arie Haan, Willy van de Kerkhof; Martien Vreijsen (46 Dick Nanninga), Kees Kist, René van de Kerkhof. Trainer: Johannes Zwartkruis

GREECE: Vasilis Konstantinou; Giannis Kyrastas, Spiros Livathinos, Kostas Iosifidis, Anthimos Kapsis (Cap), Giorgos Foiros, Hristos Ardizoglou (68 Nikos Anastopoulos), Hristos Terzanidis, Thomas Mauros, Kostas Kouis, Giorgos Kostikos (78 Hlias Galakos). Trainer: Alketas Panagoulias

Goal: Kist (67 pen)

CZECHOSLOVAKIA v GREECE **3-1** (2-1)

Stadio Olimpico, Roma 14.06.1980

Referee: Patrick Partridge (ENG) Attendance: 7,614

CZECHOSLOVAKIA: Stanislav Seman; Jozef Barmos, Anton Ondrus (Cap), Ladislav Jurkemik, Koloman Gögh; Ján Kozák, Ján Berger (24 Werner Licka), Antonín Panenka; Ladislav Vízek, Zdenek Nehoda (74 Miloslav Gajdusek), Marián Masny. Trainer: Jozef Venglos

GREECE: Vasilis Konstantinou; Giannis Kyrastas, Spiros Livathinos, Kostas Iosifidis, Anthimos Kapsis (Cap), Giorgos Foiros, Nikos Anastopoulos, Hristos Terzanidis (46 Hlias Galakos), Thomas Mauros, Kostas Kouis, Giorgos Kostikos (57 Haralampos Xanthopoulos). Trainer: Alketas Panagoulias

Goals: Panenka (5), Anastopoulos (13), Vízek (26), Nehoda (62)

WEST GERMANY v HOLLAND **3-2** (1-0)

San Paolo, Napoli 14.06.1980

Referee: Robert Wurtz (FRA) Attendance: 29,889

W. GERMANY: Harald Schumacher; Manfred Kaltz, Ulrich Stielike, Karlheinz Förster, Bernard Dietz (Cap) (75 Lothar Matthäus); Bernd Schuster, Hans-Peter Briegel, Hans Müller (66 Felix Magath); Karl-Heinz Rummenigge, Horst Hrubesch, Klaus Allofs. Trainer: Josef Derwall

HOLLAND: Piet Schrijvers; Bennie Wijnstekers, Ruud Krol (Cap), Michel Van de Korput, Hugo Hovenkamp (46 Dick Nanninga); Huub Stevens, Arie Haan, Willy van de Kerkhof; Johnny Rep, Kees Kist (70 Frans Thijssen), René van de Kerkhof. Trainer: Johannes Zwartkruis

Goals: Kl. Allofs (11, 56, 66), Rep (79 pen), Willy van de Kerkhof (86)

CZECHOSLOVAKIA v HOLLAND **1-1** (1-0)

Giuseppe Meazza, Milano 17.06.1980

Referee: Hilmi Ok (TUR) Attendance: 10,000

CZECHOSLOVAKIA: Jaroslav Netolicka; Jozef Barmos, Anton Ondrus (Cap), Rostislav Vojácek, Koloman Gogh; Ján Kozák, Ladislav Jurkemik, Antonín Panenka (89 Frantisek Stambachr); Ladislav Vízek, Zdenek Nehoda, Marián Masny (67 Werner Licka). Trainer: Jozef Venglos

HOLLAND: Piet Schrijvers; Bennie Wijnstekers, Ruud Krol (Cap), Michel Van de Korput, Hugo Hovenkamp; Willy van de Kerkhof, Frans Thijssen, Jan Poortvliet; Johnny Rep, Dick Nanninga (46 Arie Haan), René van de Kerkhof (17 Kees Kist). Trainer: Johannes Zwartkruis

Goals: Nehoda (17), Kist (60)

WEST GERMANY v GREECE **0-0**

Communale, Torino 17.06.1980

Referee: Brian McGinlay (SCO) Attendance: 16,000

W. GERMANY: Harald Schumacher; Manfred Kaltz, Ulrich Stielike, Karlheinz Förster, Bernd Förster (46 Miroslav Votava); Bernhard Cullmann (Cap), Hans-Peter Briegel, Hans Müller, Caspar Memering; Karl-Heinz Rummenigge (66 Karl Del Haye), Horst Hrubesch. Trainer: Josef Derwall

GREECE: Lenteris Poupakis; Giannis Gounaris, Haralampos Xanthopoulos, Petros Ravousis, Lakis Nikolaou; Kostas Kouis, Dimitris Nikoloudis (Cap)(65 Giorgos Koudas), Hristos Ardizoglou; Spiros Livathinos, Hlias Galakos, Thomas Mauros (79 Giorgos Kostikos). Trainer: Alketas Panagoulias

	P	W	D	L	F	A	Pts
West Germany	3	2	1	0	4	2	5
Czechoslovakia	3	1	1	1	4	3	3
Holland	3	1	1	1	4	4	3
Greece	3	0	1	2	1	4	1

GROUP II

ITALY v SPAIN 0-0

Giuseppe Meazza, Milano 12.06.1980

Referee: Károly Palotai (HUNG) Attendance: 46,816

ITALY: Dino Zoff (Cap); Claudio Gentile, Fulvio Collovati, Gaetano Scirea, Antonio Cabrini (56 Romeo Benetti II); Gabriele Oriali, Marco Tardelli, Giancarlo Antognoni; Franco Causio, Francesco Graziani, Roberto Bettega. Trainer: Vincenzo Bearzot

SPAIN: Luis Miguel ARCONADA Echarre; Miguel TENDILLO Berenguer, Bernardo Blanquetti MIGUELI, José Ramon ALESANCO Ventosa, Rafael GORDILLO Vazquez; Jesús María ZAMORA Ansorena, Enrique SAURA Gil, Juan Manuel ASENSI Ripoll (Cap); Daniel Ruiz Bazan Justa "DANI" (53 Juan Gómez Gonzalez "JUANITO"), Jesús SATRÚSTEGUI, Enrique Castro Gonzalez QUINI. Trainer: Ladislao Kubala

ENGLAND v BELGIUM 1-1 (1-1)

Stadio Comunale, Torino 12.06.1980

Referee: Heinz Aldinger (W. GER) Attendance: 15,186

ENGLAND: Raymond Clemence; Philip Neal, Philip Thompson, David Watson, Kenneth Sansom; Ray Wilkins, Kevin Keegan, Trevor Brooking, David Johnson (68 Raymond Kennedy), Anthony Woodcock, Steven Coppell (79 Terence McDermott). Trainer: Ronald Greenwood

BELGIUM: Jean-Marie Pfaff; Walter Meeuws, Eric Gerets, Luc Millecamps, Michel Renquin; Julien Cools (Cap), Wilfried Van Moer (88 Raymond Mommens), René Vandereycken, François Van der Elst; Erwin Vandenbergh, Jan Ceulemans. Trainer: Guy Thys

Goals: Wilkins (25), Ceulemans (29)

ITALY v ENGLAND 1-0 (0-0)

Stadio Comunale, Torino 15.06.1980

Referee: Nicolae Rainea (ROM) Attendance: 59,649

ITALY: Dino Zoff (Cap); Claudio Gentile, Gabriele Oriali, Romeo Benetti II, Fulvio Collovati, Gaetano Scirea, Franco Causio (88 Giuseppe Baresi), Marco Tardelli, Francesco Graziani, Giancarlo Antognoni, Roberto Bettega. Trainer: Vincenzo Bearzot

ENGLAND: Peter Shilton; Philip Neal, Kenneth Sansom; Ray Wilkins, David Watson, Philip Thompson, Kevin Keegan (Cap), Steven Coppell, Gary Birtles (75 Paul Mariner), Raymond Kennedy, Anthony Woodcock. Manager: Ronald Greenwood

Goals: Tardelli (78)

SPAIN v BELGIUM 1-2 (1-1)

Giuseppe Meazza, Milano 15.06.1980

Referee: Charles Corver (HOL) Attendance: 11,430

SPAIN: Luis Miguel ARCONADA Echarre; Miguel TENDILLO Berenguer (78 Francisco José CARRASCO Hidalgo), José Ramon ALESANCO Ventosa, Bernardo Blanquetti MIGUELI, Rafael GORDILLO Vazquez; Jesús María ZAMORA Ansorena, Juan Manuel ASENSI Ripoll (Cap)(35 Vicente Gonzalez DEL BOSQUE), Enrique SAURA Gil; Enrique Castro Gonzalez QUINI, Jesús SATRÚSTEGUI, Juan Gómez Gonzalez "JUANITO". Trainer: Ladislao Kubala

BELGIUM: Jean-Marie Pfaff; Eric Gerets, Luc Millecamps, Walter Meeuws, Michel Renquin; Julien Cools (Cap), Wilfried Van Moer (73 Raymond Mommens), René Vandereycken; François Van der Elst, Erwin Vandenbergh (81 René Verheyen), Jan Ceulemans. Trainer: Guy Thys

Goals: Gerets (16), Quini (36), Cools (64)

ENGLAND v SPAIN 2-1 (1-0)

San Paolo, Napoli 18.06.1980 Hour 17,45

Referee: Erich Linemayr (AUS) Attendance: 15,000

ENGLAND: Raymond Clemence; Vivian Anderson (85 Trevor Cherry), Michael Mills, Philip Thompson, David Watson; Ray Wilkins, Terence McDermott, Glenn Hoddle (77 Paul Mariner), Kevin Keegan (Cap), Anthony Woodcock, Trevor Brooking. Manager: Ronald Greenwood

SPAIN: Luis Miguel ARCONADA Echarre; Rafael GORDILLO Vazquez, Antonio OLMO, José Ramon ALESANCO Ventosa, Secundino Suarez Vazquez "CUNDI"; Javier Álvarez URÍA, Julio CARDEÑOSA Rodriguez (46 Daniel Ruiz Bazan Justa "DANI"), Jesús María ZAMORA Ansorena; Juan Gómez Gonzalez "JUANITO" (46 Francisco José CARRASCO Hidalgo), Carlos Alonso Gonzalez SANTILLANA (Cap), Enrique SAURA Gil. Trainer: Ladislao Kubala

Goals: Brooking (20), Dani (52 pen), Woodcock (62)

ITALY v BELGIUM 0-0

Stadio Olimpico, Roma 18.06.1980

Referee: José Antonio Silva Garrido (POR) Att: 42,318

ITALY: Dino Zoff (Cap); Claudio Gentile, Gabriele Oriali (46 Alessandro Altobelli), Romeo Benetti II, Fulvio Collovati, Gaetano Scirea, Franco Causio, Marco Tardelli, Francesco Graziani, Giancarlo Antognoni (35 Giuseppe Baresi), Roberto Bettega. Trainer: Vincenzo Bearzot

BELGIUM: Jean-Marie Pfaff; Walter Meeuws, Eric Gerets, Luc Millecamps, Michel Renquin, Julien Cools (Cap), Wilfried Van Moer (49 René Verheyen), René Vandereycken, François Van der Elst, Raymond Mommens (78 Erwin Vandenbergh), Jan Ceulemans. Trainer: Guy Thys

	P	W	D	L	F	A	Pts
Belgium	3	1	2	0	3	2	4
Italy	3	1	2	0	1	0	4
England	3	1	1	1	3	3	3
Spain	3	0	1	2	2	4	1

THIRD PLACE MATCH

CZECHOSLOVAKIA v ITALY 1-1 (0-0) (AET)

Stadio San Paolo, Napoli 21.06.1980

Referee: Erich Linemayr (AUS) Attendance: 24,652

CZECHOSLOVAKIA: Jaroslav Netolicka; Jozef Barmos, Anton Ondrus (Cap), Rostislav Vojácek, Koloman Gogh; Ján Kozák, Ladislav Jurkemik, Antonín Panenka; Ladislav Vízek (65 Miloslav Gajdusek), Zdenek Nehoda, Marián Masny. Trainer: Jozef Venglos

ITALY: Dino Zoff (Cap); Claudio Gentile, Antonio Cabrini, Giuseppe Baresi, Fulvio Collovati, Gaetano Scirea, Franco Causio, Marco Tardelli, Francesco Graziani, Roberto Bettega (83 Romeo Benetti), Alessandro Altobelli. Trainer: Vincenzo Bearzot

Goals: Jurkemik (53), Graziani (72)

Penalties: Causio (0-1), Masny (1-1), Altobelli (1-2), Nehoda (2-2), Baresi (2-3), Ondrus (3-3), Cabrini (3-4), Jurkemik (4-4), Benetti (4-5), Panenka (5-5), Graziani (5-6), Gögh (6-6), Scirea (6-7), Gajdusek (7-7), Tardelli (7-8), Kozák (8-8), Collovatti, Barmos (8-9)

FINAL

WEST GERMANY v BELGIUM 2-1 (1-0)

Stadio Olimpico, Roma 22.06.1980

Referee: Nicolae Rainea (ROM) Attendance: 47,864

W. GERMANY: Harald Schumacher; Manfred Kaltz, Ulrich Stielike, Karlheinz Förster, Bernard Dietz (Cap); Bernd Schuster, Hans-Peter Briegel (55 Bernhard Cullmann), Hans Müller; Karl-Heinz Rummenigge, Horst Hrubesch, Klaus Allofs. Trainer: Josef Derwall

BELGIUM: Jean-Marie Pfaff; Walter Meeuws, Eric Gerets, Luc Millecamps, Michel Renquin; Julien Cools (Cap), Wilfried Van Moer, René Vandereycken, François Van der Elst, Raymond Mommens, Jan Ceulemans. Trainer: Guy Thys

Goals: Hrubesch (10, 89), Vandereycken (72 pen)

Goalscorers European Football Championship 1980

7 goals: Kevin Keegan (England)

6 goals: Klaus Fischer (West Germany)

5 goals: François Van der Elst (Belgium), Marián Masny (Czechoslovakia), Klaus Allofs (West Germany)

4 goals: Robert Latchford (England), Hans Krankl (Austria), Kenneth Dalglish (Scotland), Carlos Alonso Gonzalez Santillana (Spain), Zlatko Vujovic (Yugoslavia), Martin Hoffmann, Joachim Streich (East Germany), Thomas Mauros (Greece), Atik Ismail (Finland), Robert Ian Edwards (Wales), Kees Kist (Holland), Zdenek Nehoda, Ladislav Vízek (Czechoslovakia)

3 goals: David Watson, Anthony Woodcock (England), Gerard Armstrong (N. Ireland), Gerard Daly (Rep. of Ireland), Chavdar Tzvetkov (Bulgaria), Preben Elkjær (Denmark), Walter Schachner (Austria), Tamagnini Néné (Portugal), Archibald Gemmill (Scotland), Ruud Geels (Holland), Zbigniew Boniek, Roman Ogaza (Poland), Gerd Weber (East Germany), Antonín Panenka, Anders Grönhagen (Sweden), Hlias Galakos, Dimitris Nikoloudis (Greece), Daniel Ruiz Bazan Justa "Dani" (Spain), Rummenigge (West Germany)

2 goals: Francis (England), Grealish, Stapleton (Rep. of Ireland), H. Jensen, B. Nielsen, Lerby, Simonsen (Denmark), Kreuz, Pezzey (Austria), Alberto, Gomes (Portugal), A. Gray, Mcqueen, Robertson (Scotland), Larsen-Ökland (Norway), Asensi (Spain), Kranjcar, Petrovic, Surjak (Yugoslavia), Georgescu, Răducanu, Sameş (Romania), Brandts, Metgod, Nanninga, Willy van de Kerkhof (Holland), Terlecki (Poland), Lindemann, Schnuphase (East Germany), Kozák, Stambachr (Czechoslovakia), Six (France), Borg (Sweden), Delikaris (Greece), Fekete, Tatár, Váradi (Hungary), Chesnokov (USSR), Hrubesch, Zimmermann (West Germany), Sedat (Turkey), Flynn (Wales), Vandereycken, Cools (Belgium)

1 goal: Hoddle, Barnes, Neal, Brooking, Wilkins (England), Moreland, C. Nicholl, Caskey, Spence, Anderson (N. Ireland), Martin, Givens (Rep. of Ireland), Jeliazkov, Panov, Iliev (Bulgaria), Arnesen, Røntved (Denmark), Gerets, Ceulemans, Vandenbergh, Voordeckers, Van Moer, Janssens, Vercauteren (Belgie), Welzl, Jara, Prohaska (Austria), Reinaldo, Artur, Alves (Portugal), Archibald, Jordan (Scotland), Aas, Hammer, P. Jacobsen (Norway), Villar, Saura, Del Bosque, R. Cano, Juanito, Quini (Spain), Desnica, Halilhodzic, D. Savic, Sliskovic (Yugoslavia), Augustin, Iordănescu, Mulţescu (Romania), Kaiafas, Vrahimis (Cyprus), Rep, Thijssen, René van de Kerkhof, Stevens, Peters, Wildschut, Krol, Rensenbrink (Holland), Rudy, Wieczorek, Mazur, Kusto, Lato (Poland), Häfner, Peter, Riediger (East Germany), Barberis, Heinz Hermann, Herbert Hermann, Pfister, Ponte, Tanner, Zappa (Switzerland), Gudlaugsson, P. Pétursson (Iceland), Gajdusek, Jurkemik (Czechoslovakia), Pécout, Rampillon, Lacombe, Platini, Battiston, Petit, Emon, Larios, Trésor, Gemmrich, Berdoll (France), Svensson, Backe, Cervin, Nordgren (Sweden), Braun, Michaux (Luxembourg), Anastopoulos, Ardizoglou (Greece), Pusztai, Szokolai, Tieber (Hungary), Haaskivi, Hakala, Heiskanen, Pyykkö, Nieminen, M. Toivola (Finland), Andreev, Gavrilov, Hapsalis, Shengelia, Bessonov (USSR), Bonhof, Kelsch, Kaltz, Förster (West Germany), Erhan Önal, B. Mustafa, Fatih (Turkey), Curtis, Nicholas, Deacy, P. O'sullivan, M. Thomas (Wales), Em. Farrugia, Spiteri Gonzi (Malta), Graziani, Tardelli (Italy)

Own goals: Nicholl (N. Ireland) for England, Kische (East Germany) for Holland, J. Holland (Malta) for West Germany

THE EUROPEAN FOOTBALL CHAMPIONSHIP 1984

GROUP 1

BELGIUM v SWITZERLAND 3-0 (1-0)

Brussel 06.10.1982

Referee: Paolo Bergamo (ITA) Attendance: 16,808

BELGIUM: Jean-Marie Pfaff; Eric Gerets, Walter Meeuws, Jos Daerden, Marc Baecke, Guy Vandersmissen, Ludo Coeck, Jan Ceulemans, Frankie Vercauteren, Alex Czerniatynski, Erwin Vandenbergh. Trainer: Guy Thys

SWITZERLAND: Erich Burgener; Alain Geiger, Heinz Lüdi, Charly In-Albon, Heinz Hermann, Roger Wehrli (56 Lucien Favre), Umberto Barberis, Alfred Scheiwiler (69 Erni Maissen), René Botteron, Rudolf Elsener, Claudio Sulser. Trainer: Paul Wolfisberg

Goals: Vercauteren (2), Coeck (48), Vandenberg (82)

SCOTLAND v EAST GERMANY 2-0 (0-0)

Hampden Park, Glasgow 13.10.1982

Referee: Georges Konrath (FRA) Attendance: 40,355

SCOTLAND: James Leighton; David Narey, Alan Hansen, William Miller, Francis Gray, Gordon Strachan, Graeme Souness, John Wark, Steven Archibald, Alan Brazil (71 Paul Sturrock), John Robertson. Manager: John Stein

EAST GERMANY: Bodo Rudwaleit; Norbert Trieloff, Ronald Kreer, Dirk Stahmann, Rüdiger Schnuphase (Cap), Frank Baum; Reinhard Häfner (72 Matthias Liebers), Hans-Jürgen Dörner (72 Jürgen Pommerenke), Hans-Uwe Pilz; Joachim Streich, Hans-Jürgen Riediger. Trainer: Rudolf Krause

Goals: Wark (52), Sturrock (75)

SWITZERLAND v SCOTLAND 2-0 (0-0)

Wankdorf, Bern 17.11.1982

Referee: Vojtech Christov (CZE) Attendance: 26,500

SWITZERLAND: Erich Burgener; Alain Geiger, Roger Wehrli, André Egli, Heinz Lüdi, Michel Decastel (61 Umberto Barberis), Lucien Favre, Heinz Hermann; Raimondo Ponte, Claudio Sulser, Rudolf Elsener (85 Hanspeter Zwicker). Trainer: Paul Wolfisberg

SCOTLAND: James Leighton; David Narey, Francis Gray, Graeme Souness, Alan Hansen, William Miller, John Wark, Gordon Strachan, Paul Sturrock (46 Steven Archibald), Alan Brazil, John Robertson. Manager: John Stein

Goals: Sulser (49), Egli (60)

BELGIUM v SCOTLAND 3-2 (2-2)

Heysel, Brussel 15.12.1982

Referee: Antonio da Silva Garrido (POR) Att: 48,877

BELGIUM: Jean-Marie Pfaff; Eric Gerets, Walter Meeuws, Jos Daerden, Marc Baecke, Guy Vandersmissen, Ludo Coeck, Jan Ceulemans, Frankie Vercauteren (72 René Verheyen), Erwin Vandenbergh (86 Maurits De Schrijver), François Vander Elst. Trainer: Guy Thys

SCOTLAND: James Leighton; David Narey, Francis Gray, Robert Aitken, Alexander McLeish, Alan Hansen, Gordon Strachan (77 Thomas Burns), Steven Archibald, Kenneth Dalglish, James Bett (77 Paul Sturrock), Graeme Souness. Manager: John Stein

Goals: Dalglish (13, 35), Vandenbergh (25), Vander Elst (38, 63)

SCOTLAND v SWITZERLAND 2-2 (0-1)

Hampden Park, Glasgow 30.03.1983

Referee: Charles Corver (HOL) Attendance: 36,923

SCOTLAND: James Leighton; Richard Gough, Francis Gray, Graeme Souness, Alan Hansen (.. Alexander McLeish), William Miller, John Wark, Gordon Strachan, Kenneth Dalglish, Charles Nicholas, Peter Weir. Manager: John Stein

SWITZERLAND: Erich Burgener; Alain Geiger, Roger Wehrli, André Egli, Heinz Lüdi, Michel Decastel, Lucien Favre, Heinz Hermann (.. Hanspeter Zwicker), Claudio Sulser (84 Charly In-Albon), Raimondo Ponte, Rudolf Elsener. Trainer: Paul Wolfisberg

Goals: Egli (16), Heinz Hermann (58), Wark (69), Nicholas (76)

EAST GERMANY v BELGIUM 1-2 (0-1)

Zentralstadion, Leipzig 30.03.1983

Referee: John Carpenter (IRE) Attendance: 75,000

EAST GERMANY: Bodo Rudwaleit; Norbert Trieloff, Ronald Kreer, Rüdiger Schnuphase (Cap), Dirk Stahmann; Andreas Trautmann, Hans-Jürgen Dörner, Matthias Liebers; Hans Richter (69 Martin Busse), Joachim Streich, Dieter Kühn (60 Jürgen Heun). Trainer: Rudolf Krause

BELGIUM: Jacques Munaron; Eric Gerets, Luc Millecamps, Walter Meeuws (85 Leo Clysters), Michel De Groote (46 Marc Baecke), Guy Vandersmissen, Jan Ceulemans, Ludo Coeck, Frankie Vercauteren, François Vander Elst, Erwin Vandenbergh. Trainer: Guy Thys

Goals: Van der Elst (36), Vandenbergh (69), Streich (83)

BELGIUM v EAST GERMANY 2-1 (2-1)

Heysel, Brussel 27.04.1983

Referee: Emilio Carlos Guruceta Muro (SPA) Att: 43,000

BELGIUM: Jean-Marie Pfaff; Eric Gerets, Luc Millecamps, Walter Meeuws, Michel De Groote, Guy Vandersmissen, Ludo Coeck, Frankie Vercauteren, Jan Ceulemans, François Vander Elst, Erwin Vandenbergh. Trainer: Guy Thys

EAST GERMANY: Bodo Rudwaleit; Rüdiger Schnuphase (Cap), Ronald Kreer, Dirk Stahmann, Frank Baum; Hans-Uwe Pilz (70 Rainer Ernst), Rainer Troppa, Matthias Liebers, Wolfgang Steinbach; Joachim Streich, Martin Busse (61 Hans Richter). Trainer: Rudolf Krause

Goals: Streich (9), Ceulemans (18), Coeck (38)

SWITZERLAND v EAST GERMANY 0-0

Wankdorf, Bern 04.05.1983

Referee: Rolf Ericsson (SWE) Attendance: 40,000

SWITZERLAND: Roger Berbig; Roger Wehrli, André Egli, Beat Rietmann, Charly In-Albon, Heinz Hermann, Lucien Favre, Michel Decastel, Rudolf Elsener (.. Jean-Paul Brigger), Claudio Sulser, Manfred Braschler. Trainer: Paul Wolfisberg

EAST GERMANY: Bodo Rudwaleit; Rüdiger Schnuphase (Cap), Ronald Kreer, Dirk Stahmann, Frank Baum; Rainer Troppa, Matthias Liebers (73 Jürgen Heun), Wolfgang Steinbach (61 Hans-Uwe Pilz); Andreas Bielau, Joachim Streich, Ralf Minge. Trainer: Rudolf Krause

EAST GERMANY v SWITZERLAND 3-0 (1-0)

Friedrich-Ludwig-Jahn-Sportpark, Berlin 12.10.1983

Referee: Keith Hackett (ENG) Attendance: 12,000

EAST GERMANY: Bodo Rudwaleit; Rüdiger Schnuphase (Cap), Ronald Kreer, Rainer Troppa, Uwe Zötsche; Jürgen Raab (72 Ralf Minge), Rainer Ernst, Christian Backs, Wolfgang Steinbach; Joachim Streich, Hans Richter. Trainer: Bernd Stange

SWITZERLAND: Roger Berbig; Roger Wehrli, Beat Rietmann, André Egli, Raimondo Ponte (70 Beat Sutter), Alain Geiger, Lucien Favre, Heinz Hermann, Claudio Sulser (.. Jean-Paul Brigger), Umberto Barberis, Manfred Braschler. Trainer: Paul Wolfisberg

Goals: Richter (45), Ernst (73), Streich (90)

SCOTLAND v BELGIUM 1-1 (0-1)

Hampden Park, Glasgow 12.10.1983

Referee: Enzo Barbaresco (ITA) Attendance: 23,000

SCOTLAND: James Leighton; Richard Gough, Arthur Albiston, John Wark (.. Robert Aitken), Alexander McLeish, William Miller, Kenneth Dalglish, Paul McStay, Charles Nicholas (74 Francis McGarvey), James Bett, John Robertson. Manager: John Stein

BELGIUM: Jean-Marie Pfaff; Eric Gerets, Luc Millecamps, Walter Meeuws (76 Michel De Wolf), Michel Wintacq, François Vander Elst, Ludo Coeck, Jan Ceulemans, Frankie Vercauteren, Nico Claesen, Eddy Voordeckers. Trainer: Guy Thys

Goals: Vercauteren (30), Nicholas (55)

SWITZERLAND v BELGIUM 3-1 (1-0)

Wankdorf, Bern 09.11.1983

Referee: Volker Roth (W. GER) 10,000

SWITZERLAND: Roger Berbig; Roger Wehrli, André Egli, Charly In-Albon, Heinz Lüdi, Alain Geiger, Heinz Hermann, Marco Schällibaum, Raimondo Ponte, Jean-Paul Brigger, Beat Sutter (82 Marcel Koller). Trainer: Paul Wolfisberg

BELGIUM: Jean-Marie Pfaff; Eric Gerets, Luc Millecamps, Walter Meeuws, Raymond Mommens, François Vander Elst (46 Guy Vandersmissen), Ludo Coeck (63 Nico Claesen), Frankie Vercauteren, Jan Ceulemans, Erwin Vandenbergh, Eddy Voordeckers. Trainer: Guy Thys

Goals: Schällibaum (23), Vandenbergh (63), Brigger (76), Geiger (88)

EAST GERMANY v SCOTLAND 2-1 (2-0)

Kurt-Wabbel-Stadion, Halle 16.11.1983

Referee: Franz Wöhrer (AUS) Attendance: 18,000

EAST GERMANY: Bodo Rudwaleit; Dirk Stahmann, Ronald Kreer, Rainer Troppa, Uwe Zötsche; Hans-Uwe Pilz, Rainer Ernst (87 Jürgen Raab), Christian Backs, Wolfgang Steinbach; Joachim Streich (Cap), Hans Richter. Trainer: Bernd Stange

SCOTLAND: William Thomson; Richard Gough, Arthur Albiston, John Wark, Alexander McLeish, William Miller, Gordon Strachan, Paul McStay (.. Francis McGarvey), Kenneth Dalglish, Steven Archibald, Eamonn Bannon. Manager: John Stein

Goals: Kreer (33), Streich (43), Bannon (79)

	P	W	D	L	F	A	Pts
Belgium	6	4	1	1	12	8	9
Switzerland	6	2	2	2	7	9	6
East Germany	6	2	1	3	7	7	5
Scotland	6	1	2	3	8	10	4

GROUP 2

FINLAND v POLAND 2-3 (0-2)

Vainolanniemella, Kuopio 08.09.1982

Referee: Marcel van Langenhove (BEL) Attendance: 2,845

FINLAND: Olli Huttunen; Aki Lahtinen, Pauno Kymäläinen (Cap), Mikael Granskog, Esa Pekonen; Hannu Turunen, Jukka Ikäläinen, Pasi Rautiainen, Juhani Himanka (71 Keijo Kousa); Atik Ismail (66 Ari Valvee), Ilkka Remes.
Trainer: Martti Kuusela

POLAND: Jacek Kazimierski; Stefan Majewski, Pawel Janas, Tadeusz Dolny, Jan Jalocha; Andrzej Buncol, Janusz Kupcewicz, Wlodzimierz Ciolek; Dariusz Dziekanowski (75 Wlodzimierz Mazur), Zbigniew Boniek, Wlodzimierz Smolarek (Cap). Trainer: Antoni Piechniczek

Goals: Smolarek (16 pen), Dziekanowski (28), Kupcewicz (72), Valvee (82), Kousa (84)

USSR v FINLAND 2-0 (1-0)

V.I.Lenin, Moskva 13.10.1982

Referee: Jakob Baumann (SWI) Attendance: 18,000

USSR: Renat Dasaev; Vladimir Bessonov, Aleksandr Chivadze (Cap), Anatoliy Demianenko, Sergei Baltacha, Vladimir Lozinskiy, Leonid Buriak, Andrei Bal, Sergei Andreev, Khoren Oganesian (70 Sergei Borovski), Ramaz Shengelia (28 Vadim Evtushenko). Trainer: Valeriy Lobanovski

FINLAND: Olli Huttunen; Aki Lahtinen (55 Atik Ismail), Pauno Kymäläinen, Mikael Granskog, Ilkka Remes, Hannu Turunen, Esa Pekonen, Vesa Mars, Juhani Himanka (74 Keijo Kousa), Peter Utriainen, Ari Valvee. Trainer: Martti Kuusela

Goals: Baltacha (2), Andreev (56)

FINLAND v PORTUGAL 0-2 (0-1)

Estadio Olimpico, Helsinki 22.09.1982

Referee: Klaus Scheurell (E. GER) Attendance: 3,132

FINLAND: Olli Isoaho; Aki Lahtinen, Pauno Kymäläinen, Reijo Vaittinen, Esa Pekonen, Hannu Turunen, Ilkka Remes, Pasi Rautiainen (46 Ari Valvee), Juhani Himanka (79 Keijo Kousa), Atik Ismail, Jari Parikka. Trainer: Martti Kuusela

PORTUGAL: Manuel Galrinho BENTO; Minervino José Lopes PIETRA, ANTÓNIO José BASTOS LOPES, HUMBERTO Manuel Jesus COELHO (Cap), Augusto Soares INÁCIO, António Augusto Silva VELOSO, António Luis Alves Ribeiro OLIVEIRA, João António Ferreira Resende ALVES, SHÉU Han, Tamagnini Manuel Gomes Batista NÉNÉ, Fernando Mendes Soares GOMES (74 Luis Maria Cabral NORTON MATOS). Trainer: Otto Glória

Goals: Néné (15), Oliveira (90)

POLAND v FINLAND 1-1 (1-1)

Dziesieciolecia, Warszawa 17.04.1983

Referee: Reidar Bjørnstad (NOR) Attendance: 70,000

POLAND: Józef Mlynarczyk; Stefan Majewski, Pawel Janas, Roman Wójcicki, Jan Jalocha; Andrzej Buncol, Janusz Kupcewicz, Wlodzimierz Ciolek (65 Kazimierz Buda); Wlodzimierz Smolarek (Cap), Zbigniew Boniek, Miroslaw Okonski. Trainer: Antoni Piechniczek

FINLAND: Olli Isoaho; Esa Pekonen, Pauno Kymäläinen (Cap), Mikael Granskog, Ilkka Remes (41 Aki Lahtinen); Hannu Turunen, Atik Ismail, Kari Ukkonen, Leo Houtsonen; Tuomo Hakala, Mika Lipponen (66 Ari Hjelm).
Trainer: Martti Kuusela

Goals: Smolarek (2), Janas (5 og)

PORTUGAL v POLAND 2-1 (1-0)

Estádio da Luz, Lisboa 10.10.1982

Referee: Franz Wöhrer (AUS) Attendance: 70,000

PORTUGAL: Manuel BENTO; Minervino PIETRA, HUMBERTO COELHO (Cap), ANTÓNIO BASTOS LOPES; Augusto INáCIO, António VELOSO, CARLOS MANUEL Correia dos Santos, João ALVES (35 António Manuel FRASCO Vieira); Tamagnini NÉNÉ, António OLIVEIRA (89 José Alberto COSTA), Fernando GOMES.
Trainer: Otto Martins Gloria (BRA)

POLAND: Jacek Kazimierski; Stefan Majewski (Cap), Pawel Janas, Pawel Krol, Jan Jalocha; Andrzej Buncol, Roman Wójcicki, Józef Adamiec, Zbigniew Boniek; Dariusz Dziekanowski, Wlodzimierz Mazur (46 Marek Dziuba).
Trainer: Antoni Piechniczek

Goals: Néné (2), Gomes (81), Król (90)

USSR v PORTUGAL 5-0 (2-0)

V.I.Lenin, Moskva 27.04.1983

Referee: John Hunting (ENG) Attendance: 90,000

USSR: Renat Dasaev; Vladimir Bessonov, Aleksandr Chivadze (Cap), Anatoliy Demianenko, Sergei Baltacha, Fëdor Cherenkov, Nikolai Larionov, Tengiz Sulakvelidze, Khoren Oganesian (74 Leonid Buriak), Sergei Rodionov (78 Ramaz Shengelia), Oleg Blohin. Trainer: Valeriy Lobanovski

PORTUGAL: Manuel BENTO; Minervino PIETRA, HUMBERTO COELHO (Cap), ANTÓNIO BASTOS LOPES, JOÃO Soares CARDOSO, Fernando António de Carvalho FESTAS (46 José COSTA), CARLOS MANUEL, João ALVES, JAIME Moreira PACHECO, Fernando GOMES, Tamagnini NÉNÉ. Trainer: Otto Glória

Goals: Cherenkov (16, 64), Rodionov (40), Demianenko (53), Larionov (86)

POLAND v USSR 1-1 (1-0)

Slaski, Chorzów 22.05.1983

Referee: Luigi Agnolin (ITA) Attendance: 75,000

POLAND: Józef Mlynarczyk; Stefan Majewski, Pawel Janas, Roman Wójcicki, Jan Jalocha; Adam Kensy, Jerzy Wijas, Janusz Kupcewicz (75 Andrzej Iwan), Andrzej Buncol; Zbigniew Boniek, Wlodzimierz Smolarek (81 Dariusz Dziekanowski). Trainer: Antoni Piechniczek

USSR: Renat Dasaev; Vladimir Bessonov, Aleksandr Chivadze (Cap), Anatoliy Demianenko, Sergei Baltacha, Sergei Borovski, Tengiz Sulakvelidze, Fëdor Cherenkov, Khoren Oganesian (86 Andrei Bal), Nikolai Larionov, Oleg Blohin (75 Sergei Andreev). Trainer: Valeriy Lobanovski

Goals: Boniek (19), Wojcicki (63 og)

FINLAND v USSR 0-1 (0-0)

Helsinki 01.06.1983

Referee: Dusan Krchnak (CZE) Attendance: 16,966

FINLAND: Olli Huttunen; Aki Lahtinen, Pauno Kymäläinen, Mikael Granskog, Esa Pekonen, Hannu Turunen, Leo Houtsonen, Kari Ukkonen, Pasi Rautiainen, Atik Ismail (65 Tuomo Hakala), Ari Valvee. Trainer: Martti Kuusela

USSR: Renat Dasaev; Tengiz Sulakvelidze, Aleksandr Chivadze (Cap), Anatoliy Demianenko, Sergei Baltacha (26 Andrei Bal), Nikolai Larionov, Leonid Buriak, Khoren Oganesian, Ramaz Shengelia (74 Sergei Andreev), Fëdor Cherenkov, Oleg Blohin. Trainer: Valeriy Lobanovski

Goal: Blohin (75)

PORTUGAL v FINLAND 5-0 (2-0)

Estádio José Alvalade, Lisboa 21.09.1983

Referee: Karl-Heinz Tritschler (W. GER) Attendance: 15,000

PORTUGAL: Manuel BENTO; Minervino PIETRA, António José LIMA PEREIRA, ANTÓNIO BASTOS LOPES, Augusto INACIO, JOSÉ LUIS Lopes da Costa e Silva, CALOS MANUEL, António OLIVEIRA, JAIME PACHECO (60 Paulo Jorge Santos FUTRE), Fernando GOMES, Rui Manuel Trindade JORDAO (46 Tamagnini NÉNÉ). Trainer: Fernando Cabrita

FINLAND: Pertti Alaja; Esa Pekonen, Jukka Ikäläinen, Mikael Granskog, Erkka Petaja, Hannu Turunen, Leo Houtsonen, Kari Ukkonen, Kari Virtanen, Mika Lipponen, Keijo Kousa. Trainer: Martti Kuusela

Goals: Jordao (18), Carlos Manuel (23), Ikäläinen (46 og), José Luis (82), Oliveira (87)

USSR v POLAND 2-0 (1-0)

V.I.Lenin, Moskva 09.10.1983

Referee: Johannes Jan Keizer (HOL) Attendance: 73,000

USSR: Renat Dasaev; Tengiz Sulakvelidze, Aleksandr Chivadze (Cap), Anatoliy Demianenko, Sergei Baltacha; Andrei Bal, Vadim Evtushenko (46 Aleksandr Tarkhanov), Khoren Oganesian; Iuri Gavrilov (82 Leonid Buriak), Fëdor Cherenkov, Oleg Blohin. Trainer: Valeriy Lobanovski

POLAND: Józef Mlynarczyk (Cap); Stefan Majewski, Roman Wójcicki, Pawel Król, Krzysztof Urbanowicz; Kazimierz Buda, Jerzy Wijas, Adam Kensy, Andrzej Buncol (28 Waldemar Prusik); Zbigniew Boniek, Wlodzimierz Smolarek (71 Dariusz Dziekanowski). Trainer: Antoni Piechniczek

Goals: Demianenko (10), Blohin (62)

POLAND v PORTUGAL 0-1 (0-1)

Olimpijski, Wroclaw 28.10.1983

Referee: Ulf Eriksson (SWE) Attendance: 15,000

POLAND: Józef Mlynarczyk (Cap); Stefan Majewski, Roman Wójcicki, Jerzy Wijas, Jan Jalocha; Adam Kensy (67 Andrzej Palasz), Wlodzimierz Ciolek, Waldemar Prusik, Marek Ostrowski (46 Miroslaw Okonski); Andrzej Iwan, Wlodzimierz Smolarek. Trainer: Antoni Piechniczek

PORTUGAL: Manuel BENTO; JOÃO Domingos da Silva PINTO, LIMA PEREIRA, EURICO Monteiro Gomes, Augusto INACIO; JOSÉ LUIS, CALOS MANUEL, JAIME PACHECO, José COSTA (46 José Elden Araújo Lobo Junior "LITO"); Tamagnini NÉNÉ (80 DIAMANTINO Manuel Fernandes Miranda), Fernando GOMES. Trainer: Fernando Cabrita

Goal: Carlos Manuel (31)

PORTUGAL v USSR 1-0 (1-0)

Estádio da Luz, Lisboa 13.11.1983

Referee: Georges Konrath (FRA) Attendance: 75,000

PORTUGAL: Manuel BENTO; JOÃO PINTO, LIMA PEREIRA, EURICO Gomes, Augusto INACIO, JOSÉ LUIS, CALOS MANUEL, JAIME PACHECO, Fernando Albino Sousa CHALANA (78 SHÉU Han), Fernando GOMES, Rui JORDAO (73 DIAMANTINO Miranda). Trainer: Fernando Cabrita

USSR: Renat Dasaev; Sergei Borovski, Aleksandr Chivadze (Cap), Anatoliy Demianenko, Sergei Baltacha, Andrei Bal, Sergei Rodionov (71 Vadim Evtushenko), Tengiz Sulakvelidze, Iuri Gavrilov (59 Khoren Oganesian), Fëdor Cherenkov, Oleg Blohin. Trainer: Valeriy Lobanovski

Goal: Jordao (42 pen)

	P	W	D	L	F	A	Pts
Portugal	6	5	0	1	11	6	10
USSR	6	4	1	1	11	2	9
Poland	6	1	2	3	6	9	4
Finland	6	0	1	5	3	14	1

GROUP 3

DENMARK v ENGLAND 2-2 (0-1)

Idraetsparken, København 22.09.1982

Referee: Cherles Corver (HOL) Attendance: 44,300

DENMARK: Troels Rasmussen; Ole Rasmussen, Per Røntved, Søren Busk, Ivan Nielsen, Søren Lerby, Jens J.Bertelsen, Jesper Olsen, Allan Hansen, Preben Elkjær, Lars Bastrup. Trainer: Josef Piontek

ENGLAND: Peter Shilton; Philip Neal, Kenneth Sansom, Ray Wilkins, Russell Osman, Terence Butcher, Anthony Morley, Bryan Robson, Paul Mariner, Trevor Francis, Graham Rix (83 Ricky Hill). Manager: Robert Robson

Goals: Francis (8, 81 pen), A. Hansen (69 pen), J. Olsen (90)

GREECE v ENGLAND 0-3 (0-1)

Kautatzogleio, Thessaloniki 17.11.1982

Referee: Adolf Prokop (E. GER) Attendance: 41,534

GREECE: Nikos Sargkanis; Giannis Gounaris, Anthimos Kapsis (Cap), Giorgos Foiros, Kostas Iosifidis, Petros Mihos, Spiros Livathinos, Anastasios Mitropoulos, Hristos Ardizoglou (40 Giorgos Kostikos), Nikos Anastopoulos, Thomas Mauros (77 Savvas Kofidis). Trainer: Vasilis Arhondidis

ENGLAND: Peter Shilton; Philip Neal, Kenneth Sansom, Philip Thompson, Alvin Martin, Bryan Robson, Samuel Lee, Gary Mabbutt, Paul Mariner, Anthony Woodcock, Anthony Morley. Manager: Robert Robson

Goals: Woodcock (2, 64), Lee (68)

LUXEMBOURG v GREECE 0-2 (0-2)

Stade Municipal, Luxembourg 09.10.1982

Referee: Karl-Heinz Tritschler (W. GER) Attendance: 5,000

LUXEMBOURG: Jeannot Moes (Cap); Michel Bechet (46 Romain Schreiner), Johny Clemens, Nico Rohmann, Hubert Meunier, Jean-Paul Girres (65 Marcel Di Domenico), Guy Hellers, Carlo Weis, Gilbert Dresch, Jeannot Reiter, Robert Langers. Trainer: Louis Pilot

GREECE: Nikos Sargkanis; Giannis Gounaris, Kostas Iosifidis, Giorgos Foiros, Anthimos Kapsis (Cap), Spiros Livathinos, Petros Mihos, Kostas Kouis (85 Giorgos Kostikos), Nikos Anastopoulos, Apostolos Papaioannou (62 Savvas Kofidis), Takis Dimopoulos. Trainer: Vasilis Arhondidis

Goals: Anastopoulos (6 pen, 25)

ENGLAND v LUXEMBOURG 9-0 (4-0)

Wembley, London 15.12.1982

Referee: Hreidar Jónsson (ICE) Attendance: 35,000

ENGLAND: Raymond Clemence; Philip Neal, Kenneth Sansom, Samuel Lee, Terence Butcher, Alvin Martin, Bryan Robson, Gary Mabbutt (74 Glenn Hoddle), Luther Blissett, Anthony Woodcock, Steven Coppell (67 Mark Chamberlain). Manager: Robert Robson

LUXEMBOURG: Jeannot Moes (Cap); Jean-Paul Girres, Nico Rohmann, Hubert Meunier, Johny Clemens, Marcel Bossi, Guy Hellers, Carlo Weis, Gilbert Dresch, Jeannot Reiter, Marcel Di Domenico (46 Alain Nurenberg). Trainer: Louis Pilot

Goals: Moes (18 og), Coppell (21), Woodcock (34), Blissett (44, 53, 86), Chamberlain (72), Hoddle (88), Neal (90)

LUXEMBOURG v DENMARK 1-2 (0-1)

Stade Municipal, Luxembourg 10.11.1982

Referee: Gérard Biguet (FRA) Attendance: 2,057

LUXEMBOURG: Jeannot Moes (Cap); Jean-Paul Girres, Hubert Meunier, Johny Clemens, Nico Rohmann, Guy Hellers, Carlo Weis, Robert Langers, Gilbert Dresch, Jeannot Reiter (84 Romain Schreiner), Marcel Di Domenico (73 Manou Scheitler). Trainer: Louis Pilot

DENMARK: Ole Qvist; Ole Rasmussen, Ivan Nielsen, Per Røntved, Søren Busk, Søren Lerby, Morten Olsen, John Lauridsen, Jesper Olsen (88 Morten Donnerup), Preben Elkjær (28 Klaus Berggreen), Lars Bastrup.
Trainer: Josef Piontek

Goals: Lerby (30 pen), Di Domenico (54), Berggreen (67)

LUXEMBOURG v HUNGARY 2-6 (1-2)

Stade Municipal, Luxembourg 27.03.1983

Referee: Gerard Geurds (HOL) Attendance: 4,000

LUXEMBOURG: Jeannot Moes; Romain Michaux, Marcel Bossi, Gilbert Dresch, Hubert Meunier; Jean-Paul Girres, Carlo Weis, Robert Langers, Alfred Schreiner (62 Alain Nurenberg); Romain Schreiner, Jeannot Reiter. Trainer: Louis Pilot

HUNGARY: Béla Katzirz; Zoltán Péter, Attila Kerekes, Imre Garaba, József Tóth, Péter Hannich, Tibor Nyilasi, József Póczik, László Fazekas (.. László Kiss), András Töröcsik (.. Gyula Hajszán), Gábor Pölöskei.

Goals: Reiter (3), Póczik (30, 59, 70), Nyilasi (40), Pölöskei (51), R. Schreiner (55), Hannich (57 pen)

ENGLAND v GREECE 0-0

Wembley, London 30.03.1983

Referee: Dusan Krchnak (CZE) Attendance: 50,000

ENGLAND: Peter Shilton; Philip Neal, Kenneth Sansom, Samuel Lee, Alvin Martin, Terence Butcher, Steven Coppell, Gary Mabbutt, Trevor Francis, Anthony Woodcock (72 Luther Blissett), Alan Devonshire (72 Graham Rix). Manager: Robert Robson

GREECE: Nikos Sargkanis; Giannis Gounaris (Cap), Nikos Karoulias, Giannis Gkalitsios, Petros Mihos, Haralampos Xanthopoulos, Vaggelis Kousoulakis, Anastasios Mitropoulos (76 Giannis Dontas), Kostas Kouis, Anastopoulos (85 Hristos Ardizoglou), Giorgos Kostikos. Trainer: Vasilis Arhondidis

ENGLAND v HUNGARY 2-0 (1-0)

Wembley, London 27.04.1983

Referee: Pietro D'Elia (ITA) Attendance: 60,000

ENGLAND: Peter Shilton; Philip Neal, Kenneth Sansom, Samuel Lee, Alvin Martin, Terence Butcher, Gary Mabbutt, Trevor Francis, Peter Withe, Luther Blissett, Gordon Cowans. Manager: Robert Robson

HUNGARY: Béla Katzirz; Gyözö Martos (.. Gyözö Burcsa), István Kocsis, Imre Garaba, József Tóth, Péter Hannich, Tibor Nyilasi, József Kardos, József Varga, László Kiss (.. András Töröcsik), Gyula Hajszán.

Goals: Francis (32), Withe (65)

HUNGARY v LUXEMBOURG 6-2 (3-0)

Népstadion, Budapest 17.04.1983

Referee: Edgar Azzopardi (MAL) Attendance: 15,000

HUNGARY: Béla Katzirz; Zoltán Péter, Attila Kerekes, Imre Garaba, József Tóth, Péter Hannich, Tibor Nyilasi, József Póczik (.. Gyözö Burcsa), Gyula Hajszán, László Kiss, Gábor Pölöskei (27 Lázár Szentes).

LUXEMBOURG: Jean-Paul Defrang; Romain Michaux, Marcel Bossi, Gilbert Dresch, Hubert Meunier; Jean-Paul Girres, Romain Schreiner, Carlo Weis, Alfred Schreiner (46 Alain Nurenberg); Jeannot Reiter, Théo Malget (68 Nico Wagner). Trainer: Louis Pilot

Goals: Hajszán (22), Nyilasi (34, 63), L. Kiss (38), Reiter (57), Malget (58), Szentes (61), Burcsa (66)

HUNGARY v GREECE 2-3 (1-2)

Népstadion, Budapest 15.05.1983

Referee: Eduard Sostaric (YUG) Attendance: 13,000

HUNGARY: Gábor Zsiborás; Gyözö Martos (41 Károly Jancsika), István Kocsis, Imre Garaba, József Varga, Zoltán Ebedli, József Kardos, József Póczik, Béla Bodonyi (46 László Szokolai), Tibor Nyilasi, Gyula Hajszán.

GREECE: Nikos Sargkanis; Giorgos Skartados (74 Stelios Manolas), Giannis Gkalitsios, Petros Mihos, Nikos Vamvakoulas, Vaggelis Kousoulakis (67 Hristos Ardizoglou), Giorgos Kostikos, Nikos Anastopoulos (Cap), Nikos Alavantas, Anastasios Mitropoulos, Apostolos Papaioannou. Trainer: Vasilis Arhondidis

Goals: Anastopoulos (16), Nyilasi (25), Kostikos (33), Papaioannou (51), Hajszán (89)

DENMARK v GREECE 1-0 (0-0)

Idraetsparken, København 27.04.1983

Referee: Romualdas Yushka (USSR) Attendance: 35,000

DENMARK: Ole Kjær; Ole Rasmussen, Søren Busk, Morten Olsen, Ole Madsen, Jens J.Bertelsen, John Lauridsen, Allan Simonsen (80 John Sivebaek), Jesper Olsen (46 Lars Bastrup), Preben Elkjær, Klaus Berggreen. Trainer: Josef Piontek

GREECE: Giorgos Plitsis; Nikos Vamvakoulas (80 Hristos Ardizoglou), Nikos Karoulias, Petros Mihos, Giannis Gkalitsios, Haralampos Xanthopoulos, Vaggelis Kousoulakis, Kostas Kouis (18 Giorgos Kostikos), Nikos Anastopoulos (Cap), Anastasios Mitropoulos, Apostolos Papaioannou. Trainer: Vasilis Arhondidis

Goal: Busk (76)

DENMARK v HUNGARY 3-1 (1-1)

Idraetspark, København 01.06.1983

Referee: Heinz Fahnler (AUS) Attendance: 50,000

DENMARK: Ole Kjær; Ole Rasmussen, Ivan Nielsen, Morten Olsen, Ole Madsen, Jens J.Bertelsen, John Lauridsen (14 Jesper Olsen), Allan Simonsen, Søren Lerby, Preben Elkjær (76 Kenneth Brylle), Klaus Berggreen. Trainer: Josef Piontek

HUNGARY: Béla Katzirz; Gyözö Martos, István Kocsis, Imre Garaba, József Tóth, Péter Hannich, Tibor Nyilasi, József Póczik, László Kiss (.. Lázár Szentes), András Töröcsik (.. József Kardos), Gyula Hajszán.

Goals: Elkjær (2), Nyilasi (30), J. Olsen (81), Simonsen (85 pen)

ENGLAND v DENMARK 0-1 (0-1)

Wembley, London 21.09.1983

Referee: Alexis Ponnet (BEL) Attendance: 80,000

ENGLAND: Peter Shilton; Philip Neal, Kenneth Sansom, Ray Wilkins, Russell Osman, Terence Butcher, Trevor Francis, Samuel Lee (78 Luther Blissett), Paul Mariner, John Gregory, John Barnes (68 Mark Chamberlain).
Manager: Robert Robson

DENMARK: Ole Kjær; Ole Rasmussen, Ivan Nielsen, Morten Olsen (86 Jan Mølby), Søren Busk, Søren Lerby, Jens J.Bertelsen, Jesper Olsen, Allan Simonsen, Michael Laudrup (74 Preben Elkjær), Klaus Berggreen. Trainer: Josef Piontek

Goal: Simonsen (36 pen)

HUNGARY v DENMARK 1-0 (0-0)

Népstadion, Budapest 26.10.1983

Referee: Emilio Carlos Guruceta Muro (SPA) Att: 8000

HUNGARY: Attila Kovács; József Csuhay, Gábor Köhalmi, Antal Róth, József Varga, Péter Hannich, József Kardos (.. Antal Nagy), András Töröcsik (.. László Dajka), Ferenc Csongrádi, Sándor Kiss, Gábor Pölöskei.

DENMARK: Ole Kjær; Søren Busk, Ivan Nielsen, Morten Olsen, Søren Lerby, John Lauridsen (.. Preben Elkjær), Jens J.Bertelsen, Allan Simonsen, Jesper Olsen, Klaus Berggreen, Michael Laudrup. Trainer: Josef Piontek

Goal: S. Kiss (58)

DENMARK v LUXEMBOURG 6-0 (4-0)

Idraetsparken, København 12.10.1983

Referee: Kaj John Natri (FIN) Attendance: 44,700

DENMARK: Ole Kjær; Søren Busk, Morten Olsen, Ivan Nielsen, John Lauridsen, Jens J.Bertelsen, Allan Simonsen, Jesper Olsen, Klaus Berggreen (85 Per Frimann), Michael Laudrup, Preben Elkjær (87 Flemming Christensen).
Trainer: Josef Piontek

LUXEMBOURG: Jean-Paul Defrang; Jean-Paul Girres (46 Romain Michaux), Marcel Bossi, Gilbert Dresch, Nico Wagner, Alain Nurenberg, Guy Hellers, Carlo Weis, Jean-Pierre Barboni, Jeannot Reiter, Romain Schreiner (65 Théo Malget).
Trainer: Louis Pilot

Goals: Laudrup (17, 24, 70), Elkjær (37, 58), Simonsen (42)

LUXEMBOURG v ENGLAND 0-4 (0-2)

Stade Municipal, Luxembourg 16.11.1983

Referee: Cornelis Bakker (HOL) Attendance: 12,000

LUXEMBOURG: Jean-Paul Defrang; Romain Michaux; Marcel Bossi, Gilbert Dresch, Hubert Meunier, Robert Langers, Nico Wagner, Guy Hellers, Jean-Pierre Barboni (71 Gérard Jeitz), Jeannot Reiter, Théo Malget (56 Jean-Paul Girres).
Trainer: Louis Pilot

ENGLAND: Raymond Clemence; Duxbury, Kenneth Sansom, Samuel Lee, Alvin Martin, Terence Butcher, Bryan Robson, Glenn Hoddle, Paul Mariner, Anthony Woodcock (22 John Barnes), Alan Devonshire. Manager: Robert Robson

Goals: Robson (11,56), Mariner (39), Butcher (50)

HUNGARY v ENGLAND 0-3 (0-3)

Népstadion, Budapest 12.10.1983

Referee: Bruno Galler (SWI) Attendance: 25,000

HUNGARY: Attila Kovács; Gyula Csonka, József Kardos, Imre Garaba, József Varga, Péter Hannich (.. László Szokolai), Ferenc Csongrádi, Tibor Nyilasi, Gyözö Burcsa (.. Antal Nagy), László Dajka, Gyula Hajszán.

ENGLAND: Peter Shilton; John Gregory, Kenneth Sansom, Samuel Lee, Alvin Martin, Terence Butcher, Bryan Robson, Luther Blissett (74 Peter Withe), Paul Mariner, Glenn Hoddle, Gary Mabbutt. Manager: Robert Robson

Goals: Hoddle (12), Lee (19), Mariner (40)

GREECE v DENMARK 0-2 (0-1)

Olympiako, Athina 16.11.1983

Referee: Paolo Bergamo (ITA) Attendance: 30,000

GREECE: Nikos Sargkanis; Nikos Karoulias, Giannis Damanakis (38 Dimitris Saravakos), Petros Mihos, Nikos Vamvakoulas, Nikos Alavantas, Anastasios Mitropoulos, Savvas Kofidis, Nikos Anastopoulos, Apostolos Papaioannou, Giorgos Kostikos (61 Takis Dimopoulos).
Trainer: Vasilis Arhondidis

DENMARK: Ole Kjær; Ole Rasmussen (41 John Lauridsen), Morten Olsen, Søren Busk, Ivan Nielsen, Søren Lerby, Jens J.Bertelsen, Jesper Olsen, Allan Simonsen (87 Frank Arnesen), Klaus Berggreen, Preben Elkjær. Trainer: Josef Piontek

Goals: Elkjær (16), Simonsen (47)

GREECE v HUNGARY 2-2 (1-2)

Kautatzogleio, Thessaloniki 03.12.1983

Referee: Ion Igna (ROM) Attendance: 3,000

GREECE: Giorgos Plitsis; Nikos Alavantas, Nikos Karoulias, Haralampos Xanthopoulos, Petros Mihos, Giorgos Semertzidis, Takis Dimopoulos (46 Dimitris Saravakos), Kostas Kouis, Nikos Anastopoulos, Apostolos Papaioannou (74 Savvas Kofidis), Anastasios Mitropoulos.
Trainer: Vasilis Arhondidis

HUNGARY: Attila Kovács; József Csuhay, Gábor Köhalmi, Antal Róth, József Varga, Péter Hannich (.. Gyula Hajszán), József Kardos, Ferenc Csongrádi, Béla Bodonyi, András Töröcsik, László Dajka (.. Imre Garaba).

Goals: Anastopoulos (9, 54), Kardos (12 pen), Töröcsik (34)

GREECE v LUXEMBOURG 1-0 (1-0)

Karaiskaki, Peiraias 14.12.1983

Referee: Velichko Tsonchev (BUL) Attendance: 5,000

GREECE: Nikos Sargkanis; Nikos Alavantas, Nikos Karoulias, Giannis Gkalitsios, Petros Mihos, Giorgos Semertzidis, Dimitris Saravakos, Apostolos Papaioannou (88 Savvas Kofidis), Nikos Anastopoulos, Anastasios Mitropoulos, Takis Dimopoulos (68 Batsinilas). Trainer: Vasilis Arhondidis

LUXEMBOURG: Jean-Paul Defrang; Romain Michaux, Hubert Meunier (46 Dremper), Marcel Bossi, Gilbert Dresch, Jean-Paul Girres, Guy Hellers, Nico Wagner (59 Jean Schmitz), Jean-Pierre Barboni, Robert Langers, Théo Malget.
Trainer: Louis Pilot

Goal: Saravakos (18)

	P	W	D	L	F	A	Pts
Denmark	8	6	1	1	17	5	13
England	8	5	2	1	23	3	12
Greece	8	3	2	3	8	10	8
Hungary	8	3	1	4	18	17	7
Luxembourg	8	0	0	8	5	36	0

GROUP 4

WALES v NORWAY 1-0 (1-0)

Swansea 22.09.1982

Referee: Joël Quiniou (FRA) Attendance: 4,400

WALES: Neville Southall; Christopher Marustik, Paul Price, Nigel Stevenson, Joseph Jones; Robert James, Brian Flynn, Kenneth Jackett; Michael Thomas, Alan Curtis (62 Jeremy Charles), Ian Rush. Manager: Michael England

NORWAY: Per Egil Nygård; Bjarne Berntsen, Terje Kojedal, Åge Hareide, Svein Grøndalen; Roger Albertsen, Tom Lund, Erik Solér, Arne Erlandsen (78 Stein Kollshaugen); Arne Larsen-Ökland, Hallvar Thoresen.

Goal: Rush (30)

NORWAY v YUGOSLAVIA 3-1 (1-0)

Uleval, Oslo 13.10.1982

Referee: Alojzy Jarguz (POL) Attendance: 12,264

NORWAY: Per Egil Nygård; Bjarne Berntsen, Terje Kojedal, Åge Hareide, Svein Grøndalen; Roger Albertsen, Tom Lund, Erik Solér (60 Vidar Davidsen); Hallvar Thoresen, Arne Larsen-Ökland, Arne Dokken (78 Isak Arne Refvik).

YUGOSLAVIA: Ratko Svilar; Zlatko Krmpotic, Nenad Stojkovic, Ismet Hadzic, Milan Jovin (46 Nikica Klincarski); Faruk Hadzibegic, Vladimir Petrovic, Ivan Gudelj; Safet Susic (65 Predrag Pasic), Dusan Savic, Stjepan Deveric.
Trainer: Todor Veselinovic

Goals: Lund (4), Ökland (68), Savic (75), Hareide (89)

BULGARIA v NORWAY 2-2 (1-1)

Vasil Levski, Sofia 27.10.1982

Referee: Andonios Vasaras (GRE) Attendance: 22,300

BULGARIA: Georgi Velinov; Plamen Nikolov, Angel Rangelov, Asen Mihailov, Atanas Marinov (70 Rujdi Kerimov); Georgi Iliev, Tzvedan Ionchev, Georgi Slavkov (59 Spas Djevizov); Boicho Velichkov, Stoicho Mladenov, Radoslav Zdravkov. Trainer: Ivan Vutsov

NORWAY: Per Egil Nygård; Bjarne Berntsen, Terje Kojedal, Åge Hareide (70 Vidar Davidsen), Svein Grøndalen; Kai Erik Herlovsen, Erik Solér, Arne Dokken (61 Isak Arne Refvik); Tom Lund, Arne Larsen-Ökland, Hallvar Thoresen.

Goals: Velichkov (13), Thoresen (17 pen), Ökland (67), Nikolov (68)

BULGARIA v YUGOSLAVIA 0-1 (0-1)

Vasil Levski, Sofia 17.11.1982

Referee: Paolo Casarin (ITA) Attendance: 20,000

BULGARIA: Georgi Velinov; Plamen Nikolov, Radoslav Zdravkov, Vasil Tinchev, Nikolai Grancharov, Georgi Iliev, Tzvetan Ionchev (46 Anio Sadkov), Andrei Jeliazkov, Boicho Velichkov, Plamen Markov (72 Naidenov), Spas Djevizov. Trainer: Ivan Vutsov

YUGOSLAVIA: Svilar; Slavoljub Nikolic (70 Zvjezdan Cvetkovic), Nenad Stojkovic, Ive Jerolimov, Nijaz Ferhatovic, Faruk Hadzibegic, Aleksandar Trifunovic, Zvonko Zivkovic (17 Mitar Mrkela), Ivan Gudelj, Miodrag Jesic, Stjepan Deveric. Trainer: Todor Veselinovic

Goal: N. Stojkovic (36)

NORWAY v BULGARIA 1-2 (1-1)

Ullevi, Oslo 07.09.1983

Referee: Heinz Fahnler (AUS) Attendance: 15,515

NORWAY: Tom R. Jacobsen; Erik Solér, Terje Kojedal, Åge Hareide, Svein Grøndalen; Kai Erik Herlovsen (77 Arne Erlandsen), Roger Albertsen, Anders Giske (56 Sverre Brandhaug), Vidar Davidsen; Arne Dokken, Hallvar Thoresen.

BULGARIA: Borislav Mihailov; Nikolai Arabov, Nasko Sirakov, Georgi Dimitrov, Petar Petrov; Radoslav Zdravkov, Rusi Gochev (64 Bojidar Iskrenov), Jivko Gospodinov; Antim Pehlivanov (85 Georgi Slavkov), Anio Sadkov, Stoicho Mladenov. Trainer: Ivan Vutsov

Goals: Hareide (4), Mladenov (12), Sirakov (60)

YUGOSLAVIA v WALES 4-4 (3-2)

pod Goricom, Titograd 15.12.1982

Referee: Alexis Ponnet (BEL) Attendance: 17,000

YUGOSLAVIA: Svilar; Nenad Stojković, Zvjezdan Cvetković, Aleksandar Trifunović, Nijaz Ferhatovic (82 Bosko Djurovski), Faruk Hadzibegic, Stjepan Deveric (59 Miodrag Jesic), Slavoljub Nikolic, Zlatko Kranjcar, Ivan Gudelj, Zvonko Zivkovic. Trainer: Todor Veselinovic

WALES: William David Davies; Joseph Jones, Kevin Ratcliffe, Peter Nicholas (.. Nigel Vaughan), Paul Terence Price, Kenneth Jackett, Robert James, Brian Flynn, Ian Rush, Michael Thomas (.. Jeremy Charles), John Mahoney.
Manager: Michael England

Goals: Flynn (6), Cvetkovic (14), Zivkovic (18), Kranjcar (36), Rush (39), Jesic (..), Jones (70), R. James (80)

NORWAY v WALES 0-0

Ullevaal, Oslo 21.09.1983

Referee: Vojtech Christov (CZE) Attendance: 17,575

NORWAY: Erik Thorstvedt; Svein Fjaelberg, Terje Kojedal, Åge Hareide, Svein Grøndalen; Roger Albertsen, Vidar Davidsen, Erik Solér; Hallvar Thoresen, Arne Dokken, Stein Kollshaugen.

WALES: Neville Southall; Jeffrey Hopkins, Paul Price, Kevin Ratcliffe, Joseph Jones; Peter Nicholas, Brian Flynn, Nigel Vaughan, Kenneth Jackett; Robert James, Ian Rush.
Manager: Michael England

WALES v BULGARIA 1-0 (0-0)

Racecourse Ground, Wrexham 27.04.1983

Referee: Siegfried Kirschen (E. GER) Attendance: 9,006

WALES: Neville Southall; Joseph Jones, Kevin Ratcliffe, Peter Nicholas, Paul Terence Price, Kenneth Jackett, Robert James, Brian Flynn, Ian Rush (69 Jeremy Charles), Michael Thomas, Gordon Davies. Manager: Michael England

BULGARIA: Georgi Velinov; Plamen Nikolov, Nikolai Arabov, Petar Petrov, Sasho Borisov, Radoslav Zdravkov, Tzvetan Ionchev (83 Bojidar Iskrenov), G. Iordanov (75 Georgi Slavkov), Spas Djevizov, Anio Sadkov, Stoicho Mladenov.
Trainer: Ivan Vutsov

Goal: Charles (79)

YUGOSLAVIA v NORWAY 2-1 (2-0)

JNA, Beograd 12.10.1983

Referee: Adolf Prokop (E. GER) Attendance: 10,000

YUGOSLAVIA: Zoran Simovic; Zoran Vujovic, Luka Peruzovic, Ljubomir Radanovic, Nenad Stojkovic (51 Mirza Kapetanovic); Zoran Bojovic, Blaz Sliskovic (89 Dusan Pesic), Ivan Gudelj; Zlatko Vujovic, Safet Susic, Sulejman Halilovic.
Trainer: Todor Veselinovic

NORWAY: Tom R.Jacobsen; Svein Fjaelberg, Terje Kojedal, Åge Hareide, Svein Grøndalen; Kai Erik Herlovsen, Vidar Davidsen, Erik Solér; Svein Mathisen (59 Tom Sundby), Arne Dokken, Hallvar Thoresen.

Goals: Zl. Vujovic (22), Susic (39), Thoresen (88)

BULGARIA v WALES 1-0 (0-0)

Vasil Levski, Sofia 16.11.1983

Referee: Dieter Pauly (W. GER) Attendance: 5,000

BULGARIA: Borislav Mihailov; Nasko Sirakov, Nikolai Arabov, Petar Petrov, Georgi Dimitrov, Radoslav Zdravkov, Bojidar Iskrenov, Anio Sadkov, Tzvetan Danov (46 Rusi Gochev), Jivko Gospodinov (88 Sasho Borisov), Stoicho Mladenov. Trainer: Ivan Vutsov

WALES: Neville Southall; Jeffrey Hopkins, Paul Terence Price, Kevin Ratcliffe, Joseph Jones; Brian Flynn, Peter Nicholas (59 Jeremy Charles), Michael Thomas, Nigel Vaughan, Robert James, Ian Rush. Manager: Michael England

Goal: Gochev (53)

WALES v YUGOSLAVIA 1-1 (0-0)

Ninian Park, Cardiff 14.12.1983

Referee: Erik Fredriksson (SWE) Attendance: 20,000

WALES: Neville Southall; Jeffrey Hopkins, Joseph Jones, Nigel Vaughan, Paul Terence Price, Kevin Ratcliffe, Robert James, Brian Flynn (.. Jeremy Charles), Ian Rush, Michael Thomas, Kenneth Jackett. Manager: Michael England

YUGOSLAVIA: Zoran Simovic; Zoran Vujovic, Branislav Drobnjak, Ljubomir Radanovic, Luka Peruzovic, Srecko Katanec, Zlatko Vujovic (87 Zvjezdan Cvetkovic), Ivan Gudelj, Safet Susic, Mehmed Bazdarevic, Marko Mlinarić (77 Sulejman Halilovic). Trainer: Todor Veselinovic

Goals: R. James (52), Bazdarevic (81)

YUGOSLAVIA v BULGARIA 3-2 (1-1)

Poljud, Split 21.12.1983

Referee: Augusto Lamo Castillo (SPA) Attendance: 30,000

YUGOSLAVIA: Zoran Simovic; Zoran Vujovic, Miodrag Jesic, Srecko Katanec, Luka Peruzovic, Ljubomir Radanovic, Zlatko Vujovic, Mehmed Bazdarevic, Safet Susic, Ivan Gudelj (68 Sulejman Halilovic), Marko Mlinaric.
Trainer: Todor Veselinovic

BULGARIA: Borislav Mihailov, Nasko Sirakov, Nikolai Arabov, Petar Petrov, Georgi Dimitrov, Radoslav Zdravkov, Bojidar Iskrenov, Anio Sadkov (80 Sasho Borisov), Rusi Gochev, Jivko Gospodinov, Stoicho Mladenov (75 Marinov).
Trainer: Ivan Vutsov

Goals: Iskrenov (29), Susić (31, 52), Dimitrov (61), Radanović (90)

	P	W	D	L	F	A	Pts
Yugoslavia	6	3	2	1	12	11	8
Wales	6	2	3	1	7	6	7
Bulgaria	6	2	1	3	7	8	5
Norway	6	1	2	3	7	8	4

GROUP 5

ROMANIA v CYPRUS 3-1 (2-1)

Corvinul, Hunedoara 01.05.1982

Referee: Arsen Hoxha (ALB) Attendance: 15,000

ROMANIA: Dumitru Moraru; Mircea Rednic, Costică Ştefănescu, Gino Iorgulescu, Ioan Bogdan; Aurel Ţicleanu (46 Ion Petcu), Ladislau Bölöni, Ilie Balaci; Romulus Gabor, Rodion Cămătaru, Florea Văetuş (66 Ionel Augustin).
Trainer: Mircea Lucescu

CYPRUS: Andreas Constantinou; Nikos Patikkis, Klitos Erotokritou, Stefanos Lyssandrou, George Kezos; Filippos Demetriou (75 Chrysanthos Lagos "Faketti"), Nikos Pantziaras (Cap), Stavros Papadopoulos, Theofanis Theofanous; Nikos Prokopi (26 Yiannakis Yiangoudakis), Fivos Vrahimis.
Trainer: Kostas Talianos

Goals: Văetuş (16), Cămătaru (19), Vrahimis (29), Bölöni (71)

ROMANIA v SWEDEN 2-0 (1-0)

23 August, Bucureşti 08.09.1982

Referee: Eduard Sostaric (YUG) Attendance: 50,000

ROMANIA: Dumitru Moraru; Mircea Rednic, Ioan Andonie, Gino Iorgulescu, Nicolae Ungureanu; Ladislau Bölöni, Aurel Ţicleanu, Michael Klein (85 Alexandru Custoff); Ilie Balaci (Cap), Romulus Gabor (69 Sorin Cîrţu), Dudu Georgescu.
Trainer: Mircea Lucescu

SWEDEN: Thomas Ravelli; Stig Fredriksson, Sven Dahlqvist, Glenn Hysén (80 Greger Hallén), Ingemar Erlandsson (Cap); Peter Nilsson, Hans Borg, Karl Gunnar Björklund; Thomas Larsson (86 Jan Svensson), Dan Corneliusson, Michael Andersson. Trainer: Lars Arnesson

Sent off: Nilsson (49)

Goals: Andonie (25), Klein (47)

CZECHOSLOVAKIA v SWEDEN 2-2 (0-0)

Bratislava 06.10.1982

Referee: Robert Valentine (SCO) Attendance: 14,977

CZECHOSLOVAKIA: Zdenek Hruska; Frantisek Jakubec, Jan Fiala, Ladislav Jurkemik, Jiri Ondra, Karol Brezík (46 Pavel Chaloupka), Peter Zelensky, Jan Berger, Petr Janecka, Václav Danek (77 Milan Luhovy), Lubomír Pokluda.
Trainer: Frantisek Havranek

SWEDEN: Thomas Ravelli; Andreas Ravelli, Glenn Hysén, Sven Dahlqvist, Ingemar Erlandsson, Tony Persson (61 Karl Gunnar Björklund), Robert Prytz, Michael Andersson, Jan Svensson (61 Mats Jingblad), Glenn Strömberg, Ulf Eriksson.

Goals: Janecka (51, 55), Jingblad (89), Eriksson (90)

CYPRUS v SWEDEN 0-1 (0-1)

Makarion, Nicosia 13.11.1982

Referee: Neil Midgley (ENG) Attendance: 8,000

CYPRUS: Andreas Constantinou; Nikos Patikkis, Costas Miamiliotis, Lefteris Kouis, Nikos Pantziaras (Cap), Yiannakis Yiangoudakis, Christakis Omirou Mavris (65 Panikos Hadjiloizou), Filippos Demetriou, Fivos Vrahimis (71 Costas Vasiliou), Andreas Christodoulou, Theofanis Theofanous.

SWEDEN: Thomas Ravelli; Glenn Hysén, Ingemar Erlandsson, Sten Ove Ramberg, Klas Johansson, Robert Prytz, Glenn Strömberg (73 Andreas Ravelli), Michael Andersson, Håkan Sandberg, Dan Corneliusson, Tommy Holmgren (61 Lennart Nilsson).

Goal: Corneliusson (34)

CYPRUS v ITALY 1-1 (0-0)

Tsirion, Limassol 12.02.1983

Referee: Bogdan Dochev (BUL) Attendance: 25,000

CYPRUS: Andreas Constantinou; Nikos Patikkis, George Kezos; Yiannakis Yiangoudakis, Klitos Erotokritou, Nikos Pantziaras (Cap), Christakis Omirou Mavris, Lefteris Kouis (75 Costas Vasiliou), George Savvides, Andreas Christodoulou (83 Michalis Karseras), Theofanis Theofanous.
Trainer: V. Spasov

ITALY: Dino Zoff (Cap); Claudio Gentile, Antonio Cabrini; Gabriele Oriali (46 Carlo Ancelotti), Fulvio Collovati, Gaetano Scirea; Franco Causio, Marco Tardelli, Paolo Rossi, Giancarlo Antognoni, Francesco Graziani. Trainer: Vincenzo Bearzot

Goals: Mavris (47), Patikkis (57 og)

ITALY v CZECHOSLOVAKIA 2-2 (1-1)

Stadio Giuseppe Meazza, Milano 13.11.1982

Referee: Charles Corver (HOL) Attendance: 72,386

ITALY: Dino Zoff (Cap); Giuseppe Bergomi, Claudio Gentile; Giampiero Marini, Fulvio Collovati, Gaetano Scirea; Bruno Conti, Marco Tardelli (77 Giuseppe Dossena), Paolo Rossi, Giancarlo Antognoni, Alessandro Altobelli.
Trainer: Vincenzo Bearzot

CZECHOSLOVAKIA: Ludek Miklosko; Ján Kapko, Frantisek Jakubec; Jirí Sloup, Zdenek Prokes, Jan Fiala (Cap); Petr Janecka (71 Ladislav Vízek), Pavel Chaloupka, Milan Cermák (88 Karel Jarolím), Peter Zelensky, Jaroslav Nemec.
Trainer: Frantisek Havranek

Goals: Altobelli (13), Sloup (26), Kapko (65 og), Chaloupka (70)

CYPRUS v CZECHOSLOVAKIA 1-1 (1-0)

Nicosia 27.03.1983

Referee: Stjepan Glavina (YUG) Attendance: 12,000

CYPRUS: Andreas Constantinou; Costas Miamiliotis, Nikos Pantziaras, Klitos Erotokritou, George Kezos (70 Andreas Andreou), Lefteris Kouis (72 Filippos Demetriou), Michalis Karseras, Yiannakis Yiangoudakis, Christakis Omirou Mavris, George Savvides, Theofanis Theofanous.

CZECHOSLOVAKIA: Zdenek Hruska; Stanislav Levy, Zdenek Prokes, Jan Fiala, Frantisek Jakubec, Karel Jarolím (81 Zdenek Scasny), Peter Zelensky, Pavel Chaloupka, Vlastimil Petrzela (56 Premysl Bicovsky), Milan Cermák, Ladislav Vízek.
Trainer: Frantisek Havranek

Goals: Theofanous (21), Bicovsky (59)

ITALY v ROMANIA 0-0

Stadio Comunale, Firenze 04.12.1982

Referee: Georges Konrath (FRA) Attendance: 50,478

ITALY: Dino Zoff (Cap); Claudio Gentile, Fulvio Collovati, Franco Baresi, Gabriele Oriali; Marco Tardelli, Giancarlo Antognoni, Giampiero Marini, Bruno Conti, Paolo Rossi (46 Franco Causio), Francesco Graziani (19 Alessandro Altobelli).
Trainer: Vincenzo Bearzot

ROMANIA: Silviu Lung; Mircea Rednic, Gino Iorgulescu, Costică Ştefănescu (Cap), Nicolae Ungureanu; Aurel Ţicleanu, Ladislau Bölöni, Ilie Balaci, Michael Klein; Romulus Gabor (58 Ioan Andonie), Rodion Cămătaru (85 Ionel Augustin).
Trainer: Mircea Lucescu

Sent off: Ţicleanu (55)

ROMANIA v ITALY 1-0 (1-0)

23 August, Bucureşti 16.04.1983

Referee: Michel Vautrot (FRA) Attendance: 80,000

ROMANIA: Dumitru Moraru; Mircea Rednic, Gino Iorgulescu, Costică Ştefănescu (Cap), Nicolae Ungureanu; Ionel Augustin (70 Ioan Andonie), Ladislau Bölöni, Michael Klein, Ilie Balaci; Ion Geolgău (87 Sorin Cîrţu), Rodion Cămătaru. Trainer: Mircea Lucescu

ITALY: Dino Zoff (Cap); Claudio Gentile, Fulvio Collovati, Gaetano Scirea, Antonio Cabrini, Giampiero Marini, Marco Tardelli, Giancarlo Antognoni (57 Giuseppe Dossena), Bruno Conti, Paolo Rossi, Roberto Bettega (70 Alessandro Altobelli).
Trainer: Vincenzo Bearzot

Goal: Bölöni (24)

CZECHOSLOVAKIA v CYPRUS 6-0 (3-0)

Praha 16.04.1983

Referee: Norbert Rolles (LUX) Attendance: 6,750

CZECHOSLOVAKIA: Zdenek Hruska; Frantisek Jakubec, Ladislav Jurkemik, Zdenek Prokes, Stanislas Levy, Pavel Chaloupka, Premysl Bicovsky, Milan Cermák (70 Zdenek Scasny), Ladislav Vízek, Václav Danek, Zbynek Hotovy. Trainer: Frantisek Havranek

CYPRUS: Haris Constantinou (59 Michalis Pamboris); George Kezos, Nikos Pantziaras, Klitos Erotokritou, Costas Miamiliotis, Filippos Demetriou, Lefteris Kouis, Yiannakis Yiangoudakis, Pavlos Kounnas, Theofanis Theofanous, Christakis Omirou Mavris (46 George Savvides).

Goals: Danek (3), Vízek (29, 47), Prokes (37), Jurkemik (56), Miamiliotis (72 og)

SWEDEN v ITALY 2-0 (1-0)

Nya Ullevi, Göteborg 29.05.1983

Referee: Walter Eschweiler (W. GER) Attendance: 32,860

SWEDEN: Thomas Ravelli; Ingemar Erlandsson (Cap), Glenn Hysén, Sven Dahlqvist, Stig Fredriksson; Ulf Eriksson, Glenn Strömberg, Robert Prytz (82 Sten Ove Ramberg), Tommy Holmgren; Hakan Sandberg (86 Björn Nilsson), Dan Corneliusson. Trainer: L. Arnesson

ITALY: Dino Zoff (Cap); Claudio Gentile, Antonio Cabrini; Gabriele Oriali, Fulvio Collovati, Gaetano Scirea; Bruno Conti, Marco Tardelli, Paolo Rossi, Giancarlo Antognoni (46 Giuseppe Dossena), Francesco Graziani (61 Alessandro Altobelli). Trainer: Vincenzo Bearzot

Goals: Sandberg (32), Strömberg (56)

ROMANIA v CZECHOSLOVAKIA 0-1 (0-1)

23 August, București 15.05.1983

Referee: Alexis Ponnet (BEL) Attendance: 50,000

ROMANIA: Silviu Lung; Mircea Rednic, Gino Iorgulescu, Costică Ştefănescu (Cap), Nicolae Ungureanu; Ionel Augustin, Ladislau Bölöni, Michael Klein, Ilie Balaci; Romulus Gabor (46 Ion Geolgău), Rodion Cămătaru (61 Ioan Andonie). Trainer: Mircea Lucescu

CZECHOSLOVAKIA: Zdenek Hruska; Frantisek Jakubek, Zdenek Prokes, Ladislav Jurkemik, Jan Fiala (Cap); Pavel Chaloupka, Premysl Bicovsky, Peter Zelensky (89 Ludek Kovacík), Stanislav Levy (46 Frantisek Stambacher), Petr Janecka, Ladislav Vízek. Trainer: Frantisek Havranek

Goal: Vizek (40 pen)

SWEDEN v ROMANIA 0-1 (0-1)

Rasunda, Stockholm 09.06.1983

Referee: Adolf Prokop (E. GER) Attendance: 31,474

SWEDEN: Thomas Ravelli; Ingemar Erlandsson, Glenn Hysén, Sven Dahlqvist, Stig Fredriksson; Ulf Eriksson, Glenn Strömberg, Robert Prytz (74 Sten Ove Ramberg), Tommy Holmgren; Hakan Sandberg (22 Björn Nilsson), Dan Corneliusson. Trainer: Lars Arnesson

ROMANIA: Silviu Lung; Mircea Rednic, Gino Iorgulescu, Costică Ştefănescu (Cap), Nicolae Ungureanu; Aurel Ţicleanu (72 Ionel Augustin), Ioan Andonie, Ladislau Bölöni, Michael Klein; Ilie Balaci (89 Ion Geolgău), Rodion Cămătaru. Trainer: Mircea Lucescu

Goal: Cămătaru (29)

SWEDEN v CYPRUS 5-0 (0-0)

Malmö stadium 15.05.1983

Referee: Juhani Smolander (FIN) Attendance: 19,801

SWEDEN: Thomas Ravelli; Ingemar Erlandsson (57 Andreas Ravelli), Glenn Hysén, Sven Dahlqvist, Stig Fredriksson, Robert Prytz, Sten Ove Ramberg, Ulf Eriksson, Hakan Sandberg (.. Björn Nilsson), Dan Corneliusson, Tommy Holmgren.

CYPRUS: Michalis Pamboris; Costas Miamiliotis, George Kezos, Klitos Erotokritou, Nikos Pantziaras (.. Andreas Andreou), Yiannakis Yiangoudakis, Costas Tcherkezos, Filippos Demetriou, George Savvides, Koullis Pantziaras, Theofanis Theofanous (.. Pavlos Kounnas).

Goals: Prytz (53, 76), Corneliusson (57), Hysén (61), Ravelli (72)

SWEDEN v CZECHOSLOVAKIA 1-0 (1-0)

Fotbollstadion, Solna 21.09.1983

Referee: Michel Vautrot (FRA) Attendance: 20,546

SWEDEN: Thomas Ravelli; Ingemar Erlandsson, Glenn Hysén, Sven Dahlqvist, Stig Fredriksson; Ulf Eriksson (74 Sten Ove Ramberg), Andreas Ravelli, Robert Prytz, Glenn Strömberg, Tommy Holmgren; Thomas Sunesson, Dan Corneliusson.

CZECHOSLOVAKIA: Ludek Miklosko; Frantisek Jakubec, Zdenek Prokes, Ladislav Jurkemik, Jan Fiala, Pavel Chaloupka (65 Frantisek Stambachr), Premysl Bicovsky, Peter Zelensky, Jirí Sloup, Ladislav Vízek (79 Ivo Knoflícek), Petr Janecka. Trainer: Frantisek Havranek

Goal: Corneliusson (13)

ITALY v SWEDEN 0-3 (0-2)

San Paolo, Napoli 15.10.1983

Referee: José Luis Garcia Carrion (SPA) Att: 60,086

ITALY: Ivano Bordon; Giuseppe Bergomi, Antonio Cabrini (Cap); Salvatore Bagni, Pietro Vierchowod, Franco Baresi; Bruno Conti, Carlo Ancelotti, Paolo Rossi, Giuseppe Dossena, Bruno Giordano. Trainer: Vincenzo Bearzot

SWEDEN: Thomas Ravelli; Ingemar Erlandsson (Cap), Glenn Hysén, Sven Dahlqvist, Stig Fredriksson; Ulf Eriksson, Robert Prytz, Glenn Strömberg, Tommy Holmgren (74 Andreas Ravelli); Thomas Sunesson, Dan Corneliusson (84 Mats Jingblad).

Goals: Strömberg (20, 27), Sunesson (71)

CZECHOSLOVAKIA v ROMANIA 1-1 (0-0)

Slovan, Bratislava 30.11.1983

Referee: Károly Palotay (HUNG) Attendance: 48,000

CZECHOSLOVAKIA: Zdenek Hruska; Frantisek Jakubek, Zdenek Prokes, Jan Fiala (Cap), Petr Rada; Pavel Chaloupka, Peter Zelensky, Frantisek Stambacher (72 Ladislav Jurkemik); Ladislav Vízek, Václav Danek (72 Milan Luhovy), Petr Janecka. Trainer: Frantisek Havranek

ROMANIA: Silviu Lung; Nicolae Negrilă, Costică Ştefănescu (Cap), Gino Iorgulescu, Nicolae Ungureanu; Mircea Rednic, Ladislau Bölöni, Michael Klein; Ion Geolgău, Rodion Cămătaru, Romulus Gabor (79 Ionel Augustin, 89 Alexandru Nicolae). Trainer: Mircea Lucescu

Goals: Geolgău (62), Luhovy (85)

CYPRUS v ROMANIA 0-1 (0-0)

Tsirion, Limassol 12.11.1983

Referee: Ronald Bridges (WAL) Attendance: 13,000

CYPRUS: Andreas Constantinou; Costas Miamiliotis, Nikos Pantziaras (Cap), George Kezos, Klitos Erotokritou; Marios Tsingis, George Savvidis, Yiannakis Yiangoudakis, Pavlos Kounnas (56 Christakis Omirou Mavris), Costas Foti (78 Filippos Demetriou), Theofanis Theofanous.
Trainer: Vasil Spasov

ROMANIA: Silviu Lung; Mircea Rednic, Costică Ştefănescu (Cap), Alexandru Nicolae, Nicolae Ungureanu; Aurel Ţicleanu, Gheorghe Mulţescu (46 Gheorghe Hagi), Ladislau Bölöni, Michael Klein; Rodion Cămătaru, Marcel Coraş (73 Romulus Gabor). Trainer: Mircea Lucescu

Goal: Bölöni (78)

ITALY v CYPRUS 3-1 (0-0)

Stadio Renato Curi, Perugia 22.12.1983

Referee: Oliver Donnelly (NIR) Attendance: 20,773

ITALY: Giovanni Galli; Giuseppe Bergomi, Antonio Cabrini (Cap), Franco Baresi, Pietro Vierchowod, Ubaldo Righetti (46 Fulvio Collovatti), Bruno Conti (60 Pietro Fanna), Salvatore Bagni, Paolo Rossi, Giuseppe Dossena, Alessandro Altobelli. Trainer: Vincenzo Bearzot

CYPRUS: Andreas Constantinou; Costas Miamiliotis, George Kezos; Yiannakis Yiangoudakis, Klitos Erotokritou, Nikos Pantziaras (Cap), Marios Tsingis, Lefteris Kouis (86 Pavlos Kounas), Costas Foti, Koullis Pantziaras, Theofanis Theofanous (82 Paschalis Christoforou). Trainer: V. Spasov

Goals: Altobelli (53), Tsingis (68 pen), Cabrini (82), P. Rossi (86 pen)

CZECHOSLOVAKIA v ITALY 2-0 (0-0)

Rosickeho, Praha 16.11.1983

Referee: George Courtney (ENG) Attendance: 25,000

CZECHOSLOVAKIA: Zdenek Hruska; Frantisek Jakubek, Petr Rada; Peter Zelensky, Zdenek Prokes, Jan Fiala (Cap); Petr Janecka, Pavel Chaloupka, Ladislav Vízek, Frantisek Stambachr, Václav Danek (89 Milan Luhovy).
Trainer: Frantisek Havranek

ITALY: Ivano Bordon; Giuseppe Bergomi, Antonio Cabrini; Carlo Ancelotti, Pietro Vierchowod, Ubaldo Righetti; Salvatore Bagni (75 Giancarlo Antognoni), Giuseppe Dossena, Paolo Rossi, Marco Tardelli, Bruno Giordano.
Trainer: Vincenzo Bearzot

Goals: Rada (64, 77 pen)

	P	W	D	L	F	A	Pts
Romania	8	5	2	1	9	3	12
Sweden	8	5	1	2	14	5	11
Czechoslovakia	8	3	4	1	15	7	10
Italy	8	1	3	4	6	12	5
Cyprus	8	0	2	6	4	21	2

GROUP 6

AUSTRIA v ALBANIA **5-0** (2-0)

Hanappi-stadium, Wien 22.09.1982

Referee: Iordan Zhezhov (BUL) Attendance: 10,000

AUSTRIA: Friedrich Koncilia; Bernd Krauss, Erich Obermayer (75 Ernst Baumeister), Heribert Weber, Josef Degeorgi; Herbert Prohaska (Cap), Anton Pichler (24 Karl Brauneder), Felix Gasselich; Walter Schachner, Max Hagmayr, Gernot Jurtin. Trainer: Erich Hof

ALBANIA: Ilir Luarasi; Petrit Ruçi, Arjan Hametaj, Aleko Bregu, Muhedin Targaj (Cap); Haxhi Ballgjini, Luan Vukatana, Bedri Omuri, Roland Luçi; Dashnor Bajaziti (55 Shkëlkim Muça), Agostin Kola (46 Vassilaq Zëri).
Trainer: Shyqyri Rreli

Goals: Hagmayr (24), Gasselich (45), Kola (64 og), Weber (67), Brauneder (80)

AUSTRIA v TURKEY **4-0** (3-0)

Hanappi stadium, Wien 17.11.1982

Referee: Aleksander Suchanek (POL) Attendance: 14,000

AUSTRIA: Friedrich Koncilia; Bernd Krauss, Erich Obermayer, Bruno Pezzey, Josef Degeorgi (.. Leopold Lainer); Heribert Weber, Herbert Prohaska (Cap), Felix Gasselich (12 Anton Pichler); Walter Schachner, Günter Golautschnig, Anton Polster. Trainer: Erich Hof

TURKEY: Şenol Güneş; Eren Talu, Hüsnü Özkara, Hakan Küfukçüoglu; Tuna Güneysu (.. Iskender Gönen), Arif Kocabiyik, Erdal Keser; Ali Kemal Denizci, Selçuk Yula, Şenol Çorlu, Riza Çalinbay. Trainer: Coşkun Özari

Goals: Polster (10), Pezzey (34), Prohaska (37 pen), Schachner (52)

AUSTRIA v NORTHERN IRELAND **2-0** (2-0)

Hanappi stadium, Wien 13.10.1982

Referee: Valeri Butenko (USSR) Attendance: 21,000

AUSTRIA: Friedrich Koncilia; Bernd Krauss, Erich Obermayer, Bruno Pezzey, Josef Degeorgi; Herbert Prohaska (Cap), Heribert Weber, Felix Gasselich; Walter Schachner, Max Hagmayr (70 Peter Pacult), Gernot Jurtin (.. Ernst Baumeister)
Trainer: Erich Hof

N. IRELAND: James Platt; James Nicholl, Christopher Nicholl, John McClelland, Malachy Donaghy; David McCreery, Martin O'Neill (Cap) (78 Felix Healy), Samuel McIlroy; Norman Whiteside (.. Noel Brotherson), Gerard Armstrong, William Hamilton. Manager: William Bingham

Goals: Schachner (3, 39)

NORTHERN IRELAND v WEST GERMANY **1-0** (1-0)

Belfast 17.11.1982

Referee: Rolf Nyhus (NOR) Attendance: 30,000

N. IRELAND: James Platt; James Nicholl, Malachy Donaghy, John O'Neill, John McClelland, Martin O'Neill, Noel Brotherson, Samuel McIlroy, Norman Whiteside, William Hamilton, Ian Stewart. Manager: William Bingham

W. GERMANY: Harald Schumacher; Manfred Kaltz, Ulrich Stielike, Gerhard Strack, Bernd Förster; Lothar Matthäus (.. Rudolf Völler), Bernd Schuster (72 Stefan Engels), Hans-Peter Briegel; Karl-Heinz Rummenigge (Cap), Klaus Allofs, Pierre Littbarski. Trainer: Josef Derwall

Goal: Stewart (17)

TURKEY v ALBANIA **1-0** (0-0)

Kemal Atatürk, Izmir 27.10.1982

Referee: Ion Igna (ROM) Attendance: 20,000

TURKEY: Şenol Güneş; Muzaffer Badalioglu, Eren Talu, Fatih Terim, Hakan Küfukçüoglu, Tuna Güneysu (53 Bilal Yaşar), Arif Kocabiyik, Erdal Keser, Ali Kemal Denizci, Selçuk Yula, Şenol Çorlu. Trainer: Coşkun Özari

ALBANIA: Perlat Musta; Petrit Ruçi, Arjan Hametaj, Muhedin Targaj, Arjan Bimo, Bedri Omuri, Haxhi Ballgjini, Luan Vukatana, Shkëlkim Muça (46 Arben Minga), Roland Luçi, Agostin Kola. Trainer: Shyqyri Rreli

Goal: Arif (86)

ALBANIA v NORTHERN IRELAND **0-0**

Qemal Stafa, Tiranë 15.12.1982

Referee: André Daina (SWI) Attendance: 20,000

ALBANIA: Perlat Musta; Petrit Ruçi, Arjan Hametaj, Muhedin Targaj, Arjan Bimo (46 Bedri Omuri), Haxhi Ballgjini, Luan Vukatana, Ferid Ragami, Roland Luçi (46 Shkëlkim Muça), Arben Minga, Agostin Kola.
Trainer: Shyqyri Rreli

N. IRELAND: James Platt; Malachy Donaghy, James Nicholl, John O'Neill, John McClelland, Martin O'Neill, Noel Brotherson, Samuel McIlroy, Norman Whiteside, William Hamilton, Ian Stewart. Manager: William Bingham

NORTHERN IRELAND v TURKEY 2-1 (2-0)

Belfast 30.03.1983

Referee: Alain Delmer (FRA) Attendance: 20,000

N. IRELAND: James Platt; James Nicholl, Malachy Donaghy, John O'Neill, John McClelland, Martin O'Neill, Noel Brotherson, Samuel McIlroy, Norman Whiteside, Gerard Armstrong, Ian Stewart. Manager: William Bingham

TURKEY: Eser Özaltindere; Erdogan Arica, Fatih Terim, Yusuf Altintaş, Hakan Küfukçüoglu, Eren Talu (.. Arif Kocabiyik), Raşit Çetiner, K.Hüseyin Çakiroglu, Metin Tekin, Selçuk Yula, Hasan Şengün. Trainer: Coşkun Özari

Goals: M. O'Neill (5), McClelland (17), Hasan (56)

AUSTRIA v WEST GERMANY 0-0

Prater, Wien 27.04.1983

Referee: Brian McGinlay (SCO) Attendance: 60,430

AUSTRIA: Friedrich Koncilia; Bernd Krauss, Erich Obermayer, Bruno Pezzey, Josef Degeorgi; Herbert Prohaska (Cap) (.. Leopold Lainer), Heribert Weber, Felix Gasselich (.. Ernst Baumeister), Reinhard Kienast; Walter Schachner, Johann Krankl. Trainer: Erich Hof

W. GERMANY: Harald Schumacher; Wolfgang Dremmler, Gerhard Strack, Karlheinz Förster, Hans-Peter Briegel (.. Bernd Förster); Stefan Engels, Bernd Schuster, Hans Müller (.. Wolfgang Rolff); Pierre Littbarski, Rudolf Völler, Karl Heinz Rummenigge (Cap). Trainer: Josef Derwall

ALBANIA v WEST GERMANY 1-2 (0-0)

Qemal Stafa, Tiranë 30.03.1983

Referee: Gianfranco Menegalli (ITA) Attendance: 25,000

ALBANIA: Perlat Musta; Petrit Ruçi, Muhedin Targaj, Arjan Hametaj, Arjan Bimo, Ferid Ragami, Luan Vukatana, Haxhi Ballgjini, Dashnor Bajaziti (51 Ilir Lame), Arben Minga, Agostin Kola. Trainer: Shyqyri Rreli

W. GERMANY: Harald Schumacher; Bernd Förster, Gerhard Strack, Karlheinz Förster, Jonny Otten; Stefan Engels, Hans Müller, Hans-Peter Briegel; Pierre Littbarski, Rudolf Völler (.. Norbert Meier), Karl-Heinz Rummenigge (Cap).
Trainer: Josef Derwall

Goals: Völler (54), Rummenigge (66 pen), Targaj (81 pen)

NORTHERN IRELAND v ALBANIA 1-0 (0-0)

Windsor Park, Belfast 27.04.1983

Referee: Ib Nielsen (DEN) Attendance: 14,000

N. IRELAND: Patrick Jennings; James Nicholl, John McClelland, John O'Neill, Malachy Donaghy, Martin O'Neill, Samuel McIlroy, Noel Brotherson (63 Gerald Mullan), William Hamilton, Gerard Armstrong, Ian Stewart.
Manager: William Bingham

ALBANIA: Perlat Musta; Petrit Ruçi, Arjan Hametaj, Muhedin Targaj, Kristaq Eksarko, Bedri Omuri, Sulejman Demollari, Luan Vukatana, Ilir Lame, Shkëlkim Muça (46 Sulejman Mema), Arben Minga. Trainer: Shyqyri Rreli

Goal: Stewart (54)

TURKEY v WEST GERMANY 0-3 (0-2)

Atatürk, Izmir 23.04.1983

Referee: Vojtech Christov (CZE) Attendance: 75,000

TURKEY: Şenol Güneş; Erdogan Arica, Fatih Terim, Yusuf Altintaş, Hakan Küfukçüoglu, Metin Tekin (.. Iskender Gönen), Raşit Çetiner, Erdal Keser, K. Hüseyin Çakiroglu, Selçuk Yula, Hasan Şengün. Trainer: Coşkun Özari

W. GERMANY: Harald Schumacher; Wolfgang Dremmler, Gerhard Strack, Karlheinz Förster, Hans-Peter Briegel; Stefan Engels, Bernd Schuster, Hans Müller; Pierre Littbarski (.. Wolfgang Rolff), Rudolf Völler, Karl-Heinz Rummenigge (Cap). Trainer: Josef Derwall

Goals: Rummenigge (30 pen, 71), Dremmler (34)

ALBANIA v TURKEY 1-1 (0-1)

Qemal Stafa, Tiranë 11.05.1983

Referee: Mircea Salomir (ROM) Attendance: 30,000

ALBANIA: Perlat Musta; Petrit Ruçi, Arjan Hametaj, Muhedin Targaj, Bedri Omuri, Ilir Lame, Luan Vukatana, Haxhi Ballgjini (46 Arjan Bimo), Ferid Ragami, Shkëlkim Muça (46 Pandeli Xhaho), Andrea Marko.
Trainer: Shyqyri Rreli

TURKEY: Adem Ibrahimoglu; Erdogan Arica, Fatih Terim, Yusuf Altintaş, Alpaslan Eratli, Raşit Çetiner, Ismail Kartal (.. Iskender Gönen), Metin Tekin (.. Eren Talu), Hasan Şengün, Selçuk Yula. Trainer: Coşkun Özari

Goals: Metin (34), Raşit (73 og)

ALBANIA v AUSTRIA 1-2 (0-1)

Qemal Stafa, Tiranë 08.06.1983

Referee: Laszló Padar (HUNG) Attendance: 25,000

ALBANIA: Perlat Musta; Petrit Ruçi, Arjan Hametaj, Muhedin Targaj (Cap), Arjan Bimo; Ilir Lame, Luan Vukatana, Ferid Ragami, Pandeli Xhaho (67 Andrea Marko); Arben Minga (54 Milutin Kërçiçi), Sefedin Braho.
Trainer: Shyqyri Rreli

AUSTRIA: Friedrich Koncilia; Bernd Krauss, Erich Obermayer, Anton Pichler, Leopold Lainer; Ernst Baumeister, Herbert Prohaska (Cap), Felix Gasselich (89 Gerald Willfurth); Walter Schachner, Christian Keglevits (61 Gerhard Steinkogler), Gernot Jurtin. Trainer: Erich Hof

Goals: Schachner (6, 57), Targaj (84 pen)

NORTHERN IRELAND v AUSTRIA 3-1 (1-0)

Windsor Park, Belfast 21.09.1983

Referee: Erik Fredriksson (SWE) Attendance: 41,000

N. IRELAND: Patrick Jennings; Paul Ramsey, John McClelland, Christopher Nicholl, Malachy Donaghy; Martin O'Neill (Cap), Samuel McIlroy, Ian Stewart; Gerard Armstrong, William Hamilton, Norman Whiteside.
Manager: William Bingham

AUSTRIA: Friedrich Koncilia; Bernd Krauss, Bruno Pezzey, Reinhard Kienast (68 Josef Degeorgi), Leopold Lainer; Herbert Prohaska (Cap), Heribert Weber, Felix Gasselich, Roland Gisinger (68 Gerald Willfurth); Walter Schachner, Johann Krankl. Trainer: Erich Hof

Goals: Hamilton (28), Whiteside (65), Gasselich (82), M. O'Neill (89)

WEST GERMANY v AUSTRIA 3-0 (3-0)

Park Stadium, Gelsenkirchen 05.10.1983

Referee: Luigi Agnolin (ITA) Attendance: 70,000

W. GERMANY: Harald Schumacher; Wolfgang Dremmler, Gerhard Strack, Karlheinz Förster, Hans-Peter Briegel; Wolfgang Rolff, Klaus Augenthaler, Bernd Schuster, Norbert Meier (.. Lothar Matthäus); Karl-Heinz Rummenigge (Cap), Rudolf Völler (.. Herbert Waas). Trainer: Josef Derwall

AUSTRIA: Friedrich Koncilia; Bernd Krauss (78 Johann Pregesbauer), Bruno Pezzey, Josef Degeorgi, Heribert Weber; Leopold Lainer, Herbert Prohaska (Cap), Felix Gasselich (.. Gernot Jurtin), Ernst Baumeister; Walter Schachner, Gerald Willfurth. Trainer: Erich Hof

Goals: Rummenigge (4), Völler (18, 20)

TURKEY v NORTHERN IRELAND 1-0 (1-0)

Ankara 12.10.1983

Referee: Kade Toy Attendance: 38,000

TURKEY: Adem Ibrahimoglu; Ismail Kartal, Fatih Terim, Yusuf Altintaş, Erdogan Arica, H. Ibrahim (.. Riza), Sedat Özen, Raşit Çetiner, Ilyas Tüfekçi, Hasan Şengün, Selçuk Yula.
Trainer: Coşkun Özari

N. IRELAND: Patrick Jennings; James Nicholl, Malachy Donaghy, Christopher Nicholl, John McClelland, Martin O'Neill, Brotherson (.. Cleary), Samuel McIlroy, William Hamilton (.. McCreery), Norman Whiteside, Ian Stewart.
Manager: William Bingham

Goals: Selçuk (17)

WEST GERMANY v TURKEY 5-1 (1-0)

Olympiastadion, Berlin-west 26.10.1983

Referee: Eduard Sostaric (YUG) Attendance: 35,000

W. GERMANY: Harald Schumacher; Jonny Otten, Gerhard Strack, Klaus Augenthaler, Hans-Peter Briegel (82 Matthias Herget); Lothar Matthäus, Ulrich Stielike, Norbert Meier (81 Michael Rummenigge); Pierre Littbarski, Rudolf Völler, Karl-Heinz Rummenigge (Cap). Trainer: Josef Derwall

TURKEY: Adem Ibrahimoglu; Ismail Demiriz, Fatih Terim, Yusuf Altintaş, Erdogan Arica; Sedat Özen, Raşit Çetiner, Erdal Keser, Ilyas Tüfekçi, Hasan Şengün, Selçuk Yula.
Trainer: Coşkun Özari

Goals: Völler (45, 65), Rummenigge (61, 75 pen), Stielike (66), Hasan (68)

TURKEY v AUSTRIA 3-1 (0-0)

Ali Sami Yen, Istanbul 16.11.1983

Referee: Roger Schoters (BEL) Attendance: 34,000

TURKEY: Yaşar Duran; Ismail Demiriz, Yusuf Altintaş, Fatih Terim (Cap), Erdogan Arica; Erdal Keser (.. Hasan Şengün), Raşit Çetiner, Ilyas Tüfekçi, Sedat Özen, Necdet Ergun, Selçuk Yula. Trainer: Coşkun Özari

AUSTRIA: Friedrich Koncilia; Bernd Krauss, Bruno Pezzey (Cap), Gerald Messlender, Josef Degeorgi (.. Leopold Lainer); Heinz Thonhofer, Heribert Weber, Ernst Baumeister; Walter Schachner, Gerald Willfurth (74 Peter Pacult), Christian Keglevits. Trainer: Erich Hof

Goals: Ilyas (67), Selçuk (69, 75 pen), Baumeister (70)

WEST GERMANY v NORTHERN IRELAND 0-1 (0-0)

Volksparkstadion, Hamburg 16.11.1983

Referee: Károly Palotai (HUNG) Attendance: 61,418

W. GERMANY: Harald Schumacher; Wolfgang Dremmler, Ulrich Stielike (84 Gerhard Strack), Karlheinz Förster, Hans-Peter Briegel; Lothar Matthäus, Klaus Augenthaler, Wolfgang Rolff, Norbert Meier (.. Pierre Littbarski); Karl-Heinz Rummenigge (Cap), Herbert Waas. Trainer: Josef Derwall

N. IRELAND: Patrick Jennings; James Nicholl, Gerard McElhinney, John McClelland, Malachy Donaghy, Paul Ramsey, Martin O'Neill, Gerard Armstrong, Norman Whiteside, William Hamilton, Ian Stewart.
Manager: William Bingham

Goal: Whiteside (50)

WEST GERMANY v ALBANIA 2-1 (1-1)

Ludwigsportstadion, Saarbrücken 20.11.1983

Referee: Anders Mattsson (FIN) Attendance: 40,000

W. GERMANY: Harald Schumacher; Bernd Förster, Gerhard Strack, Karlheinz Förster, Hans-Peter Briegel (34 Jonny Otten); Wolfgang Dremmler, Lothar Matthäus, Norbert Meier; Pierre Littbarski (.. Herbert Waas), Rudolf Völler, Karl-Heinz Rummenigge (Cap). Trainer: Josef Derwall

ALBANIA: Perlat Musta; Petrit Ruçi, Arjan Hametaj, Kristaq Eksarko, Bedri Omuri, Ferid Ragami, Luan Vukatana (83 Hasan Lika), Haxhi Ballgjini, Ilir Lame, Arben Minga, Genc Tomori. Trainer: Shyqyri Rreli

Goals: Tomori (22), Rummenigge (24), Strack (79)

	P	W	D	L	F	A	Pts
West Germany	8	5	1	2	15	5	11
Northern Ireland	8	5	1	2	8	5	11
Austria	8	4	1	3	15	10	9
Turkey	8	3	1	4	8	16	7
Albania	8	0	2	6	4	14	2

GROUP 7

MALTA v ICELAND 2-1 (1-0)

Stadio 'G' Celeste, Messina (ITA) 05.06.1982

Referee: Pietro D'Elia (ITA) Attendance: 1,271

MALTA: John Bonello; Constantino Consiglio, Edwin Farrugia, Norman Buttigieg, John Holland, Emmanuel Farrugia (.. M.Farrugia), Carmel Busuttil, Emmanuel Fabri, Ernest Spiteri Gonzi, Joseph Xuereb (.. Mario Schembri), George Xuereb. Trainer: Victor Scerri

ICELAND: Gudmundur Baldursson; Trausti Haraldsson, Örn Oskarsson (75 Vidar Halldórson), Marteinn Geirsson, Saevar Jónsson, Karl Thórdarson, Janus Gudlaugsson (.. Arni Sveinsson), Atli Edvaldsson, Teitur Thórdarson, Lárus Gudmundsson, Pétur Ormslev. Trainer: Jóhannes Atlason

Goals: E. Spiteri Gonzi (45), L. Fabri (48), Geirsson (51 pen)

ICELAND v HOLLAND 1-1 (0-0)

Laugardalsvöllur, Reykjavik 01.09.1982

Referee: Brian McGinlay (SCO) Attendance: 7,000

ICELAND: Thorsteinn Bjarnason; Vidar Halldórsson, Trausti Haraldsson (68 Omar Torfason), Marteinn Geirsson, Saevar Jónsson, Janus Gudlaugsson (.. Gunnar Gíslason), Arnór Gudjohnsen, Atli Edvaldsson, Lárus Gudmundsson, Pétur Ormslev, Karl Thórdarson. Trainer: Jóhannes Atlason

HOLLAND: Johannes Van Breukelen; Bennie Wijnstekers (Cap), Michel Van de Korput, Peter Boeve, Edo Ophof, Frank Rijkaard, Willy van de Kerkhof, Dick Schoenaker, Ruud Gullit, Willem Kieft, Gerald Vanenburg (.. Jurrie Koolhof).
Trainer: Cornelis Bernardus Rijvers

Goals: Atli Edvaldsson (49), Schoenaker (51)

HOLLAND v REPUBLIC OF IRELAND 2-1 (1-0)

Feyenoord, Rotterdam 22.09.1982

Referee: Ivan Gregr (CZE) Attendance: 20,500

HOLLAND: Johannes Van Breukelen; Bennie Wijnstekers (Cap), Johnny Metgod (46 René van der Kerkhof), Ronald Spelbos, Michel Van de Korput, Huub Stevens, Dick Schoenaker, Willy van de Kerkhof, Ruud Gullit, René van der Gijp, Gerald Vanenburg (80 Kees Van Kooten).
Trainer: Cornelis Bernardus Rijvers

IRELAND: Seamus McDonagh; Mark Lawrenson, Mick Martin, David O'Leary, Christopher Hughton, Gerard Daly (82 Mickey Walsh), Tony Grealish (Cap), William Brady, Anthony Galvin (75 Gary Waddock), Frank Stapleton, Michael Robinson. Trainer: Eoin Hand

Goals: Schoenaker (1), Gullit (64), Daly (79)

REPUBLIC OF IRELAND v ICELAND 2-0 (1-0)

Lansdowne Road, Dublin 13.10.1982

Referee: Paul Rion (LUX) Attendance: 20,000

IRELAND: Seamus McDonagh; Mark Lawrenson, David O'Leary, Kevin Moran, Mickey Walsh, Ronnie Whelan, Tony Grealish (Cap), Gary Waddock, William Brady (64 Kevin O'Callaghan), Frank Stapleton, Michael Robinson. Trainer: Eoin Hand

ICELAND: Thorsteinn Bjarnason; Vidar Halldórsson, Örn Oskarsson, Marteinn Geirsson, Saevar Jónsson, Gunnar Gíslason, Arnór Gudjohnsen, Atli Edvaldsson, Lárus Gudmundsson, Pétur Ormslev (42 Ragnar Margeirsson), Pétur Pétursson. Trainer: Jóhannes Atlason

Goals: Stapleton (35), Grealish (73)

SPAIN v ICELAND 1-0 (0-0)

Estadio La Rosaleda, Málaga 27.10.1982

Referee: Mario Silva (POR) Attendance: 12,000

SPAIN: Luis Miguel ARCONADA Echarre; JUAN JOSÉ Jimenez Collar, Francisco BONET Serrano, GERARDO Miranda Concepción, José Antonio CAMACHO Alfaro; Juan Antonio SEÑOR Gomez, ROBERTO Fernandez Bonilla, Rafael GORDILLO Vazquez (50 FRANCISCO López Alfaro); Juan Carlos Gómez PEDRAZA (74 Enrique MARTÍN Monreal), Carlos Alonso Gonzalez SANTILLANA, MARCOS Alonso Peña. Trainer: Miguel Muñoz

ICELAND: Thorsteinn Bjarnason; Vidar Halldórsson, Örn Oskarsson; Marteinn Geirsson, Saevar Jónsson, Omar Torfason, Arnór Gudjohnsen, Atli Edvaldsson, Sigurdur Grétarsson (.. Gunnar Gíslason), Pétur Pétursson, Arni Sveinsson (60 Heimir Karlsson). Trainer: Jóhannes Atlason

Goal: Pedraza (59)

REPUBLIC OF IRELAND v SPAIN 3-3 (1-1)

Lansdowne Road, Dublin 17.11.1982

Referee: Jan Redelfs (W. GER) Attendance: 39,000

IRELAND: Seamus McDonagh; John Devine, Mick Martin, Mark Lawrenson, Christopher Hughton; Tony Grealish (Cap) (60 Mickey Walsh), William Brady, Ashley Grimes; Kevin O'Callaghan, Frank Stapleton, Michael Robinson. Trainer: Eoin Hand

SPAIN: Luis Miguel ARCONADA Echarre; JUAN JOSÉ Jimenez Collar, Francisco BONET Serrano, Antonio MACEDA Francés, José Antonio CAMACHO Alfaro; Juan Antonio SEÑOR Gomez, VICTOR Muñoz Manrique, Rafael GORDILLO Vazquez; MARCOS Alonso Peña, Juan Carlos Gómez PEDRAZA (74 Enrique MARTÍN Monreal), Carlos Alonso Gonzalez SANTILLANA (76 ROBERTO Fernandez Bonilla). Trainer: Miguel Muñoz

Goals: Grimes (2), Maceda (31), Martin (47 og), Victor (60), Stapleton (64, 76)

MALTA v HOLLAND 0-6 (0-4)

Sportpark Tivoli-Aachen (West Germany) 19.12.1982

Referee: Dieter Pauly (W. GER) Attendance: 18,000

MALTA: John Bonello; Constantino Consiglio (46 Mario Farrugia), Edwin Farrugia, John Holland, Mario Schembri, Joseph Salerno, Emmanuel Farrugia, Emmanuel Fabri, Raymond Xuereb (.. Michael Degiorgio), Ernest Spiteri-Gonzi, George Xuereb. Trainer: Victor Scerri

HOLLAND: Piet Schrijvers; Bennie Wijnstekers (Cap), Michel Van de Korput, Hugo Hovenkamp, Edo Ophof, Peter Boeve, Dick Schoenaker, Gerald Vanenburg (.. Jurrie Koolhof), René Hofman (66 Ruud Gullit), Kees Van Kooten, Pierre Vermeulen. Trainer: Cornelis Bernardus Rijvers

Goals: Ophof (21 pen), Van Kooten (24, 71), Hovenkamp (34), Schoenaker (39, 50)

SPAIN v HOLLAND 1-0 (1-0)

Estadio Sánchez Pizjuan, Sevilla 16.02.1983

Referee: Paolo Bergamo (ITA) Attendance: 45,000

SPAIN: Luis Miguel ARCONADA Echarre; JUAN JOSÉ Jimenez Collar, Andoni GOIKOETXEA Olascoaga, Antonio MACEDA Francés, José Antonio CAMACHO Alfaro; VICTOR Muñoz Manrique, Juan Antonio SEÑOR Gomez, Rafael GORDILLO Vazquez; Francisco José CARRASCO Hidalgo, Manuel SARABIA López (88 Ricardo GALLEGO Redondo), MARCOS Alonso Peña. Trainer: Miguel Muñoz

HOLLAND: Piet Schrijvers; Bennie Wijnstekers (Cap), Ruud Krol, Ronald Spelbos, Peter Boeve, Michel Van de Korput, Johnny Metgod (43 Michel Valke), Dick Schoenaker, Hugo Hovenkamp (46 Ruud Gullit), Jurrie Koolhof, René Van der Gijp. Trainer: Cornelis Bernardus Rijvers

Goal: Señor (44 pen)

MALTA v REPUBLIC OF IRELAND 0-1 (0-0)

Ta'Qali, Valletta 30.03.1983

Referee: Adolf Mathias (AUS) Attendance: 6,487

MALTA: John Bonello; Emmanuel Farrugia, Edwin Farrugia, Mario Farrugia, Mario Schembri, John Holland, Silvio Demanuele, Raymond Xuereb, George Xuereb, Emmanuel Fabri, Michael Degiorgio. Trainer: Victor Scerri

IRELAND: Seamus McDonagh; John Devine, Mick Martin (Cap), Mark Lawrenson, Christopher Hughton, Ronnie Whelan, William Brady, Gary Waddock, Anthony Galvin (63 Kevin O'Callaghan), Frank Stapleton, Michael Robinson. Trainer: Eoin Hand

Goal: Stapleton (90)

SPAIN v REPUBLIC OF IRELAND 2-0 (0-0)

Estadio La Romareda, Zaragoza 27.04.1983

Referee: Valeri Butenko (USSR) Attendance: 45,000

SPAIN: Luis Miguel ARCONADA Echarre; JUAN JOSÉ Jimenez Collar, Antonio MACEDA Francés, Francisco BONET Serrano, José Antonio CAMACHO Alfaro; VICTOR Muñoz Manrique (46 Ricardo GALLEGO Redondo), Juan Antonio SEÑOR Gomez, Rafael GORDILLO Vazquez; MARCOS Alonso Peña, Carlos Alonso Gonzalez SANTILLANA, Francisco José CARRASCO Hidalgo (74 Hipolito RINCÓN Povedano). Trainer: Miguel Muñoz

IRELAND: Seamus McDonagh; Mark Lawrenson, Mick Martin, David O'Leary, Christopher Hughton; Ronnie Whelan (77 Gerard Daly), Tony Grealish (Cap), Ashley Grimes (57 Kevin O'Callaghan), Gary Waddock; Mickey Walsh, Frank Stapleton. Trainer: Eoin Hand

Goals: Santillana (51), Rincón (89)

MALTA v SPAIN 2-3 (1-1)

Ta'Qali, Valletta 15.05.1983

Referee: Evangelos Gianakoudakis (GRE) Att: 7,732

MALTA: John Bonello; Emmanuel Farrugia, Mario Schembri, Norman Buttigieg, Edwin Farrugia, Carmel Busuttil, Emmanuel Fabri, Joseph Salerno, Michael Degiorgio, Silvio Demanuele, Ernest Spiteri Gonzi. Trainer: Victor Scerri

SPAIN: Luis Miguel ARCONADA Echarre; Francisco BONET Serrano (50 Andoni GOIKOETXEA Olascoaga), Antonio MACEDA Francés, José Antonio CAMACHO Alfaro; Juan Antonio SEÑOR Gomez, VICTOR Muñoz Manrique, Ricardo GALLEGO Redondo, Rafael GORDILLO Vazquez; MARCOS Alonso Peña (.. Hipolito RINCÓN Povedano), Carlos Alonso Gonzalez SANTILLANA, Francisco José CARRASCO Hidalgo. Trainer: Miguel Muñoz

Goals: Señor (22), Busuttil (30, 48), Carrasco (61), Gordillo (84)

ICELAND v SPAIN 0-1 (0-1)

Laugardalsvöllur, Reykjavik 29.05.1983

Referee: Ronald Bridges (WAL) Attendance: 7,055

ICELAND: Thorsteinn Bjarnason; Vidar Halldórsson, Olafur Björnsson, Sigurdur Lárusson, Saevar Jónsson, Janus Gudlaugsson, Arnór Gudjohnsen, Ragnar Margeirsson, Lárus Gudmundsson, Pétur Pétursson (46 Omar Torfason), Gunnar Gíslason (.. Arni Sveinsson). Trainer: Jóhannes Atlason

SPAIN: Luis Miguel ARCONADA Echarre; Juan Antonio SEÑOR Gomez, Antonio MACEDA Francés, Andoni GOIKOETXEA Olascoaga, José Antonio CAMACHO Alfaro; VICTOR Muñoz Manrique, Ricardo GALLEGO Redondo, Rafael GORDILLO Vazquez; Francisco José CARRASCO Hidalgo, Carlos Alonso Gonzalez SANTILLANA (.. Manuel SARABIA López), Hipolito RINCÓN Povedano. Trainer: Miguel Muñoz

Goal: Maceda (9)

ICELAND v MALTA 1-0 (1-0)

Laugdardalsvollur, Reykjavik 05.06.1983

Referee: Alex Jacobsen (DEN) Attendance: 5,718

ICELAND: Thorsteinn Bjarnason; Vidar Halldórsson, Omar Rafnsson, Olafur Björnsson, Saevar Jónsson, Janus Gudlaugsson, Pétur Pétursson (70 Sigurdur Jónsson), Atli Edvaldsson, Lárus Gudmundsson, Petur Ormslev, Arni Sveinsson. Trainer: Jóhannes Atlason

MALTA: John Bonello; Emmanuel Farrugia, Edwin Farrugia, Norman Buttigieg, Mario Schembri, John Holland, Carmel Busuttil, Emmanuel Fabri, Silvio Demanuele (46 Ernest Spiteri Gonzi), Raymond Xuereb, Michael Degiorgio. Trainer: Victor Scerri

Goal: Atli Edvaldsson (44)

HOLLAND v ICELAND 3-0 (3-0)

Groningen 07.09.1983

Referee: Andrzej Libich (POL) Attendance: 7,000

HOLLAND: Piet Schrijvers; Bennie Wijnstekers (Cap), Ruud Gullit, Edo Ophof, Peter Boeve, Willy van de Kerkhof, Ronald Koeman (.. Michel Valke), Erwin Koeman (80 Bud Brocken), Gerald Vanenburg, Peter Houtman, Marco Van Basten. Trainer: Cornelis Bernardus Rijvers

ICELAND: Thorsteinn Bjarnason; Vidar Halldórsson, Omar Rafnsson, Jóhannes Edvaldsson, Saevar Jónsson, Pétur Ormslev, Arnór Gudjohnsen, Atli Edvaldsson, Lárus Gudmundsson (46 Asgeir Elíasson), Asgeir Sigurvinsson, Pétur Pétursson (65 Sveinbjörn Hákonarson). Trainer: Jóhannes Atlason

Goals: R. Koeman (16), Gullit (18), Houtman (21)

ICELAND v REPUBLIC OF IRELAND 0-3 (0-2)

Laugardalsvöllur, Reykjavik 21.09.1983

Referee: Gérard Biguet (FRA) Attendance: 13,706

ICELAND: Thorsteinn Bjarnason; Vidar Halldórsson, Sigurdur Lárusson, Jóhannes Edvaldsson, Saevar Jónsson, Janus Gudlaugsson, Arnór Gudjohnsen (52 Asgeir Elíasson), Atli Edvaldsson, Lárus Gudmundsson, Pétur Pétursson (81 Sigurdur Grétarsson), Pétur Ormslev. Trainer: Jóhannes Atlason

IRELAND: Seamus McDonagh; John Devine, Mark Lawrenson, Kevin Moran, Christopher Hughton, Gary Waddock, Tony Grealish (Cap), William Brady, Kevin O'Callaghan, Frank Stapleton, Michael Robinson (76 Mickey Walsh). Trainer: Eoin Hand

Goals: Waddock (17), Robinson (21), Walsh (82)

REPUBLIC OF IRELAND v HOLLAND 2-3 (2-0)

Dalymount Park, Dublin 12.10.1983

Referee: André Daina (SWI) Attendance: 35,000

IRELAND: Seamus McDonagh; John Devine, Mark Lawrenson, Kevin Moran, Christopher Hughton, Gary Waddock, William Brady, Tony Grealish (Cap) (81 Kevin Sheedy), Kevin O'Callaghan (74 Anthony Galvin), Frank Stapleton, Michael Robinson.

HOLLAND: Piet Schrijvers; Bennie Wijnstekers (Cap), Ruud Gullit, Jan Jacobus Silooy, Peter Boeve, Edo Ophof, Willy van de Kerkhof, Ronald Koeman, Adrianus Van Tiggelen (46 Bud Brocken), Gerald Vanenburg, Marco Van Basten. Trainer: Cornelis Bernardus Rijvers

Goals: Waddock (7), Brady (35 pen), Gullit (51, 75), Van Basten (77)

HOLLAND v MALTA 5-0 (2-0)

Feyenoord, Rotterdam 17.12.1983

Referee: Klaus Peschel (E. GER) Attendance: 58,000

HOLLAND: Piet Schrijvers; Bennie Wijnstekers (Cap), Ruud Gullit, Edo Ophof, Peter Boeve (.. Michel Valke), Willy van de Kerkhof, Ronald Koeman, Gerald Vanenburg, Bud Brocken, Peter Houtman, Erwin Koeman (.. Frank Rijkaard). Trainer: Cornelis Bernardus Rijvers

MALTA: John Bonello; Emmanuel Farrugia, Edwin Farrugia, Norman Buttigieg, John Holland, Mario Schembri, Raymond Farrugia (46 Alex Azzopardi), Emmanuel Fabri, Simon Tortell (46 Mario Farrugia), Michael Degiorgio, Silvio Demanuele. Trainer: Victor Scerri

Goals: Vanenburg (18), Wijnstekers (29), Rijkaard (71, 90), Houtman (81)

HOLLAND v SPAIN 2-1 (1-1)

Feyenoord, Rotterdam 16.11.1983

Referee: Michel Vautrot (FRA) Attendance: 58,000

HOLLAND: Piet Schrijvers; Bennie Wijnstekers (Cap), Ruud Gullit, Edo Ophof, Peter Boeve; Willy van de Kerkhof, Ronald Koeman, Gerald Vanenburg, Erwin Koeman, Bud Brocken, Peter Houtman. Trainer: Cornelis Bernardus Rijvers

SPAIN: Luis Miguel ARCONADA Echarre; José Vicente SÁNCHEZ Felip, Antonio MACEDA Francés, Andoni GOIKOETXEA Olascoaga, José Antonio CAMACHO Alfaro; Ricardo GALLEGO Redondo, Juan Antonio SEÑOR Gomez, Rafael GORDILLO Vazquez, Francisco GÜERRI Ballarín (67 Hipolito RINCÓN Povedano), Carlos Alonso Gonzalez SANTILLANA, Francisco José CARRASCO Hidalgo (.. MARCOS Alonso Peña). Trainer: Miguel Muñoz

Goals: Houtman (26), Santillana (41), Gullit (63)

SPAIN v MALTA 12-1 (3-1)

Estadio Benito Villamarín, Sevilla 21.12.1983

Referee: Erkan Göksel (TUR) Attendance: 25,000

SPAIN: Francisco BUYO Villalba; Juan Antonio SEÑOR Gomez, Andoni GOIKOETXEA Olascoaga, José Antonio CAMACHO Alfaro; VICTOR Muñoz Manrique, Antonio MACEDA Francés, Rafael GORDILLO Vazquez; Hipolito RINCÓN Povedano (.. MARCOS Alonso Peña), Manuel SARABIA López, Carlos Alonso Gonzalez SANTILLANA, Francisco José CARRASCO Hidalgo. Trainer: Miguel Muñoz

MALTA: John Bonello; Alex Azzopardi, Emmanuel Farrugia, John Holland, Norman Buttigieg; Emmanuele Fabri, Michael Degiorgio, Ernest Spiteri Gonzi, Raymond Farrugia (46 Mario Farrugia), Simon Tortell, Silvio Demanuele. Trainer: Victor Scerri

Goals: Santillana (16, 26, 29, 76), Demanuele (24), Rincón (47, 57, 64, 78), Maceda (62, 63), Sarabia (80), Señor (86)

REPUBLIC OF IRELAND v MALTA 8-0 (3-0)

Dalymount Park, Dublin 16.11.1983

Referee: Ole Amundsen (DEN) Attendance: 8,500

IRELAND: Patrick Bonner; Kieran O'Regan, Mark Lawrenson (81 Gary Waddock), Kevin Moran (46 James McDonagh), Christopher Hughton, Gerard Daly, Kevin Sheedy, William Brady, Kevin O'Callaghan, Frank Stapleton, Mickey Walsh.

MALTA: John Bonello; Constantino Consiglio, Alex Azzopardi, Edwin Farrugia, John Holland, Emmanuel Farrugia, Silvio Demanuele, Mario Farrugia (81 Emmanuel Fabri), Noel Attard (68 George Xuereb), Carmel Busuttil, Ernest Spiteri Gonzi. Trainer: Victor Scerri

Goals: Lawrenson (24, 53), Stapleton (27 pen), O'Callaghan (32), Sheedy (75), Brady (77, 84), Daly (85)

	P	W	D	L	F	A	Pts
Spain	8	6	1	1	24	8	13
Holland	8	6	1	1	22	6	13
Rep. of Ireland	8	4	1	3	20	10	9
Iceland	8	1	1	6	3	13	3
Malta	8	1	0	7	5	37	2

FINALS in FRANCE

GROUP I

FRANCE v DENMARK 1-0 (0-0)

Parc des Princes, Paris 12.06.1984

Referee: Volker Roth (W. GER) Attendance: 47,570

FRANCE: Joël Bats; Patrick Battiston, Yvon Le Roux (60 Jean François Domergue), Maxime Bossis, Manuel Amoros; Jean Tigana, Alain Giresse, Michel Platini (Cap), Luis Fernandez; Bernard Lacombe, Bruno Bellone. Trainer: Michel Hidalgo

DENMARK: Ole Qvist; Søren Busk, Morten Olsen (Cap), Ivan Nielsen, Søren Lerby; Klaus Berggreen, Jens Jørn Bertelsen, Allan Simonsen (46 John Lauridsen), Frank Arnesen (80 Jesper Olsen); Michael Laudrup, Preben Elkjær-Larsen. Trainer: Josef Piontek

Sent off: Amoros (87)

Goal: Platini (78)

BELGIUM v YUGOSLAVIA 2-0 (2-0)

Félix Bollaert, Lens 13.06.1984

Referee: Erik Fredriksson (SWE) Attendance: 41,774

BELGIUM: Jean-Marie Pfaff; Georges Grün, Leo Clysters (34 Paul Lambrichts), Walter De Greef, Michel De Wolf, Vincenzo Scifo, René Vandereycken, Jan Ceulemans (Cap), Frankie Vercauteren, Nico Claesen, Erwin Vandenbergh. Trainer: Guy Thys

YUGOSLAVIA: Zoran Simovic; Nenad Stojkovic, Faruk Hadzibegic, Srecko Katanec, Velimir Zajec (Cap), Mehmed Bazdarevic (60 Dragan Stojkovic), Milos Sestic, Ivan Gudelj, Zlatko Vujovic (77 Borislav Cvetkovic), Safet Susic, Sulejman Halilovic. Trainer: Todor Veselinovic

Goals: Vandenbergh (28), Grün (45)

FRANCE v BELGIUM 5-0 (3-0)

La Beaujoire, Nantes 16.06.1984

Referee: Robert Valentine (SCO) Attendance: 51,359

FRANCE: Joël Bats; Luis Fernandez, Patrick Battiston, Maxime Bossis, Jean François Domergue; Alain Giresse, Jean Tigana, Michel Platini (Cap), Bernard Genghini (79 Thierry Tusseau); Didier Six, Bernard Lacombe (65 Dominique Rocheteau). Trainer: Michel Hidalgo

BELGIUM: Jean-Marie Pfaff; Georges Grün, Walter De Greef, Paul Lambrichts, Michel De Wolf; Vincenzo Scifo (52 René Verheyen), Jan Ceulemans (Cap), René Vandereycken (46 Ludo Coeck), Frankie Vercauteren; Nico Claesen, Erwin Vandenbergh. Trainer: Guy Thys

Goals: Platini (4, 74 pen, 89), Giresse (31), Fernandez (44)

DENMARK v YUGOSLAVIA 5-0 (2-0)

Stade Gerland, Lyon 16.06.1984

Referee: Augusto Lamo Castillo (SPA) Attendance: 34,745

DENMARK: Ole Qvist; Ole Rasmussen (60 John Sivebaek), Morten Olsen (Cap), Ivan Nielsen, Søren Busk, Klaus Berggreen, Søren Lerby, Jens J.Bertelsen, Frank Arnesen (78 John Lauridsen), Michael Laudrup, Preben Elkjær-Larsen. Trainer: Josef Piontek

YUGOSLAVIA: Tomislav Ivkovic; Branko Miljus, Nenad Stojkovic, Srecko Katanec (57 Sulejman Halilovic), Velimir Zajec (Cap), Ljubomir Radanovic, Zlatko Vujovic, Ivan Gudelj, Safet Susic, Mehmed Bazdarevic (25 Dragan Stojkovic), Borislav Cvetkovic. Trainer: Todor Veselinovic

Goals: Arnesen (7, 68 pen), Berggreen (18), Elkjær-Larsen (84), Lauridsen (86)

FRANCE v YUGOSLAVIA 3-2 (0-1)

Geoffroy-Guichard, Saint-Etienne 19.06.1984

Referee: André Daina (SWI) Attendance: 45,789

FRANCE: Joël Bats; Luis Fernandez, Patrick Battiston, Maxime Bossis, Jean-François Domergue; Alain Giresse, Jean Tigana, Michel Platini (Cap), Jean-Marc Ferreri (77 Daniel Bravo); Didier Six, Dominique Rocheteau (46 Thierry Tusseau). Trainer: Michel Hidalgo

YUGOSLAVIA: Zoran Simovic; Branko Miljus, Nenad Stojkovic, Ivan Gudelj, Velimir Zajec (Cap), Ljubomir Radanovic, Milos Sestic, Dragan Stojkovic, Safet Susic, Mehmed Bazdarevic (84 Srecko Katanec), Zlatko Vujovic (60 Stjepan Deveric). Trainer: Todor Veselinovic

Goals: Sestic (31), Platini (59, 61, 76), D. Stojkovic (80 pen)

DENMARK v BELGIUM 3-2 (1-2)

La Meinau, Strasbourg 19.06.1984

Referee: Adolf Prokop (E. GER) Attendance: 36,911

DENMARK: Ole Qvist; Ole Rasmussen (57 Kenneth Brylle), Ivan Nielsen, Morten Olsen (Cap), Søren Busk, Frank Arnesen (78 John Sivebaek), Klaus Berggreen, Jens J.Bertelsen, Søren Lerby, Preben Elkjær-Larsen, Michael Laudrup. Trainer: Josef Piontek

BELGIUM: Jean-Marie Pfaff; Georges Grün, Leo Clysters, Walter De Greef, Michel De Wolf; Frankie Vercauteren (62 Eddy Voordeckers), René Vandereycken, Vincenzo Scifo, Jan Ceulemans (Cap); Nico Claesen (46 Ludo Coeck), Erwin Vandenbergh. Trainer: Guy Thys

Goals: Ceulemans (27), Vercauteren (39), Arnesen (41 pen), Brylle (60), Elkjær (84)

	P	W	D	L	F	A	Pts
France	3	3	0	0	9	2	6
Denmark	3	2	0	1	8	3	4
Belgium	3	1	0	2	4	8	2
Yugoslavia	3	0	0	3	2	10	0

GROUP II

PORTUGAL v WEST GERMANY 0-0

La Meinau, Strasbourg 14.06.1984

Referee: Romualdas Yushka (USSR) Attendance: 44,766

PORTUGAL: Manuel BENTO (Cap); JOÃO PINTO, LIMA PEREIRA, EURICO Gomes, ALVARO Monteiro Magalhaes; António Manuel FRASCO (78 António VELOSO), CARLOS MANUEL, JAIME PACHECO, António Augusto Gomes SOUSA, Fernando CHALANA; Rui JORDAO (85 Fernando GOMES). Trainer: Fernando Cabrita

W. GERMANY: Harald Schumacher; Bernd Förster, Ulrich Stielike, Karlheinz Förster, Hans-Peter Briegel; Wolfgang Rolff (67 Rudolf Bommer), Guido Buchwald (67 Lothar Matthäus), Karl-Heinz Rummenigge (Cap), Andreas Brehme; Rudolf Völler, Klaus Allofs. Trainer: Josef Derwall

SPAIN v ROMANIA 1-1 (1-1)

Geoffroy-Guichard, Saint Etienne 14.06.1984

Referee: Alexis Ponnet (BEL) Attendance: 17,012

SPAIN: Luis Miguel ARCONADA Echarre (Cap); Santiago URQUIAGA Perez, Antonio MACEDA Francés, Andoni GOIKOETXEA Olascoaga, José Antonio CAMACHO Alfaro; VICTOR Muñoz Manrique, Juan Antonio SEÑOR Gomez, Ricardo GALLEGO Redondo (73 JULIO ALBERTO Moreno Casas), Rafael GORDILLO Vazquez; Carlos Alonso Gonzalez SANTILLANA, Francisco José CARRASCO Hidalgo. Trainer: Miguel Muñoz

ROMANIA: Silviu Lung; Mircea Rednic, Gino Iorgulescu, Costică Ştefănescu, Nicolae Ungureanu; Marcel Coraş, Marin Dragnea (57 Aurel Ţicleanu), Michael Klein, Ladislau Bölöni; Rodion Cămătaru, Romulus Gabor (76 Gheorghe Hagi). Trainer: Mircea Lucescu

Goals: Carrasco (22 pen), Bölöni (35)

ROMANIA v WEST GERMANY 1-2 (0-1)

Félix Bollaert, Lens 17.06.1984

Referee: Jan Keizer (HOL) Attendance: 31,803

ROMANIA: Silviu Lung; Mircea Rednic, Ioan Andonie, Costică Ştefănescu (Cap), Nicolae Ungureanu; Marin Dragnea (62 Aurel Ţicleanu), Ladislau Bölöni, Michael Klein, Gheorghe Hagi (46 Ioan Adrian Zare); Rodion Cămătaru, Marcel Coraş. Trainer: Mircea Lucescu

W. GERMANY: Harald Schumacher; Bernd Förster, Ulrich Stielike, Karlheinz Förster (80 Guido Buchwald), Hans-Peter Briegel; Lothar Matthäus, Norbert Meier (65 Pierre Littbarski), Andreas Brehme; Karl-Heinz Rummenigge (Cap), Rudolf Völler, Klaus Allofs. Trainer: Josef Derwall

Goals: Völler (25, 67), Coraş (46)

PORTUGAL v SPAIN 1-1 (0-0)

Stade Vélodrome, Marseille 17.06.1984

Referee: Michel Vautrot (FRA) Attendance: 24,364

PORTUGAL: Manuel BENTO (Cap); JOÃO PINTO, LIMA PEREIRA, EURICO Gomes, ALVARO Magalhaes; CARLOS MANUEL, António FRASCO (77 DIAMANTINO Miranda), António SOUSA, JAIME PACHECO, Fernando CHALANA; Rui JORDAO. Trainer: Fernando Cabrita

SPAIN: Luis Miguel ARCONADA Echarre (Cap); Santiago URQUIAGA Perez (78 Juan Antonio SEÑOR Gomez), Antonio MACEDA Francés, Andoni GOIKOETXEA Olascoaga, José Antonio CAMACHO Alfaro; VICTOR Muñoz Manrique, Ricardo GALLEGO Redondo, JULIO ALBERTO Moreno Casas (69 Manuel SARABIA López), Rafael GORDILLO Vazquez; Carlos Alonso Gonzalez SANTILLANA, Francisco José CARRASCO Hidalgo. Trainer: Miguel Muñoz

Goals: Sousa (52), Santillana (73)

SPAIN v WEST GERMANY 1-0 (0-0)

Parc des Princes, Paris 20.06.1984

Referee: Vojtech Christov (CZE) Attendance: 47,691

SPAIN: Luis Miguel ARCONADA Echarre (Cap); Juan Antonio SEÑOR Gomez, Antonio MACEDA Francés, Andoni GOIKOETXEA Olascoaga (28 SALVAdor García Puig), José Antonio CAMACHO Alfaro; VICTOR Muñoz Manrique, Ricardo GALLEGO Redondo, JULIO ALBERTO Moreno Casas (81 FRANCISCO López Alfaro), Rafael GORDILLO Vazquez; Carlos Alonso Gonzalez SANTILLANA, Francisco José CARRASCO Hidalgo. Trainer: Miguel Muñoz

W. GERMANY: Harald Schumacher; Bernd Förster, Karlheinz Förster, Ulrich Stielike, Hans-Peter Briegel; Lothar Matthäus, Andreas Brehme (47 Wolfgang Rolff), Norbert Meier (60 Pierre Littbarski); Karl-Heinz Rummenigge (Cap), Rudolf Völler, Klaus Allofs. Trainer: Josef Derwall

Goal: Maceda (89)

PORTUGAL v ROMANIA 1-0 (0-0)

La Beaujoire, Nantes 20.06.1984

Referee: Heinz Fahnler (AUS) Attendance: 24,266

PORTUGAL: Manuel BENTO (Cap); JOÃO PINTO, EURICO Gomes, LIMA PEREIRA, ALVARO Magalhaes; CARLOS MANUEL (67 Tamagnini NÉNÉ), António FRASCO, António SOUSA, Fernando CHALANA (17 DIAMANTINO Miranda), Fernando GOMES, Rui JORDAO. Trainer: Fernando Cabrita

ROMANIA: Dumitru Moraru; Nicolae Negrilă, Gino Iorgulescu, Costică Ştefănescu (Cap), Nicolae Ungureanu; Mircea Irimescu (59 Romulus Gabor), Mircea Rednic, Ladislau Bölöni, Michael Klein; Rodion Cămătaru (34 Ionel Augustin), Marcel Coraş. Trainer: Mircea Lucescu

Goal: Néné (81)

	P	W	D	L	F	A	Pts
Spain	3	1	2	0	3	2	4
Portugal	3	1	2	0	2	1	4
West Germany	3	1	1	1	2	2	3
Romania	3	0	1	2	2	4	1

SEMI-FINALS

PORTUGAL v FRANCE 2-3 (0-1, 1-1) (AET)

Stade Vélodrome, Marseille 23.06.1984

Referee: Paolo Bergamo (ITA) Attendance: 54,848

FRANCE: Joël Bats; Patrick Battiston, Yvon Le Roux, Maxime Bossis, Jean François Domergue; Alain Giresse, Jean Tigana, Michel Platini (Cap), Luis Fernandez; Bernard Lacombe (66 Jean-Marc Ferreri), Didier Six (101 Bruno Bellone). Trainer: Michel Hidalgo

PORTUGAL: Manuel BENTO (Cap); JOÃO PINTO, LIMA PEREIRA, EURICO Gomes, ALVARO Magalhaes; António FRASCO, JAIME PACHECO, António SOUSA (64 Tamagnini NÉNÉ), Fernando CHALANA, Rui JORDAO, DIAMANTINO Miranda (46 Fernando GOMES). Trainer: Fernando Cabrita

Goals: Domergue (25, 115), Jordao (74, 98), Platini (119)

SPAIN v DENMARK 1-1 (0-1) (AET)

Stade Gerland, Lyon 24.06.1984

Referee: George Courtney (ENG) Attendance: 47,843

SPAIN: Luis Miguel ARCONADA Echarre (Cap); Juan Antonio SEÑOR Gomez, Antonio MACEDA Francés, SALVAdor García Puig (102 Santiago URQUIAGA Perez), José Antonio CAMACHO Alfaro; VICTOR Muñoz Manrique, Ricardo GALLEGO Redondo, JULIO ALBERTO Moreno Casas (60 Manuel SARABIA López), Rafael GORDILLO Vazquez; Carlos Alonso Gonzalez SANTILLANA, Francisco José CARRASCO Hidalgo. Trainer: Miguel Muñoz

DENMARK: Ole Qvist; John Sivebaek, Morten Olsen (Cap) (113 Kenneth Brylle-Larsen), Søren Busk, Ivan Nielsen; Frank Arnesen (68 Jesper Olsen), Søren Lerby, Jens Jørn Bertelsen, Klaus Berggreen; Michael Laudrup, Preben Elkjær-Larsen. Trainer: Josef Piontek

Sent off: Berggreen (106)

Goals: Lerby (6), Maceda (67)

Penalties: 0-1 Brylle, 1-1 Santillana, 1-2 J. Olsen, 2-2 Señor, 2-3 Laudrup, 3-3 Urquiaga, 3-4 Lerby, 4-4 Victor, Larsen, 5-4 Sarabia

FINAL

FRANCE v SPAIN 2-0 (0-0)

Parc des Princes, Paris 27.06.1984

Referee: Vojtech Christov (CZE) Attendance: 47,368

FRANCE: Joël Bats; Patrick Battiston (72 Manuel Amoros), Yvon Le Roux, Maxime Bossis, Jean-François Domergue; Alain Giresse, Jean Tigana, Michel Platini (Cap), Luis Fernandez; Bernard Lacombe (80 Bernard Genghini), Bruno Bellone. Trainer: Michel Hidalgo

SPAIN: Luis Miguel ARCONADA Echarre (Cap); Santiago URQUIAGA Perez, SALVAdor García Puig (85 ROBERTO Fernandez Bonilla), Ricardo GALLEGO Redondo, JULIO ALBERTO Moreno Casas (77 Manuel SARABIA López); Juan Antonio SEÑOR Gomez, FRANCISCO Javier López Alfaro, VICTOR Muñoz Manrique, José Antonio CAMACHO Alfaro; Carlos Alonso Gonzalez SANTILLANA, Francisco José CARRASCO Hidalgo. Trainer: Miguel Muñoz

Sent off: Le Roux (85)

Goals: Platini (57), Bellone (90)

Goalscorers European Football Championship 1984

9 goals: Michel Platini (France)

7 goals: Karl-Heinz Rummenigge, Rudolf Völler (West Germany), Carlos Alonso Gonzalez Santillana (Spain)

6 goals: Preben Elkjær Larsen (Denmark), Antonio Maceda Francés (Spain)

5 goals: Nikos Anastopoulos (Greece), Tibor Nyilasi (Hungary), Walter Schachner (Austria), Hipolito Rincón Povedano (Spain), Ruud Gullit (Holland), Frank Stapleton (Republic of Ireland), Erwin Vandenbergh (Belgium)

4 goals: Joachim Streich (East Germany), Allan Simonsen (Denmark), Dick Schoenaker (Holland), Ladislau Bölöni (Romania), Rui Jordao (Portugal)

3 goals: François Van der Elst, Frankie Vercauteren (Belgium), Michael Laudrup (Denmark), Luther Blissett, Anthony Woodcock, Trevor Francis (England), József Póczik (Hungary), Safet Susic (Yugoslavia), Dan Corneliusson, Glenn Strömberg (Sweden), Ladislav Vízek (Czechoslovakia), Selçuk Yula (Turkey), Juan Antonio Señor Gomez (Spain), Peter Houtman (Holland), William Brady (Republic of Ireland), Tamagnini Néné (Portugal), Frank Arnesen (Denmark)

2 goals: Ceulemans, Coeck (Belgium), Egli (Switzerland), Wark, Nicholas, Dalglish (Scotland), Carlos Manuel, Oliveira (Portugal), Demianenko, Blohin, Cherenkov (USSR), Smolarek (Poland), Berggreen, Lerby, J. Olsen (Denmark), Hoddle, Lee, Mariner, Robson (England), Hajszán (Hungary), Reiter (Luxembourg), R. James, Rush (Wales), Hareide, Thoresen, Ökland (Norway), Cămătaru (Romania), Prytz (Sweden), Janecka, Rada (Czechoslovakia), Altobelli (Italy), M. O'Neill, Stewart, Whiteside (N. Ireland), Gasselich (Austria), Hasan (Turkey), Targaj (Albania), Rijkaard, Van Kooten (Holland), Daly, Lawrenson, Waddock (Republic of Ireland), Atli Edvaldsson (Iceland), Busuttil (Malta), Carrasco (Spain), Domergue (France)

1 goal: Grün (Belgium), Schällibaum, Brigger, Geiger, Heinz Hermann, Sulser (Switzerland), Kreer, Richter, Ernst (East Germany), Bannon, Sturrock (Scotland), José Luis, Gomes, Sousa (Portugal), Rodionov, Larionov, Baltacha, Andreev (USSR), Boniek, Krol, Dziekanowski, Kupcewicz (Poland), Valvee, Kousa (Finland), Busk, Brylle, A. Hansen, Lauridsen (Denmark), Butcher, Withe, Coppell, Chamberlain, Neal (England), Saravakos, Kostikos, Papaioannou (Greece), Kardos, Töröcsik, S. Kiss, L. Kiss, Szentes, Burcsa, Pölöskei, Hannich (Hungary), R. Schreiner, Di Domenico, Malget (Luxembourg), Bazdarevic, Cvetkovic, Jesic, Kranjcar, Radanovic, Savic, Sestic, D. Stojkovic, N. Stojkovic, Zl. Vujovic, Zivkovic (Yugoslavia), Charles, Flynn, Jones (Wales), Iskrenov, Dimitrov, Gochev, Mladenov, Sirakov, Velichkov, Nikolov (Bulgaria), Lund (Norway), Andonie, Coraş, Geolgău, Klein, Văetuş (Romania), Sunesson, Sandberg, Hysén, Ravelli, Jingblad, Eriksson (Sweden), Luhovy, Danek, Prokes, Jurkemik, Bicovsky, Sloup, Chaloupka (Czechoslovakia), Cabrini, P. Rossi (Italy), Tsingis, Theofanous, Mavris, Vrahimis (Cyprus), Strack, Stielike, Dremmler (West Germany), Hamilton, McClelland (N. Ireland), Baumeister, Polster, Pezzey, Prohaska, Hagmayr, Weber, Brauneder (Austria), Ilyas, Metin, Arif (Turkey), Tomori (Albania), Sarabia, Gordillo, Victor, Pedraza (Spain), Vanenburg, Wijnstekers, Van Basten, R. Koeman, Ophof, Hovenkamp (Holland), O'Callaghan, Sheedy, Robinson, Walsh, Grimes, Grealish (Republic of Ireland), Geirsson (Iceland), Demanuele, E. Spiteri Gonzi, L. Fabri (Malta), Bellone, Giresse, Fernandez (France)

Own goals: Janas (Poland) for Finland, Wojcicki (Poland) for USSR, Ikalainen (Finland) for Portugal, Moes (Luxembourg) for England, Kapko (Czechoslovakia) for Italy, Patikkis (Cyprus) for Italy, Martin (Republic of Ireland) for Spain, Miamiliotis (Cyprus) for Czechoslovakia, Kola (Albania) for Austria, Raşit (Turkey) for Albania

THE EUROPEAN FOOTBALL CHAMPIONSHIP 1988

GROUP 1

ROMANIA v AUSTRIA 4-0 (1-0)

Steaua, București 10.09.1986

Referee: Gerard Biguet (FRA) Attendance: 14,000

ROMANIA: Dumitru Moraru; Ştefan Iovan, Adrian Bumbescu, Miodrag Belodedici, Mircea Rednic; Dorin Mateuţ (72 Ilie Balaci), Ladislau Bölöni (Cap), Michael Klein, Gheorghe Hagi; Victor Piţurcă (46 Marius Lăcătuş), Rodion Cămătaru. Trainer: Mircea Lucescu

AUSTRIA: Klaus Lindenberger; Heribert Weber, Gerald Messlender, Karl Brauneder (65 Peter Pacult); Leo Lainer, Reinhard Kienast (46 Jürgen Werner), Ernst Baumeister, Ewald Türmer, Josef Degeorgi; Walter Schachner (Cap), Anton Polster. Trainer: Branko Elsner

Goals: Iovan (45, 64), Lăcătuş (61), Hagi (90)

AUSTRIA v ALBANIA 3-0 (1-0)

Liebenauer, Graz 15.10.1986

Referee: Klaus Peschel (E. GER) Attendance: 5,100

AUSTRIA: Klaus Lindenberger; Gerald Piesinger, Heribert Weber (Cap), Gerald Messlender, Kari Brauneder; Manfred Zsak, Manfred Linzmaier, Jürgen Werner, Ernst Baumeister; Andreas Ogris, Anton Polster. Trainer: Branko Elsner

ALBANIA: Perlat Musta; Hysen Zmijani, Kreshnik Çipi, Rrapo Taho, Adnan Ocelli; Alfred Ferko (71 Bedri Omuri), Mirel Josa, Sulejman Demollari, Alfred Zijaj, Arben Minga (Cap), Agostin Kola. Trainer: Agron Sulaj

Goals: Ogris (19), Polster (65), Linzmaier (76)

SPAIN v ROMANIA 1-0 (0-0)

Estadio Benito Villamarin, Sevilla 12.11.1986

Referee: Jan Keizer (HOL) Attendance: 41,884

SPAIN: Andoni Zubizarreta; Miguel Porlan "Chendo", Manuel SANCHIS Hontilluelo, Juan Carlos Arteche, José Antonio Camacho (Cap); Miguel González "Michel", Ricardo Gallego (77 Juan Antonio Señor), Víctor Muñoz, Julio Alberto Moreno; Hipólito Rincón (85 ELOY Olaya), Emilio Butragueño. Trainer: Miguel Muñoz

ROMANIA: Silviu Lung; Ştefan Iovan, Adrian Bumbescu, Miodrag Belodedici, Nicolae Ungureanu; Tudorel Stoica (82 Mircea Rednic), Ladislau Bölöni (Cap), Michael Klein, Gheorghe Hagi; Marius Lăcătuş, Rodion Cămătaru (80 Gavril Balint). Trainer: Emerich Jenei

Goal: Michel (57)

ALBANIA v SPAIN 1-2 (1-0)

Qemal Stafa, Tiranë 03.12.1986

Referee: Antal Hutak (HUNG) Attendance: 20,000

ALBANIA: Perlat Musta; Hysen Zmijani, Rrapo Taho, Skender Hodja, Fatbardh Jera; Bedri Omuri, Alfred Ferko (70 Agostin Kola), Sulejman Demollari, Mirel Josa; Arben Minga (Cap), Shkëlqim Muça. Trainer: Agron Sulaj

SPAIN: Andoni Zubizarreta; Miguel Porlan CHENDO, Manuel SANCHIS Hontilluelo, Juan Carlos ARTECHE, José Antonio CAMACHO (Cap); Juan Antonio Señor (46 ELOY Olaya, Víctor Muñoz, JOAQUÍN Alonso, Miguel González MICHEL; Hipólito RINCÓN, Emilio BUTRAGUEÑO.

Goals: Muça (28), Arteche (66), Joaquín (84)

ROMANIA v ALBANIA 5-1 (3-1)

Steaua, București 25.03.1987

Referee: José Rosa dos Santos (POR) Attendance: 6,500

ROMANIA: Silviu Lung; Ştefan Iovan, Adrian Bumbescu, Miodrag Belodedici, Nicolae Ungureanu; Gheorghe Hagi (67 Mircea Rednic), Tudorel Stoica, Ladislau Bölöni (Cap), Michael Klein (63 Dorin Mateuţ); Marius Lăcătuş, Victor Piţurcă. Trainer: Emerich Jenei

ALBANIA: Perlat Musta; Hysen Zmijani, Skender Hodja, Rrapo Taho, Besnik Bilali (46 Bedri Omuri); Mirel Josa, Shkelqim Muça, Sulejman Demollari, Fatbardh Jera; Sokol Kushta (74 Alfred Ferko, Arben Minga (Cap). Trainer: Agron Sulaj

Goals: Piţurcă (2), Muça (35), Bölöni (43), Hagi (47 pen), Belodedici (54), Bumbescu (69)

AUSTRIA v SPAIN 2-3 (1-1)

Prater, Wien 01.04.1987

Referee: Bruno Galler (SWI) Attendance: 34,010

AUSTRIA: Klaus Lindenberger; Gerald Piesinger, Bruno Pezzey (Cap), Manfred Zsak, Rudolf Weinhofer (71 Alfred Roscher); Manfred Linzmaier, Jürgen Werner I, Reinhard Kienast, Ernst Baumeister; Andreas Ogris, Anton Polster. Trainer: Branko Elsner

SPAIN: Andoni Zubizarreta; Miguel Porlan "CHENDO", Genaro Andrinúa, Ricardo Gallego, José Antonio CAMACHO (Cap); Miguel González "MICHEL", VÍCTOR Muñoz, ROBERTO Fernández, Ramón CALDERÉ; Emilio Butragueño (12 ELOY Olaya, 79 Manuel SANCHIS Hontilluelo), Francisco José CARRASCO. Trainer: Miguel Muñoz

Sent off: Chendo (75)

Goals: Eloy (31, 57), Linzmaier (39), Polster (64), Carrasco (90)

ALBANIA v AUSTRIA 0-1 (0-1)

Qemal Stafa, Tiranë 29.04.1987

Referee: Gerassimos Germanakos (GRE) Att: 20,000

ALBANIA: Perlat Musta (Cap); Hysen Zmijani, Skender Hodja, Skender Gega, Bedri Omuri; Fatbardh Jera, Sulejman Demollari, Mirel Josa, Shkëlqim Muça (71 Sokol Kushta); Arben Minga, Agim Bubeqi (65 Ledi Pano).
Trainer: Agron Sulaj

AUSTRIA: Klaus Lindenberger; Gerald Piesinger, Bruno Pezzey (Cap), Manfred Zsak, Karl Brauneder; Rudolf Weinhofer (46 Robert Frind), Manfred Linzmaier, Jürgen Werner I, Ernst Baumeister; Andreas Ogris (82 Peter Pacult), Anton Polster. Trainer: Branko Elsner

Sent off: Kushta (57)

Goal: Polster (9)

ALBANIA v ROMANIA 0-1 (0-0)

Flamurtari, Vlorë 28.10.1987

Referee: Ignatius Van Swieten (HOL) Attendance: 15,000

ALBANIA: Artur Lekbello (65 Sotir Shkurti); Hysen Zmijani, Rrapo Taho, Artur Lekbello II, Roland Iljadhi; Alfred Ferko, Sulejman Demollari (46 Alfred Zijaj), Mirel Josa, Latif Gjondeda; Shkelqim Muça (Cap), Agim Bubeqi.
Trainer: Agron Sulaj

ROMANIA: Silviu Lung; Ştefan Iovan, Ioan Andonie, Miodrag Belodedici, Nicolae Ungureanu; Gheorghe Hagi (84 Mircea Rednic), Dorin Mateuţ, Ladislau Bölöni (Cap), Michael Klein; Marius Lăcătuş (88 Victor Piţurcă), Rodion Cămătaru.
Trainer: Emerich Jenei

Goal: Klein (61)

ROMANIA v SPAIN 3-1 (3-0)

Steaua, Bucureşti 29.04.1987

Referee: Alexis Ponnet (BEL) Attendance: 30,000

ROMANIA: Silviu Lung; Ştefan Iovan (78 Nicolae Negrilă), Adrian Bumbescu, Miodrag Belodedici, Nicolae Ungureanu; Dorin Mateuţ, Ladislau Bölöni (Cap), Michael Klein (88 Gavril Balint); Marius Lăcătuş, Victor Piţurcă, Gheorghe Hagi.
Trainer: Emerich Jenei

SPAIN: Andoni Zubizarreta; Genaro Andrinúa, Andoni Goikoetxea (20 JOAQUÍN Alonso), José Antonio CAMACHO (Cap) (36 Miguel Soler); Miguel González "MICHEL", VÍCTOR Muñoz (Cap), Manuel SANCHIS Hontilluelo, Ricardo Gallego, Ramón CALDERÉ; Emilio Butragueño, ELOY Olaya.
Trainer: Miguel Muñoz

Goals: Piţurcă (38), Mateuţ (43), Ungureanu (45), Calderé (81)

AUSTRIA v ROMANIA 0-0

Prater, Wien 18.11.1987

Referee: Rosario Lo Bello (ITA) Attendance: 54,117

AUSTRIA: Klaus Lindenberger; Robert Frind, Robert Pecl, Bruno Pezzey (Cap), Karl Brauneder; Peter Artner, Gerhard Rodax, Ernst Baumeister (77 Jürgen Werner I), Gerald Willfurth; Walter Schachner (81 Andreas Ogris), Anton Polster. Trainer: Branko Elsner

ROMANIA: Silviu Lung; Ştefan Iovan, Adrian Bumbescu, Miodrag Belodedici, Nicolae Ungureanu; Dorin Mateuţ (77 Tudorel Stoica), Michael Klein, Ladislau Bölöni (Cap), Gheorghe Hagi; Marius Lăcătuş, Rodion Cămătaru (65 Victor Piţurcă). Trainer: Emerich Jenei

Sent off: Belodedici (88).

SPAIN v AUSTRIA 2-0 (0-0)

Ramón Sánchez Pizjuán, Sevilla 14.10.1987

Referee: Joël Quiniou (FRA) Attendance: 59,021

SPAIN: Andoni Zubizarreta; Miguel Porlan "CHENDO", Manuel SANCHIS Hontilluelo, Genaro Andrinúa, JULIO ALBERTO Moreno; Miguel González "MICHEL" (79 Ramón CALDERÉ), VÍCTOR Muñoz, Rafael Gordillo (Cap), Juan Antonio SEÑOR; Emilio Butragueño, Francisco José CARRASCO (69 José María BAKERO).
Trainer: Miguel Muñoz

AUSTRIA: Klaus Lindenberger; Robert Frind (46 Robert Pecl), Bruno Pezzey (Cap), Gerald Messlender; Manfred Zsak, Reinhard Kienast, Ernst Baumeister (64 Manfred Linzmaier), Karl Brauneder, Gerald Willfurth; Andreas Ogris, Anton Polster. Trainer: Branko Elsner

Goals: Michel (56), Sanchis (62)

SPAIN v ALBANIA 5-0 (3-0)

Estadio Benito Villamarín, Sevilla 18.11.1987

Referee: Kurt Roethlisberger (SWI) Attendance: 45,299

SPAIN: Andoni Zubizarreta; Miguel Porlan "CHENDO", Manuel SANCHIS Hontilluelo, Andoni Goikoetxea, JULIO ALBERTO Moreno (60 Enrique Sánchez "QUIQUE"; Miguel González "MICHEL", Juan Antonio SEÑOR, VÍCTOR Muñoz (Cap), Ramón CALDERÉ (46 Francisco Llorente); Emilio Butragueño, José María BAKERO. Trainer: Miguel Muñoz

ALBANIA: Artur Lekbello; Adnan Ocelli, Rrapo Taho, Skender Gega, Artur Lekbello II (80 Alfred Zijaj); Roland Iljadhi, Mirel Josa, Sulejman Demollari, Latif Gjondeda (70 Alfred Ferko); Arben Minga (Cap), Agim Bubeqi.
Trainer: Agron Sulaj

Sent off: Chendo (74)

Goals: Bakero (6, 31), Michel (34 pen), Llorente (67), Gjondeda (74 og)

	P	W	D	L	F	A	Pts
Spain	6	5	0	1	14	6	10
Romania	6	4	1	1	13	3	9
Austria	6	2	1	3	6	9	5
Albania	6	0	0	6	2	17	0

SWITZERLAND v PORTUGAL 1-1 (1-0)

Wankdorf, Bern 29.10.1986

Referee: Siegfried Kirschen (E. GER) Attendance: 8,500

SWITZERLAND: Martin Brunner; Claude Ryf, Martin Weber, André Egli (Cap), Stefan Marini; Alain Geiger, Georges Bregy, Heinz Hermann, Thomas Bickel (62 Erni Maissen); Alain Sutter (78 Dominique Cina), Beat Sutter.
Trainer: Daniel Jeandupeux

PORTUGAL: José Alberto Ferreirinha "ZÉ BETO"; António VELOSO, Eduardo Mendez "DITO", Eduardo Luís, Fernando Mendes; Alberto Fonseca, Sheu Han (17 José Coelho), Adelino Nunes (30 Mário Jorge), Carlos Pinto "ADAO"; Jaime des Mercês, Manuel Fernandes (Cap). Trainer: Rui Seabra

Goals: Bregy (7), Manuel Fernandes (86)

GROUP 2

SWEDEN v SWITZERLAND 2-0 (1-0)

Råsunda Solna, Stockholm 24.09.1986

Referee: Vojtech Christov (CZE) Attendance: 28,046

SWEDEN: Jan Möller; Stig Fredriksson (Cap), Sven Dahlqvist, Peter Larsson, Roland Nilsson; Ulf Eriksson, Robert Prytz, Glenn Strömberg, Anders Palmér (82 Leif Engkvist); Björn Nilsson, Johnny Ekström. Trainer: Olle Nordin

SWITZERLAND: Martin Brunner; Jürg Wittwer, André Egli (Cap), Charly In-Albon, Claude Ryf; Patrice Mottiez (57 Claudio Sulser); Alain Geiger, Erni Maissen, Heinz Hermann, Thomas Bickel (79 Georges Bregy); André Halter.
Trainer: Daniel Jeandupeux

Goals: Ekström (19, 79)

PORTUGAL v SWEDEN 1-1 (0-0)

Estádio Nacional, Lisboa 12.10.1986

Referee: Keith Hackett (ENG) Attendance: 9,775

PORTUGAL: José Alberto Ferreirinha "ZÉ BETO"; António VELOSO, Eduardo Luís, Eduardo Mendez "DITO", Fernando Mendes; Jaime das Mercês, Alberto Fonseca, Adelino Nunes, Sheu Han (62 José Coelho), Carlos Pinto "ADAO" (72 Mário Jorge); Manuel Fernandes (Cap). Trainer: Rui Seabra

SWEDEN: Jan Möller; Roland Nilsson, Glenn Hysén, Peter Larsson, Stig Fredriksson (Cap); Ulf Eriksson (84 Leif Engkvist), Glenn Strömberg, Robert Prytz, Anders Palmér (75 Mats Magnusson); Johnny Ekström, Björn Nilsson.
Trainer: Olle Nordin

Goals: Strömberg (50), Coelho (66)

ITALY v SWITZERLAND 3-2 (1-1)

Giuseppe Meazza, Milano 15.11.1986

Referee: Aron Schmidhuber (W. GER) Attendance: 67,422

ITALY: Walter Zenga; Giuseppe Bergomi, Franco Baresi, Antonio Cabrini (Cap) (11 Giovanni Francini); Dario Bonetti I, Salvatore Bagni, Roberto Donadoni (41 Aldo Serena), Carlo Ancelotti; Alessandro Altobelli, Giuseppe Dossena, Gianluca Vialli. Trainer: Azeglio Vicini

SWITZERLAND: Martin Brunner; Alain Geiger; Claude Ryf, Martin Weber, Jürg Wittwer; Heinz Hermann (Cap), Georges Bregy, Urs Bamert (78 Thomas Bickel); André Halter (69 Dario Zuffi), Jean-Paul Brigger, Beat Sutter.
Trainer: Daniel Jeandupeux

Goals: Donadoni (1), Brigger (32), Altobelli (51, 85 pen), Weber (88)

MALTA v SWEDEN 0-5 (0-1)

National, Ta'Qali 16.11.1986

Referee: Lajos Hartman (HUNG) Attendance: 8,411

MALTA: Raymond Mifsud; John Joseph Aquilina (46 Alex Azzopardi), Edwin Camilleri, Martin Scicluna, John Holland (Cap); Kristian Laferla, Joseph Camilleri, Raymond Vella, Dennis Mizzi; Leonard Farrugia, Mario Schembri (75 Dennis Cauchi). Trainer: Guentcho Dobrev

SWEDEN: Jan Möller; Magnus Andersson, Glenn Hysén, Peter Larsson, Stig Fredriksson (Cap); Ulf Eriksson, Leif Engkvist, Robert Prytz, Björn Nilsson (80 Anders Palmér); Johnny Ekström, Mats Magnusson. Trainer: Olle Nordin

Goals: Hysén (25), Magnusson (69), Fredriksson (71), Ekström (82), Palmér (84)

MALTA v ITALY 0-2 (0-2)

National, Ta'Qali 06.12.1986

Referee: Ishan Tuere (TUR) Attendance: 13,191

MALTA: John Bonello; Martin Scicluna, Alfred McKay (14 Alex Azzopardi), Kristian Laferla, John Holland (Cap); John Buttigieg, Carmel Busuttil, Raymond Vella, Martin Gregory (70 Charles Scerri); Leonard Farrugia, Michael Degiorgio. Trainer: Guentcho Dobrev

ITALY: Walter Zenga; Giuseppe Bergomi, Franco Baresi, Sebastiano Nela; Riccardo Ferri, Salvatore Bagni (65 Fernando De Napoli), Roberto Donadoni, Giuseppe Dossena (74 Gianfranco Matteoli); Alessandro Altobelli (Cap), Giuseppe Giannini, Gianluca Vialli. Trainer: Azeglio Vicini

Goals: Ferri (11), Altobelli (19)

ITALY v MALTA 5-0 (5-0)

Stadio Comunale, Bergamo 24.01.1987

Referee: Stephanos Hadjistephanou (CYP) Att: 34,078

ITALY: Walter Zenga; Giuseppe Bergomi, Franco Baresi, Antonio Cabrini (Cap); Riccardo Ferri, Salvatore Bagni (56 Fernando De Napoli), Roberto Donadoni, Giuseppe Dossena (56 Gianfranco Matteoli); Alessandro Altobelli, Giuseppe Giannini, Gianluca Vialli. Trainer: Azeglio Vicini

MALTA: John Bonello; Joseph Galea, Martin Scicluna, John Holland (Cap), John Buttigieg; Kristian Laferla, Carmel Busuttil, Raymond Vella, Martin Gregory (75 Dennis Cauchi); Leonard Farrugia (34 Charles Scerri), Michael Degiorgio. Trainer: Guentcho Dobrev

Goals: Bagni (4), Bergomi (9), Altobelli (24, 35), Vialli (45)

PORTUGAL v ITALY 0-1 (0-1)

Estádio Nacional, Lisboa 14.02.1987

Referee: Michel Vautrot (FRA) Attendance: 14,195

PORTUGAL: António Jesus; António VELOSO, Eduardo Mendez "DITO", Eduardo Luís, Alvaro Magalhaes; Jaime des Mercês, Joaquim Azevedo "QUIM", António Frasco, Rui Ferreira "NASCIMENTO", Carlos Pinto "ADAO" (30 Mário Jorge); Manuel Fernandes (Cap) (55 José Coelho). Trainer: Rui Seabra

ITALY: Walter Zenga; Giuseppe Bergomi, Franco Baresi, Antonio Cabrini (Cap); Riccardo Ferri, Salvatore Bagni, Roberto Donadoni (81 Fernando De Napoli), Giuseppe Giannini; Alessandro Altobelli, Giuseppe Dossena (76 Gianfranco Matteoli), Gianluca Vialli. Trainer: Azeglio Vicini

Goal: Altobelli (40)

PORTUGAL v MALTA 2-2 (1-1)

Estádio dos Barreiros, Funchal 29.03.1987

Referee: John Kinsella (IRE) Attendance: 5,000

PORTUGAL: António Jesus; António VELOSO, Eduardo Mendez "DITO", Eduardo Luís, Alvaro Magalhaes; António Frasco (46 Rui Barros), Rui Ferreira "NASCIMENTO" (82 João Santos "SKODA"), Carlos Pinto "ADAO"; Jaime das Mercês, Manuel Fernandes (Cap), Jorge Plácido. Trainer: Júlio Pereira "JUCA"

MALTA: David Cluett; Edwin Camilleri, Alex Azzopardi, Kristian Laferla, Martin Scicluna; John Buttigieg, Carmel Busuttil (80 Mario Schembri), Raymond Vella (Cap), Dennis Mizzi; Charles Scerri, Michael Degiorgio (56 Martin Gregory). Trainer: Guentcho Dobrev (BUL)

Goals: Plácido (12, 78), Mizzi (24), Busuttil (67)

SWITZERLAND v MALTA 4-1 (3-0)

Stade de la Maladière, Neuchâtel 15.04.1987

Referee: Roger Philippi (LUX) Attendance: 5,400

SWITZERLAND: Martin Brunner; Alain Geiger; Claude Ryf, André Egli, Martin Weber (69 Thomas Bickel); Stefan Marini (81 Philippe Perret), Heinz Hermann (Cap), Georges Bregy; Dominique Cina, Jean-Paul Brigger, Alain Sutter. Trainer: Daniel Jeandupeux

MALTA: David Cluett; Edwin Camilleri (46 John Holland), Alex Azzopardi, Kristian Laferla (70 Martin Gregory), Martin Scicluna; John Buttigieg, Carmel Busuttil, Raymond Vella (Cap), Dennis Mizzi; Charles Scerri, Michael Degiorgio. Trainer: Guentcho Dobrev

Sent off: Cina (77)

Goals: Egli (6), Bregy (16, 39, 88), Busuttil (72)

SWEDEN v MALTA 1-0 (1-0)

Nya Ullevi, Göteborg 24.05.1987

Referee: Kaj Natri (FIN) Attendance: 16,165

SWEDEN: Thomas Ravelli; Andreas Ravelli, Glenn Hysén, Peter Larsson, Stig Fredriksson (Cap); Ulf Eriksson (68 Lennart Nilsson), Robert Prytz, Glenn Strömberg, Anders Limpar; Johnny Ekström (68 Stefan Pettersson), Mats Magnusson. Trainer: Olle Nordin

MALTA: David Cluett; Edwin Camilleri, Alex Azzopardi, Kristian Laferla, Martin Scicluna (35 John Holland); John Buttigieg, Martin Gregory, Raymond Vella (Cap), Dennis Mizzi; Carmel Busuttil, Michael Degiorgio (65 Charles Scerri). Trainer: Guentcho Dobrev

Goal: Ekström (13)

SWEDEN v ITALY 1-0 (1-0)

Råsunda, Solna 03.06.1987

Referee: Dieter Pauly (W. GER) Attendance: 40,070

SWEDEN: Thomas Ravelli; Roland Nilsson, Glenn Hysén, Peter Larsson, Stig Fredriksson (Cap); Ulf Eriksson (80 Andreas Ravelli), Glenn Strömberg (87 Anders Limpar), Robert Prytz, Hans Holmqvist; Johnny Ekström, Lennart Nilsson. Trainer: Olle Nordin

ITALY: Walter Zenga; Giuseppe Bergomi, Riccardo Ferri II, Giovanni Francini; Fernando De Napoli, Roberto Tricella, Roberto Mancini (46 Luigi De Agostini), Giuseppe Giannini; Alessandro Altobelli (Cap), Giuseppe Dossena, Gianluca Vialli. Trainer: Azeglio Vicini

Goal: Larsson (25)

SWITZERLAND v ITALY 0-0

Wankdorf, Bern 17.10.1987

Referee: Marcel Van Langenhove (BEL) Attendance: 29,397

SWITZERLAND: Martin Brunner; Alain Geiger; Stefan Marini, Martin Weber, Marco Schällibaum; Marcel Koller, Heinz Hermann (Cap), Thomas Bickel (57 Urs Bamert); Beat Sutter, Jean-Paul Brigger, Christophe Bonvin (56 Hanspeter Zwicker). Trainer: Daniel Jeandupeux

ITALY: Walter Zenga; Ciro Ferrara, Franco Baresi II, Antonio Cabrini (Cap); Riccardo Ferri II, Salvatore Bagni (80 Carlo Ancelotti), Roberto Donadoni, Fernando De Napoli; Alessandro Altobelli (82 Roberto Mancini), Giuseppe Giannini, Gianluca Vialli. Trainer: Azeglio Vicini

SWITZERLAND v SWEDEN 1-1 (0-0)

Stade Olympique, Lausanne 17.06.1987

Referee: Gerardus Geurds (HOL) Attendance: 7,000

SWITZERLAND: Martin Brunner; Alain Geiger; Claude Ryf, Martin Weber, Stefan Marini; Heinz Hermann (Cap), Georges Bregy (75 Urs Bamert), Marcel Koller; Christophe Bonvin (79 Alain Sutter), André Halter, Beat Sutter.
Trainer: Daniel Jeandupeux

SWEDEN: Thomas Ravelli; Roland Nilsson, Andreas Ravelli, Peter Larsson, Stig Fredriksson (Cap); Ulf Eriksson, Robert Prytz, Glenn Strömberg, Hans Holmqvist; Johnny Ekström, Lennart Nilsson (79 Mats Magnusson). Trainer: Olle Nordin

Goals: Halter (58), Ekström (60)

PORTUGAL v SWITZERLAND 0-0

Estádio das Antas, Porto 11.11.1987

Referee: Lajos Nemeth (HUNG) Attendance: 3,632

PORTUGAL: António Jesus; João Pinto (Cap), Frederico Rosa, Miguel Marques, Alvaro Magalhaes; António Frasco (46 Carlos Parente), António André, António Sousa; José Coelho, Rui Aguas (72 Carlos Pinto "ADAO"), Paulo Futre.
Trainer: Júlio Pereira "JUCA"

SWITZERLAND: Martin Brunner; Alain Geiger; Stefan Marini, Martin Weber, Marco Schällibaum; Marcel Koller (80 Philippe Perret), Heinz Hermann (Cap), Thomas Bickel; Beat Sutter, Jean-Paul Brigger (67 Hanspeter Zwicker), Christophe Bonvin. Trainer: Daniel Jeandupeux

SWEDEN v PORTUGAL 0-1 (0-1)

Råsunda, Solna 23.09.1987

Referee: Valeriy Butenko (USSR) Attendance: 28,916

SWEDEN: Thomas Ravelli; Stig Fredriksson (Cap), Glenn Hysén, Peter Larsson, Torbjörn Persson; Roland Nilsson, Robert Prytz (74 Anders Limpar), Glenn Strömberg, Björn Nilsson; Mats Magnusson (57 Lennart Nilsson), Johnny Ekström. Trainer: Olle Nordin

PORTUGAL: António Jesus; João Pinto, Miguel Marques, Pedro Venâncio, Alvaro Magalhaes; Jaime Magalhaes, António André, Oceano Cruz, António Sousa; Fernando Gomes (Cap) (85 Rui Barros), Paulo Futre. Trainer: Júlio Pereira "JUCA"

Goal: Gomes (35)

ITALY v SWEDEN 2-1 (2-1)

San Paolo, Napoli 14.11.1987

Referee: Adolf Prokop (E. GER) Attendance: 59,045

ITALY: Walter Zenga; Giuseppe Bergomi, Franco Baresi II, Giovanni Francini (26 Luigi De Agostini); Ciro Ferrara, Salvatore Bagni (89 Carlo Ancelotti), Roberto Donadoni, Fernando De Napoli; Alessandro Altobelli (Cap), Giuseppe Giannini, Gianluca Vialli. Trainer: Azeglio Vicini

SWEDEN: Thomas Ravelli; Roland Nilsson (70 Anders Limpar), Glenn Hysén (Cap), Peter Larsson, Torbjörn Persson; Jonas Thern, Glenn Strömberg, Robert Prytz, Björn Nilsson; Johnny Ekström (70 Dan Corneliusson), Stefan Pettersson.
Trainer: Olle Nordin

Goals: Vialli (27, 45), Larsson (38)

MALTA v SWITZERLAND 1-1 (0-1)

National, Ta'Qali 15.11.1987

Referee: Georges Koukoulakis (GRE) Attendance: 5,850

MALTA: David Cluett; Edwin Camilleri, Alex Azzopardi, Kristian Laferla, Martin Scicluna; John Buttigieg, Martin Gregory (58 Charles Scerri), Raymond Vella (Cap), David Carabott (78 Dennis Mizzi); Carmel Busuttil, Michael Degiorgio. Trainer: Guentcho Dobrev

SWITZERLAND: Martin Brunner; Alain Geiger; Stefan Marini, Martin Weber, Marco Schällibaum; Marcel Koller, Heinz Hermann (Cap), Thomas Bickel; Hanspeter Zwicker, Jean-Paul Brigger (86 Patrice Mottiez), Beat Sutter (75 Christophe Bonvin). Trainer: Daniel Jeandupeux

Goals: Zwicker (2), Busuttil (90)

ITALY v PORTUGAL 3-0 (1-0)

Giuseppe Meazza, Milano 05.12.1987

Referee: Jan Keizer (HOL) Attendance: 13,524

ITALY: Walter Zenga; Giuseppe Bergomi Franco Baresi II, Giovanni Francini; Riccardo Ferri II, Salvatore Bagni (61 Luigi De Agostini), Roberto Donadoni, Fernando De Napoli; Alessandro Altobelli (Cap) (68 Robert Mancini), Giuseppe Giannini, Gianluca Vialli. Trainer: Azeglio Vicini

PORTUGAL: António Jesus (69 Eduardo Lúcio); João Silva "COSTEADO", Miguel Marques, Eduardo Mendez "DITO" (Cap), Frederico Rosa, António Carvalho; Hernâni Neves, Rui Ferreira "NASCIMENTO" (55 Carlos Parente), Carlos Pinto "ADAO", Gilberto Gomes; José Coelho.
Trainer: Júlio Pereira "JUCA"

Goals: Vialli (8), Giannini (87), De Agostini (89)

MALTA v PORTUGAL 0-1 (0-0)

National, Ta'Qali 20.12.1987

Referee: Hubert Forstinger (AUS) Attendance: 4,706

MALTA: David Cluett; Edwin Camilleri, Alex Azzopardi, Kristian Laferla, Joseph Camilleri; John Buttigieg, David Carabott, Raymond Vella (Cap), Dennis Mizzi (46 Michael Degiorgio); Carmel Busuttil, Martin Gregory.
Trainer: Guentcho Dobrev

PORTUGAL: António Jesus; João Silva "COSTEADO", Miguel Marques, Eduardo Mendez "DITO" (Cap), Frederico Rosa, Fernando Mendes; Gilberto Gomes (46 António Aparício), Rui Ferreira "NASCIMENTO", Rui Barros, Carlos Pinto "ADAO"; José Coelho (83 António Carvalho).
Trainer: Júlio Pereira "JUCA"

Goal: Fredrico (74)

	P	W	D	L	F	A	Pts
Italy	8	6	1	1	16	4	13
Sweden	8	4	2	2	12	5	10
Portugal	8	2	4	2	6	8	8
Switzerland	8	1	5	2	9	9	7
Malta	8	0	2	6	4	21	2

GROUP 3

ICELAND v FRANCE 0-0

Laugardalsvöllur, Reykjavík 10.09.1986

Referee: Alan Ferguson (SCO) Attendance: 13,758

ICELAND: Bjarni Sigurdsson; Gunnar Gíslason, Saevar Jónsson, Atli Edvaldsson (Cap), Agust Már Jónsson; Omar Torfason, Ragnar Margeirsson, Asgeir Sigurvinsson, Sigurdur Jónsson; Pétur Pétursson, Arnór Gudjohnsen.
Trainer: Siegfried Held

FRANCE: Joël Bats; William Ayache, Basile Boli, Patrick Battiston (Cap), Manuel Amoros; Luis Fernandez, Jean Tigana, Philippe Vercruysse, Bernard Genghini; Yannick Stopyra, Stéphane Paille. Trainer: Henri Michel.

ICELAND v USSR 1-1 (1-1)

Laugardalsvöllur, Reykjavík 24.09.1986

Referee: Karl-Josef Assenmacher (W. GER) Att: 6,370

ICELAND: Bjarni Sigurdsson; Gunnar Gíslason, Saevar Jónsson, Atli Edvaldsson (Cap), Agust Már Jónsson; Omar Torfason, Ragnar Margeirsson, Asgeir Sigurvinsson, Sigurdur Jónsson; Pétur Pétursson, Arnór Gudjohnsen.
Trainer: Siegfried Held

USSR: Rinat Dasaev; Vladimir Bessonov, Tengiz Sulakvelidze, Oleg Kuznetsov, Anatoliy Demianenko (Cap); Vasiliy Rats, Nikolai Larionov (83 Gennadiy Litovchenko), Aleksander Zavarov, Sergei Aleinikov, Vagiz Hidiatullin (46 Sergei Rodionov); Oleg Blohin. Trainer: Valeriy Lobanovski

Goals: Gudjohnsen (30), Sulakvelidze (40)

NORWAY v EAST GERMANY 0-0

Ullevaal, Oslo 24.09.1986

Referee: Egbert Mulder (HOL) Attendance: 10,158

NORWAY: Erik Thorstvedt; Svein Fjaelberg, Terje Kojedal, Anders Giske (74 Einar Jan Aas, Per Edmund Mordt; Jan Berg, Kjetil Osvold, Kai Erik Herlovsen, Tom Sundby; Arne Larsen Ökland (Cap), Sten Glenn Haaberg (71 Arve Seland).
Trainer: Tor Røste Fossen

EAST GERMANY: René Müller (Cap); Frank Rohde; Ronald Kreer, Carsten Sänger, Uwe Zötzsche; Jörg Stübner, Rainer Ernst, Matthias Liebers, Andreas Thom; Ulf Kirsten, Frank Pastor. Trainer: Bernd Stange

FRANCE v USSR 0-2 (0-0)

Parc des Princes, Paris 11.10.1986

Referee: Paolo Casarin (ITA) Attendance: 40,496

FRANCE: Joël Bats; William Ayache, Basile Boli (87 Philippe Vercruysse), Philippe Jeannol, Manuel Amoros; Luis Fernandez, Jean Tigana, Jean-Marc Ferreri, Michel Platini (Cap); Yannick Stopyra, Jean-Pierre Papin (70 Bruno Bellone). Trainer: Henri Michel

USSR: Rinat Dasaev; Vladimir Bessonov (31 Vagiz Hidiatullin), Aleksander Chivadze, Oleg Kuznetsov, Anatoliy Demianenko (Cap); Vasiliy Rats, Pavel Iakovenko, Aleksander Zavarov, Sergei Aleinikov; Sergei Rodionov (79 Oleg Blohin), Igor Belanov. Trainer: Valeriy Lobanovski

Goals: Belanov (67), Rats (73)

EAST GERMANY v FRANCE 0-0

Zentralstadion, Leipzig 19.11.1986

Referee: George Courtney (ENG) Attendance: 54,578

EAST GERMANY: René Müller (Cap); Dirk Stahmann; Detlef Schößler, Frank Rohde; Matthias Döschner; Rico Steinmann (62 Hans Richter), Jörg Stübner, Matthias Liebers; Ulf Kirsten (77 Matthias Sammer), Frank Pastor, Andreas Thom. Trainer: Bernd Stange

FRANCE: Joël Bats; William Ayache, Basile Boli, Patrick Battiston, Manuel Amoros; Yvon Le Roux, Jean Tigana, Fabrice Poullain, Michel Platini (Cap); Yannick Stopyra, Jean-Pierre Papin (64 Bruno Bellone). Trainer: Henri Michel

USSR v NORWAY 4-0 (3-0)

Lokomotiv, Simferopol 29.10.1986

Referee: Howard King (WAL) Attendance: 26,108

USSR: Rinat Dasaev; Vladimir Bessonov, Vagiz Hidiatullin, Oleg Kuznetsov, Anatoliy Demianenko (Cap); Gennadiy Litovchenko (85 Sergei Baltacha), Pavel Iakovenko, Aleksander Zavarov (20 Oleg Blohin); Vadim Evtushenko, Sergei Rodionov, Igor Belanov. Trainer: Valeriy Lobanovski

NORWAY: Ola By Rise; Rune Bratseth, Einar Jan Aas, Anders Giske, Per Edmund Mordt (58 Sten Glenn Haaberg); Vidar Davidsen, Kai Erik Herlovsen, Kjetil Osvold, Tom Sundby; Arne Larsen Økland (Cap) (82 Per Egil Ahlsen), Jan Berg. Trainer: Tor Røste Fossen

Goals: Litovchenko (25), Belanov (29 pen), Blohin (33), Hidiatullin (54)

USSR v EAST GERMANY 2-0 (1-0)

Republikanski, Kiev 29.04.1987

Referee: Erik Fredriksson (SWE) Attendance: 76,405

USSR: Rinat Dasaev; Vladimir Bessonov, Vagiz Hidiatullin, Oleg Kuznetsov, Anatoliy Demianenko (Cap); Vasiliy Rats, Sergei Aleinikov (86 Oleg Protasov), Sergei Rodionov, Aleksander Zavarov; Aleksei Mikhailichenko (72 Pavel Iakovenko), Igor Belanov. Trainer: Valeriy Lobanovski

EAST GERMANY: René Müller (Cap); Frank Rohde; Roland Kreer, Matthias Linder, Uwe Zötzsche; Jörg Stübner (70 Marcus Wuckel), Rainer Ernst, Matthias Liebers, Jürgen Raab; Ulf Kirsten (55 Heiko Scholz), Andreas Thom. Trainer: Bernd Stange

Goals: Zavarov (41), Belanov (49)

EAST GERMANY v ICELAND 2-0 (1-0)

Ernst-Thälmann, Karl-Marx Stadt 29.10.1986

Referee: Zoran Petrovic (YUG) Attendance: 15,000

EAST GERMANY: René Müller (Cap); Frank Rohde; Detlef Schößler, Carsten Sänger (68 Dirk Stahmann), Matthias Döschner; Jörg Stübner, Rainer Ernst (85 Ralf Minge), Matthias Liebers; Ulf Kirsten, Frank Pastor, Andreas Thom. Trainer: Bernd Stange

ICELAND: Bjarni Sigurdsson; Gunnar Gíslason, Saevar Jónsson, Atli Edvaldsson (Cap), Agust Már Jónsson; Omar Torfason, Ragnar Margeirsson, Pétur Ormslev, Sigurdur Jónsson; Gudni Bergsson (75 Gudmundur Torfason), Arnór Gudjohnsen. Trainer: Siegfried Held

Goals: Thom (5), Kirsten (89)

FRANCE v ICELAND 2-0 (1-0)

Parc des Princes, Paris 29.04.1987

Referee: Frederick McKnight (NIR) Attendance: 30,000

FRANCE: Joël Bats; Jean-Christophe Thouvenel, Basile Boli, Jean-François Domergue, Manuel Amoros; Luis Fernandez, José Touré, Michel Platini (Cap), Gérald Passi; Carmelo Micchiche, Yannick Stopyra (67 Jean-Pierre Papin). Trainer: Henri Michel

ICELAND: Bjarni Sigurdsson; Gunnar Gíslason, Saevar Jónsson, Atli Edvaldsson (Cap), Agust Már Jónsson; Omar Torfason, Ragnar Margeirsson, Asgeir Sigurvinsson, Sigurdur Jónsson; Pétur Pétursson (76 Sigurdur Grétarsson), Arnór Gudjohnsen. Trainer: Siegfried Held

Goals: Micchiche (37), Stopyra (65)

NORWAY v USSR 0-1 (0-1)

Ullevaal, Oslo 03.06.1987

Referee: Marcel Van Langenhove (BEL) Attendance: 10,473

NORWAY: Erik Thorstvedt; Rune Bratseth (68 Hans Hermann Henriksen), Anders Giske, Terje Kojedal, Per Edmund Mordt; Kai Erik Herlovsen, Per Egil Ahlsen, Hallvar Thoresen (Cap), Kjetil Osvold (46 Arve Seland); Tom Sundby, Jørn Andersen. Trainer: Tor Røste Fossen

USSR: Rinat Dasaev (Cap); Tengiz Sulakvelidze, Vagiz Hidiatullin, Oleg Kuznetsov; Vasiliy Rats, Sergei Rodionov, Sergei Aleinikov, Pavel Iakovenko (68 Anatoliy Demianenko), Aleksander Zavarov; Aleksei Mikhailichenko, Igor Belanov (78 Oleg Protasov). Trainer: Valeriy Lobanovski

Goal: Zavarov (16)

USSR v FRANCE 1-1 (0-1)

V.I.Lenin, Moskva 09.09.1987

Referee: Gerassimos Germanakos (GRE) Att: 85,596

USSR: Rinat Dasaev (Cap); Viktor Losev, Vagiz Hidiatullin, Oleg Kuznetsov, Vasiliy Rats, Vadim Tischenko (46 Igor Belanov), Gennadi Litovchenko, Pavel Iakovenko, Sergei Aleinikov; Oleg Protasov, Igor Dobrovolski (70 Aleksei Mikhailichenko). Trainer: Valeriy Lobanovski

FRANCE: Joël Bats; William Ayache, Rémy Vogel, Basile Boli, Manuel Amoros; Luis Fernandez (Cap), Fabrice Poullain, José Touré (74 Jean-Philippe Rohr), Gérald Passi; Philippe Fargeon (87 Jean-Pierre Papin), Yannick Stopyra.
Trainer: Henri Michel

Goals: Touré (13), Mikhailichenko (77)

ICELAND v EAST GERMANY 0-6 (0-2)

Laugardalsvöllur, Reykjavík 03.06.1987

Referee: Henning Lund-Sørensen (DEN) Attendance: 8,758

ICELAND: Bjarni Sigurdsson; Gunnar Gíslason, Saevar Jónsson, Atli Edvaldsson (Cap), Agust Már Jónsson; Omar Torfason, Ragnar Margeirsson (86 Pétur Arnthorsson), Asgeir Sigurvinsson (75 Lárus Gudmundsson), Sigurdur Jónsson; Pétur Pétursson, Arnór Gudjohnsen. Trainer: Siegfried Held

EAST GERMANY: René Müller (Cap); Frank Rohde; Roland Kreer, Matthias Linder, Matthias Döschner; Rico Steinmann, Rainer Ernst, Jürgen Raab; Thomas Doll (77 Heiko Scholz), Ralf Minge (82 Ulf Kirsten), Andreas Thom.
Trainer: Bernd Stange

Goals: Minge (15), Thom (37, 69, 88), Doll (49), Döschner (85)

ICELAND v NORWAY 2-1 (1-1)

Laugardalsvöllur, Reykjavík 09.09.1987

Referee: Wilfred Wallace (IRE) Attendance: 5,450

ICELAND: Bjarni Sigurdsson; Gunnar Gíslason, Saevar Jónsson, Atli Edvaldsson (Cap), Vidar Thorkelsson; Olafur Thórdarson, Sigurdur Jónsson, Ragnar Margeirsson (79 Pétur Arnthorsson), Pétur Ormslev; Pétur Pétursson, Gudmundur Torfason. Trainer: Siegfried Held

NORWAY: Erik Thorstvedt; Hans Hermann Henriksen, Trond Sollied, Terje Kojedal, Per Edmund Mordt; Erik Soler (77 Jan Kristian Fjaerestad), Vegard Skogheim (74 Arne Erlandsen), Kai Erik Herlovsen (Cap), Kjetil Osvold; Jørn Andersen, Børre Meinseth. Trainer: Tord Grip

Goals: Andersen (11), Pétursson (21), Ormslev (60)

NORWAY v FRANCE 2-0 (0-0)

Ullevaal, Oslo 16.06.1987

Referee: Werner Föckler (W. GER) Attendance: 8,268

NORWAY: Erik Thorstvedt; Hans Hermann Henriksen, Terje Kojedal, Anders Giske, Per Egil Ahlsen; Jan Berg, Per Edmund Mordt, Tom Sundby, Hallvar Thoresen (Cap); Arve Seland (62 Kjetil Osvold), Jørn Andersen (89 Erik Soler).
Trainer: Tor Røste Fossen

FRANCE: Joël Bats; Jean-Christophe Thouvenel, Basile Boli, Jean-François Domergue, Manuel Amoros; Fabrice Poullain (81 Philippe Delamontagne), Jean Tigana (Cap), Jean-Marc Ferreri, Gérald Passi; Yannick Stopyra, Carmelo Micchiche (75 Philippe Fargeon). Trainer: Henri Michel

Goals: Mordt (72), Andersen (80)

NORWAY v ICELAND 0-1 (0-1)

Ullevaal, Oslo 23.09.1987

Referee: Håkan Lundgren (SWE) Attendance: 3,540

NORWAY: Erik Thorstvedt; Hans Hermann Henriksen, Rune Bratseth, Anders Giske (Cap), Per Edmund Mordt; Erik Soler, Kai Erik Herlovsen, Kjetil Osvold, Vegard Skogheim (46 Ulrich Møller); Tom Sundby (77 Jan Berg), Jørn Andersen.
Trainer: Tord Grip

ICELAND: Bjarni Sigurdsson; Gunnar Gíslason, Saevar Jónsson, Atli Edvaldsson (Cap), Vidar Thorkelsson; Olafur Thórdarson, Ragnar Margeirsson, Pétur Arnthorsson, Gudni Bergsson; Lárus Gudmundsson (85 Halldór Askelsson), Gudmundur Torfason. Trainer: Siegfried Held

Sent off: Arnthorsson (90)

Goal: Edvaldsson (31)

EAST GERMANY v USSR 1-1 (1-0)

Friedrich-Ludwig-Jahn-Sportpark, Berlin 10.10.1987

Referee: Dusan Krchnak (CZE) Attendance: 19,800

EAST GERMANY: René Müller (Cap); Uwe Zötzsche; Detlef Schößler, Ronald Kreer; Hans-Uwe Pilz (75 Jörg Stübner), Jürgen Raab (84 Ralf Minge), Matthias Liebers, Matthias Döschner; Ulf Kirsten, Andreas Thom, Thomas Doll. Trainer: Bernd Stange

USSR: Rinat Dasaev (Cap); Vladimir Bessonov, Vagiz Hidiatullin (70 Vasiliy Rats), Oleg Kuznetsov, Anatoliy Demianenko; Ivan Iaremchuk, Sergei Aleinikov, Aleksander Zavarov (60 Gennadi Litovchenko), Aleksei Mikhailichenko; Igor Dobrovolski, Oleg Protasov. Trainer: Valeriy Lobanovski

Goals: Kirsten (44), Aleinikov (80)

EAST GERMANY v NORWAY 3-1 (2-1)

Ernst-Grube, Magdeburg 28.10.1987

Referee: Friedrich Kaupe (AUS) Attendance: 7,500

EAST GERMANY: René Müller (Cap); Dirk Stahmann; Ronald Kreer, Matthias Döschner; Detlef Schößler, Hans-Uwe Pilz, Jürgen Raab, Matthias Liebers; Ulf Kirsten, Andreas Thom, Thomas Doll. Trainer: Bernd Stange

NORWAY: Lars Gaute Bø; Terje Kojedal, Erik Soler, Rune Bratseth, Anders Giske (Cap), Per Edmund Mordt; Arne Erlandsen, Ulrich Møller (62 Jan Berg), Tom Sundby; Jan Kristian Fjaerestad, Børre Meinseth.

Goals: Kirsten (14, 54), Fjaerestad (32), Thom (34)

FRANCE v NORWAY 1-1 (0-0)

Parc des Princes, Paris 14.10.1987

Referee: Joaquín Ramón Marcos (SPA) Attendance: 31,091

FRANCE: Bruno Martini; Luc Sonor, Basile Boli, Didier Sénac, Manuel Amoros; Luis Fernandez (Cap), Dominique Bijotat, José Touré; Philippe Anziani (53 Jean-Marc Ferreri), Eric Cantona, Philippe Fargeon. Trainer: Henri Michel

NORWAY: Erik Thorstvedt; Terje Kojedal, Hans Hermann Henriksen, Anders Giske (Cap), Rune Bratseth, Per Edmund Mordt; Kai Erik Herlovsen (76 Erik Soler), Kjetil Osvold, Tom Sundby; Jan Berg (79 Vegard Skogheim), Børre Meinseth. Trainer: Tord Grip

Goals: Fargeon (63), Sundby (79)

FRANCE v EAST GERMANY 0-1 (0-0)

Parc des Princes, Paris 18.11.1987

Referee: Carlos Alberto da Silva Valente (POR) Att: 18,000

FRANCE: Joël Bats; Sylvain Kastendeuch, Yvon Le Roux, Basile Boli; Manuel Amoros (Cap), Dominique Bijotat (76 Philippe Fargeon), Fabrice Poullain, Bernard Zénier, Bruno Germain; Eric Cantona, Bruno Bellone. Trainer: Henri Michel

EAST GERMANY: René Müller (Cap); Dirk Stahmann; Ronald Kreer, Matthias Döschner, Uwe Zötzsche; Hans-Uwe Pilz, Matthias Liebers, Rico Steinmann; Ulf Kirsten, Ralf Minge (61 Rainer Ernst), Andreas Thom. Trainer: Bernd Stange

Goal: Ernst (90)

USSR v ICELAND 2-0 (1-0)

Lokomotiv, Simferopol 28.10.1987

Referee: Michal Listkiewicz (POL) Attendance: 22,136

USSR: Rinat Dasaev (Cap); Vladimir Bessonov, Vagiz Hidiatullin, Alexander Bubnov, Anatoliy Demianenko; Vasiliy Rats (80 Pavel Iakovenko), Ivan Iaremchuk (71 Oleg Blohin), Gennadi Litovchenko, Sergei Aleinikov; Oleg Protasov, Igor Belanov. Trainer: Valeriy Lobanovski

ICELAND: Bjarni Sigurdsson; Gunnar Gíslason, Saevar Jónsson (80 Thorvaldur Örlygsson), Atli Edvaldsson (Cap), Vidar Thorkelsson; Omar Torfason, Ragnar Margeirsson, Gudni Bergsson, Olafur Thórdarson; Lárus Gudmundsson (69 Rúnar Kristinsson), Gudmundur Torfason. Trainer: Siegfried Held

Sent off: Arnthorsson (90)

Goals: Belanov (15), Protasov (52)

	P	W	D	L	F	A	Pts
USSR	8	5	3	0	14	3	13
East Germany	8	4	3	1	13	4	11
France	8	1	4	3	4	7	6
Iceland	8	2	2	4	4	14	6
Norway	8	1	2	5	5	12	4

GROUP 4

ENGLAND v NORTHERN IRELAND 3-0 (1-0)

Wembley, London 15.10.1986

Referee: Alphonse Constantin (BEL) Attendance: 35,300

ENGLAND: Peter Shilton; Vivian Anderson, David Watson, Terence Butcher, Kenneth Sansom; Glenn Hoddle, Bryan Robson (Cap), Stephen Hodge; Gary Lineker, Peter Beardsley (84 Antony Cottee), Christopher Waddle.
Manager: Robert Robson

N. IRELAND: Philip Hughes; Gary Fleming, Nigel Worthington, John McClelland (Cap), Alan McDonald; Malachy Donaghy, Steven Penney (74 James Quinn), David Campbell, Colin Clarke; Norman Whiteside (84 Samuel McIlroy), Ian Stewart. Manager: William Bingham

Goals: Lineker (33, 80), Waddle (78)

ENGLAND v YUGOSLAVIA 2-0 (1-0)

Wembley, London 12.11.1986

Referee: Franz Wöhrer (AUS) Attendance: 60,000

ENGLAND: Christopher Woods; Vivian Anderson, Mark Wright, Terence Butcher (Cap), Kenneth Sansom; Glenn Hoddle, Gary Mabbutt, Stephen Hodge (82 Raymond Wilkins); Gary Lineker, Peter Beardsley, Christopher Waddle (79 Trevor Steven). Manager: Robert Robson

YUGOSLAVIA: Mauro Ravnic; Zoran Vujovic, Mirsad Baljic, Refik Sabanadzovic, Marko Elzner, Faruk Hadzibegic; Srecko Katanec, Milan Jankovic; Haris Skoro (71 Semir Tuce, 73 Goran Juric), Blaz Sliskovic, Zlatko Vujovic (Cap).
Trainer: Ivan Osim

Goals: Mabbutt (21), Anderson (57)

YUGOSLAVIA v TURKEY 4-0 (2-0)

Poljud, Split 29.10.1986

Referee: Carlo Longhi (ITA) Attendance: 11,270

YUGOSLAVIA: Mauro Ravnic; Zoran Vujovic, Mirsad Baljic, Refik Sabanadzovic, Marko Elzner; Milan Jankovic, Haris Skoro (55 Dejan Savicevic), Srecko Katanec; Radmilo Mihajlovic (65 Semir Tuce), Marko Mlinarić, Zlatko Vujović (Cap). Trainer: Ivan Osim

TURKEY: Fatih Uraz; Ismail Demiriz, Yusuf Altintaş, Ismail Taniş, Erdogan Arica (Cap); Metin Tekin, Savaş Demiral, Ugur Tütüneker; Şenol Çorlu, Tanju Çolak (75 Semih Yuvakuran), Erdal Keser (70 Hasan Derviş). Trainer: Coşkun Özari

Goals: Zl. Vujovic (25, 35, 84), Savicevic (75)

NORTHERN IRELAND v ENGLAND 0-2 (0-2)

Windsor Park, Belfast 01.04.1987

Referee: Emilio Soriano Aladren (SPA) Attendance: 20,568

N. IRELAND: George Dunlop; Gary Fleming, Malachy Donaghy, John McClelland (Cap), Alan McDonald; Paul Ramsey, David Campbell (59 Daniel Wilson), David McCreery, Kevin Wilson; Norman Whiteside, Nigel Worthington.
Trainer: William Bingham

ENGLAND: Peter Shilton (46 Christopher Woods); Vivian Anderson, Mark Wright, Terence Butcher, Kenneth Sansom; Gary Mabbutt, Bryan Robson (Cap), Stephen Hodge; Gary Lineker, Peter Beardsley, Christopher Waddle.
Manager: Robert Robson

Goals: Robson (19), Waddle (43)

TURKEY v NORTHERN IRELAND 0-0

Atatürk, Izmir 12.11.1986

Referee: Dan Petrescu (ROM) Attendance: 21,919

TURKEY: Fatih Uraz; Ismail Demiriz, Yusuf Altintaş (Cap), Ismail Taniş, Kadir Akbulut; Savaş Demiral, Ugur Tütüneker, Metin Tekin; Ridvan Erler, Tanju Çolak (46 Orhan Kapucu), Şenol Çorlu. Trainer: Coşkun Özari

N. IRELAND: Philip Hughes; Malachy Donaghy, John McClelland (Cap), Alan McDonald, Nigel Worthington; Steven Penney, Daniel Wilson, David McCreery, David Campbell (74 Bernard McNally); Colin Clarke, James Quinn (77 Laurie Sánchez). Manager: William Bingham

TURKEY v ENGLAND 0-0

Atatürk, Izmir 29.04.1987

Referee: L Valeri Butenko (USSR) Attendance: 22,000

TURKEY: Fatih Uraz; Semih Yuvakuran, Ali Çoban, Erhan Önal (Cap), Ismail Demiriz, Riza Çalimbay, Savaş Demiral, Ugur Tütüneker; Hasan Dervis (87 Feyyaz Uçar), Erdal Keser, Iskender Gönen (79 Ilyas Tüfekçi). Trainer: Mustafa Denizli

ENGLAND: Christopher Woods; Vivian Anderson, Antony Adams, Gary Mabbutt, Kenneth Sansom; Glenn Hoddle, Bryan Robson (Cap), Stephen Hodge (75 John Barnes); Gary Lineker, Clive Allen (75 Mark Hateley), Christopher Waddle.
Manager: Robert Robson

NORTHERN IRELAND v YUGOSLAVIA 1-2 (1-0)

Windsor Park, Belfast 29.04.1987

Referee: Werner Föckler (W. GER) Attendance: 5,462

N. IRELAND: George Dunlop; Gary Fleming, Malachy Donaghy, John McClelland (Cap), Alan McDonald (46 Paul Ramsey); David McCreery (76 Raymond McCoy), David Campbell, Kevin Wilson, Colin Clarke; Norman Whiteside, Nigel Worthington. Trainer: William Bingham

YUGOSLAVIA: Tomislav Ivkovic; Zoran Vujovic, Mirsad Baljic, Srecko Katanec (46 Zoran Vulic), Marko Elzner, Faruk Hadzibegic; Dragan Stojkovic, Milan Jankovic; Darko Pancev, Aljosa Asanovic (77 Admir Smajic), Zlatko Vujovic (Cap). Trainer: Ivan Osim

Goals: Clarke (39), Stojkovic (48), Zl. Vujovic (79)

YUGOSLAVIA v ENGLAND 1-4 (0-4)

Crvena Zvezda, Beograd 11.11.1987

Referee: Michel Vautrot (ENG) Attendance: 49,774

YUGOSLAVIA: Mauro Ravnic (46 Vladan Radacka); Marko Elzner (27 Milan Jankovic), Zoran Vujovic, Mirsad Baljic, Faruk Hadzibegic; Srecko Katanec, Dragan Stojkovic, Mehmed Bazdarevic, Marko Mlinaric, Fadilj Vokri, Zlatko Vujovic (Cap). Trainer: Ivan Osim

ENGLAND: Peter Shilton; Gary Stevens, Antony Adams, Terence Butcher, Kenneth Sansom; Trevor Steven, Neil Webb (83 Glenn Hoddle), Bryan Robson (Cap) (75 Peter Reid); John Barnes, Peter Beardsley, Gary Lineker.
Manager: Robert Robson

Goals: Beardsley (4), Barnes (17), Robson (20), Adams (24), Katanec (81)

YUGOSLAVIA v NORTHERN IRELAND 3-0 (2-0)

Grbavica, Sarajevo 14.10.1987

Referee: Klaus Peschel (E. GER) Attendance: 14,075

YUGOSLAVIA: Mauro Ravnic; Zoran Vujovic, Mirsad Baljic, Srecko Katanec, Faruk Hadzibegic, Ljubomir Radanovic; Borislav Cvetkovic, Marko Mlinaric (76 Dragoljub Brnovic); Fadilj Vokri (76 Dejan Savicevic), Mehmed Bazdarevic, Zlatko Vujovic (Cap). Trainer: Ivan Osim

N. IRELAND: Allen McKnight; Paul Ramsey, Nigel Worthington, Malachy Donaghy, Alan McDonald; David McCreery (Cap), David Campbell (55 Anton Rogan), Daniel Wilson, Colin Clarke (48 James Quinn); Bernard McNally, Kevin Wilson. Manager: William Bingham

Goals: Vokri (13, 35), Hadzibegic (73 pen)

NORTHERN IRELAND v TURKEY 1-0 (0-0)

Windsor Park, Belfast 11.11.1987

Referee: Peter Mikkelsen (DEN) Attendance: 3,941

N. IRELAND: Allen McKnight; Paul Ramsey, Nigel Worthington, John McClelland (Cap), Alan McDonald; Malachy Donaghy, Daniel Wilson (66 David Campbell), James Quinn, Colin Clarke; Norman Whiteside, Kevin Wilson (66 Lee Doherty). Manager: William Bingham

TURKEY: Okan Gedikali; Ismail Demiriz, Gökhan Gedikali, Yusuf Altintaş (Cap), Semih Yuvakuran, Riza Çalimbay, Savaş Demiral, Uğur Tütüneker, Metin Tekin (65 Hami Mandirali), Tanju Çolak (79 Ali Çoban), Erdal Keser.
Trainer: Mustafa Denizli

Goal: Quinn (47)

ENGLAND v TURKEY 8-0 (4-0)

Wembley, London 14.10.1987

Referee: Albert Thomas (HOL) Attendance: 42,528

ENGLAND: Peter Shilton; Gary Stevens, Antony Adams, Terence Butcher, Kenneth Sansom; Trevor Steven (46 Glenn Hoddle), Neil Webb, Bryan Robson (Cap); John Barnes, Peter Beardsley (73 Cyrille Regis), Gary Lineker.
Manager: Robert Robson

TURKEY: Fatih Uraz; Riza Çalimbay, Ali Çoban, Erhan Önal (Cap), Semih Yuvakuran; Ali Gültiken (35 Savaş Demiral), Ugur Tütüneker, Muhammet Altintaş; Erdal Keser, Kayhan Kaynak, Iskender Gönen (35 Tanju Çolak).
Trainer: Mustafa Denizli

Goals: Barnes (1, 28), Lineker (8, 42, 71), Robson (59), Beardsley (62), Webb (88)

TURKEY v YUGOSLAVIA 2-3 (0-2)

Atatürk, Izmir 16.12.1987

Referee: Bruno Galler (SWI) Attendance: 4,657

TURKEY: Okan Gedikali; Riza Çalimbay, Erhan Önal, Gökhan Gedikali, Yusuf Altintaş (Cap); Ünal Karaman, Ugur Tütüneker (46 Ali Gültiken), Erdal Keser (41 Savaş Demiral); Feyyaz Uçar, Tanju Çolak, Iskender Gönen.
Trainer: Mustafa Denizli

YUGOSLAVIA: Vladan Radacka; Dragoljub Brnovic, Miodrag Krivokapic, Srecko Katanec, Faruk Hadzibegic; Ljubomir Radanovic, Admir Smajic (75 Cede Janevski), Dejan Savicevic, Dragan Jakovljevic, Mehmed Bazdarevic (Cap), Haris Skoro (80 Predrag Juric). Trainer: Ivan Osim

Goals: Radanović (6), Katanec (41), Hadzibegic (55 pen), Yusuf (64), Feyyaz (73)

	P	W	D	L	F	A	Pts
England	6	5	1	0	19	1	11
Yugoslavia	6	4	0	2	13	9	8
Northern Ireland	6	1	1	4	2	10	3
Turkey	6	0	2	4	2	16	2

GROUP 5

HUNGARY v HOLLAND 0-1 (0-0)

Népstadion, Budapest 15.10.1986

Referee: Bruno Galler (SWI) Attendance: 20,000

HUNGARY: József Szendrei; Sándor Sallai, Attila Pintér, Antal Róth (46 József Keller), Tamás Preszeller; Imre Garaba (Cap), József Kardos, Lajos Détári; Kálmán Kovács, Imre Boda (65 József Szekeres), Márton Esterházy.
Trainer: Imre Komora

HOLLAND: Johannes van Breukelen; Franklin Rijkaard, Ronald Spelbos, Adrianus van Tiggelen, Jan Jacobus Silooy; Jan Wouters, Ronald Koeman, Ruud Gullit (Cap), Johannes van't Schip; Simon Tahamata (88 Wilbert Suvrijn), Marco van Basten. Trainer: Marinus Michels

Goal: van Basten (68)

POLAND v GREECE 2-1 (2-1)

Lech, Poznán 15.10.1986

Referee: Emilio Soriano Aladren (SPA) Attendance: 31,000

POLAND: Jacek Kazimierski; Krzysztof Pawlak, Pawel Król, Marek Ostrowski; Waldemar Prusik, Waldemar Matysik (Cap), Jan Karas, Ryszard Tarasiewicz; Marek Lesniak, Dariusz Dziekanowski (46 Jan Urban), Wlodzimierz Smolarek (65 Krzysztof Baran). Trainer: Wojciech Lazarek

GREECE: Andonis Minou; Peter Xanthopoulos, Nikos Alavandas, Stelios Manolas, Peter Mihos; Kostas Mavridis (73 Kostas Batsinilas), Dimitris Saravakos, Giorgos Skartados (82 Stratos Apostolakis), Nikos Anastopoulos (Cap); Kostas Andoniou, Savas Kofidis. Trainer: Miltos Papapostolou

Goals: Dziekanowski (5 pen, 40 pen), Anastopoulos (13)

GREECE v HUNGARY 2-1 (1-0)

Olympiako, Athina 12.11.1986

Referee: Velodi Miminoshvili (USSR) Attendance: 16,666

GREECE: Andonis Minou; Stratos Apostolakis, Nikos Vamvakoulas, Stelios Manolas, Peter Mihos; Apostolos Papaioannou (64 Giorgos Skartados), Dimitris Saravakos, Kostas Andoniou, Nikos Anastopoulos (Cap); Anastasios Mitropoulos (78 Peter Xanthopoulos), Savas Kofidis.
Trainer: Miltos Papapostolou

HUNGARY: József Szendrei; Sándor Sallai, Antal Róth, Imre Garaba, Tamás Preszeller; Gyula Csonka (69 Károly Csapó), Gyözö Burcsa, Lajos Détári, Antal Nagy (Cap); Ferenc Mészáros, Márton Esterházy (46 Imre Boda).
Trainer: Imre Komora

Goals: Mitropoulos (38), Anastopoulos (65), Boda (73)

HOLLAND v POLAND 0-0

Olympisch, Amsterdam 19.11.1986

Referee: Joël Quiniou (FRA) Attendance: 52,750

HOLLAND: Johannes van Breukelen; Franklin Rijkaard, Ronald Spelbos, Adrianus van Tiggelen, Jan Jacobus Silooy; Jan Wouters, Ronald Koeman (46 Jacobus Bosman), Ruud Gullit (Cap), Johannes van't Schip; Simon Tahamata (74 René van der Gijp), Marco van Basten. Trainer: Marinus Michels

POLAND: Jacek Kazimierski; Krzysztof Pawlak, Roman Wójcicki, Pawel Król, Dariusz Wdowczyk, Waldemar Prusik, Andrzej Rudy (46 Ryszard Tarasiewicz), Jan Karas (Cap), Zbigniew Boniek; Dariusz Dziekanowski (66 Jan Urban), Wlodzimierz Smolarek. Trainer: Wojciech Lazarek

CYPRUS v GREECE 2-4 (2-1)

Makario, Nicosia 03.12.1986

Referee: Velitchko Tzonchev (BUL) Attendance: 7,528

CYPRUS: Andreas Haritou; Antonis Elia (47 Stavros Papadopoulos), Costas Miamiliotis, Demetris Misos, Nikos Pantziaras (Cap); Yiannakis Yiangoudakis, Yiannakis Ioannou, Panayiotis Marangos, George Savvides; Floros Nicolaou (75 Andreas Andreou), Evagoras Christofi.
Trainer: Panikos Iakovou

GREECE: Andonis Minou; Stratos Apostolakis, Nikos Vamvakoulas, Stelios Manolas, Peter Mihos; Apostolos Papaioannou, Dimitris Saravakos (46 Kostas Batsinilas), Kostas Andoniou, Nikos Anastopoulos (Cap); Anastasios Mitropoulos (70 Thanasis Anastasiadis), Savas Kofidis.
Trainer: Miltos Papapostolou

Goals: Andoniou (12), Christofi (28), Savvides (41), Papaioannou (47), Batsinilas (74), Anastopoulos (85 pen)

CYPRUS v HOLLAND 0-2 (0-1)

Tsirion, Limassol 21.12.1986

Referee: Ion Igna (ROM) Attendance: 7,483

CYPRUS: Andreas Haritou; Sotiris Tsikkos, Costas Miamiliotis, Demetris Misos, Avraam Socratous; Yiannakis Yiangoudakis (Cap), Pavlos Savva, Panayiotis Marangos (82 Floros Nicolaou), George Savvides; Yiannakis Ioannou, Evagoras Christofi. Trainer: Panikos Iakovou

HOLLAND: Johannes van Breukelen; Franklin Rijkaard (66 Gerald Vanenburg), Ronald Spelbos, Adrianus van Tiggelen, Jan Jacobus Silooy; Jan Wouters, Ruud Gullit (Cap), Arnoldus Mühren; René van der Gijp, Jacobus Bosman, Simon Tahamata. Trainer: Marinus Michels

Goals: Gullit (19), Bosman (73)

GREECE v CYPRUS 3-1 (0-0)

Olympiako, Athina 14.01.1987

Referee: Helmut Kohl (AUS) Attendance: 41,076

GREECE: Theologos Papadopulos; Stratos Apostolakis, Nikos Vamvakoulas, Stelios Manolas, Peter Mihos; Andreas Bonovas, Dimitris Saravakos, Kostas Andoniou, Nikos Anastopoulos (Cap); Apostolos Papaioannou (71 Anastasios Mitropoulos), Savas Kofidis (46 Kostas Batsinilas).
Trainer: Miltos Papapostolou

CYPRUS: Andreas Haritou; Charalambos Pittas, Costas Miamiliotis, Demetris Misos, Nikos Pantziaras (Cap); Yiannakis Yiangoudakis, Pavlos Savva, Panayiotis Marangos (83 Floros Nicolaou), George Savvides; Loizos Mavroudis (87 Christakis Georgiou), Evagoras Christofi.
Trainer: Panikos Iakovou

Goals: Anastopoulos (54, 66), Savva (60), Bonovas (63)

CYPRUS v HUNGARY 0-1 (0-0)

Makarion, Nicosia 08.02.1987

Referee: Dragisa Komadinic (YUG) Attendance: 4,100

CYPRUS: Andreas Haritou; George Lemesios, Charalambos Pittas, Demetris Misos, Avraam Socratous; Yiannakis Yiangoudakis (Cap), Pavlos Savva, Panayiotis Marangos (76 Floros Nicolaou), George Savvides; Loizos Mavroudis (50 Panikos Xiouroupas), Evagoras Christofi.
Trainer: Panikos Iakovou

HUNGARY: József Szendrei (Cap); Sándor Sallai, Gábor Hires, Antal Róth, Tamás Preszeller; Péter Hannich, István Varga, József Kardos, György Bognar (79 Imre Garaba), Imre Boda, Kálmán Kovács. Trainer: József Verebes

Goal: Boda (50)

HOLLAND v GREECE 1-1 (0-1)

De Kuip, Rotterdam 25.03.1987

Referee: Carlo Longhi (ITA) Attendance: 52,000

HOLLAND: Johannes van Breukelen; Ronald Koeman (71 Jacobus Bosman), Franklin Rijkaard, Ronald Spelbos, Jan Jacobus Silooy; Jan Wouters, Ruud Gullit (Cap), Arnoldus Mühren; René van der Gijp, Marco van Basten, Johannes van't Schip (82 Aron Winter). Trainer: Marinus Michels

GREECE: Theologos Papadopulos; Stratos Apostolakis (71 Peter Xanthopoulos), Nikos Vamvakoulas, Stelios Manolas, Peter Mihos; Andreas Bonovas (82 Giorgos Skartados), Dimitris Saravakos, Kostas Andoniou, Nikos Anastopoulos (Cap); Anastasios Mitropoulos, Savas Kofidis.
Trainer: Miltos Papapostolou

Goals: Saravakos (5), van Basten (55)

POLAND v CYPRUS 0-0

Lechia, Gdansk 12.04.1987

Referee: Simo Ruokonen (FIN) Attendance: 25,000

POLAND: Jacek Kazimierski; Waldemar Prusik, Pawel Król, Jerzy Wijas, Dariusz Wdowczyk; Dariusz Dziekanowski (66 Leszek Iwanicki), Jan Karas (Cap), Jan Urban; Wlodzimierz Smolarek, Jan Furtok (46 Jacek Bayer), Miroslaw Okonski.
Trainer: Wojciech Lazarek

CYPRUS: Andreas Haritou; Costas Miamiliotis, Charalambos Pittas, Nikos Pantziaras (Cap), Demetris Misos; Yiannakis Yiangoudakis, Pavlos Savva, Panayiotis Marangos, George Savvides; Floros Nicolaou, Marios Tsingis (85 Kyriakos Pantziaras). Trainer: Panikos Iakovou

GREECE v POLAND 1-0 (0-0)

Olympiako, Athina 29.04.1987

Referee: Zoran Petrovic (YUG) Attendance: 68,554

GREECE: Theologos Papadopulos; Nikos Alavandas, Nikos Vamvakoulas, Stelios Manolas, Peter Mihos; Andreas Bonovas, Dimitris Saravakos (88 Apostolos Papaioannou), Kostas Andoniou, Nikos Anastopoulos (Cap); Giorgos Skartados (73 Peter Xanthopoulos), Savas Kofidis.
Trainer: Miltos Papapostolou

POLAND: Jacek Kazimierski; Krzysztof Pawlak, Roman Wójcicki, Pawel Król, Dariusz Wdowczyk; Dariusz Dziekanowski, Waldemar Matysik (Cap), Ryszard Tarasiewicz, Marek Ostrowski (59 Waldemar Prusik); Jan Furtok (67 Marek Lesniak), Wlodzimierz Smolarek. Trainer: Wojciech Lazarek

Goal: Saravakos (52)

HOLLAND v HUNGARY **2-0** (2-0)

De Kuip, Rotterdam 29.04.1987

Referee: George Courtney (ENG) Attendance: 47,500

HOLLAND: Johannes Hiele; Ronald Koeman, Franklin Rijkaard, Adrianus van Tiggelen, Jan Jacobus Silooy; Jan Wouters, Ruud Gullit (Cap), Gerald Vanenburg, Arnoldus Mühren; Marco van Basten, Johannes van't Schip (88 René van der Gijp). Trainer: Marinus Michels

HUNGARY: József Szendrei (Cap); Sándor Sallai (40 Tibor Végh), Gábor Hires, Imre Garaba, Tamás Preszeller; Péter Hannich, József Kardos, Zoltán Péter (70 Gyözy Burcsa), Lajos Détári; József Kiprich, Kálmán Kovács.
Trainer: József Verebes

Goals: Gullit (36), Mühren (40)

HUNGARY v POLAND **5-3** (1-1)

Népstadion, Budapest 17.05.1987

Referee: Adolf Prokop (E. GER) Attendance: 5,900

HUNGARY: József Gáspár; Tibor Farkas, Gábor Hires, Attila Szalai; Sándor Rostás (46 Rezsö Kékesi), Imre Garaba (Cap), Lajos Détári, Zoltán Péter (69 Tamás Preszeller); József Kiprich, Istvan Vincze, József Szekeres.
Trainer: József Verebes

POLAND: Józef Wandzik; Krzysztof Pawlak, Roman Wójcicki, Pawel Król, Dariusz Wdowczyk; Waldemar Prusik, Waldemar Matysik (Cap), Ryszard Tarasiewicz (46 Marek Lesniak), Jan Urban (64 Kazimierz Przybys); Dariusz Marciniak, Wlodzimierz Smolarek.
Trainer: Wojciech Lazarek

Goals: Marciniak (27), Vincze (39), Smolarek (54), Détári (61 pen, 76), Péter (66), Wójcicki (81), Preszeller (83)

POLAND v HUNGARY **3-2** (1-1)

Wojska Polskiego, Warszawa 23.09.1987

Referee: Ishan Tuere (TUR) Attendance: 10,000

POLAND: Józef Wandzik; Jacek Grembocki, Józef Dankowski (46 Jaroslaw Araszkiewicz), Pawel Król, Wieslaw Cisek (66 Czeslaw Jakolcewicz); Ryszard Tarasiewicz, Andrzej Iwan, Waldemar Prusik (Cap), Jan Urban; Dariusz Dziekanowski, Marek Lesniak. Trainer: Wojciech Lazarek

HUNGARY: Péter Disztl; Arpád Toma, Sándor Sallai, Imre Garaba (Cap), Ervin Kovács, Zoltán Péter; Attila Herédi, Lajos Détári, György Bognár (81 József Fitos); Ferenc Mészáros, József Szekeres (81 György Handel). Trainer: József Garami

Goals: Dziekanowski (6), Bognár (10), Tarasiewicz (58), Lesniak (62), Mészáros (64)

HUNGARY v GREECE **3-0** (3-0)

Népstadion, Budapest 14.10.1987

Referee: Dieter Pauly (W. GER) Attendance: 15,000

HUNGARY: Péter Disztl; Sándor Sallai, Arpád Toma, Imre Garaba (Cap), Zoltán Péter; Attila Herédi, György Bognár, Lajos Détári, Ferenc Mészáros; József Kiprich, Gyula Hajszán (81 Kálmán Kovács). Trainer: József Garami

GREECE: Theologos Papadopulos; Petros Xanthopoulos (81 Stratos Apostolakis), Nikos Vamvakoulas, Stelios Manolas, Peter Mihos; Andreas Bonovas, Dimitris Saravakos, Kostas Andoniou (46 Kostas Mavridis), Nikos Anastopoulos (Cap); Anastasios Mitropoulos, Savas Kofidis.
Trainer: Miltos Papapostolou

Goals: Détári (4), Bognár (12), Mészáros (15)

POLAND v HOLLAND **0-2** (0-2)

Górnik, Zabrze 14.10.1987

Referee: Robert Valentine (SCO) Attendance: 15,000

POLAND: Marek Szczech; Kazimierz Przybys, Pawel Król, Waldemar Prusik (Cap), Marek Kostrzewa; Jan Karas (46 Czeslaw Jakolcewicz), Ryszard Tarasiewicz, Andrzej Iwan, Jan Urban; Dariusz Dziekanowski, Jaroslaw Araszkiewicz (68 Ryszard Robakiewicz). Trainer: Wojciech Lazarek

HOLLAND: Johannes van Breukelen; Ronald Koeman, Ronald Spelbos, Adrianus van Tiggelen, Jan Jacobus Silooy; Gerald Vanenburg, Hubertus van Aerle, Arnoldus Mühren, Johannes van't Schip; Ruud Gullit (Cap), Marco van Basten (80 Aron Winter). Trainer: Marinus Michels

Goals: Gullit (31, 38)

HOLLAND v CYPRUS **8-0** (4-0)

De Kuip, Rotterdam 28.10.1987

Referee: Roger Philippi (LUX) Attendance: 49,670

HOLLAND: Johannes van Breukelen; Ronald Koeman, Ronald Spelbos, Adrianus van Tiggelen, Jan Jacobus Silooy; Hubertus van Aerle, Arnoldus Mühren, Gerald Vanenburg; Jacobus Bosman, Ruud Gullit (Cap) (84 Johannes Gillhaus), Johannes van't Schip. Trainer: Marinus Michels

CYPRUS: Andreas Haritou (3 Antonis Kleftis); Charalambos Pittas, Costas Miamiliotis, Demetris Misos, Avraam Socratous; Yiannakis Yiangoudakis (Cap), Pavlos Savva, Christakis Christoforou, George Savvides; Loizos Mavroudis, Evagoras Christofi. Trainer: Takis Charalambous

Goals: Bosman (1, 38, 53, 60, 67), Gullit (20), Spelbos (40), van't Schip (47)

Haritou was injured by a smokebomb, CYPRUS left the stadium and returned after one hour. The match was awarded 3-0 to CYPRUS but, after the Dutch appealed, the match was replayed behind closed doors.

CYPRUS v POLAND 0-1 (0-0)

Tsirion, Limassol 11.11.1987

Referee: Dimitar Charlathki (BUL) Attendance: 2,497

CYPRUS: Andreas Haritou; Charalambos Pittas, Costas Miamiliotis, Christakis Christoforou, Avraam Socratous; Yiannakis Yiangoudakis (Cap), Pavlos Savva, Floros Nicolaou (75 Marios Tsingis), George Savvides; Loizos Mavroudis, Panayiotis Xiouroupas (60 George Mavroudis).
Trainer: Takis Charalambous

POLAND: Józef Wandzik; Waldemar Prusik (Cap), Pawel Król, Witold Wenclewski, Dariusz Wdowczyk; Ryszard Tarasiewicz, Andrzej Rudy, Dariusz Dziekanowski, Jan Urban (59 Krzysztof Warzycha), Marek Lesniak, Jaroslaw Araszkiewicz (46 Robert Warzycha).
Trainer: Wojciech Lazarek

Goal: Lesniak (73)

HUNGARY v CYPRUS 1-0 (0-0)

Üllöi ut, Budapest 02.12.1987

Referee: Dan Petrescu (ROM) Attendance: 3,000

HUNGARY: Péter Disztl; Sándor Sallai (Cap), Arpád Toma, Ervin Kovács, József Keller; József Fitos, Lajos Détári (80 István Vincze), György Bognár; József Kiprich, Ferenc Mészáros (46 Gyula Hajszán), Kálmán Kovács.
Trainer: József Garami

CYPRUS: George Pantziaras; Charalambos Pittas, Costas Miamiliotis, Demetris Misos, Avraam Socratous; Yiannakis Yiangoudakis (Cap), Pavlos Savva, Floros Nicolaou, Panayiotis Xiouroupas (69 George Mavroudis); Loizos Mavroudis (87 Christakis Christoforou), Marios Tsingis.
Trainer: Takis Charalambous

Goal: Kiprich (90)

HOLLAND v CYPRUS 4-0 (2-0)

Ajax, Amsterdam 09.12.1987

Referee: Ivan Gregr (CZE) Attendance: 300 (closed doors)

HOLLAND: Johannes van Breukelen; Aron Winter, Adrianus van Tiggelen, Jan Jacobus Silooy; Hubertus van Aerle, Ronald Koeman, Arnoldus Mühren, Gerald Vanenburg; Ruud Gullit (Cap), Jacobus Bosman, Johannes van't Schip.
Trainer: Marinus Michels

CYPRUS: George Pantziaras; Antonis Elia, Charalambos Pittas, Demetris Misos, Avraam Socratous; Yiannakis Yiangoudakis (Cap) (57 Ara Petrosian), Pavlos Savva, George Christodoulou, Floros Nicolaou; Loizos Mavroudis, Marios Tsingis (85 George Savva). Trainer: Takis Charalambous

Goals: Bosman (34, 45, 66), Koeman (63 pen)

GREECE v HOLLAND 0-3 (0-1)

Diagoras, Ródos 16.12.1987

Referee: Keith Hackett (ENG) Attendance: 4,000

GREECE: Hristos Mihail; Iakovos Hatziathanasiou, Lisandros Georgamlis, Pagonis Vakalopoulos, George Mitsimbonas (Cap); Giannis Kalitzakis (31 Theodoros Pahaturidis), Pavlos Papaioannou (12 Sotiris Mavromatis), Vangelis Vlahos, Thanasis Kanaras; Mihalis Ziogas, Giannis Samaras.
Trainer: Miltos Papapostolou

HOLLAND: Johannes van Breukelen; Jacob Lankhaar, Ronald Koeman (Cap), Adrianus van Tiggelen, Jacob Troost (63 Johannes de Wolf); Gerald Vanenburg, Hubertus van Aerle (63 Johannes Gillhaus), Hendrik Krüzen, Johannes van't Schip; Aron Winter, Jacobus Bosman.
Trainer: Marinus Michels

Goals: Koeman (19), Gillhaus (76, 81)

	P	W	D	L	F	A	Pts
Holland	8	6	2	0	15	1	14
Greece	8	4	1	3	12	13	9
Poland	8	3	2	3	9	11	8
Hungary	8	4	0	4	13	11	8
Cyprus	8	0	1	7	3	16	1

GROUP 6

FINLAND v WALES 1-1 (1-0)

Olympia, Helsinki 10.09.1986

Referee: Gerald Losert (AUS) Attendance: 9,840

FINLAND: Kari Laukkanen; Jari Europaeus, Esa Pekonen, Jukka Ikäläinen (Cap), Erkka Petäjä; Pasi Tauriainen, Markus Törnvall, Kari Ukkonen, Ari Hjelm; Mika Lipponen (76 Ari Valvee), Jari Rantanen. Trainer: Martti Kuusela

WALES: Martin Thomas; Kenneth Jackett, Kevin Ratcliffe (Cap), Jeremy Charles, Robert James; Peter Nicholas, Clayton Blackmore (81 Stephen Lowndes), Mark Aizelwood, David Williams (52 Neil Slatter); Ian Rush, Dean Saunders.
Manager: Harold Michael "Mike" England

Goals: Hjelm (11), Slatter (66)

CZECHOSLOVAKIA v FINLAND 3-0 (2-0)

"Za Luzánkami", Brno 15.10.1986

Referee: Gerassimos Germanakos (GRE) Att: 25,600

CZECHOSLOVAKIA: Ludek Miklosko; Stanislav Levy, Jozef Chovanec, Frantisek Straka, Jan Fiala (Cap); Karel Kula, Ivan Hasek, Lubos Kubík (76 Jirí Ondra); Petr Janecka, Tomás Skuhravy (82 Stanislav Griga), Ivo Knoflícek.
Trainer: Josef Masopust

FINLAND: Kari Laukkanen; Jari Europaeus, Esa Pekonen, Jukka Ikäläinen (Cap), Erkka Petäjä; Markus Törnvall, Kari Ukkonen, Pasi Tauriainen (34 Ari Valvee), Ari Hjelm (4 Petri Tiainen); Jari Rantanen, Mika Lipponen.
Trainer: Martti Kuusela

Sent off: Valvee (84)

Goals: Janecka (38), Knoflícek (43), Kula (67)

WALES v FINLAND 4-0 (2-0)

The Racecourse Ground, Wrexham 01.04.1987

Referee: Ignatius Van Swieten (HOL) Attendance: 7,696

WALES: Neville Southall; Kenneth Jackett, Clayton Blackmore, Patrick Van den Hauwe (11 Mark Aizelwood), Kevin Ratcliffe (Cap); David Phillips, Peter Nicholas, Robert James, Glyn Hodges; Ian Rush, Andrew Jones.
Trainer: Mike England

FINLAND: Kari Laukkanen; Jari Europaeus, Esa Pekonen, Jukka Ikäläinen (Cap), Erkka Petäjä; Hannu Turunen (70 Ismo Lius), Erik Holmgren, Pasi Tauriainen, Petri Tiainen (60 Mika Lipponen); Ari Hjelm, Jari Rantanen. Trainer: Martti Kuusela

Goals: Rush (14), Hodges (28), Phillips (64), Jones (73)

DENMARK v FINLAND 1-0 (0-0)

Idraetsparken, København 29.10.1986

Referee: Oliver Donnely (NIR) Attendance: 40,300

DENMARK: Troels Rasmussen; John Sivebaek, Søren Busk, Morten Olsen (Cap), Ivan Nielsen; Jan Mølby, Jens Jørn Bertelsen, Søren Lerby, Frank Arnesen (78 Henrik Andersen); John Eriksen, Claus Nielsen (81 Steen Tychosen).
Trainer: Josef Piontek

FINLAND: Kari Laukkanen; Jari Europaeus, Esa Pekonen, Jukka Ikäläinen (Cap), Erkka Petäjä; Petri Tiainen, Markus Törnvall (70 Pasi Tauriainen), Kari Ukkonen, Ari Hjelm; Jari Rantanen, Mika Lipponen (77 Ari Jalasvaara).
Trainer: Martti Kuusela

Goal: Bertelsen (67)

FINLAND v DENMARK 0-1 (0-0)

Olympia, Helsinki 29.04.1987

Referee: Dimitar Dimitrov (BUL) Attendance: 25,372

FINLAND: Kari Laukkanen; Jari Europaeus, Aki Lahtinen, Jukka Ikäläinen (Cap), Erkka Petäjä; Esa Pekonen, Kari Ukkonen, Petri Tiainen (65 Ari Valvee), Mika Lipponen (65 Ari Hjelm); Jari Rantanen, Ismo Lius.
Trainer: Martti Kuusela

DENMARK: Troels Rasmussen; Søren Busk; Morten Olsen (Cap), Ivan Nielsen, Jan Heintze; Klaus Berggreen (78 John Sivebaek), Jan Mølby, Jens Jørn Bertelsen, Søren Lerby (42 Lars Lunde); John Eriksen, Frank Arnesen.
Trainer: Josef Piontek

Goal: Mølby (53)

CZECHOSLOVAKIA v DENMARK 0-0

Tehelné pole, Bratislava 12.11.1986

Referee: Alexis Ponnet (BEL) Attendance: 45,000

CZECHOSLOVAKIA: Ludek Miklosko; Stanislav Levy, Jozef Chovanec, Frantisek Straka, Jan Fiala (Cap); Ivan Hasek, Lubos Kubík (75 Jirí Ondra), Karel Kula; Petr Janecka, Tomás Skuhravy (80 Stanislav Griga), Ivo Knoflícek.
Trainer: Josef Masopust

DENMARK: Troels Rasmussen; Søren Busk; Morten Olsen (Cap), Ivan Nielsen, Søren Lerby; Klaus Berggreen, Jan Mølby (46 Henrik Andersen), Jens Jørn Bertelsen, Frank Arnesen; Michael Laudrup (88 Jesper Olsen), Preben Elkjær Larsen.
Trainer: Josef Piontek

WALES v CZECHOSLOVAKIA 1-1 (0-0)

The Racecourse Ground, Wrexham 29.04.1987

Referee: Krzysztof Czemarmazowicz (POL) Att: 14,150

WALES: Neville Southall; Neil Slatter, Kevin Ratcliffe (Cap), Patrick Van den Hauwe, Clayton Blackmore; David Phillips, Robert James, Peter Nicholas, Glyn Hodges; Ian Rush, Leslie Mark Hughes (78 Andrew Jones). Trainer: Mike England

CZECHOSLOVAKIA: Ludek Miklosko; Jozef Chovanec, Frantisek Straka, Josef Novák; Ivan Hasek, Karel Kula, Lubos Kubík, Jan Fiala (Cap); Petr Janecka (88 Milan Luhovy), Tomás Skuhravy (82 Miroslav Kadlec), Ivo Knoflícek.
Trainer: Josef Masopust

Goals: Knoflícek (75), Rush (83)

DENMARK v CZECHOSLOVAKIA 1-1 (1-0)

Idraetsparken, København 03.06.1987

Referee: Claudio Pieri (ITA) Attendance: 46,600

DENMARK: Troels Rasmussen; Søren Busk; Morten Olsen (Cap), Ivan Nielsen; John Sivebaek, Jan Mølby, Jens Jørn Bertelsen, Frank Arnesen, Søren Lerby; Flemming Povlsen (67 Jesper Olsen), Preben Elkjær Larsen (87 John Eriksen). Trainer: Josef Piontek

CZECHOSLOVAKIA: Ludek Miklosko; Jozef Chovanec, Frantisek Straka, Josef Novák; Ivan Hasek, Karel Kula (83 Julius Bielik), Lubos Kubík, Jan Fiala (Cap); Petr Janecka, Tomás Skuhravy (46 Karel Jarolím), Ivo Knoflícek. Trainer: Josef Masopust

Goals: Mølby (17), Hasek (49)

DENMARK v WALES 1-0 (0-0)

Idraetsparken, København 14.10.1987

Referee: Ion Igna (ROM) Attendance: 44,500

DENMARK: Troels Rasmussen; John Sivebaek, Morten Olsen (Cap), Ivan Nielsen; Per Frimann, John Jensen, Søren Lerby, Jesper Olsen, Jan Heintze (46 Flemming Povlsen); Preben Elkjær Larsen, Michael Laudrup (85 Lars Olsen). Trainer: Josef Piontek

WALES: Edward Niedzwicki; Neil Slatter, Clayton Blackmore, Kevin Ratcliffe (Cap), Patrick Van den Hauwe; David Phillips, Robert James (72 Andrew Jones), Peter Nicholas, Kenneth Jackett (64 Glyn Hodges); Ian Rush, Leslie Mark Hughes. Trainer: Mike England

Goal: Elkjær Larsen (50)

WALES v DENMARK 1-0 (1-0)

Ninian Park, Cardiff 09.09.1987

Referee: Siegfried Kirschen (E. GER) Attendance: 20,535

WALES: Neville Southall; Neil Slatter, Clayton Blackmore, Kevin Ratcliffe (Cap), Patrick Van den Hauwe; Robert James (88 Barry Horne), David Phillips, Peter Nicholas, Andrew Jones; Leslie Mark Hughes, Glyn Hodges (71 Mark Aizelwood) Trainer: Mike England

DENMARK: Troels Rasmussen; John Sivebaek, Morten Olsen (Cap), Ivan Nielsen, Kent Nielsen, Søren Lerby; Klaus Berggreen, Jens Jørn Bertelsen, Michael Laudrup (46 John Jensen); Flemming Povlsen (66 Claus Nielsen), Preben Elkjær Larsen. Trainer: Josef Piontek

Goal: Hughes (19)

CZECHOSLOVAKIA v WALES 2-0 (1-0)

Sparta, Praha 11.11.1987

Referee: Erik Fredriksson (SWE) Attendance: 6,433

CZECHOSLOVAKIA: Ludek Miklosko; Josef Novák, Miroslav Kadlec, Frantisek Straka; Stanislav Levy, Ivan Hasek, Jozef Chovanec (Cap), Lubomír Moravcík (71 Karel Kula), Michal Bílek; Tomás Skuhravy, Ivo Knoflícek. Trainer: Josef Masopust

WALES: Neville Southall; Neil Slatter (46 Andrew Jones), Kevin Ratcliffe (Cap), Patrick Van den Hauwe, Kenneth Jackett; Geraint Williams, Peter Nicholas, Clayton Blackmore (66 Glyn Hodges), David Phillips; Ian Rush, Leslie Mark Hughes. Trainer: Mike England

Goals: Knoflícek (32), Bílek (90)

FINLAND v CZECHOSLOVAKIA 3-0 (1-0)

Olympia, Helsinki 09.09.1987

Referee: Neil Midgley (ENG) Attendance: 6,430

FINLAND: Kari Laukkanen; Jari Europaeus, Aki Lahtinen, Jukka Ikäläinen (Cap), Erkka Petäjä; Erik Holmgren, Pasi Rautiainen (63 Markku Kanerva), Petri Tiainen, Ari Hjelm; Jari Rantanen, Ismo Lius. Trainer: Martti Kuusela

CZECHOSLOVAKIA: Ludek Miklosko; Jan Fiala, Jozef Chovanec (Cap), Frantisek Straka, Josef Novák; Karel Kula (75 Pavel Chaloupka), Karel Jarolím, Lubos Kubík (64 Ivan Hasek); Petr Janecka, Tomás Skuhravy, Ivo Knoflícek. Trainer: Josef Masopust

Goals: Hjelm (28), Lius (72), Tiainen (82)

	P	W	D	L	F	A	Pts
Denmark	6	3	2	1	4	2	8
Czechoslovakia	6	2	3	1	7	5	7
Wales	6	2	2	2	7	5	6
Finland	6	1	1	4	4	10	3

GROUP 7

SCOTLAND v BULGARIA 0-0

Hampden Park, Glasgow 10.09.1986

Referee: Erik Fredriksson (SWE) Attendance: 35,076

SCOTLAND: James Leighton; Richard Gough, David Narey, William Miller (Cap), Maurice Malpas; Gordon Strachan, Paul McStay, Robert Aitken, David Cooper; Charles Nicholas (53 Kenneth Dalglish), Maurice Johnston.
Trainer: Andrew Roxburgh

BULGARIA: Borislav Mihailov; Plamen Nikolov, Georgi Dimitrov (Cap), Nikolai Iliev, Petar Petrov; Hristo Kolev, Nasko Sirakov, Plamen Simeonov (78 Georgi Karushev), Anio Sadkov; Petar Aleksandrov (87 Lachezar Tanev), Ilia Voinov.
Trainer: Hristo Mladenov

REPUBLIC OF IRELAND v SCOTLAND 0-0

Lansdowne Road, Dublin 15.10.1986

Referee: Einar Halle (NOR) Attendance: 47,500

IRELAND: Patrick Bonner; David Langan, Michael McCarthy, Kevin Moran (72 Gerard Daly), James Beglin; Paul McGrath, Raymond Houghton, William Brady, Kevin Sheedy; Frank Stapleton (Cap), John Aldridge. Trainer: Jack Charlton

SCOTLAND: James Leighton; Raymond Stewart, Richard Gough, Alan Hansen, David Narey; Paul McStay, Gordon Strachan, Robert Aitken (Cap), Murdo MacLeod; Graeme Sharp, Maurice Johnston. Trainer: Andrew Roxburgh

BELGIUM v REPUBLIC OF IRELAND 2-2 (1-1)

Heizel, Brussel 10.09.1986

Referee: Ion Igna (ROM) Attendance: 22,212

BELGIUM: Jean-Marie Pfaff; Frank Van der Elst, Georges Grün, Leo Clysters, Stéphane Demol, Patrick Vervoort; Vincenzo Scifo, Jan Ceulemans (Cap), Frank Vercauteren; Nico Claesen, Philippe Desmet. Trainer: Guy Thys

IRELAND: Patrick Bonner; David Langan, Mark Lawrenson, Kevin Moran, Christopher Hughton (82 James Beglin); Paul McGrath, Raymond Houghton, William Brady, Anthony Galvin (81 Ronald Whelan); Frank Stapleton (Cap), John Aldridge. Trainer: Jack Charlton

Goals: Claesen (14), Stapleton (18), Scifo (71), Brady (90 pen)

SCOTLAND v LUXEMBOURG 3-0 (2-0)

Hampden Park, Glasgow 12.11.1986

Referee: Eysteinn Gudmundsson (ICE) Attendance: 35,028

SCOTLAND: James Leighton; Raymond Stewart, Murdo MacLeod (64 Alistair McCoist), Richard Gough, Alan Hansen (46 Paul McStay); Patrick Nevin, Brian McClair, Robert Aitken (Cap), David Cooper; Kenneth Dalglish, Maurice Johnston.
Trainer: Andrew Roxburgh

LUXEMBOURG: John Van Rijswijck; Marcel Bossi, Gianni Di Pentima, Hubert Meunier (Cap), Laurent Schonckert; Guy Hellers, Carlo Weis, Jean-Pierre Barboni, Théo Scholten (89 Jeff Saibene); Théo Malget (79 Gérard Jeitz), Robert Langers.
Trainer: Paul Philipp

Goals: Cooper (24 pen, 38), Johnston (70)

LUXEMBOURG v BELGIUM 0-6 (0-3)

Stade Municipal, Luxembourg 14.10.1986

Referee: Krzysztof Czemarmazowicz (POL) Att: 9,534

LUXEMBOURG: John Van Rijswijck; Marcel Bossi, Hubert Meunier (Cap), Laurent Schonckert; Jean-Pierre Barboni, Jean-Paul Girres, Jeff Saibene (73 Marc Thome), Carlo Weis, Théo Malget; Robert Langers, Jeannot Reiter (58 Théo Scholten). Trainer: Paul Philipp

BELGIUM: Jacques Munaron; Leo Clysters, Eric Gerets, Stéphane Demol (50 Georges Grün), Patrick Vervoort; Vincenzo Scifo (55 Leo Van der Elst), Jan Ceulemans (Cap), Frank Vercauteren; Philippe Desmet, Nico Claesen, Erwin Vandenbergh. Trainer: Guy Thys

Goals: Gerets (5), Claesen (9, 53, 88 pen), Vercauteren (40), Ceulemans (85)

BELGIUM v BULGARIA 1-1 (0-0)

Heizel, Brussel 19.11.1986

Referee: Víctoriano Sánchez Arminio (SPA) Att: 22,780

BELGIUM: Jean-Marie Pfaff; Leo Clysters (46 Michel Renquin), Eric Gerets, Stéphane Demol, Patrick Vervoort; Vincenzo Scifo, Pierre Janssens, Jan Ceulemans (Cap), Frank Vercauteren; Nico Claesen, Philippe Desmet (56 Georges Grün). Trainer: Guy Thys

BULGARIA: Borislav Mihailov; Plamen Nikolov, Georgi Dimitrov (Cap), Nikolai Iliev, Petar Petrov; Hristo Kolev, Nasko Sirakov, Plamen Simeonov, Anio Sadkov; Petar Aleksandrov (58 Lachezar Tanev), Bojidar Iskrenov (87 Ilia Voinov). Trainer: Hristo Mladenov

Goals: Janssens (48), Tanev (63)

SCOTLAND v REPUBLIC OF IRELAND 0-1 (0-1)

Hampden Park, Glasgow 18.02.1987

Referee: Henrik van Ettekoven (HOL) Attendance: 40,081

SCOTLAND: James Leighton; Raymond Stewart, Richard Gough, Alan Hansen, Maurice Malpas (67 Alistair McCoist); Gordon Strachan, Robert Aitken (Cap), Patrick Nevin, David Cooper (46 Paul McStay); Brian McClair, Maurice Johnston. Trainer: Andrew Roxburgh

IRELAND: Patrick Bonner; Paul McGrath, Michael McCarthy, Kevin Moran, Ronald Whelan; Raymond Houghton, Mark Lawrenson, William Brady (61 John Byrne), Anthony Galvin; Frank Stapleton (Cap), John Aldridge. Trainer: Jack Charlton

Goal: Lawrenson (8)

REPUBLIC OF IRELAND v BELGIUM 0-0

Lansdowne Road, Dublin 29.04.1987

Referee: Heinz Holzmann (AUS) Attendance: 44,500

IRELAND: Patrick Bonner; John Anderson, Kevin Moran, Michael McCarthy, Ronald Whelan; Paul McGrath, William Brady (77 John Byrne), Raymond Houghton, Anthony Galvin; Frank Stapleton (Cap), John Aldridge. Trainer: Jack Charlton

BELGIUM: Jean-Marie Pfaff; Leo Clysters, Eric Gerets, Georges Grün, Philippe Albert (66 Pierre Janssens), Patrick Vervoort; Vincenzo Scifo, Jan Ceulemans (Cap), Frank Vercauteren; Nico Claesen, Philippe Desmet. Trainer: Guy Thys

BULGARIA v REPUBLIC OF IRELAND 2-1 (1-0)

Vasil Levski, Sofia 01.04.1987

Referee: Carlos Alberto da Silva Valente (POR) Att: 35,247

BULGARIA: Borislav Mihailov; Plamen Nikolov, Georgi Dimitrov (Cap), Nikolai Iliev, Krasimir Bezinski; Hristo Kolev, Nasko Sirakov, Plamen Simeonov (65 Ilia Voinov), Anio Sadkov; Lachezar Tanev, Bojidar Iskrenov (62 Petar Aleksandrov). Trainer: Hristo Mladenov

IRELAND: Patrick Bonner; John Anderson, Kevin Moran, Michael McCarthy, Christopher Hughton; Ronald Whelan, Paul McGrath, William Brady, Anthony Galvin; Frank Stapleton (Cap) (84 Niall Quinn), John Aldridge. Trainer: Jack Charlton

Goals: Sadkov (41), Stapleton (52), Tanev (81 pen)

LUXEMBOURG v BULGARIA 1-4 (0-0)

Stade Municipal, Luxembourg 30.04.1987

Referee: Gudmundur Haraldsson (ICE) Attendance: 1,920

LUXEMBOURG: John Van Rijswijck; Laurent Schonckert, Marcel Bossi, Carlo Weis, Gilbert Dresch (Cap) (72 Gérard Jeitz); Jean-Paul Girres (87 Patrick Juchem), Guy Hellers, Jean-Pierre Barboni, Robert Langers; Théo Malget, Jeannot Reiter. Trainer: Paul Philipp

BULGARIA: Borislav Mihailov; Plamen Nikolov, Georgi Dimitrov (Cap), Nikolai Iliev, Petar Petrov; Hristo Kolev, Nasko Sirakov, Plamen Simeonov (46 Petar Aleksandrov), Anio Sadkov; Lachezar Tanev, Bojidar Iskrenov (60 Georgi Iordanov). Trainer: Hristo Mladenov

Goals: Sadkov (49), Sirakov (55), Langers (59), Tanev (61), Kolev (88)

BELGIUM v SCOTLAND 4-1 (1-1)

Constant Van den Stock, Brussel 01.04.1987

Referee: Michel Vautrot (FRA) Attendance: 26,550

BELGIUM: Jean-Marie Pfaff (Cap); Leo Clysters, Georges Grün, Stéphane Demol, Patrick Vervoort; Vincenzo Scifo (73 Leo Van der Elst), Erwin Vandenbergh, Frank Van der Elst (89 Guy Vandersmissen), Frank Vercauteren; Nico Claesen, Philippe Desmet. Trainer: Guy Thys

SCOTLAND: James Leighton; Richard Gough, Paul McStay, David Narey, Maurice Malpas; Alexander McLeish, Robert Aitken (Cap), James McInally, James Bett (80 Patrick Nevin); Alistair McCoist, Paul Sturrock. Trainer: Andrew Roxburgh

Goals: Claesen (9, 55, 86), McStay (14), Vercauteren (74)

BULGARIA v LUXEMBOURG 3-0 (2-0)

Vasil Levski, Sofia 20.05.1987

Referee: Ion Crăciunescu (ROM) Attendance: 14,756

BULGARIA: Borislav Mihailov; Plamen Nikolov, Georgi Dimitrov (Cap), Nikolai Iliev, Petar Petrov; Hristo Kolev, Georgi Iordanov, Nasko Sirakov, Anio Sadkov (12 Ilia Voinov); Lachezar Tanev, Liuboslav Penev (64 Petar Aleksandrov). Trainer: Hristo Mladenov

LUXEMBOURG: John Van Rijswijck; Laurent Schonckert, Hubert Meunier (Cap), Carlo Weis, Marcel Bossi; Jean-Paul Girres, Guy Hellers, Jean-Pierre Barboni (71 Gérard Jeitz), Théo Malget; Robert Langers, Jeannot Reiter (86 Marc Thome). Trainer: Paul Philipp

Goals: Sirakov (33), Iordanov (41 pen), Kolev (57)

LUXEMBOURG v REPUBLIC OF IRELAND 0-2 (0-1)

Stade Municipal, Luxembourg 28.05.1987

Referee: Renzo Pedruzzi (SWI) Attendance: 4,955

LUXEMBOURG: John Van Rijswijck; Laurent Schonckert, Hubert Meunier (Cap), Carlo Weis, Marcel Bossi; Jean-Paul Girres (87 Marc Thome), Guy Hellers, Jean-Pierre Barboni, Théo Malget; Robert Langers, Jeannot Reiter (70 Gérard Jeitz). Trainer: Paul Philipp

IRELAND: Patrick Bonner; John Anderson (52 David Langan), Kevin Moran (46 John Byrne), Michael McCarthy, Ronald Whelan; Paul McGrath, William Brady, Raymond Houghton, Anthony Galvin; Frank Stapleton (Cap), John Aldridge. Trainer: Jack Charlton

Goals: Galvin (44), Whelan (64)

REPUBLIC OF IRELAND v BULGARIA 2-0 (0-0)

Lansdowne Road, Dublin 14.10.1987

Referee: Jan Keizer (HOL) Attendance: 22,000

IRELAND: Patrick Bonner; Paul McGrath, Michael McCarthy, Kevin Moran, Ronald Whelan; Mark Lawrenson, William Brady, Raymond Houghton, Anthony Galvin (77 Niall Quinn); Frank Stapleton (Cap), John Aldridge, John Byrne. Trainer: Jack Charlton

BULGARIA: Antonio Ananiev (56 Ilia Valov); Plamen Nikolov, Georgi Dimitrov (Cap), Nikolai Iliev, Petar Petrov; Anio Sadkov, Hristo Stoichkov, Plamen Simeonov, Nasko Sirakov; Ilia Voinov (60 Petar Aleksandrov), Bojidar Iskrenov. Trainer: Hristo Mladenov

Sent off: Brady (83)

Goals: McGrath (52), Moran (85)

REPUBLIC OF IRELAND v LUXEMBOURG 2-1 (1-1)

Lansdowne Road, Dublin 09.09.1987

Referee: Keith Cooper (WAL) Attendance: 18,000

IRELAND: Gerard Peyton; David Langan, Paul McGrath, Kevin Moran, Ashley Grimes; Ronald Whelan, William Brady, Raymond Houghton, Anthony Galvin (56 Niall Quinn); Frank Stapleton (Cap), John Byrne. Trainer: Jack Charlton

LUXEMBOURG: John Van Rijswijck; Laurent Schonckert, Hubert Meunier (Cap), Carlo Weis, Marcel Bossi; Théo Malget, Guy Hellers, Jean-Pierre Barboni (82 Gérard Jeitz), Théo Scholten (65 Gilbert Dresch); Armin Krings, Robert Langers. Trainer: Paul Philipp

Goals: Krings (29), Stapleton (31), McGrath (74)

SCOTLAND v BELGIUM 2-0 (1-0)

Hampden Park, Glasgow 14.10.1987

Referee: Paolo Casarin (ITA) Attendance: 20,052

SCOTLAND: James Leighton; Stephen Clarke, Alexander McLeish, Gary Gillespie, Maurice Malpas (53 Derek Whyte); Paul McStay, Robert Aitken (Cap), Iain Durrant, Ian Wilson; Alistair McCoist, Maurice Johnston (72 Graeme Sharp). Trainer: Andrew Roxburgh

BELGIUM: Michel Preud'homme; Leo Clysters, Eric Gerets, Georges Grün, Patrick Vervoort; Luc Beyens (55 Philippe Desmet), Frank Van der Elst, Jan Ceulemans (Cap), Frank Vercauteren; Marc Degryse, Nico Claesen. Trainer: Guy Thys

Goals: McCoist (14), McStay (79)

BULGARIA v BELGIUM 2-0 (1-0)

Vasil Levski, Sofia 23.09.1987

Referee: Karl-Heinz Tritschler (W. GER) Att: 51,000

BULGARIA: Borislav Mihailov; Plamen Nikolov, Georgi Dimitrov (Cap), Nikolai Iliev, Petar Petrov; Hristo Stoichkov (65 Georgi Iordanov), Nasko Sirakov, Anio Sadkov, Plamen Simeonov; Lachezar Tanev, Bojidar Iskrenov (80 Ilia Voinov). Trainer: Hristo Mladenov

BELGIUM: Jean-Marie Pfaff (Cap); Leo Clysters, Eric Gerets, Georges Grün, Michel Renquin; Vincenzo Scifo (70 Guy Vandersmissen), Frank Van der Elst (59 Daniel Veyt), Marc Degryse, Patrick Vervoort; Philippe Desmet, Nico Claesen. Trainer: Guy Thys

Goals: Sirakov (19), Tanev (70)

BELGIUM v LUXEMBOURG 3-0 (1-0)

Heizel, Brussel 11.11.1987

Referee: Egil Nervik (NOR) Attendance: 2,504

BELGIUM: Michel Preud'homme; Leo Clysters, Georges Grün, Pascal Plovie (46 Frank Dekenne), Raymond Mommens; Luc Beyens (71 Peter Crève), Jan Ceulemans (Cap), Paul De Mesmaecker; Marc Degryse, Marc Vanderlinden, Nico Claesen. Trainer: Guy Thys

LUXEMBOURG: John Van Rijswijck; Laurent Schonckert (65 Hubert Meunier), Carlo Weis (Cap), Marcel Bossi, Pierre Petry; Gérard Jeitz, Guy Hellers, Jean-Pierre Barboni, Théo Scholten (46 Jean-Paul Girres); Robert Langers, Jeannot Reiter. Trainer: Paul Philipp

Goals: Ceulemans (17), Degryse (56), Crève (81)

BULGARIA v SCOTLAND 0-1 (0-0)

Vasil Levski, Sofia 11.11.1987

Referee: Helmut Kohl (AUS) Attendance: 49,976

BULGARIA: Borislav Mihailov; Plamen Nikolov, Krasimir Bezinski, Nikolai Iliev, Petar Petrov; Anio Sadkov, Hristo Stoichkov, Plamen Simeonov (87 Liuboslav Penev), Nasko Sirakov (Cap); Petar Aleksandrov (44 Ilia Voinov), Bojidar Iskrenov. Trainer: Hristo Mladenov

SCOTLAND: James Leighton; Stephen Clarke, Robert Aitken (Cap), Alexander McLeish, Maurice Malpas; Gary Gillespie, Stephen Nicol, Paul McStay (57 Gary Mackay), Ian Wilson; Graeme Sharp (71 Gordon Durie), Brian McClair. Trainer: Andrew Roxburgh

Goal: Mackay (87)

LUXEMBOURG v SCOTLAND 0-0

Stade de la Frontière, Esch-sur-Alzette 02.12.1987

Referee: Manfred Neuner (W. GER) Attendance: 2,515

LUXEMBOURG: John Van Rijswijck; Hubert Meunier (Cap), Carlo Weis, Marcel Bossi, Pierre Petry; Jean-Paul Girres (87 Jeff Saibene), Gérard Jeitz, Jean-Pierre Barboni, Théo Scholten; Robert Langers, Jeannot Reiter (54 Armin Krings). Trainer: Paul Philipp

SCOTLAND: James Leighton; Maurice Malpas, Alexander McLeish, William Miller, Derek Whyte (60 Gary Mackay); Patrick Nevin (60 Kenneth Black), Paul McStay, Robert Aitken (Cap), Ian Wilson; Maurice Johnston, Graeme Sharp. Trainer: Andrew Roxburgh

	P	W	D	L	F	A	Pts
Rep. of Ireland	8	4	3	1	10	5	11
Bulgaria	8	4	2	2	12	6	10
Belgium	8	3	3	2	16	8	9
Scotland	8	3	3	2	7	5	9
Luxembourg	8	0	1	7	2	23	1

FINALS IN WEST GERMANY

GROUP 1

WEST GERMANY v ITALY 1-1 (0-0)

Rheinstadion, Düsseldorf 10.06.1988

Referee: Keith Hackett (ENG) Attendance: 68,400

W. GERMANY: Eike Immel; Jürgen Kohler, Matthias Herget, Guido Buchwald; Thomas Berthold, Pierre Littbarski, Lothar Matthäus (Cap), Andreas Brehme (76 Ulrich Borowka), Olaf Thon; Jürgen Klinsmann, Rudolf Völler (83 Dieter Eckstein). Trainer: Franz Beckenbauer

ITALY: Walter Zenga; Giuseppe Bergomi (Cap), Franco Baresi II, Riccardo Ferri II, Paolo Maldini; Roberto Donadoni, Giuseppe Giannini, Fernando De Napoli (87 Luigi De Agostini), Carlo Ancelotti; Roberto Mancini, Gianluca Vialli (90 Alessandro Altobelli). Trainer: Azeglio Vicini

Goals: Mancini (53), Brehme (56)

DENMARK v SPAIN 2-3 (1-1)

Niedersachsenstadion, Hannover 11.06.1988

Referee: Albert Thomas (HOL) Attendance: 60,366

DENMARK: Troels Rasmussen; John Sivebaek, Søren Busk, Morten Olsen (Cap) (67 Lars Olsen), Ivan Nielsen; John Helt (46 John Jensen), Michael Laudrup, Søren Lerby, Jan Heintze; Preben Elkjær Larsen, Flemming Povlsen. Trainer: Josef Piontek

SPAIN: Andoni Zubizarreta; Pedro Tomas Reñones, Genaro Andrinúa, Manuel SANCHIS Hontilluelo, José Antonio CAMACHO (Cap) (46 Miguel Soler); Miguel González "MICHEL", Ricardo Gallego, VÍCTOR Muñoz, Rafael Gordillo (88 Rafael Martín Vazquez); Emilio Butragueño, José Maria Bakero. Trainer: Miguel Muñoz

Goals: Michel (6), Laudrup (26), Butragueño (53), Gordillo (68), Povlsen (84)

WEST GERMANY v DENMARK 2-0 (1-0)

Parkstadion, Gelsenkirchen 14.06.1988

Referee: Robert Valentine (SCO) Attendance: 70,000

W. GERMANY: Eike Immel; Jürgen Kohler, Matthias Herget, Guido Buchwald (34 Ulrich Borowka); Pierre Littbarski, Wolfgang Rolff, Lothar Matthäus (Cap), Olaf Thon, Andreas Brehme; Jürgen Klinsmann, Rudolf Völler (75 Frank Mill). Trainer: Franz Beckenbauer

DENMARK: Peter Schmeichel; John Sivebaek, Lars Olsen, Ivan Nielsen; Kim Vilfort (74 Klaus Berggreen), Morten Olsen (Cap), Michael Laudrup (64 John Eriksen), Søren Lerby, Jan Heintze; Preben Elkjær Larsen, Flemming Povlsen. Trainer: Josef Piontek

Goals: Klinsmann (10), Thon (87)

ITALY v SPAIN 1-0 (0-0)

Waldstadion, Frankfurt/Main 14.06.1988

Referee: Erik Fredriksson (SWE) Attendance: 51,790

ITALY: Walter Zenga; Giuseppe Bergomi (Cap), Franco Baresi II, Riccardo Ferri II; Roberto Donadoni, Giuseppe Giannini, Fernando De Napoli, Carlo Ancelotti, Paolo Maldini; Roberto Mancini (69 Alessandro Altobelli), Gianluca Vialli (90 Luigi De Agostini). Trainer: Azeglio Vicini

SPAIN: Andoni Zubizarreta; Pedro Tomas Reñones, Genaro Andrinúa, Manuel SANCHIS Hontilluelo, Miguel Soler; Miguel González "MICHEL" (74 Aitor Beguiristain), Ricardo Gallego (68 Rafael Martín Vazquez), VÍCTOR Muñoz, Rafael Gordillo (Cap); José María Bakero, Emilio Butragueño. Trainer: Miguel Muñoz

Goal: Vialli (74)

	P	W	D	L	F	A	Pts
West Germany	3	2	1	0	5	1	5
Italy	3	2	1	0	4	1	5
Spain	3	1	0	2	3	5	2
Denmark	3	0	0	3	2	7	0

WEST GERMANY v SPAIN 2-0 (1-0)

Olympiastadion, München 17.06.1988

Referee: Michel Vautrot (FRA) Attendance: 72,308

W. GERMANY: Eike Immel; Jürgen Kohler, Matthias Herget, Ulrich Borowka; Andreas Brehme, Pierre Littbarski (63 Wolfram Wuttke), Wolfgang Rolff, Lothar Matthäus (Cap), Olaf Thon; Jürgen Klinsmann (85 Frank Mill), Rudolf Völler. Trainer: Franz Beckenbauer

SPAIN: Andoni Zubizarreta; Pedro Tomas Reñones, Genaro Andrinúa, Manuel SANCHIS Hontilluelo, José Antonio CAMACHO (Cap); Miguel González "MICHEL", Rafael Martín Vazquez, VÍCTOR Muñoz, Rafael Gordillo; José María Bakero, Emilio Butragueño (52 Julio Salinas Fernández). Trainer: Miguel Muñoz

Goals: Völler (30, 51)

ITALY v DENMARK 2-0 (0-0)

Müngersdorferstadion, Köln 17.06.1988

Referee: Bruno Galler (SWI) Attendance: 60,584

ITALY: Walter Zenga; Giuseppe Bergomi (Cap), Franco Baresi II, Riccardo Ferri II, Paolo Maldini; Roberto Donadoni (85 Luigi De Agostini), Giuseppe Giannini, Fernando De Napoli, Carlo Ancelotti; Roberto Mancini (66 Alessandro Altobelli), Gianluca Vialli. Trainer: Azeglio Vicini

DENMARK: Peter Schmeichel; Bjørn Kristensen, Lars Olsen, Ivan Nielsen; Per Friman (58 Kim Vilfort), Morten Olsen (Cap) (67 Klaus Berggreen), Michael Laudrup, John Jensen, Jan Heintze; Flemming Povlsen, John Eriksen. Trainer: Josef Piontek

Goals: Altobelli (66), De Agostini (87)

GROUP 2

ENGLAND v REPUBLIC OF IRELAND 0-1 (0-1)

Neckarstadion, Stuttgart 12.06.1988

Referee: Siegfried Kirschen (E. GER) Attendance: 55,500

ENGLAND: Peter Shilton; Gary Stevens, Anthony Adams, Mark Wright, Kenneth Sansom; Christopher Waddle, Bryan Robson (Cap), Neil Webb (61 Glenn Hoddle), John Barnes; Peter Beardsley (83 Mark Hateley), Gary Lineker. Trainer: Robert Robson

IRELAND: Patrick Bonner; Christopher Morris, Kevin Moran, Michael McCarthy, Christopher Hughton; Paul McGrath, Ronald Whelan, Raymond Houghton, Anthony Galvin (77 Kevin Sheedy); Frank Stapleton (Cap) (64 Niall Quinn), John Aldridge. Trainer: Jack Charlton

Goal: Houghton (6)

HOLLAND v USSR 0-1 (0-0)

Müngersdorfer, Köln 12.06.1988

Referee: Dieter Pauly (W. GER) Attendance: 60,500

HOLLAND: Johannes van Breukelen; Hubertus van Aerle, Franklin Rijkaard, Ronald Koeman, Adrianus van Tiggelen; Jan Wouters, Ruud Gullit (Cap), Arnoldus Mühren, Johannes van't Schip; Gerald Vanenburg (59 Marco van Basten), Jacobus Bosman. Trainer: Marinus Michels

USSR: Rinat Dasaev (Cap); Vladimir Bessonov, Vagiz Hidiatulin, Oleg Kuznetsov, Anatoli Demianenko; Gennadi Litovchenko, Aleksandr Zavarov (90 Tengiz Sulakvelidze), Aleksei Mikhailichenko, Vasiliy Rats; Igor Belanov (80 Sergei Aleinikov), Oleg Protasov. Trainer: Valeriy Lobanovski

Goal: Rats (54)

ENGLAND v HOLLAND 1-3 (0-1)

Rheinstadion, Düsseldorf 15.06.1988

Referee: Paolo Casarin (ITA) Attendance: 68,400

ENGLAND: Peter Shilton; Gary Stevens, Anthony Adams, Mark Wright, Kenneth Sansom; Trevor Steven (69 Christopher Waddle), Bryan Robson (Cap), Glenn Hoddle, John Barnes; Peter Beardsley (74 Mark Hateley), Gary Lineker. Trainer: Robert Robson

HOLLAND: Johannes van Breukelen; Hubertus van Aerle, Franklin Rijkaard, Ronald Koeman, Adrianus van Tiggelen; Jan Wouters, Ruud Gullit (Cap), Arnoldus Mühren, Erwin Koeman; Gerald Vanenburg (62 Willem Kieft), Marco van Basten (87 Wilbert Suvrijn). Trainer: Marinus Michels

Goals: van Basten (44, 72, 76), Robson (54)

REPUBLIC OF IRELAND v HOLLAND 0-1 (0-0)

Parkstadion, Gelsenkirchen 18.06.1988

Referee: Horst Brummeier (AUS) Attendance: 70,800

IRELAND: Patrick Bonner; Christopher Morris, Kevin Moran (46 Kevin Sheedy), Michael McCarthy, Christopher Hughton; Ronald Whelan, Raymond Houghton, Paul McGrath, Anthony Galvin; John Aldridge, Frank Stapleton (Cap) (84 Anthony Cascarino). Trainer: Jack Charlton

HOLLAND: Johannes van Breukelen; Hubertus van Aerle, Franklin Rijkaard, Ronald Koeman, Adrianus van Tiggelen; Jan Wouters, Ruud Gullit (Cap), Arnoldus Mühren (77 Jacobus Bosman), Erwin Koeman (50 Willem Kieft); Gerald Vanenburg, Marco van Basten. Trainer: Marinus Michels

Goal: Kieft (82)

REPUBLIC OF IRELAND v USSR 1-1 (1-0)

Niedersachsenstadion, Hannover 15.06.1988

Referee: Emilio Soriano Aladren (SPA) Attendance: 45,290

IRELAND: Patrick Bonner; Christopher Morris, Kevin Moran, Michael McCarthy, Christopher Hughton; Ronald Whelan, Raymond Houghton, Kevin Sheedy, Anthony Galvin; John Aldridge, Frank Stapleton (Cap) (81 Anthony Cascarino). Trainer: Jack Charlton

USSR: Rinat Dasaev (Cap) (69 Viktor Chanov); Tengiz Sulakvelidze (46 Sergei Gotsmanov), Vagiz Hidiatulin, Oleg Kuznetsov, Anatoli Demianenko; Sergei Aleinikov, Aleksandr Zavarov, Aleksei Mikhailichenko, Vasiliy Rats; Igor Belanov, Oleg Protasov. Trainer: Valeriy Lobanovski

Goals: Whelan (39), Protasov (75)

	P	W	D	L	F	A	Pts
USSR	3	2	1	0	5	2	5
Holland	3	2	0	1	4	2	4
Rep. of Ireland	3	1	1	1	2	2	3
England	3	0	0	3	2	7	0

ENGLAND v USSR 1-3 (1-2)

Waldstadion, Frankfurt/Main 18.06.1988

Referee: José Rosa dos Santos (POR) Attendance: 53,000

ENGLAND: Christopher Woods; Gary Stevens, David Watson, Anthony Adams, Kenneth Sansom; Trevor Steven, Stephen McMahon (53 Neil Webb), Bryan Robson (Cap), Glenn Hoddle, John Barnes; Gary Lineker (64 Mark Hateley). Trainer: Robert Robson

USSR: Rinat Dasaev (Cap); Vladimir Bessonov, Vagiz Hidiatulin, Oleg Kuznetsov; Gennadi Litovchenko, Sergei Aleinikov, Aleksandr Zavarov (86 Sergei Gotsmanov), Aleksei Mikhailichenko, Vasiliy Rats; Igor Belanov (46 Viktor Pasulko), Oleg Protasov. Trainer: Valeriy Lobanovski

Goals: Aleinikov (3), Adams (15), Mikhailichenko (28), Pasulko (72)

SEMI-FINALS

WEST GERMANY v HOLLAND 1-2 (0-0)

Volksparkstadion, Hamburg 21.06.1988

Referee: Ion Igna (ROM) Attendance: 61,330

W. GERMANY: Eike Immel; Jürgen Kohler, Matthias Herget (46 Hans Pflügler), Ulrich Borowka; Andreas Brehme, Lothar Matthäus (Cap), Wolfgang Rolff, Olaf Thon; Jürgen Klinsmann, Rudolf Völler, Frank Mill (84 Pierre Littbarski). Trainer: Franz Beckenbauer

HOLLAND: Johannes van Breukelen; Hubertus van Aerle, Franklin Rijkaard, Ronald Koeman, Adrianus van Tiggelen; Jan Wouters, Ruud Gullit (Cap), Arnoldus Mühren (59 Willem Kieft), Erwin Koeman (90 Wilbert Suvrijn); Gerald Vanenburg, Marco van Basten. Trainer: Marinus Michels

Goals: Matthäus (55 pen), R. Koeman (74), van Basten (89)

USSR v ITALY 2-0 (0-0)

Neckarstadion, Stuttgart 22.06.1988

Referee: Alexis Ponnet (BEL) Attendance: 68,000

USSR: Rinat Dasaev (Cap); Vladimir Bessonov (37 Anatoli Demianenko), Vagiz Hidiatulin, Oleg Kuznetsov; Gennadi Litovchenko, Sergei Aleinikov, Aleksandr Zavarov, Aleksei Mikhailichenko, Sergei Gotsmanov, Vasiliy Rats; Oleg Protasov. Trainer: Valeriy Lobanovski

ITALY: Walter Zenga; Giuseppe Bergomi (Cap), Franco Baresi II, Riccardo Ferri II, Paolo Maldini (64 Luigi De Agostini); Roberto Donadoni, Fernando De Napoli, Giuseppe Giannini, Carlo Ancelotti; Roberto Mancini (46 Alessandro Altobelli), Gianluca Vialli. Trainer: Azeglio Vicini

Goals: Litovchenko (60), Protasov (62)

FINAL

HOLLAND v USSR 2-0 (1-0)

Olympiastadion, München 25.06.1988

Referee: Michel Vautrot (FRA) Attendance: 72,308

HOLLAND: Johannes van Breukelen; Hubertus van Aerle, Franklin Rijkaard, Ronald Koeman, Adrianus van Tiggelen; Jan Wouters, Ruud Gullit (Cap), Arnoldus Mühren, Erwin Koeman; Gerald Vanenburg, Marco van Basten. Trainer: Marinus Michels

USSR: Rinat Dasaev (Cap); Anatoli Demianenko, Vagiz Hidiatulin, Aleksei Mikhailichenko; Gennadi Litovchenko, Sergei Aleinikov, Aleksandr Zavarov, Sergei Gotsmanov (69 Sergei Baltacha), Vasiliy Rats; Igor Belanov, Oleg Protasov (72 Viktor Pasulko). Trainer: Valeriy Lobanovski

Goals: Gullit (38), van Basten (54)

Goalscorers European Football Championship 1988

7 goals: Marco van Basten (Holland), Nico Claesen (Belgium), Alessandro Altobelli (Italy)

5 goals: Ruud Gullit (Holland), Gary Lineker (England), Nikos Anastopoulos (Greece), Johnny Ekström (Sweden), Andreas Thom (East Germany), Gianluca Vialli (Italy)

4 goals: Georges Bregy (Switzerland), Igor Belanov (USSR), Ulf Kirsten (East Germany), Zlatko Vujovic (Yugoslavia), Jacobus Johannes Bosman (Holland), Lachezar Tanev (Bulgaria), Miguel González Michel (Spain), Bryan Robson (England)

3 goals: Anton Polster (Austria), Carmel Busuttil (Malta), John Barnes, Dariusz Dziekanowski (Poland), Lajos Détári (Hungary), Ronald Koeman (Holland), Ivo Knoflícek (Czechoslovakia), Frank Stapleton (Republic of Ireland), Nasko Sirakov (Bulgaria), Oleg Protasov (USSR)

2 goals: Bakero, Eloy (Spain), Hagi, Iovan, Piţurcă (Romania), Linzmaier (Austria), Muça (Albania), Larsson (Sweden), Placido (Portugal), Aleinikov, Litovchenko, Mikhailichenko, Rats, Zavarov (USSR), Andersen (Norway), Adams, Beardsley, Waddle (England), Katanec, Hadzibegic, Vokri (Yugoslavia), Saravakos (Greece), Lesniak (Poland), Boda, Bognár, Mészáros (Hungary), Gillhaus (Holland), Mølby (Denmark), Rush (Wales), Hjelm (Finland), McGrath, Whelan (Republic of Ireland), Kolev, Sadkov (Bulgaria), Ceulemans, Vercauteren (Belgium), Cooper, McStay (Scotland), Völler (West Germany), De Agostini (Italy)

1 goal: Butragueño, Gordillo, Llorente, Sanchis, Calderé, Carrasco, Arteche, Joaquín (Spain), Klein, Mateuţ, Ungureanu, Bölöni, Belodedici, Bumbescu, Lăcătuş (Romania), Ogris (Austria), Giannini, Bagni, Bergomi, Ferri, Donadoni, Mancini (Italy), Hysén, Magnusson, Fredriksson, Palmér, Strömberg (Sweden), Fredrico, Gomes, Coelho, Manuel Fernandes (Portugal), Zwicker, Halter, Egli, Brigger, Weber (Switzerland), Mizzi (Malta), Blohin, Hidiatullin, Pasulko, Sulakvelidze (USSR), Ernst, Minge, Doll, Döschner (East Germany), Fargeon, Touré, Micchiche, Stopyra (France), Fjaerestad, Sundby, Mordt (Norway), Pétursson, Ormslev, Edvaldsson, Gudjohnsen (Iceland), Webb, Mabbutt, Anderson (England), Radanovic, Stojkovic, Savicevic (Jugos), Quinn, Clarke (N. Ireland), Yusuf, Feyyaz (Turkey), Bonovas, Andoniou, Papaioannou, Batsinilas, Mitropoulos (Greece), Tarasiewicz, Marciniak, Smolarek, Wójcicki (Poland), Kiprich, Vincze, Péter, Preszeller (Hungary), Savva, Christofi, Savvides (Cyprus), Kieft, Mühren (Holland), Laudrup, Povlsen, Elkjær Larsen, Bertelsen (Denmark), Bílek, Hasek, Janecka, Kula (Czechoslovakia), Hughes, Hodges, Phillips, Jones, Slatter (Wales), Lius, Tiainen (Finland), Moran, Galvin, Houghton, Lawrenson, Brady (Republic of Ireland), Iordanov (Bulgaria), Degryse, Crève, Janssens, Gerets, Scifo (Belgium), Mackay, McCoist, Johnston (Scotland), Krings, Langers (Luxembourg), Matthäus, Klinsmann, Thon, Brehme (West Germany)

Own goal: Gjondeda (Albania) for Spain

THE EUROPEAN FOOTBALL CHAMPIONSHIP 1992

GROUP 1

ICELAND v ALBANIA 2-0 (1-0)

Laugardalsvöllur, Reykjavík 30.05.1990

Referee: Frederick McKnight (NIR) Attendance: 6,500

ICELAND: Birkir Kristinsson; Olafur Thórdarson, Atli Edvaldsson, Gudni Bergsson, Saevar Jónsson, Thórvaldur Örlygsson (46 Kristján Jónsson), Pétur Ormslev, Sigurdur Grétarsson, Arnór Gudjohnsen, Pétur Pétursson, Gudmundur Torfason (67 Ormarr Örlygsson). Trainer: Bo Johansson

ALBANIA: Foto Strakosha; Pjerin Noga (75 Roland Iljadhi), Artur Lekbello, Naum Kove, Rudi Vata, Fatbardh Jera, Ylli Shehu (46 Arben Arbëri), Mirel Josa, Lefter Millo, Edmond Abazi, Sulejman Demollari. Trainer: Agron Sulaj

Goals: Gudjohnsen (42), Edvaldsson (88)

ICELAND v FRANCE 1-2 (0-1)

Laugardalsvöllur, Reykjavík 05.09.1990

Referee: David Syme (SCO) Attendance: 8,000

ICELAND: Bjarni Sigurdsson; Thorgrímur Thráinsson, Atli Edvaldsson, Gudni Bergsson, Saevar Jónsson, Thorvaldur Örlygsson (64 Ragnar Margeirsson), Pétur Ormslev (64 Rúnar Kristinsson), Sigurdur Grétarsson, Olafur Thórdarson, Pétur Pétursson, Arnor Gudjohnsen. Trainer: Bo Johansson

FRANCE: Bruno Martini; Manuel Amoros, Basile Boli, Franck Sauzée, Bernard Casoni, Laurent Blanc (77 Jean-Philippe Durand), Bernard Pardo, Didier Deschamps, Jean-Pierre Papin, Christian Perez, Eric Cantona (84 Luis Fernandez). Trainer: Michel Platini

Goal: Papin (12), Cantona (75), Edvaldsson (86)

CZECHOSLOVAKIA v ICELAND 1-0 (1-0)

Kosice 26.09.1990

Referee: Todor Kolev (BUL) Attendance: 35,000

CZECHOSLOVAKIA: Jan Stejskal; Miroslav Kadlec, Ján Kocián, Michal Hipp, Michal Bílek (67 Vladimír Weiss), Ivan Hasek, Lubomír Moravcík, Lubos Kubík, Václav Danek, Tomás Skuhravy, Karel Kula. Trainer: Milan Mácala

ICELAND: Bjarni Sigurdsson; Thorgrímur Thráinsson, Gudni Bergsson, Atli Edvaldsson, Saevar Jónsson, Rúnar Kristinsson (61 Kristján Jónsson), Sigurdur Grétarsson, Olafur Thórdarson, Sigurdur Jónsson, Arnor Gudjohnsen, Ragnar Margeirsson (76 Pétur Ormslev). Trainer: Bo Johansson

Goal: Danek (43)

SPAIN v ICELAND 2-1 (1-0)

Benito Villamarin, Sevilla 10.10.1990

Referee: Victor Mintoff (MAL) Attendance: 46,000

SPAIN: Andoni ZUBIZARRETA; Fernando Muñoz NANDO, Ricardo SERNA, Rafael PAZ (61 Aitor BEGUIRISTÁIN), Manuel SANCHIS, FERNANDO Gómez, Jon Andoni GOIKOETXEA, Miguel González MICHEL, Emilio BUTRAGUEÑO, Rafael MARTÍN VÁZQUEZ, CARLOS Muñoz (71 Ernesto Valverde). Trainer: Luis Suarez

ICELAND: Bjarni Sigurdsson; Thorgrímur Thráinsson, Atli Edvaldsson, Kristján Jónsson (80 Antony Gregory), Sigurdur Grétarsson, Saevar Jónsson, Gudni Bergsson, Sigurdur Jónsson (72 Pétur Ormslev), Arnor Gudjohnsen, Olafur Thórdarsson, Ragnar Margeirsson. Trainer: Bo Johansson

Goals: Butragueño (44), Carlos (64), Si. Jónsson (65)

FRANCE v CZECHOSLOVAKIA 2-1 (0-0)

Parc des Princes, Paris 13.10.1990

Referee: George Courtney (ENG) Attendance: 38,249

FRANCE: Bruno Martini; Jocelyn Angloma (52 Luis Fernandez), Jean-Philippe Durand, Basile Boli, Bernard Casoni, Franck Sauzée, Didier Deschamps, Pascal Vahirua (83 Franck Silvestre), Jean-Pierre Papin, Laurent Blanc, Eric Cantona. Trainer: Michel Platini

CZECHOSLOVAKIA: Jan Stejskal; Lubos Kubík (84 Dusan Tittel), Miroslav Kadlec, Michal Hipp, Ján Kocián, Karel Kula, Michal Bílek (80 Ladislav Pecko), Ivo Knoflícek, Jozef Chovanec, Tomás Skuhravy, Lubomír Moravcík. Trainer: Milan Mácala

Goals: Papin (59, 80), Skuhravy (87)

CZECHOSLOVAKIA v SPAIN 3-2 (1-1)

Praha 14.11.1990

Referee: Karl-Heinz Tritschler (GER) Attendance: 35,000

CZECHOSLOVAKIA: Ludek Miklosko; Michal Hipp, Miroslav Kadlec, Ivan Hasek, Michal Bílek (83 Milos Belák), Ján Kocián, Dusan Tittel, Karel Kula, Lubomír Moravcík, Václav Danek (88 Pavel Kuka), Tomás Skuhravy. Trainer: Milan Mácala

SPAIN: Andoni ZUBIZARRETA; Enrique Sánchez QUIQUE, Ricardo SERNA, Fernando Muñoz NANDO, Manuel SANCHIS, Jon Andoni GOIKOETXEA, ROBERTO Fernandez, Miguel González MICHEL (86 Guillermo AMOR), Rafael MARTÍN VÁZQUEZ, Emilio BUTRAGUEÑO, CARLOS Muñoz (60 José María BAKERO). Trainer: Luis Suarez

Goals: Danek (17,66), Roberto (29), Carlos (54), Moravcík (77)

ALBANIA v FRANCE 0-1 (0-1)

Qemal Stafa, Tiranë 17.11.1990

Referee: Bruno Galler (SWI) Attendance: 15,000

ALBANIA: Anesti Arapi; Lorenc Leskaj (46 Alfred Ferko), Genc Ibro, Skënder Hodja, Artur Lekbello, Arian Stafa, Hysen Zmijani, Sulejman Demollari, Mirel Josa, Sokol Kushta, Kujtim Majaci (56 Eduard Kaçaçi). Trainer: Agron Sulaj

FRANCE: Bruno Martini; Basile Boli, Laurent Blanc, Bernard Casoni, Christian Perez, Franck Sauzée, Didier Deschamps, Bernard Pardo, Jean-Marc Ferreri, Philippe Tibeuf (66 David Ginola), Pascal Vahirua (81 Jocelyn Angloma). Trainer: Michel Platini

Goal: Boli (23)

FRANCE v ALBANIA 5-0 (4-0)

Parc des Princes, Paris 30.03.1991

Referee: Einar Halle (NOR) Attendance: 24,181

FRANCE: Bruno Martini; Manuel Amoros, Jean-Philippe Durand, Basile Boli, Laurent Blanc, Luis Fernandez, Christophe Cocard, Franck Sauzée (73 Didier Deschamps), Jean-Pierre Papin, Pascal Vahirua (57 Pascal Baills), Eric Cantona. Trainer: Michel Platini

ALBANIA: Blendi Nallbani; Hysen Zmijani, Adnan Ocelli, Artur Lekbello, Rudi Vata, Dashnor Dume, Agim Canaj, Ilir Kepa, Josif Gjergji, Ermal Tahiri, Sulejman Demollari.

Goals: Sauzèe (1, 19), Papin (34 pen, 42), Lekbello (79 og)

SPAIN v ALBANIA 9-0 (4-0)

Benito Villamarin, Sevilla 19.12.1990

Referee: Alphonse Constantin (BEL) Attendance: 27,600

SPAIN: Andoni ZUBIZARRETA; Manuel Sánchez MANOLO, Rafael ALKORTA, Fernando Ruiz HIERRO, Manuel SANCHIS, Guillermo AMOR, Jon Andoni GOIKOETXEA (75 José María BAKERO), Miguel González MICHEL (62 Enrique Sánchez QUIQUE), Emilio Butragueño, Rafael MARTÍN VÁZQUEZ, CARLOS Muñoz. Trainer: Luis Suarez

ALBANIA: Anesti Arapi; Gjergj Dema, Artur Lekbello, Alfred Ferko (65 Mirel Josa), Genc Ibro, Hysen Zmijani, Arian Stafa, Lefter Millo, Bledar Kola (32 Sulejman Demollari), Sokol Kushta, Ermal Tahiri.

Goals: Amor (19), Carlos (22, 64), Butragueño (30, 58, 66, 75), Hierro (37), Bakero (87)

ALBANIA v CZECHOSLOVAKIA 0-2 (0-0)

Qemal Stafa, Tiranë 01.05.1991

Referee: Carlo Longhi (ITA) Attendance: 10,000

ALBANIA: Blendi Nallbani; Hysen Zmijani, Zamir Shpuza, Adnan Ocelli, Gjergj Dema, Fatos Daja, Eqerem Memushi, Dashnor Dume (74 Bledar Kola), Arben Milori, Sokol Kushta, Adrian Barballushi (65 Edmond Dosti). Trainer: Bejkush Birçe

CZECHOSLOVAKIA: Ludek Miklosko; Dusan Tittel, Miroslav Kadlec, Ivan Hasek (19 Pavel Hapál), Alois Grussmann, Karel Kula, Lubomír Moravcík, Jirí Nemec, Lubos Kubík, Roman Kukleta (85 Martin Frydek), Pavel Kuka. Trainer: Milan Mácala

Goals: Kubík (46), Kuka (66)

FRANCE v SPAIN 3-1 (1-1)

Parc des Princes, Paris 20.02.1991

Referee: Tullio Lanese (ITA) Attendance: 45,000

FRANCE: Bruno Martini; Manuel Amoros, Bernard Casoni, Basile Boli, Laurent Blanc, Bernard Pardo (51 Luis Fernandez), Jean-Philippe Durand, Franck Sauzée, Jean-Pierre Papin, Pascal Vahirua (82 Didier Deschamps), Eric Cantona. Trainer: Michel Platini

SPAIN: Andoni ZUBIZARRETA; Fernando Muñoz NANDO, Enrique Sánchez QUIQUE, Juan Francisco Rodríguez JUANITO, Manuel SANCHIS, José María BAKERO, Andoni GOIKOETXEA, Miguel González MICHEL, Emilio BUTRAGUEÑO (75 Manuel Sánchez MANOLO), Guillermo AMOR, Juan VIZCAINO (60 Miguel SOLER). Trainer: Luis Suarez

Goals: Bakero (10), Sauzée (14), Papin (58), Blanc (77)

ALBANIA v ICELAND 1-0 (0-0)

Qemal Stafa, Tiranë 26.05.1991

Referee: Sándor Varga (HUNG) Attendance: 5,000

ALBANIA: Blendi Nallbani; Eqerem Memushi (16 Mirel Josa), Artur Lekbello, Zamir Shpuza, Adnan Ocelli, Fatos Daja, Lefter Millo, Sulejman Demollari, Arben Milori, Sokol Kushta, Edmond Abazi. Trainer: Bejkush Birçe

ICELAND: Bjarni Sigurdsson; Saevar Jónsson, Gunnar Gíslason, Olafur Kristjánsson, Gudni Bergsson, Rúnar Kristinsson (62 Hlynur Stéfansson), Thorvaldur Örlygsson, Sigurdur Grétarsson, Eyjólfur Sverrisson, Olafur Thórdarson, Antony Gregory (75 Andri Marteinsson). Trainer: Bo Johansson

Goal: Abazi (56)

ICELAND v CZECHOSLOVAKIA 0-1 (0-1)

Laugardalsvöllur, Reykjavík 05.06.1991

Referee: John Spillane (IRE) Attendance: 5,000

ICELAND: Bjarni Sigurdsson; Gunnar Gíslason, Gudni Bergsson, Atli Edvaldsson, Saevar Jónsson, Rúnar Kristinsson, Thorvaldur Örlygsson, Sigurdur Grétarsson, Olafur Thórdarson, Eyjólfur Sverrisson (71 Hlynur Stéfansson), Arnor Gudjohnsen. Trainer: Bo Johansson

CZECHOSLOVAKIA: Ludek Miklosko; Alois Grussmann, Ján Kocián, Dusan Tittel, Ivan Hasek, Pavel Hapál, Lubos Kubík, Jirí Nemec, Karel Kula, Tomás Skuhravy (41 Pavel Kuka), Václav Danek (89 Ladislav Pecko). Trainer: Milan Mácala

Goal: Hasek (15)

SPAIN v FRANCE 1-2 (1-2)

Benito Villamarin, Sevilla 12.10.1991

Referee: Hubert Forstinger (AUS) Attendance: 27,500

SPAIN: Andoni ZUBIZARRETA; CRISTÓBAL Parralo, Roberto SOLOZÁBAL (46 EUSEBIO Sacristán), ABELARDO Fernández, Manuel SANCHIS, Fernando Ruiz HIERRO, Manuel Sánchez MANOLO, Ricardo González "BANGO", Emilio BUTRAGUEÑO, Rafael MARTÍN VAZQUEZ (73 ALVARO Cervera), Juan VIZCAINO. Trainer: Vicente Miera

FRANCE: Bruno Martini; Manuel Amoros, Jocelyn Angloma, Basile Boli, Laurent Blanc, Bernard Casoni, Didier Deschamps, Luis Fernandez (81 Jean-Philippe Durand), Jean-Pierre Papin, Christian Perez (62 Rémi Garde), Eric Cantona. Trainer: Michel Platini

Goals: Fernandez (12), Papin (15), Abelardo (34)

CZECHOSLOVAKIA v FRANCE 1-2 (1-0)

Tehelne pole, Bratislava 04.09.1991

Referee: Peter Mikkelsen (DEN) Attendance: 50,000

CZECHOSLOVAKIA: Ludek Miklosko; Ján Kocián, Dusan Tittel, Jirí Novotny, Pavel Hapál (81 Ivo Knoflícek), Martin Frydek (73 Ondrej Kristofík), Lubomír Moravcík, Václav Nemecek, Jirí Nemec, Ladislav Pecko, Pavel Kuka. Trainer: Milan Mácala

FRANCE: Bruno Martini; Manuel Amoros, Jocelyn Angloma (78 Jean-Philippe Durand), Basile Boli, Laurent Blanc, Bernard Casoni, Didier Deschamps, Franck Sauzée, Jean-Pierre Papin, Christophe Cocard (46 Christian Perez), Pascal Vahirua. Trainer: Michel Platini

Goals: Nemecek (19), Papin (53, 89)

CZECHOSLOVAKIA v ALBANIA 2-1 (2-0)

Míru, Olomouc 16.10.1991

Referee: Michal Listkiewicz (POL) Attendance: 2,366

CZECHOSLOVAKIA: Ludek Miklosko; Bartolomej Jurasko, Dusan Tittel, Václav Nemecek, Pavel Hapál, Lubomír Moravcík, Ludovít Lancz (46 Roman Sedlácek), Martin Frydek, Karel Kula, Václav Danek (75 Ladislav Pecko), Pavel Kuka. Trainer: Milan Mácala

ALBANIA: Foto Strakosha; Hysen Zmijani, Artur Lekbello, Salvator Kaçaj, Kreshnik Çipi, Mirel Josa, Arben Milori, Agustin Kola (52 Fatos Daja), Latif Gjondeda, Edmond Abazi, Adrian Barballushi. Trainer: Bejkush Birçe

Goals: Kula (35), Lancz (39), Zmijani (61)

ICELAND v SPAIN 2-0 (0-0)

Laugardalsvöllur, Reykjavík 25.09.1991

Referee: Cornelius Bakker (HOL) Attendance: 8,900

ICELAND: Birkir Kristinsson; Valur Valsson (46 Andri Marteinsson), Pétur Ormslev, Gudni Bergsson, Sigurdur Jónsson, Kristján Jónsson, Sigurdur Grétarsson, Eyjólfur Sverrisson, Olafur Thórdarson, Thorvaldur Örlygsson, Baldur Bjarnason (74 Hördur Magnússon). Trainer: Asgeir Eliasson

SPAIN: Andoni ZUBIZARRETA; ABELARDO Fernández, Roberto SOLOZÁBAL, EUSEBIO Sacristán, Manuel SANCHIS, Juan VIZCAÍNO, Manuel Sánchez MANOLO, Miguel González MICHEL, Emilio BUTRAGUEÑO, Rafael MARTÍN VÁZQUEZ (67 Fernando Ruiz HIERRO), Jon Andoni GOIKOETXEA. Trainer: Vicente Miera

Goals: Örlygsson (71), Sverrisson (79)

SPAIN v CZECHOSLOVAKIA 2-1 (1-0)

Benito Villamarin, Sevilla 13.11.1991

Referee: Kurt Roethlisberger (SWI) Attendance: 24,500

SPAIN: Andoni ZUBIZARRETA; ABELARDO Fernández, Miguel SOLER, Roberto SOLOZÁBAL, Manuel SANCHIS, Fernando Ruiz HIERRO, Gabriel MOYA (60 Ignacio CONTE), Miguel González MICHEL, Emilio BUTRAGUEÑO, Rafael MARTÍN VÁZQUEZ (46 Miguel Angel NADAL), Juan VIZCAÍNO. Trainer: Vicente Miera

CZECHOSLOVAKIA: Jan Stejskal; Jan Suchopárek, Milos Glonek, Lubomír Vlk (65 Alois Grussmann), Ondrej Kristofík, Václav Nemecek, Jirí Nemec, Jirí Novotny, Ladislav Pecko, Karel Kula, Peter Dubovsky (80 Radoslav Látal). Trainer: Milan Mácala

Goals: Abelardo (10), Nemecek (59), Míchel (79 pen)

FRANCE v ICELAND 3-1 (1-0)

Parc des Princes, Paris 20.11.1991

Referee: Erik Fredriksson (SWE) Attendance: 35,000

FRANCE: Bruno Martini; Manuel Amoros, Jocelyn Angloma, Bernard Casoni (46 Basile Boli), Laurent Blanc, Christian Perez, Didier Deschamps (67 Jean-Philippe Durand), Luis Fernandez, Amara Simba, Pascal Vahirua, Eric Cantona. Trainer: Michel Platini

ICELAND: Birkir Kristinsson; Kristján Jónsson, Baldur Bjarnason, Pétur Ormslev, Kristinn R.Jónsson, Thorvaldur Örlygsson, Gudni Bergsson (80 Saevar Jónsson), Valur Valsson, Arnor Gudjohnsen, Gudmundur Torfason (56 Eyjólfur Sverrisson), Sigurdur Grétarsson. Trainer: Asgeir Eliasson

Goals: Simba (42), Cantona (59, 67), Sverrisson (71)

ALBANIA v SPAIN 18.12.1991 was not played

	P	W	D	L	F	A	Pts
France	8	8	0	0	20	6	16
Czechoslovakia	8	5	0	3	12	9	10
Spain	7	3	0	4	17	12	6
Iceland	8	2	0	6	7	10	4
Albania	7	1	0	6	2	21	2

GROUP 2

SWITZERLAND v BULGARIA 2-0 (1-0)

Charmilles, Genève 12.09.1990

Referee: Guy Goethals (BEL) Attendance: 12,500

SWITZERLAND: Philipp Walker; Alain Geiger, Marc Hottiger, Dominique Herr, Peter Schepull, Heinz Hermann, Marcel Koller, Thomas Bickel, Alain Sutter (87 Blaise Piffaretti), Adrian Knup (64 Stéphane Chapuisat), Kubilay Türkyilmaz. Trainer: Uli Stielike

BULGARIA: Ilia Valov; Nikolai Iliev, Nasko Jelev, Dimitar Vasev (59 Kalin Bankov), Trifon Ivanov, Pavel Dochev, Georgi Iordanov, Kostadin Ianchev, Emil Kostadinov, Hristo Stoichkov, Krasimir Balakov (65 Nikolai Todorov). Trainer: Ivan Vutsov

Goals: Hottiger (19), Bickel (74)

SCOTLAND v ROMANIA 2-1 (1-1)

Hampden Park, Glasgow 12.09.1990

Referee: Ildefonso Urizar Azpitarte (SPA) Att: 12,801

SCOTLAND: Andy Goram; Stewart McKimmie, Maurice Malpas; Gary McAllister (72 Patrick Nevin), Brian Irvine, Alex McLeish; John Robertson, Paul McStay (Cap), Alistair McCoist, Murdo MacLeod, Robert Connor (59 Tommy Boyd). Manager: Andy Roxburgh

ROMANIA: Silviu Lung; Dan Petrescu, Michael Klein, Emil Săndoi, Iosif Rotariu, Gheorghe Popescu, Marius Lăcătuş, Dorin Mateuţ (70 Ioan Ovidiu Sabău), Rodion Cămătaru (62 Florin Răducioiu), Gheorghe Hagi, Ioan Lupescu. Trainer: Gheorghe Constantin

Goals: Cămătaru (14), Robertson (38), McCoist (75)

ROMANIA v BULGARIA 0-3 (0-1)

Steaua, Bucureşti 17.10.1990

Referee: José Rosa Dos Santos (POR) Attendance: 14,000

ROMANIA: Bogdan Stelea; Dan Petrescu, Michael Klein (46 Emil Săndoi), Ioan Andonie, Iosif Rotariu, Gheorghe Popescu, Marius Lăcătuş, Ioan Ovidiu Sabşu, Florin Răducioiu (46 Gavril Balint), Gheorghe Hagi, Ioan Lupescu. Trainer: Gheorghe Constantin

BULGARIA: Boris Mihailov; Pavel Dochev, Trifon Ivanov, Dimitar Vasev, Nikolai Iliev; Zlatko Iankov, Kostadin Ianchev, Hristo Stoichkov, Krasimir Balakov, Nasko Sirakov (75 Emil Kostadinov), Georgi Iordanov (46 Nikolai Todorov). Trainer: Ivan Vutsov

Goals: Sirakov (28), Todorov (48, 78)

SCOTLAND v SWITZERLAND 2-1 (1-0)

Hampden Park, Glasgow 17.10.1990

Referee: Esa Palsi (FIN) Attendance: 27,740

SCOTLAND: Andy Goram; Stewart McKimmie, Alex McLeish, Dave McPherson, Stephen Nicol, Gary McAllister (81 John Collins), Stuart McCall, Tommy Boyd (67 Patrick Nevin), Murdo MacLeod, Alistair McCoist, John Robertson. Manager: Andy Roxburgh

SWITZERLAND: Philipp Walker; André Egli, Dominique Herr, Peter Schepull (62 Frédéric Chassot), Blaise Piffaretti (80 Beat Sutter), Thomas Bickel, Heinz Hermann, Alain Sutter, Adrian Knup, Kubilay Türkyilmaz, Stéphane Chapuisat. Trainer: Uli Stielike

Goals: Robertson (34 pen), McAllister (51), Knup (64 pen)

BULGARIA v SCOTLAND 1-1 (0-1)

Vasil Levski, Sofia 14.11.1990

Referee: Friedrich Kaupe (AUS) Attendance: 42,000

BULGARIA: Boris Mihailov; Pavel Dochev, Dimitar Mladenov, Zlatko Iankov, Kalin Bankov, Kostadin Ianchev (55 Nikolai Todorov), Georgi Iordanov, Hristo Stoichkov, Liuboslav Penev, Nashko Sirakov, Krasimir Balakov (73 Emil Kostadinov). Trainer: Ivan Vutsov

SCOTLAND: Andy Goram; Stewart McKimmie, Maurice Malpas, Gary McAllister, Dave McPherson, Gary Gillespie, Gordon Durie (67 Patrick Nevin), James McInally, Alistair McCoist, Brian McClair, Tom Boyd.
Manager: Andy Roxburgh

Goals: McCoist (9), Todorov (71)

SAN MARINO v SWITZERLAND 0-4 (0-3)

Olimpico, Serravalle 14.11.1990

Referee: Costas Kapsos (CYP) Attendance: 931

SAN MARINO: Pier Luigi Benedettini; Marco Montironi, Bruno Muccioli (59 Ivan Matteoni), Loris Zanotti, Luca Gobbi, William Guerra, Massimo Ceccoli, Massimo Bonini (46 Ivan Toccaceli), Waldes Pasolini, Fabio Francini, Marco Macina.
Trainer: Giorgio Leoni

SWITZERLAND: Philippe Walker; Marc Hottiger, Beat Sutter, Dominique Herr, Alain Geiger, Thomas Bickel (59 Blaise Piffaretti), Adrian Knup, Heinz Hermann, Kubilay Türkyilmaz (46 Frédéric Chassot), Alain Sutter, Stéphane Chapuisat. Trainer: Uli Stielike

Goals: A. Sutter (8), Chapuisat (27), Knup (43), Chassot (85)

ROMANIA v SAN MARINO 6-0 (3-0)

National, Bucureşti 05.12.1990

Referee: Manfred Rossner (GER) Attendance: 15,000

ROMANIA: Florian Prunea; Dan Petrescu, Ştefan Iovan, Gheorghe Popescu, Mircea Rednic; Ioan Ovidiu Sabău, Ioan Lupescu (64 Constantin Stănici), Dorin Mateuţ, Ilie Dumitrescu (46 Pavel Badea); Marius Lăcătuş (Cap), Florin Răducioiu. Trainer: Mircea Rădulescu

SAN MARINO: Pier Luigi Benedettini; Paolo Conti, Ivan Toccacelli, William Guerra, Marco Montironi; Massimo Ceccoli, Loris Zanotti, Fabio Francini, Ivan Matteoni; Marco Macina (46 Giancarlo Bacciocchi); Waldes Pasolini (86 Paolo Zanotti). Trainer: Giorgio Leoni

Goals: Sabău (1), Mateuţ (18), Răducioiu (43), Lupescu (57), Badea (77), Petrescu (85)

SAN MARINO v ROMANIA 1-3 (1-2)

Olimpico, Serravalle 27.03.1991

Referee: Roger Philippi (LUX) Attendance: 745

SAN MARINO: Pier Luigi Benedettini; Claudio Canti, Bruno Muccioli, Ivan Matteoni, Luca Gobbi (74 Ivan Toccacelli), William Guerra, Massimo Ceccoli, Marco Mazza, Paolo Mazza, Fabio Francini, Waldes Pasolini (87 Marco Mularoni).
Trainer: Giorgio Leoni

ROMANIA: Florian Prunea; Dan Petrescu, Michael Klein, Emil Săndoi (46 Daniel Timofte), Ioan Lupescu, Gheorghe Popescu, Marius Lăcătuş, Ioan Ovidiu Sabău, Florin Răducioiu, Gheorghe Hagi, Dorin Mateuţ (65 Pavel Badea).
Trainer: Mircea Rădulescu

Goals: Hagi (17 pen), Pasolini (30 pen), Răducioiu (44), D. Timofte (84)

SCOTLAND v BULGARIA 1-1 (0-0)

Hampden Park, Glasgow 27.03.1991

Referee: Erik Fredriksson (SWE) Attendance: 33,119

SCOTLAND: Andy Goram; Dave McPherson, Maurice Malpas, James McInally, Richard Gough, Alex McLeish, Gordon Strachan (81 John Robertson), Brian McClair, Alistair McCoist, Paul McStay, Gordon Durie (81 John Collins).
Manager: Andy Roxburgh

BULGARIA: Boris Mihailov; Pavel Dochev, Trifon Ivanov, Ilian Kiriakov, Nikolai Iliev, Zlatko Iankov, Emil Kostadinov, Nasko Sirakov (87 Petar Aleksandrov), Liuboslav Penev, Georgi Iordanov, Krasimir Balakov (87 Lachezar Tanev).
Trainer: Ivan Vutsov

Goals: Collins (84), Kostadinov (89)

SWITZERLAND v ROMANIA 0-0

La Maladiere, Neuchâtel 03.04.1991

Referee: Gérard Biguet (FRA) Attendance: 16,000

SWITZERLAND: Stefan Huber; Marc Hottiger, Alain Geiger, Dominique Herr, Dominique Christophe Ohrel; Jean-Michel Aebi, Marcel Koller, Heinz Hermann (Cap), Christophe Bonvin (33 Thomas Bickel); Kubilay Türkyilmaz (74 Beat Sutter), Adrian Knup. Trainer: Uli Stielike

ROMANIA: Florian Prunea; Dan Petrescu, Emil Săndoi, Gheorghe Popescu, Michael Klein; Ioan Ovidiu Sabău, Ioan Lupescu, Daniel Timofte, Gheorghe Hagi (83 Dorin Mateuţ); Marius Lăcătuş (Cap), Florin Răducioiu (89 Ion Timofte).
Trainer: Mircea Rădulescu

BULGARIA v SWITZERLAND 2-3 (2-0)

Vasil Levski, Sofia 01.05.1991

Referee: Karl-Josef Assenmacher (GER) Att: 55,000

BULGARIA: Boris Mihailov; Pavel Dochev (5 Nikolai Todorov), Ilian Kiriakov, Nikolai Iliev, Trifon Ivanov, Georgi Iordanov, Nasko Sirakov (65 Lachezar Tanev), Zlatko Iankov, Emil Kostadinov, Krasimir Balakov, Liuboslav Penev. Trainer: Ivan Vutsov

SWITZERLAND: Stefan Huber; Marc Hottiger, Dominique Christophe Ohrel, Dominique Herr, André Egli, Heinz Hermann (Cap), Adrian Knup (88 Peter Schepull), Beat Sutter, Kubilay Türkyilmaz, Marcel Koller (46 Stéphane Chapuisat), Christophe Bonvin. Trainer: Uli Stielike

Goals: Kostadinov (11), Sirakov (25), Knup (59, 85), Türkyilmaz (90)

SWITZERLAND v SAN MARINO 7-0 (3-0)

Espenmoos, St.Gallen 05.06.1991

Referee: Erman Toroglu (TUR) Attendance: 12,000

SWITZERLAND: Stefan Huber; Marc Hottiger (74 Dominique Christophe Ohrel), Stéphane Chapuisat, Dominique Herr, André Egli (74 Peter Schepull), Marcel Koller, Beat Sutter, Heinz Hermann (Cap), Kubilay Türkyilmaz, Alain Sutter, Adrian Knup. Trainer: Uli Stielike

SAN MARINO: Pier Luigi Benedettini; Claudio Canti, Marco Montironi, Loris Zanotti, Luca Gobbi, William Guerra, Ivan Matteoni (46 Mauro Valentini), Marco Mazza, Nicola Bacciocchi (70 Marco Mularoni), Fabio Francini, Waldes Pasolini. Trainer: Giorgio Leoni

Goals: Knup (2, 86), Hottiger (12), B. Sutter (28), Hermann (54), Ohrel (77), Türkyilmaz (90)

SAN MARINO v SCOTLAND 0-2 (0-0)

Olimpico, Serravalle 01.05.1991

Referee: Besnik Kaimi (ALB) Attendance: 3,512

SAN MARINO: Pier Luigi Benedettini; Claudio Canti, Bruno Muccioli, Paolo Zanotti (62 Ivan Toccacelli), Luca Gobbi, William Guerra, Massimo Ceccoli, Marco Mazza, Paolo Mazza, Fabio Francini, Waldes Pasolini (78 Ivan Matteoni). Trainer: Giorgio Leoni

SCOTLAND: Andy Goram; Stewart McKimmie, Dave McPherson, Stephen Nicol (73 John Robertson), Stuart McCall, Maurice Malpas, Brian McClair (56 Patrick Nevin), Kevin Gallacher, Gary McAllister, Gordon Strachan, Gordon Durie. Manager: Andy Roxburgh

Goals: Strachan (63 pen), Durie (66)

SWITZERLAND v SCOTLAND 2-2 (2-0)

Wankdorf, Bern 11.09.1991

Referee: Tullio Lanese (ITA) Attendance: 48,000

SWITZERLAND: Stefan Huber; Marc Hottiger, Dominique Christophe Ohrel, Dominique Herr, Ciriaco Sforza, Marcel Heldmann (67 Beat Sutter), Adrian Knup, Heinz Hermann (Cap), Kubilay Türkyilmaz, Alain Sutter (60 Thomas Bickel), Stéphane Chapuisat. Trainer: Uli Stielike

SCOTLAND: Andy Goram; Stewart McKimmie (69 Brian McClair), Maurice Malpas, Stephen Nicol, Dave McPherson, Tom Boyd, Gordon Strachan, Stuart McCall, Alistair McCoist, Maurice Johnston (43 Gary McAllister), Gordon Durie. Manager: Andy Roxburgh

Goals: Chapuisat (30), Hermann (39), Durie (47), McCoist (84)

SAN MARINO v BULGARIA 0-3 (0-2)

Olimpico, Serravalle 22.05.1991

Referee: Victor Mintoff (MAL) Attendance: 612

SAN MARINO: Pier Luigi Benedettini; Claudio Canti, Marco Montironi, Bruno Muccioli, Luca Gobbi, William Guerra, Massimo Ceccoli (81 Ivan Matteoni), Marco Mazza, Paolo Mazza, Fabio Francini, Waldes Pasolini (62 Nicola Bacciocchi). Trainer: Giorgio Leoni

BULGARIA: Boris Mihailov; Emil Dimitrov, Trifon Ivanov, Ilian Kiriakov, Dean Angelov (75 Nikolai Todorov), Zlatko Iankov, Emil Kostadinov, Georgi Georgiev, Liuboslav Penev, Nasko Sirakov, Velko Iotov (57 Aleksandar Markov). Trainer: Krasimir Borisov

Goals: Ivanov (12), Sirakov (19), Penev (59 pen)

BULGARIA v SAN MARINO 4-0 (3-0)

Vasil Levski, Sofia 16.10.1991

Referee: Jiri Ulrích (CZE) Attendance: 8,000

BULGARIA: Boris Mihailov; Ilian Kiriakov, Zaprian Rakov, Radoslav Vidov, Nikolai Iliev, Zlatko Iankov, Emil Kostadinov, Hristo Stoichkov (69 Iordan Lechkov), Liuboslav Penev, Hristo Kolev (65 Ivailo Iordanov), Krasimir Balakov. Trainer: Dimitar Penev

SAN MARINO: Pier Luigi Benedettini; Ivan Toccaceli, Mauro Valentini, Ivan Matteoni, Luca Gobbi, William Guerra, Pier Angelo Manzaroli (79 Nicola Bacciocchi), Pier Domenico Della Valle, Paolo Mazza (71 Marco Mularoni), Fabio Francini, Waldes Pasolini. Trainer: Giorgio Leoni

Goals: Valentini (20 og), Stoichkov (37 pen), Iankov (41), Iliev (85)

ROMANIA v SCOTLAND 1-0 (0-0)

Steaua, București 16.10.1991

Referee: Aron Schmidhuber (GER) Attendance: 30,000

ROMANIA: Silviu Lung; Dan Petrescu, Michael Klein, Emil Săndoi, Ioan Lupescu, Gheorghe Popescu, Marius Lăcătuș, Daniel Timofte (60 Ioan Timofte), Florin Răducioiu (75 Ilie Dumitrescu), Gheorghe Hagi, Dorinel Munteanu. Trainer: Mircea Rădulescu

SCOTLAND: Andy Goram; Stewart McKimmie, Maurice Malpas, Stuart McCall, Dave McPherson, Craig Levein, Gordon Strachan, Mike Galloway (70 Roy Aitken), Brian McClair, Gordon Durie, Tom Boyd (59 Kevin Gallacher). Manager: Andy Roxburgh

Goal: Hagi (74 pen)

BULGARIA v ROMANIA 1-1 (0-1)

Vasil Levski, Sofia 20.11.1991

Referee: Peter Mikkelsen (DEN) Attendance: 20,000

BULGARIA: Boris Mihailov; Petar Hubchev, Zaprian Rakov, Ilian Kiriakov, Nikolai Iliev (56 Dimitar Mladenov), Zlatko Iankov, Emil Kostadinov (70 Ivailo Iordanov), Hristo Stoichkov, Liuboslav Penev, Nasko Sirakov, Krasimir Balakov. Trainer: Dimitar Penev

ROMANIA: Silviu Lung; Adrian Popescu, Dorinel Munteanu, Emil Săndoi (67 Ioan Timofte), Ioan Lupescu, Gheorghe Popescu, Marius Lăcătuș (60 Ilie Dumitrescu), Ioan Ovidiu Sabău, Florin Răducioiu, Gheorghe Hagi, Dorin Mateuț. Trainer: Mircea Rădulescu

Goals: A. Popescu (30), Sirakov (55)

ROMANIA v SWITZERLAND 1-0 (0-0)

Steaua, București 13.11.1991

Referee: John Blankenstein (HOL) Attendance: 30,000

ROMANIA: Silviu Lung; Adrian Popescu, Michael Klein (4 Dorinel Munteanu), Emil Săndoi, Ioan Lupescu, Gheorghe Popescu, Marius Lăcătuș, Daniel Timofte (46 Ioan Ovidiu Sabău), Florin Răducioiu, Gheorghe Hagi, Dorin Mateuț. Trainer: Mircea Rădulescu

SWITZERLAND: Stefan Huber; Marc Hottiger, Dominique Christophe Ohrel, Dominique Herr, Ciriaco Sforza, Peter Schepull, Beat Sutter (66 Christophe Bonvin), Heinz Hermann (Cap) (77 Thomas Bickel), Kubilay Türkyilmaz, Alain Sutter, Stéphane Chapuisat. Trainer: Uli Stielike

Goal: Mateuț (73)

	P	W	D	L	F	A	Pts
Scotland	8	4	3	1	14	7	11
Switzerland	8	4	2	2	19	7	10
Romania	8	4	2	2	13	7	10
Bulgaria	8	3	3	2	15	8	9
San Marino	8	0	0	8	1	33	0

SCOTLAND v SAN MARINO 4-0 (3-0)

Hampden Park, Glasgow 13.11.1991

Referee: Rune Pedersen (NOR)

SCOTLAND: Andy Goram; Dave McPherson (46 Maurice Johnston), Maurice Malpas, Gary McAllister, Richard Gough, Craig Levein (60 Kevin Gallacher), Stuart McCall, John Robertson, Alistair McCoist, Paul McStay, Gordon Durie. Manager: Andy Roxburgh

SAN MARINO: Pier Luigi Benedettini; Claudio Canti, Bruno Muccioli, Marco Mazza, Luca Gobbi (46 Marco Montironi), William Guerra, Loris Zanotti, Massimo Bonini, Paolo Mazza, Fabio Francini, Waldes Pasolini (66 Pier Angelo Manzaroli). Trainer: Giorgio Leoni

Goals: McStay (10), Gough (31), Durie (45), McCoist (62)

GROUP 3

USSR v NORWAY 2-0 (1-0)

Lenin, Moskva 12.09.1990

Referee: Hubert Forstinger (AUS) Attendance: 23,000

USSR: Aleksandr Uvarov; Andrei Chernishov, Sergei Gorlukovich, Oleg Kuznetsov, Vadim Tischenko (79 Vasili Kulkov), Igor Shalimov, Aleksei Mikhailichenko, Andrei Kanchelskis, Ivan Getsko (71 Igor Kolivanov), Oleg Protasov, Igor Dobrovolski. Trainer: Anatolyi Bîshovets

NORWAY: Erik Thorstvedt; Pål Lydersen, Tore Pedersen, Rune Bratseth, Gunnar Halle, Ørjan Berg (61 Erik Pedersen), Per-Egil Ahlsen, Tom Gulbrandsen, Jahn-Ivar Jakobsen, Jørn Andersen, Jan Age Fjørtoft (66 Tore André Dahlum). Trainer: Ingvar Stadheim

Goals: Kanchelskis (22), O. Kuznetsov (60)

NORWAY v HUNGARY 0-0

Brann, Bergen 10.10.1990

Referee: John Spillane (IRE) Attendance: 6,304

NORWAY: Erik Thorstvedt; Gunnar Halle, Tore Pedersen, Rune Bratseth, Pål Lydersen, Erik Pedersen, Per-Egil Ahlsen, Sverre Brandhaug, Jahn-Ivar Jakobsen (72 Jørn Andersen), Gøran Sørloth, Jan Age Fjørtoft (78 Tore André Dahlum). Trainer: Ingvar Stadheim

HUNGARY: Zsolt Petry; Tamás Mónos, Attila Pintér, József Szalma, Ervin Kovács, Zsolt Limperger, József Kiprich (87 Imre Fodor), István Kozma, György Bognár, Emil Lörincz, Kálmán Kovács. Trainer: Kálmán Mészöly

ITALY v USSR 0-0

Stadio Olimpico, Roma 03.11.1990

Referee: Marcel Van Langenhove (BEL) Attendance: 52,500

ITALY: Walter Zenga; Ciro Ferrara, Paolo Maldini, Franco Baresi, Riccardo Ferri, Luigi De Agostini, Massimo Crippa, Fernando De Napoli, Salvatore Schillaci (70 Aldo Serena), Roberto Mancini, Roberto Baggio. Trainer: Azeglio Vicini

USSR: Aleksandr Uvarov; Andrei Chernishov, Vasili Kulkov, Akhrik Tsveiba, Sergei Aleinikov, Igor Shalimov, Aleksei Mikhailichenko, Andrei Kanchelskis, Ivan Getsko (67 Oleg Protasov), Aleksandr Mostovoi (86 Vladimir Tatarchuk), Igor Dobrovolski. Trainer: Anatolyi Bîshovets

HUNGARY v ITALY 1-1 (1-0)

Népstadion, Budapest 17.10.1990

Referee: Bo Karlsson (SWE) Attendance: 25,000

HUNGARY: Zsolt Petry; Tamás Mónos, József Szalma, László Disztl, Zsolt Limperger, Imre Garaba (59 Imre Fodor), József Kiprich, István Kozma (86 István Urbányi), György Bognár, Emil Lörincz, Kálmán Kovács. Trainer: Kálmán Mészöly

ITALY: Walter Zenga; Giuseppe Bergomi, Luigi De Agostini, Franco Baresi, Riccardo Ferri, Giancarlo Marocchi, Roberto Donadoni, Fernando De Napoli, Salvatore Schillaci (81 Aldo Serena), Giuseppe Giannini (86 Nicola Berti), Roberto Baggio. Trainer: Azeglio Vicini

Goals: Disztl (15), Baggio (54 pen)

CYPRUS v NORWAY 0-3 (0-1)

Nicosia 14.11.1990

Referee: Zoran Petrovic (YUG) Attendance: 3,000

CYPRUS: Andreas Haritou; Yiannos Kalotheou (50 Andreas Kantilos), Costas Miamiliotis, Spiros Kastanas, Avraam Socratous, Yiannakis Yiangoudakis, George Christodoulou, Pavlos Savva, Angelos Tsolakis (75 Costas Constantinou), Floros Nicolaou, Panikos Xiourouppas. Trainer: Panikos Iacovou

NORWAY: Erik Thorstvedt; Pål Lydersen, Tore Pedersen, Rune Bratseth, Karl-Petter Løken (66 Erik Pedersen), Gunnar Halle, Sverre Brandhaug, Θyvind Leonhardsen, Lars Bohinen, Gøran Sørloth, Tore André Dahlum (79 Jan Age Fjørtoft). Trainer: Egil Olsen

Goals: Sørloth (40), Bohinen (47), Brandhaug (63)

HUNGARY v CYPRUS 4-2 (3-1)

Népstadion, Budapest 31.10.1990

Referee: Plarent Kotherja (ALB) Attendance: 3,000

HUNGARY: Zsolt Petry; Tamás Mónos, József Szalma, László Disztl, Zsolt Limperger, Imre Garaba, József Kiprich (75 Vendel Rugovics), István Kozma (57 Pál Fischer), György Bognár, Emil Lörincz, Kálmán Kovács. Trainer: Kálmán Mészöly

CYPRUS: Marios Onisiforou; Yiannos Kalotheou, Costas Miamiliotis, George Christodoulou, Avraam Socratous, Yiannakis Yiangoudakis, Andreas Kantilos (61 Angelos Tsolakis), Pavlos Savva, Spiros Kastanas, Costas Constantinou (70 Panikos Orphanides), Panikos Xiourouppas. Trainer: Panikos Iacovou

Goals: Lörincz (1), Xiourouppas (13), Christodoulou (18 og), Kiprich (20 pen, 67 pen), Tsolakis (89)

CYPRUS v ITALY 0-4 (0-3)

Tsirion, Limassol 22.12.1990

Referee: Ivan Gregr (CZE) Attendance: 10,000

CYPRUS: Marios Onisiforou; Yiannos Kalotheou, Costas Miamiliotis, George Christodoulou, Avraam Socratous, Yiannakis Yiangoudakis, Panayiotis Pounas, Pavlos Savva (56 Costas Constantinou), Angelos Tsolakis, Floros Nicolaou, Nikos Papavasiliou (64 Panikos Xiourouppas). Trainer: Panikos Iacovou

ITALY: Walter Zenga; Giuseppe Bergomi, Ciro Ferrara, Stefano Eranio, Pietro Vierchowod, Massimo Crippa, Attilio Lombardo, Nicola Berti, Salvatore Schillaci, Giancarlo Marocchi, Aldo Serena. Trainer: Azeglio Vicini

Goals: Vierchowod (13), Serena (22, 48), Lombardo (42)

CYPRUS v HUNGARY 0-2 (0-2)

Tsirion, Limassol 03.04.1991

Referee: Gerhard Kapl (AUS) Attendance: 3,000

CYPRUS: Socratis Marangos; George Constantinou, Haralambos Pittas (75 Hristakis Kasianos), Demetris Ioannou, Costas Constantinou, Yiannakis Yiangoudakis, Haralambos Christophi, Pavlos Savva (83 Andros Sotiriou), George Savvidis, Floros Nicolaou, Angelos Tsolakis. Trainer: Panikos Iacovou

HUNGARY: Zsolt Petry; Tamás Mónos, József Szalma, László Disztl, Tibor Nagy, Zsolt Limperger, József Kiprich, György Bognár, Pál Fischer (72 János Maroszán), Emil Lörincz, Kálmán Kovács. Trainer: Kálmán Mészöly

Goals: Szalma (16), Kiprich (41)

ITALY v HUNGARY 3-1 (2-0)

Arechi, Salerno 01.05.1991

Referee: Joseph Worrall (ENG) Attendance: 45,000

ITALY: Walter Zenga; Ciro Ferrara (65 Pietro Vierchowod), Paolo Maldini, Franco Baresi, Riccardo Ferri, Massimo Crippa, Roberto Donadoni (37 Stefano Eranio), Fernando De Napoli, Gianluca Vialli, Giuseppe Giannini, Roberto Mancini. Trainer: Azeglio Vicini

HUNGARY: Zsolt Petry; Tamás Mónos, László Disztl, János Paláczky (33 István Kozma), Zsolt Limperger, Imre Garaba, József Kiprich (46 József Gregor), Emil Lörincz, György Bognár, Lajos Détári, Kálmán Kovács. Trainer: Kálmán Mészöly

Goals: Donadoni (4, 21), Vialli (56), Bognár (65)

HUNGARY v USSR 0-1 (0-1)

Népstadion, Budapest 17.04.1991

Referee: Aron Schmidhuber (GER) Attendance: 40,000

HUNGARY: Zsolt Petry; Tamás Mónos, József Szalma, László Disztl, Zsolt Limperger, Imre Garaba, József Kiprich, István Kozma (62 Lajos Détári), György Bognár (70 István Vincze), Emil Lörincz, Kálmán Kovács. Trainer: Kálmán Mészöly

USSR: Aleksandr Uvarov; Andrei Chernishov, Vasili Kulkov, Akhrik Tsveiba, Dmitri Galiamin, Igor Shalimov, Aleksei Mikhailichenko, Andrei Kanchelskis, Sergei Aleinikov, Igor Kolivanov, Sergei Iuran (86 Dmitri Kuznetsov). Trainer: Anatolyi Bîshovets

Goal: Mikhailichenko (30)

USSR v CYPRUS 4-0 (1-0)

Lenin, Moskva 29.05.1991

Referee: Ştefan-Dan Petrescu (ROM) Attendance: 20,000

USSR: Aleksandr Uvarov; Andrei Chernishov, Vasili Kulkov, Aleksandr Mostovoi (74 Dmitri Kuznetsov), Dmitri Galiamin, Igor Shalimov, Aleksei Mikhailichenko, Andrei Kanchelskis, Sergei Aleinikov, Igor Kolivanov, Sergei Iuran (46 Igor Korneev). Trainer: Anatolyi Bîshovets

CYPRUS: Andreas Haritou; Yiannos Kalotheou, Haralambos Pittas, Demetris Ioannou, Floros Nicolaou, Yiannakis Yiangoudakis, Costas Costa, Haralambos Christophi, George Savvidis, George Christodoulou (84 George Constantinou), Panikos Xiouroupas (89 Pavlos Savva). Trainer: Panikos Iacovou

Goals: Mostovoi (20), Mikhailichenko (51), Korneev (83), Aleinikov (88)

NORWAY v CYPRUS 3-0 (0-0)

Ullevaal, Oslo 01.05.1991

Referee: Kaj Natri (FIN) Attendance: 7,800

NORWAY: Erik Thorstvedt; Tore Pedersen, Rune Bratseth (46 Kåre Ingebrigtsen), Pål Lydersen, Gunnar Halle (75 Erik Pedersen), Per-Egil Ahlsen, Sverre Brandhaug, Θyvind Leonhardsen, Stig Inge Bjørnebye, Gøran Sørloth, Tore André Dahlum. Trainer: Egil Olsen

CYPRUS: Andreas Haritou; Floros Nicolaou, Costas Constantinou, Demetris Ioannou, Costas Costa, Yiannos Kalotheou (77 George Constantinou), Haralambos Christophi, Yiannakis Yiangoudakis, Haralambos Pittas, George Savvidis, Panikos Xiourouppas (89 Andros Sotiriou). Trainer: Panikos Iacovou

Goals: Lydersen (49 pen), Dahlum (65), Sørloth (90)

NORWAY v ITALY 2-1 (2-0)

Ullevaal, Oslo 05.06.1991

Referee: Mario Van der Ende (HOL) Attendance: 27,500

NORWAY: Erik Thorstvedt; Pål Lydersen, Per-Egil Ahlsen, Rune Bratseth, Tore Pedersen, Karl-Petter Løken, Lars Bohinen, Kåre Ingebrigtsen, Tore André Dahlum (46 Erik Pedersen), Gøran Sørloth, Jahn-Ivar Jakobsen. Trainer: Egil Olsen

ITALY: Walter Zenga; Ciro Ferrara, Paolo Maldini, Stefano Eranio, Riccardo Ferri (90 Giuseppe Bergomi), Franco Baresi, Attilio Lombardo, Fernando De Napoli (53 Salvatore Schillaci), Gianluca Vialli, Roberto Mancini, Massimo Crippa. Trainer: Azeglio Vicini

Goals: Dahlum (4), Bohinen (25), Schillaci (79)

NORWAY v USSR 0-1 (0-0)

Ullevaal, Oslo 28.08.1991

Referee: Howard King (WAL) Attendance: 25,427

NORWAY: Erik Thorstvedt; Pål Lydersen, Tore Pedersen, Rune Bratseth, Roger Nilsen (66 Dag Riisnaes), Karl-Petter Løken, Gunnar Halle, Øivind Leonhardsen, Jahn-Ivar Jakobsen (80 Bent Skammelsrud), Gøran Sørloth, Jan Åge Fjørtoft. Trainer: Egil Olsen

USSR: Stanislav Cherchesov; Andrei Chernishov, Vasili Kulkov, Akhrik Tsveiba, Oleg Kuznetsov, Igor Shalimov, Aleksei Mikhailichenko, Andrei Kanchelskis (71 Igor Korneev), Sergei Aleinikov, Igor Kolivanov, Sergei Iuran (46 Aleksandr Mostovoi). Trainer: Anatolyi Bîshovets

Goal: Mostovoi (74)

HUNGARY v NORWAY 0-0

Rohonci út, Szombathely 30.10.1991

Referee: Gérard Biguet (FRA) Attendance: 10,000

HUNGARY: Zsolt Petry; Tibor Nagy, Attila Pintér, József Duró, Péter Lipcsei (72 Béla Illes), Emil Lörincz, Flórián Urban, István Pisont (84 Dénes Eszenyi), Pál Fischer, Lajos Détári, Kálmán Kovács. Trainer: Kálmán Mészöly

NORWAY: Frode Grodås; Tore Pedersen, Per-Egil Ahlsen, Rune Bratseth, Stig Inge Bjørnebye, Karl-Petter Løken, Kjetil Rekdal, Øivind Leonhardsen (78 Kåre Ingebrigtsen), Lars Bohinen, Gøran Sørloth (46 Jan Åge Fjørtoft), Jahn-Ivar Jakobsen. Trainer: Egil Olsen

USSR v HUNGARY 2-2 (1-1)

Lujniki, Moskva 25.09.1991

Referee: Zoran Petrovic (YUG) Attendance: 50,000

USSR: Stanislav Cherchesov; Andrei Chernishov, Vasili Kulkov, Akhrik Tsveiba (25 Oleg Kuznetsov), Dmitri Galiamin, Igor Shalimov, Aleksei Mikhailichenko, Andrei Kanchelskis, Sergei Aleinikov, Igor Kolivanov, Aleksandr Mostovoi (70 Sergei Iuran). Trainer: Anatolyi Bîshovets

HUNGARY: Zsolt Petry; Tamás Mónos (43 József Duró), László Disztl, József Szalma, Péter Lipcsei, Zsolt Limperger, József Kiprich, Emil Lörincz, István Kozma (70 Pál Fischer), Lajos Détári, Kálmán Kovács. Trainer: Kálmán Mészöly

Goals: Kiprich (11, 86), Shalimov (41 pen), Kanchelskis (48)

CYPRUS v USSR 0-3 (0-1)

Larnaca 13.11.1991

Referee: Andrew Wilson Waddell (SCO) Attendance: 4,000

CYPRUS: Andreas Haritou; Costas Costa, Haralambos Pittas, Costas Constantinou, Avraam Socratous, Neophytos Larkou, Hristos Koliandris (73 Lucas Hadjilucas), Pavlos Savva, George Savvidis (46 Andros Sotiriou), Yiannakis Ioannou, Marios Charalambous. Trainer: Andreas Michailidis

USSR: Dmitri Kharin; Andrei Chernishov, Vasili Kulkov, Akhrik Tsveiba, Dmitri Galiamin, Igor Shalimov, Aleksei Mikhailichenko, Andrei Kanchelskis, Oleg Kuznetsov, Oleg Protasov (70 Aleksandr Mostovoi), Igor Kolivanov (46 Sergei Iuran). Trainer: Anatolyi Bîshovets

Goals: Protasov (27), Iuran (79), Kanchelskis (83)

USSR v ITALY 0-0

Lenin, Moskva 12.10.1991

Referee: Bruno Galler (SWI) Attendance: 92,000

USSR: Stanislav Cherchesov; Andrei Chernishov, Vasili Kulkov, Oleg Kuznetsov (46 Akhrik Tsveiba), Dmitri Galiamin, Igor Shalimov, Aleksei Mikhailichenko, Andrei Kanchelskis, Sergei Aleinikov, Oleg Protasov (69 Dmitri Kuznetsov), Igor Kolivanov. Trainer: Anatolyi Bîshovets

ITALY: Walter Zenga; Ciro Ferrara, Paolo Maldini, Franco Baresi, Pietro Vierchowod, Massimo Crippa, Gianluigi Lentini (58 Attilio Lombardo), Fernando De Napoli, Gianluca Vialli, Giuseppe Giannini (69 Roberto Mancini), Ruggiero Rizzitelli. Trainer: Azeglio Vicini

ITALY v NORWAY 1-1 (0-0)

Luigi Ferraris, Genova 13.11.1991

Referee: Karl-Josef Assenmacher (GER) Att: 30,000

ITALY: Gianluca Pagliuca; Alessandro Costacurta, Paolo Maldini, Nicola Berti (71 Fernando De Napoli), Riccardo Ferri, Franco Baresi, Francesco Baiano (57 Ruggiero Rizzitelli), Carlo Ancelotti, Gianluca Vialli, Gianfranco Zola, Stefano Eranio. Trainer: Azeglio Vicini

NORWAY: Erik Thorstvedt; Karl-Petter Løken, Per-Egil Ahlsen, Rune Bratseth, Pål Lydersen, Ronny Johnsen (46 Jan Ove Pedersen), Kjetil Rekdal, Kåre Ingebrigtsen (83 Henning Berg), Jan Åge Fjørtoft, Gøran Sørloth, Jahn-Ivar Jakobsen. Trainer: Egil Olsen

Goals: Jakobsen (60), Rizzitelli (82)

ITALY v CYPRUS 2-0 (1-0)

Pino Zaccheria, Foggia 21.12.1991

Referee: Joaquin Ramos Marcos (SPA) Attendance: 26,000

ITALY: Walter Zenga; Dino Baggio, Paolo Maldini, Demetrio Albertini, Alessandro Costacurta, Franco Baresi, Gianfranco Zola, Nicola Berti, Gianluca Vialli (69 Francesco Baiano), Roberto Baggio (69 Pierluigi Casiraghi), Alberigo Evani.
Trainer: Azeglio Vicini

CYPRUS: Michalis Christophi; George Constantinou, Haralambos Pittas, Costas Constantinou, Floros Nicolaou, Vasos Tsagaris (55 Sakis Andreou), Hristos Koliandris, Pavlos Savva, Andros Sotiriou, Demetris Ioannou (75 Neophytos Larkou), Marios Charalambous.
Trainer: Andreas Michaelides

Goals: Vialli (27), R. Baggio (55)

	P	W	D	L	F	A	Pts
USSR	8	5	3	0	13	2	13
Italy	8	3	4	1	12	5	10
Norway	8	3	3	2	9	5	9
Hungary	8	2	4	2	10	9	8
Cyprus	8	0	0	8	2	25	0

GROUP 4

NORTHERN IRELAND v YUGOSLAVIA 0-2 (0-1)

Windsor Park, Belfast 12.09.1990

Referee: Jacob Uilenberg (HOL) Attendance: 10,000

N. IRELAND: Paul Kee; Malachy Donaghy, Nigel Worthington, Anton Rogan, Alan McDonald, Daniel Wilson, Kevin Wilson, Iain Dowie, Gerry Taggart, Kingsley Black, Robbie Dennison (66 Colin Clarke).
Manager: William Bingham

YUGOSLAVIA: Tomislav Ivkovic; Zoran Vulic, Predrag Spasic, Davor Jozic, Faruk Hadzibegic, Ilija Najdoski, Robert Prosinecki, Dejan Savicevic, Darko Pancev (87 Zeljko Petrovic), Dragan Stojkovic, Dragisa Binic.
Trainer: Ivica Osim

Goals: Pancev (37), Prosinecki (90)

FAROE ISLANDS v AUSTRIA 1-0 (0-0)

Landskrona (Sweden) 12.09.1990

Referee: Egil Nervik (NOR) Attendance: 1,265

FAROE ISLANDS: Jens Martin Knudsen; Joannes Jakobsen, Tummas Eli Hansen, Mikkjal Danielsen, J.Hansen, Allan Mørkøre, Jan Dam, Torkil Nielsen, Abraham Hansen, Kari Reynheim, Kurt Mørkøre. Trainer: Pall Gudlaugsson

AUSTRIA: Michael Konsel; Kurt Russ, Michael Streiter, Robert Pecl, Jürgen Hartmann, Manfred Linzmaier, Heinz Peischl, Andreas Herzog (61 Gerald Willfurth), Andreas Reisinger (61 Peter Pacult), Anton Polster, Gerhard Rodax.
Trainer: Josef Hickersberger

Goal: Nielsen (60)

DENMARK v FAROE ISLANDS 4-1 (2-1)

Idraetsparken, København 10.10.1990

Referee: Gudmundur Haraldsson (ICE) Attendance: 38,563

DENMARK: Peter Schmeichel; John Sivebæk, Kent Nielsen, Lars Olsen, Jan Heintze, Jan Bartram, Kim Vilfort, Lars Elstrup (73 Jens Erik Rasmussen), Flemming Povlsen, Michael Laudrup, Brian Laudrup. Trainer: Richard Møller-Nielsen

FAROE ISLANDS: Jens Martin Knudsen; Joannes Jakobsen (75 Jens Erik Rasmussen), Tummas Eli Hansen, Mikkjal Danielsen, J.Hansen, Allan Mørkøre, Torkil Nielsen, Jan Dam, Abraham Hansen, Kari Reynheim, Kurt Mørkøre.
Trainer: Pall Gudlaugsson

Goals: M. Laudrup (8, 49), A. Mørkøre (22), Elstrup (38), Povlsen (89)

NORTHERN IRELAND v DENMARK 1-1 (0-1)

Windsor Park, Belfast 17.10.1990

Referee: Roger Philippi (LUX) Attendance: 10,000

N. IRELAND: Paul Kee; Malachy Donaghy, Nigel Worthington, Gerry Taggart, Alan McDonald, Anton Rogan, Colin O'Neill (72 Stephen McBride), Daniel Wilson, Iain Dowie, Colin Clarke, Kingsley Black.
Manager: William Bingham

DENMARK: Peter Schmeichel; John Sivebæk, Kent Nielsen, Lars Olsen, John Larsen, Jan Heintze, Kim Vilfort, Jan Bartram, Michael Laudrup (80 John Helt), Brian Laudrup (70 Lars Elstrup), Flemming Povlsen.
Trainer: Richard Møller-Nielsen

Goals: Bartram (11 pen), Clarke (58)

YUGOSLAVIA v AUSTRIA 4-1 (2-1)

Beograd 31.10.1990

Referee: Aron Schmidhuber (GER) Attendance: 17,500

YUGOSLAVIA: Tomislav Ivkovic; Zoran Vulic, Predrag Spasic, Srecko Katanec (46 Robert Jarni), Davor Jozic, Faruk Hadzibegic, Robert Prosinecki, Mehmed Bazdarevic, Darko Pancev, Safet Susic (65 Zvonimir Boban), Zlatko Vujovic. Trainer: Ivica Osim

AUSTRIA: Michael Konsel; Ernst Aigner, Robert Pecl, Peter Artner, Peter Schöttel, Michael Streiter, Alfred Hörtnagl, Andreas Reisinger, Andreas Ogris (52 Peter Pacult), Andreas Herzog (46 Manfred Linzmaier), Anton Polster. Trainer: Alfred Riedl

Goals: A. Ogris (16), Pancev (31, 52, 86), Katanec (42)

AUSTRIA v NORTHERN IRELAND 0-0

Prater, Wien 14.11.1990

Referee: Gérard Biguet (FRA) Attendance: 7,000

AUSTRIA: Michael Konsel; Peter Schöttel, Peter Artner, Robert Pecl, Andreas Poiger, Manfred Linzmaier, Hainz Peischl, Gerald Willfurth, Alfred Hörtnagl, Andreas Ogris, Anton Polster (70 Peter Pacult). Trainer: Alfred Riedl

N. IRELAND: Paul Kee; Malachy Donaghy, Alan McDonald, Gerry Taggart, Nigel Worthington, Anton Rogan, Daniel Wilson, Robbie Dennison, Kingsley Black (82 Stephen Morrow), Colin Clarke (62 Iain Dowie), Kevin Wilson. Manager: William Bingham

DENMARK v YUGOSLAVIA 0-2 (0-0)

Idraetsparken, København 14.11.1990

Referee: Neil Midgley (ENG) Attendance: 39,700

DENMARK: Peter Schmeichel; John Sivebæk, Kent Nielsen, Lars Olsen, Jan Heintze, Jan Bartram, Jan Mølby (73 Lars Elstrup), Kim Vilfort, Flemming Povlsen (46 John Jensen), Michael Laudrup, Brian Laudrup. Trainer: Richard Møller-Nielsen

YUGOSLAVIA: Tomislav Ivkovic; Zoran Vulic, Predrag Spasic, Faruk Hadzibegic, Davor Jozic, Srecko Katanec, Robert Jarni, Safet Susic, Darko Pancev (12 Zvonimir Boban), Mehmed Bazdarevic, Zlatko Vujovic (88 Ilija Najdoski). Trainer: Ivica Osim

Goals: Bazdarevic (77), Jarni (84)

YUGOSLAVIA v NORTHERN IRELAND 4-1 (1-1)

Beograd 27.03.1991

Referee: Yusuf Namoglu (TÜR) Attendance: 10,750

YUGOSLAVIA: Tomislav Ivkovic; Zoran Vulic (85 Ilija Najdoski), Robert Jarni, Predrag Spasic, Zvonimir Boban, Davor Jozic, Robert Prosinecki, Mehmed Bazdarevic, Darko Pancev, Dejan Savicevic, Dragisa Binic. Trainer: Ivica Osim

N. IRELAND: Paul Kee; Gary Fleming, Anton Rogan, Malachy Donaghy, Stephen Morrow, Colin Hill, Robbie Dennison (75 Jimmy Quinn), Jim Magilton, Iain Dowie, Kevin Wilson (54 Colin Clarke), Kingsley Black. Manager: William Bingham

Goals: Binic (35), Hill (45), Pancev (47, 60, 61)

YUGOSLAVIA v DENMARK 1-2 (0-1)

Beograd 01.05.1991

Referee: Joël Quiniou (FRA) Attendance: 26,000

YUGOSLAVIA: Tomislav Ivkovic; Zoran Vulic, Robert Jarni (84 Ilija Najdoski), Predrag Spasic, Faruk Hadzibegic, Davor Jozic, Robert Prosinecki, Dejan Savicevic, Darko Pancev, Mehmed Bazdarevic, Dragisa Binic. Trainer: Ivica Osim

DENMARK: Peter Schmeichel; John Sivebæk, Kent Nielsen, Lars Olsen (54 Henrik Larsen), Bjørn Kristensen, Jan Bartram, John Jensen (82 Bjarne Goldbaek), Kim Christofte, Flemming Povlsen, Kim Vilfort, Bent Christensen. Trainer: Richard Møller-Nielsen

Goals: Christensen (32, 63), Pancev (50)

NORTHERN IRELAND v FAROE ISLANDS 1-1 (1-0)

Windsor Park, Belfast 01.05.1991

Referee: Michel Piraux (BEL) Attendance: 10,000

N. IRELAND: Paul Kee; Malachy Donaghy, Nigel Worthington, Gerry Taggart, Alan McDonald, Jim Magilton, Daniel Wilson (83 Robbie Dennison), Colin Clarke, Iain Dowie (83 Paul Williams), Kevin Wilson, Kingsley Black. Manager: William Bingham

FAROE ISLANDS: Jens Martin Knudsen; Joannes Jakobsen, Tummas Eli Hansen, Mikkjal Danielsen, Jan Allan Müller, Allan Mørkøre, Torkil Nielsen, Jan Dam, Abraham Hansen, Kari Reynheim (75 Ari Thomassen), Kurt Mørkøre. Trainer: Pall Gudlaugsson

Goals: Clarke (44), Reynheim (65)

YUGOSLAVIA v FAROE ISLANDS 7-0 (2-0)

Beograd 16.05.1991

Referee: Vasilios Nikakis (GRE) Attendance: 8,000

YUGOSLAVIA: Tomislav Ivkovic (78 Drazen Ladic); Vujadin Stanojkovic, Robert Jarni (63 Davor Suker), Zoran Vulic, Ilija Najdoski, Predrag Spasic, Robert Prosinecki, Zvonimir Boban, Darko Pancev, Dejan Savicevic, Sinisa Mihajlovic. Trainer: Ivica Osim

FAROE ISLANDS: Jens Martin Knudsen; Joannes Jakobsen, Ari Thomassen, Mikkjal Danielsen, Magni Jarnskor (50 Jan Allan Müller), Allan Mørkøre, Torkil Nielsen, Jan Dam, Kari Reynheim, Abraham Hansen, Kurt Mørkøre (15 Jakup Simun Simonsen). Trainer: Pall Gudlaugsson

Goals: Najdoski (20), Prosinecki (23), Pancev (50, 74), Vulic (65), Boban (70), Suker (86)

FAROE ISLANDS v NORTHERN IRELAND 0-5 (0-3)

Landskrona (Sweden) 11.09.1991

Referee: Simo Ruokonen (FIN) Attendance: 1,623

FAROE ISLANDS: Jens Martin Knudsen; Joannes Jakobsen (78 Kurt Mørkøre), Tummas Eli Hansen, Mikkjal Danielsen, Ari Thomassen (57 Jan Allan Müller), Allan Mørkøre, Torkil Nielsen, Jan Dam, Abraham Hansen, Kari Reynheim, Toti Jonsson. Trainer: Pall Gudlaugsson

N. IRELAND: Tommy Wright; Malachy Donaghy, Stephen Morrow, Gerry Taggart, Alan McDonald, Jim Magilton, Robbie Dennison, Kevin Wilson (68 Michael O'Neill), Iain Dowie, Colin Clarke, Kingsley Black (68 Stephen McBride). Manager: William Bingham

Goals: K. Wilson (7), Clarke (12, 48, 78 pen), McDonald (15)

AUSTRIA v FAROE ISLANDS 3-0 (1-0)

Lehen, Salzburg 22.05.1991

Referee: Loizos Loizou (CYP) Attendance: 13,000

AUSTRIA: Michael Konsel (86 Franz Wohlfahrt); Michael Baur, Kurt Russ, Heimo Pfeifenberger (24 Alfred Hörtnagl), Jürgen Hartmann, Peter Stöger, Peter Schöttel, Andreas Herzog, Michael Streiter, Arnold Wetl, Andreas Ogris. Trainer: Alfred Riedl

FAROE ISLANDS: Jens Martin Knudsen; Joannes Jakobsen, Allan Mørkøre, Mikkjal Danielsen, Tummas Eli Hansen, Jakup Simun Simonsen, Torkil Nielsen, Abraham Hansen, Jan Dam (71 Ari Thomassen), Kari Reynheim, Jens Erik Rasmussen (84 G. Mohr). Trainer: Pall Gudlaugsson

Goals: Pfeifenberger (13), Streiter (47), Wetl (64)

FAROE ISLANDS v DENMARK 0-4 (0-2)

Landskrona (Sweden) 25.09.1991

Referee: James McCluskey (SCO) Attendance: 2,589

FAROE ISLANDS: Jens Martin Knudsen (46 Kaj Leo Johannesen); Joannes Jakobsen, Tummas Eli Hansen, Mikkjal Danielsen, Kurt Mørkøre, Jan Dam, Magni Jarnskor, Toti Jonsson (82 Eyolfinn Davidsen), Abraham Hansen, Kari Reynheim, Jan Allan Müller. Trainer: Pall Gudlaugsson

DENMARK: Peter Schmeichel; John Sivebæk, Kent Nielsen, Lars Olsen, Henrik Larsen, Kim Christofte (60 Johnny Mølby), John Jensen, Kim Vilfort, Flemming Povlsen, Bent Christensen, Lars Elstrup (70 Frank Pingel). Trainer: Richard Møller-Nielsen

Goals: Christofte (2 pen), Christensen (7), Pingel (71), Vilfort (76)

DENMARK v AUSTRIA 2-1 (1-0)

Odense 05.06.1991

Referee: Michal Listkiewicz (POL) Attendance: 12,521

DENMARK: Peter Schmeichel; Kent Nielsen, Lars Olsen, Kim Vilfort, Johnny Hansen, Morten Bruun, Henrik Larsen, Brian Steen Nielsen, Claus Nielsen (46 Bjarne Goldbaek), Flemming Povlsen (78 Erik Rasmussen), Bent Christensen. Trainer: Richard Møller-Nielsen

AUSTRIA: Otto Konrad; Kurt Russ (73 Christian Prosenik), Michael Baur, Michael Streiter, Heimo Pfeifenberger, Jürgen Hartmann, Peter Schöttel (68 Alfred Hörtnagl), Andreas Herzog, Peter Stöger, Ernst Ogris, Christoph Westerthaler. Trainer: Alfred Riedl

Goals: Christensen (2, 77), E. Ogris (83)

AUSTRIA v DENMARK 0-3 (0-3)

Prater, Wien 09.10.1991

Referee: Frans Van den Wijngaert (BEL) Att: 10,000

AUSTRIA: Otto Konrad; Christian Prosenik, Michael Baur, Franz Resch, Walter Kogler, Peter Schöttel (46 Harald Gschnaidtner), Andreas Ogris, Peter Artner, Andreas Herzog, Peter Stöger, Peter Pacult. Trainer: Alfred Riedl

DENMARK: Peter Schmeichel; John Sivebæk, Kent Nielsen, Lars Olsen, Henrik Larsen (81 Brian Jensen), Kim Christofte (59 Johnny Mølby), John Jensen, Kim Vilfort, Flemming Povlsen, Bent Christensen, Lars Elstrup. Trainer: Richard Møller-Nielsen

Goals: Artner (10 og), Povlsen (16), Christensen (38)

FAROE ISLANDS v YUGOSLAVIA 0-2 (0-1)

Landskrona (Sweden) 16.10.1991

Referee: Günther Habermann (GER) Attendance: 2,485

FAROE ISLANDS: Jens Martin Knudsen; Joannes Jakobsen, Tummas Eli Hansen, Mikkjal Danielsen, Kurt Mørkøre, Jan Dam, Allan Mørkøre, Toti Jonsson, Abraham Hansen, Kari Reynheim, Jan Allan Müller (85 Eyolfinn Davidsen). Trainer: Pall Gudlaugsson

YUGOSLAVIA: Fahrudin Omerovic; Branko Brnovic, Predrag Spasic, Slavisa Jokanovic, Faruk Hadzibegic, Ilija Najdoski, Vladimir Jugovic, Dejan Savicevic, Vladan Lukic (80 Mario Stanic), Mehmet Bazdarevic, Sinisa Mihajlovic (63 Predrag Mijatovic). Trainer: Ivica Osim

Goals: Jugovic (18), Savicevic (81)

AUSTRIA v YUGOSLAVIA 0-2 (0-2)

Prater, Wien 13.11.1991

Referee: Pietro D'Elia (ITA) Attendance: 8,000

AUSTRIA: Wolfgang Knaller; Kurt Garger, Walter Kogler, Leo Lainer, Herbert Gager, Manfred Zsak, Andreas Ogris, Peter Artner, Andreas Herzog, Peter Stöger (53 Christian Keglevits), Christoph Westerthaler (73 Michael Baur). Trainer: Dietmar Constantini

YUGOSLAVIA: Fahrudin Omerovic; Budimir Vujacic, Darko Milanic, Dzoni Novak (80 Branko Brnovic), Faruk Hadzibegic, Slavisa Jokanovic, Vladan Lukic (46 Predrag Mijatovic), Dejan Savicevic, Darko Pancev, Mehmet Bazdarevic, Sinisa Mihajlovic. Trainer: Ivica Osim

Goals: Lukic (19), Savicevic (39)

NORTHERN IRELAND v AUSTRIA 2-1 (2-1)

Windsor Park, Belfast 16.10.1991

Referee: Leif Sundell (SWE) Attendance: 8,000

N. IRELAND: Tommy Wright; Malachy Donaghy, Nigel Worthington, Gerry Taggart, Colin Hill, Jim Magilton, Robbie Dennison, Kevin Wilson, Iain Dowie, Colin Clarke (46 Daniel Wilson), Kingsley Black. Manager: William Bingham

AUSTRIA: Wolfgang Knaller; Leo Lainer, Leopold Rotter, Jürgen Hartmann, Walter Kogler, Manfred Zsak, Andreas Ogris, Peter Artner, Christian Keglevits (62 Christoph Westerthaler), Peter Stöger (62 Andreas Herzog), Herbert Gager. Trainer: Dietmar Constantini

Goals: Dowie (17), Black (40), Lainer (45)

	P	W	D	L	F	A	Pts
Yugoslavia	8	7	0	1	24	4	14
Denmark	8	6	1	1	18	7	13
Northern Ireland	8	2	3	3	11	11	7
Austria	8	1	1	6	6	14	3
Faroe Islands	8	1	1	6	3	26	3

DENMARK v NORTHERN IRELAND 2-1 (2-0)

Odense 13.11.1991

Referee: Aleksei Spirin (USSR) Attendance: 10,881

DENMARK: Peter Schmeichel; John Sivebæk, Kent Nielsen, Torben Piechnik, Henrik Larsen, Lars Olsen, Kim Christofte, Kim Vilfort, Flemming Povlsen, Johnny Mølby, Lars Elstrup (52 Frank Pingel). Trainer: Richard Møller-Nielsen

N. IRELAND: Alan Fettis; Colin Hill, Nigel Worthington, Malachy Donaghy, Gerry Taggart, Jim Magilton, Stephen McBride, Kevin Wilson, Colin Clarke (67 Iain Dowie), Michael Hughes, Kingsley Black (83 Robbie Dennison). Manager: William Bingham

Goals: Povlsen (22, 37), Taggart (71)

GROUP 5

WALES v BELGIUM 3-1 (1-1)

National, Cardiff 17.10.1990

Referee: Kurt Roethlisberger (SWI) Attendance: 12,000

WALES: Neville Southall; Clayton Blackmore, Kevin Ratcliffe, Eric Young, Mark Aizlewood, Paul Bodin, Barry Horne, Peter Nicholas, Ian Rush, Mark Hughes, Dean Saunders. Manager: Terry Yorath

BELGIUM: Michel Preud'homme; Eric Gerets, Stéphane Demol, Georges Grün, Michel De Wolf, Marc Emmers, Enzo Scifo, Franky Van der Elst, Luc Nilis (75 Marc Wilmots), Bruno Versavel, Jan Ceulemans. Trainer: Guy Thys

Goals: Versavel (25), Rush (30), Saunders (83), Hughes (88)

LUXEMBOURG v GERMANY 2-3 (0-2)

Stade Municipal, Luxembourg 31.10.1990

Referee: Nielsen (DEN) Attendance: 9,500

LUXEMBOURG: John Van Rijswijck; Théo Malget, Marcel Bossi, Pierre Petry, Marc Birsens, Joël Groff, Guy Hellers, Jean-Paul Girres, Jeff Saibene (85 Gérard Jeitz), Carlo Weis, Robert Langers. Trainer: Paul Philipp

GERMANY: Bodo Illgner; Thomas Berthold, Andreas Brehme, Jürgen Kohler, Manfred Binz, Thomas Strunz, Thomas Häßler, Uwe Bein, Rudolf Völler (72 Knut Reinhardt), Lothar Matthäus, Jürgen Klinsmann. Trainer: Hubert Vogts

Goals: Klinsmann (14), Bein (30), Völler (49), Girres (57), Langers (66)

BELGIUM v WALES 1-1 (0-0)

Brussel 27.03.1991

Referee: Emilio Soriano Aladren (SPA) Attendance: 27,500

BELGIUM: Michel Preud'homme; Eric Gerets, Philippe Albert, Georges Grün, Leo Clijsters, Bruno Versavel, Franky Van der Elst, Enzo Scifo, Marc Degryse, Erwin Vandenbergh, Marc Wilmots. Trainer: Guy Thys

WALES: Neville Southall; David Phillips, Kevin Ratcliffe, Eric Young, Mark Aizlewood, Paul Bodin, Barry Horne, Peter Nicholas, Mark Hughes, Ian Rush, Dean Saunders. Manager: Terry Yorath

Goals: Degryse (48), Saunders (59)

LUXEMBOURG v WALES 0-1 (0-1)

Stade Municipal, Luxembourg 14.11.1990

Referee: Jiri Ulrich (CZE) Attendance: 7,000

LUXEMBOURG: John Van Rijswijck; Théo Malget, Marcel Bossi, Marc Birsens, Pierre Petry, Patrick Morocutti (59 Armin Krings), Guy Hellers, Jean-Paul Girres, Jeff Saibene, Carlo Weis, Robert Langers. Trainer: Paul Philipp

WALES: Neville Southall; Clayton Blackmore, Paul Bodin, Mark Aizlewood, Eric Young, Kevin Ratcliffe, Barry Horne, Peter Nicholas, Ian Rush (83 Gary Speed), Mark Hughes, Dean Saunders (89 Malcolm Allen). Manager: Terry Yorath

Goal: Rush (16)

GERMANY v BELGIUM 1-0 (1-0)

Niedersachsenstadion, Hannover 01.05.1991

Referee: Zoran Petrovic (YUG) Attendance: 56,000

GERMANY: Bodo Illgner; Stefan Reuter, Andreas Brehme, Thomas Doll, Thomas Berthold, Dietmar Beiersdorfer, Thomas Häßler, Matthias Sammer, Rudolf Völler (88 Karl-Heinz Riedle), Lothar Matthäus, Jürgen Klinsmann (77 Thomas Helmer). Trainer: Hubert Vogts

BELGIUM: Michel Preud'homme; Bertrand Crasson, Philippe Albert, Marc Emmers, Georges Grün, Franky Van der Elst, Patrick Vervoort, Bruno Versavel, Marc Degryse, Enzo Scifo, Marc Wilmots (77 Luc Nilis). Trainer: Guy Thys

Goal: Matthäus (3)

BELGIUM v LUXEMBOURG 3-0 (3-0)

Brussel 27.02.1991

Referee: Loizos Loizou (CYP) Attendance: 24,500

BELGIUM: Michel Preud'homme; Georges Grün, Marc Emmers, Philippe Albert, Bruno Versavel, Frank Dauwen, Enzo Scifo, Erwin Vandenbergh, Marc Degryse, Jan Ceulemans, Marc Wilmots. Trainer: Guy Thys

LUXEMBOURG: Paul Koch; Théo Malget (46 Gérard Jeitz), Marcel Bossi, Marc Birsens, Pierre Petry, Joël Groff (76 Denis Scuto), Guy Hellers, Jean-Paul Girres, Jeff Saibene, Carlo Weis, Armin Krings. Trainer: Paul Philipp

Goals: Vandenbergh (7), Ceulemans (17), Scifo (35)

WALES v GERMANY 1-0 (0-0)

National, Cardiff 05.06.1991

Referee: Bo Karlsson (SWE) Attendance: 38,000

WALES: Neville Southall; David Phillips, Paul Bodin, Mark Aizlewood, Andy Melville, Kevin Ratcliffe, Peter Nicholas, Dean Saunders (90 Gary Speed), Ian Rush, Mark Hughes, Barry Horne. Manager: Terry Yorath

GERMANY: Bodo Illgner; Stefan Reuter, Andreas Brehme, Jürgen Kohler, Thomas Berthold, Guido Buchwald, Thomas Helmer, Matthias Sammer (76 Stefan Effenberg), Rudolf Völler, Lothar Matthäus (46 Thomas Doll), Jürgen Klinsmann. Trainer: Hubert Vogts

Goal: Rush (67)

LUXEMBOURG v BELGIUM 0-2 (0-1)

Stade Municipal, Luxembourg 11.09.1991

Referee: Remy Harrel (FRA) Attendance: 9,000

LUXEMBOURG: John Van Rijswijck; Gérard Jeitz, Marcel Bossi, Marc Birsens, Pierre Petry, Jean-Paul Girres, Guy Hellers, Thomas Wolf, Patrick Morocutti (77 Armin Krings), Robert Langers (67 Marc Thomé), Joël Groff.
Trainer: Paul Philipp

BELGIUM: Michel Preud'homme; Georges Grün (75 Dirk Medved), Franky Van der Elst, Lorenzo Staelens, Vital Borkelmans, Patrick Vervoort, Stéphane Demol (79 Frank Dauwen), Luc Nilis, Marc Degryse, Enzo Scifo, Marc Emmers.
Trainer: Paul van Himst

Goals: Scifo (24), Degryse (48)

BELGIUM v GERMANY 0-1 (0-1)

Brussel 20.11.1991

Referee: Tullio Lanese (ITA) Attendance: 26,000

BELGIUM: Michel Preud'homme; Georges Grün, Philippe Albert, Johan Walem, Vital Borkelmans, Marc Emmers, Stéphane Demol (46 Dirk Medved), Danny Boffin, Marc Degryse, Enzo Scifo, Marc Wilmots (70 Luc Nilis).
Trainer: Paul van Himst

GERMANY: Bodo Illgner; Stefan Reuter, Andreas Brehme, Jürgen Kohler, Manfred Binz, Guido Buchwald, Andreas Möller (80 Stefan Effenberg), Thomas Doll, Rudolf Völler, Lothar Matthäus, Karl-Heinz Riedle. Trainer: Hubert Vogts

Goal: Völler (16)

GERMANY v WALES 4-1 (3-0)

Frankenstadion, Nuremberg 16.10.1991

Referee: Joël Quiniou (FRA) Attendance: 46,000

GERMANY: Bodo Illgner; Stefan Reuter, Andreas Brehme, Jürgen Kohler, Manfred Binz, Guido Buchwald, Andreas Möller, Thomas Doll (79 Stefan Effenberg), Rudolf Völler, Lothar Matthäus, Karl-Heinz Riedle (65 Thomas Häßler).
Trainer: Hubert Vogts

WALES: Neville Southall; Gavin Maguire (46 Gary Speed), Mark Bowen, Andy Melville, Eric Young (84 Ryan Giggs), Kevin Ratcliffe, Barry Horne, Dean Saunders, Ian Rush, Mark Hughes, Paul Bodin. Trainer: Terry Yorath

Goals: Möller (34), Völler (39), Riedle (45), Doll (73), Bodin (83 pen)

GERMANY v LUXEMBOURG 4-0 (2-0)

Ulrich-Haberland-Stadion, Leverkusen 18.12.1991

Referee: Zbigniew Przesmycki (POL) Attendance: 24,500

GERMANY: Bodo Illgner; Stefan Reuter, Andreas Brehme, Jürgen Kohler, Manfred Binz, Guido Buchwald, Andreas Möller (70 Uwe Bein), Thomas Doll (46 Thomas Häßler), Rudolf Völler, Lothar Matthäus, Karl-Heinz Riedle.
Trainer: Hubert Vogts

LUXEMBOURG: John Van Rijswijck; Marcel Bossi, Marc Birsens, Pierre Petry, Thomas Wolf, Jean-Paul Girres (83 Gérard Jeitz), Guy Hellers, Carlo Weis, Joël Groff (78 Luc Holtz), Robert Langers, Théo Malget. Trainer: Paul Philipp

Goals: Matthäus (15 pen), Buchwald (44), Riedle (51), Häßler (62)

WALES v LUXEMBOURG 1-0 (0-0)

National, Cardiff 13.11.1991

Referee: Sándor Puhl (HUNG) Attendance: 20,000

WALES: Neville Southall; David Phillips, Mark Bowen (72 Paul Bodin), Mark Aizlewood, Eric Young, Andy Melville (62 Ryan Giggs), Barry Horne, Peter Nicholas, Ian Rush, Mark Hughes, Gary Speed. Trainer: Terry Yorath

LUXEMBOURG: John Van Rijswijck; Marcel Bossi, Marc Birsens, Pierre Petry, Thomas Wolf, Jean-Paul Girres (88 Gérard Jeitz), Guy Hellers, Carlo Weis, Joël Groff, Robert Langers (68 Armin Krings), Théo Malget.
Trainer: Paul Philipp

Goal: Bodin (82 pen)

	P	W	D	L	F	A	Pts
Germany	6	5	0	1	13	4	10
Wales	6	4	1	1	8	6	9
Belgium	6	2	1	3	7	6	5
Luxembourg	6	0	0	6	2	14	0

GROUP 6

FINLAND v PORTUGAL 0-0

Olympiastadion, Helsinki 12.09.1990

Referee: Jozef Marko (CZE) Attendance: 10,240

FINLAND: Olavi Huttunen; Jari Rinne, Erik Holmgren, Jari Europaeus, Ari Heikkinen, Erkka Petäjä, Kimmo Tarkkio (74 Tommi Paavola), Jari Litmanen, Petri Järvinen (84 Marko Myyry), Ari Hjelm, Mika-Matti Paatelainen.
Trainer: Jukka Vakkila

PORTUGAL: SILVINO Almeida Louro; JOÃO Domingos Silva PINTO, António Augusto da Silva VELOSO, JORGE da Costa FERREIRA, Paulo Manuel VENÂNCIO, António Manuel Tavares FONSECA (64 António Manuel PACHECO Domingos), VÍTOR Manuel Araújo PANEIRA, António dos Santos ANDRÉ, JAIME Moreira PACHECO, Soares Gil RUI BARROS, José RUI Lopes AGUAS (46 Jorge Paulo CADETE Reis). Trainer: Artur Jorge

HOLLAND v GREECE 2-0 (2-0)

Feyenoord, Rotterdam 21.11.1990

Referee: Lajos Németh (HUNG) Attendance: 26,000

HOLLAND: Hans Van Breukelen; Danny Blind, Graeme Rutjes, Jan Wouters, Jerry De Jong, Gerald Vanenburg, John Van't Schip, Dennis Bergkamp (85 Aron Winter), Marco Van Basten, Richard Witschge, Bryan Roy. Trainer: Rinus Michels

GREECE: Theologis Papadopoulos, Stratos Apostolakis, Giorgos Papadopoulos, Stelios Manolas, Yannis Kalitzakis, Panayiotis Tsalouhidis, Dimitris Saravakos, Savvas Kofidis (53 Nikos Karayeoryiou), Stefanos Borbokis, Vasilis Karapialis, Nikos Tsiantakis. Trainer: Antonis Yoryadis

Goals: Bergkamp (7), Van Basten (18)

PORTUGAL v HOLLAND 1-0 (0-0)

Das Antas, Porto 17.10.1990

Referee: Siegfried Kirschen (GER) Attendance: 35,000

PORTUGAL: SILVINO Almeida Louro; JOÃO Domingos Silva PINTO, José Martins LEAL, Paulo Manuel VENÂNCIO, António Augusto da Silva VELOSO, OCEANO Andrade da Cruz, VÍTOR Manuel Araújo PANEIRA, Manuel António Couto Guimaraes "NELO" (86 CARLOS Jorge Marques Caldas XAVIER), José RUI Lopes AGUAS, José Orlando Rocha SEMEDO (90 JORGE da Costa FERREIRA), Jorge Paulo CADETE Reis. Trainer: Artur Jorge

HOLLAND: Hans Van Breukelen; Danny Blind, Frank De Boer (76 Johannes Gillhaus), Adri Van Tiggelen (60 John Van't Schip), Stan Valckx, Graeme Rutjes, Gerald Vanenburg, Richard Witschge, Marco Van Basten, Ruud Gullit, Dennis Bergkamp. Trainer: Rinus Michels

Goal: Rui Aguas (54)

GREECE v MALTA 4-0 (2-0)

Olympiako, Athina 31.10.1990

Referee: Ion Crăciunescu (ROM) Attendance: 17,500

GREECE: Theologis Papadopoulos, Stratos Apostolakis, Giorgos Papadopoulos, Stelios Manolas, Yannis Kalitzakis, Panayiotis Tsalouhidis, Dimitris Saravakos, Savvas Kofidis, Vasilis Dimitriadis (31 Stefanos Borbokis), Vasilis Karapialis, Nikos Tsiantakis. Trainer: Antonis Yoryadis

MALTA: Reginald Cini; David Carabott, Silvio Vella, Joseph Galea, Charles Scerri, John Buttigieg, Carmel Busuttil, Raymond Vella, Hubert Suda (46 Michael Degiorgio), Christian Laferla, Jesmond Zerafa. Trainer: Horst Heese

Goals: Tsiantakis (37), Karapialis (40), Saravakos (59), Borbokis (87)

MALTA v FINLAND 1-1 (0-0)

National, Ta'Qali 25.11.1990

Referee: Sadik Deda (TUR) Attendance: 6,000

MALTA: David Cluett; David Carabott, Silvio Vella, Joseph Galea, Charles Scerri, John Buttigieg, Carmel Busuttil, Raymond Vella, Christian Laferla, Michael Degiorgio, Joe Zarb (73 Hubert Suda). Trainer: Horst Heese

FINLAND: Olavi Huttunen; Jari Rinne (46 Erkka Petäjä), Ari Heikkinen, Jari Europaeus, Erik Holmgren, Marko Myyry, Jari Litmanen, Ari Hjelm, Pasi Tauriainen, Kimmo Tarkkio (75 Ari Tegelberg), Mika-Matti Paatelainen. Trainer: Jukka Vakkila

Goals: Suda (74), Holmgren (87)

MALTA v HOLLAND 0-8 (0-3)

National, Ta'Qali 19.12.1990

Referee: Rolf Blattmann (SWI) Attendance: 11,000

MALTA: David Cluett; Edwin Camilleri (46 Hubert Suda), Silvio Vella, Joseph Galea, Charles Scerri (70 Jesmond Zerafa), Christian Laferla, Carmel Busuttil, Raymond Vella, David Carabott, Michael Degiorgio, Joe Camilleri.
Trainer: Horst Heese

HOLLAND: Hans Van Breukelen; Danny Blind, Jerry De Jong, Jan Wouters, Frank De Boer, Erwin Koeman (46 Aron Winter), John Van't Schip, Dennis Bergkamp, Marco Van Basten, Ruud Gullit (71 John Van den Brom), Bryan Roy.
Trainer: Rinus Michels

Goals: Van Basten (10, 20, 25, 68, 80 pen), Winter (51), Bergkamp (58, 70)

GREECE v PORTUGAL 3-2 (1-1)

Olympiako, Athina 23.01.1991

Referee: Carlo Longhi (ITA) Attendance: 30,000

GREECE: Nikos Sarganis; Stratos Apostolakis, Giorgos Papadopoulos, Stelios Manolas, Yannis Kalitzakis, Panayiotis Tsalouhidis, Dimitris Saravakos, Savvas Kofidis (70 Giorgos Athanassiadis), Stefanos Borbokis (67 Vasilis Dimitriadis), Vasilis Karapialis, Nikos Tsiantakis.
Trainer: Antonis Yoryadis

PORTUGAL: VÍTOR Manuel Martins BAÍA; JOÃO Domingos Silva PINTO, José Martins LEAL, Paulo Manuel VENÂNCIO, António Augusto da Silva VELOSO, OCEANO Andrade da Cruz, PAULO Manuel Carvalho SOUSA, Soares Gil RUI BARROS (72 Jorge Paulo CADETE Reis), VÍTOR Manuel Araújo PANEIRA, Paulo Jorge Santos FUTRE, José RUI Lopes AGUAS. Trainer: Artur Jorge

Goals: Borbokis (7), Rui Aguas (14), Futre (62), Manolas (68), Tsalouhidis (84)

MALTA v PORTUGAL 0-1 (0-1)

National, Ta'Qali 09.02.1991

Referee: Manfred Neuner (GER) Attendance: 10,000

MALTA: David Cluett; Silvio Vella, Alex Azzopardi, Joseph Galea, Christian Laferla, John Buttigieg, Carmel Busuttil, Raymond Vella, Hubert Suda, Michael Degiorgio, Jesmond Zerafa. Trainer: Horst Heese

PORTUGAL: VÍTOR Manuel Martins BAÍA; JOÃO Domingos Silva PINTO, José Martins LEAL, Paulo Manuel VENÂNCIO, António Augusto da Silva VELOSO, OCEANO Andrade da Cruz, VÍTOR Manuel Araújo PANEIRA, Soares Gil RUI BARROS (70 Jorge Paulo CADETE Reis), José RUI Lopes AGUAS, Paulo Jorge Santos FUTRE (88 PAULO Manuel Carvalho SOUSA), José Orlando Rocha SEMEDO.
Trainer: Artur Jorge

Goal: Futre (26)

PORTUGAL v MALTA 5-0 (3-0)

Das Antas, Porto 20.02.1991

Referee: John Spillane (IRE) Attendance: 10,000

PORTUGAL: VÍTOR Manuel Martins BAÍA; JOÃO Domingos Silva PINTO (46 Jorge Paulo CADETE Reis), José Martins LEAL, Paulo Manuel VENÂNCIO (67 PAULO Sérgio Braga MADEIRA), António Augusto da Silva VELOSO, OCEANO Andrade da Cruz, VÍTOR Manuel Araújo PANEIRA, PAULO Manuel Carvalho SOUSA, José RUI Lopes AGUAS, Paulo Jorge Santos FUTRE, José Orlando Rocha SEMEDO.
Trainer: Artur Jorge

MALTA: David Cluett; Silvio Vella, Alex Azzopardi, Joe Camilleri (39 Charles Scerri), Christian Laferla, Michael Degiorgio, John Buttigieg, Raymond Vella, Carmel Busuttil, Hubert Suda (51 David Carabott), Jesmond Zerafa.
Trainer: Horst Heese

Goals: Rui Aguas (5), Leal (33), Vítor Paneira (41 pen), Scerri (48 og), Cadete (81)

HOLLAND v MALTA 1-0 (1-0)

Feyenoord, Rotterdam 13.03.1991

Referee: Dusan Krchnak (CZE) Attendance: 36,383

HOLLAND: Hans Van Breukelen; Danny Blind, Marciano Vink, Jan Wouters, Frank De Boer (46 Wim Kieft), Richard Witschge, John Van't Schip, Dennis Bergkamp, Marco Van Basten, Ruud Gullit, Bryan Roy (69 Gerald Vanenburg).
Trainer: Rinus Michels

MALTA: Reginald Cini; Edwin Camilleri, Alex Azzopardi (89 Nicholas Saliba), Joseph Brincat (85 Hubert Suda), Silvio Vella, Christian Laferla, Charles Scerri, Raymond Vella, Joe Camilleri, Michael Degiorgio, Jesmond Zerafa.
Trainer: Horst Heese

Goal: Van Basten (32 pen)

HOLLAND v FINLAND 2-0 (1-0)

Feyenoord, Rotterdam 17.04.1991

Referee: Jan Damgaard (DEN) Attendance: 27,000

HOLLAND: Hans Van Breukelen; Danny Blind, Marciano Vink, Jan Wouters, Jerry De Jong, Richard Witschge, John Van't Schip, Dennis Bergkamp (73 Wim Kieft), Marco Van Basten, Ruud Gullit, Pieter Huistra. Trainer: Rinus Michels

FINLAND: Olavi Huttunen; Erik Holmgren, Ari Heikkinen, Erkka Petäjä, Jari Europaeus, Markku Kanerva, Kari Ukkonen, Marko Myyry, Jari Litmanen (46 Ari Tegelberg), Pasi Tauriainen (89 Harri Nyyssönen), Mika-Matti Paatelainen.
Trainer: Jukka Vakkila

Goals: Van Basten (10), Gullit (77)

FINLAND v MALTA 2-0 (0-0)

Olympiastadion, Helsinki 16.05.1991

Referee: Rune Pedersen (NOR) Attendance: 5,150

FINLAND: Olavi Huttunen; Erkka Petäjä, Ari Heikkinen, Erik Holmgren, Markku Kanerva, Marko Myyry, Jari Litmanen, Kari Ukkonen, Kimmo Tarkkio (88 Pasi Tauriainen), Mika-Matti Paatelainen (74 Tommi Paavola), Petri Järvinen. Trainer: Jukka Vakkila

MALTA: Reginald Cini; Edwin Camilleri, Silvio Vella, Christian Laferla, Joseph Brincat (71 Jesmond Zerafa), John Buttigieg, Carmel Busuttil, Raymond Vella, Hubert Suda, Michael Degiorgio, Charles Scerri. Trainer: Horst Heese

Goals: Järvinen (51), Litmanen (88)

FINLAND v HOLLAND 1-1 (0-0)

Olympiastadion, Helsinki 05.06.1991

Referee: Brian McGinlay (SCO) Attendance: 21,207

FINLAND: Olavi Huttunen; Erik Holmgren, Ari Heikkinen, Erkka Petäjä, Tommi Paavola, Marko Myyry, Jari Litmanen, Kari Ukkonen (81 Ari Hjelm), Petri Järvinen, Kimmo Tarkkio, Mika-Matti Paatelainen (66 Ari Tegelberg). Trainer: Jukka Vakkila

HOLLAND: Joop Hiele; Danny Blind, Graeme Rutjes, Ronald Koeman, Frank De Boer, Jan Wouters, John Van't Schip, Richard Witschge, Marco Van Basten, Aron Winter, Pieter Huistra (75 Wim Kieft). Trainer: Rinus Michels

Goals: F. De Boer (60), Holmgren (77)

PORTUGAL v FINLAND 1-0 (1-0)

Das Antas, Porto 11.09.1991

Referee: Arturo Martino (SWI) Attendance: 30,000

PORTUGAL: VíÍTOR Manuel Martins BAÍA; JOÃO Domingos Silva PINTO I; SAMUEL António Silva Quina, FERNANDO Manuel Silva COUTO, José Martins LEAL, António Augusto da Silva VELOSO, CÉSAR Gonçalves BRITO Duarte (80 Jorge Paulo CADETE Reis), Soares Gil RUI BARROS, José RUI Lopes AGUAS (57 OCEANO Andrade da Cruz), Paulo Jorge Santos FUTRE, Manuel António Couto Guimaraes "NELO". Trainer: Carlos Queirós

FINLAND: Olavi Huttunen; Pasi Tauriainen (59 Jouko Vuorela), Erik Holmgren, Erkka Petäjä, Ari Heikkinen, Tommi Paavola, Kari Ukkonen (73 Jari Litmanen), Marko Myyry, Petri Järvinen, Kimmo Tarkkio, Mika-Matti Paatelainen. Trainer: Jukka Vakkila

Goal: César Brito (22)

FINLAND v GREECE 1-1 (0-0)

Olympiastadion, Helsinki 09.10.1991

Referee: Sergei Khusainov (USSR) Attendance: 5,225

FINLAND: Olavi Huttunen; Ari Heikkinen, Erik Holmgren, Erkka Petäjä, Marko Myyry, Petri Järvinen (63 Mika-Matti Paatelainen), Kimmo Tarkkio (82 Ari Tegelberg), Kari Ukkonen, Ari Hjelm, Jari Litmanen, Jouko Vuorela. Trainer: Jukka Vakkila

GREECE: Nikos Sarganis; Stratos Apostolakis (60 Giorgos Athanassiadis), Nikos Karayeoryiou, Giorgos Mitsibonas, Yannis Kalitzakis, Panayiotis Tsalouhidis, Dimitris Saravakos, Pavlos Papaioannou, Stefanos Borbokis (70 Giorgos Toursounidis), Vasilis Karapialis, Nikos Tsiantakis. Trainer: Antonis Yoryadis

Goals: Ukkonen (50), Tsalouhidis (74)

HOLLAND v PORTUGAL 1-0 (1-0)

Feyenoord, Rotterdam 16.10.1991

Referee: George Courtney (ENG) Attendance: 50,000

HOLLAND: Hans Van Breukelen; Danny Blind, Adri Van Tiggelen, Ronald Koeman, Erwin Koeman, Jan Wouters, Frank Rijkaard (71 Aron Winter), Dennis Bergkamp, Marco Van Basten, Ruud Gullit, Richard Witschge (81 John Van't Schip). Trainer: Rinus Michels

PORTUGAL: VÍTOR Manuel Martins BAÍA; JOÃO Domingos Silva PINTO I, José Martins LEAL, Paulo Manuel VENÂNCIO, FERNANDO Manuel Silva COUTO, Emílio Manuel Delgado PEIXE (81 CÉSAR Gonçalves BRITO Duarte), OCEANO Andrade da Cruz, Soares Gil RUI BARROS, Jorge Paulo CADETE Reis, Paulo Jorge Santos FUTRE, Manuel António Couto Guimaraes "NELO" (57 Luís Filipe Madeira FIGO). Trainer: Carlos Queirós

Goal: Ri. Witschge (21)

GREECE v FINLAND 2-0 (0-0)

Olympiako, Athina 30.10.1991

Referee: Gerhard Kapl (AUS) Attendance: 26,000

GREECE: Nikos Sarganis; Stratos Apostolakis, Nikos Karayeoryiou, Giorgos Mitsibonas, Yannis Kalitzakis, Panayiotis Tsalouhidis, Dimitris Saravakos, Pavlos Papaioannou, Giorgos Athanassiadis (46 Stefanos Borbokis), Vasilis Karapialis (73 Giorgos Toursounidis), Nikos Tsiantakis. Trainer: Antonis Yoryadis

FINLAND: Olavi Huttunen; Erik Holmgren, Ari Heikkinen, Erkka Petäjä, Jouko Vuorela (55 Mika-Matti Paatelainen), Jyrki Huhtamäki (82 Ari Tegelberg), Jari Litmanen, Kari Ukkonen, Petri Järvinen, Kimmo Tarkkio, Ari Hjelm. Trainer: Jukka Vakkila

Goals: Saravakos (50), Borbokis (52)

PORTUGAL v GREECE 1-0 (1-0)

Estadio Da Luz, Lisboa 20.11.1991

Referee: Alphonse Constantin (BEL) Attendance: 2,000

PORTUGAL: VÍTOR Manuel Martins BAÍA; JOÃO Domingos Silva PINTO I, RUI Fernando Silva BENTO, FERNANDO Manuel Silva COUTO, José Martins LEAL, Emílio Manuel Delgado PEIXE, VÍTOR Manuel Araújo PANEIRA (46 OCEANO Andrade da Cruz), Soares Gil RUI BARROS, José RUI Lopes AGUAS, JOÃO Manuel Vieira PINTO II, José Orlando Rocha SEMEDO (15 Luís Filipe Madeira FIGO). Trainer: Carlos Queirós

GREECE: Nikos Sarganis; Stratos Apostolakis, Nikos Karayeoryiou, Giorgos Mitsibonas, Yannis Kalitzakis, Panayiotis Tsalouhidis, Dimitris Saravakos, Pavlos Papaioannou (60 Giorgos Athanassiadis), Stefanos Borbokis (69 Vasilis Dimitriadis), Vasilis Karapialis, Nikos Tsiantakis. Trainer: Antonis Yoryadis

Goal: João Pinto II (16)

GREECE v HOLLAND 0-2 (0-1)

Toumbas, Thessaloniki 04.12.1991

Referee: Bo Karlsson (SWE) Attendance: 32,500

GREECE: Nikos Sarganis; Pavlos Papaioannou (46 Nikos Karayeoryiou), Kostas Lagonidis, Giorgos Mitsibonas, Yannis Kalitzakis, Panayiotis Tsalouhidis, Dimitris Saravakos, Nikos Nioblias, Nikos Tsiantakis, Vasilis Karapialis (61 Giorgos Toursounidis), Giorgos Papadopoulos.
Trainer: Antonis Yoryadis

HOLLAND: Hans Van Breukelen; Danny Blind, Adri Van Tiggelen, Ronald Koeman, Erwin Koeman, Jan Wouters, Frank Rijkaard (72 Aron Winter), Dennis Bergkamp, Marco Van Basten, Wim Kieft (85 Peter Bosz), Richard Witschge.
Trainer: Rinus Michels

Goals: Bergkamp (40), Blind (87)

MALTA v GREECE 1-1 (1-0)

National, Ta'Qali 22.12.1991

Referee: Michel Girard (FRA) Attendance: 8,000

MALTA: David Cluett; Joseph Brincat, Joseph Galea, Silvio Vella, Nicholas Saliba, Christian Laferla, Carmel Busuttil, Raymond Vella (68 Joe Camilleri), Charles Scerri (33 Stefan Sultana), Martin Gregory, Michael Degiorgio.
Trainer: Pippo Psaila

GREECE: Giorgos Plitsis; Pavlos Papaioannou, Giorgos Kapouranis, Giorgos Mitsibonas, Yannis Kalitzakis, Panayiotis Tsalouhidis, Giorgos Donis (56 Asterios Yiotsas), Spiros Maragos (54 Petros Marinakis), Vasilis Dimitriadis, Nikos Nioblias, Nikos Tsiantakis. Trainer: Antonis Yoryadis

Goals: Sultana (42), Marinakis (66)

	P	W	D	L	F	A	Pts
Holland	8	6	1	1	17	2	13
Portugal	8	5	1	2	11	4	11
Greece	8	3	2	3	11	9	8
Finland	8	1	4	3	5	8	6
Malta	8	0	2	6	2	23	2

GROUP 7

REPUBLIC OF IRELAND v TURKEY 5-0 (2-0)

Lansdowne Road, Dublin 17.10.1990

Referee: Erik Fredriksson (SWE) Attendance: 46,000

IRELAND: Pat Bonner; Dennis Irwin, Steve Staunton, Michael McCarthy, David O'Leary, Christopher Hughton, Andy Townsend (73 Kevin Moran), Raymond Houghton, Niall Quinn (66 Anthony Cascarino), John Aldridge, John Sheridan.
Manager: Jack Charlton

TURKEY: Engin Ipekoglu; Riza Çalimbay, Tugay Kerimoglu, Kemal Serdar, Gökhan Keskin, Ercan Kol (46 Tanju Çolak), Bülent Korkmaz, Oguz Çetin, Mehmet Özdilek, Hami Mandirali, Sercan Görgülü (46 Metin Tekin).
Trainer: Sepp Piontek

Goals: Aldridge (15, 57, 72 pen), O'Leary (40), Quinn (65)

ENGLAND v POLAND 2-0 (1-0)

Wembley, London 17.10.1990

Referee: Tullio Lanese (ITA) Attendance: 77,040

ENGLAND: Christopher Woods; Lee Dixon, Stuart Pearce, Paul Parker, Des Walker, Mark Wright, David Platt, Paul Gascoigne, Steve Bull (58 Peter Beardsley), Gary Lineker (58 Christopher Waddle), John Barnes. Manager: Graham Taylor

POLAND: Jozef Wandzik; Piotr Czachowski, Dariusz Wdowczyk, Roman Szewczyk, Zbigniew Kaczmarek, Janusz Nawrocki, Ryszard Tarasiewicz, Robert Warzycha, Jan Furtok (76 Krzysztof Warzycha), Roman Kosecki (86 Dariusz Kubicki), Jacek Ziober. Trainer: Andrzej Strejlau

Goals: Lineker (40 pen), Beardsley (90)

REPUBLIC OF IRELAND v ENGLAND 1-1 (1-1)

Lansdowne Road, Dublin 14.11.1990

Referee: Pietro D'Elia (ITA) Attendance: 46,000

IRELAND: Pat Bonner; Christopher Morris, Steve Staunton, Michael McCarthy, David O'Leary, Ronnald Whelan (75 Alan McLaughlin), Paul McGrath, Raymond Houghton, Niall Quinn (62 Anthony Cascarino), John Aldridge, Andy Townsend.
Manager: Jack Charlton

ENGLAND: Christopher Woods; Lee Dixon, Stuart Pearce, Antony Adams, Des Walker, Mark Wright, David Platt, Gordon Cowans, Peter Beardsley, Gary Lineker, Stephen McMahon.
Manager: Graham Taylor

Goals: Platt (67), Cascarino (80)

TURKEY v POLAND 0-1 (0-1)

Inönü, Istanbul 14.11.1990

Referee: Aleksei Spirin (USSR) Attendance: 25,000

TURKEY: Engin Ipekoglu; Bülent Korkmaz, Gökhan Keskin, Yusuf Altintas, Riza Çalimbay, Muhammet Altintas (68 Sercan Görgülü), Ünal Karaman, Oguz Çetin, Ülken Turek (68 Mehmet Özdilek), Tanju Çolak, Hami Mandirali. Trainer: Sepp Piontek

POLAND: Jozef Wandzik; Dariusz Kubicki, Zbigniew Kaczmarek, Dariusz Wdowczyk, Janusz Nawrocki, Robert Warzycha, Waldemar Prusik, Ryszard Tarasiewicz, Krzysztof Warzycha, Dariusz Dziekanowski (74 Jacek Ziober), Roman Kosecki. Trainer: Andrzej Strejlau

Goal: Dziekanowski (37)

REPUBLIC OF IRELAND v POLAND 0-0

Lansdowne Road, Dublin 01.05.1991

Referee: John Blankenstein (HOL) Attendance: 48,000

IRELAND: Pat Bonner; Dennis Irwin, Steve Staunton, David O'Leary, Kevin Moran, Andy Townsend, Paul McGrath, Raymond Houghton, Niall Quinn (71 Anthony Cascarino), John Aldridge (65 Bernie Slaven), Kevin Sheedy. Manager: Jack Charlton

POLAND: Jozef Wandzik; Czeslaw Jakolcewicz, Dariusz Wdowczyk, Piotr Soczynski, Dariusz Kubicki, Robert Warzycha, Ryszard Tarasiewicz, Piotr Czachowski, Jan Urban (88 Michal Gebura), Jan Furtok (90 Roman Kosecki), Roman Szewczyk. Trainer: Andrzej Strejlau

ENGLAND v REPUBLIC OF IRELAND 1-1 (1-1)

Wembley, London 27.03.1991

Referee: Kurt Roethlisberger (SWI) Attendance: 77,000

ENGLAND: David Seaman; Lee Dixon, Stuart Pearce, Antony Adams (46 Lee Sharpe), Des Walker, Mark Wright, Bryan Robson, David Platt, Peter Beardsley, Gary Lineker (76 Ian Wright), John Barnes. Manager: Graham Taylor

IRELAND: Pat Bonner; Dennis Irwin, Steve Staunton, David O'Leary, Kevin Moran, Andy Townsend, Paul McGrath, Raymond Houghton, Niall Quinn, John Aldridge (71 Anthony Cascarino), Kevin Sheedy. Manager: Jack Charlton

Goals: Staunton (9 og), Quinn (27)

TURKEY v ENGLAND 0-1 (0-1)

Izmir 01.05.1991

Referee: Wolf-Günter Wiesel (GER) Attendance: 25,000

TURKEY: Hayrettin Demirbas; Riza Çalimbay, Recep Çetin, Oguz Çetin, Gökhan Keskin, Ünal Karaman, Ridvan Dilmen, Muhammet Altintas, Tanju Çolak, Mehmet Özdilek, Ali Gültiken (75 Feyyaz Uçar). Trainer: Sepp Piontek

ENGLAND: David Seaman; Lee Dixon, Des Walker, Gary Pallister, Stuart Pearce, Dennis Wise, David Platt, Geoff Thomas (46 Stephen Hodge), Gary Lineker, John Barnes, Alan Smith. Manager: Graham Taylor

Goal: Wise (32)

POLAND v TURKEY 3-0 (0-0)

Wojska Polskiego, Warszawa 17.04.1991

Referee: Mircea Salomir (ROM) Attendance: 1,500

POLAND: Jozef Wandzik; Dariusz Kubicki, Czeslaw Jakolcewicz, Dariusz Wdowczyk, Robert Warzycha, Ryszard Tarasiewicz, Zbigniew Kaczmarek (64 Piotr Czachowski), Krzysztof Warzycha, Roman Kosecki, Jan Urban, Jacek Ziober (71 Piotr Soczynski). Trainer: Andrzej Strejlau

TURKEY: Engin Ipekoglu; Bülent Korkmaz, Gökhan Keskin, Riza Çalimbay, Tayfun Hut, Kemal Serdar, Feyyaz Uçar (78 Faruk Yilgit), Muhammet Altintas, Mehmet Özdilek, Abdullah Ercan (71 Osman Yildirim), Tanju Çolak. Trainer: Sepp Piontek

Goals: Tarasiewicz (75), Urban (82), Kosecki (88)

POLAND v REPUBLIC OF IRELAND 3-3 (0-1)

KKS Lech, Poznan 16.10.1991

Referee: Guy Goethals (BEL) Attendance: 17,000

POLAND: Jozef Wandzik; Dariusz Kubicki (32 Andrzej Lesiak), Piotr Czachowski, Piotr Soczynski, Dariusz Wdowczyk, Janusz Nawrocki (80 Dariusz Skrzypczak), Ryszard Tarasiewicz, Jacek Ziober, Jan Urban, Roman Kosecki, Jan Furtok. Trainer: Andrzej Strejlau

IRELAND: Pat Bonner; Dennis Irwin, Steve Staunton (56 Terry Phelan), David O'Leary, Kevin Moran, Andy Townsend, Paul McGrath, Christopher Morris, Roy Keane, Anthony Cascarino, Kevin Sheedy. Manager: Jack Charlton

Goals: McGrath (11), Czachowski (54), Townsend (62), Cascarino (68), Furtok (76), Urban (86)

ENGLAND v TURKEY 1-0 (1-0)

Wembley, London 16.10.1991

Referee: António Martín Navarette (SPA) Att: 50,896

ENGLAND: Christopher Woods; Lee Dixon, Stuart Pearce, David Batty, Des Walker, Gary Mabbutt, Bryan Robson, David Platt, Alan Smith, Gary Lineker, Christopher Waddle. Manager: Graham Taylor

TURKEY: Hayrettin Demirbas; Recep Çetin, Ogün Temizkanoglu, Gökhan Keskin, Tugay Kerimoglu, Turan Sofuoglu, Feyyaz Uçar (76 Hami Mandirali), Riza Çalimbay, Ünal Karaman, Oguz Çetin, Orhan Çikirçki. Trainer: Sepp Piontek

Goal: Smith (21)

POLAND v ENGLAND 1-1 (1-0)

KKS Lech, Poznan 13.11.1991

Referee: Hubert Forstinger (AUS) Attendance: 15,000

POLAND: Jaroslaw Bako; Robert Warzycha, Tomasz Waldoch, Piotr Soczynski, Piotr Czachowski (78 Adam Fedoruk), Roman Szewczyk, Roman Kosecki (80 Marek Rzepka), Dariusz Skrzypczak, Jan Furtok, Jan Urban, Jacek Ziober. Trainer: Andrzej Strejlau

ENGLAND: Christopher Woods; Lee Dixon, Stuart Pearce, Andy Gray (46 Alan Smith), Des Walker, Gary Mabbutt, David Platt, Geoff Thomas, David Rocastle, Gary Lineker, Andy Sinton (70 Tony Daley). Manager: Graham Taylor

Goals: Szewczyk (32), Lineker (76)

TURKEY v REPUBLIC OF IRELAND 1-3 (1-1)

Istanbul 13.11.1991

Referee: Zoran Petrovic (YUG) Attendance: 42,000

TURKEY: Hayrettin Demirbas; Recep Çetin (66 Bülent Korkmaz), Turan Sofuoglu, Gökhan Keskin, Tugay Kerimoglu, Ogün Temizkanoglu, Feyyaz Uçar (46 Ridvan Dilmen), Riza Çalimbay, Hami Mandirali, Oguz Çetin, Orhan Çikirçki. Trainer: Sepp Piontek

IRELAND: Pat Bonner; Christopher Hughton, Terry Phelan, David O'Leary, Michael McCarthy, Steve Staunton, Paul McGrath, John Byrne, Tony Cascarino, John Aldridge, Kevin Sheedy. Manager: Jack Charlton

Goals: Byrne (7, 58), Riza (12 pen), Cascarino (55)

	P	W	D	L	F	A	Pts
England	6	3	3	0	7	3	9
Rep. of Ireland	6	2	4	0	13	6	8
Poland	6	2	3	1	8	6	7
Turkey	6	0	0	6	1	14	0

FINALS IN SWEDEN

GROUP 1

SWEDEN v FRANCE 1-1 (1-0)

Rasunda, Stockholm 10.06.1992

Referee: Aleksei Spirin (CIS) Attendance: 29,860

SWEDEN: Thomas Ravelli; Roland Nilsson, Jan Eriksson, Patrik Andersson, Joachim Björklund; Klas Ingesson, Jonas Thern, Stefan Schwarz, Anders Limpar; Tomas Brolin, Kennet Andersson (73 Martin Dahlin). Trainer: Tommy Svensson.

FRANCE: Bruno Martini; Laurent Blanc, Jocelyn Anglôma (66 Luis Fernandez), Basile Boli, Bernard Casoni; Eric Cantona, Franck Sauzée, Didier Deschamps, Manuel Amoros; Jean-Pierre Papin, Pascal Vahirua (46 Christian Perez). Trainer: Michel Platini

Goals: J. Eriksson (24), Papin (58)

DENMARK v ENGLAND 0-0

Malmö stadium 11.06.1992

Referee: John Blankenstein (HOL) Attendance: 26,385

DENMARK: Peter Schmeichel; John Sivebæk, Kent Nielsen, Lars Olsen, Henrik Andersen; Kim Vilfort, John Jensen, Brian Laudrup, Kim Christofte; Bent Christensen, Flemming Povlsen. Trainer: Richard Møller-Nielsen.

ENGLAND: Christopher Woods; Keith Curle (61 Tony Daley), Martin Keown, Des Walker, Stuart Pearce; Trevor Steven, Carlton Palmer, David Platt, Paul Merson (70 Neil Webb); Gary Lineker, Alan Smith. Manager: Graham Taylor

ENGLAND v FRANCE 0-0

Malmö stadium 14.06.1992

Referee: Sándor Puhl (HUNG) Attendance: 26,535

ENGLAND: Christopher Woods; Martin Keown, Carlton Palmer, Des Walker, Stuart Pearce; Andy Sinton, Trevor Steven, David Batty, David Platt; Gary Lineker, Alan Shearer. Manager: Graham Taylor

FRANCE: Bruno Martini; Manuel Amoros, Basile Boli, Laurent Blanc, Bernard Casoni; Didier Deschamps, Luis Fernandez (74 Christian Perez), Franck Sauzée (46 Jocelyn Anglôma), Jean-Philippe Durand; Jean-Pierre Papin, Eric Cantona. Trainer: Michel Platini

SWEDEN v DENMARK 1-0 (0-0)

Rasunda, Stockholm 14.06.1992

Referee: Aron Schmidhuber (GER) Attendance: 29,902

SWEDEN: Thomas Ravelli; Roland Nilsson, Jan Eriksson, Patrik Andersson, Joachim Björklund; Klas Ingesson, Stefan Schwarz, Jonas Thern, Anders Limpar (89 Magnus Erlingmark); Tomas Brolin, Martin Dahlin (77 Johnny Ekström). Trainer: Tommy Svensson

DENMARK: Peter Schmeichel; John Sivebæk, Kent Nielsen, Lars Olsen, Henrik Andersen; Kim Vilfort, John Jensen (62 Henrik Larsen), Kim Christofte; Brian Laudrup, Flemming Povlsen, Bent Christensen (51 Torben Frank). Trainer: Richard Møller-Nielsen

Goal: Brolin (58)

SWEDEN v ENGLAND 2-1 (0-1)

Rasunda, Stockholm 17.06.1992

Referee: José Rosa dos Santos (POR) Attendance: 30,126

SWEDEN: Thomas Ravelli; Roland Nilsson, Jan Eriksson, Patrik Andersson, Joachim Björklund; Klas Ingesson, Stefan Schwarz, Jonas Thern, Anders Limpar (46 Johnny Ekström); Martin Dahlin, Tomas Brolin. Trainer: Tommy Svensson

ENGLAND: Christopher Woods; David Batty, Martin Keown, Des Walker, Stuart Pearce; Tony Daley, Carlton Palmer, Neil Webb, Andy Sinton (76 Paul Merson); David Platt, Gary Lineker (61 Alan Smith). Manager: Graham Taylor

Goals: Platt (3), J. Eriksson (51), Brolin (82)

FRANCE v DENMARK 1-2 (0-1)

Malmö stadium 17.06.1992

Referee: Hubert Forstinger (AUS) Attendance: 25,673

FRANCE: Bruno Martini; Manuel Amoros, Basile Boli, Laurent Blanc, Bernard Casoni; Didier Deschamps, Christian Perez (78 Christophe Cocard), Jean-Philippe Durand; Eric Cantona, Jean-Pierre Papin, Pascal Vahirua (46 Luis Fernandez). Trainer: Michel Platini

DENMARK: Peter Schmeichel; John Sivebæk, Kent Nielsen (63 Torben Piechnik), Lars Olsen, Henrik Andersen; Henrik Larsen, John Jensen, Kim Christofte; Brian Laudrup (67 Lars Elstrup), Torben Frank, Flemming Povlsen. Trainer: Richard Møller-Nielsen

Goals: Larsen (8), Papin (60), Elstrup (78)

	P	W	D	L	F	A	Pts
Sweden	3	2	1	0	4	2	5
Denmark	3	1	1	1	2	2	3
France	3	0	2	1	2	3	2
England	3	0	2	1	1	2	2

GROUP 2

The USSR changed their name to CIS (Confederation of Independent States) following the breakup of the Union and played the Final series under that title.

HOLLAND v SCOTLAND 1-0 (0-0)

Ullevi, Göteborg 12.06.1992

Referee: Bo Karlsson (SWE) Attendance: 35,720

HOLLAND: Hans van Breukelen; Hubertus van Aerle, Ronald Koeman, Adri van Tiggelen; Frank Rijkaard, Jan Wouters (54 Wim Jonk), Rob Witschge, Ruud Gullit, Dennis Bergkamp (85 Aron Winter); Marco van Basten, Bryan Roy. Trainer: Rinus Michels

SCOTLAND: Andy Goram; Stewart McKimmie, Richard Gough, Dave McPherson, Maurice Malpas; Stuart McCall, Gary McAllister, Paul McStay, Brian McClair (79 Duncan Ferguson); Gordon Durie, Alistair McCoist (73 Kevin Gallacher). Manager: Andrew Roxburgh

Goal: Bergkamp (76)

CIS v GERMANY 1-1 (0-0)

Idrottspark, Norrköping 12.06.1992

Referee: Gérard Biguet (FRA) Attendance: 17,410

CIS: Dmitri Harin; Oleg Kuznetsov, Andrei Chernîshov, Akhrik Tsveiba; Andrei Kanchelskis, Aleksei Mikhailichenko, Vladimir Liuty (46 Viktor Onopko), Dmitri Kuznetsov, Igor Shalimov (83 Andrei Ivanov); Igor Kolivanov, Igor Dobrovolski Trainer: Anatoli Bîshovets

GERMANY: Bodo Illgner; Manfred Binz, Stefan Reuter (63 Jürgen Klinsmann), Jürgen Kohler, Guido Buchwald, Andreas Brehme; Thomas Häßler, Stefan Effenberg, Thomas Doll; Rudolf Völler (46 Andreas Möller), Karl-Heinz Riedle. Trainer: Hans-Hubert Vogts.

Goals: Dobrovolski (62 pen), Häßler (90)

SCOTLAND v GERMANY 0-2 (0-1)

Idrottspark, Norrköping 15.06.1992

Referee: Guy Goethals (BEL) Attendance: 17,638

SCOTLAND: Andy Goram; Stewart McKimmie, Richard Gough, Dave McPherson, Maurice Malpas; Gary McAllister, Paul McStay, Stuart McCall, Brian McClair; Alistair McCoist (69 Kevin Gallacher), Gordon Durie (54 Patrick Nevin). Manager: Andrew Roxburgh

GERMANY: Bodo Illgner; Manfred Binz, Jürgen Kohler, Guido Buchwald; Thomas Häßler, Stefan Effenberg, Andreas Möller, Matthias Sammer, Andreas Brehme; Jürgen Klinsmann, Karl-Heinz Riedle (68 Stefan Reuter, 74 Michael Schulz). Trainer: Hans-Hubert Vogts.

Goals: Riedle (28), Effenberg (46)

HOLLAND v CIS 0-0

Ullevi, Göteborg 15.06.1992

Referee: Peter Mikkelsen (DEN) Attendance: 34,440

HOLLAND: Hans van Breukelen; Hubertus van Aerle, Ronald Koeman, Adri van Tiggelen; Frank Rijkaard, Jan Wouters, Rob Witschge, Ruud Gullit (70 John van't Schip), Dennis Bergkamp (79 Erik Viscaal); Marco van Basten, Bryan Roy. Trainer: Rinus Michels

CIS: Dmitri Harin; Oleg Kuznetsov, Andrei Chernîshov, Akhrik Tsveiba; Andrei Kanchelskis, Aleksei Mikhailichenko, Sergei Aleinikov (56 Dmitri Kuznetsov), Viktor Onopko; Igor Dobrovolski, Igor Kolivanov, Sergei Iuran (64 Sergei Kiriakov). Trainer: Anatoli Bîshovets

HOLLAND v GERMANY 3-1 (2-0)

Ullevi, Göteborg 18.06.1992

Referee: Pier-Luigi Pairetto (ITA) Attendance: 37,725

HOLLAND: Hans van Breukelen; Adri van Tiggelen, Ronald Koeman, Frank de Boer (61 Aron Winter); Frank Rijkaard, Jan Wouters, Rob Witschge, Ruud Gullit, Dennis Bergkamp (87 Peter Bosz); Marco van Basten, Bryan Roy. Trainer: Rinus Michels

GERMANY: Bodo Illgner; Andreas Brehme, Jürgen Kohler, Manfred Binz (46 Matthias Sammer), Michael Frontzeck; Thomas Häßler, Stefan Effenberg, Thomas Helmer, Andreas Möller; Jürgen Klinsmann, Karl-Heinz Riedle (76 Thomas Doll). Trainer: Hans-Hubert Vogts

Goals: Rijkaard (4), Witschge (14), Klinsmann (53), Bergkamp (71)

SCOTLAND v CIS 3-0 (2-0)

Idrottspark, Norrköping 18.06.1992

Referee: Kurt Roethlisberger (SWI) Attendance: 14,660

SCOTLAND: Andy Goram; Stewart McKimmie, Richard Gough, Dave McPherson, Tom Boyd; Gary McAllister, Paul McStay, Brian McClair, Stuart McCall; Kevin Gallacher (79 Patrick Nevin), Alistair McCoist (67 James McInally). Manager: Andrew Roxburgh

CIS: Dmitri Harin; Oleg Kuznetsov, Andrei Chernîshov, Kakhaber Tskhadadze; Andrei Kanchelskis, Aleksei Mikhailichenko, Igor Dobrovolski, Sergei Aleinikov (46 Dmitri Kuznetsov), Viktor Onopko; Sergei Kiriakov (46 Igor Korneev), Sergei Iuran. Trainer: Anatoli Bîshovets

Goals: McStay (6), McClair (17), McAllister (83 pen)

	P	W	D	L	F	A	Pts
Holland	3	2	1	0	4	1	5
Germany	3	1	1	1	4	4	3
Scotland	3	1	0	2	3	3	2
CIS	3	0	2	1	1	4	2

SEMI-FINALS

SWEDEN v GERMANY 2-3 (0-1)

Råsunda, Stockholm 21.06.1992

Referee: Tullio Lanese (ITA) Attendance: 28,827

SWEDEN: Thomas Ravelli; Roland Nilsson, Jan Eriksson, Joachim Björklund, Roger Ljung; Kennet Andersson, Klas Ingesson, Jonas Thern, Joakim Nilsson (59 Anders Limpar); Martin Dahlin (72 Johnny Ekström), Tomas Brolin. Trainer: Tommy Svensson

GERMANY: Bodo Illgner; Stefan Reuter, Jürgen Kohler, Thomas Helmer, Guido Buchwald, Andreas Brehme; Thomas Häßler, Stefan Effenberg, Matthias Sammer; Jürgen Klinsmann (89 Thomas Doll), Karl-Heinz Riedle. Trainer: Hans-Hubert Vogts

Goals: Häßler (10), Riedle (58, 88), Brolin (64 pen), K. Andersson (89)

HOLLAND v DENMARK 2-2 (0-0, 2-2) (AET)

Ullevi, Göteborg 22.06.1992

Referee: Emilio Soriano Aladren (SPA) Attendance: 37,450

HOLLAND: Hans van Breukelen; Adri van Tiggelen, Ronald Koeman, Frank de Boer (46 Wim Kieft); Frank Rijkaard, Jan Wouters, Rob Witschge, Ruud Gullit, Dennis Bergkamp; Marco van Basten, Bryan Roy (115 John van't Schip). Trainer: Rinus Michels

DENMARK: Peter Schmeichel; John Sivebæk, Torben Piechnik, Lars Olsen, Henrik Andersen (70 Claus Christiansen); Kim Vilfort, John Jensen, Henrik Larsen, Kim Christofte; Flemming Povlsen, Brian Laudrup (57 Lars Elstrup). Trainer: Richard Møller-Nielsen

Goals: Larsen (5, 32), Bergkamp (23), Rijkaard (85)

Penalties: R. Koeman, Bergkamp, Rijkaard, Rob Witschge; Larsen, Povlsen, Elstrup, Vilfort, Christofte. van Basten missed

FINAL

DENMARK v GERMANY 2-0 (1-0)

Ullevi, Göteborg 26.06.1992

Referee: Bruno Galler (SWI) Attendance: 37,800

DENMARK: Peter Schmeichel; John Sivebæk (66 Claus Christiansen), Torben Piechnik, Lars Olsen, Kent Nielsen; Kim Vilfort, John Jensen, Henrik Larsen, Kim Christofte; Flemming Povlsen, Brian Laudrup. Trainer: Richard Møller-Nielsen

GERMANY: Bodo Illgner; Stefan Reuter, Jürgen Kohler, Thomas Helmer, Guido Buchwald; Thomas Häßler, Stefan Effenberg (80 Andreas Thom), Matthias Sammer (46 Thomas Doll), Andreas Brehme; Jürgen Klinsmann, Karl-Heinz Riedle. Trainer: Hans-Hubert Vogts

Goals: Jensen (18), Vilfort (78)

Goalscorers European Football Championship 1992

11 goals: Jean-pierre Papin (France)

10 goals: Darko Pancev (Yugoslavia)

8 goals: Marco van Basten (Holland)

7 goals: Dennis Bergkamp (Holland)

6 goals: Adrian Knup (Switzerland), Bent Christensen (Denmark)

5 goals: Emilio Butragueño (Spain), József Kiprich (Hungary), Colin Clarke (N. Ireland), Karl-Heinz Riedle (Germany)

4 goals: Carlos Muñoz (Spain), Nasko Sirakov (Bulgaria), Alistair McCoist (Scotland), Flemming Povlsen (Denmark)

3 goals: Eric Cantona, Franck Sauzée (France), Václav Danek (Czechoslovakia), Nikolai Todorov (Bulgaria), Gordon Durie (Scotland), Andrei Kanchelskis (USSR), Ian Rush (Wales), Thomas Häßler, Rudolf Völler (Germany), Rui Aguas (Portugal), Stefanos Borbokis (Greece), John Aldridge, Tony Cascarino (Republic of Ireland), Tomas Brolin (Sweden), Henrik Larsen (Denmark)

2 goals: Hottiger, Chapuisat, Türkyilmaz, Hermann (Switzerland), Kostadinov (Bulgaria), Mcallister, McStay, Robertson (Scotland), Mateuţ, Răducioiu, Hagi (Romania), Mikhailichenko, Mostovoi (USSR), Sørloth, Bohinen, Dahlum (Norway), R. Baggio, Serena, Donadoni, Vialli (Italy), Prosinecki, Savicevic (Yugoslavia), M. Laudrup, Elstrup, Vilfort (Denmark), Saunders, Bodin (Wales), Scifo, Degryse (Belgium), Matthäus, Klinsmann (Germany), Holmgren (Finland), Futre (Portugal), Saravakos, Tsalouhidis (Greece), Lineker, Platt (England), Quinn, Byrne (Republic of Ireland), Urban (Poland), Nemecek (Czechoslovakia), Abelardo, Bakero (Spain), Sverrisson, Edvaldsson (Iceland), J. Eriksson (Sweden), Rijkaard (Holland)

1 goal: Simba, Fernandez, Blanc, Boli (France), Kula, Lancz, Hasek, Kubík, Kuka, Moravcík, Skuhravy (Czechoslovakia), Míchel, Amor, Hierro, Roberto (Spain), Örlygsson, Gudjohnsen, Si. Jónsson (Iceland), Zmijani, Abazi (Albania), Gough, Mcclair, Strachan, Collins (Scotland), B. Sutter, Ohrel, A. Sutter, Chassot, Bickel (Switzerland), A. Popescu, D. Timofte, Sabău, Lupescu, Badea, Petrescu, Cămătaru (Romania), Stoichkov, Iankov, Iliev, Ivanov, Penev (Bulgaria), Pasolini (San Marino), Protasov, Iuran, Shalimov, Korneev, Aleinikov, O. Kuznetsov (USSR), Rizzitelli, Schillaci, Vierchowod, Lombardo (Italy), Jakobsen, Lydersen, Brandhaug (Norway), Bognár, Szalma, Lörincz, Disztl (Hungary), Xiourouppas, Tsolakis (Cyprus), Lukic, Jugovic, Najdoski, Vulic, Boban, Suker, Binic, Bazdarevic, Jarni, Katanec (Yugoslavia), Christofte, Pingel, Jensen, Bartram (Denmark), Toggart, Dowie, Black, K. Wilson, McDonald, Hill (N. Ireland), Lainer, Pfeifenberger, Streiter, Wetl, A. Ogris, E. Ogris (Austria), Reynheim, A. Mørkøre, Nielsen (Faroe Islands), Buchwald, Möller, Doll, Bein, Effenberg (Germany), Hughes (Wales), Vandenbergh, Ceulemans, Versavel (Belgium), Girres, Langers (Luxembourg), Sultana, Suda (Malta), Blind, Richard Witschge, Rob Witschge, F. De Boer, Gullit, Winter (Holland), João Pinto II, César Brito, Leal, Vítor Paneira, Cadete (Portugal), Marinakis, Manolas, Tsiantakis, Karapialis (Greece), Ukkonen, Järvinen, Litmanen (Finland), Riza (Turkey), Smith, Wise, Beardsley (England), McGrath, Townsend, O'Leary (Republic of Ireland), Szewczyk, Czachowski, Furtok, Tarasiewicz, Kosecki, Dziekanowski (Poland), Dobrovolski (CIS), K. Andersson (Sweden)

Own goals: Lekbello (Albania) for France, Valentini (San Marino) for Bulgaria, Christodoulou (Cyprus) for Hungary, Artner (Austria) for Denmark, Scerri (Malta) for Portugal, Staunton (Republic of Ireland) for England

THE EUROPEAN FOOTBALL CHAMPIONSHIP 1996

GROUP 1

ISRAEL v POLAND 2-1 (1-0)

Ramat-Gan, Tel Aviv 04.09.1994

Referee: Frans Van den Wijngaert (BEL) Attendance: 3,500

ISRAEL: Boni Ginzburg; Marco Balbul, Moshe Glam, Alon Hazan, Alon Harazi, Nir Klinger, Tal Banin, Haim Revivo, Eyal Berkovitch (86 Roni Levi), Ronen Harazi, Ronny Rosenthal (89 Reuoven Atar). Trainer: Shlomo Sharf

POLAND: Józef Wandzik; Jacek Bak, Roman Szewczyk, Krzysztof Maciejewski, Tomasz Waldoch, Tomasz Lapinski, Marcin Jalocha (46 Ryszard Czerwiec), Roman Kosecki, Grzegorz Mielcarski (60 Dariusz Gesior), Wojciech Kowalczyk, Jerzy Brzeczek. Trainer: Henryk Apostel

Goals: R. Harazi (43, 58), Kosecki (80)

ROMANIA v AZERBAIJAN 3-0 (1-0)

Steaua, București 07.09.1994

Referee: Robert Sedlacek (AUS) Attendance: 10,000

ROMANIA: Bogdan Stelea (85 Dumitru Stîngaciu); Dan Petrescu, Daniel Prodan, Miodrag Belodedici, Tibor Selymes (82 Florin Cârstea); Ioan Lupescu (75 Daniel Timofte), Dorinel Munteanu, Gheorghe Popescu (Cap), Ilie Dumitrescu; Marius Lăcătuș, Florin Răducioiu.
Trainer: Anghel Iordănescu

AZERBAIJAN: Aleksander Jidkov; Fuzuli Allahverdiev, Gennadi Drozdov, Tarlan Ahmedov, Arif Asadov; Sahin Diniev, Nazim Suleimanov (Cap) (59 Vidadi Rzayev), Rasim Abusov, Samir Alekberov; Iunis Huseinov (81 Emin Agayev), Veli Kasumov. Trainer: Agasalim Mirdjavadov

Goals: Belodedici (43), Petrescu (58), Răducioiu (87)

SLOVAKIA v FRANCE 0-0

Tehelne pole, Bratislava 07.09.1994

Referee: Peter Mikkelsen (DEN) Attendance: 17,000

SLOVAKIA: Ladislav Molnar; Tomas Stupala, Marian Zeman, Milos Glonek, Vladimir Kinder, Dusan Tittel, Stefan Rusnak (80 Vladimir Weiss), Robert Tomaschek, Ondrej Kristofik, Vladislav Zvara (63 Marek Penska), Lubomir Moravcik.
Trainer: Jozef Venglos

FRANCE: Bernard Lama; Jocelyn Angloma, Eric Di Meco, Alain Roche, Laurent Blanc; Paul Le Guen, Eric Cantona (Cap), Didier Deschamps, Reynald Pedros (63 Christophe Dugarry), Youri Djorkaeff (82 Bixente Lizarazu), David Ginola.
Trainer: Aimé Jacquet

FRANCE v ROMANIA 0-0

Geoffroy Guichard, Saint Etienne 08.10.1994

Referee: Leif Sundell (SWE) Attendance: 31,744

FRANCE: Bernard Lama; Jocelyn Angloma, Bixente Lizarazu, Alain Roche, Laurent Blanc; Christian Karembeu, Eric Cantona (Cap), Marcel Desailly; Nicolas Ouédec (73 Zinedine Zidane); Patrice Loko (84 Christophe Dugarry), Reynald Pedros. Trainer: Aimé Jacquet

ROMANIA: Bogdan Stelea; Dan Petrescu, Daniel Prodan, Miodrag Belodedici, Tibor Selymes; Ioan Lupescu, Daniel Timofte (73 Marius Lăcătuș), Gheorghe Popescu, Ilie Dumitrescu; Florin Răducioiu (80 Basarab Panduru), Gheorghe Hagi (Cap). Trainer: Anghel Iordănescu

ISRAEL v SLOVAKIA 2-2 (2-2)

Ramat-Gan, Tel-Aviv 12.10.1994

Referee: John Blankenstein (HOL) Attendance: 10,000

ISRAEL: Boni Ginzburg; Marco Balbul, Moshe Glam, Alon Hazan, Alon Harazi, Nir Klinger (67 Amir Shelach), Tal Banin (61 Avi Nimni), Haim Revivo, Eyal Berkovitch, Ronen Harazi, Ronny Rosenthal. Trainer: Shlomo Sharf

SLOVAKIA: Ladislav Molnar; Tomas Stupala, Marian Zeman, Milos Glonek, Vladimir Kinder, Dusan Tittel, Vladimir Weiss (75 Ivan Kozak), Stefan Rusnak (77 Vladislav Zvara), Ondrej Kristofik, Peter Dubovsky, Lubomir Moravcik.
Trainer: Jozef Venglos

Goals: Rusnak (5), Moravcik (14), R. Harazi (25), Banin (33 pen)

POLAND v AZERBAIJAN 1-0 (1-0)

Stal, Mielec 12.10.1994

Referee: Ilka Koho (FIN) Attendance: 10,000

POLAND: Józef Wandzik; Waldemar Jaskulski, Tomasz Lapinski (79 Krzysztof Maciejewski), Sylwester Czereszewski, Tomasz Waldoch, Marek Kozminski (69 Adam Fedoruk), Piotr Swierczewski, Jerzy Brzeczek, Andrzej Juskowiak, Roman Kosecki, Krzysztof Warzycha. Trainer: Henryk Apostel

AZERBAIJAN: Aleksander Jidkov; Fuzuli Allahverdiev, Aslan Karimov, Tarlan Ahmedov, Arif Asadov; Rasim Abusov (89 Mahmud Gurbanov), Iunis Huseinov, Sahin Diniev, Khalig Mardanov, Veli Kasumov, Samir Alekberov.
Trainer: Agasalim Mirdjavadov

Goal: Juskowiak (44)

ROMANIA v SLOVAKIA 3-2 (1-0)

Steaua, Bucureşti 12.11.1994

Referee: Vadim Zhuk (BLS) Attendance: 20,000

ROMANIA: Bogdan Stelea; Dan Petrescu, Daniel Prodan, Miodrag Belodedici, Dorinel Munteanu; Ioan Lupescu, Gheorghe Popescu, Gheorghe Hagi (Cap), Ilie Dumitrescu; Marius Lăcătuş (75 Ion Vlădoiu), Florin Răducioiu (85 Daniel Timofte). Trainer: Anghel Iordănescu

SLOVAKIA: Ladislav Molnar; Tomas Stupala, Miroslav Chvila, Milos Glonek, Vladimir Kinder; Robert Tomaschek, Dusan Tittel, Ondrej Kristofik; Marek Penska (46 Jaroslav Timko), Peter Dubovsky, Lubomir Moravcik (Cap). Trainer: Jozef Venglos

Goals: Popescu (6), Hagi (47), Dubovsky (56), Chvila (80), Prodan (81)

AZERBAIJAN v FRANCE 0-2 (0-1)

Avni Aker, Trabzon (Turkey) 13.12.1994

Referee: Rune Pedersen (NOR) Attendance: 4,000

AZERBAIJAN: Aleksander Jidkov (41 Elhan Hasanov); Fuzuli Allahverdiev, Faig Cabarov, Emin Agayev, Yashar Vahabzadze, Rasim Abusov, Iunis Huseinov, Sahin Diniev, Arif Asadov (79 Vladislav Kadirov), Veli Kasumov (79 Vidadi Rzayev), Samir Alekberov. Trainer: Agasalim Mirdjavadov

FRANCE: Bernard Lama; Jocelyn Angloma, Eric Di Meco, Alain Roche, Laurent Blanc; Paul Le Guen, Eric Cantona (Cap), Marcel Desailly (71 Jean-Michel Ferri); Jean-Pierre Papin, Reynald Pedros (76 Corentin Martins), Patrice Loko. Trainer: Aimé Jacquet

Goals: Papin (25), Loko (56)

POLAND v FRANCE 0-0

Górnik, Zabrze 16.11.1994

Referee: Angelo Amendolia (ITA) Attendance: 21,000

POLAND: Józef Wandzik; Waldemar Jaskulski, Marek Swierczewski, Sylwester Czereszewski, Tomasz Waldoch, Marek Kozminski (29 Jacek Bak), Piotr Swierczewski, Henryk Baluszynski (82 Dariusz Gesior), Andrzej Juskowiak, Roman Kosecki, Krzysztof Warzycha. Trainer: Henryk Apostel

FRANCE: Bernard Lama; Jocelyn Angloma, Eric Di Meco, Alain Roche, Laurent Blanc; Paul Le Guen, Eric Cantona (Cap), Marcel Desailly; Nicolas Ouédec (76 Christophe Dugarry), Christian Karembeu, Reynald Pedros (25 Youri Djorkaeff).

ISRAEL v ROMANIA 1-1(0-0)

Ramat-Gan, Tel-Aviv 14.12.1994

Referee: Antonio Martin Navarrete (SPA) Att: 42,500

ISRAEL: Boni Ginzburg; Marco Balbul, Alon Harazi, Nir Klinger, Moshe Glam; Eyal Berkovitch, Alon Hazan, Roni Levi (76 Itzhak Zohar), Haim Revivo; Ronen Harazi (88 Amir Shelach), Ronny Rosenthal. Trainer: Shlomo Sharf

ROMANIA: Bogdan Stelea; Dan Petrescu, Daniel Prodan, Miodrag Belodedici, Tibor Selymes; Ioan Lupescu, Gheorghe Popescu, Gheorghe Hagi (Cap), Dorinel Munteanu (53 Ion Vlădoiu); Marius Lăcătuş, Ilie Dumitrescu (71 Constantin Gâlcă). Trainer: Anghel Iordănescu

Goals: Lăcătuş (69), Rosenthal (83)

AZERBAIJAN v ISRAEL 0-2 (0-1)

Avni Aker, Trabzon (Turkey) 16.11.1994

Referee: László Vagner (HUNG) Attendance: 3,000

AZERBAIJAN: Aleksander Jidkov; Fuzuli Allahverdiev, Faig Cabarov, Tarlan Ahmedov, Arif Asadov; Lev Mayorov (46 Emin Agayev), Iunis Huseinov (77 Vidadi Rzayev), Sahin Diniev, Veli Kasumov, Nazim Suleimanov, Samir Alekberov. Trainer: Agasalim Mirdjavadov

ISRAEL: Boni Ginzburg; Marco Balbul, Moshe Glam, Alon Hazan, Alon Harazi, Nir Klinger, Tal Banin, Haim Revivo, Eyal Berkovitch (65 Avi Nimni), Ronen Harazi (82 Amir Shelach), Ronny Rosenthal. Trainer: Shlomo Sharf

Goals: R. Harazi (29), Rosenthal (50)

ISRAEL v FRANCE 0-0

Ramat-Gan, Tel-Aviv 29.03.1995

Referee: James McCluskey (SCO) Attendance: 43,000

ISRAEL: Boni Ginzburg; Felix Halfon, Moshe Glam, Alon Hazan, Alon Harazi, Nir Klinger, Tal Banin, Haim Revivo, Eyal Berkovitch (64 Itzhak Zohar), Ronen Harazi, Ronny Rosenthal. Trainer: Shlomo Sharf

FRANCE: Bernard Lama; Jocelyn Angloma, Eric Di Meco, Alain Roche, Laurent Blanc; Paul Le Guen, Patrice Loko, Marcel Desailly, Ncolas Ouédec (66 David Ginola), Corentin Martins (78 Youri Djorkaeff), Reynald Pedros. Trainer: Aimé Jacquet

ROMANIA v POLAND 2-1 (1-1)

Steaua, Bucureşti 29.03.1995

Referee: Kurt Röthlisberger (SWI) Attendance: 25,000

ROMANIA: Bogdan Stelea; Dan Petrescu, Daniel Prodan, Miodrag Belodedici, Tibor Selymes; Gheorghe Popescu, Marius Lăcătuş (46 Dănuţ Lupu), Ilie Dumitrescu, Florin Răducioiu, Gheorghe Hagi (Cap) (87 Ion Vlădoiu), Dorinel Munteanu. Trainer: Anghel Iordănescu

POLAND: Józef Wandzik; Waldemar Jaskulski, Marek Swierczewski, Tomasz Waldoch; Piotr Swierczewski, Roman Kosecki (Cap), Piotr Nowak (46 Tomasz Wieszczycki), Krzysztof Warzycha, Sylwester Czereszewski (73 Tomasz Sokolowski), Andrzej Juskowiak, Henryk Baluszynski. Trainer: Henryk Apostel

Sent off: Jaskulski (74)

Goals: Juskowiak (42 pen), Răducioiu (45), Wandzik (55 og)

SLOVAKIA v AZERBAIJAN 4-1 (3-0)

Lokomotiva, Kosice 29.03.1995

Referee: Vasilios Nikakis (GRE) Attendance: 12,450

SLOVAKIA: Ladislav Molnar; Tomas Stupala, Marian Zeman, Milos Glonek, Vladimir Kinder; Dusan Tittel, Marek Penska, Ondrej Kristofik; Jaroslav Timko, Peter Dubovsky, Lubomir Moravcik (Cap) (75 Karol Prazenica). Trainer: Jozef Venglos

AZERBAIJAN: Elhan Hasanov; Arif Asadov, Yashar Vahabzadze, Faig Cabarov, Sakit Aliyev (75 Vladislav Kadirov), Rasim Abusov, Iunis Huseinov, Sahin Diniev, Veli Kasumov (68 Samir Alekberov), Nazim Suleimanov, Emin Agayev. Trainer: Agasalim Mirdjavadov

Goals: Tittel (35), Timko (40, 50), Dubovsky (45 pen), Suleimanov (80 pen)

POLAND v ISRAEL 4-3 (1-2)

Górnik, Zabrze 25.04.1995

Referee: Anders Frisk (SWE) Attendance: 5,500

POLAND: Józef Wandzik; Wojciech Kowalczyk, Marek Swierczewski, Tomasz Lapinski, Tomasz Waldoch; Marek Kozminski, Piotr Swierczewski, Piotr Nowak (46 Krzysztof Bukalski), Andrzej Juskowiak, Roman Kosecki, Henryk Baluszynski (46 Tomasz Wieszczycki). Trainer: Henryk Apostel

ISRAEL: Boni Ginzburg; Felix Halfon, Moshe Glam, Alon Hazan, Alon Harazi, Nir Klinger, Tal Banin, Haim Revivo, Eyal Berkovitch, Offer Mizrahi (71 Itzhak Zohar), Ronny Rosenthal. Trainer: Shlomo Sharf

Goals: Nowak (1), Rosenthal (37), Revivo (42), Juskowiak (50), Kowalczyk (55), Kosecki (62), Zohar (77)

FRANCE v SLOVAKIA 4-0 (2-0)

La Beaujoire, Nantes 26.04.1995

Referee: Bernd Heynemann (GER) Attendance: 26,000

FRANCE: Bernard Lama; Jocelyn Angloma, Eric Di Meco, Alain Roche, Laurent Blanc; Vincent Guérin, Didier Deschamps, Marcel Desailly, Patrice Loko, Zinedine Zidane (73 Youri Djorkaeff), David Ginola. Trainer: Aimé Jacquet

SLOVAKIA: Ladislav Molnar; Tomas Stupala, Marian Zeman, Milos Glonek, Vladimir Kinder; Dusan Tittel, Robert Tomaschek (46 Jaroslav Timko), Ondrej Kristofik, Marek Penska (74 Stefan Maixner), Peter Dubovsky, Lubomir Moravcik. Trainer: Jozef Venglos

Goals: Kristofik (27 og), Ginola (42), Blanc (58), Guérin (62)

AZERBAIJAN v ROMANIA 1-4 (1-2)

"Husseyn Avni Aker", Trabzon (Turkey) 26.04.1995

Referee: Dimitar Momirov (BUL) Attendance: 1,000

AZERBAIJAN: Elhan Hasanov; Arif Asadov, Igor Getman, Rasim Abusov, Tarlan Ahmedov (21 Yashar Vahabzadze), Faig Cabarov (76 Vladislav Kadirov), Viacheslav Lichkin, Nazim Suleimanov, Sahin Diniev; Iunis Huseinov, Samir Alekberov. Trainer: Agasalim Mirdjavadov

ROMANIA: Bogdan Stelea (85 Florin Prunea); Dan Petrescu, Daniel Prodan, Miodrag Belodedici, Tibor Selymes; Gheorghe Popescu (81 Daniel Timofte), Ioan Lupescu, Ilie Dumitrescu, Dorinel Munteanu; Marius Lăcătuş (69 Dănuţ Lupu), Florin Răducioiu. Trainer: Anghel Iordănescu

Goals: Răducioiu (1 pen, 68, 76), Suleimanov (34), Dumitrescu (38)

POLAND v SLOVAKIA 5-0 (1-0)

Górnik, Zabrze 07.06.1995

Referee: Robert Sedlacek (AUS) Attendance: 17,000

POLAND: Maciej Szczesny; Waldemar Jaskulski (73 Sylwester Czereszewski), Jacek Zielinski, Krzysztof Bukalski, Tomasz Waldoch, Marek Kozminski, Piotr Swierczewski, Piotr Nowak, Andrzej Juskowiak, Roman Kosecki, Wojciech Kowalczyk (46 Tomasz Wieszczycki). Trainer: Henryk Apostel

SLOVAKIA: Alexander Vencel; Ivan Kozak (65 Marek Penska), Marian Zeman, Milos Glonek, Karol Prazenica, Robert Tomaschek, Jan Solar, Ondrej Kristofik (70 Vladimir Weiss), Jaroslav Timko, Peter Dubovsky, Lubomir Moravcik. Trainer: Jozef Venglos

Goals: Juskowiak (10, 72), Wieszczycki (58), Kosecki (63), Nowak (69)

ROMANIA v ISRAEL 2-1 (1-0)

Steaua, București 07.06.1995

Referee: Rune Pedersen (NOR) Attendance: 20,000

ROMANIA: Bogdan Stelea; Dan Petrescu, Daniel Prodan, Miodrag Belodedici, Tibor Selymes; Dănuț Lupu (87 Basarab Panduru), Ioan Lupescu, Ilie Dumitrescu (62 Ion Vlădoiu), Dorinel Munteanu; Marius Lăcătuș, Florin Răducioiu. Trainer: Anghel Iordănescu

ISRAEL: Rafael Cohen; Felix Halfon (46 Marco Balbul, 75 Itzhak Zohar), Gadi Brumer, Amir Shelach, David Amsalem; Alon Hazan, Eyal Berkovitch, Nir Klinger, Tal Banin; Eli Driks, Offer Mizrahi. Trainer: Shlomo Sharf

Sent off: Răducioiu (67)

Goals: Lăcătuș (16), Berkovich (50), Munteanu (65)

FRANCE v AZERBAIJAN 10-0 (3-0)

Abbé-Deschamps, Auxerre 06.09.1995

Referee: Alfred Micaleff (MAL) Attendance: 15,000

FRANCE: Bernard Lama; Jocelyn Angloma (57 Lilian Thuram), Bixente Lizarazu, Marcel Desailly, Frank Leboeuf, Youri Djorkaeff, Didier Deschamps, Vincent Guérin, Christophe Dugarry (68 Christophe Cocard), Zinedine Zidane, Reynald Pedros (65 David Ginola). Trainer: Aimé Jacquet

AZERBAIJAN: Elhan Hasanov (36 Nizami Sadikov); Arif Asadov, Igor Getman, Tarlan Ahmedov, Emin Agayev, Rasim Abusov, Iunis Huseinov, Sahin Diniev, Vladislav Kadirov (74 Musvik Huseynov), Makhmud Kurbanov (46 Samir Alekberov), Viacheslav Lichkin. Trainer: Agasalim Mirdjavadov

Goals: Desailly (13), Djorkaeff (17, 78), Guérin (33), Pedros (49), Leboeuf (54, 74), Dugarry (65), Zidane (72), Cocard (90)

FRANCE v POLAND 1-1 (0-1)

Parc des Princes, Paris 16.08.1995

Referee: Manuel Diaz Vega (SPA) Attendance: 40,426

FRANCE: Bernard Lama; Jocelyn Angloma (66 Christian Karembeu), Bixente Lizarazu, Lilian Thuram, Frank Leboeuf (69 Youri Djorkaeff); Vincent Guérin, Didier Deschamps, Marcel Desailly, Christophe Dugarry, Zinedine Zidane, David Ginola (64 Reynald Pedros). Trainer: Aimé Jacquet

POLAND: Andrzej Wozniak; Tomasz Lapinski, Jacek Zielinski, Marek Kozminski, Tomasz Waldoch, Tomasz Iwan, Piotr Swierczewski, Piotr Nowak (57 Ryszard Czerwiec), Andrzej Juskowiak, Roman Kosecki (72 Pawel Wojtala), Wojciech Kowalczyk (61 Krzysztof Bukalski). Trainer: Henryk Apostel

Goals: Juskowiak (35), Djorkaeff (85)

POLAND v ROMANIA 0-0

Górnik, Zabrze 06.09.1995

Referee: Dermot Gallagher (ENG) Attendance: 25,000

POLAND: Andrzej Wozniak; Waldemar Jaskulski, Tomasz Waldoch, Jacek Zielinski, Marek Kozminski; Tomasz Iwan (76 Ryszard Czerwiec), Tomasz Wieszczycki (70 Jerzy Podbrozny), Piotr Swierczewski, Jacek Bednarz (63 Krzysztof Bukalski); Roman Kosecki (Cap), Andrzej Juskowiak. Trainer: Henryk Apostel

ROMANIA: Bogdan Stelea; Dan Petrescu, Daniel Prodan, Gheorghe Mihali, Tibor Selymes; Gheorghe Popescu (Cap), Ioan Ovidiu Sabău, Ioan Angelo Lupescu, Dorinel Munteanu (75 Constantin Gâlcă); Marius Lăcătuș (84 Ion Timofte), Ion Vlădoiu (64 Basarab Panduru). Trainer: Anghel Iordănescu

AZERBAIJAN v SLOVAKIA 0-1 (0-0)

Avni Aker, Trabzon (Turkey) 16.08.1995

Referee: Alain Hamer (LUX) Attendance: 1,000

AZERBAIJAN: Nizami Sadikov; Igor Getman, Vladislav Nosenko, Tarlan Ahmedov, Emin Agayev (71 Arif Asadov), Rasim Abusov, Iunis Huseinov, Sahin Diniev (46 Makhmud Kurbanov), Vladislav Kadirov, Viacheslav Lichkin, Samir Alekberov. Trainer: Agasalim Mirdjavadov

SLOVAKIA: Ladislav Molnar; Igor Balis (89 Karol Prazenica), Milos Sobona, Robert Tomaschek, Vladimir Kinder, Dusan Tittel, Ladislav Pecko, Julius Simon, Stefan Rusnak (58 Tibor Jancula), Peter Dubovsky, Lubomir Moravcik (78 Lubomir Faktor). Trainer: Jozef Jankech

Goals: Jancula (60)

SLOVAKIA v ISRAEL 1-0 (0-0)

Lokomotiva, Kosice 06.09.1995

Referee: Marnix Sandra (BEL) Attendance: 10,000

SLOVAKIA: Ladislav Molnar; Igor Balis (89 Rastislav Kostka), Miroslav Karhan, Jozef Juriga, Vladimir Kinder, Dusan Tittel, Ladislav Pecko, Julius Simon (80 Lubomir Faktor), Tibor Jancula (61 Stefan Rusnak), Peter Dubovsky, Lubomir Moravcik. Trainer: Jozef Jankech

ISRAEL: Rafael Cohen; Gadi Brumer, Moshe Glam, Alon Hazan, Alon Harazi, Nir Klinger (46 Ronny Rosenthal), Tal Banin, Offer Mizrahi, Eyal Berkovitch (66 Eli Driks), Haim Revivo, Amir Shelach. Trainer: Shlomo Sharf

Goal: Jancula (55)

ISRAEL v AZERBAIJAN 2-0 (1-0)

Ramat-Gan, Tel-Aviv 11.10.1995

Referee: Claude Detruche (SWI) Attendance: 5,000

ISRAEL: Boni Ginzburg; Felix Halfon, David Amsalem, Alon Hazan, Amir Shelach, Gadi Brumer, Tal Banin, Haim Revivo (87 Nir Klinger), Eyal Berkovitch (71 Itzhak Zohar), Ronen Harazi (79 Reuoven Atar), Ronny Rosenthal.
Trainer: Shlomo Sharf

AZERBAIJAN: Aleksander Jidkov; Arif Asadov, Samir Khairov (58 Emin Agayev), Tarlan Ahmedov, Yashar Vahabzade, Rasim Abusov, Viacheslav Lichkin (79 Elhan Mamedov), Vidadi Rzayev (70 Kurban Kurbanov), Vladislav Kadirov, Nazim Suleymanov, Veli Kasumov.
Trainer: Kazbek Tuayev

Goals: R. Harazi (31, 51)

FRANCE v ISRAEL 2-0 (0-0)

Michel-d'Omano, Caen 15.11.1995

Referee: Gerd Grabher (AUS) Attendance: 21,500

FRANCE: Bernard Lama; Jocelyn Angloma, Eric Di Meco (Cap) (63 Bixente Lizarazu), Christian Karembeu (90 Marc Keller), Frank Leboeuf, Vincent Guérin, Didier Deschamps, Marcel Desailly, Youri Djorkaeff, Zinedine Zidane, Michäel Madar (63 Patrice Loko). Trainer: Aimé Jacquet

ISRAEL: Rafael Cohen; Felix Halfon, Moshe Glam, Alon Hazan, Gadi Brumer, Nir Klinger (78 Itzhak Zohar), Tal Banin, Amir Shelach, Eyal Berkovitch (69 Reuoven Atar), Ronen Harazi (84 Offer Mizrahi), Ronny Rosenthal.
Trainer: Shlomo Sharf

Goals: Djorkaeff (69), Lizarazu (89)

ROMANIA v FRANCE 1-3 (0-2)

Steaua, Bucureşti 11.10.1995

Referee: Pierluigi Pairetto (ITA) Attendance: 30,000

ROMANIA: Bogdan Stelea; Dan Petrescu, Daniel Prodan, Gheorghe Mihali (46 Dănuţ Lupu), Tibor Selymes; Gheorghe Popescu, Gheorghe Hagi (63 Basarab Panduru), Ioan Angelo Lupescu, Dorinel Munteanu; Marius Lăcătuş, Ilie Dumitrescu (46 Ion Vlădoiu). Trainer: Anghel Iordănescu

FRANCE: Fabien Barthez; Jocelyn Angloma, Marcel Desailly, Frank Leboeuf, Eric Di Meco (Cap); Christian Karembeu, Didier Deschamps, Zinedine Zidane (85 Lilian Thuram), Vincent Guérin; Christophe Dugarry (63 Michäel Madar), Youri Djorkaeff (75 Bixente Lizarazu). Trainer: Aimé Jacquet

Goals: Karembeu (29), Djorkaeff (41), Lăcătuş (52), Zidane (74)

AZERBAIJAN v POLAND 0-0

Avni Aker, Trabzon (Tür) 15.11.1995

Referee: Leslie Mottram (SCO) Attendance: 1,000

AZERBAIJAN: Aleksander Jidkov; Igor Getman, Deni Gaisumov, Tarlan Ahmedov, Yashar Vahabzade, Rasim Abusov, Emin Agayev, Vidadi Rzayev (69 Kurban Kurbanov), Vladislav Kadirov (65 Makhmud Kurbanov), Nazim Suleymanov (86 Viacheslav Lichkin), Veli Kasumov. Trainer: Kazbek Tuayev

POLAND: Andrzej Wozniak; Waldemar Jaskulski, Marek Swierczewski, Tomasz Sokolowski, Tomasz Waldoch, Sylwester Czereszewski, Pawel Wojtala, Krzysztof Bukalski (71 Tomasz Lenart), Henryk Baluszynski (65 Marcin Kuzba), Ryszard Czerwiec, Slawomir Majak (46 Rafal Siadaczka).
Trainer: Wladyslaw Stachurski

SLOVAKIA v POLAND 4-1 (1-1)

Tehelné pole, Bratislava 11.10.1995

Referee: Jorge Monteiro Coroado (POR) Att: 11,000

SLOVAKIA: Ladislav Molnar; Igor Balis, Miroslav Karhan, Marian Zeman, Vladimir Kinder, Dusan Tittel, Jozef Juriga (71 Marek Ujlaky), Julius Simon, Tibor Jancula (87 Marian Bochnovic), Peter Dubovsky, Lubomir Moravcik.

POLAND: Andrzej Wozniak; Tomasz Lapinski, Jacek Zielinski, Krzysztof Bukalski, Tomasz Waldoch, Marek Kozminski (59 Jacek Bednarz), Piotr Swierczewski, Tomasz Iwan, Andrzej Juskowiak, Roman Kosecki, Henryk Baluszynski (80 Sylwester Czereszewski).
Trainer: Jozef Jankech

Sent off: Kosecki & P. Swierczewski

Goals: Juskowiak (19), Dubovsky (32 pen), Jancula (68), Ujlaky (77), Simon (83)

SLOVAKIA v ROMANIA 0-2 (0-0)

VSA, Kosice 15.11.1995

Referee: Jacobus Uilenberg (HOL) Attendance: 7,500

SLOVAKIA: Ladislav Molnar; Igor Balis, Dusan Tittel, Miroslav Karhan, Vladimir Kinder; Ladislav Pecko (46 Jozef Juriga), Robert Tomaschek, Julius Simon (78 Robert Semenik), Lubomír Moravcík (Cap), Tibor Jancula (69 Marek Ujlaky), Peter Dubovsky. Trainer: Jozef Jankech

ROMANIA: Bogdan Stelea; Dan Petrescu, Daniel Prodan, Anton Doboş, Tibor Selymes; Ioan Angelo Lupescu, Gheorghe Popescu, Gheorghe Hagi (Cap) (85 Basarab Panduru), Dorinel Munteanu; Marius Lăcătuş (73 Ilie Dumitrescu), Viorel Moldovan (88 Ion Timofte). Trainer: Anghel Iordănescu

Goals: Hagi (68), Munteanu (82)

	P	W	D	L	F	A	Pts
Romania	10	6	3	1	18	9	21
France	10	5	5	0	22	2	20
Slovakia	10	4	2	4	14	18	14
Poland	10	3	4	3	14	12	13
Israel	10	3	3	4	13	13	12
Azerbaijan	10	0	1	9	2	29	1

MACEDONIA v DENMARK 1-1 (1-0)

Gradski, Skopje 07.09.1994

Referee: Mario Van der Ende (HOL) Attendance: 25,000

MACEDONIA: Kire Trajcev; Vujadin Stanojkovic, Zoran Jovanovski, Mitko Stojkovski, Ilija Najdoski, Ljupco Markovski, Zoran Boskovski (82 Zarko Serafimovski), Bosko Djurovski, Darko Pancev, Boban Babunski (67 Dragan Kanatlarovski), Toni Micevski. Trainer: Andon Doncevski

DENMARK: Peter Schmeichel; Thomas Helveg, Marc Rieper, Lars Olsen, Jakob Friis-Hansen, Brian Steen Nielsen, John Jensen (67 Henrik Larsen), Kim Vilfort (52 Flemming Povlsen), Bent Christensen, Michael Laudrup, Brian Laudrup. Trainer: Richard Møller-Nielsen

Goals: Mi. Stojkovski (4), Povlsen (86)

GROUP 2

BELGIUM v ARMENIA 2-0 (1-0)

Brussel 07.09.1994

Referee: John Ferry (NIR)

BELGIUM: Michel Preud'homme; Régis Genaux, Michel De Wolf, Philippe Albert, Rudy Smidts, Lorenzo Staelens (76 Marc Emmers), Franky Van der Elst, Stéphane Van der Heyden (67 Danny Boffin), Marc Degryse, Luis Oliveira, Josip Weber. Trainer: Paul van Himst

ARMENIA: Armenak Petrosyan; Yervand Sukiasyan, Yervand Krbachyan, Vardan Khachatryan, Sarkys Oganesyan, Sarkis Hovsepyan, Artur Petrosyan, Razmik Grigoryan, Aramais Tonoyan, Armen Shahgeldyan (46 Arsen Avetisyan), Hamlet Mkhitaryan. Trainer: Eduard Markarov

Goals: Krbachyan (3 og), Degryse (73)

ARMENIA v CYPRUS 0-0

Razdan, Erevan 08.10.1994

Referee: Zbigniew Przesmycki (POL) Attendance: 6,000

ARMENIA: Harutyun Abramyan; Yervand Sukiasyan, Vardan Khachatryan (46 Yervand Krbachyan), Aramais Tonoyan, Sarkys Oganesyan, Harutyun Vardanyan, Artur Petrosyan, Razmik Grigoryan, Artak Adamyan, Arsen Avetisyan, Hamlet Mkhitaryan (80 Varazdat Avetisyan). Trainer: Eduard Markarov

CYPRUS: Michalis Christophi; Yiannos Kalotheou, Haralambos Pittas, Dimitris Ioannou, Louis Stephani, Andonis Zembashis, Marios Charalambous, Andros Sotiriou, Sinisa Gogic, Costas Phasouliotis (70 Costas Malekos), George Savvides. Trainer: Andreas Michaelides

CYPRUS v SPAIN 1-2 (1-2)

Tsirion, Limassol 07.09.1994

Referee: Marc Batta (FRA) Attendance: 10,000

CYPRUS: Nicos Panayiotou; Costas Costa, Haralambos Pittas, Costas Constandinou, Evagoras Christophi, Marios Charalambous, Dimitris Ioannou, Costas Phasouliotis (63 Costas Malekos), Sinisa Gogic, Andros Sotiriou, George Savvides (77 Pambos Andreou). Trainer: Andreas Michaelides

SPAIN: Andoni ZUBIZARRETA; Francisco José CAMARASA, Salvador González "VORO", Josep GUARDIOLA (64 José Luis Pérez CAMINERO), Miguel Angel NADAL, Fernando Ruiz HIERRO, Juan Antonio GOIKOETXEA, Julen GUERRERO, Francisco HIGUERA, José Emilio AMAVISCA (80 José Angel CIGANDA), SERGI Barjuán. Trainer: Javier Clemente

Goals: Higuera (18), M. Charalambous (26 og), Sotiriou (36)

DENMARK v BELGIUM 3-1 (1-1)

Idraetsparken, København 12.10.1994

Referee: Pierluigi Pairetto (ITA) Attendance: 40,075

DENMARK: Peter Schmeichel; Thomas Helveg, Marc Rieper, Lars Olsen, Jakob Friis-Hansen, Jens Risager (78 Jakob Kjeldbjerg), Brian Steen Nielsen, Kim Vilfort (71 John Jensen), Mark Strudal, Michael Laudrup, Brian Laudrup. Trainer: Richard Møller-Nielsen

BELGIUM: Gilbert Bodart; Régis Genaux, Eric Van Meir, Philippe Albert, Rudy Smidts, Vital Borkelmans (76 Luis Oliveira), Franky Van der Elst, Lorenzo Staelens, Marc Degryse, Josip Weber, Gert Verheyen. Trainer: Paul van Himst

Goals: Degryse (31), Vilfort (35), Jensen (72), Strudal (86)

MACEDONIA v SPAIN 0-2 (0-2)

Gradski, Skopje 12.10.1994

Referee: Gerd Grabher (AUS) Attendance: 30,000

MACEDONIA: Kire Trajcev (51 Danco Celeski); Vujadin Stanojkovic, Mitko Stojkovski, Bosko Djurovski, Ilija Najdoski, Zoran Jovanovski, Zoran Boskovski, Toni Savevski, Boban Babunski (39 Ljupco Markovski), Milko Djurovski (71 Zarko Serafimovski), Toni Micevski. Trainer: Andon Doncevski

SPAIN: Andoni ZUBIZARRETA, Albert FERRER, ABELARDO Fernández, Rafael ALKORTA, SERGI Barjuán, Fernando Ruiz HIERRO, José Luis Pérez CAMINERO, Miguel Angel NADAL, Julio SALINAS (64 Pedro Luis Cherubino "PIER"), Francisco HIGUERA (76 José Emilio AMAVISCA), LUIS ENRIQUE Martínez. Trainer: Javier Clemente

Goals: Salinas (16, 25)

SPAIN v DENMARK 3-0 (1-0)

Sevilla 16.11.1994

Referee: James McCluskey (SCO) Attendance: 38,000

SPAIN: Andoni ZUBIZARRETA; Albert FERRER, Alberto BELSUÉ, Rafael ALKORTA, ABELARDO Fernández, Miguel Angel NADAL, LUIS ENRIQUE Martínez, José Luis Pérez CAMINERO (72 José María BAKERO), Julio SALINAS (58 Francisco HIGUERA), DONATO Gama da Silva, SERGI Barjuán. Trainer: Javier Clemente

DENMARK: Peter Schmeichel; Thomas Helveg, Marc Rieper, Lars Olsen, Jens Risager, Jakob Friis-Hansen (65 Bent Christensen), Brian Steen Nielsen, Kim Vilfort, Mark Strudal (46 John Jensen), Michael Laudrup, Brian Laudrup. Trainer: Richard Møller-Nielsen

Goals: Nadal (41), Donato (57), Luis Enrique (87)

BELGIUM v MACEDONIA 1-1 (1-0)

Brussel 16.11.1994

Referee: Sergei Khusainov (RUS) Attendance: 17,000

BELGIUM: Michel Preud'homme; Régis Genaux, Bertrand Crasson, Danny Boffin, Rudy Smidts, Lorenzo Staelens, Franky Van der Elst, Johan Walem (69 Gilles De Bilde), Marc Degryse, Luc Nilis, Gert Verheyen. Trainer: Paul van Himst

MACEDONIA: Danco Celeski; Vujadin Stanojkovic, Zoran Jovanovski, Ilija Najdoski, Cedomir Janevski, Ljupco Markovski, Toni Micevski, Bosko Djurovski, Zoran Boskovski (87 Dragan Kanatlarovski), Milko Djurovski (80 Zarko Serafimovski), Mitko Stojkovski. Trainer: Andon Doncevski

Goals: Verheyen (31), Boskovski (50)

BELGIUM v SPAIN 1-4 (1-1)

Brussel 17.12.1994

Referee: Ahmet Çakar (TUR) Attendance: 21,000

BELGIUM: Michel Preud'homme; Régis Genaux, Philippe Albert, Bertrand Crasson, Rudy Smidts, Danny Boffin, Franky Van der Elst, Alain Bettagno (46 Gert Verheyen), Marc Degryse, Lorenzo Staelens, Gilles De Bilde. Trainer: Paul van Himst

SPAIN: Andoni ZUBIZARRETA; Alberto BELSUÉ, ABELARDO Fernández, Rafael ALKORTA, Miguel Angel NADAL, Fernando Ruiz HIERRO, LUIS ENRIQUE Martínez, Julen GUERRERO (57 Salvador González "VORO"), Julio SALINAS (70 Juan Antonio GOIKOETXEA), DONATO Gama da Silva, SERGI Barjuán. Trainer: Javier Clemente

Goals: Degryse (7), Hierro (29), Donato (57 pen), Salinas (69), Luis Enrique (90)

CYPRUS v ARMENIA 2-0 (1-0)

Tsirion, Limassol 16.11.1994

Referee: Gerald Ashby (ENG) Attendance: 8,000

CYPRUS: Michalis Christophi; Andreas Andreou, Haralambos Pittas, Dimitris Ioannou, Evagoras Christophi, Andonis Zembashis (88 George Elia), George Savvides, Louis Stephani, Sinisa Gogic, Andros Sotiriou, Costas Malekos (68 Costas Phasouliotis). Trainer: Andreas Michaelides

ARMENIA: Harutyun Abramyan; Yervand Sukiasyan, Yervand Krbachyan, Aramais Tonoyan, Sarkys Oganesyan, Harutyun Vardanyan, Artur Petrosyan, Razmik Grigoryan, Hamlet Mkhitaryan (83 Varazdat Avetisyan), Sarkis Hovsepyan, Tigran Gspeyan (68 Arsen Avetisyan). Trainer: Eduard Markarov

Goals: Sotiriou (7), Phasouliotis (88)

MACEDONIA v CYPRUS 3-0 (2-0)

Gradski, Skopje 17.12.1994

Referee: Hartmut Strampe (GER) Attendance: 16,000

MACEDONIA: Danco Celeski; Vujadin Stanojkovic, Mitko Stojkovski, Ljupco Markovski, Ilija Najdoski, Cedomir Janevski, Boban Babunski (70 Zoran Jovanovski), Bosko Djurovski, Zoran Boskovski (85 Zarko Serafimovski), Milko Djurovski, Toni Micevski. Trainer: Andon Doncevski

CYPRUS: Michalis Christophi; Yiannos Kalotheou, Marios Charalambous, Dimitris Ioannou, Evagoras Christophi, Louis Stephani, Charis Charalambous, Costas Phasouliotis, Sinisa Gogic, Andros Sotiriou (79 Pambos Andreou), George Savvides (65 Costas Malekos). Trainer: Andreas Michaelides

Goals: B. Djurovski (14, 25, 90)

CYPRUS v DENMARK 1-1 (1-1)

Tsirion, Limassol 29.03.1995

Referee: Brendan Shorte (IRE) Attendance: 15,000

CYPRUS: Nicos Panayiotou; Costas Costa, Haralambos Pittas, Dimitris Ioannou, Marios Charalambous, George Christodoulou, Yotis Engomitis, Andreas Andreou, Sinisa Gogic, Lucas Hadjilucas (87 Costas Constandinou), Marios Agathocleous. Trainer: Andreas Michaelides

DENMARK: Peter Schmeichel; Jacob Laursen, Marc Rieper, Jakob Friis-Hansen (46 Thomas Helveg), Michael Schjønberg, Jes Høgh, Brian Steen Nielsen, Peter Nielsen, Peter Rasmussen, Michael Laudrup, Brian Laudrup.
Trainer: Richard Møller-Nielsen

Goals: Schjønberg (3), Agathocleous (45)

DENMARK v MACEDONIA 1-0 (0-0)

Idraetsparken, København 26.04.1995

Referee: Karol Ihring (SVK) Attendance: 38,800

DENMARK: Peter Schmeichel; Jacob Laursen, Marc Rieper, Jes Høgh, Michael Schjønberg, Claus Thomsen, Brian Steen Nielsen, Peter Nielsen (79 Thomas Helveg), Peter Rasmussen (46 Erik Bo Andersen), Michael Laudrup, Brian Laudrup.
Trainer: Richard Møller-Nielsen

MACEDONIA: Danco Celeski; Vujadin Stanojkovic, Mitko Stojkovski, Ljupco Markovski (26 Nedzmedin Memed), Ilija Najdoski, Zoran Jovanovski, Zoran Boskovski, Bosko Djurovski, Darko Pancev, Zarko Serafimovski (77 Marjan Stojkovski), Toni Micevski. Trainer: Andon Doncevski

Goal: P. Nielsen (71)

SPAIN v BELGIUM 1-1 (1-1)

Sevilla 29.03.1995

Referee: Rémy Harrel (FRA) Attendance: 27,000

SPAIN: Andoni ZUBIZARRETA; Alberto BELSUÉ, SERGI Barjuán, ABELARDO Fernández, Miguel Angel NADAL, Fernando Ruiz HIERRO, LUIS ENRIQUE Martínez, Julen GUERRERO (37 Francisco HIGUERA), Julio SALINAS (63 Juan Antonio PIZZI), DONATO Gama da Silva, José Emilio AMAVISCA. Trainer: Javier Clemente

BELGIUM: Gilbert Bodart; Régis Genaux, Dirk Medved, Pascal Renier, Rudy Smidts, Johan Walem (70 Gert Verheyen), Emmanuel Karagiannis (83 Bertrand Crasson), Lorenzo Staelens, Marc Degryse, Gilles De Bilde, Günther Schepens.
Trainer: Paul van Himst

Goals: Guerrero (25), Degryse (26)

ARMENIA v SPAIN 0-2 (0-0)

Razdan, Erevan 26.04.1995

Referee: Adrian Porumboiu (ROM) Attendance: 40,000

ARMENIA: Harutyun Abramyan; Yervand Sukiasyan, Sarkis Hovsepyan, Aramais Tonoyan, Sarkys Oganesyan, Artur Petrosyan, Harutyun Vardanyan, Razmik Grigoryan (64 Hovanes Tahmazyan), Hamlet Mkhitaryan, Armen Shahgeldyan, Artak Adamyan (46 Arsen Avetisyan).
Trainer: Samvel Darbinyan

SPAIN: Andoni ZUBIZARRETA; Alberto BELSUÉ, Jorge OTERO, Rafael ALKORTA, Aitor CARANCA, Miguel Angel NADAL, Juan Antonio GOIKOETXEA, LUIS ENRIQUE Martínez, Juan Antonio PIZZI (57 Julio SALINAS), DONATO Gama da Silva (67 Francisco José CAMARASA), José Emilio AMAVISCA. Trainer: Javier Clemente

Goals: Amavisca (48), Goikoetxea (62)

BELGIUM v CYPRUS 2-0 (1-0)

Brussel 26.04.1995

Referee: David Elleray (ENG) Attendance: 14,000

BELGIUM: Gilbert Bodart; Dirk Medved, Georges Grün, Pascal Renier, Rudy Smidts, Lorenzo Staelens, Emmanuel Karagiannis, Luc Nilis, Marc Degryse, Gilles De Bilde (80 Michael Goossens), Günther Schepens.
Trainer: Paul van Himst

CYPRUS: Nicos Panayiotou; Yiannos Kalotheou, Haralambos Pittas, Dimitris Ioannou, Marios Charalambous, George Christodoulou, Yotis Engomitis, Andreas Andreou, Sinisa Gogic, Nicos Papavassiliou (73 Andros Sotiriou), Marios Agathocleous (62 Neophytos Larkou).
Trainer: Andreas Michaelides

Goals: Karagiannis (20), Schepens (47)

ARMENIA v MACEDONIA 2-2 (1-0)

Razdan, Erevan 10.05.1995

Referee: Christer Faellström (SWE) Attendance: 12,500

ARMENIA: Harutyun Abramyan; Yervand Sukiasyan, Sarkis Hovsepyan, Aramais Tonoyan, Sarkys Oganesyan, Harutyun Vardanyan (79 Tigran Gsepyan), Artur Petrosyan, Razmik Grigoryan, Hamlet Mkhitaryan (69 Hovanes Tahmazyan), Armen Shahgeldyan, Arsen Avetisyan.
Trainer: Samvel Darbinyan

MACEDONIA: Danco Celeski; Vujadin Stanojkovic, Mitko Stojkovski, Ljupco Markovski, Ilija Najdoski, Cedomir Janevski (59 Nedzmedin Memed), Georgi Hristov, Boban Babunski, Darko Pancev, Zarko Serafimovski, Toni Micevski (69 Dragan Kanatlarovski). Trainer: Andon Doncevski

Goals: Grigoryan (22), Shahgeldyan (51), Hristov (59), Markovski (70)

MACEDONIA v BELGIUM 0-5 (0-4)

Gradski, Skopje 07.06.1995

Referee: Ryszard Wojcik (POL) Behind closed doors

MACEDONIA: Danco Celeski; Vujadin Stanojkovic, Mitko Stojkovski, Bosko Djurovski (61 Georgi Hristov), Ilija Najdoski, Cedomir Janevski, Zoran Boskovski, Boban Babunski, Darko Pancev, Zarko Serafimovski (35 Nedzmedin Memed), Toni Micevski. Trainer: Andon Doncevski

BELGIUM: Gilbert Bodart; Régis Genaux, Georges Grün, Pascal Renier, Rudy Smidts, Lorenzo Staelens, Emmanuel Karagiannis, Bruno Versavel, Gilles De Bilde, Vincenzo Scifo, Günther Schepens (83 Philippe Léonard). Trainer: Paul van Himst

Goals: Grün (15), Scifo (18, 60), Schepens (28), Versavel (43)

SPAIN v ARMENIA 1-0 (0-0)

Sevilla 07.06.1995

Referee: Roger Philippi (LUX) Attendance: 17,000

SPAIN: Andoni ZUBIZARRETA; Alberto BELSUÉ, Agustín ARANZÁBAL Alkorta, Rafael ALKORTA, ABELARDO Fernández, Fernando Ruiz HIERRO, Juan Antonio GOIKOETXEA (46 Julio SALINAS), Julen GUERRERO (77 José Luis Pérez CAMINERO), LUIS ENRIQUE Martínez, Miguel Angel NADAL, José Emilio AMAVISCA. Trainer: Javier Clemente

ARMENIA: Harutyun Abramyan; Yervand Sukiasyan, Sarkis Hovsepyan, Aramais Tonoyan, Ara Nigoyan (70 Hakop Ter-Petrosyan), Harutyun Vardanyan, Artur Petrosyan (76 Varazdat Avetisyan), Hovanes Tahmazyan, Hamlet Mkhitaryan, Armen Shahgeldyan, Arsen Avetisyan. Trainer: Samvel Darbinyan

Goal: Hierro (63 pen)

DENMARK v CYPRUS 4-0 (0-0)

Idraetsparken, København 07.06.1995

Referee: Werner Müller (SWI) Attendance: 40,199

DENMARK: Peter Schmeichel; Jacob Laursen, Marc Rieper, Jes Høgh, Michael Schjønberg, Brian Steen Nielsen (46 Peter Rasmussen), John Jensen, Kim Vilfort (89 Erik Bo Andersen), Mikkel Beck, Michael Laudrup, Brian Laudrup. Trainer: Richard Møller-Nielsen

CYPRUS: Andros Petrides; Costas Costa, Haralambos Pittas, George Christodoulou, Marios Charalambous, Andreas Andreou, Yotis Engomitis, Neophytos Larkou, Sinisa Gogic, Lucas Hadjilucas (58 Costas Phasoulitis), Andros Sotiriou (69 Pambos Andreou). Trainer: Andreas Michaelides

Goals: Vilfort (47, 52), B. Laudrup (59), M. Laudrup (75)

ARMENIA v DENMARK 0-2 (0-1)

Razdan, Erevan 16.08.1995

Referee: Georg Dardenne (GER) Attendance: 22,000

ARMENIA: Armenak Petrosyan; Sarkis Hovsepyan, Vardan Khachatryan, Ashot Khachatryan, Sarkis Hovhannisyan, Aramais Tonoyan, Artur Petrosyan, Razmik Grigoryan, Hovanes Tahmazyan (41 Hakop Ter-Petrosyan), Armen Shahgeldyan, Arsen Avetisyan (80 Varazdat Avetisyan). Trainer: Samvel Darbinyan

DENMARK: Peter Schmeichel; Jacob Laursen, Marc Rieper, Jes Høgh, Jens Risager (85 Michael Schjønberg), Claus Thomsen, John Jensen (46 Allan Nielsen), Brian Steen Nielsen, Mikkel Beck, Michael Laudrup, Peter Rasmussen. Trainer: Richard Møller-Nielsen

Goals: M.Laudrup (33), A. Nielsen (46)

BELGIUM v DENMARK 1-3 (1-2)

Brussel 06.09.1995

Referee: Vadim Zhuk (BLS) Attendance: 40,000

BELGIUM: Gilbert Bodart; Régis Genaux, Georges Grün, Dirk Medved, Rudy Smidts (77 Pascal Renier), Lorenzo Staelens (14 Luc Nilis), Emmanuel Karagiannis, Gilles De Bilde, Marc Degryse, Vincenzo Scifo, Günther Schepens (54 Ronald Fogueene). Trainer: Paul van Himst

DENMARK: Peter Schmeichel; Jacob Laursen, Marc Rieper, Jes Høgh, Jens Risager, Claus Thomsen, Brian Steen Nielsen, Kim Vilfort, Mikkel Beck (70 Peter Rasmussen), Michael Laudrup (90 Michael Schjønberg), Brian Laudrup (76 Erik Bo Andersen). Trainer: Richard Møller-Nielsen

Goals: M. Laudrup (20), Beck (22), Grün (25), Vilfort (66)

SPAIN v CYPRUS 6-0 (1-0)

Granada 06.09.1995

Referee: Dick Jol (HOL) Attendance: 16,000

SPAIN: Andoni ZUBIZARRETA; Alberto BELSUÉ, Agustín ARANZÁBAL Alkorta, Rafael ALKORTA, Miguel Angel NADAL, Fernando Ruiz HIERRO, LUIS ENRIQUE Martínez, Julen GUERRERO (77 Javier MANJARÍN), ALFONSO Pérez (61 Juan Antonio PIZZI), José Luis Pérez CAMINERO, José Emilio AMAVISCA (53 FRANcisco Javier González). Trainer: Javier Clemente

CYPRUS: Nicos Panayiotou; Sozos Andreou, Haralambos Pittas, George Christodoulou, George Panayi, Nicos Charalambous, Dimitris Ashiotis, Andonis Andoniou (80 Pambos Andreou), Sinisa Gogic, Costas Malekkos (57 Andros Sotiriou), Lucas Hadjilucas (68 Yiannos Ioannou). Trainer: Andreas Michaelides

Goals: Guerrero (45), Alfonso (60), Pizzi (74, 79), Hierro (78), Caminero (83)

MACEDONIA v ARMENIA 1-2 (1-0)

Gradski, Skopje 06.09.1995

Referee: Vitor Manuel Melo Pereira (POR) Att: 10,000

MACEDONIA: Danco Celeski; Saso Nikolovski, Mitko Stojkovski, Ljupco Markovski, Boban Babunski, Zoran Jovanovski, Zarko Serafimovski (46 Saso Karadzov), Nedzmedin Memed (65 Dragan Veselinoski), Georgi Hristov, Toni Savevski, Toni Micevski. Trainer: Andon Doncevski

ARMENIA: Armenak Petrosyan; Tigran Gsepyan, Vardan Khachatryan, Haroutyun Vardanyan, Sarkis Hovhannisyan, Levon Stepanyan (75 Hakop Ter-Petrosyan), Artur Petrosyan (84 Ashot Khachatryan), Razmik Grigoryan (68 Varazdat Avetisyan), Hamlet Mkhitaryan, Armen Shahgeldyan, Sarkis Hovsepyan. Trainer: Samvel Darbinyan

Goals: Micevski (10), Grigoryan (61), Shahgeldyan (78)

DENMARK v SPAIN 1-1 (0-1)

Idraetsparken, København 11.10.1995

Referee: Vaclav Krondl (CZE) Attendance: 40,260

DENMARK: Peter Schmeichel; Jacob Laursen, Marc Rieper, Jes Høgh, Jens Risager, Torben Piechnik, Brian Steen Nielsen (67 Morten Wieghorst), Kim Vilfort, Mikkel Beck, Michael Laudrup, Peter Rasmussen. Trainer: Richard Møller-Nielsen

SPAIN: Andoni ZUBIZARRETA; Alberto BELSUÉ, SERGI Barjuán, Rafael ALKORTA, ABELARDO Fernández, Fernando Ruiz HIERRO, Javier MANJARÍN (61 DONATO Gama da Silva), Miguel Angel NADAL, Juan Antonio PIZZI (46 ALFONSO Pérez), José Luis Pérez CAMINERO (29 FRANcisco Javier González), LUIS ENRIQUE Martínez. Trainer: Javier Clemente

Goals: Hierro (17 pen), Vilfort (47)

ARMENIA v BELGIUM 0-2 (0-2)

Razdan, Erevan 07.10.1995

Referee: Mitko Mitrev (BUL) Attendance: 5,000

ARMENIA: Harutyun Abramyan; Yervand Soukiasyan, Vardan Khachatryan, Ashot Khachatryan, Sarkis Hovsepyan, Tigran Gsepyan, Artur Petrosyan, Razmik Grigoryan (46 Varazdat Avetisyan), Hamlet Mkhitaryan (71 Hayk Margaryan), Armen Shahgeldyan, Arsen Avetisyan.

BELGIUM: Filip De Wilde; Régis Genaux, Bertrand Crasson, Glen De Boeck, Rudy Smidts, Lorenzo Staelens, Emmanuel Karagiannis (81 Sven Vermant), Günther Schepens, Luc Nilis, Vincenzo Scifo, Gilles De Bilde (63 Michael Goossens). Trainer: Paul van Himst

Goals: Nilis (28, 38)

CYPRUS v BELGIUM 1-1 (1-0)

Tsirion, Limassol 15.11.1995

Referee: Graziano Cesari (ITA) Attendance: 8,000

CYPRUS: Nicos Panayiotou; Costas Costa, Haralambos Pittas, George Christodoulou, Marios Charalambous, Andreas Andreou, Yotis Engomitis, Sinisa Gogic (80 George Elia), Costas Malekkos (50 Neophytos Larkou), Nicos Papavassiliou, Marios Agathocleous (75 Andonis Zembashis). Trainer: Andreas Michaelides

BELGIUM: Filip De Wilde; Régis Genaux, Georges Grün, Glen De Boeck, Rudy Smidts (80 Günther Schepens), Lorenzo Staelens, Emmanuel Karagiannis (46 Michael Goosens), Danny Boffin (60 Dirk Huysmans), Marc Degryse, Luc Nilis, Gilles De Bilde. Trainer: Paul van Himst

Goals: Agathocleous (15), De Bilde (68)

CYPRUS v MACEDONIA 1-1 (0-1)

Tsirion, Limassol 11.10.1995

Referee: Irvine (NIR) Attendance: 12,000

CYPRUS: Andros Petrides; Costas Costa, Haralambos Pittas, George Christodoulou, Marios Charalambous, Yiannos Kalotheou (63 Marios Agathocleous), Yotis Engomitis (46 Nicos Papavassiliou), Andros Sotiriou (80 Neophytos Larkou), Sinisa Gogic, Costas Malekkos, George Savvides. Trainer: Andreas Michaelides

MACEDONIA: Danco Celeski; Zoran Jovanovski, Saso Karadzov, Ljupco Markovski, Saso Nikolovski, Borce Jovanovski, Dragan Veselinoski (84 Georgi Hristov), Toni Savevski, Nedzmedin Memed, Sasa Ciric, Zarko Serafimovski (77 Rade Karanfilovski). Trainer: Andon Doncevski

Goals: Jovanovski (31), Agathocleous (90)

DENMARK v ARMENIA 3-1 (2-0)

Idraetsparken, København 15.11.1995

Referee: Gilles Veissière (FRA) Attendance: 40,208

DENMARK: Peter Schmeichel; Thomas Helveg, Marc Rieper, Jes Høgh, Jens Risager, Michael Schjønberg, Brian Steen Nielsen, Kim Vilfort, Mikkel Beck, Michael Laudrup, Peter Rasmussen. Trainer: Richard Møller-Nielsen

ARMENIA: Harutyun Abramyan; Hakob Artoyan, Vardan Khachatryan, Sarkis Hovsepyan, Harutyun Vardanyan, Tigran Gsepyan (74 Yervand Krbachyan), Artur Petrosyan, Varazdat Avetisyan (70 Hayk Margaryan), Hamlet Mkhitaryan, Samvel Nikolyan, Arsen Avetisyan.

Goals: Schjønberg (20), Beck (36), Art. Petrosyan (47), M. Laudrup (58)

SPAIN v MACEDONIA 3-0 (1-0)

Elche 15.11.1995

Referee: Edgar Steinborn (GER) Attendance: 21,350

SPAIN: Andoni ZUBIZARRETA; Alberto BELSUÉ, SERGI Barjuán, Rafael ALKORTA, Miguel Angel NADAL, DONATO Gama da Silva, Javier MANJARÍN, Francisco Narváez KIKO (74 Juan Antonio GOIKOETXEA), Juan Antonio PIZZI (46 ALFONSO Pérez), José Emilio AMAVISCA (46 Albert FERRER), LUIS ENRIQUE Martínez.
Trainer: Javier Clemente

MACEDONIA: Danco Celeski; Zoran Jovanovski, Mitko Stojkovski, Zarko Serafimovski (52 Dragan Veselinoski, 78 Georgi Hristov), Boban Babunski, Jovanovski (72 Saso Nikolovski), Saso Karadzov, Nedzmedin Memed, Zoran Boskovski, Sasa Ciric, Toni Micevski.
Trainer: Andon Doncevski

Goals: Kiko (17), Manjarín (72), Amavisca (79)

	P	W	D	L	F	A	Pts
Spain	10	8	2	0	25	4	26
Denmark	10	6	3	1	19	9	21
Belgium	10	4	3	3	17	13	15
Macedonia	10	1	4	5	9	18	7
Cyprus	10	1	4	5	6	20	7
Armenia	10	1	2	7	5	17	5

GROUP 3

HUNGARY v TURKEY 2-2 (2-0)

Népstadion, Budapest 07.09.1994

Referee: Pierluigi Pairetto (ITA) Attendance: 20,000

HUNGARY: Zsolt Petry; Géza Mészöly, András Telek, József Duró (62 János Bánfi), István Kozma, Péter Lipcsei, József Kiprich (67 László Wukovics), Flórián Urban, Gábor Halmai, Lajos Détári, Kálmán Kovács. Trainer: Kálmán Mészöly

TURKEY: Engin Ipekoglu; Recep Çetin, B. Bülent Korkmaz, Gökhan Keskin (46 Arif Erdem), Ogün Temizkanoglu, Tugay Kerimoglu, Ilker Yagcioglu, Ertugrul Saglam (87 Abdullah Ercan), Hakan Sükür, Oguz Çetin, Orhan Çikrikçi.
Trainer: Fatih Terim

Goals: Kiprich (4), Halmai (45), Hakan (66), B. Bülent (70)

ICELAND v SWEDEN 0-1 (0-1)

Laugardalsvöllur, Reykjavík 07.09.1994

Referee: Leslie Mottram (SCO) Attendance: 12,000

ICELAND: Birkir Kristinsson; Sigursteinn Gíslason, Kristján Jónsson, Sigurdur Jónsson, Hlynur Stefánsson, Rúnar Kristinsson, Gudni Bergsson, Thorvaldur Örlygsson (60 Bjarki Gunnlaugsson), Arnar Gunnlaugsson, Arnór Gudjohnsen, Eyjólfur Sverrisson. Trainer: Asgeir Elíasson

SWEDEN: Thomas Ravelli; Roland Nilsson, Patrik Andersson, Joachim Björklund, Roger Ljung, Stefan Schwarz, Håkan Mild, Klas Ingesson, Kennet Andersson, Martin Dahlin (69 Henrik Larsson), Tomas Brolin.
Trainer: Tommy Svensson

Goal: Ingesson (37)

SWITZERLAND v SWEDEN 4-2 (1-1)

Wankdorf, Bern 12.10.1994

Referee: David Elleray (ENG) Attendance: 24,000

SWITZERLAND: Marco Pascolo; Marc Hottiger, Pascal Thüler, Dominique Herr, Alain Geiger, Murat Yakin (83 Stéphane Henchoz), Alain Sutter, Christophe Ohrel, Marco Grassi (67 Kubilay Türkilmaz), Ciriaco Sforza, Stéphane Chapuisat. Trainer: Roy Hodgson

SWEDEN: Thomas Ravelli; Roland Nilsson, Patrik Andersson, Joachim Björklund, Pontus Kåmark, Stefan Schwarz, Jesper Blomqvist (82 Henrik Larsson), Kennet Andersson, Jonas Thern (49 Håkan Mild), Martin Dahlin, Tomas Brolin. Trainer: Tommy Svensson

Goals: K.Andersson (5), Ohrel (37), Dahlin (61), Blomqvist (63 og), Sforza (80), Türkyilmaz (82)

TURKEY v ICELAND 5-0 (3-0)

Istanbul 12.10.1994

Referee: Nikolai Levnikov (RUS) Attendance: 20,000

TURKEY: Engin Ipekoglu (87 Rüstü Reçber); Recep Çetin, B.Bülent Korkmaz, Gökhan Keskin, Ogün Temizkanoglu, Abdullah Ercan, Arif Erdem, B.Saffet Sancakli, Hakan Sükür (61 Sergen Yalçin), Oguz Çetin, Orhan Çikrikçi (9 Mutlu Topçu). Trainer: Fatih Terim

ICELAND: Birkir Kristinsson (32 Kristján Finnbogasson); Sigursteinn Gíslason, Kristján Jónsson, Sigurdur Jónsson, Hlynur Stefánsson (85 Bjarki Gunnlaugsson), Rúnar Kristinsson, Gudni Bergsson, Thorvaldur Örlygsson, Arnar Gunnlaugsson (72 Arnar Grétarsson), Arnór Gudjohnsen, Eyjólfur Sverrisson. Trainer: Asgeir Elíasson

Goals: B. Saffet (12, 29), Hakan (30, 60), Sergen (64)

SWEDEN v HUNGARY 2-0 (1-0)

Råsunda, Solna 16.11.1994

Referee: Mario Van der Ende (HOL) Attendance: 27,571

SWEDEN: Thomas Ravelli; Roland Nilsson, Patrik Andersson, Joachim Björklund, Pontus Kåmark, Stefan Schwarz, Henrik Larsson, Kennet Andersson, Jonas Thern, Martin Dahlin, Tomas Brolin (73 Stefan Rehn). Trainer: Tommy Svensson

HUNGARY: Zsolt Petry; János Bánfi, Géza Mészöly, József Duró (76 Kálmán Kovács), István Kozma, Péter Lipcsei (59 Gábor Halmai), Lajos Détári, Flórián Urban, Emil Lörincz, József Kiprich, László Klausz. Trainer: Kálmán Mészöly

Goals: Brolin (43), Dahlin (70)

HUNGARY v SWITZERLAND 2-2 (0-0)

Népstadion, Budapest 29.03.1995

Referee: Alfred Wieser (AUS) Attendance: 15,000

HUNGARY: Zsolt Petry; Mihály Mracskó, Emil Lörincz, Géza Mészöly, István Kozma, Ervin Kovács, József Kiprich (71 Gábor Márton), Gábor Halmai, István Sallói, Béla Illés, István Vincze (78 László Klausz). Trainer: Kálmán Mészöly

SWITZERLAND: Marco Pascolo; Marc Hottiger, Walter Fernandez, Dominique Herr, Alain Geiger, Marcel Koller, Alain Sutter, Christophe Ohrel, Nestor Subiat (89 Stéphane Henchoz), Ciriaco Sforza, Thomas Bickel (64 Marco Grassi). Trainer: Roy Hodgson

Goals: Kiprich (50), Illés (72), Subiat (73, 85)

SWITZERLAND v ICELAND 1-0 (1-0)

Stade Olympique de la Pontaise, Lausanne 16.11.1994

Referee: Patrick Kelly (IRE) Attendance: 15,800

SWITZERLAND: Marco Pascolo; Marc Hottiger, Pascal Thüler, Stéphane Henchoz, Alain Geiger, Thomas Bickel, Alain Sutter, Christophe Ohrel, Marco Grassi (66 Kubilay Türkilmaz), Ciriaco Sforza, Stéphane Chapuisat. Trainer: Roy Hodgson

ICELAND: Birkir Kristinsson; Sigursteinn Gíslason (84 Haraldur Ingólfsson), Kristján Jónsson, Arnar Grétarsson (64 Bjarki Gunnlaugsson), Izudin Dadi Dervic, Rúnar Kristinsson, Gudni Bergsson, Thorvaldur Örlygsson, Arnar Gunnlaugsson, Hlynur Stefánsson, Eyjólfur Sverrisson. Trainer: Asgeir Elíasson

Goal: Bickel (45)

TURKEY v SWEDEN 2-1 (0-1)

Istanbul 29.03.1995

Referee: Alfredo Trentalange (ITA) Attendance: 25,000

TURKEY: Engin Ipekoglu; Recep Çetin, B. Bülent Korkmaz, Emre Asik, Alpay Özalan, Abdullah Ercan, Metin Tekin, Tolunay Kafkas, Hakan Sükür, Sergen Yalçin (77 Mutlu Topçu), Ertugrul Saglam (46 Oguz Çetin). Trainer: Fatih Terim

SWEDEN: Thomas Ravelli; Roland Nilsson, Patrik Andersson, Joachim Björklund, Roger Ljung, Stefan Schwarz, Henrik Larsson (78 Jesper Blomqvist), Pär Zetterberg (80 Stefan Rehn), Jonas Thern, Martin Dahlin, Kennet Andersson. Trainer: Tommy Svensson

Goals: K. Andersson (23 pen), Emre (65), Sergen (75)

TURKEY v SWITZERLAND 1-2 (1-2)

Istanbul 14.12.1994

Referee: Ion Crăciunescu (ROM) Attendance: 30,000

TURKEY: Rüstü Reçber; Recep Çetin, B. Bülent Korkmaz, Gökhan Keskin, Ogün Temizkanoglu, Abdullah Ercan, Cengiz Atilla (46 Ilker Yagcioglu), B. Saffet Sancakli, Hakan Sükür, Oguz Çetin, Arif Erdem (76 Sergen Yalçin). Trainer: Fatih Terim

SWITZERLAND: Marco Pascolo; Marc Hottiger, Pascal Thüler, Dominique Herr, Alain Geiger, Marcel Koller, Alain Sutter, Christophe Ohrel, Nestor Subiat (77 Marco Grassi), Ciriaco Sforza, Thomas Bickel (65 Christophe Bonvin). Trainer: Roy Hodgson

Goals: Koller (7), Bickel (15), Recep (40)

HUNGARY v SWEDEN 1-0 (1-0)

Népstadion, Budapest 26.04.1995

Referee: Antonio Jesus López Nieto (SPA) Att: 8,000

HUNGARY: Zoltán Végh; Mihály Mracskó, József Csábi, Géza Mészöly, István Kozma, Péter Lipcsei, Aurél Csertöi (88 Zoltán Szlezak), Gábor Halmai, István Sallói, Béla Illés, István Vincze (69 Flórián Urban). Trainer: Kálmán Mészöly

SWEDEN: Thomas Ravelli; Roland Nilsson, Patrik Andersson, Pontus Kåmark, Roger Ljung, Stefan Schwarz, Niclas Alexandersson (81 Niklas Gudmundsson), Klas Ingesson, Håkan Mild (61 Robert Andersson), Pär Zetterberg, Kennet Andersson. Trainer: Tommy Svensson

Goal: Halmai (2)

SWITZERLAND v TURKEY 1-2 (1-1)

Wankdorf, Bern 26.04.1995

Referee: Frans Van den Wijngaert (BEL) Att: 24,000

SWITZERLAND: Marco Pascolo; Marc Hottiger, Walter Fernandez (75 Marco Walker), Dominique Herr, Alain Geiger, Thomas Bickel, Alain Sutter, Christophe Ohrel, Marco Grassi, Ciriaco Sforza, Christophe Bonvin. Trainer: Roy Hodgson

TURKEY: Engin Ipekoglu; Recep Çetin, B.Bülent Korkmaz, Emre Asik, Alpay Özalan, Abdullah Ercan, Tolunay Kafkas, Ogün Temizkanoglu, Hakan Sükür, Oguz Çetin (82 Ertugrul Saglam), Sergen Yalçin (80 Suat Kaya). Trainer: Fatih Terim

Goals: Hakan (17), Hottiger (38), Ogün (55)

ICELAND v SWITZERLAND 0-2 (0-2)

Laugardalsvöllur, Reykjavík 16.08.1995

Referee: Ryszard Wojcik (POL) Attendance: 9,034

ICELAND: Birkir Kristinsson; Ólafur Adolfsson, Kristján Jónsson (88 Izudin Dadi Dervic), Sigurdur Jónsson, Bjarki Gunnlaugsson, Rúnar Kristinsson, Gudni Bergsson, Thorvaldur Örlygsson, Arnar Gunnlaugsson, Ólafur Thórdarson, Eyjólfur Sverrisson (67 Haraldur Ingólfsson). Trainer: Asgeir Elíasson

SWITZERLAND: Marco Pascolo; Marc Hottiger, Yvan Quentin, Stéphane Henchoz, Alain Geiger, Sébastian Fournier, Alain Sutter (79 Thomas Bickel), Christophe Ohrel, Adrian Knup, Ciriaco Sforza, Kubilay Türkyilmaz (85 Christophe Bonvin). Trainer: Roy Hodgson

Goals: Knup (4), Türkyilmaz (18)

SWEDEN v ICELAND 1-1 (1-1)

Råsunda, Solna 01.06.1995

Referee: Atanas Uzunov (BUL) Attendance: 26,676

SWEDEN: Thomas Ravelli; Gary Sundgren, Patrik Andersson, Jesper Mattsson, Pontus Kåmark, Stefan Schwarz, Anders Limpar (47 Henrik Larsson), Kennet Andersson, Jonas Thern, Martin Dahlin, Tomas Brolin.
Trainer: Tommy Svensson

ICELAND: Birkir Kristinsson; Ólafur Adolfsson, Kristján Jónsson, Sigurdur Jónsson, Hlynur Stefánsson, Rúnar Kristinsson, Gudni Bergsson, Thorvaldur Örlygsson, Arnar Gunnlaugsson (78 Bjarki Gunnlaugsson), Arnór Gudjohnsen (87 Ólafur Thórdarson), Eyjólfur Sverrisson.
Trainer: Asgeir Elíasson

Goals: A. Gunnlaugsson (3), Brolin (16 pen)

SWEDEN v SWITZERLAND 0-0

Gamla Ullevi, Göteborg 06.09.1995

Referee: Paolo Ceccarini (ITA) Attendance: 18,500

SWEDEN: Bengt Andersson; Pontus Kåmark, Patrik Andersson, Joachim Björklund, Mikael Nilsson, Stefan Schwarz (90 Magnus Erlingmark), Niclas Alexandersson, Kennet Andersson, Jonas Thern, Martin Dahlin, Tomas Brolin (78 Henrik Larsson). Trainer: Tommy Svensson

SWITZERLAND: Marco Pascolo; Marc Hottiger, Yvan Quentin, Stéphane Henchoz, Alain Geiger, Sébastian Fournier, Alain Sutter (46 Dominique Herr), Christophe Ohrel, Adrian Knup, Ciriaco Sforza, Kubilay Türkyilmaz (90 Marco Grassi). Trainer: Roy Hodgson

ICELAND v HUNGARY 2-1 (0-1)

Laugardalsvöllur, Reykjavik 11.06.1995

Referee: Alain Sars (FRA) Attendance: 3,573

ICELAND: Birkir Kristinsson; Ólafur Adolfsson, Kristján Jónsson, Sigurdur Jónsson, Arnar Grétarsson, Rúnar Kristinsson, Gudni Bergsson, Ólafur Thórdarson (67 Bjarki Gunnlaugsson), Arnar Gunnlaugsson, Arnór Gudjohnsen, Eyjólfur Sverrisson. Trainer: Asgeir Elíasson

HUNGARY: Zsolt Petry; Mihály Mracskó, József Csábi, Géza Mészöly, István Kozma, Péter Lipcsei, Aurél Csertöi, Gábor Halmai, István Sallói, Béla Illés (68 Gábor Márton), István Vincze (69 István Hamar). Trainer: Kálmán Mészöly

Goals: Vincze (20), Bergsson (61), S. Jónsson (67)

TURKEY v HUNGARY 2-0 (2-0)

Inönü, Istanbul 06.09.1995

Referee: Vaclav Krondl (CZE) Attendance: 30,000

TURKEY: Rüstü Reçber; Recep Çetin, Ogün Temizkanoglu, Osman Özköylü, Tugay Kerimoglu, Alpay Özalan, Abdullah Ercan, Sergen Yalçin (46 Tolunay Kafkas), Hakan Sükür (89 Bülent Uygun), Oguz Çetin, Hami Mandirali (86 Bülent Korkmaz). Trainer: Fatih Terim

HUNGARY: Zsolt Petry; Norbert Nagy (46 István Sallói), András Telek, Géza Mészöly, István Kozma, Péter Lipcsei, József Kiprich, Gábor Halmai, László Arany, Béla Illés (46 László Klausz), László Farkasházy. Trainer: Kálmán Mészöly

Goals: Hakan (9, 32)

ICELAND v TURKEY 0-0

Laugardalsvöllur, Reykjavík 11.10.1995

Referee: Hartmut Strampe (GER) Attendance: 2,308

ICELAND: Birkir Kristinsson; Sigursteinn Gíslason, Haraldur Ingólfsson (71 Hlynur Stefánsson), Kristján Jónsson (43 Arnar Grétarsson), Ólafur Adolfsson, Rúnar Kristinsson, Gudni Bergsson, Thorvaldur Örlygsson, Arnar Gunnlaugsson, Arnór Gudjohnsen, Eyjólfur Sverrisson (80 Bjarki Gunnlaugsson). Trainer: Asgeir Elíasson

TURKEY: Rüstü Reçber; Recep Çetin, Ogün Temizkanoglu, Osman Özköylü, Tugay Kerimoglu, Alpay Özalan, Hami Mandirali, Abdullah Ercan, Ertugrul Saglam, Oguz Çetin, Sergen Yalçin (74 Tolunay Kafkas). Trainer: Fatih Terim

SWEDEN v TURKEY 2-2 (1-0)

Råsunda, Solna 15.11.1995

Referee: Ryszard Wojcik (POL) Attendance: 16,350

SWEDEN: Thomas Ravelli; Teddy Lucic, Patrik Andersson, Joachim Björklund, Niclas Alexandersson, Stefan Schwarz, Håkan Mild, Christer Fursth, Jörgen Pettersson (83 Dan Sahlin), Martin Dahlin, Tomas Brolin (70 Pär Zetterberg). Trainer: Tommy Svensson

TURKEY: Rüstü Reçber; Alpay Özalan, Ogün Temizkanoglu, Osman Özköylü, Tugay Kerimoglu, Halil Ibrahim Kara (46 Kemalettin Sentürk), Tolunay Kafkas, Tayfun Korkut, Hakan Sükür, Oguz Çetin (68 Ertugrul Saglam), Oktay Derelioglu (46 Arif Erdem). Trainer: Fatih Terim

Goals: Alexandersson (25), Hakan (63), Pettersson (64), P. Andersson (72 og)

SWITZERLAND v HUNGARY 3-0 (1-0)

Hardturm, Zürich 11.10.1995

Referee: Charles Agius (MAL) Attendance: 20,000

SWITZERLAND: Marco Pascolo; Marc Hottiger, Yvan Quentin, Stéphane Henchoz, Alain Geiger, Sébastian Fournier (81 Thomas Bickel), Murat Yakin, Christophe Ohrel, Adrian Knup (89 Christophe Bonvin), Ciriaco Sforza, Kubilay Türkyilmaz (85 Alain Sutter). Trainer: Roy Hodgson

HUNGARY: Attila Hajdu; Mihály Mracskó, András Telek, Tibor Simon (24 Zoltán Jagodics), Flórián Urban, Péter Lipcsei, Gábor Halmai, Elek Nyilas (64 Tamás Mónos), Robert Jován, Béla Illés (64 László Arany), István Vincze. Trainer: Kálmán Mészöly

Goals: Türkyilmaz (23), Sforza (56), Ohrel (89)

	P	W	D	L	F	A	Pts
Switzerland	8	5	2	1	15	7	17
Turkey	8	4	3	1	16	8	15
Sweden	8	2	3	3	9	10	9
Hungary	8	2	2	4	7	13	8
Iceland	8	1	2	5	3	12	4

HUNGARY v ICELAND 1-0 (1-0)

Népstadion, Budapest 11.11.1995

Referee: Georgios Bikas (GRE) Attendance: 5,000

HUNGARY: Attila Hajdu; Tamás Mónos, József Csábi, Zoltán Szlezák, Béla Illés (89 Zalán Zombori), János Bánfi, Zoltán Bükszegi, Elek Nyilas, Ferenc Orosz (75 László Farkasházy), József Duró, István Vincze (88 Tamás Nagy). Trainer: Kálmán Mészöly

ICELAND: Birkir Kristinsson; Sigursteinn Gíslason, Kristján Jónsson, Arnar Grétarsson (79 Hlynur Stefánsson), Ólafur Adolfsson, Rúnar Kristinsson (83 Einar Thór Daníelsson), Gudni Bergsson, Thorvaldur Örlygsson, Arnar Gunnlaugsson, Arnór Gudjohnsen, Eyjólfur Sverrisson. Trainer: Asgeir Elíasson

Goal: Illés (11 pen)

GROUP 4

ESTONIA v CROATIA 0-2 (0-1)

Kadriorg, Tallinn 04.09.1994

Referee: Vaclav Krondl (CZE) Attendance: 1,250

ESTONIA: Mart Poom; Marek Lemsalu, Igor Prins, Urmas Kaljend, Toomas Kallaste, Viktor Alonen, Indro Olumets (46 Martin Reim), Dzintar Klavan, Marko Kristal, Urmas Kirs (75 Toomas Kröm), Tarmo Linnumäe. Trainer: Roman Ubakivi

CROATIA: Drazen Ladic; Dzevad Turkovic, Robert Jarni, Igor Stimac, Nikola Jerkan, Slaven Bilic, Aljosa Asanovic (88 Igor Cvitanovic), Robert Prosinecki, Davor Suker, Zvonimir Boban, Alen Boksic. Trainer: Miroslav Blazevic

Goals: Suker (45, 69)

SLOVENIA v ITALY 1-1 (1-1)

Ljudski vrt, Maribor 07.09.1994

Referee: Bernd Heynemann (GER) Attendance: 18,000

SLOVENIA: Marko Simeunovic; Marinko Galic, Darko Milanic, Robert Englaro, Alfred Jermanis, Srecko Katanec (58 Peter Binkovski), Dzoni Novak, Gregor Zidan (89 Ales Krizan), Ales Ceh, Saso Udovic, Primoz Gliha.
Trainer: Zdenko Verdenik

ITALY: Gianluca Pagliuca; Roberto Mussi, Christian Panucci, Demetrio Albertini, Alessandro Costacurta, Franco Baresi, Roberto Donadoni, Dino Baggio (55 Alberigo Evani), Pierluigi Casiraghi, Gianfranco Zola (55 Nicola Berti), Giuseppe Signori. Trainer: Arrigo Sacchi

Goals: Udovic (14), Costacurta (15)

CROATIA v LITHUANIA 2-0 (0-0)

Maksimir, Zagreb 09.10.1994

Referee: Alfred Wieser (AUS) Attendance: 12,000

CROATIA: Drazen Ladic; Nikola Jurcevic, Robert Jarni, Igor Stimac (89 Elvis Brajkovic), Nikola Jerkan, Slaven Bilic, Mladen Mladenovic, Aljosa Asanovic, Davor Suker, Zvonimir Boban, Alen Boksic (78 Ardijan Kozniku).
Trainer: Miroslav Blazevic

LITHUANIA: Gintaras Stauce; Tomas Ziukas, Andrius Tereskinas, Romas Mazeikis, Raimondas Vainoras, Viaceslavas Sukristovas, Nerijus Gudaitis, Audrius Zuta (75 Eimantas Poderis), Irmantas Stumbrys, Rolandas Vaineikis (58 Arunas Suika), Aurelijus Skarbalius. Trainer: Algimantas Liubinskas

Goals: Jerkan (56), Kozniku (81)

UKRAINE v LITHUANIA 0-2 (0-0)

Republican, Kyiv 07.09.1994

Referee: Bo Karlsson (SWE) Attendance: 25,000

UKRAINE: Dmytro Tyapushkin; Viktor Skrypnyk, Yuriy Sak (8 Sergiy Kovalets), Alexander Yevtushok, Sergiy Popov, Igor Petrov, Yevgeniy Pokhlebayev (59 Sergiy Nagornyak), Yuriy Maximov, Borys Finkel, Oleg Protasov, Sergiy Konovalov.
Trainer: Oleg Bazylevych

LITHUANIA: Gintaras Stauce; Tomas Ziukas, Viaceslavas Sukristovas, Andrius Tereskinas, Raimondas Vainoras, Rolandas Vaineikis (80 Ramunas Stonkus), Nerijus Gudaitis, Valdas Ivanauskas, Irmantas Stumbrys, Arunas Suika (55 Audrius Zuta), Aurelijus Skarbalius.
Trainer: Algimantas Liubinskas

Goals: Ivanauskas (53), Skarbalius (61)

UKRAINE v SLOVENIA 0-0

Republican, Kyiv 12.10.1994

Referee: Atanas Uzunov (BUL) Attendance: 12,000

UKRAINE: Dmytro Tyapushkin; Oleg Luzhnyi, Sergiy Diryavka, Oleg Kuznetsov, Sergiy Shmatovalenko, Sergiy Kovalets, Sergiy Lezhentsev, Alexei Mykhailychenko (75 Igor Petrov), Dmytro Mykhailenko, Viktor Leonenko, Sergiy Konovalov (65 Timerlan Guseinov). Trainer: Jozsef Szabo

SLOVENIA: Bosko Boskovic; Marinko Galic, Ales Krizan, Darko Milanic, Alfred Jermanis, Ales Ceh, Dzoni Novak (77 Vladimir Kokol), Gregor Zidan, Igor Benedejcic, Saso Udovic (63 Primoz Gliha), Matjaz Florjancic.
Trainer: Zdenko Verdenik

ESTONIA v ITALY 0-2 (0-1)

Kadriorg, Tallinn 08.10.1994

Referee: Werner Müller (SWI) Attendance: 4,000

ESTONIA: Mart Poom; Marek Lemsalu, Toomas Kallaste, Viktor Alonen, Dzintar Klavan (75 Risto Kallaste), Urmas Kaljend, Marko Kristal, Martin Reim, Toomas Kröm (68 Indro Olumets), Tarmo Linnumäe, Urmas Kirs.
Trainer: Roman Ubakivi

ITALY: Gianluca Pagliuca; Christian Panucci, Giuseppe Favalli (87 Luigi Apolloni), Alberigo Evani (83 Demetrio Albertini), Alessandro Costacurta, Paolo Maldini, Roberto Rambaudi, Dino Baggio, Pierluigi Casiraghi, Gianfranco Zola, Giuseppe Signori. Trainer: Arrigo Sacchi

Goals: Panucci (20), Casiraghi (77)

UKRAINE v ESTONIA 3-0 (2-0)

Republican, Kyiv 13.11.1994

Referee: Leon Schellings (BEL) Attendance: 500

UKRAINE: Alexander Shovkovskyi (82 Oleg Suslov); Oleg Luzhnyi, Sergiy Bezhenar, Oleg Kuznetsov, Sergiy Popov, Alexander Koval (72 Igor Petrov), Sergiy Lezhentsev, Gennadiy Lytovchenko, Gennadiy Orbu, Sergiy Skachenko (46 Timerlan Guseinov), Sergiy Konovalov. Trainer: Jozsef Szabo

ESTONIA: Rain Vessenberg; Marek Lemsalu, Urmas Kirs, Tarmo Linnumäe, Risto Kallaste, Viktor Alonen, Indro Olumets, Meelis Lindmaa, Mati Pari, Marko Kristal, Indrek Zelinski. Trainer: Roman Ubakivi

Goals: Konovalov (29), Kirs (45 og), Guseinov (72)

ITALY v CROATIA 1-2 (0-1)

La Favorita, Palermo 16.11.1994

Referee: Joël Quiniou (FRA) Attendance: 39,000

ITALY: Gianluca Pagliuca; Paolo Negro, Christian Panucci, Demetrio Albertini (55 Roberto Di Matteo), Alessandro Costacurta, Paolo Maldini, Attilio Lombardo, Dino Baggio, Pierluigi Casiraghi, Roberto Baggio, Roberto Rambaudi (46 Roberto Donadoni). Trainer: Arrigo Sacchi

CROATIA: Drazen Ladic; Elvis Brajkovic, Robert Jarni, Igor Stimac, Nikola Jerkan, Slaven Bilic, Aljosa Asanovic, Robert Prosinecki (59 Mladen Mladenovic), Davor Suker, Zvonimir Boban, Nikola Jurcevic (90 Ardijan Kozniku). Trainer: Miroslav Blazevic

Goals: Suker (32, 60), D. Baggio (90)

CROATIA v UKRAINE 4-0 (2-0)

Maksimir, Zagreb 25.03.1995

Referee: Hans-Jürgen Weber (GER) Attendance: 25,000

CROATIA: Drazen Ladic; Nikola Jurcevic (80 Goran Vlaovic), Robert Jarni, Dubravko Pavlicic, Nikola Jerkan, Slaven Bilic, Aljosa Asanovic, Robert Prosinecki, Davor Suker, Zvonimir Boban, Alen Boksic (76 Dzevad Turkovic). Trainer: Miroslav Blazevic

UKRAINE: Dmytro Tyapushkin; Oleg Luzhnyi, Andriy Telesnenko, Yuriy Bukel, Sergiy Shmatovalenko, Yuriy Martinov (46 Gennadiy Orbu), Sergei Mizin, Yuriy Kalitvintsev, Andriy Shevchenko, Viktor Leonenko, Sergiy Konovalov. Trainer: Anatoliy Konkov

Goals: Boban (13), Suker (21, 79), Prosinecki (71 pen)

SLOVENIA v LITHUANIA 1-2 (0-0)

Ljudski vrt, Maribor 16.11.1994

Referee: Karol Ihring (SVK) Attendance: 6,000

SLOVENIA: Bosko Boskovic; Marinko Galic, Ales Krizan, Robert Englaro (46 Andrej Poljsak), Alfred Jermanis, Ales Ceh, Gregor Zidan, Igor Benedejcic (46 Peter Binkovski), Zlatko Zahovic, Matjaz Florjancic, Primoz Gliha. Trainer: Zdenko Verdenik

LITHUANIA: Gintaras Stauce; Andrius Tereskinas, Viaceslavas Sukristovas, Romas Mazeikis, Raimondas Vainoras, Arunas Suika (70 Audrius Zuta), Nerijus Gudaitis, Valdas Ivanauskas, Irmantas Stumbrys, Vytautas Apanavicius, Arminas Narbekovas. Trainer: Algimantas Liubinskas

Goals: Zahovic (55), Sukristovas (64), Zuta (87)

LITHUANIA v CROATIA 0-0

Zalgiris, Vilnius 29.03.1995

Referee: Keith Burge (WAL) Attendance: 9,000

LITHUANIA: Gintaras Stauce; Tomas Ziukas, Viaceslavas Sukristovas, Ramunas Stonkus, Raimondas Vainoras, Arunas Suika, Nerijus Gudaitis, Valdas Ivanauskas, Ricardas Zdancius (69 Audrius Zuta), Aurelijus Skarbalius, Arminas Narbekovas (24 Remigijus Pocius). Trainer: Benjaminas Zelkevicius

CROATIA: Drazen Ladic; Dubravko Pavlicic (46 Mladen Mladenovic), Robert Jarni, Igor Stimac, Zvonimir Soldo, Slaven Bilic, Aljosa Asanovic, Robert Prosinecki, Davor Suker, Alen Boksic, Elvis Brajkovic. Trainer: Miroslav Blazevic

ITALY v ESTONIA 4-1 (1-0)

Arechi, Salerno 25.03.1995

Referee: Roger Philippi (LUX) Attendance: 33,000

ITALY: Angelo Peruzzi; Paolo Negro, Amedeo Carboni, Demetrio Albertini, Paolo Maldini, Lorenzo Minotti, Stefano Eranio (56 Attilio Lombardo), Dino Baggio, Alessandro Del Piero (69 Nicola Berti), Gianfranco Zola, Fabrizio Ravanelli. Trainer: Arrigo Sacchi

ESTONIA: Mart Poom; Marek Lemsalu, Urmas Kirs, Toomas Kallaste, Indro Olumets, Meelis Lindmaa, Risto Kallaste, Tarmo Linnumäe, Marko Kristal, Alari Lell (77 Mati Pari), Toomas Kröm (67 Martin Reim). Trainer: Roman Ubakivi

Goals: Zola (45, 65), Albertini (58), Reim (71), Ravanelli (82)

SLOVENIA v ESTONIA 3-0 (1-0)

Ljudski vrt, Maribor 29.03.1995

Referee: José João Mendes Pratas (POR) Att: 12,000

SLOVENIA: Bosko Boskovic; Marinko Galic, Robert Englaro, Darko Milanic, Alfred Jermanis (70 Stefan Skaper), Ales Ceh, Dzoni Novak, Gregor Zidan, Zlatko Zahovic (66 Vladimir Kokol), Matjaz Florjancic, Primoz Gliha. Trainer: Zdenko Verdenik

ESTONIA: Mart Poom; Gert Olesk, Argo Arbeiter (78 Alari Lell), Toomas Kallaste, Indro Olumets, Meelis Lindmaa, Risto Kallaste, Tarmo Linnumäe, Urmas Kirs, Martin Reim, Marko Lepik. Trainer: Roman Ubakivi

Goal: Zahovic (39), Gliha (53), Kokol (90)

UKRAINE v ITALY 0-2 (0-2)

Republican, Kyiv 29.03.1995

Referee: Sándor Puhl (HUNG) Attendance: 20,000

UKRAINE: Dmytro Tyapushkin; Oleg Luzhnyi (56 Yuriy Bukel), Andriy Telesnenko, Andriy Khomyn, Alexander Yevtushok, Gennadiy Orbu, Sergei Mizin, Yuriy Kalitvintsev, Andriy Shevchenko, Viktor Leonenko, Sergiy Konovalov (77 Yevgeniy Pokhlebayev). Trainer: Anatoliy Konkov

ITALY: Angelo Peruzzi; Antonio Benarrivo, Paolo Maldini, Demetrio Albertini, Luigi Apolloni, Lorenzo Minotti, Attilio Lombardo (73 Antonio Conte), Roberto Di Matteo, Pierluigi Casiraghi (61 Fabrizio Ravanelli), Gianfranco Zola, Nicola Berti. Trainer: Arrigo Sacchi

Goals: Lombardo (11), Zola (38)

LITHUANIA v ITALY 0-1 (0-1)

Zalgiris, Vilnius 26.04.1995

Referee: James McCluskey (SCO) Attendance: 15,000

LITHUANIA: Gintaras Stauce; Tomas Ziukas, Viaceslavas Sukristovas, Andrius Tereskinas, Raimondas Vainoras, Arunas Suika, Nerijus Gudaitis (70 Eimantas Poderis), Valdas Ivanauskas, Vytautas Apanavicius (46 Aidas Preiksaitis), Aurelijus Skarbalius, Vaidotas Slekys.
Trainer: Benjaminas Zelkevicius

ITALY: Gianluca Pagliuca; Antonio Benarrivo, Paolo Maldini, Roberto Di Matteo, Alessandro Costacurta, Lorenzo Minotti, Attilio Lombardo, Antonio Conte (22 Dino Baggio), Pierluigi Casiraghi, Gianfranco Zola, Massimo Crippa (85 Nicola Berti).
Trainer: Arrigo Sacchi

Goal: Zola (11)

CROATIA v SLOVENIA 2-0 (1-0)

Maksimir, Zagreb 26.04.1995

Referee: Oguz Sarvan (TUR) Attendance: 25,000

CROATIA: Drazen Ladic; Nikola Jurcevic (11 Tonci Gabric), Robert Jarni, Igor Stimac, Nikola Jerkan, Slaven Bilic, Aljosa Asanovic, Robert Prosinecki, Davor Suker (90 Dubravko Pavlicic), Zvonimir Boban, Alen Boksic.
Trainer: Miroslav Blazevic

SLOVENIA: Bosko Boskovic; Marinko Galic, Robert Englaro, Darko Milanic (75 Stefan Skaper), Peter Binkovski, Alfred Jermanis, Dzoni Novak, Gregor Zidan, Zlatko Zahovic (66 Vladimir Kokol), Matjaz Florjancic, Primoz Gliha.
Trainer: Zdenko Verdenik

Goals: Prosinecki (17), Suker (90)

LITHUANIA v SLOVENIA 2-1 (0-0)

Zalgiris, Vilnius 07.06.1995

Referee: László Vágner (HUNG) Attendance: 7,000

LITHUANIA: Gintaras Stauce; Tomas Ziukas, Viaceslavas Sukristovas, Ramunas Stonkus, Raimondas Vainoras, Andrius Tereskinas, Darius Maciulevicius (75 Virginijus Baltusnikas), Valdas Ivanauskas, Aidas Preiksaitis (68 Arunas Suika), Aurelijus Skarbalius, Vaidotas Slekys.
Trainer: Benjaminas Zelkevicius

SLOVENIA: Bosko Boskovic; Marinko Galic (77 Ales Krizan), Robert Englaro, Darko Milanic, Alfred Jermanis, Ales Ceh, Dzoni Novak (59 Stefan Skaper), Vladimir Kokol, Zlatko Zahovic, Matjaz Florjancic, Primoz Gliha.
Trainer: Zdenko Verdenik

Goals: Stonkus (47), Suika (70), Gliha (82)

ESTONIA v UKRAINE 0-1 (0-1)

Kadriorg, Tallinn 26.04.1995

Referee: Tore Hollung (NOR) Attendance: 1,600

ESTONIA: Mart Poom; Marek Lemsalu, Urmas Kirs, Toomas Kallaste, Indro Olumets, Viktor Alonen, Risto Kallaste, Alari Lell, Marko Kristal, Martin Reim (68 Mati Pari), Toomas Kröm (46 Martin Lepa). Trainer: Roman Ubakivi

UKRAINE: Oleg Suslov; Oleg Luzhnyi, Sergiy Diryavka, Alexander Holovko, Sergiy Shmatovalenko, Gennadiy Orbu, Igor Zhabchenko, Yuriy Maximov, Oleg Naduda (85 Alexander Yevtushok), Sergiy Nagornyak (46 Sergiy Konovalov), Timerlan Guseinov. Trainer: Anatoliy Konkov

Goal: Guseinov (17)

UKRAINE v CROATIA 1-0 (1-0)

Republican, Kyiv 11.06.1995

Referee: Kurt Röthlisberger (SWI) Attendance: 10,000

UKRAINE: Oleg Suslov; Igor Zhabchenko, Viktor Skrypnyk, Alexander Holovko, Yuriy Maximov, Gennadiy Orbu, Yevgeniy Pokhlebayev, Yuriy Kalitvintsev, Alexander Palyanytsya (77 Sergiy Nagornyak), Volodymyr Horilyi, Timerlan Guseinov (46 Pavlo Shkapenko). Trainer: Anatoliy Konkov

CROATIA: Tonci Gabric; Dubravko Pavlicic (27 Marijan Mrmic), Robert Jarni, Zvonimir Soldo, Nikola Jerkan, Slaven Bilic, Aljosa Asanovic (50 Nenad Pralija), Mladen Mladenovic, Davor Suker, Zvonimir Boban (39 Darko Butorovic), Alen Boksic. Trainer: Miroslav Blazevic

Goal: Kalitvintsev (13)

ESTONIA v SLOVENIA 1-3 (1-1)

Kadriorg, Tallinn 11.06.1995

Referee: Paul Durkin (ENG) Attendance: 2,000

ESTONIA: Mart Poom; Martin Lepa (46 Dzintar Klavan), Urmas Kirs, Toomas Kallaste, Indro Olumets, Viktor Alonen, Mati Pari, Tarmo Linnumäe, Marko Kristal, Martin Reim, Argo Arbeiter (60 Lembit Rajala). Trainer: Roman Ubakivi

SLOVENIA: Bosko Boskovic; Marinko Galic, Robert Englaro, Darko Milanic, Dzoni Novak, Alfred Jermanis (64 Matjaz Cvikl), Vladimir Kokol (46 Ales Krizan), Ales Ceh, Zlatko Zahovic, Matjaz Florjancic, Primoz Gliha.
Trainer: Zdenko Verdenik

Goals: Reim (28), Novak (37, 68), Zahovic (76)

ITALY v SLOVENIA 1-0 (1-0)

Friuli, Udine 06.09.1995

Referee: Ladislav Gadosi (SVK) Attendance: 30,000

ITALY: Angelo Peruzzi; Ciro Ferrara, Amedeo Carboni, Roberto Di Matteo, Alessandro Costacurta, Alessio Tacchinardi, Angelo Di Livio, Demetrio Albertini, Alessandro Del Piero (46 Giuseppe Signori), Gianfranco Zola (61 Roberto Baggio), Fabrizio Ravanelli (81 Dino Baggio).
Trainer: Arrigo Sacchi

SLOVENIA: Branko Zupan; Marinko Galic, Darko Milanic, Andrej Poljsak, Alfred Jermanis, Ales Ceh, Vladimir Kokol (46 Peter Binkovski), Matjaz Cvikl (78 Sandi Valentincic), Zlatko Zahovic (58 Vilijem Becaj), Saso Udovic, Primoz Gliha.
Trainer: Zdenko Verdenik

Goal: Ravanelli (13)

ESTONIA v LITHUANIA 0-1 (0-0)

Kadriorg, Tallinn 16.08.1995

Referee: Karl-Erik Nilsson (SWE) Attendance: 1,750

ESTONIA: Mart Poom; Marek Lemsalu, Urmas Kirs, Janek Kiisman (46 Arvo Kraam), Alari Lell, Risto Kallaste, Meelis Lindmaa, Martin Lepa, Marko Kristal, Martin Reim, Ivan O'Konnel-Bronin (73 Gert Olesk). Trainer: Roman Ubakivi

LITHUANIA: Gintaras Stauce; Tomas Ziukas, Viaceslavas Sukristovas, Andrius Tereskinas, Raimondas Vainoras, Arunas Suika, Darius Maciulevicius, Valdas Ivanauskas, Ramunas Stonkus, Aurelijus Skarbalius (75 Tomas Kancelskis), Vaidotas Slekys (65 Audrius Zuta). Trainer: Benjaminas Zelkevicius

Goal: Maciulevicius (48)

LITHUANIA v UKRAINE 1-3 (1-0)

Zalgiris, Vilnius 06.09.1995

Referee: Brendan Shorte (IRE) Attendance: 11,500

LITHUANIA: Gintaras Stauce; Tomas Ziukas, Viaceslavas Sukristovas, Andrius Tereskinas (68 Aidas Preiksaitis), Raimondas Vainoras, Arunas Suika, Darius Maciulevicius, Valdas Ivanauskas, Ramunas Stonkus, Aurelijus Skarbalius (77 Rimas Zvingilas), Vaidotas Slekys.
Trainer: Benjaminas Zelkevicius

UKRAINE: Oleg Suslov; Oleg Luzhnyi, Viktor Skrypnyk, Alexander Holovko, Igor Zhabchenko (68 Yevgeniy Pokhlebayev), Volodymyr Horilyi, Gennadiy Orbu, Yuriy Kalitvintsev, Sergiy Bezhenar, Andriy Gusin, Timerlan Guseinov (86 Alexander Yevtushok).
Trainer: Anatoliy Konkov

Goals: Maciulevicius (17), Guseinov (62, 72), Gusin (83)

CROATIA v ESTONIA 7-1 (4-1)

Maksimir, Zagreb 03.09.1995

Referee: Aron Huzu (ROM) Attendance: 25,000

CROATIA: Drazen Ladic (30 Marijan Mrmic); Mladen Mladenovic, Robert Jarni, Igor Stimac (83 Dzevad Turkovic), Nikola Jerkan, Slaven Bilic (75 Nenad Pralija), Mario Stanic, Robert Prosinecki, Davor Suker, Zvonimir Boban, Alen Boksic.
Trainer: Miroslav Blazevic

ESTONIA: Mart Poom; Marek Lemsalu, Urmas Kirs, Toomas Kallaste, Risto Kallaste, Janek Kiisman (43 Alari Lell), Meelis Lindmaa (76 Indro Olumets), Martin Lepa (46 Tarmo Linnumäe), Marko Kristal, Martin Reim, Lembit Rajala.
Trainer: Roman Ubakivi

Goals: Mladenovic (3), Reim (17), Suker (19 pen, 58, 89), Boksic (29), Boban (42), Stimac (82)

CROATIA v ITALY 1-1 (0-1)

Poljud, Split 08.10.1995

Referee: Jacobus Uilenberg (HOL) Attendance: 40,000

CROATIA: Drazen Ladic; Nikola Jurcevic (46 Ardijan Kozniku), Mladen Mladenovic, Igor Stimac, Nikola Jerkan, Dubravko Pavlicic, Aljosa Asanovic, Mario Stanic, Davor Suker, Zvonimir Boban, Alen Boksic.
Trainer: Miroslav Blazevic

ITALY: Luca Bucci; Ciro Ferrara (84 Antonio Benarrivo), Paolo Maldini, Roberto Di Matteo, Luigi Apolloni, Alessandro Costacurta, Angelo Di Livio, Demetrio Albertini, Alessandro Del Piero (86 Massimo Crippa), Gianfranco Zola (9 Francesco Toldo), Fabrizio Ravanelli. Trainer: Arrigo Sacchi

Goals: Albertini (29), Suker (49 pen)

LITHUANIA v ESTONIA 5-0 (4-0)

Zalgiris, Vilnius 11.10.1995

Referee: Didier Pauchard (FRA) Attendance: 2,500

LITHUANIA: Gintaras Stauce (46 Valdemaras Martinkenas); Tomas Kancelskis, Gintaras Rimkus, Ramunas Stonkus, Raimondas Vainoras, Arunas Suika (74 Rimas Zvingilas), Darius Maciulevicius, Valdas Ivanauskas, Virginijus Baltusnikas, Donatos Vencevicius, Vaidotas Slekys (46 Edgaras Jankauskas). Trainer: Benjaminas Zelkevicius

ESTONIA: Mart Poom; Gert Olesk, Martin Lepa (46 Martin Reim), Toomas Kallaste, Alari Lell (46 Marko Kristal, 79 Toomas Kröm), Indrek Zelinski, Meelis Lindmaa, Risto Kallaste, Tarmo Linnumäe, Lembit Rajala, Andres Oper. Trainer: Roman Ubakivi

Goals: Maciulevicius (5), Suika (13, 39), Slekys (44), Ivanauskas (62)

SLOVENIA v UKRAINE 3-2 (0-2)

Bezigrad, Ljubljana 11.10.1995

Referee: Alain Hamer (LUX) Attendance: 11,000

SLOVENIA: Branko Zupan; Marinko Galic, Robert Englaro, Darko Milanic, Mladen Rudonja, Ales Ceh, Dzoni Novak, Saso Udovic, Zlatko Zahovic, Matjaz Florjancic (71 Matjaz Cvikl), Primoz Gliha. Trainer: Zdenko Verdenik

UKRAINE: Oleg Suslov; Oleg Luzhnyi, Viktor Skrypnyk, Alexander Holovko, Igor Zhabchenko, Sergiy Shmatovalenko (89 Andriy Polunin), Gennadiy Orbu, Yuriy Kalitvintsev (71 Alexander Yevtushok), Sergiy Bezhenar, Andriy Gusin (46 Sergiy Nagornyak), Timerlan Guseinov. Trainer: Anatoliy Konkov

Goals: Skrypnyk (24), Guseinov (44), Udovic (53, 89), Zahovic (73)

ITALY v UKRAINE 3-1 (1-1)

San Nicola, Bari 11.11.1995

Referee: Serge Muhmenthaler (SWI) Attendance: 44,000

ITALY: Angelo Peruzzi; Antonio Benarrivo, Paolo Maldini, Roberto Di Matteo, Ciro Ferrara, Alessandro Costacurta, Dino Baggio (46 Massimo Crippa), Demetrio Albertini, Alessandro Del Piero (87 Amedeo Carboni), Gianfranco Zola (67 Marco Simone), Fabrizio Ravanelli. Trainer: Arrigo Sacchi

UKRAINE: Oleg Suslov; Oleg Luzhnyi, Viktor Skrypnyk, Sergiy Bezhenar, Volodymyr Horilyi (15 Alexander Yevtushok), Andriy Polunin, Gennadiy Orbu, Yuriy Kalitvintsev, Sergiy Nagornyak (70 Yevgeniy Pokhlebayev), Volodymyr Sharan (51 Sergiy Popov), Timerlan Guseinov. Trainer: Anatoliy Konkov

Goals: Polunin (19), Ravanelli (21, 49), Maldini (54)

ITALY v LITHUANIA 4-0 (0-0)

Giglio, Reggio Emilia 15.11.1995

Referee: Manuel Díaz Vega (SPA) Attendance: 26,000

ITALY: Angelo Peruzzi; Roberto Mussi, Paolo Maldini (72 Amedeo Carboni), Roberto Di Matteo, Ciro Ferrara, Alessandro Costacurta, Francesco Statuto (46 Gianfranco Zola), Demetrio Albertini, Pierluigi Casiraghi (46 Fabrizio Ravanelli), Alessandro Del Piero, Marco Simone. Trainer: Arrigo Sacchi

LITHUANIA: Gintaras Stauce; Tomas Ziukas, Andrius Tereskinas, Ramunas Stonkus, Raimondas Vainoras, Arunas Suika (79 Donatos Vencevicius), Darius Maciulevicius (46 Rimas Zvingilas), Valdas Ivanauskas (59 Raimondas Zutautas), Aidas Preiksaitis, Aurelijus Skarbalius, Gintaras Rimkus. Trainer: Benjaminas Zelkevicius

Goals: Suika (52 og), Zola (65, 81), Vainoras (82 og)

SLOVENIA v CROATIA 1-2 (1-1)

Bezigrad, Ljubljana 15.11.1995

Referee: Guy Goethals (BEL) Attendance: 10,000

SLOVENIA: Branko Zupan; Marinko Galic, Ales Krizan, Robert Englaro, Alfred Jermanis, Samir Zulic (62 Mladen Rudonja), Dzoni Novak, Saso Udovic, Ales Ceh, Primoz Gliha, Matjaz Florjancic (62 Matjaz Cvikl). Trainer: Zdenko Verdenik

CROATIA: Drazen Ladic; Nikola Jurcevic, Robert Jarni, Zvonimir Soldo, Nikola Jerkan, Slaven Bilic, Nenad Pralija (65 Mladen Mladenovic), Robert Prosinecki, Davor Suker, Mario Stanic, Ivica Mornar. Trainer: Miroslav Blazevic

Goals: Gliha (36), Suker (40 pen), Jurcević (55)

	P	W	D	L	F	A	Pts
Croatia	10	7	2	1	22	5	23
Italy	10	7	2	1	20	6	23
Lithuania	10	5	1	4	13	12	16
Ukraine	10	4	1	5	11	15	13
Slovenia	10	3	2	5	13	13	11
Estonia	10	0	0	10	3	31	0

GROUP 5

CZECH REPUBLIC v MALTA 6-1 (3-0)

Bazaly, Ostrava 06.09.1994

Referee: Loizos Loizou (CYP) Attendance: 10,226

CZECH REPUBLIC: Petr Kouba; Radoslav Latal (84 Petr Vesely), Jan Suchoparek, Daniel Smejkal, Lubos Kubik, Vaclav Nemecek, Jiri Nemec, Jiri Novotny, Pavel Kuka, Horst Siegl, Martin Frydek (84 Patrik Berger). Trainer: Dusan Uhrin

MALTA: David Cluett; Silvio Vella, Richard Buhagiar, Joseph Galea, Joseph Brincat, John Buttigieg, Carmel Busuttil, Nicky Saliba, Martin Gregory (81 Edwin Camilleri), Christian Laferla, Joseph Camilleri. Trainer: Pietro Ghedin

Goals: Smejkal (6 pen), Kubik (32), Siegl (35, 60, 78), Laferla (73), Berger (86)

MALTA v CZECH REPUBLIC 0-0

National, Ta'Qali 12.10.1994

Referee: Jorge Monteiro Coroado (POR) Attendance: 4,000

MALTA: David Cluett; Silvio Vella, Joseph Camilleri, Joseph Galea, Joseph Brincat, John Buttigieg, Carmel Busuttil, Nicky Saliba (75 Joe Sant Fournier), Martin Gregory, Christian Laferla, David Carabott (85 Edwin Camilleri).
Trainer: Pietro Ghedin

CZECH REPUBLIC: Pavel Srnicek; Radoslav Latal, Jan Suchoparek, Ivan Hasek, Lubos Kubik, Vaclav Nemecek (44 Miroslav Kadlec), Jiri Nemec, Jiri Novotny, Pavel Kuka, Tomas Skuhravy, Daniel Smejkal (75 Martin Frydek).
Trainer: Dusan Uhrin

LUXEMBOURG v HOLLAND 0-4 (0-1)

Stade Municipal, Luxembourg 07.09.1994

Referee: Alan Snoddy (NIR) Attendance: 8,200

LUXEMBOURG: Paul Koch; Ralph Ferron, Jeff Strasser, Marc Birsens, Thomas Wolf, Luc Holtz, Jeff Saibene, Carlo Weis, Joël Groff, Manuel Cardoni (78 Patrick Morocutti), Robert Langers (88 Dany Theis). Trainer: Paul Philipp

HOLLAND: Ed De Goey; Stan Valckx, Frank De Boer, Danny Blind, Rob Witschge, Wim Jonk, Marc Overmars, Aron Winter, Ronald De Boer, John Bosman, Bryan Roy (75 Peter Van Vossen). Trainer: Dick Advocaat

Goals: Roy (23), R. De Boer (65, 67), Jonk (90)

NORWAY v HOLLAND 1-1 (0-1)

Ullevaal, Oslo 12.10.1994

Referee: James McCluskey (SCO) Attendance: 22,293

NORWAY: Erik Thorstvedt; Pål Lydersen, Tore Pedersen, Henning Berg, Stig Inge Bjørnebye, Sigurd Rushfeldt (62 Jostein Flo), Erik Mykland, Oyvind Leonhardsen, Jan Age Fjørtoft (77 Geir Frigård), Kjetil Rekdal, Lars Bohinen.
Trainer: Egil Olsen

HOLLAND: Ed De Goey; Michael Reiziger (71 Ulrich Van Gobbel), Stan Valckx, Danny Blind, Frank De Boer, Wim Jonk, Marc Overmars, Aron Winter, Dennis Bergkamp (68 Ronald De Boer), Rob Witschge, Bryan Roy. Trainer: Guus Hiddink

Goals: Roy (21), Rekdal (52 pen)

NORWAY v BELARUS 1-0 (0-0)

Ullevaal, Oslo 07.09.1994

Referee: Guy Goethals (BEL) Attendance: 16,739

NORWAY: Frode Grodås; Pål Lydersen, Tore Pedersen, Henning Berg, Stig Inge Bjørnebye, Jostein Flo (70 Geir Frigård), Erik Mykland, Lars Bohinen (46 Oyvind Leonhardsen), Jan Age Fjørtoft, Kjetil Rekdal, Jahn Ivar Jakobsen. Trainer: Egil Olsen

BELARUS: Valeryi Shantalosov; Sergei Gurenko, Andrei Sosnitskyi, Aleksander Khatskievich, Erik Yakhimovich, Andrei Zygmantovich, Yuryi Antonovich, Mikhail Markhel, Sergei Gerasimets, Aleksander Metlitskyi, Sergei Kulanin (46 Petr Kachuro). Trainer: Sergei Borovskyi

Goal: Frigård (88)

BELARUS v LUXEMBOURG 2-0 (0-0)

Dinamo, Minsk 12.10.1994

Referee: Richard O'Hanlon (IRE) Attendance: 8,500

BELARUS: Valeryi Shantalosov; Sergei Gurenko, Pavel Rodnenok (80 Andrei Sosnitskyi), Aleksander Metlitskyi, Erik Yakhimovich, Andrei Zygmantovich, Sergei Gerasimets, Mikhail Markhel (65 Yuryi Antonovich), Sergei Aleinikov, Miroslav Romashchenko, Yuryi Shukanov.
Trainer: Sergei Borovskyi

LUXEMBOURG: Paul Koch; Ralph Ferron (82 Jean Vanek), Jeff Strasser, Marc Birsens, Thomas Wolf, Manuel Cardoni, Guy Hellers, Carlo Weis, Luc Holtz (58 Patrick Morocutti), Jeff Saibene, Stefano Fanelli. Trainer: Paul Philipp

Goals: Romashchenko (67), Gerasimets (76)

HOLLAND v CZECH REPUBLIC 0-0

Feyenoord, Rotterdam 16.11.1994

Referee: Sándor Puhl (HUNG) Attendance: 45,000

HOLLAND: Ed De Goey; Stan Valckx, Frank De Boer, Danny Blind, Rob Witschge (80 Arthur Numan), Wim Jonk, Gaston Taument, Aron Winter, Youri Mulder (71 Patrick Kluivert), Bryan Roy, Peter Van Vossen. Trainer: Guus Hiddink

CZECH REPUBLIC: Pavel Srnicek; Radoslav Latal, Jan Suchoparek, Pavel Hapal, Lubos Kubik, Miroslav Kadlec, Jiri Nemec, Michal Bilek, Pavel Kuka (90 Petr Samec), Horst Siegl, Karel Poborsky (75 Patrik Berger). Trainer: Dusan Uhrin

HOLLAND v LUXEMBOURG 5-0 (3-0)

Feyenoord, Rotterdam 14.12.1994

Referee: Daniel Roduit (SWI) Attendance: 30,000

HOLLAND: Ed De Goey; Stan Valckx, Frank De Boer, Danny Blind, Athur Numan, Wim Jonk, Marc Overmars, Aron Winter (75 Pierre Van Hooijdonk), Ronald De Boer, Youri Mulder (46 Clarence Seedorf), Bryan Roy. Trainer: Guus Hiddink

LUXEMBOURG: Paul Koch; Ralph Ferron, Jeff Strasser, Marc Birsens, Thomas Wolf, Joël Groff, Guy Hellers, Carlo Weis, Luc Holtz, Manuel Cardoni, Robert Langers (61 Dany Theis). Trainer: Paul Philipp

Goals: Mulder (7), Roy (17), Jonk (40), R. De Boer (52), Seedorf (90)

BELARUS v NORWAY 0-4 (0-2)

Dinamo, Minsk 16.11.1994

Referee: Lube Spasov (BUL) Attendance: 7,500

BELARUS: Valeryi Shantalosov; Sergei Yaskovich, Pavel Rodnenok, Aleksander Metlitskyi, Erik Yakhimovich, Andrei Zygmantovich, Yuryi Antonovich, Mikhail Markhel (46 Andrei Yusipets), Sergei Gerasimets, Miroslav Romashchenko (82 Igor Gurinovich), Yuryi Shukanov. Trainer: Sergei Borovskyi

NORWAY: Frode Grodås; Gunnar Halle, Ronny Johnsen, Henning Berg, Stig Inge Bjørnebye (42 Pål Lydersen), Sigurd Rushfeldt (78 Jahn Ivar Jakobsen), Erik Mykland, Oyvind Leonhardsen, Jan Age Fjørtoft, Kjetil Rekdal, Lars Bohinen. Trainer: Egil Olsen

Goals: H. Berg (34), Leonhardsen (40), Bohinen (52), Rekdal (83 pen)

MALTA v LUXEMBOURG 0-1 (0-0)

National, Ta'Qali 22.02.1995

Referee: Mateo Beusan (CRO) Attendance: 6,000

MALTA: David Cluett; Silvio Vella, Richard Buhagiar, Joseph Camilleri, Joseph Brincat, John Buttigieg, Carmel Busuttil, Hubert Suda (59 Charles Sciberras), Martin Gregory, Christian Laferla, David Carabott (79 Nicky Saliba). Trainer: Pietro Ghedin

LUXEMBOURG: Paul Koch; Jean Vanek, Frank Deville, Marc Birsens, Thomas Wolf, Jeff Saibene, Guy Hellers, Carlo Weis, Robert Langers (90 Sascha Schneider), Manuel Cardoni (85 Luc Holtz), Joël Groff. Trainer: Paul Philipp

Goal: Cardoni (55)

MALTA v NORWAY 0-1 (0-1)

National, Ta'Qali 14.12.1994

Referee: Gianni Beschin (ITA) Attendance: 3,000

MALTA: David Cluett; Silvio Vella, Joseph Camilleri, Michael Woods, Joseph Brincat, John Buttigieg, Carmel Busuttil, Nicky Saliba (85 Charles Scerri), Martin Gregory, Christian Laferla, David Carabott (62 Richard Buhagiar). Trainer: Pietro Ghedin

NORWAY: Frode Grodås; Gunnar Halle, Ronny Johnsen, Henning Berg, Stig Inge Bjørnebye, Jostein Flo, Erik Mykland, Sigurd Rushfeldt (82 Jahn Ivar Jakobsen), Jan Age Fjørtoft, Kjetil Rekdal, Lars Bohinen (72 Ståle Solbakken). Trainer: Egil Olsen

Goal: Fjørtoft (10)

LUXEMBOURG v NORWAY 0-2 (0-1)

Stade Municipal, Luxembourg 29.03.1995

Referee: Nikolai Levnikov (RUS) Attendance: 3,031

LUXEMBOURG: Serge Rohmann; Ralph Ferron, Jean Vanek, Marc Birsens (83 Sascha Schneider), Jeff Strasser, Frank Deville, Jeff Saibene (76 Patrick Feyder), Carlo Weis, Robert Langers, Manuel Cardoni, Joël Groff. Trainer: Paul Philipp

NORWAY: Erik Thorstvedt; Alf Inge Håland, Ronny Johnsen, Henning Berg, Stig Inge Bjørnebye, Jostein Flo (46 Gunnar Aase), Lars Bohinen, Oyvind Leonhardsen, Jan Age Fjørtoft, Kjetil Rekdal (84 Ståle Solbakken), Jahn Ivar Jakobsen. Trainer: Egil Olsen

Goals: Leonhardsen (35), Aase (77)

HOLLAND v MALTA 4-0 (1-0)

Feyenoord, Rotterdam 29.03.1995

Referee: Gylfi Orrason (ICE) Attendance: 37,000

HOLLAND: Ed De Goey; Stan Valckx, Danny Blind, Wim Jonk, Frank De Boer, Aron Winter, Marc Overmars, Clarence Seedorf, Ronald De Boer (77 Patrick Kluivert), Dennis Bergkamp, Bryan Roy (59 Eric Van de Luèr).
Trainer: Guus Hiddink

MALTA: David Cluett; Silvio Vella (89 Martin Gregory), Richard Buhagiar, Joseph Galea, Michael Woods, Joseph Camilleri, Carmel Busuttil (88 Gilbert Agius), Nicky Saliba, Joe Sant Fournier, Christian Laferla, Edwin Camilleri.
Trainer: Pietro Ghedin

Goals: Seedorf (39), Bergkamp (77 pen), Winter (80), Kluivert (85)

BELARUS v MALTA 1-1 (0-0)

Dinamo, Minsk 26.04.1995

Referee: Ladislav Gadosi (SVK) Attendance: 9,250

BELARUS: Andrei Satsunkhevich; Sergei Gurenko, Aleksander Taikov, Aleksander Metlitskyi (70 Pavel Rodnenok), Vladimir Zhuravel, Andrei Zygmantovich, Sergei Gerasimets, Andrei Yusipets (77 Petr Kachuro), Yuryi Antonovich, Igor Gurinovich, Yuryi Shukanov.
Trainer: Sergei Borovskyi

MALTA: David Cluett; Silvio Vella, David Carabott, Edwin Camilleri, Michael Woods, John Buttigieg, Carmel Busuttil (89 Lawrence Attard), Nicky Saliba, Martin Gregory (23 Gilbert Agius), Christian Laferla, Joe Sant Fournier.
Trainer: Pietro Ghedin

Goals: Taikov (57), Carabott (70)

CZECH REPUBLIC v BELARUS 4-2 (2-1)

Bazaly, Ostrava 29.03.1995

Referee: Gilles Veissière (FRA) Attendance: 5,549

CZECH REPUBLIC: Pavel Srnicek; Tomas Repka, Daniel Smejkal, Radoslav Latal, Miroslav Kadlec, Vaclav Nemecek, Pavel Hapal, Patrik Berger, Pavel Kuka, Horst Siegl (89 Petr Samec), Martin Frydek (85 Michal Bilek).
Trainer: Dusan Uhrin

BELARUS: Valeryi Shantalosov; Sergei Gurenko, Andrei Sosnitskyi, Aleksander Taikov, Erik Yakhimovich (77 Pavel Rodnenok), Andrei Zygmantovich, Sergei Gerasimets, Vladimir Zhuravel (81 Yevgenyi Kashentsev), Andrei Yusipets, Aleksander Metlitskyi, Igor Gurinovich.
Trainer: Sergei Borovskyi

Goals: Kadlec (5), Berger (17, 62), Gerasimets (44 pen), Kuka (68), Gurinovich (88)

CZECH REPUBLIC v HOLLAND 3-1 (0-1)

Praha 26.04.1995

Referee: Hellmut Krug (GER) Attendance: 17,463

CZECH REPUBLIC: Petr Kouba; Tomas Repka, Jan Suchoparek, Pavel Hapal, Miroslav Kadlec, Vaclav Nemecek, Jiri Nemec, Patrik Berger, Pavel Kuka (89 Horst Siegl), Tomas Skuhravy, Martin Frydek (46 Radoslav Latal).
Trainer: Dusan Uhrin

HOLLAND: Ed De Goey; Stan Valckx, Danny Blind, Wim Jonk, Frank De Boer, Clarence Seedorf, Arthur Numan, Aron Winter (62 Patrick Kluivert), Peter Van Vossen (46 Peter Bosz), Ronald De Boer, Marc Overmars.
Trainer: Guus Hiddink

Goals: Jonk (7), Skuhravy (49), Nemecek (58), Berger (62)

NORWAY v LUXEMBOURG 5-0 (3-0)

Ullevaal, Oslo 26.04.1995

Referee: John Ferry (NIR) Attendance: 15,124

NORWAY: Frode Grodås; Harald Brattbakk, Ronny Johnsen, Henning Berg (63 Alf Inge Håland), Roger Nilsen, Gunnar Halle, Lars Bohinen (35 Ståle Solbakken), Oyvind Leonhardsen, Jan Age Fjørtoft, Kjetil Rekdal, Jahn Ivar Jakobsen. Trainer: Egil Olsen

LUXEMBOURG: Paul Koch; Patrick Feyder, Jean Vanek, Luc Holtz (56 Dany Theis), Jeff Strasser, Frank Deville, Guy Hellers, Jeff Saibene (75 Marc Lamborelle), Robert Langers, Manuel Cardoni, Joël Groff. Trainer: Paul Philipp

Goals: Jakobsen (9), Fjørtoft (10), Brattbakk (23), H. Berg (46), Rekdal (49)

BELARUS v HOLLAND 1-0 (1-0)

Dinamo, Minsk 07.06.1995

Referee: Adrian Porumboiu (ROM) Attendance: 22,000

BELARUS: Valeryi Shantalosov; Sergei Gurenko, Andrei Dovnar (87 Yevgenyi Kashentsev), Pavel Rodnenok, Aleksander Taikov, Andrei Zygmantovich, Sergei Gerasimets, Vladimir Zhuravel, Miroslav Romashchenko (55 Yuryi Antonovich), Andrei Yusipets, Petr Kachuro.
Trainer: Sergei Borovskyi

HOLLAND: Edwin Van der Sar; Johan De Kock, Danny Blind (69 Aron Winter), Wim Jonk, Stan Valckx (65 Arthur Numan), Clarence Seedorf, Johannes Van't Schip, Edgar Davids, Patrick Kluivert, Ronald De Boer, Marc Overmars.
Trainer: Guus Hiddink

Goal: Gerasimets (27)

NORWAY v MALTA 2-0 (1-0)

Ullevaal, Oslo 07.06.1995

Referee: Zbigniew Przesmycki (POL) Attendance: 15,180

NORWAY: Erik Thorstvedt; Alf Inge Håland, Ronny Johnsen, Henning Berg, Roger Nilsen (69 Harald Brattbakk), Jostein Flo, Erik Mykland, Ståle Solbakken, Jan Age Fjørtoft, Kjetil Rekdal (83 Kåre Ingebrigtsen), Jahn Ivar Jakobsen. Trainer: Egil Olsen

MALTA: David Cluett; Silvio Vella, Richard Buhagiar (75 Edwin Camilleri), Lawrence Attard, Michael Woods, John Buttigieg (28 Nicky Saliba), Carmel Busuttil, Gilbert Agius, Joe Sant-Fournier, Christian Laferla, David Carabott. Trainer: Pietro Ghedin

Goals: Fjørtoft (43), Flo (88)

LUXEMBOURG v MALTA 1-0 (1-0)

Stade Municipal, Luxembourg 06.09.1995

Referee: Algirdas Dubinskas (LIT) Attendance: 4,700

LUXEMBOURG: Paul Koch; Jean Vanek, Frank Deville, Marc Birsens, Jeff Strasser, Jeff Saibene, Guy Hellers, Carlo Weis, Luc Holtz (84 Manuel Cardoni), Robert Langers, Joël Groff (68 Dany Theis). Trainer: Paul Philipp

MALTA: David Cluett; Jesmond Delia (27 Gilbert Agius, 89 Martin Gregory), Richard Buhagiar, Joseph Galea, Michael Woods, John Buttigieg, Carmel Busuttil, Nicky Saliba, Joe Sant-Fournier, Christian Laferla, David Carabott (46 Lawrence Attard). Trainer: Pietro Ghedin

Goal: Holtz (45)

LUXEMBOURG v CZECH REPUBLIC 1-0 (0-0)

Stade Municipal, Luxembourg 07.06.1995

Referee: John Ashman (WAL) Attendance: 1,500

LUXEMBOURG: Paul Koch; Jean Vanek, Frank Deville, Marc Birsens, Jeff Strasser, Claude Ganser (86 Manuel Cardoni), Guy Hellers, Carlo Weis, Robert Langers, Dany Theis (74 Jeff Saibene), Joël Groff. Trainer: Paul Philipp

CZECH REPUBLIC: Petr Kouba; Tomas Repka (69 Martin Frydek), Jan Suchoparek, Pavel Hapal, Miroslav Kadlec, Vaclav Nemecek, Jiri Nemec, Patrik Berger, Pavel Kuka, Tomas Skuhravy (59 Radek Drulak), Radoslav Latal. Trainer: Dusan Uhrin

Goal: Hellers (89)

HOLLAND v BELARUS 1-0 (0-0)

Feyenoord, Rotterdam 06.09.1995

Referee: Robert Sedlacek (AUS) Attendance: 17,000

HOLLAND: Edwin Van der Sar; Michael Reiziger (70 Orlando Trustfull), Danny Blind, Johan De Kock, Frank de Boer, Richard Witschge (86 Arthur Numan), Aron Winter, Ronald De Boer, René Eykelkamp (65 Youri Mulder), Dennis Bergkamp, Marc Overmars. Trainer: Guus Hiddink

BELARUS: Andrei Satsunkevich; Sergei Gurenko, Andrei Dovnar, Pavel Rodnenok, Aleksander Taikov, Andrei Zygmantovich, Sergei Gerasimets, Vladimir Zhuravel (89 Sergei Vekhtev), Miroslav Romashchenko (86 Yuri Vergeichik), Andrei Yusipets (69 Yevgeni Kashentsev), Petr Kachuro. Trainer: Sergei Borovskyi

Goal: Mulder (83)

NORWAY v CZECH REPUBLIC 1-1 (1-0)

Ullevaal, Oslo 16.08.1995

Referee: Sergei Khusainov (RUS) Attendance: 22,054

NORWAY: Erik Thorstvedt; Alf Inge Håland, Ronny Johnsen, Henning Berg, Karl-Peter Løken, Jostein Flo, Lars Bohinen, Øyvind Leonhardsen, Jan Åge Fjørtoft (80 Harald Brattbakk), Ståle Solbakken, Jahn Ivar Jakobsen (64 Geirmund Brendesaether). Trainer: Egil Olsen

CZECH REPUBLIC: Petr Kouba; Radoslav Latal (78 Karel Poborsky), Jan Suchoparek, Pavel Hapal, Miroslav Kadlec, Tomas Repka, Jiri Nemec, Patrik Berger (46 Pavel Nedved), Pavel Kuka, Radek Drulak (78 Petr Samec), Martin Frydek. Trainer: Dusan Uhrin

Goals: H. Berg (27), Suchoparek (84)

CZECH REPUBLIC v NORWAY 2-0 (1-0)

Praha 06.09.1995

Referee: Kurt Röthlisberger (SWI) Attendance: 19,522

CZECH REPUBLIC: Petr Kouba; Radoslav Latal, Jan Suchoparek, Pavel Nedved, Miroslav Kadlec, Vaclav Nemecek, Jiri Nemec, Tomas Repka, Pavel Kuka (19 Radek Drulak), Tomas Skuhravy (80 Vratislav Lokvenc), Martin Frydek (70 Karel Poborsky). Trainer: Dusan Uhrin

NORWAY: Erik Thorstvedt; Karl-Peter Løken, Ronny Johnsen, Henning Berg, Erland Johnsen, Jostein Flo, Lars Bohinen (75 Kjetil Rekdal), Øyvind Leonhardsen, Jan Åge Fjørtoft (71 Harald Brattbakk), Ståle Solbakken, Jahn Ivar Jakobsen. Trainer: Egil Olsen

Goals: Skuhravy (6 pen), Drulak (86)

BELARUS v CZECH REPUBLIC **0-2** (0-1)

Dinamo, Minsk 07.10.1995

Referee: Anders Frisk (SWE) Attendance: 20,000

BELARUS: Valeryi Shantalosov; Sergei Gurenko, Andrei Dovnar, Pavel Rodnenok, Aleksander Taikov, Andrei Yusipets (74 Vasili Baranov), Sergei Gerasimets, Vladimir Zhuravel, Valentin Belkevich, Yevgeni Kashentsev, Petr Kachuro. Trainer: Sergei Borovskyi

CZECH REPUBLIC: Petr Kouba; Radoslav Latal, Pavel Nedved (74 Patrik Berger), Pavel Hapal, Miroslav Kadlec, Vaclav Nemecek (15 Michal Hornak), Jiri Nemec, Tomas Repka, Pavel Kuka, Radek Drulak, Martin Frydek (87 Karel Poborsky). Trainer: Dusan Uhrin

Goals: Frydek (25), Berger (84)

LUXEMBOURG v BELARUS **0-0**

Stade Municipal, Luxembourg 11.10.1995

Referee: Paul Durkin (ENG) Attendance: 4,500

LUXEMBOURG: Paul Koch; Jean Vanek, Frank Deville, Marc Birsens, Jeff Strasser, Jeff Saibene, Guy Hellers, Carlo Weis, Luc Holtz (90 Marc Lamborelle), Robert Langers (81 Dany Theis), Patrick Morocutti (72 Manuel Cardoni). Trainer: Paul Philipp

BELARUS: Valeryi Shantalosov; Sergei Gurenko, Andrei Dovnar, Pavel Rodnenok, Aleksander Taikov; Andrei Yusipets, Vladimir Zhuravel, Vasili Baranov, Yevgeni Kashentsev (88 Yuri Vergeichik); Valentin Belkevich, Petr Kachuro. Trainer: Sergei Borovskyi

MALTA v HOLLAND **0-4** (0-0)

National, Ta'Qali 11.10.1995

Referee: Kim Milton Nielsen (DEN) Attendance: 8,000

MALTA: David Cluett; Lawrence Attard (70 Joseph Galea), Richard Buhagiar, Joseph Brincat, Michael Woods, Ivan Zammit, Carmel Busuttil, Nicky Saliba, Gilbert Agius (6 Joe Sant-Fournier), Christian Laferla, David Carabott. Trainer: Pietro Ghedin

HOLLAND: Edwin Van der Sar; Michael Reiziger, Danny Blind (71 Orlando Trustfull), Frank De Boer, Arthur Numan, Richard Witschge, Ronald De Boer, Clarence Seedorf, Youri Mulder (64 Glenn Helder), Patrick Kluivert, Marc Overmars. Trainer: Guus Hiddink

Goals: Overmars (53, 60, 85), Seedorf (82)

MALTA v BELARUS **0-2** (0-0)

National, Ta'Qali 12.11.1995

Referee: Talal Tokat (TUR) Attendance: 4,000

MALTA: David Cluett; Silvio Vella, Lawrence Attard, Joseph Brincat (50 Joe Sant-Fournier), Michael Woods, Ivan Zammit, Carmel Busuttil, Nicky Saliba, Gilbert Agius (63 David Carabott), Christian Laferla, Richard Buhagiar. Trainer: Pietro Ghedin

BELARUS: Valeryi Shantalosov; Sergei Gurenko, Andrei Dovnar, Oleg Khmelnitski (44 Valentin Belkevich), Aleksander Taikov, Andrei Zygmantovich (59 Andrei Yusipets), Sergei Gerasimets, Vasili Baranov, Yuri Maleyev (75 Vladimir Makovski), Alexander Metlitski, Petr Kachuro. Trainer: Sergei Borovskyi

Goals: Gerasimets (78, 82)

HOLLAND v NORWAY **3-0** (0-0)

Feyenoord, Rotterdam 15.11.1995

Referee: Dermot Gallagher (ENG) Attendance: 49,000

HOLLAND: Edwin Van der Sar; Michael Reiziger, Danny Blind, Frank De Boer, Arthur Numan, Richard Witschge (56 Edgar Davids), Marc Overmars, Clarence Seedorf, Ronald De Boer, Dennis Bergkamp (79 Youri Mulder), Glenn Helder (86 Johan De Kock). Trainer: Guus Hiddink

NORWAY: Frode Grodås; Karl-Peter Løken (62 Alf Inge Håland), Erland Johnsen, Henning Berg, Stig Inge Bjørnebye, Erik Mykland (59 Øyvind Leonhardsen), Lars Bohinen (81 Ståle Solbakken), Tore André Flo, Jan Åge Fjørtoft, Kjetil Rekdal, Jahn Ivar Jakobsen. Trainer: Egil Olsen

Goals: Seedorf (49), Mulder (87), Overmars (88)

CZECH REPUBLIC v LUXEMBOURG **3-0** (1-0)

Praha 15.11.1995

Referee: Alfred Wieser (AUS) Attendance: 22,530

CZECH REPUBLIC: Petr Kouba; Radoslav Latal, Jan Suchoparek, Pavel Hapal, Miroslav Kadlec, Vaclav Nemecek (72 Karel Poborsky), Pavel Nedved, Patrik Berger (84 Vladimir Smicer), Pavel Kuka (87 Vratislav Lokvenc), Radek Drulak, Martin Frydek. Trainer: Dusan Uhrin

LUXEMBOURG: Paul Koch; Ralph Ferron, Jean Vanek, Frank Deville (59 Dany Theis), Jeff Strasser, Luc Holtz (76 Ganser), Guy Hellers, Carlo Weis, Jeff Saibene (90 Manuel Cardoni), Robert Langers, Joël Groff. Trainer: Paul Philipp

Goals: Drulak (37, 46), Berger (57)

	P	W	D	L	F	A	Pts
Czech Republic	10	6	3	1	21	6	21
Holland	10	6	2	2	23	5	20
Norway	10	6	2	2	17	7	20
Belarus	10	3	2	5	8	13	11
Luxembourg	10	3	1	6	3	21	10
Malta	10	0	2	8	2	22	2

GROUP 6

NORTHERN IRELAND v LIECHTENSTEIN 4-1 (3-0)

Windsor Park, Belfast 20.04.1994

Referee: Roelof Luinge (HOL) Attendance: 4,500

N. IRELAND: Tommy Wright; Gary Fleming, Gerry Taggart, Malachy Donaghy, Nigel Worthington; Kevin Wilson, Jim Magilton, Steve Lomas (81 Michael O'Neill), Michael Hughes; Jimmy Quinn, Iain Dowie (78 Philip Gray).
Manager: Bryan Hamilton

LIECHTENSTEIN: Martin Oehry; Heini Stocker (68 Daniel Hasler), Christoph Frick, Wolfgang Ospelt, Roland Moser; Jürg Ritter, Alexander Quaderer, Harry Zech, Mario Frick, Daniel Telser; Christian Matt (64 Thomas Hanselmann).
Trainer: Dietrich Weise

Goals: J. Quinn (5, 33), Lomas (23), Dowie (48), Hasler (84)

NORTHERN IRELAND v PORTUGAL 1-2 (0-1)

Windsor Park Belfast 7.09.1994

Referee: Rune Pedersen (NOR) Attendance: 6,000

N. IRELAND: Alan Fettis; Gary Fleming, Nigel Worthington, Steve Morrow (81 Gerry Taggart), Alan McDonald, Steve Lomas, Keith Gillespie (81 George O'Boyle), Jim Magilton, Jimmy Quinn, Philip Gray, Michael Hughes.
Manager: Bryan Hamilton

PORTUGAL: VÍTOR Manuel Martins BAÍA; JOÃO Domingos Silva PINTO I, HÉLDER Marino Rodrigues Cristóvao, PAULO Sérgio Braga MADEIRA, João Paulo Santos "PAULINHO SANTOS", PAULO Manuel Carvalho SOUSA, Vítor Manuel Araújo "VÍTOR PANEIRA" (63 António José Santos FOLHA), José Fernando Gomes TAVARES, Luís Filipe Madeira FIGO, RUI Manuel César COSTA, Ricardo Manuel SÁ PINTO (80 DOMINGOS José Paciencia Oliveira).
Trainer: António Oliveira

Goals: Rui Costa (8), Quinn (58 pen), Domingos (81)

LIECHTENSTEIN v AUSTRIA 0-4 (0-3)

Eschen/Mauren 07.09.1994

Referee: Wieland Ziller (GER) Attendance: 5,800

LIECHTENSTEIN: Martin Heeb; Patrick Hefti, Jürgen Ospelt, Wolfgang Ospelt (28 Thomas Hanselmann), Roland Moser, Daniel Telser, Alexander Quaderer, Harry Zech (69 Christian Matt), Mario Frick, Peter Klaunzer, Daniel Hasler.
Trainer: Dietrich Weise

AUSTRIA: Franz Wohlfahrt; Wolfgang Feiersinger, Jürgen Werner, Johann Kogler, Peter Schöttel, Franz Aigner, Andreas Ogris (62 Harald Cerny), Christian Prosenik, Anton Polster, Peter Stöger, Heimo Pfeifenberger (74 Thomas Flögel).
Trainer: Herbert Prohaska

Goals: Polster (18, 45, 79), Aigner (22)

LATVIA v REPUBLIC OF IRELAND 0-3 (0-2)

Daugava, Riga 07.09.1994

Referee: Anders Frisk (SWE) Attendance: 3,000

LATVIA: Oleg Karavayev; Igor Troitsky, Vitaly Astafyev, Mikhail Zemlinsky, Yury Shevlyakov, Valentin Lobanyov, Alexey Sharando, Vadim Mikutsky (65 Alexander Yeliseyev), Vladimir Babichev, Yevgeny Milevsky (46 Igor V.Stepanov), Rolands Boulders. Trainer: Yanis Gilis

IRELAND: Alan Kelly; Gary Kelly, Dennis Irwin, Paul McGrath, Phil Babb, Jason McAteer (82 Eddie McGoldrick), Andy Townsend, John Aldridge, Niall Quinn (71 Anthony Cascarino), John Sheridan, Steve Staunton.
Manager: Jack Charlton

Goals: Aldridge (16, 75 pen), Sheridan (29)

LATVIA v PORTUGAL 1-3 (0-1)

Daugava, Riga 09.10.1994

Referee: Eric Blareau (BEL) Attendance: 1,900

LATVIA: Oleg Karavayev; Igor Troitsky, Vitaly Astafyev, Mikhail Zemlinsky, Yury Shevlyakov, Dzintars Sprogis (68 Boris Monyak), Igor V.Stepanov, Valery Ivanov, Vladimir Babichev, Alexander Glazov (46 Yevgeny Milevsky), Alexey Semyonov. Trainer: Yanis Gilis

PORTUGAL: VÍTOR Manuel Martins BAÍA; JOÃO Domingos Silva PINTO I, HÉLDER Marino Rodrigues Cristóvao, PAULO Sérgio Braga MADEIRA, Manuel António Guimaraes "NELO", PAULO Manuel Carvalho SOUSA, Vítor Manuel Araújo "VÍTOR PANEIRA" (60 PAULO Lourenço Martins ALVES), JOÃO Manuel Vieira PINTO II, Luís Filipe Madeira FIGO (81 José Fernando Gomes TAVARES), RUI Manuel César COSTA, DOMINGOS José Paciencia Oliveira.
Trainer: António Oliveira

Goals: João Pinto II (33, 72), Figo (73), Milevsky (87)

AUSTRIA v NORTHERN IRELAND **1-2** (1-2)

Ernst-Happel, Wien 12.10.1994

Referee: Antonio Jesus López Nieto (SPA) Att: 20,000

AUSTRIA: Franz Wohlfahrt; Wolfgang Feiersinger, Jürgen Werner, Johann Kogler, Peter Schöttel, Christian Prosenik (66 Heimo Pfeifenberger), Andreas Ogris (46 Ralph Hasenhüttl), Peter Artner, Anton Polster, Peter Stöger, Adolf Hütter. Trainer: Herbert Prohaska

N. IRELAND: Paul Kee; Gary Fleming, Nigel Worthington, Gerry Taggart, Alan McDonald, Steve Lomas, Keith Gillespie (56 Michael O'Neill), Jim Magilton, Iain Dowie (74 Jimmy Quinn), Philip Gray, Michael Hughes. Manager: Bryan Hamilton

Goals: Gillespie (3), Polster (25 pen), Gray (36)

REPUBLIC OF IRELAND v LIECHTENSTEIN **4-0** (3-0)

Lansdowne Road, Dublin 12.10.1994

Referee: Bragi Bergmann (ICE) Attendance: 32,980

IRELAND: Patrick Bonner; Gary Kelly, Dennis Irwin (46 Alan McLoughlin), Alan Kernaghan, Phil Babb, Jason McAteer, Eddie McGoldrick, Tommy Coyne, Niall Quinn, John Sheridan, Steve Staunton. Manager: Jack Charlton

LIECHTENSTEIN: Martin Heeb; Patrick Hefti, Jürg Ritter, Wolfgang Ospelt, Roland Moser, Daniel Telser, Thomas Hanselmann, Harry Zech, Mario Frick, Modestus Haas (78 Peter Klaunzer), Armin Heidegger (72 Christian Matt). Trainer: Dietrich Weise

Goals: Coyne (2, 4), Quinn (30, 82)

PORTUGAL v AUSTRIA **1-0** (0-0)

Lisboa 13.11.1994

Referee: Peter Mikkelsen (DEN) Attendance: 46,000

PORTUGAL: VÍTOR Manuel Martins BAÍA; JOÃO Domingos Silva PINTO I, HÉLDER Marino Rodrigues Cristóvao, OCEANO Andrade Cruz, PAULO Sérgio Braga MADEIRA, PAULO Manuel Carvalho SOUSA, Luís Filipe Madeira FIGO, JOÃO Manuel Vieira PINTO II, Ricardo Manuel SÁ PINTO (70 Vítor Manuel Araújo "VÍTOR PANEIRA"), RUI Manuel César COSTA (84 DOMINGOS José Paciencia Oliveira), João Paulo Santos "PAULINHO SANTOS". Trainer: António Oliveira

AUSTRIA: Otto Konrad; Wolfgang Feiersinger, Christian Fürstaller, Johann Kogler, Peter Schöttel, Thomas Winklhofer, Harald Cerny (71 Adolf Hütter), Peter Artner, Anton Polster, Peter Stöger, Dietmar Kühbauer (46 Christian Prosenik). Trainer: Herbert Prohaska

Goal: Figo (67)

LIECHTENSTEIN v LATVIA **0-1** (0-1)

Eschen/Mauren 15.11.1994

Referee: Piotr Werner (POL) Attendance: 1,300

LIECHTENSTEIN: Martin Heeb; Daniel Telser, Patrick Hefti, Wolfgang Ospelt, Roland Moser, Roland Hilti, Jürg Ritter, Harry Zech (59 Peter Klaunzer), Armin Heidegger (58 Ralf Oehri), Mario Frick, Daniel Hasler. Trainer: Dietrich Weise

LATVIA: Oleg Karavayev; Igor Troitsky, Vitaly Astafyev, Mikhail Zemlinsky, Yury Shevlyakov, Dzintars Sprogis, Oleg Blagonadezhdin (46 Vadim Mikutsky), Valery Ivanov, Yevgeny Milevsky, Vladimir Babichev (69 Alexey Sharando), Alexey Semyonov. Trainer: Yanis Gilis

Goal: Babichev (14)

NORTHERN IRELAND v REPUBLIC OF IRELAND **0-4** (0-3)

Windsor Park, Belfast 16.11.1994

Referee: Serge Muhmenthaler (SWI) Attendance: 10,336

NORTHERN IRELAND: Paul Kee; Gary Fleming, Nigel Worthington, Gerry Taggart, Steve Morrow, Michael O'Neill (46 Darren Patterson), Keith Gillespie (62 Kevin Wilson), Jim Magilton, Iain Dowie, Philip Gray, Michael Hughes. Manager: Bryan Hamilton

REPUBLIC OF IRELAND: Alan Kelly; Gary Kelly, Dennis Irwin, Phil Babb, Paul McGrath, Roy Keane (46 Jason McAteer), Andy Townsend, John Sheridan, Niall Quinn, John Aldridge (80 Tommy Coyne), Steve Staunton. Manager: Jack Charlton

Goals: Aldridge (6), Keane (11), Sheridan (38), Townsend (54)

PORTUGAL v LIECHTENSTEIN **8-0** (3-0)

Lisboa 18.12.1994

Referee: Lubos Pucek (CZE) Attendance: 32,000

PORTUGAL: VÍTOR Manuel Martins BAÍA; JOÃO Domingos Silva PINTO I, João Paulo Santos "PAULINHO SANTOS", OCEANO Andrade Cruz, FERNANDO Manuel Silva COUTO, Luís Filipe Madeira FIGO, Vítor Manuel Araújo "VÍTOR PANEIRA" (57 PAULO Lourenço Martins ALVES), JOÃO Manuel Vieira PINTO II (70 Carlos Alberto Oliveira SECRETÁRIO), DOMINGOS José Paciencia Oliveira, RUI Manuel César COSTA, António José Santos FOLHA. Trainer: António Oliveira

LIECHTENSTEIN: Martin Heeb; Daniel Telser, Patrick Hefti, Wolfgang Ospelt (44 Ralf Oehri), Roland Moser, Roland Hilti, Jürg Ritter, Harry Zech, Armin Heidegger, Mario Frick, Daniel Hasler (59 Christian Matt). Trainer: Dietrich Weise

Goals: Domingos (2,11), Oceano (45), João Pinto II (56), Fernando Couto (72), Folha (74), Paulo Alves (75,79)

AUSTRIA v LATVIA 5-0 (2-0)

Lehen, Salzburg 29.03.1995

Referee: Charles Agius (MAL) Attendance: 4,000

AUSTRIA: Otto Konrad; Wolfgang Feiersinger, Christian Fürstaller, Johann Kogler, Heimo Pfeifenberger, Stefan Marasek, Andreas Ogris (46 Dieter Ramusch), Peter Artner (75 Adolf Hütter), Anton Polster, Andreas Herzog, Dietmar Kühbauer. Trainer: Herbert Prohaska

LATVIA: Raimonds Laizans; Igor Troitsky, Vitaly Astafyev, Mikhail Zemlinski (66 Vadim Mikutsky), Yury Shevlyakov, Dzintars Sprogis, Oleg Blagonadezhdin, Valentin Lobanyov, Boris Monyak, Vladimir Babichev (74 Andrey Shtolcers), Vitaly Teplov. Trainer: Yanis Gilis

Goals: Herzog (17, 59), Pfeifenberger (40), Polster (71 pen, 90)

REPUBLIC OF IRELAND v NORTHERN IRELAND 1-1 (0-0)

Lansdowne Road, Dublin 29.03.1995

Referee: Mario Van der Ende (HOL) Attendance: 32,200

REPUBLIC OF IRELAND: Alan Kelly; Gary Kelly, Dennis Irwin, Phil Babb, Paul McGrath, Roy Keane, Andy Townsend, David Kelly (74 Jason McAteer), Niall Quinn (82 Anthony Cascarino), John Sheridan, Steve Staunton.
Manager: Jack Charlton

NORTHERN IRELAND: Alan Fettis; Darren Patterson, Nigel Worthington, Gerry Taggart, Alan McDonald, Steve Morrow, Keith Gillespie, Jim Magilton, Iain Dowie, Colin Hill, Michael Hughes. Manager: Bryan Hamilton

Goals: N. Quinn (47), Dowie (72)

AUSTRIA v LIECHTENSTEIN 7-0 (3-0)

Lehen, Salzburg 26.04.1995

Referee: Vasiliy Melnichuk (UKR) Attendance: 5,500

AUSTRIA: Otto Konrad; Dieter Ramusch, Wolfgang Feiersinger, Johann Kogler, Christian Fürstaller (72 Adolf Hütter), Stefan Marasek, Herfried Sabitzer (70 Marcus Pürk), Peter Artner, Anton Polster, Andreas Herzog, Dietmar Kühbauer. Trainer: Herbert Prohaska

LIECHTENSTEIN: Martin Oehry; Heini Stocker, Jürgen Ospelt, Jürg Ritter (65 Christian Matt), Roland Moser, Daniel Telser, Roland Hilti, Harry Zech, Alex Burgmaier, Ralf Oehri (46 Patrick Marxer), Daniel Hasler. Trainer: Dietrich Weise

Goals: Kühbauer (8), Polster (11, 53 pen), Sabitzer (17), Pürk (84), Hütter (87, 90)

REPUBLIC OF IRELAND v PORTUGAL 1-0 (1-0)

Lansdowne Road, Dublin 26.04.1995

Referee: Angelo Amendolia (ITA) Attendance: 25,000

IRELAND: Alan Kelly; Gary Kelly, Dennis Irwin, Phil Babb, Paul McGrath, Raymond Houghton (84 Jeff Kenna), Andy Townsend, John Aldridge (84 Anthony Cascarino), Niall Quinn, John Sheridan, Steve Staunton.
Manager: Jack Charlton

PORTUGAL: VÍTOR Manuel Martins BAÍA; JOÃO Domingos Silva PINTO I, JORGE Paulo COSTA Almeida, HÉLDER Marino Rodrigues Cristóvao (64 António José Santos FOLHA), FERNANDO Manuel Silva COUTO, PAULO Manuel Carvalho SOUSA, Luís Filipe Madeira FIGO (76 PEDRO Alexandre Santos BARBOSA), JOÃO Manuel Vieira PINTO II, DOMINGOS José Paciencia Oliveira, RUI Manuel César COSTA, João Paulo Santos "PAULINHO SANTOS".
Trainer: António Oliveira

Goal: Vítor Baía (45 og)

LATVIA v NORTHERN IRELAND 0-1 (0-0)

Daugava, Riga 26.04.1995

Referee: Finn Lambek (DEN) Attendance: 1,500

LATVIA: Raimonds Laizans; Igor Troitsky, Vitaly Astafyev, Mikhail Zemlinsky, Yury Shevlyakov, Dzintars Sprogis, Igor N. Stepanov, Oleg Blagonadezhdin (31 Rikhards Butkus, 72 Boris Monyak), Vitaly Teplov, Vladimir Babichev, Alexander Yeliseyev. Trainer: Yanis Gilis

N. IRELAND: Alan Fettis; Darren Patterson, Nigel Worthington, Barry Hunter, Alan McDonald, Colin Hill, Keith Gillespie (78 George O'Boyle), Kevin Wilson, Iain Dowie (80 Jimmy Quinn), Kevin Horlock, Michael Hughes.
Manager: Bryan Hamilton

Goal: Dowie (67 pen)

LIECHTENSTEIN v REPUBLIC OF IRELAND 0-0

Eschen/Mauren 03.06.1995

Referee: Charles Agius (MAL) Attendance: 4,500

LIECHTENSTEIN: Martin Heeb; Thomas Hanselmann, Jürgen Ospelt (31 Jürgen Zech), Wolfgang Ospelt (64 Patrick Marxer), Daniel Hasler, Daniel Telser, Jürg Ritter, Roland Hilti, Mario Frick, Harry Zech, Alex Burgmaier.
Trainer: Dietrich Weise

IRELAND: Alan Kelly; Gary Kelly, Dennis Irwin, Phil Babb, Paul McGrath, Ronald Whelan, Jason McAteer (73 Jeff Kenna), John Aldridge, Niall Quinn (60 Anthony Cascarino), John Sheridan, Steve Staunton. Manager: Jack Charlton

PORTUGAL v LATVIA 3-2 (3-0)

Das Antas, Porto 03.06.1995

Referee: Zoran Petrovic (YUG) Attendance: 40,000

PORTUGAL: VÍTOR Manuel Martins BAÍA; Fernando NÉLSON Jesus Alves (79 PEDRO Alexandre Santos BARBOSA), João Paulo Santos "PAULINHO SANTOS", JORGE Paulo COSTA Almeida, FERNANDO Manuel Silva COUTO, PAULO Manuel Carvalho SOUSA (46 Paulo Jorge Santos FUTRE), Luís Filipe Madeira FIGO, Carlos Alberto Oliveira SECRETÁRIO, DOMINGOS José Paciencia Oliveira, RUI Manuel César COSTA, António José Santos FOLHA. Trainer: António Oliveira

LATVIA: Raimonds Laizans; Igor Troitsky, Vitaly Astafyev, Mikhail Zemlinsky, Yury Shevlyakov, Boris Monyak, Valery Ivanov, Armands Zeiberlinsh, Vitas Rimkus, Vitaly Teplov (61 Dzintars Sprogis), Imants Bleidelis (38 Vladimir Babichev). Trainer: Yanis Gilis

Goals: Figo (5), Secretário (19), Domingos (21), Rimkus (51, 85)

NORTHERN IRELAND v LATVIA 1-2 (1-0)

Windsor Park, Belfast 07.06.1995

Referee: Juan Ansuategui Roca (SPA) Attendance: 6,000

N. IRELAND: Alan Fettis; Pat McGibbon (46 Darren Patterson), Nigel Worthington, Gerry Taggart, Alan McDonald, Steve Morrow, Gerard McMahon, Jim Magilton, Iain Dowie, Keith Rowland (64 Keith Gillespie), Michael Hughes. Manager: Bryan Hamilton

LATVIA: Raimonds Laizans; Igor Troitsky, Vitaly Astafyev, Dzintars Sprogis, Artur Zakreshevsky, Boris Monyak, Valery Ivanov, Armands Zeiberlinsh, Vitas Rimkus (70 Alexander Yeliseyev), Vladimir Babichev (82 Vitaly Teplov), Imants Bleidelis. Trainer: Yanis Gilis

Goals: Dowie (44), Zeiberlinsh (59), Astafyev (62)

REPUBLIC OF IRELAND v AUSTRIA 1-3 (0-0)

Lansdowne Road, Dublin 11.06.1995

Referee: Markus Merk (GER) Attendance: 33,000

IRELAND: Alan Kelly; Gary Kelly, Dennis Irwin, Phil Babb, Paul McGrath, Ronald Whelan, Tommy Coyne, Raymond Houghton, Niall Quinn (56 Anthony Cascarino), John Sheridan, Steve Staunton (46 Jeff Kenna). Manager: Jack Charlton

AUSTRIA: Michael Konsel; Anton Pfeffer, Peter Schöttel, Johann Kogler, Christian Fürstaller, Stefan Marasek, Heimo Pfeienberger (82 Adolf Hütter), Christian Prosenik, Anton Polster, Dietmar Kühbauer, Dieter Ramusch (72 Andreas Ogris). Trainer: Herbert Prohaska

Goals: Houghton (67), Polster (70, 80), Ogris (74)

LIECHTENSTEIN v PORTUGAL 0-7 (0-3)

Eschen/Mauren 15.08.1995

Referee: Dragutin Poljak (CRO) Attendance: 2,500

LIECHTENSTEIN: Martin Heeb; Thomas Hanselmann, Jürgen Zech, Roland Moser, Daniel Hasler, Daniel Telser (67 Ralf Oehri), Heini Stocker (46 Patrick Marxer), Roland Hilti, Mario Frick, Harry Zech, Peter Klaunzer (46 Christoph Frick). Trainer: Dietrich Weise

PORTUGAL: ALFREDO da Silva Castro (82 RUI Manuel Silva CORREIA); DIMAS Manuel Marques Teixeira (55 PAULO Lourenço Martins ALVES), JORGE Paulo COSTA Almeida, OCEANO Andrade Cruz (46 Ricardo Manuel SÁ PINTO), FERNANDO Manuel Silva COUTO, João Paulo Santos "PAULINHO SANTOS", Carlos Alberto Oliveira SECRETÁRIO, Soares Gil RUI BARROS, DOMINGOS José Paciencia Oliveira, RUI Manuel César COSTA, António José Santos FOLHA. Trainer: António Oliveira

Goals: Domingos (25), Paulinho Santos (33), Rui Costa (41, 71 pen), Paulo Alves (67, 73, 90)

LATVIA v AUSTRIA 3-2 (1-0)

Daugava, Riga 16.08.1995

Referee: Ilka Koho (FIN) Attendance: 2,000

LATVIA: Raimonds Laizans; Igor Troitsky, Vitaly Astafyev, Mikhail Zemlinsky, Yury Shevlyakov, Imants Bleidelis, Valery Ivanov, Armands Zeiberlinsh, Vitas Rimkus, Vladimir Babichev (75 Alexander Yeliseyev), Artur Zakreshevsky (82 Boris Monyak). Trainer: Yanis Gilis

AUSTRIA: Otto Konrad; Anton Pfeffer, Peter Schöttel, Johann Kogler (46 Markus Schopp), Walter Kogler, Stefan Marasek, Andreas Ogris (64 Peter Stöger), Christian Prosenik (64 Dieter Ramusch), Anton Polster, Wolfgang Feiersinger, Heimo Pfeienberger. Trainer: Herbert Prohaska

Goals: Rimkus (11, 59), Polster (69), Ramusch (78), Zeiberlinsh (88)

PORTUGAL v NORTHERN IRELAND 1-1 (0-0)

Das Antas, Porto 03.09.1995

Referee: Rémy Harrel (FRA) Attendance: 50,000

PORTUGAL: VÍTOR Manuel Martins BAÍA; Carlos Alberto Oliveira SECRETÁRIO, JORGE Paulo COSTA Almeida (74 Soares Gil RUI BARROS), OCEANO Andrade Cruz, FERNANDO Manuel Silva COUTO, PAULO Manuel Carvalho SOUSA, Luís Filipe Madeira FIGO, João Paulo Santos "PAULINHO SANTOS", DOMINGOS José Paciencia Oliveira, RUI Manuel César COSTA (82 PAULO Lourenço Martins ALVES), António José Santos FOLHA. Trainer: António Oliveira

N. IRELAND: Alan Fettis; Steve Morrow, Nigel Worthington, Colin Hill, Barry Hunter, Steve Lomas, Keith Gillespie, Jim Magilton (79 Keith Rowland), Iain Dowie (76 Philip Gray), Neil Lennon, Michael Hughes. Manager: Bryan Hamilton

Goals: Domingos (47), Hughes (67)

AUSTRIA v REPUBLIC OF IRELAND 3-1 (1-0)

Ernst-Happel, Wien 06.09.1995

Referee: Ahmet Çakar (TUR) Attendance: 24,000

AUSTRIA: Michael Konsel; Markus Schopp, Peter Schöttel, Anton Pfeffer, Christian Fürstaller, Stefan Marasek, Heimo Pfeifenberger, Dietmar Kühbauer, Anton Polster (79 Harald Cerny), Andreas Herzog, Peter Stöger.
Trainer: Herbert Prohaska

IRELAND: Alan Kelly; Gary Kelly, Dennis Irwin, Alan Kernaghan, Paul McGrath, Roy Keane, Andy Townsend, Raymond Houghton (67 Anthony Cascarino), Niall Quinn, John Sheridan, Mark Kennedy. Manager: Jack Charlton

Goals: Stöger (3, 64, 77), McGrath (74)

REPUBLIC OF IRELAND v LATVIA 2-1 (0-0)

Lansdowne Road, Dublin 11.10.1995

Referee: Fernández Marín (SPA) Attendance: 33,000

IRELAND: Alan Kelly; Gary Kelly, Terry Phelan, Phil Babb, Paul McGrath, Jeff Kenna, Andy Townsend, Jason McAteer, Niall Quinn, John Aldridge (79 David Kelly, 84 Mark Kennedy), Steve Staunton. Manager: Jack Charlton

LATVIA: Oleg Karavayev; Igor Troitsky, Vitaly Astafyev, Mikhail Zemlinsky, Yury Shevlyakov, Igor N.Stepanov, Valery Ivanov, Armands Zeiberlinsh, Vitas Rimkus, Vladimir Babichev (73 Alexander Yeliseyev), Artur Zakreshevsky.
Trainer: Yanis Gilis

Goals: Aldridge (61 pen, 64), Rimkus (78)

LATVIA v LIECHTENSTEIN 1-0 (0-0)

Daugava, Riga 06.09.1995

Referee: Tom Henning Ovrebo (NOR) Attendance: 3,800

LATVIA: Oleg Karavayev; Igor Troitsky, Vitaly Astafyev, Mikhail Zemlinsky, Yury Shevlyakov, Imants Bleidelis (28 Rolands Boulders), Valery Ivanov, Armands Zeiberlinsh, Vitas Rimkus, Vladimir Babichev (75 Yury Karashauskas), Boris Monyak. Trainer: Yanis Gilis

LIECHTENSTEIN: Martin Heeb; Christoph Frick, Jürgen Zech, Ralf Oehri (63 Herbert Bicker), Daniel Hasler, Daniel Telser, Heini Stocker (85 Peter Klaunzer), Roland Hilti, Harry Schädler, Mario Frick, Patrik Marxer (73 Daniel Frick).
Trainer: Dietrich Weise

Goals: Zeiberlinsh (83)

LIECHTENSTEIN v NORTHERN IRELAND 0-4 (0-1)

Eschen/Mauren 11.10.1995

Referee: Lubos Michel (SVK) Attendance: 1,100

LIECHTENSTEIN: Martin Oehri; Patrik Hefti, Christoph Frick (78 Thomas Hanselmann), Roland Hilti (66 Jürgen Ospelt), Daniel Hasler, Peter Klaunzer, Daniel Telser, Heini Stocker (46 Rolf Sele), Franz Schädler, Harry Zech, Ralf Oehri.
Trainer: Dietrich Weise

N. IRELAND: Alan Fettis (75 Trevor Wood); Steve Lomas, Nigel Worthington, Colin Hill, Barry Hunter, Neil Lennon, Gerard McMahon (80 Pat McGibbon), Michael O'Neill, Jimmy Quinn, Philip Gray, Michael Hughes (90 Keith Rowland).
Manager: Bryan Hamilton

Goals: O'Neill (36), McMahon (49), Ji. Quinn (55 pen), Gray (72)

AUSTRIA v PORTUGAL 1-1 (1-0)

Ernst-Happel, Wien 11.10.1995

Referee: Nikolai Levnikov (RUS) Attendance: 44,000

AUSTRIA: Michael Konsel; Markus Schopp, Peter Schöttel, Anton Pfeffer, Wolfgang Feiersinger, Stefan Marasek, Heimo Pfeifenberger, Dietmar Kühbauer, Anton Polster (83 Harald Cerny), Andreas Herzog, Peter Stöger.
Trainer: Herbert Prohaska

PORTUGAL: VíTOR Manuel Martins BAÍA; Fernando NÉLSON Jesus Alves, HÉLDER Marino Rodrigues Cristóvao, OCEANO Andrade Cruz, JORGE Paulo COSTA Almeida, PAULO Manuel Carvalho SOUSA, Carlos Alberto Oliveira SECRETÁRIO (59 Ricardo Manuel SÁ PINTO), JOÃO Manuel Vieira PINTO (46 António José Santos FOLHA), DOMINGOS José Paciencia Oliveira (72 DOMINGUEZ), RUI Manuel César COSTA, João Paulo Santos "PAULINHO SANTOS".
Trainer: António Oliveira

Goals: Stöger (21), Paulinho Santos (49)

NORTHERN IRELAND v AUSTRIA 5-3 (2-0)

Windsor Park, Belfast 15.11.1995

Referee: Leif Sundell (SWE) Attendance: 8,400

N. IRELAND: Alan Fettis; Steve Lomas, Nigel Worthington, Barry Hunter, Colin Hill, Neil Lennon, Keith Gillespie, Michael O'Neill, Iain Dowie (81 Jimmy Quinn), Philip Gray (78 Alan McDonald), Michael Hughes. Manager: Bryan Hamilton

AUSTRIA: Michael Konsel; Markus Schopp, Walter Kogler, Anton Pfeffer, Wolfgang Feiersinger, Stefan Marasek, Heimo Pfeifenberger, Andreas Herzog (46 Arnold Wetl), Anton Polster, Dietmar Kühbauer (46 Christian Stumpf), Peter Stöger. Trainer: Herbert Prohaska

Goals: O'Neill (27, 78), Dowie (32 pen), Hunter (53), Schopp (56), Gray (64), Stumpf (70), Wetl (80)

PORTUGAL v REPUBLIC OF IRELAND 3-0 (0-0)

Lisboa 15.11.1995

Referee: Paolo Ceccarini (ITA) Attendance: 80,000

PORTUGAL: VÍTOR Manuel Martins BAÍA (85 Adelino Augusto Barros NENO); Carlos Alberto Oliveira SECRETÁRIO, HÉLDER Marino Rodrigues Cristóvao, OCEANO Andrade Cruz, FERNANDO Manuel Silva COUTO, PAULO Manuel Carvalho SOUSA, Luís Filipe Madeira FIGO, JOÃO Manuel Vieira PINTO (68 Jorge Paulo CADETE Reis), DOMINGOS José Paciencia Oliveira (72 António José Santos FOLHA), RUI Manuel César COSTA, João Paulo Santos "PAULINHO SANTOS". Trainer: António Oliveira

IRELAND: Alan Kelly; Gary Kelly, Dennis Irwin, Phil Babb, Paul McGrath, Jason McAteer, Mark Kennedy (75 Anthony Cascarino), Jeff Kenna, Niall Quinn, John Aldridge, Steve Staunton (78 Alan Kernaghan). Manager: Jack Charlton

Goals: Rui Costa (59), Hélder (74), Cadete (89)

	P	W	D	L	F	A	Pts
Portugal	10	7	2	1	29	7	23
Rep. of Ireland	10	5	2	3	17	11	17
North. Ireland	10	5	2	3	20	15	17
Austria	10	5	1	4	29	14	16
Latvia	10	4	0	6	11	20	12
Liechtenstein	10	0	1	9	1	40	1

GROUP 7

WALES v ALBANIA 2-0 (1-0)

Arms Park, Cardiff 07.09.1994

Referee: Gianni Beschin (ITA) Attendance: 6,500

WALES: Neville Southall; Adrian Williams, Andy Melville, Chris Coleman, Paul Bodin; David Phillips, Jeremy Goss (74 Mark Pembridge), Gary Speed; Nathan Blake (80 Iwan Roberts), Ian Rush, Ryan Giggs. Manager: Mike Smith

ALBANIA: Foto Strakosha; Agustin Kola (52 Indrit Fortuzi), Ilir Shulku, Arian Xhumba, Rudi Vata, Salvator Kaçaj, Ylli Shehu (81 Edmond Dosti), Arian Bellai, Bledar Kola, Ledio Pano, Sulejman Demollari. Trainer: Neptun Bajko

Goals: Coleman (9), Giggs (67)

GEORGIA v MOLDOVA 0-1 (0-1)

Boris Paichadze, Tbilisi 07.09.1994

Referee: Ahmet Çakar (TUR) Attendance: 40,000

GEORGIA: Irakli Zoidze; Georgi Nemsadze, Kakhi Tskhadadze, Murtaz Shelia, Mihail Kavelashvili, Rezo Arveladze (70 Zaza Revishvili), Archil Arveladze, Gocha Jamarauli, Gija Guruli (46 Gela Inalishvili), Georgi Kinkladze, Shota Arveladze. Trainer: Aleksandr Chivadze

MOLDOVA: Vasile Coşelev; Serghei Secu, Serghei Nani, Serghei Stroenco, Valeriu Pogorelov, Andrei Stroenco (55 Radu Rebeja), Igor Oprea, Alexandru Curtianu, Serghei Belous, Alexandru Spiridon (81 Vladimir Kosse), Serghei Cleşcenco. Trainer: Ion Caras

Goal: Oprea (40)

BULGARIA v GEORGIA 2-0 (0-0)

Vasil Levski, Sofia 12.10.1994

Referee: Ladislav Gadosi (SVK) Attendance: 45,000

BULGARIA: Dimitar Popov; Ilian Kiriakov, Trifon Ivanov, Tsanko Tsvetanov, Petar Hubchev, Zlatko Iankov, Daniel Borimirov (54 Emil Kostadinov), Hristo Stoichkov, Iordan Lechkov, Nasko Sirakov (67 Liuboslav Penev), Krasimir Balakov. Trainer: Dimitar Penev

GEORGIA: Akaki Devadze; Zaza Revishvili, Kakhi Tskhadadze, Murtaz Shelia, Georgi Chikhradze, Dimitri Kudinov, Georgi Nemsadze (72 Gela Inalishvili), Kakhi Gogichaishvili, Temur Ketsbaia, Georgi Kinkladze, Shota Arveladze (78 Gija Guruli). Trainer: Aleksandr Chivadze

Goals: Kostadinov (55, 62)

MOLDOVA v WALES 3-2 (2-1)

Republican, Chişinău 12.10.1994

Referee: István Vad (HUNG) Attendance: 18,000

MOLDOVA: Vasile Coşelev; Serghei Secu, Serghei Belous (86 Emil Caras), Valeriu Pogorelov, Radu Rebeja, Serghei Stroenco, Igor Oprea, Alexandru Curtianu, Serghei Nani, Alexandru Spiridon, Iurie Miterev (46 Vladimir Kosse).
Trainer: Ion Caras

WALES: Neville Southall; Kit Symons, Mark Bowen, Adrian Williams, Chris Coleman, David Phillips, Barry Horne, Mark Pembridge, Iwan Roberts, Nathan Blake (87 Andy Melville), Gary Speed. Manager: Mike Smith

Goals: Speed (6), Belous (8), Secu (20), Blake (69), Pogorelov (78)

ALBANIA v GERMANY 1-2 (1-1)

Qemal Stafa, Tirana 16.11.1994

Referee: Vasiliy Melnichuk (UKR) Attendance: 23,000

ALBANIA: Foto Strakosha; Hysen Zmijani (65 Ledio Pano), Artur Lekbello, Arian Xhumba, Rudi Vata, Salvator Kaçaj, Sokol Kushta, Arian Bellai, Lefter Millo, Altin Rraklli, Sulejman Demollari (56 Bledar Kola). Trainer: Neptun Bajko

GERMANY: Andreas Köpke; Stefan Reuter, Ralf Weber (83 Dirk Schuster), Jürgen Kohler, Thomas Berthold, Dieter Eilts, Andreas Möller, Matthias Sammer (46 Thomas Strunz), Jürgen Klinsmann, Lothar Matthäus, Ulf Kirsten. Trainer: Hubert Vogts

Goals: Klinsmann (18), Zmijani (34), Kirsten (46)

ALBANIA v GEORGIA 0-1 (0-1)

Qemal Stafa, Tirana 14.12.1994

Referee: László Molnár (HUNG) Attendance: 15,000

ALBANIA: Foto Strakosha; Gjergj Dema, Salvator Kaçaj, Arian Xhumba, Rudi Vata (30 Ilir Shulku), Artur Lekbello (46 Saimir Malko), Indrit Fortuzi, Arian Bellai, Bledar Kola, Altin Rrakli, Sulejman Demollari. Trainer: Neptun Bajko

GEORGIA: Akaki Devadze; Zaza Revishvili, Dimitri Kudinov, Murtaz Shelia, Georgi Chikhradze, Kakhi Gogichaishvili (63 Mihail Jishkariani), Gela Inalishvili, Gocha Gogrichiani, Temur Ketsbaia, Georgi Kinkladze, Shota Arveladze (75 Gocha Jamarauli). Trainer: Aleksandr Chivadze

Goal: S. Arveladze (19)

BULGARIA v MOLDOVA 4-1 (1-0)

Vasil Levski, Sofia 16.11.1994

Referee: Denis McArdle (IRE) Attendance: 50,000

BULGARIA: Borislav Mihailov; Ilian Kiriakov, Trifon Ivanov, Petar Hubchev, Tsanko Tsvetanov, Krasimir Balakov, Ivailo Iordanov, Iordan Lechkov (86 Stanimir Stoilov), Hristo Stoichkov, Emil Kostadinov, Liuboslav Penev (80 Nasko Sirakov). Trainer: Dimitar Penev

MOLDOVA: Vasile Coşelev; Serghei Secu, Serghei Belous, Serghei Stroenco, Valeriu Pogorelov, Radu Rebeja, Alexandru Curtianu (82 Vladimir Kosse), Alexandru Spiridon, Serghei Nani, Igor Oprea, Serghei Cleşcenco. Trainer: Ion Caras

Goals: Stoichkov (45, 85), Cleşcenco (60), Balakov (64), Kostadinov (87)

WALES v BULGARIA 0-3 (0-2)

Arms Park, Cardiff 14.12.1994

Referee: Leif Sundell (SWE) Attendance: 20,000

WALES: Neville Southall; Mark Bowen, Mark Aizlewood, Vinnie Jones, Chris Coleman, Andy Melville, David Phillips, Dean Saunders, Ian Rush, Mark Hughes, Gary Speed. Manager: Mike Smith

BULGARIA: Borislav Mihailov; Emil Kremenliev, Trifon Ivanov, Tsanko Tsvetanov, Zlatko Iankov, Ivailo Iordanov, Emil Kostadinov (74 Ilian Kiriakov), Hristo Stoichkov, Liuboslav Penev (74 Nasko Sirakov), Krasimir Balakov, Iordan Lechkov. Trainer: Dimitar Penev

Goals: Ivanov (5), Kostadinov (16), Stoichkov (51)

GEORGIA v WALES 5-0 (2-0)

Boris Paichadze, Tbilisi 16.11.1994

Referee: Alain Sars (FRA) Attendance: 45,000

GEORGIA: Akaki Devadze; Zaza Revishvili, Kakhi Tskhadadze, Murtaz Shelia, Georgi Chikhradze, Kakhi Gogichaishvili, Georgi Nemsadze (42 Gela Inalishvili), Gocha Gogrichiani, Temur Ketsbaia (75 Mihail Kavelashvili), Georgi Kinkladze, Shota Arveladze. Trainer: Aleksandr Chivadze

WALES: Neville Southall; Alan Neilson (46 Kit Symons), Mark Bowen, Andy Melville, Chris Coleman, David Phillips, Barry Horne, Dean Saunders, Ian Rush, Mark Hughes, Gary Speed. Manager: Mike Smith

Goals: Ketsbaia (31, 49), Kinkladze (41), Gogrichiani (59), S. Arveladze (67)

MOLDOVA v GERMANY 0-3 (0-2)

Republican, Chişinău 14.12.1994

Referee: Jef van Vliet (HOL) Attendance: 25,000

MOLDOVA: Vasile Coşelev; Serghei Secu, Serghei Belous, Valeriu Pogorelov, Serghei Stroenco, Radu Rebeja (81 Ion Testimiţanu), Igor Oprea (58 Vladimir Gaidamaşciuc), Alexandru Curtianu, Serghei Nani, Alexandru Spiridon, Serghei Cleşcenco. Trainer: Ion Caras

GERMANY: Andreas Köpke; Stefan Reuter, Ralf Weber, Thomas Helmer, Thomas Berthold, Matthias Sammer, Andreas Möller (79 Stefan Kuntz), Thomas Hässler, Jürgen Klinsmann, Lothar Matthäus, Ulf Kirsten (69 Thomas Strunz). Trainer: Hubert Vogts

Goals: Kirsten (6), Klinsmann (38), Matthäus (71)

GERMANY v ALBANIA 2-1 (2-0)

Fritz-Walter, Kaiserslautern 18.12.1994

Referee: Svend Erik Christensen (DEN) Att: 20,310

GERMANY: Andreas Köpke; Stefan Reuter, Ralf Weber, Thomas Helmer, Thomas Berthold, Mathias Sammer, Andreas Möller, Thomas Hässler (78 Thomas Strunz), Jürgen Klinsmann, Lothar Matthäus, Ulf Kirsten (59 Stefan Kuntz). Trainer: Hubert Vogts

ALBANIA: Foto Strakosha; Hysen Zmijani, Ilir Shulku, Arian Xhumba, Gjergj Dema, Salvator Kaçaj, Saimir Malko, Arian Bellai, Bledar Kola (59 Alvaro Zalla), Altin Rraklli, Sulejman Demollari. Trainer: Neptun Bajko

Goals: Matthäus (8 pen), Klinsmann (17), Rrakli (58)

GEORGIA v GERMANY 0-2 (0-2)

Boris Paichadze, Tbilisi 29.03.1995

Referee: Martin Bodenham (ENG) Attendance: 75,000

GEORGIA: Akaki Devadze; Zaza Revishvili, Kakhi Tskhadadze, Murtaz Shelia, Georgi Chikhradze, Kakhi Gogichaishvili, Dimitri Kudinov, Gocha Jamarauli (64 Gocha Gogrichiani), Rezo Arveladze (77 Mihail Kavelashvili), Georgi Kinkladze, Shota Arveladze. Trainer: Aleksandr Chivadze

GERMANY: Andreas Köpke; Stefan Reuter, Ralf Weber (46 Steffen Freund), Jürgen Kohler, Thomas Helmer, Markus Babbel, Dieter Eilts, Mario Basler, Jürgen Klinsmann, Andreas Möller, Heiko Herrlich. Trainer: Hubert Vogts

Goals: Klinsmann (24, 45)

ALBANIA v MOLDOVA 3-0 (2-0)

Qemal Stafa, Tiranë 29.03.1995

Referee: Urs Meier (SWI) Attendance: 15,000

ALBANIA: Foto Strakosha (80 Blendi Nallbani); Saimir Malko, Ilir Shulku, Arian Xhumba (69 Indrit Fortuzi), Rudi Vata, Salvator Kaçaj, Sokol Kushta (75 Edmond Dalipi), Arian Bellai, Edmond Abazi, Altin Rraklli, Sulejman Demollari. Trainer: Neptun Bajko

MOLDOVA: Vasile Coşelev; Sergei Secu, Serghei Belous, Valeriu Pogorelov, Vladimir Gaidamaşciuc (66 Andrei Stroenco), Serghei Stroenco, Igor Oprea, Alexandru Curtianu (73 Emil Caras), Serghei Nani, Alexandru Spiridon, Serghei Cleşcenco. Trainer: Ion Caras

Goals: Kushta (31, 79), Kaçaj (41)

GERMANY v WALES 1-1 (1-1)

Rheinstadion, Düsseldorf 26.04.1995

Referee: José García-Aranda Encinar (SPA) Att: 43,461

GERMANY: Andreas Köpke; Stefan Reuter, Ralf Weber, Steffen Freund, Markus Babbel, Christian Ziege (86 Stefan Kuntz), Dieter Eilts, Mario Basler (76 Mehmet Scholl), Jürgen Klinsmann, Thomas Hässler, Heiko Herrlich. Trainer: Hubert Vogts

WALES: Neville Southall; David Phillips, Mark Bowen, Vinnie Jones, Kit Symons, Chris Coleman (46 Adrian Williams), Barry Horne, Dean Saunders, Ian Rush, Mark Hughes (89 John Hartson), Gary Speed. Manager: Mike Smith

Goals: Saunders (8), Herrlich (42)

BULGARIA v WALES 3-1 (1-0)

Vasil Levski, Sofia 29.03.1995

Referee: Michel Piraux (BEL) Attendance: 65,000

BULGARIA: Borislav Mihailov; Emil Kremenliev, Trifon Ivanov, Tsanko Tsvetanov (65 Ilian Kiriakov), Petar Hubchev, Zlatko Iankov, Emil Kostadinov, Hristo Stoichkov, Liuboslav Penev, Krasimir Balakov, Iordan Lechkov. Trainer: Dimitar Penev

WALES: Neville Southall; David Phillips, Mark Bowen, Vinnie Jones (78 John Cornforth), Kit Symons, Chris Coleman, Barry Horne, Dean Saunders, John Hartson, Gary Speed, Ryan Giggs. Manager: Mike Smith

Goals: Balakov (37), Penev (70, 82), Saunders (83)

GEORGIA v ALBANIA 2-0 (2-0)

Boris Paichadze, Tbilisi 26.04.1995

Referee: Roelof Luinge (HOL) Attendance: 25,000

GEORGIA: Akaki Devadze; Georgi Gudushauri, Dimitri Kudinov, Murtaz Shelia (70 Nugzar Lobjanidze), Georgi Chikhradze, Kakhi Gogichaishvili, Gela Inalishvili, Gocha Jamarauli, Temur Ketsbaia, David Kizilashvili (59 Archil Arveladze), Shota Arveladze. Trainer: Aleksandr Chivadze

ALBANIA: Foto Strakosha; Ardian Mema, Saimir Malko, Arian Xhumba, Rudi Vata, Salvator Kaçaj, Sokol Kushta (83 Edmond Dosti), Indrit Fortuzi (57 Sokol Prenga), Edmond Dalipi, Altin Rraklli, Sulejman Demollari. Trainer: Neptun Bajko

Goals: S. Arveladze (2), Ketsbaia (42)

MOLDOVA v BULGARIA 0-3 (0-1)

Republican, Chişinău 26.04.1995

Referee: Jiri Ulrich (CZE) Attendance: 18,000

MOLDOVA: Vasile Coşelev; Sergei Secu, Oleg Fistican, Valeriu Pogorelov, Emil Caras (66 Vladimir Gaidamaşciuc); Radu Rebeja, Igor Oprea (83 Boris Cebotari), Serghei Belous, Serghei Nani; Alexandru Curtianu, Serghei Cleşcenco. Trainer: Ion Caras

BULGARIA: Borislav Mihailov; Emil Kremenliev (81 Ilian Kiriakov), Trifon Ivanov, Tsanko Tsvetanov, Petar Hubchev; Zlatko Iankov, Ivailo Iordanov, Hristo Stoichkov (76 Petar Mikhtarski), Iordan Lechkov; Liuboslav Penev, Krasimir Balakov. Trainer: Dimitar Penev

Goals: Balakov (29), Stoichkov (57, 67)

WALES v GEORGIA 0-1 (0-0)

Arms Park, Cardiff 07.06.1995

Referee: Ilka Koho (FIN) Attendance: 6,500

WALES: Neville Southall; David Phillips, Mark Bowen, Vinnie Jones, Kit Symons, Adrian Williams, Barry Horne, Dean Saunders (82 Mark Pembridge), Ian Rush, Mark Hughes (82 John Hartson), John Cornforth. Manager: Mike Smith

GEORGIA: Akaki Devadze; Besik Beradze, Kakhi Tskhadadze, Murtaz Shelia, Georgi Chikhradze, Kakhi Gogichaishvili, Gela Inalishvili, Mihail Kavelashvili (73 Levan Tskitishvili), Temur Ketsbaia, Georgi Kinkladze, Shota Arveladze (86 Georgi Kilasonia). Trainer: Aleksandr Chivadze

Goal: Kinkladze (72)

MOLDOVA v ALBANIA 2-3 (2-2)

Republican, Chişinău 07.06.1995

Referee: Leon Schellings (BEL) Attendance: 8,000

MOLDOVA: Evgheni Ivanov; Sergei Secu, Oleg Fistican, Valeriu Pogorelov, Radu Rebeja (73 Vladimir Kosse), Serghei Stroenco, Andrei Stroenco, Serghei Belous (55 Iurie Miterev), Serghei Nani, Alexandru Curtianu, Serghei Cleşcenco. Trainer: Ion Caras

ALBANIA: Foto Strakosha; Artan Bano, Ilir Shulku, Saimir Malko, Rudi Vata, Salvator Kaçaj, Sokol Kushta, Arian Bellai, Bledar Kola, Altin Rraklli (87 Sokol Prenga), Sulejman Demollari (81 Ledio Pano). Trainer: Neptun Bajko

Goals: Kushta (7), Curtianu (10), Cleşcenco (15), Bellai (25), Vata (71)

ALBANIA v BULGARIA 1-1 (1-1)

Qemal Stafa, Tirana 06.09.1995

Referee: Charles Agius (MAL) Attendance: 10,000

ALBANIA: Foto Strakosha; Edmond Abazi, Ilir Shulku, Arian Xhumba, Rudi Vata, Artur Lekbello, Sokol Kushta, Arian Bellai, Bledar Kola (65 Ylli Shehu, 88 Ledio Pano), Altin Rraklli, Kliton Bozgo (86 Sulejman Demollari). Trainer: Neptun Bajko

BULGARIA: Borislav Mihailov; Emil Kremenliev, Trifon Ivanov, Tsanko Tsvetanov, Petar Hubchev; Daniel Borimirov, Emil Kostadinov, Hristo Stoichkov, Liuboslav Penev (75 Nasko Sirakov), Krasimir Balakov, Iordan Lechkov (75 Krasimir Chomakov). Trainer: Dimitar Penev

Goals: Stoichkov (8), Rraklli (15)

BULGARIA v GERMANY 3-2 (1-2)

Vasil Levski, Sofia 07.06.1995

Referee: Pierluigi Pairetto (ITA) Attendance: 60,000

BULGARIA: Borislav Mihailov; Emil Kremenliev, Trifon Ivanov, Tsanko Tsvetanov, Petar Hubchev; Zlatko Iankov, Ivailo Iordanov (63 Emil Kostadinov), Hristo Stoichkov, Liuboslav Penev, Krasimir Balakov, Iordan Lechkov (81 Nasko Sirakov). Trainer: Dimitar Penev

GERMANY: Andreas Köpke; Stefan Reuter, Thomas Strunz (90 Ulf Kirsten), Markus Babbel, Thomas Helmer, Matthias Sammer, Dieter Eilts, Mario Basler (81 Andreas Möller), Jürgen Klinsmann, Thomas Hässler, Heiko Herrlich. Trainer: Hubert Vogts

Goals: Klinsmann (18), Strunz (44), Stoichkov (45 pen, 66 pen), Kostadinov (69)

GERMANY v GEORGIA 4-1 (1-1)

Frankenstadion, Nuremberg 06.09.1995

Referee: James McCluskey (SCO) Attendance: 40,000

GERMANY: Oliver Kahn; Markus Babbel, Christian Ziege, Jürgen Kohler, Thomas Helmer, Steffen Freund, Andreas Möller, Thomas Strunz, Jürgen Klinsmann, Thomas Hässler, Ulf Kirsten. Trainer: Hubert Vogts

GEORGIA: Akaki Devadze; Gocha Gujabidze, Dimitri Kudinov, Murtaz Shelia, Georgi Chikhradze, Kakhi Gogichaishvili (68 Archil Arveladze), Georgi Nemsadze, Mihail Kavelashvili (46 Georgi Kilasonia), Temur Ketsbaia, Georgi Kinkladze, Shota Arveladze. Trainer: Aleksandr Chivadze

Goals: Ketsbaia (28), Möller (38), Ziege (56), Kirsten (62), Babbel (72)

WALES v MOLDOVA 1-0 (0-0)

Arms Park, Cardiff 06.09.1995

Referee: Gylfi Orrason (ICE) Attendance: 5,000

WALES: Neville Southall; Mark Bowen, Chris Coleman, Adrian Williams, Kit Symons, Mark Pembridge, Barry Horne, Lee Nogan (46 David Phillips), Ian Rush (69 John Hartson), Mark Hughes, Gary Speed. Trainer: Bobby Gould

MOLDOVA: Evgheni Ivanov; Oleg Fistican, Ion Testimiţanu, Vitali Culibaba, Radu Rebeja (84 Vadim Gavriliuc), Serghei Stroenco, Igor Oprea, Serghei Belous, Serghei Nani (76 Alexandru Suharev), Boris Cebotari, Serghei Cleşcenco. Trainer: Ion Caras

Sent off: Fistican (88)

Goal: Speed (55)

WALES v GERMANY 1-2 (0-0)

Arms Park, Cardiff 11.10.1995

Referee: Ion Crăciunescu (ROM) Attendance: 25,000

WALES: Neville Southall; Stephen Jenkins (71 Paul Mardon), Mark Bowen, Kit Symons, Andy Melville, Mark Pembridge (82 Geraint Williams), Barry Horne, Dean Saunders, Nathan Blake (82 Glyn Hodges), Gary Speed, Ryan Giggs. Trainer: Bobby Gould

GERMANY: Andreas Köpke; Markus Babbel (46 Christian Wörns), Christian Ziege, Steffen Freund, Thomas Helmer, Matthias Sammer, Andreas Möller, Dieter Eilts, Jürgen Klinsmann, Thomas Hässler, Heiko Herrlich (74 Stefan Kuntz). Trainer: Hubert Vogts

Goals: Melville (75 og), Helmer (78 og), Klinsmann (81)

BULGARIA v ALBANIA 3-0 (1-0)

Vasil Levski, Sofia 07.10.1995

Referee: Juha Hirviniemi (FIN) Attendance: 35,000

BULGARIA: Borislav Mihailov; Emil Kremenliev, Trifon Ivanov, Tsanko Tsvetanov, Zlatko Iankov, Ilian Kiriakov (88 Daniel Borimirov), Emil Kostadinov (86 Nasko Sirakov), Hristo Stoichkov, Liuboslav Penev, Krasimir Balakov, Iordan Lechkov. Trainer: Dimitar Penev

ALBANIA: Foto Strakosha; Hysen Zmijani, Saimir Malko, Arian Xhumba, Ilir Shulku, Gjergj Dema, Sokol Kushta, Arian Bellai, Bledar Kola, Altin Rraklli, Edmond Abazi (85 Sulejman Demollari). Trainer: Neptun Bajko

Goals: Lechkov (13), Kostadinov (82, 84)

GEORGIA v BULGARIA 2-1 (1-0)

Boris Paichadze, Tbilisi 11.10.1995

Referee: Urs Meier (SWI) Attendance: 45,000

GEORGIA: Irakli Zoidze; Georgi Gudushauri (82 Besik Beradze), Dimitri Kudinov, Murtaz Shelia, Georgi Chikhradze, Kakhi Gogichaishvili, Georgi Nemsadze, Gocha Jamarauli (74 Georgi Kilasonia), Archil Arveladze (46 Mihail Kavelashvili), Georgi Kinkladze, Shota Arveladze. Trainer: Aleksandr Chivadze

BULGARIA: Borislav Mihailov; Ilian Kiriakov, Trifon Ivanov (58 Krasimir Chomakov), Tsanko Tsvetanov, Zlatko Iankov, Nasko Sirakov (58 Daniel Borimirov), Emil Kostadinov, Hristo Stoichkov, Liuboslav Penev, Krasimir Balakov, Iordan Lechkov. Trainer: Dimitar Penev

Goals: S. Arveladze (1), Kinkladze (47 pen), Stoichkov (87)

GERMANY v MOLDOVA 6-1 (3-0)

Ulrich Haberland, Leverkusen 08.10.1995

Referee: Zygmunt Ziober (POL) Attendance: 28,500

GERMANY: Andreas Köpke; Markus Babbel, Christian Ziege, Steffen Freund, Thomas Helmer, Matthias Sammer (83 Christian Wörns), Andreas Möller (78 Mehmet Scholl), Dieter Eilts, Jürgen Klinsmann, Thomas Hässler, Heiko Herrlich (74 Fredi Bobic). Trainer: Hubert Vogts

MOLDOVA: Evgheni Ivanov; Sergiu Secu, Ion Testimiţanu, Vitali Culibaba, Radu Rebeja, Serghei Stroenco, Igor Oprea (86 Vadim Gavriliuc), Serghei Belous, Serghei Nani (60 Iurie Miterev), Alexandru Curtianu, Serghei Cleşcenco. Trainer: Ion Caras

Goals: S.Stroenco (15 og), Helmer (18), Sammer (24, 72), Möller (47, 61), Rebeja (80)

ALBANIA v WALES 1-1 (1-1)

Qemal Stafa, Tirana 15.11.1995

Referee: David Suheil (ISR) Attendance: 5,500

ALBANIA: Foto Strakosha; Hysen Zmijani, Ilir Shulku, Gjergj Dema (83 Arben Milori), Rudi Vata, Artur Lekbello, Sokol Kushta (57 Bushi), Saimir Malko, Kliton Bozgo (78 Alvaro Zalla), Altin Rraklli, Ledio Pano. Trainer: Neptun Bajko

WALES: Neville Southall; Stephen Jenkins, Mark Bowen, David Phillips, Eric Young, Andy Melville, Gareth Taylor (84 John Robinson), Ceri Hughes (63 Robbie Savage), Dean Saunders, Mark Pembridge, Ryan Giggs. Manager: Bobby Gould

Goals: Kushta (3 pen), Pembridge (43)

GERMANY v BULGARIA 3-1 (0-0)

Olimpiastadion, Berlin 15.11.1995

Referee: Vasilios Nikakis (GRE) Attendance: 75,841

GERMANY: Andreas Köpke; Markus Babbel, Steffen Freund, Jürgen Kohler (46 Thomas Strunz), Thomas Helmer, Matthias Sammer, Dieter Eilts, Mario Basler, Jürgen Klinsmann, Thomas Hässler (88 Stefan Reuter), Stefan Kuntz (82 Fredi Bobic). Trainer: Hubert Vogts

BULGARIA: Dimitar Popov; Emil Kremenliev, Valentin Dartilov, Tsanko Tsvetanov, Gosho Ginchev, Zlatko Iankov, Emil Kostadinov, Hristo Stoichkov, Liuboslav Penev (86 Nasko Sirakov), Krasimir Balakov (82 Daniel Borimirov), Iordan Lechkov (62 Ilian Kiriakov). Trainer: Dimitar Penev

Goals: Stoichkov (47), Klinsmann (50, 77 pen), Hässler (56)

MOLDOVA v GEORGIA 3-2 (2-0)

Republican, Chişinău 15.11.1995

Referee: Mario van der Ende (HOL) Attendance: 7,000

MOLDOVA: Vasile Coşelev; Sergiu Secu, Ion Testimiţanu, Vitali Culibaba, Serghei Belous, Serghei Nani, Igor Oprea (52 Alexandru Suharev), Serghei Kirilov (74 Vadim Gavriliuc), Iurie Miterev, Alexandru Curtianu (72 Boris Cebotari), Serghei Cleşcenco. Trainer: Ion Caras

GEORGIA: Irakli Zoidze; Georgi Gudushauri (63 David Janashia), Dimitri Kudinov, Besik Beradze, Georgi Chikhradze, Kakhi Gogichaishvili, Levan Tskitishvili, Gocha Jamarauli (60 Mamuka Machavariani), Temur Ketsbaia, Georgi Kinkladze, Shota Arveladze. Trainer: Aleksandr Chivadze

Sent off: Chikhradze (40)

Goals: Testimiţanu (5 pen), Miterev (17, 68), Janashia (66), Culibaba (77 og)

	P	W	D	L	F	A	Pts
Germany	10	8	1	1	27	10	25
Bulgaria	10	7	1	2	24	10	22
Georgia	10	5	0	5	14	13	15
Moldova	10	3	0	7	11	27	9
Wales	10	2	2	6	9	19	8
Albania	10	2	2	6	10	16	8

GROUP 8

FINLAND v SCOTLAND 0-2 (0-1)

Olympiastadion, Helsinki 07.09.1994

Referee: Ryszard Wojcik (POL) Attendance: 12,845

FINLAND: Petri Jakonen; Janne Mäkelä, Markku Kanerva, Aki Hyryläinen, Antti Heinola (30 Erik Holmgren), Kim Suominen, Rami Rantanen (41 Petri Järvinen), Janne Lindberg, Ari Hjelm, Jari Litmanen, Mika-Matti Paatelainen. Trainer: Tommy Lindholm

SCOTLAND: Andy Goram; Stewart McKimmie, Tom Boyd, Alan McLaren, Colin Hendry, Craig Levein (78 Stuart McCall), Andy Walker (65 Eoin Jess), Paul McStay, Duncan Shearer, Gary McAllister, John Collins. Manager: Craig Brown

Goals: Shearer (29), Collins (66)

FAROE ISLANDS v GREECE 1-5 (0-2)

Svangaskard, Toftir 07.09.1994

Referee: Michel Piraux (BEL) Attendance: 2,412

FAROE ISLANDS: Jens Martin Knudsen; Tummas Eli Hansen, Jens Christian Hansen, Abraham Hansen, Oli Johannesen, Jan Dam, Allan Mørkøre (84 Jens Erik Rasmussen), Magni Jarnskor, Jan Allan Müller, Todi Jonsson, Øssur Hansen (54 Henning Jarnskor). Trainer: Allan Simonsen

GREECE: Hristos Karkamanis; Efstratios Apostolakis, Kiriakos Karataidis, Kostas Pavlopoulos, Yannis Kallitzakis, Panayotis Tsalouhidis, Dimitris Saravakos, Hristos Kostis (79 Dimitris Markos), Minas Hantzidis (82 Theodoros Zagorakis), Vassilis Tsartas, Alexandros Alexandris. Trainer: Kostas Polihroniou

Goals: Saravakos (12), Tsalouhidis (17, 87), Alexandris (55, 60), Apostolakis (89 og)

GREECE v FINLAND 4-0 (1-0)

Kautatzogleio, Thessaloniki 12.10.1994

Referee: Philippe Leduc (FRA) Attendance: 30,000

GREECE: Ilias Atmatsidis; Efstratios Apostolakis, Mihalis Kassapis, Nikos Dabizas, Yannis Kallitzakis, Panayotis Tsalouhidis, Theodoros Zagorakis, Dimitris Markos (64 Yorgos Toursounidis), Nikos Mahlas, Vassilis Tsartas, Zissis Vrizas (42 Daniel Batista). Trainer: Kostas Polihroniou

FINLAND: Petri Jakonen; Janne Mäkelä, Markku Kanerva, Aki Hyryläinen, Antti Heinola (31 Erik Holmgren), Kim Suominen, Petri Järvinen (73 Antti Sumiala), Janne Lindberg, Ari Hjelm, Jari Litmanen, Mika-Matti Paatelainen. Trainer: Tommy Lindholm

Goals: Markos (23), Batista (69), Mahlas (76, 90)

SCOTLAND v FAROE ISLANDS 5-1 (3-0)

Hampden Park, Glasgow 12.10.1994

Referee: Terje Hauge (NOR) Attendance: 20,885

SCOTLAND: Andy Goram; Stewart McKimmie, Tom Boyd, Alan McLaren, Colin Hendry (58 Billy McKinlay), Craig Levein, Patrick Nevin, Paul McStay, John McGinlay, Scott Booth (70 Andy Walker), John Collins.
Manager: Craig Brown

FAROE ISLANDS: Jens Martin Knudsen; Jens Christian Hansen, Tummas Eli Hansen, Oli Johannesen, Øssur Hansen, Jan Dam (54 Djoni Joensen), Magni Jarnskor, Kurt Mørkøre (71 Janus Rasmussen), Jan Allan Müller, Todi Jonsson, Henning Jarnskor. Trainer: Allan Simonsen

Goals: McGinlay (4), Booth (34), Collins (40, 72), McKinlay (61), Müller (75)

GREECE v SAN MARINO 2-0 (1-0)

Olympiako, Athina 16.11.1994

Referee: Chaim Lipkovitch (ISR) Attendance: 13,500

GREECE: Ilias Atmatsidis; Efstratios Apostolakis, Mihalis Kassapis, Nikos Dabizas, Yannis Kallitzakis, Spiros Maragos (46 Kostas Frantzeskos), Theodoros Zagorakis, Yorgos Toursounidis, Nikos Mahlas, Vassilis Tsartas, Zissis Vrizas (70 Daniel Batista). Trainer: Kostas Polihroniou

SAN MARINO: Pier Luigi Benedettini; Luca Gobbi, Mirco Gennari (46 Claudio Canti), Pier Domenico Della Valle (75 Bryan Gasperoni), Mauro Valentini, William Guerra, Pierangelo Manzaroli, Fabio Francini, Nicola Bacciocchi, Massimo Bonini, Davide Gualtieri. Trainer: Giorgio Leoni

Goals: Mahlas (20), Frantzeskos (84)

RUSSIA v SAN MARINO 4-0 (1-0)

Luzhniki, Moskva 12.10.1994

Referee: Alain Hamer (LUX) Attendance: 20,000

RUSSIA: Stanislav Cherchesov; Vasili Kulkov (62 Omari Tetradze), Yuri Nikiforov, Ilya Tsymbalar (56 Igor Kolyvanov), Igor Shalimov, Valeri Karpin, Viktor Onopko, Andrei Kanchelskis, Andrei Pyatnitski, Dmitri Radchenko, Sergei Kiryakov. Trainer: Oleg Romantsev

SAN MARINO: Pier Luigi Benedettini; Luca Gobbi, Mirco Gennari, Marco Mazza, Mauro Valentini, William Guerra (21 Pier Domenico Della Valle), Pierangelo Manzaroli, Ivan Matteoni, Nicola Bacciocchi, Massimo Bonini, Fabio Francini (61 Claudio Canti). Trainer: Giorgio Leoni

Goals: Karpin (43), Kolyvanov (64), Nikiforov (65), Radchenko (67)

SCOTLAND v RUSSIA 1-1 (1-1)

Hampden Park, Glasgow 16.11.1994

Referee: Bo Karlsson (SWE) Attendance: 31,254

SCOTLAND: Andy Goram; Stewart McKimmie, Tom Boyd, Stuart McCall, Alan McLaren, Craig Levein, Scott Booth, Billy McKinlay (83 Patrick Nevin), John McGinlay (63 John Spencer), Gary McAllister, John Collins.
Manager: Craig Brown

RUSSIA: Stanislav Cherchesov; Vasili Kulkov, Yuri Nikiforov, Sergei Gorlukovich, Igor Shalimov, Valeri Karpin, Viktor Onopko, Andrei Kanchelskis, Andrei Pyatnitski (75 Omari Tetradze), Dmitri Radchenko, Vladislav Radimov.
Trainer: Oleg Romantsev

Goals: Booth (19), Radchenko (26)

FINLAND v FAROE ISLANDS 5-0 (1-0)

Olympiastadion, Helsinki 16.11.1994

Referee: Gylfi Orrason (ICE) Attendance: 5,000

FINLAND: Kari Laukkanen; Janne Mäkelä, Markku Kanerva, Anders Eriksson, Petri Helin, Janne Lindberg (78 Marko Rajamäki), Antti Sumiala (88 Jukka Ruhanen), Kari Ukkonen, Ari Hjelm, Jari Litmanen, Mika-Matti Paatelainen.
Trainer: Jukka Ikäläinen

FAROE ISLANDS: Jens Martin Knudsen; Oli Johannesen, Tummas Eli Hansen, Janus Rasmussen, Øssur Hansen (76 Jens Erik Rasmussen), Kurt Mørkøre, Magni Jarnskor, Henning Jarnskor, Jan Allan Müller, Todi Jonsson, Djoni Joensen.
Trainer: Allan Simonsen

Goals: Sumiala (37), Litmanen (53 pen, 72), Paatelainen (75, 85)

FINLAND v SAN MARINO 4-1 (2-1)

Olympiastadion, Helsinki 14.12.1994

Referee: Hermann Albrecht (GER) Attendance: 3,140

FINLAND: Kari Laukkanen; Janne Mäkelä, Markku Kanerva, Anders Eriksson, Petri Helin (74 Marko Myyry), Janne Lindberg, Antti Sumiala, Kari Ukkonen, Ari Hjelm, Jari Litmanen, Mika-Matti Paatelainen. Trainer: Jukka Ikäläinen

SAN MARINO: Pier Luigi Benedettini; Claudio Canti, Mirco Gennari, Bryan Gasperoni, Luca Gobbi, William Guerra, Pierangelo Manzaroli, Pier Domenico Della Valle, Nicola Bacciocchi (86 Claudio Peverani), Massimo Bonini, Marco Marco Mularoni (60 Davide Gualtieri).
Trainer: Giorgio Leoni

Goals: Paatelainen (24, 30, 86, 90), Della Valle (34)

GREECE v SCOTLAND 1-0 (1-0)

Olympiako, Athina 18.12.1994

Referee: John Blankenstein (HOL) Attendance: 20,000

GREECE: Ilias Atmatsidis; Efstratios Apostolakis, Mihalis Kassapis, Mihalis Vlahos, Yannis Kallitzakis, Panayotis Tsalouhidis, Theodoros Zagorakis, Nikos Nioblias (88 Theofilos Karassavidis), Nikos Mahlas, Yorgos Toursounidis, Alexandros Alexandris (72 Spiros Maragos). Trainer: Kostas Polihroniou

SCOTLAND: Andy Goram (77 James Leighton); Stewart McKimmie, Tom Boyd, Stuart McCall, Colin Hendry, Alan McLaren, John McGinlay, Billy McKinlay (46 John Spencer), Duncan Ferguson, Gary McAllister, John Collins. Manager: Craig Brown

Goal: Apostolakis (18 pen)

GREECE v RUSSIA 0-3 (0-1)

Kautatzogleio, Thessaloniki 26.04.1995

Referee: Loris Stafoggia (ITA) Attendance: 45,000

GREECE: Ilias Atmatsidis; Efstratios Apostolakis, Mihalis Kassapis, Nikos Dabizas, Yannis Kallitzakis, Panayotis Tsalouhidis, Theodoros Zagorakis, Nikos Nioblias (46 Vassilis Tsartas), Nikos Mahlas (59 Thamistoklis Nikolaidis), Yorgos Toursounidis, Yorgos Donis. Trainer: Kostas Polihroniou

RUSSIA: Dmitri Kharin; Vasili Kulkov, Yuri Nikiforov, Yuri Kovtun, Dmitri Khlestov, Valeri Karpin, Viktor Onopko, Andrei Pyatnitski (46 Sergei Kiryakov), Igor Dobrovolski, Dmitri Radchenko (77 Aleksandr Mostovoi), Vladimir Beschastnykh. Trainer: Oleg Romantsev

Goals: Nikiforov (36), Zagorakis (78 og), Beschastnykh (79)

SAN MARINO v FINLAND 0-2 (0-1)

Olimpico, Serravalle 29.03.1995

Referee: David Suheil (ISR) Attendance: 824

SAN MARINO: Pier Luigi Benedettini; Luca Gobbi, Mirco Gennari, Marco Mazza (70 Ivan Matteoni), Mauro Valentini, William Guerra, Pierangelo Manzaroli, Fabio Francini, Paolo Montagna (75 Davide Gualtieri), Massimo Bonini, Marco Mularoni. Trainer: Giorgio Leoni

FINLAND: Kari Laukkanen; Janne Mäkelä, Kari Ukkonen, Anders Eriksson, Petri Helin, Janne Lindberg, Antti Sumiala, Marko Myyry (83 Sami Hyypiä), Ari Hjelm, Jari Litmanen, Petri Järvinen (76 Marko Rajamäki). Trainer: Jukka Ikäläinen

Goals: Litmanen (45), Sumiala (65)

SAN MARINO v SCOTLAND 0-2 (0-1)

Olimpico, Serravalle 26.04.1995

Referee: Loizos Loizou (CYP) Attendance: 1,738

SAN MARINO: Pier Luigi Benedettini; Claudio Canti, Mirco Gennari, Marco Mazza, Luca Gobbi, William Guerra, Pierangelo Manzaroli, Pier Domenico Della Valle, Nicola Bacciocchi, Massimo Bonini (46 Ivan Matteoni), Marco Mularoni (73 Davide Gualtieri). Trainer: Giorgio Leoni

SCOTLAND: James Leighton; Colin Calderwood, Tom Boyd, Alan McLaren, Colin Hendry, Darren Jackson, Patrick Nevin (78 Billy McKinlay), Duncan Shearer (67 John Spencer), John McGinlay, Gary McAllister, John Collins. Manager: Craig Brown

Goals: Collins (19), Calderwood (85)

RUSSIA v SCOTLAND 0-0

Luzhniki, Moskva 29.03.1995

Referee: Hartmut Strampe (GER) Attendance: 27,500

RUSSIA: Dmitri Kharin; Dmitri Khlestov, Yuri Nikiforov, Yuri Kovtun, Igor Shalimov (70 Vladislav Radimov), Valeri Karpin, Viktor Onopko, Andrei Kanchelskis, Igor Dobrovolski, Dmitri Radchenko (56 Nikolai Pisarev), Sergei Kiryakov. Trainer: Oleg Romantsev

SCOTLAND: James Leighton; Stewart McKimmie, Tom Boyd, Alan McLaren, Colin Hendry, Colin Calderwood, Darren Jackson (77 Duncan Shearer), Paul McStay, John McGinlay (83 Billy McKinlay), Gary McAllister, John Collins. Manager: Craig Brown

FAROE ISLANDS v FINLAND 0-4 (0-0)

Svangaskard, Toftir 26.04.1995

Referee: Alan Howells (WAL) Attendance: 1,000

FAROE ISLANDS: Jens Martin Knudsen; Oli Johannesen, Jens Christian Hansen, Janus Rasmussen, Kurt Mørkøre, Allan Mørkøre, Magni Jarnskor (80 Henning Jarnskor), Øssur Hansen, Allan Joensen, Todi Jonsson, Julian Johnsson. Trainer: Allan Simonsen

FINLAND: Kari Laukannen; Janne Mäkelä, Kari Ukkonen, Anders Eriksson, Petri Helin, Janne Lindberg (82 Kim Suominen), Antti Sumiala (60 Joonas Kolkka), Sami Hyypiä, Ari Hjelm, Jari Litmanen, Mika-Matti Paatelainen. Trainer: Jukka Ikäläinen

Goals: Hjelm (55), Paatelainen (75), Lindberg (78), Helin (83)

RUSSIA v FAROE ISLANDS 3-0 (0-0)

Luzhniki, Moskva 06.05.1995

Referee: Sergo Kvaratskhelia (GEO) Attendance: 9,500

RUSSIA: Stanislav Cherchesov; Dmitri Khlestov, Yuri Nikiforov, Yuri Kovtun, Omari Tetradze, Valeri Kechinov, Viktor Onopko, Dmitri Cheryshev, Andrei Pyatnitski (22 Vladimir Lebed), Nikolai Pisarev, Mukhsin Mukhamadiev. Trainer: Oleg Romantsev

FAROE ISLANDS: Jens Martin Knudsen; Oli Johannesen, Jens Christian Hansen, Janus Rasmussen, Kurt Mørkøre, Allan Joensen, Magni Jarnskor, Øssur Hansen, Henning Jarnskor (69 Djoni Joensen), Todi Jonsson, Jens Erik Rasmussen. Trainer: Allan Simonsen

Goals: Kechinov (53), Pisarev (72), Mukhamadiev (80)

FAROE ISLANDS v SCOTLAND 0-2 (0-2)

Svangaskard, Toftir 07.06.1995

Referee: Vladimir Hrinak (SVK) Attendance: 3,881

FAROE ISLANDS: Jens Martin Knudsen; Oli Johannesen, Tummas Eli Hansen, Janus Rasmussen, Jens Christian Hansen, Øssur Hansen, Magni Jarnskor (63 Allan Joensen), Julian Johnsson, Henning Jarnskor, Todi Jonsson, Jens Erik Rasmussen (74 Jan Allan Müller). Trainer: Allan Simonsen

SCOTLAND: James Leighton; Stewart McKimmie, Rob McKinnon, Alan McLaren, Colin Calderwood, Craig Burley, Darren Jackson, Billy McKinlay, John McGinlay (75 Scott Gemmill), John Collins, Duncan Shearer (86 John Robertson). Manager: Craig Brown

Goals: McKinlay (25), McGinlay (29)

FAROE ISLANDS v SAN MARINO 3-0 (2-0)

Svangaskard, Toftir 25.05.1995

Referee: Brendan Shorte (IRE) Attendance: 3,450

FAROE ISLANDS: Jens Martin Knudsen; Oli Johannesen, Jens Christian Hansen, Janus Rasmussen, Kurt Mørkøre, Øssur Hansen, Magni Jarnskor, Julian Johnsson, Henning Jarnskor, Todi Jonsson, Jens Erik Rasmussen. Trainer: Allan Simonsen

SAN MARINO: Pier Luigi Benedettini; Luca Gobbi, Mirco Gennari, Bryan Gasperoni, Mauro Valentini, Claudio Canti, Pierangelo Manzaroli, Fabio Francini, Nicola Bacciocchi, Massimo Bonini (57 Andrea Ugolini), Marco Mularoni. Trainer: Giorgio Leoni

Goals: J.C. Hansen (7), J.E. Rasmussen (9), Johnsson (62)

FINLAND v GREECE 2-1 (1-1)

Olympiastadion, Helsinki 11.06.1995

Referee: Hellmut Krug (GER) Attendance: 10,500

FINLAND: Kari Laukannen; Janne Mäkelä, Marko Tuomela, Erik Holmgren, Petri Helin, Janne Lindberg, Antti Sumiala (63 Petri Järvinen), Marko Myyry, Ari Hjelm, Jari Litmanen, Mika-Matti Paatelainen (86 Petri Tiainen). Trainer: Jukka Ikäläinen

GREECE: Nikos Mihopoulos; Efstratios Apostolakis, Mihalis Kassapis, Nikos Dabizas, Alexandros Alexiou, Panayotis Tsalouhidis, Theodoros Zagorakis, Themistoklis Nikolaidis, Dimitris Markos (58 Daniel Batista), Vassilis Tsartas (70 Nikos Mahlas), Yorgos Donis. Trainer: Kostas Polihroniou

Goals: Nikolaidis (6), Litmanen (44 pen), Hjelm (55)

SAN MARINO v RUSSIA 0-7 (0-2)

Olimpico, Serravalle 07.06.1995

Referee: Karel Bohunek (CZE) Attendance: 1,450

SAN MARINO: Pier Luigi Benedettini; Luca Gobbi, Mirco Gennari, Marco Mazza, Mauro Valentini, William Guerra, Pierangelo Manzaroli, Pier Domenico Della Valle (63 Claudio Canti), Nicola Bacciocchi, Fabio Francini, Paolo Montagna (77 Massimo Bonini). Trainer: Giorgio Leoni

RUSSIA: Stanislav Cherchesov; Vasili Kulkov, Omari Tetradze, Yuri Kovtun, Igor Shalimov, Valeri Karpin, Viktor Onopko, Igor Kolyvanov, Vladimir Beschastnykh, Igor Dobrovolski (60 Dmitri Radchenko), Sergei Kiryakov (86 Dmitri Cheryshev). Trainer: Oleg Romantsev

Goals: Dobrovolski (20 pen), Gobbi (38 og), Kiryakov (48), Shalimov (49), Beschastnykh (59), Kolyvanov (64), Cheryshev (86)

FINLAND v RUSSIA 0-6 (0-3)

Olympiastadion, Helsinki 16.08.1995

Referee: Sándor Puhl (HUNG) Attendance: 14,200

FINLAND: Kari Laukannen; Janne Mäkelä (46 Kim Suominen), Markku Kanerva, Erik Holmgren, Rami Nieminen, Janne Lindberg, Antti Sumiala, Rami Rantanen (65 Tommi Grönlund), Ari Hjelm, Petri Tiainen, Mika-Matti Paatelainen (46 Petri Järvinen). Trainer: Jukka Ikäläinen

RUSSIA: Dmitri Kharin (82 Stanislav Cherchesov); Yuri Kovtun, Yuri Nikiforov, Ilya Tsymbalar, Dmitri Khlestov, Valeri Karpin (61 Andrei Kanchelskis), Viktor Onopko, Vasili Kulkov, Aleksandr Mostovoi, Dmitri Radchenko (68 Sergei Kiryakov), Igor Kolyvanov. Trainer: Oleg Romantsev

Goals: Kulkov (32, 49), Karpin (39), Radchenko (42), Kolyvanov (67, 69)

SCOTLAND v GREECE 1-0 (0-0)

Hampden Park, Glasgow 16.08.1995

Referee: Peter Mikkelsen (DEN) Attendance: 34,910

SCOTLAND: James Leighton; Stewart McKimmie, Tom Boyd, Stuart McCall, Colin Calderwood, Tosh McKinlay, Duncan Shearer (71 Alistair McCoist), Craig Burley, Darren Jackson (73 John Robertson), Gary McAllister, John Collins. Manager: Craig Brown

GREECE: Ilias Atmatsidis; Efstratios Apostolakis, Kiriakos Karataidis, Yannis Kallitzakis, Nikos Dabizas, Panayotis Tsalouhidis, Theodoros Zagorakis (79 Yorgos H.Yoryadis), Daniel Batista (49 Alexandros Alexandris), Zissis Vrizas (30 Nikos Mahlas), Vassilis Tsartas, Mihalis Kassapis. Trainer: Kostas Polihroniou

Goal: McCoist (72)

SCOTLAND v FINLAND 1-0 (1-0)

Hampden Park, Glasgow 06.09.1995

Referee: Vasiliy Melnichuk (UKR) Attendance: 35,505

SCOTLAND: James Leighton; Stewart McKimmie (88 Billy McKinlay), Tom Boyd, Colin Calderwood, Colin Hendry, Tosh McKinlay, John Spencer (75 Alistair McCoist), Alan McLaren, Scott Booth (80 Darren Jackson), Gary McAllister, John Collins. Manager: Craig Brown

FINLAND: Kari Laukannen; Kari Rissanen, Markku Kanerva, Erik Holmgren, Kim Suominen, Janne Lindberg, Rami Nieminen (64 Tommi Grönlund), Marko Myyry, Ari Hjelm, Jari Litmanen, Petri Järvinen. Trainer: Jukka Ikäläinen

Goal: Booth (10)

SAN MARINO v GREECE 0-4 (0-2)

Olimpico, Serravalle 06.09.1995

Referee: Milan Mitrovic (SVN) Attendance: 1,000

SAN MARINO: Stefano Muccioli; Luca Gobbi, Mirco Gennari, Marco Mazza, Ivan Matteoni, William Guerra, Pierangelo Manzaroli (89 Claudio Peverani), Pier Domenico Della Valle, Nicola Bacciocchi, Marco Mularoni (79 Paolo Montagna), Fabio Francini (76 Claudio Canti). Trainer: Giorgio Leoni

GREECE: Ilias Atmatsidis; Efstratios Apostolakis, Kiriakos Karataidis, Marinos Ouzounidis, Nikos Dabizas, Panayotis Tsalouhidis, Theodoros Zagorakis, Themistoklis Nikolaidis (46 Alexandros Alexandris), Nikos Mahlas (79 Daniel Batista), Yorgos H. Yoryadis (58 Grigoris Yorgatos), Yorgos Donis. Trainer: Kostas Polihroniou

Goals: Tsalouhidis (6), Y.H. Yoryadis (31), Alexandris (59), Donis (80)

FAROE ISLANDS v RUSSIA 2-5 (1-1)

Svangaskard, Toftir 06.09.1995

Referee: Alan Snoddy (NIR) Attendance: 1,852

FAROE ISLANDS: Jens Martin Knudsen; Oli Johannesen, Tummas Eli Hansen (81 Allan Joensen), Janus Rasmussen, Jens Christian Hansen, Øssur Hansen, Kurt Mørkøre, Julian Johnsson, Jan Allan Müller (72 Jens Erik Rasmussen), Todi Jonsson, Henning Jarnskor. Trainer: Allan Simonsen

RUSSIA: Stanislav Cherchesov; Yuri Kovtun, Yuri Nikiforov, Ilya Tsymbalar, Igor Shalimov, Andrei Kanchelskis (58 Vladimir Beschastnykh), Viktor Onopko, Vasili Kulkov (65 Ramiz Mamedov), Aleksandr Mostovoi, Dmitri Radchenko (46 Sergei Kiryakov), Igor Kolyvanov.

Goals: Mostovoi (10 pen), H. Jarnskor (12), Jonsson (55), Kiryakov (60), Kolyvanov (65), Tsymbalar (83), Shalimov (88)

SAN MARINO v FAROE ISLANDS 1-3 (0-2)

Olimpico, Serravalle 11.10.1995

Referee: Roland Beck (LIE) Attendance: 1,000

SAN MARINO: Stefano Muccioli; Vittorio Valentini, Mirco Gennari, Ivan Matteoni (75 Claudio Peverani), Mauro Valentini, William Guerra, Pierangelo Manzaroli, Marco Mazza (57 Marco Mularoni), Nicola Bacciocchi, Fabio Francini, Paolo Montagna (81 Bryan Gasperoni). Trainer: Giorgio Leoni

FAROE ISLANDS: Jens Martin Knudsen; Andreas F.Hansen, Jens Christian Hansen, Janus Rasmussen, Henning Jarnskor (88 Harley Bertholdsen), Allan Mørkøre, Magni Jarnskor, Øssur Hansen (81 Kari Reynheim), Jan Allan Müller, Todi Jonsson (75 John Petersen), Jan Dam. Trainer: Allan Simonsen

Goals: Jonsson (42, 44, 59), M. Valentini (55)

RUSSIA v GREECE 2-1 (1-0)

Luzhniki, Moskva 11.10.1995

Referee: Gerd Grabher (AUS) Attendance: 65,000

RUSSIA: Dmitri Kharin; Yuri Kovtun, Yuri Nikiforov, Ilya Tsymbalar (61 Dmitri Radchenko), Dmitri Khlestov, Valeri Karpin (76 Igor Shalimov), Viktor Onopko, Vasili Kulkov, Aleksandr Mostovoi, Sergei Yuran (46 Sergei Kiryakov), Igor Kolyvanov. Trainer: Oleg Romantsev

GREECE: Nikos Mihopoulos; Efstratios Apostolakis, Mihalis Kassapis, Marinos Ouzounidis, Yannis Kallitzakis (46 Nikos Dabizas), Panayotis Tsalouhidis, Theodoros Zagorakis, Alexandros Alexandris, Daniel Batista (66 Nikos Mahlas), Vassilis Tsartas (46 Grigoris Yorgatos), Yorgos Donis. Trainer: Kostas Polihroniou

Goals: Ouzounidis (38 og), Tsalouhidis (64), Onopko (72)

GREECE v FAROE ISLANDS 5-0 (0-0)

OFI, Iraklion 15.11.1995

Referee: Mitko Mitrev (BUL) Attendance: 11,000

GREECE: Ilias Atmatsidis; Efstratios Apostolakis, Mihalis Kassapis, Marinos Ouzounidis, Nikos Dabizas, Panayotis Tsalouhidis (46 Themistoklis Nikolaidis), Theodoros Zagorakis (70 Kostas Konstantinidis), Alexandros Alexandris (75 Yorgos H.Yoryadis), Nikos Mahlas, Vassilis Tsartas, Yorgos Donis. Trainer: Kostas Polihroniou

FAROE ISLANDS: Jakup Mikkelsen; Oli Johannesen, Tummas Eli Hansen, Jens Christian Hansen, Øssur Hansen (90 Harley Bertholdsen), Allan Mørkøre, Magni Jarnskor, Henning Jarnskor, Jan Allan Müller (83 John Petersen), Kari Reynheim (55 Julian Johnsson), Jan Dam. Trainer: Allan Simonsen

Goals: Alexandris (59), Nikolaidis (62), Mahlas (66), Donis (76), Tsartas (80)

SCOTLAND v SAN MARINO 5-0 (2-0)

Hampden Park, Glasgow 15.11.1995

Referee: Karel Bohunek (CZE) Attendance: 30,306

SCOTLAND: James Leighton; Alan McLaren, Tom Boyd, Colin Calderwood, Colin Hendry, Scot Gemmill, Patrick Nevin, Scott Booth (66 Darren Jackson), Eoin Jess, Gary McAllister (48 Alistair McCoist), John Collins (59 Billy McKinlay). Manager: Craig Brown

SAN MARINO: Stefano Muccioli; Federico Moroni, Mirco Gennari, Marco Mazza (82 Pier Domenico Della Valle), Mauro Valentini, William Guerra (71 Paolo Montagna), Pierangelo Manzaroli, Ivan Matteoni, Nicola Bacciocchi, Marco Mularoni (52 Claudio Canti), Fabio Francini. Trainer: Giorgio Leoni

Goals: Jess (30), Booth (45), McCoist (49), Nevin (71), Francini (90 og)

RUSSIA v FINLAND 3-1 (1-1)

Luzhniki, Moskva 15.11.1995

Referee: Markus Merk (GER) Attendance: 3,500

RUSSIA: Stanislav Cherchesov; Ramiz Mamedov (46 Igor Dobrovolski), Yuri Nikiforov, Ilya Tsymbalar, Dmitri Khlestov, Valeri Karpin (75 Andrei Kanchelskis), Viktor Onopko, Vasili Kulkov, Aleksandr Mostovoi, Sergei Yuran, Dmitri Radchenko (62 Sergei Kiryakov). Trainer: Oleg Romantsev

FINLAND: Antti Niemi; Kari Rissanen, Jussi Nuorela, Aki Hyryläinen, Rami Nieminen, Janne Lindberg, Antti Sumiala (76 Jokke Kangaskorpi), Kim Suominen (88 Harri Ylönen), Ari Hjelm, Marko Myyry, Tommi Grönlund (70 Jarkko Koskinen). Trainer: Jukka Ikäläinen

Goals: Radchenko (40), Suominen (44), Kulkov (55), Kiryakov (71)

	P	W	D	L	F	A	Pts
Russia	10	8	2	0	34	5	26
Scotland	10	7	2	1	19	3	23
Greece	10	6	0	4	23	9	18
Finland	10	5	0	5	18	18	15
Faroe Islands	10	2	0	8	10	35	6
San Marino	10	0	0	10	2	36	0

QUALIFICATION PLAY-OFF

HOLLAND v REPUBLIC OF IRELAND 2-0 (1-0)

Anfield, Liverpool 13.12.1995

Referee: Vadim Zhuk (BLS) Attendance: 35,000

HOLLAND: Edwin Van der Sar; Michael Reiziger, Danny Blind, Clarence Seedorf, Winston Bogarde, Ronald De Boer, Marc Overmars, Edgar Davids, Patrick Kluivert, Dennis Bergkamp (57 Johan De Kock), Glenn Helder (80 Aron Winter). Trainer: Guus Hiddink

IRELAND: Alan Kelly; Gary Kelly, Dennis Irwin, Phil Babb, Paul McGrath, Jeff Kenna, Andy Townsend (50 Jason McAteer), John Aldridge (72 Alan Kernaghan), Anthony Cascarino, John Sheridan, Terry Phelan.
Manager: Jack Charlton

Goals: Kluivert (29, 88)

FINALS IN ENGLAND

GROUP A

ENGLAND v SWITZERLAND 1-1 (1-0)

Wembley, London 08.06.1996

Referee: Manuel Díaz Vega (SPA) Attendance: 76,567

ENGLAND: David Seaman; Gary Neville, Antony Adams, Gareth Southgate, Stuart Pearce; Darren Anderton, Paul Ince, Paul Gascoigne (77 David Platt), Steve McManaman (69 Steve Stone); Teddy Sheringham (69 Nick Barmby), Alan Shearer.
Manager: Terry Venables

SWITZERLAND: Marco Pascolo; Sébastien Jeanneret, Ramon Vega, Stéphane Henchoz, Yvan Quentin; Johann Vogel, Alain Geiger (67 Marcel Koller), Ciriaco Sforza, Christophe Bonvin (69 Stéphane Chapuisat); Marco Grassi, Kubilay Türkyilmaz. Trainer: Artur Jorge

Goals: Shearer (23), Türkyilmaz (82 pen)

HOLLAND v SCOTLAND 0-0

Villa Park, Birmingham 11.06.1996

Referee: Leif Sundell (SWE) Attendance: 34,363

HOLLAND: Edwin Van der Sar; Michael Reiziger, Danny Blind, Winston Bogarde; Ronald De Boer (68 Aron Winter), Edgar Davids, Clarence Seedorf, Richard Witschge (78 Philip Cocu), Gaston Taument (63 Patrick Kluivert), Dennis Bergkamp, Jordi Cruijff. Trainer: Guus Hiddink

SCOTLAND: Andy Goram; Stewart McKimmie (85 Craig Burley), Colin Calderwood, Colin Hendry, Tom Boyd; Kevin Gallacher (56 Billy McKinlay), Stuart McCall, Gary McAllister, John Collins; Scott Booth (46 John Spencer), Gordon Durie. Manager: Craig Brown

SWITZERLAND v HOLLAND 0-2 (0-0)

Villa Park, Birmingham 13.06.1996

Referee: Atanas Uzunov (BUL) Attendance: 36,800

SWITZERLAND: Marco Pascolo; Sébastien Jeanneret (68 Alexandre Comisetti), Ramon Vega, Stéphane Henchoz, Yvan Quentin; Marc Hottiger, Ciriaco Sforza, Johann Vogel; Kubilay Türkyilmaz, Marco Grassi, Stéphane Chapuisat. Trainer: Artur Jorge

HOLLAND: Edwin Van der Sar; Michael Reiziger, Danny Blind, Winston Bogarde; Ronald De Boer (80 Edgar Davids), Aron Winter, Clarence Seedorf (26 Johan De Kock), Richard Witschge; Jordi Cruijff (84 Patrick Kluivert), Dennis Bergkamp, Peter Hoekstra. Trainer: Guus Hiddink

Goals: Cruijff (66), Bergkamp (79)

SCOTLAND v ENGLAND 0-2 (0-0)

Wembley, London 15.06.1996

Referee: Pierluigi Pairetto (ITA) Attendance: 76,864

SCOTLAND: Andy Goram; Stewart McKimmie, Colin Calderwood, Colin Hendry, Tom Boyd; John Collins, Stuart McCall, Gary McAllister, Tosh McKinlay (82 Craig Burley); John Spencer (67 Alistair McCoist), Gordon Durie (87 Eoin Jess). Manager: Craig Brown

ENGLAND: David Seaman; Gary Neville, Antony Adams, Gareth Southgate, Stuart Pearce (46 Jamie Redknapp, 85 Sol Campbell); Darren Anderton, Paul Ince (80 Steve Stone), Paul Gascoigne, Steve McManaman; Teddy Sheringham, Alan Shearer. Manager: Terry Venables

Goals: Shearer (52), Gascoigne (79)

SCOTLAND v SWITZERLAND 1-0 (1-0)

Villa Park, Birmingham 18.06.1996

Referee: Vaclav Krondl (CZE) Attendance: 34,926

SCOTLAND: Andy Goram; Craig Burley, Colin Calderwood, Colin Hendry, Tom Boyd; John Collins, Stuart McCall, Gary McAllister, Tosh McKinlay (60 Scott Booth); Alistair McCoist (84 John Spencer), Gordon Durie. Manager: Craig Brown

SWITZERLAND: Marco Pascolo; Marc Hottiger, Ramon Vega, Stéphane Henchoz, Yvan Quentin (80 Alexandre Comisetti); Johann Vogel, Marcel Koller (46 Raphaël Wicky), Ciriaco Sforza; Kubilay Türkyilmaz, Christophe Bonvin, Stéphane Chapuisat. Trainer: Artur Jorge

Goal: McCoist (36)

HOLLAND v ENGLAND 1-4 (0-1)

Wembley, London 18.06.1996

Referee: Gerd Grabher (AUS) Attendance: 76,798

ENGLAND: David Seaman; Gary Neville, Antony Adams, Gareth Southgate, Stuart Pearce; Steve McManaman, Paul Ince (68 David Platt), Paul Gascoigne, Darren Anderton; Teddy Sheringham (76 Nick Barmby), Alan Shearer (76 Robbie Fowler). Manager: Terry Venables

HOLLAND: Edwin Van der Sar; Michael Reiziger, Danny Blind, Winston Bogarde; Aron Winter, Clarence Seedorf, Ronald De Boer (72 Patrick Kluivert), Richard Witschge (46 Johan De Kock); Jordi Cruijff, Dennis Bergkamp, Peter Hoekstra. Trainer: Guus Hiddink

Goals: Shearer (23 pen, 57), Sheringham (51, 62), Kluivert (78)

	P	W	D	L	F	A	Pts
England	3	2	1	0	7	2	7
Holland	3	1	1	1	3	4	4
Scotland	3	1	1	1	1	2	4
Switzerland	3	0	1	2	1	4	1

GROUP B

SPAIN v BULGARIA 1-1 (0-0)

Elland Road, Leeds 09.06.1996

Referee: Paolo Ceccarini (ITA) Attendance: 24,006

SPAIN: Andoni ZUBIZARRETA; Alberto BELSUÉ, Rafael ALKORTA, ABELARDO Fernández, SERGI Barjuán; José Luis Pérez CAMINERO (82 DONATO Gama da Silva), Fernando Ruiz HIERRO, Julen GUERRERO (52 José Emilio AMAVISCA), Guillermo AMOR (73 ALFONSO Pérez), LUIS ENRIQUE Martínez; Juan Antonio PIZZI.
Trainer: Javier Clemente

BULGARIA: Borislav Mihailov; Radostin Kishishev, Petar Hubchev, Trifon Ivanov, Ilian Kiriakov (70 Tsanko Tsvetanov); Iordan Lechkov, Zlatko Iankov, Krasimir Balakov; Emil Kostadinov (71 Ivailo Iordanov), Liuboslav Penev (77 Daniel Borimirov), Hristo Stoichkov. Trainer: Dimitar Penev

Goals: Stoichkov (65 pen), Alfonso (74)

ROMANIA v FRANCE 0-1 (0-1)

St.James Park, Newcastle 10.06.1996

Referee: Hellmut Krug (GER) Attendance: 26,323

ROMANIA: Bogdan Stelea; Dan Petrescu (77 Iulian Filipescu), Gheorghe Mihali, Miodrag Belodedici, Tibor Selymes; Ioan Lupescu, Gheorghe Popescu, Gheorghe Hagi (Cap), Dorinel Munteanu; Marius Lăcătuş (56 Adrian Ilie), Florin Răducioiu (46 Viorel Moldovan).
Trainer: Anghel Iordănescu

FRANCE: Bernard Lama; Lilian Thuram, Marcel Desailly, Laurent Blanc, Eric Di Meco (67 Bixente Lizarazu); Christian Karembeu, Didier Deschamps (Cap), Zinedine Zidane (79 Alain Roche), Vincent Guérin; Youri Djorkaeff, Christophe Dugarry (67 Patrice Loko). Trainer: Aimé Jacquet

Goal: Dugarry (24)

ROMANIA v BULGARIA 0-1 (0-1)

St.James Park, Newcastle 13.06.1996

Referee: Peter Mikkelsen (DEN) Attendance: 19,107

ROMANIA: Bogdan Stelea; Dan Petrescu, Daniel Prodan, Miodrag Belodedici, Tibor Selymes; Ioan Lupescu (46 Constantin Gâlcă), Gheorghe Popescu (56 Adrian Ilie), Gheorghe Hagi (Cap), Dorinel Munteanu; Marius Lăcătuş (46 Viorel Moldovan), Florin Răducioiu.
Trainer: Anghel Iordănescu

BULGARIA: Borislav Mihailov (Cap); Radostin Kishishev, Trifon Ivanov, Zlatko Iankov, Tsanko Tsvetanov; Iordan Lechkov (89 Boncho Genchev), Ivailo Iordanov, Krasimir Balakov; Emil Kostadinov (31 Daniel Borimirov), Liuboslav Penev (72 Nasko Sirakov), Hristo Stoichkov.
Trainer: Dimitar Penev

Goal: Stoichkov (3)

FRANCE v SPAIN 1-1 (0-0)

Elland Road, Leeds 15.06.1996

Referee: Vadim Zhuk (BLS) Attendance: 35,626

FRANCE: Bernard Lama; Jocelyn Angloma (65 Alain Roche), Laurent Blanc, Marcel Desailly, Bixente Lizarazu; Christian Karembeu, Youri Djorkaeff, Didier Deschamps, Zinedine Zidane, Vincent Guérin (81 Lilian Thuram); Patrice Loko (74 Christophe Dugarry). Trainer: Aimé Jacquet

SPAIN: Andoni ZUBIZARRETA (Cap); Jorge OTERO (59 Francisco Narváez KIKO), Rafael ALKORTA, Juan Manuel LÓPEZ, ABELARDO Fernández, SERGI Barjuán; José Emilio AMAVISCA, Fernando Ruiz HIERRO, José Luis Pérez CAMINERO, LUIS ENRIQUE Martínez (55 Javier MANJARÍN); ALFONSO Pérez (83 Julio SALINAS).
Trainer: Javier Clemente

Goals: Djorkaeff (48), Caminero (85)

FRANCE v BULGARIA 3-1 (1-0)

St.James Park, Newcastle 18.06.1996

Referee: Dermot Gallagher (ENG) & Paul Durkin (ENG)

Attendance: 26,976

FRANCE: Bernard Lama; Lilian Thuram, Laurent Blanc, Marcel Desailly, Bixente Lizarazu; Christian Karembeu, Youri Djorkaeff, Didier Deschamps, Zinedine Zidane (62 Reynald Pedros), Vincent Guérin; Christophe Dugarry (70 Patrice Loko). Trainer: Aimé Jacquet

BULGARIA: Borislav Mihailov (Cap); Emil Kremenliev, Petar Hubchev, Trifon Ivanov, Tsanko Tsvetanov; Iordan Lechkov, Zlatko Iankov (78 Daniel Borimirov), Krasimir Balakov (82 Georgi Donkov), Ivailo Iordanov; Liuboslav Penev, Hristo Stoichkov. Trainer: Dimitar Penev

Goals: Blanc (20), Penev (62og), Stoichkov (68), Loko (90)

The referee Dermott Gallagher limped off with a leg injury was replaced by Paul Durkin in the 27th minute.

ROMANIA v SPAIN 1-2 (1-1)

Elland Road, Leeds 18.06.1996

Referee: Ahmet Çakar (TUR) Attendance: 32,719

ROMANIA: Florin Prunea; Dan Petrescu, Daniel Prodan (86 Ioan Lupescu), Anton Doboş, Tibor Selymes; Ovidiu Stângă, Gheorghe Popescu, Constantin Gâlcă, Gheorghe Hagi (Cap); Florin Răducioiu (78 Ion Vlădoiu), Adrian Ilie (66 Dorinel Munteanu). Trainer: Anghel Iordănescu

SPAIN: Andoni ZUBIZARRETA (Cap); Juan Manuel LÓPEZ, Rafael ALKORTA, ABELARDO Fernández (63 Guillermo AMOR), SERGI Barjuán; Javier MANJARÍN, Fernando Ruiz HIERRO, Miguel Angel NADAL, José Emilio AMAVISCA (72 Julen GUERRERO), Francisco Narváez KIKO, Juan Antonio PIZZI (57 ALFONSO Pérez). Trainer: Javier Clemente

Goals: Manjarín (10), Răducioiu (30), Amor (84)

	P	W	D	L	F	A	Pts
France	3	2	1	0	5	2	7
Spain	3	1	2	0	4	3	5
Bulgaria	3	1	1	1	3	4	4
Romania	3	0	0	3	1	4	0

GROUP C

GERMANY v CZECH REPUBLIC 2-0 (2-0)

Old Trafford, Manchester 09.06.1996

Referee: David Elleray (ENG) Attendance: 37,500

GERMANY: Andreas Köpke; Jürgen Kohler (14 Markus Babbel), Matthias Sammer, Thomas Helmer; Stefan Reuter, Thomas Hässler, Dieter Eilts, Andreas Möller, Christian Ziege; Fredi Bobic (65 Thomas Strunz), Stefan Kuntz (83 Oliver Bierhoff). Trainer: Hubert Vogts

CZECH REPUBLIC: Petr Kouba; Michal Hornak, Miroslav Kadlec, Jan Suchoparek; Radoslav Latal, Martin Frydek (46 Patrik Berger), Radek Bejbl, Pavel Nedved, Jiri Nemec; Karel Poborsky (46 Radek Drulak), Pavel Kuka.
Trainer: Dusan Uhrin

Goals: Ziege (26), Möller (32)

ITALY v RUSSIA 2-1 (1-1)

Anfield, Liverpool 11.06.1996

Referee: Leslie Mottram (SCO) Attendance: 35,120

ITALY: Angelo Peruzzi; Roberto Mussi, Luigi Apolloni, Alessandro Costacurta, Paolo Maldini; Angelo Di Livio (62 Diego Fuser), Roberto Di Matteo, Demetrio Albertini, Alessandro Del Piero (46 Roberto Donadoni); Gianfranco Zola, Pierluigi Casiraghi (80 Fabrizio Ravanelli).
Trainer: Arrigo Sacchi

RUSSIA: Stanislav Cherchesov; Omari Tetradze, Yevgeni Bushmanov (46 Igor Yanovski), Viktor Onopko, Yuri Kovtun; Andrei Kanchelskis, Valeri Karpin (63 Sergei Kiryakov), Vladislav Radimov, Aleksandr Mostovoi, Ilya Tsymbalar (71 Igor Dobrovolski); Igor Kolyvanov. Trainer: Oleg Romantsev

Goals: Casiraghi (5, 52), Tsymbalar (20)

CZECH REPUBLIC v ITALY 2-1 (2-1)

Anfield, Liverpool 14.06.1996

Referee: Antonio Jesus López Nieto (SPA) Att: 37,320

CZECH REPUBLIC: Petr Kouba; Michal Hornak, Miroslav Kadlec, Jan Suchoparek; Radoslav Latal (88 Vaclav Nemecek), Pavel Nedved, Radek Bejbl, Patrik Berger (64 Vladimir Smicer), Jiri Nemec; Karel Poborsky, Pavel Kuka.
Trainer: Dusan Uhrin

ITALY: Angelo Peruzzi; Roberto Mussi, Luigi Apolloni, Alessandro Costacurta, Paolo Maldini; Diego Fuser, Demetrio Albertini, Dino Baggio (39 Amedeo Carboni), Roberto Donadoni; Enrico Chiesa (78 Gianfranco Zola), Fabrizio Ravanelli (58 Pierluigi Casiraghi). Trainer: Arrigo Sacchi

Goals: Nedved (5), Chiesa (18), Bejbl (36)

RUSSIA v GERMANY 0-3 (0-0)

Old Trafford, Manchester 16.06.1996

Referee: Kim Milton Nielsen (DEN) Attendance: 50,670

RUSSIA: Dmitri Kharin; Yuri Kovtun, Yuri Nikiforov, Viktor Onopko; Omari Tetradze, Andrei Kanchelskis, Vladislav Radimov (46 Valeri Karpin), Aleksandr Mostovoi, Dmitri Khokhlov (66 Igor Simutenkov), Ilya Tsymbalar; Igor Kolyvanov. Trainer: Oleg Romantsev

GERMANY: Andreas Köpke; Markus Babbel, Matthias Sammer, Thomas Helmer; Stefan Reuter, Thomas Hässler (67 Steffen Freund), Dieter Eilts, Andreas Möller (87 Thomas Strunz), Christian Ziege; Jürgen Klinsmann, Oliver Bierhoff (85 Stefan Kuntz). Trainer: Hubert Vogts

Goals: Sammer (56), Klinsmann (77, 90)

CZECH REPUBLIC v RUSSIA 3-3 (2-0)

Anfield, Liverpool 19.06.1996

Referee: Anders Frisk (SWE) Attendance: 21,128

CZECH REPUBLIC: Petr Kouba; Michal Hornak, Lubos Kubik, Jan Suchoparek; Radoslav Latal, Pavel Nedved, Radek Bejbl, Patrik Berger (90 Vaclav Nemecek), Jiri Nemec; Karel Poborsky, Pavel Kuka (64 Vladimir Smicer).
Trainer: Dusan Uhrin

RUSSIA: Stanislav Cherchesov; Sergei Gorlukovich, Yuri Nikiforov, Omari Tetradze; Valeri Karpin, Vladislav Radimov, Igor Yanovski, Dmitri Khokhlov, Ilya Tsymbalar (67 Igor Shalimov); Igor Kolyvanov (46 Aleksandr Mostovoi), Igor Simutenkov (46 Vladimir Beschastnykh).
Trainer: Oleg Romantsev

Goals: Suchoparek (7), Kuka (19), Mostovoi (49), Tetradze (54), Beschastnykh (85), Smicer (89)

ITALY v GERMANY 0-0

Old Trafford, Manchester 19.06.1996

Referee: Guy Goethals (BEL) Attendance: 53,740

ITALY: Angelo Peruzzi; Roberto Mussi, Alessandro Costacurta, Paolo Maldini, Amedeo Carboni (78 Moreno Torricelli); Diego Fuser (81 Angelo Di Livio), Demetrio Albertini, Roberto Di Matteo (68 Enrico Chiesa), Roberto Donadoni; Gianfranco Zola, Pierluigi Casiraghi. Trainer: Arrigo Sacchi

GERMANY: Andreas Köpke; Steffen Freund, Matthias Sammer, Thomas Helmer; Thomas Strunz, Thomas Hässler, Dieter Eilts, Andreas Möller (89 Marco Bode), Christian Ziege; Jürgen Klinsmann, Fredi Bobic. Trainer: Hubert Vogts

	P	W	D	L	F	A	Pts
Germany	3	2	1	0	5	0	7
Czech Republic	3	1	1	1	5	6	4
Italy	3	1	1	1	3	3	4
Russia	3	0	1	2	4	8	1

GROUP D

DENMARK v PORTUGAL 1-1 (1-0)

Hillsborough, Sheffield 09.06.1996

Referee: Mario Van der Ende (HOL) Attendance: 34,993

DENMARK: Peter Schmeichel; Thomas Helveg, Jes Høgh, Marc Rieper, Jens Risager; Henrik Larsen (90 Kim Vilfort), Claus Thomsen (83 Torben Piechnik), Michael Laudrup, Brian Steen Nielsen; Brian Laudrup, Mikkel Beck. Trainer: Richard Møller-Nielsen

PORTUGAL: VÍTOR Manuel Martins BAÍA; João Paulo Santos "PAULINHO SANTOS", FERNANDO Manuel Silva COUTO, HÉLDER Marino Rodrigues Cristóvao, DIMAS Manuel Marques Teixeira; OCEANO Andrade Cruz (37 António José Santos FOLHA), PAULO Manuel Carvalho SOUSA (79 José Fernando Gomes TAVARES), RUI Manuel César COSTA, Luís Filipe Madeira FIGO (63 DOMINGOS José Paciencia Oliveira); Ricardo Manuel SÁ PINTO, JOÃO Manuel Vieira PINTO. Trainer: António Oliveira

Goals: B. Laudrup (22), Sá Pinto (53)

TURKEY v CROATIA 0-1 (0-0)

City Ground, Nottingham 11.06.1996

Referee: Serge Muhmenthaler (SWI) Attendance: 22,460

TURKEY: Rüstü Reçber; Vedat Inceefe, Rahim Zafer, Alpay Özalan; Ogün Temizkanoglu, Tolunay Kafkas (88 Saffet Akyüz), Sergen Yalçin, Tugay Kerimoglu, Abdullah Ercan; Arif Erdem (82 Hami Mandirali), Hakan Sükür. Trainer: Fatih Terim

CROATIA: Drazen Ladic; Slaven Bilic, Nikola Jerkan, Igor Stimac; Mario Stanic, Robert Prosinecki, Zvonimir Boban (48 Zvonimir Soldo), Aljosa Asanovic, Robert Jarni; Alen Boksic (72 Goran Vlaovic), Davor Suker (89 Dubravko Pavlicic). Trainer: Miroslav Blazevic

Goal: Vlaovic (85)

PORTUGAL v TURKEY 1-0 (0-0)

City Ground, Nottingham 13.06.1996

Referee: Sándor Puhl (HUNG) Attendance: 22,670

PORTUGAL: VÍTOR Manuel Martins BAÍA; João Paulo Santos "PAULINHO SANTOS", FERNANDO Manuel Silva COUTO, HÉLDER Marino Rodrigues Cristóvao, DIMAS Manuel Marques Teixeira; Luís Filipe Madeira FIGO, PAULO Manuel Carvalho SOUSA, RUI Manuel César COSTA, António José Santos FOLHA (46 José Fernando Gomes TAVARES); Ricardo Manuel SÁ PINTO (65 Jorge Paulo CADETE Reis), JOÃO Manuel Vieira PINTO (77 PORFÍRIO). Trainer: António Oliveira

TURKEY: Rüstü Reçber; Recep Çetin, Vedat Inceefe, Ogün Temizkanoglu (46 Rahim Zafer), Alpay Özalan; Oguz Çetin (69 Arif Erdem), Sergen Yalçin, Tugay Kerimoglu, Abdullah Ercan; Saffet Akyüz (62 Tolunay Kafkas), Hakan Sükür. Trainer: Fatih Terim

Goal: Fernando Couto (66)

CROATIA v DENMARK 3-0 (0-0)

Hillsborough, Sheffield 16.06.1996

Referee: Marc Batta (FRA) Attendance: 33,671

CROATIA: Drazen Ladic; Slaven Bilic, Nikola Jerkan, Igor Stimac; Mario Stanic, Robert Prosinecki (88 Mladen Mladenovic), Zvonimir Boban (82 Zvonimir Soldo), Aljosa Asanovic, Robert Jarni; Goran Vlaovic (82 Nikola Jurcevic), Davor Suker. Trainer: Miroslav Blazevic

DENMARK: Peter Schmeichel; Thomas Helveg (46 Jacob Laursen), Claus Thomsen, Jes Høgh, Marc Rieper; Henrik Larsen (69 Stig Tøfting), Kim Vilfort (58 Mikkel Beck), Michael Laudrup, Michael Schjønberg, Brian Steen Nielsen; Brian Laudrup. Trainer: Richard Møller-Nielsen

Goals: Suker (53 pen, 89), Boban (80)

CROATIA v PORTUGAL 0-3 (0-2)

City Ground, Nottingham 19.06.1996

Referee: Bernd Heynemann (GER) Attendance: 20,484

CROATIA: Marijan Mrmic; Dario Simic, Slaven Bilic, Dubravko Pavlicic, Zvonimir Soldo; Nikola Jurcevic, Mladen Mladenovic (46 Zvonimir Boban), Robert Prosinecki (46 Aljosa Asanovic), Robert Jarni; Goran Vlaovic, Igor Pamic (46 Davor Suker). Trainer: Miroslav Blazevic

PORTUGAL: VÍTOR Manuel Martins BAÍA; Carlos Alberto Oliveira SECRETÁRIO, FERNANDO Manuel Silva COUTO, HÉLDER Marino Rodrigues Cristóvao, DIMAS Manuel Marques Teixeira; OCEANO Andrade Cruz, PAULO Manuel Carvalho SOUSA (70 José Fernando Gomes TAVARES), RUI Manuel César COSTA (61 PEDRO Alexandre Santos BARBOSA), Luís Filipe Madeira FIGO; Ricardo Manuel SÁ PINTO (46 DOMINGOS José Paciencia Oliveira), JOÃO Manuel Vieira PINTO. Trainer: António Oliveira

Goals: Figo (4), João Pinto II (33), Domingos (83)

TURKEY v DENMARK 0-3 (0-0)

Hillsborough, Sheffield 19.06.1996

Referee: Nikolai Levnikov (RUS) Attendance: 28,951

TURKEY: Rüstü Reçber; Recep Çetin (68 Bülent Korkmaz), Vedat Inceefe, Ogün Temizkanoglu, Alpay Özalan; Tayfun Korkut, Tugay Kerimoglu, Orhan Çikrikçi (68 Saffet Akyüz), Abdullah Ercan; Hami Mandirali, Hakan Sükür (46 Arif Erdem). Trainer: Fatih Terim

DENMARK: Peter Schmeichel; Thomas Helveg, Jes Høgh, Claus Thomsen, Marc Rieper; Allan Nielsen, Michael Laudrup, Michael Schjønberg (46 Henrik Larsen), Brian Steen Nielsen; Brian Laudrup, Erik Bo Andersen (89 Søren Andersen). Trainer: Richard Møller-Nielsen

Goals: B. Laudrup (50, 84), A. Nielsen (69)

	P	W	D	L	F	A	Pts
Portugal	3	2	1	0	5	1	7
Croatia	3	2	0	1	4	3	6
Denmark	3	1	1	1	4	4	4
Turkey	3	0	0	3	0	5	0

QUARTER-FINALS

ENGLAND v SPAIN 0-0 (AET)

Wembley, London 22.06.1996

Referee: Marc Batta (FRA) Attendance: 75,447

ENGLAND: David Seaman; Gary Neville, Antony Adams, Gareth Southgate, Stuart Pearce; Steve McManaman (109 Steve Stone), David Platt, Paul Gascoigne, Darren Anderton (109 Nick Barmby), Teddy Sheringham (109 Robbie Fowler), Alan Shearer. Manager: Terry Venables

SPAIN: Andoni ZUBIZARRETA (Cap); Alberto BELSUÉ, Rafael ALKORTA (74 Juan Manuel LÓPEZ), ABELARDO Fernández, SERGI Barjuán; Javier MANJARÍN (46 José Luis Pérez CAMINERO), Fernando Ruiz HIERRO, Miguel Angel NADAL, Guillermo AMOR; Francisco Narváez KIKO, Julio SALINAS (46 ALFONSO Pérez). Trainer: Javier Clemente

Penalties: 1-0 Shearer, Hierro (hits bar), 2-0 Platt, 2-1 Amor, 3-1 Pearce, 3-2 Belsué, 4-2 Gascoigne, Nadal (saved)

FRANCE v HOLLAND 0-0 (AET)

Anfield, Liverpool 22.06.1996

Referee: Antonio Jesus López Nieto (SPA) Att: 37,465

FRANCE: Bernard Lama; Lilian Thuram, Laurent Blanc, Marcel Desailly, Bixente Lizarazu; Christian Karembeu, Youri Djorkaeff, Didier Deschamps, Zinedine Zidane, Vincent Guérin; Patrice Loko (62 Christophe Dugarry; 80 Reynald Pedros). Trainer: Aimé Jacquet

HOLLAND: Edwin Van der Sar; Michael Reiziger, Danny Blind, Johan De Kock, Winston Bogarde; Ronald De Boer, Richard Witschge (80 Youri Mulder); Jordi Cruijff (69 Aron Winter), Dennis Bergkamp (60 Clarence Seedorf), Patrick Kluivert, Philip Cocu. Trainer: Guus Hiddink

Penalties: 0-1 De Kock, 1-1 Zidane, 1-2 R. De Boer, 2-2 Djorkaeff, 2-3 Kluivert, 3-3 Lizarazu, Seedorf (missed), 4-3 Guérin, 4-4 Blind, 5-4 Blanc

GERMANY v CROATIA 2-1 (1-0)

Old Trafford, Manchester 23.06.1996

Referee: Leif Sundell (SWE) Attendance: 43,412

GERMANY: Andreas Köpke; Markus Babbel, Matthias Sammer, Thomas Helmer; Stefan Reuter, Mehmet Scholl (88 Thomas Hässler), Dieter Eilts, Andreas Möller, Christian Ziege; Jürgen Klinsmann (39 Steffen Freund), Fredi Bobic (46 Stefan Kuntz). Trainer: Hubert Vogts

CROATIA: Drazen Ladic; Igor Stimac, Nikola Jerkan, Slaven Bilic; Mario Stanic, Nikola Jurcevic (78 Mladen Mladenovic), Zvonimir Boban, Aljosa Asanovic, Robert Jarni; Goran Vlaovic, Davor Suker. Trainer: Miroslav Blazevic

Goals: Klinsmann (21 pen), Suker (51), Sammer (59)

PORTUGAL v CZECH REPUBLIC 0-1 (0-0)

Villa Park, Birmingham 23.06.1996

Referee: Hellmut Krug (GER) Attendance: 26,832

PORTUGAL: VÍTOR Manuel Martins BAÍA; Carlos Alberto Oliveira SECRETÁRIO, FERNANDO Manuel Silva COUTO, HÉLDER Marino Rodrigues Cristóvao, DIMAS Manuel Marques Teixeira; Luís Filipe Madeira FIGO (83 Jorge Paulo CADETE Reis), OCEANO Andrade Cruz (65 António José Santos FOLHA), PAULO Manuel Carvalho SOUSA, RUI Manuel César COSTA; Ricardo Manuel SÁ PINTO (46 DOMINGOS José Paciencia Oliveira), JOÃO Manuel Vieira PINTO. Trainer: António Oliveira

CZECH REPUBLIC: Petr Kouba; Michal Hornak, Miroslav Kadlec, Jan Suchoparek; Radoslav Latal, Karel Poborsky, Radek Bejbl, Vaclav Nemecek (90 Patrik Berger), Jiri Nemec; Vladimir Smicer (85 Lubos Kubik), Pavel Kuka. Trainer: Dusan Uhrin

Goal: Poborsky (53)

CZECH REPUBLIC v FRANCE 0-0 (AET)

Old Trafford, Manchester 26.06.1996

Referee: Leslie Mottram (SCO) Attendance: 43,877

CZECH REPUBLIC: Petr Kouba; Michal Hornak, Miroslav Kadlec, Karel Rada; Karel Poborsky, Pavel Novotny, Vaclav Nemecek, Pavel Nedved, Jiri Nemec (84 Lubos Kubik); Vladimir Smicer (46 Patrik Berger), Radek Drulak (70 Martin Kotulek). Trainer: Dusan Uhrin

FRANCE: Bernard Lama; Lilian Thuram (83 Jocelyn Angloma), Laurent Blanc, Alain Roche, Bixente Lizarazu; Sabri Lamouchi (62 Reynald Pedros), Youri Djorkaeff, Marcel Desailly, Zinedine Zidane, Vincent Guérin; Patrice Loko. Trainer: Aimé Jacquet

Penalties: 1-0 Zidane, 1-1 Kubik, 2-1 Djorkaeff, 2-2 Nedved, 3-2 Lizarazu, 3-3 Berger, 4-3 Guérin, 4-4 Poborsky, 5-4 Blanc, 5-5 Rada, Pedros (missed), 5-6 Kadlec

SEMI-FINALS

GERMANY v ENGLAND 1-1 (1-1) (AET)

Wembley, London 26.06.1996

Referee: Sándor Puhl (HUNG) Attendance: 75,862

GERMANY: Andreas Köpke; Markus Babbel, Matthias Sammer, Thomas Helmer (110 Marco Bode); Stefan Reuter, Mehmet Scholl (77 Thomas Hässler), Steffen Freund (118 Thomas Strunz), Dieter Eilts, Andreas Möller, Christian Ziege; Stefan Kuntz. Trainer: Hubert Vogts

ENGLAND: David Seaman; Gareth Southgate, Antony Adams, Stuart Pearce; Darren Anderton, David Platt, Paul Ince, Paul Gascoigne, Steve McManaman; Teddy Sheringham, Alan Shearer. Manager: Terry Venables

Goals: Shearer (3), Kuntz (16)

Penalties: 0-1 Shearer, 1-1 Hassler, 1-2 Platt, 2-2 Strunz, 2-3 Pearce, 3-3 Reuter, 3-4 Gascoigne, 4-4 Ziege, 4-5 Sheringham, 5-5 Kuntz, Southgate (saved), 6-5 Möller

FINAL

GERMANY v CZECH REPUBLIC 2-1 (0-0, 1-1) (AET)

Wembley, London 30.06.1996

Referee: Pierluigi Pairetto (ITA) Attendance: 73,611

GERMANY: Andreas Köpke; Markus Babbel, Matthias Sammer, Thomas Helmer; Thomas Strunz, Thomas Hässler, Dieter Eilts (46 Marco Bode), Mehmet Scholl (69 Oliver Bierhoff), Christian Ziege; Jürgen Klinsmann, Stefan Kuntz. Trainer: Hubert Vogts

CZECH REPUBLIC: Petr Kouba; Michal Hornak, Karel Rada, Miroslav Kadlec, Jan Suchoparek; Karel Poborsky (88 Vladimir Smicer), Pavel Nedved, Radek Bejbl, Patrik Berger, Jiri Nemec; Pavel Kuka. Trainer: Dusan Uhrin

Goals: Berger (58 pen), Bierhoff (73,95)

The Match was won by Oliver Bierhoff's "Golden Goal" in the 95th minute.

Goalscorers European Football Championship 1996

15 goals: Davor Suker (Croatia)

13 goals: Hristo Stoichkov (Bulgaria)

12 goals: Jürgen Klinsmann (Germany)

11 goals: Anton Polster (Austria)

7 goals: Andrzej Juskowiak (Poland), Hakan Sükür (Turkey), Patrik Berger (Czech Republic), Domingos José Paciencia Oliveira (Portugal), Emil Kostadinov (Bulgaria), Mika-Matti Paatelainen (Finland)

6 goals: Florin Răducioiu (Romania), Youri Djorkaeff (France), Ronen Harazi (Israel), Gianfranco Zola (Italy)

5 goals: Kim Vilfort (Denmark), Timerlan Guseinov (Ukraine), Sergei Gerasimets (Belarus), Paulo Alves (Portugal), John Aldridge (Republic of Ireland), Iain Dowie (N. Ireland), Vitas Rimkus (Latvia), Alan Shearer (England), Igor Kolyvanov (Russia)

4 goals: Fernando Ruiz Hierro (Spain), Brian Laudrup, Michael Laudrup (Denmark), Marc Degryse (Belgium), Kubilay Türkyilmaz (Switzerland), Fabrizio Ravanelli (Italy), Zlatko Zahovic (Slovenia), Patrick Kluivert, Marc Overmars, Clarence Seedorf (Holland), Luís Filipe Madeira Figo, João Manuel Vieira Pinto II, Rui Costa (Portugal), Jimmy Quinn (N. Ireland), Peter Stöger (Austria), Andreas Möller, Matthias Sammer (Germany), Shota Arveladze, Temur Ketsbaia (Georgia), Sokol Kushta (Albania), Todi Jonsson (Faroe Islands), Jari Litmanen (Finland), Alexandros Alexandris, Nikos Mahlas, Panayotis Tsalouhidis (Greece), Scott Booth, John Collins (Scotland), Dmitri Radchenko (Russia)

3 goals: Marius Lăcătuş (Romania), Peter Dubovsky, Tibor Jancula (Slovakia), Roman Kosecki (Poland), Ronny Rosenthal (Israel), Julio Salinas (Spain), Bosko Djurovski (Macedonia), Marios Agathocleous (Cyprus), Zvonimir Boban (Croatia), Pierluigi Casiraghi (Italy), Darius Maciulevicius, Arunas Suika (Lithuania), Martin Reim (Estonia), Primoz Gliha, Saso Udovic (Slovenia), Radek Drulak, Horst Siegl (Czech Republic), Ronald De Boer, Wim Jonk, Youri Mulder, Bryan Roy (Holland), Henning Berg, Jan Age Fjørtoft, Kjetil Rekdal (Norway), Niall Quinn (Republic of Ireland), Philip Gray, Michael O'Neill (N. Ireland), Armands Zeiberlinsh (Latvia), Ulf Kirsten (Germany), Krasimir Balakov (Bulgaria), Georgi Kinkladze (Georgia), Alistair McCoist (Scotland), Vladimir Beschastnykh, Sergei Kiryakov, Vasili Kulkov (Russia)

2 goals: Hagi, Munteanu (Romania), Blanc, Guérin, Leboeuf, Loko, Dugarry, Zidane (France), Timko (Slovakia), Nowak (Poland), Suleimanov (Azerbaijan), Alfonso, Amavisca, Caminero, Donato, Guerrero, Luis Enrique, Manjarín, Pizzi (Spain), Beck, A. Nielsen, Schjønberg (Denmark), Grün, Nilis, Schepens, Scifo (Belgium), Sotiriou (Cyprus), Grigoryan, Shahgeldyan (Armenia), Bickel, Ohrel, Sforza, Subiat (Switzerland), Saffet, Sergen (Turkey), K. Andersson, Brolin, Dahlin (Sweden), Halmai, Illés, Kiprich (Hungary), Prosinecki (Croatia), Albertini (Italy), Ivanauskas (Lithuania), Novak (Slovenia), Kuka, Skuhravy, Suchoparek (Czech Republic), Bergkamp (Holland), Leonhardsen (Norway), Fernando Couto, Paulinho Santos (Portugal), Coyne, Sheridan (Republic of Ireland), Hütter, Herzog (Austria), Bierhoff, Matthäus, Ziege (Germany), Penev (Bulgaria), Cleşcenco, Miterev (Moldova), Saunders, Speed (Wales), Rraklli (Albania), Hjelm, Sumiala (Finland), Nikolaidis, Donis (Greece), McKinlay, McGinlay (Scotland), Sheringham (England), Karpin, Mostovoi, Nikiforov, Shalimov, Tsymbalar (Russia)

2 goals: Dumitrescu, Popescu, Prodan, Belodedici, Petrescu (Romania), Cocard, Papin, Ginola, Desailly, Lizarazu, Karembeu, Pedros (France), Ujlaky, Simon, Tittel, Chvila, Rusnak, Moravcik (Slovakia), Wieszczycki, Kowalczyk (Poland), Berkovich, Revivo, Zohar, Banin (Israel), Amor, Goikoetxea, Higuera, Kiko, Nadal (Spain), Jensen, P. Nielsen, Povlsen, Strudal (Denmark), De Bilde, Versavel, Karagiannis, Verheyen (Belgium), Jovanovski, Micevski, Hristov, Markovski, Boskovski, Mi. Stojkovski (Macedonia), Phasouliotis (Cyprus), Art. Petrosyan (Armenia), Knup, Hottiger, Koller (Switzerland), Ogün, Emre, Recep, B. Bülent (Turkey), Alexandersson, Pettersson, Ingesson (Sweden), Vincze (Hungary), A. Gunnlaugsson, Bergsson, S. Jónsson (Iceland), Vlaovic, Jurcevic, Mladenovic, Boksic, Stimac, Jerkan, Kozniku (Croatia), Maldini, Lombardo, D. Baggio, Panucci, Costacurta, Chiesa (Italy), Slekys, Stonkus, Sukristovas, Zuta, Skarbalius (Lithuania), Polunin, Skrypnyk, Gusin, Kalitvintsev, Konovalov (Ukraine), Kokol (Slovenia), Frydek, Nemecek, Kadlec, Smejkal, Kubik, Nedved, Bejbl, Smicer, Poborsky (Czech Republic), Winter, Cruijff (Holland), Flo, Jakobsen, Brattbakk, Aase, Bohinen, Frigård (Norway), Taikov, Gurinovich, Romashchenko (Belarus), Holtz, Hellers, Cardoni (Luxembourg), Carabott, Laferla (Malta), Cadete, Folha, Hélder, Oceano, Sá Pinto, Secretário (Portugal), Houghton, McGrath, Keane, Townsend (Republic of Ireland), D. Hasler (Liechtenstein), Hunter, Mcmahon, Hughes, Gillespie, Lomas (N. Ireland), Astafyev, Babichev, Milevsky (Latvia), Schopp, Stumpf, Wetl, Ramusch, Ogris, Kühbauer, Sabitzer, Pürk, Pfeifenberger, Aigner (Austria), Babbel, Hässler, Helmer, Herrlich, Kuntz, Strunz (Germany), Lechkov, Ivanov (Bulgaria), Janashia, Gogrichiani (Georgia), Testimiţanu, Rebeja, Curtianu, Belous, Secu, Pogorelov, Oprea (Moldova), Pembridge, Blake, Coleman, Giggs (Wales), Bellai, Vata, Kaçaj, Zmijani (Albania), M. Valentini, Della Valle (San Marino), H. Jarnskor, J.C. Hansen, J.E. Rasmussen, Johnsson, Müller (Faroe Islands), Suominen, Lindberg, Helin (Finland), Tsartas, Y.H. Yoryadis, Apostolakis, Frantzeskos, Markos, Batista, Saravakos (Greece), Jess, Nevin, Calderwood, Shearer (Scotland), Gascoigne (England), Onopko, Dobrovolski, Cheryshev, Kechinov, Pisarev, Mukhamadiev, Tetradze (Russia)

Own goals: Wandzik (Poland) for Romania, Kristofik (Slovakia) & Penev (Bulgaria) for France, Krbachyan (Armenia) for Belgium, M. Charalambous (Cyprus) for Spain, Blomqvist (Sweden) for Switzerland, P. Andersson (Sweden) for Turkey, Suika & Vainoras (Lithuania) for Italy, Kirs (Estonia) for Ukraine, Vítor Baía (Portugal) for Republic of Ireland, Helmer (Germany) for Wales, Melville (Wales) & S. Stroenco (Moldova) for Germany, Culibaba (Moldova) for Georgia, Apostolakis (Greece) for Faroe Islands, Francini (San Marino) for Scotland, Gobbi (San Marino), Ouzounidis (Greece) & Zagorakis (Greece) for Russia

THE EUROPEAN FOOTBALL CHAMPIONSHIP 2000

GROUP 1

WALES v ITALY 0-2 (0-1)

Anfield, Liverpool 05.09.1998

Referee: Terje Hauge (NOR) Attendance: 23,160

WALES: Paul Jones; John Robinson, Darren Barnard, Kit Symons, Adrian Williams, Chris Coleman; Andy Johnson, Gary Speed, Mark Hughes (80 Robbie Savage); Nathan Blake (65 Dean Saunders), Ryan Giggs. Manager: Bobby Gould

ITALY: Angelo Peruzzi; Christian Panucci, Gianluca Pessotto, Fabio Cannavaro, Mark Iuliano; Dino Baggio, Diego Fuser, Demetrio Albertini (66 Luigi Di Biagio), Eusebio Di Francesco (85 Michele Serena); Christian Vieri, Alessandro Del Piero (74 Roberto Baggio). Trainer: Dino Zoff

Goals: Fuser (19), Vieri (77)

BELARUS v DENMARK 0-0

Republican, Minsk 05.09.1998

Referee: Georg Dardenne (GER) Attendance: 35,000

BELARUS: Andrei Satsunkevich; Erik Yakhimovich, Andrei Lavrik, Andrei Ostrovskiy, Sergei Shtanyuk, Myroslav Romaschenko (39 Vyacheslav Gerashchenko); Sergei Gurenko, Alexandr Khatskevich, Vasily Baranov, Valentin Belkevich, Vladimir Makovskiy (88 Maxym Romaschenko). Trainer: Mikhail Vergeyenko

DENMARK: Peter Schmeichel; Ole Tobiasen, Marc Rieper, Jes Høgh, Jan Heintze; Thomas Helveg, Allan Nielsen, Claus Thomsen, Jon Dahl Tomasson (81 Søren Frederiksen); Martin Jørgensen (67 Thomas Gravesen), Peter Møller (67 Søren Andersen). Trainer: Bo Johansson

ITALY v SWITZERLAND 2-0 (1-0)

Friuli, Udine 10.10.1998

Referee: Alain Sars (FRA) Attendance: 35,247

ITALY: Gianluigi Buffon; Christian Panucci, Fabio Cannavaro, Paolo Maldini, Moreno Torricelli; Diego Fuser, Demetrio Albertini, Dino Baggio, Eusebio Di Francesco (63 Jonathan Bachini); Alessandro Del Piero (69 Francesco Totti), Filippo Inzaghi. Trainer: Dino Zoff

SWITZERLAND: Andreas Hilfiker; Régis Rothenbühler, Stéphane Henchoz, Ramon Vega, Stefan Wolf (65 Frédéric Chassot), Johann Vogel; Patrick Müller, Raphaël Wicky (86 Fabio Celestini), Ciriaco Sforza; Stéphane Chapuisat, David Sesa. Trainer: Gilbert Gress

Goals: Del Piero (19, 61)

DENMARK v WALES 1-2 (0-0)

Idraetsparken, København 10.10.1998

Referee: Sándor Piller (HUNG) Attendance: 36,000

DENMARK: Mogens Krogh; Ole Tobiasen, Marc Rieper, Jes Høgh, Jan Heintze; Thomas Helveg, Brian Steen Nielsen, Per Frandsen (76 Thomas Gravesen), Martin Jørgensen; Søren Frederiksen, Mikkel Beck (65 Ebbe Sand).
Trainer: Bo Johansson

WALES: Paul Jones; Kit Symons, Adrian Williams, Chris Coleman; Robbie Savage, Darren Barnard, Andy Johnson (54 Mark Pembridge), Mark Hughes, Gary Speed; Dean Saunders (81 John Robinson), Nathan Blake (69 Craig Bellamy).
Manager: Bobby Gould

Goals: Frederiksen (58), Williams (59), Bellamy (86)

WALES v BELARUS 3-2 (1-0)

Cardiff 14.10.1998

Referee: Lawrence Sammut (MAL) Attendance: 7,813

WALES: Paul Jones; Chris Coleman, Kit Symons, Robbie Savage; Darren Barnard, John Robinson, Andy Johnson, Mark Hughes, Mark Pembridge; Dean Saunders, Nathan Blake.
Manager: Robert Gould

BELARUS: Andrei Satsunkevich; Erik Yakhimovich, Andrei Lavrik, Sergei Shtanyuk, Andrei Ostrovskiy; Vyacheslav Gerashchenko (88 Maxym Romaschenko), Alexandr Khatskevich, Vasily Baranov (69 Sergei Gerasimets), Sergei Gurenko; Valentin Belkevich, Vladimir Makovskiy (72 Petr Kachuro). Trainer: Mikhail Vergeyenko

Goals: Robinson (14), Gurenko (20), Belkevich (48), Coleman (53), Symons (84)

SWITZERLAND v DENMARK 1-1 (0-0)

Zürich 14.10.1998

Referee: Miroslav Radoman (YUG) Attendance: 12,500

SWITZERLAND: Andreas Hilfiker; Stéphane Henchoz, Sébastien Jeanneret (76 Régis Rothenbühler), Ciriaco Sforza; Johann Vogel, Sébastien Fournier, David Sesa (89 Bernt Haas), Raphaël Wicky, Patrick Müller (77 Franco Di Jorio); Fabio Celestini, Stéphane Chapuisat. Trainer: Gilbert Gress

DENMARK: Mogens Krogh; Ole Tobiasen, Marc Rieper, Jes Høgh, Jan Heintze; Thomas Helveg, Brian Steen Nielsen, Per Frandsen (59 Søren Colding), Martin Jørgensen; Søren Frederiksen (61 Ebbe Sand), Jon Dahl Tomasson (77 Mikkel Beck). Trainer: Bo Johansson

Goals: Chapuisat (57), Tobiasen (90)

DENMARK v ITALY 1-2 (0-1)

Idraetsparken, København 27.03.1999

Referee: António Jesús López Nieto (SPA) Att: 41,429

DENMARK: Peter Schmeichel; Bjarne Goldbaek (83 Søren Colding), Jes Høgh, René Henriksen, Jan Heintze; Thomas Helveg, Claus Thomsen, Allan Nielsen (77 Stig Tøfting), Martin Jørgensen; Jesper Grønkjaer (53 Miklos Molnar), Ebbe Sand. Trainer: Bo Johansson

ITALY: Gianluigi Buffon; Christian Panucci, Alessandro Nesta, Fabio Cannavaro, Paolo Maldini; Diego Fuser (46 Antonio Conte), Dino Baggio, Luigi Di Biagio, Eusebio Di Francesco; Enrico Chiesa (63 Francesco Totti), Filippo Inzaghi. Trainer: Dino Zoff

Goals: Inzaghi (1), Sand (57), Conte (69)

ITALY v BELARUS 1-1 (1-1)

Stadio Del Conero, Ancona 31.03.1999

Referee: Michel Piraux (BEL) Attendance: 20,735

ITALY: Gianluigi Buffon; Christian Panucci, Fabio Cannavaro, Alessandro Nesta, Paolo Maldini; Antonio Conte, Luigi Di Biagio (46 Giuliano Giannichedda), Dino Baggio, Francesco Totti (46 Eusebio Di Francesco); Enrico Chiesa (64 Roberto Baggio), Filippo Inzaghi. Trainer: Dino Zoff

BELARUS: Gennadiy Tumilovich; Andrei Lavrik, Erik Yakhimovich, Alexandr Lukhvich, Sergei Gurenko; Andrei Ostrovskiy, Valentin Belkevich, Myroslav Romaschenko, Radislav Orlovskiy; Vasily Baranov, Vladimir Makovskiy. Trainer: Mikhail Vergeyenko

Goals: Belkevich (24), Inzaghi (31 pen)

BELARUS v SWITZERLAND 0-1 (0-0)

Minsk 27.03.1999

Referee: Oguz Sarvan (TUR) Attendance: 35,000

BELARUS: Gennadiy Tumilovich; Erik Yakhimovich, Andrei Lavrik, Sergei Gurenko, Alexandr Lukhvich; Vyacheslav Gerashchenko (85 Vadim Skripchenko), Alexandr Khatskevich, Valentin Belkevich, Vasily Baranov (59 Alexandr Chaika); Vladimir Makovskiy (86 Andrei Ostrovskiy), Myroslav Romaschenko. Trainer: Mikhail Vergeyenko

SWITZERLAND: Martin Brunner; Sébastien Fournier, Stéphane Henchoz, Marc Hodel, Sébastien Jeanneret; Stéphane Chapuisat, Raphaël Wicky (66 Patrick Müller), David Sesa (73 Patrick De Napoli); Alexandre Comisetti, Ciriaco Sforza, Johann Vogel. Trainer: Gilbert Gress

Goal: Fournier (72)

DENMARK v BELARUS 1-0 (1-0)

Idraetsparken, København 05.06.1999

Referee: Lucilio Cardoso Cortes Baptista (POR) Att: 24,876

DENMARK: Peter Schmeichel; Søren Colding, René Henriksen, Jes Høgh, Jan Heintze; Bjarne Goldbaek, Allan Nielsen, Stig Tøfting (67 Brian Steen Nielsen), Jesper Grønkjaer; Martin Jørgensen, Ebbe Sand (78 Miklos Molnar). Trainer: Bo Johansson

BELARUS: Gennadiy Tumilovich; Erik Yakhimovich, Andrei Lavrik, Alexandr Lukhvich, Andrei Ostrovskiy (46 Maxym Romaschenko); Sergei Gurenko, Alexandr Khatskevich (70 Alexandr Kulchiy), Radislav Orlovskiy, Valentin Belkevich; Vladimir Makovskiy (85 Nikolai Ryndyuk), Vasily Baranov. Trainer: Mikhail Vergeyenko

Goal: Heintze (22)

SWITZERLAND v WALES 2-0 (1-0)

Hardturm, Zürich 31.03.1999

Referee: Miroslav Liba (CZE) Attendance: 13,500

SWITZERLAND: Martin Brunner; Stéphane Henchoz, Sébastien Jeanneret, Stefan Wolf, Raphaël Wicky, Sébastien Fournier; Ciriaco Sforza, Johann Vogel, Patrick Müller; Stéphane Chapuisat, Alexandre Comisetti (68 Patrick Bühlmann). Trainer: Gilbert Gress

WALES: Paul Jones (26 Mark Crossley); John Robinson, Kit Symons, Chris Coleman, Mark Pembridge; Andy Johnson, Mark Hughes (74 Craig Bellamy), Gary Speed, Robbie Savage; Dean Saunders, Nathan Blake (64 John Hartson). Manager: Robert Gould

Goal: Chapuisat (4, 71)

ITALY v WALES 4-0 (3-0)

Stadio Renato Dall'Ara, Bologna 05.06.1999

Referee: Edgar Steinborn (GER) Attendance: 15,500

ITALY: Gianluigi Buffon; Christian Panucci, Paolo Negro, Fabio Cannavaro, Paolo Maldini; Diego Fuser (69 Angelo di Livio), Antonio Conte, Demetrio Albertini, Eusebio Di Francesco; Christian Vieri (46 Vincenzo Montella), Filippo Inzaghi (80 Enrico Chiesa). Trainer: Dino Zoff

WALES: Paul Jones; Adrian Williams, Andy Melville, Robert Page; John Robinson (78 Steve Jenkins), Craig Bellamy (79 Mark Pembridge), Gary Speed, Mark Hughes, Darren Barnard; Ryan Giggs, Dean Saunders (46 John Hartson). Manager: Robert Gould

Goals: Vieri (7), Inzaghi (37), Maldini (40), Chiesa (89)

SWITZERLAND v ITALY 0-0

Stade Olympique de al Pontaise, Lausanne 09.06.1999

Referee: Graham Poll (ENG) Attendance: 16,000

SWITZERLAND: Stefan Huber; Sébastien Jeanneret (76 Franco Di Jorio), Régis Rothenbühler, Patrick Müller, Marc Hodel; Johann Vogel, David Sesa, Raphaël Wicky (69 Bernt Haas), Ciriaco Sforza, Alexandre Comisetti (55 Fabio Celestini); Stéphane Chapuisat. Trainer: Gilbert Gress

ITALY: Gianluigi Buffon; Christian Panucci (69 Giuseppe Pancaro), Paolo Maldini, Demetrio Albertini, Fabio Cannavaro; Paolo Negro, Diego Fuser (60 Angelo di Livio), Antonio Conte, Eusebio Di Francesco; Filippo Inzaghi, Christian Vieri (60 Enrico Chiesa). Trainer: Dino Zoff

DENMARK v SWITZERLAND 2-1 (0-0)

Idraetsparken, København 04.09.1999

Referee: Ryszard Wojcik (POL) Attendance: 41,667

DENMARK: Peter Schmeichel; Thomas Helveg, René Henriksen, Jes Høgh, Jan Heintze; Bjarne Goldbaek (51 Søren Colding), Stig Tøfting, Allan Nielsen (80 Brian Steen Nielsen), Martin Jørgensen; Ebbe Sand (88 Morten Wieghorst), Jon Dahl Tomasson.

SWITZERLAND: Stefan Huber; Patrick Müller, Marc Hodel, Raphaël Wicky (90 Thomas Wyss); Sébastien Jeanneret, Johann Vogel, Ciriaco Sforza, Franco Di Jorio (60 Kubilay Türkyilmaz); David Sesa (78 Sascha Müller), Stéphane Chapuisat, Patrick Bühlmann.

Goals: A. Nielsen (54), Türkyilmaz (79), Tomasson (81)

WALES v DENMARK 0-2 (0-0)

Anfield, Liverpool 09.06.1999

Referee: Armand Ancion (BEL) Attendance: 10,956

WALES: Paul Jones; Steve Jenkins, Darren Barnard (90 Andrew Legg), John Robinson (85 Mark Pembridge), Andy Melville; Chris Coleman, Gary Speed, Dean Saunders, Ryan Giggs; John Hartson (87 Craig Bellamy), Mark Hughes. Managers: Neville Southall & Mark Hughes

DENMARK: Peter Schmeichel; Søren Colding, René Henriksen, Jes Høgh, Jan Heintze; Bjarne Goldbaek, Allan Nielsen (81 Stig Tøfting), Jesper Grønkjaer, Ebbe Sand; Miklos Molnar (70 Jon Dahl Tomasson), Martin Jørgensen (89 Per Frandsen). Trainer: Bo Johansson

Goals: Tomasson (84), Tøfting (90 pen)

ITALY v DENMARK 2-3 (2-1)

Stadio San Paolo, Napoli 08.09.1999

Referee: Dick Jol (HOL) Attendance: 46,919

ITALY: Gianluigi Buffon; Christian Panucci, Alessandro Nesta, Fabio Cannavaro, Giuseppe Pancaro; Diego Fuser, Dino Baggio (46 Giuliano Giannichedda), Demetrio Albertini, Eusebio Di Francesco (70 Antonio Conte); Filippo Inzaghi, Christian Vieri (77 Francesco Totti).

DENMARK: Peter Schmeichel; Søren Colding, Jes Høgh, René Henriksen, Jan Heintze; Thomas Helveg (52 Bjarne Goldbaek), Allan Nielsen, Stig Tøfting (52 Morten Wieghorst), Martin Jørgensen, Jon Dahl Tomasson (85 Michael Schjønberg); Ebbe Sand.

Sent off: Wieghorst (81), Giannichedda (87)

Goals: Fuser (10), Vieri (34), Jørgensen (39 pen), Wieghorst (57), Tomasson (63)

BELARUS v WALES 1-2 (1-1)

Republican, Minsk 04.09.1999

Referee: Tom Henning Øvrebø (NOR) Attendance: 25,000

BELARUS: Gennadiy Tumilovich; Igor Tarlovskiy, Andrei Lavrik, Alexandr Lukhvich, Andrei Ostrovskiy; Sergei Gurenko, Vasily Baranov, Alexandr Chaika, Alexandr Kulchiy; Vladimir Makovskiy, Radislav Orlovskiy (60 Myroslav Romaschenko).

WALES: Paul Jones; Robert Page, Chris Coleman, Andy Melville, Darren Barnard; John Robinson, Mark Pembridge (81 Carl Robinson), Gary Speed, Nathan Blake; Ryan Giggs, Dean Saunders.

Goals: Baranov (30), Saunders (42), Giggs (86)

SWITZERLAND v BELARUS 2-0 (0-0)

Lausanne 08.09.1999

Referee: Leslie Irvine (NIR) Attendance: 12,000

SWITZERLAND: Stefan Huber; Patrick Müller (78 Stefan Wolf), Stéphane Henchoz, Marc Hodel; Raphaël Wicky, Johann Vogel, Ciriaco Sforza, Franco Di Jorio; Patrick Bühlmann (71 David Sesa), Stéphane Chapuisat (63 Alexandre Comisetti), Kubilay Türkyilmaz.

BELARUS: Youri Afanasenko; Erik Yakhimovich, Andrei Lavrik, Alexandr Lukhvich, Andrei Ostrovskiy; Sergei Gurenko, Alexandr Chaika, Alexandr Kulchiy (55 Petr Kachuro), Igor Tarlovskiy; Vasily Baranov, Vladimir Makovskiy (69 Maxym Romaschenko).

Goals: Türkyilmaz (68, 86 pen)

WALES v SWITZERLAND 0-2 (0-1)

Wrexham 09.10.1999

Referee: Spiridon Papadakos (GRE) Attendance: 5,064

WALES: Paul Jones; Mark Delaney, Robert Page, Chris Coleman, Darren Barnard; John Robinson, Robbie Savage, Gary Speed, John Oster (77 Matthew Jones); Dean Saunders (66 John Hartson), Nathan Blake (77 Iwan Roberts).

SWITZERLAND: Pascal Zuberbühler; Stéphane Henchoz, Marc Hodel, Christophe Jaquet (70 Thomas Wyss); Bernt Haas, Johann Vogel, David Sesa, Franco Di Jorio; Sébastien Jeanneret, Alexandre Rey (66 Alexandre Comisetti), Patrick Bühlmann.

Goals: Rey (16), Bühlmann (59)

BELARUS v ITALY 0-0

Republican, Minsk 09.10.1999

Referee: Claude Colombo (FRA) Attendance: 32,000

BELARUS: Valeriy Shantalosov; Sergei Gurenko, Alexandr Lukhvich, Erik Yakhimovich, Igor Tarlovskiy, Radislav Orlovskiy; Myroslav Romaschenko (46 Vladimir Makovskiy), Andrei Ostrovskiy, Alexandr Chaika, Vasily Baranov; Sergei Gerasimets (77 Alexandr Kulchiy).

ITALY: Gianluigi Buffon; Christian Panucci, Alessandro Nesta, Fabio Cannavaro, Paolo Maldini; Francesco Moriero, Antonio Conte, Luigi Di Biagio, Gian Luca Zambrotta; Filippo Inzaghi, Christian Vieri (82 Alessandro Del Piero).

	P	W	D	L	F	A	Pts
Italy	8	4	3	1	13	5	15
Denmark	8	4	2	2	11	8	14
(vs Switzerland	*2*	*1*	*1*	*0*	*3*	*2*	*4)*
Switzerland	8	4	2	2	9	5	14
(vs Denmark)	*2*	*0*	*1*	*1*	*2*	*3*	*1)*
Wales	8	3	0	5	7	16	9
Belarus	8	0	3	5	4	10	3

GROUP 2

GEORGIA v ALBANIA 1-0 (0-0)

Boris Paichadze, Tbilisi 05.09.1998

Referee: Claude Détruche (SWI) Attendance: 25,000

GEORGIA: David Gvaramadze; Kakhi Kaladze, Levan Tskitishvili, Levan Silagadze (43 Giorgi Kiknadze), Mamuka Tsereteli; Levan Kobiashvili, Georgi Nemsadze, Gocha Jamarauli, Temur Ketsbaia (54 Zaza Janashia); Giorgi Kinkladze, Aleksandre Iashvili (62 Archil Arveladze).
Trainer: Vladimir Gutsaev

ALBANIA: Foto Strakosha; Altin Lala, Ilir Shulku, Arian Xhumba, Rudi Vata; Luan Pinari, Altin Haxhi, Alban Bushi (74 Alpin Gallo), Bledar Kola; Altin Rrakli, Igli Tare (68 Arian Peço, 86 Artur Maxhuni). Trainer: Astrit Hafizi

Sent off: Pinari (72), Janashia (80)

Goal: A. Arveladze (65)

GREECE v SLOVENIA 2-2 (0-1)

Olympiako Spiros Louis, Athina 06.09.1998

Referee: Alfredo Trentalange (ITA) Attendance: 28,908

GREECE: Ilias Atmatsidis; Michalis Kasapis (78 Grigoris Yeorgatos), Nikolaos Dabizas, Ioanis Kalitzakis, Vasilios Borbokis (83 Nikolaos Liberopoulos); Theodoros Zagorakis, Vasilios Tsartas (46 Konstantinos Frantzeskos), Dimitrios Markos; Marinos Ouzounidis, Nikolaos Mahlas, Themistoklis Nikolaidis. Trainer: Anghel Iordănescu

SLOVENIA: Marko Simeunovic; Darko Milanic, Marinko Galic, Aleksander Knavs, Dzoni Novak; Ales Ceh, Saso Udovic (46 Robert Englaro), Zlatko Zahovic, Milan Osterc (68 Ermin Siljak, 71 Milenko Acimovic); Mladen Rudonja, Miran Pavlin.
Trainer: Srecko Katanec

Goals: Zahovic (19, 73), Mahlas (55 pen), Frantzeskos (58)

NORWAY v LATVIA 1-3 (1-1)

Oslo 06.09.1998

Referee: Serghei Shmolik (BLS) Attendance: 11,030

NORWAY: Espen Baardsen; Vegard Heggem (60 Henning Berg), Ronny Johnsen, Erik Hoftun, Stig Inge Bjørnebye; Petter Rudi (80 Håvard Flo), Kjetil Rekdal, Ståle Solbakken, Frank Strandli; Tore André Flo, Ole Gunnar Solskjær (62 Jostein Flo).
Trainer: Nils-Johan Semb

LATVIA: Oleg Karavayev; Yury Laizans (51 Victor Lukashevich), Artur Zakreshevsky, Mikhail Zemlinsky, Valentin Lobanyov; Alexey Sharando (73 Rolands Boulders), Valery Ivanov, Imants Bleidelis, Marian Pakhar (81 Alexander Isakov); Vladimir Babichev, Andrey Shtolcers.
Trainer: Revaz Dzodzuashvili

Goals: Pakhar (11), Solbakken (17), Shtolcers (53), Zemlinsky (64 pen)

SLOVENIA v NORWAY 1-2 (1-1)

Ljubljana 10.10.1998

Referee: Andres Schluchter (SWI) Attendance: 6,200

SLOVENIA: Marko Simeunovic; Darko Milanic, Marinko Galic, Dzoni Novak, Aleksander Knavs; Ales Ceh, Saso Udovic (64 Milenko Acimovic), Zlatko Zahovic, Milan Osterc (46 Robert Englaro); Mladen Rudonja, Miran Pavlin. Trainer: Srecko Katanec

NORWAY: Frode Grodås; Alf Inge Håland, Erik Hoftun, Henning Berg, Stig Inge Bjørnebye; Jostein Flo, Vegard Heggem (85 Vidar Riseth), Ståle Solbakken, Kjetil Rekdal; Tore André Flo (90 Sigurd Rushfeldt), Roar Strand (46 Daniel Berg Hestad). Trainer: Nils-Johan Semb

Goals: Zahovic (24), T.A. Flo (45), Rekdal (80)

GREECE v GEORGIA 3-0 (3-0)

Olympiako Spiros Louis, Athina 14.10.1998

Referee: Atanas Uzunov (BUL) Attendance: 15,000

GREECE: Ilias Atmatsidis; Nikolaos Dabizas, Grigoris Yeorgatos, Marinos Ouzounidis, Ioanis Kalitzakis; Ilias Poursanidis, Theodoros Zagorakis, Konstantinos Frantzeskos (74 Vasilios Tsartas), Dimitrios Markos; Nikolaos Mahlas (82 Dimitrios Mavrogenidis), Nikolaos Liberopoulos (69 Stylianos Yanakopoulos). Trainer: Anghel Iordănescu

GEORGIA: Nikoloz Togonidze; Murtaz Shelia, Kakhi Kaladze, Levan Kobiashvili, Gela Shekiladze, Mikheil Kavelashvili (59 Georgi Gakhokidze); Georgi Nemsadze, Gocha Jamarauli, Temur Ketsbaia; Giorgi Kinkladze, Shota Arveladze. Trainer: Vladimir Gutsaev

Goals: Mahlas (13), Liberopoulos (15), Ouzounidis (36)

LATVIA v GEORGIA 1-0 (1-0)

Riga 10.10.1998

Referee: Constantin Zotta (ROM) Attendance: 3,500

LATVIA: Oleg Karavayev; Victor Lukashevich, Vitaly Astafyev (76 Alexander Isakov), Mikhail Zemlinsky, Valentin Lobanyov; Alexey Sharando, Valery Ivanov, Imants Bleidelis (51 Yury Laizans), Marian Pakhar (89 Rolands Boulders); Vladimir Babichev, Andrey Shtolcers.
Trainer: Revaz Dzodzuashvili

GEORGIA: David Gvaramadze; Kakhi Kaladze, Giorgi Gakhokidze (61 Giorgi Demetradze), Mikheil Kavelashvili, Gela Shekiladze; Levan Kobiashvili, Georgi Nemsadze, Gocha Jamarauli, Temur Ketsbaia; Giorgi Kinkladze, Shota Arveladze.
Trainer: Vladimir Gutsaev

Goal: Shtolcers (2)

SLOVENIA v LATVIA 1-0 (0-0)

Ljudski vrt, Maribor 14.10.1998

Referee: Karen Nalbandian (ARM) Attendance: 3,292

SLOVENIA: Marko Simeunovic; Robert Englaro, Mladen Rudonja, Darko Milanic, Marinko Galic; Aleksander Knavs (46 Primoz Gliha), Dzoni Novak, Miran Pavlin, Saso Udovic (88 Zeljko Milinovic); Zlatko Zahovic, Rudi Istenic (65 Milenko Acimovic). Trainer: Srecko Katanec

LATVIA: Oleg Karavayev; Victor Lukashevich, Vitaly Astafyev (78 Rolands Boulders), Mikhail Zemlinsky, Valentin Lobanyov; Alexey Sharando, Valery Ivanov (87 Vitas Rimkus), Imants Bleidelis (51 Mikhail Mikholap), Marian Pakhar; Alexander Isakov, Andrey Shtolcers.
Trainer: Revaz Dzodzuashvili

Goal: Udovic (85)

NORWAY v ALBANIA 2-2 (0-1)

Oslo 14.10.1998

Referee: Gerd Grabher (AUS) Attendance: 17,700

NORWAY: Frode Grodås; Alf Inge Håland (57 Steffen Iversen), Erik Hoftun, Henning Berg, Stig Inge Bjørnebye; Ståle Solbakken (89 Sigurd Rushfeldt), Vegard Heggem, Kjetil Rekdal, Roar Strand; Jostein Flo (57 Ole Gunnar Solskjær), Tore André Flo. Trainer: Nils-Johan Semb

ALBANIA: Foto Strakosha; Altin Lala, Ilir Shulku, Arian Xhumba, Ervin Fakaj; Rudi Vata, Altin Haxhi, Alban Bushi (84 Mahir Halili), Bledar Kola (89 Edmond Dalipi); Altin Rrakli, Igli Tare. Trainer: Astrit Hafizi

Goals: Bushi (37), Tare (52), Rekdal (82 pen), Berg (87)

ALBANIA v GREECE 0-0

Qemal Stafa, Tiranë 18.11.1998

Referee: Victor-José Esquinas Torres (SPA) Att: 18,670

ALBANIA: Foto Strakosha; Ervin Fakaj, Arian Xhumba, Rudi Vata, Ilir Shulku; Edmond Dalipi (53 Mahir Halili), Altin Haxhi, Alban Bushi, Bledar Kola; Altin Rrakli, Igli Tare.
Trainer: Astrit Hafizi

GREECE: Ilias Atmatsidis; Nikolaos Dabizas (89 Leonidas Vokolos), Dimitrios Markos, Marinos Ouzounidis, Ioanis Kalitzakis; Ilias Poursanidis, Theodoros Zagorakis, Konstantinos Frantzeskos (46 Nikolaos Liberopoulos), Grigoris Yeorgatos; Nikolaos Mahlas, Themistoklis Nikolaidis (70 Konstantinos Konstantinidis).
Trainer: Anghel Iordănescu

GREECE v NORWAY 0-2 (0-1)

Olympiako Spiros Louis, Athina 27.03.1999

Referee: Leslie Irvine (NIR) Attendance: 42,572

GREECE: Ilias Atmatsidis; Dimitrios Markos (54 Nikolaos Mahlas), Marinos Ouzounidis, Nikolaos Dabizas, Giorgos Anatolakis; Ilias Poursanidis, Theodoros Zagorakis (46 Dimitrios Mavrogenidis), Stylianos Yanakopoulos, Grigoris Yeorgatos; Nikolaos Liberopoulos (75 Konstantinos Frantzeskos), Themistoklis Nikolaidis.
Trainer: Anghel Iordănescu

NORWAY: Thomas Myhre; Vegard Heggem, Ronny Johnsen, Henning Berg, André Bergdølmo (65 Gunnar Halle); Roar Strand (59 Lars Bohinen), Erik Mykland, Ståle Solbakken, Steffen Iversen; Ole Gunnar Solskjær (88 John Carew), Petter Rudi. Trainer: Nils Johan Semb

Goals: Solskjaer (38, 87)

GEORGIA v SLOVENIA 1-1 (1-0)

Boris Paichadze, Tbilisi 27.03.1999

Referee: Alain Hamer (LUX) Attendance: 20,000

GEORGIA: Soso Grishikashvili; Kakhi Kaladze, Gia Chkhaidze, Georgi Balashvili, Mamuka Tsereteli; Rati Aleksidze (46 Giorgi Kinkladze), Georgi Nemsadze, Gocha Jamarauli (82 Georgi Daraselia), Levan Kobiashvili; Zaza Janashia, Georgi Demetradze (73 Mikheil Kavelashvili).
Trainer: Vladimir Gutsaev

SLOVENIA: Marko Simeunovic; Amir Karic, Spasoje Bulajic, Darko Milanic, Aleksander Knavs; Zeljko Milinovic, Mladen Rudonja (90 Zeljko Mitrakovic), Ales Ceh, Saso Udovic (60 Milenko Acimovic); Zlatko Zahovic, Miran Pavlin (77 Rudi Istenic). Trainer: Srecko Katanec

Goals: Z. Janashia (42), Knavs (52)

LATVIA v GREECE 0-0

Daugava, Riga 31.03.1999

Referee: Knud-Erik Fisker (DEN) Attendance: 3,200

LATVIA: Oleg Karavayev; Victor Lukashevich, Vitaly Astafyev, Mikhail Zemlinsky, Valentin Lobanyov; Alexey Sharando (62 Igor Stepanov), Valery Ivanov (29 Alexander Isakov), Oleg Blagonadezhdin, Marian Pakhar; Mikhail Mikholap (46 Rolands Boulders), Andrey Shtolcers.
Trainer: Revaz Dzodzuashvili

GREECE: Ilias Atmatsidis; Michalis Kasapis, Marinos Ouzounidis, Nikolaos Dabizas, Dimitrios Mavrogenidis; Ilias Poursanidis, Nikolaos Liberopoulos, Grigoris Yeorgatos (74 Konstantinos Frantzeskos), Stylianos Yanakopoulos (74 Theodoros Zagorakis); Nikolaos Mahlas (80 Ioanis Anastasiou), Themistoklis Nikolaidis.
Trainer: Vasilios Daniel

LATVIA v ALBANIA 0-0

Riga 28.04.1999

Referee: Eric Romain (SWI) Attendance: 2,600

LATVIA: Oleg Karavayev; Igor Stepanov (84 Alexey Sharando), Alexander Isakov, Victor Lukashevich, Valentin Lobanyov; Oleg Blagonadezhdin, Valery Ivanov, Rolands Boulders; Andrey Rubins, Mikhail Mikholap (69 Victor Dobretsov), Andrey Shtolcers (60 Yury Laizans).
Trainer: Revaz Dzodzuashvili

ALBANIA: Foto Strakosha; Altin Lala, Ilir Shulku, Arian Xhumba, Rudi Vata (78 Redi Jupi Bashkim); Ervin Fakaj, Altin Haxhi, Alban Bushi (86 Mahir Halili); Bledar Kola, Altin Rrakli (81 Edmond Dalipi), Igli Tare. Trainer: Astrit Hafizi

GEORGIA v NORWAY 1-4 (0-4)

Boris Paichadze, Tbilisi 28.04.1999

Referee: Sándor Puhl (HUNG) Attendance: 15,000

GEORGIA: Nikoloz Togonidze; Kakhi Kaladze, Givi Didava, Gela Shekiladze (46 Zurab Popkhadze), Mamuka Tsereteli; Aleksandre Rekhviashvili (82 Giorgi Kiknadze), Georgi Nemsadze, Gocha Jamarauli; Temur Ketsbaia (46 Georgi Demetradze), Zaza Janashia, Levan Kobiashvili.
Trainer: Vladimir Gutsaev

NORWAY: Thomas Myhre; André Bergdølmo, Erik Hoftun, Alf Inge Håland, Tore Pedersen; Steffen Iversen, Erik Mykland, Ståle Solbakken; Tore André Flo (87 John Carew), Ole Gunnar Solskjær (46 Roar Strand), Petter Rudi (83 Vidar Riseth).
Trainer: Nils-Johan Semb

Goals: Iversen (15), T.A. Flo (26, 37), Solskjær (34), Z. Janashia (57)

NORWAY v GEORGIA 1-0 (1-0)

Oslo 30.05.1999

Referee: Luc Huyghe (BEL) Attendance: 18,236

NORWAY: Frode Olsen; Vegard Heggem, Tore Pedersen, Erik Hoftun; André Bergdømo, Steffen Iversen (85 Tore André Dahlum), Ståle Solbakken, Erik Mykland; Øyvind Leonhardsen (46 Petter Rudi), Vidar Riseth (70 Kjetil Rekdal), Tore André Flo. Trainer: Nils-Johan Semb

GEORGIA: David Gvaramadze; Valter Guchua (62 David Chichveishvili), Kakhi Kaladze, Givi Didava (46 Zurab Popkhadze), Mamuka Tsereteli; Levan Tskitishvili, Georgi Nemsadze, Gocha Jamarauli, Temur Ketsbaia, Mikheil Kavelashvili; Georgi Demetradze (77 Mikheil Ashvetia).
Trainer: Johan Boskamp

Goal: Iversen (4)

ALBANIA v NORWAY 1-2 (1-1)

Tiranë 05.06.1999

Referee: Livio Bazzolini (ITA) Attendance: 16,000

ALBANIA: Foto Strakosha; Altin Lala, Ilir Shulku, Arian Xhumba, Rudi Vata; Ervin Fakaj (62 Arian Bellai), Altin Haxhi, Alban Bushi, Bledar Kola (69 Albert Duro); Altin Rrakli (80 Erjon Bogdani), Igli Tare. Trainer: Astrit Hafizi

NORWAY: Frode Olsen; André Bergdølmo, Tore Pedersen (62 Bjørn Otto Bragstad), Erik Hoftun, Alf Inge Håland; Steffen Iversen, Ståle Solbakken (89 Vidar Riseth), Kjetil Rekdal, Erik Mykland, Petter Rudi (78 Tore André Dahlum); Tore André Flo. Trainer: Nils-Johan Semb

Goals: Iversen (3), Tare (16), T.A. Flo (83)

ALBANIA v SLOVENIA 0-1 (0-1)

Tiranë 09.06.1999

Referee: Adrian Stoica (ROM) Attendance: 8,000

ALBANIA: Foto Strakosha; Altin Lala, Ilir Shulku, Arian Xhumba, Rudi Vata; Albert Duro, Arian Bellai, Alban Bushi, Erjon Bogdani (73 Edmond Dalipi); Altin Rrakli (46 Mahir Halili), Igli Tare. Trainer: Astrit Hafizi

SLOVENIA: Marko Simeunovic; Zeljko Milinovic, Amir Karic, Marinko Galic, Aleksander Knavs; Dzoni Novak, Ales Ceh, Saso Udovic (65 Milenko Acimovic), Zlatko Zahovic, Miran Pavlin; Milan Osterc (82 Rudy Istenic). Trainer: Srecko Katanec

Goal: Zahovic (26 pen)

LATVIA v SLOVENIA 1-2 (1-2)

Riga 05.06.1999

Referee: Juan Manuel Brito Arceo (SPA) Attendance: 2,500

LATVIA: Alexander Kolinko; Victor Lukashevich, Vitaly Astafyev (41 Andrey Rubins), Mikhail Zemlinsky, Valentin Lobanyov (43 Igor Korablyov); Alexey Sharando (59 Imants Bleidelis), Yury Laizans, Andrey Shtolcers, Vladimir Babichev; Marian Pakhar, Mikhail Mikholap.
Trainer: Revaz Dzodzuashvili

SLOVENIA: Marko Simeunovic; Mladen Rudonja (88 Milan Osterc), Zeljko Milinovic, Amir Karic, Marinko Galic; Aleksander Knavs, Dzoni Novak, Ales Ceh, Saso Udovic (65 Milenko Acimovic); Zlatko Zahovic, Miran Pavlin (78 Rudi Istenic). Trainer: Srecko Katanec

Goals: Pakhar (18), Zahovic (25, 42 pen)

GREECE v LATVIA 1-2 (1-1)

Olympiako Spiros Louis, Athina 09.06.1999

Referee: Lubomir Pucek (CZE) Attendance: 15,000

GREECE: Ilias Atmatsidis; Dimitrios Mavrogenidis, Michalis Kasapis, Marinos Ouzounidis, Giorgos Anatolakis; Andreas Zikos, Theodoros Zagorakis, Konstantinos Frantzeskos (61 Ioanis Anastasiou), Grigoris Yeorgatos (72 Dimitrios Markos); Nikolaos Mahlas, Andreas Niniadis (80 Nikolaos Frousos).
Trainer: Vasilios Daniel

LATVIA: Alexander Kolinko; Victor Lukashevich, Mikhail Zemlinsky, Valentin Lobanyov, Igor Korablyov; Yury Laizans, Andrey Rubins (64 Alexander Zhizhmanov), Vladimir Babichev, Vitaly Astafyev (54 Imants Bleidelis); Marian Pakhar, Maris Verpakovsky (46 Mikhail Mikholap).
Trainer: Revaz Dzodzuashvili

Goals: Verpakovsky (24), Niniadis (38 pen), Zemlinsky (90 pen)

GEORGIA v GREECE 1-2 (0-0)

Boris Paichadze, Tbilisi 05.06.1999

Referee: William Young (SCO) Attendance: 7,000

GEORGIA: David Gvaramadze; David Chichveishvili (9 Givi Didava), Otar Khizaneishvili, Badri Akhvlediani (65 Zurab Khizanishvili), Mamuka Tsereteli; Levan Tskitishvili (56 Rati Aleksidze), Georgi Nemsadze, Gocha Jamarauli, Temur Ketsbaia; Mikheil Ashvetia, Levan Kobiashvili.
Trainer: Johan Boskamp

GREECE: Ilias Atmatsidis; Dimitrios Mavrogenidis, Michalis Kasapis, Marinos Ouzounidis, Giorgos Anatolakis; Ilias Poursanidis, Theodoros Zagorakis (80 Konstantinos Frantzeskos), Konstantinos Konstantinidis (46 Nikolaos Frousos), Andreas Niniadis; Nikolaos Mahlas, Grigoris Yeorgatos (61 Ioanis Anastasiou). Trainer: Vasilios Daniel

Goals: Ketsbaia (55), Frantzeskos (85), Mahlas (90)

SLOVENIA v ALBANIA 2-0 (0-0)

Bezigrad, Ljubljana 18.08.1999

Referee: Paulo Paraty da Silva (POR) Attendance: 8,000

SLOVENIA: Mladen Dabanovic; Darko Milanic (61 Zeljko Milinovic), Marinko Galic, Aleksander Knavs; Dzoni Novak (90 Rudy Istenic), Ales Ceh, Zlatko Zahovic, Miran Pavlin; Milan Osterc, Mladen Rudonja, Saso Udovic (46 Milenko Acimovic).

ALBANIA: Foto Strakosha; Luan Pinari, Ilir Shulku, Arian Xhumba, Rudi Vata; Arian Bellai, Altin Haxhi, Edvin Murati (59 Mahir Halili), Bledar Kola; Altin Rrakli (60 Erjon Bogdani), Igli Tare.

Goals: Zahovic (49), Osterc (80)

NORWAY v GREECE 1-0 (1-0)

Ullevaal, Oslo 04.09.1999 Oslo

Referee: Markus Merk (GER) Attendance: 24,133

NORWAY: Frode Olsen; Henning Berg, André Bergdølmo, Erik Hoftun, Vegard Heggem; Steffen Iversen, Øyvind Leonhardsen (73 Vidar Riseth), Erik Mykland, Bent Skammelsrud; Tore André Flo, Ole Gunnar Solskjær (67 Petter Rudi).

GREECE: Ilias Atmatsidis; Dimitrios Mavrogenidis, Michalis Kasapis, Nikolaos Dabizas, Marinos Ouzounidis; Ilias Poursanidis, Theodoros Zagorakis (49 Nikolaos Mahlas), Andreas Niniadis (46 Stylianos Yanakopoulos), Grigoris Yeorgatos; Nikolaos Liberopoulos, Themistoklis Nikolaidis.

Goal: Leonhardsen (34)

GEORGIA v LATVIA 2-2 (1-0)

Boris Paichadze, Tbilisi 08.09.1999

Referee: Miroslav Radoman (YUG) Attendance: 4,500

GEORGIA: David Gvaramadze; Kakhi Kaladze, Levan Tskitishvili (70 Tengiz Sichinava), Givi Didava, Mamuka Tsereteli; Gela Shekiladze, Georgi Nemsadze, Gocha Jamarauli, Mikheil Kavelashvili (75 Archil Arveladze); Levan Kobiashvili, Shota Arveladze (72 Georgi Demetradze).

LATVIA: Alexander Kolinko; Igor Stepanov, Yury Laizans (83 Rolands Boulders), Mikhail Zemlinsky, Valentin Lobanyov; Andrey Rubins, Valery Ivanov, Imants Bleidelis, Alexander Isakov (60 Vladimir Babichev); Marian Pakhar, Andrey Shtolcers (74 Alexey Sharando).

Sent off: Tsereteli (80)

Goals: S. Arveladze (30), Kavelashvili (52), Bleidelis (62), Stepanov (90)

ALBANIA v LATVIA 3-3 (1-1)

Tiranë 04.09.1999

Referee: Alain Hamer (LUX) Attendance: 4,000

ALBANIA: Foto Strakosha; Altin Lala, Ilir Shulku, Arian Xhumba, Rudi Vata; Ervin Fakaj (73 Erjon Bogdani), Altin Haxhi, Alban Bushi, Arian Bellai; Edvin Murati (46 Edmond Dalipi), Igli Tare (77 Devi Muka).

LATVIA: Alexander Kolinko; Igor Stepanov, Vitaly Astafyev (81 Vladimir Babichev), Mikhail Zemlinsky, Valentin Lobanyov; Victor Lukashevich, Valery Ivanov (61 Oleg Blagonadezhdin), Imants Bleidelis, Andrey Rubins; Andrey Shtolcers (84 Rolands Boulders), Mikhail Mikholap.

Sent off: Lukashevich (86)

Goals: Astafyev (20, 62), Bushi (29, 78), Shtolcers (70), Muka (90)

NORWAY v SLOVENIA 4-0 (3-0)

Ullevaal, Oslo 08.09.1999

Referee: Gilles Veissière (FRA) Attendance: 24,288

NORWAY: Frode Olsen; André Bergdølmo, Erik Hoftun, Henning Berg, Vegard Heggem; Steffen Iversen, Erik Mykland, Øyvind Leonhardsen, Ole Gunnar Solskjær (78 Vidar Riseth), Bent Skammelsrud (76 Jan Derek Sørensen); Tore André Flo (87 Andreas Lund).

SLOVENIA: Marko Simeunović (46 Mladen Dabanovic); Milan Osterc (83 Milenko Acimovic), Mladen Rudonja, Zeljko Milinovic, Rudi Istenić; Aleksander Knavs, Dzoni Novak, Ales Ceh, Miran Pavlin; Saso Udović (41 Amir Karić), Zlatko Zahovic.

Sent off: Istenić (55)

Goals: Istenic (15 og), Iversen (17), Solskjær (30), Leonhardsen (67)

SLOVENIA v GEORGIA 2-1 (0-0)

Ljubljana 04.09.1999

Referee: Jan Wegereef (HOL) Attendance: 8,500

SLOVENIA: Marko Simeunovic; Marinko Galic, Zeljko Milinovic, Aleksander Knavs, Dzoni Novak; Ales Ceh, Mladen Rudonja, Zlatko Zahovic (90 Rudy Istenic), Miran Pavlin; Milan Osterc (46 Milenko Acimovic), Saso Udovic (75 Amir Karic).

GEORGIA: David Gvaramadze; Levan Kobiashvili, Levan Tskitishvili, Givi Didava, Tengiz Sichinava; Badri Akhvlediani (46 Gela Shekiladze), Kakhi Kaladze, Mikhail Potskhveria, Mikheil Kavelashvili; Archil Arveladze, Shota Arveladze.

Goals: Acimovic (48), S. Arveladze (55), Zahovic (80)

GREECE v ALBANIA 2-0 (1-0)

Olympiako Spiros Louis, Athina 06.10.1999

Referee: Valentin Ivanov (RUS) Attendance: 8,000

GREECE: Ilias Atmatsidis; Georgios Amanatidis, Grigoris Yeorgatos (66 Konstantinos Konstantinidis), Nikolaos Dabizas; Marinos Ouzounidis, Ilias Poursanidis, Theodoros Zagorakis (46 George Georgiadis), Andreas Zikos, Vasilios Tsartas (75 Andreas Niniadis); Nikolaos Mahlas, Themistoklis Nikolaidis.

ALBANIA: Foto Strakosha; Altin Lala, Arian Bellai (84 Erjon Bogdani), Arian Xhumba, Rudi Vata; Edvin Murati (55 Albert Duro), Altin Haxhi, Alban Bushi, Bledar Kola; Altin Rrakli, Igli Tare (67 Devi Muka).

Goals: Tsartas (1), Georgiadis (87)

LATVIA v NORWAY 1-2 (0-0)

Riga 09.10.1999

Referee: Dietmar Drabek (AUS) Attendance: 3,000

LATVIA: Alexander Kolinko; Victor Lukashevich (80 Yury Laizans), Mikhail Zemlinsky, Valentin Lobanyov, Oleg Blagonadezhdin; Imants Bleidelis, Valery Ivanov, Vitaly Astafyev, Andrey Rubins; Andrey Shtolcers, Marian Pakhar.

NORWAY: Frode Olsen; Vegard Heggem, Henning Berg, Erik Hoftun, André Bergdølmo; Steffen Iversen (46 Andreas Lund), Øyvind Leonhardsen, Bent Skammelsrud, Erik Mykland (80 Ståle Solbakken), Ole Gunnar Solskjær (89 Vidar Riseth); Tore André Flo.

Goals: Solskjær (52), Pakhar (53), T.A. Flo (86)

	P	W	D	L	F	A	Pts
Norway	10	8	1	1	21	9	25
Slovenia	10	5	2	3	12	14	17
Greece	10	4	3	3	13	8	15
Latvia	10	3	4	3	13	12	13
Albania	10	1	4	5	8	14	7
Georgia	10	1	2	7	8	18	5

ALBANIA v GEORGIA 2-1 (2-0)

Tiranë 09.10.1999

Referee: Alfred Micallef (MAL) Attendance: 3,000

ALBANIA: Arian Beqaj; Albert Duro, Ilir Shulku, Arian Xhumba, Rudi Vata; Ervin Fakaj, Altin Lala, Alban Bushi (54 Edvin Murati), Bledar Kola; Altin Rrakli (75 Devi Muka), Igli Tare (90 Erjon Bogdani).

GEORGIA: Grigori Tchanturia; Levan Kobiashvili, Georgi Gakhokidze, Givi Didava, Gela Shekiladze; David Chichveishvili, Georgi Nemsadze, Gocha Jamarauli, Kakhi Kaladze; Archil Arveladze (83 David Janashia), Shota Arveladze.

Goals: Rrakli (30), Kola (36), S. Arveladze (52)

SLOVENIA v GREECE 0-3 (0-2)

Ljudski vrt, Maribor 09.10.1999

Referee: Gamal Ghandour (EGY) Attendance: 2,500

SLOVENIA: Marko Simeunovic; Edo Bajrektarevic, Mladen Rudonja, Muamer Vugdalic (84 Robert Englaro), Marinko Galic; Simon Seslar, Dzoni Novak, Ales Ceh, Saso Udovic (46 Amir Karic); Milenko Acimovic, Ante Simundza (60 Milan Osterc).

GREECE: Ilias Atmatsidis; Georgios Amanatidis, Andreas Zikos, Nikolaos Dabizas, Paraskevas Antzas (71 Theodoros Zagorakis); Ilias Poursanidis, George Georgiadis, Konstantinos Konstantinidis, Nikolaos Liberopoulos; Vasilios Tsartas (69 Andreas Niniadis), Themistoklis Nikolaidis (75 Nikolaos Mahlas).

Goals: Tsartas (39), Georgiadis (43), Nikolaidis (73)

GROUP 3

TURKEY v NORTHERN IRELAND 3-0 (1-0)

Ali Sami Yen, Istanbul 05.09.1998

Referee: Ryszard Wojcik (POL) Attendance: 19,840

TURKEY: Reçber Rüstü; Mert Korkmaz, Saffet Akbas, Tayfur Havutçu, Alpay Özalan; Abdullah Ercan, Okan Buruk (87 Arif Erdem), Tugay Kerimoglu (74 Oguz Çetin), Sergen Yalçin; Hakan Şükür, Oktay Derelioglu (79 Hami Mandirali). Trainer: Mustafa Denizli

N. IRELAND: Alan Fettis; Aaron Hughes, Colin Hill, Steve Morrow, Kevin Horlock; Keith Rowland (46 James Quinn), Philip Mulryne, Keith Gillespie (74 Jim Whitley), Neil Lennon; Iain Dowie, Michael Hughes. Trainer: Lawrie McMenemy

Goals: Oktay (17, 58), Tayfur (51 pen)

FINLAND v MOLDOVA 3-2 (2-2)

Olimpic, Helsinki 05.09.1998

Referee: Graham Barber (ENG) Attendance: 18,716

FINLAND: Antti Niemi; Harri Ylönen, Marko Tuomela, Sami Hyypiä, Tommi Kautonen, Aarno Turpeinen (46 Juha Reini), Jarkko Wiss, Jonatan Johansson (80 Antti Sumiala), Mika-Matti Paatelainen, Jari Litmanen (Cap), Joonas Kolkka (73 Sami Mahlio). Trainer: Richard Møller-Nielsen

MOLDOVA: Vasili Coşelev; Oleg Fistican (76 Ivan Tabanov); Radu Rebeja (46 Ghenadie Puşca), Ion Testimiţanu, Alexandru Guzun, Serghei Stroenco, Alexandru Curtianu (Cap), Igor Oprea, Vladimir Gaidamaşciuc, Sergiu Epureanu (71 Alexandr Suharev), Sergiu Cleşcenco. Trainer: Ivan Danilianţ

Sent off: Puşca (89).

Goals: Kolkka (8), Oprea (10, 12), Johansson (45), Paatelainen (63)

TURKEY v GERMANY 1-0 (0-0)

Bursa 10.10.1998

Referee: Hugh Dallas (SCO) Attendance: 17,505

TURKEY: Reçber Rüştü; Ogün Temizkanoglu (88 Hakan Ünsal), Fatih Akyel, Alpay Özalan; Tayfur Havutçu, Abdullah Ercan, Mert Korkmaz, Tugay Kerimoglu (60 Oktay Derelioglu), Sergen Yalçin (80 Saffet Akbas), Tayfun Korkut; Hakan Şükür. Trainer: Mustafa Denizli

GERMANY: Oliver Kahn; Markus Babbel, Marko Rehmer, Jens Nowotny; Jörg Heinrich (75 Oliver Neuville), Stefan Beinlich, Jens Jeremies, Carsten Ramelow, Lars Ricken (80 Marco Bode); Oliver Bierhoff, Ulf Kirsten. Trainer: Erich Ribbek

Sent off: Tayfun (71)

Goal: Hakan Şükür (70)

TURKEY v FINLAND 1-3 (0-1)

Istanbul 14.10.1998

Referee: Vaclav Krondl (CZE) Attendance: 20,420

TURKEY: Reçber Rüstü; Fatih Akyel, Ogün Temizkanoglu, Alpay Özalan; Tayfur Havutçu, Abdullah Ercan, Okan Buruk (46 Hami Mandirali), Tugay Kerimoglu (46 Mert Korkmaz), Sergen Yalçin (83 Hasan Sas); Hakan Şükür, Oktay Derelioglu. Trainer: Mustafa Denizli

FINLAND: Antti Niemi; Harri Ylönen, Marko Tuomela, Sami Hyypiä, Tommi Kautonen, Juha Reini; Aki Riihilahti (76 Simo Valakari), Jari Ilola, Jari Litmanen; Mika-Matti Paatelainen (46 Joonas Kolkka), Jonatan Johansson (89 Jarmo Saastamoinen). Trainer: Richard Møller-Nielsen

Goals: Paatelainen (5), Johansson (51), Ogün (73), Litmanen (90)

NORTHERN IRELAND v FINLAND 1-0 (1-0)

Belfast 10.10.1998

Referee: Zoran Arsic (YUG) Attendance: 10,200

N. IRELAND: Alan Fettis; Aaron Hughes, Kevin Horlock, Darren Patterson, Steve Morrow; Keith Gillespie (70 Jon McCarthy), Neil Lennon, Keith Rowland (88 James Quinn), Philip Mulryne; Iain Dowie (79 George O'Boyle), Michael Hughes. Manager: Lawrie McMenemy

FINLAND: Antti Niemi; Harri Ylönen, Juka Reini, Sami Hyypiä, Tommi Kautonen; Simo Valakari, Jari Ilola, Aki Riihilahti (76 Jari Litmanen), Joonas Kolkka; Mika-Matti Paatelainen, Jonatan Johansson. Trainer: Richard Møller-Nielsen

Goal: Rowland (36)

NORTHERN IRELAND v MOLDOVA 2-2 (0-1)

Windsor Park, Belfast 18.11.1998

Referee: Vladimir Hrinak (SVK) Attendance: 11,137

N. IRELAND: Alan Fettis; Danny Griffin, Peter Kennedy, Steve Lomas (Cap), Darren Patterson, Steve Morrow, Keith Gillespie (87 Jon McCarthy), Neil Lennon, Iain Dowie, Michael Hughes, Keith Rowland (78 Phil Gray). Manager: Lawrie McMenemy

MOLDOVA: Serghei Dinov; Oleg Fistican, Radu Rebeja, Ion Testimiţanu (85 Vitali Maevici), Alexandru Guzun (71 Ghenadie Puşca), Serghei Stroenco, Alexandru Curtianu, Gheorghe Stratulat (50 Alexandr Suharev), Sergiu Epureanu, Vladimir Gaidamaşciuc, Sergiu Cleşcenco. Trainer: Ivan Danilianţ

Sent off: Curtianu (66)

Goals: Gaidamaşciuc (23), Dowie (49), Testimiţanu (58), Lennon (63)

MOLDOVA v GERMANY 1-3 (1-3)

Republican, Chişinău 14.10.1998

Referee: Juan Antonio Marín Fernández (SPA) Att: 6,500

MOLDOVA: Vasili Coşelev; Oleg Fistican, Radu Rebeja, Ion Testimiţanu, Alexandru Guzun, Serghei Stroenco, Alexandru Curtianu (52 Alexandr Suharev), Igor Oprea, Vladimir Gaidamaşciuc, Sergiu Epureanu, Sergiu Cleşcenco. Trainer: Ivan Danilianţ

GERMANY: Oliver Kahn; Markus Babbel, Marko Rehmer, Michael Tarnat, Jens Nowotny, Christian Nerlinger, Carsten Ramelow, Stefan Beinlich (81 Dariusz Wosz), Lars Ricken (53 Oliver Neuville), Oliver Bierhoff (Cap), Ulf Kirsten (73 Carsten Jancker). Trainer: Erich Ribbek

Sent off: Oprea (84)

Goals: Guzun (6), Kirsten (19, 36), Bierhoff (38)

NORTHERN IRELAND v GERMANY 0-3 (0-2)

Belfast 27.03.1999

Referee: Graziano Cesari (ITA) Attendance: 14,270

N. IRELAND: Maik Taylor; Darren Patterson, Mark Williams, Steve Lomas, Kevin Horlock; Keith Gillespie (84 Jon McCarthy), Neil Lennon (68 Danny Sonner), Steve Morrow, Michael Hughes; Iain Dowie, Keith Rowland (68 Peter Kennedy). Manager: Lawrie McMenemy

GERMANY: Oliver Kahn; Lothar Matthäus (46 Jens Nowotny), Christian Wörns, Markus Babbel, Jörg Heinrich; Thomas Strunz, Dietmar Hamann, Jens Jeremies, Marco Bode (78 Michael Preetz); Oliver Bierhoff, Oliver Neuville (68 Carsten Jancker). Trainer: Erich Ribbeck

Goals: Bode (11, 43), Hamann (62)

TURKEY v MOLDOVA 2-0 (1-0)

Ali Sami Yen, Istanbul 27.03.1999

Referee: Konrad Plautz (AUS) Attendance: 19,454

TURKEY: Rüştu Reçber; Fatih Akyel, Ogün Temizkanoglu, Tayfur Havutçu, Alpay Özalan; Abdullah Ercan, Okan Buruk, Tugay Kerimoglu (85 Ayhan Akman), Hakan Şükür, Sergen Yalçin, Oktay Derelioglu (25 Hami Mandirali, 75 Arif Erdem). Trainer: Mustafa Denizli

MOLDOVA: Serghei Dinov; Oleg Fistican, Radu Rebeja, Ivan Tabanov, Alexandru Guzun; Serghei Stroenco, Oleg Şişchin, Gheorghe Stratulat, Vladimir Gaidamaşciuc; Sergiu Epureanu, Sergiu Cleşcenco (80 Alexandru Suharev). Trainer: Ivan Danilianţ (8)

Sent off: Şişchin (61)

Goals: Hakan Şükür (34), Sergen (90)

GERMANY v MOLDOVA 6-1 (3-0)

Leverkusen 05.06.1999

Referee: Jorge Manuel Monteiro Coroado (POR) Attendance: 21,000

GERMANY: Oliver Kahn; Jens Nowotny, Lothar Matthäus (75 Markus Babbel), Jörg Heinrich; Thomas Strunz, Jens Jeremies (46 Mehmet Scholl), Dietmar Hamann, Marco Bode; Oliver Neuville, Oliver Bierhoff, Ulf Kirsten (54 Carsten Ramelow). Trainer: Erich Ribbeck

MOLDOVA: Serghei Dinov; Oleg Fistican, Serghei Stroenco, Vitalie Maevici (55 Gheorghe Stratulat), Alexandru Guzun; Alexandru Curtianu, Radu Rebeja, Igor Oprea, Vladimir Gaidamaşciuc (75 Serghei Belous); Sergiu Epureanu, Sergiu Cleşcenco (81 Oleg Şişchin). Trainer: Ivan Danilianţ (10)

Goals: Bierhoff (2, 56, 82), Kirsten (27), Bode (38), Scholl (71), Stratulat (76)

MOLDOVA v NORTHERN IRELAND 0-0

Republican, Chişinău 31.03.1999

Referee: Edo Trivkovic (CRO) Attendance: 9,000

MOLDOVA: Serghei Dinov; Oleg Fistican, Adrian Sosnovschi, Alexandru Guzun, Radu Rebeja; Serghei Stroenco, Alexandru Suharev, Igor Oprea (90 Gheorghe Stratulat), Vladimir Gaidamaşciuc, Sergiu Epureanu, Sergiu Cleşcenco. Trainer: Ivan Danilianţ

N. IRELAND: Maik Taylor; Darren Patterson (63 Aaron Hughes), Kevin Horlock, Steve Lomas, Mark Williams, Steve Morrow, Keith Gillespie, Neil Lennon, Iain Dowie, Michael Hughes, Stephen Robinson. Manager: Lawrie McMenemy

FINLAND v TURKEY 2-4 (2-2)

Olimpic, Helsinki 05.06.1999

Referee: Dick Jol (HOL) Attendance: 36,042

FINLAND: Antti Niemi; Harri Ylönen, Toni Kuivasto, Sami Hyypiä, Hannu Tihinen; Aki Riihilahti, Joonas Kolkka, Simo Valakari, Jonatan Johansson; Mika-Matti Paatelainen, Jari Litmanen. Trainer: Richard Møller-Nielsen

TURKEY: Reçber Rüştü; Ali Eren Beserler, Fatih Akyel, Saffet Akbas, Alpay Özalan, Abdullah Ercan (90 Hakan Ünsal); Tayfur Havutçu, Tayfun Korkut, Ayhan Akman (74 Tugay Kerimoglu); Hakan Şükür, Sergen Yalçin (89 Ümit Davala). Trainer: Mustafa Denizli

Goals: Tihinen (10), Paatelainen (14), Tayfur (25, 84), Hakan Şükür (34, 87)

GERMANY v FINLAND 2-0 (2-0)

Nürnberg 31.03.1999

Referee: Sergei Khusainov (RUS) Attendance: 40,758

GERMANY: Oliver Kahn; Markus Babbel, Lothar Matthäus, Christian Wörns; Thomas Strunz, Dietmar Hamann (72 Jens Nowotny), Jens Jeremies, Jörg Heinrich; Oliver Neuville (65 Ulf Kirsten), Oliver Bierhoff, Marco Bode (76 Carsten Jancker). Trainer: Erich Ribbeck

FINLAND: Antti Niemi; Tomi Kinnunen, Harri Ylönen, Sami Hyypiä, Juka Reini (89 Mika Lehkosuo), Tommi Kautonen (72 Joonas Kolkka); Jari Ilola, Jari Litmanen, Aki Riihilahti; Jonatan Johansson, Mika-Matti Paatelainen (46 Jarmo Saastamoinen). Trainer: Richard Møller-Nielsen

Goals: Jeremies (31), Neuville (36)

MOLDOVA v FINLAND 0-0

Republican, Chişinău 09.06.1999

Referee: Fiorenzo Treossi (ITA) Attendance: 8,000

MOLDOVA: Serghei Dinov; Oleg Fistican, Serghei Stroenco, Oleg Şişkin (75 Serghei Belous), Alexandru Guzun; Alexandru Curtianu, Radu Rebeja, Sergiu Epureanu, Gheorghe Stratulat, Igor Oprea; Alexandru Suharev (89 Serghei Kirilov). Trainer: Ivan Danilianţ

FINLAND: Antti Niemi; Juha Reini (86 Mika Lehkosuo), Sami Hyypiä, Harri Ylönen, Hannu Tihinen (46 Tommi Kautonen); Joonas Kolkka, Aki Riihilahti, Simo Valakari, Jari Ilola; Jonatan Johansson (61 Mikael Forsell), Mika-Matti Paatelainen. Trainer: Richard Møller-Nielsen

NORTHERN IRELAND v TURKEY 0-3 (0-1)

Windsor Park, Belfast 04.09.1999

Referee: Alain Sars (FRA) Attendance: 7,270

N. IRELAND: Maik Taylor; Aaron Hughes, Kevin Horlock, Steve Lomas, Mark Williams; Barry Hunter, Jon McCarthy (63 Keith Gillespie), Neil Lennon, Michael Hughes; Iain Dowie (77 James Quinn), Peter Kennedy.

TURKEY: Recber Rüstü; Ali Eren Beserler, Ogün Temizkanoglu, Tayfur Havutçu, Alpay Özalan; Arif Erdem (79 Okan Buruk), Abdullah Ercan (75 Hakan Ünsal), Tugay Kerimoglu, Sergen Yalçin (90 Ümit Karan); Hakan Şükür, Tayfun Korkut.

Goals: Erdem (45, 46, 48)

FINLAND v GERMANY 1-2 (0-2)

Olimpic, Helsinki 04.09.1999

Referee: Antonio López Nieto (SPA) Attendance: 20,184

FINLAND: Antti Niemi (46 Pasi Laaksonen); Jarmo Saastamoinen, Sami Hyypiä, Toni Kuivasto, Harri Ylönen (46 Shefki Kuqi); Janne Salli, Jarkko Wiss, Aki Riihilahti, Teemu Tainio; Jonatan Johansson, Mika Kottila.

GERMANY: Jens Lehmann; Markus Babbel, Thomas Linke, Jens Nowotny, Lothar Matthäus; Jens Jeremies, Mehmet Scholl (79 Christian Nerlinger), Oliver Neuville (85 Thomas Strunz); Oliver Bierhoff, Ulf Kirsten (32 Bernd Schneider), Christian Ziege.

Goals: Bierhoff (2, 17), Salli (63)

MOLDOVA v TURKEY 1-1 (1-0)

Republican, Chişinău 08.09.1999

Referee: Andreas Schluster (SWI) Attendance: 10,000

MOLDOVA: Serghei Dinov; Oleg Fistican, Vadim Boreţ, Alexandru Guzun (78 Oleg Şişchin), Radu Rebeja; Iuri Osipenco, Serghei Stroenco, Igor Oprea, Sergiu Epureanu; Vladimir Gaidamaşciuc (46 Gheorghe Stratulat), Sergiu Cleşcenco (82 Serghei Kirilov). Trainer: Ivan Danilianţ

TURKEY: Rüştu Reçber; Ali Eren Beserler, Fatih Akyel (46 Tugay Kerimoglu), Alpay Özalan, Ogün Temizkanoglu; Okan Buruk (46 Ayhan Akman), Tayfur Havutçu, Sergen Yalçin (87 Ümit Davala), Hakan Ünsal; Arif Erdem, Hakan Şükür. Trainer: Mustafa Denizli

Goals: Epureanu (3), Tayfur (76)

GERMANY v NORTHERN IRELAND 4-0 (4-0)

Westfalenstadion, Dortmund 08.09.1999

Referee: Georgios Bikas (GRE) Attendance: 41,000

GERMANY: Jens Lehmann; Thomas Linke, Lothar Matthäus, Markus Babbel (30 Thomas Strunz); Jens Jeremies, Jens Nowotny (46 Christian Wörns), Mehmet Scholl, Christian Ziege; Oliver Neuville (67 Bernd Schneider), Oliver Bierhoff, Marco Bode.

N. IRELAND: Maik Taylor; Ian Nolan, Mark Williams, Steve Morrow, Kevin Horlock; Neil Lennon (46 Keith Gillespie), Steve Lomas, Michael Hughes, Jon McCarthy, Peter Kennedy; Iain Dowie (46 James Quinn).

Goals: Bierhoff (3), Ziege (16, 33, 45)

GERMANY v TURKEY 0-0

Olimpiastadion, München 09.10.1999

Referee: Pierluigi Collina (ITA) Attendance: 63,572

GERMANY: Oliver Kahn; Markus Babbel, Lothar Matthäus, Thomas Linke; Bernd Schneider (89 Mustafa Dogan), Dietmar Hamann (46 Christian Nerlinger), Jens Jeremies, Christian Ziege (76 Marco Bode); Oliver Neuville, Oliver Bierhoff, Mehmet Scholl.

TURKEY: Recber Rüstü; Oguz Çetin, Fatih Akyel, Alpay Özalan, Ali Eren Beserler; Okan Buruk (72 Arif Erdem), Tayfur Havutçu (85 Oktay Derelioglu), Tayfun Korkut, Abdullah Ercan (69 Ergün Penbe), Sergen Yalçin; Hakan Şükür.

FINLAND v NORTHERN IRELAND 4-1 (1-0)

Olimpic, Helsinki 09.10.1999

Referee: Amand Ancion (BEL) Attendance: 8,217

FINLAND: Jani Viander; Mika Lehkosuo, Toni Kuivasto, Sami Hyypiä, Hannu Tihinen; Jarkko Wiss (86 Simo Valakari), Joonas Kolkka, Aki Riihilahti (86 Sami Ylä-Jussila), Jari Litmanen; Mika-Matti Paatelainen, Jonatan Johansson.

N. IRELAND: Maik Taylor; Iain Jenkins (79 Jim Whitley), Mark Williams, Steven Morrow, Ian Nolan; Jon McCarthy, Jeff Whitley, Neil Lennon, Peter Kennedy; Michael Hughes (74 Damien Johnson), James Quinn (68 Adrian Coote).

Goals: Johansson (9), Jeff Whitley (59), Hyypiä (63), Kolkka (73, 83)

	P	W	D	L	F	A	Pts
Germany	8	6	1	1	20	4	19
Turkey	8	5	2	1	15	6	17
Finland	8	3	1	4	13	13	10
Northern Ireland	8	1	2	5	4	19	5
Moldova	8	0	4	4	7	17	4

GROUP 4

ICELAND v FRANCE 1-1 (1-1)

Laugardalsvöllur, Reykjavik 05.09.1998

Referee: Eric Blareau (BEL) Attendance: 10,500

ICELAND: Birkir Kristinsson; Pétur Marteinsson, Lárus Orri Sigurdsson, Audun Helgason, Hermann Hreidarsson, Eyjólfur Sverrisson; Rúnar Kristinsson, Helgi Kolvidsson, Thórdur Gudjónsson; Arnar Gunnlaugsson (70 Stefán Thórdarson), Ríkhardur Dadason. Trainer: Gudjón Thórdarson

FRANCE: Fabien Barthez; Christian Karembeu, Frank Leboeuf, Lilian Thuram, Bixente Lizarazu; Didier Deschamps, Zinedine Zidane, Youri Djorkaeff; Robert Pires, Christophe Dugarry (67 Thierry Henry), Lilian Laslandes.
Trainer: Roger Lemerre

Goals: Dadason (33), Dugarry (36)

UKRAINE v RUSSIA 3-2 (2-0)

Dinamo, Kyiv 5.09.1998

Referee: Markus Merk (GER) Attendance: 82,100

UKRAINE: Olexandr Shovkovskyi; Andriy Gusin, Olexandr Holovko, Volodymyr Mykytyn, Vladyslav Vashchuk; Yuriy Dmitrulin, Serhiy Popov, Serhiy Kovalev (87 Valeriy Kriventsov); Serhiy Skachenko (46 Yuriy Kalitvintsev), Andriy Shevchenko, Serhiy Rebrov. Trainer: Jozsef Szabo

RUSSIA: Dmitriy Kharin; Yuriy Kovtun, Igor Chugaynov, Valeriy Minko, Igor Yanovskiy, Yevgeniy Varlamov; Andrei Kanchelskis (71 Valeriy Karpin), Sergei Semak (73 Stanislav Cherchesov), Viktor Onopko, Dmitriy Alenichev (64 Aleksandr Mostovoi); Igor Kolyvanov.
Trainer: Anatoliy Byshovets **Sent off**: Kharin (73)

Goals: Popov (14), Skachenko (24), Varlamov (67), Rebrov (75 pen), Onopko (87)

ARMENIA v ANDORRA 3-1 (1-0)

Razdan, Erevan 05.09.1998

Referee: Richard O'Hanlon (IRE) Attendance: 8,000

ARMENIA: Roman Berezovski; Yervand Sukiasyan, Yervand Krbashyan, Sarkis Hovsepyan, Tigran Hovhannisyan (83 Felix Khodgoyan); Harutyun Vardanyan, Albert Sarkisyan, Ara Adamyan, Artak Adamyan (86 Tigran Gspeyan); Armen Shahgeldyan, Garnik Avalyan (69 Tigran Yesayan).
Trainer: Suren Barsegyan

ANDORRA: Jesús Luis ÁLVAREZ de Fulate "KOLDO"; Francisco Javier RAMIREZ Palomo, José Manuel GARCIA Luena "TXEMA", Angel MARTIN GARCIA, Antonio LIMA SOLA; Jordi ESCURA Aixas, Genis GARCIA Iscla, Óscar SONEJEE Masánd, Juli SÁNCHEZ Soto; Jesús Julián LUCENDO Heredia, Justo RUIZ Gonzalez.
Trainer: Manuel Miluir

Goals: Avalyan (40), Yesayan (71, 90), Lucendo (86 pen)

ANDORRA v UKRAINE 0-2 (0-2)

Andorra la Vella 10.10.1998

Referee: Antin Guetsov (BUL) Attendance: 850

ANDORRA: Jesús Luis ÁLVAREZ de Fulate "KOLDO"; Francisco Javier RAMIREZ Palomo, José Manuel GARCIA Luena "TXEMA", Genis GARCIA Iscla, Ildefons LIMA SOLA, Juli SÁNCHEZ Soto (88 Manuel JIMENEZ Soria); Antonio LIMA SOLA, Agusti POL Perez, Óscar SONEJEE Masánd, Emiliano GONZALEZ Árquez, Justo RUIZ Gonzalez.
Trainer: Manuel Miluir

UKRAINE: Olexandr Shovkovskyi; Oleh Luzhnyi, Volodymyr Mykytyn (46 Serhiy Kovalev), Olexandr Holovko, Vladyslav Vashchuk; Serhiy Popov, Andriy Gusin, Vitaliy Kosovskyi; Yuriy Maximov (52 Valeriy Kriventsov), Andriy Shevchenko (70 Dmytro Mykhailenko), Serhiy Rebrov.
Trainer: Jozsef Szabo

Goals: Kosovskyi (30), Rebrov (43)

RUSSIA v FRANCE 2-3 (1-2)

Moskva 10.10.1998

Referee: Piero Ceccarini (ITA) Attendance: 50,000

RUSSIA: Sergei Ovchinnikov; Dmitriy Khlestov, Viktor Onopko, Yevgeniy Varlamov, Igor Yanovskiy; Valeriy Karpin, Dmitriy Alenichev (70 Sergei Semak), Yegor Titov, Aleksandr Mostovoi, Andrei Tikhonov; Vladimir Beschastnykh (63 Aleksei Gerasimenko). Trainer: Anatoli Byshovets

FRANCE: Bernard Lama; Lilian Thuram, Laurent Blanc, Marcel Desailly, Bixente Lizarazu; Robert Pires, Didier Deschamps, Emmanuel Petit (46 Alain Boghossian), Zinedine Zidane; Youri Djorkaeff (54 Patrick Vieira), Nicolas Anelka (88 Tony Vairelles). Trainer: Roger Lemerre

Goals: Anelka (13), Pirés (29), Yanovskiy (45), Mostovoi (56), Boghossian (81)

ARMENIA v ICELAND 0-0

Erevan 10.10.1998

Referee: Morgan Norman (SWE) Attendance: 15,000

ARMENIA: Roman Berezovski; Yervand Sukiasyan, Vardan Khachatryan, Sarkis Hovsepyan, Albert Sarkisyan; Harutyun Vardanyan, Artur Petrosyan (81 Tigran Hovhannisyan), Artak Adamyan, Eric Assadourian (62 Tigran Yesayan); Armen Shahgeldyan, Karapet Mikaelyan. Trainer: Suren Barsegyan

ICELAND: Birkir Kristinsson; Audun Helgason, Hermann Hreidarsson, Siggi Jónsson, Lárus Orri Sigurdsson; Rúnar Kristinsson, Helgi Kolvidsson, Steinar Adolfsson, Arnar Gunnlaugsson; Thórdur Gudjónsson, Ríkhardur Dadason.
Trainer: Gudjón Thórdarson

UKRAINE v ARMENIA 2-0 (1-0)

Republican, Kyiv 14.10.1998

Referee: Marcel Lică (ROM) Attendance: 14,850

UKRAINE: Olexandr Shovkovskyi; Oleh Luzhnyi, Yuriy Dmitrulin, Olexandr Holovko, Vladyslav Vashchuk; Serhiy Popov (75 Yuriy Maximov), Serhiy Skachenko (61 Serhiy Kovalev), Andriy Gusin, Vitaliy Kosovskyi; Andriy Shevchenko (78 Valeriy Kriventsov), Serhiy Rebrov. Trainer: Jozsef Szabo

ARMENIA: Roman Berezovski; Yervand Sukiasyan, Vardan Khachatryan, Sarkis Hovsepyan, Yervand Krbashyan (85 Tigran Hovhannisyan); Harutyun Vardanyan, Artur Petrosyan, Ara Adamyan, Armen Shahgeldyan; Eric Assadourian (73 Tigran Yesayan), Karapet Mikaelyan (65 Garnik Avalyan). Trainer: Suren Barsegyan

Goals: Skachenko (32), Gusin (80)

FRANCE v ANDORRA 2-0 (0-0)

St.Denis, Paris 14.10.1998

Referee: Dani Koren (ISR) Attendance: 75,000

FRANCE: Bernard Lama; Frank Leboeuf, Laurent Blanc, Bixente Lizarazu, Youri Djorkaeff (82 Alain Boghossian), Tony Vairelles; Vincent Candela, Didier Deschamps, Zinedine Zidane, Christophe Dugarry (71 Robert Pires), David Trézéguet (71 Nicolas Anelka). Trainer: Roger Lemerre

ANDORRA: Jesús Luis ÁLVAREZ de Fulate "KOLDO"; Francisco Javier RAMIREZ Palomo (80 Juli SÁNCHEZ Soto), José Manuel GARCIA Luena "TXEMA", Angel MARTIN GARCIA, Antonio LIMA SOLA, Ildefons LIMA SOLA; Agusti POL Perez, Óscar SONEJEE Masánd, Jesús Julián LUCENDO Heredia (88 Manuel JIMENEZ Soria), Justo RUIZ Gonzalez; Emiliano GONZALEZ Árquez. Trainer: Manuel Miluir

Goals: Candela (53), Djorkaeff (61)

ICELAND v RUSSIA 1-0 (0-0)

Laugardalsvöllur, Reykjavík 14.10.1998

Referee: René Temmink (HOL) Attendance: 3,345

ICELAND: Birkir Kristinsson; Audun Helgason, Hermann Hreidarsson, Siggi Jónsson, Lárus Orri Sigurdsson; Rúnar Kristinsson, Helgi Kolvidsson (87 Stefán Thórdarson), Steinar Adolfsson, Arnar Gunnlaugsson; Thórdur Gudjónsson (5 Helgi Sigurdsson), Ríkhardur Dadason.
Trainer: Gudjón Thórdarson

RUSSIA: Stanislav Cherchesov; Yuriy Kovtun, Yevgeniy Varlamov, Aleksei Smertin, Igor Yanovskiy; Igor Shalimov, Viktor Onopko, Valeriy Karpin (58 Dmitriy Khokhlov), Yegor Titov, Andrei Tikhonov (12 Aleksei Igonin); Aleksandr Mostovoi. Trainer: Anatoli Byshovets

Sent off: Smertin (74)

Goal: Kovtun (86 og)

ANDORRA v ICELAND 0-2 (0-0)

Andorra-la-Vella 27.03.1999

Referee: Charles Agius (MAL) Attendance: 1,000

ANDORRA: Jesús Luis ÁLVAREZ de Fulate "KOLDO"; Francisco Javier RAMIREZ Palomo (77 Emiliano GONZALEZ Árquez), José Manuel GARCIA Luena "TXEMA", Angel MARTIN GARCIA, Ildefons LIMA SOLA, Agusti POL Perez; Óscar SONEJEE Masánd, Manuel JIMENEZ Soria (63 Juli SÁNCHEZ Soto), Jesús Julián LUCENDO Heredia, Antonio LIMA SOLA; Justo RUIZ Gonzalez (82 Richard IMBERNON RIOS). Trainer: Manuel Miluir

ICELAND: Birkir Kristinsson; Audun Helgason, Brynjar Gunnarsson (71 Hermann Hreidarsson), Siggi Jónsson, Steinar Adolfsson; Rúnar Kristinsson, Arnar Gunnlaugsson (81 Tryggvi Gudmundsson), Eyjólfur Sverrisson (60 Arnar Gretarsson), Stefán Thórdarson; Thórdur Gudjónsson, Helgi Sigurdsson. Trainer: Gudjón Thorsarson

Goals: E. Sverrisson (57), Adolfsson (66)

ARMENIA v RUSSIA 0-3 (0-1)

Erevan 27.03.1999

Referee: Terje Hauge (NOR) Attendance: 10,000

ARMENIA: Roman Berezovski; Artur Mkrchyan, Yervand Krbashyan (64 Haik Harutyunyan), Sarkis Hovsepyan, Sarkis Hovhannisyan; Harutyun Vardanyan, Artur Petrosyan, Artur Voskanyan (78 Manuk Kakosyan), Albert Sarkisyan; Armen Shahgeldyan, Karapet Mikaelyan (82 Tigran Yesayan). Trainer: Suren Barsegyan

RUSSIA: Aleksandr Filimonov; Dmitriy Khlestov, Yuriy Drozdov, Ilya Tsymbalar, Igor Yanovskiy; Dmitriy Alenichev (64 Andrei Tikhonov), Viktor Onopko, Valeriy Karpin, Yegor Titov; Sergei Yuran (86 Dmitriy Khokhlov), Aleksandr Panov (46 Vladimir Beschastnykh). Trainer: Oleg Romantsev

Goals: Karpin (7, 63 pen), Beschastnykh (90)

FRANCE v UKRAINE 0-0

Saint Denis, Paris 27.03.1999

Referee: Günther Benkö (AUS) Attendance: 78,500

FRANCE: Fabien Barthez; Lilian Thuram, Bixente Lizarazu, Emmanuel Petit (78 Alain Boghossian), Laurent Blanc; Youri Djorkaeff, Didier Deschamps, Marcel Desailly; Nicolas Anelka, Robert Pires (84 Vikash Dhorasoo), Christophe Dugarry (69 Sylvain Wiltord). Trainer: Roger Lemerre

UKRAINE: Olexandr Shovkovskyi; Oleh Luzhnyi, Volodymyr Mykytyn, Olexandr Holovko, Vladyslav Vashchuk; Andriy Gusin (86 Viktor Skrypnyk), Serhiy Popov, Serhiy Kovalev (55 Vitaliy Kosovskyi), Serhiy Skachenko (69 Yuriy Maximov); Andriy Shevchenko, Serhiy Rebrov. Trainer: Jozsef Szabo

FRANCE v ARMENIA 2-0 (2-0)

Saint Denis, Paris 31.03.1999

Referee: Georgios Bikas (GRE) Attendance: 78,852

FRANCE: Fabien Barthez; Lilian Thuram (79 Christian Karembeu), Laurent Blanc, Marcel Desailly, Alain Boghossian; Patrick Vieira, Didier Deschamps, Youri Djorkaeff (69 Robert Pires), Christophe Dugarry (46 David Trézéguet); Nicolas Anelka, Sylvain Wiltord. Trainer: Roger Lemerre

ARMENIA: Roman Berezovski; Artur Mkrchyan (40 Vardan Khachatryan), Sarkis Hovsepyan, Harutyun Vardanyan, Artur Voskanyan (77 Aram Hairapetyan); Yervand Sukiasyan, Armen Shahgeldyan (53 Tigran Yesayan), Sarkis Hovhannisyan, Artur Petrosyan; Albert Sarkisyan, Karapet Mikaelyan. Trainer: Suren Barsegyan

Goals: Wiltord (1), Dugarry (45)

RUSSIA v ANDORRA 6-1 (3-0)

Moskva 31.03.1999

Referee: Mikko Vuorela (FIN) Attendance: 20,000

RUSSIA: Aleksandr Filimonov; Dmitriy Khlestov, Aleksei Smertin, Ilya Tsymbalar, Vadim Yevseyev (46 Andrei Tikhonov); Dmitriy Alenichev, Viktor Onopko, Valeriy Karpin, Yegor Titov; Aleksandr Shirko, Vladimir Beschastnykh. Trainer: Oleg Romantsev

ANDORRA: Jesús Luis ÁLVAREZ de Fulate "KOLDO"; ALONSO JUNAS (57 Emiliano GONZALEZ Árquez), Ildefons LIMA SOLA, José Manuel GARCIA Luena "TXEMA", Angel MARTIN GARCIA; Antonio LIMA SOLA, Agusti POL Perez, Justo RUIZ Gonzalez, Óscar SONEJEE Masánd, Manuel JIMENEZ Soria; Jesús Julián LUCENDO Heredia (65 Juli SÁNCHEZ Soto). Trainer: Manuel Miluir

Goals: Titov (8), Beschastnykh (12, 62), Onopko (42), Tsymbalar (50), Juli Sánchez (72), Alenichev (89)

UKRAINE v ICELAND 1-1 (0-0)

Republican, Kyiv 31.03.1999

Referee: Dani Koren (ISR) Attendance: 50,000

UKRAINE: Olexandr Shovkovskyi; Oleh Luzhnyi, Olexandr Holovko, Vladyslav Vashchuk, Volodymyr Mykytyn; Andriy Gusin, Serhiy Popov (75 Yuriy Kalitvintsev), Serhiy Skachenko (46 Yuriy Maximov), Vitaliy Kosovskyi; Serhiy Rebrov, Andriy Shevchenko. Trainer: Jozsef Szabo

ICELAND: Birkir Kristinsson; Audun Helgason, Lárus Orri Sigurdsson, Siggi Jónsson, Steinar Adolfsson; Rúnar Kristinsson (80 Helgi Kolvidsson), Hermann Hreidarsson, Eyjólfur Sverrisson, Helgi Sigurdsson (86 Sverrir Sverrisson); Thórdur Gudjónsson, Brynjar Gunnarsson. Trainer: Gudjón Thórdarson

Goals: Vashchuk (59), L. Sigurdsson (66)

ICELAND v ARMENIA 2-0 (1-0)

Laugardalsvöllur, Reykjavík 05.06.1999

Referee: Mikka Peltola (FIN) Attendance: 5,565

ICELAND: Birkir Kristinsson; Audun Helgason (72 Helgi Kolvidsson), Hermann Hreidarsson, Siggi Jónsson, Pétur Marteinsson; Brynjar Gunnarsson, Rúnar Kristinsson, Eyjólfur Sverrisson, Ríkhardur Dadason (69 Heidar Helguson); Helgi Sigurdsson (81 Einar Thór Daníelsson), Thórdur Gudjónsson. Trainer: Gudjón Thórdarson

ARMENIA: Roman Berezovski; Yervand Sukiasyan (65 Artur Mkrchyan), Vardan Khachatryan, Sarkis Hovsepyan, Harutyun Vardanyan, Haik Harutyunyan; Artur Voskanyan (84 Karen Grigoryan), Artur Petrosyan (75 Aram Hairapetyan), Albert Sarkisyan; Armen Shahgeldyan, Karapet Mikaelyan. Trainer: Suren Barsegyan

Goals: Dadason (30), R. Kristinsson (46)

UKRAINE v ANDORRA 4-0 (2-0)

Republican, Kyiv 05.06.1999

Referee: Andreas Georgiou (GRE) Attendance: 45,000

UKRAINE: Valeriy Vorobiov; Oleh Luzhnyi, Volodymyr Mykytyn (69 Serhiy Mizin), Olexandr Holovko, Vladyslav Vashchuk, Yuriy Dmitrulin (80 Roman Maxymyuk), Eduard Tsykhmeistruk; Serhiy Popov, Andriy Gusin; Andriy Shevchenko (74 Serhiy Skachenko), Serhiy Rebrov. Trainer: Jozsef Szabo

ANDORRA: Jesús Luis ÁLVAREZ de Fulate "KOLDO"; Agusti POL Perez, Angel MARTIN GARCIA (53 Jesús Julián LUCENDO Heredia), José Manuel GARCIA Luena "TXEMA", Antonio LIMA SOLA, Ildefons LIMA SOLA; Emiliano GONZALEZ Árquez, Óscar SONEJEE Masánd, Francisco Javier RAMIREZ Palomo; Juli SÁNCHEZ Soto, Justo RUIZ Gonzalez. Trainer: Manuel Miluir

Goals: Popov (38), Rebrov (41), Dmitrulin (56), Gusin (89)

FRANCE v RUSSIA 2-3 (0-1)

Saint-Denis, Paris 05.06.1999

Referee: Paul Anthony Durkin (ENG) Attendance: 78,788

FRANCE: Fabien Barthez; Vincent Candela (88 Robert Pires), Lilian Thuram, Emmanuel Petit, Laurent Blanc; Youri Djorkaeff (90 Alain Boghossian), Didier Deschamps, Marcel Desailly; Nicolas Anelka, Sylvain Wiltord, Christophe Dugarry (57 Patrick Vieira). Trainer: Roger Lemerre

RUSSIA: Aleksandr Filimonov; Dmitriy Khlestov, Yevgeniy Varlamov, Sergei Semak (59 Vladimir Beschastnykh), Aleksei Smertin; Aleksandr Mostovoi (25 Dmitriy Khokhlov), Viktor Onopko, Aleksandr Panov; Valeriy Karpin, Yegor Titov, Andrei Tikhonov (71 Ilya Tsymbalar). Trainer: Oleg Romantsev

Goals: Panov (40, 75), Petit (48), Wiltord (54), Karpin (85)

RUSSIA v ICELAND 1-0 (1-0)

Moskva 09.06.1999

Referee: Metin Tokat (TUR) Attendance: 36,000

RUSSIA: Aleksandr Filimonov; Dmitriy Khlestov, Yevgeniy Varlamov (55 Igor Yanovskiy), Sergei Semak (46 Viktor Bulatov), Aleksei Smertin; Vladimir Beschastnykh (70 Ilya Tsymbalar), Viktor Onopko, Valeriy Karpin, Dmitriy Khokhlov; Aleksandr Panov, Andrei Tikhonov. Trainer: Oleg Romantsev

ICELAND: Birkir Kristinsson; Audun Helgason, Hermann Hreidarsson (59 Steinar Adolfsson), Siggi Jónsson (46 Helgi Kolvidsson); Pétur Marteinsson, Eyjólfur Sverrisson, Lárus Orri Sigurdsson, Thórdur Gudjónsson, Rúnar Kristinsson; Brynjar Gunnarsson (80 Heidar Helguson), Ríkhardur Dadason. Trainer: Gudjón Thórdarson

Goal: Karpin (44)

ARMENIA v UKRAINE 0-0

Erevan 09.06.1999

Referee: Robert Boggi (ITA) Attendance: 10,000

ARMENIA: Roman Berezovski; Tigran Petrosyan (66 Karen Grigoryan), Vardan Khachatryan, Sarkis Hovsepyan, Sarkis Hovhannisyan (46 Haik Harutyunyan), Harutyun Vardanyan; Artur Petrosyan, Artur Voskanyan, Albert Sarkisyan; Armen Shahgeldyan, Karapet Mikaelyan (46 Artur Mkrchyan). Trainer: Suren Barsegyan

UKRAINE: Valeriy Vorobiov; Oleh Luzhnyi, Volodymyr Mykytyn, Olexandr Holovko, Vladyslav Vashchuk; Yuriy Dmitrulin, Eduard Tsykhmeistruk, Serhiy Popov (36 Serhiy Konovalov), Andriy Gusin; Andriy Shevchenko (82 Vasyl Kardash), Serhiy Rebrov (70 Serhiy Skachenko). Trainer: Jozsef Szabo

ANDORRA v FRANCE 0-1 (0-0)

Montjuic Olympic Stadium, Barcelona 09.06.1999

Referee: Michael Ross (NIR) Attendance: 7,600

ANDORRA: Jesús Luis ÁLVAREZ de Fulate "KOLDO"; Agusti POL Perez, José Manuel GARCIA Luena "TXEMA" (70 Roberto JONAS), Francisco Javier RAMIREZ Palomo, Antonio LIMA SOLA, Ildefons LIMA SOLA; Emiliano GONZALEZ Árquez, Óscar SONEJEE Masánd, Justo RUIZ Gonzalez, Jesús Julián LUCENDO Heredia (77 Angel MARTIN GARCIA); Manuel JIMENEZ Soria (89 Genis GARCIA Iscla). Trainer: Manuel Miluir

FRANCE: Ulrich Ramé; Vincent Candela, Emmanuel Petit (56 Patrick Vieira), Frank Leboeuf; Christian Karembeu, Alain Boghossian, Vikash Dhorasoo (61 Robert Pires), Marcel Desailly, Christophe Dugarry; Nicolas Anelka, Sylvain Wiltord. Trainer: Roger Lemerre

Sent off: I. Lima (86), Dugarry (25)

Goal: Leboeuf (85 pen)

UKRAINE v FRANCE 0-0

Republican, Kyiv 04.09.1999

Referee: Hugh Dallas (SCO) Attendance: 70,000

UKRAINE: Olexandr Shovkovskyi; Oleh Luzhnyi, Serhiy Popov, Olexandr Holovko, Vladyslav Vashchuk; Yuriy Dmitrulin (46 Volodymyr Mykytyn), Andriy Gusin (81 Eduard Tsykhmeistruk), Yuriy Maximov (67 Serhiy Konovalov), Vitaliy Kosovskyi; Andriy Shevchenko, Serhiy Rebrov.

FRANCE: Fabien Barthez; Lilian Thuram, Marcel Desailly, Laurent Blanc, Bixente Lizarazu; Patrick Vieira, Didier Deschamps, Christian Karembeu, Zinedine Zidane; Youri Djorkaeff (69 Robert Pires), Nicolas Anelka (52 Lilian Laslandes).

RUSSIA v ARMENIA 2-0 (1-0)

Moskva 04.09.1999

Referee: Charles Agius (MAL) Attendance: 36,000

RUSSIA: Aleksandr Filimonov; Dmitriy Khlestov, Viktor Onopko, Aleksei Smertin, Dmitriy Alenichev; Dmitriy Khokhlov, Valeriy Karpin, Andrei Tikhonov (73 Igor Yanovskiy), Yegor Titov (80 Sergei Semak); Vladimir Beschastnykh, Aleksandr Panov (79 Aleksandr Shirko).

ARMENIA: Roman Berezovski; Artur Mkrchyan, Vardan Khachatryan, Sarkis Hovsepyan, Sarkis Hovhannisyan; Harutyun Vardanyan, Romik Khachatryan (85 Tigran Petrosyan), Haik Harutyunyan, Artur Voskanyan; Armen Shahgeldyan (77 Alekhandro Devani), Karapet Mikaelyan.

Goals: Beschastnykh (8 pen), Karpin (70)

ICELAND v ANDORRA 3-0 (2-0)

Laugardalsvöllur, Reykjavík 04.09.1999

Referee: Miroslav Liba (CZE) Attendance: 5,210

ICELAND: Birkir Kristinsson; Audun Helgason, Hermann Hreidarsson, Siggi Jónsson, Lárus Orri Sigurdsson (26 Arnar Vidarsson); Bjarni Gudjónsson, Brynjar Gunnarsson, Tryggvi Gudmundsson, Helgi Sigurdsson (57 Heidar Helguson); Thórdur Gudjónsson, Ríkhardur Dadason (77 Eidur Gudjohnsen).

ANDORRA: Jesús Luis ÁLVAREZ de Fulate "KOLDO"; Angel MARTIN GARCIA (61 Armand Godoy), Jordi ESCURA Aixas, Francisco Javier RAMIREZ Palomo, José Manuel GARCIA Luena "TXEMA"; Óscar SONEJEE Masánd, Agusti Pol Perez (90 David Buxo), Emiliano GONZALEZ Árquez, Manuel JIMENEZ Soria; Juli SÁNCHEZ Soto, Alex Godoy (67 Genis GARCIA Iscla).

Goals: T. Gudjónsson (29), Hreidarsson (32), Gudjohnsen (90)

ANDORRA v RUSSIA 1-2 (1-1)

Andorra-la-Vella 08.09.1999

Referee: Jørn West Larsen (DEN) Attendance: 1,000

ANDORRA: Jesús Luis ÁLVAREZ de Fulate "KOLDO"; Francisco Javier RAMIREZ Palomo, Jordi ESCURA Aixas, José Manuel GARCIA Luena "TXEMA", Ildefons LIMA SOLA; Óscar SONEJEE Masánd, Emiliano GONZALEZ Árquez, Alex Godoy (59 Agusti Pol Perez), Juli SÁNCHEZ Soto (89 Armand Godoy); Manuel JIMENEZ Soria, Justo RUIZ Gonzalez.

RUSSIA: Aleksandr Filimonov; Dmitriy Khlestov, Aleksei Smertin, Viktor Onopko; Dmitriy Khokhlov (55 Artem Bezrodniy), Dmitriy Alenichev (61 Igor Yanovskiy), Valeriy Karpin, Yegor Titov, Andrei Tikhonov; Vladimir Beschastnykh (46 Aleksandr Panov), Aleksandr Shirko.

Goals: Onopko (22, 57), Justo Ruiz (39 pen)

ARMENIA v FRANCE 2-3 (1-1)

Erevan 08.09.1999

Referee: Atanas Ouzounov (BUL) Attendance: 18,000

ARMENIA: Roman Berezovski; Vardan Khachatryan, Sarkis Hovsepyan, Romik Khachatryan (75 Yervand Sukiasyan), Artur Mkrchyan; Haik Harutyunyan (65 Karen Grigoryan), Artur Petrosyan, Albert Sarkisyan, Tigran Yesayan; Armen Shahgeldyan, Karapet Mikaelyan (68 Alekhandro Devani).

FRANCE: Fabien Barthez; Bixente Lizarazu, Laurent Blanc, Marcel Desailly, Lilian Thuram; Didier Deschamps, Christian Karembeu, Zinedine Zidane (73 Frédéric Déhu); Youri Djorkaeff, Lilian Laslandes, Sylvain Wiltord (63 Laurent Robert).

Sent off: Déhu (89)

Goals: Mikaelyan (6), Djorkaeff (45 pen), Zidane (67), Laslandes (74), Shahgeldyan (90 pen)

ICELAND v UKRAINE 0-1 (0-1)

Laugardalsvöllur, Reykjavík 08.09.1999

Referee: Vítor Manuel Melo Pereira (POR) Att: 7,000

ICELAND: Birkir Kristinsson; Audun Helgason, Hermann Hreidarsson, Siggi Jónsson (85 Arnar Vidarsson), Lárus Orri Sigurdsson; Rúnar Kristinsson, Brynjar Gunnarsson, Helgi Kolvidsson (59 Heidar Helguson), Pétur Marteinsson; Thórdur Gudjónsson, Ríkhardur Dadason (73 Eidur Gudjohnsen).

UKRAINE: Olexandr Shovkovskyi; Oleh Luzhnyi (80 Volodymyr Mykytyn), Olexandr Holovko, Vladyslav Vashchuk, Yuriy Dmitrulin; Serhiy Popov, Yuriy Maximov, Serhiy Konovalov (66 Eduard Tsykhmeistruk), Vitaliy Kosovskyi; Andriy Shevchenko, Serhiy Rebrov.

Goal: Rebrov (43 pen)

RUSSIA v UKRAINE 1-1 (0-0)

Moskva 09.10.1999

Referee: David Elleray (Eng) Attendance: 80,000

RUSSIA: Aleksandr Filimonov; Dmitriy Khlestov, Dmitriy Khokhlov, Aleksei Smertin, Dmitriy Alenichev; Yuri Drozdov, Viktor Onopko, Valeriy Karpin, Yegor Titov; Aleksandr Panov (80 Sergei Semak), Andrei Tikhonov (60 Vladimir Beschastnykh).

UKRAINE: Olexandr Shovkovskyi; Oleh Luzhnyi, Olexandr Holovko, Vladyslav Vashchuk, Serhiy Mizin; Yuriy Dmitrulin (78 Serhiy Kovalev), Yuriy Maximov (76 Guennadiy Moroz), Andriy Gusin, Serhiy Skachenko (42 Volodymyr Mykytyn); Andriy Shevchenko, Serhiy Rebrov

Goals: Karpin (76), Shevchenko (88)

FRANCE v ICELAND 3-2 (2-0)

Stade de France, Paris 09.10.1999

Referee: Bernd Heynemann (GER) Attendance: 78,391

FRANCE: Bernard Lama; Bixente Lizarazu, Marcel Desailly, Laurent Blanc, Lilian Thuram; Didier Deschamps, Alain Boghossian (90 Patrick Vieira), Zinedine Zidane, Youri Djorkaeff; Sylvain Wiltord (83 Tony Vairelles), Lilian Laslandes (64 David Trézéguet).

ICELAND: Birkir Kristinsson; Eyjólfur Sverrisson, Audun Helgason, Lárus Orri Sigurdsson, Pétur Marteinsson (81 Helgi Kolvidsson), Hermann Hreidarsson; Brynjar Gunnarsson, Thórdur Gudjónsson, Rúnar Kristinsson; Helgi Sigurdsson (65 Heidar Helguson), Ríkhardur Dadason (53 Eidur Gudjohnsen).

Goals: Dadason (18 og), Djorkaeff (38), Sverrisson (48), Gunnarsson (56), Trézéguet (71)

ANDORRA v ARMENIA 0-3 (0-1)

Andorra la Vella 09.10.1999

Referee: Peter Jones (ENG) Attendance: 700

ANDORRA: Jesús Luis ÁLVAREZ de Fulate "KOLDO"; Francisco Javier RAMIREZ Palomo, Jordi ESCURA Aixas, Óscar SONEJEE Masánd, Genis GARCIA Iscla (58 Roberto Jonas Alonso); Antonio LIMA SOLA, Alex Godoy (46 Agusti Pol Perez), Emiliano GONZALEZ Árquez (62 Xavier Soria), Manuel JIMENEZ Soria; Juli SÁNCHEZ Soto, Justo RUIZ Gonzalez.

ARMENIA: Harutyun Abrahamyan; Yervand Sukiasyan, Artur Voskanyan, Artur Mkrchyan, Harutyun Vardanyan, Romik Khachatryan; Tigran Petrosyan (79 Ara Hakopyan), Artur Petrosyan (82 Yervand Krbashyan), Albert Sarkisyan; Armen Shahgeldyan (78 Artur Minasyan), Tigran Yesayan.

Sent off: Sarkisyan (31)

Goals: Petrosyan (26), Yesayan (59), Shahgeldyan (63)

	P	W	D	L	F	A	Pts
France	10	6	3	1	17	10	21
Ukraine	10	5	5	0	14	4	20
Russia	10	6	1	3	22	12	19
Iceland	10	4	3	3	12	7	15
Armenia	10	2	2	6	8	15	8
Andorra	10	0	0	10	3	28	0

GROUP 5

SWEDEN v ENGLAND 2-1 (2-1)

Råsunda, Solna 05.09.1998

Referee: Pierluigi Collina (ITA) Attendance: 35,394

SWEDEN: Magnus Hedman; Roland Nilsson, Patrick Andersson, Joachim Björklund, Pontus Kåmark (83 Teddy Lucic); Stefan Schwarz, Andreas Andersson (89 Daniel Andersson), Johan Mjällby, Fredrik Ljungberg; Henryk Larsson, Jörgen Pettersson. Trainer: Tommy Söderberg

ENGLAND: David Seaman; Sol Campbell (74 Paul Merson), Graeme Le Saux, Tony Adams, Gareth Southgate, Darren Anderton (42 Robert Lee); Paul Ince, Jamie Redknapp, Paul Scholes (87 Teddy Sheringham); Alan Shearer, Michael Owen. Manager: Glenn Hoddle

Sent off: Ince (66)

Goals: Shearer (2), A. Andersson (32), Mjällby (33)

BULGARIA v POLAND 0-3 (0-2)

Neftochimik, Burgas 06.09.1998

Referee: Marc Batta (FRA) Attendance: 20,000

BULGARIA: Zdravko Zdravkov; Radostin Kishishev, Zlatomir Zagorcic (50 Ivailo Petkov), Milen Petkov (46 Mitko Trendafilov), Ivailo Iordanov, Gosho Ginchev; Georgi Bachev, Daniel Borimirov (46 Ilia Gruev), Zakhari Sirakov; Doncho Donev, Hristo Stoichkov. Trainer: Hristo Bonev

POLAND: Kazimierz Sidorczuk; Jacek Bak, Tomasz Lapinski, Rafal Siadaczka, Jacek Zielinski; Tomasz Hajto (79 Tomasz Klos), Piotr Swierczewski (68 Radoslaw Michalski), Tomasz Iwan, Jerzy Brzeczek; Sylwester Czereszewski, Miroslaw Trzeciak (80 Andrzej Juskowiak). Trainer: Janusz Wojcik

Goals: Czereszewski (19, 45), Iwan (47)

POLAND v LUXEMBOURG 3-0 (2-0)

Wojska Polskiego, Warszawa 10.10.1998

Referee: Bujar Pregia (ALB) Attendance: 8,000

POLAND: Adam Matysek; Krzysztof Ratajczyk (69 Rafal Siadaczka), Jacek Zielinski, Tomasz Lapinski; Tomasz Hajto (62 Slawomir Majak), Jerzy Brzeczek, Piotr Swierczewski, Sylwester Czereszewski (75 Jacek Bak); Tomasz Iwan, Miroslaw Trzeciak, Andrzej Juskowiak.
Trainer: Janusz Wojcik

LUXEMBOURG: Paul Koch; Ralph Ferron, Nicolas Funck, Jeff Strasser, Marc Birsens; Daniel Theis (46 Frank Deville), Luc Holtz (69 Eugène Afrika), Jeff Saibene, Marcel Christophe (63 Serge Thill); Laurent Deville, Manuel Cardoni.
Trainer: Paul Philipp

Sent off: Birsens (30)

Goals: Brzeczek (19), Juskowiak (33), Trzeciak (64)

ENGLAND v BULGARIA 0-0

Wembley, London 10.10.1998

Referee: László Vágner (HUNG) Attendance: 72,974

ENGLAND: David Seaman; Gary Neville, Sol Campbell, Gareth Southgate, Darren Anderton (67 David Batty), Andy Hinchcliffe (35 Graeme Le Saux); Robert Lee, Jamie Redknapp, Paul Scholes (76 Teddy Sheringham); Alan Shearer, Michael Owen. Manager: Glenn Hoddle

BULGARIA: Zdravko Zdravkov; Radostin Kishishev, Valentin Naidenov, Ivailo Iordanov, Zlatko Iankov, Rosen Kirilov, Zlatomir Zagorcic; Ilian Iliev (62 Ilia Gruev), Milen Petkov; Hristo Stoichkov (60 Georgi Bachev), Marian Hristov (90 Georgi Ivanov). Trainer: Dimitar Dimitrov

BULGARIA v SWEDEN 0-1 (0-0)

Burgas 14.10.1998

Referee: Bernd Heynemann (GER) Attendance: 12,000

BULGARIA: Zdravko Zdravkov; Zlatomir Zagorcic, Valentin Naidenov (69 Georgi Ivanov), Ivailo Petkov; Ivailo Iordanov, Zlatko Iankov, Rosen Kirilov (18 Velian Parushev), Milen Petkov, Ilian Iliev (60 Georgi Bachev); Hristo Stoichkov, Marian Hristov. Trainer: Dimitar Dimitrov

SWEDEN: Magnus Hedman; Roland Nilsson, Patrick Andersson, Joachim Björklund, Teddy Lucic (76 Gary Sundgren); Stefan Schwarz, Håkan Mild, Johan Mjällby, Fredrik Ljungberg; Henryk Larsson (88 Magnus Erlingmark), Martin Åslund (71 Jesper Blomqvist).
Trainer: Tommy Sönderberg

Goal: Larsson (62)

LUXEMBOURG v ENGLAND 0-3 (0-2)

Stade Municipal, Luxembourg 14.10.1998

Referee: Sotirios Vorgias (GRE) Attendance: 8,054

LUXEMBOURG: Paul Koch; Ralph Ferron, Nicolas Funck, Jeff Strasser, Frank Deville (85 Christian Alverdi); Laurent Deville, Jeff Saibene, Daniel Theis (61 Luc Holtz), Manuel Cardoni, Patrick Posing; Marcel Christophe (78 Paolo Amodio). Trainer: Paul Philipp

ENGLAND: David Seaman; Rio Ferdinand, Phillip Neville, David Batty, Darren Anderton (63 Robert Lee); Sol Campbell, Gareth Southgate, David Beckham, Paul Scholes (76 Ian Wright); Alan Shearer, Michael Owen.
Trainer: Glenn Hoddle

Goals: Owen (19), Shearer (40 pen), Southgate (90)

LUXEMBOURG v BULGARIA 0-2 (0-2)

Stade Municipal, Luxembourg 31.03.1999

Referee: Milan Mitrovic (SVN) Attendance: 3,004

LUXEMBOURG: Philippe Felgen; Ralph Ferron (76 Luc Holtz), Laurent Deville, Marc Birsens, Jeff Strasser; Jeff Saibene, Daniel Theis (89 Frank Deville), Jean-Pierre Vanek, Patrick Posing (46 Mikhail Zaritski), Manuel Cardoni; Marcel Christophe. Trainer: Paul Philipp

BULGARIA: Zdravko Zdravkov; Radostin Kishishev, Georgi Markov, Ilian Stoianov (46 Ivailo Petkov); Ivailo Iordanov, Zlatko Iankov, Stilian Petrov, Hristo Stoichkov (78 Svetoslav Todorov), Hristo Iovov (77 Georgi Ivanov); Milen Petkov, Ilian Iliev. Trainer: Dimitar Dimitrov

Goals: Stoichkov (18), Iordanov (38)

SWEDEN v LUXEMBOURG 2-0 (1-0)

Göteborg 27.03.1999

Referee: Vasili Melnichuk (UKR) Attendance: 37,728

SWEDEN: Magnus Hedman; Pontus Kåmark (68 Teddy Lucic), Patrick Andersson, Joachim Björklund, Gary Sundgren; Stefan Schwarz, Niclas Alexandersson, Johan Mjällby, Fredrik Ljungberg (79 Daniel Andersson); Henryk Larsson, Kennet Andersson. Trainer: Tommy Söderberg

LUXEMBOURG: Philippe Felgen; Ralph Ferron, Nicolas Funck, Marc Birsens, Jeff Strasser; Jeff Saibene (89 Frank Deville), Daniel Theis (69 Luc Holtz), Jean-Pierre Vanek, Laurent Deville; Manuel Cardoni, Marcel Christophe (81 Mikhail Zaritski). Trainer: Pierre Philipp

Goals: Mjällby (35), Larsson (86)

POLAND v SWEDEN 0-1 (0-1)

Slaski, Chorzów 31.03.1999

Referee: Markus Merk (GER) Attendance: 30,000

POLAND: Kazimierz Sidorczuk; Rafal Siadaczka (82 Dariusz Adamczuk), Jacek Zielinski, Tomasz Lapinski, Tomasz Waldoch; Slawomir Majak (68 Wojciech Kowalczyk), Radoslaw Michalski (88 Jacek Bak), Tomasz Iwan, Jerzy Brzeczek; Andrzej Juskowiak, Miroslaw Trzeciak.
Trainer: Janusz Wojcik

SWEDEN: Magnus Hedman; Pontus Kåmark, Patrick Andersson, Joachim Björklund, Teddy Lucic; Stefan Schwarz, Håkan Mild (73 Niclas Alexandersson), Fredrik Ljungberg, Johan Mjällby; Henryk Larsson (89 Jörgen Pettersson), Kennet Andersson. Trainer: Tommy Söderberg

Goal: Ljundberg (36)

ENGLAND v POLAND 3-1 (2-1)

Wembley, London 27.03.1999

Referee: Vitor Manuel Melo Pereira (POR) Att: 72,000

ENGLAND: David Seaman; Gary Neville, Graeme Le Saux, Martin Keown, Sol Campbell; Tim Sherwood, David Beckham (78 Phillip Neville), Paul Scholes (84 Jamie Redknapp), Steve McManaman (69 Ray Parlour); Alan Shearer, Andy Cole.
Manager: Kevin Keegan

POLAND: Adam Matysek; Jacek Bak, Tomasz Lapinski, Krzysztof Ratajczyk, Jacek Zielinski; Tomasz Hajto, Piotr Swierczewski (46 Tomasz Klos), Tomasz Iwan, Jerzy Brzeczek; Rafal Siadaczka (67 Wojciech Kowalczyk), Miroslaw Trzeciak (84 Andrzej Juskowiak). Trainer: Janusz Wojcik

Goals: Scholes (11, 21, 70), Brzeczek (27)

POLAND v BULGARIA 2-0 (1-0)

Wojska Polskiego, Warszawa 04.06.1999

Referee: Stefano Braschi (ITA) Attendance: 6,200

POLAND: Adam Matysek; Tomasz Waldoch, Tomasz Lapinski, Rafal Siadaczka, Jacek Zielinski; Tomasz Hajto (80 Slawomir Majak), Radoslaw Michalski, Tomasz Iwan, Artur Wichniarek (59 Thomas Frankowski); Krzysztof Nowak (74 Jerzy Brzeczek), Miroslaw Trzeciak. Trainer: Janusz Wojcik

BULGARIA: Dimitar Ivankov; Radostin Kishishev, Zlatomir Zagorcic, Ivailo Petkov (80 Ilian Iliev), Georgi Markov; Rosen Kirilov, Stilian Petrov, Hristo Iovov (62 Georgi Bachev), Stanimir Stoilov; Hristo Stoichkov (63 Georgi Ivanov), Milen Petkov. Trainer: Dimitar Dimitrov

Goals: Hajto (15), Iwan (62)

ENGLAND v SWEDEN 0-0

Wembley, London 05.06.1999

Referee: José Maria Garcia-Aranda Encinar (SPA)

Attendance: 74,000

ENGLAND: David Seaman; Phillip Neville, Graeme Le Saux (46 Michael Gray), Tim Sherwood, Martin Keown (35 Rio Ferdinand); Sol Campbell, David Beckham (75 Ray Parlour), David Batty, Paul Scholes; Alan Shearer, Andy Cole. Manager: Kevin Keegan

SWEDEN: Magnus Hedman; Roland Nilsson, Patrick Andersson, Joachim Björklund, Pontus Kåmark; Stefan Schwarz, Håkan Mild (7 Niclas Alexandersson), Johan Mjällby (82 Daniel Andersson), Fredrik Ljungberg; Henryk Larsson (69 Magnus Svensson), Kennet Andersson. Trainer: Tommy Söderberg

Sent off: Scholes (51)

BULGARIA v ENGLAND 1-1 (1-1)

Sofia 09.06.1999

Referee: Mario van der Ende (HOL) Attendance: 25,000

BULGARIA: Dimitar Ivankov; Radostin Kishishev, Zlatomir Zagorcic, Stanimir Stoilov, Georgi Markov, Rosen Kirilov; Ilian Iliev (60 Daniel Borimirov), Milen Petkov, Stilian Petrov; Hristo Iovov (46 Martin Petrov), Hristo Stoichkov (73 Georgi Bachev). Trainer: Dimitar Dimitrov

ENGLAND: David Seaman; Phillip Neville, Michael Gray, Jonathon Woodgate (64 Ray Parlour), Gareth Southgate; Sol Campbell, Jamie Redknapp, David Batty; Alan Shearer, Teddy Sheringham, Robbie Fowler (81 Emile Heskey). Manager: Kevin Keegan

Sent off: M. Petrov (58)

Goals: Shearer (15), Markov (18)

LUXEMBOURG v POLAND 2-3 (0-2)

Stade Josef Henri Barthel, Luxembourg 09.06.1999

Referee: Valentin Ivanov (RUS) Attendance: 2,800

LUXEMBOURG: Philippe Felgen; Jean-Pierre Vanek, Nicolas Funck, Marc Birsens, Jeff Strasser; Jeff Saibene (85 Christian Alverdi), Daniel Theis (46 Sacha Schneider), Frank Deville, Mikhail Zaritski (66 Patrick Posing), Manuel Cardoni; Marcel Christophe. Trainer: Paul Philipp

POLAND: Adam Matysek; Tomasz Waldoch, Tomasz Lapinski, Rafal Siadaczka, Tomasz Klos; Tomasz Hajto (66 Jerzy Brzeczek), Radoslaw Michalski, Tomasz Iwan, Krzysztof Nowak; Artur Wichniarek (87 Slawomir Majak), Miroslaw Trzeciak. Trainer: Janusz Wojcik

Goals: Siadaczka (22), Wichniarek (45), Iwan (68), Birsens (76), Vanek (82)

ENGLAND v LUXEMBOURG 6-0 (5-0)

Wembley, London 04.09.1999

Referee: Sergei Shmolik (BLS) Attendance: 68,772

ENGLAND: Nigel Martyn; Kieron Dyer (46 Gary Neville), Stuart Pearce, Martin Keown, Tony Adams (65 Phillip Neville); Ray Parlour, David Batty, David Beckham (65 Michael Owen), Steve McManaman; Alan Shearer, Robbie Fowler. Manager: Kevin Keegan

LUXEMBOURG: Philippe Felgen; Ralph Ferron, Marc Birsens, Manuel Schauls, Jean-Pierre Vanek; Jeff Saibene, Patrick Posing (83 Frank Deville), Sacha Schneider (46 Christian Alverdi), Daniel Theis; Marcel Christophe (63 Mikhail Zaritski), Nicolas Funck.

Goals: Shearer (12 pen, 28, 34), McManaman (30, 44), Owen (90)

SWEDEN v BULGARIA 1-0 (0-0)

Stockholm 04.09.1999

Referee: Dani Koren (ISR) Attendance: 35,640

SWEDEN: Magnus Hedman; Roland Nilsson, Patrick Andersson, Joachim Björklund, Pontus Kåmark; Daniel Andersson, Håkan Mild (83 Magnus Svensson), Johan Mjällby, Fredrik Ljungberg (63 Niclas Alexandersson); Henryk Larsson, Kennet Andersson. Trainer: Tommy Söderberg

BULGARIA: Dimitar Ivankov; Stanimir Stoilov (89 Ilia Gruev), Zlatomir Zagorcic (26 Zlatko Iankov), Ivailo Petkov, Georgi Markov; Rosen Kirilov, Daniel Borimirov, Stilian Petrov, Marian Hristov; Milen Petkov, Svetoslav Todorov (46 Hristo Iovov).

Sent off: Petkov (60)

Goal: Alexandersson (65)

LUXEMBOURG v SWEDEN 0-1 (0-1)

Stade Municipal, Luxembourg 08.09.1999

Referee: Attila Hanacsek (HUNG) Attendance: 4,228

LUXEMBOURG: Philippe Felgen; Jean-Pierre Vanek, Manuel Schauls, Marc Birsens, Nicolas Funck; Jeff Strasser, Jeff Saibene (87 Luc Holtz), Christian Alverdi (74 Daniel Theis), Sacha Schneider (46 Mikhail Zaritski), Patrick Posing; Marcel Christophe.

SWEDEN: Magnus Hedman; Roland Nilsson, Patrick Andersson, Johan Mjällby, Teddy Lucic; Stefan Schwarz (81 Daniel Andersson), Niclas Alexandersson, Häkan Mild, Magnus Svensson (46 Pär Zetterberg); Henryk Larsson, Kennet Andersson. Trainer: Tommy Söderberg

Goal: Alexandersson (39)

POLAND v ENGLAND 0-0

Wojska Polskiego, Warszawa 08.09.1999

Referee: Günter Benkö (AUS) Attendance: 14,000

POLAND: Adam Matysek; Jacek Zielinski, Tomasz Klos (90 Jacek Bak), Tomasz Waldoch, Tomasz Hajto; Radoslaw Michalski, Krzysztof Nowak, Radoslav Gilewicz (64 Andrzej Juskowiak), Rafal Siadaczka; Tomasz Iwan, Miroslaw Trzeciak (59 Piotr Swierczewski). Trainer: Janusz Wojcik

ENGLAND: Nigel Martyn; Gary Neville (14 Phillip Neville), Stuart Pearce, Martin Keown, Tony Adams; David Batty, David Beckham, Paul Scholes, Steve McManaman (80 Kieron Dyer); Robbie Fowler (66 Michael Owen), Alan Shearer. Manager: Kevin Keegan

Sent off: Batty (84)

SWEDEN v POLAND 2-0 (0-0)

Råsunda, Stockholm 09.10.1999

Referee: Urs Meier (SWI) Attendance: 35,037

SWEDEN: Magnus Hedman; Roland Nilsson (46 Gary Sundgren), Patrick Andersson, Joachim Björklund, Pontus Kåmark; Stefan Schwarz, Niclas Alexandersson, Johan Mjällby; Fredrik Ljungberg (83 Håkan Mild), Kennet Andersson, Henryk Larsson. Trainer: Tommy Söderberg

POLAND: Adam Matysek; Tomasz Klos, Tomasz Waldoch, Rafal Siadaczka, Jacek Zielinski; Tomasz Hajto, Piotr Swierczewski (89 Artur Wichniarek), Radoslaw Michalski, Miroslaw Trzeciak; Andrzej Juskowiak (81 Pawel Kryszalowicz), Sylwester Czereszewski (73 Krzysztof Nowak). Trainer: Janusz Wojcik

Goals: K. Andersson (64), Larsson (90)

BULGARIA v LUXEMBOURG 3-0 (1-0)

Sofia 10.10.1999

Referee: Ladislav Gadosi (SVK) Attendance: 4,000

BULGARIA: Zdravko Zdravkov; Zlatomir Zagorcic (84 Biser Ivanov), Stanimir Stoilov, Ivailo Petkov, Ivailo Yordanov; Georgi Markov, Daniel Borimirov, Stilian Petrov; Marian Hristov (64 Svetoslav Todorov), Alexandar Alexandrov, Georgi Bachev (51 R. Hristov).

LUXEMBOURG: Philippe Felgen; Jean-Pierre Vanek, Manuel Schauls, Marc Birsens, Jeff Strasser, Jeff Saibene; Christian Alverdi (71 Daniel Theis), Patrick Posing (59 Frank Deville), Manuel Cardoni (85 Luc Holtz), Mikhail Zaritski; Marcel Christophe.

Goals: Borimirov (40), Petkov (68), Hristov (78)

	P	W	D	L	F	A	Pts
Sweden	8	7	1	0	10	1	22
England	8	3	4	1	14	4	13
(vs Poland	*2*	*1*	*1*	*0*	*3*	*1*	*4)*
Poland	8	4	1	3	12	8	13
(vs England	*2*	*0*	*1*	*1*	*1*	*3*	*1)*
Bulgaria	8	2	2	4	6	8	8
Luxembourg	8	0	0	8	2	23	0

GROUP 6

AUSTRIA v ISRAEL 1-1 (1-0)

Ernst Happel, Wien 05.09.1998

Referee: Anders Frisk (SWE) Attendance: 20,000

AUSTRIA: Franz Wohlfahrt; Wolfgang Feiersinger, Peter Schöttel (72 Martin Hiden), Anton Pfeffer; Harald Cerny (74 Peter Stöger), Dietmar Kühbauer, Roman Mählich, Hannes Reinmayr, Martin Amerhauser; Ivica Vastic, Mario Haas (71 Christian Mayrleb). Trainer: Herbert Prohaska

ISRAEL: Rafael Cohen; Ran Ben Shimon, Alon Harazi, Amir Shelach (46 Alon Mizrahi), David Amsalem, Arik Benado; Yossi Abuksis (46 Avi Nimni), Eyal Berkovic, Walid Badir; Haim Revivo, Ronen Harazi (61 Najwan Ghrayeb). Trainer: Shlomo Sharf

Sent off: Amsalem (58)

Goals: Reinmayr (7), Nimni (69 pen)

CYPRUS v SPAIN 3-2 (1-0)

Larnaca 05.09.1998

Referee: Serghei Khusainov (RUS) Attendance: 1,876

CYPRUS: Nicos Panayiotou; Panayotis Engomitis, Charalambos Pittas, Dimitris Ioannou (85 Ioakim Ioakim), Marios Charalambous, Costas Costa; Vassos Melanarkitis, Milenko Spoljaric, Marios Christodoulou; Sinisa Gogic (61 Marios Agathokleous), Kostas Malekkos (55 Panikos Pounas). Trainer: Panikos Georgiou

SPAIN: Santiago Cañizares; Sergio Barjúan "SERGI", Miguel Angel Nadal (66 Guillermo Amor), Rafael Alkorta, MÍCHEL SALGADO Fernández; RAÚL González, ALFONSO Pérez (38 Francisco Narváez "KIKO"), LUIS ENRIQUE Martínez, Fernando Ruiz Hierro; Fernando Morientes, Joseba ETXEBERRÍA Lizardi (60 Santiago Ezquerro). Trainer: Javier Clemente Lázaro

Goals: Engomitis (44), Gogic (48), Raúl (72), Spoljaric (76), Morientes (84)

CYPRUS v AUSTRIA 0-3 (0-0)

Larnaca 10.10.1998

Referee: Fernand Meese (FRA) Attendance: 12,000

CYPRUS: Nicos Panayiotou; Costas Costa, Panayotis Engomitis, Dimitris Ioannou, Marios Charalambous; Charalambos Pittas (67 Nicolas Georgiou), Marios Christodoulou, Milenko Spoljaric, Vassos Melanarkitis (67 Panayiotis Pounas); Marios Agathocleus (46 Yiannakis Okkas), Sinisa Gogic. Trainer: Panikos Georgiou

AUSTRIA: Franz Wohlfahrt; Peter Schöttel, Martin Hiden, Anton Pfeffer, Harald Cerny; Dietmar Kühbauer, Roman Mählich, Hannes Reinmayr (78 Peter Stöger), Arnold Wetl; Mario Haas (78 Christian Mayrleb), Ivica Vastic (82 Eduard Glieder). Trainer: Herbert Prohaska

Sent off: Ioannou (33)

Goals: Cerny (53, 61), Reinmayr (74)

SAN MARINO v ISRAEL 0-5 (0-3)

Olimpico, Serravalle 10.10.1998

Referee: Asim Khudiev (AZE) Attendance: 872

SAN MARINO: Federico Gasperoni; Mirco Gennari, Mauro Marani, Mauro Valentini, Simone Bacciocchi (56 Vittorio Valentini), William Guerra; Riccardo Muccioli, Pier Domenico Della Valle (67 Fabio Francini), Paolo Montagna (80 Davide Gualtieri), Ivan Matteoni; Andy Selva.
Trainer: Gian Paolo Mazza

ISRAEL: Rafael Cohen; Alon Harazi, Najwan Ghrayeb, Arik Benado (69 Amir Shelach), Ran Ben Shimon; Jan Telasnikov, Walid Badir, Haim Revivo, Eyal Berkovic (72 Offer Shitrit), Avi Nimni (61 Tal Banin); Alon Mizrahi. Trainer: Shlomo Sharf

Goals: Revivo (16), Nimni (18, 57), Mizrahi (31), Ghrayeb (82)

SAN MARINO v AUSTRIA 1-4 (0-0)

Olimpico, Serravale 14.10.1998

Referee: Valeriy Onufer (UKR) Attendance: 872

SAN MARINO: Federico Gasperoni; Mirco Gennari, Mauro Marani, Mauro Valentini (80 Pier Domenico Della Valle), Simone Bacciocchi; Fabio Francini (69 Vittorio Valentini), William Guerra, Riccardo Muccioli, Andrea Ugolini (62 Paolo Montagna); Ivan Matteoni, Andy Selva.
Trainer: Gian Paolo Mazza

AUSTRIA: Franz Wohlfahrt; Peter Schöttel, Anton Pfeffer, Martin Hiden; Andreas Heraf, Dietmar Kühbauer, Hannes Reinmayr (46 Christian Mayrleb), Arnold Wetl, Harald Cerny; Ivica Vastic (70 Peter Stöger), Mario Haas (66 Eduard Glieder).
Trainer: Herbert Prohaska

Goals: Vastic (58), Mayrleb (64), Hiden (68), Glieder (76), Selva (80 pen)

ISRAEL v SPAIN 1-2 (0-0)

Ramat-Gan, Tel Aviv 14.10.1998

Referee: David Elleray (ENG) Attendance: 37,000

ISRAEL: Rafael Cohen; Alon Harazi, Arik Benado, Ran Ben Shimon, Alon Hazan (75 Tal Banin); Najwan Ghrayeb, Jan Telasnikov (58 Alon Mizrahi), Eyal Berkovic, Avi Nimni, Walid Badir; Haim Revivo. Trainer: Shlomo Sharf

SPAIN: Santiago Cañizares; MÍCHEL SALGADO Fernández, Agustín ARANZÁBAL Alkorta, Rafael Alkorta, Fernando Ruiz Hierro; Vicente Engonga, Bittor Alkiza, LUIS ENRIQUE Martínez, Francisco Javier DE PEDRO (73 Joseba ETXEBERRÍA Lizardi); Francisco Narváez "KIKO" (88 Ismaël Urzaíz), RAÚL González (89 Marcos Vales).
Trainer: José António Camacho

Goals: Hazan (63), Hierro (65), Etxeberría (77)

SAN MARINO v CYPRUS 0-1 (0-1)

Olimpico, Serravalle 18.11.1998

Referee: John McDermott (IRE) Attendance: 600

SAN MARINO: Federico Gasperoni; Mirco Gennari, Mauro Marani, Vittorio Valentini, Mauro Valentini, William Guerra; Ivan Matteoni (75 Fabio Francini), Riccardo Muccioli (83 Luciano Mularoni), Bryan Gasperoni; Paolo Montagna (66 Nicola Bacciocchi), Andrea Ugolini.
Trainer: Gian Paolo Mazza

CYPRUS: Nicos Panayiotou; Andreas Sofocleous, Charalambos Pittas, Yiotis Panayiotou, Marios Charalambous; Vassos Melanarkitis, Panayotis Engomitis, Milenko Spoljaric, Marios Agathokleous (73 Yiannos Ioannou); Sinisa Gogic (86 Yiannakis Okkas), Kostas Malekkos (73 Michalis Andreas Constantinou). Trainer: Panikos Georgiou

Goal: Spoljaric (41)

CYPRUS v SAN MARINO 4-0 (3-0)

Limassol 10.02.1999

Referee: Roland Beck (LIE) Attendance: 3,000

CYPRUS: Nicos Panayiotou; Ioakim Ioakim, George Theodotou, Marios Charalambous, Marios Christodoulou; Charalambos Pittas, Vassos Melanarkitis, Milenko Spoljaric, Sinisa Gogic (83 Yiannakis Okkas); Michalis Andreas Constantinou (83 Yiannos Ioannou), Kostas Malekkos (90 Aristos Aristocleous). Trainer: Panikos Georgiou

SAN MARINO: Federico Gasperoni; Mirco Gennari, Mauro Marani (86 Damiano Vannucci), Luca Gobbi, Vittorio Valentini; William Guerra, Ermanno Zonzini, Pier Domenico Della Valle (69 Pier-Angelo Manzaroli), Andrea Ugolini (46 Nicola Bacciocchi); Luciano Mularoni, Andy Selva.
Trainer: Gian Paolo Mazza

Goals: Melanarkitis (18), Constantinou (32, 45), Christodoulou (89)

SPAIN v AUSTRIA 9-0 (5-0)

Luis Casanova, Valencia 27.03.1999

Referee: Gilles Veissière (FRA) Attendance: 45,000

SPAIN: Santiago Cañizares; MÍCHEL SALGADO Fernández, Sergio Barjuán SERGI, MARCELINO Elena, Fernando Ruiz Hierro; Francisco Javier González "FRAN", Joseba ETXEBERRÍA Lizardi (83 Daniel García "DANI"), Juan Carlos VALERON (72 Gaizka Mendieta), Josep Guardiola; Ismaël Urzaíz (60 Pedro Manuel Munitis), RAÚL González.
Trainer: Josá Antonio Camacho

AUSTRIA: Franz Wohlfahrt; Wolfgang Feiersinger (53 Walter Kogler), Harald Cerny, Anton Pfeffer, Peter Schöttel; Roman Mählich, Günther Neukirchner, Arnold Wetl, Christian Prosenik (58 Hannes Reinmayr); Mario Haas (70 Christian Mayrleb), Andreas Herzog. Trainer: Herbert Prohaska

Goals: Raúl (5, 17, 48, 73), Urzaíz (29, 45), Hierro (35 pen), Wetl (76 og), Fran (85)

ISRAEL v CYPRUS 3-0 (1-0)

Ramat Gan, Tel Aviv 28.03.1999

Referee: Marcel Lică (ROM) Attendance: 32,000

ISRAEL: Nir Davidovich; Alon Harazi, Najwan Ghrayeb, Amir Shelach, Walid Badir (46 Offer Talker); Arik Benado, Tal Banin, Haim Revivo (85 Avi Tikva), Eyal Berkovic; Ronen Harazi (46 Alon Mizrahi), Avi Nimni. Trainer: Shlomo Sharf

CYPRUS: Nicos Panayiotou; George Theodotou, Charalambos Pittas, Dimitris Ioannou, Marios Charalambous; Vassos Melanarkitis, Michlis Andreas Constantinou (66 Yiannakis Okkas), Milenko Spoljaric (79 Marios Agathokleous), Andreas Sofocleous; Kostas Malekkos (46 Charis Nicolaou), Marios Christodoulou.
Trainer: Panikos Georgiou

Goals: Banin (11), Mizrahi (47, 53)

SAN MARINO v SPAIN 0-6 (0-2)

Olimpico, Serravalle 31.03.1999

Referee: Goran Maric (CRO) Attendance: 2,500

SAN MARINO: Federico Gasperoni; Mirco Gennari, Vittorio Valentini, Mauro Valentini, Luca Gobbi (50 Simone Della Balda); Mauro Marani, Pier-Angelo Manzaroli, Bryan Gasperoni (75 Riccardo Muccioli), Ermanno Zonzini; Andy Selva, Paolo Montagna (60 Davide Gualtieri).
Trainer: Gian Paolo Mazza

SPAIN: Santiago Cañizares; MÍCHEL SALGADO Fernández, Francisco Jímenez "PACO", MARCELINO Elena, Sergio Barjuán SERGI; Joseba ETXEBERRÍA Lizardi, Josep Guardiola (69 Vicente Engonga), Juan Carlos Valerón (77 Iván Helguera), Francisco Javier González "FRAN"; Ismaël Urzaíz (61 Daniel García "DANI"), RAÚL González.
Trainer: José António Camacho

Goals: Fran (20), Raúl (45, 59, 66), Urzaíz (49), Etxeberría (73)

AUSTRIA v SAN MARINO 7-0 (3-0)

Graz 28.04.1999

Referee: Kyros Vasaras (GRE) Attendance: 15,400

AUSTRIA: Franz Wohlfahrt; Harald Cerny (70 Richard Kitzbichler), Thomas Winklhofer (78 Klaus Rohseano), Markus Schopp (70 Eduard Glieder), Wolfgang Feiersinger; Günther Neukirchner, Christian Mayrleb, Andreas Herzog, Christian Prosenik; Ivica Vastic, Martin Amerhauser.
Trainer: Otto Baric

SAN MARINO: Federico Gasperoni; Mirco Gennari (46 Simone Bacciocchi), Damiano Vannucci, Luca Gobbi, William Guerra; Simone Della Balda, Bryan Gasperoni (15 Pier-Angelo Manzaroli), Riccardo Muccioli, Paolo Montagna (79 Nicola Bacciocchi); Andy Selva, Ermanno Zonzini.
Trainer: Gian-Paolo Mazza

Goals: Mayrleb (24, 53), Vastic (43, 44, 84), Amerhauser (71), Herzog (82 pen)

SPAIN v SAN MARINO 9-0 (4-0)

Villareal 05.06.1999

Referee: Gerard Perry (IRE) Attendance: 16,000

SPAIN: Santiago Cañizares; MÍCHEL SALGADO Fernández (67 Pedro Manuel Munitis), Agustín ARANZÁBAL Alkorta, Josep Guardiola; MARCELINO Elena, Fernando Ruiz Hierro, LUIS ENRIQUE Martínez, Julen Guerrero (80 Gaizka Mendieta); Joseba ETXEBERRÍA Lizardi, Fernando Morientes, RAÚL González (67 Ismaël Urzaíz).
Trainer: José Antonio Camacho

SAN MARINO: Federico Gasperoni; Pier Domenico Della Valle, Simone Della Balda, William Guerra, Mirco Gennari (90 Damiano Vannucci); Luca Gobbi, Ermanno Zonzini, Pier-Angelo Manzaroli (75 Mauro Valentini), Paolo Montagna (58 Andrea Ugolini), Mauro Marani; Nicola Bacciocchi.
Trainer: Gian Paolo Mazza

Goals: Hierro (8 pen), Luis Enrique (22, 71, 75), Etxeberría (25, 45), Raúl (61), Gennari (89 og), Mendieta (90)

ISRAEL v AUSTRIA 5-0 (2-0)

Ramat-Gan, Tel Aviv 06.06.1999

Referee: Lubos Michel (SVK) Attendance: 45,000

ISRAEL: Nir Davidovich; Arik Benado, Amir Shelach, Najwan Ghrayeb, Alon Harazi; Yossi Abuksis (82 Idan Tal), Tal Banin, Alon Hazan, Eyal Berkovic (79 Avi Tikva); Alon Mizrahi (77 Nir Sivilia), Haim Revivo. Trainer: Shlomo Sharf

AUSTRIA: Franz Wohlfahrt; Zoran Barisic, Thomas Winklhofer, Walter Kogler; Harald Cerny, Roman Mählich, Günther Neukirchner, Andreas Herzog, Martin Amerhauser (46 Christian Prosenik); Christian Mayrleb (67 Mario Haas), Ivica Vastic (57 Eduard Glieder). Trainer: Otto Baric

Goals: Berkovic (26, 48), Revivo (45), Mizrahi (54), Ghrayeb (75)

CYPRUS v ISRAEL 3-2 (1-1)

Limassol 05.09.1999

Referee: Graham Barber (Eng) Attendance: 16,000

CYPRUS: Nicos Panayiotou; Costas Costa, Charalambos Pittas, Costas Kaiafas (80 Aristos Aristocleous), Marios Charalambous; Vassos Melanarkitis, Panayotis Engomitis, Milenko Spoljaric, Nicodemos Papavasiliou (64 Marios Christodoulou); Sinisa Gogic (72 Michlis Andreas Constantinou), Yiannakis Okkas.

ISRAEL: Nir Davidovich; Alon Harazi, Najwan Ghrayeb, Amir Shelach (64 Nir Sivilia), Arik Benado; Alon Hazan, Tal Banin, Haim Revivo, Yossi Abuksis (58 Yossi Benayoun); Eyal Berkovic (18 Walid Badir), Alon Mizrahi.
Trainer: Shlomo Sharf

Goals: Engomitis (27), Badir (31), Spoljaric (53, 86 pen), Benayoun (82)

AUSTRIA v SPAIN 1-3 (0-1)

Wien 04.09.1999

Referee: Michel Piraux (BEL) Attendance: 27,000

AUSTRIA: Alex Manninger; Michael Hatz, Michael Streiter, Thomas Winklhofer; Robert Ibertsberger, Dietmar Kühbauer, Roman Mählich (60 Markus Schopp), Roland Kirchler (68 Markus Weissenberger); Harald Cerny, Ivica Vastic, Christian Mayrleb.

SPAIN: Santiago Cañizares; MÍCHEL SALGADO Fernández, Fernando Ruiz Hierro, Francisco Jímenez "PACO", Sergio Barjúan "SERGI"; Joseba ETXEBERRÍA Lizardi (81 Gaizka Mendieta), Josep Guardiola, Juan Carlos Valerón (72 Vicente Engonga), LUIS ENRIQUE Martínez; Fernando Morientes (88 Julen Guerrero), RAÚL González.
Trainer: José António Camacho

Goals: Raúl (22), Hierro (49 og, 56), Luis Enrique (88)

ISRAEL v SAN MARINO 8-0 (3-0)

Tel Aviv 08.09.1999

Referee: Ilhami Kaplan (TUR) Attendance: 25,078

ISRAEL: Nir Davidovich; Alon Harazi, David Amsalem, Offer Talker, Arik Benado (65 Alon Halfon); Alon Hazan, Jan Telasnikov, Haim Revivo; Yossi Benayoun, Avi Tikva (61 Yossi Abuksis), Alon Mizrahi (46 Nir Sivilia).
Trainer: Shlomo Sharf

SAN MARINO: Federico Gasperoni; Fabrizio Pelliccioni, Mirco Gennari, Simone Bacciocchi, Marco Tomassoni; Simone Della Balda, Nicola Bacciocchi (58 Roberto Selva), Bryan Gasperoni, Andy Selva; Paolo Montagna (80 Marco De Luigi), Ermanno Zonzini (74 Pier Domenico Della Valle).
Trainer: Gian Paolo Mazza

Sent off: Selva (75)

Goals: Benayoun (25, 46, 70), Mizrahi (38), Revivo (40, 68), Sivilia (84), Abuksis (89)

SPAIN v CYPRUS 8-0 (5-0)

Badajoz 08.09.1999

Referee: Alfredo Trentalange (ITA) Attendance: 15,000

SPAIN: Santiago Cañizares (77 Antonio Jiménez "TONI"); MÍCHEL SALGADO Fernández, CÉSAR MARTÍN Villar, Fernando Ruiz Hierro, Agustín ARANZÁBAL Alkorta; Joseba ETXEBERRÍA Lizardi (46 Pedro Manuel Munitis), Josep Guardiola, Julen Guerrero, LUIS ENRIQUE Martínez (61 Gaizka Mendieta); RAÚL González, Ismaël Urzaíz.
Trainer: José António Camacho

CYPRUS: Nicos Panayiotou; Costas Costa, Charis Nicolaou (46 Aristos Aristocleous), Loukas Louka, Charalambos Pittas (46 George Theodotou); Vassos Melanarkitis, Panayotis Engomitis, George Christodoulou, Nicodemos Papavasiliou; Sinisa Gogic (88 Michalis Andreas Constantinou), Yiannakis Okkas.

Goals: Urzaíz (20, 25, 38), Guerrero (33, 42, 56), César (82), Hierro (88)

SPAIN v ISRAEL 3-0 (2-0)

Albacete 10.10.1999

Referee: Hellmut Krug (GER) Attendance: 12,000

SPAIN: Antonio Jiménez "TONI"; MÍCHEL SALGADO Fernández, Fernando Ruiz Hierro (23 CÉSAR MARTÍN Villar), Francisco Jímenez "PACO", Sergio Barjuán SERGI; Joseba ETXEBERRÍA Lizardi, Josep Guardiola, Julen Guerrero (70 Gaizka Mendieta), LUIS ENRIQUE Martínez; RAÚL González, Fernando Morientes (78 Ismaël Urzaíz).
Trainer: José António Camacho

ISRAEL: Dudu Avate; Alon Hazan (83 Jan Telasnikov), Arik Benado (50 Alon Halfon), Shimon Gershon, Amir Shelach, David Amsalem; Tal Banin, Haim Revivo, Eyal Berkovic (68 Yossi Benayoun), Idan Tal; Amir Torjman.

Goals: Morientes (30), César (37), Raúl (53)

AUSTRIA v CYPRUS 3-1 (2-0)

Wien 10.10.1999

Referee: Livio Bazzoli (ITA) Attendance: 10,000

AUSTRIA: Alex Manninger; Ivica Vastic, Thomas Winklhofer, Günther Neukirchner (46 Andreas Herzog); Harald Cerny (74 Jürgen Kauz), Dietmar Kühbauer, Robert Ibertsberger, Markus Weissenberger (83 Gerd Wimmer), Roland Kirchler; Eduard Glieder, Christian Mayrleb.

CYPRUS: Nicos Panayiotou; Costas Costa, Marios Charalambous, Kimis Alexandrou; Panayotis Engomitis, Costas Kaiafas, Vassos Melanarkitis (82 Marios Dimitriou), Milenko Spoljaric, Marios Christodoulou; Sinisa Gogic (26 Marios Agathokleous), Yiannakis Okkas (46 George Theodotou).

Sent off: Kaiafas (31), Spoljaric (45), Ibertsberger (75)

Goals: Glieder (5), Vastic (23), Costa (63), Herzog (81)

	P	W	D	L	F	A	Pts
Spain	8	7	0	1	42	5	21
Israel	8	4	1	3	25	9	13
(vs Austria	*2*	*1*	*1*	*0*	*6*	*1*	*4)*
Austria	8	4	1	3	19	20	13
(vs Israel	*2*	*0*	*1*	*1*	*1*	*6*	*1)*
Cyprus	8	4	0	4	12	21	12
San Marino	8	0	0	8	1	44	0

GROUP 7

ROMANIA v LIECHTENSTEIN 7-0 (4-0)

Steaua, Bucureşti 02.09.1998

Referee: Salem Prolic (BOS) Attendance: 4,000

ROMANIA: Bogdan Stelea (82 Bogdan Lobonţ); Dan Petrescu, Gheorghe Popescu (Cap), Florin Bătrânu, Cosmin Marius Contra; Florentin Petre, Constantin Gâlcă, Cătălin Munteanu (71 Ioan Ovidiu Sabău), Dorinel Munteanu; Viorel Moldovan, Adrian Ilie (68 Dumitru Adrian Mihalcea). Trainer: Victor Piţurcă

LIECHTENSTEIN: Martin Oehry; Christof Ritter, Thomas Hanselmann, Harry Zech (Cap), Patrick Hefti, Modestus Haas (46 Martin Stocklasa); Thomas Beck, Hansjörg Lingg (61 Marco Büchel), Michael Stocklasa, Ralf Oehri; Martin Telser (88 Marco Ender). Trainer: Ralf Loose

Goals: Popescu (17), C. Munteanu (29), Ilie (31, 44, 51), Moldovan (54), Haas (59 og)

SLOVAKIA v AZERBAIJAN 3-0 (3-0)

Scremel, Kosice 05.09.1998

Referee: Alan Snoddy (NIR) Attendance: 3,243

SLOVAKIA: Alexander Vencel; Stanislav Varga, Dusan Tittel, Marek Spilar; Miroslav Sovic, Robert Tomaschek, Peter Dubovsky (62 Vladislav Zvara), Lubomír Moravcík, Vladimir Kinder; Jozef Majoros (82 Marek Ujlaky), Martin Fabus (62 Tibor Jancula). Trainer: Jozef Jankech

AZERBAIJAN: Dmitriy Kramarenko; Emin Agaev, Deni Gaysumov, Faik Jabbarov, Vyacheslav Lychkin; Kurban Kurbanov (66 Vidadi Rzayev), Arif Asadov, Rasim Abusov, Narvik Sirkhaev; Nazim Suleymanov (46 Rufat Kuliev), Velli Kasumov. Trainer: Vagif Sadigov

Goals: Fabus (17), Dubovsky (25 pen), Moravcik (39)

HUNGARY v PORTUGAL 1-3 (1-0)

Népstadion, Budapest 06.09.1998

Referee: Urs Meier (SWI) Attendance: 50,000

HUNGARY: Gábor Király; Csaba Fehér (78 Zoltán Kovács), Pál Lakos, János Hrutka, János Mátyus; Krisztián Lisztes (46 Pál Dárdai), Gábor Halmai, Béla Illés; Tibor Dombi (78 György Korsós), Ferenc Horváth, István Hamar. Trainer: Bertalan Bicskei

PORTUGAL: VÍTOR Manuel Martins BAÍA; Carlos Alberto Oliveira SECRETÁRIO, PAULO Sérgio Braga MADEIRA, JORGE Paulo COSTA Almeida, DIMAS Manuel Marques Teixeira; "FIGO" Luis Filipe Madeira Caeiro, PAULO Jorge Gomes BENTO, RUI Manuel César COSTA, João Paulo Maio PAULINHO SANTOS; JOÃO Manuel Vieira PINTO, Ricardo Manuel da Silva SÁ PINTO. Trainer: HUMBERTO COELHO

Goals: Horváth (32), Sá Pinto (56, 75), Rui Costa (84)

PORTUGAL v ROMANIA 0-1 (0-0)

Das Antas, Porto 10.10.1998

Referee: Helmut Krug (GER) Attendance: 37,354

PORTUGAL: VÍTOR Manuel Martins BAÍA (Cap); ABEL Luis da Silva Costa XAVIER (87 DANIel Cruz Carvalho), FERNANDO Manuel Silva COUTO, JORGE Paulo COSTA Almeida, DIMAS Manuel Marques Teixeira; PAULO Jorge Gomes BENTO (70 SÉRGIO Paulo Marceneiro CONCEIÇAO), João Paulo Maio PAULINHO SANTOS, RUI Manuel César COSTA, "FIGO" Luis Filipe Madeira Caeiro; Ricardo Manuel da Silva SÁ PINTO, JOÃO Manuel Vieira PINTO (80 NUNO GOMES Miguel Soares Pereira Ribeiro). Trainer: HUMBERTO Manuel de Jesus COELHO

ROMANIA: Bogdan Stelea; Dan Petrescu (85 Cosmin Contra), Iulian Filipescu, Gheorghe Popescu (Cap), Liviu Ciobotariu, Dorinel Munteanu; Florentin Petre, Cătălin Munteanu (62 Ioan Lupescu), Constantin Gâlcă, Laurenţiu Roşu; Viorel Moldovan (90 Dumitru Mihalcea). Trainer: Victor Piţurcă **Sent off**: Roşu (64).

Goal: D. Munteanu (90)

LIECHTENSTEIN v SLOVAKIA 0-4 (0-3)

Eschen-Mauren 10.10.1998

Referee: Vladimir Antonov (MOL) Attendance: 2,500

LIECHTENSTEIN: Martin Oehry; Christof Ritter, Thomas Hanselmann, Harry Zech, Patrick Hefti (76 Hansjörg Lingg); Daniel Hasler, Ralf Oehri (46 Jörgen Ospelt), Michael Stocklasa, Modestus Haas (33 Martin Stocklasa), Mario Frick; Martin Telser. Trainer: Ralf Loose

SLOVAKIA: Alexander Vencel; Stanislav Varga (65 Milan Timko), Dusan Tittel, Marek Spilár; Miroslav Sovic, Peter Dubovsky, Robert Tomaschek, Lubomír Moravcík, Vladimír Kinder (30 Ivan Kozák); Jozef Majoros, Martin Fabus (61 Tibor Jancula). Trainer: Jozef Jankech

Goals: Sovic (3), Dubovsky (13), Tomaschek (36, 61)

AZERBAIJAN v HUNGARY 0-4 (0-0)

Tofik Bakhramov, Baku 10.10.1998

Referee: Stéphane Bre (FRA) Attendance: 7,500

AZERBAIJAN: Dmitriy Kramarenko (60 Alexander Zhidkov); Emin Agaev, Deni Gaysumov, Aslan Kerimov, Vyacheslav Lychkin; Rasim Abusov, Arif Asadov (52 Ilkhan Mamedov), Vidadi Rzayev, Kurban Kurbanov; Elshan Kambarov (58 Velli Kasumov), Narvik Sirkhaev. Trainer: Kazbek Tuaev **Sent off**: Lychkin (60)

HUNGARY: Gábor Király; János Hrutka, Csaba Fehér, János Mátyus, Vilmos Sebök (65 György Korsós); István Pisont, Krisztián Lisztes (75 Tibor Dombi), Pál Dárdai, Ferenc Horváth (6 Miklós Fehér); Béla Illés, István Hamar. Trainer: Bertalan Bicskei

Goals: Dárdai (59), Illés (84 pen), Pisont (89), M. Fehér (90)

HUNGARY v ROMANIA 1-1 (0-0)

Népstadion, Budapest 14.10.1998

Referee: Kim Milton Nielsen (DEN) Attendance: 40,000

HUNGARY: Gábor Király; Csaba Fehér, János Hrutka, Vilmos Sebök, János Mátyus; Gábor Egressy (77 Krisztián Lisztes), István Pisont, Béla Illés (Cap), Pál Dárdai, István Hamar (69 Nórbert Tóth); Miklós Fehér (75 Ferenc Hámori). Trainer: Bertalan Bicskei

ROMANIA: Bogdan Stelea; Dan Petrescu, Liviu Ciobotariu, Gheorghe Popescu (Cap), Iulian Filipescu; Florentin Petre (69 Denis Şerban), Ioan Lupescu, Constantin Gâlcă, Gheorghe Craioveanu (75 Cătălin Munteanu), Dorinel Munteanu; Viorel Moldovan (80 Dumitru Mihalcea). Trainer: Victor Piţurcă

Sent off: Hamori (86), Filipescu (90)

Goals: Moldovan (50), Hrutka (83)

SLOVAKIA v PORTUGAL 0-3 (0-2)

Tehelne pole, Bratislava 14.10.1998

Referee: Oguz Sarvan (TUR) Attendance: 22,059

SLOVAKIA: Alexander Vencel; Marek Spilár, Dusan Tittel, Robert Tomaschek, Stanislav Varga; Miroslav Sovic (82 Attila Pinte), Vladimír Kinder (46 Ivan Kozák), Peter Dubovsky, Lubomír Moravcík; Jozef Majoros, Martin Fabus (57 Szilárd Németh). Trainer: Jozef Jankech

PORTUGAL: VÍTOR Manuel Martins BAÍA (Cap); ABEL Luis da Silva Costa XAVIER, JORGE Paulo COSTA Almeida, FERNANDO Manuel Silva COUTO, DIMAS Manuel Marques Teixeira; João Paulo Maio PAULINHO SANTOS, PAULO Jorge Gomes BENTO, RUI Manuel César COSTA (66 Francisco DA COSTA); "FIGO" Luis Filipe Madeira Caeiro (89 Nuno Gonçalves da Rocha CAPUCHO); JOÃO Manuel Vieira PINTO (46 SÉRGIO Paulo Marceneiro CONCEIÇAO), Ricardo Manuel da Silva SÁ PINTO.
Trainer: HUMBERTO Manuel de Jesus COELHO

Goals: João Pinto (16, 33), Abel Xavier (70)

LIECHTENSTEIN v AZERBAIJAN 2-1 (0-0)

Vaduz 14.10.1998

Referee: Herbert Barr (NIR) Attendance: 1,900

LIECHTENSTEIN: Peter Jehle; Christof Ritter, Harry Zech, Daniel Hasler, Martin Stocklasa; Herbert Bicker (67 Jörgen Ospelt), Hansjörg Lingg, Michael Stocklasa, Thomas Beck (74 Marco Büchel); Mario Frick, Martin Telser.
Trainer: Ralf Loose

AZERBAIJAN: Alexander Zhidkov; Ilgham Yadullayev, Deni Gaysumov, Emin Agaev; Aslan Kerimov, Rasim Abusov (79 Rufat Kuliev), Makhmud Kurbanov (25 Nazim Suleymanov), Vidadi Rzayev; Kurban Kurbanov, Elshan Kambarov (51 Ilkhan Mamedov), Narvik Sirkhaev. Trainer: Kazbek Tuaev

Goals: M. Frick (47), M. Telser (49), K. Kurbanov (59)

PORTUGAL v AZERBAIJAN 7-0 (2-0)

Guimaraes 26.03.1999

Referee: Jacek Granat (POL) Attendance: 14,650

PORTUGAL: VÍTOR Manuel Martins BAÍA (77 PEDRO Manuel ESPINHA Ferreira); Carlos Alberto Oliveira SECRETÁRIO, PAULO Sérgio Braga MADEIRA, FERNANDO Manuel Silva COUTO, DIMAS Manuel Marques Teixeira; PAULO Manuel Carvalho SOUSA, RUI Manuel César COSTA (83 PEDRO Alexandre dos Santos BARBOSA), SÉRGIO Paulo Marceneiro CONCEIÇAO; "FIGO" Luis Filipe Madeira Caeiro (73 Pedro Miguel Resende PAULETA), JOÃO Manuel Vieira PINTO, Ricardo Manuel da Silva SÁ PINTO.
Trainer: HUMBERTO Manuel de Jesus COELHO

AZERBAIJAN: Dmitriy Kramarenko; Rasim Abusov, Tarlan Akhmedov, Emin Agaev, Alexei Stukas; Arif Asadov, Bakhtiyar Musayev (67 Vidadi Rzayev), Narvik Sirkhaev, Vyacheslav Lychkin; Kurban Kurbanov, Elshan Kambarov (72 Vadim Vasilyev). Trainer: Akhmed Aleskerov

Sent off: Abusov (67)

Goals: Sá Pinto (28), João Pinto (36, 71), Paulo Madeira (67), Sérgio Conceiçao (75), Pauleta (82, 83)

HUNGARY v LIECHTENSTEIN 5-0 (3-0)

Üllöi út, Budapest 27.03.1999

Referee: Kostas Kapitanis (CYP) Attendance: 9,534

HUNGARY: Gábor Király; György Korsós, Vilmos Sebök, János Hrutka (78 József Somogyi), János Mátyus; István Pisont, Gábor Halmai, Béla Illés; József Sebök (71 Tibor Dombi), Miklós Fehér, Norbert Tóth (76 István Hamar).
Trainer: Bertalan Bicskei

LIECHTENSTEIN: Peter Jehle; Hansjörg Lingg (74 Patrick Burgmeier), Daniel Hasler, Christof Ritter, Thomas Hanselmann (46 Patrick Hefti), Martin Stocklasa; Albert Wohlwend, Martin Telser, Matthias Beck (77 Jürgen Ospelt); Michael Stocklasa, Mario Frick. Trainer: Ralf Loose

Goals: J. Sebök (17), V. Sebök (33, 42, 85 pen), Illés (74)

ROMANIA v SLOVAKIA 0-0

"Lia Manoliu", Bucureşti 27.03.1999

Referee: Graham Barber (ENG) Attendance: 22,000

ROMANIA: Bogdan Stelea; Dan Petrescu, Florin Bătrânu, Gheorghe Popescu (Cap), Dorinel Munteanu; Florentin Petre, Constantin Gâlcă, Cătălin Munteanu (68 Ioan Lupescu), Laurenţiu Roşu; Viorel Moldovan (72 Gheorghe Craioveanu), Adrian Ilie. Trainer: Victor Piţurcă

SLOVAKIA: Miroslav König; Roman Kratochvíl, Marián Zeman, Stanislav Varga, Miroslav Karhan; Igor Balis, Tibor Zátek (76 Peter Dzurik), Róbert Tomaschek (Cap), Vladimír Labant; Peter Dubovsky (86 Marian Suchancok), Jozef Majoros (70 Peter Slicho). Trainer: Jozef Adamec

Sent off: Labant (80)

AZERBAIJAN v ROMANIA 0-1 (0-0)

Tofik Bakhramov, Baku 31.03.1999

Referee: Roelof Luinge (HOL) Attendance: 10,000

AZERBAIJAN: Gusein Magomedov; Vladimir Poshekhontsev, Tarlan Akhmedov (Cap), Aslan Kerimov, Emin Agaev (76 Rufat Kuliev); Narvik Sirkhaev, Vyacheslav Lychkin, Arif Asadov, Makhmud Kurbanov (66 Vidadi Rzayev), Zaur Tagizade (68 Elshan Kambarov), Kurban Kurbanov. Trainer: Akhmed Aleskerov

ROMANIA: Bogdan Lobonţ; Cosmin Contra, Iulian Filipescu, Liviu Ciobotariu, Dorinel Munteanu; Florentin Petre, Ioan Lupescu, Constantin Gâlcă, Laurenţiu Roşu (74 Daniel Florea), Gheorghe Craioveanu (89 Dumitru Mihalcea), Viorel Moldovan. Trainer: Victor Piţurcă

Goal: Petre (49)

SLOVAKIA v HUNGARY 0-0

Slovan, Bratislava 31.03.1999

Referee: Claude Colombo (FRA) Attendance: 19,452

SLOVAKIA: Miroslav König; Roman Kratochvíl, Marian Zeman (14 Peter Dzurik), Stanislav Varga, Miroslav Karhan; Igor Balis, Robert Tomaschek, Tibor Zátek (79 Norbert Hrncar), Attila Pinte (83 Peter Slicho); Peter Dubovsky, Jozef Majoros. Trainer: Jozef Adamec

HUNGARY: Gábor Király; György Korsós, János Hrutka, Vilmos Sebök, János Mátyus; István Pisont, Gábor Halmai, Béla Illés; József Sebök (55 Tibor Dombi); Miklós Fehér (64 István Hamar), Norbert Tóth. Trainer: Bertalan Bicskei

LIECHTENSTEIN v PORTUGAL 0-5 (0-1)

Vaduz 31.03.1999

Referee: Gylfi Thor Orrason (ICE) Attendance: 3,000

LIECHTENSTEIN: Peter Jehle; Christof Ritter, Thomas Hanselmann (84 Jürgen Ospelt), Martin Stocklasa, Hansjörg Lingg; Daniel Hasler, Christoph Frick, Albert Wohlwend (82 Patrick Burgmaier), Michael Stocklasa (66 Matthias Beck), Martin Telser; Mario Frick. Trainer: Ralf Loose

PORTUGAL: VÍTOR Manuel Martins BAÍA; Carlos Alberto Oliveira SECRETÁRIO, PAULO Sérgio Braga MADEIRA, FERNANDO Manuel Silva COUTO, DIMAS Manuel Marques Teixeira; PAULO Manuel Carvalho SOUSA, SÉRGIO Paulo Marceneiro CONCEIÇAO (88 Nuno Gonçalves da Rocha CAPUCHO), RUI Manuel César COSTA; "FIGO" Luis Filipe Madeira Caeiro, JOÃO Manuel Vieira PINTO (75 NUNO GOMES Miguel Soares Pereira Ribeiro), Ricardo Manuel da Silva SÁ PINTO (62 Pedro Miguel Resende PAULETA). Trainer: HUMBERTO Manuel de Jesus COELHO

Goals: Rui Costa (15 pen, 79), Figo (49), Paulo Madeira (54, 61)

ROMANIA v HUNGARY 2-0 (2-0)

Steaua, Bucureşti 05.06.1999

Referee: Rune Pedersen (NOR) Attendnce: 25,000

ROMANIA: Bogdan Lobonţ; Dan Petrescu, Iulian Filipescu, Gheorghe Popescu, Ştefan Dumitru Nanu; Florentin Petre, Gheorghe Hagi (Cap) (46 Ioan Lupescu), Constantin Gâlcă, Dorinel Munteanu; Viorel Moldovan (60 Ioan Viorel Ganea), Adrian Ilie (87 Gheorghe Craioveanu). Trainer: Victor Piţurcă

HUNGARY: Gábor Király; Vilmos Sebök, János Mátyus, János Hrutka, György Korsós; József Sebök (76 Miklós Herczeg), Gábor Halmai, Béla Illés (Cap) (81 Sándor Preisinger), Pál Dárdai; Miklós Fehér (46 István Pisont), Gábor Egressy. Trainer: Bertalan Bicskei

Goals: Ilie (3), Munteanu (15)

PORTUGAL v SLOVAKIA 1-0 (0-0)

Lisboa 05.06.1999

Referee: Claus Bo Larsen (DEN) Attendance: 25,000

PORTUGAL: VÍTOR Manuel Martins BAÍA; ABEL Luis da Silva Costa XAVIER (31 SÉRGIO Paulo Marceneiro CONCEIÇAO), FERNANDO Manuel Silva COUTO, PAULO Sérgio Braga MADEIRA, DIMAS Manuel Marques Teixeira; PAULO Jorge Gomes BENTO, PAULO Manuel Carvalho SOUSA, RUI Manuel César COSTA; "FIGO" Luis Filipe Madeira Caeiro (90 PEDRO Alexandre dos Santos BARBOSA), JOÃO Manuel Vieira PINTO (61 Nuno Gonçalves da Rocha CAPUCHO), Ricardo Manuel da Silva SÁ PINTO. Trainer: HUMBERTO Manuel de Jesus COELHO

SLOVAKIA: Miroslav König; Roman Kratochvíl, Milan Timko, Stanislav Varga, Miroslav Karhan; Attila Pinte (66 Peter Slicho), Robert Tomaschek, Vladislav Zvara (30 Jozef Valachovic), Vladimír Labant; Peter Dubovsky, Jozef Majoros (84 Vladimir Kozuch). Trainer: Jozef Adamec

Goal: Capucho (62)

AZERBAIJAN v LIECHTENSTEIN 4-0 (2-0)

Tofik Bakhramov, Baku 05.06.1999

Referee: Knut Stadsgård (DEN) Attendance: 8,500

AZERBAIJAN: Dmitriy Kramarenko; Ilgham Yadullayev, Tarlan Akhmedov, Emin Agaev, Vyacheslav Lychkin (74 Alexei Stukas); Aslan Kerimov, Makhmud Kurbanov, Zaur Tagizade (68 Mirbagir Isaev), Narvik Sirkhaev; Kurban Kurbanov, Vadim Vasilyev (61 Elmir Khankishiev). Trainer: Akhmed Aleskerov

LIECHTENSTEIN: Peter Jehle; Hansjörg Lingg, Christof Ritter, Harry Zech, Martin Stocklasa; Michael Stocklasa (74 Albert Wohlwend), Christoph Frick, Herbert Bicker (59 Matthias Beck), Daniel Hasler; Martin Telser, Harald Benz (46 Thomas Beck). Trainer: Ralf Loose

Goals: K. Kurbanov (16), Lychkin (42), Tagizade (60), Isaev (73)

ROMANIA v AZERBAIJAN 4-0 (2-0)

Steaua, București 09.06.1999

Referee: Zelijko Siric (CRO) Attendance: 10,000

ROMANIA: Bogdan Lobonţ; Dan Petrescu, Iulian Filipescu, Gheorghe Popescu (Cap), Ştefan Dumitru Nanu; Florentin Petre (66 Viorel Moldovan), Ioan Lupescu, Constantin Gâlcă, Dorinel Munteanu; Ioan Viorel Ganea (60 Gheorghe Craioveanu), Ion Vlădoiu (77 Laurenţiu Roşu). Trainer: Victor Piţurcă

AZERBAIJAN: Dmitriy Kramarenko; Emin Agaev (70 Igor Getman), Vladimir Poshekhontsev, Tarlan Akhmedov (Cap), Ilgham Yadullayev, Aslan Kerimov; Narvik Sirkhaev, Vyacheslav Lychkin (81 Vadim Vasilyev), Makhmud Kurbanov (61 Bakhtiyar Musayev), Zaur Tagizade, Kurban Kurbanov. Trainer: Akhmed Aleskerov

Goals: Ganea (35), Munteanu (44 pen), Vlădoiu (48), Roşu (90)

HUNGARY v SLOVAKIA 0-1 (0-0)

ETO, Györ 09.06.1999

Referee: Manuel Diaz Vega (SPA) Attendance: 18,000

HUNGARY: Gábor Király; György Korsós, János Hrutka, Vilmos Sebök, János Mátyus; Pál Dárdai, Gábor Halmai (73 István Pisont), József Somogyi (78 Sándor Preisinger), Béla Illés; József Sebök, Gábor Egressy (60 Tibor Dombi). Trainer: Bertalan Bicskei

SLOVAKIA: Miroslav König; Roman Kratochvíl, Milan Timko, Stanislav Varga, Miroslav Karhan; Attila Pinte, Jozef Valachovic, Vladislav Zvara (82 Peter Dzurik), Peter Németh, Vladimír Labant; Martin Fabus. Trainer: Jozef Adamec

Goal: Fabus (53)

PORTUGAL v LIECHTENSTEIN 8-0 (3-0)

Coimbra 09.06.1999

Referee: Dietmar Drabek (AUS) Attendance: 25,000

PORTUGAL: VÍTOR Manuel Martins BAÍA; Carlos Alberto Oliveira SECRETÁRIO (15 Nuno Gonçalves da Rocha CAPUCHO), FERNANDO Manuel Silva COUTO, PAULO Sérgio Braga MADEIRA, DIMAS Manuel Marques Teixeira; PAULO Manuel Carvalho SOUSA (63 PEDRO Alexandre dos Santos BARBOSA), SÉRGIO Paulo Marceneiro CONCEIÇAO, RUI Manuel César COSTA; "FIGO" Luis Filipe Madeira Caeiro, JOÃO Manuel Vieira PINTO, Ricardo Manuel da Silva SÁ PINTO. Trainer: HUMBERTO Manuel de Jesus COELHO

LIECHTENSTEIN: Peter Jehle; Jürgen Ospelt, Daniel Hasler, Christof Ritter, Harry Zech, Daniel Telser (53 Hansjörg Lingg); Albert Wohlwend, Martin Telser (75 Marco Büchel), Michael Stocklasa (66 Patrick Burgmeier); Herbert Bicker, Thomas Beck. Trainer: Ralf Loose

Goals: Sá Pinto (27, 44, 52), João Pinto (39, 60, 69), Rui Costa (81, 90 pen)

AZERBAIJAN v PORTUGAL 1-1 (0-0)

Tofik Bakhramov, Baku 03.09.1999

Referee: Dermot Gallagher (ENG) Attendance: 8,000

AZERBAIJAN: Dmitriy Kramarenko; Emin Agaev, Vladimir Poshekhontsev, Tarlan Akhmedov, Vyacheslav Lychkin (90 Alexei Stukas), Igor Getman, Kamal Kuliev, Zaur Tagizade, Bakhtiyar Musayev (58 Makhmud Kurbanov), Vadim Vasilyev (54 Elshan Kambarov), Adagim Niftaliyev. Trainer: Akhmed Aleskerov

PORTUGAL: VÍTOR Manuel Martins BAÍA; Carlos Alberto Oliveira SECRETÁRIO, DIMAS Manuel Marques Teixeira, PAULO Sérgio Braga MADEIRA, FERNANDO Manuel Silva COUTO, PAULO Manuel Carvalho SOUSA (67 Nuno Gonçalves da Rocha CAPUCHO), "FIGO" Luis Filipe Madeira Caeiro, JOÃO Manuel Vieira PINTO, Ricardo Manuel da Silva SÁ PINTO (46 SÉRGIO Paulo Marceneiro CONCEIÇAO), RUI Manuel César COSTA, PAULO Jorge Gomes BENTO (30 Pedro Miguel Resende PAULETA). Trainer: HUMBERTO Manuel de Jesus COELHO.

Sent off: Tagizade (84)

Goals: Tagizade (51), Figo (90)

SLOVAKIA v ROMANIA 1-5 (1-2)

Slovan, Bratislava 04.09.1999

Referee: Graziano Cesari (ITA) Attendance: 8,000

SLOVAKIA: Miroslav König; Miroslav Karhan, Peter Németh, Roman Kratochvil (74 Jaroslav Hrabal), Stanislav Varga (Cap), Vladimir Labant, Jozef Valachovic, Igor Balis (67 Tibor Jancula), Szilárd Németh, Vladimir Janocko, Martin Fabus (81 Marek Ujlaky). Trainer: Jozef Adamec

ROMANIA: Bogdan Stelea; Dan Petrescu, Liviu Ciobotariu, Iulian Filipescu, Constantin Gâlcă, Gheorghe Popescu, Ioan Ovidiu Sabău (83 Ovidiu Stângă), Dorinel Munteanu, Ioan Viorel Ganea (58 Viorel Moldovan), Gheorghe Hagi (Cap) (75 Ioan Lupescu), Adrian Ilie. Trainer: Victor Piţurcă

Goals: Ilie (6), Labant (21 pen), Hagi (30), Ciobotariu (66), Moldovan (88, 90)

LIECHTENSTEIN v HUNGARY 0-0

Rheinpark, Vaduz 04.09.1999

Referee: Sten Kaldma (EST) Attendance: 1,800

LIECHTENSTEIN: Peter Jehle; Jürgen Ospelt, Martin Stocklasa, Patrick Hefti, Harry Zech, Michael Stocklasa, Martin Telser (66 Christof Ritter), Thomas Beck (82 Herbert Bicker), Frédéric Gigon, Mario Frick (90 Matthias Beck), Daniel Hasler. Trainer: Ralf Loose

HUNGARY: Gábor Király; Gábor Egressy, János Mátyus, Vilmos Sebök, György Korsós, Gábor Halmai, Tibor Dombi (60 Thomas Sowunmi), Ferenc Horváth (75 Miklós Herczeg), Béla Illés, Pál Dárdai, Csaba Fehér (46 Miklós Lendvai). Trainer: Bertalan Bicskei

SLOVAKIA v LIECHTENSTEIN 2-0 (1-0)

Slovan, Bratislava 08.09.1999

Referee: Andreas Georgiou (CYP) Attendance: 3,052

SLOVAKIA: Kamil Susko; Miroslav Karhan, Vladimír Janocko (41 Jaroslav Hrabal), Peter Dzurik, Stanislav Varga, Vladimír Labant, Jozef Valachovic, Igor Balis, Szilárd Németh (76 Vladimir Kozuch), Marek Ujlaky, Martin Fabus (61 Peter Németh). Trainer: Jozef Adamec

LIECHTENSTEIN: Peter Jehle; Jürgen Ospelt, Martin Stocklasa, Christof Ritter, Harry Zech, Michael Stocklasa, Thomas Beck, Mario Frick (12 Marco Buchel, 57 Matthias Beck), Daniel Hasler, Martin Telser, Frédéric Gigon (57 Albert Wohlwend). Trainer: Ralf Loose

Sent off: Valachovic (36)

Goals: S. Nemeth (4), Karhan (55)

HUNGARY v AZERBAIJAN 3-0 (1-0)

Népstadion, Budapest 08.09.1999

Referee: Saso Lazarevski (MAC) Attendance: 2,910

HUNGARY: Gábor Király; János Hrutka, György Korsós, János Mátyus, Vilmos Sebök, Gábor Halmai, Miklós Lendvai, Gábor Egressy, Thomas Sowunmi (89 Akos Füzi), Béla Illés, Miklós Herczeg (74 Ferenc Horváth).
Trainer: Bertalan Bicskei

AZERBAIJAN: Jahangir Gassan; Igor Getman, Vladimir Poshekhontsev, Arif Asadov, Vyacheslav Lychkin (68 Alexei Stukas), Aslan Kerimov (60 Elshan Kambarov), Kamal Kuliev, Ilgham Yadullayev, Bakhtiyar Musayev, Vadim Vasilyev (90 Farrukh Ismailov), Adagim Nyftaliev.
Trainer: Akhmed Aleskerov

Goals: V. Sebök (28), Egressy (51), Sowunmi (55)

ROMANIA v PORTUGAL 1-1 (1-1)

Steaua, Bucureşti 08.09.1999

Referee: Hartmut Strampe (GER) Attendance: 24,000

ROMANIA: Bogdan Stelea; Dan Petrescu (46 Ştefan Dumitru Nanu), Liviu Ciobotariu, Iulian Filipescu, Constantin Gâlcă, Gheorghe Popescu, Ioan Ovidiu Sabău, Dorinel Munteanu, Viorel Moldovan (69 Ioan Lupescu), Gheorghe Hagi (Cap), Adrian Ilie (85 Ioan Viorel Ganea). Trainer: Victor Piţurcă

PORTUGAL: VÍTOR Manuel Martins BAÍA (Cap); RUI Fernando Pereira BENTO, DIMAS Manuel Marques Teixeira, FERNANDO Manuel Silva COUTO, PAULO Sérgio Braga MADEIRA, PAULO Jorge Gomes BENTO, RUI Manuel César COSTA, PAULO Manuel Carvalho de SOUSA (67 SÉRGIO Paulo Marceneiro CONCEIÇAO), FIGO Luis Filipe Madeira, Ricardo Manuel da Silva SÁ PINTO, JOÃO Manuel Vieira PINTO (82 Pedro Miguel Resende PAULETA).
Trainer: HUMBERTO Manuel de Jesus COELHO

Goals: Hagi (37), Figo (45)

PORTUGAL v HUNGARY 3-0 (2-0)

Da Luz, Lisboa 09.10.1999

Referee: Kim Milton Nielsen (DEN) Attendance: 65,000

PORTUGAL: VÍTOR Manuel Martins BAÍA; Carlos Alberto Oliveira SECRETÁRIO (46 ABEL Luis da Silva Costa XAVIER), PAULO Sérgio Braga MADEIRA, JORGE Paulo COSTA Almeida, DIMAS Manuel Marques Teixeira, PAULO Manuel Carvalho de SOUSA, RUI Manuel César COSTA (84 PAULO Jorge Gomes BENTO), FIGO Luis Filipe Madeira, SÉRGIO Paulo Marceneiro CONCEIÇAO, JOÃO Manuel Vieira PINTO (89 Ricardo Manuel da Silva SÁ PINTO), Pedro Miguel Resende PAULETA.
Trainer: HUMBERTO Manuel de Jesus COELHO

HUNGARY: Gábor Király; Pál Lakos, György Korsós, Attila Dragoner, Gábor Halmai, János Mátyus; István Pisont (24 Pál Dárdai), Thomas Sowunmi (83 Zoltán Kovács), Miklós Lendvai, Gábor Egressy; Ferenc Horváth (75 Attila Kuttor). Trainer: Bertalan Bicskei

Sent off: Pauleta (41).

Goals: Rui Costa (15 pen), João Pinto (16), Abel Xavier (58)

LIECHTENSTEIN v ROMANIA 0-3 (0-1)

Rheinpark, Vaduz 09.10.1999

Referee: Andrei Butenko (RUS) Attendance: 2,900

LIECHTENSTEIN: Peter Jehle; Jürgen Ospelt, Martin Stocklasa, Patrick Hefti, Harry Zech, Christof Ritter, Christoph Frick (Cap) (89 Albert Wohlwend), Mario Frick (90 Matthias Beck), Frédéric Gigon, Martin Telser (69 Herbert Bicker), Thomas Beck. Trainer: Ralf Loose

ROMANIA: Bogdan Stelea; Dan Petrescu, Ştefan Dumitru Nanu, Liviu Ciobotariu, Constantin Gâlcă (75 Ioan Lupescu); Gheorghe Popescu, Florentin Petre, Laurenţiu Roşu, Viorel Moldovan (62 Ioan Viorel Ganea); Gheorghe Hagi (Cap) (77 Ovidiu Stângă), Adrian Ilie. Trainer: Victor Piţurcă

Sent off: T. Beck (53)

Goals: Roşu (26), Ganea (65, 73)

AZERBAIJAN v SLOVAKIA 0-1 (0-0)

Tofik Bakhramov, Baku 09.10.1999

Referee: Kyros Vassaras (GRE) Attendance: 8,000

AZERBAIJAN: Dmitriy Kramarenko; Igor Getman, Emin Agaev (80 Aslan Kerimov), Vladimir Poshekhontsev, Tarlan Akhmedov, Mirbagir Isaev (56 Farrukh Ismailov), Ilgham Yadullayev, Elshan Kambarov (46 Vyacheslav Lychkin), Bakhtiyar Musayev, Vadim Vasilyev, Adagim Niftaliev. Trainer: Akhmed Aleskerov

SLOVAKIA: Kamil Susko; Stanislav Varga, Ivan Kozák, Marián Suchancok, Roman Kratochvíl, Vladimír Labant (90 Attila Pinte), Milan Timko, Martin Fabus, Miroslav Karhan (86 Marian Zeman), Peter Németh, Vladimir Janocko (84 Vladimir Kozuch).

Goal: Labant (70)

	P	W	D	L	F	A	Pts
Romania	10	7	3	0	25	3	24
Portugal	10	7	2	1	32	4	23
Slovakia	10	5	2	3	12	9	17
Hungary	10	3	3	4	14	10	12
Azerbaijan	10	1	1	8	6	26	4
Liechtenstein	10	1	1	8	2	39	4

GROUP 8

REPUBLIC OF IRELAND v CROATIA 2-0 (2-0)

Lansdowne Road, Dublin 05.09.1998

Referee: Vítor Manuel Melo Pereira (POR) Att: 34,000

IRELAND: Shay Given; Denis Irwin, Steve Staunton, Phil Babb, Kenny Cunningham; Roy Keane, Jason McAteer, Mark Kinsella, Damien Duff (46 Jeff Kenna); Keith O'Neill (5 Anthony Cascarino), Robbie Keane (61 Lee Carsley). Manager: Mick McCarthy

CROATIA: Drazen Ladic; Dario Simic, Igor Stimac, Zvonimir Soldo (77 Mario Tokic); Aljosa Asanovic, Zvonimir Boban, Krunoslav Jurcic, Igor Tudor (65 Petar Krpan), Robert Jarni; Silvio Maric (46 Igor Pamic), Mario Stanic. Manager: Miroslav Blazevic

Sent off: Stanic (70), Jurcic (72)

Goals: Irwin (4 pen), Roy Keane (15)

MACEDONIA v MALTA 4-0 (1-0)

Gradski, Skopje 06.09.1998

Referee: Jan Wegereef (HOL) Attendance: 4,000

MACEDONIA: Petar Milosevski; Mitko Stojkovski (80 Vlatko Gosev), Goce Sedloski, Igor Nikolovski (78 Dzevdet Šainovski), Goran Stavrevski; Goran Lazarevski, Milan Stojanoski (70 Artim Sakiri), Toni Micevski, Srdjan Zaharievski; Risto Bozinov, Viktor Trenevski. Trainer: Djoko Hadzievski

MALTA: Mario Muscat; Brian Said, Jeffrey Chetcuti, Jonathan Magri Overend, Darren Debono; David Camilleri, Carmel Busuttil, Gilbert Agius (70 Hubert Suda), Noel Turner; Joseph Brincat, Antoine Zahra (78 David Carabott). Trainer: Josef Ilic

Goals: Bozinov (20, 48), Sakiri (75, 80)

MALTA v CROATIA 1-4 (1-0)

National, Ta'Qali 10.10.1998

Referee: Bohdan Benedik (SVK) Attendance: 1,573

MALTA: Mario Muscat; Gilbert Agius (55 Ivan Zammit), Jeffrey Chetcuti, Michael Spiteri, Darren Debono; John Buttigieg, Carmel Busuttil, David Camilleri, Hubert Suda (57 Noel Turner); Joseph Brincat, Antoine Zahra (78 Paul Sixsmith). Trainer: Josef Ilic

CROATIA: Drazen Ladic; Dario Simic (81 Mario Tokic), Zvonimir Soldo, Igor Tudor; Danijel Saric, Robert Jarni (88 Mario Cvitanovic), Aljosa Asanovic, Silvio Maric, Zvonimir Boban; Davor Suker, Jurica Vucko (16 Davor Vugrinec). Trainer: Miroslav Blazevic

Goals: Suda (28 pen), D. Simic (54), Vugrinec (67, 74), Suker (80)

REPUBLIC OF IRELAND v MALTA 5-0 (2-0)

Lansdowne Road, Dublin 14.10.1998

Referee: Roy Helge Olsen (NOR) Attendance: 34,500

IRELAND: Shay Given; Jeff Kenna, Steve Staunton, Kenny Cunningham, Gary Breen; Roy Keane, Jason McAteer (85 Lee Carsley), Mark Kinsella, Damien Duff; Niall Quinn (73 Anthony Cascarino), Robbie Keane (82 Mark Kennedy). Trainer: Mick McCarthy

MALTA: Reggie Cini; Jeffrey Chetcuti, Michael Spiteri, Darren Debono, John Buttigieg, David Carabott; Paul Sixsmith (77 David Camilleri), Noel Turner, Joseph Brincat; Hubert Suda (66 Gilbert Agius), Antoine Zahra (70 Ivan Zammit). Trainer: Josef Ilic

Goals: Rob Keane (16, 19), Roy Keane (53), Quinn (62), Breen (81)

YUGOSLAVIA v REPUBLIC OF IRELAND 1-0 (0-0)

Beograd 18.11.1998

Referee: Karl-Erik Nilsson (SWE) Attendance: 28,250

YUGOSLAVIA: Ivica Kralj; Goran Djorovic, Miroslav Djukic, Sinisa Mihajlovic; Jovan Stankovic, Slavisa Jokanovic, Dejan Stankovic, Vladimir Jugovic (85 Nenad Grozdic), Dragan Stojkovic (46 Darko Kovacevic); Predrag Mijatovic, Savo Milosevic (77 Ljubinko Drulovic). Trainer: Milan Zivadinovic

IRELAND: Shay Given; Denis Irwin, Steve Staunton, Gary Breen, Kenny Cunningham; Roy Keane, Jason McAteer (83 Keith O'Neill), Mark Kinsella, Alan McLoughlin (73 David Connolly), Damien Duff; Niall Quinn (72 Anthony Cascarino). Trainer: Mick McCarthy

Goal: Mijatovic (64)

CROATIA v MACEDONIA 3-2 (2-1)

Maksimir, Zagreb 14.10.1998

Referee: Nikolai Levnikov (RUS) Attedance: 20,000

CROATIA: Drazen Ladic; Igor Stimac, Dario Simic, Igor Tudor; Mario Stanic (81 Krunoslav Jurcic), Robert Jarni, Zvonimir Soldo, Aljosa Asanovic (62 Danijel Saric), Zvonimir Boban; Silvio Maric, Davor Suker. Trainer: Miroslav Blazevic

MACEDONIA: Petar Milosevski; Goce Sedloski, Igor Nikolovski (78 Milan Stojanoski), Goran Stavrevski, Toni Micevski (46 Vlatko Gosev); Dzevdet Sainovski, Goran Lazarevski (60 Risto Bozinov), Srdjan Zaharievski, Viktor Trenevski; Sasa Ciric, Artim Sakiri. Trainer: Djoko Hadzievski

Goals: Ciric (2), Suker (16), Boban (45, 70), Sainovski (55)

MALTA v YUGOSLAVIA 0-3 (0-1)

National, Ta'Qali 10.02.1999

Referee: Pascal Garibian (FRA) Attendance: 1,781

MALTA: Ernest Barry; Brian Said, Noel Turner, Michael Spiteri, David Camilleri (73 Paul Sixsmith); John Buttigieg, Carmel Busuttil, Nicholas Saliba, David Carabott; Chucks Nwoko (82 Michael Cutajar), Gilbert Agius (59 Graham Bencini). Trainer: Josef Ilic

YUGOSLAVIA: Ivica Kralj; Zoran Mirkovic, Goran Djorovic, Slavisa Jokanovic, Miroslav Djukic; Jovan Stankovic (75 Djordje Tomic), Albert Nadj, Darko Kovacevic (70 Savo Milosevic), Sinisa Mihajlovic; Predrag Mijatovic, Dejan Stankovic (87 Nenad Grozdic). Trainer: Milan Zivadinovic

Goals: Nadj (22, 55), Milosevic (90)

MALTA v MACEDONIA 1-2 (0-0)

National, Ta'Qali 18.11.1998

Referee: Serghei Shmolik (BLS) Attendance: 1,295

MALTA: Mario Muscat; Paul Sixsmith, David Camilleri, Michael Spiteri, John Buttigieg; Darren Debono, Carmel Busuttil, Joseph Brincat, Nicholas Saliba (67 Noel Turner); Michael Cutajar (59 Gilbert Agius), Chucks Nwoko (54 David Carabott). Trainer: Josef Ilic

MACEDONIA: Petar Milosevski; Boban Babunski, Igor Nikolovski, Goce Sedloski, Dragan Veselinovski; Goran Stavrevski, Srdjan Zaharievski, Toni Micevski, Risto Bozinov (65 Viktor Trenevski); Dzevdet Sainovski, Artim Sakiri. Trainer: Djoko Hadzievski

Goals: Nikoloski (49), Zaharievski (62), Sixsmith (69)

MACEDONIA v CROATIA 1-1 (0-1)

Gradski, Skopje 05.06.1999

Referee: Hugh Dallas (SCO) Attendance: 12,000

MACEDONIA: Petar Milosevski; Dzevdet Sainovski, Goran Stavrevski, Milan Stojanoski, Igor Nikolovski; Boban Babunski (75 Srdjan Zaharievski), Vanco Trajcov (75 Georgi Hristov), Toni Micevski, Viktor Trenevski (46 Risto Bozinov); Sasa Ciric, Artim Sakiri. Trainer: Djoko Hadzievski

CROATIA: Drazen Ladic; Danijel Saric, Robert Jarni, Zvonimir Soldo, Goran Juric; Dario Simic, Aljosa Asanovic (87 Igor Biscan), Davor Vugrinec (64 Goran Vlaovic), Zvonimir Boban; Davor Suker, Alen Boksic (19 Milan Rapaic). Trainer: Miroslav Blazevic

Goals: Suker (19), Hristov (80)

YUGOSLAVIA v MALTA 4-1 (1-1)

Thessaloniki 08.06.1999

Referee: Morgan Norman (SWE) Attendance: 2,000

YUGOSLAVIA: Ivica Kralj; Zoran Mirkovic, Goran Djorovic, Miroslav Djukic, Nisa Saveljic, Albert Nadj (46 Savo Milosevic); Slavisa Jokanovic, Dragan Stojkovic (77 Ljubinko Drulovic), Dejan Stankovic (63 Nenad Grozdic); Predrag Mijatovic, Darko Kovacevic. Trainer: Milan Zivadinovic

MALTA: Ernest Barry; Jeffrey Chetcuti, Richard Buhagiar (80 Michael Cutajar), Darren Debono; Brian Said, John Buttigieg, Carmel Busuttil, Nicholas Saliba, David Camilleri (64 Joseph Brincat); David Carabott, Chucks Nwoko (83 Stefan Sultana). Trainer: Josef Ilic

Goals: Saliba (8), Mijatović (34), Milosević (49, 90), D. Kovacević (75)

CROATIA v MALTA 2-1 (1-0)

Maksimir, Zagreb 21.08.1999

Referee: Atanas Uzunov (BUL) Attendance: 20,000

CROATIA: Marijan Mrmic; Zvonimir Soldo, Igor Stimac, Dario Simic; Igor Biscan, Aljosa Asanovic, Josip Simic (46 Goran Vlaovic); Milan Rapaic, Mario Stanic (46 Alen Boksic), Davor Suker, Zvonimir Boban (17 Danijel Saric). Trainer: Miroslav Blazevic

MALTA: Ernest Barry; Silvio Vella, Darren Debono; Brian Said, David Camilleri, Carmel Busuttil (73 Ifanyi Okonikwo), Nicholas Saliba, Joseph Brincat; David Carabott, Chuks Nwoko (90 Adrian Mifsud), Gilbert Agius (85 Stefan Sultana). Trainer: Josef Ilic

Goals: Stanic (34), Soldo (55), Carabott (61)

REPUBLIC OF IRELAND v MACEDONIA 1-0 (0-0)

Lansdowne Road, Dublin 09.06.1999

Referee: Urs Maier (SWI) Attendance: 28,108

IRELAND: Alan Kelly; Stephen Carr, Denis Irwin, Lee Carsley, Kenny Cunningham; Gary Breen, Mark Kennedy, Mark Kinsella, Damien Duff (62 Kevin Kilbane); Niall Quinn (81 David Connolly), Robbie Keane (67 Anthony Cascarino). Manager: Mick McCarthy

MACEDONIA: Petar Milosevski; Dzevdet Sainovski (70 Goce Sedloski), Goran Stavrevski, Milan Stojanoski, Igor Nikolovski; Boban Babunski, Vanco Trajcov (46 Nedzmedin Memedi), Toni Micevski, Artim Sakiri; Sasa Ciric, Viktor Trenevski (76 Georgi Hristov). Trainer: Dzoko Hadzievski

Goal: Quinn (65)

REPUBLIC OF IRELAND v YUGOSLAVIA 2-1 (0-0)

Lansdowne Road, Dublin 01.09.1999

Referee: Pierluigi Collina (ITA) Attendance: 31,400

IRELAND: Alan Kelly; Denis Irwin (65 Stephen Carr), Kenny Cunningham, Gary Breen, Steve Staunton; Mark Kennedy, Roy Keane (69 Lee Carsley), Mark Kinsella, Kevin Kilbane; Robbie Keane, Niall Quinn (79 Anthony Cascarino). Manager: Mick McCarthy

YUGOSLAVIA: Aleksander Kocic; Slobodan Komljenovic, Miroslav Djukic, Sinisa Mihajlovic (69 Nisa Saveljic), Drazen Bolic; Dejan Govedarica, Albert Nadj (76 Darko Kovacevic), Dejan Stankovic, Dejan Savicevic (54 Ljubinko Drulovic); Predrag Mijatovic, Savo Milosevic. Trainer: Vujadin Boskov

Goals: Robbie Keane (54), Stankovic (61), Kennedy (70)

YUGOSLAVIA v CROATIA 0-0

Beograd 18.08.1999

Referee: Kim Milton Nielsen (DEN) Attedance: 52,600

YUGOSLAVIA: Aleksander Kocic; Slavisa Jokanovic, Sinisa Mihajlovic, Miroslav Djukic; Zoran Mirkovic, Dejan Stankovic, Jovan Stankovic, Albert Nadj, Goran Djorovic (46 Ljubinko Drulovic); Darko Kovacevic (66 Savo Milosevic), Predrag Mijatovic.

CROATIA: Drazen Ladic; Zvonimir Soldo, Dario Simic, Igor Stimac; Robert Jarni, Robert Kovac, Aljosa Asanovic, Krunoslav Jurcic; .Zvonimir Boban (81 Igor Biscan), Mario Stanic (46 Milan Rapaic), Davor Suker.

CROATIA v REPUBLIC OF IRELAND 1-0 (0-0)

Maksimir, Zagreb 04.09.1999

Referee: Manuel Diaz Vega (SPA) Attendance: 30,000

CROATIA: Drazen Ladic; Dario Simic, Robert Jarni, Zvonimir Soldo, Igor Stimac; Slaven Bilic (46 Tomislav Rukavina), Aljosa Asanovic, Mario Stanic (84 Josip Simic); Davor Suker, Milan Rapaic, Robert Kovac,

IRELAND: Alan Kelly; Stephen Carr, Steve Staunton, Gary Breen, Kenny Cunningham; Lee Carsley, Gary Kelly (72 Ian Harte), Mark Kinsella, Alan McLoughlin; Anthony Cascarino (82 Niall Quinn), Damien Duff (58 Kevin Kilbane).

Goal: Suker (90)

YUGOSLAVIA v MACEDONIA 3-1 (1-0)

Beograd 05.09.1999

Referee: Anders Frisk (SWE) Attendance: 22,000

YUGOSLAVIA: Ivica Kralj; Zoran Mirkovic, Slavisa Jokanovic, Miroslav Djukic, Mladen Krstajic; Nisa Saveljic, Dejan Stankovic (75 Dejan Govedarica), Predrag Mijatovic, Dragan Stojkovic (66 Dejan Savicevic); Savo Milosevic (82 Darko Kovacevic), Ljubinko Drulovic.

MACEDONIA: Petar Milosevski; Goran Stavrevski, Zoran Jovanovski (59 Zarko Serafimovski), Goran Lazarevski, Boban Babunski; Toni Savevski, Dragan Veselinovski, Toni Micevski (53 Marjan Gerasimovski), Sasa Ciric (77 Nedzmedin Memedi); Georgi Hristov, Artim Sakiri.

Goals: Stojkovic (37, 54), Ciric (64 pen), Savicevic (77)

MALTA v REPUBLIC OF IRELAND 2-3 (0-2)

National, Ta'Qali 08.09.1999

Referee: Sorin Corpodean (ROM) Attendance: 4,018

MALTA: Ernest Barry; Brian Said, Jeffrey Chetcuti (23 Richard Buhagiar), Darren Debono; David Carabott, John Buttigieg (29 Silvio Vella), Carmel Busuttil, Nicholas Saliba, David Camilleri; Chuks Nwoko, Gilbert Agius (67 Daniel Theuma). Trainer: Josef Ilic

IRELAND: Alan Kelly; Stephen Carr, Steve Staunton, Gary Breen (75 Ian Harte), Kenny Cunningham; Lee Carsley, Kevin Kilbane (65 Damien Duff), Mark Kinsella, Mark Kennedy (54 Alan McLoughlin); Niall Quinn, Robbie Keane.

Goals: Robbie Keane (12), Breen (20), Said (61), Carabott (68 pen), Staunton (72)

MACEDONIA v YUGOSLAVIA 2-4 (0-4)

Gradski, Skopje 08.09.1999

Referee: Lubos Michel (SVK) Attendance: 13,000

MACEDONIA: Petar Milosevski; Goran Stavrevski, Zoran Jovanovski, Goran Lazarevski, Boban Babunski, Dragan Veselinovski (40 Zarko Serafimovski); Toni Savevski (46 Marjan Gerasimovski), Toni Micevski (40 Dzevdet Sainovski), Sasa Ciric; Georgi Hristov, Artim Sakiri.

YUGOSLAVIA: Ivica Kralj; Zoran Mirkovic (46 Slobodan Komljenovic), Mladen Krstajic, Miroslav Djukic, Sinisa Mihajlovic; Slavisa Jokanovic, Dejan Stankovic, Ljubinko Drulovic, Dragan Stojkovic (46 Dejan Savicevic); Predrag Mijatovic, Savo Milosevic (82 Darko Kovacevic).

Goals: Milosevic (1), Babunski (4 og), Stankovic (14), Drulovic (38), Sakiri (60), Ciric (90)

MACEDONIA v REPUBLIC OF IRELAND 1-1 (0-1)

Gradski, Skopje 09.10.1999

Referee: Juan Antonio Fernández Marín (SPA) Att: 14,000

MACEDONIA: Antoni Filevski; Goran Stavrevski, Zoran Jovanovski (70 Srdjan Zaharievski), Goce Sedloski, Boban Babunski; Marjan Gerasimovski, Milan Stojanoski (56 Argend Bekiri), Toni Savevski, Goran Stanik (79 Nedzmedin Memedi); Georgi Hristov, Dzevdet Sainovski.

IRELAND: Alan Kelly; Denis Irwin, Kenny Cunningham, Gary Breen, Steve Staunton; Gary Kelly, Mark Kinsella, Alan McLoughlin, Mark Kennedy (87 Mathew Holland); Niall Quinn (79 Anthony Cascarino), Robbie Keane (68 Keith O'Neill)

Goals: Quinn (18), Stavrevski (90)

CROATIA v YUGOSLAVIA 2-2 (1-2)

Maksimir, Zagreb 09.10.1999

Referee: José Manuel Garcia-Aranda (SPA) Att: 39,000

CROATIA: Drazen Ladic; Goran Juric, Robert Kovac (62 Igor Biscan), Igor Tudor (83 Milan Rapaic), Tomislav Rukavina; Zvonimir Soldo, Mario Stanic, Aljosa Asanovic, Robert Jarni; Alen Boksic (75 Josip Simic), Davor Suker.

YUGOSLAVIA: Ivica Kralj; Zoran Mirkovic, Miroslav Djukic, Sinisa Mihajlovic, Goran Djorovic; Slavisa Jokanovic, Dragan Stojkovic (53 Drazen Bolic), Dejan Stankovic, Albert Nadj (56 Ljubinko Drulovic); Predrag Mijatovic (74 Dejan Savicevic), Savo Milosevic.

Sent off: Mirkovic (41)

Goals: Boksic (20), Mijatovic (26), Stankovic (31), Stanic (47)

	P	W	D	L	F	A	Pts
Yugoslavia	8	5	2	1	18	8	17
Rep. of Ireland	8	5	1	2	14	6	16
Croatia	8	4	3	1	13	9	15
Macedonia	8	2	2	4	13	14	8
Malta	8	0	0	8	6	27	0

GROUP 9

ESTONIA v FAROE ISLANDS 5-0 (2-0)

Kadriorg, Tallinn 04.06.1998

Referee: Martin Ingvarsson (SWE) Attedance: 3,500

ESTONIA: Mart Poom; Urmas Kirs, Janek Meet, Sergei Hohlov-Simson, Marek Lemsalu; Martin Reim, Andres Oper, Sergei Terehhov, Kristen Viikmäe (80 Ivan O'Konnel-Bronin); Indrek Zelinski, Marko Kristal. Trainer: Teitur Thordarsson

FAROE ISLANDS: Jens Martin Knudsen; Jens Kristian Hansen, Pol Thorsteinsson (84 Uni Arge), Jan Dam, Øssur Hansen; Todi Jonsson (84 Henning Jarnskor), Oli Johannesen, Jan Allan Møller (41 Jakup Mikkelsen), Allan Mørkøre; Julian Johnsson, John Petersen. Trainer: Alan Simonsen

Sent off: Knudsen (40).

Goals: Viikmäe (13), Reim (43 pen), Terehhov (77), Oper (87), Kirs (90)

BOSNIA HERZEGOVINA v FAROE ISLANDS 1-0 (0-0)

Olimpijski, Sarajevo 19.08.1998

Referee: Tomasz Mikulski (POL) Attendance: 20,000

BOSNIA HERZEGOVINA: Mirsad Dedic; Sead Kapetanovic, Mirsad Varesanovic, Mirsad Hibic, Sergei Barbarez (75 Jasmin Mujdza); Muhamed Konjic, Sead Halilovic, Hasan Salihamidzic (81 Nermin Sabic); Elvir Bolic (65 Edin Mujcin), Meho Kodro, Elvir Baljic. Trainer: Dzemaludin Musovic

FAROE ISLANDS: Jakup Mikkelsen; Hans Frodi Hansen, Pol Thorsteinsson, Oli Johannesen, Jens Kristian Hansen; Henning Jarnskor, Samal Joensen, Julian Johnsson, Allan Mørkøre; Uni Arge (77 Jakup a Borg), John Petersen.
Trainer: Allan Simonsen

Goal: Baljic (65)

LITHUANIA v SCOTLAND 0-0

Zalgiris, Vilnius 05.09.1998

Referee: Constantin Zotta (ROM) Attendance: 5,000

LITHUANIA: Gintaras Stauce; Gediminas Sugzda (61 Orestas Buitkus), Deividas Semberas, Raimondas Zutautas, Virginijus Baltusnikas; Tomas Zvirgzdauskas, Grazvydas Mikulenas (90 Vaidotas Slekys), Andrius Skerla, Aidas Preiksaitis; Aurelijus Skarbalius, Edgaras Jankauskas.
Trainer: Kestutis Latoza

SCOTLAND: James Leighton; Matt Elliott, Colin Calderwood (70 Callum Davidson), Colin Hendry, Thomas Boyd; Christian Dailly, Paul Lambert, Kevin Gallacher, John Collins; Alistair McCoist (82 Neil McCann), Darren Jackson (56 Barry Ferguson). Manager: Craig Brown

BOSNIA HERZEGOVINA v ESTONIA 1-1 (0-1)

Olimpijski, Sarajevo 05.09.1998

Referee: Charles Agius (MAL) Attendance: 14,750

BOSNIA HERZEGOVINA: Mirsad Dedic; Sead Kapetanovic, Jasmin Mujdza (65 Nermin Sabic), Muhamed Konjic, Mirsad Varesanovic; Mirsad Hibic, Suad Katana (55 Edin Mujcin), Sead Halilovic (77 Elvir Bolic), Sergei Barbarez; Hasan Salihamidzic, Elvir Baljic. Trainer: Dzemaludin Musovic

ESTONIA: Mart Poom; Maksim Smirnov, Urmas Kirs, Sergei Hohlov-Simson, Urmas Rooba (80 Janek Meet); Viktor Alonen, Sergei Terehhov, Andres Oper, Martin Reim; Marko Kristal, Indrek Zelinski (80 Kristen Viikmäe).
Trainer: Teitur Thordarsson

Goals: Hibic (28 og), Barbarez (75 pen)

FAROE ISLANDS v CZECH REPUBLIC 0-1 (0-0)

Svangaskard, Toftir 06.09.1998

Referee: Juha Hirviniemi (FIN) Attendance: 2,589

FAROE ISLANDS: Jakup Mikkelsen; Hans Frodi Hansen, Pol Thorsteinsson, Oli Johannesen, Jens Kristian Hansen; Henning Jarnskor, Uni Arge (78 Magni Jarnskor), Julian Johnsson, Allan Mørkøre, Todi Jonsson; John Petersen.
Trainer: Allan Simonsen

CZECH REPUBLIC: Tomás Postulka; Karel Rada, Tomás Votava, Martin Cizek (55 Patrik Berger), Jan Suchopárek; Jirí Nemec, Vratislav Lokvenc, Radek Bejbl (81 Radoslav Latal), Pavel Nedved; Karel Poborsky (81 Radek Sloncik), Vladimir Smicer. Trainer: Josef Chovanec

Sent off: Nedved (86)

Goal: Smicer (84)

BOSNIA HERZEGOVINA v CZECH REPUBLIC 1-3 (0-1)

Olimpijski, Sarajevo 10.10.1998

Referee: Domenico Messina (ITA) Attendance: 20,000

BOSNIA HERZEGOVINA: Mirsad Dedic; Mirsad Varesanovic, Sead Kapetanovic, Muhamed Konjic, Suad Katana; Mirsad Hibic, Edin Mujcin (62 Marko Topic), Sead Halilovic, Sergei Barbarez; Hasan Salihamidzic (64 Enes Demirovic), Elvir Baljic (69 Bakir Besirevic).
Trainer: Dzemaludin Musovic

CZECH REPUBLIC: Tomás Postulka; Radoslav Latal, Jan Suchopárek, Tomás Repka, Tomás Votava; Miroslav Baranek (71 Karel Rada), Radek Bejbl, Jirí Nemec, Patrik Berger; Vladimir Smicer (85 Radek Sloncik), Vratislav Lokvenc (80 Pavel Kuka). Trainer: Jozef Chovanec

Goals: Baranek (12), Smicer (59), Topic (88), Kuka (90)

LITHUANIA v FAROE ISLANDS 0-0

Zalgiris, Vilnius 10.10.1998

Referee: Charles Schaak (LUX) Attendance: 800

LITHUANIA: Gintaras Stauce; Andrius Skerla, Saulius Mikalajunas (74 Rimantas Zvingilas), Raimondas Zutautas, Virginijus Baltusnikas; Tomas Zvirgzdauskas, Grazvydas Mikulenas (46 Orestas Buitkus), Aurelijus Skarbalius, Aidas Preiksaitis; Valdas Ivanauskas, Edgaras Jankauskas. Trainer: Kestutis Latoza

FAROE ISLANDS: Jakup Mikkelsen; Oli Johannesen, Jens Kristian Hansen, Pol Thorsteinsson, Hans Frodi Hansen; Samal Joensen, Henning Jarnskor, Julian Johnsson, Uni Arge (88 Jakup a Borg); Todi Jonsson, John Petersen. Trainer: Allan Simonsen

SCOTLAND v ESTONIA 3-2 (0-1)

Tynecastle stadium, Edinburgh 10.10.1998

Referee: Joaquim Bento-Marques (POR) Att: 16,930

SCOTLAND: James Leighton; David Weir, Thomas Boyd, Colin Calderwood (56 Simon Donnelly), Colin Hendry; Callum Davidson, Kevin Gallacher (18 Darren Jackson), Billy McKinlay, Allan Johnston; Alistair McCoist (70 William Dodds), Ian Durrant. Manager: Craig Brown

ESTONIA: Mart Poom; Sergei Hohlov-Simson, Urmas Kirs, Urmas Rooba, Viktor Alonen; Martin Reim, Maksim Smirnov, Sergei Terehhov, Marko Kristal; Andres Oper, Indrek Zelinski (88 Kristen Viikmäe). Trainer: Teitur Thordarsson

Sent off: Kristal (83)

Goals: Hohlov-Simson (35, 78 og), Dodds (70, 84), Smirnov (76)

LITHUANIA v BOSNIA HERZEGOVINA 4-2 (1-1)

Zalgiris, Vilnius 14.10.1998

Referee: Manfred Schüttengruber (AUS) Attendance: 1,000

LITHUANIA: Gintaras Stauce; Andrius Skerla, Dainius Gleveckas, Tomas Zvirgzdauskas, Saulius Mikalajunas (87 Virginijus Baltusnikas); Raimondas Zutautas, Deividas Semberas, Aurelijus Skarbalius (64 Rimantas Zvingilas), Aidas Preiksaitis; Valdas Ivanauskas, Edgaras Jankauskas (80 Tomas Danilevicius). Trainer: Kestutis Latoza

BOSNIA HERZEGOVINA: Mirsad Dedic; Mirsad Varesanovic, Sead Kapetanovic (80 Jasmin Mujdza), Muhamed Konjic, Suad Katana (75 Marko Topic); Edin Ramcic, Edin Mujcin (80 Bakir Besirevic), Sead Halilovic, Sergei Barbarez; Hasan Salihamidzic, Elvir Baljic. Trainer: Dzemaludin Musovic

Sent off: Baljic (70)

Goals: Konjic (4), Ivanauskas (10, 67, 75), Baljic (68), Baltusnikas (90)

SCOTLAND v FAROE ISLANDS 2-1 (2-0)

Pittodrie, Aberdeen 14.10.1998

Referee: Kostas Kapitanis (GRE) Attendance: 18,517

SCOTLAND: Neil Sullivan; Matt Elliott, Colin Hendry, Callum Davidson, Thomas Boyd; David Weir, Billy McKinlay (46 Ian Durrant), Craig Burley; Allan Johnston (80 Stephen Glass), Simon Donnelly, William Dodds. Manager: Craig Brown

FAROE ISLANDS: Jakup Mikkelsen; Oli Johannesen, Jens Kristian Hansen, Pol Thorsteinsson, Hans Frodi Hansen; Julian Johnsson, Henning Jarnskor (81 John Hansen), Todi Jonsson, Uni Arge (69 Jakup a Borg); Samal Joensen, John Petersen. Trainer: Allan Simonsen

Goals: Burley (22), Dodds (45), Petersen (86 pen)

CZECH REPUBLIC v ESTONIA 4-1 (4-0)

Teplice 14.10.1998

Referee: Eyjolfur Olafsson (ICE) Attendance: 13,123

CZECH REPUBLIC: Tomás Postulka; Tomás Votava (53 Karel Rada), Jan Suchopárek, Tomás Repka, Radoslav Latal; Pavel Nedved, Radek Bejbl (80 Martin Cizek), Patrik Berger, Jirí Nemec; Vladimir Smicer, Vratislav Lokvenc (61 Pavel Kuka). Trainer: Josef Chovanec

ESTONIA: Mart Poom; Janek Meet, Sergei Hohlov-Simson, Martin Reim, Urmas Rooba; Kristen Viikmäe (46 Raivo Nommik), Maksim Smirnov (46 Argo Arbeiter), Viktor Alonen, Sergei Terehhov (62 Ivan O'Konnel-Bronin); Andres Oper, Indrek Zelinski. Trainer: Teitur Thordarsson

Goals: Nedved (8), Berger (21, 41), Lokvenc (45), Arbeiter (90)

CZECH REPUBLIC v LITHUANIA 2-0 (1-0)

Teplice 27.03.1999

Referee: Attila Juhos (HUNG) Attendance: 14,658

CZECH REPUBLIC: Pavel Srnicek; Jan Suchopárek, Michal Hornák, Tomás Repka; Karel Poborsky (63 Pavel Kuka), Pavel Nedved, Martin Hasek, Jirí Nemec, Patrik Berger; Vratislav Lokvenc (71 Jan Koller), Vladimir Smicer (80 Miroslav Baranek). Trainer: Jozef Chovanek

LITHUANIA: Gintaras Stauce; Raimondas Vainoras, Andrius Skerla, Tomas Zvirgzdauskas, Deividas Semberas; Aurelijus Skarbalius, Aidas Preiksaitis, Saulius Mikalajunas (78 Grazvydas Mikulenas), Darius Zutautas; Edgaras Jankauskas (67 Rimantas Zvingilas), Valdas Ivanauskas (83 Orestas Buitkus). Trainer: Kestutis Latoza

Goals: Hornak (10), Berger (74 pen)

LITHUANIA v ESTONIA 1-2 (0-0)

Zalgiris, Vilnius 31.03.1999

Referee: Alfredo Trentalange (ITA) Attendance: 3,000

LITHUANIA: Gintaras Stauce; Raimondas Vainoras, Andrius Skerla, Tomas Zvirgzdauskas, Deividas Semberas; Aurelijus Skarbalius (36 Dainius Gleveckas, 56 Orestas Buitkus), Aidas Preiksaitis, Saulius Mikalajunas, Raimondas Zutautas; Darius Maciulevicius, Grazvydas Mikulenas (46 Arturas Fomenka). Trainer: Kestutis Latoza

ESTONIA: Mart Poom; Marek Lemsalu, Urmas Kirs, Sergei Hohlov-Simson, Erko Saviauk; Mark Shvets (70 Marko Kristal), Sergei Terehhov, Andres Oper (67 Indrek Zelinski), Maksim Smirnov (90 Viktor Alonen); Martin Reim, Kristen Viikmäe. Trainer: Teitur Thordarsson

Goals: Terehhov (49, 77), Fomenka (83)

BOSNIA HERZEGOVINA v LITHUANIA 2-0 (1-0)

Olimpijski, Sarajevo 05.06.1999

Referee: Arturo Dauden Ibañez (SPA) Attendance: 6,100

BOSNIA HERZEGOVINA: Mirsad Dedic; Edin Smajic, Sead Kapetanovic, Mirsad Varesanovic, Mirsad Hibic; Bakir Besirevic, Senad Repuh (85 Elvir Bolic), Nermin Sabic; Meho Kodro (79 Edin Mujcin), Hasan Salihamidzic, Marko Topic (86 Almir Turkovic). Trainer: Faruk Hadzibegic

LITHUANIA: Pavelas Leusas; Andrius Skerla, Marius Skinderis, Darius Gvildys, Tomas Kancelskis; Tomas Zvirgzdauskas, Saulius Mikalajunas, Valdas Ivanauskas, Aidas Preiksaitis; Deividas Semberas (64 Grazvydas Mikulenas), Darius Maciulevicius (46 Arturas Fomenka). Trainer: Kestutis Latoza

Sent off: Salilhamidzic (67), Gvildys (82)

Goals: Kodro (26 pen), Bolic (90)

SCOTLAND v CZECH REPUBLIC 1-2 (0-2)

Celtic Park, Glasgow 31.03.1999

Referee: Kim-Milton Nielsen (DEN) Attendance: 44,513

SCOTLAND: Neil Sullivan; David Weir, Thomas Boyd, Paul Lambert, Matt Elliott; Callum Davidson (52 Allan Johnston), David Hopkin, Craig Burley, Gary McAllister (64 Don Hutchison); Eoin Jess, Neil McCann. Manager: Craig Brown

CZECH REPUBLIC: Pavel Srnicek; Tomás Votava, Jan Suchopárek, Pavel Nedved, Michal Hornak; Martin Hasek, Jirí Nemec, Karel Poborsky (76 Karel Rada), Vratislav Lokvenc (70 Pavel Kuka); Vladimir Smicer (84 Miroslav Baranek), Patrik Berger. Trainer: Jozef Chovanec

Goals: Elliott (27 og), Smicer (35), Jess (68)

ESTONIA v CZECH REPUBLIC 0-2 (0-1)

Tallinn 05.06.1999

Referee: Juan Ansuategui Roca (SPA) Attendance: 2,900

ESTONIA: Mart Poom; Marek Lemsalu, Urmas Kirs, Sergei Hohlov-Simson, Erko Saviauk; Viktor Alonen (65 Maksim Smirnov, 74 Ivan O'Konnel-Bronin), Sergei Terehhov (80 Mark Shvets), Andres Oper, Martin Reim; Marko Kristal, Kristen Viikmäe. Trainer: Teitur Thordarsson

CZECH REPUBLIC: Pavel Srnicek; Michal Hornak, Jan Suchopárek, Tomás Repka; Martin Hasek, Jirí Nemec, Karel Poborsky, Patrik Berger, Pavel Nedved (86 Tomás Galasek); Vladimir Smicer (65 Pavel Kuka), Vratislav Lokvenc (70 Jan Koller). Trainer: Jozef Chovanec

Goals: Berger (45), Koller (83)

FAROE ISLANDS v SCOTLAND 1-1 (0-1)

Svangaskard, Toftir 05.06.1999

Referee: Philippe Kalt (FRA) Attendance: 4,500

FAROE ISLANDS: Jakup Mikkelsen; Oli Johannesen, Øssur Hansen (86 John Hansen), Pol Thorsteinsson, Hans Frodi Hansen; Samal Joensen, Julian Johnsson, Joannes Joensen (69 Jakup a Borg), Allan Mørkøre; Todi Jonsson, John Petersen (82 Uni Arge). Trainer: Allan Simonsen

SCOTLAND: Neil Sullivan; David Weir, Colin Calderwood, Matt Elliott, Thomas Boyd; Callum Davidson, William Dodds, Paul Lambert, Kevin Gallacher (89 Eoin Jess); Ian Durrant (46 Colin Cameron), Allan Johnston (86 Scot Gemmill). Manager: Craig Brown

Sent off: Elliot (45)

Goals: Johnston (38), H.F. Hansen (90)

CZECH REPUBLIC v SCOTLAND 3-2 (0-1)

Sparta, Praha 09.06.1999

Referee: Hellmut Krug (W. GER) Attendance: 21,000

CZECH REPUBLIC: Pavel Srnicek; Tomás Repka, Jan Suchopárek, Michal Hornak; Martin Hasek (61 Miroslav Baranek), Jirí Nemec, Pavel Nedved, Karel Poborsky (69 Jan Koller), Vratislav Lokvenc (69 Pavel Kuka); Vladimir Smicer, Patrik Berger. Trainer: Jozef Chovanec

SCOTLAND: Neil Sullivan; David Weir, Thomas Boyd, Colin Calderwood, Paul Ritchie; Callum Davidson, William Dodds, Paul Lambert, Ian Durrant (71 Eoin Jess); Kevin Gallacher, Allan Johnston. Manager: Craig Brown

Goals: Ritchie (30), Johnston (63), Repka (65), Kuka (75), Koller (87)

FAROE ISLANDS v BOSNIA HERZEGOVINA 2-2 (1-1)

Svangaskard, Toftir 09.06.1999

Referee: Peter Jones (ENG) Attendance: 4,600

FAROE ISLANDS: Jakup Mikkelsen; Oli Johannesen, Julian Johnsson, Pol Thorsteinsson, Samal Joensen; Hans Frodi Hansen, Øssur Hansen (65 Henning Jarnskor), Allan Mørkøre, Uni Arge (87 Joannes Joensen); Todi Jonsson, John Petersen. Trainer: Allan Simonsen

BOSNIA HERZEGOVINA: Mirsad Dedic; Edin Smajic, Bakir Besirevic, Mirsad Varesanovic, Mirsad Hibic; Almir Turkovic (63 Omer Joldic), Senad Repuh (78 Adnan Osmanhodzic), Nermin Sabic, Elvir Bolic; Edin Mujcin, Marko Topic (85 Samir Muratovic). Trainer: Faruk Hadzibegic

Goals: Bolic (13, 49), Arge (38, 47)

FAROE ISLANDS v ESTONIA 0-2 (0-2)

Svangaskard, Toftir 04.09.1999

Referee: Edo Trivkovic (CRO) Attendance: 2,300

FAROE ISLANDS: Jakup Mikkelsen; Hans Frodi Hansen, Jens Kristian Hansen, Pol Thorsteinsson (75 Øssur Hansen), Oli Johannesen, Samal Joensen (87 Henning Jarnskor), Julian Johnsson, Todi Jonsson, Allan Mørkøre, Uni Arge (87 Jakup a Borg), John Petersen.

ESTONIA: Mart Poom; Raio Piiroja, Urmas Kirs, Sergei Hohlov-Simson, Erko Saviauk (80 Marek Lemsalu); Viktor Alonen, Sergei Terehhov, Aivar Anniste (67 Ivan O'Konnel-Bronin), Marko Kristal; Martin Reim, Indrek Zelinski (75 Dmitri Ustritski).

Goals: Reim (88), Piiroja (90)

ESTONIA v LITHUANIA 1-2 (1-0)

Tallinn 09.06.1999

Referee: Hermann Albrecht (GER) Attendance: 2,000

ESTONIA: Mart Poom; Marek Lemsalu, Urmas Kirs, Urmas Kaal, Kristen Viikmäe; Viktor Alonen, Sergei Terehhov (75 Ivan O'Konnel-Bronin), Marko Kristal (80 Mark Shvets), Martin Reim; Andres Oper, Indrek Zelinski. Trainer: Teitur Thordarsson

LITHUANIA: Pavelas Leusas; Andrius Skerla, Tomas Zvirgzdauskas, Raimondas Zutautas, Marius Skinderis; Aurelijus Skarbalius, Darius Zutautas (46 Darius Maciulevicius), Valdas Ivanauskas (88 Aidas Preiksaitis), Saulius Mikalajunas; Tomas Ramelis, Tomas Razanauskas. Trainer: Kestutis Latoza

Goals: Oper (8), Ramelis (51), Maciulevicius (56)

LITHUANIA v CZECH REPUBLIC 0-4 (0-0)

Zalgiris, Vilnius 04.09.1999

Referee: Jacek Granat (Pol) Attendance: 3,000

LITHUANIA: Gintaras Stauce; Donatas Vencevicius, Andrius Tereskinas, Tomas Razanauskas, Saulius Mikalajunas, Darius Zutautas, Tomas Zvirgzdauskas, Deividas Semberas (55 Andrius Skerla), Valdas Ivanauskas (38 Tomas Ramelis), Aidas Preiksaitis (81 Tomas Danilevicius), Edgaras Jankauskas.

CZECH REPUBLIC: Pavel Srnicek; Pavel Nedved (75 Miroslav Baranek), Karel Rada, Tomás Repka, Marek Nikl, Jirí Nemec (71 Pavel Horvath), Patrik Berger, Pavel Kuka, Radek Bejbl, Karel Poborsky (74 Radek Sloncik), Jan Koller.

Sent off: Jankauskas (20)

Goals: Nedved (60, 63), Koller (69, 90)

BOSNIA HERZEGOVINA v SCOTLAND 1-2 (1-2)

Kosevo, Sarajevo 04.09.1999

Referee: Nikolai Levnikov (RUS) Attendance: 26,000

BOSNIA HERZEGOVINA: Mirsad Dedic; Omer Joldic (77 Senad Repuh), Jasmin Mujdza (77 Enes Demirovic), Muhamed Konjic (60 Edin Mujcin), Mirsad Hibic; Bakir Besirevic, Elvir Bolic, Sead Halilovic, Sergei Barbarez; Meho Kodro, Marko Topic.

SCOTLAND: Neil Sullivan; David Weir, David Hopkin, Colin Calderwood (46 Christian Dailly), Colin Hendry, Barry Ferguson (69 Ian Durrant), William Dodds, Craig Burley, Neil McCann (74 Kevin Gallacher), Don Hutchison, John Collins.

Goals: Hutchison (13), Bolic (23), Dodds (45)

FAROE ISLANDS v LITHUANIA 0-1 (0-0)

Torshavn 08.09.1999

Referee: Eric Romain (BEL) Attendance: 450

FAROE ISLANDS: Jakup Mikkelsen; Oli Johannesen, Jens Kristian Hansen, Pol Thorsteinsson, Hans Frodi Hansen, Øssur Hansen, Henning Jarnskor (84 Hedin a Lakjuni), Julian Johnsson (65 Frodi Benjaminsen), Allan Mørkøre, Todi Jonsson, Uni Arge (46 Jakup a Borg).

LITHUANIA: Gintaras Stauce (79 Rodimanskas); Darius Zutautas, Donatas Vencevicius, Andrius Tereskinas, Tomas Razanauskas (77 Andrius Skerla), Tomas Zvirgzdauskas, Deividas Semberas, Saulius Mikalajunas, Aidas Preiksaitis, Marius Skinderis, Tomas Ramelis.

Goal: Ramelis (55)

ESTONIA v SCOTLAND 0-0

Kadriorg, Tallinn 08.09.1999

Referee: Fritz Stuchlik (AUS) Attendance: 5,000

ESTONIA: Mart Poom; Raio Piiroja, Urmas Kirs, Sergei Hohlov-Simson, Erko Saviauk; Aivar Anniste, Sergei Terehhov, Marko Kristal, Martin Reim; Andres Oper, Ivan O'Konnel-Bronin (46 Indrek Zelinski).

SCOTLAND: Neil Sullivan; David Weir, Callum Davidson, Christian Dailly, Colin Hendry, Ian Durrant (68 Barry Ferguson), William Dodds, Craig Burley, Allan Johnston (56 Neil McCann), Don Hutchison, John Collins.

ESTONIA v BOSNIA HERZEGOVINA 1-4 (1-1)

Tallinn 09.10.1999

Referee: Roelof Luinge (HOL) Attendance: 1,200

ESTONIA: Martin Kaalma; Raio Piiroja, Urmas Kirs, Sergei Hohlov-Simson, Aivar Anniste (61 Erko Saviauk); Viktor Alonen, Sergei Terehhov (74 Ivan O'Konnel-Bronin), Andres Oper, Indrek Zelinski (40 Kristen Viikmäe); Marko Kristal, Martin Reim.

BOSNIA HERZEGOVINA: Adnan Guso; Omer Joldić, Sead Kapetanović, Faruk Hujdurović, Mirsad Varesanović; Bakir Besirević, Faruk Ihtijarević, Nermin Sabić (60 Samir Duro), Marko Topić; Elvir Bolić (80 Edin Mujcin), Elvir Baljić (89 Alen Avdić).

Goals: Oper (4), Baljic (42, 57, 67, 87)

CZECH REPUBLIC v BOSNIA HERZEGOVINA 3-0 (1-0)

Teplice 08.09.1999

Referee: Karl-Erik Nilsson (SWE) Attendance: 10,125

CZECH REPUBLIC: Pavel Srnicek; Tomás Repka, Jan Suchopárek, Pavel Nedved, Marek Nikl, Radek Bejbl, Jirí Nemec, Karel Poborsky, Pavel Kuka (79 Miroslav Baranek), Jan Koller (57 Vratislav Lokvenc), Patrik Berger.

BOSNIA HERZEGOVINA: Mirsad Dedic; Omer Joldic (71 Senad Repuh), Muhamed Konjic, Mirsad Hibic; Bakir Besirevic, Marko Topic (71 Enes Demirovic), Mirsad Varesanovic, Nermin Sabic; Faruk Ihtijarevic (71 Elvir Bolic), Sergei Barbarez, Meho Kodro.

Goals: Koller (26), Berger (59 pen), Poborsky (67)

CZECH REPUBLIC v FAROE ISLANDS 2-0 (1-0)

Praha 09.10.1999

Referee: Marcel Lică (ROM) Attendance: 21,362

CZECH REPUBLIC: Pavel Srnicek; Karel Rada, Jan Suchopárek (74 Pavel Verbir), Tomás Repka; Karel Poborsky, Miroslav Baranek (59 Michal Hornak), Radek Bejbl (66 Pavel Horvath), Patrik Berger, Jirí Nemec; Jan Koller, Vladimir Smicer.

FAROE ISLANDS: Jens Martin Knudsen; Pol Thorsteinsson, Jens Kristian Hansen, Oli Johannesen, Hans Frodi Hansen; Allan Mørkøre, Samal Joensen, Julian Johnsson, Henning Jarnskor (89 Øssur Hansen), John Petersen (72 Rogvi Jakobsen), Todi Jonsson.

Sent off: Berger (59), Thorsteinsson (59), Knudsen (60)

Goals: Koller (11), Verbir (84)

SCOTLAND v BOSNIA HERZEGOVINA 1-0 (1-0)

Ibox, Glasgow 05.10.1999

Referee: Leif Sundell (SWE) Attendance: 30,574

SCOTLAND: Neil Sullivan; Callum Davidson, David Weir, Paul Lambert, Colin Hendry (37 Colin Calderwood), Kevin Gallacher (80 Mark Burchill), Christian Dailly, William Dodds (90 Gary McSwegan), David Hopkin, John Collins, Craig Burley.

BOSNIA HERZEGOVINA: Adnan Guso; Sead Kapetanovic, Bakir Besirevic, Faruk Hujdurovic, Mirsad Varesanovic; Faruk Ihtijarevic (77 Marko Topic), Nermin Sabic, Elvir Bolic, Sergei Barbarez; Edin Mujcin (83 Alen Avdic), Elvir Baljic.

Goal: Collins (26 pen)

SCOTLAND v LITHUANIA 3-0 (0-0)

Hampden, Glasgow 09.10.1999

Referee: Stéphane Bré (FRA) Attendance: 22,059

SCOTLAND: Jonathan Gould; David Weir, Callum Davidson, Paul Lambert, Brian O'Neil; Paul Ritchie, Christian Dailly, Craig Burley (46 Colin Cameron), Gary McSwegan (82 Kevin Gallacher); Mark Burchill (79 William Dodds), Don Hutchison.

LITHUANIA: Pavelas Leusas; Andrius Skerla, Marius Skinderis, Andrius Tereskinas (65 Arturas Fomenka), Darius Zutautas, Tomas Zvirgzdauskas; Irmantas Stumbrys (54 Darius Maciulevicius), Saulius Mikalajunas, Tomas Razanauskas, Grazvydas Mikulenas; Vidas Dancenko (54 Donatas Vencevicius).

Goals: Hutchison (48), McSwegan (49), Cameron (89)

	P	W	D	L	F	A	Pts
Czech Republic	10	10	0	0	26	5	30
Scotland	10	5	3	2	15	10	18
Bosnia-Herzeg.	10	3	2	5	14	17	11
(vs Lith. + Eston.	*4*	*2*	*1*	*1*	*9*	*6*	*7)*
Lithuania	10	3	2	5	8	16	11
(vs Bosnia + Est.	*4*	*2*	*0*	*2*	*7*	*7*	*6)*
Estonia	10	3	2	5	15	17	11
(vs Bos. + Lith.	*4*	*1*	*1*	*2*	*5*	*8*	*4)*
Faroe Islands	10	0	3	7	4	17	3

Tie-breaker rules for the EC2000 qualifying groups to be applied when two (or more) teams finish equal on points:

1) Points in mutual encounters between those teams.

2) Goal difference in mutual encounters between those teams.

3) Away goals in mutual encounters between those teams.

4) Total goal difference (against all other teams)

5) Total goals scored (against all other teams)

6) Total away goals scored (against all other teams)

7) Fair play

Note on qualifying 2nd placed teams:

The best second place finisher (computed by records against teams finishing first, third and fourth) qualifies automatically; the other eight enter a random draw for two-legged playoff matches from which four more countries qualify

QUALIFICATION PLAY-OFFS

SCOTLAND v ENGLAND 0-2 (0-2)

Hampden Park, Glasgow 13.11.1999

Referee: Manuel Diaz Vega (SPA) Attendance: 52,000

SCOTLAND: Neil Sullivan; David Weir, Paul Ritchie, Christian Dailly, Colin Hendry; Barry Ferguson, William Dodds, Craig Burley, John Collins; Kevin Gallacher (82 Mark Burchill), Don Hutchison.

ENGLAND: David Seaman; Sol Campbell, Phillip Neville, Paul Ince, Tony Adams, Martin Keown; David Beckham, Paul Scholes, Jamie Redknapp; Alan Shearer, Michael Owen (67 Andy Cole). Manager: Kevin Keegan

Goals: Scholes (21, 42)

ENGLAND v SCOTLAND 0-1 (0-1)

Wembley, London 17.11.1999

Referee: Pierluigi Collina (ITA) Attendance: 75,848

ENGLAND: David Seaman; Sol Campbell, Phillip Neville, Paul Ince, Tony Adams, Gareth Southgate; David Beckham, Paul Scholes (89 Ray Parlour), Jamie Redknapp; Alan Shearer, Michael Owen (63 Emile Heskey). Manager: Kevin Keegan

SCOTLAND: Neil Sullivan; David Weir, Callum Davidson, Christian Dailly, Colin Hendry; Barry Ferguson, William Dodds, Craig Burley, John Collins; Neil McCann (74 Mark Burchill), Don Hutchison.

Goal: Hutchison (39)

ISRAEL v DENMARK 0-5 (0-2)

Ramat Gan 13.11.1999

Referee: David Elleray (ENG) Attendance: 43,000

ISRAEL: Dudu Avate; Ran Ben Shimon (38 Idan Tal), Alon Harazi, David Amsalem, Arik Benado; Yossi Abuksis (38 Yossi Benayoun), Tal Banin (79 Jan Telasnikov), Alon Hazan, Haim Revivo; Amir Torjman, Eyal Berkovic. Trainer: Shlomo Sharf

DENMARK: Peter Schmeichel; Stig Tøfting (79 Bjarne Goldbaek), René Henriksen, Jes Høgh, Jan Heintze; Thomas Helveg, Brian Steen Nielsen, Jesper Grønkjær, Ebbe Sand; Jon Dahl Tomasson (79 Søren Andersen), Martin Jørgensen (86 Michael Schjønberg).

Sent off: Revivo (57)

Goals: Tomasson (2, 34), Tøfting (66), Jørgensen (69), B.S. Nielsen (72)

DENMARK v ISRAEL 3-0 (2-0)

Idraetsparken, København 17.11.1999

Referee: Vítor Manuel Melo Pereira (POR) Att: 41,186

DENMARK: Peter Schmeichel (19 Thomas Sorensen); Thomas Helveg (71 Jacob Laursen), René Henriksen, Jes Høgh, Jan Heintze; Martin Jørgensen, Stig Tøfting, Brian Steen Nielsen, Jesper Grønkjær (82 Michael Schjønberg); Jon Dahl Tomasson, Ebbe Sand.

ISRAEL: Shavit Elimelech; Alon Harazi, David Amsalem (43 Walid Badir), Amir Shelach, Offer Talker; Alon Hazan, Tal Banin, Idan Tal (28 Jan Telasnikov), Eyal Berkovic, Yossi Benayoun (73 Shimon Gershon); Amir Torjman. Trainer: Shlomo Sharf

Goals: Sand (4), B.S. Nielsen (15), Tomasson (64)

REPUBLIC OF IRELAND v TURKEY 1-1 (0-0)

Landsdowne Road, Dublin 13.11.1999

Referee: Anders Frisk (SWE) Attendance: 33,610

IRELAND: Alan Kelly (61 Dean Kiely); Stephen Carr, Denis Irwin, Gary Breen, Kenny Cunningham; Roy Keane, Rory Delap (53 Damien Duff), Lee Carsley, Kevin Kilbane; Anthony Cascarino (75 David Connolly), Robbie Keane.

TURKEY: Reçber Rüstü; Ali Eren Beserler, Ogün Temizkanoglu, Tayfur Havutçu, Alpay Özalan; Abdullah Ercan, Tayfun Korkut, Ümit Davala (46 Arif Erdem), Hakan Unsal (67 Tugay Kerimoglu); Hakan Şükür, Sergen Yalçin (85 Mert Korkmaz).

Goals: Robbie Keane (79), Tayfur (83 pen)

TURKEY v REPUBLIC OF IRELAND 0-0

Bursa 17.11.1999

Referee: Gilles Veissière (FRA) Attendance: 19,900

TURKEY: Reçber Rüştü (38 Engin Ipekoglu); Ali Eren Beserler, Ogün Temizkanoglu, Tayfur Havutçu, Alpay Özalan; Arif Erdem (83 Ümit Davala), Abdullah Ercan, Okan Buruk, Hakan Şükür; Sergen Yalçin, Tayfun Korkut (46 Fatih Akyel).

IRELAND: Dean Kiely; Stephen Carr (5 Jeff Kenna, 79 Anthony Cascarino), Kenny Cunningham, Gary Breen, Denis Irwin; Rory Delap, Mark Kinsella, Roy Keane, Kevin Kilbane; Niall Quinn, David Connolly (70 Damien Duff).

SLOVENIA v UKRAINE 2-1 (0-1)

Ljubljana 13.11.1999

Referee: Urs Meier (SWI) Attendance: 8,000

SLOVENIA: Mladen Dabanovic; Amir Karic, Mladen Rudonja, Darko Milanic (73 Milan Osterc), Zeljko Milinovic; Aleksander Knavs, Dzoni Novak, Ales Ceh, Miran Pavlin; Saso Udovic (46 Milenko Acimovic), Zlatko Zahovic.

UKRAINE: Olexandr Shovkovskyi; Dmitri Parfenov, Andriy Gusin, Alexander Holovko, Vladyslav Vashchuk; Yuriy Dmitrulin, Sergiy Kandaurov (56 Vasyl Kardash), Serhiy Popov, Vitaliy Kosovskyi; Andriy Shevchenko, Serhiy Rebrov.

Sent off: Parfenov (60), Gusin (88)

Goals: Shevchenko (33), Zahovic (53), Acimovic (84)

UKRAINE v SLOVENIA 1-1 (0-0)

Olympiyski, Kyiv 17.11.1999

Referee: Bernd Heynemann (GER) Attendance: 52,800

UKRAINE: Olexandr Shovkovskyi; Oleh Luzhnyi, Vladyslav Vashchuk, Alexander Holovko, Yuriy Dmitrulin; Serhiy Fedorov, Vitaliy Kosovskyi (73 Serhiy Popov), Sergiy Kandaurov (46 Serhiy Kovalev), Serhiy Skachenko (57 Gennadiy Moroz); Serhiy Rebrov, Andriy Shevchenko.

SLOVENIA: Mladen Dabanovic; Marinko Galic, Darko Milanic, Zeljko Milinovic, Dzoni Novak; Amir Karic (73 Milan Osterc), Ales Ceh, Miran Pavlin, Zlatko Zahovic; Saso Udovic (57 Milenko Acimovic), Mladen Rudonja.

Goals: Rebrov (67 pen), Pavlin (77)

FINALS in BELGIUM and HOLLAND

GROUP A

GERMANY v ROMANIA 1-1 (1-1)

Liege 12.06.2000

Referee: Kim Milton Nielsen (DEN) Attendance: 28,500

GERMANY: Oliver Kahn; Thomas Linke (46 Marko Rehmer), Lothar Matthäus (77 Sebastian Deisler), Jens Nowotny; Markus Babbel, Mehmet Scholl, Jens Jeremies, Thomas Hässler (73 Dietmar Hamann), Christian Ziege; Paulo Roberto Rink, Oliver Bierhoff. Trainer: Erich Ribbeck

ROMANIA: Bogdan Stelea; Liviu Ciobotariu, Gheorghe Popescu, Iulian Filipescu, Cristian Chivu; Dan Petrescu (69 Cosmin Contra), Constantin Gâlcă, Dorinel Munteanu, Gheorghe Hagi (73 Adrian Mutu); Viorel Moldovan (85 Ioan Lupescu), Adrian Ilie. Trainer: Emerich Ienei

Goals: Moldovan (5), Scholl (28)

PORTUGAL v ENGLAND 3-2 (2-2)

Philips, Eindhoven 12.06.2000

Referee: Anders Frisk (SWE) Attendance: 33,000

PORTUGAL: VÍTOR Manuel Martins BAÍA; ABEL Luis da Silva Costa XAVIER, FERNANDO Manuel Silva COUTO, JORGE Paulo COSTA Almeida, DIMAS Manuel Marques Teixeira; FIGO Luis Filipe Madeira, José Luís da Cruz VIDIGAL, RUI Manuel César COSTA (85 Roberto Deus Severo BETO), PAULO Jorge Gomes BENTO; NUNO GOMES Miguel Soares Pereira Ribeiro (90 Nuno Gonçalves da Rocha CAPUCHO), JOÃO Manuel Vieira PINTO (76 SÉRGIO Paulo Marceneiro CONCEIÇAO).
Trainer: HUMBERTO Manuel de Jesus COELHO.

ENGLAND: David Seaman; Gary Neville, Tony Adams (82 Martin Keown), Sol Campbell, Phillip Neville; David Beckham, Paul Ince, Paul Scholes, Steve McManaman (58 Dennis Wise); Alan Shearer, Michael Owen (46 Emile Heskey).
Trainer: Kevin Keegan

Goals: Scholes (3), McManaman (18), Figo (22), João Pinto (37), Nuno Gomes (59)

ENGLAND v GERMANY 1-0 (0-0)

Stade Communal, Charleroi 17.06.2000

Referee: Pierluigi Collina (ITA) Attendance: 30,000

ENGLAND: David Seaman; Gary Neville, Martin Keown, Sol Campbell, Philip Neville; David Beckham, Paul Ince, Paul Scholes (72 Nick Barmby), Dennis Wise; Alan Shearer, Michael Owen (61 Steven Gerrard). Trainer: Kevin Keegan

GERMANY: Oliver Kahn; Markus Babbel, Lothar Matthäus, Jens Nowotny; Sebastian Deisler (72 Michael Ballack), Dietmar Hamann, Mehmet Scholl, Jens Jeremies (78 Marco Bode), Christian Ziege; Carsten Jancker, Ulf Kirsten (70 Paulo Roberto Rink. Trainer: Erich Ribbeck

Goal: Shearer (53)

ROMANIA v PORTUGAL 0-1 (0-0)

Gelre Dome, Arnhem 17.06.2000

Referee: Gilles Veissière (FRA) Attendance: 24,000

ROMANIA: Bogdan Stelea; Cosmin Contra, Gheorghe Popescu, Iulian Filipescu, Cristian Chivu; Dan Petrescu (64 Florentin Petre), Constantin Gâlcă, Gheorghe Hagi, Dorinel Munteanu; Adrian Ilie (78 Laurentiu Roşu), Viorel Moldovan (69 Ionel Ganea). Trainer: Emerich Ienei

PORTUGAL: VÍTOR Manuel Martins BAÍA; Carlos Alberto Oliveira SECRETÁRIO, FERNANDO Manuel Silva COUTO, JORGE Paulo COSTA Almeida, DIMAS Manuel Marques Teixeira; PAULO Jorge Gomes BENTO, RUI Manuel César COSTA (87 Francisco DA COSTA), José Luís da Cruz VIDIGAL; FIGO Luis Filipe Madeira, NUNO GOMES Miguel Soares Pereira Ribeiro (57 Ricardo Manuel da Silva SÁ PINTO), JOÃO Manuel Vieira PINTO (57 SÉRGIO Paulo Marceneiro CONCEIÇAO).
Trainer: HUMBERTO Manuel de Jesus COELHO

Goal: Da Costa (90)

ENGLAND v ROMANIA 2-3 (2-1)

Stade Communal, Cherleroi 20.06.2000

Referee: Urs Meier (SWI) Attendance: 27,000

ENGLAND: Nigel Martyn; Gary Neville, Phillip Neville, Sol Campbell, Martin Keown; David Beckham, Paul Scholes (81 Gareth Southgate), Paul Ince, Dennis Wise (75 Nick Barmby); Alan Shearer, Michael Owen (66 Emile Heskey).
Trainer: Kevin Keegan

ROMANIA: Bogdan Stelea; Iulian Filipescu, Cosmin Contra, Gheorghe Popescu (31 Miodrag Belodedici); Dan Petrescu, Adrian Mutu, Dorinel Munteanu, Christian Chivu, Constantin Galca (68 Laurentiu Roşu); Viorel Moldovan, Adrian Ilie (74 Ionel Gane). Trainer: Emerich Ienei

Goals: Chivu (22), Shearer (41 pen), Owen (45), D. Munteanu (48), Ganea (89 pen)

PORTUGAL v GERMANY 3-0 (1-0)

Feyenoord, Rotterdam 20.06.2000

Referee: Dick Jol (HOL) Attendance: 45,000

PORTUGAL: PEDRO Manuel ESPINHA Ferreira (90 JoaQUIM Sampaio Silva); RUI JORGE De Sousa, Roberto Deus Severo BETO, FERNANDO Manuel Silva COUTO, Francisco DA COSTA; Nuno Gonçalves da Rocha CAPUCHO, JORGE Paulo COSTA Almeida, PAULO Manuel SOUSA (72 José Luís da Cruz VIDIGAL), SÉRGIO Paulo Marceneiro CONCEIÇAO; Pedro Miguel PAULETA (67 NUNO GOMES Miguel Soares Pereira Ribeiro), Ricardo Manuel da Silva SÁ PINTO.
Trainer: HUMBERTO Manuel de Jesus COELHO

GERMANY: Oliver Kahn; Marko Rehmer, Lothar Matthäus, Jens Nowotny; Sebastian Deisler, Michael Ballack (46 Paulo Roberto Rink), Mehmet Scholl (60 Thomas Hässler), Dietmar Hamann, Thomas Linke; Carsten Jancker (69 Ulf Kirsten), Marco Bode. Trainer: Erich Ribbeck

Goals: Sergio Conceiçao (35, 54, 71)

	P	W	D	L	F	A	Pts
Portugal	3	3	0	0	7	2	9
Romania	3	1	1	1	4	4	4
England	3	1	0	2	5	6	3
Germany	3	0	1	2	1	5	1

ITALY v BELGIUM 2-0 (1-0)

Stade Roi Baudouin, Brussel 14.06.2000

Referee: Jos Maria Garca Aranda (SPA) Att: 46,000

ITALY: Francesco Toldo; Fabio Cannavaro, Alessandro Nesta, Mark Iuliano; Gian Luca Zambrotta, Antonio Conte, Demetrio Albertini, Stefano Fiore (83 Massimo Ambrosini), Paolo Maldini; Filippo Inzaghi (77 Marco Delvecchio), Francesco Totti (64 Alessandro Del Piero). Trainer: Dino Zoff

BELGIUM: Filip de Wilde; Eric Deflandre, Joos Valgaeren, Lorenzo Staelens, Nico van Kerckhoven (45 Marc Hendrickx); Gert Verheyen (67 Mbo Mpenza), Yves Vanderhaeghe, Marc Wilmots, Bart Goor; Emile Mpenza, Branko Strupar (58 Luc Nilis). Trainer: Robert Waseige

Goals: Totti (6), Fiore (66)

GROUP B

BELGIUM v SWEDEN 2-1 (1-0)

Stade Roi Baudouin, Brussel 10.06.2000

Referee: Markus Merk (GER) Attendance: 50,000

BELGIUM: Filip de Wilde; Eric Deflandre, Lorenzo Staelens, Joos Valgaeren, Philippe Léonard (72 Nico van Kerckhoven); Gert Verheyen (88 Jacky Peeters), Yves Vanderhaeghe, Marc Wilmots, Bart Goor; Branko Strupar (69 Luc Nilis), Emile Mpenza. Trainer: Robert Waseige

SWEDEN: Magnus Hedman; Roland Nilsson (46 Teddy Lucic), Patrick Andersson 81', Joachim Björklund, Olof Mellberg; Niclas Alexandersson, Johan Mjällby, Daniel Andersson (70 Yksel Osmanovski), Fredrik Ljungberg; Kennet Andersson, Jörgen Pettersson (50 Henryk Larsson). Trainers: Tommy Söderberg & Lars Lagerback

Sent off: P. Andersson (81)

Goals: Goor (43), Mpenza (46), Mjällby (53)

SWEDEN v TURKEY 0-0

Philips, Eindhoven 15.06.2000

Referee: Dick Jol (HOL) Attendance: 27,000

SWEDEN: Magnus Hedman; Teddy Lucic, Joachim Björklund, Olof Mellberg, Gary Sundgren; Håkan Mild, Johan Mjällby, Fredrik Ljungberg, Niclas Alexandersson (63 Anders Andersson); Henryk Larsson (78 Magnus Svensson), Kennet Andersson (46 Jörgen Pettersson).
Trainers: Tommy Söderberg & Lars Lagerback

TURKEY: Reçber Rüstü; Alpay Özalan, Ogün Temizkanoglu (59 Tugay Kerimoglu), Fatih Akyel, Hakan Ünsal; Ümit Davala (45 Tayfun Korkut), Okan Buruk, Mustafa Izzet (58 Sergen Yalçin), Suat Kaya, Arif Erdem; Hakan Şükür.
Trainer: Mustafa Denizli

TURKEY v ITALY 1-2 (0-0)

Gelre Dome, Arnhem 11.06.2000

Referee: Hugh Dallas (SCO) Attendance: 28,000

TURKEY: Reçber Rüstü; Alpay Özalan, Ogün Temizkanoglu, Fatih Akyel; Tayfur Havutçu, Tayfun Korkut, Ümit Davala (76 Tugay Kerimoglu), Okan Buruk (89 Ergün Penbe), Abdullah Erkan; Sergen Yalçin (81 Arif Erdem), Hakan Şükür. Trainer: Mustafa Denizli

ITALY: Francesco Toldo; Fabio Cannavaro, Alessandro Nesta, Paolo Maldini; Gian Luca Zambrotta, Antonio Conte, Demetrio Albertini, Stefano Fiore (75 Alessandro Del Piero), Gianluca Pessotto (62 Mark Iuliano); Filippo Inzaghi, Francesco Totti (83 Angelo di Livio). Trainer: Dino Zoff

Goals: Conte (52), Okan (61), Inzaghi (70 pen)

TURKEY v BELGIUM 2-0 (1-0)

Stade Roi Baudouin, Brussel 19.06.2000

Referee: Kim Milton Nielsen (DEN) from 41st minute Günter Benkö (AUS) Attendance: 45,000

TURKEY: Reçber Rüstü; Fatih Akyel, Ogün Temizkanoglu, Alpay Özalan; Tayfun Korkut, Okan Buruk (77 Ergün Penbe), Tugay Kerimoglu (37 Tayfur Havutçu), Suat Kaya, Abdullah Erkan; Hakan Şükür, Arif Erdem (87 Osman Özköylü). Trainer: Mustafa Denizli

BELGIUM: Filip de Wilde; Eric Deflandre, Lorenzo Staelens, Joos Valgaeren, Nico van Kerckhoven; Gert Verheyen (63 Branko Strupar), Yves Vanderhaeghe, Marc Wilmots, Bart Goor (59 Marc Hendrickx); Luc Nilis (77 Gilles de Bilde), Emile Mpenza. Trainer: Robert Waseige

Sent off: de Wilde (84)

Goals: Hakan Şükür (45, 70)

ITALY v SWEDEN 2-1 (1-0)

Philips, Eindhoven 19.06.2000

Referee: Vtor Manuel Melo Pereira (POR) Att: 26,000

ITALY: Francesco Toldo; Ciro Ferrara, Paolo Maldini (42 Alessandro Nesta), Mark Iuliano (46 Fabio Cannavaro), Angelo di Livio (64 Stefano Fiore), Paolo Negro; Massimo Ambrosini, Luigi Di Biagio, Gianluca Pessotto; Vincenzo Montella, Alessandro Del Piero. Trainer: Dino Zoff

SWEDEN: Magnus Hedman; Patrick Andersson, Joachim Björklund, Tomas Gustafsson (75 Kennet Andersson), Olof Mellberg; Håkan Mild, Fredrik Ljungberg, Johan Mjällby (56 Daniel Andersson), Yksel Osmanovski; Henryk Larsson, Magnus Svensson (52 Niclas Alexandersson). Trainers: Tommy Söderberg & Lars Lagerback

Goals: Di Biagio (39), H. Larsson (77), Del Piero (88)

YUGOSLAVIA v SLOVENIA 3-3 (0-1)

Stade Communal, Charleroi 13.06.2000

Referee: Vítor Manuel Melo Pereira (POR) Att: 20,000

YUGOSLAVIA: Ivica Kralj; Ivan Dudic, Miroslav Djukic, Sinisa Mihajlovic, Albert Nadj; Iovan Stankovic (36 Dragan Stojkovic), Ljubinko Drulovic, Slavisa Jokanovic, Vladimir Jugovic; Predrag Mijatovic (82 Mateja Kezman), Darko Kovacevic (52 Savo Milosevic). Trainer: Vujadin Boskov

SLOVENIA: Mladen Dabanovic; Marinko Galic, Darko Milanic, Zeljko Milinovic; Djoni Novak, Aleš Ceh, Miran Pavlin (74 Zoran Pavlovic), Amir Karic (78 Milan Osterc), Mladen Rudonja; Zlatko Zahovic, Sašo Udovic (64 Milenko Acimovic). Trainer: Srecko Katanec

Sent off: Mihajlovic (59)

Goals: Zahovic (23, 57), Pavlin (52), Milosevic (67, 73), Drulovic (70)

	P	W	D	L	F	A	Pts
Italy	3	3	0	0	6	2	9
Turkey	3	1	1	1	3	2	4
Belgium	3	1	0	2	2	5	3
Sweden	3	0	1	2	2	4	1

GROUP C

SPAIN v NORWAY 0-1 (0-0)

Feyenoord Rotterdam 13.06.2000

Referee: Gamal El Ghandour (EGY) Attendance: 45,000

SPAIN: José Molina; MÍCHEL SALGADO Fernández, Fernándo Ruiz Hierro, Francisco Jímcncz "PACO", Agustín ARANZÁBAL Alkorta; Joseba ETXEBERRÍA Lizardi (72 ALFONSO Pérez), Josep Guardiola, Juan Carlos Valerón (81 Iván Helguera), FRAN Gonzalez (72 Gaizka Mendieta); Ismaël Urzaíz, RAÚL González. Trainer: José Antonio Camacho

NORWAY: Thomas Myhre; Vegard Heggem, Henning Berg (59 Dan Eggen), Björn Otto Bragstad, André Bergdølmo; Steffen Iversen (90 Vidar Riseth), Eirik Bakke, Bent Skammelsrud, Erik Mykland, Ole Gunnar Solskjær; Tore André Flo (71 John Carew). Trainer: Nils Johan Semb

Goal: Iversen (66)

SLOVENIA v SPAIN 1-2 (0-1)

Amsterdan Arena 18.06.2000

Referee: Markus Merk (GER) Attendance: 45,000

SLOVENIA: Mladen Dabanovic; Darko Milanic (68 Aleksander Knavs), Marinko Galic, Zeljko Milinovic; Djoni Novak, Aleš Ceh, Miran Pavlin (82 Milenko Acimovic), Amir Karic, Mladen Rudonja; Zlatko Zahovic, Sašo Udovic (46 Milan Osterc). Trainer: Srecko Katanec

SPAIN: Santiago Cañizares; MÍCHEL SALGADO Fernández, Fernándo Ruiz Hierro, ABELARDO Fernandez, Agustín ARANZÁBAL Alkorta; Joseba ETXEBERRÍA Lizardi, Josep Guardiola (81 Iván Helguera), Juan Carlos Valerón (89 Vicente Engonga), Gaizka Mendieta; ALFONSO Pérez (71 Ismaël Urzaíz), RAÚL González. Trainer: Josá Antonio Camacho

Goals: Raúl (4), Zahovic (59), Etxeberría (60)

NORWAY v YUGOSLAVIA 0-1 (0-1)

Sclessin, Liège 18.06.2000

Referee: Hugh Dallas (SCO) Attendance: 27,000

NORWAY: Thomas Myhre; Vegard Heggem (35 Stig Inge Bjørnebye), Dan Eggen, Bjørn Otto Bragstad, André Bergdølmo; Steffen Iversen (71 John Carew), Eirik Bakke (76 Roar Strand), Bent Skammelsrud, Erik Mykland, Ole Gunnar Solskjær; Tore André Flo. Trainer: Nils Johan Semb

YUGOSLAVIA: Ivica Kralj; Slobodan Komljenovic, Miroslav Djukic, Nisa Saveljic, Goran Djorovic; Dragan Stojkovic (84 Albert Nadj), Slavisa Jokanovic (89 Dejan Govedarica), Ljubinko Drulovic, Vladimir Jugovic; Savo Milosevic, Predrag Mijatovic (87 Mateja Kezman). Trainer: Vujadin Boskov

Sent off: Kezman (88)

Goal: Milosevic (8)

SLOVENIA v NORWAY 0-0

Gelre Dome, Arnhem 21.06.2000

Referee: Graham Poll (ENG) Attendance: 22,000

SLOVENIA: Mladen Dabanovic; Aleksander Knavs, Marinko Galic (83 Milenko Acimovic), Zeljko Milinovic; Djoni Novak, Aleš Ceh, Miran Pavlin, Amir Karic, Mladen Rudonja; Ermin Šiljak (86 Milan Osterc), Zlatko Zahovic.
Trainer: Srecko Katanec

NORWAY: Thomas Myhre; André Bergdølmo, Dan Eggen, Bjørn Otto Bragstad, Stig Inge Bjørnebye; Erik Mykland, Ståle Solbakken; Steffen Iversen, Tore André Flo, John Carew (61 Eirik Bakke, 82 Roar Strand), Ole Gunnar Solskjær.
Trainer: Nils Johan Semb

YUGOSLAVIA v SPAIN 3-4 (1-1)

Jan Breydel, Brugge 21.06.2000

Referee: Gilles Veissière (FRA) Attendance: 24,000

YUGOSLAVIA: Ivica Kralj; Slobodan Komljenovic, Miroslav Djukic, Sinisa Mihajlovic, Goran Djorovic (12 Iovan Stankovic); Dragan Stojkovic (68 Nisa Saveljic), Slavisa Jokanovic 63', Vladimir Jugovic (46 Dejan Govedarica), Ljubinko Drulovic; Savo Milosevic, Predrag Mijatovic.
Trainer: Vujadin Boskov

SPAIN: Santiago Cañizares; MÍCHEL SALGADO Fernández (46 Pedro Munitis), ABELARDO Fernandez, Francisco Jímenez "PACO" (64 Ismaël Urzaíz), Sergi; Gaizka Mendieta, Josep Guardiola, Iván Helguera, FRAN Gonzalez (22 Joseba ETXEBERRÍA Lizardi); RAÚL González, ALFONSO Pérez.
Trainer: José Antonio Camacho

Sent off: Jokanovic (63)

Goals: Milosević (30), Alfonso (39, 90), Govedarica (51), Munitis (52), Komljenovic (75), Mendieta (90 pen)

	P	W	D	L	F	A	Pts
Spain	3	2	0	1	6	5	6
Yugoslavia	3	1	1	1	7	7	4
Norway	3	1	1	1	1	1	4
Slovenia	3	0	2	1	4	5	2

GROUP D

FRANCE v DENMARK 3-0 (1-0)

Jan Breydel, Brugge 11.06.2000

Referee: Günter Benkö (AUS) Attendance: 29,000

FRANCE: Fabien Barthez; Lilian Thuram, Laurent Blanc, Marcel Desailly, Bixente Lizarazu; Youri Djorkaeff (58 Patrick Vieira), Didier Deschamps, Zinedine Zidane, Emmanuel Petit; Thierry Henry, Nicolas Anelka (81 Sylvain Wiltord).
Trainer: Roger Lemerre

DENMARK: Peter Schmeichel; Søren Colding, Michael Schjønberg, René Henriksen, Jan Heintze; Morten Bisgaard (72 Martin Jørgensen), Allan Nielsen, Stig Tøfting (72 Thomas Gravesen), Jesper Grønkjær; Ebbe Sand, Jon Dahl Tomasson (79 Mikkel Beck). Trainer: Bo Johansson

Goals: Blanc (16), Henry (64), Wiltord (90)

HOLLAND v CZECH REPUBLIC 1-0 (0-0)

Amsterdam ArenA 11.06.2000

Referee: Pierluigi Collina (ITA) Attendance: 50,000

HOLLAND: Edwin van der Sar; Michael Reiziger, Jaap Stam (75 Bert Konterman), Frank de Boer, Giovanni van Bronckhorst; Clarence Seedorf (57 Ronald de Boer), Phillip Cocu, Edgar Davids, Boudewijn Zenden (78 Marc Overmars); Dennis Bergkamp, Patrick Kluivert. Trainer: Frank Rijkaard

CZECH REPUBLIC: Pavel Srnícek; Radoslav Látal (70 Radek Bejbl), Karel Rada, Tomáš Repka, Petr Gabriel; Karel Poborsky, Pavel Nedved (90 Vratislav Lokvenc), Jirí Nemec, Tomáš Rosický, Vladimir Šmicer (83 Pavel Kuka); Jan Koller.
Trainer: Jozef Chovanec

Sent off: Látal (90)

Goal: Frank de Boer (89 pen)

CZECH REPUBLIC v FRANCE 1-2 (1-1)

Jan Breydel, Brugge 16.06.2000

Referee: Graham Poll (ENG) Attendance: 28,000

CZECH REPUBLIC: Pavel Srnícek; Tomáš Repka, Karel Rada, Petr Gabriel (46 Milan Fukal); Karel Poborsky, Radek Bejbl (49 Vratislav Lokvenc), Jirí Nemec, Tomáš Rosický (62 Marek Jankulovski), Pavel Nedved; Vladimir Šmicer, Jan Koller. Trainer: Jozef Chovanec

FRANCE: Fabien Barthez; Lilian Thuram, Laurent Blanc, Marcel Desailly, Vincent Candela; Didier Deschamps, Zinedine Zidane, Emmanuel Petit (46 Youri Djorkaeff); Patrick Vieira, Nicolas Anelka (55 Christophe Dugarry), Thierry Henry (90 Sylvain Wiltord). Trainer: Roger Lemerre

Goals: Henry (7), Poborsky (35 pen), Djorkaeff (60)

DENMARK v HOLLAND 0-3 (0-0)

Feyenoord, Rotterdam 16.06.2000

Referee: Urs Meier (SWI) Attendance: 50,000

DENMARK: Peter Schmeichel; Søren Colding, René Henriksen, Michael Schjønberg (82 Thomas Helveg), Jan Heintze; Morten Bisgaard, Allan Nielsen (61 Stig Tøfting), Thomas Gravesen (67 Brian Steen Nielsen), Jesper Grønkjær; Jon Dahl Tomasson, Ebbe Sand. Trainer: Bo Johansson

HOLLAND: Edwin van der Sar (90 Sander Westerveld); Michael Reiziger, Bert Konterman, Frank de Boer, Giovanni van Bronckhorst; Boudewijn Zenden, Phillip Cocu, Edgar Davids, Marc Overmars (61 Ronald de Boer); Dennis Bergkamp (76 Aron Winter), Patrick Kluivert. Trainer: Frank Rijkaard

Goals: Kluivert (57), R. de Boer (66), Zenden (77)

FRANCE v HOLLAND 2-3 (2-1)

Amsterdam ArenA 21.06.2000

Referee: Anders Frisk (SWE) Attendance: 50,000

FRANCE: Bernard Lama; Christian Karembeu, Marcel Desailly, Frank Leboeuf, Vincent Candela; Christophe Dugarry (68 Youri Djorkaeff), Patrick Vieira (90 Didier Deschamps), Johan Micoud, Robert Pires; David Trézéguet, Sylvain Wiltord (80 Nicolas Anelka). Trainer: Roger Lemerre

HOLLAND: Sander Westerveld; Paul Bosvelt, Jaap Stam, Frank de Boer, Arthur Numan; Boudewijn Zenden, Edgar Davids, Phillip Cocu, Marc Overmars (89 Peter van Vossen); Dennis Bergkamp (78 Aron Winter), Patrick Kluivert (60 Roy Makaay). Trainer: Frank Rijkaard

Goals: Dugarry (8), Kluivert (14), Trézéguet (31), Frank de Boer (51), Zenden (59)

DENMARK v CZECH REPUBLIC 0-2 (0-0)

Sclessin, Liège 21.06.2000

Referee: Gamal El Ghandour (EGY) Attendance: 20,000

DENMARK: Peter Schmeichel; Thomas Helveg, René Henriksen, Michael Schjønberg, Jan Heintze (68 Søren Colding); Stig Tøfting, Brian Steen Nielsen, Bjarne Goldbæk, Jesper Grønkjær; Mikkel Beck (74 Miklos Molnar), Jon Dahl Tomasson. Trainer: Bo Johansson

CZECH REPUBLIC: Pavel Srnícek; Tomáš Repka, Karel Rada, Milan Fukal; Karel Poborsky, Radek Bejbl (62 Marek Jankulovski), Patrik Berger, Jirí Nemec, Pavel Nedved; Jan Koller (74 Pavel Kuka), Vladimir Šmicer (79 Vratislav Lokvenc). Trainer: Jozef Chovanec

Goals: Šmicer (64, 67)

	P	W	D	L	F	A	Pts
Holland	3	3	0	0	7	2	9
France	3	2	0	1	7	4	6
Czech Republic	3	1	0	2	3	3	3
Denmark	3	0	0	3	0	8	0

QUARTER-FINALS

TURKEY v PORTUGAL 0-2 (0-1)

Amsterdam ArenA 24.06.2000

Referee: Dick Jol (HOL) Attendance: 45,000

TURKEY: Reçber Rüstü; Ogün Temizkanoglu (84 Sergen Yalçin), Fatih Akyel, Hakan Ünsal; Tayfun Korkut, Okan Buruk (62 Oktay Derelioglu), Tayfur Havutçu, Ergün Penbe, Alpay Özalan; Hakan Şükür, Arif Erdem (62 Suat Kaya). Trainer: Mustafa Denizli

PORTUGAL: VÍTOR Manuel Martins BAÍA; SÉRGIO Paulo Marceneiro CONCEIÇAO, FERNANDO Manuel Silva COUTO, JORGE Paulo COSTA Almeida, DIMAS Manuel Marques Teixeira; Francisco DA COSTA (46 PAULO Manuel SOUSA), RUI Manuel César COSTA (87 Nuno Gonçalves da Rocha CAPUCHO), FIGO Luis Filipe Madeira, PAULO Jorge Gomes BENTO; JOÃO Manuel Vieira PINTO, NUNO GOMES Miguel Soares Pereira Ribeiro (74 Ricardo Manuel da Silva SÁ PINTO). Trainer: HUMBERTO Manuel de Jesus COELHO

Sent off: Alpay Özalan (29)

Goals: Nuno Gomes (44, 56)

ITALY v ROMANIA 2-0 (2-0)

Stade Roi Baudouin, Brussel 24.06.2000

Referee: Vítor Manuel Melo Pereira (POR) Att: 40,000

ITALY: Francesco Toldo; Fabio Cannavaro, Alessandro Nesta, Mark Iuliano; Gian Luca Zambrotta, Antonio Conte (55 Luigi Di Biagio), Demetrio Albertini, Stefano Fiore, Paolo Maldini (46 Gianluca Pessotto); Francesco Totti (75 Alessandro Del Piero), Filippo Inzaghi. Trainer: Dino Zoff

ROMANIA: Bogdan Stelea; Iulian Filipescu, Miodrag Belodedici, Liviu Ciobotariu; Florentin Petre, Constantin Gâlcă (68 Ioan Lupescu), Dorinel Munteanu, Gheorghe Hagi, Cristian Chivu; Adrian Mutu, Viorel Moldovan (54 Ionel Ganea). Trainer: Emeric Ienei

Sent off: Hagi (59)

Goals: Totti (33), Inzaghi (43)

HOLLAND v YUGOSLAVIA 6-1 (2-0)

Feyenoord, Rotterdam 25.06.2000

Referee: José Maria García Aranda (SPA) Att: 50,000

HOLLAND: Edwin van der Sar (65 Sander Westerveld); Paul Bosvelt, Frank de Boer, Jaap Stam, Arthur Numan; Marc Overmars, Phillip Cocu, Edgar Davids, Boudewijn Zenden (80 Ronald de Boer); Dennis Bergkamp, Patrick Kluivert (60 Roy Makaay). Trainer: Frank Rijkaard

YUGOSLAVIA: Ivica Kralj; Slobodan Komljenović, Nisa Saveljić (56 Iovan Stanković), Sinisa Mihajlović, Miroslav Djukić; Dragan Stojković (52 Dejan Stanković), Dejan Govedarica, Vladimir Jugović, Ljubinko Drulović (70 Darko Kovacević); Predrag Mijatović, Savo Milosević. Trainer: Vujadin Boskov

Goals: Kluivert (24, 38, 54), Govedarica (51 og), Overmars (78, 90), Milosević (90)

SPAIN v FRANCE 1-2 (1-2)

Jan Breydel, Brugge 25.06.2000

Referee: Pierluigi Collina (ITA) Attendance: 30,000

SPAIN: Santiago Cañizares; MÍCHEL SALGADO Fernández, Francisco Jímenez "PACO", ABELARDO Fernandez, Agustín ARANZÁBAL Alkorta; Gaizka Mendieta (57 Ismaël Urzaíz), Josep Guardiola, Iván Helguera (77 GERARD Lopez), Pedro Munitis (73 Joseba ETXEBERRÍA Lizardi); RAÚL González, ALFONSO Pérez. Trainer: José Antonio Camacho

FRANCE: Fabien Barthez; Lilian Thuram, Marcel Desailly, Laurent Blanc, Bixente Lizarazu; Patrick Vieira, Didier Deschamps, Zinedine Zidane, Youri Djorkaeff; Christophe Dugarry, Thierry Henry (81 Nicolas Anelka). Trainer: Roger Lemerre

Goals: Zidane (32), Mendieta (38 pen), Djorkaeff (42)

SEMI-FINALS

FRANCE v PORTUGAL 2-1 (0-1) (AET)

Stade Roi Baudouin, Brussel 28.06.2000

Referee: Günter Benkö (AUS) Attendance: 50,000

FRANCE: Fabien Barthez; Lilian Thuram, Laurent Blanc, Marcel Desailly, Bixente Lizarazu; Patrick Vieira, Zinedine Zidane, Didier Deschamps, Emmanuel Petit (87 Robert Pires); Nicolas Anelka (72 Sylvain Wiltord), Thierry Henry (105 David Trézéguet). Trainer: Roger Lemerre

PORTUGAL: VÍTOR Manuel Martins BAÍA; ABEL Luis da Silva Costa XAVIER, FERNANDO Manuel Silva COUTO, DIMAS Manuel Marques Teixeira (91 RUI JORGE De Sousa), JORGE Paulo COSTA Almeida; SÉRGIO Paulo Marceneiro CONCEIÇAO, RUI Manuel César COSTA (78 JOÃO Manuel Vieira PINTO), José Luís da Cruz VIDIGAL (61 PAULO Jorge Gomes BENTO), Francisco DA COSTA, FIGO Luis Filipe Madeira; NUNO GOMES Miguel Soares Pereira Ribeiro. Trainer: HUMBERTO Manuel de Jesus COELHO

Sent off: Nuno Gomes (117)

Goals: Nuno Gomes (19), Henry (51), Zidane (117 pen)

The match was won by Zidane's golden goal

ITALY v HOLLAND 0-0

Amsterdam ArenA 29.06.2000

Referee: Markus Merk (GER) Attendance: 50,000

ITALY: Francesco Toldo; Fabio Cannavaro, Alessandro Nesta, Mark Iuliano; Gian Luca Zambrotta, Demetrio Albertini (78 Gianluca Pessotto), , Luigi Di Biagio, Stefano Fiore (83 Francesco Totti), Paolo Maldini; Filippo Inzaghi (67 Marco Delvecchio), Alessandro Del Piero. Trainer: Dino Zoff

HOLLAND: Edwin van der Sar; Paul Bosvelt, Jaap Stam, Frank de Boer, Giovanni van Bronckhorst; Marc Overmars, Phillip Cocu (95 Aron Winter), Edgar Davids, Boudewijn Zenden (77 Peter van Vossen); Patrick Kluivert, Dennis Bergkamp (87 Clarence Seedorf). Trainer: Frank Rijkaard

Sent off: Zambrotta

Penalties: 1-0 Di Biagio, F. de Boer (saved), 2-0 Pessotto, Stam (missed), 3-0 Totti, 3-1 Kluivert, Maldini (saved), Bosvelt (saved)

FINAL

FRANCE v ITALY 2-1 (0-0, 1-1) (AET)

Feyenoord, Rotterdam 02.07.2000

Referee: Anders Frisk (SWE) Attendance: 50,000

FRANCE: Fabien Barthez; Bixente Lizarazu (86 Robert Pires), Marcel Desailly, Laurent Blanc, Lilian Thuram; Zinedine Zidane, Didier Deschamps, Patrick Vieira, Youri Djorkaeff (76 David Trézéguet); Thierry Henry, Christophe Dugarry (58 Sylvain Wiltord). Trainer: Roger Lemerre

ITALY: Francesco Toldo; Mark Iuliano, Alessandro Nesta, Fabio Cannavaro, Paolo Maldini; Gianluca Pessotto, Demetrio Albertini, Luigi Di Biagio (65 Massimo Ambrosini), Stefano Fiore (53 Alessandro Del Piero); Marco Delvecchio (86 Vincenzo Montella), Francesco Totti. Trainer: Dino Zoff

Goals: Delvecchio (55), Wiltord (90), Trézéguet (103)

The match was won by Trézéguet's golden goal

Goalscorers European Football Championship 2000

12 goals: Zlatko Zahovic (Slovenia), Raúl González (Spain)

9 goals: João Manuel Vieira Pinto (Portugal), Savo Milosevic (Yugoslavia)

8 goals: Alan Shearer (England)

7 goals: Oliver Bierhoff (Germany)

6 goals: Jon Dahl Tomasson (Denmark), Hakan Şükür (Turkey), Valeriy Karpin (Russia), Paul Scholes (England), Ismaël Urzaíz (Spain), Rui Manuel César Costa, Ricardo Manuel Da Silva Sá Pinto (Portugal), Adrian Ilie (Romania), Elvir Baljic (Bosnia), Jan Koller (Czech Republic)

5 goals: Tore André Flo, Steffen Iversen, Ole Gunnar Solskjær (Norway), Filippo Inzaghi (Italy), Tayfur Havutçu (Turkey), Serhiy Rebrov (Ukraine), Youri Djorkaeff (France), Ivica Vastic (Austria), Alon Mizrahi (Israel), Joseba Etxeberría Lizardi, Fernándo Ruiz Hierro (Spain), Viorel Moldovan (Romania), Robbie Keane (Republic of Ireland), Patrik Berger, Vladimir Smicer (Czech Republic), Patrick Kluivert (Holland)

4 goals: Vladimir Beschastnykh, Viktor Onopko (Russia), Sylvain Wiltord (France), Henryk Larsson (Sweden), Milenko Spoljaric (Cyprus), Yossi Benayoun, Haim Revivo (Israel), Luis Enrique Martínez (Spain), Vilmos Sebök (Hungary), Figo Luis Filipe Madeira, Sérgio Paulo Marceneiro Conceiçao, Nuno Gomes Miguel Soares Pereira Ribeiro (Portugal), Ioan Viorel Ganea, Dorinel Munteanu (Romania), Davor Suker (Croatia), Elvir Bolic (Bosnia), William Dodds (Scotland)

3 goals: Stéphane Chapuisat, Kubilay Türkyilmaz (Switzerland), Shota Arveladze (Georgia), Alban Bushi (Albania), Marian Pakhar, Andrey Shtolcers (Latvia), Nikolaos Mahlas (Greece), Jonatan Johansson, Joonas Kolkka, Mika-Matti Paatelainen (Finland), Alessandro Del Piero, Christian Vieri (Italy), Marco Bode, Ulf Kirsten, Christian Ziege (Germany), Arif Erdem (Turkey), Tigran Yesayan (Armenia), Christophe Dugarry, Thierry Henry, David Trézéguet, Zinedine Zidane (France), Tomasz Iwan (Poland), Steve McManaman, Michael Owen (England), Johan Mjällby (Sweden), Christian Mayrleb (Austria), Avi Nimni (Israel), Julen Guerrero, Gaizka Mendieta (Spain), Paulo Sérgio Braga Madeira (Portugal), Sasa Ciric, Artim Sakiri (Macedonia), Niall Quinn (Republic of Ireland), Andres Oper, Sergei Terehhov (Estonia), Valdas Ivanauskas (Lithuania), Don Hutchison (Scotland), Predrag Mijatovic, Dejan Stankovic (Yugoslavia), Pavel Nedved (Czech Republic)

2 goals: Belkevich (Belarus), Tøfting, B.S. Nielsen, Sand, Jørgensen (Denmark), Z. Janashia (Georgia), Tare (Albania), Astafyev, Zemlinsky (Latvia), Tsartas, Frantzeskos, Georgiadis (Greece), Acimovic, Pavlin (Slovenia), Leonhardsen, Rekdal (Norway), Oprea (Moldova), Conte, Fuser, Totti (Italy), Scholl (Germany), Oktay (Turkey), Shahgeldyan (Armenia), Dadason, Sverrisson (Iceland), Panov (Russia), Gusin, Popov, Shevchenko, Skachenko (Ukraine), Czereszewski, Brzeczek (Poland), Alexandersson (Sweden), Constantinou, Engomitis (Cyprus), Cerny, Glieder, Herzog, Reinmayr (Austria), Berkovic, Ghrayeb (Israel), Fran, Alfonso, César, Morientes (Spain), Tagizade, K. Kurbanov (Azerbaijan), Illés (Hungary), Fabus, Dubovsky, Tomaschek, Labant (Slovakia), Pauleta, Abel Xavier (Portugal), Roşu (Romania), Carabott (Malta), Bozinov (Macedonia), Boban, Vugrinec, Stanic (Croatia), Breen, Roy Keane (Republic of Ireland), Arge (Faroe Islands), Reim (Estonia), Ramelis (Lithuania), Johnston (Scotland), Stojkovic, Nadj, Drulovic (Yugoslavia), Kuka, Poborsky (Czech Republic), Frank De Boer, Zenden, Overmars (Holland)

1 goal: Baranov, Gurenko (Belarus), Bellamy, Coleman, Giggs, Robinson, Saunders, Symons, Williams (Wales), Rey, Bühlmann, Fournier (Switzerland), Wieghorst, A. Nielsen, Heintze, Frederiksen (Denmark), Kavelashvili, Ketsbaia, A. Arveladze (Georgia), Rrakli, Kola, Muka (Albania), Bleidelis, Stepanov, Verpakovsky (Latvia), Nikolaidis, Niniadis, Liberopoulos, Ouzounidis (Greece), Osterc, Knavs, Udovic (Slovenia), Solbakken, Berg (Norway), Epureanu, Stratulat, Gaidamaşciuc, Testimiţanu, Guzun (Moldova), Jeff Whitley, Dowie, Lennon, Rowland (N. Ireland), Hyypiä, Salli, Tihinen, Litmanen (Finland), Maldini, Chiesa, Fiore, Di Biagio, Delvecchio (Italy), Jeremies, Neuville, Hamann (Germany), Sergen, Ogün, Okan (Turkey), Juli Sánchez, Justo Ruiz, Lucendo (Andorra), Petrosyan, Mikaelyan, Avalyan (Armenia), Adolfsson, Gunnarsson, T. Gudjónsson, Hreidarsson, Gudjohnsen, R. Kristinsson, L. Sigurdsson (Iceland), Titov, Tsymbalar, Alenichev, Yanovskiy, Mostovoi, Varlamov (Russia), Dmitrulin, Vashchuk, Kosovskyi (Ukraine), Laslandes, Leboeuf, Petit, Candela, Anelka, Pirés, Boghossian, Blanc (France), Birsens, Vanek (Luxembourg), Borimirov, Petkov, Hristov, Markov, Stoichkov, Iordanov (Bulgaria),

Siadaczka, Wichniarek, Hajto, Juskowiak, Trzeciak (Poland), Southgate (England), A. Andersson, Ljundberg, K. Andersson (Sweden), Selva (San Marino), Costa, Melanarkitis, Christodoulou, Gogic (Cyprus), Amerhauser, Hiden (Austria), Banin, Hazan, Sivilia, Abuksis, Badir (Israel), Munitis (Spain), M. Frick, M. Telser (Liechtenstein), Lychkin, Isaev (Azerbaijan), Egressy, Sowunmi, J. Sebök, Hrutka, Dárdai, Pisont, M. Fehér, Horváth (Hungary), S. Nemeth, Karhan, Sovic, Moravcik (Slovakia), Capucho, Da Costa (Portugal), Hagi, Ciobotariu, C. Munteanu, Vlădoiu, Petre, Popescu, Chivu (Romania), Said, Saliba, Suda, Sixsmith (Malta), Stavrevski, Hristov, Nikoloski, Zaharievski, Sainovski (Macedonia), Boksic, Soldo, D. Simic (Croatia), Staunton, Kennedy, Irwin (Republic of Ireland), H.F. Hansen, Petersen (Faroe Islands), Piiroja, Hohlov-Simson, Smirnov, Viikmäe, Kirs, Arbeiter (Estonia), Maciulevicius, Fomenka, Baltusnikas (Lithuania), Kodro, Konjic, Topic, Barbarez (Bosnia), McSwegan, Cameron, Collins, Ritchie, Burley, Jess (Scotland), Goor, Mpenza (Belgium), Savicevic, D. Kovacevic, Govedarica, Komljenovic (Yugoslavia), Verbír, Repka, Jess, Lokvenc, Hornak, Baranek (Czech Republic), R. De Boer (Holland)

Own goals: Istenic (Slovenia) for Norway, Kovtun (Russia) for Iceland, Dadason (Iceland) for France, Wetl (Austria) for Spain, Gennari (San Marino) for Spain, Hierro (Spain) for Austria, Haas (Liechtenstein) for Romania, Babunski (Macedonia) for Yugoslavia, Hibic (Bosnia Herzegovina) for Estonia, Hohlov-Simson (Estonia) for Scotland, Elliott (Scotland) for Czech Republic, Govedarica (Yugoslavia) for Holland

THE EUROPEAN FOOTBALL CHAMPIONSHIP 2004

GROUP 1

CYPRUS v FRANCE 1-2 (1-1)

GSP, Nicosia 07.09.2002

Referee: Herbert Fandel (GER) Attendance: 11,898

CYPRUS: Nicos Panagiotou; Petros Konnafis, Ioakim Ioakim, Dimitris Daskalakis (68 Hrysis Mihael), Nikos Nicolaou (74 Marios Agathocleous), Panagiotou Spyrou, Giorgos Theodotou, Marinos Satsias, Giannaki Okkas, Kostas Kaiafas, Rainer Rauffmann (62 Giasoumas Giasoumi).
Trainer: Moca Vukotić

FRANCE: Grégory Coupet, Patrick Vieira, Philippe Christanval, Claude Makélèle, Marcel Desailly, Djibril Cissé, Zinedine Zidane, Sylvain Wiltord (79 Olivier Kapo), Mickäel Silvestre, Lilian Thuram, Steve Marlet (70 Sidney Govou).
Trainer: Jacques Santini

Goals: Okkas (14), Cissé (39), Wiltord (51)

SLOVENIA v MALTA 3-0 (1-0)

Central, Ljubljana 7.09.2002

Referee: Giorgos Borovilos (GRE) Attendance: 8,211

SLOVENIA: Marko Simeunović; Amir Karić, Muamer Vugdalić, Spasoje Bulajić, Aleksander Knavs, Goran Šukalo (74 Saša Gajser), Ermin Šiljak (90 Ermin Raković), Zlatko Zahović, Miran Pavlin, Sebastjan Cimirotić, Milenko Acimović (86 Aleksander Radosavljević). Trainer: Bojan Prašnikar

MALTA: Mario Muscat; Brian Said, Jeffrey Chetcuti, David Carabott, Darren Debono, Luke Dimech, Gilbert Agius, Stefan Giglio, Mifsud (88 Mifsud), George Mallia (71 Daniel Bogdanović), Chucks Nwoko. Trainer: Siegfried Held

Goals: Debono (37 og), Šiljak (59), Cimirotić (90)

FRANCE v SLOVENIA 5-0 (2-0)

Stade de France, Paris 12.10.2002

Referee: Kim Milton Nielsen (DEN) Attendance: 77,619

FRANCE: Fabien Barthez, Lilian Thuram (84 Willy Sagnol), Marcel Desailly, William Gallas, Mickäel Silvestre, Patrick Vieira, Claude Makélèle, Sylvain Wiltord (87 Bruno Cheyrou), Zinedine Zidane, Steve Marlet (80 Sidney Govou), Thierry Henry. Trainer: Jacques Santini

SLOVENIA: Marko Simeunović, Amir Karić (88 Suad Fileković), Muamer Vugdalić, Fabijan Cipot, Goran Šukalo, Aleksander Radosavljević, Ermin Šiljak, Zlatko Zahović, Miran Pavlin, Saša Gajser, Sebastjan Cimirotić.
Trainer: Bojan Prašnikar **Sent off**: Gajser (90)

Goals: Vieira (10), Marlet (35, 64), Wiltord (79), Govou (86)

MALTA v ISRAEL 0-2 (0-0)

National, Ta'Qali 12.10.2002

Referee: Sergei Shebek (UKR) Attendance: 4,000

MALTA: Mario Muscat; Brian Said, Jeffrey Chetcuti, David Carabott, Darren Debono, Luke Dimech, Gilbert Agius (83 George Mallia), Noel Turner, Michael Mifsud, Joe Brincat (74 Adrian Mifsud), Chucks Nwoko (64 Daniel Bogdanovic). Trainer: Siegfried Held

ISRAEL: Dudu Awat; Avishai Zano, Walid Badir, Arik Benado, Assi Domb, Adoram Keissy, Tal Banin, Heim Revivo, Pini Balili (70 Yossi Benayoun), Eyal Berkovich (89 Avi Nimni), Idan Tal (82 Ygal Antebi). Trainer: Avraham Grant

Goals: Balili (56), Revivo (77)

CYPRUS v ISRAEL 1-1 (0-1)

Tsirion, Limassol 29.03.2003

Referee: Thomas Michael McCurry (SCO) Att: 5,000

CYPRUS: Nicos Panagiotou; Petros Konnafis, Ioakim Ioakim (46 Nikos Nikolaou, 76 Demetris Daskalakis), Panagiotou Spyrou, Giorgos Theodotou, Vladan, Giannakis Okkas, Mihalis Konstantinou, Kostas Kaiafas, Stelios Okkarides, Giotis Engomitis (60 Rainer Rauffmann). Trainer: Moca Vukotić

ISRAEL: Dudu Awat; Alon Harazi, Tal Ben Haim, Arik Benado, Walid Badir (83 Josef Abukasis), Adoram Keise, Tal Banin, Haim Revivo, Omri Afek (72 Yossi Benayoun), Michael Zandberg (66 Avi Nimny), Idan Tal. Trainer: Avraham Grant

Goals: Afek (2), Rauffmann (61)

MALTA v FRANCE 0-4 (0-2)

National, Ta'Qali 16.10.2002

Referees: Alexandru Dan Tudor (ROM) Attendance: 12,360

MALTA: Mario Muscat; Brian Said, Jeffrey Chetcuti, David Carabott, Darren Debono (87 Miguel Mifsud), Luke Dimech, Gilbert Agius, Stefan Giglio, Michael Mifsud, Joe Brincat (69 George Mallia), Chucks Nwoko (46 Daniel Bogdanovic). Trainer: Siegfried Held

FRANCE: Fabien Barthez, Patrick Vieira (70 Olivier Dacourt), Claude Makélélé, Marcel Desailly, Zinedine Zidane, Sylvain Wiltord, Thierry Henry (78 Eric Carrière), Mickäel Silvestre, Lilian Thuram, William Gallas (84 Philippe Mexes), Steve Marlet. Trainer: Jacques Santini

Goals: Henry (25, 35), Wiltord (59), Carrière (84)

FRANCE v MALTA 6-0 (2-0)

Félix Bollaert, Lens 29.03.2003

Referee: Emil Bozinovski (MAC) Attendance: 40,775

FRANCE: Fabien Barthez, Lilian Thuram (65 Willy Sagnol), William Gallas, Mickäel Silvestre, Bixente Lizarazu, Claude Makélélé, Benoît Pedretti, Zinedine Zidane, Sylvain Wiltord (75 Sidney Govou), Thierry Henry (80 Jérôme Rothen), David Trezeguet. Trainer: Jacques Santini

MALTA: Mario Muscat; Ian Ciantar, Carlo Mamo (71 Jeffrey Chetcuti), David Carabott, Brian Said, Luke Dimech, Daniel Bogdanovic (62 Noel Turner), Simon Vella, Miguel Mifsud, George Mallia, Chucks Nwoko. Trainer: Siegfried Held

Goals: Wiltord (36), Henry (38, 54), Zidane (57, 81 pen), Trezeguet (70)

CYPRUS v MALTA 2-1 (0-0)

GSP, Nicosia 20.11.2002

Referee: Anton Genov (BUL) Attendance: 9,758

CYPRUS: Nicos Panagiotou; Petros Konnafis, Ioakim Ioakim, Panagiotou Spyrou, Giorgos Theodotou, Marinos Satsias (61 Hrysis Mihael), Giannakis Okkas, Kostas Kaiafas, Mihalis Konstantinou (66 Nikos Nicolaou), Stelios Okkarides, Rainer Rauffmann (71 Giasoumas Giasoumi).
Trainer: Moca Vukotić

MALTA: Mario Muscat; Brian Said, Jeffrey Chetcuti, David Carabott, Carlo Mamo (74 Miguel Mifsud), Gilbert Agius, Stefan Giglio (80 Daniel Theuma), Michael Mifsud, Adrian Mifsud (61 George Mallia), Daniel Bogdanovic.
Trainer: Siegfried Held

Goals: Rauffmann (50), Okkas (74), M. Mifsud (90)

SLOVENIA v CYPRUS 4-1 (4-1)

Central, Ljubljana 02.04.2003

Referee: Paulo Manuel GOMES COSTA (POR) Att: 7,000

SLOVENIA: Marko Simeunović, Fabijan Cipot, Amir Karić, Muamer Vugdalić, Spasoje Bulajić, Goran Šukalo, Nastja Ceh, Ermin Šiljak (90 Ermin Raković), Zlatko Zahović, Miran Pavlin, Robert Koren (85 Anton Zlogar).
Trainer: Bojan Prašnikar

CYPRUS: Nicos Panagiotou; Petros Konnafis (46 Ioakim Ioakim), Demetris Daskalakis, Panagiotou Spyrou (75 Giorgos Constantinou), Giorgos Theodotou, Vladan, Giannakis Okkas, Kostas Kaiafas, Mihalis Konstantinou, Stelios Okkarides, Rainer Rauffmann (46 Haralambides).
Trainer: Moca Vukotić

Goals: Šiljak (5, 14), Konstantinou (10), Zahović (39 pen), Ceh (43)

ISRAEL v FRANCE 1-2 (1-2)

Renzo Barbera, Palermo 02.04.2003

Referee: Graham Barber (ENG) Attendance: 2,455

ISRAEL: Dudu Awat; Alon Harazi, Omri Afek, Arik Benado, Tal Ben Haim, Adoram Keise, Tal Banin (70 Yossi Benayoun), Haim Revivo, Amir Torjman (46 Michael Zandberg), Josef Abukasis, Idan Tal (66 Walid Badir). Trainer: Avraham Grant

FRANCE: Fabien Barthez, Lilian Thuram, William Gallas, Mickäel Silvestre, Bixente Lizarazu, Claude Makélélé, Patrick Vieira, Zinedine Zidane, Sylvain Wiltord (65 Sidney Govou), David Trezeguet (70 Djibril Cissé), Thierry Henry. Trainer: Jacques Santini

Goals: Afek (1), Trezeguet (22), Zidane (45)

ISRAEL v SLOVENIA 0-0

Atatürk, Antalya 07.06.2003

Referee: Massimo Busacca (SWI) Attendance: 1,750

ISRAEL: Shavit Elimelech, Tal Ben-Haim, Arik Benado, Josef Abukasis (86 Shai Holtzman), Yossi Benayoun, Idan Tal (77 Walid Badir), Haim Revivo, Omri Afek (71 Michael Zandberg), Adoram Keisi, Avi Nimny, Yaish Zano.
Trainer: Avraham Grant

SLOVENIA: Marko Simeunović; Fabijan Cipot, Amir Karić, Muamer Vugdalić, Aleksander Knavs, Goran Šukalo, Ermin Šiljak, Zlatko Zahović, Miran Pavlin, Saša Gajser (71 Robert Koren), Milenko Acimović (86 Matej Snofl).
Trainer: Bojan Prašnikar

ISRAEL v CYPRUS 2-0 (0-0)

Renzo Barbera, Palermo 30.04.2003

Referee: Michal Benes (CZE) Attendance: 2,500

ISRAEL: Shavit Elimelech; Zano, Omri Afek, Arik Benado, Tal Ben Haim, Adoram Keise, Tal Banin (84 Walid Badir), Haim Revivo, Amir Torjman (52 Yossi Benayou), Josef Abukasis, Michael Zandberg (67 Holtsman). Trainer: Avraham Grant

CYPRUS: Nicos Panagiotou; Petros Konnafis, Germanou, Nikolaou, Giorgos Theodotou, Nicolaou (89 Giasoumi), Giannakis Okkas, Mihalis Konstantinou, Stelios Okkarides, Engomitis (80 Michael), Vladan (62 Kaiafas).
Trainer: Moca Vukotić

Goals: Badir (88), Holtsman (90+5)

MALTA v CYPRUS 1-2 (0-1)

National, Ta'Qali 07.06.2003

Referee: Bernhard Brugger (AUS) Attendance: 3,000

MALTA: Saviour Darmanin; William Camenzuli, Simon Vella, David Carabott, Brian Said (86 Daniel Bogdanovic), Luke Dimech, Noel Turner, Stefan Giglio, Michael Mifsud, George Mallia (66 Gilbert Agius), Chucks Nwoko (23 Mario Muscat). Trainer: Siegfried Held

CYPRUS: Nicos Panagiotou; Petros Konnafis, Daskalakis (65 Foukaris), Ilia, Satsias, Giannakis Okkas (78 Giasoumi), Mihalis Konstantinou, Michael, Stelios Okkarides, Haralambidis (90+1 Garpozis), Hritodoulou.
Trainer: Moca Vukotić

Sent off: Darmanin (23)

Goals: Konstantinou (23 pen, 52), Dimech (72)

MALTA v SLOVENIA 1-3 (0-2)

National, Ta'Qali 30.04.2003

Referee: Attila Hanacsek (HUNG) Attendance: 5,000

MALTA: Mario Muscat; Ian Ciantar, Simon Vella, David Carabott, Brian Said, Luke Dimech, Noel Turner, Stefan Giglio (70 William Camenzul), Michael Mifsud, George Mallia, Chucks Nwoko (63 Daniel Bogdanovic).
Trainer: Siegfried Held

SLOVENIA: Marko Simeunović; Fabijan Cipot, Amir Karić, Muamer Vugdalić, Oslaj (61 Matej Snofl), Goran Šukalo, Nastja Ceh, Ermin Šiljak (90 Ermin Raković), Zlatko Zahović, Miran Pavlin, Saša Gajser (78 Robert Koren).
Trainer: Bojan Prašnikar

Goals: Zahović (15), Šiljak (36, 57), M. Mifsud (90+1)

FRANCE v CYPRUS 5-0 (3-0)

Stade de France, Paris 06.09.2003

Referee: Leslie Irvine (NIR) Attendance: 58,000

FRANCE: Fabien Barthez, Lilian Thuram (65 Willy Sagnol), Marcel Desailly, Mickäel Silvestre, Bixente Lizarazu, Claude Makélélé, Patrick Vieira (71 Olivier Dacourt), Robert Pires, Sylvain Wiltord, David Trezeguet, Thierry Henry (78 Steve Marlet). Trainer: Jacques Santini

CYPRUS: Nikos Panagiotou; Petros Konnafis (46 Ioakim Ioakim), Nikos Nikolaou, Stelios Okkarides, Giorgos Theodotou, Marinos Satsias, Giannakis Okkas, Kostas Kaiafas, Mihalis Konstantinou (67 Giasoumas Giasoumi), Nikolaos Georgiou, Giotis Engomitis (59 Hrysis Mihael).
Trainer: Momcilo Vukotić

Goals: Trezeguet (7, 81), Wiltord (20, 41), Henry (60)

SLOVENIA v ISRAEL 3-1 (2-0)

Central, Ljubljana 06.09.2003

Referee: Herbert Fandel (GER) Attendance: 8,000

SLOVENIA: Marko Simeunović; Fabijan Cipot, Amir Karić, Matej Snofl, Aleksander Knavs, Goran Šukalo, Nastja Ceh (90+3 Mladen Rudonja), Ermin Šiljak (64 Sebastjan Cimirotić), Zlatko Zahović, Adem Kapić (84 Simon Sešlar), Milenko Acimović. Trainer: Bojan Prašnikar

ISRAEL: Shavit Elimelech; Alon Harazi, Tal Ben Haim, Ariel Banad, Adoram Keise (46 Pini Balili), Haim Revivo, Avi Nimny, Josef Abukasis (77 Walid Badir), Idan Tal, Eyal Berkovic, Yossi Benayoun. Trainer: Avraham Grant

Sent off: Nimny (87), Ben Haim (90)

Goals: Šiljak (35), Knavs (37), Haim Revivo (69), Ceh (78)

ISRAEL v MALTA 2-2 (1-0)

Atatürk, Antalya 10.09.2003

Referee: Eric Blareau (BEL) Attendance: 600

ISRAEL: Shavit Elimelech; Alon Harazi, Arik Benado, Shimon Gershon, Michael Zandberg, Haim Revivo, Josef Abukasis, Eyal Berkovic, Idan Tal, Pini Balili, Walid Badir. Trainer: Avraham Grant

MALTA: Mario Muscat; Etienne Barbara, Jeffrey Chetcuti, David Carabott, Brian Said, William Camenzuli, Noel Turner, Stefan Giglio (79 Daniel Theuma), Michael Mifsud, Daniel Bogdanovic (69 Michael Ganea), Chucks Nwoko (88 Adrian Mifsud). Trainer: Siegfried Held

Goals: Haim Revivo (16), Michael Mifsud (51 pen), Carabott (52), Balili (78)

SLOVENIA v FRANCE 0-2 (0-1)

Central, Ljubljana 10.09.2003

Referee: Domenico Messina (ITA) Attendance: 8,211

SLOVENIA: Marko Simeunović; Fabijan Cipot, Amir Karić, Muamer Vugdalić (83 Matej Snofl), Aleksander Knavs, Goran Šukalo (55 Adem Kapić), Nastja Ceh, Ermin Šiljak, Zlatko Zahović (65 Sebastjan Cimirotić), Miran Pavlin, Milenko Acimović. Trainer: Bojan Prašnikar

FRANCE: Fabien Barthez, Lilian Thuram, Marcel Desailly, Mickäel Silvestre, Bixente Lizarazu, Claude Makélélé, Patrick Vieira, Zinedine Zidane (79 Robert Pires), Sylvain Wiltord (75 Willy Sagnol), David Trezeguet (69 Olivier Dacourt), Thierry Henry. Trainer: Jacques Santini

Sent off: Makelele (67)

Goals: Trezeguet (9), Dacourt (71)

CYPRUS v SLOVENIA 2-2 (0-2)

Tsirion, Limassol 11.10.2003

Referee: Tom Henning Ovrebo (NOR) Attendance: 2,346

CYPRUS: Nikos Panagiotou; Nikos Georgiou, Georgiou (77 Lambrou), Nikos Nikolaou, Marios Ilia, Stelios Okkarides, Giasoumas Giasoumi, Giotis Engomitis (46 Eleftherakis Eleftheriou), Mihalis Konstantinou (1 Elias Haralambous), Michael Morphis, Nikos Nikolaou. Trainer: Momcilo Vukotić

SLOVENIA: Marko Simeunović; Fabijan Cipot (24 Spasoje Bulajić), Muamer Vugdalić, Aleksander Knavs (1 Matej Snofl), Goran Šukalo, Nastja Ceh, Ermin Šiljak, Miran Pavlin, Mladen Rudonja (85 Robert Koren), Adem Kapić, Milenko Acimović. Trainer: Bojan Prašnikar

Goals: Šiljak (11, 41), Georgiou (71), Giasoumi (81)

FRANCE v ISRAEL 3-0 (3-0)

Stade de France, Paris 11.10.2003

Referee: Cosimo Bolognino (ITA) Attendance: 56,000

FRANCE: Fabien Barthez, Réveillère, Bixente Lizarazu, Jean-Alain Boumsong, Robert Pires (85 Ludovic Giuly), Zinedine Zidane, Thierry Henry (76 Djibril Cissé), Lilian Thuram, Olivier Dacourt, Benoît Pedretti, David Trezeguet (85 Steve Marlet). Trainer: Jacques Santini

ISRAEL: Nir Davidovitch; Alon Harazi, Arik Benado, Shimon Gershon, Adoram Keise, Haim Revivo, Walid Badir (75 Kfir Udi), Idan Tal, Zitoni (88 Pini Balili), Yossi Benayoun, Michael Zandberg (46 Josef Abukasis). Trainer: Avraham Grant

Goals: Henry (9), Trezeguet (24), Boumsong (42)

	P	W	D	L	F	A	Pts
France	8	8	0	0	29	2	24
Slovenia	8	4	2	2	15	12	14
Israel	8	2	3	3	9	11	9
Cyprus	8	2	2	4	9	18	8
Malta	8	0	1	7	5	24	1

GROUP 2

NORWAY v DENMARK 2-2 (0-1)

Ullevål, Oslo 07.09.2002

Referee: Hugh Dallas (SCO) Attendance: 25,114

NORWAY: Frode Grodås; André Bergdølmo, Ronny Johnsen, Henning Berg, Christer Basma, Steffen Iversen, Trond Andersen (77 John Carew), Øyvind Leonhardsen (77 Roar Strand), Eirik Bakke (88 Svindal Larsen), Ole Gunnar Solskjaer, John Arne Riise. Trainer: Nils Johan Semb

DENMARK: Thomas Sørensen, Christian Poulsen, Steven Lustü, Martin Laursen, Niclas Jensen, Thomas Helveg, Thomas Gravesen, Jesper Grønkjaer (70 Claus Jensen), Jon Dahl Tomasson (90+2 Per Nielsen), Dennis Rommedahl (59 Jan Michaelsen), Ebbe Sand. Trainer: Morten Olsen

Goals: Tomasson (23, 72), Riise (54), Carew (90+3)

BOSNIA HERZEGOVINA v ROMANIA 0-3 (0-3)

Koševo, Sarajevo 07.09.2002

Referee: Lucilio CARDOSO CORTEZ BATISTA (POR) Attendance: 4,500

BOSNIA HERZEGOVINA: Tomislav Piplica; Mirsad Bešlija (41 Senad Brkić), Vedin Mušić, Mirsad Hibić, Munever Rižvić, Asmir Ikanović (37 Jasmin Hurić), Ahmedin Hota, Samir Muratović, Hasan Salihamidžić, Zlatan Bajramović (46 Bruno Akrapović), Siniša Mulina. Trainer: Blaz Slišković

ROMANIA: Bogdan Stelea (33 Bogdan Argeş Vintilă); Cosmin Marius Contra, Matei Mirel Rădoi, Dorinel Munteanu, Cristian Chivu, Gheorghe Popescu (Cap), Paul Constantin Codrea (84 Tiberiu Ghioane), Vlad Munteanu, Ionel Ganea, Adrian Mutu, Marius Constantin Niculae (66 Florin Cernat). Trainer: Anghel Iordănescu

Goals: Chivu (7), D. Munteanu (8), Ganea (27)

DENMARK v LUXEMBOURG 2-0 (0-0)

Idraetsparken, København 12.10.2002

Referee: Ferenc Bede (HUN) Attendance: 40,259

DENMARK: Skov-Jensen; Kasper Bøgelund, René Henriksen, Christian Poulsen, Niclas Jensen, Claus Jensen, Thomas Gravesen, Dennis Rommedahl (67 Røll Larsen), Jon Dahl Tomasson, Martin Jørgensen (75 Peter Lovenkrands), Ebbe Sand. Trainer: Morten Olsen

LUXEMBOURG: Alija Besic; Ralph Ferron, Frank Deville, Eric Hoffmann, Jeff Strasser, Sébastien Remy (83 Nico Funck), Claude Reiter, Luc Holtz (83 Sven Di Domenico), Fons Leweck, Manuel Cardoni, Gordon Braun (79 Daniel Huss). Trainer: Allan Simonsen

Goals: Tomasson (52 pen), Ebbe Sand (72)

ROMANIA v NORWAY 0-1 (0-0)

Steaua, Bucureşti 12.10.2002

Referee: Valentin Ivanov (RUS) Attendance: 21,000

ROMANIA: Bogdan Argeş Vintilă; Cosmin Marius Contra, Matei Mirel Rădoi, Răzvan Dincă Raţ, Cristian Chivu, Gheorghe Popescu (Cap), Paul Codrea, Dorinel Munteanu (85 Daniel Pancu), Ioan Viorel Ganea (63 Adrian Ilie), Adrian Mutu, Dinu Viorel Moldovan (63 Marius Niculae). Trainer: Anghel Iordănescu

NORWAY: Thomas Myhre; André Bergdølmo, Claus Lundekvam, Henning Berg, Christer Basma, Steffen Iversen, John Carew (78 Øyvind Leonhardsen), Trond Andersen, Eirik Bakke, Ole Gunnar Solskjaer (90 Sigurd Rushfeldt), John Arne Riise. Trainer: Nils Johan Semb

Goal: Iversen (83)

NORWAY v BOSNIA HERZEGOVINA 2-0 (2-0)

Ullevål, Oslo 16.10.2002

Referee: Michal Benes (CZE) Attendance: 24,169

NORWAY: Frode Olsen; André Bergdølmo, Claus Lundekvam, Henning Berg, Christer Basma, Steffen Iversen, Trond Andersen (90 Svindal Larsen), Øyvind Leonhardsen (65 John Carew), Eirik Bakke, Ole Gunnar Solskjaer (90 Sigurd Rushfeldt), John Arne Riise. Trainer: Nils Johan Semb

BOSNIA HERZEGOVINA: Almir Tolja; Spomenko Bosnjak (65 Edin Mujcin), Sasa Papac, Mirsad Hibić, Zlatan Bajramović, Muhamed Konjić, Vedin Mušić, Nermin Sabić (57 Jasmin Hurić), Vladan Grujić, Hasan Salihamidzić (84 Nenad Misković), Elvir Baljić. Trainer: Blaz Slišković

Goals: Lundekvam (7), Riise (27)

LUXEMBOURG v ROMANIA 0-7 (0-4)

Stade Municipal Josy Barthel, Luxembourg 16.10.2002

Referee: Romans Lajuks (LAT) Attendance: 2,056

LUXEMBOURG: Alija Besic; Ralph Ferron, Frank Deville, Eric Hoffmann, Jeff Strasser, Sébastien Remy, Claude Reiter, Luc Holtz (76 Sacha Rohmann), Fons Leweck, Manuel Cardoni (60 Sacha Schneider), Gordon Braun (71 Daniel Huss). Trainer: Allan Simonsen

ROMANIA: Bogdan Argeş Vintilă; Cosmin Marius Contra, Matei Mirel Rădoi, Răzvan Dincă Raţ, Ilie Iulian Miu, Gheorghe Popescu, Paul Codrea (36 Tiberiu Ghioane), Dorinel Munteanu, Dinu Viorel Moldovan (69 Florin Cernat), Adrian Ilie, Ioan Viorel Ganea (46 Daniel Pancu). Trainer: Anghel Iordănescu

Goals: Moldovan (2, 5), Rădoi (24), Contra (45, 47, 86), Ghioane (80)

BOSNIA HERZEGOVINA v LUXEMBOURG 2-0 (0-0)

Bilino Polje, Zenica 29.03.2003

Referee: Jouni Hyytiä (FIN) Attendance: 12,000

BOSNIA HERZEGOVINA: Kennan Hasagić; Bulend Bišcević (68 Dzemal Berberović), Vedin Music, Muhamed Konjić, Zlatan Bajramović, Haris Alihodzić, Elvir Bolić (81 Almir Turković), Mirsad Bešlija (79 Mirko Hrgović), Sergej Barbarez, Vladan Grujić, Elvir Baljić. Trainer: Blaz Slišković

LUXEMBOURG: Alija Besic; René Peters, Ben Federspiel, Eric Hoffmann, Jeff Strasser, Sébastien Remy, Manou Schauls, Gregory Molitor, Gordon Braun (88 Sacha Schneider), Fons Leweck (77 Sven Di Domenico), Marcel Christophe (85 Daniel Huss). Trainer: Allan Simonsen

Goals: Bolić (53), Barbarez (79)

ROMANIA v DENMARK 2-5 (1-1)

Naţional, Bucureşti 29.03.2003

Referee: Manuel Enrique MEJUTO GONZÁLEZ (SPA) Attendance: 50,300

ROMANIA: Bogdan Lobonţ; Cosmin Marius Contra, Matei Mirel Rădoi, Iulian Sebastian Filipescu, Cristian Chivu, Gheorghe Popescu (Cap), Paul Constantin Codrea (62 Laurenţiu Aurelian Reghecampf), Dorinel Munteanu, Ioan Viorel Ganea, Adrian Mutu, Daniel Pancu (68 Florin Bratu). Trainer: Anghel Iordănescu

DENMARK: Thomas Sørensen; Thomas Rytter (35 Jan Michaelsen), René Henriksen, Martin Laursen, Niclas Jensen, Christian Poulsen (67 Morten Wieghorst), Thomas Gravesen, Peter Lovenkrands (46 Martin Jørgensen), Jon Dahl Tomasson, Dennis Rommedahl, Ebbe Sand. Trainer: Morten Olsen

Goals: Mutu (5), Rommedahl (9, 90+1), Munteanu (47), Gravesen (53), Tomasson (71), Contra (73 og)

LUXEMBOURG v NORWAY 0-2 (0-0)

Josy Barthel, Luxembourg 02.04.2003

Referee: Ivan Dobrinov (BUL) Attendance: 3,000

LUXEMBOURG: Alija Besic; René Peters, Ben Federspiel, Eric Hoffmann, Jeff Strasser, Sébastien Remy, Manou Schauls, Gregory Molitor, Gordon Braun (76 Sacha Schneider), Fons Leweck (90+2 Gilles Engeldinger), Marcel Christophe (83 Daniel Huss). Trainer: Allan Simonsen

NORWAY: Frode Olsen; André Bergdølmo, Ronny Johnsen, Henning Berg, Christer Basma, Petter Rudi (46 Jo Tessem), Trond Andersen, Eirik Bakke (86 Svindal Larsen), Tore André Flo (46 Sigurd Rushfeldt), Ole Gunnar Solskjaer, John Arne Riise. Trainer: Nils Johan Semb

Goals: Rushfeldt (58), Solskjaer (73)

DENMARK v BOSNIA HERZEGOVINA 0-2 (0-2)

Parken, København 02.04.2003

Referee: Anton Stredak (SVK) Attendance: 30,845

DENMARK: Thomas Sørensen; Jan Michaelsen, René Henriksen, Martin Albrechtsen, Niclas Jensen (80 Per Frandsen), Claus Jensen (59 Morten Weighorst), Thomas Gravesen, Dennis Rommedahl, Jon Dahl Tomasson (84 Soren Berg), Martin Jørgensen, Ebbe Sand. Trainer: Morten Olsen

BOSNIA HERZEGOVINA: Kennan Hasagić; Dzemal Berberović, Vedin Music, Muhamed Konjić, Zlatan Bajramović, Mirsad Hibić, Mirsad Bešlija (83 Sinisa Mulina), Bulend Bišcević, Sergej Barbarez, Mirko Hrgović (67 Vladan Grujić), Elvir Baljić (76 Blatnak). Trainer: Blaz Slišković

Goals: Barbarez (23), Baljić (29)

DENMARK v NORWAY 1-0 (1-0)

Parken, København 07.06.2003

Referee: Graham Poll (ENG) Attendance: 41,824

DENMARK: Thomas Sørensen; Morten Weighorst, René Henriksen, Martin Laursen, Niclas Jensen, Thomas Helveg, Thomas Gravesen, Jesper Grønkjaer (71 Dennis Rommedahl), Claus Jensen (62 Røll Larsen), Martin Jørgensen (84 Per Nielsen), Ebbe Sand. Trainer: Morten Olsen

NORWAY: Frode Olsen; Christer Basma, Ronny Johnsen, Claus Lundekvam, Steffen Iversen, John Carew, Trond Andersen (46 Andre Bergdølmo), Ole Gunnar Solskjaer (90 Haavard Flo), Eirik Bakke, Øyvind Leonhardsen (62 Tore André Flo), John Arne Riise. Trainer: Nils Johan Semb

Goal: Grønkjaer (6)

ROMANIA v BOSNIA HERZEGOVINA 2-0 (0-0)

Ion Oblemenco, Craiova 07.06.2003

Referee: Ruud Bossen (HOL) Attendance: 25,292

ROMANIA: Bogdan Lobonţ; Cosmin Marius Contra, Răzvan Dincă Raţ, Adrian Iencsi, Cristian Chivu, Matei Mirel Rădoi, Paul Constantin Codrea (65 Zeno Marius Bundea), Daniel Pancu, Ioan Viorel Ganea, Adrian Mutu (86 Miu), Adrian Ilie (78 Florin Costin Şoavă). Trainer: Anghel Iordănescu

BOSNIA HERZEGOVINA: Kennan Hasagić; Dzemal Berberović (78 Blatnak), Vedin Music, Muhamed Konjić, Zlatan Bajramović, Mirsad Hibić, Bolić, Mirsad Bešlija (50 Bartolović), Sergej Barbarez, Vladan Grujić, Hrgović. Trainer: Blaz Slišković

Goals: Mutu (46), Ganea (88)

LUXEMBOURG v DENMARK 0-2 (0-1)

Josy Barthel, Luxembourg 11.06.2003

Referee: Yuri Baskakov (RUS) Attendance: 6,869

LUXEMBOURG: Alija Besic; Claude Reiter, Ben Federspiel, Manuel Schauls, Jeff Strasser, Sébastien Remy, Fons Leweck, Gregory Molitor, Patrick Posing, Manuel Cardoni, Gordon Braun (71 Marcel Christophe). Trainer: Allan Simonsen

DENMARK: Thomas Sørensen; Morten Weighorst (53 Røll Larsen), René Henriksen, Martin Laursen, Niclas Jensen, Kasper Bøgelund, Thomas Gravesen, Jesper Grønkjaer (64 Dennis Rommedahl), Claus Jensen, Martin Jørgensen, Ebbe Sand (74 Morten Skoubo). Trainer: Morten Olsen

Goals: C. Jensen (22), Gravesen (50)

NORWAY v ROMANIA 1-1 (0-0)

Ullevål, Oslo 11.06.2003

Referee: Lubos Michel (SVK) Attendance: 24,890

NORWAY: Frode Olsen; André Bergdølmo, Ronny Johnsen, Henning Berg (Cap) (85 Claus Lundekvam), Christer Basma, Frode Johnsen (70 Tore André Flo), John Carew (81 Steffen Iversen), Eirik Bakke, Trond Andersen, Ole Gunnar Solskjaer, John Arne Riise. Trainer: Nils Johan Semb

ROMANIA: Bogdan Lobonţ; Cosmin Marius Contra, Răzvan Dincă Raţ, Adrian Mihai Iencsi, Cristian Eugen Chivu, Matei Mirel Rădoi, Florin Costin Şoavă, Daniel Gabriel Pancu (86 Florin Daniel Bratu), Ioan Viorel Ganea, Adrian Mutu, Adrian Bucurel Ilie (46 Alin Tudor Stoica).
Trainer: Anghel Iordănescu

Goals: Ganea (64), Solskjaer (78 pen)

BOSNIA HERZEGOVINA v NORWAY 1-0 (0-0)

Bilino Polje, Zenica 06.09.2003

Referee: Stéphane Bre (FRA) Attendance: 18,000

BOSNIA HERZEGOVINA: Kennan Hasagić; Emir Spahić, Sasa Papac, Muhamed Konjić, Zlatan Bajramović, Mirsad Hibić, Elvir Bolić, Vladan Grujić, Sergej Barbarez (89 Bulend Bišcević), Hasan Salihamidzić (65 Mirsad Bešlija), Vedin Musić (69 Mirko Hrgović). Trainer: Blaz Slišković

NORWAY: Espen Johnsen; André Bergdølmo, Ronny Johnsen, Henning Berg, Christer Basma, Roar Strand (88 Jan Gunnar Solli), John Carew (73 Tore André Flo), Martin Andresen, Brede Hangeland, Ole Gunnar Solskjaer, John Arne Riise. Trainer: Nils Johan Semb

Goal: Bajramović (87)

ROMANIA v LUXEMBOURG 4-0 (3-0)

Astra, Ploieşti 06.09.2003

Referee: Alon Yefet (ISR) Attendance: 4,500

ROMANIA: Bogdan Ionuţ Lobonţ; Flavius Vladimir Stoican, Mihai Adrian Iencsi, Cristian Eugen Chivu (Cap) (46 Florin Costin Şoavă), Răzvan Dincă Raţ; Florentin Dumitru, Mirel Matei Rădoi, Daniel Gabriel Pancu (76 Alin Tudor Adi Stoica), Dorinel Ionel Munteanu; Ioan Viorel Ganea, Adrian Mutu (46 Florin Daniel Bratu). Trainer: Anghel Iordănescu

LUXEMBOURG: Alija Besic; Rene Peters, Manou Schauls, Eric Hoffmann, Ben Federspiel; Alphonse Leweck, Claude Reiter, Jeff Strasser, Sebastien Remy; Gordon Braun (85 Daniel Huss), Manuel Cardoni (Cap) (85 Paul Mannon).
Trainer: Allan Simonsen

Goals: Mutu (39), Pancu (42), Ganea (43), Bratu (78)

LUXEMBOURG v BOSNIA HERZEGOVINA 0-1 (0-1)

Josy Barthel, Luxembourg 10.09.2003

Referee: Kostas Kapitanis (CYP) Attendance: 3,425

LUXEMBOURG: Alija Besic; Rene Peters, Ben Federspiel (55 Gilles Engeldinger), Eric Hoffmann, Jeff Strasser, Sebastien Remy, Manou Schauls, Claude Reiter, Alphonse Leweck, Gordon Braun (22 Paul Mannon), Daniel Huss.
Trainer: Allan Simonsen

BOSNIA HERZEGOVINA: Kennan Hasagić; Emir Spahić, Almir Turković, Muhamed Konjić, Zlatan Bajramović, Mirsad Hibić, Elvir Bolić (62 Mirsad Bešlija), Jasmin Hurić (62 Bulend Bišcević), Sergej Barbarez, Hasan Salihamidzić, Mirko Hrgović (78 Sasa Papac). Trainer: Blaz Slišković

Goal: Barbarez (35)

DENMARK v ROMANIA 2-2 (1-0)

"Parken", København 10.09.2003

Referee: Urs Meier (SWI) Attendance: 42,049

DENMARK: Thomas Sørensen; Thomas Helveg, Martin Laursen, René Henriksen (Cap), Niclas Jensen; Thomas Gravesen, Morten Weighorst (63 Christian Poulsen), Jesper Grønkjaer (80 Dennis Rommedahl); Martin Jørgensen, Jon Dahl Tomasson (55 Claus Jensen), Ebbe Sand.
Trainer: Morten Olsen

ROMANIA: Bogdan Ionuţ Lobonţ; Flavius Vladimir Stoican, Mihai Adrian Iencsi, Cristian Eugen Chivu (Cap), Răzvan Dincă Raţ; Florentin Dumitru (70 Florin Lucian Cernat), Mirel Matei Rădoi, Dorinel Ionel Munteanu, Daniel Gabriel Pancu; Ioan Viorel Ganea (67 Florin Daniel Bratu), Adrian Mutu (90+2 Alin Tudor Adi Stoica). Trainer: Anghel Iordănescu

Goals: Tomasson (34 pen), Mutu (62), Pancu (71), Laursen (90+5)

NORWAY v LUXEMBOURG **1-0** (1-0)

Ullevål, Oslo 11.10.2003

Referee: Zsolt Szabo (HUNG) Attendance: 22,255

NORWAY: Espen Johnsen; John Arne Riise, Claus Lundekvam, Henning Berg, Christer Basma, Roar Strand, Fredrik Winsnes (80 Trond Andersen), Martin Andresen, Tore André Flo (84 Sigurd Rushfeldt), Svindal Larsen, Harald Martin Brattbakk. Trainer: Nils Johan Semb

LUXEMBOURG: Alija Besic; Rene Peters, Eric Hoffmann, Jeff Strasser, Sebastien Remy, Manou Schauls, Paul Mannon (72 Sven Di Domenico), Alphonse Leweck, Gordon Braun, Daniel Huss, Stephane Gillet. Trainer: Allan Simonsen

Goal: T.A. Flo (18)

BOSNIA HERZEGOVINA v DENMARK **1-1** (1-1)

Koševo, Sarajevo 11.10.2003

Referee: Graham Barber (ENG) Attendance: 35,630

BOSNIA HERZEGOVINA: Kennan Hasagić; Emir Spahić (45 Elvir Baljić), Vedin Music, Muhamed Konjić (80 Mirko Hrgović), Zlatan Bajramović (86 Bulend Bišcević), Mirsad Hibić, Elvir Bolić, Vladan Grujić, Sergej Barbarez, Hasan Salihamidzić, Mirsad Bešlija. Trainer: Blaz Slišković

DENMARK: Thomas Sørensen; Morten Weighorst, René Henriksen (Cap), Martin Laursen, Niclas Jensen (90+3 Per Nielsen), Thomas Helveg, Thomas Gravesen, Jesper Grønkjaer (85 Røll Larsen), Martin Jørgensen (57 Dennis Rommedahl), Jon Dahl Tomasson, Christian Poulsen.
Trainer: Morten Olsen

Sent off: Gravesen (90+2)

Goals: Jørgensen (12), Bolić (39)

	P	W	D	L	F	A	Pts
Denmark	8	4	3	1	15	9	15
Norway	8	4	2	2	9	5	14
Romania	8	4	2	2	21	9	14
Bosnia Herz.	8	4	1	3	7	8	13
Luxembourg	8	0	0	8	0	21	0

GROUP 3

AUSTRIA v MOLDOVA **2-0** (2-0)

Ernst Happel, Wien 07.09.2002

Referee: Stuart Dougal (SCO) Attendance: 25,114

AUSTRIA: Alex Manninger; Ernst Dospel, Michael Baur, Martin Hiden, Jürgen Panis, René Aufhauser, Markus Schopp (58 Gerd Wimmer), Thomas Flögel, Ivic Vastic (81 Michael Wagner), Andreas Herzog (Cap), Roman Wallner (68 Roland Linz). Trainer: Johann Hans Krankl

MOLDOVA: Evgeni Hmaruc, Alexandr Covalenco, Radu Rebeja, Ghenadie Olexici, Andrian Sosnovschi, Iurie Priganiuc (68 Vadim Boreţ), Victor Berco (46 Valeri Catînsus), Sergei Rogaciov, Stanislav Ivanov, Serghei Cleşcenco, Evghenie Boicenco (46 Boris Cebotari). Trainer: Victor Pasulko

Goals: Herzog (4 pen, 30 pen)

HOLLAND v BELARUS **3-0** (2-0)

Philips, Eindhoven 07.09.2002

Referee: Graham Barber (ENG) Attendance: 34,103

HOLLAND: Edwin van der Sar; Fernando Ricksen, Jaap Stam, Frank de Boer, Boudewijn Zenden, Mark van Bommel, Andy van der Meyde, Phillip Cocu, Ruud van Nistelrooij (69 Jimmy Floyd Hasselbaink), Patrick Kluivert, Edgar Davids (69 Raphael van der Vaart, 81 Michael Reiziger).
Trainer: Dick Advocaat

BELARUS: Valeri Shantalosov (86 Vasiliy Khomutovski); Aleksandr Kulchiy, Andrei Ostrovski, Aliaksandr Lukhvich, Sergei Shtanyuk, Sergei Gurenko, Alexandr Khatskevich (80 Piotr Kachura), Maksim Romashchenko, Sergei Omelyanchuk (75 Vladimir Shuneiko), Aleksandr Gleb, Vitali Kutuzov.
Trainer: Eduard Malofeev

Sent off: Romashchenko (82)

Goals: Davids (34), Kluivert (36), Hasselbaink (72)

MOLDOVA v CZECH REPUBLIC **0-2** (0-0)

Republican, Chişinău 12.10.2002

Referee: Leslie Irvine (NIR) Attendance: 3,000

MOLDOVA: Evgeni Hmaruc; Alexandr Covalenco, Radu Rebeja, Ghenadie Puşcă, Andrian Sosnovschi, Ghenadie Olexici, Valeri Catînsus, Boris Cebotari, Sergei Rogaciov (71 Alexandru Budanov), Vadim Boreţ (65 Stanislav Ivanov), Serghei Cleşcenco (46 Evghenii Patula).
Trainer: Viktor Pasulko **Sent off**: Sosnovschi (69)

CZECH REPUBLIC: Petr Cech; Zdenek Grygera, Marek Jankulovski, Rene Bolf, Tomáš Ujfaluši, Tomáš Galásek (55 Jirí Jarošik), Stepan Vachousek (87 Richard Dostálek), Karel Poborský, Jan Koller, Tomáš Rosický (81 Vratislav Lokvenc), Jirí Štajner. Trainer: Karel Brückner

Goals: Jankulovski (69 pen), Rosický (79)

BELARUS v AUSTRIA 0-2 (0-0)

Dinamo, Minsk 12.10.2002

Referee: Eric Poulat (FRA) Attendance: 23,000

BELARUS: Gennadi Tumilovich; Aleksandr Kulchiy, Andrii Ostrovski, Alexander Lukhvich, Sergei Shtanyuk, Sergei Gurenko, Alexander Khatskevich, Sergei Yaskovich (51 Sergei Omelyanchuk), Vladimir Shuneiko (64 Roman Vasilyuk), Aleksandr Gleb, Vitali Kutuzov (83 Nikolai Ryndyuk). Trainer: Eduard Malofeev

AUSTRIA: Alex Manninger, Ernst Dospel, Michael Baur, Martin Hiden, Bozo Kovacevic (90 René Aufhauser), Markus Schopp, Harald Cerny, Thomas Flögel, Roman Wallner (75 Muhammet Akagündüz), Michael Wagner, Volkan Kahraman (82 Andreas Herzog). Trainer: Johann Hans Krankl

Sent off: Lukkvich (84)

Goals: Schopp (57), Akagündüz (90)

BELARUS v MOLDOVA 2-1 (1-1)

Dinamo, Minsk 29.03.2003

Referee: Johan Verbist (BEL) Attendance: 8,000

BELARUS: Gennadi Tumilovich; Aleksandr Kulchiy, Andrei Ostrovski, Sergei Omelyanchuk, Andrei Lavrik, Sergei Gurenko, Alexander Khatskevich, Valentin Belkevich, Vladimir Shuneiko, Aleksandr Gleb (80 Maksim Romashchenko), Vitali Kutuzov (88 Denis Kovba). Trainer: Eduard Malofeev

MOLDOVA: Evgeni Hmaruc; Alexandr Covalenco, Radu Rebeja, Ion Testimiţanu, Valeri Catînsus, Iurie Priganiuc, Serghei Covalciuc, Ghenadie Olexici, Serghei Rogaciov (26 Alexandru Popovici, 62 Victor Berco), Boris Cebotari (80 Alexandru Golban), Serghei Cleşcenco. Trainer: Viktor Pasulko

Goals: Cebotari (14), Kutuzov (43), Gurenko (58)

CZECH REPUBLIC v BELARUS 2-0 (2-0)

Na Stínadlech, Teplice 16.10.2002

Referee: Helmut Fleischer (GER) Attendance: 12,860

CZECH REPUBLIC: Petr Cech; Martin Jiránek (86 Zdenek Grygera), Tomáš Ujfaluši, Tomáš Galásek, Rene Bolf, Marek Jankulovski, Milan Baroš, Karel Poborský, Jan Koller (57 Stepan Vachousek), Tomáš Rosický (90 Jirí Jarošik), Pavel Nedved. Trainer: Karel Brückner

BELARUS: Gennadi Tumilovich; Aleksandr Kulchiy, Vladimir Shuneiko (46 Sergei Omelyanchuk), Aliaksandr Khrapkouski, Sergei Shtanyuk, Sergei Gurenko, Alexander Khatskevich, Sergei Yashkovich (26 Andrei Lavrik), Maxym Romashchenko, Aleksandr Gleb (70 Nikolai Ryndyuk), Vitali Kutuzov. Trainer: Eduard Malofeev

Goals: Poborský (6), Baroš (23)

HOLLAND v CZECH REPUBLIC 1-1 (0-0)

Feyenoord, Rotterdam 29.03.2003

Referee: Kim Milton Nielsen (DEN) Attendance: 51,480

HOLLAND: Ronald Waterreus; Fernando Ricksen, Jaap Stam, Frank de Boer, Giovanni van Bronckhorst (40 Rafael van der Vaart), Clarence Seedorf, Mark van Bommel, Edgar Davids, Boudewijn Zenden, Ruud van Nistelrooij (81 Roy Makaay), Patrick Kluivert. Trainer: Dick Advocaat

CZECH REPUBLIC: Petr Cech; Zdenek Grygera, Tomáš Ujfaluši, Tomáš Galásek, Rene Bolf, Marek Jankulovski, Vladimír Šmicer (79 Martin Jiránek), Tomáš Rosický (68 Milan Baroš), Pavel Nedved, Karel Poborský, Jan Koller (88 Vratislav Lokvenc). Trainer: Karel Bruckner

Goals: van Nistelrooij (46), Koller (68)

AUSTRIA v HOLLAND 0-3 (0-3)

Ernst Happel, Wien 16.10.2002

Referee: Pierluigi Collina (ITA) Attendance: 46,300

AUSTRIA: Alex Manninger; Ernst Dospel, Michael Baur, Martin Hiden, Michael Wagner, Markus Schopp, Harald Cerny, Thomas Flögel, Roman Wallner (80 Paul Scharner), Andreas Herzog (46 René Aufhauser), Markus Weissenberger (76 Muhammet Akagündüz). Trainer: Johann Hans Krankl

HOLLAND: Edwin van der Sar; Fernando Ricksen, Jaap Stam, Frank de Boer, Boudewijn Zenden (69 Wilfred Bouma), Mark van Bommel (77 Ronald de Boer), Clarence Seedorf, Philip Cocu, Roy Makaay (80 Jimmy Floyd Hasselbaink), Patrick Kluivert, Edgar Davids. Trainer: Dick Advocaat

Sent off: Hiden (77)

Goals: Seedorf (16), Cocu (20), Makaay (30)

CZECH REPUBLIC v AUSTRIA 4-0 (2-0)

Letná, Praha 02.04.2003

Referee: Antonio Jesus LOPEZ NIETO (SPA) Att: 21,472

CZECH REPUBLIC: Petr Cech; Zdenek Grygera, Tomáš Ujfaluši, Tomáš Galásek, Rene Bolf, Marek Jankulovski, Vladimír Šmicer (63 Tomáš Rosický), Karel Poborský, Jan Koller (79 Vratislav Lokvenc), Pavel Nedved (74 Stepan Vachousek), Milan Baroš. Trainer: Karel Bruckner

AUSTRIA: Thomas Mandl; Paul Scharner, Mario Hieblinger, Stranzl, Emanuel Pogatetz, René Aufhauser, Markus Schopp, Thomas Flögel, Mario Haas (63 Ernst Dospel), Andreas Herzog (53 Bozo Kovacevic), Markus Weissenberger. Trainer: Johann Hans Krankl

Sent off: Kovacevic (56)

Goals: Nedved (19), Koller (32, 62), Jankulovski (57 pen)

MOLDOVA v HOLLAND 1-2 (1-1)

Sheriff, Tiraspol 02.04.2003

Referee: Alain Sars (FRA) Attendance: 12,500

MOLDOVA: Evgeni Hmaruc; Alexandru Covalenco, Ghenadie Olexici, Ion Testimiţanu, Valeri Catînsus, Iurie Priganiuc, Serghei Covalciuc (80 Victor Berco), Stanislav Ivanov, Vadim Boreţ, Boris Cebotari (86 Serghei Pogreban), Serghei Cleşcenco (63 Alexandru Golban). Trainer: Viktor Pasulko

HOLLAND: Ronald Waterreus; Michael Reiziger, Jaap Stam (63 Fernando Ricksen), Frank de Boer, Mark van Bommel, Edgar Davids, Clarence Seedorf (67 Ronald de Boer), Rafael van der Vaart (75 Pierre van Hooijdonk), Ruud van Nistelrooij, Patrick Kluivert, Boudewijn Zenden. Trainer: Dick Advocaat

Goals: Boreţ (17), van Nistelrooij (37), van Bommel (84)

CZECH REPUBLIC v MOLDOVA 5-0 (1-0)

Ander, Olomouc 11.06.2003

Referee: Kristinn Jakobsson (ICE) Attendance: 12,100

CZECH REPUBLIC: Petr Cech; Zdenek Grygera, Tomáš Ujfaluši, Tomáš Galásek, Rene Bolf, Marek Jankulovski, Vladimír Šmicer (59 Milan Baroš), Karel Poborský (65 Štajner), Jan Koller (80 Vratislav Lokvenc), Tomáš Rosický, Pavel Nedved. Trainer: Karel Bruckner

MOLDOVA: Evgenii Hmaruc; Serghei Covalenco, Ghenadie Olexici, Ivan Testemiţanu, Valeriu Catînsus, Iurie Priganiuc, Serghei Covalciuc (83 Pogreban), Stanislav Ivanov, Vadim Boreţ, Cebotari (76 Viorel Frunză), Serghei Rogaciov (76 Eugen Patula). Trainer: Viktor Pasulko

Sent off: Priganiuc (79)

Goals: Šmicer (41), Koller (73 pen), Štajner (82), Lokvenc (88, 90)

MOLDOVA v AUSTRIA 1-0 (0-0)

Sheriff, Tiraspol 07.06.2003

Referee: Joaquim Paulo PARATY DA SILVA (POR) Attendance: 2,000

MOLDOVA: Evgenii Hmaruc; Boris Cebotari, Ghenadie Olexici, Ivan Testimiţanu, Valeriu Catînsus, Iurie Priganiuc, Serghei Covalciuc, Stanislav Ivanov, Vadim Boreţ (68 Liviu Andriuţă), Viorel Frunză (85 Eduard Valuta), Serghei Rogaciov (78 Eugen Patula). Trainer: Viktor Pasulko

AUSTRIA: Thomas Mandl; Paul Scharner (80 Thomas Eder), Anton Ehmann, Ernst Dospel (56 Harald Cerny), Martin Stranzl, René Aufhauser, Markus Schopp, Thomas Flögel, Mario Haas, Michael Wagner (70 Roman Wallner), Roland Kirchler. Trainer: Johann Hans Krankl

Goal: Frunză (60)

AUSTRIA v BELARUS 5-0 (1-0)

Tivoli Neu, Innsbruck 11.06.2003

Referee: Peter Fröjdfeldt (SWE) Attendance: 8,100

AUSTRIA: Thomas Mandl (86 Payer); Paul Scharner, Anton Ehmann, Ernst Dospel, Martin Stranzl (46 Hieblinger), René Aufhauser, Cerny, Thomas Flögel, Mario Haas (61 Wallner), Michael Wagner, Roland Kirchler. Trainer: Johann Hans Krankl

BELARUS: Gennadi Tumilovich; Aleksandr Kulchiy, Andrei Ostrovski, Lukhvich, Shtanyuk (66 Khrapkouski), Sergei Gurenko, Omelyanchuk, Valentin Belkevich (55 Kovba), Maksim Romashchenko, Andrei Lavrik, Vitali Kutuzov (46 Vasilyuk). Trainer: Eduard Malofeev

Goals: Aufhauser (33), Haas (47), Kirchler (53), Wallner (62), Cerny (70)

BELARUS v HOLLAND 0-2 (0-0)

Dinamo, Minsk 07.06.2003

Referee: Tom Henning Ovrebo (NOR) Attendance: 28,500

BELARUS: Gennadi Tumilovich; Aleksandr Kulchiy, Andrei Ostrovski, Lukhvich, Shtanyuk (90+1 Omelyanchuk), Sergei Gurenko, Vladimir Shuneiko (75 Kovba), Valentin Belkevich, Maksim Romashchenko (51 Gleb), Andrei Lavrik, Vitali Kutuzov. Trainer: Eduard Malofeev

HOLLAND: van der Sar; Michael Reiziger (46 Bosvelt), Jaap Stam, Frank de Boer, van Bronckhorst (61 Overmars), Mark van Bommel, Clarence Seedorf, Cocu, Ruud van Nistelrooij (75 van der Vaart), Patrick Kluivert, Boudewijn Zenden. Trainer: Dick Advocaat

Goals: Overmars (62), Kluivert (68)

HOLLAND v AUSTRIA 3-1 (1-1)

Feyenoord, Rotterdam 06.09.2003

Referee: Eric Poulat (FRA) Attendance: 48,000

HOLLAND: Edwin van der Sar; Michael Reiziger, Jaap Stam, Frank de Boer, Boudewijn Zenden (46 Marc Overmars), Phillip Cocu, Andy van der Meyde (71 Arjen Robben), Mark van Bommel, Patrick Kluivert, Rafael van der Vaart (83 Ronald Waterreus), Edgar Davids (46 Pierre van Hooijdonk). Trainer: Dick Advocaat

AUSTRIA: Thomas Mandl; Martin Hiden, Anton Ehmann, Emanuel Pogatetz, Ernst Dospel, René Aufhauser, Markus Schopp, Thomas Flögel, Edi Glieder (65 Roland Kirchler), Andreas Ivanschitz, Roland Kollmann (65 Mario Haas). Trainer: Johann Hans Krankl

Goals: van der Vaart (29), Pogatetz (32), Kluivert (60), Cocu (62)

BELARUS v CZECH REPUBLIC 1-3 (1-1)

Dinamo, Minsk 06.09.2003

Referee: Thomas Michael McCurry (SCO)
Attendance: 28,000

BELARUS: Gennadi Tumilovich; Aleksandr Kulchiy, Andrei Ostrovski, Aleksandr Lukhvich, Siarhei Shtanyuk, Sergei Gurenko (82 Vitali Volodenkov), Rauneika (90+3 Aliaksandr Khrapkouski), Vitali Kutuzov (56 Aleksandr Gleb), Maksim Romashchenko, Geraschenko, Bulyga.
Trainer: Eduard Malofeev

CZECH REPUBLIC: Petr Cech; Zdenek Grygera, Tomáš Ujfaluši, Rene Bolf, Marek Jankulovski, Karel Poborský, Jan Koller, Tomáš Rosický (83 Stepan Vachousek), Pavel Nedved, Milan Baroš (66 Tomáš Hübschman), Roman Týce (35 Vladimír Šmicer). Trainer: Karel Bruckner

Goals: Bulyga (14), Nedved (37), Baroš (54), Šmicer (85)

CZECH REPUBLIC v HOLLAND 3-1 (2-0)

Toyota Arena, Praha 10.09.2003

Referee: Lucilio CARDOSO CORTEZ BATISTA (POR)
Attendance: 18,356

CZECH REPUBLIC: Petr Cech; Zdenek Grygera (25 Tomáš Hübschman), Tomáš Ujfaluši, Tomáš Galásek, Rene Bolf, Vladimír Šmicer (81 Stepan Vachousek), Karel Poborský, Jan Koller, Tomáš Rosický (60 Milan Baroš), Pavel Nedved, Martin Jiránek. Trainer: Karel Bruckner

HOLLAND: Edwin van der Sar; Michael Reiziger, Jaap Stam, Frank de Boer (46 André Ooijer), Phillip Cocu, Mark van Bommel, Marc Overmars (20 Paul Bosvelt), Edgar Davids, Ruud van Nistelrooij (71 Pierre van Hooijdonk), Patrick Kluivert, Rafael van der Vaart. Trainer: Dick Advocaat

Sent off: Davids (14)

Goals: Koller (15 pen), Poborský (38), van der Vaart (62), Baroš (90+4)

MOLDOVA v BELARUS 2-1 (1-0)

Sheriff, Tiraspol 10.09.2003

Referee: Dejan Delević (YUG) Attendance: 7,000

MOLDOVA: Evgeni Hmaruc; Alexandru Covalenco (74 Alexei Savinov), Ghenadie Olexici (69 Vadim Boreţ), Victor Barîşev, Valeri Catînsus, Eduard Valuta, Sergei Covalciuc, Stanislav Ivanov, Serghei Rogaciov, Boris Cebotari, Sergei Dadu (67 Serghei Cleşcenco). Trainer: Viktor Pasulko

BELARUS: Gennadi Tumilovich; Aleksandr Kulchiy, Andrei Ostrovski, Aleksandr Lukhvich, Siarhei Shtanyuk (42 Sergei Omelyanchuk), Sergei Gurenko, Rauneika, Gerashchenko, Bulyga, Maksim Romashchenko (63 Roman Vasilyuk), Vitali Kutuzov (50 Vitali Volodenkov). Trainer: Eduard Malofeev

Goals: Dadu (26), Covalciuc (88), Vasilyuk (90 pen)

HOLLAND v MOLDOVA 5-0 (1-0)

Philips, Eindhoven 11.10.2003

Referee: Zeljko Sirić (CRO) Attendance: 25,000

HOLLAND: Edwin van der Sar; Michael Reiziger, Jaap Stam (32 Roy Makaay), André Ooijer, Giovanni van Bronckhorst, Phillip Cocu, Andy van der Meyde, Sneijder, Patrick Kluivert (70 Pierre van Hooijdonck), Rafael van der Vaart, Marc Overmars (64 Arjen Robben). Trainer: Dick Advocaat

MOLDOVA: Evgeni Hmaruc; Alexandru Covalenco (62 Ivan Testimiţanu), Alexei Savinov, Eduard Valuta, Valeri Catînsus, Iurie Priganiuc, Sergei Covalciuc, Stanislav Ivanov (81 Iuri Miterev), Victor Barîşev, Boris Cebotari, Sergei Dadu (74 Alexandru Golban). Trainer: Viktor Pasulko

Goals: Kluivert (43), Sneijder (50), van Hooijdonk (73 pen), van der Vaart (79), Robben (88)

AUSTRIA v CZECH REPUBLIC 2-3 (0-1)

Ernst Happel, Wien 11.10.2003

Referee: Giorgos Kasnaferis (GRE) Attendance: 32,350

AUSTRIA: Thomas Mandl; Standfest, Martin Stranzl, Martin Hiden, Emanuel Pogatetz, Muhammet Akagündüz, Markus Schopp, Thomas Flögel (67 Michael Wagner), Edi Glieder (67 Ernst Dospel), Andreas Ivanschitz, Mario Haas (76 Roland Linz). Trainer: Johann Hans Krankl

CZECH REPUBLIC: Petr Cech; Petrouš, Tomáš Galásek, Rene Bolf, Marek Jankulovski (82 Vorisek), Heinz (67 Jan Koller), Jirí Štajner, Pavel Nedved, Vratislav Lokvenc, Stepan Vachousek, Martin Jiránek (41 Roman Týce).
Trainer: Karel Bruckner

Sent off: Schopp (65)

Goals: Jankulovski (26), Haas (49), Ivanschitz (77), Vachousek (78), Koller (90+2)

	P	W	D	L	F	A	Pts
Czech Republic	8	7	1	0	23	5	22
Holland	8	6	1	1	20	6	19
Austria	8	3	0	5	12	14	9
Moldova	8	2	0	6	5	19	6
Belarus	8	1	0	7	4	20	3

GROUP 4

SAN MARINO v POLAND 0-2 (0-0)

Serravalle 07.09.2002

Referee: Paul McKeon (IRE) Attendance: 2,210

SAN MARINO: Federico Gasperoni; Miko Gennari, Mauro Marani, Nicola Albani, Ivan Matteoni, Simone Bacciocchi, Lorenzo Moretti (70 Ermanno Zonzini), Michele Marani, Andrea Ugolini (78 Marco de Luigi), Andy Selva, Damiano Vannucci (83 Roberto Selva). Trainer: Giampaolo Mazza

POLAND: Pawel Kowalewski, Arkadiusz Glowacki, Mariusz Kukielka, Kamil Kosowski, Tomasz Kos, Jacek Bak, Pawel Kaczorowski, Artur Wichniarek (46 Tomasz Dawidowski), Maciej Zurawski, Radoslaw Kaluzny (60 Marcin Zewlakow), Emmanuel Olisadebe (80 Mariusz Lewandowski). Trainer: Zbigniew Boniek

Goals: Kaczorowski (75), Kukielka (88)

POLAND v LATVIA 0-1 (0-1)

Wojska Polskiego, Warszawa 12.10.2002

Referee: Massimo Busacca (SWI) Attendance: 12,000

POLAND: Jerzy Dudek; Krzysztof Ratajczyk, Mariusz Kukielka, Michal Zewlakow (46 Lukasz Surma), Jacek Zielinski, Tomasz Hajto, Tomasz Dawidowski, Artur Wichniarek (46 Marcin Zewlaow), Maciej Zurawski, Mariusz Lewandowski, Kamil Kosowski (63 Marcin Mieciel). Trainer: Zbigniew Boniek

LATVIA: Aleksandrs Kolinko; Igors Stepanovs, Vitalis Astafjevs, Mihails Zemlinskis, Juris Laizans, Oleg Blagonadezdins, Aleksandrs Isakovs, Imants Bleidelis, Marians Pahars (59 Andrejs Prohorenkovs), Andrejs Rubins, Maris Verpakovskis (89 Andrejs Štolcers). Trainer: Aleksandrs Starkovs

Goal: Laizans (29)

LATVIA v SWEDEN 0-0

Skonto, Riga 07.09.2002

Referee: Frank de Bleeckere (BEL) Attendance: 8,207

LATVIA: Aleksandrs Kolinko; Igors Stepanovs, Vitalijs Astafjevs, Mihails Zemlinskis, Juris Laizans, Oleg Blagonadezdins, Aleksandrs Isakovs, Imants Bleidelis, Maris Pahars (80 Andrejs Štolcers), Andrejs Rubins, Maris Verpakovskis. Trainer: Aleksandrs Starkovs

SWEDEN: Magnus Hedman; Olof Mellberg, Andreas Jakobsson, Michael Svensson, Tomas Antonelius, Tobias Linderoth, Niclas Alexandersson, Pontus Farnerud (56 Mattias Jonson), Magnus Svensson (79 Johansson), Marcus Allbäck, Zlatan Ibrahimovic (65 Kim Källström). Trainer: Lars Lagerbäck

HUNGARY v SAN MARINO 3-0 (0-0)

Megyeri úti, Budapest 16.10.2002

Referee: Gylfi Thor Orrason (ICE) Attendance: 8,000

HUNGARY: Gábor Király; Csaba Fehér, Attila Dragóner, Zsolt Löw, Gábor Gyepes, Flórián Urbán, Attila Tököli, Pál Dárdai (78 Miklós Fehér), Krisztián Kenesei (46 Zoltán Gera), Krisztián Lisztes (84 Vasile Miriuță), Péter Lipcsei. Trainer: Imre Gellei

SAN MARINO: Federico Gasperoni; Miko Gennari, Carlo Valentini (81 Ermanno Zonzini), Nicola Albani, Luca Gobbi, Simone Bacciocchi, Lorenzo Moretti (55 Roberto Selva), Michele Marani, Riccardo Muccioli (73 Paolo Montagna), Andy Selva, Damiano Vannucci. Trainer: Giampaolo Mazza

Goals: Gera (49, 60, 85)

SWEDEN v HUNGARY 1-1 (0-1)

Råsunda, Solna 12.10.2002

Referee: Wolfgang Stark (GER) Attendance: 35,084

SWEDEN: Andreas Isaksson; Olof Mellberg, Andreas Jakobsson, Michael Svensson, Tomas Antonelius (67 Mattias Jonson), Tobias Linderoth, Niclas Alexandersson (59 Kim Källström), Anders Svensson, Fredrik Ljungberg, Andreas Andersson, Zlatan Ibrahimovic (78 Marcus Allbäck). Trainer: Lars Lagerbäck

HUNGARY: Gábor Király; Csaba Fehér, Attila Dragóner, Zsolt Löw, Gábor Gyepes, Flórián Urbán, Attila Tököli (59 Miklós Fehér), Pál Dárdai, Krisztián Kenesei (70 Zoltán Gera), Krisztián Lisztes, Péter Lipcsei. Trainer: Imre Gellei

Goals: Kenesei (5), Ibrahimovic (76)

SAN MARINO v LATVIA 0-1 (0-0)

Olimpico, Serravalle 20.11.2002

Referee: Asim Khudiev (AZE) Attendance: 600

SAN MARINO: Federico Gasperoni, Carlo Valentini, Miko Gennari (86 Nicola Albani), Simone Bacciocchi, Ivan Matteoni, Luca Gobbi, Riccardo Muccioli, Michele Marani (53 Ermanno Zonzini), Paolo Montagna (59 Marco de Luigi), Andy Selva, Damiano Vannucci. Trainer: Giampaolo Mazza

LATVIA: Aleksandrs Kolinko; Igors Stepanovs, Vitalijs Astafjevs, Mihails Zemlinskis, Vladimir Kolesnicenko (57 Andrejs Prohorenkovs), Oleg Blagonadezdins, Aleksandrs Isakovs, Imants Bleidelis (46 Andrejs Štolcers), Marians Pahars, Andrey Rubins, Maris Verpakovskis (63 Mikhail Mikholaps). Trainer: Aleksandrs Starkovs

Goal: C. Valentini (89 og)

POLAND v HUNGARY 0-0

National Slaski, Chorzów 29.03.2003

Referee: Massimo de Santis (ITA) Attendance: 49,000

POLAND: Jerzy Dudek; Miroslaw Szymkowiak, Maciej Stolarczyk, Kamil Kosowski, Jacek Bak, Piotr Swierczewski, Tomasz Hajto, Marcin Kuzba, Radoslaw Kaluzny, Emmanuel Olisadebe, Marcin Zajac (72 Tomasz Dawidowski). Trainer: Zbigniew Boniek

HUNGARY: Gábor Király; Csaba Fehér, Flórián Urbán, Attila Dragóner, Tamás Juhár, Péter Lipcsei, Pál Dárdai, Krisztián Lisztes, Zsolt Löw, Attila Tököli (84 Zoltán Böör), Krisztián Kenesei (69 Jozsef Sebök). Trainer: Imre Gellei

POLAND v SAN MARINO 5-0 (2-0)

Mosir, Ostrowiec Swietokrzyski 02.04.2003

Referee: Loizos Loizou (CYP) Attendance: 6,000

POLAND: Jerzy Dudek; Burkhadt, Jacek Zielinski, Miroslaw Sznaucer, Kamil Kosowski, Jacek Bak (64 Wasilewski), Miroslaw Szymkowiak, Zajac (46 Bartosz Karwan), Maciej Zurawski, Marcin Kuzba, Emmanuel Olisadebe (39 Jacek Krzynówek). Trainer: Pawel Janas

SAN MARINO: Federico Gasperoni, Ermanno Zonzini (68 Brian Gasperoni), Mauro Marani, Simone Bacciocchi, Ivan Matteoni, Nicola Albani, Lorenzo Moretti, Riccardo Muccioli, Paolo Montagna (76 Marco de Luigi), Andy Selva (90 Andrea Ugolini), Damiano Vannucci. Trainer: Giampaolo Mazza

Goals: Szymkowiak (4), Kosowski (26), Kuzba (54, 90+3), Karwan (81)

HUNGARY v SWEDEN 1-2 (0-1)

Ferénc Puskas, Budapest 02.04.2003

Referee: Lucilio CARDOSO CORTEZ BATISTA (POR) Attendance: 28,000

HUNGARY: Gábor Király; Csaba Fehér, Attila Dragóner, Zsolt Löw, Tamás Juhár, Flórián Urbán (61 László Bodnár), Attila Tököli (67 József Sebök), Pál Dárdai, Krisztián Kenesei, Krisztián Lisztes, Péter Lipcsei (79 Zoltán Böör). Trainer: Imre Gellei

SWEDEN: Andreas Isaksson; Teddy Lucic, Olof Mellberg, Michael Svensson, Erik Edman, Johan Mjällby, Andreas Andersson, Anders Svensson (61 Kim Källström), Fredrik Ljungberg, Marcus Allbäck (90+2 Matias Jonson), Henrik Larsson. Trainer: Lars Lagerbäck

Goals: Allbäck (34, 66), Lisztes (65)

LATVIA v SAN MARINO 3-0 (2-0)

Skonto, Riga 30.04.2003

Referee: Hubert Byrne (IRE) Attendance: 7,500

LATVIA: Aleksandrs Kolinko; Igors N. Stepanovs, Zirnis, Mihails Zemlinskis, Juris Laizans, Andrejs Prohorenkovs, Aleksandrs Isakovs, Imants Bleidelis (83 Viktors Dobrecovs), Maris Verpakovskis (60 Vits Rimkus), Andrey Rubins, Mikhail Mikholaps (78 Andrejs Štolcers). Trainer: Aleksandrs Starkovs

SAN MARINO: Federico Gasperoni, Federico Valentini, Gennari, Simone Bacciocchi, Ivan Matteoni, Nicola Albani, Riccardo Muccioli (90 Brian Gasperoni), Mauro Marani, Paolo Montagna (64 de Luigi), Andy Selva, Damiano Vannucci. Trainer: Giampaolo Mazza

Goals: Prohorenkovs (9), Bleidelis (20, 74)

HUNGARY v LATVIA 3-1 (0-1)

Ferénc Puskas, Budapest 07.06.2003

Referee: Markus Merk (GER) Attendance: 5,000

HUNGARY: Zoltán Vegh; Csaba Fehér, Attila Dragóner (38 Zoltán Gera), Zsolt Löw, Tamás Juhár, Flórián Urbán, Imre Szabics, Pál Dárdai, Krisztián Kenesei (64 Miklos Lendvai), Krisztián Lisztes (77 Zoltán Böör), Péter Lipcsei. Trainer: Imre Gellei

LATVIA: Aleksandrs Kolinko; Igors N. Stepanovs, Vitalijs Astafjevs (76 Igors Semjonovs), Mihails Zemlinskis, Juris Laizans, Olegs Blagonadezdins, Aleksandrs Isakovs, Imants Bleidelis (78 Andrejs Štolcers), Maris Verpakovskis, Andrey Rubins, Valentins Lobanovs (73 Mihails Miholaps). Trainer: Aleksandrs Starkovs

Sent off: Juhár (61)

Goals: Verpakovskis (38), Szabics (51, 58), Gera (87)

SAN MARINO v SWEDEN 0-6 (0-1)

Seravalle 07.06.2003

Referee: Dejan Delević (SRBM) Attendance: 2,184

SAN MARINO: Federico Gasperoni, Carlo Valentini (66 Zonzini), Gennari, Nicola Albani, Simone Bacciocchi, Ivan Matteoni, Brian Gasperoni, Moretti (86 Roberto Selva), Paolo Montagna, Andy Selva, Damiano Vannucci (77 de Luigi). Trainer: Giampaolo Mazza

SWEDEN: Andreas Isaksson; Teddy Lucic, Olof Mellberg, Andreas Jakobsson, Erik Edman, Johan Mjällby (73 Andreas Johansson), Andreas Andersson, Kim Källström (57 Anders Svensson), Fredrik Ljungberg (73 Mikael Nilsson), Marcus Allbäck, Matias Jonson. Trainer: Lars Lagerbäck

Goals: Jonson (16, 60, 70), Allbäck (49, 85), Ljungberg (55)

SWEDEN v POLAND 3-0 (2-0)

Råsunda, Solna 11.06.2003

Referee: Gilles Veissiere (FRA) Attendance: 35,220

SWEDEN: Andreas Isaksson; Teddy Lucic (87 Michael Svensson), Olof Mellberg, Andreas Jakobsson, Erik Edman; Mikael Nilsson, Johan Mjällby, Anders Svensson, Fredrik Ljungberg; Marcus Allbäck, Matias Jonson (69 Magnus Svensson). Trainer: Lars Lagerbäck

POLAND: Jerzy Dudek; Marcin Baszczyński (46 Tomasz Kłos), Tomasz Hajto, Jacek Bąk, Maciej Stolarczyk; Tomasz Dawidowski, Mirosław Szymkowiak (76 Marcin Burkhardt), Tomasz Zdebel, Kamil Kosowski (64 Marcin Zając), Jacek Krzyńowek; Artur Wichniarek. Trainer: Paweł Janas

Goals: Anders Svensson (15, 70), Allbäck (43)

SAN MARINO v HUNGARY 0-5 (0-2)

Serravalle 11.06.2003

Referee: Kenneth William Clark (SCO) Attendance: 1,000

SAN MARINO: Federico Gasperoni; Carlo Valentini, Michele Marani, Nicola Albani, Simone Bacciocchi, Ivan Matteoni, Brian Gasperoni, Ermanno Zonzini, Marco de Luigi (73 Paulo Montagna), Andy Selva, Damiano Vannucci (65 Manolo Gennari). Trainer: Giampaolo Mazza

HUNGARY: Zoltán Vegh; Bodog, Attila Dragóner, Zsolt Löw, Tamás Szekeres (55 Akos Füzi), Péter Lipcsei (73 Miklos Lendvai), Imre Szabics, Pál Dárdai (78 Gábor Zavadszky), Krisztián Kenesei, Krisztián Lisztes, Zoltán Böör. Trainer: Imre Gellei

Goals: Böör (5), Lisztes (21, 81), Kenesei (60), Szabics (77)

LATVIA v POLAND 0-2 (0-2)

Skonto, Riga 06.09.2003

Referee: Kyros Vassaras (GRE) Attendance: 8,207

LATVIA: Aleksandrs Kolinko; Aleksandrs Isakovs, Mihalis Zemlinskis, Igors Stepanovs, Olegs Blagonadeždins; Imants Bleidelis, Juris Laizans, Valentins Lobanovs, Andrejs Rubins (77 Igors Semjonovs); Maris Verpakovskis (82 Andrejs Stolcers), Andrejs Prohorenkovs (80 Vits Rimkus). Trainer: Aleksadrs Starkovs

POLAND: Jerzy Dudek; Tomasz Kłos, Tomasz Hajto, Jacek Bąk, Krzysztof Ratajczyk; Mariusz Lewandowski (68 Kamil Kosowski), Mirosław Szymkowiak (88 Tomasz Zdebel), Radosław Sobolewski, Jacek Krzynówek; Maciej Żurawski, Paweł Kryszałowicz (46 Marek Saganowski). Trainer: Paweł Janas

Sent off: Laizans (60)

Goals: Szymkowiak (36), Klos (39)

SWEDEN v SAN MARINO 5-0 (1-0)

Ullevi, Göteborg 06.09.2003

Referee: Stefan Messner (AUS) Attendance: 31,098

SWEDEN: Andreas Isaksson; Teddy Lucic, Olof Mellberg, Michael Svensson, Erik Edman; Andreas Jakobsson (64 Tobias Linderoth), Mikael Nilsson, Anders Svensson (64 Andreas Johansson), Kim Källström, Zlatan Ibrahimovic, Mattias Jonson (72 Niklas Skoog). Trainer: Lars Lagerbäck

SAN MARINO: Federico Gasperoni, Carlo Valentini, Mirko Gennari (25 Luca Nanni), Nicola Albani, Simone Bacciocchi, Ivan Matteoni, Michele Marani, Lorenzo Moretti (84 Roberto Selva), Paolo Montagna, Gasperoni (8 Ermanno Zonzini), Damiano Vannucci. Trainer: Giampaolo Mazza

Goals: Jonson (32), Jakobsson (48), Ibrahimovic (53, 81), Källström (66 pen)

POLAND v SWEDEN 0-2 (0-2)

Slaski, Chorzów 10.09.2003

Referee: Michael Riley (ENG) Attendance: 20,000

POLAND: Jerzy Dudek; Tomasz Klos, Radoslaw Sobolewski, Michal Zewlakov, Miroslaw Szymkowiak, Jacek Bak, Tomasz Hajto, Jacek Krzynówek (69 Kamil Kosowski), Mariusz Lewandowski, Marek Saganowski (65 Grzegorz Rasiak), Maciej Zurawski (74 Pawel Kryszalowicz). Trainer: Pawel Janas

SWEDEN: Andreas Isaksson; Teddy Lucic, Olof Mellberg, Michael Svensson, Erik Edman; Andreas Jakobsson, Mikael Nilsson, Anders Svensson, Fredrik Ljungberg, Marcus Allbäck (89 Zlatan Ibrahimovic), Mattias Jonson (86 Andreas Andersson). Trainer: Lars Lagerbäck

Sent off: Hajto (63)

Goals: Nilsson (3), Mellberg (37)

LATVIA v HUNGARY 3-1 (2-0)

Skonto, Riga 10.09.2003

Referee: Claus Bo Larsen (DEN) Attendance: 7,500

LATVIA: Aleksandrs Kolinko; Igors N. Stepanovs, Vitalis Astafjevs, Mihails Zemlinskis, Valentins Lobanovs, Olegs Blagonadezdins, Dzintars Zirnis, Imants Bleidelis, Maris Verpakovskis (89 Vladimirs Kolesnicenko), Andrey Rubins, Vits Rimkus (76 Igors Semjonovs). Trainer: Aleksandrs Starkovs

HUNGARY: Gábor Kiraly; Csaba Fehér (46 Tamás Szekeres), Attila Dragóner, Zsolt Löw (46 Zoltán Böör), Tamás Juhár, Péter Lipcsei, Imre Szabics, Pál Dárdai, Miklós Fehér, Krisztián Lisztes, Zoltán Gera (85 Zoltán Kovács). Trainer: Imre Gellei

Goals: Verpakovskis (38, 51), Astafjevs (42), Lisztes (53)

SWEDEN v LATVIA 0-1 (0-1)

Råsunda, Solna 11.10.2003

Referee: Massimo de Santis (ITA) Attendance: 32,095

SWEDEN: Andreas Isaksson; Teddy Lucic (46 Mikael Dorsin), Olof Mellberg, Michael Svensson, Andreas Andersson (81 Andreas Johansson), Andreas Jakobsson, Mikael Nilsson, Anders Svensson, Kim Källström (64 Zlatan Ibrahimovic), Marcus Allbäck, Mattias Jonson. Trainer: Lars Lagerbäck

LATVIA: Aleksandrs Kolinko; Igors N. Stepanovs, Vitalis Astafjevs, Mihails Zemlinskis, Valentins Lobanovs, Olegs Blagonadezdins, Dzintars Zirnis, Imants Bleidelis, Maris Verpakovskis (88 Andrejs Štolcers), Andrey Rubins (81 Jurgis Pucinskis), Vits Rimkus (74 Aleksandrs Isakovs). Trainer: Aleksandrs Starkovs

Sent off: Zirnis (72)

Goal: Verpakovskis (22)

HUNGARY v POLAND 1-2 (0-1)

Ferénc Puskas, Budapest 11.10.2003

Referee: Manuel Enrique Mejuto Gonzalez (SPA) Att: 15,500

HUNGARY: Gábor Kiraly; Tamas Bodog, Attila Dragóner, Tamas Juhár; Zoltán Böör, Peter Lipcsei (46 Zoltán Gera), Krisztian Lisztes, Pal Dárdai, Akos Füzi; Miklós Fehér (64 Krisztian Kenesei), Imre Szabics. Trainer: Imre Gellei

POLAND: Jerzy Dudek; Tomasz Klos, Jacek Bak, Tomasz Rzasa; Jacek Krzynówek, Sebastian Mila (52 Kamil Kosowski), Radoslaw Sobolewski, Miroslaw Szymkowiak (85 Mariusz Lewandowski), Michal Zewlakow; Andrzej Niedzielan (88 Marek Saganowski), Grzegorz Rasiak. Trainer: Pawel Janas

Goals: Niedzielan (11, 62), Szabics (49)

	P	W	D	L	F	A	Pts
Sweden	8	5	2	1	19	3	17
Latvia	8	5	1	2	10	6	16
Poland	8	4	1	3	11	7	13
Hungary	8	3	2	3	15	9	11
San Marino	8	0	0	8	0	30	0

GROUP 5

FAROE ISLANDS v SCOTLAND 2-2 (2-0)

Toftír 07.09.2002

Referee: Jacek Granat (POL) Attendance: 4,000

FAROE ISLANDS: Jens Martin Knudsen; Oli Johannesen, Jens Hansen, Pol Thorsteinson, Jón Jacobsen, Hjalgrim Elttør (89 Hedin á Lakjuni), Frodi Benjaminsen, Julian Johnsson, Jakup a Borg, John Petersen (80 Andrew av Fløtum), Jacobsen (75 Jacobsen). Trainer: Henrik Larsen

SCOTLAND: Robert Douglas; Maurice Ross (76 Graham Alexander), Stephen Crainey, Christian Dailly, David Weir, Barry Ferguson, Paul Dickov (46 Steven Crawford), Scott Dobie (83 Steven Thompson), Kevin Kyle, Paul Lambert, Allan Johnston. Trainer: Hans-Hubert Vogts

Goals: John Petersen (7, 13), Lambert (62), Ferguson (83)

LITHUANIA v GERMANY 0-2 (0-1)

S. Darius & S. Girenas Sport C, Kaunas 07.09.2002

Referee: Graham Poll (ENG) Attendance: 8,419

LITHUANIA: Gintaras Stauce; Marius Stankevicius, Ignas Dedura, Dainius Gleveckas, Aurelijus Skarbalijus, Deividas Semberas, Raimondas Zutautas, Saulius Mikalajunas, Edgaras Jankauskas (77 Arturas Fomenko), Tomas Razanauskas (71 Igoris Morinas), Robertas Poškus.
Trainer: Benjaminas Zelkevicius

GERMANY: Oliver Kahn; Thomas Linke, Jörg Böhme, Christoph Metzelder, Carsten Ramelow, Dietmar Hamann, Torsten Frings, Michael Ballack, Carsten Jancker (68 Oliver Neuville), Bernd Schneider (85 Jens Jeremies), Miroslav Klose.
Trainer: Rudi Völler

Goals: Ballack (25), Stankevicius (58 og)

LITHUANIA v FAROE ISLANDS 2-0 (2-0)

S. Darius & S. Girenas Sport Club, Kaunas 12.10.2002

Referee: Dejan Delević (YUG) Attendance: 4,000

LITHUANIA: Gintaras Stauce; Andrius Skerla, Rolandas Dziaukstas, Dainius Gleveckas, Aurelijus Skarbalijus, Deividas Cesnauskis (77 Giedrius Slavickas, 84 Marius Stankevicius), Raimondas Zutautas (75 Nerijus Barasa), Saulius Mikalajunas, Arturas Fomenko, Tomas Razanauskas, Robertas Poškus.
Trainer: Benjaminas Zelkevicius

FAROE ISLANDS: Jakup Mikkelsen; Oli Johannesen, Jens Hansen, Pol Thorsteinsson (75 Jóhannis Joensen), Jón Jacobsen, Øssur Hansen, Frodi Benjaminsen, Johnsson (70 Rógvi Jacobsen), Jakup a Borg, John Petersen, Christian Jacobsen (62 Andrew av Fløtum). Trainer: Henrik Larsen

Goals: Razanauskas (23 pen), Poškus (37)

ICELAND v SCOTLAND 0-2 (0-1)

Laugardalsvöllur, Reykjavík 12.10.2002

Referee: Alain Sars (FRA) Attendance: 6,000

ICELAND: Árni Gautur Arason; Bjarni Thorsteinsson, Arnar Vidarsson (66 Marel Baldvinsson), Brynjar Gunnarsson, Larus Sigurdsson, Runar Kristinsson, Hermann Hreidarsson, Ívar Ingimarsson, Eidur Gudjohnsen, Helgi Sigurdsson (46 Heidar Helgason), Haukur Gudnason (75 Thórdur Gudjónsson). Trainer: Atli Edvaldsson

SCOTLAND: Robert Douglas, Maurice Ross, Lee Wilkie, Stephen Pressley, Christian Dailly, Barry Ferguson, Jackie McNamara (35 Callum Davidson), Steven Crawford, Steven Thompson (87 Scott Severin), Paul Lambert, Gary Naysmith (90 Russell Anderson). Trainer: Hans-Hubert Vogts

Goals: Dailly (7), Naysmith (63)

GERMANY v LITHUANIA 1-1 (1-0)

Frankenstadion, Nürnberg 29.03.2003

Referee: Victor José ESQUINAS TORRES (SPA) Att: 40,556

GERMANY: Oliver Kahn; Arne Friedrich, Tobias Rau (82 Paul Freier), Christian Wörns, Carsten Ramelow, Dietmar Hamann, Torsten Frings, Jörg Böhme (46 Marko Rehmer), Fredi Bobic (71 Kevin Kuranyi), Bernd Schneider, Miroslav Klose. Trainer: Rudi Völler

LITHUANIA: Gintaras Stauce; Deividas Semberas, Ignas Dedura, Nerijus Barasa, Vadim Petrenko (86 Rolandas Dziaukstas), Tomas Zvirgzdauskas, Igoris Morinas, Saulius Mikalajunas, Edgaras Jankauskas (90+4 Arturas Fomenko), Tomas Razanauskas, Arunas Pukelevicius (46 Darius Maciulevicius). Trainer: Benjaminas Zelkevicius

Goals: Ramelow (7), Razanauskas (72)

GERMANY v FAROE ISLANDS 2-1 (1-1)

Niedersachsenstadion, Hannover 16.10.2002

Referee: Dani Koren (ISR) Attendance: 36,692

GERMANY: Oliver Kahn; Arne Friedrich, Christian Wörns, Carsten Ramelow (46 Paul Freier), Torsten Frings, Dietmar Hamann, Carsten Jancker (69 Oliver Neuville), Bernd Schneider (87 Sebastian Kehl), Miroslav Klose, Michael Ballack, Jens Jeremies. Trainer: Rudi Völler

FAROE ISLANDS: Jakup Mikkelsen; Oli Johannesen, Jens Hansen, Pol Thorsteinson, Jón Jacobsen, Øssur Hansen, Frodi Benjaminsen, Sjúrdur Jacobsen, Jakup a Borg (71 Hjalgrim Elttør), John Petersen (87 Helgi Petersen), Andrew av Fløtum (77 Christian Jacobsen). Trainer: Henrik Larsen

Goals: Ballack (1 pen), Friedrich (45 og), Klose (59)

SCOTLAND v ICELAND 2-1 (1-0)

Hampden Park, Glasgow 29.03.2003

Referee: Rene Temmink (HOL) Attendance: 37,548

SCOTLAND: Robert Douglas; Graham Alexander, Lee Wilkie, Stephen Pressley, Christian Dailly, Barry Ferguson, Steven Crawford, Paul Lambert, Kenny Miller (82 Jackie McNamara), Don Hutchinson (66 Callum Davidson), Gary Naysmith. Trainer: Hans-Hubert Vogts

ICELAND: Árni Gautur Arason; Bjarni Thorsteinsson, Arnar Vidarsson (83 Helgi Sigurdsson), Larus Sigurdsson, Brynjar Gunnarsson, Runar Kristinsson, Gudni Bergsson, Ívar Ingimarsson, Eidur Gudjohnsen, Johannes Gudjonsson, Arnar Gretarsson. Trainer: Atli Edvaldsson

Goals: Miller (11), Gudjohnsen (48), Wilkie (70)

ICELAND v LITHUANIA 3-0 (0-0)

Laugardalsvöllur, Reykjavík 16.10.2002

Referee: Grzegorz Gilewski (POL) Attendance: 3,500

ICELAND: Árni Gautur Arason; Bjarni Thorsteinsson (37 Bjarni Gudjónsson), Arnar Vidarsson, Johannes Gudjonsson (75 Helgi Sigurdsson), Brynjar Gunnarsson, Ólafur Stígsson (65 Gylfi Einarsson), Hermann Hreidarsson, Ívar Ingimarsson, Eidur Gudjohnsen, Heidar Helgason, Haukur Gudnason. Trainer: Atli Edvaldsson

LITHUANIA: Gintaras Stauce; Andrius Skerla, Rolandas Dziaukstas, Dainius Gleveckas, Marius Stankevicius, Deividas Cesnauskis, Nerijus Barasa, Saulius Mikalajunas, Arturas Fomenko, Tomas Razanauskas, Robertas Poškus. Trainer: Benjaminas Zelkevicius

Sent off: Cesnauskis (21)

Goals: H. Helgason (50), Gudjohnsen (60, 73)

LITHUANIA v SCOTLAND 1-0 (0-0)

S. Darius & S. Girenas Sport C, Kaunas 02.04.2003

Referee: Fritz Stuchlik (AUS) Attendance: 6,400

LITHUANIA: Gintaras Stauce; Deividas Semberas, Ignas Dedura, Nerijus Barasa, Vadim Petrenko (71 Darius Maciulevicius), Tomas Zvirgzdauskas, Igoris Morinas, Saulius Mikalajunas (89 Orestas Buitkus), Edgaras Jankauskas (63 Arturas Fomenko), Tomas Razanauskas, Dainius Gleveckas. Trainer: Benjaminas Zelkevicius

SCOTLAND: Paul Gallacher; Graham Alexander, Lee Wilkie, Christian Dailly, Stephen Pressley, Jackie McNamara (78 Andy Gray), Steven Crawford (57 Paul Devlin), Paul Lambert, Kenny Miller, Don Hutchinson (84 Colin Cameron), Gary Naysmith. Trainer: Hans-Hubert Vogts

Goal: Razanauskas (74 pen)

SCOTLAND v GERMANY 1-1 (0-1)

Hampden Park, Glasgow 07.06.2003

Referee: Domenico Messina (ITA) Attendance: 48,037

SCOTLAND: Robert Douglas; Maurice Ross (76 Jackie McNamara), Gary Naysmith, Christian Dailly, Steven Pressley, Andy Webster, Paul Devlin (62 Gavin Rae), Paul Lambert, Kenny Miller (90 Steven Thompson), Steven Crawford, Colin Cameron. Trainer: Hans-Hubert Vogts

GERMANY: Oliver Kahn; Arne Friedrich, Tobias Rau (57 Paul Freier), Christian Wörns, Carsten Ramelow, Torsten Frings, Fredi Bobic, Bernd Schneider (87 Sebastian Kehl), Miroslav Klose (76 Oliver Neuville), Michael Ballack, Jens Jeremies. Trainer: Rudi Völler

Goals: Bobic (23), Miller (70)

ICELAND v FAROE ISLANDS 2-1 (0-0)

Laugardalsvöllur, Reykjavík 07.06.2003

Referee: Miroslav Liba (CZE) Attendance: 6,038

ICELAND: Árni Gautur Arason; Larus Sigurdsson (76 Gretarsson), Arnar Vidarsson, Larus Sigurdsson, Hreidarsson, Runar Kristinsson, Gudni Bergsson, Johannes Gudjonsson, Eidur Gudjohnsen, Thordur Gudjónsson, Helgi Sigurdsson (76 Tryggvi Gudmundsson). Trainer: Atli Edvaldsson

FAROE ISLANDS: Jakup Mikkelsen; Christian Jacobsen, Pól Thorsteinsson (80 Jóhannis Joensen), Súni Olsen, Jón Jacobsen, Jann Ingi Petersen (62 Helgi Petersem), Frodi Benjaminsen, Rógvi Jacobsen, Jakup a Borg, John Petersen, Andrew av Fløtum (65 Hjalgrím Elttør).
Trainer: Henrik Larsen

Goals: H. Sigurdsson (51), R. Jacobsen (63), T. Gudmundsson (90+2)

FAROE ISLANDS v GERMANY 0-2 (0-0)

Tórsvøllur, Tórshavn 11.06.2003

Referee: Jan Wegereef (HOL) Attendance: 6,500

FAROE ISLANDS: Jakup Mikkelsen; Óli Johannesen, Jóhannis Joensen, Pól Thorsteinson, Jón Jacobsen, Rógvi Jacobsen, Frodi Benjaminsen, Julian Johnsson, Jakup a Borg (61 Hjalgrím Elttør), John Petersen, Christian Jacobsen (77 Jann Ingi Petersen).
Trainer: Henrik Larsen

GERMANY: Oliver Kahn (46 Rost); Arne Friedrich, Tobias Rau (71 Hartmann), Christian Wörns, Carsten Ramelow, Freier, Neuville, Kehl, Fredi Bobic, Bernd Schneider, Jens Jeremies (65 Klose). Trainer: Rudi Völler

Goals: Klose (89), Bobic (90+2)

LITHUANIA v ICELAND 0-3 (0-0)

S. Darius & S. Girenas Sport C, Kaunas 11.06.2003

Referee: Sorin Corpodean (ROM) Attendance: 8,419

LITHUANIA: Gintaras Stauce; Deividas Semberas, Ignas Dedura, Nerijus Barasa (71 Darius Maciulevicius), Vadim Petrenko, Tomas Zvirgzdauskas, Raimondas Zutautas (63 Darius Danilevicius), Igoris Morinas, Edgaras Jankauskas (76 Olegas Guscinas), Tomas Razanauskas, Aurelius Skarbalius. Trainer: Algimantas Liubinskas. **Sent off**: Semberas (85)

ICELAND: Árni Gautur Arason; Brynjar Gunnarsson, Arnar Vidarsson (90 Indridi Sigurdsson), Larus Sigurdsson, Hreidarsson, Runar Kristinsson, Gudni Bergsson, Johannes Gudjonsson (88 Arnar Gretarsson), Eidur Gudjohnsen, Thordur Gudjónsson, Helgi Sigurdsson (81 Tryggvi Gudmundsson). Trainer: Atli Edvaldsson

Goals: T. Gudjónsson (60), Gudjohnsen (71), Hreidarsson (90+3)

FAROE ISLANDS v ICELAND 1-2 (0-1)

Tórsvøllur, Tórshavn 20.08.2003

Referee: Eduardo ITURRALDE GONZÁLEZ (SPA)
Attendance: 3,416

FAROE ISLANDS: Jakup Mikkelsen; Jann Ingi Petersen, Pól Thorsteinson (80 Jóhannis Joensen), Jón Jacobsen, Súni Olsen, Rógvi Jacobsen, Julian Johnsson, Christian Jacobsen, John Petersen (80 Helgi Petersen), Andrew Fløtum (56 Hjalgrím Elttør), Óli Johannesen. Trainer: Henrik Larsen

ICELAND: Árni Gautur Arason; Olafur Bjarnason, Arnar Vidarsson, Johannes Gudjonsson, Petur Marteinsson, Runar Kristinsson (78 Heidar Helgason), Hermann Hreidarsson, Brynjar Gunnarsson (71 Arnar Gretarsson), Eidur Gudjohnsen, Thordur Gudjónsson, Helgi Sigurdsson (86 Helgi Sigurdsson). Trainer: Atli Edvaldsson

Goals: Gudjohnsen (6), R. Jacobsen (65), Marteinsson (70)

SCOTLAND v FAROE ISLANDS 3-1 (2-1)

Hampden Park, Glasgow 06.09.2003

Referee: Darko Ceferin (SVN) Attendance: 40,901

SCOTLAND: Robert Douglas; Jackie McNamara, Gary Naysmith, Andy Webster, Lee Wilkie, Barry Ferguson, Paul Devlin (58 James McFadden), Colin Cameron, Paul Dickov (67 Gavin Rae), Steven Crawford (75 Steven Thompson), Neil McCann. Trainer: Hans-Hubert Vogts

FAROE ISLANDS: Jakup Mikkelsen; Petersen, Pól Thorsteinson, Jón Jacobsen, Rógvi Jacobsen, Fródi Benjaminsen, Julian Johnsson (84 Atli Danielsen), Jákup á Borg (84 Christian Lamhauge Holst), John Petersen, Helgi Petersen (65 Tor-Ingar Akselsen), Óli Johannesen.
Trainer: Henrik Larsen

Goals: McCann (8), Johnsson (35), Dickov (45), McFadden (73)

ICELAND v GERMANY 0-0

Laugardalsvöllur, Reykjavík 06.09.2003

Referee: Paul Allaerts (BEL) Attendance: 7,035

ICELAND: Árni Gautur Arason; Olafur Bjarnason, Indridi Sigurdsson (84 Arnar Vidarsson), Larus Sigurdsson, Petur Marteinsson (75 Arnar Gretarsson), Runar Kristinsson, Hermann Hreidarsson, Johannes Gudjonsson, Eidur Gudjohnsen, Thordur Gudjónsson, Heidar Helgason (78 Helgi Sigurdsson). Trainer: Atli Edvaldsson

GERMANY: Oliver Kahn, Christian Rahn, Arne Friedrich (61 Michael Hartmann), Christian Wörns, Carsten Ramelow, Frank Baumann, Oliver Neuville (46 Kevin Kuranyi), Sebastian Kehl, Bernd Schneider (70 Sebastian Deisler), Miroslav Klose, Michael Ballack. Trainer: Rudi Völler

GERMANY v SCOTLAND 2-1 (1-0)

Westfalenstadion, Dortmund 10.09.2003

Referee: Anders Frisk (SWE) Attendance: 67,000

GERMANY: Oliver Kahn, Arne Friedrich, Marko Rehmer, Christian Wörns, Carsten Ramelow, Frank Baumann, Fredi Bobic (74 Miroslav Klose), Bernd Schneider (79 Sebastian Kehl), Michael Ballack, Tobias Rau, Kevin Kuranyi. Trainer: Rudi Völler

SCOTLAND: Robert Douglas; Jackie McNamara, Gary Naysmith, Christian Dailly, Stephen Pressley, Barry Ferguson, James McFadden (53 Gavin Rae), Colin Cameron, Steven Thompson, Neil McCann, Paul Lambert (46 Maurice Ross). Trainer: Hans-Hubert Vogts

Sent off: Ross (66)

Goals: Bobic (25), Ballack (50 pen), McCann (60)

FAROE ISLANDS v LITHUANIA 1-3 (1-1)

Tofta, Toftír 10.09.2003

Referee: Edo Trivković (CRO) Attendance: 2,175

FAROE ISLANDS: Jens Knudsen; Hans Hansen, Súni Olsen, Pól Thorsteinson (50 Rógvi Jacobsen), Jón Jacobsen, Jann Ingi Petersen, Fródi Benjaminsen, Julian Johnsson (85 Atli Danielsen), Jákup á Borg (77 Tor-Ingar Akselsen), John Petersen, Christian Jacobsen. Trainer: Henrik Larsen

LITHUANIA: Eduardas Kurskis; Rolandas Dziaukstas, Ignas Dedura, Nerijus Barasa, Deividas Cesnauskis, Tomas Zvirgzdauskas, Igoris Morinas (77 Aurimas Kucys), Edgaras Cesnauskis, Edgaras Jankauskas, Elimantas Poderis (46 Tomas Tamosauskas), Donatas Vencevicius (90 Dimitrijus Guscinas). Trainer: Algimantas Liubinskas

Goals: Morinas (22, 57), Olsen (42), Vencevicius (88)

SCOTLAND v LITHUANIA 1-0 (0-0)

Hampden Park, Glasgow 11.10.2003

Referee: Claude Colombo (FRA) Attendance: 50,343

SCOTLAND: Robert Douglas; Jackie McNamara, Gary Naysmith, Christian Dailly, Stephen Pressley, Barry Ferguson, Gavin Rae, Colin Cameron (66 Darren Fletcher), Kenny Miller (66 Don Hutchison), Steven Crawford, James McFadden (90 Graham Alexander). Trainer: Hans-Hubert Vogts

LITHUANIA: Gintaras Stauce; Rolandas Dziaukstas, Ignas Dedura, Nerijus Barasa, Darius Regelskis (87 Ricardas Beniusis), Tomas Zvirgzdauskas, Donatas Vencevicius (82 Darius Maciulevicius), Giedruis Barevicius (46 Edgaras Cesnauskis), Aurelius Skarbalijus, Tomas Razanauskas, Robertas Poškus. Trainer: Algimantas Liubinskas

Goal: Fletcher (70)

GERMANY v ICELAND 3-0 (1-0)

AOL Arena, Hamburg 11.10.2003

Referee: Valentin Ivanov (RUS) Attendance: 50,785

GERMANY: Oliver Kahn, Arne Friedrich, Christian Rahn, Christian Wörns, Carsten Ramelow, Frank Baumann, Andreas Hinkel, Fredi Bobic (70 Miroslav Klose), Bernd Schneider, Michael Ballack, Kevin Kuranyi (85 Oliver Neuville). Trainer: Rudi Völler

ICELAND: Árni Gautur Arason; Olafur Bjarnason, Arnar Vidarsson, Ivar Ingimarsson, Larus Sigurdsson (66 Rikhardur Dadason), Runar Kristinsson, Hermann Hreidarsson, Arnar Gretarsson, Eidur Gudjohnsen, Thordur Gudjónsson, Helgi Sigurdsson (80 Brynjar Gunnarsson). Trainer: Asgeir Sigurvinsson

Goals: Ballack (9), Bobic (59), Kuranyi (79)

	P	W	D	L	F	A	Pts
Germany	8	5	3	0	13	4	18
Scotland	8	4	2	2	12	8	14
Iceland	8	4	1	3	11	9	13
Lithuania	8	3	1	4	7	11	10
Faroe Islands	8	0	1	7	7	18	1

GROUP 6

ARMENIA v UKRAINE 2-2 (0-2)

Republican, Erevan 07.09.2002

Referee: Mikko Vuorela (FIN) Attendance: 9,000

ARMENIA: Roman Berezovsky; Artur Mkrtchyan (60 Albert Sarkisyan), Artak Minasyan (46 Artur Voskanyan), Sarkis Hovsepyan, Harutyun Vardanyan, Romik Khachatryan, Artur Petrosyan, Khose Bilibio, Karen Dokhoyan, Artavazd Karamyan, Arman Karamyan (71 Andrej Movsesyan). Trainer: Óscar López

UKRAINE: Vitaly Reva; Oleh Luzhny, Andriy Nesmachniy, Anatoliy Tymoshchuk, Serhiy Serebrennikov, Serhiy Kormiltsev, Andriy Husin (65 Roman Maksymyuk, 90+3 Serhiy Popov), Hennadiy Zubov (69 Olexandr Spivak), Andriy Vorobey, Vladimir Yezerskyy, Gennadiy Moroz. Trainer: Leonid Buriak

Sent off: Yezerskyi (90+3)

Goals: Serebrennikov (2), Zubov (33), Petrosyan (73), Sarkisyan (90+3)

GREECE v SPAIN 0-2 (0-1)

Apostolos Nikolaidis, Athina 07.09.2002

Referee: Markus Merk (GER) Attendance: 17,134

GREECE: Antonis Nikopolidis; Hristos Patsatzoglou, Takis Fyssas (72 Zisis Vryzas), Nikos Dabizas, Traianos Dellas, Kostas Konstantinidis (40 Giorgos Karagounis), Theodoros Zagorakis (46 Aggelis Basinas), Stelios Giannakopoulos, Angelos Charisteas, Vasilis Tsartas, Themistoklis Nikolaidis. Trainer: Otto Rehhagel

SPAIN: IKER CASILLAS Fernández, MÍCHEL SALGADO Fernández, RAÚL BRAVO Sanfelix, José Antonio GARCÍA CALVO, Carlos MARCHENA López, IVÁN HELGUERA Bujía, RAÚL González Blanco (Cap), JOAQUÍN Sánchez Rodríguez (59 Gaizka MENDIETA Zabala), Juan Carlos VALERÓN Santana (87 CÉSAR MARTÍN Villar), Xavier Hernández Creus "XAVI" (59 Rubén BARAJA Vegas), VICENTE Rodríguez Guillén. Trainer: José Ignacio SÁEZ "IÑAKI"

Goals: Raúl González (8), Valerón (77)

SPAIN v NORTHERN IRELAND 3-0 (1-0)

Carlos Belmonte, Albacete 12.10.2002

Referee: Lubos Michel (SVK) Attendance: 16,000

SPAIN: IKER CASILLAS Fernández, MÍCHEL SALGADO Fernández, RAÚL BRAVO Sanfelix, José María Gutiérrez Hernández "GUTI" (83 Jesús Capitán Prado "CAPI"), Carles PUYOL Saforcada, IVÁN HELGUERA Bujía, RAÚL González Blanco (Cap) (63 Fernando MORIENTES Sánchez), Rubén BARAJA Vegas, JOAQUÍN Sánchez Rodríguez (76 Gaizka MENDIETA Zabala), Xavier Hernández Creus "XAVI", VICENTE Rodríguez Guillén. Trainer: José Ignacio SÁEZ "IÑAKI"

N. IRELAND: Maik Taylor; Aaron Hughes, George McCartney, Gerry Taggart (69 Grant McCann), Colin Murdock, Steve Lomas, Keith Gillespie, Philip Mulryne, Damien Johnson, Paul McVeigh (65 David Healy), Kevin Horlock (65 Michael Hughes). Trainer: Samuel McIlroy

Goals: Baraja (19, 89), Guti (59)

UKRAINE v GREECE 2-0 (0-0)

Oliympiskyi, Kyiv 12.10.2002

Referee: Rene Temmink (HOL) Attendance: 55,000

UKRAINE: Vitaly Reva; Oleh Luzhny, Mykhailo Starostiak, Anatoliy Tymoschuk, Andriy Husin, Serhiy Kormiltsev (71 Serhiy Rebrov), Serhiy Serebrennikov (24 Andriy Voronin), Hennadiy Zubov, Gennadiy Moroz (25 Olexandr Radchenko), Maxym Kalynichenko, Andriy Vorobey. Trainer: Leonid Buriak

GREECE: Antonis Nikopolidis; Giourkas Seitaridis, Stelios Venetidis, Nikos Dabizas, Traianos Dellas, Vasilis Lakis (66 Stelios Giannakopoulos), Theodoros Zagorakis (69 Angelos Basinas), Giorgos Karagounis, Angelos Charisteas, Vasilis Tsartas, Themistoklis Nikolaidis (66 Zizis Vryzas). Trainer: Otto Rehhagel

Goals: Vorobey (51), Voronin (90)

GREECE v ARMENIA 2-0 (1-0)

Apostolos Nikolaidis, Athina 16.10.2002

Referee: Darko Ceferin (SVN) Attendance: 6,000

GREECE: Antonis Nikopolidis; Giourkas Seitaridis, Stelios Venetidis (60 Zizis Vryzas), Nikos Dabizas, Traianos Dellas, Angelos Basinas, Giorgos Georgiadis (46 Stelios Giannakopoulos), Pantelis Kafes, Angelos Charisteas, Vasilis Tsartas (46 Theodoros Zagorakis), Themistoklis Nikolaidis. Trainer: Otto Rehhagel

ARMENIA: Roman Berezovsky; Albert Sarkisyan (82 Eghishin Melikyan), Khose Bilibio, Sarkis Hovsepyan, Harutyun Vardanyan, Romik Khachatryan (46 Artak Minasyan), Artur Petrosyan, Artur Voskanyan, Karen Dokhoyan, Artavazd Karamyan, Arman Karamyan (66 Artur Mkhitaryan). Trainer: Oskar Lopez

Goals: Nikolaidis (2, 59)

NORTHERN IRELAND v UKRAINE 0-0

Windsor Park, Belfast 16.10.2002

Referee: Cosimo Bolognino (ITA) Attendance: 9,288

N. IRELAND: Maik Taylor; Steve Lomas (Cap), Kevin Horlock, George McCartney, Aaron Hughes, Damien Johnson (83 Colin Murdock), Keith Gillespie, Philip Mulryne (90 Grant McCann), David Healy, Paul McVeigh (65 Andy Kirk), Michael Hughes. Trainer: Samuel McIlroy

UKRAINE: Vitaliy Reva; Oleh Luzhny, Mykhailo Starostiak, Anatoliy Tymoschuk, Serhiy Kormiltsev (89 Vitaliy Lysytskyy), Andriy Husin, Andriy Voronin, Maxym Kalynichenko (54 Serhiy Rebrov), Hennadiy Zubov, Andriy Vorobey (76 Olexandr Melaschenko), Olexandr Radchenko. Trainer: Leonid Buryak

ARMENIA v NORTHERN IRELAND 1-0 (0-0)

Republican, Erevan 29.03.2003

Referee: Roland Beck (LIE) Attendance: 10,321

ARMENIA: Roman Berezovsky; Eghishin Melikyan, Karen Dokhoyan, Sarkis Hovsepyan, Harutyun Vardanyan, Khose Bilibio, Artur Petrosyan (89 Hamlet Mkhitaryan), Artur Voskanyan, Albert Sarkisyan (88 Artur Mkrtchyan), Artavazd Karamyan, Arman Karamyan (87 Agvan Mkrtchyan). Trainer: Oskar Lopez

N. IRELAND: Maik Taylor; Aaron Hughes, Grant McCann, Mark Williams, Steve Lomas, Keith Gillespie, Damien Johnson, David Healy, James Quinn (71 Stuart Elliott), Paul McKnight, Christopher Baird. Trainer: Samuel McIlroy

Goal: Petrosyan (86)

UKRAINE v SPAIN 2-2 (1-0)

Olimpiyski, Kyiv 29.03.2003

Referee: Michael Riley (ENG) Attendance: 82,000

UKRAINE: Olexandr Shovkovskiy; Andriy Nesmachniy, Serhiy Fedorov, Anatoliy Tymoschuk, Serhiy Kormiltsev (63 Maksym Kalininchenko), Dmytrulin, Andriy Shevchenko (67 Serhiy Serebrennikov), Andriy Husin, Horshkov, Andriy Voronin, Andriy Vorobey. Trainer: Leonid Buryak

SPAIN: IKER CASILLAS Fernández, MÍCHEL SALGADO Fernández, Agustín ARANZÁBAL Alkorta, Carlos MARCHENA López, CÉSAR MARTÍN Villar, David ALBELDA Aliques (66 Xavier Hernández Creus "XAVI"), RAÚL González Blanco, Rubén BARAJA Vegas, José María Gutiérrez Hernández "GUTI" (66 Juan Carlos VALERÓN Santana), VICENTE Rodríguez Guillén (78 DIEGO TRISTÁN Herrera), Joseba ETXEBERRÍA Lizardi. Trainer: José Ignacio SÁEZ RUIZ "IÑAKI"

Goals: Voronin (11), Raúl (84), Etxeberría (87), Horshkov (90+2)

NORTHERN IRELAND v GREECE 0-2 (0-1)

Windsor Park, Belfast 02.04.2003

Referee: Grzegorz Gilewski (POL) Attendance: 7,196

N. IRELAND: Maik Taylor; Aaron Hughes, George McCartney, Craigan, Mark Williams, Steve Lomas, Keith Gillespie, Damien Johnson, David Healy (67 Andrew Kirk), James Quinn, Grant McCann (67 Paul McVeigh). Trainer: Samuel McIlroy

GREECE: Antonis Nikopolidis; Stelios Giannakopoulos, Stelios Venetidis (70 Takis Fyssas), Nikos Dabizas, Sotiris Kyrgiakos, Konstantinos Konstantinidis, Theodoros Zagorakis, Giorgos Karagounis, Angelos Charisteas, Vasilis Tsartas (75 Pantelis Kafes), Themistoklis Nikolaidis (41 Zisis Vryzas). Trainer: Otto Rehhagel

Sent off: Quinn (38), Gillespie (69)

Goals: Charisteas (3, 55)

SPAIN v ARMENIA 3-0 (0-0)

Antonio Amilivia, León 02.04.2003

Referee: Alon Yefet (ISR) Attendance: 13,000

SPAIN: IKER CASILLAS Fernández, MÍCHEL SALGADO Fernández, RAÚL BRAVO Sanfelix, David ALBELDA Aliques, Carlos MARCHENA López, IVÁN HELGUERA Bujía, RAÚL González Blanco, Xavier Hernández Creus "XAVI" (53 VICENTE Rodríguez Guillén), Juan Carlos VALERÓN Santana (64 Rubén BARAJA Vegas), DIEGO TRISTÁN Herrera, Joseba ETXEBERRÍA Lizardi (41 JOAQUÍN SÁNCHEZ Rodríguez). Trainer: José Ignacio SÁEZ RUIZ "IÑAKI"

ARMENIA: Roman Berezovsky; Eghishin Melikyan, Karen Dokhoyan, Sarkis Hovsepyan, Harutyun Vardanyan, Romik Khachatryan (83 Vardan Minasyan), Artur Petrosyan (80 Hamlet Mkhitaryan), Artur Voskanyan, Albert Sarkisyan, Artavazd Karamyan (90+3 Khose Bilibio), Arman Karamyan. Trainer: Mihai Stoichiţă

Goals: Diego Tristán (64), Iván Helguera (69), Joaquín Sánchez (90+3)

SPAIN v GREECE 0-1 (0-1)

La Romareda, Zaragoza 07.06.2003

Referee: Alain Sars (FRA) Attendance: 30,000

SPAIN: IKER CASILLAS Fernández, MÍCHEL SALGADO Fernández, RAÚL BRAVO Sanfelix, Carlos MARCHENA López (76 SERGIO), PUYOL, IVÁN HELGUERA Bujía, RAÚL González Blanco, Juan Carlos VALERÓN Santana, MORIENTES, VICENTE Rodríguez Guillén (57 DE PEDRO), Joseba ETXEBERRÍA Lizardi (57 Joaquín SÁNCHEZ). Trainer: José Ignacio SÁEZ RUIZ "IÑAKI"

GREECE: Antonis Nikopolidis; Seitaridis, Stelios Venetidis, Nikos Dabizas, Dellas, Kapsis, Theodoros Zagorakis, Zisis Vryzas, Angelos Charisteas (34 Lakis), Vasilis Tsartas (36 Karagounis), Stelios Giannakopoulos. Trainer: Otto Rehhagel **Sent off**: Venetidis (82)

Goal: Giannakopoulos (42)

UKRAINE v ARMENIA 4-3 (1-1)

Ukraine, Lviv 07.06.2003

Referee: Hermann Albrecht (GER) Attendance: 28,000

UKRAINE: Shutkov; Luzhny, Serhiy Fedorov, Andriy Nesmachniy, Popov (65 Kalinichenko), Andriy Shevchenko, Andriy Vorobey, Horshkov, Andriy Voronin, Rebrov (81 Venhlinskyy), Zakarliuka (59 Radchenko). Trainer: Leonid Buryak

ARMENIA: Roman Berezovsky; Partsikian, Karen Dokhoyan, Sarkis Hovsepyan, Harutyun Vardanyan, Romik Khachatryan, Artur Petrosyan (80 Bilibio), Artur Voskanyan, Albert Sarkisyan, Artavazd Karamyan, Arman Karamyan (87 Harutyunian). Trainer: Mihai Stoichiţă

Goals: Sarkisyan (14 pen, 52), Horshkov (28), Shevchenko (66 pen, 73), Petrosyan (74), Fedorov (90+2)

NORTHERN IRELAND v SPAIN 0-0

Windsor Park, Cardiff 11.06.2003

Referee: Claus Bo Larsen (DEN) Attendance: 11,365

N. IRELAND: Maik Taylor; Baird, Kennedy, Aaron Hughes, George McCartney, Griffin, Doherty (80 Toner), Damien Johnson, David Healy, Smith (90 Williams), Jones (73 McVeigh). Trainer: Samuel McIlroy

SPAIN: IKER CASILLAS Fernández, Carlos MARCHENA López, JUANFRAN, SERGIO (66 Joaquín SÁNCHEZ), Carles PUYOL Saforcada, IVÁN HELGUERA Bujía, RAÚL González Blanco, Rubén BARAJA Vegas, Juan Carlos VALERÓN Santana, VICENTE Rodríguez Guillén (66 Fernando MORIENTES Sánchez), Joseba ETXEBERRÍA Lizardi (79 DE PEDRO). Trainer: José Ignacio SÁEZ RUIZ "IÑAKI"

GREECE v UKRAINE 1-0 (0-0)

Apostolos Nikolaidis, Athina 11.06.2003

Referee: Frank de Bleeckere (BEL) Attendance: 15,000

GREECE: Antonis Nikopolidis; Seitaridis, Takis Fyssas, Nikos Dabizas, Dellas, Kapsis, Theodoros Zagorakis (71 Tsartas), Vryzas (46 Charisteas), Lakis (66 Houtos), Giorgos Karagounis, Giannakopoulos. Trainer: Otto Rehhagel

UKRAINE: Olexandr Shovkovskiy; Andriy Nesmachniy, Serhiy Fedorov, Holovko, Anatoliy Tymoschuk, Shevchuk, Andriy Shevchenko, Andriy Husin, Zakarliuka (88 Kalinichenko), Andriy Voronin (90 Pukanych), Rebrov (61 Vorobey). Trainer: Leonid Buryak

Goal: Charisteas (86)

ARMENIA v GREECE 0-1 (0-1)

Republikan, Erevan 06.09.2003

Referee: Rene Temmink (HOL) Attendance: 6,500

ARMENIA: Roman Berezovsky; Eghishe Melikyan, Khose Bilibio, Tudor Marian Zeciu, Harutyun Vardanyan, Romik Khachatryan, Artur Petrosyan, Artur Voskanyan (88 Ara Hakobyan), Albert Sarkisyan, Artavazd Karamyan, Arman Karamyan (64 Andrey Movsisyan). Trainer: Mihai Stoichiţă

GREECE: Antonis Nikopolidis; Giourkas Seitaridis, Takis Fyssas, Paraskevas Antzas, Traianos Dellas, Angelos Basinas, Mihalis Kapsis, Zisis Vryzas, Angelos Charisteas, Giorgos Karagounis (84 Theodoros Zagorakis), Stilianos Giannakopoulos (67 Giorgos Georgiadis). Trainer: Otto Rehhagel

Goal: Vryzas (36)

UKRAINE v NORTHERN IRELAND 0-0

Centralny, Donetsk 06.09.2003

Referee: Wolfgang Stark (GER) Attendance: 24,000

UKRAINE: Olexandr Shovkovskiy; Serhiy Fedorov, Olexandr Horshkov, Oleg Luzhny, Andriy Nesmachniy, Anatoliy Tymoschuk, Serhiy Rebrov (72 Olexandr Melaschenko), Andriy Husin (16 Oleg Gusev), Gennadiy Zubov, Andriy Voronin, Andriy Vorobey. Trainer: Leonid Buryak

N. IRELAND: Maik Taylor; Christopher Baird, Peter Kennedy, George McCartney, Danny Griffin, Keith Gillespie, Damien Johnson, David Healy (62 Andrew Kirk), Tommy Doherty (67 Philip Mulryne), Michael Hughes (81 Stephen Jones), Aaron Hughes. Trainer: Samuel McIlroy

NORTHERN IRELAND v ARMENIA 0-1 (0-1)

Windsor Park Belfast 10.09.2003

Referee: Anton Stredak (SVK) Attendance: 8,616

N. IRELAND: Maik Taylor; Christopher Baird, Grant McCann, George McCartney, Danny Griffin, Keith Gillespie (29 Stephen Jones), Damien Johnson, David Healy (78 Paul McVeigh), Andy Smith, Tommy Doherty (29 Philip Mulryne), Aaron Hughes. Trainer: Samuel McIlroy

ARMENIA: Roman Berezovsky; Eghishe Melikyan, Khose Bilibio, Sargis Hovsepyan, Tudor Marian Zeciu, Romik Khachatryan, Artur Petrosyan (13 Arman Karamyan), Artur Voskanyan, Albert Sarkisyan, Artavazd Karamyan (87 Eduard Partsikian), Andrey Movsisyan (75 Ara Hakobyan). Trainer: Mihai Stoichiţă

Goal: Ar. Karamyan (29)

SPAIN v UKRAINE 2-1 (0-0)

Manuel Martínez Valero Elche 10.09.2003

Referee: Terje Hauge (NOR) Attendance: 38,000

SPAIN: IKER CASILLAS Fernández, MÍCHEL SALGADO Fernández, JUANITO, Carlos MARCHENA López, Carles PUYOL Saforcada, Xabier "XABI" ALONSO Olona, RAÚL González Blanco, Rubén BARAJA Vegas, FERNANDO José TORRES Sanz (65 José Antonio REYES CALDERÓN), VICENTE Rodríguez Guillén (64 Juan Carlos VALERÓN Santana), Joseba ETXEBERRÍA Lizardi.
Trainer: José Ignacio SÁEZ RUIZ "IÑAKI"

UKRAINE: Olexandr Shovkovskiy; Oleg Luzhny, Serhiy Fedorov, Anatoliy Tymoschuk, Andriy Nesmachniy, Yuri Dmytrulin (65 Gennadiy Zubov), Andriy Shevchenko, Serhiy Popov (19 Serhiy Serebrennikov), Andriy Voronin (52 Oleg Gusev), Andriy Vorobey, Olexandr Horshkov.
Trainer: Leonid Buryak

Goals: Raúl (59, 71), Shevchenko (84)

GREECE v NORTHERN IRELAND 1-0 (0-0)

Apostolos Nikolaidis, Athina 11.10.2003

Referee: Lucilio Cardoso Cortez Batisa (POR) Att: 15,500

GREECE: Antonis Nikopolidis; Giourkas Seitaridis, Takis Fyssas, Nikos Dabizas (46 Themistoklis Nikolaidis), Traianos Dellas, Angelos Basinas (90 Theodoros Zagorakis), Paraskevas Antzas, Zisis Vryzas, Angelos Charisteas (46 Stylianos Venetidis), Vasilis Tsiartas, Stilianos Giannakopoulos.
Trainer: Otto Rehhagel

N. IRELAND: Maik Taylor; Christopher Baird, Peter Kennedy, George McCartney, Aaron Hughes, Danny Griffin (88 Stephen Jones), Keith Gillespie (64 Andy Smith), Jeff Whitley, David Healy, Michael Hughes, Stuart Elliott (70 Colin Murdock). Trainer: Samuel McIlroy

Sent off: McCartney (69)

Goal: Tsiartas (69 pen)

ARMENIA v SPAIN 0-4 (0-1)

Vazgen Sargsyan, Erevan 11.10.2003

Referee: Urs Meier (SWI) Attendance: 15,000

ARMENIA: Roman Berezovsky; Eghishe Melikyan, Karen Dokhoyan, Sargis Hovsepyan, Harutyun Vardanyan, Romik Khachatryan, Tudor Marian Zeciu, Artur Voskanyan, Albert Sarkisyan, Artavazd Karamyan, Arman Karamyan.
Trainer: Mihai Stoichiță

SPAIN: IKER CASILLAS Fernández, MÍCHEL SALGADO Fernández, Carlos MARCHENA López, David ALBELDA, Carles PUYOL Saforcada, IVÁN HELGUERA Bujía, RAÚL González Blanco (78 LUQUE), Rubén BARAJA Vegas (66 Xabier "XABI" ALONSO Olona), Juan Carlos VALERÓN Santana, VICENTE Rodríguez Guillén (62 José Antonio REYES CALDERÓN), Joseba ETXEBERRÍA Lizardi.
Trainer: José Ignacio SÁEZ RUIZ "IÑAKI"

Goals: Valerón (7), Raúl (76), Reyes Calderón (87, 90)

	P	W	D	L	F	A	Pts
Greece	8	6	0	2	8	4	18
Spain	8	5	2	1	16	4	17
Ukraine	8	2	4	2	11	10	10
Armenia	8	2	1	5	7	16	7
Northern Ireland	8	0	3	5	0	8	3

GROUP 7

TURKEY v SLOVAKIA 3-0 (2-0)

Ali Sami Yen 07.09.2002

Referees: Antonio Jesus LOPEZ NIETO (SPA) Att: 20,000

TURKEY: Rüştü Reçber; Emre Belözoglu (78 Cihan Haspolati), Bülent Korkmaz, Fatih Akyel, Alpay Özalan, Arif Erdem, Okan Buruk (63 Nihat Kahveci), Tugay Kerimoglu, Akin Serhat (87 Ümit Davala), Yildiray Bastürk, Hakan Ünsal.
Trainer: Şenol Günes

SLOVAKIA: Juraj Bucek, Miroslav Karhan, Marek Spilár, Marian Cisovsky, Peter Dzúrik, Vladimir Labant (61 Rastislav Michalík), Karol Kisel, Jozef Kozlej (55 Luboš Reiter), Vratislav Gresko (72 Peter Hlinka), Vladimir Janocko, Robert Vittek.
Trainer: Ladislav Jurkemik

Goals: Akin Serhat (14), Arif Erdem (45, 65)

LIECHTENSTEIN v MACEDONIA 1-1 (0-1)

Rheinpark, Vaduz 08.09.2002

Referee: Vitaliy Godulyan (UKR) Attendance: 2,300

LIECHTENSTEIN: Peter Jehle; Christof Ritter, Frédéric Gigon (83 Patrick Burgmaier), Daniel Hasler, Michael Stocklasa, Martin Stocklasa, Martin Telser (83 Fabio D'Elia), Andreas Gerster, Thomas Beck, Mario Frick, Matthias Beck (46 Ronny Büchel). Trainer: Ralf Loose

MACEDONIA: Petar Milosevski; Braga de Jesus (85 Boban Grncarov), Robert Petrov, Goce Sedloski, Igor Nikolovski, Igor Mitrevski, Velice Šumulikoski, Goran Pandev (70 Aco Stojkov), Georgi Hristov (58 Robert Popov), Artim Sakiri, Aleksandar Mitrevski. Trainer: Nikola Ilievski

Goals: Hristov (7), Michael Stocklasa (90+3)

SLOVAKIA v ENGLAND 1-2 (1-0)

SK Slovan Bratislava 12.10.2002

Referee: Domenico Messina (ITA) Attendance: 30,000

SLOVAKIA: Miroslav König; Martin Petras, Miroslav Karhan, Peter Hlinka, Peter Dzúrik (Cap), Marian Zeman, Attila Pinte (85 Jozef Kozlej), Szilárd Nemeth, Vladimír Leitner, Vladimír Janocko (85 Marek Mintál), Robert Vittek (78 Luboš Reiter). Trainer: Ladislav Jurkemik

ENGLAND: David Seaman; Gary Neville, Ashley Cole, Steven Gerrard (74 Kieron Dyer), Jonathan Woodgate, Gareth Southgate, David Beckham, Paul Scholes, Emile Heskey (90 Alan Smith), Michael Owen (80 Owen Hargreaves), Nicky Butt. Trainer: Sven-Göran Eriksson

Goals: Nemeth (24), Beckham (64), Owen (79)

ENGLAND v MACEDONIA 2-2 (2-2)

Saint Mary's, Southampton 16.10.2002

Referee: Arturo DAUDEN IBAÑEZ (SPA) Att: 32,095

ENGLAND: David Seaman; Gary Neville, Ashley Cole, Steven Gerrard (55 Nicky Butt), Jonathan Woodgate, Sol Campbell, David Beckham, Paul Scholes, Alan Smith, Michael Owen, Wayne Bridge (58 Darius Vassell).
Trainer: Sven-Göran Eriksson

MACEDONIA: Petar Milosevski, Robert Popov, Robert Petrov, Goce Sedloski, Aleksandar Vasoski, Velice Šumulikoski, Vanco Trajanov (90 Milan Stojanoski), Aleksandar Mitrevski, Goce Toleski (61 Goran Pandev), Artim Sakiri, Vlatko Grozdanovski. Trainer: Nikola Ilievski

Sent off: Smith (89)

Goals: Sakiri (11), Beckham (14), Trajanov (25), Gerrard (36)

MACEDONIA v TURKEY 1-2 (1-1)

Gradski, Skopje 12.10.2002

Referee: Knud Erik Fisker (DEN) Attendance: 12,000

MACEDONIA: Petar Milosevski; Igor Mitrevski, Aleksandar Vasoski, Goce Sedloski, Milan Stojanoski (46 Robert Petrov), Aleksandar Mitrevski, Vanco Trajanov (65 Dragan Nacevski), Velice Šumulikoski, Georgi Hristov, Artim Sakiri, Vlatko Grozdanovski. Trainer: Nikola Ilievski

TURKEY: Rüştü Reçber; Emre Belözoglu, Bülent Korlmaz, Fatih Akyel, Alpay Özalan, Arif Erdem (46 Akin Serhat), Okan Buruk (82 Ümit Davala), Tugay Kerimoglu (46 Hasan Şaş), Nihat Kahveci, Ümit Özat, Ergün Penbe.
Trainer: Senol Güneş

Goals: Grozdanovski (2), Okan Buruk (29), Nihat (53)

LIECHTENSTEIN v ENGLAND 0-2 (0-1)

Rheinpark, Vaduz 29.03.2003

Referee: Giorgos Kasnaferis (GRE) Attendance: 3,548

LIECHTENSTEIN: Peter Jehle; Martin Telser, Fabio D'Elia, Daniel Hasler, Michael Stocklasa, Martin Stocklasa, Harald Zech (67 Franz Burgmeier), Ronny Büchel (86 Matthias Beck), Thomas Beck, Mario Frick (82 Thomas Nigg), Andreas Gerster.
Trainer: Ralf Loose

ENGLAND: David James; Gary Neville, Wayne Bridge, Steven Gerrard (66 Nicky Butt), Rio Ferdinand, Gareth Southgate, David Beckham (70 Danny Murphy), Paul Scholes, Emile Heskey (80 Wayne Rooney), Michael Owen, Kieron Dyer.
Trainer: Sven-Göran Eriksson

Goals: Owen (28), Beckham (53)

TURKEY v LIECHTENSTEIN 5-0 (3-0)

Ali Sami Yen, Istanbul 16.10.2002

Referee: Yuri Baskakov (RUS) Attendance: 18,000

TURKEY: Rüştü Reçber; Emre Belözoglu, Bülent Korkmaz (46 Fatih Akyel), Ümit Davala, Alpay Özalan, Arif Erdem, Okan Buruk (60 Hakan Ünsal), Tugay Kerimoglu, Nihat Kahveci, Ilhan Mansiz (79 Akin Serhat), Ergün Penbe.
Trainer: Şenol Güneş

LIECHTENSTEIN: Peter Jehle; Martin Telser, Fabio D'Elia, Daniel Hasler, Michael Stocklasa, Martin Stocklasa (79 Matthias Beck), Thomas Nigg (72 Patrick Burgmaier), Ronny Büchel (85 Jürgen Ospelt), Thomas Beck, Mario Frick, Andreas Gerster. Trainer: Ralf Loose

Goals: Okan (7), Ümit (14), Ilhan (23), Akin (81, 90)

MACEDONIA v SLOVAKIA 0-2 (0-1)

City, Skopje 29.03.2003

Referee: Laurent Duhamel (FRA) Attendance: 10,000

MACEDONIA: Petar Milosevski; Aguinaldo Braga de Jesus, Goran Lazarevski (81 Aco Stojkov), Goce Sedloski, Igor Mitrevski, Velice Šumulikoski (51 Ilco Naumoski), Igor Jancevski, Mile Krstev, Saso Krstev (61 Vlatko Grozdanovski), Artim Sakiri, Goran Pandev. Trainer: Nikola Ilievski

SLOVAKIA: Miroslav König; Martin Petras, Maros Klimpl, Peter Hlinka, Miroslav Karhan (89 Michal Hanek), Igor Demo (80 Labant), Vladimír Leitner, Szilárd Nemeth (75 Luboš Reiter), Rastislav Michalík, Vladimír Janocko, Robert Vittek.
Trainer: Ladislav Jurkemik

Goals: Petras (28), Reiter (90+3)

ENGLAND v TURKEY 2-0 (0-0)

Stadium of Light, Sunderland 02.04.2003

Referee: Urs Meier (SWI) Attendance: 47,667

ENGLAND: David James; Gary Neville, Wayne Bridge, Steven Gerrard, Rio Ferdinand, Sol Campbell, David Beckham, Paul Scholes, Wayne Rooney (89 Kieron Dyer), Michael Owen (58 Darius Vassell), Nicky Butt. Trainer: Sven-Göran Eriksson

TURKEY: Rüştü Reçber; Emre Belözoglu, Bülent Korkmaz, Fatih Akyel (79 Hakan Şükür), Alpay Özalan, Ergün Penbe, Okan Buruk (59 Ümit Davala), Tugay Kerimoglu, Ilhan Mansiz, Yildiray Bastürk (70 Hasan Şaş), Nihat Kahveci. Trainer: Şenol Günes

Goals: Vassell (75), Beckham (90+2 pen)

MACEDONIA v LIECHTENSTEIN 3-1 (1-1)

City Skopje 07.06.2003

Referee: Jaroslav Jara (CZE) Attendance: 1,500

MACEDONIA: Petar Milosevski; Velice Šumulikoski, Sasko Lazarevski, Goce Sedloski, Aleksander Vasoski, Aleksander Mitrevski, Aco Stojkov, Vanco Trajanov (59 Igor Jancevski), Ilco Naumoski (46 Dragan Dimitrovski), Artim Sakiri (55 Alexsandar Bajevski), Mile Krstev. Trainer: Nikola Ilievski

LIECHTENSTEIN: Peter Jehle; Jürgen Ospelt, Sandro Maierhofer (89 Mario Wolfinger), Daniel Hasler, Frédéric Gigon, Andreas Gerster, Martin Telser, Fabio d'Elia, Matthias Beck (89 Franz-Josef Vogt), Mario Frick, Roger Beck (79 Claudio Alabor). Trainer: Ralf Loose

Goals: Beck (20), Sedloski (39 pen), Krstev (52), Stojkov (82)

SLOVAKIA v LIECHTENSTEIN 4-0 (1-0)

FC Spartak, Trnava 02.04.2003

Referee: Darko Ceferin (SVN) Played behind closed doors

SLOVAKIA: Miroslav König; Martin Petras, Maros Klimpl, Peter Hlinka, Miroslav Karhan, Igor Demo (68 Vladimír Labant), Vladimír Leitner, Jozef Kozlej (46 Szilárd Nemeth), Rastislav Michalík (81 Marek Mintál), Vladimír Janocko, Luboš Reiter. Trainer: Ladislav Jurkemik

LIECHTENSTEIN: Peter Jehle; Martin Telser, Fabio D'Elia, Daniel Hasler, Michael Stocklasa, Martin Stocklasa, Franz Burgmeier, Ronny Büchel (71 Frédéric Gigon), Thomas Beck, Mario Frick (60 Thomas Nigg), Andreas Gerster (85 Jürgen Ospelt). Trainer: Ralf Loose

Goals: Reiter (18), Nemeth (51, 64), Janocko (90)

ENGLAND v SLOVAKIA 2-1 (0-1)

BT Cellnet Riverside, Middlesbrough 11.06.2003

Referee: Wolfgang Stark (GER) Attendance: 35,000

ENGLAND: David James; Danny Mills (43 Owen Hargreaves), Ashley Cole, Steven Gerrard, Matthew Upson, Gareth Southgate, Frank Lampard, Paul Scholes, Wayne Rooney (58 Darius Vassell), Michael Owen, Philip Neville. Trainer: Sven-Göran Eriksson

SLOVAKIA: Miroslav König; Martin Petras, Michal Hanek, Marian Zeman, Radoslav Zábavník, Igor Demo (55 Marek Mintál), Vladimír Labant (39 Ondrej Debnar), Szilárd Nemeth (76 Lubos Reiter), Rastislav Michalík, Vladimír Janocko, Robert Vittek. Trainer: Ladislav Jurkemik

Goals: Janocko (31), Owen (62 pen, 73)

SLOVAKIA v TURKEY 0-1 (0-1)

SK Slova, Bratislava 07.06.2003

Referee: Terje Hauge (NOR) Attendance: 15,000

SLOVAKIA: Miroslav König; Maros Klimpl, Marian Zeman, Peter Hlinka (46 Robert Vittek), Vladimír Labant, Igor Demo, Martin Petras, Miroslav Karhan (71 Marek Mintál), Vladimír Janocko, Rastislav Michalík (77 Karol Kisel), Szilárd Nemeth. Trainer: Ladislav Jurkemik

TURKEY: Rüştü Reçber; Fatih Akyel, Bülent Korkmaz, Alpay Özalan, Ergün Penbe, Okan Buruk (59 Tayfun Korkut), Tugay Kerimoglu, Emre Belözoglu (90 Ibrahim Üzülmez), Yildiray Bastürk (80 Volkan Arslan), Hakan Şükür, Nihat Kahveci. Trainer: Şenol Günes

Goal: Nihat Kahveci (12)

TURKEY v MACEDONIA 3-2 (1-2)

Inönü, Istanbul 11.06.2003

Referee: Roberto Rosetti (ITA) Attendance: 20,000

TURKEY: Rüştü Reçber; Emre Belözoglu (Gökdeniz Karadeniz), Fatih Akyel, Bülent Korkmaz, Alpay Özalan, Ergün Penbe, Tayfun Korkut, Tugay Kerimoglu, Hakan Şükür (78 Arif Erdem), Ibrahim Üzülmez, Nihat Kahveci. Trainer: Şenol Günes

MACEDONIA: Petar Milosevski; Risto Bozinovski (76 Goce Toleski), Aleksander Vasoski, Goce Sedloski, Igor Jancevski (70 Goran Stankovski), Aleksander Mitrevski, Aco Stojkov, Velice Šumulikoski, Vlatko Grozdanovski (52 Arben Nuhiji), Artim Sakiri, Goran Lazarevski. Trainer: Nikola Ilievski

Goals: Grozdanovski (23), Nihat (26), Sakiri (28), Karadeniz (47), Hakan Sükür (59)

LIECHTENSTEIN v TURKEY 0-3 (0-2)

Rheinpark, Vaduz 06.09.2003

Referee: Dick van Egmond (HOL) Attendance: 3,548

LIECHTENSTEIN: Peter Jehle; Martin Telser, Michael Stocklasa (83 Sandro Maierhofer), Daniel Hasler, Christof Ritter, Martin Stocklasa, Thomas Beck (60 Matthias Beck), Andreas Gerster, Fabio d'Elia, Mario Frick, Franz Burgmeier (60 Ronny Büchel). Trainer: Ralf Loose

TURKEY: Rüştü Reçber; Ümit Davala, Bülent Korkmaz (63 Deniz Baris), Ibrahim Üzülmez, Alpay Özalan, Ergün Penbe, Okan Buruk (75 Gökdeniz Karadeniz), Tugay Kerimoglu, Hakan Şükür, Tuncay Sanli, Tümer Metin (63 Hasan Şaş). Trainer: Şenol Günes

Goals: T. Metin (14), O. Buruk (41), H. Şükür (50)

SLOVAKIA v MACEDONIA 1-1 (1-0)

Mestsky Sportovy, Zilina 10.09.2003

Referee: Leif Sundell (SWE) Attendance: 2,286

SLOVAKIA: Miroslav König; Martin Petras, Vladimír Labant, Maros Klimpl, Radoslav Zábavník, Branislav Labant, Martin Durica (71 Karol Kisel), Szilárd Nemeth, Tomáš Oravec, Vladimír Janocko (90 Dušan Sninský), Marek Mintál. Trainer: Ladislav Jurkemik

MACEDONIA: Petar Milosevski; Goran Stavrevski, Goce Sedloski, Igor Mitrevski, Milan Stojanoski, Igor Jancevski, Goran Pandev (73 Dimitar Kapinovski), Vanco Trajanov, Vlatko Grozdanovski, Artim Sakiri, Ilco Naumoski (38 Draganco Dimitrovski). Trainer: Nikola Ilievski

Goals: Nemeth (25), Dimitrovski (62)

MACEDONIA v ENGLAND 1-2 (1-0)

Gradski, Skopje 06.09.2003

Referee: Frank de Bleeckere (BEL) Attendance: 20,500

MACEDONIA: Petar Milosevski; Igor Mitrevski, Milan Stojanoski, Velice Šumulikoski, Vlatko Grozdanovski (56 Aguinaldo Braga de Jesus), Vanco Trajanov, Goran Pandev (47 Igor Gjuzelov), Artim Sakiri, Ilco Naumoski, Georgi Hristov (88 Draganco Dimitrovski), Goran Stavrevski. Trainer: Nikola Ilievski

ENGLAND: David James; Gary Neville, Ashley Cole, Owen Hargreaves, John Terry, Sol Campbell, David Beckham, Frank Lampard (46 Emile Heskey), Wayne Rooney (74 Phil Neville), Michael Owen (84 Kieron Dyer), Nicky Butt. Trainer: Sven-Göran Eriksson

Goals: Hristov (28), Rooney (52), Beckham (63)

TURKEY v ENGLAND 0-0

Şükrü Saraçioglu, Istanbul 11.10.2003

Referee: Pierluigi Collina (ITA) Attendance: 42,000

TURKEY: Rüştü Reçber; Ibrahim Üzülmez, Bülent Korkmaz, Fatih Akyel, Alpay Özalan, Emre Belözoglu (80 Ergün Penbe), Okan Buruk (68 Ilhan Mansiz), Tugay Kerimoglu, Hakan Şükür, Nihat Kahveci, Sergen Yalçin (61 Tuncay Sanli). Trainer: Şenol Günes

ENGLAND: David James; Gary Neville, Ashley Cole, Steven Gerrard, John Terry, Sol Campbell, David Beckham, Paul Scholes (90+1 Frank Lampard), Wayne Rooney (72 Kieron Dyer), Emile Heskey (76 Darius Vassell), Nicky Butt. Trainer: Sven-Göran Eriksson

ENGLAND v LIECHTENSTEIN 2-0 (0-0)

Old Trafford, Manchester 10.09.2003

Referee: Knud Erik Fisker (DEN) Attendance: 64,931

ENGLAND: David James; Gary Neville, Matthew Upson, John Terry, Wayne Bridge, David Beckham (57 Owen Hargreaves), Steven Gerrard (57 Phil Neville), Frank Lampard, Wayne Rooney (67 Joe Cole), James Beattie, Michael Owen. Trainer: Sven-Göran Eriksson

LIECHTENSTEIN: Peter Jehle; Martin Telser, Michael Stocklasa (46 Sandro Maierhofer), Daniel Hasler, Christof Ritter, Martin Stocklasa, Matthias Beck (56 Thomas Beck), Andreas Gerster, Fabio d'Elia (71 Ronny Büchel), Mario Frick, Franz Burgmeier. Trainer: Ralf Loose

Goals: Owen (46), Rooney (50)

LIECHTENSTEIN v SLOVAKIA 0-2 (0-1)

Rheinpark, Vaduz 11.10.2003

Referee: Jouni Hyytiä (FIN) Attendance: 800

LIECHTENSTEIN: Martin Heeb; Martin Telser, Sandro Maierhofer, Daniel Hasler, Michael Stocklasa, Christof Ritter, Thomas Beck (46 Roger Beck), Matthias Beck (46 Raphael Rohrer), Fabio d'Elia (76 Ronny Büchel), Mario Frick, Franz Burgmeier. Trainer: Ralf Loose

SLOVAKIA: Miroslav König; Maros Klimpl, Vladimír Leitner, Vladimír Labant, Stanislav Varga, Radoslav Zábavník, Karol Kisel (46 Rudolf Urban), Szilárd Nemeth (76 Tomáš Oravec), Rastislav Michalík (84 Peter Babnic), Vladimír Janocko, Robert Vittek. Trainer: Ladislav Jurkemik

Goals: Vittek (40, 56)

	P	W	D	L	F	A	Pts
England	8	6	2	0	14	5	20
Turkey	8	6	1	1	17	5	19
Slovakia	8	3	1	4	11	9	10
Macedonia	8	1	3	4	11	14	6
Liechtenstein	8	0	1	7	2	22	1

GROUP 8

CROATIA v ESTONIA 0-0

Gradski vrt, Osijek 07.09.2002

Referee: Juan Antonio FERNANDEZ MARIN (SPA) Attendance: 10,000

CROATIA: Stipe Pletikosa; Boris Zivković, Marko Babić, Dario Šimić, Mario Tokić, Filip Tapalović, Davor Vugrinec, Daniel Šarić (79 Stjepan Tomas), Ivica Olić, Silvio Marić (46 Milan Rapaić), Tomislav Marić (60 Mladen Petrić). Trainer: Otto Barić

ESTONIA: Mart Poom; Teet Allas, Andrei Stepanov, Raio Piiroja, Erko Saviauk, Martin Reim, Meelis Rooba, Marko Kristal, Indrek Zelinski, Andres Oper, Joel Lindpere (59 Urmas Rooba). Trainer: Arnoldus Dick Pijpers

BELGIUM v BULGARIA 0-2 (0-1)

Roi Baudouin, Brussel 07.09.2002

Referee: Terje Hauge (NOR) Attendance: 20,000

BELGIUM: Geert de Vlieger; Stijn Vreven, Daniel van Buyten, Timmy Simons, Peter Vanderheyden (64 Bob Peeters), Yves Vanderhaeghe, Gaetan Englebert (53 Mbo Mpenza), Bart Goor, Emile Mpenza (70 Bernd Thijs), Walter Baseggio, Wesley Sonck. Trainer: Aimé Antheunis

BULGARIA: Zdravko Zdravkov, Radostin Kishishev, Rosen Kirilov, Ivailo Petkov, Martin Petrov, Georgi Peev (83 Georgi Petkov), Stilian Petrov, Milen Petkov (90 Zlatomir Zagorcic), Zoran Jankovic (77 Georgi Chilikov), Krasimir Balakov, Predrag Pazin. Trainer: Plamen Markov

Goals: Jankovic (17), Stilian Petrov (63)

ANDORRA v BELGIUM 0-1 (0-0)

Estadio Communal, Andorra La Vella 12.10.2002

Referee: Karen Nalbandyan (ARM) Attendance: 700

ANDORRA: Jesús Luis "KOLDO" ÁLVAREZ de Fulate; José AYALA, Manuel "TXEMA" GARCÍA (66 Jordi ESCURA Aixas), Roberto JONÁS Alonso, Antonio LIMA Sola, Juli FERNÁNDEZ, EMILIANO González Árquez, Manolo JIMÉNEZ, Óscar SONEJEE Masán, Juli SÁNCHEZ Soto (7 FERNANDO SILVA), Justo RUIZ González.
Trainer: David Rodrigo

BELGIUM: Geert de Vlieger; Olivier de Cock, Joos Valgaeren, Timmy Simons, Didier Dheedene, Yves Vanderhaeghe, Thomas Buffel, Bart Goor, Wesley Sonck (89 Tom Soetaers), Walter Baseggio (82 Bernd Thijs), Joris van Houdt.
Trainer: Aimé Antheunis

Goal: Sonck (61)

BULGARIA v CROATIA 2-0 (2-0)

Vasil Levski 12.10.2002

Referee: Anders Frisk (SWE) Attendance: 43,000

BULGARIA: Zdravko Zdravkov; Radostin Kishishev, Rosen Kirilov, Ivailo Petkov, Dimitar Berbatov (39 Georgi Chilikov), Zoran Jankovic, Krasimir Balakov, Georgi Peev (90 Georgi Ivanov "Gonzo"), Martin Petrov (66 Georgi Petrov), Predrag Pazin, Stilian Petrov. Trainer: Plamen Markov

CROATIA: Stipe Pletikosa; Dario Šimić (46 Silvio Marić), Stjepan Tomas, Robert Kovac, Igor Tudor, Boris Zivković, Davor Vugrinec, Jerko Leko, Mario Stanić, Milan Rapaić (46 Ivica Olić), Alen Bokšić. Trainer: Otto Barić

Goals: S. Petrov (22), Berbatov (37)

ESTONIA v BELGIUM 0-1 (0-1)

A Le Coq Arena, Tallinn 16.10.2002

Referee: Michael Riley (ENG) Attendance: 2,500

ESTONIA: Mart Poom; Teet Allas, Andrei Stepanov, Raio Piiroja, Urmas Rooba, Martin Reim, Aivar Anniste (46 Kert Haavistu), Marko Kristal (83 Joel Lindpere), Indrek Zelinski, Andres Oper, Sergei Terehhov (60 Kristen Viikmäe). Trainer: Arnoldus Dick Pijpers

BELGIUM: Geert de Vlieger; Oliver de Cock, Joos Valgaeren, Timmy Simons, Didier Dheedene, Yves Vanderhaeghe, Thomas Buffel (89 Joris van Hout), Bart Goor, Wesley Sonck, Walter Baseggio, Peter van Houdt. Trainer: Aimé Antheunis

Goal: Sonck (2)

BULGARIA v ANDORRA 2-1 (1-0)

Vasil Levski, Sofia 16.10.2002

Referee: Ceri Richards (WAL) Attendance: 42,000

BULGARIA: Zdravko Zdravkov; Radostin Kishishev, Rosen Kirilov, Ivailo Petkov, Zoran Jankovic (77 Georgi Ivanov "Gonzo"), Krasimir Balakov (Cap) (62 Svetoslav Petrov), Georgi Peev, Georgi Chilikov, Martin Petrov (75 Vladimir Manchev), Predrag Pazin, Stilian Petrov.
Trainer: Plamen Markov

ANDORRA: Jesús Luis "KOLDO" ÁLVAREZ de Fulate; José AYALA, Jordi ESCURA Aixas, Roberto JONÁS Alonso, Antonio LIMA Sola, Ildefons LIMA Sola, EMILIANO González Árquez (64 FERNANDO SILVA), Óscar SONEJEE Masán, Juli FERNÁNDEZ, Manolo JIMÉNEZ (80 Marc PUJOL), Justo RUIZ González. Trainer: David Rodrigo

Goals: Chilikov (37), Balakov (58), Antonio Lima (80)

CROATIA v ANDORRA 2-0 (2-0)

NK Varteks, Varazdin 02.04.2003

Referee: Marian Salomir (ROM) Attendance: 8,500

CROATIA: Stipe Pletikosa; Dario Šimić, Josip Šimunić (46 Niko Kovac), Robert Kovac, Igor Tudor, Boris Zivković, Milan Rapaić (65 Marko Babić), Jerko Leko, Dado Pršo, Danijel Hrman, Tomislav Marić (46 Mario Stanić).
Trainer: Otto Barić

ANDORRA: Jesús Luis "KOLDO" ÁLVAREZ de Fulate; José AYALA, Manuel "TXEMA" GARCÍA, Roberto JONÁS Alonso, Juli FERNÁNDEZ, Óscar SONEJEE Masán, Emiliano GONZÁLEZ (90+1 Alain Montwani), Marc PUJOL, AGUSTI POL (84 Jesus LUCENDO), Manolo JIMÉNEZ (54 Jordi ESCURA), JULÍ SÁNCHEZ. Trainer: David Rodrigo

Goals: Rapaic (10 pen, 43)

CROATIA v BELGIUM 4-0 (1-0)

Maksimir, Zagreb 29.03.2003

Referee: Herbert Fandel (GER) Attendance: 25,000

CROATIA: Stipe Pletikosa; Dario Šimić, Josip Šimunić, Robert Kovac, Igor Tudor (77 Niko Kovac), Boris Zivković, Milan Rapaić, Giovanni Rosso (46 Jerko Leko), Dado Pršo (71 Mario Stanić), Darijo Srna, Tomislav Marić.
Trainer: Otto Barić

BELGIUM: Franky Vandendriessche; Oliver de Cock (56 Eric Deflandre), Timmy Simons, Daniel van Buyten, Peter van der Heyden, Joos Valgaeren (67 Jelle van Damme), Gaëtan Englebert (55 Walter Baseggio), Bart Goor, Wesley Sonck, Thomas Buffel, Mbo Mpenza. Trainer: Aimé Antheunis

Goals: Srna (9), Pršo (55), To. Marić (70), Leko (76)

ANDORRA v ESTONIA 0-2 (0-1)

Comunal, Andorra la Vella 30.04.2003

Referee: Ali Aydin (TUR) Attendance: 500

ANDORRA: Jesús Luis "KOLDO" ÁLVAREZ de Fulate; José AYALA (90 FERNANDO SILVA), Manuel "TXEMA" GARCÍA, Jordi ESCURA, Juli FERNÁNDEZ, Óscar SONEJEE Masán, EMILIANO González Árquez, Marc PUJOL (80 Felix ALVAREZ), Manolo JIMÉNEZ (71 Jesus LUCENDO), JULÍ SÁNCHEZ, Justo RUIZ González.
Trainer: David RODRIGO

ESTONIA: Mart Poom; Teet Allas, Andrei Stepanov, Marek Lemsalu, Urmas Rooba, Martin Reim, Kert Haavistu (68 Ott Reinumäe), Marko Kristal, Indrek Zelinski, Kristen Viikmäe (89 Meelis Rooba), Sergei Terehhov (55 Joel Lindpere).
Trainer: Arnoldus Dick Pijpers

Goals: Zelinski (26, 74)

ESTONIA v BULGARIA 0-0

A Le Coq Arena, Tallinn 02.04.2003

Referee: Konrad Plautz (AUS) Attendance: 4,000

ESTONIA: Mart Poom; Teet Allas, Marek Lemsalu, Enar Jääger, Urmas Rooba, Liivo Leetma, Kert Haavistu (62 Ott Reinumäe), Marko Kristal, Indrek Zelinski (56 Kristen Viikmäe), Andres Oper, Sergei Terehhov.
Trainer: Arnoldus Dick Pijpers

BULGARIA: Zdravko Zdravkov; Radostin Kishishev, Rosen Kirilov, Ivailo Petkov, Dimitar Berbatov, Zoran Jankovic (46 Svetoslav Todorov), Krasimir Balakov, Georgi Peev, Martin Petrov (71 Milen Petkov), Predrag Pazin, Stilian Petrov.
Trainer: Plamen Markov

BULGARIA v BELGIUM 2-2 (0-1)

Vassil Levski, Sofia 07.06.2003

Referee: Pierluigi Collina (ITA) Attendance: 42,000

BULGARIA: Zdravko Zdravkov; Martin Stankov, Rosen Kirilov, Milen Petkov, Daniel Borimirov, Dimitar Berbatov (54 Svetoslav Todorov), Marian Hristov (73 Vladimir Manchev), Velizar Dimitrov (80 Alexandar Alexandrov), Martin Petrov, Stilian Petrov, Ilian Stoianov. Trainer: Plamen Markov

BELGIUM: Geert de Vlieger; Eric Deflandre, Timmy Simons, Daniel van Buyten, Didier Dheedene, Philippe Clement, Walter Baseggio, Bart Goor, Wesley Sonck (74 Emile Mpenza), Thomas Buffel, Mbo Mpenza. Trainer: Aimé Antheunis

Goals: S. Petrov (31 og), Berbatov (52), Clement (56), Todorov (71 pen)

ESTONIA v ANDORRA 2-0 (2-0)

A le coq Arena, Tallinn 07.06.2003

Referee: Attila Juhos (HUN) Attendance: 3,500

ESTONIA: Mart Poom; Teet Allas, Andrei Stepanov, Raio Piiroja, Urmas Rooba (49 Erko Saviauk), Liivo Leetma, Kert Haavistu (70 Meelis Rooba), Marko Kristal, Kristen Viikmäe, Vjatsheslav Zahovaiko, Joel Lindpere (89 Ott Reinumäe). Trainer: Arnoldus Dick Pijpers

ANDORRA: Jesús Luis "KOLDO" ÁLVAREZ de Fulate; Jordi ESCURA, Manuel "TXEMA" GARCÍA, Juli FERNÁNDEZ, Antonio LIMA, Ildefons LIMA, Emiliano GONZÁLEZ (83 FERNANDO SILVA), Julí SÁNCHEZ, Manolo JIMÉNEZ (52 Marc PUJOL), Óscar SONEJEE Masán, Justo RUÍZ. Trainer: David RODRIGO

Goals: Allas (22), Viikmäe (31)

ESTONIA v CROATIA 0-1 (0-0)

A le coq Arena, Tallinn 11.06.2003

Referee: Alain Hamer (LUX) Attendance: 7,000

ESTONIA: Mart Poom; Teet Allas (82 Vjatsheslav Zahovaiko), Andrei Stepanov, Raio Piiroja, Urmas Rooba, Liivo Leetma, Meelis Rooba (71 Ott Reinumäe), Marko Kristal, Indrek Zelinski, Andres Oper, Joel Lindpere (83 Marek Lemsalu). Trainer: Arnoldus Dick Pijpers

CROATIA: Stipe Pletikosa; Dario Šimić (60 Tomislav Marić), Josip Šimunić, Marko Babić (73 Jerko Leko), Stjepan Tomas, Boris Zivković, Milan Rapaić (79 Giovanni Rosso), Darijo Srna, Dado Pršo, Niko Kovac, Ivica Olić. Trainer: Otto Barić

Goal: N. Kovac (76)

BELGIUM v ANDORRA 3-0 (2-0)

Jules Ottenstadion, Gand 11.06.2003

Referee: Siarhei Shmolik (BLS) Attendance: 12,000

BELGIUM: Geert de Vlieger; Oliver de Cock, Timmy Simons, Daniel van Buyten, Didier Dheedene (79 Peter van der Heyden), Philippe Clement, Walter Baseggio, Bart Goor (84 Tom Soetaers), Wesley Sonck, Thomas Buffel (74 Martens), Mbo Mpenza. Trainer: Aimé Antheunis

ANDORRA: Jesús Luis "KOLDO" ÁLVAREZ de Fulate; José AYALA, Manuel "TXEMA" GARCÍA, Roberto JONÁS, Antonio LIMA, Ildefons LIMA, Emiliano GONZÁLEZ (72 Felix ALVAREZ), JULÍ SÁNCHEZ (59 Jordi ESCURA), Juli FERNÁNDEZ, Óscar SONEJEE Masán (82 Jesus LUCENDO), Marc PUJOL. Trainer: David RODRIGO

Goals: Goor (21, 69), Sonck (45)

BULGARIA v ESTONIA 2-0 (1-0)

Vasil Levski, Sofia 06.09.2003

Referee: Franz-Xaver Wack (GER) Attendance: 25,128

BULGARIA: Dimitar Ivankov; Daniel Borimirov, Rosen Kirilov, Ilian Stoianov (87 Zhivko Zhelev), Ivailo Petkov, Georgi Petrov, Velizar Dimitrov (71 Georgi Peev), Zoran Jankovic (62 Nikolai Krastev), Martin Petrov, Dimitar Berbatov, Marian Hristov. Trainer: Plamen Markov

ESTONIA: Mart Poom; Teet Allas, Andrei Stepanov, Enar Jääger, Urmas Rooba, Liivo Leetma, Meelis Rooba (60 Ott Reinumäe), Marko Kristal, Kristen Viikmäe, Andres Oper, Joel Lindpere (75 Ragnar Klavan). Trainer: Arnoldus Dick Pijpers

Sent off: Oper (70)

Goals: M. Petrov (16), Berbatov (66)

ANDORRA v CROATIA 0-3 (0-2)

Comunal Andorra La Vella 06.09.2003

Referee: Miroslav Liba (CZE) Attendance: 800

ANDORRA: Jesús Luis "KOLDO" ÁLVAREZ de Fulate; Francesco RAMIREZ, Manuel "TXEMA" GARCÍA, Roberto JONÁS (68 Genis GARCÍA), Ildefons LIMA, Juli FERNÁNDEZ, José AYALA, Julí SÁNCHEZ (72 Manolo JIMÉNEZ), Óscar SONEJEE Masán, Emiliano GONZÁLEZ (49 FERNANDO SILVA), Justo RUÍZ. Trainer: David RODRIGO

CROATIA: Stipe Pletikosa; Dario Šimić, Josip Šimunić, Stjepan Tomas, Robert Kovac, Jerko Leko (46 Igor Tudor), Milan Rapaić, Giovanni Rosso, Ivica Mornar, Niko Kovac (32 Jurica Vranješ), Ivica Olić (57 Dado Pršo). Trainer: Otto Barić

Goals: N. Kovac (4), Šimunić (16), Rosso (71)

BELGIUM v CROATIA 2-1 (2-1)

Roi Baudouin, Brussel 10.09.2003

Referee: Graham Poll (ENG) Attendance: 35,000

BELGIUM: Geert de Vlieger; Eric Deflandre, Timmy Simons, Daniel van Buyten, Jelle van Damme, Walter Baseggio, Bart Goor, Wesley Sonck (90 Tom Soetaers), Thomas Buffel (88 Sandy Martens), Jonathan Walasiak, Philippe Clement. Trainer: Aimé Antheunis

CROATIA: Stipe Pletikosa; Dario Šimić, Josip Šimunić, Stjepan Tomas, Robert Kovac, Boris Zivković, Milan Rapaić (78 Silvio Marić), Giovani Rosso (65 Darijo Srna), Ivica Mornar, Niko Kovac, Ivica Olić (46 Dado Pršo). Trainer: Otto Barić

Sent off: Šimunić (74)

Goals: Sonck (34, 42), Šimić (36)

ANDORRA v BULGARIA 0-3 (0-2)

Comunal Andorra La Vella 10.09.2003

Referee: Tomasz Mikulski, (POL) Attendance: 899

ANDORRA: Jesús Luis "KOLDO" ÁLVAREZ de Fulate; Francesco RAMIREZ, Manuel "TXEMA" GARCÍA, Roberto JONÁS (60 JULÍ SÁNCHEZ), Antonio LIMA, Óscar SONEJEE Masán, José AYALA (80 Jordi ESCURA), Manolo JIMÉNEZ, Juli FERNÁNDEZ, Marc PUJOL, Justo RUIZ (90 Jesus LUCENDO). Trainer: David RODRIGO

BULGARIA: Dimitar Ivankov; Rosen Kirilov, Ivailo Petkov, Daniel Borimirov, Zoran Jankovic (59 Velizar Dimitrov), Dimitar Berbatov, Georgi Peev (63 Vladimir Manchev), Marian Hristov, Martin Petrov, Predrag Pazin, Stilian Petrov. Trainer: Plamen Markov

Sent off: Ramirez (85)

Goals: Berbatov (10, 23), Hristov (58)

CROATIA v BULGARIA 1-0 (0-0)

Maksimir, Zagreb 11.10.2003

Referee: Gilles Veissiere (FRA) Attendance: 37,000

CROATIA: Stipe Pletikosa; Dario Šimić, Jurica Vranješ, Robert Kovac, Igor Tudor, Boris Zivković, Milan Rapaić (54 Marko Babić), Darijo Srna (46 Ivica Olić), Dado Pršo, Jerko Leko, Ivica Mornar (76 Giovanni Rosso). Trainer: Otto Barić

BULGARIA: Zdravko Zdravkov; Nikolai Krastev, Rosen Kirilov, Ivailo Petkov, Daniel Borimirov, Velizar Dimitrov (62 Vladimir Manchev), Georgi Peev (72 Zoran Jankovic), Marian Hristov, Predrag Pazin, Stilian Petrov. Trainer: Plamen Markov

Goal: Olić (48)

BELGIUM v ESTONIA 2-0 (1-0)

Sclessin, Liège 11.10.2003

Referee: Massimo Busacca (SWI) Attendance: 26,000

BELGIUM: Geert de Vlieger; Eric Deflandre, Timmy Simons, Daniel van Buyten, Jelle van Damme (56 Olivier Deschacht), Philippe Clement, Walter Baseggio, Bart Goor, Wesley Sonck (80 Emile Mpenza), Thomas Buffel (87 Cedric Roussel), Mbo Mpenza. Trainer: Aimé Antheunis

ESTONIA: Mart Poom; Enar Jääger, Marek Lemsalu, Raio Piiroja, Urmas Rooba, Ott Reinumäe, Kert Haavistu (77 Vjatseslav Zahovaiko), Martin Reim, Kristen Viikmäe, Meelis Rooba, Ragnar Klavan. Trainer: Arnoldus Dick Pijpers

Goals: Piiroja (41 og), Buffel (60)

	P	W	D	L	F	A	Pts
Bulgaria	8	5	2	1	13	4	17
Croatia	8	5	1	2	12	4	16
Belgium	8	5	1	2	11	9	16
Estonia	8	2	2	4	4	6	8
Andorra	8	0	0	8	1	18	0

GROUP 9

FINLAND v WALES 0-2 (0-1)

Olympic, Helsinki 07.09.2002

Referee: Konrad Plautz (AUS) Attendance: 35,833

FINLAND: Antti Niemi; Ville Nylund (69 Jonatan Johansson), Janne Saarinen (78 Peter Kopteff), Sami Hyypiä, Hannu Tihinen, Aki Riihilahti, Mika Nurmela (86 Mika Kottila), Teemu Tainio, Shefki Kuqi, Jari Litmanen, Joonas Kolkka. Trainer: Antti Muurinen

WALES: Paul Jones; Mark Delaney, Gary Speed, Andrew Melville, Daniel Gabbidon, Mark Pembridge, Robbie Savage, Andy Johnson (76 Craig Bellamy), John Hartson, Simon Davies, Ryan Giggs. Trainer: Mark Hughes

Goals: Hartson (30), Davies (72)

AZERBAIJAN v ITALY 0-2 (0-1)

Tofig Bakhramov, Baku 07.09.2002

Referee: Kyros Vassaras (GRE) Attendance: 37,000

AZERBAIJAN: Dmitriy Kramarenko; Kamal Guliyev, Aslan Kerimov, Tarlan Akhmedov, Emin Guliyev, Emin Imamaliev, Makhmud Gurbanov (68 Bakhtiar Musayev), Samir Aliyev (88 Nadir Nabiev), Gurban Gurbanov (90 Farrukh Ismaylov), Rashad Sadhikov, Emin Agaev. Trainer: Vagyf Sadygov

ITALY: Gianluigi Buffon; Christian Panucci, Alessandro Nesta, Fabio Cannavaro, Francesco Coco, Luigi di Biagio (57 Massimo Ambrosini), Damiano Tommasi, Gennaro Gattuso, Alessandro del Piero, Filippo Inzaghi (78 Andrea Pirlo), Christian Vieri (57 Vincenzo Montella). Trainer: Giovanni Trappatoni

Goals: Akhmedov (32 og), del Piero (63)

FINLAND v AZERBAIJAN 3-0 (1-0)

Olympic, Helsinki 12.10.2002

Referee: Alain Hamer (LUX) Attendance: 11,853

FINLAND: Antti Niemi; Petri Pasanen, Janne Saarinen, Sami Hyypiä (79 Toni Kuivasto), Hannu Tihinen, Aki Riihilahti, Mika Nurmela, Teemu Tainio (74 Jarkko Wiss), Antti Sumiala (85 Shefki Kuqi), Jari Litmanen, Joonas Kolkka. Trainer: Antti Muurinen

AZERBAIJAN: Jahanjir Hasanzade; Emin Agaev, Aslan Kerimov, Tarlan Akhmedov, Emin Guliyev, Kamal Guliyev, Mahmud Gurbanov (65 Rashad Sadikhov), Emin Imamaliev (83 Vadim Vasilyev), Gurban Gurbanov, Samir Aliyev, Ramiz Mammadov (90 Fizuli Mammedov). Trainer: Vagif Sadykov

Goals: Akhmedov (14 og), Tihinen (59), Hyypiä (71)

SERBIA MONTENEGRO v FINLAND 2-0 (0-0)

FK Crvena Zvezda, Beograd 16.10.2002

Referee: Dick van Egmond (HOL) Attendance: 25,000

SERBIA MONTENEGRO: Dragoslav Jevrić; Zoran Njegus (46 Mladen Krstajić), Ivica Dragutinović, Nemanja Vidić, Igor Duljaj, Nikola Lazetić, Predrag Mijatović, Dejan Stanković, Sinisa Mihajlović, Mateja Kezman (62 Nenad Brnović), Darko Kovacević (71 Savo Milosević). Trainer: Dejan Savicević

FINLAND: Antti Niemi; Petri Pasanen (63 Juha Reini), Janne Saarinen, Sami Hyypiä, Toni Kuivasto, Aki Riihilahti, Mika Nurmela, Teemu Tainio (82 Shefki Kuqi), Antti Sumiala (57 Jonatan Johansson), Jari Litmanen, Joonas Kolkka. Trainer: Antti Muurinen

Sent off: Reini (83)

Goals: Kovacević (56), Mihajlović (84 pen)

ITALY v SERBIA MONTENEGRO 1-1 (1-0)

San Paolo, Napoli 12.10.2002

Referee: Manuel Enrique MEJUTO GONZÁLEZ (SPA) Attendance: 50,000

ITALY: Gianluigi Buffon; Christian Panucci, Luciano Zauri (81 Massimo Oddo), Gennaro Gattuso, Fabio Cannavaro, Alessandro Nesta, Alessandro Del Piero, Christiano Doni (46 Vincenzo Montella), Filippo Inzaghi, Andrea Pirlo (78 Massimo Ambrosini), Damiano Tommasi. Trainer: Giovanni Trapattoni

SERBIA MONTENEGRO: Dragoslav Jevrić; Zoran Mirković (10 Igor Duljaj), Ivica Dragutinović, Nemanja Vidić, Mladen Krstajić, Goran Trobok, Nikola Lazetić, Predrag Mijatović (65 Mateja Kezman), Dejan Stanković, Sinisa Mihajlović, Darko Kovacević (73 Savo Milosević). Trainer: Dejan Savicević

Goals: Mijatović (29), Del Piero (40)

AZERBAIJAN v WALES 0-2 (0-1)

Tofig Bakhramov, Baku 20.11.2002

Referee: Luc Huyghe (BEL) Attendance: 15,000

AZERBAIJAN: Djakhangir Hasanzade; Aslan Kerimov (46 Fizuli Mammedov), Ilgam Yadullayev, Tarlan Akhmedov (76 Arif Asadov), Adam Niftaliev, Rashad Sadikhov, Makhmud Gurbanov (64 Farukh Ismaylov), Emin Imamaliev, Gurban Gurbanov, Vadim Vasilyev, Samir Aliyev. Trainer: Asker Abdullayev

WALES: Paul Jones; Mark Delaney (73 Rhys Weston), Darren Barnard, Andrew Melville, Robert Page, Gary Speed, Carl Robinson (90 Paul Trollope), Robert Earnshaw (90 Neil Roberts), John Hartson, Simon Davies, Ryan Giggs. Trainer: Mark Hughes

Goals: Speed (10), Hartson (70)

WALES v ITALY 2-1 (1-1)

Millenium, Cardiff 16.10.2002

Referee: Gilles Veissiere (FRA) Attendance: 70,000

WALES: Paul Jones; Mark Delaney, Andrew Melville, Daniel Gabbidon, Gary Speed, Simon Davies, Robbie Savage, Craig Bellamy (90 Nathan Blake), Mark Pembridge, Ryan Giggs, John Hartson. Manager: Mark Hughes

ITALY: Gianluigi Buffon; Christian Panucci, Luciano Zauri, Luigi Di Biagio (64 Gennaro Gattuso, 84 Massimo Marazzina), Fabio Cannavaro, Alessandro Nesta, Alessandro Del Piero, Massimo Ambrosini, Andrea Pirlo, Vincenzo Montella (69 Massimo Maccarone), Damiano Tommasi. Trainer: Giovanni Trapattoni

Goals: Davies (11), Del Piero (32), Bellamy (70)

SERBIA MONTENEGRO v AZERBAIJAN 2-2 (1-0)

Gradski, Podgorica 12.02.2003

Referee: Jacek Granat (POL) Attendance: 16,038

SERBIA MONTENEGRO: Dragoslav Jevrić; Nenad Djordjević, Goran Bunjevcević, Milan Dudić, Branko Bosković, Nikola Lazetić (74 Marković), Predrag Mijatović (70 Danijel Ljuboja), Savo Milosević, Dejan Stanković, Zvonimir Vukić, Mateja Kezman (59 Igor Duljaj). Trainer: Dejan Savicević

AZERBAIJAN: Djakhangir Hasanzade; Kamal Guliyev, Rashad Sadikhov, Emin Guliyev, Tarlan Akhmedov, Mahmud Gurbanov (90 Fizuli Mamedov), Emin Imamaliev, Farrukh Ismaylov (55 Ruslan Musayev), Samir Aliyev (87 Mamedov). Trainer: Asker Abdullayev

Goals: Mijatović (33 pen), Lazetić (52), Gurbanov (58, 77)

ITALY v FINLAND 2-0 (2-0)

Renzo Barbera, Palermo 29.03.2003

Referee: Valentin Ivanov (RUS) Attendance: 34,074

ITALY: Gianluigi Buffon; Christian Panucci, Gianluca Zambrotta, Cristiano Zanetti, Fabio Cannavaro, Alessandro Nesta, Mauro Camoranesi, Simone Perrotta, Christian Vieri (82 Bernardo Corradi), Francesco Totti (87 Fabrizio Miccoli), Marco Delvecchio (68 Alessandro Birindelli). Trainer: Giovanni Trapattoni

FINLAND: Antti Niemi; Petri Pasanen, Janne Saarinen, Sami Hyypiä, Hannu Tihinen, Aki Riihilahti (36 Jonatan Johansson), Mika Nurmela (75 Peter Kopteff), Jari Ilola, Mikael Forssell, Teemu Tainio, Joonas Kolkka. Trainer: Antti Muurinen

Goals: Vieri (5, 22)

FINLAND v ITALY 0-2 (0-1)

Olympic, Helsinki 11.06.2003

Referee: Zeljko Sirić (CRO) Attendance: 36,850

FINLAND: Jussi Jääskelainen; Petri Pasanen, Janne Saarinen, Sami Hyypiä, Hannu Tihinen, Simo Valakari (82 Aki Riihilahti), Mika Nurmela (69 Peter Kopteff), Mika Väyrynen, Mikael Forssell, Jari Litmanen, Joonas Kolkka (78 Jonatan Johansson). Trainer: Antti Muurinen

ITALY: Gianluigi Buffon; Christian Panucci, Gianluca Zambrotta, Cristiano Zanetti, Fabio Cannavaro (90 Nicola Legrottaglie), Alessandro Nesta, Alessandro del Piero, Simone Perrotta, Bernardo Corradi (85 Marco Delvecchio), Francesco Totti, Stefano Fiore (83 Masimo Oddo). Trainer: Giovanni Trappatoni

Goals: Totti (32), del Piero (73)

WALES v AZERBAIJAN 4-0 (3-0)

Millenium, Cardiff 29.03.2003

Referee: Ohilippe Leuba (SWI) Attendance: 72,500

WALES: Paul Jones; Gary Speed (45 Paul Trollope), Andrew Melville, Robert Page, Mark Pembridge, Robbie Savage (19 Carl Robinson), Craig Bellamy (72 Robert Edwards), John Hartson, Simon Davies, Ryan Giggs, John Oster. Trainer: Mark Hughes

AZERBAIJAN: Djakhangir Hasanzade; Tarlan Akhmedov, Kamal Guliyev, Samir Aliyev (78 Zaur Tagizade), Emin Guliyev (46 Ilham Yadullayev), Aftandil Hajiev (46 Fizuli Mamedov), Mahmud Gurbanov, Ramiz Mamedov, Gurbanov, Emin Imamaliev, Ruslan Musayev. Trainer: Asker Abdullayev

Goals: Bellamy (1), Speed (40), Hartson (44), Giggs (52)

AZERBAIJAN v SERBIA MONTENEGRO 2-1 (0-1)

Shafa, Baku 11.06.2003

Referee: Knud Erik Fisker (DEN) Attendance: 5,000

AZERBAIJAN: Dmitri Kramarenko; Emin Agaev (84 Zaur Tagizade), Aslan Kerimov, Tarlan Akhmedov, Emin Guliyev, Kamal Guliyev, Makhmud Gurbanov, Gurban Gurbanov (90+3 Ilgam Yadullayev), Rashad Sadikhov, Samir Aliyev, Ruslan Musayev (53 Farrukh Ismaylov). Trainer: Asker Abdullayev

SERBIA MONTENEGRO: Dragoslav Jevrić (46 Dragon Zilić); Zoran Mirković, Nikola Malbasa, Zoran Njegus, Nenad Djordjević, Predrag Mijatović (68 Nenad Kovacević), Zvonimir Vukić, Igor Duljaj (89 Savo Milosević), Darko Kovacević, Branko Bosković, Mladen Krstajić. Trainer: Dejan Savicević

Goals: Bosković (27), Gurbanov (87 pen), Ismaylov (90)

FINLAND v SERBIA MONTENEGRO 3-0 (2-0)

Olympic, Helsinki 07.06.2003

Referee: Claude Colombo (FRA) Attendance: 17,343

FINLAND: Jussi Jääskelainen; Petri Pasanen, Janne Saarinen, Sami Hyypiä, Hannu Tihinen, Simo Valakari, Mika Nurmela (87 Aki Riihilahti), Mika Väyrynen, Mikael Forssell (79 Shefki Kuqi), Jari Litmanen, Joonas Kolkka (66 Peter Kopteff). Trainer: Antti Muurinen

SERBIA MONTENEGRO: Dragoslav Jevrić; Zoran Mirković (80 Nenad Kovacević), Boban Dmitrović, Nemanja Vidić, Predrag Mijatović (46 Zvonimir Vukić), Savo Milosević (46 Nenad Jestrović), Sinisa Mihajlović, Igor Duljaj, Slobodan Marković, Darko Kovacević, Mladen Krstajić. Trainer: Dejan Savicević

Sent off: Mihajlović (26)

Goals: Hyypiä (19), Kolkka (45), Forssell (56)

SERBIA MONTENEGRO v WALES 1-0 (0-0)

Crvena Zvezda, Beograd 20.08.2003

Referee: Anders Frisk (SWE) Attendance: 25,000

SERBIA MONTENEGRO: Dragoslav Jevrić; Ivica Dragutinović, Dragan Mladenović, Dejan Stefanović, Goran Gavrancić, Zvonimir Vukić (67 Saša Ilić), Mateja Kezman, Dejan Stanković (81 Predrag Djordjević), Darko Kovacević, Mladen Krstajić, Milivoje Cirković. Trainer: Ilija Petković

WALES: Paul Jones; Mark Delaney, Gary Speed, Daniel Gabbidon, Robert Page, Mark Pembridge, Robbie Savage, Craig Bellamy, Nathan Blake (78 Robert Earnshaw), Simon Davies, Ryan Giggs. Trainer: Mark Hughes

Goal: Mladenović (73)

ITALY v WALES 4-0 (0-0)

Giuseppe Meazza, Milano 06.09.2003

Referee: Markus Merk (GER) Attendance: 68,000

ITALY: Gianluigi Buffon; Christian Panucci (58 Massimo Oddo), Gianluca Zambrotta, Cristiano Zanetti, Fabio Cannavaro, Alessandro Nesta, Alessandro del Piero, Simone Perrotta (86 Stefano Fiore), Christian Vieri, Filippo Inzaghi (74 Gennaro Gattuso), Mauro Camoranesi.
Trainer: Giovanni Trappatoni

WALES: Paul Jones; Mark Delaney, Gary Speed, Jason Koumas (71 Robert Earnshaw), Robert Page, Mark Pembridge, Robbie Savage, Craig Bellamy, John Hartson (82 Nathan Blake), Simon Davies, Ryan Giggs. Trainer: Mark Hughes

Goals: Inzaghi (59, 63, 70), del Piero (76 pen)

SERBIA MONTENEGRO v ITALY 1-1 (0-1)

Crvena Zvezda, Beograd 10.09.2003

Referee: Alain Hamer (LUX) Attendance: 35,000

SERBIA MONTENEGRO: Dragoslav Jevrić; Milivoje Cirković, Ivica Dragutinović (70 Branko Bosković), Dragan Mladenović, Dejan Stefanović, Goran Gavrancić, Saša Ilić, Mateja Kezman (59 Danijel Ljuboja), Savo Milosević, Predrag Djordjević, Mladen Krstajić. Trainer: Ilija Petković

ITALY: Gianluigi Buffon; Christian Panucci, Gianluca Zambrotta, Alessio Tacchinardi, Fabio Cannavaro, Alessandro Nesta, Alessandro del Piero, Simone Perrotta, Christian Vieri (79 Bernardo Corradi), Filippo Inzaghi (64 Stefano Fiore), Mauro Camoranesi (51 Gennaro Gattuso).
Trainer: Giovanni Trappatoni

Goals: Inzaghi (22), S. Ilić (82)

AZERBAIJAN v FINLAND 1-2 (0-0)

Shafa, Baku 06.09.2003

Referee: Vladimir Hrinak (SVK) Attendance: 7,500

AZERBAIJAN: Dmitriy Kramarenko; Emin Agaev (11 Ruslan Musayev), Tarlan Akhmedov, Emin Guliyev, Kamal Guliyev, Mahmud Gurbanov, Ilham Yadullayev, Rashad Sadikhov, Farrukh Ismaylov, Samir Aliyev (46 Emin Imamaliyev), Vadim Vasilyev (60 Zaur Tagizade). Trainer: Asker Abdullayev

SUOMI: Antti Niemi; Janne Saarinen, Sami Hyypiä, Petri Pasanen, Mika Väyrynen (85 Aki Riihilahti), Mika Nurmela, Teemu Tainio (85 Simo Valakari), Mikael Forssell, Jonatan Johansson (46 Peter Kopteff), Joonas Kolkka, Juha Reini.
Trainer: Antti Muurinen

Sent off: Akhmedov (42)

Goals: Tainio (52), Nurmela (74), Ismaylov (88)

ITALY v AZERBAIJAN 4-0 (2-0)

Oreste Granillo, Regio Calabria 11.10.2003

Referee: Stuart Dougal (SCO) Attendance: 30,000

ITALY: Gianluigi Buffon; Massimo Oddo, Alessandro Nesta (77 Matteo Ferrari), Fabio Cannavaro, Gianluca Zambrotta, Mauro Camoranesi, Simone Perrotta, Cristiano Zanetti, Francesco Totti, Christian Vieri (54 Marco di Vaio), Filippo Inzaghi. Trainer: Giovanni Trappatoni

AZERBAIJAN: Dmitriy Kramarenko (55 Jahangir Hasanzade); Rufat Guliyev, Aslan Kerimov, Ilham Yadullayev, Emin Agaev, Zaur Tagizade (74 Vadim Vasilyev), Mahmud Gurbanov (82 Ramiz Mamedov), Rashad Sadikhov, Emin Guliyev, Samir Aliyev, Emin Imamaliev.
Trainer: Asker Abdullayev

Goals: Vieri (16), Inzaghi (24, 87), di Vaio (64)

WALES v FINLAND 1-1 (1-0)

Millenium, Cardiff 10.09.2003

Referee: Arturo DAUDEN IBAÑEZ (SPA)
Attendance: 72,500

WALES: Paul Jones; Rhys Weston (72 Carl Robinson), Gary Speed, Andy Melville, Robert Page, Mark Pembridge, Jason Koumas, Robert Earnshaw, John Hartson (82 Nathan Blake), Simon Davies, Ryan Giggs. Trainer: Mark Hughes

FINLAND: Antti Niemi; Petri Pasanen (82 Peter Kopteff), Janne Saarinen (46 Juha Reini), Sami Hyypiä, Hannu Tihinen, Aki Riihilahti, Mika Nurmela, Teemu Tainio, Mikael Forssell, Mika Väyrynen (58 Shefki Kuqi), Joonas Kolkka.
Trainer: Antti Muurinen

Sent off: Koumas (64)

Goals: Davies (3), Forssell (78)

WALES v SERBIA MONTENEGRO 2-3 (1-1)

Millenium, Cardiff 11.10.2003

Referee: Fritz Stuchlik (AUS) Attendance: 72,514

WALES: Paul Jones; Mark Delaney, Gary Speed, Daniel Gabbidon, Rhys Weston (67 Robert Edwards), Carl Robinson, Robert Earnshaw, Craig Bellamy, John Hartson (86 Nathan Blake), Darren Barnard, Ryan Giggs. Trainer: Mark Hughes

SERBIA MONTENEGRO: Dragoslav Jevrić; Goran Bunjevcević, Milivoje Cirković, Goran Gavrancić, Mateja Kezman (60 Savo Milosević), Dragan Sarac, Branko Bosković, Nenad Djordjević, Darko Kovacević, Zvonimir Vukić, Danijel Ljuboja. Trainer: Ilija Petković

Goals: Vukić (6), Hartson (26), Milosević (82), Gavrancić (88), Earnshaw (90+1)

	P	W	D	L	F	A	Pts
Italy	8	5	2	1	17	4	17
Wales	8	4	1	3	13	10	13
Serbia & Monten.	8	3	3	2	11	11	12
Finland	8	3	1	4	9	10	10
Azerbaijan	8	1	1	6	5	20	4

GROUP 10

RUSSIA v REPUBLIC OF IRELAND 4-2 (2-0)

Lokomotiv, Moskva 07.09.2002

Referee: Claude Colombo (FRA) Attendance: 23,000

RUSSIA: Sergey Ovchinnikov; Gennadi Nizhegorodov, Sergei Ignashevitch, Evgeni Aldonin, Sergei Semak (75 Dmitri Khokhlov), Igor Yanovski, Rolan Gusev (29 Andrei Solomatin), Andrei Kariaka, Dmitri Loskov, Viktor Onopko, Vladimir Beschastnykh (46 Aleksandr Kerzhakov).
Trainer: Valeri Gazzaev

IRELAND: Shay Given; Steve Finnan, Ian Harte, Kenny Cunnigham, Gary Breen, Matt Holland, Jason McAteer (65 Gary Doherty), Mark Kinsella, Kevin Kilbane (86 Phil Babb), Damien Duff (17 Clinton Morrison), Robbie Keane.
Trainer: Mick McCarthy

Goals: Kariaka (20), Beschastnykh (24), Doherty (69), Kerzhakov (71), Morrison (76), Babb (88 og)

SWITZERLAND v GEORGIA 4-1 (1-0)

Saint Jakob Park, Basel 08.09.2002

Referee: Vladimir Hrinak (SVK) Attendance: 20,500

SWITZERLAND: Jörg Stiel; Bernt Haas, Joël Magnin (82 Bruno Berner), Stéphane Henchoz, Murat Yakin, Johann Vogel (68 Fabio Celestini), Ricardo Cabañas, Patrick Müller, Alexander Frei, Hakan Yakin (73 Raphaël Wicky), Stéphane Chapuisat. Trainer: Jakob Kuhn

GEORGIA: David Gvaramadze; Levan Kobiashvili, Gela Shekiladze, Kakhi Kaladze, Edik Sadjaia (46 Aleksandre Rekhviashvili, 84 Mikheil Kavelashvili), Levan Tskitishvili, Giorgi Nemsadze, Gocha Jamarauli, Giorgi Demetradze, Giorgi Kinkladze (46 Vladimer Burduli), Archil Arveladze.
Trainer: Alexandr Chivadze

Goals: Frei (37), A. Arveladze (62), Hakan Yakin (63), Müller (74), Chapuisat (81)

ALBANIA v SWITZERLAND 1-1 (0-1)

Qemal Stafa, Tiranë 12.10.2002

Referee: Orhan Erdemir (TUR) Attendance: 15,000

ALBANIA: Foto Strakosha; Geri Çipi, Arian Xhumba, Edvin Murati, Klodian Duro (88 Elvis Sina), Besnik Hasi, Altin Lala, Fatmir Vata, Igli Tare (71 Florian Myrtaj), Erion Bogdani, Altin Haxhi. Trainer: Giuseppe Dossena

SWITZERLAND: Jörg Stiel; Bernt Haas, Joël Magnin, Patrick Müller, Murat Yakin, Johann Vogel, Ricardo Cabañas (80 Mario Cantaluppi), Raphaël Wicky, Alex Frei, Hakan Yakin (63 Fabio Celestini), Stéphane Chapuisat (84 Leonard Thurre).
Trainer: Jakob Kuhn

Goals: Murat Yakin (37), Murati (68)

GEORGIA v RUSSIA

Lokomotiv, Tbilisi 12.10.2002

Referee: Tom Henning Ovrebo (NOR)

GEORGIA: Giorgi Lomaia; Aleksandre Rekhviashvili, Giorgi Shashiashvili, Kakhi Kaladze, Aleksandr Amisulashvili, Givi Didava, Levan Tskitishvili, Vladimer Burduli, Aleksandre Iashvili, Levan Kobiashvili, Shota Arveladze (25 Giorgi Demetradze). Trainer: Aleksandr Chivadze

RUSSIA: Sergey Ovchinnikov; Gennadi Nizhegorodov, Sergei Ignashevich, Aleksei Smertin, Sergei Semak, Igor Yanovski, Viktor Onopko, Rolan Gusev, Andrei Solomatin, Dmitri Loskov, Vladimir Beschastnykh. Trainer: Valery Gazzaev

Match abandoned due failure of floodlights

REPUBLIC OF IRELAND v SWITZERLAND 1-2 (0-1)

Lansdowne Road, Dublin 16.10.2002

Referee: Rune Pedersen (NOR) Attendance: 35,000

IRELAND: Shay Given; Gary Kelly, Ian Harte (86 Gary Doherty), Kenny Cunningham, Gary Breen, Matt Holland, Colin Healy, Mark Kinsella, Damien Duff (83 Thomas Butler), Robbie Keane, Kevin Kilbane (62 Clinton Morrison).
Trainer: Michael McCarthy

SWITZERLAND: Jörg Stiel; Bernt Haas, Joël Magnin, Patrick Müller, Murat Yakin, Johann Vogel, Ricardo Cabañas, Raphaël Wicky (85 Mario Cantaluppi), Alex Frei (71 Leonard Thurre), Hakan Yakin (85 Fabio Celestini), Stéphane Chapuisat.
Trainer: Jakob Kuhn

Goals: H. Yakin (45), Magnin (78 og), Celestini (87)

RUSSIA v ALBANIA 4-1 (2-1)

Centralnyi, Volgograd 16.10.2002

Referee: Leif Sundell (SWE) Attendance: 18,000

RUSSIA: Sergey Ovchinnikov; Gennadi Nizhegorodov, Sergei Ignashevich, Aleksei Smertin, Sergei Semak, Igor Yanovski, Viktor Onopko, Rolan Gusev (79 Vadim Evseev), Andrei Solomatin, Dmitri Loskov (46 Evgeni Aldonin), Aleksandr Kerzhakov (64 Denis Popov). Trainer: Valery Gazzaev

ALBANIA: Foto Strakosha; Geri Çipi, Arian Xhumba, Ervin Fakaj, Edvin Murati, Besnik Hasi, Altin Lala, Klodian Duro, Fatmir Vata (60 Elvis Sina), Igli Tare (69 Florian Myrtaj), Altin Xahhi (56 Alban Bushi). Trainer: Giuseppe Dossena

Goals: Kerzhakov (3), Duro (13), Semak (42, 55), Onopko (52)

GEORGIA v REPUBLIC OF IRELAND 1-2 (0-1)

Lokomotiv, Tbilisi 29.03.2003

Referee: Kyros Vassaras (GRE) Attendance: 15,000

GEORGIA: Giorgi Lomaia; Khizaneishvili, Giorgi Shashiashvili, Aleksandr Amisulashvili, Levan Kobiashvili, Levan Tskitishvili, Georgi Nemsadze, Gocha Jamarauli, Temur Ketsbaia (46 Georgi Demetradze), Georgi Kinkladze (72 Givi Didava), Aleksandre Iashvili. Trainer: Aleksandr Chivadze

IRELAND: Shay Given; Stephen Carr, Kenny Cunningham, Gary Breen, John O'Shea, Matt Holland, Damien Duff, Mark Kinsella, Gary Doherty, Lee Carsley, Kevin Kilbane. Trainer: Brian Kerr

Goals: Duff (18), Kobiashvili (62), Doherty (84)

ALBANIA v RUSSIA 3-1 (1-0)

Loro Borici, Shkoder 29.03.2003

Referee: Paul Allaerts (BEL) Attendance: 16,000

ALBANIA: Foto Strakosha; Ardit Beqiri, Geri Çipi, Ardian Aliaj, Altin Lala, Besnik Hasi, Klodian Duro, Ervin Skela (83 Nevil Dede), Edvin Murati (67 Arian Bellai), Igli Tare, Altin Rrakli (70 Florian Myrtaj). Trainer: Giuseppe Dossena

RUSSIA: Sergey Ovchinnikov; Gennadi Nizhegorodov, Sergei Ignashevich, Aleksei Smertin (72 Igor Yanovski), Sergei Semak, Aleksei Berezoutski, Evgeni Aldonin, Rolan Gusev (54 Vladimir Beschastnykh), Aleksandr Tochilin (46 Andrei Kariaka), Dmitri Loskov, Aleksandr Kerzhakov. Trainer: Valery Gazzaev

Goals: Rraklli (20), Kariaka (76), Lala (79), Tare (82)

ALBANIA v REPUBLIC OF IRELAND 0-0

Qemal Stafa, Tirana 02.04.2003

Referee: Stefano Farina (ITA) Attendance: 20,000

ALBANIA: Foto Strakosha; Ardit Beqiri, Geri Çipi, Ardian Aliaj, Altin Lala, Besnik Hasi, Klodian Duro, Ervin Skela (85 Alban Bushi), Edvin Murati (66 Arian Bellai), Igli Tare, Altin Rrakli (69 Florian Myrtaj). Trainer: Hans-Peter Briegel

IRELAND: Shay Given; Stephen Carr, John O'Shea, Matt Holland, Mark Kinsella, Gary Breen, Kenny Cunningham, Lee Carsley, Damien Duff, Kevin Kilbane, Robbie Keane (66 Gary Doherty). Trainer: Brian Kerr

GEORGIA v SWITZERLAND 0-0

Lokomotiv, Tbilisi 02.04.2003

Referee: Edo Trivković (CRO) Attendance: 7,000

GEORGIA: Giorgi Lomaia; Otar Khizaneishvili, Zurab Khizaneishvili, Aleksandr Rekhviashvili, Kvirkvelia, Revaz Kemoklidze, Georgi Nemsadze (48 Givi Didava), Levan Tskitishvili, Aleksandre Iashvili (48 Shota Arveladze), Levan Kobiashvili, Georgi Demetradze (72 Mikheil Ashvetia). Trainer: Aleksandr Chivadze

SWITZERLAND: Pascal Zuberbühler; Bernt Haas, Bruno Berner, Patrick Müller, Murat Yakin, Johann Vogel, Ricardo Cabañas (67 Mario Cantaluppi), Raphaël Wicky, Alex Frei (59 Fabio Celestini), Hakan Yakin (90 Léonard Turre), Stéphane Chapuisat. Trainer: Jakob Kuhn

GEORGIA v RUSSIA 1-0 (1-0)

Lokomotiv, Tbilisi 30.04.2003

Referee: Franz-Xaver Wack (GER) Behind closed doors

GEORGIA: Giorgi Lomaia; Otar Khizaneishvili, Zurab Khizaneishvili, Kakha Kaladze, David Kvirkvelia, Levan Tskitishvili, Georgi Nemsadze, Vladimir Burduli (80 Giorgi Shashiashvili), Malkhaz Asatiani (75 Givi Didava), Georgi Demetradze, Mikheil Ashvetia (84 Rati Aleksidze). Trainer: Aleksandr Chivadze

RUSSIA: Mandrikin; Gennadi Nizhegorodov, Sergei Ignashevich (14 Denis Evsikov), Aleksei Smertin, Sergei Semak, Evgeni Aldonin (79 Dmitri Sychev), Viktor Onopko, Dmitri Alenichev, Egor Titov, Marat Izmailov (46 Aleksandr Kerzhakov), Andrei Kariaka.
Trainer: Valery Gazzaev

Goal: Asatiani (11)

SWITZERLAND v RUSSIA 2-2 (2-1)

Saint Jakob Park, Basel 07.06.2003

Referee: Arturo DAUDEN IBAÑEZ (SPA) Att: 30,500

SWITZERLAND: Jorg Stiel; Bernt Haas, Ludovic Magnin (61 Bruno Berner), Patrick Müller (82 Stéphane Henchoz), Murat Yakin, Fabio Celestini, Ricardo Cabañas, Raphaël Wicky (71 Johann Vogel), Alex Frei, Hakan Yakin, Stéphane Chapuisat. Trainer: Jakob Kuhn

RUSSIA: Sergey Ovchinnikov; Vasili Berezoutski, Yuri Kovtun, Aleksei Smertin, Sergei Semak (82 Denis Evsikov), Sergei Ignashevich, Igor Yanovski, Rolan Gusev, Evgeni Aldonin, Denis Popov (46 Dmitri Sychev), Andrei Kariaka (52 Bistrov). Trainer: Valery Gazzaev

Goals: Frei (14, 16), Ignashevich (24, 68 pen)

SWITZERLAND v ALBANIA 3-2 (2-1)

Stade de Genève 11.06.2003

Referee: Stephen Graham Bennett (ENG) Att: 26,000

SWITZERLAND: Jorg Stiel; Bernt Haas, Bruno Berner, Stéphane Henchoz (75 Marco Zwyssig), Murat Yakin, Johann Vogel, Ricardo Cabañas, Raphaël Wicky (64 Christophe Spycher), Alex Frei (83 Fabio Celestini), Hakan Yakin, Stéphane Chapuisat. Trainer: Jakob Kuhn

ALBANIA: Foto Strakosha; Ardit Beqiri, Geri Çipi, Ardian Aliaj, Altin Lala, Klodian Duro, Besnik Hasi (64 Lorik Cana), Ervin Skela, Arian Bellai (62 Altin Rraklli), Igli Tare, Alban Bushi. Trainer: Hans-Peter Briegel

Goals: Haas (10), Lala (22), Frei (32), Cabanas (71), Skela (86 pen)

REPUBLIC OF IRELAND v ALBANIA 2-1 (1-1)

Lansdowne Road, Dublin 07.06.2003

Referee: Tomasz Mikulski (POL) Attendance: 33,000

IRELAND: Shay Given; Stephen Carr, John O'Shea, Gary Breen, Kenny Cunningham, Matt Holland, Damien Duff, Mark Kinsella (55 Carsley), Connolly (65 Gary Doherty), Robbie Keane, Kevin Kilbane (76 Reid). Trainer: Brian Kerr

ALBANIA: Foto Strakosha (79 Arjan Beqaj); Elvin Beqiri, Geri Çipi, Klodian Duro, Besnik Hasi, Edvin Murati (58 Arian Bellai), Altin Lala, Ervin Skela, Ardian Aliaj, Altin Rraklli (85 Florian Myrtaj), Igli Tare. Trainer: Hans-Peter Briegel

Goals: Keane (6), Skela (7), Aliaj (90+2 og)

REPUBLIC OF IRELAND v RUSSIA 1-1 (1-1)

Lansdowne Road, Dublin 06.09.2003

Referee: Lubos Michel (SVK) Attendance: 36,000

IRELAND: Shay Given; Stephen Carr, John O'Shea (26 Ian Harte), Gary Breen, Kenny Cunningham, Matt Holland, Lee Carsley (45 Steven Reid), Colin Healy, Damien Duff, Clinton Morrison (73 Gary Doherty), Kevin Kilbane. Trainer: Brian Kerr

RUSSIA: Sergey Ovchinnikov; Vadim Evseev, Aleksei Smertin, Dmitri Alenichev (39 Evgeni Aldonin), Sergei Ignashevich, Viktor Onopko, Rolan Gusev, Dmitri Bulykin, Aleksandr Mostovoi, Valery Essipov (34 Aleksandr Kerzhakov), Dmitri Sennikov. Trainer: Valery Gazzaev

Goals: Duff (35), Ignashevich (42)

REPUBLIC OF IRELAND v GEORGIA 2-0 (1-0)

Lansdowne Road, Dublin 11.06.2003

Referee: Eduardo ITURRALDE GONZÁLEZ (SPA) Attendance: 36,000

IRELAND: Shay Given; Stephen Carr, John O'Shea, Gary Breen, Kenny Cunningham, Matt Holland, Lee Carsley, Colin Healy (86 Mark Kinsella), Gary Doherty (89 Alan Lee), Robbie Keane, Kevin Kilbane. Trainer: Brian Kerr

GEORGIA: Giorgi Lomaia; Otar Khizanishvili, Zurab Khizaneishvili, Kakha Kaladze, Aleksandr Amisulashvili, Givi Didava (77 Rati Aleksidze), Aleksandr Rekhviashvili, Vladimir Burduli, Malkhaz Asatiani, Georgi Demetradze (61 Vitaly Daraselia), Shota Arveladze. Trainer: Ivan Šušak

Goals: Doherty (43), Keane (59)

GEORGIA v ALBANIA 3-0 (3-0)

Boris Paichadze, Tbilisi 06.09.2003

Referee: Nicolai Vollquartz (DEN) Attendance: 18,000

GEORGIA: Giorgi Lomaia; Otar Khizanishvili, Revaz Kemoklidze, Vladimir Burduli (70 Aleksandr Rekhviashvili), Dato Kvirkvelia, Levan Kobiashvili, Georgi Nemsadze, Mikheil Ashvetia, Aleksandr Iashvili, Gocha Jamarauli (58 Malkhaz Asatiani), Shota Arveladze (60 Georgi Demetradze). Trainer: Ivan Šušak

ALBANIA: Foto Strakosha; Nevil Dede (10 Redi Jupi), Geri Çipi, Besnik Hasi, Lorik Cana, Ardian Aliaj, Arian Bellai (46 Klodian Duro), Edvin Murati, Ervin Skela, Mehmet Dragusha, Alban Bushi (61 Igli Tare). Trainer: Hans-Peter Briegel

Goals: S. Arveladze (8, 43), Ashvetia (17)

RUSSIA v SWITZERLAND 4-1 (2-1)

Lokomotiv, Moskva 10.09.2003

Referee: Pierluigi Collina (ITA) Attendance: 29,000

RUSSIA: Sergey Ovchinnikov; Vladislav Radimov, Andrei Solomatin (46 Dmitri Sennikov), Aleksei Smertin, Andrei Kariaka, Sergei Ignashevich, Viktor Onopko, Rolan Gusev (55 Marat Izmailov), Dmitri Bulykin, Aleksandr Mostovoi, Aleksandr Kerzhakov (77 Dmitri Sytchev).
Trainer: Valery Gazzaev

SWITZERLAND: Pascal Zuberbühler; Remo Meyer, Bruno Berner, Stéphane Henchoz, Murat Yakin, Johann Vogel, Ricardo Cabañas, Patrick Müller (63 Benjamin Huggel), Alexander Frei, Fabio Celestini, Stéphane Chapuisat.
Trainer: Jakob Kuhn

Sent off: Cabanas (88)

Goals: Frei (13), Bulykin (20, 33, 59), Mostovoi (72)

SWITZERLAND v REPUBLIC OF IRELAND 2-0 (1-0)

St. Jakob-Park, Basel 11.10.2003

Referee: Anders Frisk (SWE) Attendance: 31,006

SWITZERLAND: Jörg Stiel; Bernt Haas, Christoph Spycher, Patrick Müller, Murat Yakin, Johann Vogel, Benjamin Huggel, Raphaël Wicky, Alexander Frei (90+1 Stéphane Henchoz), Hakan Yakin (55 Fabio Celestini), Stéphane Chapuisat (68 Streller). Trainer: Jakob Kuhn

IRELAND: Shay Given; Stephen Carr, Ian Harte, John O'Shea, Gary Breen, Matt Holland (74 Mark Kinsella), Damien Duff, Colin Healy, David Connolly (58 Clinton Morrison), Robbie Keane, Kevin Kilbane (74 Steve Finnan). Trainer: Brian Kerr

Goals: H. Yakin (6), Frei (60)

ALBANIA v GEORGIA 3-1 (0-0)

Qemal Stafa, Tirana 10.09.2003

Referee: Marian Salomir (ROM) Attendance: 10,500

ALBANIA: Foto Strakosha; Arjan Beqaj, Geri Çipi, Besnik Hasi, Lorik Cana (85 Devis Mukaj), Edvin Murati (18 Altin Haxhi), Blendi Shkembi, Altin Rraklli (58 Alban Bushi), Ardian Aliaj, Igli Tare, Klodian Duro.
Trainer: Hans-Peter Briegel

GEORGIA: Giorgi Lomaia; Otar Khizanishvili, Revaz Kemoklidze (40 Aleksandr Rekhviashvili), Givi Didava (54 Georgi Kinkladze), Dato Kvirkvelia, Levan Kobiashvili, Georgi Nemsadze, Mikheil Ashvetia, Aleksandr Iashvili (54 Georgi Demetradze), Gocha Jamarauli, Shota Arveladze.
Trainer: Ivan Šušak

Goals: Hasi (51), Tare (53), A. Arveladze (62), Bushi (80)

	P	W	D	L	F	A	Pts
Switzerland	8	4	3	1	15	11	15
Russia	8	4	2	2	19	12	14
Rep. of Ireland	8	3	2	3	10	11	11
Albania	8	2	2	4	11	15	8
Georgia	8	2	1	5	8	14	7

RUSSIA v GEORGIA 3-1 (2-1)

Lokomotiv, Moskva 11.10.2003

Referee: Konrad Plautz (AUS) Attendance: 30,000

RUSSIA: Sergey Ovchinnikov; Vadim Evseev, Dmitri Sennikov, Yegor Titov, Andrei Kariaka (45 Marat Izmailov), Sergei Ignashevich, Viktor Onopko, Rolan Gusev (63 Evgeni Aldonin), Dmitri Bulykin, Aleksandr Mostovoi, Aleksandr Kerzhakov (56 Dmitri Sytchev). Trainer: Valery Gazzaev

GEORGIA: Giorgi Lomaia; Otar Khizanishvili, Revaz Kemoklidze, Levan Kobiashvili, Dato Kvirkvelia, Levan Tskitishvili (54 Malkhaz Asatiani), Georgi Nemsadze, Mikheil Ashvetia (58 Vitali Daraselia), Aleksandr Iashvili, Gocha Jamarauli, Georgi Demetradze. Trainer: Ivan Šušak

Goals: Iashvili (3), Bulykin (29), Titov (45+2), Sytchev (73)

QUALIFICATION PLAY-OFFS

SCOTLAND v HOLLAND 1-0 (1-0)

Hampden Park, Glasgow 15.11.2003

Referee: Terje Hauge (NOR) Attendance: 50,670

SCOTLAND: Robert Douglas; Jackie McNamara, Gary Naysmith, Stephen Pressley, Lee Wilkie, Barry Ferguson, Darren Fletcher, Christian Dailly, Paul Dickov (66 Kenny Miller), James McFadden, Neil McCann (71 Stephen Pearson).
Trainer: Hans-Hubert Vogts

HOLLAND: Edwin Van der Sar; André Ooijer, Jaap Stam, Frank de Boer, Giovanni van Bronckhorst (46 Clarence Seedorf), Phillip Cocu, Andy van der Meyde, Edgar Davids (61 Rafael van der Vaart), Ruud Van Nistelrooij, Patrick Kluivert (77 Roy Makaay), Marc Overmars. Trainer: Dick Advocaat

Goal: McFadden (22)

HOLLAND v SCOTLAND 6-0 (3-0)

ArenA, Amsterdam 19.11.2003

Referee: Lubos Michel (SVK) Attendance: 52,000

HOLLAND: Edwin Van der Sar; André Ooijer (46 Frank de Boer), Michael Reiziger, Philip Cocu, Edgar Davids, Wesley Sneijder, Rafael van der Vaart, Wilfred Bouma (67 Clarence Seedorf), Marc Overmars, Andy van der Meyde, Ruud Van Nistelrooij (76 Patrick Kluivert).
Trainer: Dick Advocaat

SCOTLAND: Robert Douglas; Jackie McNamara, Gary Naysmith (46 Maurice Ross), Steven Pressley, Lee Wilkie, Barry Ferguson, Darren Fletcher, Neil McCann (62 Kenny Miller), Gavin Rae, Paul Dickov (45 Stevie Crawford), James McFadden. Trainer: Hans-Hubert Vogts

Goals: Sneijder (13), Ooijer (32), Van Nistelrooij (36, 50, 66), Frank de Boer (64)

CROATIA v SLOVENIA 1-1 (1-1)

Maskimir, Zagreb 15.11.2003

Referee: Markus Merk (GER) Attendance: 35,000

CROATIA: Stipe Pletikosa; Dario Šimić, Neretljak, Stjepan Tomas, Igor Tudor, Boris Zivković (59 Darijo Srna), Ivica Mornar, Jerko Leko (46 Giovani Rosso), Dado Pršo, Niko Kovac, Ivica Olić (46 Milan Rapaić). Trainer: Otto Barić

SLOVENIA: Mladen Dabanović; Fabijan Cipot, Amir Karić, Muamer Vugdalić, Aleksander Knavs, Goran Šukalo, Nastja Ceh (87 Spasoje Bulajić), Ermin Šiljak (90 Bostjan Cesar), Zlatko Zahović, Miran Pavlin, Milenko Acimović (75 Adem Kapić). Trainer: Bojan Prašnikar

Goals: Pršo (5), Šiljak (22)

LATVIA v TURKEY 1-0 (1-0)

Skonto Riga 15.11.2003

Referee: Gilles Veissiere (FRA) Attendance: 10,000

LATVIA: Aleksandrs Kolinko; Igors N. Stepanovs, Vitalis Astafjevs, Valentins Lobanovs, Juris Laizans, Aleksandrs Isakovs, Imants Bleidelis, Maris Verpakovskis (89 Vladimirs Kolesnicenko), Andrey Rubins (82 Jurgis Pucinskis), Vits Rimkus (86 Andrejs Stolcers), Korablovs.
Trainer: Aleksandrs Starkovs.

TURKEY: Rüştü Reçber; Emre Asik, Bülent Korkmaz, Fatih Akyel, Ergün Penbe, Emre Belözoglu, Okan Buruk (84 Gökdeniz Karadeniz), Tugay Kerimoglu (87 Tümer Metin), Ilhan Mansiz, Nihat Kahveci (77 Deniz Baris), Ibrahim Üzülmez. Trainer: Senol Günes.

Sent off: Emre Asik (73)

Goal: Verpakovskis (29)

SLOVENIA v CROATIA 0-1 (0-0)

Central, Ljubljana 19.11.2003

Referee: Urs Meier (SWI) Attendance: 10,000

SLOVENIA: Mladen Dabanović; Fabijan Cipot (87 Mladen Dabanović), Aleksander Knavs, Muamer Vugdalić, Milenko Acimović, Nastja Ceh, Amir Karić, Miran Pavlin, Goran Šukalo (66 Ermin Raković), Zlatko Zahović, Mladen Rudonja (46 Adem Kapić). Trainer: Bojan Prašnikar

CROATIA: Stipe Pletikosa; Josip Simunic (53 Marko Babic), Igor Tudor, Boris Zivković, Robert Kovac, Nico Kovac, Milan Rapaić (66 Stjepan Tomas), Giovani Rosso, Darijo Srna, Dado Pršo (75 Jerko Leko), Tomislav Sokota. Trainer: Otto Barić

Sent off: Tudor (58)

Goal: Pršo (60)

TURKEY v LATVIA 2-2 (1-0)

Inönü, Istanbul 19.11.2003

Referee: Anders Frisk (SWE) Attendance: 24,000

TURKEY: Ömer Çatkiç; Deniz Baris, Bülent Korkmaz, Ibrahim Üzülmez, Ümit Davala (81 Hasan Şaş), Emre Belözoglu, Tümer Metin (60 Gökdeniz Karadeniz), Tugay Kerimoglu (80 Tuncay Sanli), Ilhan Mansiz, Nihat Kahveci, Hakan Şükür. Trainer: Senol Günes

LATVIA: Aleksandrs Kolinko; Aleksandrs Isakovs, Igors N. Stepanovs, Mihails Zemlinskis, Dzintars Zirnis, Vitalis Astafjevs, Imants Bleidelis, Juris Laizans, Andrey Rubins, Maris Verpakovskis (90 Marian Pahars), Vits Rimkus (79 Andrejs Stolcers). Trainer: Aleksandrs Starkovs.

Goals: Ilhan Mansiz (20), Hakan Şükür (64), Laizans (66), Verpakovskis (77)

RUSSIA v WALES 0-0

Lokomotiv, Moscow 15.11.2003

Referee: Lucilio Cardoso Cortez Batista (POR) Att: 29,000

RUSSIA: Sergey Ovchinnikov; Vadim Evseev, Dmitri Sennikov, Aleksei Smertin (59 Rolan Gusev), Dmitri Alenichev, Sergei Ignashevitch, Viktor Onopko, Dmitri Loskov, Dmitri Bulykin, Aleksandr Mostovoi, Dmitri Sytchev (46 Marat Izmailov). Trainer: Gueorgui Yartsev

WALES: Paul Jones, Mark Delaney, Darren Barnard, Andrew Melville, Daniel Gabbidon, Andy Johnson, Robbie Savage, Jason Koumas, John Hartson (83 Nathan Blake), Gary Speed, Ryan Giggs. Manager: Mark Hughes

WALES v RUSSIA 0-1 (0-1)

Millennium Stadium, Cardiff 19.11.2003

Referee: Manuel Enrique Mejuto Gonzalez (SPA)
Attendance: 73,062

WALES: Paul Jones; Mark Delaney, Daniel Gabbidon, Andrew Melville, Darren Barnard, Ryan Giggs, Andy Johnson (58 Robert Earnshaw), Jason Koumas (74 Nathan Blake), Robbie Savage, Gary Speed, John Hartson. Manager: Mark Hughes

RUSSIA: Viacheslav Malafeev, Dmitri Alenichev, Vadim Evseev, Sergei Ignashevich, Viktor Onopko, Dmitri Sennikov, Rolan Gusev, Marat Izmailov, Aleksei Smertin, Egor Titov (59 Vladislav Radimov), Dmitri Bulykin.
Trainer: Gueorgui Yartsev

Goal: Evseev (22)

SPAIN v NORWAY 2-1 (1-1)

Mestalla, Valencia 15.11.2003

Referee: Graham Poll (ENG) Attendance: 53,000

SPAIN: IKER CASILLAS Fernández; MÍCHEL SALGADO Fernández, Carlos MARCHENA López, David ALBELDA, Carles PUYOL Saforcada, IVÁN HELGUERA Bujía, RAÚL González Blanco, Rubén BARAJA Vegas, FERNANDO José TORRES Sanz (69 Juan Carlos VALERÓN Santana), José Antonio REYES CALDERÓN (78 VICENTE Rodríguez Guillén), Joseba ETXEBERRÍA Lizardi (78 Joaquín SÁNCHEZ). Trainer: José Ignacio SÁEZ RUIZ "IÑAKI"

NORWAY: Espen Johnsen, John Arne Riise, Claus Lundekvam, Henning Berg, Christer Basma, Roar Strand (24 Harald Martin Brattbakk), Jan Gunnar Solli, Martin Andresen (57 Runar Berg), Tore André Flo, Trond Andersen, Steffen Iversen (78 Frode Johnsen). Trainer: Nils Johan Semb

Goals: Iversen (14), Raúl (21), Berg (85 og)

NORWAY v SPAIN 0-3 (0-1)

Ullevål, Oslo 19.11.2003

Referee: Pierluigi Collina (ITA) Attendance: 25,100

NORWAY: Espen Johnsen (61 Frode Olsen); Trond Andersen (46 Haavard Flo), Christer Basma, Ronny Johnsen, Claus Lundekvam, John Arne Riise, Jan Gunnar Solli, Stale Stensaas, Martin Andresen (73 Frode Johnsen), Tore Andre Flo, Steffen Iversen. Trainer: Nils Johan Semb

SPAIN: IKER CASILLAS Fernández; CÉSAR MARTÍN Villar, Carles PUYOL Saforcada, MÍCHEL SALGADO Fernández, David ALBELDA (84 Rubén BARAJA Vegas), Xabier "XABI" ALONSO Olona, IVÁN HELGUERA Bujía, Juan Carlos VALERÓN Santana (73 José María Gutiérrez Hernández "GUTI"), VICENTE Rodríguez Guillén, Joseba ETXEBERRÍA Lizardi (77 Joaquín SÁNCHEZ), RAÚL González Blanco.
Trainer: José Ignacio SÁEZ RUIZ "IÑAKI"

Goals: Raúl (34), Vicente (49), Etxeberría (56)

FINALS in PORTUGAL

GROUP A

PORTUGAL v GREECE 1-2 (0-1)

Dragão, Porto 12.06.2004

Referee: Pierluigi Collina (ITA) Attendance: 53,000

PORTUGAL: RICARDO Alexandre Martins Soares Pereira; PAULO Renato Rebocho FERREIRA, FERNANDO Manuel Silva COUTO (Cap), JORGE Manuel Almeida Gomes de ANDRADE, RUI JORGE Sousa Dias Macedo Oliveira, Francisco José Rodrigues Costa "COSTINHA" (66 NUNO Miguel Soares Ribeiro "GOMES"), Nuno Ricardo Oliveira Ribeiro "MANICHE", Luís Filipe Madeira Caeiro "FIGO", RUI Manuel César COSTA (46 Anderson Luís de Sousa "DECO"), SIMÃO Pedro Fonseca Sabrosa (46 CRISTIANO RONALDO Santos Aveiro), Pedro Miguel Carreiro Resende "PAULETA". Coach: Luiz Felipe SCOLARI

GREECE: Antonis Nikopolidis; Giourkas Seitaridis, Mihalis Kapsis, Traianos Dellas, Panagiotis Fyssas, Stelios Giannakopoulos (68 Demis Nikolaidis), Theodoros Zagorakis (Cap), Angelos Basinas, Giorgos Karagounis (46 Konstantinos Katsouranis), Zissis Vryzas, Angelos Charisteas (74 Vasilis Lakis).
Trainer: Otto Rehhagel

Goals: Karagounis (7), Basinas (51 pen), C. Ronaldo (90+3)

SPAIN v RUSSIA 1-0 (0-0)

Algarve, Faro 12.06.2004

Referee: Urs Meier (SWI) Attendance: 30,000

SPAIN: Iker CASILLAS Fernández; Carles PUYOL Saforcada, IVÁN HELGUERA Bujía, Carlos MARCHENA López, RAÚL BRAVO Sanfelix; Rubén BARAJA Vegas (59 Xabier "XABI" ALONSO Olona), David ALBELDA Aliqués; Joseba ETXEBERRÍA Lizardi, RAÚL González Blanco (Cap) (78 FERNANDO José TORRES Sanz), VICENTE Fernández Pujante; Fernando MORIENTES Sánchez (59 Juan Carlos VALERÓN Santana).
Trainer: José Ignacio SÁEZ RUIZ "IÑAKI"

RUSSIA: Sergei Ovchinnikov; Vadim Evseev, Roman Sharonov, Alexei Smertin (Cap), Dimitriy Sennikov; Evgeni Aldonin (68 Dmitri Sytchev), Rolan Gusev (46 Vladislav Radimov), Dmitri Alenichev, Alexandr Mostovoi, Marat Izmailov (74 Andrei Kariaka); Dmitri Bulykin. Trainer: Georgi Yartsev

Sent off: Sharonov (88)

Goal: Valeron (60)

GREECE v SPAIN 1-1 (0-1)

Bessa, Porto 16.06.2004

Referee: Lubos Michel (SVK) Attendance: 25,444

GREECE: Antonis Nikopolidis, Giourkas Seitaridis, Mihalis Kapsis, Traianos Dellas, Panagiotis Fyssas (86 Stelios Venetidis), Giorgos Karagounis (53 Vasilis Tsartas), Theodoros Zagorakis (Cap), Konstantinos Katsouranis, Stelios Giannakopoulos (49 Demis Nikolaidis), Zissis Vryzas, Angelos Charisteas.
Trainer: Otto Rehhagel

SPAIN: Iker CASILLAS Fernández; Carles PUYOL Saforcada, IVÁN HELGUERA Bujía, Carlos MARCHENA López, RAÚL BRAVO Sanfelix, Joseba ETXEBERRÍA Lizardi (46 JOAQUÍN Sánchez Rodríguez), David ALBELDA Aliqués, Rubén BARAJA Vegas, VICENTE Fernández Pujante, RAÚL González Blanco (80 FERNANDO José TORRES Sanz), Fernando MORIENTES Sánchez (65 Juan Carlos VALERÓN Santana).
Trainer: José Ignacio SÁEZ RUIZ "IÑAKI"

Goals: Morientes (28), Charisteas (66)

RUSSIA v PORTUGAL 0-2 (0-1)

Da Luz, Lisboa 16.06.2004

Referee: Terje Hauge (NOR) Attendance: 65,000

RUSSIA: Sergei Ovchinnikov; Vadim Evseev, Alexei Bugaev, Alexei Smertin (Cap), Dimitriy Sennikov, Evgeni Aldonin (45+2 Vyacheslav Malafeev), Marat Izmailov (72 Vladimir Bistrov), Dmitri Loskov, Andrei Kariaka (79 Dmitri Bulykin), Dmitri Alenichev, Alexandr Kerzhakov. Trainer: Georgi Yartsev

PORTUGAL: RICARDO Alexandre Martins Soares Pereira; Luís MIGUEL Brito Garcia Monteiro, JORGE Manuel Almeida Gomes de ANDRADE, RICARDO Alberto Silveira CARVALHO, NUNO Jorge Pereira Silva VALENTE, Francisco José Rodrigues Costa "COSTINHA", Luís Filipe Madeira Caeiro "FIGO" (Cap), Nuno Ricardo Oliveira Ribeiro "MANICHE", Anderson Luís de Sousa "DECO", SIMÃO Pedro Fonseca Sabrosa (63 RUI Manuel César COSTA), Pedro Miguel Carreiro Resende "PAULETA" (57 NUNO Miguel Soares Ribeiro "GOMES"). Trainer: Luiz Felipe SCOLARI

Sent off: Ovchinnikov (45)

Goals: Maniche (7), Rui Costa (89)

SPAIN v PORTUGAL 0-1 (0-0)

José Alvalade, Lisboa 20.06.2004

Referee: Anders Frisk (SWE) Attendance: 47,500

SPAIN: Iker CASILLAS Fernández; Carles PUYOL Saforcada, IVÁN HELGUERA Bujía, Juan Gutiérrez Moreno "JUANITO" (80 Fernando MORIENTES Sánchez), RAÚL BRAVO Sanfelix, JOAQUÍN Sánchez Rodríguez (72 Alberto LUQUE Martos), Xabier "XABI" ALONSO Olona, David ALBELDA Aliqués (66 Rubén BARAJA Vegas), VICENTE Fernández Pujante, FERNANDO José TORRES Sanz, RAÚL González Blanco (Cap). Trainer: José Ignacio SÁEZ RUIZ "IÑAKI"

PORTUGAL: RICARDO Alexandre Martins Soares Pereira; Luís MIGUEL Brito Garcia Monteiro, RICARDO Alberto Silveira CARVALHO, JORGE Manuel Almeida Gomes de ANDRADE, NUNO Jorge Pereira Silva VALENTE, Luís Filipe Madeira Caeiro "FIGO" (Cap) (78 Armando Gonçalves Teixeira "PETIT"), Nuno Ricardo Oliveira Ribeiro "MANICHE", Francisco José Rodrigues Costa "COSTINHA", Anderson Luís de Sousa "DECO", CRISTIANO RONALDO Santos Aveiro (84 FERNANDO Manuel Silva COUTO), Pedro Miguel Carreiro Resende "PAULETA" (46 NUNO Miguel Soares Ribeiro "GOMES"). Trainer: Luiz Felipe Scolari

Goal: Nuno Gomes (57)

RUSSIA v GREECE 2-1 (2-1)

Algarve, Faro 20.06.2004

Referee: Gilles Veissière (FRA) Attendance: 28,000

RUSSIA: Vyacheslav Malafeev; Alexandr Aniukov, Alexei Bugaev, Roman Sharonov (55 Dimitriy Sennikov), Vadim Evseev, Rolan Gusev, Vladislav Radimov, Andrei Kariaka (46 Igor Semshov), Dmitri Alenichev (Cap), Dmitri Bulykin (46 Dmitri Sytchev), Dmitri Kirichenko. Trainer: Georgi Yartsev

GREECE: Antonis Nikopolidis; Giourkas Seitaridis, Mihalis Kapsis, Traianos Dellas, Stelios Venetidis, Konstantinos Katsouranis, Theodoros Zagorakis (Cap), Angelos Basinas (42 Vasilsi Tsartas), Dimitris Papadopoulos (70 Demis Nikolaidis), Angelos Charisteas, Zissis Vryzas. Trainer: Otto Rehhagel

Goals: Kirichenko (2), Bulykin (17), Vryzas (43)

	P	W	D	L	F	A	Pts
Portugal	3	2	0	1	4	2	6
Greece	3	1	1	1	4	4	4
Spain	3	1	1	1	2	2	4
Russia	3	1	0	2	2	4	3

If points are level, advancement is decided by:

1) Head-to-head points
2) Head-to-head goal difference
3) Head-to-head goals scored
4) Overall goal difference
5) Overall goals scored
6) UEFA coefficient
7) Fair Play
8) Draw

GROUP B

SWITZERLAND v CROATIA 0-0

Dr. Magalhães Pessoa, Leiria 13.06.2004

Referee: Lucilio Cardoso Cortes Batista (POR)
Attendance: 30,000

SWITZERLAND: Jörg Stiel; Bernt Haas, Patrick Müller, Murat Yakin, Christoph Spycher, Benjamin Huggel, Johann Vogel, Raphael Wicky (82 Stephane Henchoz), Hakan Yakin (Cap) (86 Daniel Gygax), Alexander Frei, Stephane Chapuisat. Trainer: Kobi Kuhn

CROATIA: Tomislav Butina; Dario Simic (60 Darijo Srna), Josip Simunic, Robert Kovac, Boris Zivkovic (Cap), Ivica Mornar, Niko Kovac, Nenad Bjelica (73 Dovani Rosso), Ivica Olic (46 Milan Rapaic), Dado Prso, Tomislav Sokota. Trainer: Otto Baric

Sent off: Vogel (50)

FRANCE v ENGLAND 2-1 (0-1)

Da Luz, Lisboa 13.06.2004

Referee: Markus Merk (GER) Attendance: 65,000

FRANCE: Fabien Barthez; William Gallas, Lilian Thuram, Mickael Silvestre (79 Willy Sagnol), Bixente Lizarazu, Robert Pires (75 Sylvain Wiltord), Claude Makelele, Patrick Vieira, Zinedine Zidane (Cap), David Trezeguet, Thierry Henry.
Trainer: Jacques Santini

ENGLAND: David James; Gary Neville, Sol Campbell, Ledley King, Ashley Cole, David Beckham (Cap), Steven Gerrard, Frank Lampard, Paul Scholes (76 Owen Hargreaves), Wayne Rooney (76 Emile Heskey), Michael Owen (70 Darius Vassell).
Manager: Sven Göran Eriksson

Goals: Lampard (38), Zidane (90+1, 90+3 pen)

ENGLAND v SWITZERLAND 3-0 (1-0)

Municipal, Coimbra 17.06.2004

Referee: Valentin Ivanov (RUS) Attendance: 30,000

ENGLAND: David James; Gary Neville, Sol Campbell, John Terry, Ashley Cole, David Beckham (Cap), Frank Lampard, Steven Gerrard, Paul Scholes (70 Owen Hargreaves), Michael Owen (72 Darius Vassell), Wayne Rooney (83 Kieron Dyer).
Manager: Sven Göran Eriksson

SWITZERLAND: Jörg Stiel; Bernt Haas, Murat Yakin (Cap), Patrick Müller, Christoph Spycher, Benjamin Huggel, Fabio Celestini (53 Ricardo Cabanas), Raphael Wicky, Hakan Yakin (83 Johann Vonlanthen), Alexander Frei, Stephane Chapuisat (46 Daniel Gygax). Trainer: Jakob Kuhn

Sent off: Haas (60)

Goals: Rooney (23, 75), Gerrard (82)

CROATIA v FRANCE 2-2 (0-1)

Dr. Magalhaes Pessoa, Leiria 17.06.2004

Referee: Kim Milton Nielsen (DEN) Attendance: 29,000

CROATIA: Tomislav Butina; Dario Simic (Cap), Robert Kovac, Igor Tudor, Josip Simunic, Dovani Rosso, Nenad Bjelica (68 Jerko Leko), Niko Kovac, Milan Rapaic, Dado Prso, Tomislav Sokota (73 Ivica Olic). Trainer: Otto Baric

FRANCE: Fabien Barthez; William Gallas (81 Willy Sagnol), Lilian Thuram, Marcel Desailly (Cap), Mickael Silvestre, Sylvain Wiltord (70 Robert Pires), Patrick Vieira, Olivier Dacourt (79 Benoit Pedretti), Zinedine Zidane, David Trezeguet, Thierry Henry.
Trainer: Jacques Santini

Goals: Zidane (22), Rapaic (48 pen), Prso (52), Trezeguet (64)

CROATIA v ENGLAND 2-4 (1-2)

Da Luz, Lisboa 21.06.2004

Referee: Pierluigi Collina (ITA) Attendance: 50,000

CROATIA: Tomislav Butina; Dario Simic (67 Darijo Srna), Igor Tudor, Robert Kovac (46 Ivica Mornar), Josip Simunic, Dovani Rosso, Boris Zivkovic (Cap), Niko Kovac, Milan Rapaic (55 Ivica Olic), Dado Prso, Tomislav Sokota.
Trainer: Otto Baric

ENGLAND: David James; Gary Neville, John Terry, Sol Campbell, Ashley Cole, David Beckham (Cap), Frank Lampard (84 Philip Neville), Steven Gerrard, Paul Scholes (70 Ledley King), Michael Owen, Wayne Rooney (72 Darius Vassell).
Manager: Sven Göran Eriksson

Goals: N. Kovac (5), Scholes (40), Rooney (45+1, 68), Tudor (73), Lampard (79)

SWITZERLAND v FRANCE 1-3 (1-1)

Municipal, Coimbra 21.06.2004

Referee: Lubos Michel (SVK) Attendance: 30,000

SWITZERLAND: Jörg Stiel; Stephane Henchoz (86 Ludovic Magnin), Murat Yakin (Cap), Patrick Müller, Christoph Spycher, Ricardo Cabanas, Johann Vogel, Raphael Wicky, Hakan Yakin (60 Benjamin Huggel), Daniel Gygax (86 Milaim Rama), Johann Vonlanthen. Trainer: Kobi Kuhn

FRANCE: Fabien Barthez; Willy Sagnol (46 William Gallas), Lilian Thuram, Mickael Silvestre, Bixente Lizarazu, Zinedine Zidane (Cap), Claude Makelele, Patrick Vieira, Robert Pires, David Trezeguet (75 Louis Saha), Thierry Henry.
Trainer: Jacques Santini

Goals: Zidane (20), Vonlanthen (26), Henry (76, 84)

	P	W	D	L	F	A	Pts
France	3	2	1	0	7	4	7
England	3	2	0	1	8	4	6
Croatia	3	0	2	1	4	6	2
Switzerland	3	0	1	2	1	6	1

GROUP C

DENMARK v ITALY 0-0

Dr. Afonso Henriques, Guimarães 14.06.2004

Referee: Manuel Mejuto Gonzáles (SPA) Att: 30,000

DENMARK: Thomas Sørensen; Thomas Helveg, Martin Laursen, Rene Henriksen (Cap), Niclas Jensen, Dennis Rommedahl, Daniel Jensen, Christian Poulsen (76 Brian Priske), Martin Jørgensen (72 Kenneth Perez), Jon Dahl Tomasson, Ebbe Sand (68 Claus Jensen).
Trainer: Morten Olsen

ITALY: Gianluigi Buffon; Christian Panucci, Alessandro Nesta, Fabio Cannavaro (Cap), Gianluca Zambrotta, Simone Perrotta, Cristiano Zanetti (57 Gennaro Gattuso), Marco Camoranesi (67 Stefano Fiore), Francesco Totti, Alessandro del Piero (63 Andrea Cassano), Christian Vieri.
Trainer: Giovanni Trapattoni

SWEDEN v BULGARIA 5-0 (1-0)

José Alvalade, Lisboa 14.06.2004

Referee: Michael Riley (Eng) Attendance: 52,000

SWEDEN: Andreas Isaksson; Teddy Lucici (41 Christian Wilhelmsson), Olof Mellberg (Cap), Andreas Jakobsson, Erik Edman, Mikael Nilsson, Tobias Linderoth, Fredrik Ljungberg, Anders Svensson (76 Kim Källström), Henrik Larsson, Zlatan Ibrahimovic (82 Marcus Allbäck).
Trainers: Tommy Söderberg and Lars Lagerback

BULGARIA: Zdravko Zdravkov; Vladimir Ivanov, Rosen Kirilov, Predrag Pazin, Ivailo Petkov, Georgi Peev, Stilian Petrov (Cap), Marian Hristov, Martin Petrov (84 Zdravko Lazarov), Zoran Jankovic (62 Velizar Dimitrov), Dimitar Berbatov (76 Vladimir Manchev). Trainer: Plamen Markov

Goals: Ljungberg (32), Larsson (57, 58), Ibrahimovic (78 pen), Allback (90+1)

BULGARIA v DENMARK 0-2 (0-0)

Municipal, Braga 18.06.2004

Referee: Lucilio Cardoso Cortez Batista (POR)
Attendance: 30,000

BULGARIA: Zdravko Zdravkov; Vladimir Ivanov (51 Zdravko Lazarov), Rosen Kirilov, Ilian Stoianov, Ivailo Petkov (40 Zlatomir Zagorcic), Georgi Peev, Stilian Petrov (Cap), Marian Hristov, Martin Petrov, Zoran Jankovic (81 Milen Petkov), Dimitar Berbatov. Trainer: Plamen Markov

DENMARK: Thomas Sørensen; Thomas Helveg, Martin Laursen, Rene Henriksen (Cap), Niclas Jensen, Dennis Rommedahl (23 Jesper Grønkjaer), Daniel Jensen, Thomas Gravesen, Martin Jørgensen (72 Claus Jensen), Jon Dahl Tomasson, Ebbe Sand. Trainer: Morten Olsen

Sent off: Stilian Petrov (83)

Goals: Tomasson (51), Grønkjaer (90+2)

ITALY v SWEDEN 1-1 (1-0)

Dragão, Porto 18.06.2004

Referee: Urs Meier (SWI) Attendance: 49,000

ITALY: Gianluigi Buffon; Christian Panucci, Alessandro Nesta, Fabio Cannavaro (Cap), Gianluca Zambrotta, Gennaro Gattuso (76 Giuseppe Favalli), Andrea Pirlo, Simone Perrotta, Andrea Cassano (70 Stefano Fiore), Alessandro del Piero (82 Marco Camoranesi), Christian Vieri.
Trainer: Giovanni Trapattoni

SWEDEN: Andreas Isaksson; Mikael Nilsson, Olof Mellberg, Andreas Jakobsson, Erik Edman (77 Marcus Allbäck), Christian Wilhelmsson (67 Mattias Jonson), Tobias Linderoth, Fredrik Ljungberg, Anders Svensson (55 Kim Källström), Henrik Larsson, Zlatan Ibrahimovic.
Trainers: Tommy Söderberg & Lars Lagerback

Goals: Cassano (37), Ibrahimovic (85)

ITALY v BULGARIA 2-1 (0-1)

Dr. Afonso Henriques, Guimarães 22.06.2004

Referee: Valentin Ivanov (RUS) Attendance: 27,000

ITALY: Gianluigi Buffon; Christian Panucci, Marco Materazzi (83 Marco di Vaio), Alessandro Nesta, Gianluca Zambrotta, Stefano Fiore, Andrea Pirlo, Simone Perrotta (68 Massimo Oddo), Andrea Cassano, Alessandro del Piero (Cap), Bernardo Corradi (54 Christian Vieri). Trainer: Giovanni Trapattoni

BULGARIA: Zdravko Zdravkov (Cap); Daniel Borimirov, Zlatomir Zagorcic, Predrag Pazin (64 Kiril Kotev), Ilian Stoianov, Zdravko Lazarov, Milen Petkov, Marian Hristov (79 Velizar Dimitrov), Martin Petrov, Zoran Jankovic (46 Valeri Bozhinov), Dimitar Berbatov. Trainer: Plamen Markov

Goals: M. Petrov (45 pen), Perrotta (48), Cassano (90+4)

DENMARK v SWEDEN 2-2 (1-0)

Do Bessa, Porto 22.06.2004

Referee: Markus Merk (GER) Attendance: 25,000

DENMARK: Sørensen Thomas Sørensen; Thomas Helveg, Martin Laursen, Rene Henriksen (Cap), Niclas Jensen (46 Kasper Bøgelung), Daniel Jensen (66 Christian Poulsen), Thomas Gravesen, Jesper Grønkjaer, Jon Dahl Tomasson, Martin Jørgensen (66 Dennis Rommedahl), Ebbe Sand. Trainer: Morten Olsen

SWEDEN: Andreas Isaksson; Mikael Nilsson, Olof Mellberg (Cap), Andreas Jakobsson, Erik Edman, Mattias Jonson, Anders Andersson (80 Marcus Allbäck), Kim Källström (72 Christian Wilhelmsson), Fredrik Ljungberg, Zlatan Ibrahimovic, Henrik Larsson.
Trainers: Tommy Söderberg & Lars Lagerback

Goals: Tomasson (28, 66), Larsson (47 pen), Jonson (89)

	P	W	D	L	F	A	Pts
Sweden	3	1	2	0	8	3	5
Denmark	3	1	2	0	4	2	5
Italy	3	1	2	0	3	2	5
Bulgaria	3	0	0	3	1	9	0

GROUP D

CZECH REPUBLIC v LATVIA 2-1 (0-1)

Municipal, Aveiro 15.06.2004

Referee: Gilles Veissière (FRA) Attendance: 65,000

CZECH REPUBLIC: Petr Cech; Zdenek Grygera (56 Marek Heinz), René Bolf, Tomas Ujfalusi, Marek Jankulovski, Karel Poborsky, Martin Galasek (64 Vladimir Smicer), Tomas Rosicky, Pavel Nedved (Cap), Jan Koller, Milan Baros (87 Martin Jiranek). Trainer: Karel Bruckner

LATVIA: Aleksandrs Kolinko; Aleksandrs Isakovs, Igors Stepanovs, Mihails Zemlinskis, Olegs Blagonadezdins, Imants Bleidelis, Vitalis Astafjevs (Cap), Valentins Lobanovs (90 Vits Rimkus), Andrejs Rubins, Andrejs Prohorenkovs (72 Juris Laizans), Maris Verpakovskis (81 Marians Pahars).
Trainer: Aleksandrs Starkovs

Goals: Verpakovskis (45+1), Baros (73), Heinz (85)

GERMANY v HOLLAND 1-1 (1-0)

Dragão, Porto 15.06.2004

Referee: Anders Frisk (SWE) Attendance: 52,000

GERMANY: Oliver Kahn; Arne Friedrich, Christian Wörns, Jens Nowotny, Philipp Lahm, Frank Baumann, Dietmar Hamann, Bernd Schneider (68 Bastian Schweinsteiger), Michael Ballack, Torsten Frings (78 Fabian Ernst), Kevin Kuranyi (85 Fredi Bobici). Trainer: Rudolf Völler

HOLLAND: Edwin van der Sar; Johnny Heitinga (74 Pierre van Hooijdonk), Jaap Stam, Wilfred Bouma, Giovanni van Bronckhorst, Rafael van der Vaart, Phillip Cocu, Edgar Davids (46 Wesley Sneijder), Andy van der Meyde, Ruud van Nistelrooy, Boudewijn Zenden (46 Marc Overmars).
Trainer: Dick Advocaat

Goals: Frings (30), van Nistelrooy (80)

LATVIA v GERMANY 0-0

Do Bessa, Porto 19.06.2004

Referee: Michael Riley (ENG) Attendance: 28,000

LATVIA: Aleksandrs Kolinko; Aleksandrs Isakovs, Igors Stepanovs, Mihails Zemlinskis, Olegs Blagonadezdins, Imants Bleidelis, Vitalis Astafjevs, Valentins Lobanovs (70 Juris Laizans), Andrejs Rubins; Maris Verpakovskis (90+2 Dzintars Zirnis), Andrejs Prokhorenkovs (67 Marians Pahars).
Trainer: Alexandrs Starkovs

GERMANY: Oliver Kahn; Arne Friedrich, Christian Wörns, Philipp Lahm, Frank Baumann; Bernd Schneider (46 Bastian Schweinsteiger), Dietmar Hamann, Michael Ballack, Torsten Frings; Fredi Bobici (67 Miroslav Klose), Kevin Kuranyi (78 Thomas Brdaric). Trainer: Rudolf Völler

HOLLAND v CZECH REPUBLIC 2-3 (2-1)

Municipal, Aveiro 19.06.2004

Referee: Manuel Enrique MEJUTO GONZÁLEZ (SPA)
Attendance: 30,000

HOLLAND: Edwin van der Sar; Johnny Heitinga, Jaap Stam, Wilfred Bouma, Giovanni van Bronkhorst; Clarence Seedorf (86 Rafael van der Vaart), Phillip Cocu, Edgar Davids; Andy van der Meyde (79 Michael Reiziger), Ruud van Nistelrooy, Arjen Robben (59 Paul Bosvelt). Trainer: Dick Advocaat

CZECH REPUBLIC: Petr Cech; Zdenek Grygera (25 Vladimir Smicer), Tomas Ujfalusi, Martin Jiranek, Marek Jankulovski; Karel Poborsky, Martin Galasek (62 Marek Heinz), Tomas Rosicky, Pavel Nedved (Cap), Jan Koller (75 Marek Rozenhal), Milan Baros. Trainer: Karel Brückner

Sent off: Heitinga (75)

Goals: Bouma (4), van Nistelrooy (19), Koller (23), Baros (71), Smicer (88)

GERMANY v CZECH REPUBLIC 1-2 (1-1)

José Alvalade, Lisboa 23.06.2004

Referee: Terje Hauge (NOR) Attendance: 46,849

GERMANY: Oliver Kahn (Cap); Arne Friedrich, Christian Wörns, Jens Nowotny, Torsten Frings (46 Lukas Podolski), Dietmar Hamann (79 Miroslav Klose), Philipp Lahm, Bernd Schneider, Bastian Schweinsteiger (86 Jens Jeremies), Michael Ballack, Kevin Kuranyi. Trainer: Rudolf Völler

CZECH REPUBLIC: Jaromir Blazek; Martin Jiranek, René Bolf, Marek Rozenhal, Pavel Mares, Jaroslav Plasil (70 Karel Poborsky), Martin Galasek (Cap) (46 Tomas Hübschman), Roman Tyce, Stepan Vachousek, Marek Heinz, Vratislav Lokvenc (59 Milan Baros). Trainer: Karel Brückner

Goals: Ballack (21), Heinz (30), Baros (77)

HOLLAND v LATVIA 3-0 (2-0)

Municipal, Braga 23.06.2004

Referee: Kim Milton Nielsen (DEN) Attendance: 25,000

HOLLAND: Edwin van der Saar, Michael Reiziger, Jaap Stam, Frank de Boer (Cap), Giovanni van Bronkhorst, Clarence Seedorf, Phillip Cocu, Edgar Davids (77 Wesley Sneijder), Andy van der Meyde (62 Marc Overmars),Ruud van Nistelrooy (70 Roy Makaay), Arjen Robben.
Trainer: Dick Advocaat

LATVIA: Aleksandrs Kolinko; Aleksandrs Isakovs, Igors Stepanovs, Mihails Zemlinskis, Olegs Blagonadezdins, Imants Bleidelis (83 Andrejs Stolcers), Valentins Lobanovs, Vitalis Astafjevs (Cap), Andrejs Rubins, Andrejs Prohorenkovs (74 Juris Laizans), Maris Verpakovskis (62 Marians Pahars).
Trainer: Aleksandr Starkovs

Goals: van Nisterooy (27 pen, 35), Makaay (83)

	P	W	D	L	F	A	Pts
Czech Republic	3	3	0	0	7	4	9
Holland	3	1	1	1	6	4	4
Germany	3	0	2	1	2	3	2
Latvia	3	0	1	2	1	5	1

QUARTER FINALS

PORTUGAL v ENGLAND 2-2 (0-1, 1-1) (AET)

Da Luz, Lisboa 24.06.2004

Referee: Urs Meier (SWI) Attendance: 65,000

PORTUGAL: RICARDO Alexandre Martins Soares Pereira; Luís MIGUEL Brito Garcia Monteiro (79 RUI Manuel César COSTA), JORGE Manuel Almeida Gomes de ANDRADE, RICARDO Alberto Silveira CARVALHO, NUNO Jorge Pereira Silva VALENTE; Nuno Ricardo Oliveira Ribeiro "MANICHE", Francisco José Rodrigues Costa "COSTINHA" (63 SIMÃO Pedro Fonseca Sabrosa), Anderson Luís de Sousa "DECO"; Luís Filipe Madeira Caeiro "FIGO" (Cap) (75 HELDER Manuel Marques POSTIGA), NUNO Miguel Soares Ribeiro "GOMES", CRISTIANO RONALDO Santos Aveiro.
Trainer: Luiz Felipe SCOLARI

ENGLAND: David James; Gary Neville, John Terry, Sol Campbell, Ashley Cole; David Beckham, Frank Lampard, Steven Gerrard (82 Owen Hargreaves), Paul Scholes (57 Philip Neville); Michael Owen, Wayne Rooney (27 Darius Vassell).
Manager: Sven Göran Eriksson

Goals: Owen (3), Helder Postiga (83), Rui Costa (110), Lampard (115)

Penalties: Beckham (missed), 0-1 Deco, 1-1 Owen, 1-2 Simão, 2-2 Lampard, Rui Costa (missed), 2-3 Terry, 3-3 Cristiano Ronaldo, 3-4 Hargreaves, 4-4 Maniche, 4-5 A. Cole, 5-5 Helder Postiga, Vassell (saved), 6-5 Ricardo

FRANCE v GREECE 0-1 (0-0)

José Alvalade, Lisboa 25.06.2004

Referee: Anders Frisk (SWE) Attendance: 45,400

FRANCE: Fabien Barthez; William Gallas, Lilian Thuram, Mickael Silvestre, Bixente Lizarazu, Zinedine Zidane (Cap), Claude Makelele, Olivier Dacourt (73 Sylvain Wiltord), Robert Pires (79 Jérôme Rothen), David Trezeguet (73 Louis Saha), Thierry Henry. Trainer: Jacques Santini

GREECE: Antonis Nikopolidis; Giourkas Seitaridis, Mihalis Kapsis, Traianos Dellas, Panagiotis Fyssas, Giorgos Karagounis, Theodoros Zagorakis (Cap), Angelos Basinas (84 Vasilis Tsartas), Konstantinos Katsouranis, Angelos Charisteas, Demis Nikolaidis (61 Vasilsi Lakis). Trainer: Otto Rehhagel

Goal: Charisteas (65)

SWEDEN v HOLLAND 0-0 (AET)

Algarve, Faro 26.06.2004

Referee: Lubos Michel (SVK) Attendance: 30,000

SWEDEN: Andreas Isaksson; Alexander Östlund, Olof Mellberg (Cap), Andreas Jakobsson, Mikael Nilsson, Mattias Jonson (65 Christian Wilhelmsson), Tobias Linderoth, Anders Svensson (81 Kim Källström), Fredrik Ljungberg, Zlatan Ibrahimovic, Henrik Larsson.
Trainers: Tommy Söderberg & Lars Lagerback

HOLLAND: Edwin van der Saar, Michael Reiziger, Jaap Stam, Frank de Boer (Cap) (35 Wilfred Bouma), Giovanni van Bronkhorst, Edgar Davids (61 Johnny Heitinga), Clarence Seedorf, Phillip Cocu, Andy van der Meyde (87 Roy Makaay), Ruud van Nistelrooy, Arjen Robben. Trainer: Dick Advocaat

Penalties: Källström 1-0, van Nistelrooy 1-1, Larsson 2-1, Heitinga 2-2, Ibrahimovic (miss), Reiziger 2-3, Ljungberg 3-3, Cocu (miss), Wilhelmsson 4-3, Makaay 4-4, Mellberg (saved), Robben 4-5

CZECH REPUBLIC v DENMARK 3-0 (0-0)

Dragão, Porto 27.06.2004

Referee: Valentin Ivanov (RUS) Attendance: 45,000

CZECH REPUBLIC: Petr Cech; Martin Jiranek (39 Zdenek Grygera), René Bolf (65 Marek Rozenhal), Tomas Ujfalusi, Marek Jankulovski, Karel Poborsky, Martin Galasek, Tomas Rosicky, Pavel Nedved (Cap), Jan Koller, Milan Baros (70 Marek Heinz). Trainer: Karel Bruckner

DENMARK: Thomas Sørensen; Thomas Helveg, Martin Laursen, Rene Henriksen (Cap), Kasper Bøgelund, Christian Poulsen, Claus Jensen (71 Ole Madsen), Thomas Gravesen, Jesper Grønkjaer (78 Dennis Rommedahl), Jon Dahl Tomasson, Martin Jørgensen (85 Peter Lovenkrands).
Trainer: Morten Olsen

Goals: Koller (49), Baros (63, 65)

SEMI-FINALS

PORTUGAL v HOLLAND 2-1 (1-0)

Da Luz, Lisboa 30.06.2004

Referee: Anders Frisk (SWE) Attendance: 52,000

PORTUGAL: RICARDO Alexandre Martins Soares Pereira; Luís MIGUEL Brito Garcia Monteiro, JORGE Manuel Almeida Gomes de ANDRADE, RICARDO Alberto Silveira CARVALHO, NUNO Jorge Pereira Silva VALENTE; CRISTIANO RONALDO Santos Aveiro (68 Armando Gonçalves Teixeira "PETIT"), Nuno Ricardo Oliveira Ribeiro "MANICHE" (88 FERNANDO Manuel Silva COUTO), Anderson Luís de Sousa "DECO", Francisco José Rodrigues Costa "COSTINHA"; Luís Filipe Madeira Caeiro "FIGO" (Cap), Pedro Miguel Carreiro Resende "PAULETA" (75 NUNO Miguel Soares Ribeiro "GOMES"). Trainer: Luiz Felipe SCOLARI

HOLLAND: Edwin van der Saar, Michael Reiziger, Jaap Stam, Wilfred Bouma (58 Rafael van der Vaart), Giovanni van Bronkhorst, Edgar Davids, Clarence Seedorf, Phillip Cocu (Cap), Marc Overmars (46 Roy Makaay), Ruud van Nistelrooy, Arjen Robben (81 van Hooijdonk). Trainer: Dick Advocaat

Goals: C. Ronaldo (26), Maniche (58), Andrade (63 og)

CZECH REPUBLIC v GREECE 0-1 (0-0, 0-0) (AET)

Dragão, Porto 01.07.2004

Referee: Pierluigi Collina (ITA) Attendance: 45,000

GREECE: Antonis Nikopolidis; Giourkas Seitaridis, Mihalis Kapsis, Traianos Dellas, Panagiotis Fyssas, Giorgos Karagounis, Theodoros Zagorakis (Cap), Konstantinos Katsouranis, Angelos Basinas (71 Stelios Giannakopoulos), Angelos Charisteas, Zissis Vryzas (91 Vasilis Tsartas).
Trainer: Otto Rehhagel

CZECH REPUBLIC: Petr Cech; Zdenek Grygera, Tomas Ujfalusi, René Bolf, Marek Jankulovski, Karel Poborský, Martin Galasek, Tomas Rosicky, Pavel Nedved (Cap) (40 Vladimir Smicer), Jan Koller, Milan Baros. Trainer: Karel Bruckner

Goal: Dellas (105+1) "Silver Goal"

FINAL

PORTUGAL v GREECE 0-1 (0-0)

Da Luz, Lisboa 04.07.2004

Referee: Markus Merk (GER) Attendance: 62,865

PORTUGAL: RICARDO Alexandre Martins Soares Pereira; Luís MIGUEL Brito Garcia Monteiro (43 PAULO Renato Rebocho FERREIRA), JORGE Manuel Almeida Gomes de ANDRADE, RICARDO Alberto Silveira CARVALHO, NUNO Jorge Pereira Silva VALENTE; CRISTIANO RONALDO Santos Aveiro, Nuno Ricardo Oliveira Ribeiro "MANICHE", Anderson Luís de Sousa "DECO", Francisco José Rodrigues Costa "COSTINHA" (60 RUI Manuel César COSTA); Luís Filipe Madeira Caeiro "FIGO" (Cap), Pedro Miguel Carreiro Resende "PAULETA" (74 NUNO Miguel Soares Ribeiro "GOMES").
Trainer: Luiz Felipe SCOLARI

GREECE: Antonis Nikopolidis; Giourkas Seitaridis, Mihalis Kapsis, Traianos Dellas, Panagiotis Fyssas, Theodoros Zagorakis (Cap), Konstantinos Katsouranis, Angelos Basinas Stelios Giannakopoulos (76 Stelios Venetidis), Angelos Charisteas, Zissis Vryzas (81 Dimitrios Papadopoulos).
Trainer: Otto Rehhagel

Goal: Charisteas (57)

Goalscorers European Football Championship 2004

9 goals: Ermin Šiljak (Slovenia), Ruud van Nistelrooij (Holland)

8 goals: Thierry Henry (France), Jon Dahl Tomasson (Denmark), Milan Baros, Jan Koller (Czech Republic)

7 goals: Zinedine Zidane, David Trezeguet (France), Maris Verpakovskis (Latvia), RAÚL González Blanco (Spain)

6 goals: Sylvain Wiltord (France), Angelos Charisteas (Greece), Michael Owen, Wayne Rooney (England), Filippo Inzaghi (Italy), Alexander Frei (Switzerland), Marcus Allbäck (Sweden)

5 goals: Zlatan Ibrahimovic, Mattias Jonson (Sweden), Michael Ballack (Germany), Eidur Gudjohnsen (Iceland), David Beckham (England), Wesley Sonck (Belgium), Alessandro del Piero (Italy), Dimitar Berbatov (Bulgaria), Dmitri Bulykin (Russia)

4 goals: Ionel Ganea, Adrian Mutu (Romania), Patrick Kluivert (Holland), Zoltán Gera, Krisztián Lisztes, Imre Szabics (Hungary), Fredi Bobic (Germany), Szilárd Nemeth (Slovakia), Dado Pršo (Croatia), John Hartson (Wales)

3 goals: Heim Revivo (Israel), Michael Mifsud (Malta), Mihalis Konstantinou (Cyprus), Cosmin Marius Contra (Romania), Sergej Barbarez (Bosnia-Herzegovina), Marek Jankulovski, Vladimír Šmicer (Czech Republic), Rafael van der Vaart (Holland), Henrik Larsson (Sweden), Tomas Razanauskas (Lithuania), Artur Petrosyan, Albert Sarkisyan (Armenia), Juan Carlos VALERÓN Santana (Spain), Andriy Shevchenko (Ukraine), Akin Serhat, Nihat Kahveci, Hakan Şükür (Turkey), Frank Lampard (England), Milan Rapaić, Niko Kovac (Croatia), Simon Davies (Wales), Mahmud Gurbonov (Azerbaijan), Christian Vieri (Italy), Gary Doherty (Republic of Ireland), Hakan Yakin (Switzerland), Sergei Ignashevich (Russia)

2 goals: Giannaki Okkas, Rainer Rauffmann (Cyprus), Steve Marlet (France), Pini Balili, Omri Afek (Israel), Zlatko Zahović, Nastja Ceh (Slovenia), John Arne Riise, Steffen Iversen, Ole Gunnar Solskjaer (Norway), Dorinel Munteanu, Dinu Viorel Moldovan, Daniel Gabriel Pancu (Romania), Elvir Bolić (Bosnia-Herzegovina), Dennis Rommedahl, Thomas Gravesen, Jesper Grønkjaer (Denmark), Andreas Herzog, Mario Haas (Austria), Karel Poborský, Pavel Nedved, Vratislav Lokvenc, Marek Heinz (Czech Republic), Philip Cocu, Roy Makaay, Wesley Sneijder (Holland), Krisztián Kenesei (Hungary), Juris Laizans, Imants Bleidelis (Latvia), Miroslaw Szymkowiak, Marcin Kuzba, Andrzej Niedzielan (Poland), Fredrik Ljungberg (Sweden), John Petersen, Rógvi Jacobsen (Faroe Islands), Miroslav Klose (Germany), Kenny Miller, Neil McCann, James McFadden (Scotland), Igoris Morinas (Lithuania), Rubén BARAJA Vegas, Joseba ETXEBERRÍA Lizardi, José Antonio REYES CALDERÓN (Spain), Andriy Voronin, Olexandr Horshkov (Ukraine), Themistoklis Nikolaidis, Zisis Vryzas (Greece), CRISTIANO RONALDO, Nuno Ricardo Oliveira Ribeiro "MANICHE", RUI Manuel César COSTA (Portugal), Arif Erdem, Okan Buruk, Ilhan Mansiz (Turkey), Georgi Hristov, Vlatko Grozdanovski, Artim Sakiri (Macedonia), Steven Gerrard (England), Luboš Reiter, Vladimír Janocko, Robert Vittek (Slovakia), Stilian Petrov, Martin Petrov (Bulgaria), Indrek Zelinski (Estonia), Bart Goor (Belgium), Sami Hyypiä, Mikael Forssell (Finland), Predrag Mijatović (Serbia-Montenegro), Craig Bellamy, Gary Speed (Wales), Farrukh Ismaylov (Azerbaijan), Andrea Cassano (Italy), Andrei Kariaka, Aleksandr Kerzhakov, Sergei Semak (Russia), Archil Arveladze, Shota Arveladze (Georgia), Damien Duff, Robbie Keane (Republic of Ireland), Altin Lala, Igli Tare, Ervin Skela (Albania)

1 goal: Djibril Cissé, Patrick Vieira, Sidney Govou, Eric Carrière, Olivier Dacourt, Alain Boumsong (France), Sebastjan Cimirotić (Slovenia), Walid Badir, Holtsman (Israel), Luke Dimech (Malta), Aleksander Knavs (Slovenia), David Carabott (Malta), Stavros Georgiou, Giasoumas Giasoumi (Cyprus), John Carew, Claus Lundekvam, Sigurd Rushfeldt, Tore André Flo (Norway), Cristian Chivu, Matei Mirel Rădoi, Tiberiu Ghioane, Florin Daniel Bratu (Romania), Ebbe Sand, Claus Jensen, Martin Laursen, Martin Jørgensen (Denmark), Elvir Baljić, Zlatan Bajramović (Bosnia-Herzegovina), Edgar Davids, Jimmy Floyd Hasselbaink, Clarence Seedorf, Mark van Bommel, Marc Overmars, Pierre van Hooijdonck, Arjen Robben, André Ooijer, Frank de Boer, Wilfred Bouma (Holland), Tomáš Rosický, Štajner, Stepan Vachousek (Czech Republic), Markus Schopp, Muhammet Akagündüz, René Aufhauser, Roland Kirchler, Wallner, Cerny, Emanuel Pogatetz, Andreas Ivanschitz (Austria), Boris Cebotari, Vadim Boreț, Viorel Frunză, Sergei Dadu, Sergei Covalciuc (Moldova), Vitali Kutuzov, Sergei Gurenko, Bulyga, Roman Vasilyuk (Belarus), Pawel Kaczorowski, Mariusz Kukielka, Kamil Kosowski, Batosz Karwan, Tomasz Kłos (Poland), Andrejs Prohorenkovs, Vitalis Astafjevs (Latvia), Anders Svensson, Andreas Jakobsson, Kim Källström, Mikael Nilsson, Olog Mellberg (Sweden), Zoltán Böör (Hungary), Paul Lambert, Barry Ferguson, Christian Dailly, Gary Naysmith, Lee Wilkie, Paul Dickov, Darren Fletcher (Scotland), Robertas Poškus, Donatas Vencevicius (Lithuania), Heidar Helgason, Helgi Sigurdsson, Tryggvi Gudmundsson, Thordur Gudjónsson, Hermann Hreidarsson, Petur Marteinsson (Iceland), Carsten Ramelow, Kevin Kuranyi, Torsten Frings (Germany), Julian Jonsson, Súni Olsen (Faroe Islands), Serhiy Serebrennikov, Hennadiy Zubov, Andriy Vorobey, Serhiy Fedorov (Ukraine), José María Gutiérrez Hernández "GUTI", DIEGO TRISTÁN Herrera, IVÁN HELGUERA Bujía, JOAQUÍN SÁNCHEZ Rodríguez, VICENTE Rodríguez Guillén, Fernando MORIENTES Sánchez (Spain), Stelios Giannakopoulos, Vasilis Tsiartas, Giorgos Karagounis, Angelos Basinas, Traianos Dellas (Greece), Arman Karamyan (Armenia), NUNO Miguel Soares Ribeiro "GOMES", HELDER Manuel Marques POSTIGA (Portugal), Michael Stocklasa, Roger Beck (Liechtenstein), Okan Buruk, Ümit Davala, Gökdeniz Karadeniz, Tümer Metin (Turkey), Vanco Trajanov, Goce Sedloski, Mile Krstev, Aco Stojkov, Draganco Dimitrovski (Macedonia), Martin Petras (Slovakia), Darius Vassell, Paul Scholes (England),

1 goal (continued): Zoran Jankovic, Georgi Chilikov, Krasimir Balakov, Svetoslav Todorov, Marian Hristov (Bulgaria), Antonio Lima Sola (Andorra), Darijo Srna, Tomislav Marić, Jerko Leko, Josip Šimunić, Giovanni Rosso, Dario Šimić, Ivica Olić, Igor Tudor (Croatia), Philippe Clement, Thomas Buffel (Belgium), Teet Allas, Kristen Viikmäe (Estonia), Hannu Tihinen, Joonas Kolkka, Teemu Tainio, Mika Nurmela (Finland), Darko Kovacević, Sinisa Mihajlović, Nikola Lazetić, Branko Bosković, Dragan Mladenović, Saša Ilić, Zvonimir Vukić, Savo Milosević, Goran Gavrancić (Serbia-Montenegro), Ryan Giggs, Robert Earnshaw (Wales), Francesco Totti, Marco di Vaio, Simone Perrotta (Italy), Vladimir Beschastnykh, Viktor Onopko, Aleksandr Mostovoi, Yegor Titov, Dmitri Sytchev, Vadim Evseev, Dmitri Kirichenko (Russia), Clinton Morrison (Republic of Ireland), Patrick Müller, Stéphane Chapuisat, Murat Yakin, Fabio Celestini, Bernt Haas, Ricardo Cabañas, Johann Vonlanthen (Switzerland), Edvin Murati, Klodian Duro, Altin Rrakli, Besnik Hasi, Alban Bushi (Albania), Levan Kobiashvili, Malkhaz Asatiani, Mikheil Ashvetia, Aleksandr Iashvili (Georgia)

Own goals: Darren Debono (Malta) for Slovenia, Carlo Valentini (San Marino) for Latvia, Marius Stankevicius (Lithuania) for Germany, Arne Friedrich (Germany) for Faroe Islands, Stilian Petrov (Bulgaria) for Belgium, Raio Piiroja (Estonia) for Belgium, Phil Babb (Rep. of Ireland) for Russia, Joël Magnin (Switzerland) for Republic of Ireland, Ardian Aliaj (Albania) for Republic of Ireland, Henning Berg (Norway) for Spain, JORGE Manuel Almeida Gomes de ANDRADE (Portugal) for Holland, Cosmin Marius Contra (Romania) for Denmark.

2 Own goals: Tarlan Akhmedov (Azerbaijan) for Italy and Finland

THE EUROPEAN FOOTBALL CHAMPIONSHIP 2008

GROUP 1

BELGIUM v KAZAKHSTAN 0-0

Constant Vanden Stock, Brussels 16.08.2006

Referee: Mark Courtney (NIR) Attendance: 20,000

BELGIUM: Stijn Stijnen, Thomas Vermaelen, Timmy Simons, Daniel Van Buyten, Vincent Kompany (38 Stein Huysegems), Jelle Van Damme (60 Luigi Pieroni), Carl Hoefkens (74 Anthony Vanden Borre), Bart Goor, Thomas Buffel, Karel Geraerts, Moussa Dembélé. Trainer: René Vandereycken

KAZAKHSTAN: David Loria, Aleksandr Kuchma, Samat Smakov, Egor Azovskiy, Andrei Karpovich (54 Andrei Travin), Eduard Sergienko, Nikita Khokhlov, Dmitriy Byakov, Ruslan Baltiyev, Maksim Zhalmagambetov, Nurbol Zhumaskaliyev. Trainer: Arno Pijpers

SERBIA v AZERBAIJAN 1-0 (0-0)

FK Crvena Zvezda, Beograd 02.09.2006

Ref: Knut Kircher (GER) Att: Played behind closed doors

SERBIA: Vladimir Stojković, Marjan Marković, Milan Stepanov, Mladen Krstajić, Aleksandar Luković, Igor Duljaj, Ognjen Koroman (64 Saša Ilić), Dejan Stanković, Danko Lazović (74 Ivan Ergić), Marko Pantelić (81 Danijel Ljuboja), Nikola Žigić. Trainer: Javier Clemente

AZERBAIJAN: Farhad Veliyev, Zaur Hasimov, Ruslan Abbasov, Aslan Kerimov, Sergei Sokolov, Elmar Baxsiyev, Andre Ladaga (77 Vagif Dzavadov), Yuri Muzika (62 Ilgar Gurbanov), Emin Imamaliev, Aleksandr Chertoganov, Farrukh Ismaylov (72 Samir Musaev). Trainer: Sahin Diniev

Goal: Žigić (72)

POLAND v FINLAND 1-3 (0-0)

The Krzyszkowiak, Bydgoszcz 02.09.2006

Referee: Laurent Duhamel (FRA) Attendance: 15,000

POLAND: Jerzy Dudek, Marcin Wasilewski, Arkadiusz Glowacki, Jacek Bak, Michal Zewlakow, Jakub Blaszczykowski (46 Ireneusz Jelen), Miroslaw Szymkowiak (46 Euzebiusz Smolarek), Arkadiusz Radomski, Jacek Krzynówek, Maciej Zurawski, Tomasz Frankowski (73 Lukasz Gargula). Trainer: Leo Beenhakker

FINLAND: Jussi Jääskeläinen, Hannu Tihinen, Sami Hyypiä, Toni Kallio, Teemu Tainio, Petri Pasanen, Markus Heikkinen, Joonas Kolkka (79 Mika Nurmela), Jari Litmanen (87 Mikael Forssell), Jonatan Johansson (67 Alexei Eremenko Jr.), Mika Väyrynen. Trainer: Roy Hodgson

Sent off: Arkadiusz Glowacki (75)

Goals: Litmanen (54, 76 pen), Väyrynen (84), Gargula (89)

AZERBAIJAN v KAZAKHSTAN 1-1 (1-1)

Tofikh Bakhramov, Baku 06.09.2006

Referee: Zsolt Szabó (HUN) Attendance: 18,000

AZERBAIJAN: Farhad Veliyev, Aslan Kerimov, Sergei Sokolov (58 Yuri Muzika), Ruslan Abbasov (46 Rail Melikov), Andre Ladaga, Ceyhun Sultanov (65 Samir Musaev), Aleksandr Chertoganov, Emin Imamaliev, Vagif Dzavadov, Ilgar Gurbanov, Leandro Gomes. Trainer: Sahin Diniyev

KAZAKHSTAN: David Loria, Egor Azovskiy, Aleksandr Kuchma, Maksim Zhalmagambetov, Samat Smakov, Andrei Karpovich (66 Andrei Travin), Eduard Sergienko, Nikita Khokhlov, Dmitriy Byakov, Ruslan Baltiyev, Nurbol Zhumaskaliyev (74 Kairat Utabaev). Trainer: Arno Pijpers

Goals: Ladaga (16), Byakov (36)

FINLAND v PORTUGAL 1-1 (1-1)

Olympiastadion, Helsinki 06.09.2006

Referee: Konrad Plautz (AUS) Attendance: 38,000

FINLAND: Jussi Jääskeläinen, Toni Kallio, Sami Hyypiä, Hannu Tihinen, Petri Pasanen, Joonas Kolkka (81 Alexei Eremenko Jr.), Teemu Tainio, Mika Väyrynen, Jari Litmanen, Markus Heikkinen, Jonatan Johansson (63 Shefki Kuqi). Trainer: Roy Hodgson

PORTUGAL: RICARDO Pereira, MARCO CANEIRA, RICARDO COSTA, RICARDO CARVALHO, NUNO VALENTE, Francisco Costa "COSTINHA", Armando Teixeira "PETIT", Anderson Souza "DECO" (85 TIAGO Mendes), Luís Cunha "NANI" (56 RICARDO ROCHA), CRISTIANO RONALDO, NUNO GOMES (75 JOÃO MOUTINHO). Trainer: Luiz Felipe Scolari

Sent off: Ricardo Costa (53)

Goals: Johansson (22), Nuno Gomes (42)

POLAND v SERBIA 1-1 (1-0)

Wojska Polskiego, Warsaw 06.09.2006

Referee: Graham Poll (ENG) Attendance: 5,500

POLAND: Wojciech Kowalewski, Pawel Golanski (72 Marcin Wasilewski), Mariusz Jop, Jacek Bak, Michal Zewlakow, Ireneusz Jelen (73 Jakub Blaszczykowski), Mariusz Lewandowski, Arkadiusz Radomski, Jacek Krzynówek, Maciej Zurawski, Radoslaw Matusiak. Trainer: Leo Beenhakker

SERBIA: Vladimir Stojković, Marjan Marković, Milan Stepanov, Milan Biševac, Mladen Krstajić, Igor Duljaj (67 Ivan Ergić), Nenad Kovačević, Dejan Stanković, Aleksandar Trišović (60 Danko Lazović), Marko Pantelić (82 Ognjen Koroman), Nikola Žigić. Trainer: Javier Clemente

Goals: Matusiak (30), Lazović (71)

ARMENIA v BELGIUM 0-1 (0-1)

Republican, Yerevan 06.09.2006

Referee: Gerald Lehner (AUS) Attendance: 8,000

ARMENIA: Gevorg Kasparov, Sargis Hovsepyan, Robert Arzumanyan, Karen Dokhoyan, Egishe Melikyan, Romik Khachatryan, Karen Aleksanyan, Agvan Mkrtchyan (76 Arman Karamyan), Hamlet Mkhitaryan (81 Galust Petrosyan), Samvel Melkonyan, Armen Shahgeldyan (72 Aram Hakobyan). Trainer: Ian Porterfield

BELGIUM: Stijn Stijnen, Carl Hoefkens, Timmy Simons, Jelle Van Damme, Daniel Van Buyten, Koen Daerden (66 Bart Goor), Gaëtan Englebert, Pieter Collen (59 Anthony Vanden Borre), Karel Geraerts, Moussa Dembélé (77 Steven Defour), Luigi Pieroni. Trainer: René Vandereycken

Goal: Van Buyten (41)

SERBIA v BELGIUM 1-0 (0-0)

FK Crvena Zvezda, Beograd 07.10.2006

Referee: Domenico Messina (ITA) Attendance: 30,000

SERBIA: Vladimir Stojković, Marjan Marković, Nemanja Vidić, Mladen Krstajić, Ivica Dragutinović, Nenad Kovačević, Dejan Stanković, Ognjen Koroman (71 Ivan Ergić), Aleksandar Trišović (58 Danko Lazović), Marko Pantelić (90 Igor Duljaj), Nikola Žigić. Trainer: Javier Clemente

BELGIUM: Stijn Stijnen, Vincent Kompany, Carl Hoefkens, Timmy Simons, Thomas Vermaelen, Daniel Van Buyten, Karel Geraerts, Gaby Mudingayi (75 Luigi Pieroni), Bart Goor (84 Kevin Vandenbergh), Emile Mpenza, Moussa Dembélé (62 Mbo Mpenza). Trainer: René Vandereycken

Goal: Žigić (54)

PORTUGAL v AZERBAIJAN 3-0 (2-0)

Bessa XXI, Porto 07.10.2006

Referee: Mark Halsey (ENG) Attendance: 18,000

PORTUGAL: RICARDO Pereira, MIGUEL Monteiro, RICARDO CARVALHO, RICARDO ROCHA, NUNO VALENTE (46 MARCO CANEIRA), Francisco Costa "COSTINHA", Nuno Ribeiro "MANICHE" (64 TIAGO Mendes), Anderson Souza "DECO", CRISTIANO RONALDO (73 Luís Cunha "NANI"), NUNO GOMES, SIMÃO Sabrosa. Trainer: Luiz Felipe Scolari

AZERBAIJAN: Farhad Veliyev, Zaur Hasimov, Ernani Pereira, Sergei Sokolov, Aslan Kerimov, Andre Ladaga, Aleksandr Chertoganov, Emin Imamaliev, Yuri Muzika (66 Ilgar Gurbanov), Ceyhun Sultanov (64 Farrukh Ismaylov), Leandro Gomes (76 Vagif Dzavadov). Trainer: Sahin Diniyev

Goals: Cristiano Ronaldo (25, 63), Ricardo Carvalho (31)

ARMENIA v FINLAND 0-0

Republican, Erevan 07.10.2006

Referee: Damir Skomina (SLO) Attendance: 8,000

ARMENIA: Gevorg Kasparov, Sargis Hovsepyan, Robert Arzumanyan, Karen Dokhoyan, Egishe Melikyan, Samvel Melkonyan, Armen Tigranyan, Karen Aleksanyan (54 Aram Hakobyan), Arman Karamyan (46 Agvan Mkrtchyan), Armen Shahgeldyan, Edgar Manucharyan (78 Ara Hakobyan). Trainer: Ian Porterfield

FINLAND: Jussi Jääskeläinen, Petri Pasanen, Sami Hyypiä, Hannu Tihinen, Mika Väyrynen (73 Mika Nurmela), Jari Litmanen, Joonas Kolkka, Shefki Kuqi (66 Mikael Forssell), Toni Kallio, Jonatan Johansson (83 Aki Riihilahti), Markus Heikkinen. Trainer: Roy Hodgson

KAZAKHSTAN v POLAND 0-1 (0-0)

Centralny, Almaty 07.10.2006

Referee: Edo Trivković (CRO) Attendance: 20,000

KAZAKHSTAN: David Loria, Egor Azovskiy, Aleksandr Kuchma, Maksim Zhalmagambetov, Samat Smakov, Andrei Karpovich (59 Andrei Travin), Eduard Sergienko (81 Sergey Larin), Nikita Khokhlov, Dmitriy Byakov, Nurbol Zhumaskaliyev, Kairat Utabaev (68 Kairat Ashirbekov). Trainer: Arno Pijpers

POLAND: Wojciech Kowalewski, Grzegorz Bronowicki, Pawel Golanski, Jakub Blaszczykowski (87 Rafal Grzelak), Jacek Bak, Euzebiusz Smolarek, Radoslaw Sobolewski, Maciej Zurawski (71 Radoslaw Matusiak), Grzegorz Rasiak, Arkadiusz Radomski, Mariusz Lewandowski (30 Przemyslaw Kazmierczak). Trainer: Leo Beenhakker

Goal: Smolarek (52)

SERBIA v ARMENIA 3-0 (0-0)

FK Crvena Zvezda, Beograd 11.10.2006

Referee: Giorgos Kasnaferis (GRE) Attendance: 20,000

SERBIA: Vladimir Stojković, Ivica Dragutinović, Milan Stepanov, Mladen Krstajić, Igor Duljaj, Nenad Kovačević, Dejan Stanković, Ognjen Koroman (72 Ivan Ergić), Aleksandar Trišović (46 Saša Ilić), Marko Pantelić (46 Danko Lazović), Nikola Žigić. Trainer: Javier Clemente

ARMENIA: Gevorg Kasparov, Sargis Hovsepyan, Robert Arzumanyan, Karen Dokhoyan, Rafael Nazaryan, Egishe Melikyan, Samvel Melkonyan, Agvan Mkrtchyan, Aram Hakobyan (69 Arthur Minasyan), Edgar Manucharyan (79 Armen Tigranyan), Armen Shahgeldyan (65 Nshan Erzrumyan). Trainer: Ian Porterfield

Sent off: Rafael Nazaryan (76)

Goals: Stanković (54 pen), Lazović (62), Žigić (90)

POLAND v PORTUGAL 2-1 (2-0)

Slaski, Chorzow 11.10.2006

Referee: Wolfgang Stark (GER) Attendance: 40,000

POLAND: Wojciech Kowalewski, Grzegorz Bronowicki, Pawel Golanski, Jacek Bak, Mariusz Lewandowski, Jakub Blaszczykowski (65 Jacek Krzynowek), Euzebiusz Smolarek, Radoslaw Sobolewski, Arkadiusz Radomski, Maciej Zurawski, Grzegorz Rasiak (73 Radoslaw Matusiak). Trainer: Leo Beenhakker

PORTUGAL: RICARDO Pereira, MIGUEL Monteiro, NUNO VALENTE, RICARDO CARVALHO, RICARDO ROCHA, Anderson Souza "DECO" (83 Nuno Ribeiro "MANICHE"), Armando Teixeira "PETIT" (68 Luís Cunha "NANI"), Francisco Costa "COSTINHA" (46 TIAGO Mendes), SIMÃO Sabrosa, NUNO GOMES, CRISTIANO RONALDO. Trainer: Luiz Felipe Scolari

Goals: Smolarek (9, 18), Nuno Gomes (90)

BELGIUM v AZERBAIJAN 3-0 (1-0)

Constant Vanden Stock Stadium, Brussels 11.10.2006

Referee: Romans Lajuks (LAT) Attendance: 12,000

BELGIUM: Stijn Stijnen, Timmy Simons, Thomas Vermaelen, Anthony Vanden Borre (77 Mbo Mpenza), Philippe Léonard, Daniel Van Buyten, Carl Hoefkens, Karel Geraerts, Bart Goor, Emile Mpenza (70 Moussa Dembélé), Kevin Vandenbergh (86 Luigi Pieroni). Trainer: René Vandereycken

AZERBAIJAN: Farhad Veliyev, Zaur Hasimov (76 Vugar Nadyrov), Sergei Sokolov, Aslan Kerimov, Ernani Pereira, Andre Ladaga, Yuri Muzika (33 Ilgar Gurbanov), Ceyhun Sultanov (55 Vagif Dzavadov), Emin Imamaliev, Aleksandr Chertoganov, Leandro Gomes. Trainer: Sahin Diniyev

Sent off: Moussa Dembélé (87)

Goals: Simons (24 pen), Vandenbergh (47), Dembélé (82)

KAZAKHSTAN v FINLAND 0-2 (0-1)

Centralny, Almaty 11.10.2006

Referee: Athanassios Briakos (GRE) Attendance: 17,000

KAZAKHSTAN: David Loria, Samat Smakov, Aleksandr Kuchma, Maksim Zhalmagambetov, Egor Azovskiy, Ruslan Baltiyev, Nikita Khokhlov, Andrei Travin (82 Maksim Azovskiy), Eduard Sergienko (76 Sergey Larin), Nurbol Zhumaskaliyev (63 Kairat Ashirbekov), Dmitriy Byakov. Trainer: Arno Pijpers

FINLAND: Jussi Jääskeläinen, Petri Pasanen, Sami Hyypiä, Hannu Tihinen, Jari Litmanen, Joonas Kolkka, Jari Ilola, Mika Väyrynen (90 Aki Riihilahti), Mika Nurmela, Mikael Forssell (72 Shefki Kuqi), Toni Kallio. Trainer: Roy Hodgson

Goals: Litmanen (27), Hyypiä (65)

FINLAND v ARMENIA 1-0 (1-0)

Finnair, Helsinki 15.11.2006

Referee: Craig Thomson (SCO) Attendance: 9,500

FINLAND: Jussi Jääskeläinen, Sami Hyypiä, Ari Nyman, Hannu Tihinen, Markus Heikkinen, Toni Kallio, Joonas Kolkka, Alexei Eremenko Jr (88 Shefki Kuqi), Mika Väyrynen (47 Jari Ilola), Jonatan Johansson, Mika Nurmela. Trainer: Roy Hodgson

ARMENIA: Gevorg Kasparov, Karen Dokhoyan (46 Valeri Aleksanyan), Sargis Hovsepyan, Aleksandr Tadevosyan, Levon Pachajyan, Hamlet Mkhitaryan (75 Ara Hakobyan), Romik Khachatryan, Agvan Mkrtchyan, Artavazd Karamyan, Robert Zebelyan (78 Arman Karamyan), Armen Shahgeldyan. Trainer: Ian Porterfield

Goal: Nurmela (10)

BELGIUM v POLAND 0-1 (0-1)

Roi Baudouin, Brussels 15.11.2006

Referee: Stuart Dougal (SCO) Attendance: 46,000

BELGIUM: Stijn Stijnen, Thomas Vermaelen, Timmy Simons, Daniel Van Buyten, Carl Hoefkens, Philippe Léonard (80 Gaby Mudingayi), Anthony Vanden Borre (46 Stein Huysegems), Bart Goor, Karel Geraerts, Emile Mpenza, Kevin Vandenbergh (62 Luigi Pieroni). Trainer: René Vandereycken

POLAND: Artur Boruc, Dariusz Dudka (79 Rafal Murawski), Grzegorz Bronowicki, Marcin Wasilewski, Jacek Bak, Michal Zewlakow, Radoslaw Sobolewski, Jakub Blaszczykowski, Euzebiusz Smolarek, Maciej Zurawski (62 Lukasz Gargula), Radoslaw Matusiak (89 Przemyslaw Kazmierczak). Trainer: Leo Beenhakker

Goal: Matusiak (19)

PORTUGAL v KAZAKHSTAN 3-0 (2-0)

Cidade de Coimbra, Coimbra 15.11.2006

Referee: René Rogalla (SWI) Attendance: 25,000

PORTUGAL: RICARDO Pereira, MIGUEL Monteiro, PAULO FERREIRA, RICARDO CARVALHO, António Leonel "TONEL" (77 JORGE ANDRADE), TIAGO Mendes, Anderson Souza "DECO" (63 CARLOS MARTINS), RAUL MEIRELES, CRISTIANO RONALDO (58 RICARDO QUARESMA), SIMÃO Sabrosa, NUNO GOMES. Trainer: Luiz Felipe Scolari

KAZAKHSTAN: David Loria, Aleksandr Kuchma, Maksim Zhalmagambetov, Samat Smakov, Egor Azovskiy, Andrei Travin, Eduard Sergienko (74 Sergey Larin), Nikita Khokhlov, Dmitriy Byakov, Ruslan Baltiyev, Nurbol Zhumaskaliyev. Trainer: Arno Pijpers

Goals: Simão (8, 86), Cristiano Ronaldo (30)

POLAND v AZERBAIJAN 5-0 (3-0)

Wojska Polskiego, Warsaw 24.03.2007

Referee: Kristinn Jakobsson (ISL) Attendance: 14,000

POLAND: Artur Boruc, Marcin Wasilewski, Dariusz Dudka, Jacek Bak, Michal Zewlakow, Wojciech Lobodzinski, Lukasz Gargula, Mariusz Lewandowski, Jacek Krzynówek (79 Ireneusz Jelen), Maciej Zurawski, Radoslaw Matusiak (69 Przemyslaw Kazmierczak). Trainer: Leo Beenhakker

AZERBAIJAN: Jahangir Hasanzade, Aslan Kerimov, Samir Abbasov, Ernani Pereira, Elmar Baxsiyev, Ilgar Gurbanov, Emin Imamaliev (65 Murad Agakisiyev), Kanan Kerimov (67 Vagif Dzavadov), Aleksandr Chertoganov, Leandro Gomes (62 Andre Ladaga), Branimir Subašić. Trainer: Shahin Diniyev

Goals: Bak (3), Dudka (6), Lobodzinski (34), Krzynówek (58), Kazmierczak (84)

KAZAKHSTAN v SERBIA 2-1 (0-0)

Tcentralny, Almaty 24.03.2007

Referee: Vladimír Hriňák (SVK) Attendance: 15,000

KAZAKHSTAN: David Loria, Samat Smakov, Aleksandr Kuchma, Maksim Zhalmagambetov, Farkhadbek Irismetov, Sergey Skorykh, Eduard Sergienko (58 Anton Chichulin), Ruslan Baltiyev, Murat Suyumagambetov (80 Andrey Finonchenko), Nurbol Zhumaskaliyev, Kairat Ashirbekov (71 Dmitriy Byakov). Trainer: Arno Pijpers

SERBIA: Vladimir Stojković, Marjan Marković, Milan Stepanov, Nemanja Vidić, Duško Tošic, Nenad Kovačević, Ivan Ergić (70 Ognjen Koroman), Boško Janković, Miloš Krasic, Marko Pantelić (69 Danko Lazović), Nikola Žigić. Trainer: Javier Clemente

Sent off: Nikola Žigić (90)

Goals: Ashirbekov (47), Zhumaskaliyev (61), Žigić (68)

PORTUGAL v BELGIUM 4-0 (0-0)

José Alvalade, Lisbon 24.03.2007

Referee: Kyros Vassaras (GRE) Attendance: 47,000

PORTUGAL: RICARDO Pereira, MIGUEL Monteiro, RICARDO CARVALHO, JORGE ANDRADE, PAULO FERREIRA, TIAGO Mendes, Armando Teixeira "PETIT" (76 FERNANDO MEIRA), JOÃO MOUTINHO, CRISTIANO RONALDO (78 HUGO VIANA), NUNO GOMES, RICARDO QUARESMA (70 Luís Cunha "NANI"). Trainer: Luiz Felipe Scolari

BELGIUM: Stijn Stijnen, Carl Hoefkens (64 François Sterchele), Philippe Clément, Daniel Van Buyten, Peter Van der Heyden, Marouane Fellaini, Gaby Mudingayi, Mark De Man, Steven Defour, Maarten Martens (56 Thomas Chatelle), Mbo Mpenza (81 Jelle van Damme). Trainer: René Vandereycken

Goals: Nuno Gomes (53), Cristiano Ronaldo (55, 75), Ricardo Quaresma (69)

AZERBAIJAN v FINLAND 1-0 (0-0)

Republic Stadium, Baku 28.03.2007

Referee: Domenico Messina (ITA) Attendance: 14,000

AZERBAIJAN: Farhad Veliyev, Ernani Pereira, Andre Ladaga (66 Emin Imamaliev), Ramin Guliyev, Aslan Kerimov, Samir Abbasov, Ceyhun Sultanov (76 Ilgar Gurbanov), Leandro Gomes (10 Vugar Nadyrov), Murad Agakisiyev, Branimir Subašic, Aleksandr Chertoganov. Trainer: Shahin Diniyev

FINLAND: Jussi Jääskeläinen, Petri Pasanen, Sami Hyypiä, Hannu Tihinen, Mika Väyrynen, Jari Litmanen, Joonas Kolkka (85 Shefki Kuqi), Toni Kallio, Alexei Eremenko Jr, Jonatan Johansson (86 Mikael Forssell), Markus Heikkinen. Trainer: Roy Hodgson

Goal: Imamaliev (83)

POLAND v ARMENIA 1-0 (1-0)

Kielce Stadium, Kielce 28.03.2007

Referee: Alberto Undiano Mallenco (SPA) Att: 15,500

POLAND: Artur Boruc, Dariusz Dudka, Jacek Bak, Marcin Wasilewski, Michal Zewlakow, Jacek Krzynówek (83 Ireneusz Jelen), Jakub Blaszczykowski, Mariusz Lewandowski, Lukasz Gargula, Maciej Zurawski, Przemyslaw Kazmierczak (61 Radoslaw Sobolewski). Trainer: Leo Beenhakker

ARMENIA: Roman Berezovsky, Egishe Melikyan, Karen Dokhoyan, Sargis Hovsepyan, Robert Arzumanyan, Romik Khachatryan, Rafael Nazaryan (46 Edgar Manucharyan), Artavazd Karamyan (68 Samvel Melkonyan), Levon Pachajyan, Armen Shahgeldyan (75 Hamlet Mkhitaryan), Robert Zebelyan. Trainer: Ian Porterfield

Goal: Zurawski (26)

SERBIA v PORTUGAL 1-1 (1-1)

FK Crvena Zvezda, Beograd 28.03.2007

Referee: Bertrand Layec (FRA) Attendance: 51,000

SERBIA: Vladimir Stojković, Duško Tošic (84 Danko Lazović), Nemanja Vidić, Ivica Dragutinović, Mladen Krstajić, Igor Duljaj, Boško Janković (64 Ognjen Koroman), Nenad Kovačević, Miloš Krasić, Dejan Stanković (78 Marjan Marković), Marko Pantelić. Trainer: Javier Clemente

PORTUGAL: RICARDO Pereira, PAULO FERREIRA, JORGE ANDRADE, MIGUEL Monteiro (72 MARCO CANEIRA), RICARDO CARVALHO, Armando Teixeira "PETIT", JOÃO MOUTINHO (77 RAUL MEIRELES), TIAGO Mendes, CRISTIANO RONALDO, NUNO GOMES (82 RICARDO QUARESMA), SIMÃO Sabrosa. Trainer: Luiz Felipe Scolari

Goals: Tiago (5), Janković (37)

KAZAKHSTAN v ARMENIA 1-2 (0-2)

Tcentralny, Almaty 02.06.2007

Referee: Pavel Kralovec (CZE) Attendance: 17,100

KAZAKHSTAN: David Loria, Samat Smakov, Aleksandr Kuchma, Maksim Zhalmagambetov, Farkhadbek Irismetov, Anton Chichulin, Eduard Sergienko (36 Dmitri Byakov), Ruslan Baltiyev, Zhambyl Kukeyev (57 Murat Tleshev), Murat Suyumagambetov, Nurbol Zhumaskaliyev (78 Oleg Kornienko). Trainer: Arno Pijpers

ARMENIA: Gevorg Kasparov, Sargis Hovsepyan, Robert Arzumanyan, Aleksandr Tadevosyan, Agvan Mkrtchyan, Vahagn Minasyan, Ararat Arakelyan (80 Aram Hakobyan), Artur Voskanyan, Egishe Melikyan, Hamlet Mkhitaryan (75 Armen Shahgeldyan), Samvel Melkonya (90 Arman Karamyan). Trainer: Ian Porterfield

Goals: Arzumanyan (31), Hovsepyan (39 pen), Baltiyev (88 pen)

FINLAND v SERBIA 0-2 (0-1)

Olympiastadion, Helsinki 02.06.2007

Referee: Manuel Mejuto González (SPA) Att: 33,615

FINLAND: Jussi Jääskeläinen, Toni Kallio, Sami Hyypiä, Hannu Tihinen, Petri Pasanen, Markus Heikkinen, Jari Ilola, Mika Väyrynen, Teemu Tainio (28 Joonas Kolkka), Shefki Kuqi (70 Jari Litmanen), Mikael Forssell (62 Jonatan Johansson). Trainer: Roy Hodgson

SERBIA: Vladimir Stojković, Ivica Dragutinović, Mladen Krstajić, Nemanja Vidić, Antonio Rukavina, Dejan Stanković, Nenad Kovačević, Zdravko Kuzmanović, Boško Janković (67 Danko Lazović), Marko Pantelić (60 Milan Jovanović), Miloš Krasic (85 Igor Duljaj). Trainer: Javier Clemente

Goals: Janković (3), Jovanović (86)

BELGIUM v PORTUGAL 1-2 (0-1)

Roi Baudouin, Brussels 02.06.2007

Referee: Martin Hansson (SWE) Attendance: 45,585

BELGIUM: Stijn Stijnen, Marouane Fellaini, Timmy Simons, Carl Hoefkens (46 Mark De Man), Thomas Vermaelen, Philippe Clément, Jan Vertonghen, Gaby Mudingayi (76 Karel Geraerts), Emile Mpenza, François Sterchele (61 Tom De Mul), Steven Defour. Trainer: René Vandereycken

PORTUGAL: RICARDO Pereira, JORGE ANDRADE, PAULO FERREIRA, FERNANDO MEIRA, MIGUEL Monteiro (53 José Bosingwa), Anderson Souza "DECO", Armando Teixeira "PETIT", TIAGO Mendes, HÉLDER POSTIGA (79 HUGO ALMEIDA), Luís Cunha "NANI" (86 Sergio Valente "DUDA"), RICARDO QUARESMA. Trainer: Luiz Felipe Scolari

Sent off: Hugo Almeida (90)

Goals: Nani (43), Fellaini (55), Hélder Postiga (64)

AZERBAIJAN v POLAND 1-3 (1-0)

Tofikh Bakhramov, Baku 02.06.2007

Referee: Costas Kapitanis (CYP) Attendance: 4,500

AZERBAIJAN: Farhad Veliyev, Ramin Guliyev, Samir Abbasov, Emin Guliyev, Alim Gurbanov (65 Ilgar Gurbanov), Emin Imamaliev (70 Zaur Hasimov), Aleksandr Chertoganov, Aslan Kerimov, Khagani Mamedov (53 Vagif Dzavadov), Ramazan Abbasov, Branimir Subašić.
Trainer: Shahin Diniyev

POLAND: Artur Boruc, Marcin Wasilewski, Dariusz Dudka, Jacek Bak, Michal Zewlakow, Jakub Blaszczykowski (57 Wojciech Lobodzinski), Mariusz Lewandowski, Jacek Krzynówek, Euzebiusz Smolarek, Grzegorz Rasiak (81 Radoslaw Sobolewski), Maciej Zurawski (57 Marek Saganowski). Trainer: Leo Beenhakker

Goals: Subašić (6), Smolarek (63), Krzynowek (66, 90)

ARMENIA v POLAND 1-0 (0-0)

Republican, Yerevan 06.06.2007

Referee: Pavel Cristian Balaj (ROM) Attendance: 12,500

ARMENIA: Gevorg Kasparov, Sargis Hovsepyan, Robert Arzumanyan, Egishe Melikyan, Vahagn Minasyan (78 Levon Pachajyan), Aleksandr Tadevosyan, Agvan Mkrtchyan, Artur Voskanyan, Ararat Arakelyan, Hamlet Mkhitaryan (70 Arman Karamyan), Armen Shahgeldyan (46 Aram Hakobyan).
Trainer: Ian Porterfield

POLAND: Artur Boruc, Dariusz Dudka, Grzegorz Bronowicki, Marcin Wasilewski, Michal Zewlakow, Mariusz Lewandowski, Jacek Bak (65 Radoslaw Sobolewski), Euzebiusz Smolarek (60 Maciej Zurawski), Jacek Krzynówek, Wojciech Lobodzinski (60 Jakub Blaszczykowski), Marek Saganowski.
Trainer: Leo Beenhakker

Goal: Mkhitaryan (66)

KAZAKHSTAN v AZERBAIJAN 1-1 (0-1)

Centralny, Almaty 06.06.2007

Referee: Albert Toussaint (LUX) Attendance: 11,800

KAZAKHSTAN: David Loria, Samat Smakov, Aleksandr Kuchma, Maksim Zhalmagambetov, Farkhadbek Irismetov, Anton Chichulin, Ruslan Baltiyev, Andrei Karpovich, Sergey Ostapenko (79 Murat Tleshev), Dmitriy Byakov, Nurbol Zhumaskaliyev (90 Kairat Utabaev). Trainer: Arno Pijpers

AZERBAIJAN: Jahangir Hasanzade, Zaur Hasimov, Emin Guliyev, Ramin Guliyev, Samir Abbasov, Ceyhun Sultanov (74 Alim Gurbanov), Aleksandr Chertoganov, Ramazan Abbasov, Branimir Subašic, Vugar Nadyrov (84 Khagani Mamedov), Aslan Kerimov (58 Emin Imamaliev).
Trainer: Sahin Diniyev

Sent off: Maksim Zhalmagambetov (45)

Goals: Nadyrov (30), Baltiyev (53)

FINLAND v KAZAKHSTAN 2-1 (1-1)

Ratina, Tampere 22.08.2007

Referee: Viktor Kassai (HUN) Attendance: 13,000

FINLAND: Jussi Jääskeläinen, Toni Kallio, Sami Hyypiä, Hannu Tihinen, Petri Pasanen, Roman Eremenko (46 Daniel Sjolund), Markus Heikkinen, Joonas Kolkka (88 Mika Nurmela), Teemu Tainio (76 Aki Riihilahti), Alexei Eremenko Jr, Jonatan Johansson. Trainer: Roy Hodgson

KAZAKHSTAN: David Loria, Egor Azovskiy, Aleksandr Kuchma, Samat Smakov, Farkhadbek Irismetov, Sergey Skorykh (69 Anton Chichulin), Sergey Larin (78 Kairat Ashirbekov), Ruslan Baltiyev, Nurbol Zhumaskaliyev, Dmitriy Byakov, Sergey Ostapenko (70 Murat Suyumagambetov).
Trainer: Arno Pijpers

Goals: Eremenko Jr (13), Byakov (23), Tainio (61)

FINLAND v BELGIUM 2-0 (1-0)

Olympiastadion, Helsinki 06.06.2007

Referee: Mike Riley (ENG) Attendance: 34,818

FINLAND: Jussi Jääskeläinen, Toni Kallio, Petri Pasanen, Ari Nyman, Hannu Tihinen, Joonas Kolkka (88 Mika Nurmela), Markus Heikkinen, Roman Eremenko, Mika Väyrynen, Alexei Eremenko Jr (89 Mikael Forssell), Jonatan Johansson.
Trainer: Roy Hodgson

BELGIUM: Stijn Stijnen, Thomas Vermaelen (46 Maarten Maertens), Timmy Simons, Philippe Clément, Mark De Man, Jelle Van Damme, Jan Vertonghen, Marouane Fellaini, Steven Defour, Tom De Mul (55 Faris Haroun), Emile Mpenza (86 François Sterchele). Trainer: René Vandereycken

Sent off: Marouane Fellaini (Belgium)

Goals: Johansson (27), Eremenko Jr (71)

BELGIUM v SERBIA 3-2 (2-0)

Roi Baudouin, Brussels 22.08.2007

Referee: Terje Hauge (NOR) Attendance: 19,202

BELGIUM: Stijn Stijnen, Timmy Simons, Carl Hoefkens, Thomas Vermaelen, Vincent Kompany, Gaby Mudingayi, Bart Goor, Karel Geraerts, Kevin Mirallas (67 Anthony Vanden Borre), Moussa Dembélé (89 Nicolas Lombaerts), Steven Defour (86 Mbo Mpenza). Trainer: René Vandereycken

SERBIA: Vladimir Stojković, Antonio Rukavina, Nemanja Vidić, Mladen Krstajić, Ivica Dragutinović, Nenad Kovačević, Zdravko Kuzmanović, Boško Janković, Ognjen Koroman (56 Milos Krasić), Danko Lazović (70 Milan Smiljanić), Marko Pantelić (56 Milan Jovanović). Trainer: Javier Clemente

Goals: Dembélé (10, 88), Mirallas (30), Kuzmanović (73, 90)

ARMENIA v PORTUGAL 1-1 (1-1)

Republican, Erevan 22.08.2007

Referee: Claus Bo Larsen (DEN) Attendance: 15,550

ARMENIA: Roman Berezovsky, Sargis Hovsepyan, Robert Arzumanyan, Aleksandr Tadevosyan, Agvan Mkrtchyan, Levon Pachajyan, Artur Voskanyan, Ararat Arakelyan, Artavazd Karamyan (70 Egishe Melikyan), Hamlet Mkhitaryan (59 Gevorg Ghazaryan), Samvel Melkonyan (90 Romik Khachatryan). Trainer: Ian Porterfield

PORTUGAL: RICARDO Pereira, MIGUEL Monteiro, FERNANDO MEIRA, JORGE ANDRADE (76 BRUNO ALVES), PAULO FERREIRA, RAUL MEIRELES, TIAGO Mendes, Anderson Souza "DECO", CRISTIANO RONALDO, HÉLDER POSTIGA (61 NUNO GOMES), SIMÃO Sabrosa (63 RICARDO QUARESMA). Trainer: Luiz Felipe Scolari

Goals: Arzumanyan (11), Cristiano Ronaldo (37)

SERBIA v FINLAND 0-0

FK Crvena Zvezda, Beograd 08.09.2007

Referee: Eric Braamhaar (HOL) Attendance: 15,000

SERBIA: Vladimir Stojković, Antonio Rukavina, Branislav Ivanović, Ivica Dragutinović, Duško Tošić (53 Zoran Tosić), Nenad Kovačević, Zdravko Kuzmanović, Dejan Stanković, Boško Janković (54 Milan Jovanović), Miloš Krasić, Danko Lazović (62 Nikola Žigić). Trainer: Javier Clemente

FINLAND: Jussi Jääskeläinen, Petri Pasanen, Sami Hyypiä, Hannu Tihinen, Toni Kuivasto, Mika Nurmela, Teemu Tainio, Markus Heikkinen, Alexei Eremenko Jr (74 Mikael Forssell), Daniel Sjölund, Jonatan Johansson (78 Jarkko Wiss). Trainer: Roy Hodgson

PORTUGAL v POLAND 2-2 (0-1)

Estádio do Sport Lisboa e Benfica, Lisbon 08.09.2007

Referee: Roberto Rosetti (ITA) Attendance: 55,000

PORTUGAL: RICARDO Pereira, José Bosingwa, FERNANDO MEIRA, BRUNO ALVES, MARCO CANEIRA, Anderson Souza "DECO", Nuno Ribeiro "MANICHE", Armando Teixeira "PETIT", CRISTIANO RONALDO, NUNO GOMES (69 RICARDO QUARESMA), SIMÃO Sabrosa (81 JOÃO MOUTINHO). Trainer: Luiz Felipe Scolari

POLAND: Artur Boruc, Marcin Wasilewski, Mariusz Jop, Michal Zewlakow, Grzegorz Bronowicki (55 Pawel Golanski), Jakub Blaszczykowski, Mariusz Lewandowski, Dariusz Dudka, Euzebiusz Smolarek (73 Wojciech Lobodzinski), Jacek Krzynówek, Maciej Zurawski (56 Radoslaw Matusiak). Trainer: Leo Beenhakker

Goals: Lewandowski (44), Maniche (50), Cristiano Ronaldo (73), Krzynowek (88)

FINLAND v POLAND 0-0

Olympiastadion, Helsinki 12.09.2007

Referee: Herbert Fandel (GER) Attendance: 34,000

FINLAND: Jussi Jääskeläinen, Toni Kuivasto, Sami Hyypiä, Hannu Tihinen, Petri Pasanen, Daniel Sjölund, Markus Heikkinen (90 Jarkko Wiss), Teemu Tainio, Joonas Kolkka, Alexei Eremenko Jr, Jonatan Johansson (72 Mikael Forssell). Trainer: Roy Hodgson

POLAND: Artur Boruc, Pawel Golanski, Mariusz Jop, Michal Zewlakow, Jakub Blaszczykowski, Dariusz Dudka, Radoslaw Sobolewski, Mariusz Lewandowski, Euzebiusz Smolarek (80 Maciej Zurawski), Jacek Krzynówek, Grzegorz Rasiak (65 Marek Saganowski). Trainer: Leo Beenhakker

KAZAKHSTAN v BELGIUM 2-2 (1-2)

Centralny, Almaty 12.09.2007

Referee: Alexandru Dan Tudor (ROM) Attendance: 18,000

KAZAKHSTAN: David Loria, Egor Azovskiy (66 Dmitri Lyapkin), Samat Smakov, Farkhadbek Irismetov, Aleksandr Kuchma, Sergey Larin (73 Murat Suyumagambetov), Sergey Skorykh, Andrei Karpovich, Nurbol Zhumaskaliyev, Sergey Ostapenko, Dmitriy Byakov. Trainer: Arno Pijpers

BELGIUM: Stijn Stijnen, Timmy Simons, Vincent Kompany, Carl Hoefkens, Thomas Vermaelen, Bart Goor (84 Mbo Mpenza), Marouane Fellaini, Karel Geraerts (77 Faris Haroun), Steven Defour, Kevin Mirallas (63 Jan Vertonghen), Moussa Dembélé. Trainer: René Vandereycken

Goals: Geraerts (13), Mirallas (24), Byakov (39), Smakov (77 pen)

PORTUGAL v SERBIA 1-1 (1-0)

José Alvalade, Lisboa 12.09.2007

Referee: Markus Merk (GER) Attendance: 53,000

PORTUGAL: RICARDO Pereira, PAULO FERREIRA, FERNANDO MEIRA, BRUNO ALVES, Armando Teixeira "PETIT", José Bosingwa, Anderson Souza "DECO" (77 JOÃO MOUTINHO), Nuno Ribeiro "MANICHE" (83 RAUL MEIRELES), CRISTIANO RONALDO, NUNO GOMES (65 RICARDO QUARESMA), SIMÃO Sabrosa. Trainer: Luiz Felipe Scolari

SERBIA: Vladimir Stojković, Antonio Rukavina, Ivica Dragutinović, Nemanja Vidić, Branislav Ivanović, Zoran Tošic (61 Nikola Žigić), Dejan Stanković, Nenad Kovačević, Miloš Krasic (61 Marko Pantelić), Zdravko Kuzmanović (71 Igor Duljaj), Milan Jovanović. Trainer: Javier Clemente

Sent off: Ivica Dragutinović (90)

Goals: SIMÃO Sabrosa (11), Ivanović (88)

ARMENIA v SERBIA 0-0

Republican, Erevan 13.10.2007

Referee: Stefan Johannesson (SWE) Attendance: 10,000

ARMENIA: Roman Berezovsky, Sargis Hovsepyan, Robert Arzumanyan, Karen Dokhoyan, Aleksandr Tadevosyan, Levon Pachajyan, Artur Voskanyan (70 Romik Khachatryan), Ararat Arakelyan, Artavazd Karamyan, Hamlet Mkhitaryan (82 Aram Hakobyan), Samvel Melkonyan (62 Robert Zebelyan). Trainer: Vardan Minasyan

SERBIA: Vladimir Stojković, Antonio Rukavina, Branislav Ivanović, Milan Stepanov, Duško Tošić, Nenad Kovačević, Zdravko Kuzmanović (61 Zoran Tosić), Dejan Stanković, Miloš Krasić (73 Bosko Janković), Marko Pantelić (62 Danko Lazović), Nikola Žigić. Trainer: Javier Clemente

AZERBAIJAN v PORTUGAL 0-2 (0-2)

Tofikh Bakhramov, Baku 13.10.2007

Referee: Ivan Bebek (CRO) Attendance: 30,000

AZERBAIJAN: Farhad Veliyev, Elvin Aliyev, Samir Abbasov, Aslan Kerimov, Sasha Yunisoglu, Emin Guliyev, Aleksandr Chertoganov, Emin Imamaliev (7 Zaur Hasimov), Ilgar Gurbanov (56 Khagani Mamedov), Branimir Subašić, Samir Aliyev (73 Alim Gurbanov). Trainer: Sahin Diniyev

PORTUGAL: RICARDO Pereira, BRUNO ALVES, PAULO FERREIRA, MIGUEL Monteiro (75 JORGE RIBEIRO), RICARDO CARVALHO, Nuno Ribeiro "MANICHE", Anderson Souza "DECO", MIGUEL VELOSO, CRISTIANO RONALDO, RICARDO QUARESMA (70 Luís Cunha "NANI"), HUGO ALMEIDA. Trainer: Flávio Teixeira

Sent off: Aslan Kerimov (29)

Goals: Bruno Alves (12), Hugo Almeida (45)

POLAND v KAZAKHSTAN 3-1 (0-1)

Legia, Warsaw 13.10.2007

Referee: Espen Berntsen (NOR) Attendance: 12,000

POLAND: Artur Boruc, Mariusz Jop, Grzegorz Bronowicki, Dariusz Dudka, Jacek Bak, Euzebiusz Smolarek, Jacek Krzynówek, Marek Saganowski (46 Maciej Zurawski), Michal Zewlakow (46 Marcin Wasilewski), Wojciech Lobodzinski (80 Kamil Kosowski), Mariusz Lewandowski.
Trainer: Leo Beenhakker

KAZAKHSTAN: David Loria, Dmitri Lyapkin, Aleksandr Kuchma, Samat Smakov, Kairat Nurdauletov, Sergey Skorykh (81 Andrei Karpovich), Ruslan Baltiyev, Nurbol Zhumaskaliyev, Sergey Larin (73 Murat Suyumagambetov), Sergey Ostapenko, Dmitriy Byakov (85 Kairat Ashirbekov).
Trainer: Arno Pijpers

Goals: Byakov (20), Smolarek (56, 65, 66)

KAZAKHSTAN v PORTUGAL 1-2 (0-0)

Centralny, Almaty 17.10.2007

Referee: Jan W. Wegereef (HOL) Attendance: 18,500

KAZAKHSTAN: David Loria, Samat Smakov, Maksim Zhalmagambetov, Farkhadbek Irismetov, Aleksandr Kuchma, Sergey Larin (37 Dmitri Lyapkin), Sergey Skorykh, Andrei Karpovich (86 Kairat Nurdauletov), Nurbol Zhumaskaliyev, Sergey Ostapenko, Dmitriy Byakov. Trainer: Arno Pijpers

PORTUGAL: RICARDO Pereira, MIGUEL Monteiro, RICARDO CARVALHO, BRUNO ALVES, PAULO FERREIRA, Nuno Ribeiro "MANICHE" (59 Luís Cunha "NANI"), Anderson Souza "DECO", MIGUEL VELOSO, RICARDO QUARESMA (82 JOÃO MOUTINHO), HUGO ALMEIDA (63 Ariza Makukula), CRISTIANO RONALDO.
Trainer: Flávio Teixeira

Goals: Makukula (84), Cristiano Ronaldo (88), Byakov (90)

BELGIUM v FINLAND 0-0

Roi Baudouin, Brussels 13.10.2007

Referee: Costas Kapitanis (CYP) Attendance: 4,100

BELGIUM: Stijn Stijnen, Nicolas Lombaerts, Daniel Van Buyten, Vincent Kompany, Guillaume Gillet, Timmy Simons, Gaby Mudingayi, Faris Haroun (67 Bart Goor), Christophe Grégoire (67 Wesley Sonck), Kevin Mirallas (84 François Sterchele), Moussa Dembélé. Trainer: René Vandereycken

FINLAND: Jussi Jääskeläinen, Sami Hyypiä, Petri Pasanen, Hannu Tihinen, Toni Kallio, Alexei Eremenko Jr, Roman Eremenko, Aki Riihilahti, Jonatan Johansson (88 Shefki Kuqi), Joonas Kolkka, Daniel Sjölund (90 Mika Nurmela).
Trainer: Roy Hodgson

BELGIUM v ARMENIA 3-0 (0-0)

Roi Baudouin, Brussels 17.10.2007

Referee: Johannes Valgeirsson (ISL) Attendance: 14,800

BELGIUM: Stijn Stijnen, Nicolas Lombaerts (83 Jan Vertonghen), Daniel Van Buyten (60 Vincent Kompany), Timmy Simons, Gill Swerts, Steven Defour, Marouane Fellaini, Bart Goor, Karel Geraerts, Moussa Dembélé, Kevin Mirallas (46 Wesley Sonck). Trainer: René Vandereycken

ARMENIA: Gevorg Kasparov, Aleksandr Tadevosyan (82 Agvan Mkrtchyan), Sargis Hovsepyan, Robert Arzumanyan, Karen Dokhoyan, Ararat Arakelyan, Romik Khachatryan (57 Aram Hakobyan), Levon Pachajyan, Artur Voskanyan, Samvel Melkonyan (70 Robert Zebelyan), Artavazd Karamyan.
Trainer: Vardan Minasyan

Goals: Sonck (63), Dembélé (69), Geraerts (76)

AZERBAIJAN v SERBIA 1-6 (1-4)

Tofikh Bakhramov, Baku 17.10.2007

Referee: Thomas Einwaller (AUS) Attendance: 9,000

AZERBAIJAN: Farhad Veliyev (46 Jahangir Hasanzade), Samir Abbasov, Ramin Guliyev, Zaur Hasimov (50 Elmar Bakshiev), Ceyhun Sultanov (69 Farrukh Ismaylov), Emin Guliyev, Alim Gurbanov, Aleksandr Chertoganov, Ramazan Abbasov, Samir Aliyev, Branimir Subašić.
Trainer: Sahin Diniyev

SERBIA: Vladimir Stojković, Milan Biševac, Branislav Ivanović, Antonio Rukavina, Duško Tošic, Zoran Tošic, Igor Duljaj, Boško Janković (68 Danko Lazović), Nenad Kovačević (65 Milan Jovanović), Zdravko Kuzmanović, Nikola Žigić (73 Marko Pantelić). Trainer: Javier Clemente

Goals: D. Tosic (4), Žigić (17, 42), Aliyev (26), Janković (41), Jovanović (75), Lazović (81)

PORTUGAL v ARMENIA 1-0 (1-0)

Dr. Magalhães Pessoa, Leiria 17.11.2007

Referee: Mike Riley (ENG) Attendance: 23,000

PORTUGAL: RICARDO Pereira, José Bosingwa, FERNANDO MEIRA, BRUNO ALVES, MARCO CANEIRA, MIGUEL VELOSO, Nuno Ribeiro "MANICHE", CRISTIANO RONALDO, SIMÃO Sabrosa (77 Luís Cunha "NANI"), RICARDO QUARESMA (60 MANUEL FERNANDES), HUGO ALMEIDA (68 Ariza Makukula). Trainer: Flávio Teixeira

ARMENIA: Roman Berezovsky, Sargis Hovsepyan, Robert Arzumanyan, Karen Dokhoyan, Aleksandr Tadevosyan, Ararat Arakelyan, Artur Voskanyan, Romik Khachatryan (59 Hamlet Mkhitaryan), Samvel Melkonyan (63 Edgar Manucharyan), Levon Pachajyan, Artavazd Karamyan (76 Agvan Mkrtchyan).
Trainer: Vardan Minasyan

Goal: Hugo Almeida (42)

FINLAND v AZERBAIJAN 2-1 (0-0)

Olympiastadion, Helsinki 17.11.2007

Referee: Alain Hamer (LUX) Attendance: 10,300

FINLAND: Jussi Jääskeläinen, Petri Pasanen, Sami Hyypiä, Hannu Tihinen, Toni Kallio (66 Mika Vayrynen), Joonas Kolkka, Roman Eremenko (80 Shefki Kuqi), Teemu Tainio, Daniel Sjölund, Mikael Forssell, Jonatan Johansson (59 Jari Litmanen). Trainer: Roy Hodgson

AZERBAIJAN: Farhad Veliyev, Samir Abbasov, Usima Nduka (46 Elvin Aliyev), Sasha Yunisoglu, Rashad F. Sadygov, Zaur Tagizade, Makhmud Gurbonov, Branimir Subašic, Zaur Ramazanov, Ramin Guliyev (61 Andre Ladaga), Jemshid Maharramov. Trainer: Gjokica Hadzievski

Goals: M. Gurbonov (63), Forssell (79), Kuqi (86)

ARMENIA v KAZAKHSTAN 0-1 (0-0)

Republican, Erevan 21.11.2007

Referee: Fredy Fautrel (FRA) Attendance: 8,000

ARMENIA: Roman Berezovsky, Sargis Hovsepyan, Robert Arzumanyan, Karen Dokhoyan, Aleksandr Tadevosyan, Ararat Arakelyan (56 Romik Khachatrayan), Artur Voskanyan (80 Gevorg Ghazaryan), Artavazd Karamyan, Hamlet Mkhitaryan, Levon Pachajyan, Samvel Melkonyan (59 Edgar Manucharyan). Trainer: Vardan Minasyan

KAZAKHSTAN: David Loria, Kairat Nurdauletov, Aleksandr Kuchma, Maksim Zhalmagambetov, Farkhadbek Irismetov, Ruslan Baltiyev, Sergey Larin (61 Dmitri Lyapkin), Sergey Skorykh, Nurbol Zhumaskaliyev, Sergey Ostapenko, Dmitriy Byakov. Trainer: Arno Pijpers

Goal: Ostapenko (64)

POLAND v BELGIUM 2-0 (1-0)

Slaski, Chorzow 17.11.2007

Referee: Claus Bo Larsen (DEN) Attendance: 47,000

POLAND: Artur Boruc, Michal Zewlakow, Jacek Bak, Marcin Wasilewski, Grzegorz Bronowicki, Wojciech Lobodzinski (46 Jakub Blaszczykowski), Radoslaw Sobolewski, Jacek Krzynówek, Mariusz Lewandowski, Euzebiusz Smolarek (85 Kamil Kosowski), Maciej Zurawski (82 Rafal Murawski).
Trainer: Leo Beenhakker

BELGIUM: Stijn Stijnen, Jan Vertonghen, Daniel Van Buyten, Vincent Kompany, Guillaume Gillet, Bart Goor, Faris Haroun (84 Karel Geraerts), Marouane Fellaini, Steven Defour (61 Luigi Pieroni), Moussa Dembélé, Kevin Mirallas (76 Stein Huysegems). Trainer: René Vandereycken

Goals: Smolarek (45, 49)

PORTUGAL v FINLAND 0-0

Estádio do Dragão, Porto 21.11.2007

Referee: Luboš Michel (SVK) Attendance: 50,000

PORTUGAL: RICARDO Pereira, José Bosingwa, PEPE, BRUNO ALVES, MARCO CANEIRA, FERNANDO MEIRA, MIGUEL VELOSO, Nuno Ribeiro "MANICHE" (73 Raul Meireles), CRISTIANO RONALDO, NUNO GOMES (77 Ariza Makukula), RICARDO QUARESMA (84 Luís Cunha "NANI").
Trainer: Luiz Felipe Scolari

FINLAND: Jussi Jääskeläinen, Sami Hyypiä, Toni Kallio, Petri Pasanen, Hannu Tihinen, Markus Heikkinen, Joonas Kolkka (75 Jonatan Johansson), Jari Litmanen (67 Mika Vayrynen), Daniel Sjölund, Teemu Tainio (69 Roman Eremenko), Mikael Forssell. Trainer: Roy Hodgson

SERBIA v POLAND 2-2 (0-1)

FK Crvena Zvezda, Beograd 21.11.2007

Referee: Massimo Busacca (SWI) Attendance: 20,000

SERBIA: Vlada Avramov, Antonio Rukavina, Branislav Ivanović, Mladen Krstajić (64 Dusko Tosić), Ivica Dragutinović, Zdravko Kuzmanović, Nenad Kovačević, Igor Duljaj (46 Danko Lazović), Miloš Krasic (76 Bosko Janković), Milan Jovanović, Nikola Žigic. Trainer: Javier Clemente

POLAND: Lukasz Fabianski, Marcin Wasilewski, Jacek Bak (77 Michal Zewlakow), Mariusz Jop, Jakub Wawrzyniak, Wojciech Lobodzinski, Mariusz Lewandowski, Grzegorz Bronowicki, Rafal Murawski, Kamil Kosowski (19 Tomasz Zahorski), Grzegorz Rasiak (46 Radoslaw Matusiak). Trainer: Leo Beenhakker

Goals: Murawski (28), Matusiak (46), Žigić (68), Lazović (70)

AZERBAIJAN v BELGIUM 0-1 (0-0)

Tofikh Bakhramov, Baku 21.11.2007

Referee: Asaf Kenan (ISR) Attendance: 17,000

AZERBAIJAN: Farhad Veliyev, Rail Melikov, Samir Abbasov, Rashad F. Sadygov, Ramin Guliyev, Makhmud Gurbonov, Aslan Kerimov (84 Khagani Mamedov), Jemshid Maharramov (77 Anatoli Ponomarev), Zaur Tagizade (70 Leandro Gomes), Zaur Ramazanov, Branimir Subašić. Trainer: Gjokica Hadzievski

BELGIUM: Brian Vandenbussche, Jelle Van Damme, Daniel Van Buyten, Guillaume Gillet, Jan Vertonghen, Marouane Fellaini, Christophe Grégoire (68 Bart Goor), Gill Swerts, Karel Geraerts (46 Steven Defour), Moussa Dembélé, Luigi Pieroni (81 Kevin Mirallas). Trainer: René Vandereycken

Goal: Pieroni (52)

SERBIA v KAZAKHSTAN 1-0 (0-0)

FK Partizan, Beograd 24.11.2007

Referee: Kyros Vassaras (GRE)

SERBIA: Vlada Avramov, Ivan Stevanović, Djordje Tutoric, Branislav Ivanović, Dušan Andjelković, Gojko Kacar, Igor Duljaj, Miloš Krasic (24 Bosko Janković), Milan Jovanović (63 Stefan Babović), Nikola Žigic (80 Ljubomir Fejsa), Ranko Despotović. Trainer: Javier Clemente

KAZAKHSTAN: David Loria, Samat Smakov, Sergey Skorykh, Maksim Zhalmagambetov, Kairat Nurdauletov, Dmitri Lyapkin (83 Nurbol Zhumaskaliyev), Farkhadbek Irismetov, Ruslan Baltiyev (86 Kairat Ashirbekov), Andrei Karpovich, Dmitriy Byakov, Murat Suyumagambetov (73 Sergey Ostapenko). Trainer: Arno Pijpers

Goal: Ostapenko (79 own goal)

	P	W	D	L	F	A	Pts
Poland	14	8	4	2	24	12	28
Portugal	14	7	6	1	24	10	27
Serbia	14	6	6	2	22	11	24
Finland	14	6	6	2	13	7	24
Belgium	14	5	3	6	14	16	18
Kazakhstan	14	2	4	8	11	21	10
Armenia	12	2	3	7	4	13	9
Azerbaijan	12	1	2	9	6	28	5

GROUP 2

FAROE ISLANDS v GEORGIA 0-6 (0-3)

Toftir, Toftir 16.08.2006

Referee: Michael Ross (NIR) Attendance: 1,000

FAROE ISLANDS: Jákup Mikkelsen, Janus Joensen, Atli Danielsen, Óli Johannesen, Claus Bech Jørgensen (45 Pauli Hansen), Fródi Benjaminsen, Jákup á Borg, Kári Nielsen, Símun Samuelsen (60 Hans Pauli Samuelsen), Christian Høgni Jacobsen, Rógvi Jacobsen (71 Jónhard Frederiksberg). Trainer: Jógvan Martin Olsen

GEORGIA: Grigol Chanturia, Giorgi Shashiashvili, Malkhaz Asatiani, Ilia Kandelaki (66 David Kvirkvelia), Levan Kobiashvili, Kakhaber Aladashvili (71 Giorgi Gakhokidze), Gogita Gogua (57 Giorgi Demetradze), Jaba Kankava, David Mujiri, Aleksandr Iashvili, Shota Arveladze. Trainer: Klaus Toppmöller

Goals: Mujiri (16), Iashvili (18), Arveladze (37, 62, 82), Kobiashvili (51 pen)

SCOTLAND v FAROE ISLANDS 6-0 (5-0)

Celtic Park, Glasgow 02.09.2006

Referee: Igor Egorov (RUS) Attendance: 50,000

SCOTLAND: Craig Gordon, Christian Dailly, David Weir, Steven Pressley, Gary Naysmith, Darren Fletcher (46 Gary Stewart Teale), Paul Hartley, Nigel Quashie (84 Scott Severin), Kenny Miller (61 Garry O'Connor), Kris Boyd, James McFadden. Trainer: Walter Smith

FAROE ISLANDS: Jákup Mikkelsen, Pauli Hansen, Óli Johannesen, Atli Danielsen, Janus Joensen, Fródi Benjaminsen, Julian Johnsson (76 Simun Samuelsen), Jákup á Borg, Jónhard Frederiksberg (60 Hanus Thorleifson), Christian Høgni Jacobsen, Rógvi Jacobsen (84 Kári Nielsen). Trainer: Jógvan Martin Olsen

Goals: Fletcher (7), McFadden (10), Boyd (24 pen, 38), Miller (30 pen), O'Connor (85)

GEORGIA v FRANCE 0-3 (0-2)

Boris Paichadze, Tbilisi 02.09.2006

Referee: Jan Wegereef (HOL) Attendance: 60,000

GEORGIA: Grigol Chanturia, Zurab Khizanishvili, Levan Kobiashvili, Malkhaz Asatiani, Jaba Kankava, Kakhaber Aladashvili (39 Ilia Kandelaki), Gogita Gogua, Aleksandr Iashvili (46 David Kvirkvelia), Giorgi Demetradze, David Mujiri (82 Zurab Mentesashvili), Shota Arveladze. Trainer: Klaus Toppmöller

FRANCE: Grégory Coupet, Willy Sagnol, Lilian Thuram, William Gallas, Éric Abidal, Patrick Vieira, Claude Makélélé (58 Rio Antonio Mavuba), Franck Ribéry (69 Sidney Govou), Florent Malouda, Louis Saha (86 Sylvain Wiltord), Thierry Henry. Trainer: Raymond Domenech

Goals: Malouda (7), Saha (16), Asatiani (46 own goal)

LITHUANIA v SCOTLAND 1-2 (0-0)

S. Darius & S. Girenas, Kaunas 06.09.2006

Referee: Vladimír Hrinák (SVK) Attendance: 7,000

LITHUANIA: Zydrunas Karčemarskas, Marius Stankevičius, Rolandas Džiaukštas, Andrius Skerla, Tomas Žvirgždauskas, Mantas Savenas (50 Tomas Tamošaukas), Mindaugas Kalonas, Saulius Mikoliunas (66 Tadas Labukas), Aidas Preikšaitis (81 Darius Miceika), Robertas Poškus, Tomas Danilevičius. Trainer: Algimantas Liubinskas

SCOTLAND: Craig Gordon, Christian Dailly, David Weir, Gary Caldwell, Gary Naysmith, Steven Pressley, Darren Fletcher, Nigel Quashie (43 Kris Boyd), James McFadden (21 Graham Alexander), Paul Hartley (88 Scott Severin), Kenny Miller. Trainer: Walter Smith

Goals: Dailly (46), Miller (62), Miceika (85)

ITALY v LITHUANIA 1-1 (1-1)

San Paolo, Napoli 02.09.2006

Referee: Martin Hansson (SWE) Attendance: 50,000

ITALY: Gianluigi Buffon, Massimo Oddo, Fabio Cannavaro, Andrea Barzagli, Fabio Grosso, Andrea Pirlo, Daniele De Rossi (61 Marco Marchionni), Gennaro Gattuso, Simone Perrotta (72 Alberto Gilardino), Antonio Cassano, Filippo Inzaghi (86 David Di Michele). Trainer: Roberto Donadoni

LITHUANIA: Zydrunas Karčemarskas, Marius Stankevičius, Rolandas Džiaukštas, Andrius Skerla, Aidas Preikšaitis, Tomas Žvirgždauskas, Mantas Savenas (65 Mindaugas Kalonas), Saulius Mikoliunas (82 Tomas Tamošaukas), Deividas Česnauskis, Robertas Poškus (79 Tadas Labukas), Tomas Danilevičius. Trainer: Algimantas Liubinskas

Goals: Danilevičius (21), Inzaghi (30)

FRANCE v ITALY 3-1 (2-1)

Stade de France, Paris 06.09.2006

Referee: Herbert Fandel (GER) Attendance: 78,800

FRANCE: Grégory Coupet, Willy Sagnol, William Gallas, Lilian Thuram, Éric Abidal, Franck Ribéry (88 Louis Saha), Patrick Vieira, Claude Makélélé, Florent Malouda, Sidney Govou (75 Sylvain Wiltord), Thierry Henry. Trainer: Raymond Domenech

ITALY: Gianluigi Buffon, Gianluca Zambrotta, Fabio Cannavaro, Andrea Barzagli, Fabio Grosso, Franco Semioli (54 David Di Michele), Andrea Pirlo, Gennaro Gattuso, Simone Perrotta, Antonio Cassano (73 Filippo Inzaghi), Alberto Gilardino (87 Daniele De Rossi). Trainer: Roberto Donadoni

Goals: Govou (2, 55), Henry (18), Gilardino (20)

UKRAINE v GEORGIA 3-2 (1-1)

Olyimpiyskiy, Kiev 06.09.2006

Referee: Jaroslav Jára (CZE) Attendance: 25,000

UKRAINE: Olexandr Shovkovskiy, Andriy Nesmachniy, Andriy Rusol, Anatoliy Tymoschuk, Ruslan Rotan, Oleh Shelayev, Oleh Gusev, Serhiy Rebrov (57 Andriy Voronin), Andriy Gusin (46 Volodymyr Yezerskiy), Serhiy Tkachenko (63 Andriy Vorobey), Andriy Shevchenko. Trainer: Oleh Blokhin

GEORGIA: Grigol Chanturia, Levan Kobiashvili, Malkhaz Asatiani, Zurab Khizanishvili, David Imedashvili (35 Ilia Kandelaki), Jaba Kankava, Gogita Gogua, David Kvirkvelia (85 David Mujiri), Zurab Menteshashvili (81 Mikheil Ashvetia), Giorgi Demetradze, Shota Arveladze. Trainer: Klaus Toppmöller

Goals: Shevchenko (31), Arveladze (38), Demetradze (61), Rotan (61), Rusol (80)

FAROE ISLANDS v LITHUANIA 0-1 (0-0)

Tórsvøllur, Torshavn 07.10.2006

Referee: Anthony Buttimer (IRL) Attendance: 2,000

FAROE ISLANDS: Jákup Mikkelsen, Vagnur Mortensen, Atli Danielsen, Mikkjal Thomassen, Fródi Benjaminsen, Pauli Hansen (90 Arnbjørn Hansen), Jákup á Borg, Marni Djurhuus, Símun Samuelsen (73 Jónhard Frederiksberg), Rógvi Jacobsen (81 Kári Nielsen), Christian Høgni Jacobsen. Trainer: Jøgvan Martin Olsen

LITHUANIA: Zydrunas Karčemarskas, Marius Stankevičius, Gediminas Paulauskas, Andrius Skerla, Tomas Žvirgždauskas, Mantas Savenas (46 Mindaugas Kalonas), Darius Miceika, Deividas Česnauskis, Saulius Mikoliunas (62 Vitalijus Kavaliauskas), Tomas Danilevičius, Robertas Poškus (70 Ricardas Beniušis). Trainer: Algimantas Liubinskas

Goal: Skerla (89)

SCOTLAND v FRANCE 1-0 (0-0)

Hampden Park, Glasgow 07.10.2006

Referee: Massimo Busacca (SWI) Attendance: 50,500

SCOTLAND: Craig Gordon, Christian Dailly, Steven Pressley, David Weir, Graham Alexander, Darren Fletcher, Barry Ferguson, Gary Caldwell, Paul Hartley, Lee McCulloch (58 Gary Stewart Teale), James McFadden (72 Gary O'Connor). Trainer: Walter Smith

FRANCE: Grégory Coupet, Éric Abidal, Lilian Thuram, Jean-Alain Boumsong, Willy Sagnol, Franck Ribéry (74 Sylvain Wiltord), Patrick Vieira, Claude Makélélé, Florent Malouda, David Trezeguet (62 Louis Saha), Thierry Henry. Trainer: Raymond Domenech

Goal: Caldwell (67)

ITALY v UKRAINE 2-0 (0-0)

Stadio Olimpico, Roma 07.10.2006

Referee: Kyros Vassaras (GRE) Attendance: 49,100

ITALY: Gianluigi Buffon, Massimo Oddo, Fabio Cannavaro, Marco Materazzi, Gianluca Zambrotta, Gennaro Gattuso, Andrea Pirlo, Daniele De Rossi, Vincenzo Iaquinta (76 Mauro Camoranesi), Luca Toni (85 Filippo Inzaghi), Alessandro Del Piero (62 Antonio Di Natale). Trainer: Roberto Donadoni

UKRAINE: Olexandr Shovkovskiy, Andriy Rusol, Bohdan Shershun, Volodymyr Yezerskiy, Andriy Nesmachniy, Serhiy Nazarenko (59 Maxym Kalynychenko), Oleh Gusev, Oleh Shelayev, Anatoliy Tymoschuk, Andriy Vorobey (73 Artem Milevskiy), Andriy Voronin. Trainer: Oleh Blokhin

Goals: Oddo (71 pen), Toni (79)

UKRAINE v SCOTLAND 2-0 (0-0)

NSC Olympiyskiy, Kiev 11.10.2006

Referee: Martin Hansson (SWE) Attendance: 55,000

UKRAINE: Olexandr Shovkovskiy, Andriy Nesmachniy, Vyacheslav Sviderskiy, Olexandr Kucher, Andriy Rusol, Anatoliy Tymoschuk, Oleh Shelayev, Oleh Gusev (62 Artem Milevskiy), Maxym Kalynychenko (76 Andriy Vorobey), Andriy Shevchenko, Andriy Voronin (90 Bohdan Shershun). Trainer: Oleh Blokhin

SCOTLAND: Craig Gordon, Robbie Neilson (86 Stephen McManus), David Weir, Steven Pressley, Graham Alexander, Gary Caldwell, Barry Ferguson, Darren Fletcher, Paul Hartley, Kenny Miller, James McFadden (73 Kris Boyd). Trainer: Walter Smith

Sent off: Steven Pressley (86)

Goals: Kucher (60), Shevchenko (90 pen)

FRANCE v FAROE ISLANDS 5-0 (1-0)

Bonal, Sochaux-Montbéliard 11.10.2006

Referee: Sorin Corpodean (ROM) Attendance: 19,300

FRANCE: Mickaël Landreau, Willy Sagnol (79 François Clerc), William Gallas, Lilian Thuram, Julien Escudé, Franck Ribéry, Patrick Vieira, Jérémy Toulalan, Florent Malouda, Louis Saha (61 David Trezeguet), Thierry Henry (61 Nicolas Anelka). Trainer: Raymond Domenech

FAROE ISLANDS: Jákup Mikkelsen, Marni Djurhuus, Vagnur Mortensen, Atli Danielsen, Símun Samuelsen, Rógvi Jacobsen, Fródi Benjaminsen, Mikkjal Thomassen, Jákup á Borg (87 Jonhard Frederiksberg), Christian Høgni Jacobsen, Pauli Hansen (47 Kári Nielsen). Trainer: Jøgvan Martin Olsen

Goals: Saha (1), Henry (22), Anelka (77), Trezeguet (78, 84)

GEORGIA v ITALY 1-3 (1-1)

Boris Paichadze, Tbilisi 11.10.2006

Referee: Michael Riley (ENG) Attendance: 50,000

GEORGIA: Giorgi Lomaia, Zurab Khizanishvili, Otar Khizaneishvili, Kakha Kaladze, Giorgi Shashiashvili, Jaba Kankava, Levan Tskitishvili (74 Ilia Kandelaki), Zurab Menteshashvili, Otar Martsvaladze (85 Vasil Gigiadze), David Kvirkvelia, 32 Mikheil Ashvetia (70 Aleksandr Iashvili). Trainer: Klaus Toppmöller

ITALY: Gianluigi Buffon, Massimo Oddo, Fabio Cannavaro (74 Marco Materazzi), Alessandro Nesta, Andrea Pirlo (64 Stefano Mauri), Daniele De Rossi, Simone Perrotta, Gianluca Zambrotta, Mauro Camoranesi (87 Vincenzo Iaquinta), Luca Toni, Antonio Di Natale. Trainer: Roberto Donadoni

Sent off: Jaba Kankava (60)

Goals: De Rossi (18), Shashiashvili (26), Camoranesi (63), Perrotta (71)

SCOTLAND v GEORGIA 2-1 (1-1)

Hampden Park, Glasgow 24.03.2007

Referee: Nicolai Vollquartz (DEN) Attendance: 50,900

SCOTLAND: Craig Gordon, Graham Alexander, David Weir, Stephen McManus, Gary Naysmith, Gary Stewart Teale (60 Scott Brown), Barry Ferguson, Paul Hartley, Lee McCulloch, Kenny Miller (90 Shaun Maloney), Kris Boyd (76 Craig Beattie). Trainer: Alexander McLeish

GEORGIA: Giorgi Lomaia, Giorgi Shashiashvili, Zurab Khizanishvili, Lasha Salukvadze, Zaal Eliava, Vladimer Burduli (57 David Siradze), Levan Tskitishvili (90 David Mujiri), Zurab Menteshashvili (46 Gogita Gogua), Levan Kobiashvili, Giorgi Demetradze, Shota Arveladze. Trainer: Klaus Toppmöller

Goals: Boyd (11), Arveladze (41), Beattie (87)

FAROE ISLANDS v UKRAINE 0-2 (0-1)

Toftir, Toftir 24.03.2007

Referee: Damir Skomina (SVN) Attendance: 717

FAROE ISLANDS: Jákup Mikkelsen, Súni Olsen (74 Tem Hansen), Marni Djurhuus, Atli Danielsen, Simun Samuelsen (66 Christian Lamhauge Holst), Rógvi Jacobsen, Fródi Benjaminsen, Mikkjal Thomassen (78 Sámal Joensen), Jákup á Borg, Christian Høgni Jacobsen, Óli Johannesen.
Trainer: Jógvan Martin Olsen

UKRAINE: Olexandr Shovkovskiy, Volodymyr Yezerskiy, Dmytro Chygrynskiy, Andriy Rusol, Andriy Nesmachniy, Oleh Gusev (60 Andriy Vorobey), Anatoliy Tymoschuk (82 Oleh Shelayev), Taras Mikhalik, Maxym Kalynychenko, Olexiy Bielik, Andriy Voronin (75 Serhiy Nazarenko).
Trainer: Oleh Blokhin

Goals: Yezerskiy (20), Gusev (57)

GEORGIA v FAROE ISLANDS 3-1 (1-0)

Boris Paichadze, Tbilisi 28.03.2007

Referee: Pavel Saliy (KAZ) Attendance: 15,000

GEORGIA: Giorgi Lomaia, David Kvirkvelia, Levan Tskitishvili, Aleksandr Iashvili, Levan Kobiashvili (61 Zurab Mentesashvili), David Mujiri, Jaba Kankava, Lasha Salukvadze, Giorgi Demetradze, Giorgi Shashiashvili, David Siradze.
Trainer: Klaus Toppmöller

FAROE ISLANDS: Jákup Mikkelsen, Súni Olsen, Marni Djurhuus, Atli Danielsen, Rógvi Jacobsen, Fródi Benjaminsen, Mikkjal Thomassen, Jákup á Borg (86 Simun Samuelsen), Christian Høgni Jacobsen, Andrew av Fløtum (43 Christian Lamhauge Holst), Óli Johannesen.
Trainer: Jógvan Martin Olsen

Sent off: Frodi Benjaminsen (63)

Goals: Siradze (26), Iashvili (46, 90 pen), Rog. Jacobsen (57)

LITHUANIA v FRANCE 0-1 (0-0)

S. Darius & S. Girenas, Kaunas 24.03.2007

Referee: Howard Webb (ENG) Attendance: 8,000

LITHUANIA: Zydrunas Karčemarskas, Arunas Klimavicius, Andrius Skerla, Tomas Žvirgždauskas, Gediminas Paulauskas, Deividas Šemberas, Igoris Morinas (82 Ricardas Beniušis), Mantas Savenas (77 Mindaugas Kalonas), Marius Stankevičius, Robertas Poškus (86 Tomas Radzinevičius), Tomas Danilevičius. Trainer: Algimantas Liubinskas

FRANCE: Grégory Coupet, Willy Sagnol, Lilian Thuram, William Gallas, Éric Abidal, Florent Malouda (89 Abou Diaby), Claude Makélélé, Jérémy Toulalan, Lassana Diarra, Sidney Govou (62 Djibril Cissé), Nicolas Anelka.
Trainer: Raymond Domenech

Goal: Anelka (73)

ITALY v SCOTLAND 2-0 (1-0)

San Nicola, Bari 28.03.2007

Referee: Frank De Bleeckere (BEL) Attendance: 37,500

ITALY: Gianluigi Buffon, Massimo Oddo, Fabio Cannavaro, Marco Materazzi, Gianluca Zambrotta, Gennaro Gattuso, Daniele De Rossi, Mauro Camoranesi, Simone Perrotta (77 Andrea Pirlo), Antonio Di Natale (66 Alessandro Del Piero), Luca Toni (87 Fabio Quagliarella).
Trainer: Roberto Donadoni

SCOTLAND: Craig Gordon, Graham Alexander, Gary Naysmith, David Weir, Stephen McManus, Barry Ferguson, Gary Stewart Teale (66 Shaun Maloney), Paul Hartley, Scott Brown (86 Craig Beattie), Lee McCulloch (81 Kris Boyd), Kenny Miller. Trainer: Alexander McLeish

Goals: Toni (12, 70)

UKRAINE v LITHUANIA 1-0 (0-0)

Chornomorets, Odessa 28.03.2007

Referee: Florian Meyer (GER) Attendance: 28,000

UKRAINE: Olexandr Shovkovskiy, Andriy Nesmachniy, Olexandr Kucher, Volodymyr Yezerskiy, Andriy Rusol, Oleh Gusev (79 Andriy Vorobey), Anatoliy Tymoschuk, Maxym Kalynychenko (82 Dmytro Chygrynskiy), Taras Mikhalik (70 Oleh Shelayev), Andriy Shevchenko, Andriy Voronin.
Trainer: Oleh Blokhin

LITHUANIA: Paulius Grybauskas, Deividas Šemberas, Arunas Klimavičius, Gediminas Paulauskas, Marius Stankevičius, Andrius Skerla, Tomas Žvirgždauskas, Mantas Savenas (51 Mindaugas Kalonas), Igoris Morinas (56 Andrius Gedgaudas), Robertas Poškus (64 Tomas Radzinevičius), Tomas Danilevičius. Trainer: Algimantas Liubinskas

Goal: Gusev (47)

FAROE ISLANDS v ITALY 1-2 (0-1)

Tórsvøllur, Torshavn 02.06.2007

Referee: Robert Malek (POL) Attendance: 5,987

FAROE ISLANDS: Jákup Mikkelsen, Atli Danielsen, Marni Djurhuus, Jón Rói Jacobsen, Óli Johannesen, Jákup á Borg (73 Simun Samuelsen), Mikkjal Thomassen, Súni Olsen, Christian Høgni Jacobsen, Rógvi Jacobsen, Andrew av Fløtum (56 Christian Lamhauge Holst). Trainer: Jógvan Martin Olsen

ITALY: Gianluigi Buffon, Massimo Oddo, Max Tonetto, Fabio Cannavaro, Marco Materazzi (66 Andrea Barzagli), Aimo Diana, Gennaro Gattuso, Andrea Pirlo, Alessandro Del Piero, Tommaso Rocchi (86 Fabio Quagliarella), Filippo Inzaghi (58 Cristiano Lucarelli). Trainer: Roberto Donadoni

Goals: Inzaghi (12, 48), Róg. Jacobsen (77)

LITHUANIA v GEORGIA 1-0 (0-0)

S. Darius & S. Girenas, Kaunas 02.06.2007

Referee: Claudio Circhetta (SWI) Attendance: 6,000

LITHUANIA: Zydrunas Karčemarskas, Deividas Šemberas, Marius Stankevičius, Andrius Skerla, Tomas Žvirgždauskas, Arunas Klimavicius, Gediminas Paulauskas, Mantas Savenas (55 Mindaugas Kalonas), Igoris Morinas (62 Saulius Mikoliunas), Ričardas Beniušis (75 Tadas Labukas), Tomas Danilevičius. Trainer: Algimantas Liubinskas

GEORGIA: Giorgi Lomaia, Otar Khizaneishvili, Kakha Kaladze, Zaal Eliava, Levan Kobiashvili, Zurab Khizanishvili, Levan Tskitishvili (80 David Mujiri), Zurab Menteshashvili (64 Otar Martsvaladze), David Kvirkvelia, Aleksandr Iashvili, Giorgi Demetradze. Trainer: Klaus Toppmöller

Goal: Mikoliunas (78)

FRANCE v UKRAINE 2-0 (0-0)

Stade de France, Paris 02.06.2007

Referee: Luis Medina Cantalejo (SPA) Attendance: 80,051

FRANCE: Grégory Coupet, Éric Abidal, William Gallas, François Clerc, Lilian Thuram, Claude Makélélé, Florent Malouda, Jérémy Toulalan, Samir Nasri (81 Lassana Diarra), Franck Ribéry, Nicolas Anelka (77 Djibril Cissé). Trainer: Raymond Domenech

UKRAINE: Olexandr Shovkovskiy, Andriy Nesmachniy, Volodymyr Yezerskiy (78 Evgen Levchenko), Andriy Rusol, Dmytro Chygrynskiy, Olexiy Gay, Anatoliy Tymoschuk, Oleh Gusev, Taras Mikhalik, Maxym Kalynychenko (64 Ruslan Rotan), Andriy Voronin (72 Andriy Vorobey). Trainer: Oleh Blokhin

Goals: Ribéry (57), Anelka (71)

FAROE ISLANDS v SCOTLAND 0-2 (0-2)

Toftir, Toftir 06.06.2007

Referee: Giorgos Kasnaferis (GRE) Attendance: 4,600

FAROE ISLANDS: Jákup Mikkelsen, Atli Danielsen, Jón Rói Jacobsen, Óli Johannesen (36 Marni Djurhuus, 77 Simun Samuelsen), Fródi Benjaminsen, Mikkjal Thomassen, Jákup á Borg (82 Andrew av Fløtum), Súni Olsen, Rógvi Jacobsen, Christian Høgni Jacobsen, Christian Lamhauge Holst. Trainer: Jógvan Martin Olsen

SCOTLAND: Craig Gordon, Graham Alexander, David Weir, Stephen McManus, Gary Naysmith, Paul Hartley, Barry Ferguson, Darren Fletcher (68 Gary Stewart Teale), Shaun Maloney (77 Charles Adam), Garry O'Connor, Kris Boyd (83 Steven Naismith). Trainer: Alexander McLeish

Goals: Maloney (31), O'Connor (35)

FRANCE v GEORGIA 1-0 (1-0)

Abbé-Deschamps, Auxerre 06.06.2007

Referee: Lucilio Cardoso Cortez Batista (POR) Att: 21,000

FRANCE: Mickaël Landreau, Éric Abidal, François Clerc, William Gallas, Claude Makélélé, Florent Malouda (65 Djibril Cissé), Samir Nasri, Franck Ribéry (90 Sidney Govou), Lilian Thuram, Jérémy Toulalan, Nicolas Anelka (89 Karim Benzema). Trainer: Raymond Domenech

GEORGIA: Giorgi Lomaia, Otar Khizaneishvili, Kakha Kaladze, Zurab Khizanishvili, Mate Ghvinianidze, Lasha Salukvadze (12 David Mujiri), Zaal Eliava (62 Otar Martsvaladze), David Kvirkvelia, Jaba Kankava (85 Giorgi Shashiashvili), Vladimer Burduli, Aleksandr Iashvili. Trainer: Klaus Toppmöller

Goal: Nasri (33)

LITHUANIA v ITALY 0-2 (0-2)

S. Darius & S. Girenas, Kaunas 06.06.2007

Referee: Pieter Vink (HOL) Attendance: 7,000

LITHUANIA: Paulius Grybauskas, Deividas Šemberas, Marius Stankevičius, Andrius Skerla, Tomas Žvirgždauskas, Arunas Klimavčius, Gediminas Paulauskas (46 Andrius Gedgaudas), Mantas Savenas (61 Tadas Labukas), Mindaugas Kalonas, Igoris Morinas (39 Saulius Mikoliunas), Tomas Danilevičius. Trainer: Algimantas Liubinskas

ITALY: Gianluigi Buffon, Massimo Oddo, Fabio Cannavaro, Marco Materazzi, Gianluca Zambrotta, Andrea Pirlo, Daniele De Rossi (65 Gennaro Gattuso), Simone Perrotta (71 Massimo Ambrosini), Fabio Quagliarella, Filippo Inzaghi, Antonio Di Natale (74 Alessandro Del Piero). Trainer: Roberto Donadoni

Goals: Quagliarella (31, 45)

SCOTLAND v LITHUANIA 3-1 (1-0)

Hampden Park, Glasgow 08.09.2007

Referee: Damir Skomina (SVN) Attendance: 51,000

SCOTLAND: Craig Gordon, Alan Hutton, David Weir, Stephen McManus, James McEveley, Gary Stewart Teale (69 James McFadden), Scott Brown, Darren Fletcher, Lee McCulloch (76 Shaun Maloney), Kris Boyd, Garry O'Connor (76 Craig Beattie). Trainer: Alexander McLeish

LITHUANIA: Zydrunas Karčemarskas, Marius Stankevičius (56 Edgaras Jankauskas), Andrius Skerla, Tomas Žvirgždauskas, Arunas Klimavicius, Deividas Šemberas, Mindaugas Kalonas, Deividas Česnauskis, Igoris Morinas (46 Saulius Mikoliunas), Tomas Danilevičius, Andrius Velicka (46 Audrius Ksanavicius). Trainer: Algimantas Liubinskas

Goals: Boyd (31), Danilevičius (61 pen), McManus (77), McFadden (83)

GEORGIA v UKRAINE 1-1 (0-1)

Boris Paichadze, Tbilisi 08.09.2007

Referee: Alain Hamer (LUX) Attendance: 25,000

GEORGIA: Giorgi Lomaia, Mate Ghvinianidze, Kakha Kaladze, Malkhaz Asatiani, Lasha Salukvadze, Levan Tskitishvili, Zurab Menteshashvili (79 Dimitri Tatanashvili), Lasha Jakobia (62 David Siradze), Giorgi Demetradze, Aleksandr Iashvili (62 Levan Kenia), Otar Martsvaladze. Trainer: Klaus Toppmöller

UKRAINE: Olexandr Shovkovskiy, Volodymyr Yezerskiy, Andriy Rusol, Olexandr Kucher, Anatoliy Tymoschuk, Ruslan Rotan (80 Olexiy Gay), Serhiy Nazarenko, Oleh Gusev, Oleh Shelayev (90 Olexander Gladkiy), Andriy Shevchenko, Andriy Voronin (72 Maxym Kalynychenko). Trainer: Oleh Blokhin

Goals: Shelayev (9), Siradze (89)

ITALY v FRANCE 0-0

Stadio Giuseppe Meazza, Milano 08.09.2007

Referee: Luboš Michel (SVK) Attendance: 80,000

ITALY: Gianluigi Buffon, Massimo Oddo, Fabio Cannavaro, Andrea Barzagli, Gianluca Zambrotta, Daniele De Rossi, Gennaro Gattuso, Andrea Pirlo, Mauro Camoranesi (58 Simone Perrotta), Alessandro Del Piero (83 Antonio Di Natale), Filippo Inzaghi (65 Cristiano Lucarelli). Trainer: Roberto Donadoni

FRANCE: Mickaël Landreau, Lassana Diarra, Lilian Thuram, Julien Escudé, Éric Abidal, Franck Ribéry (86 Jeremy Toulalan), Claude Makélélé, Patrick Vieira, Florent Malouda, Thierry Henry, Nicolas Anelka. Trainer: Pierre Mankowski

LITHUANIA v FAROE ISLANDS 2-1 (1-0)

S. Darius & S. Girenas, Kaunas 12.09.2007

Referee: Tsvetan Georgiev (BUL) Attendance: 4,000

LITHUANIA: Zydrunas Karčemarskas, Deividas Šemberas, Arunas Klimavicius, Andrius Skerla, Vidas Alunderis, Kestutis Ivaskevicius, Saulius Mikoliunas (32 Andrius Velicka), Deividas Česnauskis (31 Mindaugas Kalonas), Audrius Ksanavicius, Edgaras Jankauskas (83 Aurimas Kucys), Tomas Danilevičius. Trainer: Algimantas Liubinskas

FAROE ISLANDS: Jákup Mikkelsen, Fródi Benjaminsen, Atli Danielsen, Christian Lamhauge Holst (74 Hans Pauli Samuelsen), Jón Jacobsen, Mikkjal Thomassen, Símun Samuelsen, Christian Høgni Jacobsen (81 Andrew Fløtum), Súni Olsen (63 Pauli Hansen), Jákup á Borg, Rógvi Jacobsen. Trainer: Jógvan Martin Olsen

Goals: Jankauskas (8), Danilevičius (53), Róg. Jacobsen (90)

FRANCE v SCOTLAND 0-1 (0-0)

Parc des Princes, Paris 12.09.2007

Referee: Konrad Plautz (AUS) Attendance: 42,000

FRANCE: Mickaël Landreau, Lassana Diarra, Lilian Thuram, Julien Escudé, Éric Abidal (77 Karim Benzema), Franck Ribéry, Patrick Vieira (69 Samir Nasri), Claude Makélélé, Florent Malouda, David Trezeguet, Nicolas Anelka. Trainer: Raymond Domenech

SCOTLAND: Craig Gordon, Alan Hutton, Stephen McManus, David Weir, Graham Alexander, Lee McCulloch, Barry Ferguson, Darren Fletcher (26 Stephen Pearson), Scott Brown, Paul Hartley, James McFadden (76 Garry O'Connor). Trainer: Alexander McLeish

Goal: McFadden (64)

UKRAINE v ITALY 1-2 (0-1)

NSC Olympiyskiy Stadium, Kiev 12.09.2007

Referee: Howard Webb (ENG) Attendance: 42,000

UKRAINE: Olexandr Shovkovskiy, Olexandr Kucher, Volodymyr Yezerskiy, Andriy Rusol, Oleh Shelayev, Oleh Gusev (88 Artem Milevskiy), Maxym Kalynychenko (60 Andriy Voronin), Anatoliy Tymoschuk, Olexiy Gay, Serhiy Nazarenko (69 Olexandr Gladkiy), Andriy Shevchenko. Trainer: Oleh Blokhin

ITALY: Gianluigi Buffon, Christian Panucci, Fabio Cannavaro, Andrea Barzagli, Gianluca Zambrotta, Mauro Camoranesi (78 Massimo Oddo), Massimo Ambrosini, Andrea Pirlo, Simone Perrotta (68 Alberto Aquilani), Vincenzo Iaquinta (85 Fabio Quagliarella), Antonio Di Natale. Trainer: Roberto Donadoni

Goals: Di Natale (41, 77), Shevchenko (71)

SCOTLAND v UKRAINE 3-1 (2-1)

Hampden Park, Glasgow 13.10.2007

Referee: Pieter Vink (HOL) Attendance: 51,400

SCOTLAND: Craig Gordon, Alan Hutton, David Weir, Stephen McManus, Gary Naysmith, Scott Brown (76 Shaun Maloney), Barry Ferguson, Stephen Pearson, Lee McCulloch (60 Christian Dailly), James McFadden (80 Garry O'Connor), Kenny Miller. Trainer: Alexander McLeish

UKRAINE: Olexandr Shovkovskiy, Andriy Nesmachniy, Volodymyr Yezerskiy, Dmytro Chygrynskiy, Olexandr Kucher, Oleh Gusev (46 Ruslan Rotan), Anatoliy Tymoschuk (73 Oleh Shelayev), Olexandr Gladkiy, Andriy Vorobey (62 Serhiy Nazarenko), Andriy Shevchenko, Andriy Voronin. Trainer: Oleh Blokhin

Goals: K. Miller (4), McCulloch (10), Shevchenko (24), McFadden (68)

FAROE ISLANDS v FRANCE 0-6 (0-2)

Tórsvøllur, Torshavn 13.10.2007

Referee: Gabriele Rossi (SMR) Attendance: 8,100

FAROE ISLANDS: Jákup Mikkelsen, Christian Jacobsen, Jón Rói Jacobsen, Fródi Benjaminsen, Einar Hansen, Símun Samuelsen (84 Andrew Fløtum), Súni Olsen, Mikkjal Thomassen (78 Rokur Jespersen), Hjalgrím Elttør (46 Bergur Midjord), Rógvi Jacobsen, Christian Lamhauge Holst.
Trainer: Jógvan Martin Olsen

FRANCE: Mickaël Landreau, Bacary Sagna, Éric Abidal, Lilian Thuram, Patrice Evra, Jérôme Rothen, Claude Makélélé (73 Lassana Diarra), Jérémy Toulalan, Franck Ribéry (64 Hatem Ben Arfa), Nicolas Anelka (46 Karim Benzema), Thierry Henry. Trainer: Raymond Domenech

Goals: Anelka (6), Henry (8), Benzema (50), Rothen (66), Benzema (80), Ben Arfa (90)

FRANCE v LITHUANIA 2-0 (0-0)

La Beaujoire, Nantes 17.10.2007

Referee: Viktor Kassai (HUN) Attendance: 36,400

FRANCE: Mickaël Landreau, Lassana Diarra (69 Hatem Ben Arfa), Lilian Thuram, William Gallas, Éric Abidal, Jérémy Toulalan, Claude Makélélé, Florent Malouda, Franck Ribéry, Thierry Henry, Karim Benzema.
Trainer: Raymond Domenech

LITHUANIA: Zydrunas Karčemarskas, Arunas Klimavicius, Ignas Dedura, Andrius Skerla, Tomas Žvirgždauskas, Aurimas Kucys (84 Andrius Velicka), Audrius Ksanavičius (77 Tadas Labukas), Mindaugas Kalonas (63 Mantas Savenas), Igoris Morinas, Tomas Danilevičius, Edgaras Jankauskas.
Trainer: Algimantas Liubinskas

Goals: Henry (80, 81)

ITALY v GEORGIA 2-0 (1-0)

Luigi Ferraris, Genova 13.10.2007

Referee: Carlos Megía Dávila (SPA) Attendance: 23,100

ITALY: Gianluigi Buffon, Massimo Oddo, Christian Panucci, Andrea Barzagli, Fabio Grosso, Andrea Pirlo, Gennaro Gattuso, Massimo Ambrosini (88 Stefano Mauri), Fabio Quagliarella (72 Pasquale Foggia), Antonio Di Natale, Luca Toni.
Trainer: Roberto Donadoni

GEORGIA: Giorgi Lomaia, Georgi Shashiashvili (60 David Siradze), Lasha Salukvadze, Malkhaz Asatiani, Zurab Khizanishvili, David Kvirkvelia, Levan Tskitishvili, Zurab Menteshashvili, Jaba Kankava, Levan Mchedlidze (60 Levan Kenia), Giorgi Demetradze (85 Lasha Jakobia).
Trainer: Klaus Toppmöller

Goals: Pirlo (44), Grosso (84)

UKRAINE v FAROE ISLANDS 5-0 (3-0)

NSC Olympiyskiy Stadium, Kiev 17.10.2007

Referee: Haim Jakov (ISR) Attendance: 3,000

UKRAINE: Andriy Pyatov, Andriy Nesmachniy, Andriy Rusol, Dmytro Chygrynskiy, Olexiy Gai, Serhiy Nazarenko, Anatoliy Tymoschuk (69 Olexandr Grytsay), Oleh Gusev (62 Andriy Vorobey), Maxym Kalynychenko, Olexandr Gladkiy (46 Artem Milevskiy), Andriy Voronin.
Trainer: Oleh Blokhin

FAROE ISLANDS: Jákup Mikkelsen, Atli Danielsen, Einar Hansen, Óli Hansen, Jón Rói Jacobsen, Jóhan Davidsen, Mikkjal Thomassen (8 Tem Hansen), Christian Lamhauge Holst (75 Andrew av Fløtum), Christian Høgni Jacobsen (89 Hanus Thorleifson), Símun Samuelsen, Rógvi Jacobsen.
Trainer: Jógvan Martin Olsen

Goals: Kalynychenko (40, 49), Gusev (43,45), Vorobey (64)

GEORGIA v SCOTLAND 2-0 (1-0)

Boris Paichadze, Tbilisi 17.10.2007

Referee: Knut Kircher (GER) Attendance: 55,500

GEORGIA: Giorgi Makaridze, Georgi Shashiashvili, Malkhaz Asatiani, Lasha Salukvadze, Zurab Khizanishvili, Jaba Kankava, Zurab Menteshashvili, Levan Kenia (79 Ilia Kandelaki), David Kvirkvelia, David Siradze (89 Lasha Jakobia), Levan Mchedlidze (85 Alexandre Kvakhadze).
Trainer: Klaus Toppmöller

SCOTLAND: Craig Gordon, Greame Murty, Stephen McManus, David Weir, Graham Alexander, Darren Fletcher, Barry Ferguson, Stephen Pearson (66 Kris Boyd), Shaun Maloney, Kenny Miller (66 Craig Beattie), James McFadden.
Trainer: Alexander McLeish

Goals: Mchedlidze (16), Siradze (64)

SCOTLAND v ITALY 1-2 (0-1)

Hampden Park, Glasgow 17.11.2007

Referee: Manuel Mejuto González (SPA) Att: 53,300

SCOTLAND: Craig Gordon, Alan Hutton, David Weir, Stephen McManus, Gary Naysmith, Scott Brown (74 Kenny Miller), Darren Fletcher, Paul Hartley, Barry Ferguson, Lee McCulloch (90 Kris Boyd), James McFadden.
Trainer: Alexander McLeish

ITALY: Gianluigi Buffon, Christian Panucci, Fabio Cannavaro, Andrea Barzagli, Gianluca Zambrotta, Mauro Camoranesi (82 Giorgio Chiellini), Gennaro Gattuso (86 Daniele De Rossi), Andrea Pirlo, Massimo Ambrosini, Antonio Di Natale (68 Vincenzo Iaquinta), Luca Toni. Trainer: Roberto Donadoni

Goals: Toni (2), Ferguson (65), Panucci (89)

LITHUANIA v UKRAINE 2-0 (1-0)

S. Darius & S. Girenas, Kaunas 17.11.2007

Referee: David Malcolm (NIR) Attendance: 3,000

LITHUANIA: Zydrunas Karčemarskas, Gediminas Paulauskas, Arunas Klimavicius, Marius Stankevičius, Ignas Dedura, Andrius Skerla, Tomas Žvirgždauskas, Tadas Papeckys (17 Igoris Morinas), Mantas Savenas, Tomas Danilevičius (82 Andrius Velicka), Edgaras Jankauskas (90 Mindaugas Kalonas). Trainer: Algimantas Liubinskas

UKRAINE: Olexandr Shovkovskiy (44 Andriy Pyatov), Dmytro Chygrynskiy, Vladyslav Vaschuk, Oleh Shelayev (72 Serhiy Nazarenko), Volodymyr Yezerskiy, Olexiy Gai, Anatoliy Tymoschuk, Oleh Gusev, Ruslan Rotan, Andriy Shevchenko, Andriy Voronin (69 Artem Milevskiy). Trainer: Oleh Blokhin

Goals: Savenas (41), Danilevičius (67)

GEORGIA v LITHUANIA 0-2 (0-0)

Boris Paichadze, Tbilisi 21.11.2007

Referee: Aleksandar Stavrev (MKD)

GEORGIA: Giorgi Makaridze, Lasha Salukvadze, Malkhaz Asatiani, Kakha Kaladze, David Kvirkvelia, Jaba Kankava, Levan Tskitishvili, Zurab Menteshashvili (31 Otar Marsvaladze), Levan Kenia, Levan Mchedlidze, David Siradze (75 Nickolas Gelashvili). Trainer: Klaus Toppmöller

LITHUANIA: Žydrunas Karčemarskas, Marius Stankevičius, Tomas Žvirgždauskas, Andrius Skerla, Gediminas Paulauskas, Ignas Dedura, Vidas Alunderis, Audrius Ksanavičius, Mantas Savenas (67 Mindaugas Kalonas), Saulius Mikoliunas (76 Igoris Morinas), Edgaras Jankauskas (52 Andrius Velicka). Trainer: Algimantas Liubinskas

Goals: Ksanavicius (52, 90)

ITALY v FAROE ISLANDS 3-1 (3-0)

Alberto Braglia, Modena 21.11.2007

Referee: Florian Meyer (GER) Attendance: 19,000

ITALY: Marco Amelia, Massimo Oddo, Fabio Cannavaro (53 Daniele Bonera), Giorgio Chiellini, Fabio Grosso, Daniele De Rossi, Massimo Ambrosini (58 Fabio Quagliarella), Simone Perrotta, Vincenzo Iaquinta, Raffaele Palladino, Luca Toni (74 Alberto Gilardino). Trainer: Roberto Donadoni

FAROE ISLANDS: Jákup Mikkelsen, Jóhan Davidsen, Fródi Benjaminsen, Jón Rói Jacobsen, Einar Hansen, Atli Danielsen, Súni Olsen, Rógvi Jacobsen, Símun Samuelsen (75 Hanus Thorleifson), Christian Høgni Jacobsen, Christian Lamhauge Holst (86 Andrew av Fløtum). Trainer: Jógvan Martin Olsen

Goals: Benjaminsen (11 own goal), Toni (36), Chiellini (41), Róg. Jacobsen (83)

UKRAINE v FRANCE 2-2 (1-2)

NSC Olympiyskiy Stadium, Kiev 21.11.2007

Referee: Tom Henning Øvrebø (NOR) Attendance: 30,000

UKRAINE: Andriy Pyatov, Vladyslav Vaschuk, Olexandr Grytsay, Olexandr Romanchuk (81 Volodymyr Yezerskiy), Serhiy Fedorov, Anatoliy Tymoschuk, Oleh Gusev (90 Artem Milevskiy), Ruslan Rotan, Olexiy Gai, Andriy Shevchenko, Andriy Voronin (84 Oleh Shelayev). Trainer: Oleh Blokhin

FRANCE: Sébastien Frey, François Clerc, William Gallas, Lilian Thuram, Éric Abidal, Franck Ribéry (89 Hatem Ben Arfa), Claude Makélélé, Lassana Diarra, Sidney Govou, Thierry Henry, Karim Benzema (46 Samir Nasri). Trainer: Raymond Domenech

Goals: Voronin (14), Henry (20), Govou (34), Shevchenko (46)

	P	W	D	L	F	A	Pts
Italy	12	9	2	1	22	9	29
France	12	8	2	2	25	5	26
Scotland	12	8	0	4	21	12	24
Ukraine	12	5	2	5	18	16	17
Lithuania	12	5	1	6	11	13	16
Georgia	12	3	1	8	16	19	10
Faroe Islands	12	0	0	12	4	43	0

GROUP 3

MALTA v BOSNIA-HERZEGOVINA 2-5 (1-3)

National, Ta' Qali 02.09.2006

Referee: Thomas Vejlgaard (DEN) Attendance: 5,000

MALTA: Justin Haber, Ian Ciantar (46 Ivan Woods), Ian Azzopardi, Brian Said, Luke Dimech, Gilbert Agius (82 Gareth Sciberras), Claude Mattocks (65 Peter Pullicino), Michael Mifsud, Andre Schembri, Jamie Pace, Kevin Sammut. Trainer: Dusan Fitzel

BOSNIA-HERZEGOVINA: Kenan Hasagić, Džemal Berberović, Vedin Musić, Emir Spahić, Zlatan Bajramović, Saša Papac (61 Ninoslav Milenković), Sergej Barbarez (66 Vladan Grujić), Zvjezdan Misimović, Zlatan Muslimović, Mirko Hrgović, Mladen Bartolović (53 Mirsad Bešlija). Trainer: Blaz Slišković

Goals: Barbarez (4), Pace (6), M. Hrgović (10), Bartolović (45), Muslimović (48), Misimović (50), Mifsud (85)

HUNGARY v NORWAY 1-4 (0-3)

Megyeri úti, Budapest 02.09.2006

Referee: Eric Braamhaar (HOL) Attendance: 15,000

HUNGARY: Gábor Király, Csaba Fehér, Zsolt Löw, Roland Juhász (66 Vilmos Vanczák), László Éger, Thomas Sowunmi (80 Sandor Torghelle), Balázs Molnár, Pál Dárdai, András Horváth (61 Zoltan Kiss), Zoltán Gera, Szabolcs Huszti. Trainer: Péter Bozsik

NORWAY: Thomas Myhre, Anders Rambekk, Erik Hagen, Brede Hangeland, Marius Johnson, Fredrik Strømstad (62 Daniel Omoya Braaten), Martin Andersen, Kristofer Hæstad (85 Tommy Svindal Larsen), Morten Gamst Pedersen, Ole Gunnar Solskjær, John Carew (76 Steffen Iversen). Trainer: Åge Hareide

Goals: Solskjær (15, 54), Strømstad (32), Gamst Pedersen (41), Gera (90 pen)

MOLDOVA v GREECE 0-1 (0-0)

Zimbru, Chişinău 02.09.2006

Referee: Matteo Trefoloni (ITA) Attendance: 8,000

MOLDOVA: Sergei Paşcenco, Serghei Laşcencov, Andrei Corneencov, Ivan Testimiţanu, Serghei Epureanu (65 Serghei Cleşcenco), Radu Rebeja, Serghei Covalciuc, Ghenadie Olexici, Victor Berco, Serghei Rogaciov (78 Serghei Dadu), Stanislav Ivanov. Trainer: Anatoli Teslev

GREECE: Antonios Nikopolidis, Giourkas Seitaridis, Panagiotis Fyssas, Traianos Dellas (89 Giorgos Anatolakis), Sotiris Kyrgiakos, Kostas Katsouranis, Angelos Basinas, Theodoros Zagorakis (46 Dimitris Salpingidis), Giorgos Karagounis, Angelos Charisteas (46 Nikos Liberopoulos), Ioannis Amanatidis. Trainer: Otto Rehhagel

Goal: Liberopoulos (77)

NORWAY v MOLDOVA 2-0 (0-0)

Ullevål, Oslo 06.09.2006

Referee: Hristo Ristoskov (BUL) Attendance: 23,900

NORWAY: Thomas Myhre, Erik Hagen, Brede Hangeland, Marius Johnsen (65 Steffen Iversen), Fredrik Strømstad (90 Tommy Svindal Larsen), Martin Andersen, Morten Gamst Pedersen, Anders Rambekk, Kristofer Hæstad, John Carew, Frode Johnsen (46 Ole Gunnar Solskjær). Trainer: Åge Hareide

MOLDOVA: Sergei Paşcenco, Serghei Laşcencov (77 Serghei Cleşcenco), Andrei Corneencov, Ivan Testimiţanu, Radu Rebeja, Alexandu Epureanu, Serghei Covalciuc, Stanislav Ivanov, Victor Berco, Serghei Rogaciov (72 Serghei Dadu), Ghenadie Olexici. Trainer: Anatoli Teslev

Sent off: Victor Berco (46)

Goals: Strømstad (73), Iversen (79)

TURKEY v MALTA 2-0 (0-0)

Commerzbank Arena, Frankfurt am Main 06.09.2006

Referee: Bernardino González Vázquez (SPA)
Attendance: Played behind closed doors

TURKEY: Rüştü Reçber, Mehmet Topuz, Can Arat, Gökhan Zan, Mehmet Aurelio, Fatih Tekke (46 Nihat Kahveci), Yildiray Baştürk (46 Arda Turan), Tümer Metin, Ergün Penbe, Hakan Şükür (81 Nuri Şahin), Hamit Altintop. Trainer: Fatih Terim

MALTA: Justin Haber, Ian Ciantar, Stephen Wellman, Brian Said, Luke Dimech, Gilbert Agius (87 Gareth Sciberras), Kevin Sammut (81 Peter Pullicino), Michael Mifsud, Ivan Woods, Andre Schembri (89 Terence Scerri), Jamie Pace. Trainer: Dušan Fitzel

Goals: Nihat (56), Tümer (77)

BOSNIA-HERZEGOVINA v HUNGARY 1-3 (0-1)

Bilino Polje, Zenica 06.09.2006

Referee: Costas Kapitanis (CYP) Attendance: 13,000

BOSNIA-HERZEGOVINA: Kenan Hasagić, Emir Spahić, Vedin Musić (46 Ninoslav Milenković), Saša Papac, Sergej Barbarez, Dušan Kerkez, Zlatan Bajramović, Mirko Hrgović (73 Mirsad Bešlija), Mladen Bartolović (63 Vule Trivunović), Zvjezdan Misimović, Elvir Bolić. Trainer: Blaz Slišković

HUNGARY: Gábor Király, Csaba Fehér (82 Zoltan Kiss), Zsolt Löw (65 Roland Juhász), Sándor Torghelle (90 Péter Kabát), László Éger, Balázs Tóth, Balázs Molnár, Pál Dárdai, Szabolcs Huszti, Zoltán Gera, Vilmos Vanczák. Trainer: Péter Bozsik

Sent off: Emir Spahic (39)

Goals: Huszti (36 pen), Gera (46), Dárdai (49), Misimović (64 pen)

MOLDOVA v BOSNIA-HERZEGOVINA 2-2 (2-0)

Zimbru, Chişinău 07.10.2006

Referee: Hervé Piccirillo (FRA) Attendance: 10,000

MOLDOVA: Serghei Paşcenco, Serghei Laşcencov, Valeriu Catînsus, Alexandru Gaţcan (90 Serghei Cleşcenco), Alexandru Epureanu, Ghenadie Olexici, Ivan Testimiţanu, Radu Rebeja, Stanislav Ivanov, Serghei Epureanu (72 Andrei Corneencov), Serghei Rogaciov (71 Serghei Dadu). Trainer: Anatoli Teslev

BOSNIA-HERZEGOVINA: Kenan Hasagić, Vule Trivunović, Saša Papac, Velimir Vidić, Dalibor Šilić, Zlatan Bajramović (77 Vladan Grujić), Mirko Hrgović (83 Sulejman Smajić), Sergej Barbarez, Zvjezdan Misimović, Dario Damjanović (46 Ivica Grlić), Mladen Bartolović. Trainer: Blaz Sliškovic

Goals: Rogaciov (13, 32 pen), Misimović (62), Grlić (68)

HUNGARY v TURKEY **0-1** (0-1)

Ferenc Puskás, Budapest 07.10.2006

Referee: Alain Hamer (LUX) Attendance: 6,500

HUNGARY: Gábor Király, Csaba Fehér, Vilmos Vanczák, Roland Juhász, László Éger, Balázs Tóth, Péter Halmosi (46 Peter Kabat, 76 Ádám Komlosi), Pál Dárdai, Sándor Torghelle (80 Imre Szabics), Zoltán Gera, Szabolcs Huszti. Trainer: Péter Bozsik

TURKEY: Rüştü Reçber, Hamit Altintop, Servet Çetin, Gökhan Zan, Mehmet Aurelio, Gökdeniz Karadeniz (63 Huseyin Çimşir), Arda Turan (88 Mehmet Topuz), Ibrahim Üzülmez, Sabri Sarioğlu, Tuncay Şanli (90 Can Arat), Hakan Şükür. Trainer: Fatih Terim

Goal: Tuncay (41)

GREECE v NORWAY **1-0** (1-0)

Giorgos Karaiskakis Stadium, Athens 07.10.2006

Referee: Luboš Michel (SVK) Attendance: 22,000

GREECE: Antonios Nikopolidis, Giourkas Seitaridis, Panagiotis Fyssas, Giorgos Anatolakis, Sotiris Kyrgiakos, Angelos Basinas, Kostas Katsouranis, Giorgos Karagounis (90 Christos Patsatzoglou), Stelios Giannakopoulos (46 Angelos Charisteas), Giorgos Samaras, Nikos Liberopoulos (71 Ioannis Amanatidis). Trainer: Otto Rehhagel

NORWAY: Thomas Myhre, Anders Rambekk (85 Ole Martin Årst), Erik Hagen, Brede Hangeland, John Arne Riise, Fredrik Strømstad (61 Daniel Omoya Braaten), Martin Andresen, Kristofer Hæstad, Morten Gamst Pedersen, Steffen Iversen, Ole Gunnar Solskjær. Trainer: Åge Hareide

Goal: Katsouranis (33)

MALTA v HUNGARY **2-1** (1-1)

National, Ta' Qali 11.10.2006

Referee: Johny Ver Eecke (BEL) Attendance: 5,000

MALTA: Justin Haber, Kenneth Scicluna, Stephen Wellman, Brian Said, Luke Dimech, George Mallia (64 Andrew Cohen), Kevin Sammut, Jamie Pace, Andre Schembri (72 Terence Scerri), Michael Mifsud, Gilbert Agius (82 Peter Pullicino). Trainer: Dušan Fitzel

HUNGARY: Gábor Király, Csaba Fehér (76 Peter Halmosi), Balázs Tóth, Roland Juhász, Vilmos Vanczák, Leandro de Almeida (46 Zoltan Kiss), Szabolcs Huszti, Pál Dárdai, Sándor Torghelle, Imre Szabics (60 Peter Czvitkovics), Zoltán Gera. Trainer: Péter Bozsik

Goals: Schembri (14, 53), Torghelle (19)

TURKEY v MOLDOVA **5-0** (3-0)

Commerzbank Arena, Frankfurt am Main 11.10.2006

Referee: Nicolai Vollquartz (DEN)
Attendance: Played behind closed doors

TURKEY: Rüştü Reçber, Servet Çetin, Hamit Altintop, Gökhan Zan, Mehmet Aurelio, Gökdeniz Karadeniz (60 Tümer Metin), Arda Turan (72 Nihat Kahveci), Ibrahim Üzülmez, Sabri Sarioğlu, Tuncay Şanli, Hakan Şükür (81 Halil Altintop). Trainer: Fatih Terim

MOLDOVA: Serghei Paşcenco, Alexandru Epureanu (46 Andrei Corneencov), Ivan Testimiţanu, Valeriu Catînsus, Ghenadie Olexici, Alexandru Gaţcan, Serghei Epureanu (63 Serghei Dadu), Serghei Covalciuc, Stanislav Ivanov, Radu Rebeja, Serghei Rogaciov. Trainer: Anatoli Teslev

Goals: Hakan Şukur (35, 37 pen, 43, 73), Tuncay (68)

BOSNIA-HERZEGOVINA v GREECE **0-4** (0-1)

Bilino Polje, Zenica 11.10.2006

Referee: Yuri Baskakov (RUS) Attendance: 11,000

BOSNIA-HERZEGOVINA: Kenan Hasagić (46 Almir Tolja), Dalibor Šilić (69 Senajid Ibričić), Branimir Bajić, Zlatan Bajramović, Saša Papac, Ivicia Grlić (61 Vladan Grujić), Zvjezdan Misimović, Sergej Barbarez, Mirko Hrgović, Mladen Bartolović, Alen Škoro. Trainer: Blaz Sliškovic

GREECE: Antonios Nikopolidis, Giorgos Anatolakis, Sotiris Kyrgiakos, Panagiotis Fyssas, Giourkas Seitaridis (57 Christos Patsatzoglou), Kostas Katsouranis, Giorgos Karagounis (36 Georgios Alexopoulos), Stelios Giannakopoulos (85 Ioannis Amanatidis), Angelos Basinas, Giorgos Samaras, Angelos Charisteas. Trainer: Otto Rehhagel

Sent off: Saša Papac (50)

Goals: Charisteas (8 pen), Patsatzoglou (78), Samaras (81), Katsouranis (90)

MOLDOVA v MALTA **1-1** (0-0)

Zimbru, Chişinău 24.03.2007

Referee: Vusal Aliyev (AZE) Attendance: 10,000

MOLDOVA: Serghei Paşcenco, Victor Golovatenco, Alexandru Epureanu, Ghenadie Olexici, Vitalie Bordian, Radu Rebeja, Victor Comleonoc, Serghei Namaşco (81 Serghei Dadu), Viorel Frunză (74 Serghei Alexeev), Igor Bugaiov, Denis Zmeu (63 Stanislav Ivanov). Trainer: Igor Dobrovolskiy

MALTA: Justin Haber, Brian Said, Roderick Briffa, Luke Dimech, Gilbert Agius, Michael Mifsud (90 Gareth Sciberras), Ivan Woods (77 Kevin Sammut), George Mallia, Andre Schembri (70 Daniel Bogdanovic), Kenneth Scicluna, Jamie Pace. Trainer: Dušan Fitzel

Sent off: Luke Dimech (84), Serghei Dadu (84)

Goals: Mallia (73), Epureanu (85)

NORWAY v BOSNIA-HERZEGOVINA 1-2 (0-2)

Ullevål, Oslo 24.03.2007

Referee: Michael Riley (ENG) Attendance: 16,987

NORWAY: Thomas Myhre, Erik Hagen, Brede Hangeland, John Arne Riise, Fredrik Strømstad (62 Christian Grindheim), Martin Andresen, John Carew, Morten Gamst Pedersen, Kristofer Hæstad, Frode Johnsen (46 Steffen Iversen), Jarl André Storbæk (79 Simen Brenne). Trainer: Åge Hareide

BOSNIA-HERZEGOVINA: Adnan Gušo, Mirko Hrgović, Džemal Berberović (58 Vedin Music), Safet Nadarević (46 Ivan Radeljić), Branimir Bajić, Branislav Krunić, Dario Damjanović, Zlatan Muslimović, Zvjezdan Misimović, Vedad Ibišević, Adnan Čustović (82 Darko Maletić). Trainer: Fuad Muzurović

Goals: Misimović (18), Muslimović (33), Carew (50 pen)

MALTA v GREECE 0-1 (0-0)

National, Ta' Qali 28.03.2007

Referee: Pedro Proenca Oliveira Alves Garcia (POR)
Attendance: 15,000

MALTA: Justin Haber, Ian Azzopardi, Brian Said, Roderick Briffa, Kenneth Scicluna, Gilbert Agius, George Mallia (89 Etienne Barbara), Kevin Sammut, Jamie Pace, Michael Mifsud, Andre Schembri (71 Daniel Bogdanovic). Trainer: Dušan Fitzel

GREECE: Kostas Chalkias, Traianos Dellas (83 Giorgos Anatolakis), Loukas Vintra, Sotiris Kyrgiakos, Michalis Kapsis, Vassilis Torosidis, Angelos Basinas, Giorgos Karagounis, Kostas Katsouranis, Theofanis Gekas (90 Giorgos Samaras), Dimitris Salpingidis (64 Nikos Liberopoulos). Trainer: Otto Rehhagel

Sent off: Roderick Briffa (69)

Goal: Basinas (66 pen)

GREECE v TURKEY 1-4 (1-1)

Giorgos Karaiskakis Stadium, Athens 24.03.2007

Referee: Wolfgang Stark (GER) Attendance: 33,000

GREECE: Antonios Nikopolidis, Traianos Dellas, Sotiris Kyrgiakos, Giourkas Seitaridis, Panagiotis Fyssas (56 Vassilis Torosidis), Kostas Katsouranis, Angelos Basinas, Giorgos Karagounis, Stelios Giannakopoulos (72 Ioannis Amanatidis), Angelos Charisteas (63 Theofanis Gekas), Giorgos Samaras. Trainer: Otto Rehhagel

TURKEY: Volkan Demirel, Servet Çetin, Hamit Altintop, Gökhan Zan, Ibrahim Üzülmez (19 Volkan Yaman), Mehmet Aurelio, Tümer Metin (80 Gökdeniz Karadeniz), Sabri Sarioğlu, Gökhan Ünal (57 Huseyin Çimşir), Hakan Şükür, Tuncay Şanli. Trainer: Fatih Terim

Goals: Kyrgiakos (5), Tuncay (27), Gökhan Ünal (55), Tümer (70), Gökdeniz (81)

TURKEY v NORWAY 2-2 (0-2)

Commerzbank Arena, Frankfurt am Main 28.03.2007

Referee: Stefano Farina (ITA)
Attendance: Played behind closed doors

TURKEY: Volkan Demirel, Sabri Sarioğlu, Servet Çetin, Emre Aşik, Hamit Altintop, Tümer Metin (46 Volkan Yaman), Emre Belözoğlu, Gökdeniz Karadeniz (79 Mehmet Yildiz), Mehmet Aurelio, Hakan Şükür (90 Huseyin Çimşir), Tuncay Şanli. Trainer: Fatih Terim

NORWAY: Thomas Myhre, John Arne Riise, Erik Hagen, Brede Hangeland, Jarl André Storbæk, Fredrik Strømstad, Martin Andresen, Kristofer Hæstad (57 Per Ciljan Skjelbred), Simen Brenne (82 Erik Nevland), Thorstein Helstad (63 Daniel Fredheim Holm), John Carew. Trainer: Åge Hareide

Goals: Brenne (31), Andresen (40), Hamit (72, 90)

HUNGARY v MOLDOVA 2-0 (1-0)

Megyeri úti, Budapest 28.03.2007

Referee: Martin Ingvarsson (SWE) Attendance: 5,000

HUNGARY: Zoltán Végh, Csaba Csizmadia, Boldizsár Bodor, Roland Juhász, Béla Balogh (36 Tamás Vaskó), Balázs Tóth, Krisztián Vadócz, Dániel Tőzsér, Tamás Priskin (88 Tibor Tisza), Tamás Hajnal (64 Szabolcs Huszti), Zoltán Gera. Trainer: Peter Várhidi

MOLDOVA: Serghei Paşcenco, Victor Golovatenco, Andrei Cojocari, Ghenadie Olexici, Alexandru Epureanu, Stanislav Ivanov (46 Serghei Namaşco), Andrei Corneencov, Vitalie Bordian, Victor Comleonoc (66 Denis Zmeu), Viorel Frunză (46 Serghei Alexeev), Igor Bugaiov. Trainer: Igor Dobrovolskiy

Goals: Priskin (9), Gera (63)

BOSNIA-HERZEGOVINA v TURKEY 3-2 (2-2)

Olympic Stadium Asim Ferhatovic Hase, Sarajevo 02.06.2007

Referee: Peter Fröjdfeldt (SWE) Attendance: 20,000

BOSNIA-HERZEGOVINA: Adnan Gušo, Branimir Bajić, Vedin Music, Ivan Radeljić, Dario Damjanović, Elvir Rahimić, Mirko Hrgović, Zvjezdan Misimović, Darko Maletić (82 Adnan Čustović), Zlatan Muslimović (90 Boris Pandza), Edin Džeko (61 Zajko Zeba). Trainer: Fuad Muzurović

TURKEY: Rüştü Reçber, Hamit Altintop, Servet Çetin, Gökhan Zan, Ibrahim Üzülmez, Mehmet Aurelio, Sabri Sarioğlu (77 Ümit Karan), Gökdeniz Karadeniz (46 Huseyin Çimşir), Arda Turan (62 Yildiray Baştürk), Tuncay Şanli, Hakan Şükür. Trainer: Fatih Terim

Goals: Hakan Şükür (13), Muslimović (27), Sabri (39), Džeko (47), Čustović (87)

NORWAY v MALTA 4-0 (1-0)

Ullevål, Oslo 02.06.2007

Referee: Jacek Granat (POL) Attendance: 16,364

NORWAY: Håkon André Opdal, Erik Hagen, John Arne Riise, Bjørn Helge Riise, Martin Andresen, Kristofer Hæstad (82 Daniel Omoya Braaten), Steffen Iversen, John Carew (72 Thorstein Helstad), Morten Gamst Pedersen (62 Simen Brenne), Jarl André Storbæk, Brede Hangeland.
Trainer: Åge Hareide

MALTA: Mario Muscat, Ian Azzopardi, Brian Said, Stephen Wellman, Kenneth Scicluna, Gilbert Agius, Kevin Sammut (46 Ivan Woods), George Mallia, Jamie Pace, Michael Mifsud (83 Etienne Barbara), Andre Schembri (69 Daniel Bogdanovic).
Trainer: Dušan Fitzel

Goals: Hæstad (31), Helstad (73), Iversen (79), John Arne Riise (90)

BOSNIA-HERZEGOVINA v MALTA 1-0 (1-0)

Olympic Stadium Asim Ferhatovic Hase, Sarajevo 06.06.2007

Referee: Ceri Richards (WAL) Attendance: 15,000

BOSNIA-HERZEGOVINA: Adnan Gušo, Vedin Musić (90 Veldin Muharemović), Mirko Hrgović, Boris Pandža, Ivan Radeljić, Darko Maletić (80 Mladen Bartolović), Dario Damjanović, Zvjezdan Misimović, Elvir Rahimić, Zlatan Muslimović, Edin Džeko (57 Zajko Zeba).
Trainer: Fuad Muzurovic

MALTA: Mario Muscat, Ian Azzopardi, Brian Said, Daniel Bogdanovic (65 Andre Schembri), Luke Dimech, Gilbert Agius, Roderick Briffa, Michael Mifsud, Ivan Woods (70 George Mallia), Kenneth Scicluna, Jamie Pace (82 Etienne Barbara). Trainer: Dušan Fitzel

Goal: Muslimović (6)

GREECE v HUNGARY 2-0 (2-0)

Pankritio, Heraklion 02.06.2007

Referee: Claus Bo Larsen (DEN) Attendance: 16,000

GREECE: Kostas Chalkias, Giourkas Seitaridis, Vassilis Torosidis, Giorgos Anatolakis (52 Christos Patsatzoglou), Sotiris Kyrgiakos, Kostas Katsouranis, Giorgos Karagounis, Angelos Basinas, Theofanis Gekas, Ioannis Amanatidis (87 Nikos Liberopoulos), Angelos Charisteas (79 Stelios Giannakopoulos). Trainer: Otto Rehhagel

HUNGARY: Zoltán Végh, Szabolcs Balajcza, Boldizsár Bodor (40 Vilmos Vanczak), Roland Juhász, Béla Balogh, Balázs Tóth, Krisztián Vadócz (73 Zoltan Szelesi), Dániel Tőzsér, Tamás Priskin (79 Balázs Dzsudzsak), Tamás Hajnal, Zoltán Gera.
Trainer: Peter Várhidi

Goals: Gekas (16), Seitaridis (29)

GREECE v MOLDOVA 2-1 (1-0)

Pankritio, Heraklion 06.06.2007

Referee: Jan Wegereef (HOL) Attendance: 22,000

GREECE: Antonios Nikopolidis, Giourkas Seitaridis, Ioannis Goumas, Sotiris Kyrgiakos, Christos Patsatzoglou (80 Stelios Giannakopoulos), Vassilis Torosidis, Giorgos Karagounis, Kostas Katsouranis, Ioannis Amanatidis (71 Giorgos Samaras), Angelos Charisteas, Theofanis Gekas (63 Nikos Liberopoulos).
Trainer: Otto Rehhagel

MOLDOVA: Nicolae Calancea, Alexandru Epureanu, Victor Golovatenco, Valeriu Catînsus, Serghei Namaşco, Vitalie Bordian, Victor Comleonoc (82 Igor Tigirlas), Nicolae Josan, Alexandru Gaţcan, Serghei Alexeev (64 Viorel Frunză), Igor Bugaiov (50 Denis Zmeu). Trainer: Igor Dobrovolskiy

Goals: Charisteas (30), Frunză (80), Liberopoloulos (90)

NORWAY v HUNGARY 4-0 (1-0)

Ullevål, Oslo 06.06.2007

Referee: Eduardo Iturralde González (SPA) Att: 19,198

NORWAY: Håkon André Opdal, Jarl André Storbæk, Erik Hagen, Brede Hangeland, John Arne Riise, Bjørn Helge Riise, Martin Andresen, Christian Grindheim (46 Kristofer Hæstad), Steffen Iversen (46 Daniel Omoya Braaten), John Carew, Morten Gamst Pedersen (82 Thorstein Helstad).
Trainer: Åge Hareide

HUNGARY: Zoltán Végh, Zoltán Szélesi, Roland Juhász, Béla Balogh, Vilmos Vanczák, Ákos Buzsáky (83 Krisztián Vadócz), Balázs Tóth, Dániel Tőzsér, Zoltán Gera, Tamás Priskin (71 Tibor Tisza), Tamás Hajnal. Trainer: Peter Várhidi

Goals: Iversen (22), Braaten (57), Carew (60, 78)

HUNGARY v BOSNIA-HERZEGOVINA 1-0 (1-0)

Sóstói, Szekesfehervar 08.09.2007

Referee: Matteo Simone Trefoloni (ITA) Att: 11,000

HUNGARY: Márton Fülöp, Vilmos Vanczák, Tamás Vaskó, Roland Juhász, Zoltán Szélesi, Ádám Vass, Dániel Tozsér, Zoltán Gera, Tamás Hajnal (72 Csaba Csizmandia), Balázs Dzsudzsák (90 Peter Halmosi), Róbert Feczesin (85 Attila Filkor). Trainer: Peter Várhidi

BOSNIA-HERZEGOVINA: Adnan Gušo, Džemal Berberović, Branimir Bajić, Ivan Radeljić, Darko Maletić (79 Mario Bozić), Elvir Rahimić, Zvjezdan Misimović, Mirko Hrgović (84 Adnan Čustović), Zlatan Muslimović, Vedad Ibišević (67 Edin Džeko), Dragan Blatnjak. Trainer: Fuad Muzurović

Goal: Gera (39 pen)

MALTA v TURKEY 2-2 (1-1)

National, Ta' Qali 08.09.2007

Referee: Stefan Messner (AUS) Attendance: 18,000

MALTA: Justin Haber, Ian Azzopardi, Brian Said, Luke Dimech, Roderick Briffa (88 Kevin Sammut), Kenneth Scicluna, Gilbert Agius, Jamie Pace, Michael Mifsud, Ivan Woods (83 George Mallia), Andre Schembri (90 Terence Scerri). Trainer: Dušan Fitzel

TURKEY: Hakan Arikan, Servet Çetin, Ibrahim Toraman, Hamit Altintop, Ibrahim Üzülmez, Sabri Sarioğlu (52 Gokdeniz Karadeniz), Emre Belözoğlu, Arda Turan (30 Ayhan Akman), Tuncay Şanli (66 Deniz Baris), Halil Altintop, Hakan Şükür. Trainer: Fatih Terim

Goals: Said (41), Halil Altintop (45), Schembri (76), Servet Çetin (78)

BOSNIA-HERZEGOVINA v MOLDOVA 0-1 (0-1)

Olympic Stadium Asim Ferhatovic Hase, Sarajevo 12.09.2007

Referee: Jouni Hyytiä (FIN) Attendance: 4,000

BOSNIA-HERZEGOVINA: Adnan Gušo, Džemal Berberović, Branimir Bajić, Safet Nadarević, Ivan Radelji (46 Vedad Ibisević), Elvir Rahimić, Darko Maletić (78 Adnan Čustović), Zajko Zeba (46 Dario Damjanović), Dragan Blatnjak, Zlatan Muslimović, Edin Džeko. Trainer: Fuad Muzurović

MOLDOVA: Nicolae Calancea, Alexandru Epureanu, Serghei Laşcencov, Victor Golovatenco, Radu Rebeja, Victor Comleonoc (63 Serghei Namaşco), Andrei Corneencov, Alexandru Gaţcan (85 Nicolae Josan), Vitalie Bordian, Igor Bugaev, Anatolie Doros (73 Serghei Rogaciov).
Trainer: Igor Dobrovolskiy

Goal: Bugaev (22)

MOLDOVA v NORWAY 0-1 (0-0)

Zimbru, Chişinău 08.09.2007

Referee: Robert Malek (POL) Attendance: 15,000

MOLDOVA: Serghei Paşcenco, Ghenadie Olexici (78 Serghei Rogaciov), Radu Rebeja, Alexandru Epureanu, Serghei Laşcencov, Vitalie Bordian, Alexandru Gaţcan (66 Alexandru Suvorov), Denis Zmeu, Victor Comleonoc, Igor Bugaev, Viorel Frunză. Trainer: Igor Dobrovolskiy

NORWAY: Håkon André Opdal, Jarl André Storbæk, Kjetil Wæhler (66 Vidar Riseth), Brede Hangeland, John Arne Riise, Bjørn Helge Riise, Martin Andresen, Christian Grindheim, Steffen Iversen (68 Thorstein Helstad), John Carew, Morten Gamst Pedersen. Trainer: Åge Hareide

Goal: Iversen (49)

TURKEY v HUNGARY 3-0 (0-0)

Inönü, Istanbul 12.09.2007

Referee: Stuart Dougal (SCO) Attendance: 28,000

TURKEY: Hakan Arikan, Emre Aşik, Hamit Altintop, Servet Çetin, Ibrahim Üzülmez, Mehmet Aurelio, Gökdeniz Karadeniz (61 Halil Altintop), Ayhan Akman (67 Serdar Ozkan), Tuncay Şanli, Gökhan Ünal, Nihat Kahveci (46 Emre Belozoglu). Trainer: Fatih Terim

HUNGARY: Márton Fülöp (71 Janos Balogh), Roland Juhász, Zoltán Szélesi, Vilmos Vanczák, Csaba Csizmadia, Tamás Vaskó, Ádám Vass, Zoltán Gera, Balázs Dzsudzsák (82 Peter Halmosi), Tamás Hajnal, Tamás Priskin (66 Balázs Tóth).
Trainer: Peter Várhidi

Sent off: Zoltan Gera (63)

Goals: Gökhan (68), Aurelio (72), Halil Altintop (90)

NORWAY v GREECE 2-2 (2-2)

Ullevål, Oslo 12.09.2007

Referee: Massimo Busacca (SWI) Attendance: 24,000

NORWAY: Håkon André Opdal, Erik Hagen, Brede Hangeland, Martin Andresen, John Arne Riise, Morten Gamst Pedersen, Bjørn Helge Riise (90 Frode Kippe), Jan Gunnar Solli (70 Thorstein Helstad), Jarl André Storbæk, John Carew, Steffen Iversen (80 Vidar Riseth). Trainer: Åge Hareide

GREECE: Kostas Chalkias, Giourkas Seitaridis (64 Paraskevas Antzas), Christos Patsatzoglou, Sotiris Kyrgiakos, Traianos Dellas, Angelos Basinas (76 Giorgos Samaras), Giorgos Karagounis, Vassilis Torossidis, Kostas Katsouranis, Dimitris Salpingidis (46 Nikos Liberopoulos), Theofanis Gekas. Trainer: Otto Rehhagel

Goals: Kyrgiakos (7, 30), Carew (15), J.A. Riise (39)

HUNGARY v MALTA 2-0 (1-0)

Megyeri úti, Budapest 13.10.2007

Referee: Karen Nalbandyan (ARM) Attendance: 7,600

HUNGARY: Márton Fülöp, Zoltán Szélesi, Tamás Vaskó, Roland Juhász, Béla Balogh, Ádám Vass, Dániel Tozsér, Zoltán Gera, Attila Filkor (75 Akos Buzsaky), Róbert Feczesin (83 Peter Rajczi), Balázs Dzsudzsák (87 Leandro de Almeida).
Trainer: Peter Várhidi

MALTA: Justin Haber, Ian Azzopardi, Brian Said, Kenneth Scicluna, Luke Dimech, Roderick Briffa, Kevin Sammut (66 Udochuckwu Nwoko), George Mallia, Michael Mifsud, Ivan Woods (90 Roderick Bajada), Andre Schembri (83 Terence Scerri). Trainer: Dušan Fitzel

Goals: Feczesin (34), Tozsér (78)

MOLDOVA v TURKEY 1-1 (1-0)

Zimbru, Chişinău 13.10.2007

Referee: Martin Atkinson (ENG) Attendance: 10,500

MOLDOVA: Nicolae Calancea, Victor Golovatenco, Alexandru Epureanu, Alexei Savinov, Andrei Corneencov, Vitalie Bordian, Nicolae Josan, Denis Zmeu (67 Serghei Namaşco), Alexandru Gaţcan (89 Ghenadie Olexici), Victor Comleonoc, Viorel Frunză (86 Denis Calincov).
Trainer: Igor Dobrovolskiy

TURKEY: Hakan Arikan (17 Volkan Demirel), Servet Çetin, Gökhan Zan, Ibrahim Üzülmez, Emre Belözoğlu, Mehmet Topuz, Mehmet Aurelio, Arda Turan (69 Tümer Metin), Selçuk Inan (46 Ümit Karan), Tuncay Şanli, Gökhan Ünal.
Trainer: Fatih Terim

Goals: Frunză (11), Ümit Karan (63)

GREECE v BOSNIA-HERZEGOVINA 3-2 (1-0)

OAKA Spyro Louis, Athens 13.10.2007

Referee: Grzegorz Gilewski (POL) Attendance: 15,000

GREECE: Antonios Nikopolidis, Traianos Dellas, Sotiris Kyrgiakos, Christos Patsatzoglou, Vassilis Torosidis, Angelos Basinas, Giorgos Karagounis, Kostas Katsouranis, Ioannis Amanatidis (70 Stelios Giannakopoulos), Theofanis Gekas (81 Paraskevas Antzas), Angelos Charisteas (69 Nikos Liberopoulos). Trainer: Otto Rehhagel

BOSNIA-HERZEGOVINA: Adnan Gušo, Džemal Berberović, Branimir Bajić, Safet Nadarević, Branislav Krunić (46 Vedad Ibisević), Zvjezdan Misimović (82 Sejad Salihović), Mirko Hrgović, Admir Vladavić, Elvir Rahimić, Dragan Blatnjak (62 Samir Merzić), Zlatan Muslimović.
Trainer: Fuad Muzurović

Sent off: Mirko Hrgovic (56)

Goals: Charisteas (10), M. Hrgović (54), Gekas (58), Liberopoulos (73), Ibiševic (90)

TURKEY v GREECE 0-1 (0-0)

Ali Sami Yen, Istanbul 17.10.2007

Referee: Manuel Mejuto González (SPA) Att: 24,000

TURKEY: Volkan Demirel, Servet Çetin, Gökhan Zan, Hamit Altintop, Emre Belözoğlu (71 Arda Turan), Ibrahim Üzülmez, Mehmet Aurelio, Gökdeniz Karadeniz (65 Hakan Şükür), Ümit Karan (46 Tümer Metin), Gökhan Ünal, Tuncay Şanli.
Trainer: Fatih Terim

GREECE: Kostas Chalkias, Traianos Dellas, Sotiris Kyrgiakos, Paraskevas Antzas, Giourkas Seitaridis, Vassilis Torosidis, Giorgos Karagounis, Angelos Basinas, Angelos Charisteas (59 Giorgos Samaras), Ioannis Amanatidis, Theofanis Gekas (56 Nikos Liberopoulos). Trainer: Otto Rehhagel

Goal: Amanatidis (79)

BOSNIA-HERZEGOVINA v NORWAY 0-2 (0-1)

Koševo, Sarajevo 17.10.2007

Referee: Stéphane Lannoy (FRA) Attendance: 15,000

BOSNIA-HERZEGOVINA: Adnan Gušo, Džemal Berberović, Samir Merzić, Branimir Bajić, Branislav Krunić, Dragan Blatnjak (46 Vedad Ibisević), Zlatan Muslimović (46 Edin Džeko), Zvjezdan Misimović, Darko Maletić (78 Veldin Muharemović), Safet Nadarević, Sejad Salihović.
Trainer: Fuad Muzurović

NORWAY: Håkon André Opdal, Jarl André Storbæk, Brede Hangeland, Erik Hagen, John Arne Riise, Bjørn Helge Riise (90 John Anders Bjorkoy), Martin Andresen, Christian Grindheim (58 Sigurd Rushfeldt), Jan Gunnar Solli, Thorstein Helstad (76 Daniel Braaten), Morten Gamst Pedersen.
Trainer: Åge Hareide

Goals: Hagen (5), B. Riise (74)

MALTA v MOLDOVA 2-3 (0-3)

National, Ta' Qali 17.10.2007

Referee: Igorj Ishchenko (UKR) Attendance: 10,000

MALTA: Justin Haber, Kenneth Scicluna (46 Terence Scerri), Ian Azzopardi (90 Udochukwu Nwoko), Brian Said, Luke Dimech, Roderick Briffa, Jamie Pace, George Mallia, Ivan Woods, Andre Schembri (46 Andrew Cohen), Michael Mifsud.
Trainer: Dušan Fitzel

MOLDOVA: Serghei Paşcenco, Victor Golovatenco, Serghei Stroenco, Serghei Laşcencov, Andrei Corneencov, Vitalie Bordian, Nicolae Josan, Alexandru Gaţcan (77 Denis Zmeu), Victor Comlenoc (69 Serghei Namaşco), Viorel Frunză (83 Anatolie Doros), Igor Bugaev. Trainer: Igor Dobrovolski

Sent off: Victor Golovatenco (88)

Goals: Bugaev (24 pen), Frunză (31, 35), Scerri (71), Michael Mifsud (84 pen)

MOLDOVA v HUNGARY 3-0 (2-0)

Zimbru, Chişinău 17.11.2007

Referee: Pavel Královec (CZE) Attendance: 6,500

MOLDOVA: Stanislav Namaşco, Serghei Laşcencov, Radu Rebeja, Alexandru Epureanu, Vitalie Bordian, Serghei Namaşco, Evgheni Cebotari (50 Semion Bulgaru), Denis Zmeu (90 Ghenadie Olexici), Nicolae Josan, Igor Bugaev, Denis Calincov (64 Serghei Alexeev). Trainer: Igor Dobrovolski

HUNGARY: Márton Fülöp, Zoltán Szélesi, Tamás Vaskó, Csaba Csizmadia, Vilmos Vanczák, Zoltán Gera, Dániel Tozsér (38 Akos Buzsaky), Tamás Hajnal, Krisztián Vadócz (39 Bela Balogh), Balázs Dzsudzsák (71 Robert Feczesin), Tamás Priskin. Trainer: Peter Várhidi

Goals: Bugaev (13), Josan (23), Alexeev (86)

NORWAY v TURKEY **1-2** (1-1)

Ullevål, Oslo 17.11.2007

Referee: Markus Merk (GER) Attendance: 23,800

NORWAY: Håkon André Opdal, Jarl André Storbæk (88 Sigurd Rushfeldt), Erik Hagen, Brede Hangeland, John Arne Riise, Bjørn Helge Riise, Alexander Tettey, Kristofer Hæstad (68 Per Ciljan Skjelbred), Steffen Iversen (84 Thorstein Helstad), John Carew, Morten Gamst Pedersen.
Trainer: Åge Hareide

TURKEY: Volkan Demirel, Ibrahim Kas (15 Gökhan Gonul), Emre Aşik, Servet Çetin, Hakan Balta, Hamit Altintop, Mehmet Aurelio, Emre Belözoğlu, Arda Turan (87 Tuncay Şanli), Nihat Kahveci, Semih Sentürk (67 Yusuf Simsek).
Trainer: Fatih Terim

Goals: Hagen (12), Emre Belözoğlu (31), Nihat Kahveci (59)

GREECE v MALTA **5-0** (1-0)

OAKA Spyro Louis, Athens 17.11.2007

Referee: Sten Kaldma (EST) Attendance: 31,300

GREECE: Antonios Nikopolidis, Christos Patsatzoglou, Traianos Dellas, Sotiris Kyrgiakos, Vassilis Torosidis (48 Nikos Spiropoulos), Angelos Basinas, Kostas Katsouranis, Giorgos Karagounis (70 Alexandros Tziolis), Stelios Giannakopoulos (46 Nikos Liberopoulos), Theofanis Gekas, Ioannis Amanatidis. Trainer: Otto Rehhagel

MALTA: Justin Haber, Josef Mifsud, Roderick Briffa, Brian Said, Ian Azzopardi, Peter Pullicino, Jamie Pace, Kevin Sammut (61 Andrew Cohen), Udochukwu Nwoko, Andre Schembri (68 Terence Scerri), Michael Mifsud (78 Gareth Sciberras). Trainer: Dušan Fitzel

Goals: Gekas (32), Basinas (54), Amanatidis (61), Gekas (72, 74)

MALTA v NORWAY **1-4** (0-3)

National, Ta' Qali 21.11.2007

Referee: Yuri Baskakov (RUS) Attendance: 6,000

MALTA: Justin Haber, Ian Azzopardi, Luke Dimech, Stephen Wellmen, Roderick Briffa, Udochukwu Nwoko (86 Andrew Cohen), Peter Pullicino, Ivan Woods (83 Etienne Barbara), Jamie Pace, Andre Schembri, Michael Mifsud (87 Terence Scerri). Trainer: Dušan Fitzel

NORWAY: Håkon André Opdal, Jarl André Storbæk, Erik Hagen, Brede Hangeland, John Arne Riise, Bjørn Helge Riise (75 Kristofer Hæstad), Vidar Riseth, Per Ciljan Skjelbred, Steffen Iversen (84 Sigurd Rushfeldt), John Carew (68 Thorstein Helstad), Morten Gamst Pedersen.
Trainer: Åge Hareide

Sent off: Andre Schembri (68)

Goals: Iversen (25, 27 pen, 45), Michael Mifsud (53), Pedersen (75)

HUNGARY v GREECE **1-2** (1-1)

Ferenc Puskás, Budapest 21.11.2007

Referee: Robert Styles (ENG) Attendance: 32,300

HUNGARY: Márton Fülöp, Zoltán Szélesi, Tamás Vaskó, Roland Juhász, Vilmos Vanczák, Ádám Vass, Dániel Tozsér (86 Leandro de Almeida), Ákos Buzsáky, Tamás Hajnal (79 Attila Filkor), Péter Halmosi (83 Robert Feczesin), Tamás Priskin.
Trainer: Peter Várhidi

GREECE: Kostas Chalkias (46 Antonios Nikopolidis), Christos Patsatzoglou, Michalis Kapsis, Loukas Vintra, Sotiris Kyrgiakos, Angelos Basinas, Alexandros Tziolis (46 Giorgos Samaras), Giorgos Karagounis, Kostas Katsouranis, Theofanis Gekas (84 Ioannis Amanatidis), Dimitris Salpingidis.
Trainer: Otto Rehhagel

Goals: Buzsaky (7), Vanczak (22 own goal), Basinas (59 pen)

TURKEY v BOSNIA-HERZEGOVINA **1-0** (1-0)

Ali Sami Yen, Istanbul 21.11.2007

Referee: Eric Braamhaar (HOL) Attendance: 25,500

TURKEY: Rüştü Reçber, Gökhan Gönül, Emre Aşik, Servet Çetin, Hakan Balta, Hamit Altintop, Mehmet Aurelio, Emre Belözoğlu, Arda Turan (76 Tuncay Şanli), Nihat Kahveci (90 Gökdeniz Karadeniz), Semih Sentürk (61 Sabri Sarioğlu).
Trainer: Fatih Terim

BOSNIA-HERZEGOVINA: Adnan Gušo, Senidad Ibričić (75 Vedad Ibišević), Safet Nadarević, Džemal Berberović, Samir Merzić (89 Veldin Muharemović), Branimir Bajić, Branislav Krunić, Darko Maletić, Zvjezdan Misimović, Elvir Rahimić, Edin Džeko (83 Sejad Salihović). Trainer: Fuad Muzurović

Goal: Nihat Kahveci (43)

	P	W	D	L	F	A	Pts
Greece	12	10	1	1	25	10	31
Turkey	12	7	3	2	25	11	24
Norway	12	7	2	3	27	11	23
Bosnia-Herz.	12	4	1	7	16	22	13
Moldova	12	3	3	6	12	19	12
Hungary	12	4	0	8	11	22	12
Malta	12	1	2	9	10	31	5

GROUP 4

CZECH REPUBLIC v WALES 2-1 (0-0)

Na Stínadlech, Teplice 02.09.2006

Referee: Jonas Eriksson (SWE) Attendance: 16,200

CZECH REPUBLIC: Petr Čech, Tomáš Ujfaluši, Martin Jiránek, David Rozehnal, Marek Jankulovski, Jiří Štajner (45 Libor Sionko), Tomáš Galásek (87 Radoslav Kovac), Tomáš Rosický, Jaroslav Plašil, Marek Kulic (75 David Lafata), Jan Koller. Trainer: Karel Brückner

WALES: Paul Douglas Jones, Mark Delaney (78 David Cotterill), Danny Gabbidon, James Collins, Sam Ricketts (79 Robert Earnshaw), Carl Robinson, Carl Fletcher (46 Joe Ledley), Simon Davies, Ryan Giggs, Craig Bellamy, Lewin Nyatanga. Trainer: John Toshack

Goals: Lafata (76, 89), Jiranek (85 own goal)

SLOVAKIA v CYPRUS 6-1 (3-0)

Tehelné Pole, Bratislava 02.09.2006

Referee: Oleh Orekhov (UKR) Attendance: 5,000

SLOVAKIA: Kamil Čontofalský, Radoslav Zábavník (46 Filip Hološko), Martin Škrtel, Ján Durica, Marek Čech, Peter Hlinka, Miroslav Karhan, Dušan Švento, Marek Mintál, Szilárd Németh (46 Matej Krajčik), Filip Šebo (56 Ivan Hodúr). Trainer: Dušan Galis

CYPRUS: Michalis Morfis, Giorgos Theodotou, Lambros Lambrou, Loukas Louka (67 Christos Theofilou), Chrysostomous Michail, Kostas Charalambides, Konstantinos Makridis, Alexandros Garpozis (46 Simos Krassas), Yiannis Okkas, Yiasemakis Yiasoumi, Nektarios Alexandrou (46 Marios Elia). Trainer: Angelos Anastasiadis

Goals: Škrtel (9), Mintál (33, 56), Sebo (43, 49), Karhan (52), Yiasoumi (90)

GERMANY v REPUBLIC OF IRELAND 1-0 (0-0)

Gottlieb-Daimler, Stuttgart 02.09.2006

Referee: Luis Medina Cantalejo (SPA) Attendance: 53,200

GERMANY: Jens Lehmann, Philipp Lahm, Arne Friedrich, Manuel Friedrich, Marcel Jansen, Bernd Schneider (83 Tim Borowski), Torsten Frings, Michael Ballack, Bastian Schweinsteiger, Lukas Podolski (76 Oliver Neuville), Miroslav Klose. Trainer: Joachim Löw

REPUBLIC OF IRELAND: Shay Given, Stephen Carr, Andy O'Brien, Richard Dunne, Kevin Kilbane (83 Alan O'Brien), Steve Finnan, Steven Reid, John O'Shea, Damien Duff (77 Aiden McGeady), Kevin Doyle (79 Stephen Elliott), Robbie Keane. Trainer: Stephen Staunton

Goal: Podolski (57)

SLOVAKIA v CZECH REPUBLIC 0-3 (0-2)

Tehelné Pole, Bratislava 06.09.2006

Referee: Stephen Bennett (ENG) Attendance: 24,000

SLOVAKIA: Kamil Čontofalský, Peter Hlinka, Martin Škrtel, Ján Durica, Jozef Valachovič (46 Ivan Hodúr), Dušan Švento, Marek Čech (24 Szilard Nemeth), Matej Krajčík, Miroslav Karhan, Marek Mintál, Filip Šebo (46 Filip Hološko). Trainer: Dušan Galis

CZECH REPUBLIC: Petr Čech, Marek Jankulovski, Martin Jiránek, Tomáš Ujfaluši, David Rozehnal, Jan Polák (72 Radoslav Kováč), Tomáš Galásek, Libor Sionko (77 Jiří Štajner), Tomáš Rosický, Jaroslav Plašil, Jan Koller. Trainer: Karel Brückner

Goals: Sionko (10, 21), Koller (57)

SAN MARINO v GERMANY 0-13 (0-6)

Olimpico, Serravalle 06.09.2006

Referee: Selçuk Dereli (TUR) Attendance: 5,000

SAN MARINO: Aldo Simoncini, Nicola Albani, Alessandro Della Valle, Simone Bacciocchi, Mirko Palazzi, Carlo Valentini, Damiano Vannucci (68 Davide Simoncini), Michele Marani, Marco Domeniconi (46 Giovanni Bonini), Manuel Marani (78 Mattia Masi), Andy Selva. Trainer: Giampaolo Mazza

GERMANY: Jens Lehmann, Marcel Jansen, Arne Friedrich, Philipp Lahm, Bastian Schweinsteiger, Torsten Frings (62 Thomas Hitzlsperger), Michael Ballack (46 David Odonkor), Bernd Schneider, Manuel Friedrich, Miroslav Klose (46 Gerald Asamoah), Lukas Podolski. Trainer: Joachim Löw

Goals: Podolski (11, 43, 64, 72), Schweinsteiger (28, 47), Klose (30, 46), Ballack (35), Hitzlsperger (66, 73), M. Friedrich (87), Schneider (90 pen)

WALES v SLOVAKIA 1-5 (1-3)

Millennium, Cardiff 07.10.2006

Referee: Dick van Egmond (HOL) Attendance: 28,500

WALES: Paul Jones, Richard Duffy, Gareth Bale, Danny Gabbidon, Lewin Nyatanga, Carl Robinson, Robert Edwards (58 Joe Ledley), Jason Koumas, Simon Davies (88 David Cotterill), Craig Bellamy, Robert Earnshaw (46 Paul Parry). Trainer: John Toshack

SLOVAKIA: Kamil Čontofalský, Ján Kozák, Roman Kratochvíl, Martin Petráš, Stanislav Varga, Miroslav Karhan (67 Matej Krajčik), Marek Mintál (71 Ivan Hodúr), Róbert Vittek (77 Filip Hološko), Peter Petráš, Dušan Švento, Ján Durica. Trainer: Dušan Galis

Goals: Svento (14), Mintál (32, 38), Bale (37), Karhan (51), Vittek (59)

CZECH REPUBLIC v SAN MARINO **7-0** (4-0)

U Nisy, Liberec 07.10.2006

Referee: Vusal Aliyev (AZE) Attendance: 9,500

CZECH REPUBLIC: Petr Čech, Tomáš Ujfaluši, Zdeněk Grygera, David Rozehnal (46 Tomáš Zápotočný), Marek Jankulovski, David Jarolím, Jan Polák, Tomáš Rosický (63 Jaroslav Plašil), Milan Baroš, Marek Kulič (46 David Lafata), Jan Koller. Trainer: Karel Brückner

SAN MARINO: Federico Valentini, Nicola Albani, Alessandro Della Valle, Simone Bacciocchi, Matteo Andreini (82 Paolo Mariotti), Carlo Valentini, Damiano Vannucci, Mattia Masi (69 Federico Crescentini), Marco Domeniconi, Michele Moretti (54 Michele Marani), Andy Selva.
Trainer: Giampaolo Mazza

Goals: Kulič (15), Polák (22), Baroš (28, 68), Koller (43, 52), Jarolím (49)

CYPRUS v REPUBLIC OF IRELAND **5-2** (2-2)

GSP, Nicosia 07.10.2006

Referee: Lucílio Batista (POR) Attendance: 7,000

CYPRUS: Michalis Morfis, Marinos Satsias, Lambros Lambrou, Loukas Louka, Giorgos Theodotou, Chrysostomous Michail (46 Kostas Charalambides), Alexandros Garpozis (77 Ilias Charalambous), Konstantinos Makridis, Yiannis Okkas (86 Yiasemakis Yiasoumi), Michalis Konstantinou, Stathis Aloneftis. Trainer: Angelos Anastasiadis

REPUBLIC OF IRELAND: Paddy Kenny, Steve Finnan, John O'Shea, Andy O'Brien (71 Alan Lee), Richard Dunne, Kevin Kilbane, Aiden McGeady (80 Alan O'Brien), Stephen Ireland (83 Jonathan Douglas), Clinton Morrisson, Robbie Keane, Damien Duff. Trainer: Steve Staunton

Sent off: Richard Dunne (78)

Goals: Ireland (8), M. Konstantinou (10, 50 pen), Garpozis (16), Dunne (44), Charalambides (60, 75)

REPUBLIC OF IRELAND v CZECH REPUBLIC **1-1** (0-0)

Lansdowne Road, Dublin 11.10.2006

Referee: Bertrand Layec (FRA) Attendance: 35,500

REPUBLIC OF IRELAND: Wayne Henderson, Stephen Kelly, Paul McShane, John O'Shea, Steve Finnan, Lee Carsley, Andy Reid (72 Alan Quinn), Jonathan Douglas, Kevin Kilbane (79 Alan O'Brien), Damien Duff, Robbie Keane.
Trainer: Steve Staunton

CZECH REPUBLIC: Petr Čech, Jan Polák, Tomáš Ujfaluši, Radoslav Kováč, Marek Jankulovski, Martin Jiránek, Tomáš Rosický, Jaroslav Plašil (85 Zdeněk Grygera), David Rozehnal, Jan Koller, Milan Baroš (82 David Jarolím).
Trainer: Karel Brückner

Goals: Kilbane (62), Koller (64)

WALES v CYPRUS **3-1** (2-0)

Millennium, Cardiff 11.10.2006

Referee: Jacek Granat (POL) Attendance: 20,500

WALES: Lewis Price, Richard Duffy (78 Robert Edwards), Danny Gabbidon, Lewin Nyatanga, Gareth Bale, Craig Morgan, Carl Robinson, Jason Koumas (76 Joe Ledley), Simon Davies, Craig Bellamy (90 Paul Parry), Robert Earnshaw.
Trainer: John Toshack

CYPRUS: Michalis Morfis, Giorgos Theodotou, Lambros Lambrou, Loukas Louka, Marinos Satsias (83 Yiasemakis Yiasoumi), Chrysostomous Michail (46 Kostas Charalambides), Alexandros Garpozis (46 Ilias Charalambous), Konstantinos Makridis, Stathis Aloneftis, Michalis Konstantinou, Yiannis Okkas.
Trainer: Angelos Anastasiadis

Goals: Koumas (33), Earnshaw (39), Bellamy (72), Okkas (83)

SLOVAKIA v GERMANY **1-4** (0-3)

Tehelné Pole, Bratislava 11.10.2006

Referee: Terje Hauge (NOR) Attendance: 21,000

SLOVAKIA: Kamil Čontofalský, Peter Petráš (73 Filip Hološko), Stanislav Varga, Martin Škrtel, Ján Durica, Miroslav Karhan, Martin Petráš, Dušan Švento, Ján Kozák (65 Ivan Hodúr), Marek Mintál, Róbert Vittek. Trainer: Dušan Galis

GERMANY: Jens Lehmann, Arne Friedrich, Manuel Friedrich, Clemens Fritz, Philipp Lahm, Michael Ballack, Torsten Frings, Bernd Schneider (75 David Odonkor), Bastian Schweinsteiger (77 Piotr Trochowski), Miroslav Klose, Lukas Podolski (85 Mike Hanke). Trainer: Joachim Löw

Goals: Podolski (13, 72), Ballack (25), Schweinsteiger (36), Varga (58)

REPUBLIC OF IRELAND v SAN MARINO **5-0** (3-0)

Lansdowne Road, Dublin 15.11.2006

Referee: Lassin Isaksen (FAR) Attendance: 34,000

REPUBLIC OF IRELAND: Shay Given, Steve Finnan, Paul McShane, Richard Dunne, John O'Shea, Lee Carsley (50 Jonathan Douglas), Kevin Kilbane (79 Alan Lee), Andy Reid, Damien Duff, Kevin Doyle (63 Aiden McGeady), Robbie Keane. Trainer: Steve Staunton

SAN MARINO: Federico Valentini, Matteo Bugli, Nicola Albani, Simone Bacciocchi, Davide Simoncini (81 Giovanni Bonini), Damiano Vannucci (72 Federico Crescentini), Carlo Valentini, Matteo Andreini, Paolo Mariotti (59 Michele Marani), Manuel Marani, Andy Selva.
Trainer: Giampaolo Mazza

Goals: A. Reid (7), Doyle (24), Keane (31, 58 pen, 85)

CYPRUS v GERMANY 1-1 (1-1)

GSP, Nicosia 15.11.2006

Referee: Peter Fröjdfeldt (SWE) Attendance: 12,000

CYPRUS: Antonis Georgallides, Marios Elia, Lambros Lambrou, Loukas Louka, Giorgos Theodotou (79 Ilias Charalambous), Konstantinos Makridis, Kostas Charalambides, Chrysostomous Michail (68 Simos Krassas), Yiannis Okkas (72 Charis Nicolaou), Stathis Aloneftis, Michalis Konstantinou. Trainer: Angelos Anastasiadis

GERMANY: Timo Hildebrand, Arne Friedrich, Philipp Lahm, Bastian Schweinsteiger, Torsten Frings, Michael Ballack, Clemens Fritz, Manuel Friedrich, David Odonkor (79 Thomas Hitzlsperger), Miroslav Klose, Oliver Neuville (62 Mike Hanke). Trainer: Joachim Löw

Goals: Ballack (16), Okkas (43)

SAN MARINO v REPUBLIC OF IRELAND 1-2 (0-0)

Olimpico, Serravalle 07.02.2007

Referee: Peter Rasmussen (DEN) Attendance: 3,300

SAN MARINO: Aldo Simoncini, Carlo Valentini, Manuel Marani, Nicola Albani, Davide Simoncini, Riccardo Muccioli, Giovanni Bonini (74 Damiano Vannucci), Marco Domeniconi (84 Matteo Bugli), Michele Marani, Andy Selva, Alex Gasperoni (66 Matteo Andreini). Trainer: Giampaolo Mazza

REPUBLIC OF IRELAND: Wayne Henderson, Steve Finnan, Richard Dunne, John O'Shea (46 Paul McShane), Ian Harte (71 Stephen Hunt), Damien Duff, Lee Carsley, Stephen Ireland, Kevin Kilbane, Shane Long (76 Anthony Stokes), Robbie Keane. Trainer: Stephen Staunton

Goals: Kilbane (49), Manuel Marani (82), Ireland (90)

REPUBLIC OF IRELAND v WALES 1-0 (0-0)

Croke Park, Dublin 24.03.2007

Referee: Terje Hauge (NOR) Attendance: 75,300

REPUBLIC OF IRELAND: Shay Given, Steve Finnan, Paul McShane, Richard Dunne, John O'Shea, Jonathan Douglas (80 Stephen Hunt), Lee Carsley, Stephen Ireland (59 Kevin Doyle), Kevin Kilbane, Robbie Keane (88 Aiden McGeady), Damien Duff. Trainer: Stephen Staunton

WALES: Danny Coyne, Sam Ricketts, Gareth Bale (74 Danny Collins), James Collins, Steve Evans, Lewin Nyatanga, Joe Ledley (46 Carl Fletcher), Carl Robinson (90 Jermaine Mauric Easter), Simon Davies, Ryan Giggs, Craig Bellamy. Trainer: John Toshack

Goal: Ireland (39)

CYPRUS v SLOVAKIA 1-3 (1-0)

GSP, Nicosia 24.03.2007

Referee: Gerald Lehner (AUS) Attendance: 2,696

CYPRUS: Michalis Morfis, Marinos Satsias, Lambros Lambrou, Loukas Louka, Giorgos Theodotou (43 Antonis Georgallides), Chrysostomous Michail, Konstantinos Charalambidis, Alexandros Garpozis (66 Ilias Charalambous), Konstantinos Makridis (58 Marios Elia), Yiasemakis Yiasoumi, Stathis Aloneftis. Trainer: Angelos Anastasiadis

SLOVAKIA: Kamil Čontofalský, Peter Šinglár (46 Igor Žofčak), Martin Škrtel, Ján Durica, Vratislav Greško, Balázs Borbély, Matej Krajčík, Dušan Švento, Marek Sapara (68 Ján Kozák), Róbert Vittek, Martin Jakubko (79 Stanislav Šesták). Trainer: Dušan Galis

Sent off: Michalis Morfis (42)

Goals: Aloneftis (45), Vittek (54), Škrtel (67), Jakubko (77)

CZECH REPUBLIC v GERMANY 1-2 (0-1)

Sparta, Praha 24.03.2007

Referee: Roberto Rosetti (ITA) Attendance: 17,821

CZECH REPUBLIC: Petr Čech, Tomáš Ujfaluši (84 Stanislav Vlček), Martin Jiránek, David Rozehnal, Marek Jankulovski, Libor Sionko (46 Jaroslav Plašil), Tomáš Rosický, Tomáš Galásek (62 Marek Kulič), Jan Polák, Jan Koller, Milan Baroš. Trainer: Karel Brückner

GERMANY: Jens Lehmann, Philipp Lahm, Per Mertesacker, Christoph Metzelder, Marcel Jansen, Bernd Schneider, Torsten Frings, Michael Ballack, Bastian Schweinsteiger, Lukas Podolski (89 Thomas Hitzlsperger), Kevin Kuranyi. Trainer: Joachim Löw

Goals: Kuranyi (42, 62), Baroš (77)

CZECH REPUBLIC v CYPRUS 1-0 (1-0)

U Nisy, Liberec 28.03.2007

Referee: Ivan Bebek (CRO) Attendance: 9,310

CZECH REPUBLIC: Petr Čech, Tomáš Ujfaluši, Zdeněk Grygera (12 Radoslav Kováč, 27 Martin Jiranek), David Rozehnal, Marek Jankulovski, Tomáš Galásek, Tomáš Rosický, Jan Polák, David Jarolím, Jan Koller, Milan Baroš (77 Jaroslav Plašil). Trainer: Karel Brückner

CYPRUS: Antonis Georgallides, Marinos Satsias, Lambros Lambrou, Giorgos Theodotou, Paraskevas Christou, Marios Elia (76 Ilias Charalambous), Kostas Charalambidis (75 Simos Krassas), Konstantinos Makridis, Yiasemakis Yiasoumi (72 Kyriakos Chailis), Yiannis Okkas, Stathis Aloneftis. Trainer: Angelos Anastasiadis

Goal: Kováč (22)

REPUBLIC OF IRELAND v SLOVAKIA 1-0 (1-0)

Croke Park, Dublin 28.03.2007

Referee: Yuri Baskakov (RUS) Attendance: 71,300

REPUBLIC OF IRELAND: Shay Given, John O'Shea, Steve Finnan, Paul McShane, Richard Dunne, Lee Carsley, Stephen Ireland (70 Stephen Hunt), Aiden McGeady (87 Alan Quinn), Kevin Kilbane, Damien Duff, Kevin Doyle (74 Shane Long). Trainer: Stephen Staunton

SLOVAKIA: Kamil Čontofalský, Peter Šinglár (79 Stanislav Šesták), Martin Škrtel, Maroš Klimpl, Vratislav Greško, Dušan Švento (87 Lubomir Michalík), Igor Žofčák, Balázs Borbély, Marek Sapara (72 Filip Hološko), Róbert Vittek, Martin Jakubko. Trainer: Ján Kocian

Goal: Doyle (13)

WALES v SAN MARINO 3-0 (2-0)

Millennium, Cardiff 28.03.2007

Referee: Ararat Tchagharyan (ARM) Attendance: 18,750

WALES: Danny Coyne, Sam Ricketts, Steve Evans (63 Lewin Nyatanga), James Collins, Gareth Bale, Carl Fletcher, Jason Koumas, Simon Davies, Ryan Giggs (73 Paul Parry), Craig Bellamy, Jermaine Mauric Easter (46 David Cotterill). Trainer: John Toshack

SAN MARINO: Aldo Simoncini, Carlo Valentini (85 Alan Toccaceli), Matteo Andreini, Nicola Albani, Riccardo Muccioli, Simone Bacciocchi, Cristian Negri (79 Federico Nanni), Marco Domeniconi (67 Matteo Bugli), Manuel Marani, Andy Selva, Alex Gasperoni. Trainer: Giampaolo Mazza

Goals: Giggs (3), Bale (20), Koumas (63 pen)

WALES v CZECH REPUBLIC 0-0

Millennium, Cardiff 02.06.2007

Referee: Paul Allaerts (BEL) Attendance: 30,700

WALES: Wayne Robert Hennessey, Sam Ricketts, Lewin Nyatanga, Danny Gabbidon, James Collins, Carl Robinson, Joe Ledley, Jason Koumas, Simon Davies, Ryan Giggs (89 Robert Earnshaw), Craig Bellamy. Trainer: John Toshack

CZECH REPUBLIC: Petr Čech, Tomáš Ujfaluši, Radoslav Kováč, Marek Jankulovski, David Rozehnal, Jan Polák (65 David Jarolím), Tomáš Sivok (83 Marek Matějovský), Tomáš Rosický, Jaroslav Plašil, Jan Koller, Milan Baroš (46 Marek Kulič). Trainer: Karel Brückner

GERMANY v SAN MARINO 6-0 (1-0)

Frankenstadion, Nuremberg 02.06.2007

Referee: Jouni Hyytiä (FIN) Attendance: 44,000

GERMANY: Jens Lehmann, Philipp Lahm (70 Patrick Helmes), Per Mertesacker, Christoph Metzelder, Marcell Jansen, Torsten Frings, Thomas Hitzlsperger, Bernd Schneider, Roberto Hilbert (59 Clemens Fritz), Miroslav Klose, Kevin Kuranyi (59 Mario Gomez). Trainer: Joachim Löw

SAN MARINO: Aldo Simoncini, Carlo Valentini, Damiano Vannucci, Nicola Albani, Alessandro Della Valle, Davide Simoncini, Simone Bacciocchi, Cristian Negri (69 Giovanni Bonini), Matteo Bugli (85 Fabio Vitaioli), Alex Gasperoni, Manuel Marani (76 Marco Domeniconi). Trainer: Giampaolo Mazza

Sent off: Davide Simoncini (54)

Goals: Kuranyi (45), Jansen (52), Frings (56 pen), Gomez (63, 65), Fritz (67)

GERMANY v SLOVAKIA 2-1 (2-1)

Arena Hamburg, Hamburg 06.06.2007

Referee: Olegário Benquerença (POR) Attendance: 51,000

GERMANY: Jens Lehmann, Marcell Jansen, Philipp Lahm, Per Mertesacker, Christoph Metzelder, Clemens Fritz, Torsten Frings, Thomas Hitzlsperger, Bernd Schneider (90 Simon Rolfes), Miroslav Klose (74 Piotr Trochowski), Kevin Kuranyi (65 Mario Gomez). Trainer: Joachim Löw

SLOVAKIA: Kamil Čontofalský, Martin Škrtel, Marek Hamsik, Ján Durica, Maroš Klimpl, Dušan Švento, Zdeno Štrba (83 Tomáš Oravec), Matej Krajčík, Marek Sapara (65 Filip Hološko), Stanislav Šesták (65 Igor Žofčák), Róbert Vittek. Trainer: Ján Kocian

Goals: Durica (10 own goal), Metzelder (20 own goal), Hitzlsperger (43)

SAN MARINO v CYPRUS 0-1 (0-0)

Olimpico, Serravalle 22.08.2007

Referee: Albano Janku (ALB) Attendance: 552

SAN MARINO: Aldo Simoncini, Carlo Valentini, Damiano Vannucci, Nicola Albani, Alessandro Della Valle, Gianluca Bollini (77 Nicola Ciacci), Giovanni Bonini (84 Federico Nanni), Matteo Bugli, Fabio Bollini (63 Matteo Andreini), Manuel Marani, Andy Selva. Trainer: Giampaolo Mazza

CYPRUS: Antonis Georgallides, Giorgos Theodotou, Paraskevas Christou, Lambros Lambrou, Christakis Marangos (24 Marios Nikolaou), Stathis Aloneftis, Chrysostomous Michail, Alexandros Garpozis (86 Ilias Charalambous), Yiasemakis Yiasoumi (55 Kostas Charalambidis), Yiannis Okkas, Michalis Konstantinou. Trainer: Angelos Anastasiadis

Goal: Okkas (54)

WALES v GERMANY **0-2** (0-1)

Millennium, Cardiff 08.09.2007

Referee: Manuel Mejuto González (SPA) Att: 31,000

WALES: Wayne Robert Hennessey, Sam Ricketts, Danny Gabbidon, James Collins, Lewin Nyatanga, Joe Ledley (46 Robert Earnshaw), Gareth Bale, Jason Koumas (67 Carl Fletcher), Carl Robinson, Simon Davies (79 Andrew Crofts), Freddy Eastwood. Trainer: John Toshack

GERMANY: Jens Lehmann, Arne Friedrich, Per Mertesacker, Christoph Metzelder, Christian Pander (46 Piotr Trochowski), Roberto Hilbert, Thomas Hitzlsperger, Bastian Schweinsteiger, Marcell Jansen, Kevin Kuranyi (72 Lukas Podolski), Miroslav Klose (87 Patrick Helmes). Trainer: Joachim Löw

Goals: Klose (5, 60)

SAN MARINO v CZECH REPUBLIC **0-3** (0-1)

Olimpico, Serravalle 08.09.2007

Referee: Dejan Filipovic (SRB) Attendance: 3,000

SAN MARINO: Aldo Simoncini, Carlo Valentini, Damiano Vannucci, Davide Simoncini, Alessandro Della Valle, Gianluca Bollini (82 Paolo Mariotti), Matteo Bugli (67 Fabio Vitaioli), Fabio Bollini (58 Matteo Andreini), Manuel Marani, Andy Selva, Giovanni Bonini. Trainer: Giampaolo Mazza

CZECH REPUBLIC: Petr Čech, Tomáš Ujfaluši, David Rozehnal, Radoslav Kováč, Marek Jankulovski, Tomáš Galásek (80 Jaroslav Plašil), Tomáš Rosický, David Jarolím (69 Jan Polák), Marek Kulič (56 Stanislav Vlček), Martin Fenin, Jan Koller. Trainer: Karel Brückner

Sent off: Alessandro Della Valle (64)

Goals: Rosický (33), Jankulovski (75), Koller (90)

SLOVAKIA v REPUBLIC OF IRELAND **2-2** (1-1)

Tehelné Pole, Bratislava 08.09.2007

Referee: Stefano Farina (ITA) Attendance: 12,400

SLOVAKIA: Štefan Senecký, Vratislav Greško, Marek Čech, Ján Durica, Maroš Klimpl, Matej Krajčík, Marek Hamšik, Marek Sapara (71 Filip Šebo), Marek Mintál, Filip Hološko, Stanislav Šesták (65 Branislav Obzera). Trainer: Ján Kocian

REPUBLIC OF IRELAND: Shay Given, John O'Shea, Stephen Kelly, Paul McShane, Richard Dunne, Lee Carsley, Aiden McGeady (61 Darron Gibson), Stephen Ireland (76 Jonathan Douglas), Kevin Kilbane, Kevin Doyle (89 Daryl Murphy), Robbie Keane. Trainer: Stephen Staunton

Goals: Ireland (7), Klimpl (37), Doyle (57), Čech (90)

SLOVAKIA v WALES **2-5** (1-3)

Antona Malatinského, Trnava 12.09.2007

Referee: Laurent Duhamel (FRA) Attendance: 5,500

SLOVAKIA: Štefan Senecký, Vratislav Greško (64 Igor Žofčák), Maroš Klimpl, Ján Durica, Marek Čech, Marek Hamšík, Peter Petráš, Marek Sapara, Marek Mintál, Stanislav Šesták (46 Branislav Obzera), Filip Hološko.
Trainer: Ján Kocian

WALES: Wayne Robert Hennessey, Sam Ricketts, Danny Gabbidon, Craig Morgan, James Collins, Gareth Bale, Simon Davies, Carl Robinson, Joe Ledley (85 David Vaughan), Craig Bellamy, Freddy Eastwood (73 Carl Fletcher).
Trainer: John Toshack

Goals: Mintál (12, 57), Eastwood (22), Bellamy (34, 41), Durica (78 own goal), S. Davies (90)

CYPRUS v SAN MARINO **3-0** (2-0)

GSP, Nicosia 12.09.2007

Referee: Alexey Kulbakov (BLR) Attendance: 600

CYPRUS: Antonis Georgallides, Ilias Charalambous (65 Alexandros Garpozis), Stelios Okkarides, Paraskevas Christou, Chrysostomous Michail, Marios Elia (76 Giorgos Theodotou), Konstantinos Makridis, Marios Nikolaou, Yiannis Okkas (46 Yiasemakis Yiasoumi), Michalis Konstantinou, Stathis Aloneftis. Trainer: Angelos Anastasiadis

SAN MARINO: Federico Valentini, Carlo Valentini, Damiano Vannucci, Fabio Vitaioli, Nicola Albani (81 Giacomo Benedettini), Fabio Bollini, Matteo Andreini, Matteo Bugli, Manuel Marani (87 Federico Nanni), Andy Selva, Giovanni Bonini (73 Paolo Mariotti). Trainer: Giampaolo Mazza

Goals: Makridis (15), Aloneftis (41, 90)

CZECH REPUBLIC v REPUBLIC OF IRELAND **1-0** (1-0)

Sparta Stadium, Praha 12.09.2007

Referee: Kyros Vassaras (GRE) Attendance: 16,700

CZECH REPUBLIC: Petr Čech, Tomáš Ujfaluši, David Rozehnal, Radoslav Kováč, Marek Jankulovski, Libor Sionko (74 Stanislav Vlček), Tomáš Galásek (46 Tomas Sivok), Tomáš Rosický, Jan Polák, Jaroslav Plašil, Milan Baroš (89 David Jarolím). Trainer: Karel Brückner

REPUBLIC OF IRELAND: Shay Given, Stephen Kelly, Paul McShane, Richard Dunne, John O'Shea (38 Stephen Hunt), Aiden McGeady (62 Shane Long), Lee Carsley (82 Andrew Keogh), Andy Reid, Kevin Kilbane, Kevin Doyle, Robbie Keane. Trainer: Stephen Staunton

Sent off: Steven Hunt (61)

Goal: Jankulovski (15)

SLOVAKIA v SAN MARINO 7-0 (3-0)

Športová hala Dubnica, Dubnica nad Vahom 13.10.2007

Referee: Luc Wilmes (LUX) Attendance: 2,600

SLOVAKIA: Kamil Čontofalský, Martin Škrtel, Matej Krajcík, Ján Durica, Ottó Szabó, Marek Sapara (79 Andrej Hesek), Marek Čech, Marek Hamšík, Ján Kozák, Stanislav Šesták (60 Blazej Vasčák), Filip Hološko (71 Filip Šebo). Trainer: Ján Kocian

SAN MARINO: Federico Valentini, Matteo Andreini, Damiano Vannucci, Fabio Vitaioli, Nicola Albani, Alessandro Della Valle, Gianluca Bollini (57 Giacomo Benedettini), Carlo Valentini, Matteo Bugli (68 Luca Bonifaci), Manuel Marani (85 Marco De Luigi), Federico Nanni. Trainer: Giampaolo Mazza

Goals: Hamšík (24), Šesták (32, 57), Sapara (37), Skrtel (51), Hološko (54), Durica (76 pen)

SAN MARINO v WALES 1-2 (0-2)

Olimpico, Serravalle 17.10.2007

Referee: Anthony Zammit (MLT) Attendance: 1,300

SAN MARINO: Aldo Simoncini, Carlo Valentini, Damiano Vannucci (76 Matteo Bugli), Nicola Albani, Alessandro Della Valle, Luca Bonifazi (62 Giovanni Bonini), Davide Simoncini, Riccardo Muccioli, Matteo Andreini, Marco De Luigi (80 Matteo Vitaioli), Andy Selva. Trainer: Giampaolo Mazza

WALES: Lewis Price, Gareth Bale, Neal Eardley, Danny Gabbidon, Lewin Nyatanga, Carl Robinson, David Vaughan (62 Sam Ricketts), Simon Davies, Joe Ledley, Robert Earnshaw, Craig Bellamy. Trainer: John Toshack

Sent off: Nicola Albani (85)

Goals: Earnshaw (13), Ledley (36), A. Selva (73)

CYPRUS v WALES 3-1 (0-1)

GSP, Nicosia 13.10.2007

Referee: Carlo Bertolini (SWI) Attendance: 8,500

CYPRUS: Antonis Georgallides, Stelios Okkarides, Marinos Satsias (71 Christos Marangos), Marios Elia (63 Kostas Charalambidis), Chrysostomous Michail (46 Yiasemakis Yiasoumi), Paraskevas Christou, Alexandros Garpozis, Konstantinos Makridis, Marios Nikolaou, Stathis Aloneftis, Yiannis Okkas. Trainer: Angelos Anastasiadis

WALES: Danny Coyne, Sam Ricketts (73 Jermaine Maurice Easter), James Collins (44 Craig Morgan), Danny Gabbidon, Gareth Bale, Lewin Nyatanga, Joe Ledley, Carl Robinson, Simon Davies, Craig Bellamy, Freddy Eastwood (58 Robert Earnshaw). Trainer: John Toshack

Goals: Collins (21), Okkas (59, 68), Charalampidis (79)

REPUBLIC OF IRELAND v CYPRUS 1-1 (0-0)

Croke Park, Dublin 17.10.2007

Referee: Mikko Vuorela (FIN) Attendance: 54,900

REPUBLIC OF IRELAND: Shay Given, Steve Finnan, Kevin Kilbane, Paul McShane, John O'Shea, Joseph O'Brien (46 Liam Miller), Andy Reid, Andrew Keogh (63 Aiden McGeady), Kevin Doyle, Robbie Keane, Stephen Hunt (74 Jonathan Douglas). Trainer: Stephen Staunton

CYPRUS: Antonis Georgallides, Marinos Satsias (69 Christos Marangos), Stelios Okkarides, Paraskevas Christou, Kostas Charalambidis, Marios Elia, Alexandros Garpozis, Konstantinos Makridis (82 Christis Theofilou), Marios Nikolaou, Yiannis Okkas, Yiasoumi Yiasoumi (73 Chrysostomous Michail). Trainer: Angelos Anastasiadis

Sent off: Marios Elia (90)

Goals: Okkarides (78), Finnan (88)

REPUBLIC OF IRELAND v GERMANY 0-0

Croke Park, Dublin 13.10.2007

Referee: Martin Hansson (SWE) Attendance: 67,500

REPUBLIC OF IRELAND: Shay Given, Stephen Kelly, Richard Dunne, Joseph O'Brien, Steve Finnan, Lee Carsley, Andy Reid, Kevin Kilbane (90 Daryl Murphy), Andrew Keogh (78 Aiden McGeady), Kevin Doyle (70 Shane Long), Robbie Keane. Trainer: Stephen Staunton

GERMANY: Jens Lehmann, Arne Friedrich, Clemens Fritz, Marcell Jansen, Per Mertesacker, Christoph Metzelder, Torsten Frings, Bastian Schweinsteiger (18 Simon Rolfes), Piotr Trochowski (88 Gonzalo Castro), Mario Gómez (64 Lukas Podolski), Kevin Kuranyi. Trainer: Joachim Löw

GERMANY v CZECH REPUBLIC 0-3 (0-2)

Fußball Arena München, Munich 17.10.2007

Referee: Howard Webb (ENG) Attendance: 66,400

GERMANY: Timo Hildebrand, Marcell Jansen, Arne Friedrich, Per Mertesacker, Christoph Metzelder (46 Clemens Fritz), Bastian Schweinsteiger (65 Mario Gomez), Torsten Frings, Piotr Trochowski (46 Simon Rolfes), David Odonkor, Kevin Kuranyi, Lukas Podolski. Trainer: Joachim Löw

CZECH REPUBLIC: Petr Čech, Radoslav Kováč, David Rozehnal, Tomáš Ujfaluši, Zdeněk Pospech, Tomáš Galásek, Daniel Pudil (73 Marek Kulic), Marek Matejovský, Libor Sionko (58 Stanislav Vlček), Jaroslav Plašil, Jan Koller (79 Martin Fenin). Trainer: Karel Brückner

Goals: Sionko (2), Matejovsky (23), Plašil (63)

WALES v REPUBLIC OF IRELAND 2-2 (1-1)

Millennium, Cardiff 17.11.2007

Referee: Oleh Oriekhov (UKR) Attendance: 24,600

WALES: Wayne Robert Hennessey, Neal Eardley (81 David Cotterill), James Collins, Danny Gabbidon, Christopher Gunter, Joe Ledley, Jason Koumas, Carl Robinson (37 David Edwards), Carl Fletcher, Simon Davies, Freddy Eastwood (60 Jermaine Maurice Easter). Trainer: John Toshack

REPUBLIC OF IRELAND: Shay Given, Steve Finnan, Paul McShane, John O'Shea, Kevin Kilbane, Aiden McGeady, Lee Carsley, Liam Miller (60 Stephen Hunt), Andy Reid (87 Darren Potter), Kevin Doyle, Robbie Keane. Trainer: Donald Givens

Goals: Koumas (23, 89 pen), Keane (31), Doyle (60)

CYPRUS v CZECH REPUBLIC 0-2 (0-1)

GSP, Nicosia 21.11.2007

Referee: Levan Paniashvili (GEO) Attendance: 5,200

CYPRUS: Antonis Georgallides, Paraskevas Christou, Lambros Lambrou, Marios Nikolaou (56 Elias Charlambous), Alexandros Garpozis, Kostas Charalambidis (62 Yiasoumi Yiasoumi), Konstantinos Makridis (84 Chrysostomous Michail), Marinos Satsias, Stathis Aloneftis, Yiannis Okkas, Michalis Konstantinou. Trainer: Angelos Anastasiadis

CZECH REPUBLIC: Daniel Zítka, Zdeněk Pospech, Radoslav Kováč, David Rozehnal, Michal Kadlec, Jaroslav Plašil (87 Jiří Kladrubsky), Tomáš Galásek, Marek Matějovský, Daniel Pudil, Marek Kulic (57 Milan Baroš), Jan Koller (76 Martin Fenin). Trainer: Karel Brückner

Goals: Pudil (11), Koller (74)

GERMANY v CYPRUS 4-0 (2-0)

AWD-Arena, Hannover 17.11.2007

Referee: Peter Rasmussen (DEN) Attendance: 44,500

GERMANY: Jens Lehmann, Philipp Lahm, Christoph Metzelder, Per Mertesacker, Arne Friedrich, Piotr Trochowski (66 Tim Borowski), Thomas Hitzlsperger, Clemens Fritz (77 Roberto Hilbert), Lukas Podolski, Mario Gómez (73 Mike Hanke), Miroslav Klose. Trainer: Joachim Löw

CYPRUS: Antonis Georgallides, Lambros Lambrou, Giorgos Theodotou (27 Marios Nikolaou), Paraskevas Christou, Alexandros Garpozis, Yiannis Okkas, Kostas Charalampidis (46 Christis Theofilou), Marinos Satsias, Stathis Aloneftis, Konstantinos Makridis, Michalis Konstantinou (68 Yiasemakis Yiasoumi). Trainer: Angelos Anastasiadis

Goals: Fritz (2), Klose (20), Podolski (53), Hitzlsperger (82)

GERMANY v WALES 0-0

Commerzbank Arena, Frankfurt am Main 21.11.2007

Referee: Pavel Cristian Balaj (ROM) Attendance: 49,300

GERMANY: Jens Lehmann, Gonzalo Castro (56 Roberto Hilbert), Per Mertesacker, Christoph Metzelder, Philipp Lahm, Clemens Fritz, Tim Borowski, Thomas Hitzlsperger (46 Simon Rolfes), Lukas Podolski, Mario Gómez (71 Oliver Neuville), Miroslav Klose. Trainer: Joachim Löw

WALES: Wayne Robert Hennessey, Sam Ricketts, Danny Gabbidon, James Collins, Lewin Nyatanga, Christopher Gunter, Carl Fletcher, Simon Davies, David Edwards (90 Andrew Crofts), Joe Ledley, Robert Earnshaw (56 Jermaine Maurice Easter). Trainer: John Toshack

CZECH REPUBLIC v SLOVAKIA 3-1 (1-0)

Sparta, Praha 17.11.2007

Referee: Tony Asumaa (FIN) Attendance: 15,700

CZECH REPUBLIC: Jaromír Blazek, Zdeněk Pospech, Radoslav Kováč, David Rozehnal, Zdeněk Grygera (46 Michal Kadlec), Jan Polák (86 Marek Matějovský), Tomáš Galásek, Tomáš Rosický, Jaroslav Plašil, Jan Koller, Milan Baroš (70 Marek Kulic). Trainer: Karel Brückner

SLOVAKIA: Kamil Čontofalský, Matej Krajcík, Martin Škrtel, Lubomír Michalík, Marek Čech, Zdeno Štrba, Karol Kisel (88 Juraj Halenar), Marek Sapara, Ján Kozák, Marek Hamšík (58 Filip Hološko), Marek Mintál (67 Stanislav Šesták). Trainer: Ján Kocian

Goals: Grygera (13), Kulic (76), Kadlec (79 own goal), Rosický (83)

SAN MARINO v SLOVAKIA 0-5 (0-1)

Olimpico, Serravalle 21.11.2007

Referee: Andrejs Sipailo (LVA) Attendance: 500

SAN MARINO: Federico Valentini, Carlo Valentini, Mauro Marani (84 Matteo Andreini), Davide Simoncini, Alessandro Della Valle, Gianluca Bollini (61 Maicol Berretti), Michele Marani, Riccardo Muccioli, Damiano Vannucci, Manuel Marani, Andy Selva (50 Marco De Luigi). Trainer: Giampaolo Mazza

SLOVAKIA: Štefan Senecký, Matej Krajcík (63 Peter Petráš), Lubomír Michalík, Tomas Hubocan, Marek Čech, Balázs Borbély, Marek Hamšík, Karol Kisel (46 Otto Szabo), Ján Kozák, Stanislav Šesták (75 Juraj Halenar), Filip Hološko. Trainer: Ján Kocian

Goals: Michalík (42), Hološko (51, 57), Hamšik (53), Čech (83)

	P	W	D	L	F	A	Pts
Czech Republic	12	9	2	1	27	5	29
Germany	12	8	3	1	35	7	27
Ireland	12	4	5	3	17	14	17
Slovakia	12	5	1	6	33	23	16
Wales	12	4	3	5	18	19	15
Cyprus	12	4	2	6	17	24	14
San Marino	12	0	0	12	2	57	0

GROUP 5

ESTONIA v MACEDONIA 0-1 (0-0)

A Le Coq Arena, Tallinn 16.08.2006

Referee: Kristinn Jakobsson (ISL) Attendance: 5,000

ESTONIA: Mart Poom, Enar Jääger, Andrei Stepanov, Raio Piiroja, Dmitri Kruglov, Aleksandr Dmitrijev, Sergei Terehhov, Ragnar Klavan, Joel Lindpere (74 Tarmo Neemelo), Andrei Sidorenkov (67 Ingemar Teever), Kristen Viikmäe (90 Alo Bärengrub). Trainer: Jelle Goes

MACEDONIA: Jane Nikolovski, Vlade Lazarevski, Robert Petrov (85 Aleksandar Vasoski), Goce Sedloski, Igor Mitreski, Nikolče Noveski, Velice Šumulikoski, Igor Jančevski, Goran Pandev (80 Darko Tasevski), Ilčo Naumoski (71 Aco Stojkov), Goran Maznov. Trainer: Srecko Katanec

Goal: Sedloski (73)

ENGLAND v ANDORRA 5-0 (3-0)

Old Trafford, Manchester 02.09.2006

Referee: Bernhard Brugger (AUS) Attendance: 56,300

ENGLAND: Paul Robinson, Phil Neville (65 Aaron Lennon), Wes Brown, John Terry, Ashley Cole, Steven Gerrard, Owen Hargreaves, Frank Lampard, Stewart Downing (64 Kieran Richardson), Peter Crouch, Jermain Defoe (71 Andrew Johnson). Trainer: Steve McClaren

ANDORRA: Jesús Álvarez "Koldo", Antoni Lima, José Manuel García Txema, José Manuel Ayala, Óscar Sonejee, Javier Martin Sánchez (46 Juli Sánchez), Toni Sivera (77 Genís García), Marcio Vieira, Fernando Silva, Marc Pujol (49 Manolo Jiménez), Justo Ruíz. Trainer: David Rodrigo

Goals: Crouch (5, 66), Gerrard (13), Defoe (38, 47)

ESTONIA v ISRAEL 0-1 (0-1)

A Le Coq Arena, Tallinn 02.09.2006

Referee: Johan Verbist (BEL) Attendance: 5,000

ESTONIA: Mart Poom, Enar Jääger, Andrei Stepanov, Raio Piiroja, Dmitri Kruglov, Sergei Terehhov, Ragnar Klavan, Aleksandr Dmitrijev (85 Ingemar Teever), Kristen Viikmäe (69 Konstantin Vassiljev), Tarmo Neemelo (85 Alo Bärengrub), Andres Oper. Trainer: Jelle Goes

ISRAEL: Dudu Awat, Shimon Gershon, Tal Ben Haim, Yossi Benayoun, Michael Zandberg (60 Amit Ben Shoshan), Omri Afek, Walid Badir, Idan Tal, Yaniv Katan (72 Gal Alberman), Yoav Ziv, Roberto Colautti. Trainer: Dror Kashtan

Goal: Colautti (8)

ISRAEL v ANDORRA 4-1 (3-0)

De Goffert, Nijmegen 06.09.2006

Referee: Siniša Zrnic (BHZ)
Attendance: Played behind closed doors on neutral ground

ISRAEL: Dudu Awat, Omri Afek, Tal Ben Haim, Shimon Gershon, Yoav Ziv, Idan Tal, Walid Badir (76 Gal Alberman), Yossi Benayoun (69 Omer Golan), Amit Ben Shoshan, Yaniv Katan (62 Toto Adurans Tamuz), Roberto Colautti. Trainer: Dror Kashtan

ANDORRA: Jesús Álvarez "Koldo", Marc Bernaus, José Manuel García Txema, Antoni Lima, José Manuel Ayala, Fernando Silva, Óscar Sonejee, Marcio Vieira (67 Sergio Moreno), Manolo Jiménez, Marc Pujol (46 Genís García), Justo Ruíz (54 Juli Fernández). Trainer: David Rodrigo

Sent off: Fernando Silva (77)

Goals: Benayoun (9), Ben Shoshan (11), Gershon (43 pen), Tamuz (69), Fernández (84)

RUSSIA v CROATIA 0-0

Lokomotiv, Moscow 06.09.2006

Referee: Manuel Enrique Mejuto González (SPA)
Attendance: 28,000

RUSSIA: Igor Akinfeev, Sergei Ignashevich, Aleksandr Anyukov, Denis Kolodon, Aleksei Berezutski, Marat Izmailov, Evgeni Aldonin, Igor Semshov, Diniyar Bilyaletdinov, Roman Pavlyuchenko (53 Pavel Pogrebnyak), Andrei Arshavin. Trainer: Guus Hiddink

CROATIA: Stipe Pletikosa, Robert Kovač, Vedran Čorluka, Goran Sablić, Anthony Šerić, Niko Kovač, Luka Modrić, Niko Kranjčar, Milan Rapaić (58 Mladen Petrić), Ivan Klasnić (88 Marko Babić), Eduardo da Silva (71 Jerko Leko). Trainer: Slaven Bilić

MACEDONIA v ENGLAND 0-1 (0-0)

Gradski, Skopje 06.09.2006

Referee: Bertrand Layec (FRA) Attendance: 16,600

MACEDONIA: Jane Nikolovski, Nikolce Noveski, Robert Petrov, Goce Sedloski, Igor Mitreski, Vlade Lazarevski, Igor Jančevski (52 Darko Tasevski), Velice Šumulikoski, Ilčo Naumoski (74 Artim Šakiri), Goran Maznov (56 Aco Stojkov), Goran Pandev. Trainer: Srecko Katanec

ENGLAND: Paul Robinson, Phil Neville, John Terry, Rio Ferdinand, Ashley Cole, Steven Gerrard, Owen Hargreaves, Frank Lampard (84 Michael Carrick), Stewart Downing, Peter Crouch (87 Andrew Johnson), Jermain Defoe (76 Aaron Lennon). Trainer: Steve McClaren

Goal: Crouch (46)

CROATIA v ANDORRA 7-0 (2-0)

Maksimir, Zagreb 07.10.2006

Referee: Anthony Zammit (MLT) Attendance: 15,000

CROATIA: Stipe Pletikosa, Dario Šimić, Josip Šimunić, Robert Kovač, Vedran Čorluka, Niko Kovač (69 Jerko Leko), Luka Modrić, Ivan Klasnić, Niko Kranjčar, Mladen Petrić (60 Boško Balaban), Eduardo da Silva (64 Marko Babić). Trainer: Slaven Bilić

ANDORRA: Jesús Álvarez "Koldo", José Manuel Ayala, Jordi Rubio, Óscar Sonejee, Juli Fernández, Jordi Escura, Genís García (68 Manolo Jiménez), Marcio Vieira, Juli Sánchez (53 Juan Carlos Toscano), Marc Pujol, Toni Sivera (60 Justo Ruíz). Trainer: David Rodrigo

Goals: Petrić (12, 37, 48, 50), Klasnić (58), Balaban (62), Modrić (83)

ENGLAND v MACEDONIA 0-0

Old Trafford, Manchester 07.10.2006

Referee: Markus Merk (GER) Attendance: 72,100

ENGLAND: Paul Robinson, Gary Neville, John Terry, Ledley King, Ashley Cole, Steven Gerrard, Frank Lampard, Michael Carrick, Stewart Downing (70 Shaun Wright-Phillips), Wayne Rooney (74 Jermain Defoe), Peter Crouch. Trainer: Steve McClaren

MACEDONIA: Jane Nikolovski, Nikolce Noveski, Robert Petrov, Goce Sedloski, Vlade Lazarevski, Igor Mitreski, Aleksandar Mitreski, Velice Šumulikoski, Goran Maznov, Ilčo Naumoski (46 Aco Stojkov), Goran Pandev (83 Darko Tasevski). Trainer: Srecko Katanec

ANDORRA v MACEDONIA 0-3 (0-3)

Estadi Comunal, Andorra La Vella 11.10.2006

Referee: Lasha Silagava (GEO) Attendance: 350

ANDORRA: Jesús Álvarez "Koldo", José Manuel García Txema, José Manuel Ayala, Óscar Sonejee, Jordi Rubio, Genís García, Marcio Vieira, Marc Pujol (87 Manolo Jiménez), Marc Bernaus, Toni Sivera, Juan Carlos Toscano (34 Justo Ruíz). Trainer: David Rodrigo

MACEDONIA: Jane Nikolovski, Nikolce Noveski, Igor Mitreski, Goce Sedloski, Robert Petrov (70 Artim Šakiri), Aleksandar Mitreski, Velice Šumulikoski, Vlade Lazarevski, Ilčo Naumoski (32 Aco Stojkov), Goran Pandev (55 Darko Tasevski), Goran Maznov. Trainer: Srecko Katanec

Sent off: Antoni Sivera (26)

Goals: Pandev (13), Noveski (16), Naumoski (31)

RUSSIA v ISRAEL 1-1 (1-0)

Dinamo, Moscow 07.10.2006

Referee: Florian Meyer (GER) Attendance: 22,000

RUSSIA: Igor Akinfeev, Vasili Berezutskiy, Sergei Ignashevich, Aleksandr Anyukov, Aleksei Berezutskiy, Aleksei Smertin, Evgeni Aldonin, Andrei Arshavin, Diniyar Bilyaletdinov (30 Aleksandr Kerzhakov), Yuriy Zhirkov (77 Igor Semshov), Pavel Pogrebnyak (57 Marat Izmailov). Trainer: Guus Hiddink

ISRAEL: Dudu Awat, Tal Ben Haim, Shimon Gershon (46 Tomer Ben-Yosef), Adoram Keissy, Rahamin Klemi Saban (46 Amit Ben Shoshan), Omri Afek, Walid Badir, Idan Tal, Yossi Benayoun (75 Toto Adurans Tamuz), Gal Alberman, Roberto Colautti. Trainer: Dror Kashtan

Goals: Arshavin (5), Ben Shoshan (84)

CROATIA v ENGLAND 2-0 (0-0)

Maksimir, Zagreb 11.10.2006

Referee: Roberto Rosetti (ITA) Attendance: 34,500

CROATIA: Stipe Pletikosa, Dario Šimic, Josip Šimunić, Robert Kovač, Vedran Čorluka, Milan Rapaić (76 Ivica Olić), Niko Kovač, Luka Modrić, Niko Kranjčar (89 Marko Babić), Eduardo da Silva (81 Jerko Leko), Mladen Petrić. Trainer: Slaven Bilić

ENGLAND: Paul Robinson, Jamie Carragher (73 Shaun Wright-Phillips), Rio Ferdinand, John Terry, Gary Neville, Michael Carrick, Scott Parker (72 Jermain Defoe), Frank Lampard, Ashley Cole, Wayne Rooney, Peter Crouch (72 Kieran Richardson). Trainer: Steve McClaren

Goals: Eduardo (61), G. Neville (69 own goal)

RUSSIA v ESTONIA 2-0 (0-0)

Petrovsky, St Petersburg 11.10.2006

Referee: Eric Braamhaar (HOL) Attendance: 21,500

RUSSIA: Igor Akinfeev, Aleksei Berezutskiy, Vasili Berezutskiy, Sergei Ignashevich, Aleksandr Anyukov, Vladimir Bystrov, Egor Titov, Diniyar Bilyaletdinov (90 Ivan Saenko), Evgeni Aldonin (74 Dmitri Sychev), Andrei Arshavin, Aleksandr Kerzhakov (46 Pavel Pogrebnyak). Trainer: Guus Hiddink

ESTONIA: Mart Poom, Teet Allas (81 Ats Purje), Enar Jääger, Andrei Stepanov, Raio Piiroja, Dmitri Kruglov, Sergei Terehhov (81 Andrei Sidorenkov), Aleksandr Dmitrijev, Ragnar Klavan, Ingemar Teever (81 Vladislav Gussev), Andres Oper. Trainer: Jelle Goes

Sent off: Raio Piiroja (90)

Goals: Pogrebnyak (78), Sychev (88)

CROATIA v MACEDONIA 2-1 (0-1)

Maksimir, Zagreb 24.03.2007

Referee: Konrad Plautz (AUS) Attendance: 33,000

CROATIA: Stipe Pletikosa, Dario Šimić, Josip Šimunić, Vedran Čorluka, Milan Rapaić (46 Darijo Srna), Marko Babić, Boško Balaban (79 Igor Budan), Niko Kovač, Luka Modrić, Niko Kranjčar, Eduardo da Silva. Trainer: Slaven Bilić

MACEDONIA: Jane Nikoloski, Nikolce Noveski, Robert Popov, Goce Sedloski, Vlade Lazarevski, Aleksandar Mitreski (77 Igor Jančevski), Velice Šumulikoski, Goran Maznov (71 Miroslav Vajs), Ilčo Naumoski (60 Darko Tasevski), Goran Pandev, Aleksandar Vasoski. Trainer: Srecko Katanec

Sent off: Goce Sedloski (68)

Goals: Sedloski (36), Srna (58), Eduardo (88)

MACEDONIA v RUSSIA 0-2 (0-2)

Gradski, Skopje 15.11.2006

Referee: Paul Allaerts (BEL) Attendance: 16,500

MACEDONIA: Jane Nikoloski, Nikolce Noveski, Robert Petrov, Goce Sedloski, Igor Mitreski, Vlade Lazarevski, Velice Šumulikoski, Artim Šakiri (35 Darko Tasevski), Aleksandar Mitreski (46 Igor Jancevski, 71 Vlatko Grozdanovski), Goran Maznov, Aco Stojkov. Trainer: Srecko Katanec

RUSSIA: Igor Akinfeev, Vasili Berezutskiy, Aleksei Berezutskiy, Denis Kolodin, Vladimir Bystrov, Diniyar Bilyaletdinov, Igor Semshov, Yuri Zhirkov, Egor Titov, Andrei Arshavin (90 Roman Pavlyuchenko), Pavel Pogrebnyak (57 Dmitri Sychev). Trainer: Guus Hiddink

Goals: Bystrov (18), Arshavin (32)

ISRAEL v ENGLAND 0-0

Ramat Gan, Tel-Aviv 24.03.2007

Referee: Tom Henning Øvrebø (NOR) Attendance: 41,500

ISRAEL: Dudu Awat, Tal Ben Haim, Shimon Gershon, Yoav Ziv, Arik Benado, Yuval Shpungin, Walid Badir, Yossi Benayoun, Amit Ben Shoshan (87 Gal Alberman), Toto Adurans Tamuz (75 Elyaniv Barda), Pini Balali (69 Ben Sahar). Trainer: Dror Kashtan

ENGLAND: Paul Robinson, Phil Neville (72 Micah Richards), Rio Ferdinand, John Terry, Jamie Carragher, Steven Gerrard, Frank Lampard, Owen Hargreaves, Aaron Lennon (83 Stewart Downing), Wayne Rooney, Andrew Johnson (80 Jermain Defoe). Trainer: Stephen McClaren

ISRAEL v CROATIA 3-4 (1-2)

Ramat Gan, Tel-Aviv 15.11.2006

Referee: Eduardo Iturralde González (SPA) Att: 35,000

ISRAEL: Dudu Awat, Omri Afek, Tal Ben Haim, Tomer Ben-Yosef, Adoram Keissy, Gal Alberman, Walid Badir (46 Toto Adurans Tamuz), Idan Tal, Yaniv Katan (59 Amit Ben Shoshan), Yossi Benayoun, Roberto Colautti. Trainer: Dror Kashtan

CROATIA: Vedran Runje, Vedran Čorluka, Dario Šimić, Robert Kovač, Josip Šimunić, Darijo Srna (88 Ivica Olić), Niko Kovač, Luka Modrić, Niko Kranjčar (70 Marko Babić), Eduardo da Silva (81 Jerko Leko), Mladen Petrić. Trainer: Slaven Bilić

Goals: Colautti (8, 89), Srna (35 pen), Eduardo (39, 54, 72), Benayoun (68)

ESTONIA v RUSSIA 0-2 (0-0)

A Le Coq Arena, Tallin 24.03.2007

Referee: Darko Ceferin (SVN) Attendance: 11,000

ESTONIA: Mart Poom, Tihhon Šišov (80 Tarmo Neemelo), Marek Lemsalu, Dmitri Kruglov, Andrei Stepanov, Aleksandr Dmitrijev, Liivo Leetma (69 Tarmo Kink), Joel Lindpere, Ragnar Klavan, Andres Oper, Sergei Terehhov (52 Gert Kams). Trainer: Jelle Goes

RUSSIA: Igor Akinfeev, Roman Shishkin, Sergei Ignashevich, Aleksandr Anyukov, Dmitri Torbinskiy, Diniyar Bilyaletdinov, Konstantin Zyryanov, Yuri Zhirkov, Vladimir Bystrov (90 Ivan Saenko), Aleksandr Kerzhakov (83 Dmitri Sychev), Andrei Arshavin. Trainer: Guus Hiddink

Goals: Kerzhakov (66, 78)

ISRAEL v ESTONIA **4-0** (2-0)

Ramat Gan, Tel-Aviv 28.03.2007

Referee: Cüneyt Cakir (TUR) Attendance: 23,658

ISRAEL: Dudu Awat, Yuval Shpungin, Tal Ben Haim, Shimon Gershon, Yoav Ziv, Idan Tal (87 Salim Toema), Walid Badir, Yossi Benayoun, Amit Ben Shoshan (70 Gal Alberman), Toto Adurans Tamuz (64 Ben Sahar), Roberto Colautti. Trainer: Dror Kashtan

ESTONIA: Mart Poom, Tihhon Šišov, Marek Lemsalu, Alo Bärengrub, Andres Oper, Dmitri Kruglov, Aleksandr Dmitrijev, Taavi Rähn (39 Tarmo Kink), Joel Lindpere (80 Gert Kams), Ragnar Klavan, Tarmo Neemelo (61 Oliver Konsa). Trainer: Jelle Goes

Goals: Tal (19), Colautti (29), Sahar (77, 80)

MACEDONIA v ISRAEL **1-2** (1-2)

Gradski, Skopje 02.06.2007

Referee: Knut Kircher (GER) Attendance: 16,000

MACEDONIA: Jane Nikoloski, Nikolce Noveski, Robert Petrov, Vlade Lazarevski (46 Vlatko Grozdanovski), Igor Mitreski, Aleksandar Vasoski, Velice Šumulikoski, Darko Tasevski, Ilčo Naumoski (46 Stevica Ristić), Goran Pandev (55 Artim Položani), Aco Stojkov. Trainer: Srecko Katanec

ISRAEL: Dudu Awat, Yuval Shpungin, Yoav Ziv, Arik Benado, Walid Badir, Idan Tal, Pini Balali (61 Ben Sahar), Gal Alberman, Roberto Colautt (81 Omer Golan), Barak Itzhaki (76 Michael Zandberg), Dekel Keinan. Trainer: Dror Kashtan

Goals: Itzhaki (11), Stojkov (13), Colautti (44)

ANDORRA v ENGLAND **0-3** (0-0)

Olímpico de Montjuic, Barcelona 28.03.2007

Referee: Bruno Miguel Duarte Paixao (POR) Att: 12,800

ANDORRA: Jesús Álvarez "Koldo", Óscar Sonejee, Antoni Lima, José Manuel Ayala, Marc Bernaus, Jordi Escura, Marcio Vieira, Genís García, Justo Ruíz (85 Juli Fernández), Marc Pujol (69 Francisco Martínez), Juan Carlos Toscano (90 Sergio Moreno). Trainer: David Rodrigo

ENGLAND: Paul Robinson, Micah Richards (61 Kieron Dyer), John Terry, Rio Ferdinand, Ashley Cole, Aaron Lennon, Owen Hargreaves, Steven Gerrard, Stewart Downing, Andrew Johnson (79 David Nugent), Wayne Rooney (61 Jermain Defoe). Trainer: Stephen McClaren

Goals: Gerrard (54, 76), Nugent (89)

ESTONIA v CROATIA **0-1** (0-1)

A Le Coq Arena, Tallinn 02.06.2007

Referee: Viktor Kassai (HUN) Attendance: 10,000

ESTONIA: Mart Poom, Enar Jääger, Andrei Stepanov, Raio Piiroja, Dmitri Kruglov, Aleksandr Dmitrijev, Joel Lindpere (78 Tarmo Kink), Ragnar Klavan, Konstantin Vassiljev, Oliver Konsa (71 Tarmo Neemelo), Vladimir Voskoboinikov. Trainer: Jelle Goes

CROATIA: Stipe Pletikosa, Josip Šimunić, Robert Kovač, Vedran Čorluka, Marko Babić, Niko Kovač, Darijo Srna, Luka Modrić, Niko Kranjčar (74 Jerko Leko), Mladen Petrić (54 Ivica Olić), Eduardo da Silva (84 Boško Balaban). Trainer: Slaven Bilić

Goal: Eduardo (32)

RUSSIA v ANDORRA **4-0** (2-0)

Petrovsky, Sankt Petersburg 02.06.2007

Referee: Tommy Skjerven (NOR) Attendance: 21,000

RUSSIA: Vyacheslav Malafeev, Vasili Berezutski, Sergei Ignashevich, Aleksei Berezutski (46 Aleksandr Anyukov), Vladimir Bystrov, Konstantin Zyryanov, Dmitri Torbinskiy, Igor Semshov, Yuri Zhirkov (57 Viktor Budyanski), Andrei Arshavin, Aleksandr Kerzhakov (54 Dmitri Sychev). Trainer: Guus Hiddink

ANDORRA: Jesús Álvarez "Koldo", José Manuel García Txema, Òscar Alfonso Da Cunha (57 Juli Sánchez), Marc Bernaus, José Manuel Ayala, Jordi Escura, Marcio Vieira, Marc Pujol, Manolo Jiménez (73 Xavier Andorra), Justo Ruíz, Sergio Moreno (88 Álex Somoza). Trainer: David Rodrigo

Goals: Kerzhakov (8, 16, 49), Sychev (71)

ANDORRA v ISRAEL **0-2** (0-1)

Comunal, Andorra La Vella 06.06.2007

Referee: Ian Stokes (IRL) Attendance: 618

ANDORRA: Jesús Álvarez "Koldo", Ildefons Lima, José Manuel García Txema (61 Oscar Sonejee), Antoni Lima, José Manuel Ayala, Jordi Escura, Genís García, Marcio Vieira, Marc Bernaus, Justo Ruíz, Juan Carlos Toscano (77 Juli Sánchez). Trainer: David Rodrigo

ISRAEL: Dudu Awat, Yoav Ziv, Arik Benado, Avi Yehiel, Dedi Ben Dayan, Idan Tal, Yossi Benayoun, Gal Alberman (71 Walid Badir), Toto Tamuz (77 Yaniv Katan), Roberto Colautti (86 Omer Golan), Barak Itzhaki. Trainer: Dror Kashtan

Goals: Tamuz (37), Colautti (53)

CROATIA v RUSSIA 0-0

Maksimir, Zagreb 06.06.2007

Referee: Luboš Michel (SVK) Attendance: 38,000

CROATIA: Stipe Pletikosa, Vedran Čorluka, Dario Šimić, Robert Kovač, Josip Šimunić, Darijo Srna (8 Jerko Leko), Niko Kovač, Luka Modrić, Niko Kranjčar (66 Mladen Petrić), Eduardo da Silva, Ivica Olić (83 Marko Babić). Trainer: Slaven Bilić

RUSSIA: Vyacheslav Malafeev, Vasili Berezutski, Sergei Ignashevich, Aleksei Berezutski, Vladimir Bystrov (61 Ivan Saenko), Aleksandr Anyukov, Yuriy Zhirkov, Igor Semshov, Viktor Budyanski (46 Dmitri Torbinskiy), Andrei Arshavin, Aleksandr Kerzhakov (73 Dmitri Sychev). Trainer: Guus Hiddink

ESTONIA v ENGLAND 0-3 (0-1)

A Le Coq Arena, Tallinn 06.06.2007

Referee: Grzegorz Gilewski (POL) Attendance: 10,500

ESTONIA: Mart Poom, Enar Jääger, Andrei Stepanov, Dmitri Kruglov, Ragnar Klavan, Aleksandr Dmitrijev, Joel Lindpere, Konstantin Vassiljev, Oliver Konsa (46 Tarmo Neemelo), Vladimir Voskoboinikov, Sergei Terehhov (64 Tarmo Kink). Trainer: Jelle Goes

ENGLAND: Paul Robinson, Wes Brown, John Terry, Ledley King, Wayne Bridge, David Beckham (68 Kieron Dyer), Steven Gerrard, Frank Lampard, Joe Cole (75 Stewart Downing), Peter Crouch, Michael Owen (88 Jermaine Jenas). Trainer: Stephen McClaren

Goals: J. Cole (37), Crouch (54), Owen (62)

ESTONIA v ANDORRA 2-1 (1-0)

A Le Coq Arena, Tallinn 22.08.2007

Referee: Adrian Mccourt (NIR) Attendance: 10,000

ESTONIA: Mart Poom, Enar Jääger, Andrei Stepanov, Raio Piiroja, Dmitri Kruglov, Martin Reim, Aleksandr Dmitrijev, Ragnar Klavan, Joel Lindpere, Indrek Zelinski, Vladimir Voskoboinikov (46 Tarmo Kink). Trainer: Viggo Jensen

ANDORRA: Jesús Álvarez "Koldo", José Manuel García Txema, Óscar Sonejee, Antoni Lima, Ildefons Lima, Jordi Escura, José Manuel Ayala (88 Genís García), Marc Pujol (79 Juli Sánchez), Toni Sivera (53 Juan Carlos Toscano Beltran), Marcio Vieira, Fernando Silva. Trainer: David Rodrigo

Sent off: Ragnar Klavan (45), Indrek Zelinski (90)

Goals: Piiroja (34), Silva (82), Zelinski (90)

ENGLAND v ISRAEL 3-0 (1-0)

Wembley, London 08.09.2007

Referee: Pieter Vink (HOL) Attendance: 85,400

ENGLAND: Paul Robinson, Micah Richards, Rio Ferdinand, John Terry, Ashley Cole, Shaun Wright-Phillips (83 David Bentley), Steven Gerrard (71 Phil Neville), Gareth Barry, Joe Cole, Emile Heskey (71 Andrew Johnson), Michael Owen. Trainer: Stephen McClaren

ISRAEL: Dudu Awat, Yuval Shpungin, Tal Ben Haim, Shimon Gershon, Yoav Ziv, Yossi Benayoun, Walid Badir, Arik Benado (57 Omwer Golan), Idan Tal, Yaniv Katan, Barak Itzhaki (46 Toto Tamuz). Trainer: Dror Kashtan

Goals: Wright-Phillips (20), Owen (49), Richards (66)

RUSSIA v MACEDONIA 3-0 (1-0)

Lokomotiv Stadium, Moscow 08.09.2007

Referee: Tom Henning Øvrebø (NOR) Attendance: 26,000

RUSSIA: Vladimir Gabulov, Vasili Berezutski, Sergei Ignashevich, Aleksei Berezutski, Vladimir Bystrov (89 Aleksandr Anyukov), Igor Semshov, Konstantin Zyrianov, Diniyar Bilyaletdinov, Andrei Arshavin, Roman Pavlyuchenko (66 Aleksandr Kerzhakov), Dmitri Sychev (70 Vyacheslav Malafeev). Trainer: Guus Hiddink

MACEDONIA: Petar Milosevski, Goran Popov, Vlade Lazarevski, Goce Sedloski, Igor Mitreski, Aleksandar Mitreski (46 Vanco Trajanov), Velice Šumulikoski, Darko Tasevski, Aleksandar Vasoski (88 Goce Toleski), Goran Pandev, Aco Stojkov (46 Goran Maznov). Trainer: Srecko Katanec

Sent off: Vladimir Gabulov (70)

Goals: V. Berezutski (8), Arshavin (84), Kerzhakov (88)

CROATIA v ESTONIA 2-0 (2-0)

Maksimir, Zagreb 08.09.2007

Referee: Jérôme Laperrière (SWI) Attendance: 19,000

CROATIA: Stipe Pletikosa, Dario Šimić, Josip Šimunić, Robert Kovač, Vedran Čorluka, Niko Kovač, Darijo Srna (81 Marko Babić), Luka Modrić, Niko Kranjčar (60 Ivan Rakitić), Mladen Petrić (70 Ivica Olić), Eduardo da Silva. Trainer: Slaven Bilić

ESTONIA: Pavel Londak, Teet Allas, Andrei Stepanov, Raio Piiroja, Urmas Rooba (84 Aivar Anniste), Taavi Rähn, Aleksandr Dmitrijev, Dmitri Kruglov, Joel Lindpere (90 Martin Reim), Tarmo Kink (80 Kaimar Saag), Andres Oper. Trainer: Viggo Jensen

Goals: Eduardo (39, 45)

ANDORRA v CROATIA 0-6 (0-3)

Estadi Comunal, Andorra La Vella 12.09.2007

Referee: Olivier Thual (FRA) Attendance: 200

ANDORRA: Jesús Álvarez "Koldo", Antoni Lima, José Manuel García Txema, Óscar Sonejee, José Manuel Ayala, Toni Sivera (59 Xavi Andorra), Genís García, Justo Ruíz (82 Alex Somoza), Manolo Jiménez, Fernando Silva (57 Sergio Moreno), Marcio Vieira. Trainer: David Rodrigo

CROATIA: Vedran Runje, Darijo Srna, Robert Kovač, Vedran Čorluka, Dario Knezević, Niko Kranjčar, Luka Modrić (46 Boško Balaban), Jerko Leko, Marko Babic, Mladen Petrić (46 Danijel Pranjić), Eduardo da Silva (62 Ivan Rakitić). Trainer: Slaven Bilić

Sent off: Genís García (77)

Goals: Srna (34), Petrić (38, 44), Krancjar (49), Eduardo (55), Rakitić (64)

ENGLAND v ESTONIA 3-0 (3-0)

Wembley, London 13.10.2007

Referee: Nicolai Vollquartz (DEN) Attendance : 86,700

ENGLAND: Paul Robinson, Micah Richards, Sol Campbell, Rio Ferdinand (46 Jolean Lescott), Ashley Cole (49 Phil Neville), Shaun Wright-Phillips, Steven Gerrard, Gareth Barry, Joe Cole, Wayne Rooney, Michael Owen (70 Frank Lampard). Trainer: Stephen McClaren

ESTONIA: Mart Poom, Dmitri Kruglov, Andrei Stepanov, Raio Piiroja, Enar Jääger, Taavi Rähn, Ragnar Klavan, Aleksandr Dmitrijev, Joel Lindpere, Tarmo Kink (62 Kristen Viikmae), Kaimar Saag. Trainer: Viggo Jensen

Goals: Wright-Phillips (11), Rooney (32), Rahn (33 own goal)

ENGLAND v RUSSIA 3-0 (2-0)

Wembley, London 12.09.2007

Referee: Martin Hansson (SWE) Attendance: 86,100

ENGLAND: Paul Robinson, Micah Richards, Rio Ferdinand, John Terry, Ashley Cole, Shaun Wright-Phillips, Gareth Barry, Steven Gerrard, Joe Cole (87 Phil Neville), Emile Heskey (80 Peter Crouch), Michael Owen (90 Stewart Downing). Trainer: Stephen McClaren

RUSSIA: Vyacheslav Malafeev, Vasili Berezutski, Sergei Ignashevich, Aleksei Berezutski, Aleksandr Anyukov (80 Aleksandr Kerzhakov), Diniyar Bilyaletdinov, Yuri Zhirkov, Igor Semshov (40 Vladimir Bystrov), Dmitri Sychev (63 Roman Pavlyuchenko), Andrei Arshavin, Konstantin Zyryanov. Trainer: Guus Hiddink

Goals: Owen (7, 31), Ferdinand (84)

CROATIA v ISRAEL 1-0 (0-0)

Maksimir, Zagreb 13.10.2007

Referee: Wolfgang Stark (GER) Attendance: 30,000

CROATIA: Stipe Pletikosa, Dario Šimić, Josip Šimunić, Robert Kovač, Vedran Čorluka, Darijo Srna, Luka Modrić, Jerko Leko, Ivica Olić (81 Ivan Rakitić), Niko Kranjčar (46 Danijel Pranjić), Eduardo da Silva. Trainer: Slaven Bilić

ISRAEL: Nir Davidovich, Eyal Meshumar, Shimon Gershon, Tal Ben Haim, Ygal Antebi, Aviram Baruchya (58 Omer Golan), Gal Alberman, Yossi Benayoun, Pini Balali (67 Toto Tamuz), Elyaniv Barda (75 Moshe Ohayon), Tamir Cohen. Trainer: Dror Kashtan

Goal: Eduardo (52)

MACEDONIA v ESTONIA 1-1 (1-1)

Gradski, Skopje 12.09.2007

Referee: Leontios Trattou (CYP) Attendance: 5,000

MACEDONIA: Petar Milosevski, Vlade Lazarevski, Goce Sedloski, Nikolce Noveski, Aleksandar Vasoski, Vlatko Grozdanovski, Vanco Trajanov (46 Artim Polozani), Velice Šumulikoski, Goran Maznov, Darko Tasevski, Aco Stojkov (81 Goce Toleski). Trainer: Srecko Katanec

ESTONIA: Pavel Londak, Enar Jääger, Andrei Stepanov, Raio Piiroja, Dmitri Kruglov, Taavi Rähn (62 Martin Reim), Aleksandr Dmitrijev, Ragnar Klavan, Joel Lindpere, Andres Oper (90 Aivar Anniste), Kaimar Saag (79 Tarmo Kink). Trainer: Viggo Jensen

Goals: Piiroja (17), Maznov (30)

ANDORRA v ESTONIA 0-2 (0-1)

Comunal, Andorra La Vella 17.11.2007

Referee: William Collum (SCO) Attendance: 200

ANDORRA: Jesús Álvarez "Koldo", Emili Garcia (46 Marcio Vieira), Jordi Rubio, Óscar Sonejee, Antoni Lima, Ildefons Lima (81 Justo Ruiz), Manolo Jiménez, José Manuel Ayala, Sergio Moreno (70 Juan Carlos Toscano Beltran), Marc Pujol, Toni Sivera. Trainer: David Rodrigo

ESTONIA: Pavel Londak, Enar Jääger, Dmitri Kruglov (84 Konstantin Vassiljev), Raio Piiroja, Andrei Stepanov, Aleksandr Dmitrijev, Ragnar Klavan, Joel Lindpere, Martin Reim (68 Taijo Teniste), Kaimar Saag, Andres Oper (46 Tarmo Kink). Trainer: Viggo Jensen

Goals: Oper (31), Lindpere (60)

RUSSIA v ENGLAND 2-1 (0-1)

Luzhniki, Moskva 17.10.2007

Referee: Luis Medina Cantalejo (SPA) Attendance: 80,000

RUSSIA: Vladimir Gabulov, Aleksei Berezutski, Sergei Ignashevich, Vasili Berezutski (46 Dmitri Torbinskiy), Aleksandr Anyukov, Konstantin Zyrianov, Igor Semshov, Diniyar Bilyaletdinov, Yuri Zhirkov, Andrei Arshavin (90 Denis Kolodin), Aleksandr Kerzhakov (58 Roman Pavlyuchenko). Trainer: Guus Hiddink

ENGLAND: Paul Robinson, Micah Richards, Rio Ferdinand, Sol Campbell, Jolean Lescott (79 Frank Lampard), Shaun Wright-Phillips (80 Stewart Downing), Steven Gerrard, Gareth Barry, Joe Cole (80 Peter Crouch), Wayne Rooney, Michael Owen. Trainer: Stephen McClaren

Goals: Rooney (29), Pavlyuchenko (69 pen, 73)

ISRAEL v RUSSIA 2-1 (1-0)

Ramat Gan, Tel-Aviv 17.11.2007

Referee: Stefano Farina (ITA) Attendance: 37,500

ISRAEL: Dudu Awat, Yuval Shpungin, Dekel Keinan, Tal Ben Haim, Yoav Ziv, Tamir Cohen, Gal Alberman, Barak Itzhaki (62 Amit Ben Shoshan), Maor Bar Buzaglo (64 Moshe Ohayon), Elyaniv Barda, Ben Sahar (69 Omer Golan). Trainer: Dror Kashtan

RUSSIA: Vladimir Gabulov, Aleksei Berezutski, Sergei Ignashevich, Vasili Berezutski (68 Pavel Pogrebnyak), Aleksandr Anyukov, Konstantin Zyrianov, Igor Semshov (30 Dmitri Torbinskiy), Diniyar Bilyaletdinov, Yuri Zhirkov, Andrei Arshavin, Roman Pavlyuchenko (52 Dmitri Sychev). Trainer: Guus Hiddink

Goals: Barda (10), Bilyaletdinov (61), Golan (90)

MACEDONIA v ANDORRA 3-0 (2-0)

Gradski, Skopje 17.10.2007

Referee: Paulius Malzinskas (LTU) Attendance: 18,000

MACEDONIA: Tome Pacovski, Vlade Lazarevski, Nikolce Noveski, Goce Sedloski, Igor Mitreski, Goran Popov, Velice Šumulikoski, Darko Tasevski (84 Vanco Trajanov), Goran Maznov (62 Stevica Ristić), Ilčo Naumoski (75 Artim Položani), Goran Pandev. Trainer: Srecko Katanec

ANDORRA: Jesús Álvarez "Koldo", Óscar Sonejee, Julià Fernández, Ildefons Lima, José Manuel Ayala, Jordi Escura, Marc Pujol, Justo Ruíz (63 Xavier Andorra), Manolo Jiménez (78 Alex Somoza), Marcio Vieira, Juan Carlos Toscano Beltrán (82 Gabriel Riera). Trainer: David Rodrigo

Goals: Naumoski (30), Sedloski (44), Pandev (59)

ISRAEL v MACEDONIA 1-0 (1-0)

Ramat Gan, Tel-Aviv 21.11.2007

Referee: Tomasz Mikulski (POL) Attendance: 2,800

ISRAEL: Dudu Awat, Yuval Shpungin, Dekel Keinan, Tal Ben Haim, Yoav Ziv, Moshe Ohayon, Tamir Cohen, Maor Bar Buzaglo (46 Amit Ben Shoshan), Barak Itzhaki (72 Aviram Baruchyan), Elyaniv Barda, Roberto Colautti (55 Ben Sahar). Trainer: Dror Kashtan

MACEDONIA: Petar Milosevski, Nikolce Noveski, Goran Popov, Goce Sedloski, Igor Mitreski, Vlatko Grozdanovski (66 Slavco Georgievski), Velice Šumulikoski, Vlade Lazarevski, Goran Maznov (60 Stevica Ristić), Darko Tasevski (46 Artim Polozani), Aco Stojkov. Trainer: Srecko Katanec

Goal: Barda (35)

MACEDONIA v CROATIA 2-0 (0-0)

Gradski, Skopje 17.11.2007

Referee: Frank De Bleeckere (BEL) Attendance: 18,000

MACEDONIA: Petar Milosevski, Nikolce Noveski, Igor Mitreski, Goran Popov, Goce Sedloski (88 Boban Grncarov), Vlade Lazarevski, Darko Tasevski, Vlatko Grozdanovski, Velice Šumulikoski, Goran Maznov, Ilčo Naumoski (78 Artim Položani). Trainer: Srecko Katanec

CROATIA: Stipe Pletikosa, Dario Šimić, Josip Šimunić, Robert Kovač, Vedran Čorluka, Niko Kovač, Darijo Srna, Luka Modrić, Niko Kranjčar (75 Ognjen Vukojević), Mladen Petrić (42 Marijo Mandzukić), Eduardo da Silva (54 Ivica Olić). Trainer: Slaven Bilić

Goals: Maznov (71), Naumoski (78)

ENGLAND v CROATIA 2-3 (0-2)

Wembley, London 21.11.2007

Referee: Peter Fröjdfeldt (SWE) Attendance: 88,100

ENGLAND: Scott Carson, Micah Richards, Sol Campbell, Jolean Lescott, Wayne Bridge, Shaun Wright-Phillips (46 David Beckham), Steven Gerrard, Gareth Barry (46 Jermain Defoe), Frank Lampard, Joe Cole (80 Darren Bent), Peter Crouch. Trainer: Stephen McClaren

CROATIA: Stipe Pletikosa, Vedran Čorluka, Dario Šimić, Robert Kovač, Josip Šimunić, Darijo Srna, Luka Modrić, Niko Kovač, Niko Kranjčar (75 Danijel Pranjić), Ivica Olić (84 Ivan Rakitić), Eduardo da Silva (69 Mladen Petrić). Trainer: Slaven Bilić

Goals: Krančjar (8), Olić (14), Lampard (56 pen), Crouch (65), Petrić (77)

ANDORRA v RUSSIA 0-1 (0-1)

Estadi Comunal, Andorra La Vella 21.11.2007

Referee: Terje Hauge (NOR) Attendance: 500

ANDORRA: Jesús Álvarez "Koldo" (46 Jose Antonio Gomes), Antoni Lima, Ildefons Lima, Óscar Sonejee (83 Gabriel Riera), Marc Bernaus, Jordi Escura, Manolo Jiménez, Toni Sivera, Sergio Moreno, Justo Ruíz, Marcio Vieira (50 Xavier Andorra). Trainer: David Rodrigo

RUSSIA: Vladimir Gabulov, Aleksandr Anyukov, Aleksei Berezutski, Vasili Berezutski (38 Dmitri Torbinskiy), Denis Kolodin, Diniyar Bilyaletdinov, Yuri Zhirkov, Konstantin Zyrianov, Andrei Arshavin, Aleksandr Kerzhakov, Dmitri Sychev. Trainer: Guus Hiddink

Sent off: Andrei Arshavin (84)

Goal: Sychev (39)

	P	W	D	L	F	A	Pts
Croatia	12	9	2	1	28	8	29
Russia	12	7	3	2	18	7	24
England	12	7	2	3	24	7	23
Israel	12	7	2	3	20	12	23
Macedonia	12	4	2	6	12	12	14
Estonia	12	2	1	9	5	21	7
Andorra	12	0	0	12	2	42	0

GROUP 6

NORTHERN IRELAND v ICELAND 0-3 (0-3)

Windsor Park, Belfast 02.09.2006

Referee: Tommy Skjerven (NOR) Attendance: 15,000

NORTHERN IRELAND: Maik Taylor, Christopher Baird, Tony Capaldi (76 Michael Duff), Aaron Hughes, Stephen James Craigan, Sammy Clingan, Keith Gillespie, Stuart Elliott (63 Kyle Lafferty), Steve Davis, David Healy, James Quinn (83 Warren Feeney). Trainer: Lawrie Sanchez

ICELAND: Árni Gautur Arason, Grétar Rafn Steinsson, Indridi Sigurdsson, Ívar Ingimarsson, Hermann Hreidarsson, Brynjar Björn Gunnarsson (75 Stefán Gíslason), Kári Árnason (55 Helgi Valur Daníelsson), Jóhannes Karl Gudjónsson, Eidur Smári Gudjohnsen, Hannes Sigurdsson (64 Hjálmar Jónsson), Gunnar Heidar Thorvaldsson. Trainer: Eyjölfur Sverrisson

Goals: Thorvaldsson (13), Hreidarsson (20), Gudjohnsen (37)

LATVIA v SWEDEN 0-1 (0-1)

Skonto, Riga 02.09.2006

Referee: Darko Ceferin (SLO) Attendance: 9,000

LATVIA: Aleksandrs Kolinko, Igors Stepanovs, Vitalis Astafjevs, Dzintars Zirnis (83 Girts Karlsons), Jurijs Laizans (84 Aleksejs Višnakovs), Maris Smirnovs, Imants Bleidelis, Maris Verpakovskis, Andrejs Rubins, Andrejs Prohorenkovs (57 Marians Pahars), Oskars Klava. Trainer: Jurijs Andrejevs

SWEDEN: Rami Shaaban, Mikael Nilsson, Olof Mellberg, Petter Hansson, Erik Edman, Tobias Linderoth, Niclas Alexandersson, Kim Källström (71 Anders Svensson), Fredrik Ljungberg, Zlatan Ibrahimović, Johan Elmander (81 Christian Wilhelmsson). Trainer: Lars Lagerbäck

Goal: Källström (38)

SPAIN v LIECHTENSTEIN 4-0 (2-0)

El Vivero, Badajoz 02.09.2006

Referee: Emil Bozinovski (MKD) Attendance: 15,000

SPAIN: Iker Casillas, Sergio Ramos, Carles Puyol, Pablo Ibáñez, Mariano Pernía, David Albelda (69 Borja Oubiña), Xabi Alonso, Cesc Fábregas (63 Andrés Iniesta), Raúl González, Fernando Torres, David Villa (63 Luis García Sanz). Trainer: Luis Aragonés

LIECHTENSTEIN: Peter Jehle, Martin Telser (56 Benjamin Fischer), Sandro Maierhofer, Daniel Hasler, Martin Stocklasa, Franz Burgmeier, Martin Büchel, Marco Ritzberger, Fabio D'Elia, Thomas Beck (69 Roger Beck), Mario Frick (86 Raphaël Rohrer). Trainer: Martin Andermatt

Goals: Torres (20), Villa (45, 62), Luis García Sanz (66)

ICELAND v DENMARK 0-2 (0-2)

Laugardalsvöllur, Reykjavik 06.09.2006

Referee: Nikolai Ivanov (RUS) Attendance: 10,000

ICELAND: Árni Gautur Arason, Grétar Rafn Steinsson, Indridi Sigurdsson, Hermann Hreidarsson, Ívar Ingimarsson, Hjálmar Jónsson (66 Veigar Páll Gunnarsson), Brynjar Björn Gunnarsson (76 Stefán Gíslason), Kári Árnason (82 Arnar Thór Vidarsson), Jóhannes Karl Gudjónsson, Eidur Smári Gudjohnsen, Gunnar Heidar Thorvaldsson.
Trainer: Eyjólfur Sverrisson

DENMARK: Thomas Sørensen, Lars Jacobsen, Michael Gravgaard, Daniel Agger, Christian Bager Poulsen, Thomas Kahlenberg (81 Claus Jensen), Thomas Gravesen (70 Daniel Jensen), Jan Kristiansen, Jon Dahl Tomasson, Martin Jørgensen (90 Thomas Helveg), Dennis Rommedahl.
Trainer: Morten Olsen

Goals: Rommedahl (5), Tomasson (33)

SWEDEN v LIECHTENSTEIN 3-1 (1-1)

Ullevi, Gothenburg 06.09.2006

Referee: Veaceslav Banari (MOL) Attendance: 17,735

SWEDEN: Rami Shaaban, Mikael Nilsson, Petter Hansson, Teddy Lucic, Erik Edman, Tobias Linderoth, Niclas Alexandersson, Kim Källström (57 Anders Svensson), Fredrik Ljungberg, Marcus Allbäck, Johan Elmander (82 Markus Rosenberg). Trainer: Lars Lagerbäck

LIECHTENSTEIN: Peter Jehle, Daniel Hasler, Christof Ritter, Sandro Maierhofer (89 Fabio D'Elia), Martin Büchel, Martin Stocklasa, Benjamin Fischer (55 Ronny Büchel), Daniel Frick, Marco Ritzberger, Thomas Beck (42 Franz Burgmeier), Mario Frick. Trainer: Martin Andermatt

Goals: Allbäck (2, 69), M. Frick (27), Rosenberg (89)

NORTHERN IRELAND v SPAIN 3-2 (1-1)

Windsor Park, Belfast 06.09.2006

Referee: Frank De Bleeckere (BEL) Attendance: 14,500

NORTHERN IRELAND: Roy Carroll (12 Maik Taylor), Michael Duff, Aaron Hughes, Stephen James Craigan, Jonny Evans, Keith Gillespie, Sammy Clingan, Steve Davis, Christopher Baird, David Healy (85 Warren Feeney), Kyle Lafferty (54 James Quinn). Trainer: Lawrie Sanchez

SPAIN: Iker Casillas, Sergio Ramos (46 Míchel Salgado), Carles Puyol, Pablo Ibáñez, Antonio López, David Albelda (29 Cesc Fábregas), Xavi Hernández, Xabi Alonso, Fernando Torres (63 Luis García Sanz), David Villa, Raúl González. Trainer: Luis Aragonés

Goals: Xavi (14), Healy (20, 64, 80), Villa (52)

SWEDEN v SPAIN 2-0 (1-0)

Råsunda, Solna 07.10.2006

Referee: Stephen Bennett (ENG) Attendance: 38,000

SWEDEN: Rami Shaaban, Mikael Nilsson, Olof Mellberg, Petter Hansson, Erik Edman, Tobias Linderoth, Niclas Alexandersson, Fredrik Ljungberg (56 Christian Wilhelmsson), Anders Svensson (75 Kim Källstrom), Johan Elmander (77 Daniel Andersson), Marcus Allbäck. Trainer: Lars Lagerbäck

SPAIN: Iker Casillas, Sergio Ramos, Carles Puyol, Juanito Gutiérrez, Juan Capdevila (52 Antonio Puerta), David Albelda, Miguel Ángel Angulo (59 Luis García Sanz), Cesc Fábregas (46 Andrés Iniesta), Xavi Hernández, David Villa, Fernando Torres. Trainer: Luis Aragonés

Goals: Elmander (10), Allbäck (82)

DENMARK v NORTHERN IRELAND 0-0

Parken Stadium, Copenhagen 07.10.2006

Referee: Konrad Plautz (AUS) Attendance: 41,482

DENMARK: Thomas Sørensen (68 Jesper Christiansen), Lars Jacobsen, Michael Gravgaard, Daniel Agger, Niclas Jensen (73 Nicklas Bendtner), Daniel Jensen, Christian Bager Poulsen, Thomas Kahlenberg, Jon Dahl Tomasson, Martin Jørgensen, Peter Løvenkrands (55 Claus Jensen).
Trainer: Morten Olsen

NORTHERN IRELAND: Maik Taylor, Michael Duff, Aaron Hughes, Stephen James Craigan, Christopher Baird, Sammy Clingan (56 Damien Johnson), Steven Davis, Jonny Evans, Keith Gillespie, Kyle Lafferty (63 Steve Jones), David Healy (84 Warren Feeney). Trainer: Lawrie Sanchez

LATVIA v ICELAND 4-0 (3-0)

Skonto, Riga 07.10.2006

Referee: Alan Kelly (IRL) Attendance: 6,800

LATVIA: Aleksandrs Kolinko, Igors Stepanovs, Vitalis Astafjevs, Dzintars Zirnis, Jurijs Laizans, Oskars Klava (82 Denis Kačanovs), Maris Smirnovs, Imants Bleidelis (46 Aleksejs Višnakovs), Maris Verpakovskis (57 Marians Pahars), Genadijs Solonicins, Girts Karlsons.
Trainer: Jurijs Andrejevs

ICELAND: Árni Gautur Arason, Grétar Rafn Steinsson, Kristján Sigurdsson, Stefán Gíslason, Ívar Ingimarsson, Hannes Sigurdsson (71 Emil Hallfredsson), Hermann Hreidarsson, Brynjar Björn Gunnarsson, Eidur Smári Gudjohnsen, Jóhannes Karl Gudjónsson (46 Veigar Páll Gunnarsson), Kári Árnason (42 Helgi Valur Daníelsson).
Trainer: Eyjólfur Sverrisson

Goals: Karlsons (14), Verpakovskis (15, 25), Višnakovs (52)

ICELAND v SWEDEN 1-2 (1-1)

Laugardalsvöllur, Reykjavik 11.10.2006

Referee: Grzegorz Gilewski (POL) Attendance: 8,700

ICELAND: Árni Gautur Arason, Ívar Ingimarsson, Grétar Rafn Steinsson, Hermann Hreidarsson, Kristján Örn Sigurdsson, Indridi Sigurdsson (51 Hjálmar Jónsson), Jóhannes Karl Gudjónsson (81 Marel Jóhann Baldvinsson), Arnar Thór Vidarsson, Emil Hallfredsson, Hannes Sigurdsson, Eidur Smári Gudjohnsen. Trainer: Eyjólfur Sverrisson

SWEDEN: Rami Shaaban, Mikael Nilsson, Mikael Antonsson, Petter Hansson, Erik Edman, Niclas Alexandersson, Daniel Andersson, Kim Källström, Christian Wilhelmsson, Marcus Allbäck (79 Markus Rosenberg), Johan Elmander (90 Daniel Majstorovic). Trainer: Lars Lagerbäck

Goals: Vidarsson (6), Källström (8), Wilhelmsson (59)

NORTHERN IRELAND v LATVIA 1-0 (1-0)

Windsor Park, Belfast 11.10.2006

Referee: Helmut Fleischer (GER) Attendance: 14,500

NORTHERN IRELAND: Maik Taylor, Christopher Baird, Stephen James Craigan, Aaron Hughes, Jonny Evans, Keith Gillespie, Steve Davis, Damien Johnson, Sammy Clingan, David Healy (90 Warren Feeney), Kyle Lafferty (87 James Quinn). Trainer: Lawrie Sanchez

LATVIA: Aleksandrs Kolinko, Igors Stepanovs, Vitalis Astafjevs, Dzintars Zirnis, Jurijs Laizans, Denis Kačanovs, Genadijs Solonicins (84 Aleksejs Višnakovs), Maris Smirnovs (46 Kaspars Gorkšs), Maris Verpakovskis (78 Gatis Kalnins), Girts Karlsons, Marians Pahars. Trainer: Jurijs Andrejevs

Goal: Healy (35)

LIECHTENSTEIN v DENMARK 0-4 (0-2)

Rheinpark, Vaduz 11.10.2006

Referee: Ceri Richards (WAL) Attendance: 2,700

LIECHTENSTEIN: Peter Jehle, Martin Telser, Daniel Hasler, Christof Ritter, Martin Stocklasa, Benjamin Fischer (80 Fabio D'Elia), Thomas Beck (63 Marco Ritzberger), Mario Frick, Franz Burgmeier (62 Daniel Frick), Martin Büchel, Yves Oehri. Trainer: Martin Andermatt

DENMARK: Jesper Christiansen, Christian Bager Poulsen, Michael Gravgaard, Daniel Agger, Niclas Jensen, Lars Jacobsen, Daniel Jensen (46 Dennis Sørensen), Thomas Kahlenberg (64 Claus Jensen), Jon Dahl Tomasson, Martin Jørgensen, Dennis Rommedahl (78 Michael Krohn-Dehli). Trainer: Morten Olsen

Goals: D. Jensen (29), Gravgaard (32), Tomasson (51, 64)

LIECHTENSTEIN v NORTHERN IRELAND 1-4 (0-0)

Rheinpark, Vaduz 24.03.2007

Referee: Oleh Oriekhov (UKR) Attendance: 4,340

LIECHTENSTEIN: Peter Jehle, Yves Oehri (68 Martin Telser), Martin Stocklasa, Christof Ritter, Michael Stocklasa, Martin Büchel, Ronny Büchel (86 Daniel Frick), Franz Burgmeier, Thomas Beck, Mario Frick, Raphaël Rohrer (82 Stefan Büchel). Trainer: Hans-Peter Zaugg

NORTHERN IRELAND: Maik Taylor, Michael Duff, Stephen James Craigan, Aaron Hughes, Damien Johnson, Chris Brunt (68 Grant McCann), Keith Gillespie, Jonny Evans, Steve Davis, Kyle Lafferty (56 Warren Feeney), David Healy (82 Steve Jones). Trainer: Lawrie Sanchez

Goals: Healy (52, 75, 83), Burgmeier (89), McCann (90)

SPAIN v DENMARK 2-1 (1-0)

Santiago Bernabéu, Madrid 24.03.2007

Referee: Massimo Busacca (SWI) Attendance: 75,000

SPAIN: Iker Casillas, Javi Navarro, Carlos Marchena, Juan Capdevila, Ángel López, Xavi Hernández (60 Xabi Alonso), Andrés Iniesta, David Silva, David Albelda, Fernando Morientes (64 Fernando Torres), David Villa (76 Miguel Ángel Angulo). Trainer: Luis Aragonés

DENMARK: Thomas Sørensen, Daniel Agger, Michael Gravgaard, Lars Jacobsen, Niclas Jensen, Christian Bager Poulsen, Daniel Jensen, Thomas Kahlenberg (60 Jesper Grønkjær), Dennis Rommedahl, Martin Jørgensen (38 Leon Andreasen, 73 Nicklas Bendtner), Jon Dahl Tomasson. Trainer: Morten Olsen

Sent off: Niclas Jensen (20)

Goals: Morientes (34), Villa (46), Gravgaard (49)

LIECHTENSTEIN v LATVIA 1-0 (1-0)

Rheinpark, Vaduz 28.03.2007

Referee: Serge Gumienny (BEL) Attendance: 1,680

LIECHTENSTEIN: Peter Jehle, Martin Telser, Martin Stocklasa, Daniel Hasler, Michael Stocklasa, Martin Büchel, Ronny Büchel, Franz Burgmeier, Mario Frick, Thomas Beck (76 Benjamin Fischer), Raphaël Rohrer (90 Stefan Büchel). Trainer: Hans-Peter Zaugg

LATVIA: Aleksandrs Kolinko, Denis Kačanovs, Kaspars Gorkšs (79 Andrejs Prohorenkovs), Igors Stepanovs, Oskars Klava, Imants Bleidelis, Viktors Morozs (61 Andrei Pereplotkins), Jurijs Laizans, Aleksejs Višnakovs, Maris Verpakovskis (46 Girts Karlsons), Marians Pahars. Trainer: Jurijs Andrejevs

Goal: M. Frick (17)

NORTHERN IRELAND v SWEDEN 2-1 (1-1)

Windsor Park, Belfast 28.03.2007

Referee: Eric Braamhaar (HOL) Attendance: 14,500

NORTHERN IRELAND: Maik Taylor, Michael Duff, Aaron Hughes, Stephen James Craigan, Jonny Evans, Damien Johnson, Grant McCann, Steven Davis, Chris Brunt (90 Ivan Sproule), David Healy (87 Sean Webb), Warren Feeney (79 Kyle Lafferty). Trainer: Lawrie Sanchez

SWEDEN: Andreas Isaksson, Mikael Nilsson, Olof Mellberg (69 Daniel Majstorovic), Petter Hansson, Erik Edman, Niclas Alexandersson (61 Christian Wilhelmsson), Daniel Andersson, Anders Svensson (46 Kim Källstrom), Fredrik Ljungberg, Zlatan Ibrahimović, Johan Elmander. Trainer: Lars Lagerbäck

Goals: Elmander (26), Healy (31, 58)

SPAIN v ICELAND 1-0 (0-0)

Son Moix, Palma de Mallorca 28.03.2007

Referee: Laurent Duhamel (FRA) Attendance: 17,000

SPAIN: Iker Casillas, Sergio Ramos, Carlos Marchena, Carles Puyol, Juan Capdevila (46 Miguel Ángel Angulo), Andrés Iniesta, David Albelda (78 Xabi Alonso), Xavi Hernández, David Silva, David Villa, Fernando Morientes (43 Fernando Torres). Trainer: Luis Aragonés

ICELAND: Árni Gautur Arason, Kristján Örn Sigurdsson, Ólafur Örn Bjarnason, Ívar Ingimarsson, Gunnar Thór Gunnarsson, Grétar Rafn Steinsson, Arnar Thór Vidarsson (83 Hannes Sigurdsson), Brynjar Björn Gunnarsson, Emil Hallfredsson (74 Indridi Sigurdsson), Veigar Páll Gunnarsson (56 Stefán Gíslason), Eidur Smári Gudjohnsen. Trainer: Eyjölfur Sverrisson

Goal: Iniesta (81)

ICELAND v LIECHTENSTEIN 1-1 (1-0)

Laugardalsvöllur, Reykjavik 02.06.2007

Referee: Sten Kaldma (EST) Attendance: 5,000

ICELAND: Árni Gautur Arason, Grétar Rafn Steinsson, Gunnar Thór Gunnarsson, Kristján Örn Sigurdsson, Ívar Ingimarsson, Stefán Gíslason, Emil Hallfredsson (82 Théodór Elmar Bjarnason), Brynjar Björn Gunnarsson, Matthías Gudmundsson (70 Birkir Már Saevarsson), Veigar Páll Gunnarsson (72 Hannes Sigurdsson), Eidur Smári Gudjohnsen. Trainer: Eyjölfur Sverrisson

LIECHTENSTEIN: Peter Jehle, Michael Stocklasa, Daniel Hasler, Martin Stocklasa, Marco Ritzberger, Ronny Büchel, Franz Burgmeier (78 Daniel Frick), Thomas Beck (87 Roger Beck), Mario Frick, Raphaël Rohrer (85 Wolfgang Kieber), Daniel Steuble. Trainer: Hans-Peter Zaugg

Goals: B. Gunnarsson (27), Rohrer (69)

LATVIA v SPAIN 0-2 (0-1)

Skonto, Riga 02.06.2007

Referee: Craig Alexander Thomson (SCO) Att: 9,500

LATVIA: Aleksandrs Kolinko, Dzintars Zirnis, Oskars Klava, Deniss Ivanovs, Arturs Zakreševskis, Andrejs Rubins (65 Genadijs Solonicins), Vitalis Astafjevs, Jurijs Laizans, Imants Bleidelis (85 Andrejs Pereplotkins), Maris Verpakovskis, Girts Karlsons (89 Aleksandrs Cauna).
Trainer: Aleksandrs Starkovs

SPAIN: Iker Casillas, Carles Puyol, Sergio Ramos, Carlos Marchena, David Albelda (66 Xabi Alonso), Andrés Iniesta, Xavi Hernández, Miguel Ángel Angulo (46 JOAQUÍN Sánchez), Juan Capdevila, David Villa, LUIS GARCÍA Fernández (55 Roberto Soldado). Trainer: Luis Aragonés

Goals: Villa (45), Xavi (60)

DENMARK v SWEDEN 3-3 (0-3)

Parken, København 02.06.2007

Referee: Herbert Fandel (GER)

DENMARK: Thomas Sørensen, Lars Jacobsen, Michael Gravgaard, Daniel Agger, Jan Kristiansen (35 Leon Andreasen), Christian Bager Poulsen, Daniel Jensen (63 Jesper Grønkjær), Dennis Rommedahl, Thomas Kahlenberg (46 Nicklas Bendtner), Martin Jørgensen, Jon Dahl Tomasson.
Trainer: Morten Olsen

SWEDEN: Andreas Isaksson, Niclas Alexandersson, Olof Mellberg, Petter Hansson, Mikael Nilsson, Christian Wilhelmsson, Tobias Linderoth, Anders Svensson, Fredrik Ljungberg, Marcus Allbäck (80 Kennedy Bakircioglü), Johan Elmander (74 Markus Rosenberg). Trainer: Lars Lagerbäck

Sent off: Poulsen (89)

Goals: Elmander (7, 26), Hansson (23), Agger (34), Tomasson (62), Andreasen (75)

The match was abandoned in the 89th minute after a Danish spectator came on to the pitch and assaulted the referee. At the time, the score stood at 3-3 but the match was awarded to Sweden with a 3-0 scoreline.

SWEDEN v ICELAND 5-0 (3-0)

Råsunda, Solna 06.06.2007

Referee: Alain Hamer (LUX) Attendance: 33,400

SWEDEN: Andreas Isaksson, Niclas Alexandersson, Olof Mellberg, Petter Hansson, Mikael Nilsson (57 Max von Schlebrügge), Christian Wilhelmsson, Tobias Linderoth (62 Daniel Andersson), Anders Svensson, Fredrik Ljungberg, Markus Rosenberg, Marcus Allbäck (73 Zlatan Ibrahimović).
Trainer: Lars Lagerbäck

ICELAND: Árni Gautur Arason, Grétar Rafn Steinsson (90 Kristjan Örn Sigurdsson), Gunnar Thór Gunnarsson, Ólafur Örn Bjarnason, Ívar Ingimarsson, Théodór Elmar Bjarnason, Arnar Thór Vidarsson, Emil Hallfredsson (53 Hjálmar Jónsson), Brynjar Björn Gunnarsson, Hannes Sigurdsson, Birkir Már Saevarsson (65 Matthías Gudmundsson).
Trainer: Eyjölfur Sverrisson

Goals: Allbäck (11, 51), Svensson (42), Mellberg (45), Rosenberg (50)

LIECHTENSTEIN v SPAIN 0-2 (0-2)

Rheinpark, Vaduz 06.06.2007

Referee: Nikolay Ivanov (RUS) Attendance: 5,739

LIECHTENSTEIN: Peter Jehle, Michael Stocklasa (29 Martin Telser), Daniel Hasler, Martin Stocklasa, Marco Ritzberger, Ronny Büchel, Franz Burgmeier, Michele Polverino, Raphaël Rohrer (59 Daniel Frick), Mario Frick, Thomas Beck (82 Roger Beck). Trainer: Hans-Peter Zaugg

SPAIN: José Manuel Reina, Javi Navarro, Carlos Marchena, Sergio Ramos, Juan Capdevila (52 Antonio López), Xabi Alonso, Andrés Iniesta, JOAQUÍN Sánchez, Cesc Fábregas (67 Luis García Fernández), David Silva (77 Roberto Soldado), David Villa. Trainer: Luis Aragonés

Goals: Villa (8, 14)

LATVIA v DENMARK 0-2 (0-2)

Skonto, Riga 06.06.2007

Referee: Matteo Simone Trefoloni (ITA) Attendance: 7,500

LATVIA: Aleksandrs Kolinko, Dzintars Zirnis, Oskars Klava, Deniss Ivanovs, Igors Stepanovs, Andrejs Rubins (75 Aleksandrs Cauna), Vitalis Astafjevs, Jurijs Laizans, Imants Bleidelis (66 Genadijs Solonicins), Maris Verpakovskis, Girts Karlsons (61 Marians Pahars). Trainer: Aleksandrs Starkovs

DENMARK: Thomas Sørensen, Lars Jacobsen, Martin Laursen, Daniel Agger, Niclas Jensen, Daniel Jensen, Martin Jørgensen, Jon Dahl Tomasson, Dennis Rommedahl (46 Thomas Kahlenberg), Nicklas Bendtner (60 Rasmus Würtz), Jesper Grønkjær. Trainer: Morten Olsen

Goals: Rommedahl (15, 17)

NORTHERN IRELAND v LIECHTENSTEIN 3-1 (2-0)

Windsor Park, Belfast 22.08.2007

Referee: Radek Matejek (CZE) Attendance: 13,000

NORTHERN IRELAND: Maik Taylor, Michael Duff, George McCartney, Christopher Baird, Stephen James Craigan, Gary Clinghan, Keith Gillespie (85 Stephen Jones), Steven Davis, Kyle Lafferty (75 Warren Feeney), David Healy, Chris Brunt (62 Stuart Elliott). Trainer: Nigel Worthington

LIECHTENSTEIN: Peter Jehle, Michael Stocklasa (38 Yves Oehri), Martin Stocklasa, Martin Telser, Fabio D'Elia, Michele Polverino, Ronny Büchel, Daniel Frick, Christoph Biedermann (62 Stefan Büchel), Raphaël Rohrer (74 Roger Beck), Mario Frick. Trainer: Hans-Peter Zaugg

Goals: Healy (5, 35), Lafferty (56), M. Frick (89)

LATVIA v NORTHERN IRELAND 1-0 (0-0)

Skonto, Riga 08.09.2007

Referee: Pedro Proença (POR) Attendance: 7,500

LATVIA: Andris Vanins, Dzintars Zirnis, Kaspars Gorkšs, Oskars Klava, Deniss Ivanovs, Imants Bleidelis, Jurijs Laizans, Vitalis Astafjevs, Andrejs Rubins, Maris Verpakovskis (90 Kristaps Blanks), Girts Karlsons (72 Vits Rimkus). Trainer: Aleksandrs Starkovs

NORTHERN IRELAND: Maik Taylor, Christopher Baird, Michael Duff, Jonny Evans, George McCartney, Keith Gillespie, Gary Clinghan, Steven Davis, Stuart Elliott (66 Chris Brunt), David Healy, Kyle Lafferty (72 Warren Feeney). Trainer: Nigel Worthington

Goal: Baird (56 own goal)

ICELAND v SPAIN 1-1 (1-0)

Laugardalsvöllur, Reykjavik 08.09.2007

Referee: Wolfgang Stark (GER) Attendance: 9,500

ICELAND: Árni Gautur Arason, Kristján Sigurdsson, Ragnar Sigurdsson, Ívar Ingimarsson, Hermann Hreidarsson, Grétar Rafn Steinsson, Arnar Thór Vidarsson (69 Olafur Ingi Skulason), Jóhannes Karl Gudjónsson (79 Baldur Adalsteinsson), Emil Hallfredsson, Kári Árnason, Gunnar Heidar Thorvaldsson (88 Ármann Smári Björnsson). Trainer: Eyjölfur Sverrisson

SPAIN: Iker Casillas, Sergio Ramos, Carlos Marchena, Juanito Gutiérrez, Mariano Pernía (26 David Albelda), Joaquín Sánchez (69 Luis Garcia Fernández), Xabi Alonso, Xavi Hernández, David Silva, Fernando Torres (57 Andrés Iniesta), David Villa. Trainer: Luis Aragonés

Sent off: Xabi Alonso (20)

Goals: Hallfredsson (40), Iniesta (86)

SWEDEN v DENMARK 0-0

Råsunda, Solna 08.09.2007

Referee: Frank De Bleeckere (BEL) Attendance: 33,000

SWEDEN: Andreas Isaksson, Mikael Nilsson, Olof Mellberg, Petter Hansson, Erik Edman, Niclas Alexandersson, Tobias Linderoth, Anders Svensson (69 Kim Källstrom), Christian Wilhelmsson (57 Kennedy Bakircioglu), Zlatan Ibrahimović (89 Rade Prica), Johan Elmander. Trainer: Lars Lagerbäck

DENMARK: Thomas Sørensen, Leon Andreasen (81 Peter Lovenkrands), Martin Laursen, Daniel Agger, Niclas Jensen, Thomas Helveg, Daniel Jensen, Dennis Rommedahl, Thomas Kahlenberg (54 Nicklas Bendtner), Jon Dahl Tomasson (90 Michael Gravgaard), Jesper Grønkjær. Trainer: Morten Olsen

ICELAND v NORTHERN IRELAND 2-1 (1-0)

Laugardalsvöllur, Reykjavik 12.09.2007

Referee: Yuri Baskakov (RUS) Attendance: 2,500

ICELAND: Árni Gautur Arason, Kristján Sigurdsson, Ragnar Sigurdsson, Ívar Ingimarsson, Hermann Hreidarsson, Kári Árnason (87 Asgeir Asgeirsson), Arnar Thór Vidarsson, Grétar Rafn Steinsson, Emil Hallfredsson, Gunnar Heidar Thorvaldsson (79 Olafur Ingi Skulason), Ármann Björnsson (53 Eidur Smári Gudjohnsen). Trainer: Eyjölfur Sverrisson

NORTHERN IRELAND: Maik Taylor, Christopher Baird, Michael Duff, Jonny Evans, George McCartney, Keith Gillespie, Gary Clinghan, Steven Davis (79 Grant McCann), Chris Brunt (83 Stephen Jones), David Healy, Warren Feeney. Trainer: Nigel Worthington

Goals: Ar. Bjornsson (6), Healy (72 pen), Gillespie (90 own goal)

DENMARK v LIECHTENSTEIN 4-0 (4-0)

Atletion, Aarhus 12.09.2007

Referee: Mark Clattenburg (ENG) Attendance: 20,000

DENMARK: Thomas Sørensen, Martin Laursen, Daniel Agger (28 Michael Gravgaard), Niclas Jensen, Thomas Helveg, Leon Andreasen, Jesper Grønkjær (46 Thomas Kahlenberg), Morten Nordstrand, Jon Dahl Tomasson (68 Peter Lovenkrands), Dennis Rommedahl, Esben Hansen. Trainer: Morten Olsen

LIECHTENSTEIN: Peter Jehle, Martin Telser, Martin Stocklasa, Marco Ritzberger (46 Thomas Beck), Yves Oehri (46 Daniel Frick), Ronny Büchel, Franz Burgmeier, Fabio D'Elia, Raphaël Rohrer, Michele Polverino, Mario Frick (84 Roger Beck). Trainer: Hans-Peter Zaugg

Goals: Nordstrand (3, 36), Laursen (12), Tomasson (18)

SPAIN v LATVIA 2-0 (1-0)

Nuevo Carlos Tartiere, Oviedo 12.09.2007

Referee: Alon Yefet (ISR) Attendance: 25,000

SPAIN: Iker Casillas, Sergio Ramos, Carlos Marchena, Juanito Gutiérrez, Mariano Pernía, JOAQUÍN Sánchez (77 Miguel Ángel Angulo), David Albelda, Xavi Hernández, David Silva (69 Cesc Fábregas), Fernando Torres, David Villa (48 Andrés Iniesta). Trainer: Luis Aragonés

LATVIA: Andris Vanins, Dzintars Zirnis, Oskars Klava, Kaspars Gorkšs, Deniss Ivanovs, Imants Bleidelis (74 Aleksejs Višnakovs), Vitalis Astafjevs, Jurijs Laizans, Andrejs Rubins, Girts Karlsons (63 Marians Pahars), Maris Verpakovskis (88 Kristaps Blanks). Trainer: Aleksandrs Starkovs

Goals: Xavi (13), Torres (85)

ICELAND v LATVIA 2-4 (1-3)

Laugardalsvöllur, Reykjavik 13.10.2007

Referee: Michael Leslie Dean (ENG) Attendance: 5,900

ICELAND: Árni Gautur Arason, Kristján Sigurdsson (86 Ármann Smári Björnsson), Hjálmar Jónsson, Ragnar Sigurdsson, Ívar Ingimarsson, Grétar Rafn Steinsson (25 Kári Árnason), Brynjar Björn Gunnarsson, Jóhannes Karl Gudjónsson, Emil Hallfredsson, Gunnar Heidar Thorvaldsson (65 Hannes Sigurdsson), Eidur Smári Gudjohnsen. Trainer: Eyjölfur Sverrisson

LATVIA: Andris Vanins, Oskars Klava, Kaspars Gorkšs, Deniss Ivanovs, Dzintars Zirnis, Vitalis Astafjevs, Jurijs Laizans, Genadijs Solonicins, Aleksejs Višnakovs (90 Jurijs Zigajevs), Girts Karlsons (59 Vits Rimkus), Maris Verpakovskis (78 Marians Pahars). Trainer: Aleksandrs Starkovs

Goals: Gudjohnsen (4), Klava (27), Laizans (31), Verpakovskis (37, 46), Gudjohnsen (52)

LIECHTENSTEIN v SWEDEN 0-3 (0-2)

Rheinpark, Vaduz 13.10.2007

Referee: Paolo Dondarini (ITA) Attendance: 4,100

LIECHTENSTEIN: Peter Jehle, Martin Telser, Yves Oehri, Daniel Hasler, Franz Burgmeier (59 Daniel Steuble), Ronny Büchel, Martin Büchel (61 Andreas Gerster), Thomas Beck, Mario Frick (74 Roger Beck), Raphaël Rohrer, Daniel Frick (60 Benjamin Fischer). Trainer: Hans-Peter Zaugg

SWEDEN: Andreas Isaksson, Matias Concha, Petter Hansson, Daniel Majstorovic, Erik Edman, Christian Wilhelmsson, Tobias Linderoth (70 Daniel Andersson), Anders Svensson, Fredrik Ljungberg (39 Kim Källstrom), Marcus Allbäck, Johan Elmander. Trainer: Lars Lagerbäck

Goals: Ljungberg (19), Wilhelmsson (29), A. Svensson (56)

DENMARK v SPAIN 1-3 (0-2)

Atletion, Aarhus 13.10.2007

Referee: Luboš Michel (SVK) Attendance: 19,800

DENMARK: Thomas Sørensen, Thomas Helveg, Martin Laursen, Ulrik Laursen, Niclas Jensen (79 Kenneth Perez), Christian Bager Poulsen, Daniel Jensen, Leon Andreasen (46 Nicklas Bendtner), Dennis Rommedahl, Jon Dahl Tomasson, Jesper Grønkjær (65 Thomas Kahlenberg). Trainer: Morten Olsen

SPAIN: Iker Casillas, Carlos Marchena, Sergio Ramos, Juan Capdevila, Raúl Albiol, David Albelda (64 Pablo Ibáñez), Xavi Hernández, Andrés Iniesta, JOAQUÍN Sánchez (69 Albert Riera), Cesc Fábregas (78 Luis García Fernández), Raúl Tamudo. Trainer: Luis Aragonés

Goals: Tamudo (14), Sergio Ramos (40), Tomasson (87), Riera (89)

LIECHTENSTEIN v ICELAND 3-0 (1-0)

Rheinpark, Vaduz 17.10.2007

Referee: Christoforos Zografos (GRE) Attendance: 2,600

LIECHTENSTEIN: Peter Jehle, Martin Telser, Daniel Hasler, Martin Stocklasa, Yves Oehri, Ronny Büchel, Andreas Gerster, Franz Burgmeier, Benjamin Fischer (62 Thomas Beck), Raphaël Rohrer (68 Roger Beck), Mario Frick (90 Fabio D'Elia). Trainer: Hans-Peter Zaugg

ICELAND: Árni Gautur Arason, Hermann Hreidarsson, Kristján Sigurdsson, Ívar Ingimarsson, Ragnar Sigurdsson, Jóhannes Karl Gudjónsson (58 Ármann Smári Bjornsson), Emil Hallfredsson, Arnar Thór Vidarsson, Brynjar Björn Gunnarsson (85 Asgei Asgeirsson), Gunnar Heidar Thorvaldsson (71 Helgi Sigurdsson), Eidur Smári Gudjohnsen. Trainer: Eyjölfur Sverrisson

Goals: M. Frick (28), T. Beck (80, 82)

DENMARK v LATVIA 3-1 (2-0)

Parken, Copenhagen 17.10.2007

Referee: Cüneyt Cakir (TUR) Attendance: 19,000

DENMARK: Thomas Sørensen, Martin Laursen, Ulrik Laursen (32 Leon Andreasen), Chris Sørensen, Thomas Helveg, Christian Bager Poulsen (71 Jesper Grønkjær), Daniel Jensen, Thomas Kahlenberg, Dennis Rommedahl, Nicklas Bendtner, Jon Dahl Tomasson. Trainer: Morten Olsen

LATVIA: Andris Vanins, Oskars Klava, Deniss Ivanovs, Dzintars Zirnis, Kaspars Gorkšs, Vitalis Astafjevs, Jurijs Laizans, Aleksejs Višnakovs (78 Jurijs Zigajevs), Genadijs Solonicins, Vits Rimkus (63 Andrejs Butriks), Marians Pahars (90 Denis Kačanovs). Trainer: Aleksandrs Starkovs

Goals: Tomasson (7 pen), U. Laursen (27), Gorkšs (80), Rommedahl (90)

SWEDEN v NORTHERN IRELAND 1-1 (1-0)

Råsunda, Solna 17.10.2007

Referee: Bertrand Layec (FRA) Attendance: 33,100

SWEDEN: Andreas Isaksson, Matias Concha, Olof Mellberg, Petter Hansson, Erik Edman, Tobias Linderoth, Anders Svensson, Christian Wilhelmsson (46 Mikael Nilsson), Kim Källström (85 Andreas Johansson), Zlatan Ibrahimovic, Johan Elmander (73 Marcus Allbäck). Trainer: Lars Lagerbäck

NORTHERN IRELAND: Maik Taylor, Gareth McAuley, Aaron Hughes, George McCartney (87 Tony Capaldi), Stephen James Craigan, Steven Davis, Gary Clinghan, Chris Brunt, David Healy, Ivan Sproule, Kyle Lafferty.
Trainer: Nigel Worthington

Goals: Mellberg (15), Lafferty (72)

LATVIA v LIECHTENSTEIN 4-1 (2-1)

Skonto, Riga 17.11.2007

Referee: Svein Oddvar Moen (NOR) Attendance: 4,800

LATVIA: Andris Vanins, Kaspars Gorkšs, Oskars Klava, Dzintars Zirnis, Deniss Ivanovs, Imants Bleidelis (82 Aleksejs Višnakovs), Jurijs Laizans, Vitalis Astafjevs, Andrejs Rubins, Girts Karlsons (71 Marians Pahars), Maris Verpakovskis (77 Vits Rimkus). Trainer: Aleksandrs Starkovs

LIECHTENSTEIN: Peter Jehle, Marco Ritzberger, Martin Stocklasa, Fabio D'Elia, Daniel Hasler, Ronny Büchel (80 Martin Büchel), Andreas Gerster, Franz Burgmeier, Raphaël Rohrer (72 Daniel Frick), Mario Frick, Benjamin Fischer (71 Roger Beck). Trainer: Hans-Peter Zaugg

Goals: Zirnis (13 own goal), G. Karlsons (14), Verpakovskis (30), Laizans (63), Višnakovs (87)

NORTHERN IRELAND v DENMARK 2-1 (0-0)

Windsor Park, Belfast 17.11.2007

Referee: Pieter Vink (HOL) Attendance: 14,500

NORTHERN IRELAND: Maik Taylor, Gareth McAuley, Jonny Evans, Aaron Hughes, Stephen James Craigan, Gary Clinghan, Keith Gillespie (74 Ivan Sproule), Steven Davis, Chris Brunt, David Healy, Warren Feeney (85 Christopher Baird). Trainer: Nigel Worthington

DENMARK: Thomas Sørensen, Brian Priske (72 Rasmus Wurtz), Chris Sørensen, Martin Laursen, Per Krøldrup, Christian Bager Poulsen, Leon Andreasen, Thomas Kahlenberg (46 Dennis Sørensen), Dennis Rommedahl, Martin Jørgensen (79 Simon Poulsen), Nicklas Bendtner.
Trainer: Morten Olsen

Goals: Bendtner (51), Feeney (62), Healy (80)

SPAIN v SWEDEN 3-0 (2-0)

Santiago Bernabéu, Madrid 17.11.2007

Referee: Roberto Rosetti (ITA) Attendance: 73,000

SPAIN: Iker Casillas, Sergio Ramos, Carles Puyol, Carlos Marchena, Juan Capdevila, Andrés Iniesta (52 JOAQUÍN Sánchez), Cesc Fábregas, David Albelda, Xavi Hernández, David Silva (66 Albert Riera), David Villa (52 Raul Tamudo).
Trainer: Luis Aragonés

SWEDEN: Andreas Isaksson, Mikael Nilsson, Olof Mellberg, Petter Hansson, Erik Edman, Christian Wilhelmsson (79 Kennedy Bakircioglu), Daniel Andersson (46 Kim Källstrom), Anders Svensson, Fredrik Ljungberg, Zlatan Ibrahimović, Markus Rosenberg (60 Markus Allbäck).
Trainer: Lars Lagerbäck

Goals: Capdevila (14), Iniesta (39), Sergio Ramos (65)

SPAIN v NORTHERN IRELAND 1-0 (0-0)

Gran Canaria, Las Palmas de Gran Canaria 21.11.2007

Referee: Herbert Fandel (GER) Attendance: 31,000

SPAIN: José Manuel Reina, Sergio Ramos, Raúl Albiol, Pablo Ibáñez, Mariano Pernía, Andrés Iniesta, Xavi Hernández (67 David Villa), Cesc Fábregas (47 JOAQUÍN Sánchez), Marcos Senna, David Silva, Daniel Güiza (57 Raúl Tamudo). Trainer: Luis Aragonés

NORTHERN IRELAND: Maik Taylor, Gareth McAuley, Stephen James Craigan, Aaron Hughes, Christopher Baird, Ivan Sproule (46 Stephen Robinson), Gary Clinghan, Steven Davis, Chris Brunt (59 Kyle Lafferty), David Healy, Warren Feeney (72 Martin Paterson). Trainer: Nigel Worthington

Goal: Xavi (52)

	P	W	D	L	F	A	Pts
Spain	12	9	1	2	23	8	28
Sweden	12	8	2	2	23	9	26
N. Ireland	12	6	2	4	17	14	20
Denmark	12	6	2	4	21	11	20
Latvia	12	4	0	8	15	17	12
Iceland	12	2	2	8	10	27	8
Liechtenstein	12	2	1	9	9	32	7

DENMARK v ICELAND 3-0 (2-0)

Parken Stadium, Copenhagen 21.11.2007

Referee: Olegário Benquerença (POR) Attendance: 15,393

DENMARK: Thomas Sørensen, William Kvist, Ulrik Laursen, Per Krøldrup, Chris Sørensen, Dennis Rommedahl (73 Simon Poulsen), Daniel Jensen, Christian Bager Poulsen, Martin Jørgensen (53 Thomas Kahlenberg), Nicklas Bendtner (84 Søren Larsen), Jon Dahl Tomasson. Trainer: Morten Olsen

ICELAND: Árni Gautur Arason, Grétar Rafn Steinsson, Kristján Sigurdsson (7 Sverrir Gardarsson), Hermann Hreidarsson, Ragnar Sigurdsson, Théodór Elmar Bjarnason, Brynjar Björn Gunnarsson, Stefán Gíslason, Emil Hallfredsson (73 Eggert Gunnthor Jónnson), Veigar Páll Gunnarsson (84 Asgeir Asgeirsson), Gunnar Heidar Thorvaldsson. Trainer: Olafur Johannesson

Goals: Bendtner (34), Tomasson (44), Kahlenberg (59)

SWEDEN v LATVIA 2-1 (1-1)

Råsunda, Solna 21.11.2007

Referee: Wolfgang Stark (GER) Attendance: 26,000

SWEDEN: Andreas Isaksson, Mikael Nilsson, Olof Mellberg, Daniel Majstorovic, Erik Edman, Christian Wilhelmsson, Kim Källström, Anders Svensson, Fredrik Ljungberg, Zlatan Ibrahimovic, Marcus Allbäck. Trainer: Lars Lagerbäck

LATVIA: Aleksandrs Kolinko, Kaspars Gorkšs, Igors Stepanovs, Deniss Ivanovs, Dzintars Zirnis, Andrejs Rubins, Jurijs Laizans, Vitalis Astafjevs (49 Genadijs Solonicins), Imants Bleidelis (43 Aleksejs Višnakovs), Girts Karlsons (62 Marians Pahars), Maris Verpakovskis. Trainer: Aleksandrs Starkovs

Goals: Allbäck (1), Laizans (26), Källstrom (57)

GROUP 7

BELARUS v ALBANIA 2-2 (2-1)

Dinamo, Minsk 02.09.2006

Referee: Tony Asumaa (FIN) Attendance: 30,000

BELARUS: Vasiliy Khomutovskiy, Aleksandr Kulchiy, Vladimir Korytko, Sergei Omelyanchuk, Sergei Shtaniuk, Viacheslav Hleb (64 Vitaliy Bulyga), Timofei Kalachev (84 Vitaliy Lanko), Denis Kovba, Maksim Romashchenko, Aleksandr Hleb, Vitaliy Kutuzov. Trainer: Yuri Puntus

ALBANIA: Ilion Lika, Armend Dallku, Besnik Hasi, Adrian Aliaj (46 Debatik Curri), Elvin Beqiri, Altin Haxhi, Altin Lala (84 Devis Muka), Lorik Cana, Ervin Skela (73 Edmond Kapllani), Igli Tare, Erjon Bogdani. Trainer: Otto Barić

Goals: Kalachev (2), Skela (7 pen), Romashchenko (24), Hasi (86)

LUXEMBOURG v NETHERLANDS 0-1 (0-1)

Josy Barthel, Luxembourg 02.09.2006

Referee: João Ferreira (POR) Attendance: 8,000

LUXEMBOURG: Jonathan Joubert, Jeff Strasser, Eric Hoffmann, Claude Reiter, Kim Kintziger, Gilles Bettmer, Aurélien Joachim, Claudio Lombardelli (83 Ben Federspiel), Mario Mutsch, Sébastien Remy, Carlos Ferreira (88 Daniel Huss). Trainer: Guy Hellers

NETHERLANDS: Edwin van der Sar, John Heitinga, André Ooijer (46 Urby Emanuelson), Joris Mathijsen, Tim de Cler, Stijn Schaars (46 Jan Vennegoor of Hesselink), Theo Janssen, Denny Landzaat, Klaas Jan Huntelaar, Robin van Persie (77 Ryan Babel), Dirk Kuyt. Trainer: Marco van Basten

Goal: Mathijsen (18)

ROMANIA v BULGARIA 2-2 (1-0)

Farul, Constanța 02.09.2006

Referee: Stefano Farina (ITA) Attendance: 15,000

ROMANIA: Bogdan Lobonț, Cosmin Contra, Răzvan Raț, Gabriel Tamaş, Cristian Chivu, Paul Codrea, Florentin Petre (71 Bănel Nicoliță), Nicolae Dică (59 Răzvan Cociş), Ciprian Marica, Adrian Mutu, Laurențiu Roşu (79 Vasile Maftei). Trainer: Victor Pițurcă

BULGARIA: Georgi Petkov, Aleksandar Tunchev, Stanislav Angelov, Elin Topuzakov, Lucio Wagner, Stilian Petrov, Radostin Kishishev (46 Chavdar Yankov), Martin Petrov, Zoran Janković, Dimitar Berbatov (62 Valeri Bozhinov), Georgi Peev (46 Blagoy Georgiev). Trainer: Hristo Stoichkov

Sent off: Gabriel Tamaş (90)

Goals: Roşu (46), Marica (55), M. Petrov (82, 84)

NETHERLANDS v BELARUS 3-0 (1-0)

PSV, Eindhoven 06.09.2006

Referee: Howard Webb (ENG) Attendance: 27,000

NETHERLANDS: Edwin van der Sar, John Heitinga (67 Khalid Boulahrouz), André Ooijer, Joris Mathijsen, Giovanni van Bronckhorst, Nigel de Jong, Wesley Sneijder, Denny Landzaat (68 Stijn Schaars), Klaas Jan Huntelaar (76 Ryan Babel), Robin van Persie, Dirk Kuyt.
Trainer: Marco van Basten

BELARUS: Vasiliy Khomutovskiy, Aleksandr Yurevich, Sergei Shtaniuk, Sergei Omelyanchuk, Dmitriy Lentsevich, Timofei Kalachev (73 Vitaliy Lanko), Denis Kovba, Vladimir Korytko (46 Oleg Strakhanovich), Maksim Romashchenko (69 Artem Kontsevoy), Aleksandr Hleb, Sergei Kornilenko.
Trainer: Yuri Puntus

Goals: Van Persie (33, 78), Kuyt (90)

ALBANIA v ROMANIA 0-2 (0-0)

Qemal Stafa, Tirana 06.09.2006

Referee: Olegário Benquerença (POR) Attendance: 10,000

ALBANIA: Arjan Beqaj, Elvin Beqiri, Armend Dallku, Lorik Cana, Besnik Hasi, Ervin Skela (64 Adrian Aliaj), Altin Lala (78 Devis Muka), Igli Tare, Erjon Bogdani (62 Bekim Kastrati), Altin Haxhi, Debatik Curri. Trainer: Otto Barić

ROMANIA: Bogdan Lobonț, Cosmin Contra, Răzvan Raț, Sorin Ghionea, Cristian Chivu, Paul Codrea, Florentin Petre, Nicolae Dică, Ciprian Marica (78 Ioan Ganea), Adrian Mutu (85 Bănel Nicoliță), Laurențiu Roşu (89 Andrei Mărgăritescu). Trainer: Victor Pițurcă

Goals: Dică (65), Mutu (75 pen)

ROMANIA v BELARUS 3-1 (2-1)

Steaua, Bucureşti 07.10.2006

Referee: Alberto Undiano (SPA) Attendance: 28,000

ROMANIA: Dănuț Coman, Răzvan Raț, Gabriel Tamaş, Cristian Chivu, Florentin Petre, Ciprian Marica (90 Claudiu Niculescu), Adrian Mutu (72 Mugurel Buga), Laurențiu Roşu, Dorin Goian, Petre Marin, Nicolae Dică (86 Răzvan Cociş).
Trainer: Victor Pițurcă

BELARUS: Vladimir Gayev, Aleksandr Kulchiy (65 Oleg Strakhanovich), Dmitriy Lentsevich, Sergei Omelyanchuk, Sergei Shtaniuk, Timofei Kalachev (50 Vyacheslav Hleb), Aleksandr Hleb, Sergei Gurenko, Maksim Romashchenko, Sergei Kornilenko (66 Vladimir Korytko), Aleksandr Yurevich.
Trainer: Yuri Puntus

Goals: Mutu (7), Marica (10), Kornilenko (20), Goian (76)

BULGARIA v SLOVENIA 3-0 (0-0)

Vassil Levski, Sofia 06.09.2006

Referee: Claus Bo Larsen (DEN) Attendance: 10,000

BULGARIA: Dimitar Ivankov, Stanislav Angelov, Lucio Wagner, Aleksandar Tunchev, Elin Topuzakov, Stilian Petrov, Chavdar Yankov (69 Radostin Kishishev), Blagoy Georgiev (53 Dimitar Telkiyski), Martin Petrov, Valeri Bozhinov (60 Hristo Yovov), Zoran Janković. Trainer: Hristo Stoichkov

SLOVENIA: Borut Mavrič, Branko Ilič, Aleksander Knavs, Bojan Jokič, Boštjan Cesar, Anton Žlogar, Robert Koren (76 Klemen Lavrič), Andrej Komac, Milenko Ačimovič, Valter Birsa (80 Borut Semler), Milivoje Novakovič.
Trainer: Branko Oblak

Goals: Bozhinov (58), M. Petrov (72), Telkiyski (81)

SLOVENIA v LUXEMBOURG 2-0 (2-0)

Arena Petrol, Celje 07.10.2006

Referee: Panicos Kailis (CYP) Attendance: 3,500

SLOVENIA: Borut Mavrič, Branko Ilič, Matej Mavrič, Boštjan Cesar, Bojan Jokič, Nastja Čeh, Milenko Ačimovič (75 Andrej Komac), Valter Birsa, Robert Koren, Milivoje Novakovič, Klemen Lavrič (85 Miran Burgič). Trainer: Branko Oblak

LUXEMBOURG: Jonathan Joubert (72 Stephane Gillet), Kim Kintziger, Eric Hoffmann, Claude Reiter, René Peters, Jeff Strasser, Gilles Bettmer, Aurélien Joachim (66 Daniel Huss), Claudio Lombardelli (42 Charles Leweck), Sébastien Remy, Mario Mutsch. Trainer: Guy Hellers

Goals: Novakovič (30), Koren (44)

BULGARIA v NETHERLANDS 1-1 (1-0)

Vasil Levski National Stadium, Sofia 07.10.2006

Referee: Tom Henning Øvrebø (NOR) Attendance: 30,600

BULGARIA: Dimitar Ivankov, Stanislav Angelov, Elin Topuzakov, Valentin Iliev, Lucio Wagner, Radostin Kishishev, Chavdar Yankov (82 Zoran Janković), Hristo Yovov (54 Dimitar Telkiyski), Stilian Petrov, Martin Petrov (64 Valeri Bozhinov), Dimitar Berbatov. Trainer: Hristo Stoichkov

NETHERLANDS: Edwin van der Sar, Khalid Boulahrouz, André Ooijer, Joris Mathijsen, Giovanni van Bronckhorst, Nigel de Jong, Denny Landzaat, Wesley Sneijder (90 Stijn Schaars), Robin van Persie, Dirk Kuyt (16 Ryan Babel), Arjen Robben. Trainer: Marco van Basten

Goals: M. Petrov (12), Van Persie (62)

NETHERLANDS v ALBANIA 2-1 (2-0)

Amsterdam ArenA, Amsterdam 11.10.2006

Referee: Alon Yefet (ISR) Attendance: 40,000

NETHERLANDS: Edwin van der Sar, Khalid Boulahrouz, André Ooijer, Joris Mathijsen, Giovanni van Bronckhorst (68 Urby Emanuelson), Nigel de Jong (50 Stijn Schaars), Wesley Sneijder (80 Tim de Cler), Denny Landzaat, Ryan Babel, Robin van Persie, Arjen Robben. Trainer: Marco van Basten

ALBANIA: Arjan Beqaj, Nevil Dede, Armend Dallku, Adrian Aliaj (65 Edvin Murati), Besnik Hasi, Altin Haxhi, Debatik Curri, Ervin Skela, Altin Lala (46 Devis Muka), Igli Tare, Erjon Bogdani (79 Besart Berisha). Trainer: Otto Barić

Goals: Van Persie (15), Beqaj (42 own goal), Curri (67)

BELARUS v SLOVENIA 4-2 (1-2)

Dinamo, Minsk 11.10.2006

Referee: Viktor Kassai (HUN) Attendance: 23,000

BELARUS: Vladimir Gayev, Sergei Omelyanchuk, Sergei Shtaniuk, Sergei Gurenko, Aleksandr Kulchiy, Denis Kovba, Timofei Kalachev, Maksim Romashchenko (50 Vladimir Korytko), Aleksandr Hleb, Vyacheslav Hleb (69 Oleg Strakhanovich), Sergei Kornilenko (90 Artem Kontsevoy). Trainer: Yuri Puntus

SLOVENIA: Borut Mavrič, Branko Ilič, Bojan Jokič, Boštjan Cesar, Matej Mavrič, Robert Koren, Milenko Ačimovič (70 Andrej Komac), Anton Žlogar, Valter Birsa, Milivoje Novakovič (82 Miran Burgič), Klemen Lavrič. Trainer: Branko Oblak

Goals: Kovba (18), Cesar (19), Lavrič (43), Kornilenko (52, 60), Korytko (85)

LUXEMBOURG v BELARUS 1-2 (0-1)

Josy Barthel, Luxembourg 24.03.2007

Referee: Mark Steven Whitby (WAL) Attendance: 3,150

LUXEMBOURG: Jonathan Joubert, Jeff Strasser, Eric Hoffmann, Claude Reiter, Kim Kintziger, René Peters, Gilles Bettmer, Ben Payal (67 Carlos Ferreira), Claudio Lombardelli (58 Jérôme Bigard), Sébastien Remy, Dan Collette (64 Chris Sagramola). Trainer: Guy Hellers

BELARUS: Yuriy Zhevnov, Aleksandr Yurevich, Sergei Shtaniuk, Aleksandr Kulchiy, Vladimir Korytko, Oleg Strakhanovich (58 Artem Chelyadinski), Aleksandr Hleb, Timofei Kalachev, Vyacheslav Hleb, Sergei Kornilenko (74 Gennadiy Bliznyuk), Vitaliy Kutuzov (80 Artem Radkov). Trainer: Yuri Puntus

Goals: Kalachev (25), Kutuzov (54), Sagramola (68)

LUXEMBOURG v BULGARIA 0-1 (0-1)

Josy Barthel, Luxembourg 11.10.2006

Referee: Novo Panic (BIH) Attendance: 3,200

LUXEMBOURG: Stéphane Gillet, Claude Reiter, Jeff Strasser, Kim Kintziger, René Peters (61 Ben Payal), Gilles Bettmer, Mario Mutsch, Sébastien Remy, Aurélien Joachim (52 Daniel Huss), Claudio Lombardelli (69 Charles Leweck), Carlos Ferreira. Trainer: Guy Hellers

BULGARIA: Dimitar Ivankov, Stanislav Angelov, Aleksandar Tunchev, Elin Topuzakov, Lucio Wagner, Chavdar Yankov (77 Radostin Kishishev), Zdravko Lazarov (46 Hristo Yovov), Stilian Petrov, Dimitar Telkiyski, Valeri Bozhinov (68 Zoran Janković), Dimitar Berbatov. Trainer: Hristo Stoichkov

Goal: Tunchev (26)

ALBANIA v SLOVENIA 0-0

Loro Boriçi, Shkoder 24.03.2007

Referee: Joseph Attard (MLT) Attendance: 12,000

ALBANIA: Arjan Beqaj, Armend Dallku, Elvin Beqiri, Nevil Dede, Lorik Cana, Altin Haxhi, Altin Lala, Klodian Duro, Devis Muka (86 Besart Berisha), Edmond Kapllani (58 Alban Bushi), Erjon Bogdani (89 Hamdi Salihi). Trainer: Otto Barić

SLOVENIA: Samir Handanovič, Matej Mavrič, Bojan Jokič, Boštjan Cesar, Branko Ilič, Robert Koren, Anton Žlogar, Andrej Komac (90 Fabijan Cipot), Nastja Čeh (80 Milenko Ačimovič), Klemen Lavrič, Ermin Rakovič (63 Valter Birsa). Trainer: Matjaž Kek

NETHERLANDS v ROMANIA 0-0

De Kuip, Rotterdam 24.03.2007

Referee: Markus Merk (GER) Attendance: 49,000

NETHERLANDS: Maarten Stekelenburg, Kew Jaliens, Wilfred Bouma, Joris Mathijsen, Giovanni van Bronckhorst, Denny Landzaat (79 Urby Emanuelson), Wesley Sneijder, Ryan Babel, Rafael van der Vaart (86 Clarence Seedorf), Klaas Jan Huntelaar, Arjen Robben. Trainer: Marco van Basten

ROMANIA: Bogdan Lobonţ, Cosmin Contra, Dorin Goian, Gabriel Tamaş, Răzvan Raţ (78 Ştefan Radu), Răzvan Cociş, Bănel Nicoliţă, Mirel Rădoi, Paul Codrea (87 Laurenţiu Roşu), Ciprian Marica (64 Daniel Niculae), Adrian Mutu. Trainer: Victor Piţurcă

SLOVENIA v NETHERLANDS 0-1 (0-0)

Arena Petrol, Celje 28.03.2007

Referee: Manuel Mejuto González (SPA) Attendance: 9,500

SLOVENIA: Samir Handanovič, Branko Ilič, Bojan Jokič, Matej Mavrič, Boštjan Cesar, Nastja Čeh, Andrej Komac, Robert Koren, Milenko Ačimovič (61 Goran Šukalo), Klemen Lavrič (83 Valter Birsa), Ermin Rakovič (65 Milivoje Novakovič). Trainer: Matjaž Kek

NETHERLANDS: Edwin van der Sar, John Heitinga (74 Demy de Zeeuw), Joris Mathijsen, Wilfred Bouma, Urby Emanuelson, Ibrahim Afellay (85 Clarence Seedorf), Ryan Babel (73 Danny Koevermans), Giovanni van Bronckhorst, Dirk Kuyt, Wesley Sneijder, Arjen Robben. Trainer: Marco van Basten

Goal: Van Bronckhorst (86)

BULGARIA v ALBANIA 0-0

Vasil Levski National Stadium, Sofia 28.03.2007

Referee: Jonas Eriksson (SWE) Attendance: 25,000

BULGARIA: Dimitar Ivankov, Radostin Kishishev, Aleksandar Tunchev, Igor Tomašić, Lucio Wagner, Chavdar Yankov, Stilian Petrov, Georgi Peev (65 Valeri Bozhinov), Hristo Yovov (46 Dimitar Telkiyski), Zoran Janković (46 Svetoslav Todorov), Dimitar Berbatov. Trainer: Hristo Stoitchkov

ALBANIA: Arjan Beqaj, Armend Dallku, Nevil Dede, Elvin Beqiri, Debatik Curri, Altin Lala, Klodian Duro (68 Ervin Bulku), Altin Haxhi (54 Edmond Kapllani), Lorik Cana, Besart Berisha (79 Alban Bushi), Erjon Bogdani. Trainer: Otto Barić

ALBANIA v LUXEMBOURG 2-0 (1-0)

Qemal Stafa, Tirana 02.06.2007

Referee: Lasha Silagava (GEO) Attendance: 8,000

ALBANIA: Arjan Beqaj, Debatik Curri, Armend Dallku, Lorik Cana, Alban Bushi (76 Hamdi Salihi), Edmond Kapllani, Klodian Duro, Besart Berisha (46 Devis Muka), Ervin Skela, Altin Haxhi (74 Kristi Vangjeli), Nevil Dede. Trainer: Otto Barić

LUXEMBOURG: Jonathan Joubert, Kim Kintziger, Jérôme Bigard (60 Daniel Da Mota), Eric Hoffmann, Jeff Strasser, René Peters, Gilles Bettmer, Ben Payal (82 Carlos Ferreira), Dan Collette (70 Chris Sagramola), Sébastien Remy, Mario Mutsch. Trainer: Guy Hellers

Goals: Kapllani (38), Haxhi (57)

ROMANIA v LUXEMBOURG 3-0 (1-0)

Ceahlaul, Piatra Neamt 28.03.2007

Referee: Romans Lajuks (LVA) Attendance: 12,000

ROMANIA: Bogdan Lobonţ, Cosmin Contra, Gabriel Tamaş (87 Dorel Stoica), Dorin Goian, Ştefan Radu, Mirel Rădoi, Ianis Zicu, Laurenţiu Roşu (53 Adrian Cristea), Răzvan Cociş, Daniel Niculae (65 Ciprian Marica), Adrian Mutu. Trainer: Victor Piţurcă

LUXEMBOURG: Jonathan Joubert, Jeff Strasser, Jérôme Bigard, Eric Hoffmann, Claude Reiter, René Peters, Gilles Bettmer (50 Ben Payal), Claudio Lombardelli (81 Carlos Ferreira), Sébastien Remy, Mario Mutsch, Dan Collette (49 Chris Sagramola). Trainer: Guy Hellers

Goals: Mutu (26), Contra (56), Marica (90)

SLOVENIA v ROMANIA 1-2 (0-0)

Arena Petrol, Celje 02.06.2007

Referee: Stuart Dougal (SCO) Attendance: 7,000

SLOVENIA: Samir Handanovič, Boštjan Cesar, Branko Ilič, Bojan Jokič, Matej Mavrič, Goran Šukalo (80 Dare Vršič), Nastja Čeh, Andrej Komac, Robert Koren (53 Valter Birsa), Klemen Lavrič, Ermin Rakovič (61 Milivoje Novakovič). Trainer: Matjaž Kek

ROMANIA: Bogdan Lobonţ, Cristian Chivu, Cosmin Contra, Răzvan Raţ, Gabriel Tamaş, Paul Codrea, Bănel Nicoliţă, Laurenţiu Roşu (63 Ianis Zicu), Ciprian Marica (74 Daniel Niculae), Adrian Mutu, Dorel Stoica (77 Gabriel Mureşan). Trainer: Victor Piţurcă

Sent off: Boštjan Cesar (80), Daniel Niculae (80)

Goals: Tamaş (52), Nicoliţă (69), Vršič (90)

BELARUS v BULGARIA 0-2 (0-1)

Dinamo, Minsk 02.06.2007

Referee: Jaroslav Jara (CZE) Attendance: 29,000

BELARUS: Yuriy Zhevnov, Sergei Omelyanchuk (71 Oleg Strakhanovich), Sergei Shtaniuk, Yan Tigorev, Aleksandr Kulchiy, Timofei Kalachev, Vladimir Korytko, Denis Kovba, Aleksandr Hleb, Sergei Kornilenko (59 Roman Vasilyuk), Vitaliy Kutuzov (46 Vyacheslav Hleb). Trainer: Yuri Puntus

BULGARIA: Dimitar Ivankov, Aleksandar Tunchev, Igor Tomašić, Stanislav Angelov (90 Valeri Domovchiyski), Lucio Wagner, Dimitar Telkiyski, Radostin Kishishev, Stilian Petrov, Hristo Yovov (77 Vladimir Manchev), Martin Petrov (88 Tsvetan Genkov), Dimitar Berbatov.
Trainer: Stanimir Stoilov

Goals: Berbatov (28, 46)

ROMANIA v SLOVENIA 2-0 (1-0)

Dan Paltinisanu, Timisoara 06.06.2007

Referee: Alon Yefet (ISR) Attendance: 22,000

ROMANIA: Bogdan Lobonţ, Răzvan Raţ, Gabriel Tamaş, Dorin Goian, Cosmin Contra, Ianis Zicu (60 Laurenţiu Roşu), Cristian Chivu, Paul Codrea (78 Mihăiţă Pleşan), Florentin Petre (75 Bănel Nicoliţă), Ciprian Marica, Adrian Mutu.
Trainer: Victor Piţurcă

SLOVENIA: Samir Handanovič, Matej Mavrič, Mitja Mörec, Bojan Jokič (84 Suad Filekovič), Branko Ilič, Nastja Čeh, Andrej Komac, Dare Vršič, Anton Žlogar (77 Goran Šukalo), Klemen Lavrič, Valter Birsa (54 Milivoje Novakovič).
Trainer: Matjaž Kek

Goals: Mutu (40), Contra (70)

BULGARIA v BELARUS 2-1 (2-1)

Vasil Levski National Stadium, Sofia 06.06.2007

Referee: Kristinn Jakobsson (ISL) Attendance: 10,227

BULGARIA: Dimitar Ivankov, Radostin Kishishev, Aleksandar Tunchev, Igor Tomašić, Lucio Wagner, Chavdar Yankov (90 Zahari Sirakov), Stilian Petrov, Dimitar Telkiyski, Hristo Yovov (68 Stanislav Angelov), Dimitar Berbatov, Martin Petrov (81 Vladimir Manchev). Trainer: Stanimir Stoilov

BELARUS: Yuriy Zhevnov, Sergei Shtaniuk, Artem Radkov, Yan Tigorev, Aleksandr Yurevich, Timofei Kalachev (44 Vitaliy Kutuzov), Vladimir Korytko, Denis Kovba, Aleksandr Hleb, Oleg Strakhanovich (64 Vyacheslav Hleb), Roman Vasilyuk (55 Sergei Kornilenko). Trainer: Yuri Puntus

Goals: Vasilyuk (5 pen), M. Petrov (10), Yankov (40)

LUXEMBOURG v SLOVENIA 0-3 (0-2)

Josy Barthel, Luxembourg 08.09.2007

Referee: Sergiy Berezka (UKR) Attendance: 2,000

LUXEMBOURG: Jonathan Joubert, Jérôme Bigard, Eric Hoffmann, Jeff Strasser, Jeremie Peiffer (52 Daniel Da Mota), Claudio Lombardelli (46 Ben Payal), Carlos Ferreira, Gilles Bettmer, Mario Mutsch, René Peters, Daniel Huss (63 Joel Kitenge). Trainer: Guy Hellers

SLOVENIA: Samir Handanovič, Mišo Brecko, Mitja Mörec, Anton Žlogar (82 Fabijan Cipot), Aleš Kokot, Andraz Kirm (64 Andrej Komac), Robert Koren, Dalibor Stevanovič, Dare Vršič (78 Rene Mihelič), Milivoje Novakovič, Klemen Lavrič.
Trainer: Matjaž Kek

Goals: Lavrič (7, 47), Novakovič (37)

LUXEMBOURG v ALBANIA 0-3 (0-2)

Josy Barthel, Luxembourg 06.06.2007

Referee: Paulius Malzinskas (LTU) Attendance: 4,325

LUXEMBOURG: Jonathan Joubert, Jeff Strasser, Jérôme Bigard (46 Claudio Lombardelli), Eric Hoffmann, Kim Kintziger, Ben Payal (64 Daniel Da Mota), René Peters, Gilles Bettmer, Sébastien Remy, Mario Mutsch, Dan Collette (79 Chris Sagramola). Trainer: Guy Hellers

ALBANIA: Arjan Beqaj, Nevil Dede, Altin Haxhi, Armend Dallku, Debatik Curri, Ervin Skela (60 Klodian Duro), Lorik Cana, Devis Muka (77 Daniel Xhafa), Edmond Kapllani, Alban Bushi (67 Besart Berisha), Erjon Bogdani.
Trainer: Otto Barić

Goals: Skela (25), Kapllani (36, 72)

BELARUS v ROMANIA 1-3 (1-2)

Dinamo, Minsk 08.09.2007

Referee: Peter Fröjdfeldt (SWE) Attendance: 19,300

BELARUS: Vasiliy Khomutovskiy, Vladimir Korytko, Artem Radkov, Pavel Plaskonny, Yan Tigorev, Timofei Kalachev (77 Aleksei Skverniuk), Maksim Romashchenko, Aleksandr Hleb, Igor Stasevich, Sergei Kornilenko, Vitali Rodionov (61 Roman Vasilyuk). Trainer: Bernd Stange

ROMANIA: Bogdan Lobonţ, Răzvan Raţ, Cristian Chivu, Dorin Goian, Petre Marin, Paul Codrea (90 Eugen Trică), Ovidiu Petre, Bănel Nicoliţă, Nicolae Dică (67 Dorinel Munteanu), Adrian Mutu, Sergiu Radu (56 Florentin Petre).
Trainer: Victor Piţurcă

Goals: Mutu (16, 77 pen), Romashchenko (20), Dică (42)

NETHERLANDS v BULGARIA 2-0 (1-0)

Amsterdam ArenA, Amsterdam 08.09.2007

Referee: Luis Medina Cantalejo (SPA) Attendance: 50,000

NETHERLANDS: Edwin van der Sar, Mario Melchiot (57 Khalid Boulahrouz), Joris Mathijsen, Wilfred Bouma, Giovanni van Bronckhorst, John Heitinga, Wesley Sneijder (73 Clarence Seedorf), Demy de Zeeuw (81 Nigel de Jong), Ryan Babel, Ruud van Nistelrooy, Robin van Persie.
Trainer: Marco van Basten

BULGARIA: Dimitar Ivankov, Lucio Wagner (78 Chavdar Yankov), Radostin Kishishev, Aleksandar Tunchev, Igor Tomašić, Stanislav Angelov, Georgi Peev (60 Ivelin Popov), Martin Petrov, Stilian Petrov, Dimitar Telkiyski (68 Velizar Dimitrov), Dimitar Berbatov. Trainer: Dimitar Penev

Goals: Sneijder (22), Van Nistelrooy (58)

ALBANIA v NETHERLANDS 0-1 (0-0)

Qemal Stafa, Tirana 12.09.2007

Referee: Mike Riley (ENG) Attendance: 20,000

ALBANIA: Arjan Beqaj, Armend Dallku, Nevil Dede, Debatik Curri, Kristi Vangjeli, Klodian Duro (69 Altin Haxhi), Altin Lala, Lorik Cana, Devis Muka, Erjon Bogdani (83 Ervin Bulku), Edmond Kapllani (46 Alban Bushi).
Trainer: Otto Barić

NETHERLANDS: Edwin van der Sar, Mario Melchiot, Joris Mathijsen, Wilfred Bouma (63 Urby Emanuelson), André Ooijer, Demy de Zeeuw, Wesley Sneijder, Giovanni van Bronckhorst, Ryan Babel (75 Dirk Kuyt), Ruud van Nistelrooy, Robin van Persie (46 Rafael Van der Vaart).
Trainer: Marco van Basten

Sent off: Lorik Cana (87)

Goal: Van Nistelrooy (90)

SLOVENIA v BELARUS 1-0 (1-0)

Arena Petrol, Celje 12.09.2007

Referee: Veaceslav Banari (MDA) Attendance: 4,000

SLOVENIA: Samir Handanovič, Branko Ilič (82 Mišo Brecko), Bojan Jokič, Mitja Mörec, Fabijan Cipot, Robert Koren, Andraz Kirm, Dalibor Stevanovič (75 Luka Zinko), Valter Birsa (67 Dare Vršič), Milivoje Novakovič, Klemen Lavrič. Trainer: Matjaž Kek

BELARUS: Vladimir Gaev, Yan Tigorev, Artem Radkov, Pavel Plaskonny, Timofei Kalachev, Igor Stasevich, Maksim Romashchenko, Aleksandr Hleb, Sergei Kornilenko (46 Vitali Rodionov), Vladimir Korytko (89 Nikolai Kashevski), Gennadiy Bliznyuk (74 Egor Filipenko).
Trainer: Bernd Stange

Sent off: Artem Radkov (70)

Goal: Lavrič (3 pen)

BELARUS v LUXEMBOURG 0-1 (0-0)

Tsentralny, Gomel 13.10.2007

Referee: Michael Svendsen (DEN) Attendance: 14,000

BELARUS: Yuriy Zhevnov (69 Vasiliy Khomutovskiy), Sergei Omelyanchuk, Igor Stasevich (62 Timofei Kalachev), Egor Filipenko, Pavel Plaskonny, Vladimir Korytko, Aleksei Skverniuk, Maksim Romashchenko, Aleksandr Hleb, Sergei Kornilenko, Andrei Voronkov (77 Vitali Rodionov).
Trainer: Bernd Stange

LUXEMBOURG: Jonathan Joubert, Benoit Lang, Kim Kinziger, Jean Wagner, René Peters, Ben Payal (76 Carlos Ferreira), Gilles Bettmer, Claudio Lombardelli (45 Fons Leweck), Sébastien Remy, Mario Mutsch, Joël Kitenge (61 Daniel Da Mota). Trainer: Guy Hellers

Goal: F. Leweck (90)

BULGARIA v LUXEMBOURG 3-0 (2-0)

Vasil Levski National Stadium, Sofia 12.09.2007

Referee: Bülent Demirlek (TUR) Attendance: 8,000

BULGARIA: Georgi Petkov, Aleksandar Tunchev, Igor Tomašić, Petar Zanev, Stanislav Angelov, Ivelin Popov (74 Martin Kouchev), Radostin Kishishev, Stilian Petrov (60 Chavdar Yankov), Velizar Dimitrov, Dimitar Berbatov, Martin Petrov (66 Hristo Yovov). Trainer: Dimitar Penev

LUXEMBOURG: Jonathan Joubert, Jérôme Bigard, Kim Kinziger, Eric Hoffmann, Jeremie Peiffer (46 Dan Collette), Jeff Strasser, René Peters, Gilles Bettmer (83 Daniel Da Mota), Sébastien Remy, Mario Mutsch, Daniel Huss (46 Ben Payal).
Trainer: Guy Hellers

Goals: Berbatov (27, 28), M. Petrov (54 pen)

ROMANIA v NETHERLANDS 1-0 (0-0)

Farul, Constanța 13.10.2007

Referee: Kyros Vassaras (GRE) Attendance: 13,000

ROMANIA: Bogdan Lobonţ, Dorin Goian, George Ogăraru, Răzvan Raţ, Gabriel Tamaş, Cristian Chivu, Bănel Nicoliţă, Paul Codrea, Ovidiu Petre, Ciprian Marica (70 Daniel Niculae), Adrian Mutu. Trainer: Victor Piţurcă

NETHERLANDS: Maarten Stekelenburg, Giovanni van Bronckhorst, John Heitinga (68 Kew Jaliens), André Ooijer (84 Danny Koevermans), Joris Mathijsen, Wilfred Bouma, Demy de Zeeuw, Rafael van der Vaart, Clarence Seedorf, Ruud van Nistelrooy, Arjen Robben (78 Ryan Babel).
Trainer: Marco van Basten

Goal: Goian (71)

SLOVENIA v ALBANIA 0-0

Arena Petrol, Celje 13.10.2007

Referee: Duarte Nuno Pereira Gomes (POR)
Attendance: 4,600

SLOVENIA: Samir Handanovič, Mišo Brecko, Bojan Jokič (77 Branko Ilič), Mitja Mörec, Fabijan Cipot, Anton Žlogar, Andraz Kirm, Robert Koren, Valter Birsa (81 Rene Mihelič), Milivoje Novakovič (61 Dejan Rusič), Klemen Lavrič.
Trainer: Matjaž Kek

ALBANIA: Arjan Beqaj, Kristi Vangjeli, Debatik Curri, Nevil Dede, Blerim Rrustemi, Altin Haxhi (60 Devis Muka), Altin Lala, Ervin Bulku, Klodian Duro (77 Alban Bushi), Ervin Skela (90 Jahmir Hyka), Erjon Bogdani. Trainer: Otto Barić

ALBANIA v BULGARIA 1-1 (1-0)

Qemal Stafa, Tirana 17.10.2007

Referee: Fritz Stuchlik (AUS) Attendance: 8,000

ALBANIA: Arjan Beqaj, Debatik Curri, Armend Dallku, Nevil Dede, Kristi Vangeli, Klodian Duro, Altin Haxhi (46 Devis Muka), Altin Lala, Ervin Skela, Hamdi Salihi (73 Ervin Bulku), Erjon Bogdani. Trainer: Otto Barić

BULGARIA: Georgi Petkov, Radostin Kishishev, Igor Tomašić, Valentin Iliev, Lucio Wagner, Stanislav Angelov, Stilian Petrov (46 Blagoy Georgiev), Dimitar Telkiyski (46 Chavdar Yankov), Ivelin Popov (72 Hristo Yovov), Martin Petrov, Dimitar Berbatov. Trainer: Dimitar Penev

Goals: Kishishev (32 own goal), Berbatov (87)

LUXEMBOURG v ROMANIA 0-2 (0-1)

Josy Barthel, Luxembourg 17.10.2007

Referee: Felix Brych (GER) Attendance: 3,600

LUXEMBOURG: Stéphane Gillet, Benoit Lang, Jean Wagner, Kim Kinziger, Eric Hoffmann, Mario Mutsch, Ben Payal (68 Fons Leweck), René Peters, Gilles Bettmer (49 Carlos Ferreira), Sébastien Remy, Joël Kitenge (57 Daniel Da Mota).
Trainer: Guy Hellers

ROMANIA: Bogdan Lobonţ, George Ogăraru, Gabriel Tamaş, Dorin Goian, Răzvan Raţ, Florentin Petre, Andrei Mărgăritescu, Cristian Chivu (87 Ovidiu Petre), Ciprian Marica, Nicolae Dică (68 Adrian Cristea), Daniel Niculae (76 Florin Bratu). Trainer: Victor Piţurcă

Goals: F. Petre (42), Marica (61)

BULGARIA v ROMANIA 1-0 (1-0)

Vasil Levski National, Sofia 17.11.2007

Referee: Konrad Plautz (AUS) Attendance: 15,000

BULGARIA: Dimitar Ivankov, Zhivko Milanov, Igor Tomašic, Aleksandar Tunchev, Petar Zanev, Blagoy Georgiev, Stilian Petrov, Hristo Yovov (83 Dimitar Telkiyski), Velizar Dimitrov, Martin Petrov (90 Zdravko Lazarov), Dimitar Berbatov.
Trainer: Dimitar Penev

ROMANIA: Bogdan Lobonţ, George Ogăraru, Gabriel Tamaş (58 Răzvan Cociş), Dorin Goian, Răzvan Raţ, Paul Codrea (82 Eugen Trică), Ovidiu Petre, Cristian Chivu, Bănel Nicoliţă, Ionuţ Mazilu (65 Ciprian Marica), Daniel Niculae.
Trainer: Victor Piţurcă

Goal: V. Dimitrov (6)

NETHERLANDS v SLOVENIA 2-0 (1-0)

PSV, Eindhoven 17.10.2007

Referee: Nicola Rizzoli (ITA) Attendance: 35,000

NETHERLANDS: Maarten Stekelenburg, Kew Jaliens, John Heitinga, Wilfred Bouma, Urby Emanuelson, Wesley Sneijder, Demy de Zeeuw, Clarence Seedorf, Robin van Persie (59 Andre Ooijer), Klaas Jan Huntelaar, Rafael van der Vaart (29 Arjen Robben, 62 Ryan Babel). Trainer: Marco van Basten

SLOVENIA: Samir Handanovič, Boštjan Cesar, Robert Koren, Mitja Mörec, Mišo Brecko, Anton Žlogar, Andraz Kirm (81 Bojan Jokič), Klemen Lavrič, Valter Birsa (67 Milivoje Novakovič), Branko Ilič, Andrej Komac (85 Zlatan Ljubijankič). Trainer: Matjaž Kek

Goals: Sneijder (14), Huntelaar (86)

ALBANIA v BELARUS 2-4 (2-2)

Qemal Stafa, Tirana 17.11.2007

Referee: Bülent Demirlek (TUR) Attendance: 5,000

ALBANIA: Arjan Beqaj, Debatik Curri, Nevil Dede, Altin Lala (75 Alban Bushi), Blerim Rrustemi (38 Kristi Vangeli), Ervin Skela, Lorik Cana, Armend Dallku, Klodian Duro, Erjon Bogdani, Edmond Kapllani (74 Hamdi Salihi).
Trainer: Slavko Kovacic.

BELARUS: Yuriy Zhevnov, Sergei Omelyanchuk, Egor Filipenko, Pavel Plaskonny (65 Aleksei Skverniuk), Roman Kirenkin, Aleksandr Kulchiy, Timofei Kalachev (75 Vladimir Korytko), Maksim Romashchenko, Aleksandr Hleb, Vitaliy Bulyga, Vitaliy Kutuzov (90 Sergei Kornilenko).
Trainer: Bernd Stange

Goals: Romashchenko (28, 63 pen), Bogdani (39), Kapllani (43), Kutuzov (45, 54)

NETHERLANDS v LUXEMBOURG 1-0 (1-0)

De Kuip, Rotterdam 17.11.2007

Referee: Martin Hansson (SWE) Attendance: 49,000

NETHERLANDS: Edwin van der Sar, Mario Melchiot, Joris Mathijsen, Wilfred Bouma, Demy de Zeeuw, Giovanni van Bronckhorst, Rafael van der Vaart, Wesley Sneijder, Clarence Seedorf (77 Urby Emanuelson), Ruud van Nistelrooy (46 Dirk Kuyt), Danny Koevermans (84 Ryan Babel).
Trainer: Marco van Basten

LUXEMBOURG: Jonathan Joubert, Kim Kinziger, Eric Hoffmann, Jean Wagner, Jeff Strasser, Mario Mutsch, René Peters, Ben Payal, Gilles Bettmer (66 Fons Leweck), Sébastien Remy, Joël Kitenge (50 Aurélien Joachim).
Trainer: Guy Hellers

Goal: Koevermans (43)

ROMANIA v ALBANIA 6-1 (1-0)

Naţional, Bucureşti 21.11.2007

Referee: Edo Trivkovic (CRO) Attendance: 25,000

ROMANIA: Bogdan Lobonţ, George Ogăraru, Gabriel Tamaş (78 Marius Constantin), Dorin Goian, Răzvan Raţ, Florentin Petre (65 Gheorghe Bucur), Andrei Mărgăritescu, Răzvan Cociş, Daniel Niculae, Ciprian Marica (73 Ionuţ Mazilu), Nicolae Dică. Trainer: Victor Piţurcă

ALBANIA: Arjan Beqaj, Debatik Curri, Nevil Dede, Kristi Vangjeli (41 Edmond Kapllani), Andi Lila, Altin Haxhi, Altin Lala, Ervin Bulku, Klodian Duro (78 Jahmir Hyka), Ervin Skela, Erjon Bogdani (83 Elis Bakaj). Trainer: Slavko Kovacic

Sent off: Debatik Curri (61), Nevil Dede (70)

Goals: Dică (22, 73 pen), Tamaş (53), D. Niculae (63, 68), Kapllani (64), Marica (71 pen)

SLOVENIA v BULGARIA 0-2 (0-0)

Arena Petrol, Celje 21.11.2007

Referee: Howard Webb (ENG) Attendance: 3,600

SLOVENIA: Samir Handanovič, Bojan Jokič, Mitja Mörec, Boštjan Cesar, Mišo Brecko, Anton Žlogar, Robert Koren, Dalibor Stevanovič (56 Andrej Komac), Andraž Kirm, Valter Birsa (49 Branko Ilič), Klemen Lavrič (65 Milivoje Novakovič).
Trainer: Matjaž Kek

BULGARIA: Dimitar Ivankov, Zhivko Milanov (46 Iordan Todorov), Igor Tomašić, Aleksandar Tunchev, Stanislav Angelov, Blagoy Georgiev, Stilian Petrov (46 Dimitar Telkiyski), Hristo Yovov (76 Zdravko Lazarov), Velizar Dimitrov, Martin Petrov, Dimitar Berbatov.
Trainer: Dimitar Penev

Sent off: Bojan Jokič (45)

Goals: Georgiev (81), Berbatov (84)

BELARUS v NETHERLANDS 2-1 (0-0)

Dinamo, Minsk 21.11.2007

Referee: Bertrand Layec (FRA) Attendance: 19,000

BELARUS: Yuriy Zhevnov, Sergei Omelyanchuk (90 Igor Stasevich), Egor Filipenko, Roman Kirenkin, Aleksei Skverniuk, Vladimir Korytko, Aleksandr Hleb (46 Nikolai Kashevski), Aleksandr Kulchiy, Maksim Romashchenko, Vitaliy Kutuzov, Vitaliy Bulyga (85 Sergei Kornilenko).
Trainer: Bernd Stange

NETHERLANDS: Maarten Stekelenburg, Mario Melchiot, Joris Mathijsen, André Ooijer, Wilfred Bouma, Wesley Sneijder (46 Dirk Kuyt), Rafael van der Vaart, Giovanni van Bronckhorst (66 Orlando Engelaar), Demy de Zeeuw (69 Nigel de Jong), Ryan Babel, Danny Koevermans.
Trainer: Marco van Basten

Goals: Bulyga (49), Korytko (65), Van der Vaart (89)

	P	W	D	L	F	A	Pts
Romania	12	9	2	1	26	7	29
Netherlands	12	8	2	2	15	5	26
Bulgaria	12	7	4	1	18	7	25
Belarus	12	4	1	7	17	23	13
Albania	12	2	5	5	12	18	11
Slovenia	12	3	2	7	9	16	11
Luxembourg	12	1	0	11	2	23	3

FINAL TOURNAMENT IN SWITZERLAND AND AUSTRIA

GROUP A

SWITZERLAND v CZECH REPUBLIC 0-1 (0-0)

St. Jakob-Park, Basel 07.06.2008

Referee: Roberto Rosetti (ITA) Attendance: 42,500

SWITZERLAND: Diego Benaglio, Ludovic Magnin, Philippe Senderos, Stephan Lichtsteiner (75 Johan Vonlanthen), Gökhan Inler, Alexander Frei (46 Hakan Yakin), Marco Streller, Gelson Fernandes, Tranquillo Barnetta, Valon Behrami (84 Eren Derdiyok), Patrick Müller.
Trainer: Jakob Kuhn

CZECH REPUBLIC: Petr Čech, Zdeněk Grygera, Jan Polák, Tomáš Galásek, Marek Jankulovski, Libor Sionko (83 Stanislav Vlček), Jan Koller (56 Václav Svěrkoš), David Jarolím (87 Radoslav Kováč), Jaroslav Plašil, Tomáš Ujfaluši, David Rozehnal. Trainer: Karel Brückner

Goal: Svěrkoš (71)

PORTUGAL v TURKEY 2-0 (0-0)

Stade de Genève, Genève 07.06.2008

Referee: Herbert Fandel (GER) Attendance: 30,084

PORTUGAL: RICARDO Pereira, José Bosingwa, PEPE, Ricardo Carvalho, Paulo Ferreira, Anderson Souza "DECO" (90 Fernando Meira), Armando Petit, João Moutinho, Simão Sabrosa (81 Raul Meireles), Cristiano Ronaldo, Nuno Gomes (69 Nani). Trainer: Luiz Felipe Scolari

TURKEY: Volkan Demirel, Hamit Altintop (76 Semih Şentürk), Gökhan Zen (55 Emre Aşik), Servet Cetin, Hakan Balta, Mevlut Erdinc (46 Sabri Sarioglu), Emre Belezoglu, Kazim Kazim, Mehmet Aurelio, Tuncay Şanli, Nihat Kahveci. Trainer: Fatih Terim

Goals: Pepe (61), Raul Meireles (90+3)

CZECH REPUBLIC v PORTUGAL 1-3 (1-1)

Stade de Geneve, Genève 11.06.2008

Referee: Kyros Vassaras (GRE) Attendance: 30,084

CZECH REPUBLIC: Petr Čech, Zdeněk Grygera, Tomáš Ujfaluši, David Rozehnal, Marek Jankulovski, Libor Sionko, Jan Polák, Marek Matějovský (68 Stanislav Vlček), Tomáš Galásek (73 Jan Koller), Jaroslav Plašil (85 David Jarolím), Milan Baroš. Trainer: Karel Brückner

PORTUGAL: RICARDO Pereira, José Bosingwa, PEPE, Ricardo Carvalho, Paulo Ferreira, Armando Petit, Anderson Souza "DECO", João Moutinho (75 Fernando Meira), Simão Sabrosa (80 Ricardo Quaresma), Nuno Gomes (79 Hugo Almeida), Cristiano Ronaldo. Trainer: Luiz Felipe Scolari

Goals: Sionko (17), Anderson Souza "DECO" (8), Cristiano Ronaldo (63), Ricardo Quaresma (90+1)

SWITZERLAND v TURKEY 1-2 (1-0)

St.Jakob Park, Basel 11.06.2008

Referee: Luboš Michel (SVK) Attendance: 42,500

SWITZERLAND: Diego Benaglio, Stephan Lichtsteiner, Patrick Mueller, Philippe Senderos, Ludovic Magnin, Valon Behrami, Gokhan Inler, Gelson Fernandes (76 Ricardo Cabanas), Tranquillo Barnetta (66 Johan Vonlanthen), Hakan Yakin (86 Daniel Gygax), Eren Derdiyok.
Trainer: Jakob Kuhn

TURKEY: Volkan Demirel, Hamit Altintop, Emre Aşik, Servet Cetin, Hakan Balta, Gokdeniz Karadeniz (46 Mehmet Topal), Tumer Metin (46 Semih Şenturk), Mehmet Aurelio, Arda Turan, Tuncay Şanli, Nihat Kahveci (85 Kazim Kazim).
Trainer: Fatih Terim

Goals: Hakan Yakin (32), Semih Şenturk (57), Arda Turan (90)

TURKEY v CZECH REPUBLIC 3-2 (0-1)

Stade de Geneve, Genève 15.06.2008

Referee: Peter Frojdfeldt (SWE) Attendance: 30,084

TURKEY: Volkan Demirel, Hamit Altintop, Emre Gungor (63 Emre Aşik), Servet Cetin, Hakan Balta, Tuncay Şanli, Mehmet Topal (57 Kazim Kazim), Mehmet Aurelio, Arda Turan, Semih Şenturk (46 Sabri Sarioglu), Nihat Kahveci.
Trainer: Fatih Terim

CZECH REPUBLIC: Petr Čech, Zdeněk Grygera, Tomáš Ujfaluši, David Rozehnal, Marek Jankulovski, Libor Sionko (84 Stanislav Vlček), Jan Polák, Marek Matějovský (39 David Jarolím), Tomáš Galásek, Jaroslav Plašil (80 Michal Kadlec), Jan Koller. Trainer: Karel Brückner

Sent off: Volkan (90+3)

Goals: Arda Turan (75), Nihat Kahveci (88, 89), Koller (34), Plasil (62)

SWITZERLAND v PORTUGAL 2-0 (0-0)

St.Jakob Park, Basel 15.06.2008

Referee: Konrad Plautz (AUS) Attendance: 42,500

SWITZERLAND: Pascal Zuberbuehler, Stephan Lichtsteiner (83 Stephane Grichting), Patrick Mueller, Philippe Senderos, Ludovic Magnin, Valon Behrami, Gelson Fernandes, Gokhan Inler, Johan Vonlanthen (61 Tranquillo Barnetta), Hakan Yakin (86 Ricardo Cabanas), Eren Derdiyok. Trainer: Jakob Kuhn

PORTUGAL: RICARDO Pereira, Miguel (71 João Moutinho), Pepe, Bruno Alves, Paulo Ferreira (41 Jorge Riberiro), Fernando Meira, Miguel Veloso, Raul Meireles, Nani, Ricardo Quaresma, Helder Postiga (74 Hugo Almeida).
Trainer: Luiz Felipe Scolari

Goals: Murat Yakin (71, 83 pen)

	P	W	D	L	F	A	Pts
Portugal	3	2	0	1	5	3	6
Turkey	3	2	0	1	5	5	6
Switzerland	3	1	0	2	3	3	3
Czech Republic	3	1	0	2	4	6	3

GROUP B

AUSTRIA v CROATIA **0-1** (0-1)

Ernst-Happel, Wien 08.06.2008

Referee: Pieter Vink (HOL) Attendance: 51,428

AUSTRIA: Jürgen Macho, Sebastian Prödl, Martin Stranzl, Emanuel Pogatetz, René Aufhauser, Jürgen Säumel (61 Ivica Vastic), Joachim Standfest, Andreas Ivanschitz, Ronald Gercaliu (69 Ümit Korkmaz), Martin Harnik, Roland Linz (74 Roman Kienast). Trainer: Josef Hickersberger

CROATIA: Stipe Pletikosa, Vedran Čorluka, Robert Kovač, Josip Šimunić, Danijel Pranjić, Darijo Srna, Niko Kovač, Luka Modrić, Niko Kranjčar (61 Dario Knežević), Ivica Olić (83 Ognjen Vukojević), Mladen Petrić (72 Igor Budan). Trainer: Slaven Bilić

Goal: Modric (4 pen)

GERMANY v POLAND **2-0** (1-0)

Wörtherseestadion, Klagenfurt 08.06.2008

Referee: Tom Henning Øvrebø (NOR) Attendance: 30,461

GERMANY: Jens Lehmann, Philipp Lahm, Per Mertesacker, Christoph Metzelder, Marcell Jansen, Clemens Fritz (55 Bastian Schweinsteiger), Torsten Frings, Michael Ballack, Lukas Podolski, Mario Gómez García (75 Thomas Hitzlsperger), Miroslav Klose (90 Kevin Dennis Kurányi). Trainer: Joachim Löw

POLAND: Artur Boruc, Marcin Wasilewski, Michał Żewłakow, Jacek Bąk, Paweł Golański (75 Marek Saganowski), Wojciech Łobodziński (65 Łukasz Piszczek), Dariusz Dudka, Mariusz Lewandowski, Maciej Żurawski (46 Roger), Jacek Krzynówek, Euzebiusz Smolarek. Trainer: Leo Beenhakker

Goals: Podolski (20, 72)

CROATIA v GERMANY **2-1** (1-0)

Wörtherseestadion, Klagenfurt 12.06.2008

Referee: Frank de Bleeckere (BEL) Attendance: 30,461

CROATIA: Stipe Pletikosa, Vedran Čorluka, Robert Kovač, Josip Šimunić, Danijel Pranjić, Darijo Srna (80 Jerko Leko), Niko Kovač, Niko Kranjčar (85 Dario Knežević), Luka Modrić, Ivan Rakitić, Ivica Olić (72 Mladen Petrić). Trainer: Slaven Bilić

GERMANY: Jens Lehmann, Philipp Lahm, Per Mertesacker, Christoph Metzelder, Marcell Jansen (46 David Odonkor), Clemens Fritz (82 Kevin Dennis Kurányi), Torsten Frings, Michael Ballack, Lukas Podolski, Mario Gómez García (65 Bastian Schweinsteiger), Miroslav Klose. Trainer: Joachim Löw

Goals: Srna (24), Olic (62), Podolski (79)

AUSTRIA v POLAND **1-1** (0-1)

Ernst Happel, Wien 12.06.2008

Referee: Howard Melton Webb (ENG) Attendance: 51,428

AUSTRIA: Jürgen Macho, György Garics, Sebastian Proedl, Martin Stranzl, Emanuel Pogatetz, Christoph Leitgeb, Rene Aufhauser (74 Jürgen Saeumel), Andreas Ivanschitz (64 Ivica Vastic), Ümit Korkmaz, Martin Harnik, Roland Linz (64 Roman Kienast). Trainer: Josef Hickersberger

POLAND: Artur Boruc, Marcin Wasilewski, Jacek Bąk, Mariusz Jop (46 Paweł Golański), Michał Żewłakow, Euzebiusz Smolarek, Mariusz Lewandowski, Dariusz Dudka, Jacek Krzynówek, Roger Guerreiro (82 Rafał Murawski), Marek Saganowski (80 Wojciech Łobodziński). Trainer: Leo Beenhakker

Goals: Guerreiro (30), Vastic (90 pen)

AUSTRIA v GERMANY **0-1** (0-0)

Ernst Happel, Wien 16.06.2008

Referee: Manuel Mejuto González (SPA) Att: 51,428

AUSTRIA: Jürgen Macho, Martin Stranzl, Martin Hiden (55 Christoph Leitgeb), Emanuel Pogatetz, György Garics, Rene Aufhauser (63 Jürgen Säumel), Andreas Ivanschitz, Christian Fuchs, Martin Harnik (67 Roman Kienast), Erwin Hoffer, Ümit Korkmaz. Trainer: Josef Hickersberger

GERMANY: Jens Lehmann, Arne Friederich, Per Mertesacker, Christoph Metzelder, Philipp Lahm, Clemens Fritz (90 Tim Borowski), Torsten Frings, Michael Ballack, Lukas Podolski (83 Oliver Neuville), Miroslav Klose, Mario Gómez García (60 Thomas Hitzlsperger). Trainer: Joachim Löw

Goal: Ballack (48)

POLAND v CROATIA **0-1** (0-0)

Worthersee, Klagenfurt 16.06.2008

Referee: Kyros Vassaras (GRE) Attendance: 30,461

POLAND: Artur Boruc, Marcin Wasilewski, Dariusz Dudka, Michał Żewłakow, Jakub Wawrzyniak, Wojciech Łobodziński (55 Euzebiusz Smolarek), Rafał Murawski, Mariusz Lewandowski (46 Adam Kokoszka), Jacek Krzynówek, Roger, Marek Saganowski (68 Tomasz Zahorski). Trainer: Leo Beenhakker

CROATIA: Vedran Runje, Dario Simić, Hrvoje Vejić, Dario Knežević (27 Vedran Čorluka), Danijel Pranjić, Jerko Leko, Ognjen Vukojević, Nikola Pokrivač, Ivan Rakitić, Ivan Klasnić (75 Nikola Kalinić), Mladen Petrić (75 Niko Kranjčar). Trainer: Slaven Bilić

Goal: Klasnic (53)

	P	W	D	L	F	A	Pts
Croatia	3	3	0	0	4	1	9
Germany	3	2	0	1	4	2	6
Austria	3	0	1	2	1	3	1
Poland	3	0	1	2	1	4	1

GROUP C

ROMANIA v FRANCE 0-0

Letzigrund, Zürich *09.06.2008*

Referee: Manuel Mejuto González (SPA) Att: 30,585

ROMANIA: Bogdan Lobonţ, Cosmin Contra, Gabriel Tamaş, Dorin Goian, Răzvan Raţ, Răzvan Cociş (64 Paul Codrea), Mirel Rădoi (90 Nicolae Dică), Cristian Chivu, Bănel Nicoliţă, Adrian Mutu (78 Marius Niculae), Daniel Niculae. Trainer: Victor Piţurcă

FRANCE: Grégory Coupet, Willy Sagnol, Lilian Thuram, William Gallas, Éric Abidal, Franck Ribéry, Jérémy Toulalan, Claude Makélélé, Florent Malouda, Nicolas Anelka (72 Bafétimbi Gomis), Karim Benzema (78 Samir Nasri). Trainer: Raymond Domenech

NETHERLANDS v ITALY 3-0 (**2**-0)

Stade de Suisse, Bern *09.06.2008*

Referee: Peter Frojdfeldt (SWE) Attendance: 31,783

NETHERLANDS: Edwin van der Sar, Khalid Boulahrouz (77 Johnny Heitinga), André Ooijer, Joris Mathijsen, Giovanni van Bronckhorst, Nigel de Jong, Orlando Engelaar, Dirk Kuyt (81 Ibrahim Afellay), Rafael Van der Vaart, Wesley Sneijder, Ruud van Nistelrooy (70 Robin van Persie). Trainer: Marco van Basten

ITALY: Gianluigi Buffon, Christian Panucci, Andrea Barzagli, Marco Materazzi (55 Fabio Grosso), Gianluca Zambrotta, Massimo Ambrosini, Andrea Pirlo, Gennaro Gattuso, Mauro Camoranesi (75 Antonio Cassano), Antonio Di Natale (64 Alessandro Del Piero), Luca Toni. Trainer: Roberto Donadoni

Goals: Van Nistelrooy (26), Sneijder (31), van Bronckhorst (79)

ITALY v ROMANIA 1-1 (0-0)

Letzigrund, Zürich *13.06.2008*

Referee: Tom Henning Øvrebø (NOR) Attendance: 30,585

ITALY: Gianluigi Buffon, Gianluca Zambrotta, Christian Panucci, Giorgio Chiellini, Fabio Grosso, Simone Perrotta (58 Antonio Cassano), Daniele De Rossi, Andrea Pirlo, Mauro Camoranesi (85 Massimo Ambrosini), Alessandro Del Piero, (77 Fabio Quagliarella), Luca Toni. Trainer: Roberto Donadoni

ROMANIA: Bogdan Lobonţ, Cosmin Contra, Gabriel Tamaş, Dorin Goian, Răzvan Raţ, Paul Codrea, Mirel Rădoi (25 Nicolae Dică), Cristian Chivu, Florentin Petre (60 Bănel Nicoliţă), Adrian Mutu (88 Răzvan Cociş), Daniel Niculae. Trainer: Victor Piţurcă

Goals: Panucci (57), Mutu (55)

NETHERLANDS v FRANCE 4-1 (1-0)

Stade de Suisse, Bern *13.06.2008*

Referee: Herbert Fandel (GER) Attendance: 31,783

NETHERLANDS: Edwin van der Sar, Khalid Boulahrouz, André Ooijer, Joris Mathijsen, Giovanni van Bronckhorst, Orlando Engelaar (46 Arjen Robben), Dirk Kuyt (56 Robin van Persie), Rafael van der Vaart (78 Wilfred Bouma), Wesley Sneijder, Ruud van Nistelrooy. Trainer: Marco van Basten

FRANCE: Gregory Coupet, Willy Sagnol, Lilian Thuram (cap.), William Gallas, Patrice Evra, Jeremy Toulalan, Claude Makélélé, Sidney Govou (75 Nicolas Anelka), Franck Ribéry, Florent Malouda (60 Bagetibis Gomis), Thierry Henry. Trainer: Raymond Domenech

Goals: Kuyt (24), Van Persie (59), Robben (72), Sneijder (90), Henry (71)

FRANCE v ITALY 0-2 (0-1)

Letzigrund, Zürich *17.06.2008*

Referee: Luboš Michel (SVK) Attendance: 31,500

FRANCE: Gregory Coupet, François Clerc, William Gallas, Eric Abidal, Patrice Evra, Sidney Govou (66 Nicolas Anelka), Jeremy Toulalan, Claude Makélélé, Franck Ribery (10 Samir Nasri, 26 Jean-Alain Boumsong), Thierry Henry, Karim Benzema. Trainer: Raymond Domenech

ITALY: Gianluigi Buffon, Gianluca Zambrotta, Giorgio Chiellini, Christian Panucci, Fabio Grosso, Andrea Pirlo (55 Massimo Ambrosini), Daniele De Rossi, Gennaro Gattuso (82 Alberto Aquilani), Simone Perrotta (64 Mauro Camoranessi), Luca Toni, Antonio Cassano. Trainer: Roberto Donadoni

Goals: Pirlo (25), Henry (62 own goal)

NETHERLANDS v ROMANIA 2-0 (0-0)

Stade de Suisse, Bern 17.06.2008

Referee: Massimo Busacca (SWI) Attendance: 30,777

NETHERLANDS: Maarten Stekelenburg, Khalid Boulahrouz (58 Mario Melchiot), John Heitinga, Wilfred Bouma, Tim de Cler, Demy de Zeeuw, Orlando Engelaar, Ibrahim Afellay, Robin van Persie, Klaas-Jan Huntelaar (83 Jan Vennegoor of Hesselink), Arjen Robben (62 Dirk Kuyt). Trainer: Marco van Basten

ROMANIA: Bogdan Lobonţ, Cosmin Contra, Gabriel Tamaş, Sorin Ghionea, Răzvan Raţ, Paul Codrea (72 Nicolae Dică), Cristian Chivu, Răzvan Cociş, Bănel Nicoliţă (82 Florentin Petre), Adrian Mutu, Marius Niculae (59 Daniel Niculae). Trainer: Victor Piţurcă.

Goals: Huntelaar (55), van Persie (87)

	P	W	D	L	F	A	Pts
Netherlands	3	3	0	0	9	1	9
Italy	3	1	1	1	3	4	4
Romania	3	0	2	1	1	3	2
France	3	0	1	2	1	6	1

GROUP D

SPAIN v RUSSIA 4-1 (2-0)

Tivoli Neu, Innsbruck 10.06.2008

Referee: Konrad Plautz (AUS) Attendance: 30,772

SPAIN: Iker Casillas, Sergio Ramos, Carles Puyol, Carlos Marchena, Joan Capdevila, David Silva (78 Xabi Alonso), Marcos Senna, Xavi Hernández, Andres Iniesta (63 Santi Cazorla), Fernando Torres (54 Cesc Fabregas), David Villa. Trainer: Luis Aragonés

RUSSIA: Igor Akinfeev, Aleksandr Aniukov, Denis Kolodin, Roman Shirokov, Yuri Zhirkov, Konstantin Zyryanov, Serghei Semak, Igor Semshov (58 Dmitri Torbinski), Dmitri Sychev (46 Vladimir Bistrov, 70 Roman Adamov), Diniar Bilialetdinov, Roman Pavliucenko. Trainer: Guus Hiddink

Goals: David Villa (20, 45, 75), Fabregas (90), Pavlyucenko (82)

GREECE v SWEDEN 0-2 (0-0)

Wals-Siezenheim, Salzburg 10.06.2008

Referee: Massimo Busacca (SWI) Attendance: 30,883

GREECE: Antonis Nikopolidis, Giourkas Seitaridis, Sotiris Kyrgiakos, Paraskevas Antzas, Traianos Dellas (70 Ioannis Amanatidis), Vassilis Torosidis, Angelos Charisteas, Angelos Basinas, Costas Katsouranis, Giorgos Karagounis, Theofanis Gekas (46 Giorgos Samaras). Trainer: Otto Rehhagel

SWEDEN: Andreas Isaksson, Niclas Alexandersson (74 Fredrik Stoor), Olof Mellberg, Petter Hansson, Mikael Nilsson, Christian Wilhelmsson (78 Markus Rosenberg), Anders Svensson, Fredrik Ljungberg, Henrik Larsson, Daniel Andersson, Zlatan Ibrahimović (71 Johan Elmander). Trainer: Lars Lagerbäck

Goals: Ibrahimovic (67), Hansson (72)

SWEDEN v SPAIN 1-2 (1-1)

Tivoli Neu, Innsbruck 14.06.2008

Referee: Pieter Vink (HOL) Attendance: 30,772

SWEDEN: Andreas Isaksson, Fredrik Stoor, Olof Mellberg, Petter Hansson, Mikael Nilsson, Anders Svensson, Daniel Andersson, Fredrik Ljungberg, Johan Elmander (79 Sebastian Larsson), Zlatan Ibrahimović (46 Markus Rosenberg), Henrik Larsson (87 Kim Källström). Trainer: Lars Lagerbäck

SPAIN: Iker Casillas, Sergio Ramos, Carles Puyol (24 Raul Albiol), Carlos Marchena, Joan Capdevila, Marcos Senna, Andres Iniesta (59 Santi Cazorla), Xavi Hernández (58 Cesc Fabregas), David Silva, David Villa, Fernando Torres. Trainer: Luis Aragonés

Goals: Ibrahimović (34), Torres (15), Villa (90+2)

GREECE v RUSSIA 0-1 (0-1)

Wals-Siezenheim, Salzburg 14.06.2008

Referee: Roberto Rosetti (ITA) Attendance: 30,883

GREECE: Antonis Nikopolidis, Giourkas Seitaridis (40 Giorgos Karagounis), Traianos Dellas, Sotiris Kyrgiakos, Vassilis Torosidis, Costas Katsouranis, Angelos Basinas, Christos Patsatzoglou, Angelos Charisteas, Nikos Liberopoulos (61 Theofanis Gekas), Ioannis Amanatidis (80 Stelios Giannakopoulos). Trainer: Otto Rehhagel

RUSSIA: Igor Akinfeev, Aleksandr Aniukov, Denis Kolodin, Serghei Ignashevich, Yuri Zhirkov (87 Vasili Berezutski), Serghei Semak, Dmitri Torbinski, Konstantin Zyryanov, Igor Semshov, Diniar Bilialetdinov (70 Ivan Saenko), Roman Pavliucenko. Trainer: Guus Hiddink

Goal: Zyryanov (33)

RUSSIA v SWEDEN 2-0 (1-0)

Tivoli Neu, Innsbruck 18.06.2008

Referee: Frank De Bleeckere (BEL) Attendance: 30,772

RUSSIA: Igor Akinfeev, Alexandr Aniukov, Denis Kolodin, Serghei Ignashevich, Yuri Zhirkov, Serghei Semak, Konstantin Zyryanov, Igor Semshov, Diniar Bilialetdinov (65 Igor Saenko), Andrei Arshavin, Roman Pavliucenko (90 Vladimir Bystrov). Trainer: Guus Hiddink

SWEDEN: Andreas Isaksson, Fredrik Stoor, Olof Mellberg, Petter Hansson, Mikael Nilsson (79 Marcus Allback), Johan Elmander, Anders Svensson, Daniel Andersson (56 Kim Källström), Fredrik Ljungberg, Zlatan Ibrahimović, Henrik Larsson. Trainer: Lars Lagerbäck

Goals: Pavliucenko (24), Arshavin (50)

GREECE v SPAIN 1-2 (1-0)

Wals-Siezenheim, Salzburg 18.06.2008

Referee: Howard Webb (ENG) Attendance: 30,883

GREECE: Antonis Nikopolidis, Loukas Vintra, Sotiris Kyrgiakos (65 Paraskevas Antzas), Traianos Dellas, Nikos Spyropoulos, Angelos Basinas, Costas Katsouranis, Dimitris Salpigidis (85 Stelios Giannakopoulos), Giorgos Karagounis (74 Alexis Tziolis), Yannis Amanatidis, Angelos Charisteas. Trainer: Otto Rehhagel

SPAIN: José Manuel Reina, Alvaro Arbeloa, Juanito Gutiérrez, Raúl Albiol, Fernando Navarro, Xabi Alonso, Ruben de la Red, Cesc Fábregas, Sergio García, Andres Iniesta (58 Santi Cazorla), Daniel Güiza. Trainer: Luis Aragonés

Goals: Charisteas (42), Ruben de la Red (61), Güiza (88)

	P	W	D	L	F	A	Pts
Spain	3	3	0	0	8	3	9
Russia	3	2	0	1	4	4	6
Sweden	3	1	0	2	3	4	3
Greece	3	0	0	3	1	5	0

QUARTER-FINALS

PORTUGAL v GERMANY 2-3 (1-2)

St Jakobs Park, Basel 19.06.2008

Referee: Peter Frojdfeldt (SWE) Attendance: 42,500

PORTUGAL: RICARDO Pereira, José Bosingwa, PEPE, Ricardo Carvalho, Paulo Ferreira, João Moutinho (31 Raul Meireles), Armando Petit (73 Helder Postiga), Anderson Souza "DECO", Cristiano Ronaldo, Nuno Gomes (67 Nani), Simão Sabrosa. Trainer: Luiz Felipe Scolari

GERMANY: Jens Lehmann, Arne Friedrich, Per Mertesacker, Christoph Metzelder, Philipp Lahm, Bastian Schweinsteiger (83 Clemens Fritz), Simon Rolfes, Michael Ballack, Thomas Hitzlsperger (73 Tim Borowski), Miroslav Klose (89 Marcell Jansen), Lukas Podolski. Trainer: Joachim Löw

Goals: Nuno Gomes (40), Helder Postiga (87), Schweinsteiger (22), Klose (28), Ballack (61)

CROATIA v TURKEY 1-1 (0-0, 0-0) (AET)

Ernst Happel, Wien 20.06.2008

Referee: Roberto Rosetti (ITA) Attendance: 51,428

CROATIA: Stipe Pletikosa, Vedran Čorluka, Josip Simunić, Robert Kovač, Danijel Pranjić, Darijo Srna, Niko Kovač, Luka Modrić, Ivan Rakitić, Niko Kranjčar (65 Mladen Petrić), Ivica Olić (97 Ivan Klasnić). Trainer: Slaven Bilić

TURKEY: Ruştu Recber, Sabri Sarioglu, Emre Aşik, Gokhan Zan, Hakan Balta, Hamit Altintop, Tuncay Şanli, Mehmet Topal (77 Semih Şenturk), Arda Turan, Kazim Kazim (61 Ugur Boral), Nihat Kahveci (117 Gokdeniz Karadeniz). Trainer: Fatih Terim

Goals: Klasnić (117), Şenturk (120)

Penalties: Modrić (miss), Turan 0-1, Srna 1-1, Şenturk 1-2, Rakitić (miss), Hamit Altintop 1-3, Petrić (miss)

NETHERLANDS v RUSSIA 1-3 (0-0, 1-1) (AET)

St.Jakobs Park, Basel 21.06.2008

Referee: Luboš Michel (SVK) Attendance: 42,500

NETHERLANDS: Edwin van der Sar, Khalid Boulahrouz (54 Johnny Heitinga), André Ooijer, Joris Mathijsen, Giovanni van Bronckhorst, Rafael van der Vaart, Nigel de Jong, Orlando Engelaar (63 Ibrahim Afellay), Wesley Sneijder, Dirk Kuyt (46 Robin van Persie), Ruud van Nistelrooy. Trainer: Marco van Basten

RUSSIA: Igor Akinfeev, Aleksandr Aniukov, Denis Kolodin, Serghei Ignashevich, Yuri Jirkov, Konstantin Zîrianov, Andrei Arshavin Serghei Semak, Igor Semshov (81 Dmitri Torbinski), Roman Pavliucenko (114 Dmitri Sychev), Ivan Saenko (69 Diniar Bilialetdinov). Trainer: Guus Hiddink

Goals: van Nistelrooy (86), Pavliucenko (56), Torbinski (112), Arshavin (116)

SPAIN v ITALY 0-0 (AET)

Ernst Happel, Wien 22.06.2008

Referee: Herbert Fandel (GER) Attendance: 51,428

SPAIN: Iker Casillas, Sergio Ramos, Carles Puyol, Carlos Marchena, Joan Capdevila, Marcos Senna, Andres Iniesta (59 Santi Cazorla), Xavi Hernández (60 Cesc Fábregas), David Silva, David Villa, Fernando Torres (85 Daniel Güiza). Trainer: Luis Aragonés

ITALY: Gianluigi Buffon, Gianluca Zambrotta, Christian Panucci, Giorgio Chiellini, Fabio Grosso, Alberto Aquilani (108 Alessandro Del Piero), Daniele De Rossi, Massimo Ambrosini, Simone Perrotta (68 Mauro Camoranesi), Antonio Cassano (75 Antonio Di Natale), Luca Toni. Trainer: Roberto Donadoni

Penalties: Villa 1-0, Grosso 1-1, Cazorla 2-1, De Rossi (miss), Marcos Senna 3-1, Camoranesi 3-2, Güiza (miss), Di Natale (miss), Fabregas 4-2.

SEMI-FINALS

GERMANY v TURKEY 3-2 (1-1)

St. Jakobs Park, Basel 25.06.2008

Referee: Massimo Busacca (SWI) Attendance: 42,000

GERMANY: Jens Lehmann, Arne Friedrich, Per Mertesacker, Christoph Metzelder, Philipp Lahm, Bastian Schweinsteiger, Simon Rolfes (46 Torsten Frings), Michael Ballack, Thomas Hitzlsperger, Lukas Podolski, Miroslav Klose (90+2 Marcell Janssen). Trainer: Joachim Löw

TURKEY: Ruştu Recber, Sabri Sarioglu, Mehmet Topal, Gokhan Zan, Hakan Balta, Kazim Kazim (90+1 Tumer Metin), Hamit Altintop, Mehmet Aurelio, Ayhan Akman (81 Mevlut Erdinc), Ugur Boral (84 Gokdeniz Karadeniz), Semih Şenturk. Trainer: Fatih Terim

Goals: Schweinsteiger (26), Klose (79), Lahm (90), Ugur Boral (22), Semih Şenturk (86)

RUSSIA v SPAIN 0-3 (0-0)

Ernst Happel, Wien 26.06.2008

Referee: Frank De Bleeckere (BEL) Attendance: 50,000

RUSSIA: Igor Akinfeev, Aleksandr Aniukov, Vasili Berezuțki, Serghei Ignaşevici, Iuri Jirkov, Konstantin Zîrianov, Sergei Semak, Igor Semshov (56 Diniar Bilialetdinov), Ivan Saenko (57 Dmitri Sychev), Andrei Arshavin, Roman Pavliucenko. Trainer: Guus Hiddink

SPAIN: Iker Casillas, Sergio Ramos, Carles Puyol, Carlos Marchena, Joan Capdevila, Marcos Senna, Andres Iniesta, Xavi Hernández (69 Xabi Alonso 69), David Silva, David Villa (35 Cesc Fábregas), Fernando Torres (69 Daniel Güiza). Trainer: Luis Aragones.

Goals: Xavi (50), Güiza (73), Silva (82)

FINAL

SPAIN v GERMANY 1-0 (1-0)

Ernst Happel, Wien 29.06.2008

Referee: Roberto Rosetti (ITA) Attendance: 50,000

GERMANY: Jens Lehmann, Arne Friedrich, Per Mertesacker, Christoph Metzelder, Philipp Lahm (46 Marcell Jansen), Bastian Schweinsteiger, Torsten Frings, Michael Ballack, Thomas Hitzlsperger (58 Kevin Kuranyi), Lukas Podolski, Miroslav Klose (79 Mario Gomez). Trainer: Joachim Löw

SPAIN: Iker Casillas, Sergio Ramos, Carles Puyol, Carlos Marchena, Joan Capdevila, Marcos Senna, Andres Iniesta, Xavi Hernández, Cesc Fábregas (64 Xabi Alonso), David Silva (66 Santi Cazorla), Fernando Torres (78 Dani Güiza). Trainer: Luis Aragones

Goal: Fernando Torres (33)

Goalscorers European Football Championship 2008

13 goals: David Healy (Northern Ireland).

11 goals: Lukas Podolski (Germany), David Villa (Spain).

10 goals: Eduardo da Silva (Croatia).

9 goals: Euzebiusz Smolarek (Poland), Cristiano Ronaldo (Portugal).

7 goals: Mladen Petrić (Croatia), Jan Koller (Czech Republic), Jon Dahl Tomasson (Denmark), Thierry Henry (France), Miroslav Klose (Germany), Steffen Iversen (Norway), Nikola Žigić (Serbia), Adrian Mutu (Romania).

6 goals: Dimitar Berbatov, Martin Petrov (Bulgaria), Roberto Colautti (Israel), Robin van Persie (Netherlands), Aleksandr Kerzhakov (Russia), Mintál (Slovakia), Markus Allbäck (Sweden).

5 goals: Edmond Kapllani (Albania), Yiannis Okkas (Cyprus), Crouch (England), Shota Arveladze (Georgia), Michael Ballack, Bastian Schweinsteiger (Germany), Theofanis Gekas (Greece), Luca Toni (Italy), Dimitriy Byakov (Kazakhstan), Maris Verpakovskis (Latvia), Ciprian Marica (Romania), Andrei Arshavin, Roman Pavlyuchenko (Russia), Xavi Hernández (Spain), Hakan Şükür, Nihat Kahveci (Turkey), Andriy Shevchenko (Ukraine).

4 goals: Maksim Romashchenko (Belarus), Moussa Dembélé (Belgium), Misimović, Muslimović (Bosnia Herzegovina), Darijo Srna (Croatia), Sionko (Czech Republic), Dennis Rommedahl (Denmark), Rógvi Jacobsen (Faroe Islands), Nicolas Anelka (France), Thomas Hitzlsperger (Germany), Angelos Charisteas (Greece), Zoltán Gera (Hungary),

Kevin Doyle, Stephen Ireland, Robbie Keane (Ireland), Mario Frick (Liechtenstein), Tomas Danilevičius (Lithuania), Viorel Frunză (Moldova), Wesley Sneijder, Ruud van Nistelrooy (Netherlands), Carew (Norway), Jacek Krzynówek (Poland), Nuno Gomes (Portugal), Nicolae Dică (Romania), Kris Boyd, James McFadden (Scotland), Danko Lazović (Serbia), Klemen Lavrič (Slovenia), Fernando Torres (Spain), Oleh Gusev (Ukraine), Jason Koumas (Wales).

3 goals: Sergei Kornilenko, Vitaliy Kutuzov (Belarus), Ivan Klasnić (Croatia), Stathis Aloneftis, Kostas Charalambides (Cyprus), Milan Baroš (Czech Republic), Steven Gerrard, Michael Owen (England), Jari Litmanen (Finland), Sidney Govou (France), Aleksandr Iashvili, Sotiris Kyrgiakos, David Siradze (Georgia), Kevin Kuranyi (Germany), Angelos Basinas, Nikos Liberopoulos (Greece), Eidur Gudjohnsen (Iceland), Filippo Inzaghi (Italy), Jurijs Laizans (Latvia), Naumoski, Sedloski (Macedonia), Michael Mifsud, Andre Schembri (Malta), Bugaev (Moldova), Radoslaw Matusiak (Poland), Simão Sabrosa (Portugal), Sychev (Russia), Kenny Miller (Scotland), Boško Janković (Serbia), Filip Hološko, Martin Škrtel (Slovakia), Iniesta (Spain), Källstrom (Sweden), Hakan Yakin (Switzerland), Semih Senturk, Tuncay Sanli (Turkey), Craig Bellamy (Wales).

2 goals: Skela (Albania), Arzumanyan (Armenia), Kalachev, Korytko (Belarus), Geraerts, Miralles (Belgium), M. Hrgović (Bosnia Herzegovina), Kranjčar, Modrić, Olić (Croatia), M. Konstantinou (Cyprus), Jankulovski, Kulič, Lafata, Plašil, Rosický (Czech), Bendtner, Gravgaard, Nordstrand (Denmark), Defoe, Rooney, Wright-Phillips (England), Piiroja (Estonia), Eremenko Jr, Johansson (Finland), Benzema, Saha, Trezeguet (France), Fritz, Gomez (Germany), Amanatidis, Katsouranis (Greece), Kilbane (Ireland), Barda, Ben Shoshan, Benayoun, Sahar, Tamuz (Israel), Panucci, Pirlo, Quagliarella, Di Natale (Italy), Baltiyev (Kazakhstan), G.Karlsons, Višnakovs (Latvia), T. Beck (Liechtenstein), Ksanavičius (Lithuania), Maznov, Pandev (Macedonia), Rogaciov (Moldova), Huntelaar, Kuyt, van Bronckhorst (Netherlands), Lafferty (N. Ireland), Hagen, Gamst Pedersen, J.A. Riise, Strømstad, Solskjær (Norway), Hélder Postiga, Hugo Almeida, Quaresma (Portugal), Contra, Goian, D.Niculae, Tamaş (Romania), O'Connor (Scotland), Jovanović, Kuzmanović (Serbia), Čech, Hamšík, Karhan, Sebo, Šesták, Vittek (Slovakia), Novakovič (Slovenia), Güiza, Sergio Ramos (Spain), Elmander, Ibrahimovic, Mellberg, Rosenberg, A. Svensson, Wilhelmsson (Sweden), Gökhan Ünal, Halil Altintop, Hamit Altintop, Tümer Metin, Arda Turan (Turkey), Kalynychenko (Ukraine), Bale, Earnshaw (Wales).

1 goal: Bogdani, Haxhi, Curri, Hasi (Albania), Silva, Fernández (Andorra), Hovsepyan, Mkhitaryan (Armenia), Ivica Vastic (Austria), Aliyev, M. Gurbonov, Imamaliev, Ladaga, Nadyrov, Subašić (Azerbaijan), Bulyga, Vasilyuk, Kovba (Belarus), Fellaini, Pieroni, Simons, Sonck, Vandenbergh, Van Buyten (Belgium), Ibiševic, Džeko, Čustović, Barbarez, Bartolović, Grlić (Bosnia Herzegovina), Georgiev, V. Dimitrov, Tunchev, Bozhinov, Telkiyski, Yankov (Bulgaria), Rakitić, Balaban (Croatia), Okkarides, Makridis, Garpozis, Yiasoumi (Cyprus), Pudil, Grygera, Matejovsky, Kováč, Polák, Jarolím, Svěrkoš (Czech Republic), Kahlenberg, U. Laursen, M. Laursen, D. Jensen (Denmark), Lampard, Ferdinand, Nugent, Ricahrds, Cole (England), Oper, Lindpere, Zelinski (Estonia), Forssell, Kuqi, Tainio, Gargula, Hyypiä, Nurmela, Väyrynen (Finland), Malouda, Ribéry, Nasri, Rothen, Ben Arfa (France), Mujiri, Kobiashvili, Demetradze, Shashiashvili, Mchedlidze (Georgia), Jansen, Lahm, Frings, M. Friedrich, Schneider (Germany), Seitaridis, Patsatzoglou, Samaras (Greece), Buzsaky, Feczesin, Tozsér, Priskin, Torghelle, Huszti, Dárdai (Hungary), Ar. Björnsson, Hallfredsson, B. Gunnarsson, Vidarsson, Thorvaldsson, Hreidarsson (Iceland), Finnan, A. Reid, Dunne (Ireland), Golan, Itzhaki, Tal, Gershon (Israel), Gilardino, Oddo, De Rossi, Camoranesi, Perrotta, Grosso, Chiellini (Italy), Ashirbekov, Ostapenko, Smakov, Zhumaskaliyev (Kazakhstan), Gorkšs, Klava (Latvia), Rohrer, F. Burgmeier (Liechtenstein), Miceika, Skerla, Mikoliunas, Jankauskas, Savenas (Lithuania), F. Leweck, Sagramola (Luxembourg), Stojkov, Noveski (Macedonia), Scerri, Said, Mallia, Pace (Malta), Josan, Alexeev, Epureanu (Moldova), Van der Vaart, Koevermans, Mathijsen, Robben (Netherlands), Feeney, McCann (Northern Ireland), B. Riise, Braaten, Hæstad, Helstad, Brenne, Andresen (Norway), Bak, Dudka, Guerreiro, Lewandowski, Lobodzinski, Kazmierczak, Murawski, Zurawski (Poland), Bruno Alves, Deco, Makukula, Maniche, Nani, Pepe, Meireles, Ricardo Carvalho, Tiago (Portugal), Nicoliţă, Roşu, F. Petre (Romania), V. Berezutski, Bilyaletdinov, Bystrov, Pogrebnyak, Torbinski, Zyryanov (Russia), A. Selva, Marani (San Marino), Dailly, Caldwell, Beattie, Maloney, McManus, McCulloch, Ferguson, Fletcher (Scotland), Ivanović, Stanković, Tosić (Serbia), Michalík, Sapara, Durica, Klimpl, Jakubko, Varga, Svento (Slovakia), Vršič, Cesar, Koren (Slovenia), Capdevila, De la Red, Fabregas, Tamudo, Riera, Morientes, Luis García Sanz, Silva (Spain), Hansson, Ljungberg (Sweden), Emre Belözoğlu, Ugur Boral, Ümit Karan, Aurelio, Çetin, Sabri, Gökdeniz (Turkey), Rotan, Rusol, Kucher, Yezerskiy, Shelayev, Vorobey, Voronin (Ukraine), Ledley, Collins, Eastwood, S. Davies, Giggs (Wales).

Own goals: Kishishev (Bulgaria) for Albania, G. Neville (England) for Croatia, Rahn (Estonia) for England, Asatiani (Georgia) for France, Durica (Slovakia) for Germany, Gillespie (N. Ireland) for Iceland, Vanczak (Hungary) for Greece, Benjaminsen (Faroe), Thierry Henry (France) both for Italy, Baird (N. Ireland) for Latvia, Zirnis (Latvia) for Liechtenstein, Beqaj (Albania) for Netherlands, Ostapenko (Kazakhstan) for Serbia, Metzelder (Germany), Kadlec (Czech) both for Slovakia, Jiranek (Czech Rep), Durica (Slovakia) both for Wales.

THE EUROPEAN FOOTBALL CHAMPIONSHIP 2012

QUALIFIERS – GROUP A

BELGIUM v GERMANY 0-1 (0-0)

Roi Baudouin, Brussel 03.09.2010

Referee: Terje Hauge (NOR) Attendance: 41,126

BELGIUM: Logan Bailly, Toby Alderweireld, Daniel Van Buyten, Vincent Kompany, Thomas Vermaelen, Marouane Fellaini, Timmy Simons (83 Jelle Vossen), Jan Vertonghen, Moussa Dembélé, Romelu Lukaku (73 Christian Benteke), Eden Hazard (73 Steven Defour). Trainer: Georges Leekens

GERMANY: Manuel Neuer, Philipp Lahm, Per Mertesacker, Holger Badstuber, Marcell Jansen (46 Heiko Westermann), Sami Khedira, Bastian Schweinsteiger, Thomas Müller, Mesut Özil (88 Cacau), Lukas Podolski (70 Toni Kroos), Miroslav Klose. Trainer: Joachim Löw

Goal: Miroslav Klose (51)

KAZAKHSTAN v TURKEY 0-3 (0-2)

Astana Arena 03.09.2010

Referee: István Vad (HUN) Attendance: 15,800

KAZAKHSTAN: Andrei Sidelnikov, Aleksandr Kirov, Renat Abdulin, Aleksandr Kislitsyn (85 Mikhail Rozhkov), Andrei Karpovich (64 Denis Radionov), Sergei Ostapenko (71 Gleb Maltsev), Nurbol Zhumaskaliyev, Azat Nurgaliyev, Genrikh Shmidtgal, Aleksei Popov, Maksim Azovski. Trainer: Bernd Storck

TURKEY: Onur Kivrak, Servet Çetin, Hakan Balta, Emre Belözöglu, Hamit Altintop, Nihat Kahveci (82 Selçuk Inan), Tuncay Şanli (80 Halil Altintop), Arda Turan, Mehmet Aurélio (89 Colin Kazim Richards), Ömer Erdoğan, Sabri Sarioğlu. Trainer: Guus Hiddink

Goals: Arda Turan (24), Hamit Altintop (26), Nihat Kahveci (76)

AUSTRIA v KAZAKHSTAN 2-0 (0-0)

Stadion Salzburg 07.09.2010

Referee: Marijo Strahonja (CRO) Attendance: 22,500

AUSTRIA: Jurgen Macho, Franz Schiemer, Emanuel Pogatetz, Christian Fuchs, Jakob Jantscher (66 David Alaba), Veli Kavlak, Sebastian Prödl, Ekrem Dag, Martin Harnik (66 Erwin Hoffer), Roland Linz, Marc Janko (78 Stefan Maierhofer). Trainer: Dietmar Constantini

KAZAKHSTAN: Andrei Sidelnikov, Kazbek Geteriyev, Aleksandr Kirov, Renat Abdulin, Aleksandr Kislitsyn (75 Mikhail Rozhkov), Andrei Karpovich, Evgeni Averchenko, Gleb Maltsev (46 Sergei Khizhnichenko), Nurbol Zhumaskaliyev, Azat Nurgaliyev (59 Maksim Azovski), Aleksei Popov. Trainer: Bernd Storck

Goals: Roland Linz (90+1), Erwin Hoffer (90+2)\

GERMANY v AZERBAIJAN 6-1 (3-0)

Müngersdorfer, Köln 07.09.2010

Referee: Markus Strömbergtsson (SWE) Attendance: 43,751

GERMANY: Manuel Neuer, Sascha Riether, Per Mertesacker (11 Heiko Westermann), Holger Badstuber, Phillip Lahm, Bastian Schweinsteiger (78 Cacau), Sami Khedira, Thomas Müller (61 Marko Marin), Mesut Özil, Lukas Podolski, Miroslav Klose. Trainer: Joachim Löw

AZERBAIJAN: Kamran Agayev, Maksim Medvedev, Raşad Ferhad Sadyqov, Sasha Yunisoğlu (56 Vurgun Huseynov), Elnur Allahverdiyev, Samir Abbasov, Mahir Şükürov, Vugar Nadyrov (85 Araz Abdullayev), Rail Mälikov, Alexandr Chertoganov (64. Raşad Abulfaz Sadyqov), Vagif Cavadov. Trainer: Berti Vogts

Goals: Heiko Westermann (28), Lukas Podolski (45+1), Miroslav Klose (45+2, 90+2), Raşad Ferhad Sadyqov (53 own goal), Vagif Cavadov (53), Holger Badstuber (86)

TURKEY v BELGIUM 3-2 (0-1)

Şükrü Saraçoglu, Istanbul 07.09.2010

Referee: Damir Skomina (SVN) Attendance: 43,538

TURKEY: Onur Kivrak, Servet Çetin, Ismail Köybaşi, Emre Belözoğlu, Hamit Altintop, Tuncay Şanli (82 Selçuk Şahin), Arda Turan, Mehmet Aurélio, Ömer Erdoğan, Selcuk Inan (71 Semih Şentürk), Sabri Sarioğlu (73 Gökhan Gönül). Trainer: Guus Hiddink

BELGIUM:: Logan Bailly, Toby Alderweireld, Daniel Van Buyten, Vincent Kompany, Thomas Vermaelen, Timmy Simons, Guillaume Gillet (82 Hazard), Jan Vertonghen, Romelu Lukaku (76 Witsel), Marouane Fellaini, Moussa Dembélé (64 Kevin Mirallas). Trainer: Georges Leekens

Goals: Daniel Van Buyten (28, 69), Hamit Altintop (48), Semih Şentürk (66), Arda Turan (78)

AUSTRIA v AZERBAIJAN 3-0 (1-0)

Ernst Happel, Wien 08.10.2010

Referee: Nicolai Vollquartz (DEN) Attendance: 26,500

AUSTRIA: Jürgen Macho, Franz Schiemer, Christian Fuchs, Zlatko Junuzović (78 Julian Baumgartlinger), Marko Arnautovic, Sebastian Prödl, Paul Scharner, Florian Klein, Martin Harnik (55 Veli Kavlak), Roland Linz (59 Erwin Hoffer), Stefan Maierhofer. Trainer: Dietmar Constantini

AZERBAIJAN: Kamran Agayev, Rail Mälikov, Saşa Yunisoğlu, Mahir Şükürov, Elnur Allahverdiyev, Vagif Cavadov (74 Raşad Abulfaz Sadyqov), Samir Abbasov, Elvin Mämädov (59 Vugar Nadyrov), Rauf Äliyev, Raşad Ferhad Sadyqov, Rahid Ämirquliyev. Trainer: Berti Vogts

Goals: Sebastian Prödl (3), Marko Arnautovic (53, 90+2)

GERMANY v TURKEY 3-0 (1-0)

Olympiastadion, Berlin 08.10.2010

Referee: Howard Webb (ENG) Attendance: 74,244

GERMANY: Manuel Neuer, Heiko Westermann, Sami Khedira, Mesut Özil (90 Marko Marin), Lukas Podolski (86 Christian Träsch), Miroslav Klose (90 Cacau), Thomas Müller, Holger Badstuber, Philipp Lahm, Per Mertesacker, Toni Kroos. Trainer: Joachim Löw

TURKEY: Volkan Demirel, Servet Çetin, Ömer Erdoğan, Emre Belözoğlu, Hamit Altintop, Gökhan Gönül, Özer Hurmaci, Mehmet Aurélio (25 Tuncay Şanli), Nuri Şahin (78 Sercan Yildirim), Halil Altintop (63. Semih Şentürk), Sabri Sarioğlu. Trainer: Guus Hiddink

Goals: Miroslav Klose (42, 87), Mesut Özil (79)

BELGIUM v AUSTRIA 4-4 (1-2)

Roi Baudouin, Brussel 12.10.2010

Referee: Mike Dean (ENG) Attendance: 24,231

BELGIUM: Logan Bailly, Toby Alderweireld (46 Dedryck Boyata), Vincent Kompany, Jan Vertonghen, Timmy Simons (73 Romelu Lukaku), Axel Witsel, Marouane Fellaini (81 Eden Hazard), Marvin Ogunjimi, Jelle Vossen, Jonathan Legear, Nicolas Lombaerts. Coach: Georges Leekens

AUSTRIA: Jürgen Macho, Franz Schierner, Christian Fuchs, Zlatko Junuzovic (72 Yasin Pehlivan), Marko Arnautovic (88 Martin Harnik), Veli Kavlak (56 Erwin Hoffer), Julian Baumgartlinger, Sebastian Prödl, Paul Scharner, Florian Klein, Stefan Maierhofer. Trainer: Dietmar Constantini

Sent off: Scharner (68)

Goals: Jelle Vossen (11), Franz Schierner (14, 62), Marko Arnautovic (29), Marouane Fellaini (47), Marvin Ogunjimi (87), Nicolas Lombaerts (90), Martin Harnik (90+3)

KAZAKHSTAN v BELGIUM 0-2 (0-0)

Astana Arena, Astana 08.10.2010

Referee: Marcin Borski (POL) Attendance: 8,500

KAZAKHSTAN: Andrei Sidelnikov, Kazbek Geteriyev, Aleksandr Kirov, Renat Abdulin, Aleksandr Kislitsyn, Andrei Karpovich, Nurbol Zhumaskaliyev (87 Evgeni Averchenko), Sergei Khizhnichenko, Azat Nurgaliyev (74 Mikhail Rozhkov), Heinrich Schmidtgal, Aleksei Popov. Coach: Bernd Storck

BELGIUM: Logan Bailly, Toby Alderweireld, Daniel van Buyten, Nicolas Lombaerts, Olivier Deschacht, Timmy Simons, Axel Witsel, Marouane Fellaini, Romelu Lukaku (46 Marvin Ogunjimi), Jelle Vossen, Jelle Van Damme (79 Jonathan Legear). Coach: Georges Leekens

Sent off: Kislitsyn (68)

Goals: Marvin Ogunjimi (52, 70)

KAZAKHSTAN v GERMANY 0-3 (0-0)

Astana Arena, Astana 12.10.2010

Referee: Alexandru Tudor (ROM) Attendance: 18,000

KAZAKHSTAN: Andrei Sidelnikov, Kazbek Geteriyev, Aleksandr Kirov, Renat Abdulin, Nurbol Zhumaskaliyev, Sergei Khizhnichenko (79 Andrey Finonchenko), Azat Nurgaliyev (63 Evgeni Averchenko), Heinrich Schmidtgal, Alexey Popov, Maksim Azovski, Farkhadbek Irismetov (68 Mikhail Rozhkov). Trainer: Bernd Storck

GERMANY: Manuel Neuer, Heiko Westermann, Sami Khedira, Mesut Özil (79 Cacau), Lukas Podolski, Miroslav Klose (55 Mario Gomez), Thomas Müller (71 Marko Marin), Heiko Badstuber, Philipp Lahm, Per Mertesacker, Toni Kroos. Trainer: Joachim Low

Goals: M. Klose (48), Mario Gomez (76), Lukas Podolski (85)

AZERBAIJAN v TURKEY 1-0 (1-0)

Tofiq Bähramov-Republican stadium, Baku 12.10.2010

Referee: Alexandru Deconu (ROM) Attendance: 29,500

AZERBAIJAN: Kamran Ağayev, Rail Mälilov (46 Aleksandr Chertoganov), Saša Yunisoğlu, Mahir Şükürov, Elnur Allahverdiyev, Vagif Cavadov (85 Vurgun Hüseynov), Raşad F. Sadiqov, Ruslan Abişov, Vüqar Nadirov, Rahid Ämirquliyev, Farid Quliyev (71 Rauf Äliyev). Trainer: Berti Vogts

TURKEY: Volkan Demirel, Servet Çetin, Hakan Balta, Emre Belözoğlu, Hamit Altintop, Gökhan Gönul, Semih Şentürk, Tuncay Şanli (62 Sercan Yildirim), Özer Hurmaci (46 Nihat Kahveci), Selçuk Inan (82 Halil Altintop), Ibrahim Toraman. Coach: Guus Hiddink

Goals: Raşad F. Sadiqov (38)

AUSTRIA v BELGIUM 0-2 (0-1)

Ernst-Happel-Stadion, Wien 25.03.2011

Referee: Vladislav Bezborodov (RUS) Attendance: 45,000

AUSTRIA: Jürgen Macho, Aleksandar Dragović, Emanuel Pogatetz, Christian Fuchs, David Alaba (54 Yasin Pehlivan), Zlatko Junuzovic (69 Ümit Korkmaz), Marko Arnautovic, Ekrem Dağ, Julian Baumgartlinger, Martin Harnik, Marc Janko (54 Stefan Maierhofer). Trainer: Dietmar Constantini

BELGIUM: Simon Mignolet, Laurent Ciman, Daniel van Buyten, Vincent Kompany, Jan Vertonghen, Timmy Simons, Nacer Chadli, Steven Defour, Marvin Ogunjimi (80 Kevin Mirallas), Axel Witsel, Moussa Dembélé.
Trainer: Georges Leekens

Goals: Axel Witsel (6, 50)

GERMANY v KAZAKHSTAN 4-0 (3-0)

Fritz- Walter-Stadion, Kaiserslautern 26.03.2011

Referee: Stavrev (MKD) Attendance: 47,849

GERMANY: Manuel Neuer, Denis Aogo, Sami Khedira, (78 Toni Kroos), Mesut Özil, Lukas Podolski (65 Mario Gomez), Miroslav Klose, Thomas Müller (78 Mario Götze), Holger Badstuber, Philipp Lahm, Per Mertesacker.
Trainer: Joachim Low

KAZAKHSTAN: David Loria, Vladislav Chernyshev, Renat Abdulin, Anton Chichulin, Farkhadbek Irismetov, Sergei Khizhnichenko, Nurbol Zhumaskaliyev (46 Maksat Baizhanov), Ulan Konysbayev, Azat Nurgaliyev (60 Zhambyl Kukeev), Kairat Nurdauletov, Kazbek Geteriyev (81 Sergey Ostapenko). Trainer: Miroslav Beranek

Goals: Miroslav Klose (3, 88), Thomas Müller (25, 43)

TURKEY v AUSTRIA 2-0 (1-0)

Istanbul, Şükrü Saracoğlu 29.03.2011

Referee: Pavel Kralovec (CZE) Attendance: 40,420

TURKEY: Volkan Demirel, Servet Çetin, Hakan Balta, Serdar Kesimal, Hamit Altintop, Gökhan Gönül, Selçuk Inan, Mehmet Ekici (63 Mehmet Topuz), Arda Turan (89 Mehmet Topal), Burak Yilmaz (72 Semih Şentürk), Nuri Şahin.
Trainer: Guus Hiddink

AUSTRIA: Jürgen Macho, Aleksandar Dragović, Emanuel Pogatetz, Christian Fuchs, Yasin Pehlivan (57 Ümit Korkmaz), David Alaba, Ekrem Dağ, Julian Baumgartlinger (46 Erwin Hoffer), Paul Scharner, Martin Harnik (69 Marko Arnautovic), Stefan Maierhofer. Trainer: Dietmar Constantini

Goals: Arda Turan (28), Gökhan Gönül (78)

BELGIUM v AZERBAIJAN 4-1 (3-1)

Roi Baudouin Brussel 29.03.2011

Referee: Daniel Stålhammar (SWE) Attendance: 34,985

BELGIUM: Simon Mignolet, Laurent Ciman, Daniel van Buyten (80 Jelle van Damme), Nicolas Lombaerts, Jan Vertonghen, Timmy Simons, Nacer Chadli, Steven Defour (90 Vadis Odjida-Ofoe), Jelle Vossen, Axel Witsel, Moussa Dembélé (64 Eden Hazard). Trainer: Georges Leekens

AZERBAIJAN: Kamran Ägayev, Rail Mälikov, Mahir Şükürov, Vagif Cavadov (76 Vüqar Nadirov), Aleksandr Chertoganov, Elvin Mämädov (78 Cavid Hüseynov), Rauf Äliyev, Räşad F. Sadiqov, Ruslan Abişov, Rahid Ämirquliyev, Vladimir Levin.
Trainer: Berti Vogts.

Goals: Jan Vertonghen (12), Ruslan Abişov (16), Timmy Simons (32 pen), Nacer Chadli (45+1), Jelle Vossen (74)

AUSTRIA v GERMANY 1-2 (0-1)

Ernst-Happel, Wien 03.06.2011

Referee: Massimo Busacca (ITA) Attendance: 47,500

AUSTRIA: Christian Gratzel, Emanuel Pogatetz, Christian Fuchs, Stefan Kulovits, David Alaba, Erwin Hoffer (88 Marc Janko), Ekrem Dag (66 Zlatko Junuzovic), Julian Baumgartlinger, Paul Scharner, Florian Klein, Martin Harnik (81 Daniel Royer). Trainer: Dietmar Constantini

GERMANY: Manuel Neuer, Marcel Schmelzer, Arne Friedrich, Mats Hummels, Sami Khedira (69 Holger Badstuber), Mesut Özil, Lukas Podolski (67 Andre Schürrle), Thomas Müller, Philipp Lahm, Toni Kroos (90 Denis Aogo), Mario Gomez. Trainer: Joachim Löw

Goals: Mario Gomez (44, 90), Arne Friedrich (50 own goal)

BELGIUM v TURKEY 1-1 (1-1)

Roi Baudouin, Brussel 03.06.2011

Referee: Nicola Rizzoli (ITA) Attendance: 44,185

BELGIUM: Simon Mignolet, Toby Alderweireld, Vincent Kompany, Nicolas Lombaerts, Jan Vertonghen (46 Thomas Vermaelen), Timmy Simons, Nacer Chadli, Steven Defour (88 Jelle Vossen), Marvin Ogunjimi, Axel Witsel, Eden Hazard (60 Dries Mertens). Trainer: Georges Leekens

TURKEY: Volkan Demirel, Servet Çetin, Serdar Kesimal, Emre Belözoğlu, Selçuk Inan (78 Mehmet Topal), Çaglar Birinci, Arda Turan (85 Semih Şentürk), Burak Yilmaz (76 Mehmet Ekici), Kazim Kazim, Selçuk Şahin, Sabri Sarioğlu.
Trainer: Guus Hiddink

Goals: Marvin Ogunjimi (4), Burak Yilmaz (22)

KAZAKHSTAN v AZERBAIJAN 2-1 (0-0)

Astana Arena, Astana 03.06.2011

Referee: Euan Norris (SCO) Attendance: 10,000

KAZAKHSTAN: Roman Nesterenko, Yuri Logvinenko (65 Mikhail Rozhkov), Mukhtar Mukhtarov, Kairat Nurdauletov, Kazbek Geteriyev, Samat Smakov, Heinrich Schmidtgal, Marat Khairullin (82 Aleksandr Kirov), Ulan Konysbayev, Sergei Gridin, Sergei Ostapenko (79 Sergei Khizinichenko).
Trainer: Miroslav Beránek

AZERBAIJAN: Kamran Ägayev, Rail Mälikov, Raşad A. Sadiqov, Vagif Cavadov, Rauf Äliyev (79 Murad Hüseynov), Raşad A. Sadiqov, Ruslan Abişov, Cavid Hüseynov (61 Vüqar Nadirov), Maksim Medvedev, Vladimir Levin, Afran Ismayilov.
Trainer: Bent Vogts

Goals: Sergei Gridin (57, 68), Vüqar Nadirov (63)

AZERBAIJAN v GERMANY 1-3 (0-2)

Tofiq Bährramov, Baku 07.06.2011

Referee: Koukoulakis (GRE) Attendance: 25,000

AZERBAIJAN: Kamran Agayev, Rail Mälikov, Elnur Allahverdiyev, Vagif Cavadov (71 Murad Hüseynov), Alexandr Chertoganov (86 Raşad Abulfaz Sadyqov), Vurgun Hüseynov, Raşad Ferhad Sadyqov, Ruslan Abişov, Vugar Nadirov, Rahid Ämirquliyev, Afran Ismaylov (58 Arif Isayev). Trainer: Berti Vogts

GERMANY: Manuel Neuer, Denis Aogo, Mats Hummels, Mesut Özil (81 Mario Götze), Lukas Podolski (76 Andre Schürrle), Thomas Müller (88 Lewis Holtby), Holger Badstuber, Philipp Lahm, Toni Kroos, Benedikt Höwedes, Mario Gomez. Trainer: Joachim Löw

Goals: Mesut Özil (30), Mario Gomez (41), Murad Hüseynov (89), Andre Schürrle (90+3)

AZERBAIJAN v BELGIUM 1-1 (0-0)

Tofig Bahramov Republican stadium, Baku 02.09.2011

Referee: Lee Probert (ENG) Attendance: 9,300

AZERBAIJAN: Kamran Agayev, Mahir Şukurov, Elnur Ällahverdiyev, Vagif Cavadov, Aleksandr Chertoganov (83 Branimir Subašić), Rauf Äliyev, Vurgun Hüseynov, Raşad F. Sadyqov, Ruslan Abişov (63 Rahid Ämirguliyev), Agil Nabiyev, Afran Ismayilov (58 Elşan Mämädov). Trainer: Berti Vogts

BELGIUM: Simon Mignolet, Toby Alderweireld, Jan Vertonghen, Vincent Kompany, Nicolas Lombaerts, Timmy Simons, Eden Hazard, Marouane Fellaini, Romelu Lukaku (61 Igor De Camargo), Axel Witsel, Dries Mertens. Trainer: Georges Leekens

Goals: Timmy Simons (55 pen), Rauf Äliyev (86)

TURKEY v KAZAKHSTAN 2-1 (1-0)

Turk Telekom Arena, Istanbul 02.09.2011

Referee: Clément Turpin (FRA) Attendance: 47,756

TURKEY: Volkan Demirel, Hakan Balta, Serdar Kesimal, Emre Belözoğlu (60 Gökhan Töre), Selçuk Inan, Mehmet Ekici (51 Selcuk Şahin), Arda Turan, Egemen Korkmaz, Burak Yilmaz, Colin Kazim Richards (82 Umut Bulut), Sabri Sarioğlu. Trainer: Guus Hiddink

KAZAKHSTAN: Aleksandr Mokin, Aleksandr Kirov, Yuri Logvinenko, Mukhtar Mukhtarov, Mark Gurman, Kairat Nurdauletov, Heinrich Schmidtgal, Marat Khairullin (67 Sergei Ostapenko), Ulan Konysbayev (86 Tanat Nusserbayev), Marat Shakhmetov (82 Maksat Bayzhanov), Sergei Gridin. Trainer: Miroslav Beránek

Sent off: Inan (90+2)

Goals: Burak Yilmaz (31), Ulan Konysbayev (55), Arda Turan (90+6)

GERMANY v AUSTRIA 6-2 (3-1)

Arena AufSchalke, Gelsenkirchen 02.09.2011

Referee: Paulo Tagliavento (ITA) Attendance: 53,313

GERMANY: Manuel Neuer, Benedikt Höwedes (46 Jerome Boateng), Mats Hummels, Holger Badstuber, Phillip Lahm, Bastian Schweinsteiger, Toni Kroos (85 Mario Götze), Thomas Müller, Mesut Özil, Lukas Podolski (74 Andre Schürrle), Miroslav Klose. Trainer: Joachim Löw

AUSTRIA: Christian Gratzel, Florian Klein, Franz Schiemer, Emanuel Pogatetz, Christian Fuchs, Ekrem Dağ, Julian Baumgartlinger, David Alaba, Daniel Royer (73 Erwin Hoffer), Martin Harnik, Marko Arnautovic. Trainer: Dietmar Constantini

Goals: Miroslav Klose (8), Mesut Özil (23, 47), Lukas Podolski (28), Marko Arnautovic (42), Martin Harnik (51), Andre Schürrle (84), Mario Götze (89)

AZERBAIJAN v KAZAHSTAN 3-2 (0-1)

Tofiq Bakhramov Tepublican, Baku 06.09.2011

Referee: Anders Hermansen (DEN) Attendance: 9,112

AZERBAIJAN: Kamran Agayev, Mahir Şukurov, Vagif Cavadov, Aleksandr Chertoganov (46 Branimir Subašic), Rauf Äliyev, Vurgun Hüseynov, Raşad F. Sadyqov, Agil Nabiyev (13 Sasa Yunisoğlu), Rahid Ämirguliyev, Ufuk Budak, Afran Ismayilov (87 Ruslan Abişov). Trainer: Berti Vogts

KAZAKHSTAN: Aleksandr Mokin, Aleksandr Kirov, Yuri Logvinenko, Mark Gurman, Kairat Nurdauletov, Zhambyl Kukeyev (59 Marat Khairullin), Ulan Konysbayev, Marat Shakhmetov (70 Serikzhan Muzhikov), Sergei Gridin, Sergei Ostapenko, Mikhail Rozhkov (77 Vitali Yevstigneev). Trainer: Miroslav Beránek

Goals: Sergei Ostapenko (20), Rauf Äliyev (53), Mahir Şukurov (62 pen), Vagif Cavadov (68), Vitali Yevstgneev (77)

AUSTRIA v TURKEY 0-0

Ernst-Happel-Stadion, Wien 06.09.2011

Referee: Alberto Undiano Mallenco (SPA) Att: 47,500

AUSTRIA: Pascal Grünwald, Emanuel Pogatetz, Christian Fuchs, Marko Arnautovic (90+3 Stefan Maierhofer), David Alaba, Ekrem Dağ, Julian Baumgartlinger, Paul Scharner, Daniel Royer (67 Erwin Hoffer), Martin Harnik, Franz Schiemer. Trainer: Dietmar Constantini

TURKEY: Volkan Demirel, Servet Çetin, Hakan Balta, Yekta Kurtuluş, Egemen Korkmaz, Umut Bulut, Arda Turan,, Mehmet Topal, Burak Yilmaz (90+3 Gökhan Töre), Selçuk Şahin, Sabri Sarioğlu. Trainer: Guus Hiddink

AZERBAIJAN v AUSTRIA 1-4 (0-1)

Dalga Stadium, Baku 07.10.2010

Referee: Stephan Studer (SWI) Attendance: 6,000

AZERBAIJAN: Kamran Agayev, Sasa Yunisoğlu, Elnur Allahverdiyev, Raşad A. Sadyqov (46 Rahid Ämirguliyev), Vagif Cavadov (57 Vüqar Nadirov), Rauf Äliyev, Vurgun Hüseynov, Raşad F. Sadyqov, Ruslan Abişov, Ufuk Budak, Afran Ismayilov. Trainer: Berti Vogts

AUSTRIA: Pascal Grünwald, Aleksandr Dragović, Christian Fuchs, Andreas Ivanschitz (73 Daniel Royer), Marko Arnautovic (66 Zlatko Junuzovic), David Alaba, Ekrem Dağ, Julian Baumgartlinger, Sebastian Prödl, Paul Scharner, Marc Janko (88 Philipp Hosiner). Trainer: Willibald Ruttensteiner

Sent off: Yunisoğlu (27)

Goals: Andreas Ivanschitz (34), Marc Janko (52, 62), Vüqar Nadirov (74), Zlatko Junuzovic (90+1)

GERMANY v BELGIUM 3-1 (2-0)

Esprit Arena, Düsseldorf 11.10.2011

Referee: Svein Oddvar Moen (NOR) Attendance: 48,483

GERMANY: Manuel Neuer, Benedikt Höwedes, Mats Hummels, Per Mertesacker, Philipp Lahm (84 Ilkay Gündogan), Sami Khedira, Thomas Müller (71 Marco Reus), Mesut Özil, Toni Kroos, Andre Schürrle, Mario Gomez (76 Cacau). Trainer: Joachim Löw

BELGIUM: Simon Mignolet, Laurent Ciman, Vincent Kompany, Jan Vertonghen, Nicolas Lombaerts, Marouane Fellaini, Timmy Simons, Moussa Dembelé (64 Dries Mertens), Axel Witsel, Eden Hazard, Marvin Ogunjimi (46. Romelu Lukaku). Trainer: Georges Leekens

Goals: Mesut Özil (30), Andre Schürrle (33), Mario Gomez (48), Marouane Fellaini (86)

BELGIUM v KAZAKHSTAN 4-1 (2-0)

Roi Baudouin, Brussel 07.10.2011

Referee: Milorad Mažić (SRB) Attendance: 29,758

BELGIUM: Simon Mignolet, Laurent Ciman, Daniel van Buyten, Vincent Kompany, Jan Vertonghen, Timmy Simons (75 Steven Defour), Dries Mertens, Axel Witsel, Igor De Camargo (73 Marvin Ogunjimi), Eden Hazard (63 Vadis Odjidja), Moussa Dembélé. Trainer: Georges Leekens

KAZAKHSTAN: Vladimir Loginovskiy, Aleksandr Kirov, Mukhtar Mukhtarov, Zhambyl Kukeyev (61 Kairat Nurdauletov), Andrei Karpovich (75 Marat Shakhmetov), Serikzhan Muzhikov, Daurenbek Tazhimbetov (57 Sergei Ostapenko), Nurtas Kurgulin, Sergei Khizhnichenko, Mikhail Rozhkov, Vitali Yevstigneev. Trainer: Miroslav Beránek

Sent off: Kurgulin (59)

Goals: Timmy Simons (40 pen), Eden Hazard (43), Vincent Kompany (49), Kairat Nurdauletov (86 pen), Marvin Ogunjimi (84)

KAZAKHSTAN v AUSTRIA 0-0

Astana Arena, Astana 11.10.2011

Referee: Hannes Kaasik (EST) Attendance: 11,000

KAZAKHSTAN: Andrei Sidelnikov, Aleksandr Kirov, Mukhtar Mukhtarov, Mark Gurman (77 Vitali Yevstigneev), Kairat Nurdauletov, Heinrich Schmidtgal, Marat Khairullin, Azat Nurgaliyev (46 Serikzhan Muzhikov), Sergei Gridin, Sergei Ostapenko, Mikhail Rozhkov.
Trainer: Miroslav Beránek

AUSTRIA: Pascal Grünwald, Aleksandr Dragović, Christian Fuchs, Andreas Ivanschitz (66 Zlatko Junuzovic), Marko Arnautovic (83 Stefan Maierhofer), David Alaba, Ekrem Dağ, Sebastian Prödl, Paul Scharner, Stefan Kulovits (74 Veli Kavlak), Marc Janko. Trainer: Willibald Ruttensteiner

TURKEY v GERMANY 1-3 (0-1)

Turk Telekom Arena, Istanbul 07.10.2011

Referee: Martin Atkinson (ENG) Attendance: 49,532

TURKEY: Volkan Demirel, Gökhan Gönül, Servet Çetin, Egemen Korkmaz, Hakan Balta, Mehmet Aurelio (86 Umut Bulut), Selçuk Inan (46 Gökhan Töre), Hamit Altintop, Arda Turan (70 Colin Kazim-Richards), Sabri Sarioğlu, Burak Yilmaz. Trainer: Guus Hiddink

GERMANY: Manuel Neuer, Jérôme Boateng (74. Benedikt Höwedes), Per Mertesacker, Holger Badstuber, Philipp Lahm, Bastian Schweinsteiger, Sami Khedira, Thomas Müller, Mario Götze (90 Marco Reus), Lukas Podolski (62 Andre Schürrle), Mario Gomez. Trainer: Joachim Löw

Goals: Mario Gomez (35), Thomas Müller (66), Hakan Balta (79), Bastian Schweinsteiger (86 pen)

TURKEY v AZERBAIJAN 1-0 (0-0)

Turk Telekom Arena, Istanbul 11.10.2011

Referee: Peter Rasmussen (DEN) Attendance: 32,174

TURKEY: Sinan Bolat, Hakan Balta, Gökhan Zan, Emre Belözoğlu (78 Gökhan Töre), Hamit Altintop, Arda Turan, Mehmet Topal, Burak Yilmaz (88 Umut Bulut), Colin Kazim Richards (58 Selçuk Inan), Egemen Korkmaz, Sabri Sarioğlu. Trainer: Guus Hiddink

AZERBAIJAN: Kamran Agayev, Mahir Şukurov, Aleksandr Chertoganov, Branimir Subašic, Vurgun Hüseynov, Raşad F. Sadyqov, Ruslan Abişov, Vüqar Nadirov, Ufuk Budak (90+3 Rahid Ämirguliyev), Vladimir Levin, Afran Ismayilov (46 Elshan Mämmädov, 85 Arif Isaev). Trainer: Berti Vogts

Goal: Burak Yilmaz (60)

	P	W	D	L	F	A	Pts
Germany	10	10	0	0	34	7	30
Turkey	10	5	2	3	13	11	17
Belgium	10	4	3	3	21	15	15
Austria	10	3	3	4	16	17	12
Azerbaijan	10	2	1	7	10	26	7
Kazakhstan	10	1	1	8	6	24	4

SLOVAKIA v MACEDONIA 1-0 (0-0)

Pasienky, Bratislava 03.09.2010

Referee: Claudio Circhetta (SWI) Attendance: 5,980

SLOVAKIA: Ján Mucha, Peter Pekarík (90 Jakub Sylvestr), Martin Škrtel, Vladimír Weiss (61 Erik Jendrišek), Zdeno Štrba, Miroslav Stoch, Marek Sapara, Filip Hološko, Tomáš Hubočan, Kornel Saláta (76 Juraj Kucka), Marek Hamšík. Trainer: Vladimír Weiss

MACEDONIA: Edin Nuredinovski, Vance Sikov, Goran Popov, Nikolce Noveski, Igor Mitreski, Slavčo Georgievski, Ivan Tričkovski (80 Boban Grncarov), Velice Sumulikoski, Goran Pandev, Ilco Naumoski (61 Stevica Ristic), Filip Despotovski (73 Aleksandr Lazevski). Trainer: Mirsad Jonuz

Sent off: Sikov (85)

Goal: Filip Hološko (90+1)

GROUP B

ANDORRA v RUSSIA 0-2 (0-1)

Estadi Comunal, Andorra la Vella 03.09.2010

Referee: Marco Borg (MLT) Attendance: 1,100

ANDORRA: José Antonio Gómes, Jordi Rubio (57 Ivan Lorenzo), Marc Bernaus, Fernando Silva, Ildefons Lima, Marc Pujol (88 Daniel Mejías), Marcio Vieira, Sebastià Gómez, Sergi Moreno (76 Manolo Jiménez), Cristian Martínez, Josep Ayala. Trainer: Jesús Álvarez

RUSSIA: Igor Akinfeev, Aleksandr Anyukov, Vasili Berezutski, Sergei Ignashevich, Diniyar Bilyaletdinov, Igor Semshov, Roman Shirokov, Konstantin Zyryanov, Pavel Pogrebnyak (85 Roman Pavlyuchenko), Andrey Arshavin, Vladimir Bystrov (60 Alan Dzagoev). Trainer: Dick Advocaat

Goals: Pavel Pogrebnyak (14, 64 pen)

RUSSIA v SLOVAKIA 0-1 (0-1)

Lokomotiv, Moskva 07.09.2010

Referee: Frank de Bleeckere (BEL) Attendance: 27,052

RUSSIA: Igor Akinfeev, Aleksandr Anyukov, Vasili Berezutski, Sergei Ignashevich (81 Diniyar Bilyaletdinov), Yuri Zhirkov, Igor Semshov (61 Vladimir Bystrov), Roman Shirokov, Konstantin Zyryanov, Pavel Pogrebnyak (71 Roman Pavlyuchenko), Andrey Arshavin, Alan Dzagoev. Trainer: Dick Advocaat

SLOVAKIA: Ján Mucha, Martin Škrtel, Radoslav Zabavník, Miroslav Karhan (73 Marek Sapara), Zdeno Štrba, Miroslav Stoch (90+2 Mário Pečalka), Filip Hološko, Tomáš Hubočan, Kornel Saláta, Marek Hamšík, Juraj Kucka (58 Erik Jendrišek). Trainer: Vladimír Weiss

Goal: Miroslav Stoch (27)

ARMENIA v REPUBLIC OF IRELAND 0-1 (0-0)

Republican, Erevan 03.09.2011

Referee: Zsolt Szabó (HUN) Attendance: 8,600

ARMENIA: Roman Berezovski, Karlen Mkrtchyan, Sargis Hovsepyan, Robert Arzumanyan, Ararat Arakelyan, Artur Edigaryan (68 Davit Manoyan 68), Edgar Malakyan (79 Edgar Manucharyan), Yura Movsisyan, Levon Pachajyan, Artak Edigaryan (71 Hovhannes Hambardzumyan), Henrik Mkhitaryan. Trainer: Vardan Minasyan

IRELAND: Shay Given, Sean St Ledger, Kevin Kilbane, John O'Shea, Richard Dunne, Glenn Whelan, Liam Lawrence, Paul Green, Kevin Doyle, Robbie Keane (85 Andrew Keogh), Aiden McGeady (68 Keith Fahey). Trainer: Giovanni Trapattoni

Goal: Keith Fahey (76)

MACEDONIA v ARMENIA 2-2 (1-1)

National Arena Filip II Macedonian, Skopje 07.09.2010

Referee: Espen Berndtsen (NOR) Attendance: 9,000

MACEDONIA: Edin Nuredinovski, Aleksandar Todorovski, Goran Popov, Nikolce Noveski, Igor Mitreski, Slavčo Georgievski (67 Filip Despotovski), Ivan Tričkovski, Velice Sumulikoski, Stevica Ristic (62 Ilco Naumoski), Goran Pandev, Mario Gjurovski (75 Baže Ilijoski). Trainer: Vlatko Kostov

ARMENIA: Roman Berezovski, Karlen Mkrtchyan (90+2 Hrayr Mkoyan), Sargis Hovsepyan, Robert Arzumanyan, Ararat Arakelyan, Davit Manoyan, Edgar Malakyan (60 Edgar Manucharyan), Yura Movsisyan, Levon Pachajyan (70 Artur Edigaryan), Artak Edigaryan, Henrik Mkhitaryan. Trainer: Vardan Minasyan

Goals: Yura Movsisyan (41), Mario Gjurovski (42), Edgar Manucharyan (90+1), Ilco Naumoski (90+6 pen)

REPUBLIC OF IRELAND v ANDORRA 3-1 (2-1)

Dublin Arena 07.09.2010

Referee: Leontios Trattou (CYP) Attendance: 40,283

IRELAND: Shay Given, Sean St Ledger, Kevin Kilbane, John O'Shea (75 Stephen Kelly), Richard Dunne, Glenn Whelan (61 Darron Gibson), Liam Lawrence, Paul Green, Kevin Doyle (82 Andrew Keogh), Robbie Keane, Aiden McGeady. Trainer: Giovanni Trapattoni

ANDORRA: José Antonio Gómes, Marc Bernaus, Fernando Silva, Ildefons Lima, Marc Pujol (86 Oscar Sonejee), Marcio Vieira, Sebastià Gómez, Sergio Moreno (59 Manolo Jiménez), Cristian Martínez, Josep Ayala (71 Xavi Andorrá), Jordi Escura. Trainer: Jesús Álvarez

Goals: Kevin Kilbane (15), Kevin Doyle (41), Cristian Martínez (45), Robbie Keane (54)

REPUBLIC OF IRELAND v RUSSIA 2-3 (0-2)

Dublin Arena 08.10.2010

Referee: Kevin Blom (HOL) Attendance: 50,411

IRELAND: Shay Given, Sean St Ledger, Kevin Kilbane, John O'Shea, Richard Dunne, Glenn Whelan (66 Darron Gibson), Liam Lawrence (62 Shane Long), Paul Green, Kevin Doyle (71 Keith Fahey), Robbie Keane, Aiden McGeady. Trainer: Giovanni Trapattoni

RUSSIA: Igor Akinfeev, Aleksandr Anyukov, Vasili Berezutski, Sergei Ignashevich, Yuri Zhirkov, Roman Shirokov, Igor Denisov, Konstantin Zyryanov (68 Igor Semshov), Aleksandr Kerzhakov (80 Pavel Pogrebnyak), Andrey Arshavin, Alan Dzagoev (85 Aleksei Berezutski). Trainer: Dick Advocaat

Goals: Aleksandr Kerzhakov (11), Alan Dzagoev (29), Roman Shirokov (50), Robbie Keane (72 pen), Shane Long (78)

ARMENIA v SLOVAKIA 3-1 (1-1)

Republican, Erevan 08.10.2010

Referee: Daniele Orsato (ITA) Attendance: 8,500

ARMENIA: Roman Berezovski, Karlen Mkrtchyan, Sargis Hovsepyan, Robert Arzumanyan (79 Ararat Arakelyan), Marcos Pizzelli (72 Artur Edigaryan), Gevorg Ghazaryan, Yura Movsisyan, Hrayr Mkoyan, Levon Pachajyan (46 Edgar Manucharyan), Artak Edigaryan, Henrik Mkhitaryan. Trainer: Vardan Minasyan

SLOVAKIA: Ján Mucha, Peter Pekarík, Martin Škrtel, Radoslav Zabavník (81 Filip Šebo), Miroslav Karhan, Vladimír Weiss, Stanislav Šesták, Miroslav Stoch (57 Filip Hološko), Kamil Kopúnek (57 Juraj Kucka), Kornel Saláta, Marek Hamšík. Trainer: Vladimír Weiss

Goals: Yura Movsisyan 23, Vladimir Weiss (37), Gevorg Ghazaryan (50), Henrik Mkhitaryan (89)

ARMENIA v ANDORRA 4-0 (3-0)

Republican, Erevan 12.10.2010

Referee: Tomasz Mikulski (POL) Attendance: 12,000

ARMENIA: Roman Berezovski, Sargis Hovsepyan, Robert Arzumanyan, Artur Edigaryan, Marcos Pizzelli (83 Artur Yuspashyan), Gevorg Ghazaryan (67 Edgar Malakyan), Edgar Manucharyan, Yura Movsisyan (53 Hovhannes Goharyan), Hrayr Mkoyan, Artak Edigaryan, Henrik Mkhitaryan. Trainer: Vardan Minasyan

ANDORRA: José Antonio Gómes, Marc Bernaus, Fernando Silva, Ildefons Lima, Cristian Martínez (87 Jordi Rubio), Marcio Vieira, Sebastiàn Gómez, Sergio Moreno (51 Manolo Jiménez), Marc Vales (64 Xavi Andorrá), Josep Ayala, Jordi Escura. Trainer: Jesús Álvarez

Goals: Gevorg Ghazaryan (4), Henrik Mkhitaryan (16), Yura Movsisyan (33), Marcos Pizzelli (52)

ANDORRA v MACEDONIA 0-2 (0-1)

Estadi Comunal, Andorra la Vella 08.10.2010

Referee: Gediminas Mažeika (LIT) Attendance: 550

ANDORRA: José Antonio Gómes, Marc Bernaus, Fernando Silva, Cristian Martínez (74 Manolo Jiménez), Marcio Vieira, Sebastiàn Gómez, Sergio Moreno, Daniel Mejías (62 Ivan Lorenzo), Josep Ayala (86 Samir Bousenine), Jordi Escura, Marc Vales. Trainer: Jesús Álvarez

MACEDONIA: Edin Nuredinovski, Vance Sikov, Nikolce Noveski, Igor Mitreski, Slavčo Georgievski (34 Mario Gjurovski), Ivan Tričkovski, Velice Sumulikoski (83 Boban Grncarov), Stevica Ristic, Ilco Naumoski (73 Adim Ibraimi), Filip Despotovski, Vlade Lazarevski. Trainer: Mirsad Jonuz

Goals: Ilco Naumoski (42), Vance Sikov (60)

SLOVAKIA v REPUBLIC OF IRELAND 1-1 (1-1)

Štadión MŠK, Žilina 12.10.2010

Referee: Alberto Undiano Mallenco (SPA) Att: 10,892

SLOVAKIA: Ján Mucha, Ján Ďurica, Radoslav Zabavník, Miroslav Karhan, Vladimír Weiss (70 Miroslav Stoch), Stanislav Šesták (70 Filip Hološko), Tomáš Hubočan, Kornel Saláta, Marek Hamšík, Erik Jendrišek (84 Tomáš Oravec), Juraj Kucka. Trainer: Vladimír Weiss

IRELAND: Shay Given, Sean St Ledger, Kevin Kilbane, John O'Shea, Richard Dunne, Glenn Whelan, Keith Fahey (71 Andrew Keogh), Paul Green (42 Darron Gibson), Shane Long, Robbie Keane, Aiden McGeady. Trainer: Giovanni Trapattoni

Goals: Sean St Ledger (16), Ďurica (36)

MACEDONIA v RUSSIA 0-1 (0-1)

National Arena Filip II Macedonian, Skopje 12.10.2010

Referee: Stefan Johannesson (SWE) Attendance: 10,500

MACEDONIA: Edin Nuredinovski, Vance Sikov, Nikolce Noveski, Igor Mitreski, Ivan Tričkovski, Velice Sumulikoski, Mario Gjurovski (79 Armend Alimi), Ilco Naumoski, Filip Despotovski (78 Slavčo Georgievski), Aleksandr Lazevski, Adim Ibraimi (49 Stevica Ristic). Trainer: Mirsad Jonuz

RUSSIA: Igor Akinfeev, Aleksandr Anyukov, Vasili Berezutski, Sergei Ignashevich, Yuri Zhirkov, Roman Shirokov, Igor Denisov, Konstantin Zyryanov, Aleksandr Kerzhakov (79 Pavel Pogrebnyak), Andrey Arshavin (81 Vladimir Bystrov), Alan Dzagoev (61 Aleksei Berezutski). Trainer: Dick Advocaat

Goal: Aleksandr Kerzhakov (8)

REPUBLIC OF IRELAND v MACEDONIA 2-1 (2-1)

Dublin Arena 26.03.2011

Referee: István Vad (HUN) Attendance: 33,200

IRELAND: Keiren Westwood, Kevin Foley, Kevin Kilbane, Darren O'Dea, Richard Dunne, Glenn Whelan, Aiden McGeady, Darron Gibson (77 Keith Fahey), Kevin Doyle (20 Shane Long), Robbie Keane (87 James McCarthy), Damien Duff. Trainer: Giovanni Trapattoni

MACEDONIA: Edin Nuredinovski, Vance Sikov, Goran Popov, Nikolce Noveski, Ivan Tričkovski, Velice Sumulikoski, Goran Pandev, Ilco Naumoski (68 Stevica Ristic), Boban Grncarov, Darko Tasevski (61 Mario Gjurovski), Muhamed Demiri (84 Slavčo Georgievski). Trainer: Mirsad Jonuz

Goals: Aiden McGeady (2), Robbie Keane (21), Ivan Tričkovski (45)

ARMENIA v RUSSIA 0-0

Republican, Erevan 26.03.2011

Referee: Craig Thomson (SCO) Attendance: 14,800

ARMENIA: Roman Berezovski, Levon Hayrapetyan (67 Artak Edigaryan), Sargis Hovsepyan, Robert Arzumanyan, Karlen Mkrtchyan, Marcos Pizzelli (57 Artur Edigaryan), Edgar Malakyan (49 Edgar Manucharyan), Gevorg Ghazaryan, Yura Movsisyan, Hrayr Mkoyan, Henrik Mkhitaryan. Trainer: Vardan Minasyan

RUSSIA: Igor Akinfeev, Roman Shishkin, Vasili Berezutski, Sergei Ignashevich, Yuri Zhirkov, Roman Shirokov, Igor Denisov, Konstantin Zyryanov, Aleksandr Kerzhakov (78 Pavel Pogrebnyak), Andrey Arshavin (90 Diniyar Bilyaletdinov), Alan Dzagoev. Trainer: Dick Advocaat

RUSSIA v ARMENIA 3-1 (1-1)

Stadion Petrovski, St Petersburg (RUS) 04.06.2011

Referee: Stéphane Lannoy (FRA) Attendance: 18,000

RUSSIA: Igor Akinfeev, Aleksandr Anyukov (75 Renat Yanbaev), Vasili Berezutski, Sergei Ignashevich, Yuri Zhirkov, Igor Semshov (69 Denis Glushakov), Igor Denisov, Konstantin Zyryanov (82 Alan Dzagoev), Roman Pavlyuchenko, Andrey Arshavin, Dmitri Torbinski. Trainer: Dick Advocaat

ARMENIA: Roman Berezovski, Levon Hayrapetyan, Sargis Hovsepyan, Robert Arzumanyan, Karlen Mkrtchyan (90 Artak Edigaryan), Marcos Pizzelli (67 Artur Edigaryan), Gevorg Ghazaryan, Yura Movsisyan, Hrayr Mkoyan, Henrik Mkhitaryan, Levon Pachajyan (57 Edgar Manucharyan). Trainer: Vardan Minasyan

Goals: Marcos Pizzelli (25), Roman Pavlyuchenko (26, 59, 73 pen)

ANDORRA v SLOVAKIA 0-1 (0-1)

Estadi Comunal, Andorra la Vella 26.03.2011

Referee: Menashe Masiah (ISR) Attendance: 850

ANDORRA: José Antonio Gómes, Jordi Rubio, Marc Bernaus, Emili Garcia, Ildefons Lima, Cristian Martínez, Sebastiàn Gómez (72 Marcio Vieira), Manolo Jiménez (87 Oscar Sonejee), Sergio Moreno, Marc Vales, Josep Ayala (81 Juli Sánchez). Trainer: Jesús Álvarez

SLOVAKIA: Ján Mucha, Peter Pekarík, Martin Škrtel, Ján Ďurica, Róbert Vittek (78 Juraj Piroska), Miroslav Stoch (90 Kornel Saláta), Marek Hamšík, Erik Jendrišek (87 Filip Hološko), Filip Lukšík, Tomáš Kóňa, Filip Šebo. Trainer: Vladimír Weiss

Goal: Filip Šebo (21)

SLOVAKIA v ANDORRA 1-0 (0-0)

Štadión Pasienky, Bratislava 04.06.2011

Referee: Lorenc Jemini (ALB) Attendance: 4,300

SLOVAKIA: Marián Kello, Ján Ďurica, Marek Čech (83 Kornel Saláta), Miroslav Karhan, Róbert Jež, Róbert Vittek, Filip Hološko (74 Igor Žofčák), Tomáš Hubočan, Marek Hamšík, Juraj Kucka (46 Stanislav Šesták), Filip Šebo. Trainer: Vladimír Weiss

ANDORRA: José Antonio Gómes, Jordi Rubio, Marc Bernaus, Emili Garcia, Ildefons Lima, Marcio Vieira, Manolo Jiménez (86 Joaquim Salvat), Fernando Silva (63 Sebastiàn Gómez), Cristian Martínez, Marc Vales, Josep Ayala (16 Xavi Andorrá). Trainer: Jesús Álvarez

Goal: Miroslav Karhan (63)

MACEDONIA v REPUBLIC OF IRELAND 0-2 (0-2)

National Arena Filip II Macedonian, Skopje 04.06.2011

Referee: Florian Meyer (GER) Attendance: 29,500

MACEDONIA: Martin Bogatinov, Boban Grncarov, Goran Popov, Nikolce Noveski, Vance Sikov, Ivan Tričkovski, Velice Sumulikoski, Muhamed Demiri (72 Dusan Savik), Goran Pandev, Ilco Naumoski (10 Feran Hasani), Filip Despotovski (57 Mario Gjurovski). Trainer: Mirsad Jonuz

IRELAND: Shay Given, Stephen Kelly, Kevin Kilbane, John O'Shea, Darren O'Dea, Glenn Whelan, Aiden McGeady, Keith Andrews, Simon Cox (65 Shane Long), Robbie Keane, Stephen Hunt. Trainer: Giovanni Trapattoni

Goals: Robbie Keane (8, 37)

REPUBLIC OF IRELAND v SLOVAKIA 0-0

Dublin Arena 02.09.2011

Referee: Pedro Proença (POR) Attendance: 35,480

IRELAND: Shay Given, Sean St Ledger, Stephen Ward, John O'Shea, Richard Dunne, Glenn Whelan, Aiden McGeady (85 Stephen Hunt), Keith Andrews, Kevin Doyle (64 Simon Cox), Robbie Keane, Damien Duff. Trainer: Giovanni Trapattoni

SLOVAKIA: Ján Mucha, Peter Pekarík, Martin Škrtel, Ján Ďurica, Marek Čech, Miroslav Karhan, Vladimír Weiss (86 Erik Jendrišek), Miroslav Stoch, Filip Hološko (88 Róbert Vittek), Marek Hamšík, Juraj Kucka (77 Karim Guédé). Trainer: Vladimír Weiss

ANDORRA v ARMENIA 0-3 (0-1)

Estadi Comunal, Andorra la Vella 02.09.2011

Referee: Alexander Kostadinov (BUL) Attendance: 750

ANDORRA: José Antonio Gómes, Cristian Martínez, Marc Bernaus, Emili Garcia, Ildefons Lima, Marc Pujol, Fernando Silva (72 Sebastiàn Gómez), Sergio Moreno (81 Marcio Vieira), Marc Vales, Josep Ayala (87 Juli Sánchez), Jordi Rubio. Trainer: Jesús Álvarez

ARMENIA: Roman Berezovski, Sargis Hovsepyan, Karlen Mkrtchyan, Marcos Pizzelli (83 Artur Edigaryan), Gevorg Ghazaryan (89 Zaven Badoyan), Artur Sarkisov, Hrayr Mkoyan, Valeri Aleksanyan, Henrik Mkhitaryan, Levon Hayrapetyan, Edgar Manucharyan (78 Edgar Malakyan). Trainer: Vardan Minasyan

Sent off: Lima (90)

Goals: Marcos Pizzelli (35), Gevorg Ghazaryan (75), Henrik Mkhitaryan (90+1 pen)

RUSSIA v REPUBLIC OF IRELAND 0-0

Luzhniki, Moskva 06.09.2011

Referee: Felix Brych (GER) Attendance: 49,515

RUSSIA: Vyacheslav Malafeev, Aleksandr Anyukov, Vasili Berezutski, Sergei Ignashevich, Aleksei Berezutski, Igor Semshov, Roman Shirokov, Konstantin Zyryanov, Aleksandr Kerzhakov (54 Roman Pavlyuchenko), Andrey Arshavin, Yuri Zhirkov (76 Diniyar Bilyaletdinov). Trainer: Dick Advocaat

IRELAND: Shay Given, Stephen Kelly, Stephen Ward, Darren O'Dea, Richard Dunne, Glenn Whelan, Aiden McGeady, Keith Andrews, Kevin Doyle (59 Simon Cox), Robbie Keane, Damien Duff (67 Stephen Hunt). Trainer: Giovanni Trapattoni

RUSSIA v MACEDONIA 1-0 (1-0)

Luzhniki, Moskva 02.09.2011

Referee: Bülent Yıldırım (TUR) Attendance: 31,028

RUSSIA: Vyacheslav Malafeev, Aleksandr Anyukov, Vasili Berezutski, Aleksei Berezutski, Yuri Zhirkov, Igor Semshov (46 Roman Pavlyuchenko), Igor Denisov, Roman Shirokov, Aleksandr Kerzhakov (88 Denis Glushakov), Andrey Arshavin, Konstantin Zyryanov (60 Dmitri Torbinski). Trainer: Dick Advocaat

MACEDONIA: Martin Bogatinov, Vance Sikov, Goran Popov, Nikolce Noveski, Ivan Tričkovski, Velice Sumulikoski (85 Muarem Muarem), Muhamed Demiri, Goran Pandev, Agim Ibraimi, Daniel Georgievski (66 Feran Hasani), Mirko Ivanovski (75 Aleksandar Trajkovski). Trainer: John Toshack

Sent off: Pandev (90+5)

Goal: Igor Semshov (41)

MACEDONIA v ANDORRA 1-0 (0-0)

National Arena Filip II Macedonian, Skopje 06.09.2011

Referee: Mark Steven Whitby (WAL) Attendance: 5,000

MACEDONIA: Martin Bogatinov, Goran Popov, Vance Sikov, Ivan Tričkovski, Velice Sumulikoski, Daniel Georgievski, Daniel Mojsov, Muarem Muarem (77 Muhamed Huseini), Feran Hasani (68 Samir Fazli), Agim Ibraimi (46 Aleksandar Trajkovski), Mirko Ivanovski. Trainer: John Toshack

ANDORRA: José Antonio Gómes, Cristian Martínez, Marc Bernaus, Oscar Sonejee, Emili Garcia, Marcio Vieira (83 Marc García), Fernando Silva (74 Sebastiàn Gómez), Sergio Moreno, Marc Vales, Josep Ayala, Jordi Rubio (26 Alexandre Gutierrez). Trainer: Jesús Álvarez

Goal: Mirko Ivanovski (59)

SLOVAKIA v ARMENIA 0-4 (0-0)

Štadión pod Dubňom, Zilina 06.09.2011

Referee: Marcin Borski (POL) Attendance: 7,238

SLOVAKIA: Ján Mucha, Peter Pekarík, Martin Škrtel, Ján Ďurica, Marek Čech (78 Erik Jendrišek), Miroslav Karhan, Vladimír Weiss (71 Stanislav Šesták), Miroslav Stoch, Filip Hološko, Marek Hamšík, Karim Guédé (55 Róbert Jež). Trainer: Vladimír Weiss

ARMENIA: Roman Berezovski, Sargis Hovsepyan, Karlen Mkrtchyan, Artur Edigaryan (90+2 Artur Yuspashyan), Marcos Pizzelli (73 Edgar Manucharyan), Gevorg Ghazaryan, Yura Movsisyan (85 Artur Sarkisov), Hrayr Mkoyan, Valeri Aleksanyan, Henrik Mkhitaryan, Levon Hayrapetyan. Trainer: Vardan Minasyan

Goals: Yura Movsisyan (57), Henrik Mkhitaryan (70), Gevorg Ghazaryan (80), Artur Sarkisov (90+1)

ARMENIA v MACEDONIA 4-1 (2-0)

Republican, Erevan 07.10.2011

Referee: Robert Schörgenhofer (AUS) Attendance: 14,403

ARMENIA: Roman Berezovski, Artur Yuspashyan, Sargis Hovsepyan, Karlen Mkrtchyan (75 Artur Sarkisov), Artur Edigaryan, Marcos Pizzelli (63 Edgar Manucharyan), Gevorg Ghazaryan (83 Edgar Malakyan), Yura Movsisyan, Valeri Aleksanyan, Henrik Mkhitaryan, Levon Hayrapetyan. Trainer: Vardan Minasyan

MACEDONIA: Martin Bogatinov, Vance Sikov, Goran Popov, Nikolce Noveski, Ivan Tričkovski, Velice Sumulikoski, Muhamed Demiri, Muarem Muarem (46 Mario Gjurovski), Filip Ivanovski (60 Igor Mitreski), Georgievski (51 Vlade Lazarevski), Ivanovski. Trainer: John Toshack

Sent off: Sumulikoski (53)

Goals: Marcos Pizzelli (28), Henrik Mkhitaryan (34), Gevorg Ghazaryan (69), Vance Sikov (86), Artur Sarkisov (90+1)

SLOVAKIA v RUSSIA 0-1 (0-0)

Štadión pod Dubňom, Zilina 07.10.2011

Referee: Jonas Eriksson (SWE) Attendance: 10,087

SLOVAKIA: Ján Mucha, Peter Pekarík, Martin Škrtel, Ján Ďurica, Miroslav Karhan (86 Filip Šebo), Miroslav Stoch, Filip Hološko (73 Vladimír Weiss), Tomáš Hubočan, Marek Hamšík, Erik Jendrišek, Juraj Kucka (73 Karim Guédé). Trainer: Vladimír Weiss

RUSSIA: Vyacheslav Malafeev, Aleksandr Anyukov, Vasili Berezutski, Sergei Ignashevich, Yuri Zhirkov (90+4 Aleksei Berezutski), Roman Shirokov, Igor Denisov, Konstantin Zyryanov, Roman Pavlyuchenko (87 Pavel Pogrebnyak), Andrey Arshavin, Alan Dzagoev (90+3 Aleksandr Samedov). Trainer: Dick Advocaat

Goal: Alan Dzagoev (71)

ANDORRA v REPUBLIC OF IRELAND 0-2 (0-2)

Estadi Comunal, Andorra la Vella 07.10.2011

Referee: Libor Kovařik (CZE) Attendance: 860

ANDORRA: José Antonio Gómes, Cristian Martínez, Marc Bernaus, Emili Garcia, Ildefons Lima (81 Oscar Sonejee), Marc Pujol (60 Edu Peppe), Marcio Vieira, Fernando Silva, Sergio Moreno, Josep Ayala, Alexandre Gutierrez (78 Ivan Lorenzo). Trainer: Jesús Álvarez

IRELAND: Shay Given, Sean St Ledger, Stephen Ward, John O'Shea, Darren O'Dea, Glenn Whelan (65 Keith Fahey), Aiden McGeady, Keith Andrews, Kevin Doyle (71 Shane Long), Robbie Keane, Damien Duff (75 Stephen Hunt). Trainer: Giovanni Trapattoni

Goals: Kevin Doyle (8), Aiden McGeady (20)

RUSSIA v ANDORRA 6-0 (4-0)

Luzhniki, Moskva 11.10.2011

Referee: Eli Hacmon (ISR) Attendance: 38,790

RUSSIA: Vyacheslav Malafeev, Roman Shishkin, Vasili Berezutski, Sergei Ignashevich, Aleksei Berezutski, Igor Semshov (72 Diniyar Bilyaletdinov), Igor Denisov, Roman Pavlyuchenko (73 Pavel Pogrebnyak), Andrey Arshavin, Alan Dzagoev, Denis Glushakov (80 Aleksandr Samedov). Trainer: Dick Advocaat

ANDORRA: José Antonio Gómes, Marc Bernaus, Emili Garcia, Ildefons Lima, Marc Pujol (85 Juli Sánchez), Marcio Vieira, Sergio Moreno, Edu Peppe (79 Ivan Lorenzo), Sebastiàn Gómez (70 Fernando Silva), Marc Vales, Alexandre Gutierrez. Trainer: Jesús Álvarez

Goals: Alan Dzagoev (5, 44), Sergei Ignashevich (26), Roman Pavlyuchenko (30), Denis Glushakov (59), Diniyar Bilyaletdinov (78)

REPUBLIC OF IRELAND v ARMENIA 2-1 (1-0)

Dublin Arena 11.10.2011

Referee: Eduardo Iturralde González (SPA) Att: 45,200

IRELAND: Shay Given, Sean St Ledger, Stephen Kelly, John O'Shea, Richard Dunne, Glenn Whelan (76 Keith Fahey), Aiden McGeady (67 Stephen Hunt), Keith Andrews, Kevin Doyle, Simon Cox (80 Jon Walters), Damien Duff. Trainer: Giovanni Trapattoni

ARMENIA: Roman Berezovski, Sargis Hovsepyan, Karlen Mkrtchyan, Marcos Pizzelli (53 Edgar Manucharyan), Edgar Malakyan (28 Arsen Petrosyan), Gevorg Ghazaryan (62 Artur Sarkisov), Yura Movsisyan, Hrayr Mkoyan, Valeri Aleksanyan, Henrik Mkhitaryan, Levon Hayrapetyan. Trainer: Vardan Minasyan

Sent off: Doyle (81), Berezovski (26)

Goals: Valeri Aleksanyan (43 own goal), Richard Dunne (59), Henrik Mkhitaryan (62)

MACEDONIA v SLOVAKIA 1-1 (0-0)

National Arena Filip II Macedonian, Skopje 11.10.2011

Referee: Tony Chapron (FRA) Attendance: 4,100

MACEDONIA: Martin Bogatinov, Vance Sikov, Nikolce Noveski, Ivan Tričkovski, Muhamed Demiri, Mario Gjurovski, Samir Fazli (84 Aleksandar Trajkovski), Vlatko Grozdanoski (46 Robert Petrov), Vlade Lazarevski, Daniel Mojsov, Aleksandar Lazevski (64 Filip Ivanovski). Trainer: John Toshack

SLOVAKIA: Ján Mucha, Peter Pekarík, Vladimír Weiss, Róbert Jež (88 Peter Grajciar), Juraj Piroska (87 Filip Hološko), Lubomir Michalik, Tomáš Hubočan (46 Marek Čech), Kornel Saláta, Marek Hamšík, Erik Jendrišek, Juraj Kucka. Trainer: Vladimír Weiss

Goals: Juraj Piroska (54), Nikolce Noveski (79)

	P	W	D	L	F	A	Pts
Russia	10	7	2	1	17	4	23
Eire	10	6	3	1	15	7	21
Armenia	10	5	2	3	22	10	17
Slovakia	10	4	3	3	7	10	15
Macedonia	10	2	2	6	8	14	8
Andorra	10	0	0	10	1	25	0

GROUP C

ESTONIA v FAROE ISLANDS 2-1 (0-1)

Lilleküla, Tallinn 11.08.2010

Referee: Ante Vučemilović (CRO) Attendance: 5,470

ESTONIA: Sergei Pareiko, Raio Piiroja, Dmitri Kruglov (70 Sander Post), Aleksandr Dmitrijev, Sander Puri (76 Ats Purje), Andres Oper (62 Kaimar Saag), Tarmo Kink, Konstantin Vassiljev, Ragnar Klavan, Enar Jääger, Alo Barengrub. Trainer: Tarmo Rüütli

FAROE ISLANDS: Gunnar Nielsen, Jónas Tór Næs, Johan Davidsen, Atli Gregersen, Hendrik Rubeksen, Jan Ingi Petersen (85 Bogi Løkin), Fródi Benjaminsen, Símun Samuelsen (74 Jústinus Hansen), Jákup Borg (67 Rógvi Poulsen), Christian Lamhauge Holst, Jóan Edmundsson. Trainer: Brian Kerr

Goals: Jóan Edmundsson (28), Kaimar Saag (90+1), Raio Piiroja (90+3)

FAROE ISLANDS v SERBIA 0-3 (0-2)

Tórsvøllur, Torshavn 03.09.2011

Referee: Albert Toussaint (LUX) Attendance: 1,847

FAROE ISLANDS: Gunnar Nielsen, Daniel Udsen (46 Christian Mouritsen), Hendrik Rubeksen, Johan Davidsen, Atli Gregersen, Jónas Tór Næs, Fródi Benjaminsen, Jann Ingi Petersen (73 Jústinus Hansen), Símun Samuelsen, Christian Lamhauge Holst (79 Arnbjørn Hansen), Jóan Edmundsson. Trainer: Brian Kerr

SERBIA: Andjelko Djuričić, Antonio Rukavina, Nemanja Vidić, Danko Lazović (83 Miloš Ninković), Dejan Stanković (58 Radoslav Petrović), Milan Jovanović, Ivan Obradović (46 Aleksandr Luković), Miloš Krasić, Nikola Žigić, Neven Subotić, Zdravko Kuzmanović. Trainer: Rešad Kunovac

Goals: Danko Lazović (14), Dejan Stanković (18), Nikola Žigić (90+1)

ESTONIA v ITALY 1-2 (1-0)

Lilleküla, Tallinn 03.09.2010

Referee: Carlos Velasco Carballo (SPA) Attendance: 8,600

ESTONIA: Sergei Pareiko, Taavi Rähn, Raio Piiroja, Dmitri Kruglov (82 Tarmo Kink), Aleksandr Dmitrijev, Sander Puri (77 Ats Purje), Sergei Zenjov (63 Kaimar Saag), Martin Vunk, Konstantin Vassiljev, Ragnar Klavan, Enar Jääger. Trainer: Tarmo Rüütli

ITALY: Salvatore Sirigu, Cristian Molinaro, Giorgio Chiellini, Daniele De Rossi, Simone Pepe (60 Fabio Quagliarella), Giampaolo Pazzini, Antonio Cassano (80 Luca Antonelli), Mattia Cassani, Riccardo Montolivo (75 Angelo Palombo), Leonardo Bonucci, Andrea Pirlo. Trainer: Cesare Prandelli

Goals: Sergei Zenjov (31), Antonio Cassano (60), Leonardo Bonucci (63)

SLOVENIA v NORTHERN IRELAND 0-1 (0-0)

Ljudski vrt, Maribor 03.09.2010

Referee: Cristian Balaj (ROM) Attendance: 12,000

SLOVENIA: Samir Handanovič, Miso Brečko, Boštjan Cesar, Robert Koren, Zlatan Ljubijankič (88 Tim Matavž), Valter Birsa, Milivoje Novakovič (74 Zlatko Dedič), Bojan Jokić, Andraž Kirm (74 Josip Iličić), Aleksandar Radosavljevič, Matej Mavrič. Trainer: Matjaž Kek

NORTHERN IRELAND: Maik Taylor, Gareth McAuley, Craig Cathcart, Stephen Craigan, Chris Baird, Steven Davis, Grant McCann (67 Corry Evans), David Healy (67 Kyle Lafferty), Warren Feeney, Chris Brunt (89 Jonny Gorman), Aaron Hughes. Trainer: Nigel Worthington

Goal: Corry Evans (70)

SERBIA v SLOVENIA 1-1 (0-0)

Stadion FK Crvena zvezda, Belgrade 07.09.2010

Referee: Olegário Benquerença (POR) Attendance: 24,028

SERBIA: Andjelko Djuričić, Antonio Rukavina, Nemanja Vidić, Zoran Tošić (46 Miloš Krasić), Danko Lazović, Dejan Stanković (71 Gojko Kačar), Aleksandr Luković, Milan Jovanović (64 Miloš Ninković), Nikola Žigić, Neven Subotić, Zdravko Kuzmanović. Trainer: Rešad Kunovac

SLOVENIA: Samir Handanovič, Mišo Brečko, Boštjan Cesar, Robert Koren, Valter Birsa (78 Josip Iličić), Milivoje Novakovič, Bojan Jokić, Zlatko Dedič (77 Zlatan Ljubijankič), Andraž Kirm (89 Dalibor Stevanović), Aleksandar Radosavljevič, Matej Mavrič. Trainer: Matjaž Kek

Goals: Milivoje Novakovič (63), Nikola Žigić (86)

ITALY v FAROE ISLANDS 5-0 (3-0)

Stadio Artemio Franchi, Firenze 07.09.2010

Referee: Aleksei Kulbakov (BLR) Attendance: 19,266

ITALY: Emiliano Viviano, Lorenzo De Silvestri, Giorgio Chiellini, Daniele De Rossi (76 Angelo Palombo), Antonio Cassano, Alberto Gilardino (59 Giampaolo Pazzini), Luca Antonelli, Riccardo Montolivo, Leonardo Bonucci, Andrea Pirlo, Giuseppe Rossi (59 Fabio Quagliarella).
Trainer: Cesare Prandelli

FAROE ISLANDS: Gunnar Nielsen, Bogi Løkin (74 Jónas Tór Næs), Hendrik Rubeksen, Atli Gregersen, Egil á Bø, Jóhan Davidsen, Fródi Benjaminsen, Jann Ingi Petersen, Christian Mouritsen (74 Christian Lamhauge Holst), Símun Samuelsen, Jóan Edmundsson (89 Daniel Udsen). Trainer: Brian Kerr

Goals: Alberto Gilardino (11), Daniele De Rossi (22), Antonio Cassano (27), Fabio Quagliarella (81), Andrea Pirlo (90)

SERBIA v ESTONIA 1-3 (0-0)

FK Partizan, Beograd 08.10.2010

Referee: Maksim Layushkin (RUS) Attendance: 12,000

SERBIA: Vladimir Stojković, Marko Lomić, Gojko Kačar (46 Miloš Ninković), Nemanja Vidić, Branislav Ivanović, Dejan Stanković, Aleksandr Luković, Milan Jovanović (46 Zoran Tošić), Miloš Krasić, Nikola Žigić, Zdravko Kuzmanović (79 Danko Lazović). Trainer: Vladimir Petrović

ESTONIA: Sergei Pareiko, Taavi Rähn, Raio Piiroja, Dmitri Kruglov, Aleksandr Dmitrijev, Sander Puri (70 Ats Purje), Tarmo Kink (64 Kaimar Saag), Sergei Zenjov (87 Martin Vunk), Konstantin Vassiljev, Ragnar Klavan, Enar Jääger.
Trainer: Tarmo Rüütli

Goals: Nikola Žigić (60), Tarmo Kink (63), Konstantin Vassiljev (73), Aleksandr Luković (90+1 own goal)

NORTHERN IRELAND v ITALY 0-0

Windsor Park, Belfast 08.10.2010

Referee: Tony Chapron (FRA) Attendance: 15,200

NORTHERN IRELAND: Maik Taylor, Gareth McAuley, Jonny Evans, Stephen Craigan, Chris Baird, Steven Davis, Grant McCann (80 Corry Evans), David Healy (66 Kyle Lafferty), Warren Feeney, Chris Brunt (71 Niall McGinn), Aaron Hughes. Trainer: Nigel Worthington

ITALY: Emiliano Viviano, Domenico Criscito, Giorgio Chiellini, Daniele De Rossi, Stefano Mauri (79 Claudio Marchisio), Simone Pepe (84 Giuseppe Rossi), Antonio Cassano, Marco Borriello (74 Giampaolo Pazzini), Mattian Cassani, Andrea Pirlo, Leonardo Bonucci.
Trainer: Cesare Prandelli

SLOVENIA v FAROE ISLANDS 5-1 (2-0)

ŠRC Stožice, Ljubljana 08.10.2010

Referee: Stanislav Todorov (BUL) Attendance: 15,750

SLOVENIA: Samir Handanovič, Mišo Brečko, Marko Šuler, Boštjan Cesar, Robert Koren, Valter Birsa (51 Andraž Kirm), Milivoje Novakovič (73 Zlatko Dedič), Bojan Jokić, Aleksandar Radosavljevič (59 Armin Bačinović), Josip Iličić, Tim Matavž.
Trainer: Matjaž Kek

FAROE ISLANDS: Jákup Mikkelsen, Hendrik Rubeksen, Jónas Tór Næs, Atli Gregersen, Egil á Bø, Jústinus Hansen, Fródi Benjaminsen, Bogi Løkin (41 Hjalgrim Elttør), Daniel Udsen (81 Jann Ingi Petersen), Christian Lamhauge Holst (81 Christian Mouritsen), Jóan Edmundsson.
Trainer: Brian Kerr

Goals: Tim Matavž (25, 36, 65), Milivoje Novakovič (72 pen), Zlatko Dedič (84), Christian Mouritsen (90+3)

FAROE ISLANDS v NORTHERN IRELAND 1-1 (0-0)

Svangaskard Stadion, Toftir 12.10.2010

Referee: Cyril Zimmermann (SWI) Attendance: 1,921

FAROE ISLANDS: Jákup Mikkelsen, Jónas Tór Næs, Erling Jacobsen, Jóhan Davidsen, Atli Gregersen, Daniel Udsen (68 Jann Ingi Petersen), Fródi Benjaminsen, Símun Samuelsen (78 Arnbjørn Hansen), Christian Lamhauge Holst (85 Jústinus Hansen), Jóan Edmundsson, Hjalgrim Elttør.
Trainer: Brian Kerr

NORTHERN IRELAND: Maik Taylor, Gareth McAuley, Jonny Evans, Stephen Craigan, Chris Baird, Steven Davis, Niall McGinn (83 Corry Evans), Kyle Lafferty, Warren Feeney (50 David Healy), Chris Brunt, Aaron Hughes.
Trainer: Nigel Worthington

Goals: Christian Lamhauge Holst (60), Kyle Lafferty (76)

ESTONIA v SLOVENIA 0-1 (0-0)

Lilleküla Stadium, Tallinn 12.10.2010

Referee: Tommy Skjerven (NOR) Attendance: 5,722

ESTONIA: Sergei Pareiko, Taavi Rähn (55 Kari Palatu), Dmitri Kruglov, Aleksandr Dmitrijev, Sander Puri (69 Ats Purje), Tarmo Kink (59 Sergei Zenjov), Konstantin Vassiljev, Ragnar Klavan, Enar Jääger, Kaimar Saag, Andrei Sidorenkov. Trainer: Tarmo Rüütli

SLOVENIA: Samir Handanovič, Mišo Brečko, Marko Šuler, Boštjan Cesar, Robert Koren, Valter Birsa (90+1 Zlatan Ljubijankič), Milivoje Novakovič, Bojan Jokić, Aleksandar Radosavljevič, Josip Iličić (67 Andraž Kirm), Tim Matavž (53 Zlatko Dedič). Trainer: Matjaž Kek

Goal: Andrei Sidorenkov (67 own goal)

ITALY v SERBIA awarded 3-0

Stadio Luigi Ferraris, Genoa 12.10.2010

Referee: Craig Thomson (SCO) Attendance: 28,000

ITALY: Emiliano Viviano, Domenico Criscito, Giorgio Chiellini, Stefano Mauri, Claudio Marchisio, Antonio Cassano, Angelo Palombo, Gianluca Zambrotta, Giampaolo Pazzini, Andrea Pirlo, Leonardo Bonucci. Trainer: Cesare Prandelli

SERBIA: Željko Brkić, Gojko Kačar, Branislav Ivanović, Zoran Tošić, Dragan Mrdja, Dejan Stanković, Aleksandr Luković, Miloš Krasić, Neven Subotić, Slobodan Rajković, Zdravko Kuzmanović. Trainer: Vladimir Petrović

The match was abandoned after six minutes due to disturbances in the crowd and the game was subsequently awarded to Italy with a 3-0 scoreline.

SERBIA v NORTHERN IRELAND 2-1 (0-1)

Stadion FK Crvena zvezda, Beograd 25.03.2011

Referee: Serge Gumienny (BEL) Attendance: 350

SERBIA: Željko Brkić, Aleksandar Kolarov, Milan Biševac, Branislav Ivanović, Zoran Tošić, Adem Ljajić (46 Milan Jovanović), Marko Pantelić, Dejan Stanković, Nenad Milijaš (46 Miloš Ninković), Miloš Krasić (86 Radosav Petrović), Neven Subotić. Trainer: Vladimir Petrović

NORTHERN IRELAND: Lee Camp, Craig Cathcart, Jonny Evans (86 Pat McCourt), Gareth McAuley, Chris Baird, Corry Evans, Sammy Clingan, Jonny Gorman (78 Warren Feeney), Kyle Lafferty (46 David Healy), Chris Brunt, Aaron Hughes. Trainer: Nigel Worthington

Goals: Gareth McAuley (40), Marko Pantelić (65), Zoran Tošić (74)

SLOVENIA v ITALY 0-1 (0-0)

ŠRC Stožice, Ljubljana 25.03.2011

Referee: Felix Brych (GER) Attendance: 15,790

SLOVENIA: Samir Handanovič, Mišo Brečko (70 Siniša Andjelković), Marko Šuler, Boštjan Cesar, Robert Koren, Valter Birsa (74 Josip Iličić), Milivoje Novakovič, Bojan Jokić, Zlatko Dedič (56 Zlatan Ljubijankič), Andraž Kirm, Aleksandar Radosavljevič. Trainer: Matjaž Kek

ITALY: Gianluigi Buffon, Christian Maggio, Giorgio Chiellini, Thiago Motta, Stefano Mauri (63 Antonio Nocerino), Giampaolo Pazzini, Antonio Cassano (74 Giuseppe Rossi), Alberto Aquilani, Federico Balzaretti, Riccardo Montolivo (87 Claudio Marchisio), Leonardo Bonucci. Trainer: Cesare Prandelli

Goal: Thiago Motta (73)

ESTONIA v SERBIA 1-1 (0-1)

Lilleküla Stadium, Tallinn 29.03.2011

Referee: Bas Nijhuis (HOL) Attendance: 5,185

ESTONIA: Sergei Pareiko, Taavi Rähn, Raio Piiroja, Dmitri Kruglov, Aleksandr Dmitrijev, Sander Puri (29 Ats Purje), Konstantin Vassiljev, Ragnar Klavan, Enar Jääger, Jarmo Ahjupera (55 Andres Oper), Kaimar Saag (66 Tarmo Kink). Trainer: Tarmo Rüütli

SERBIA: Željko Brkić, Aleksandar Kolarov, Milan Biševac, Nemanja Vidić, Branislav Ivanović, Zoran Tošić, Marko Pantelić, Nenad Milijaš, Milan Jovanović (74 Nikola Žigić), Radosav Petrović, Miloš Ninković (14 Veseljko Trivunović). Trainer: Vladimir Petrović

Goals: Marko Pantelić (38), Konstantin Vassiljev (84)

NORTHERN IRELAND v SLOVENIA 0-0

Windsor Park, Belfast 29.03.2011

Referee: Björn Kuipers (HOL) Attendance: 14,200

NORTHERN IRELAND: Lee Camp, Craig Cathcart, Jonny Evans, Gareth McAuley, Stephen Craigan, Chris Baird, Corry Evans (90+1 Liam Boyce), Sammy Clingan, Warren Feeney (82 Pat McCourt), Chris Brunt, Grant McCann (72 Joan McQuoid). Trainer: Nigel Worthington

SLOVENIA: Samir Handanovič, Mišo Brečko, Marko Šuler, Robert Koren, Valter Birsa, Milivoje Novakovič (84 Zlatko Dedič), Bojan Jokić, Armin Bačinović (90 Goran Šukalo), Andraž Kirm, Josip Iličić (29 Zlatan Ljubijankič), Matej Mavrič. Trainer: Matjaž Kek

FAROE ISLANDS v SLOVENIA 0-2 (0-1)

Svangaskard Stadion, Toftir 03.06.2011

Referee: Oliver Drachta (AUS) Attendance: 974

FAROE ISLANDS: Jákup Mikkelsen, Jónas Tór Næs (81 Súni Olsen), Einar Hansen, Jóhan Davidsen, Rógvi Baldvinsson, Daniel Udsen (45+2 Atli Danielsen), Fródi Benjaminsen, Pól Jóhannus Justinussen, Hjalgrím Elttør, Jóan Edmundsson, Christian Lamhauge Holst (75 Christian Mouritsen).

SLOVENIA: Samir Handanovič, Mišo Brečko, Marko Šuler, Boštjan Cesar, Robert Koren, Valter Birsa (47 Matej Mavrič), Milivoje Novakovič (55 Zlatan Ljubijankič), Bojan Jokić, Josip Iličić, Armin Bačinović, Tim Matavž (76 Andraž Kirm). Trainer: Matjaž Kek

Sent off: Šuler (25)

Goals: Tim Matavž (29), Rógvi Baldvinsson (47 own goal)

ITALY v ESTONIA 3-0 (2-0)

Alberto Braglia, Modena 03.06.2011

Referee: Alexandru Dan Tudor (ROM) Attendance: 19,434

ITALY: Gianluigi Buffon, Christian Maggio, Giorgio Chiellini, Federico Balzaretti, Claudio Marchisio, Antonio Cassano (65 Giampaolo Pazzini), Alberto Aquilani (24 Antonio Nocerino), Andrea Ranocchia, Riccardo Montolivo, Andrea Pirlo, Giuseppe Rossi (79 Sebastian Giovinco). Trainer: Cesare Prandelli

ESTONIA: Sergei Pareiko, Taijo Teniste (58 Kaimar Saag), Taavi Rähn, Raio Piiroja, Dmitri Kruglov, Sander Puri, Tarmo Kink (79 Gert Kams), Sergei Zenjov (58 Jarmo Ahjupera), Martin Vunk, Ragnar Klavan, Enar Jääger. Trainer: Tarmo Rüütli

Goals: Giuseppe Rossi (21), Antonio Cassano (39), Giampaolo Pazzini (68)

FAROE ISLANDS v ESTONIA 2-0 (1-0)

Svangaskard Stadion, Toftir 07.06.2011

Referee: Antti Munukka (FIN) Attendance: 1,715

FAROE ISLANDS: Jákup Mikkelsen, Jónas Tór Næs, Einar Hansen, Atli Gregersen, Rógvi Baldvinsson, Atli Danielsen, Fródi Benjaminsen, Hjalgrim Elttør (90+1 Súni Olsen), Pól Jóhannus Justinussen, Aarnbjørn Hansen (69 Símun Samuelsen), Christian Lamhauge Holst (85 Christian Mouritsen). Trainer: Brian Kerr

ESTONIA: Sergei Pareiko, Taavi Rähn, Raio Piiroja, Dmitri Kruglov, Sander Puri, Tarmo Kink, Sergei Zenjov, Konstantin Vassiljev, Enar Jääger, Jarmo Ahjupera (66 Gert Kams), Kaimar Saag (82 Sergei Mošnikov). Trainer: Tarmo Rüütli

Sent off: Justinussen (89), Puri (57)

Goals: Fródi Benjaminsen (43 pen), Aarnbjørn Hansen (47)

NORTHERN IRELAND v FAROE ISLANDS 4-0 (1-0)

Windsor Park, Belfast 10.08.2011

Referee: Emir Alecković (BIH) Attendance: 13,183

NORTHERN IRELAND: Lee Camp, Chris Baird, Jonny Evans, Gareth McAuley (46 Craig Cathcart), Sammy Clingan, Corry Evans (59 Niall McGinn), Steven Davis, David Healy (83 Jamie Ward), Pat McCourt, Grant McCann, Aaron Hughes. Trainer: Nigel Worthington

FAROE ISLANDS: Jákup Mikkelsen, Jónas Tór Næs, Jóhan Davidsen, Rógvi Baldvinsson, Atli Gregersen, Daniel Udsen, Fródi Benjaminsen, Súni Olsen (75 Atli Danielsen), Christian Lamhauge Holst (68 Arnbjørn Hansen), Jóan Edmundsson, Hjalgrim Elttør (75 Christian Mouritsen). Trainer: Brian Kerr

Goals: Aaron Hughes (5), Steven Davis (66), Pat McCourt (71, 88)

NORTHERN IRELAND v SERBIA 0-1 (0-0)

Windsor Park, Belfast 02.09.2011

Referee: Thomas Einwaller (AUS) Attendance: 15,148

NORTHERN IRELAND: Lee Camp, Craig Cathcart, Jonny Evans, Gareth McAuley, Corry Evans (59 Niall McGinn), Chris Baird, Steven Davis, David Healy (84 Josh McQuoid), Chris Brunt, Grant McCann (71 Warren Feeney), Aaron Hughes. Trainer: Nigel Worthington

SERBIA: Bojan Jorgačević, Branislav Ivanović, Zoran Tošić (78 Adem Ljajić), Marko Pantelić, Dejan Stanković, Aleksandar Kolarov, Milan Jovanović, Miloš Ninković (74 Radosav Petrović), Neven Subotić, Zdravko Kuzmanović (90 Ljubomir Fejsa), Slobodan Rajković. Trainer: Vladimir Petrović

Goal: Marko Pantelić (67)

SLOVENIA v ESTONIA 1-2 (0-1)

ŠRC Stožice, Ljubljana 02.09.2011

Referee: Stephan Studer (SWI) Attendance: 15,480

SLOVENIA: Samir Handanovič, Mišo Brečko, Boštjan Cesar, Branko Ilič, Robert Koren, Valter Birsa, Milivoje Novakovič (56 Zlatan Ljubijankič), Bojan Jokić, Aleksandar Radosavljevič (56 Dare Vršič), Josip Iličić (81 Nejc Pečnik), Tim Matavž. Trainer: Matjaž Kek

ESTONIA: Sergei Pareiko, Taavi Rähn, Raio Piiroja (74 Andrei Stepanov), Dmitri Kruglov (69 Ats Purje), Aleksandr Dmitrijev, Sergei Zenjov (61 Jarmo Ahjupera), Martin Vunk, Konstantin Vassiljev, Ragnar Klavan, Enar Jääger, Taijo Teniste. Trainer: Tarmo Rüütli

Goals: Konstantin Vassiljev (29 pen), Tim Matavž (78), Ats Purje (81)

FAROE ISLANDS v ITALY 0-1 (0-1)

Tórsvøllur, Torshavn 02.09.2011

Referee: Tamás Bognar (HUN) Attendance: 5,654

FAROE ISLANDS: René Tórgard, Jónas Tór Næs, Johan Davidsen, Rógvi Baldvinsson, Atli Gregersen, Pól Jóhannus Justinussen (87 Símun Samuelsen), Fródi Benjaminsen, Súni Olsen (76 Atli Danielsen), Christian Lamhauge Holst (87 Christian Mouritsen), Jóan Edmundsson, Hjalgrim Elttør. Trainer: Brian Kerr

ITALY: Gianluigi Buffon, Christian Maggio, Giorgio Chiellini, Domenico Criscito, Daniele De Rossi, Thiago Motta (73 Alberto Aquilani), Antonio Cassano (85 Mario Balotelli), Andrea Ranocchia, Riccardo Montolivo, Andrea Pirlo, Giuseppe Rossi (59 Giampaolo Pazzini). Trainer: Cesare Prandelli

Goal: Antonio Cassano (11)

ITALY v SLOVENIA 1-0 (0-0)

Stadio Artemio Franchi, Firenze 06.09.2011

Referee: Svein Oddvar Moen (NOR) Attendance: 18,000

ITALY: Gianluigi Buffon, Giorgio Chiellini, Daniele De Rossi, Federico Balzaretti, Antonio Cassano (61 Giampaolo Pazzini), Thiago Motta (46 Claudio Marchisio), Andrea Ranocchia, Mattian Cassani, Riccardo Montolivo (76 Mario Balotelli), Andrea Pirlo, Giuseppe Rossi. Trainer: Cesare Prandelli

SLOVENIA: Samir Handanovič, Mišo Brečko, Marko Šuler, Boštjan Cesar, Robert Koren, Valter Birsa (56 Josip Iličić), Milivoje Novakovič, Bojan Jokić, Andraž Kirm (87 Zlatko Dedič), Aleksandar Radosavljević, Dare Vršič (75 Nejc Pečnik). Trainer: Matjaž Kek

Goal: Giampaolo Pazzini (85)

ESTONIA v NORTHERN IRELAND 4-1 (2-1)

Lilleküla Stadium, Tallinn 06.09.2011

Referee: Daniel Stålhammar (SWE) Attendance: 8,660

ESTONIA: Sergei Pareiko, Taavi Rähn, Raio Piiroja, Dmitri Kruglov, Sander Puri (63 Ats Purje), Tarmo Kink (88 Kaimar Saag), Martin Vunk, Konstantin Vassiljev, Ragnar Klavan, Enar Jääger, Jarmo Ahjupera (53 Sergei Zenjov). Trainer: Tarmo Rüütli

NORTHERN IRELAND: Lee Camp, Chris Baird, Craig Cathcart, Gareth McAuley, Sammy Clingan, Steven Davis, David Healy (65 Josh McQuoid), Chris Brunt, Grant McCann, Niall McGinn (65 Warren Feeney), Aaron Hughes. Trainer: Nigel Worthington

Goals: Martin Vunk (28), Tarmo Kink (32), Raio Piiroja (40 own goal), Sergei Zenjov (60), Kaimar Saag (90+3)

SERBIA v ITALY 1-1 (1-1)

Stadion FK Crvena zvezda, Beograd 07.10.2011

Referee: Pedro Proença (POR) Attendance: 35,000

SERBIA: Bojan Jorgačević, Branislav Ivanović, Zoran Tošić, Marko Pantelić, Dejan Stanković (87 Milan Jovanović), Aleksandar Kolarov, Ljubomir Fejsa (46 Radosav Petrović), Miloš Krasić (76 Nikola Žigić), Miloš Ninković, Neven Subotić, Slobodan Rajković. Trainer: Vladimir Petrović

ITALY: Gianluigi Buffon, Christian Maggio, Giorgio Chiellini, Daniele De Rossi, Claudio Marchisio (70 Antonio Nocerino), Antonio Cassano (67 Sebastian Giovinco), Andrea Barzagli, Riccardo Montolivo (82 Alberto Aquilani), Leonardo Bonucci, Andrea Pirlo, Giuseppe Rossi. Trainer: Cesare Prandelli

Goals: Claudio Marchisio (2), Branislav Ivanović (26)

SERBIA v FAROE ISLANDS 3-1 (2-1)

FK Partizan, Beograd 06.09.2011

Referee: Arman Amirkhanyan (ARM) Attendance: 7,500

SERBIA: Bojan Jorgačević, Milan Biševac (45 Nenad Tomović), Branislav Ivanović, Zoran Tošić, Marko Pantelić, Dejan Stanković (46 Radosav Petrović), Aleksandar Kolarov, Milan Jovanović, Miloš Ninković (82 Ljubomir Fejsa), Neven Subotić, Zdravko Kuzmanović. Trainer: Vladimir Petrović

FAROES ISLANDS: René Tórgard, Jónas Tór Næs, Johan Davidsen, Rógvi Baldvinsson, Atli Gregersen, Atli Danielsen, Fródi Benjaminsen, Símun Samuelsen (73 Pól Jóhannus Justinussen), Christian Lamhauge Holst (78 Christian Mouritsen), Jóan Edmundsson, Hjalgrím Elttør.

Goals: Milan Jovanović (6), Zoran Tošić (22), Fródi Benjaminsen (37), Zdravko Kuzmanović (69)

NORTHERN IRELAND v ESTONIA 1-2 (1-0)

Windsor Park, Belfast 07.10.2011

Referee: Manuel Gräfe (GER) Attendance: 12,604

NORTHERN IRELAND: Lee Camp, Lee Hodson, Craig Cathcart, Gareth McAuley, Chris Baird, Sammy Clingan (32 Corry Evans), Pat McCourt, Steven Davis, Kyle Lafferty (69 Warren Feeney), Grant McCann (83 David Healy), Chris Brunt. Trainer: Nigel Worthington

ESTONIA: Sergei Pareiko, Raio Piiroja, Dmitri Kruglov, Aleksandr Dmitrijev, Sander Puri (57 Ats Purje), Tarmo Kink (65 Konstantin Vassiljev), Martin Vunk, Ragnar Klavan, Enar Jääger, Jarmo Ahjupera (46 Sergei Zenjov), Andrei Stepanov. Trainer: Tarmo Rüütli

Goals: Steven Davis (22), Konstantin Vassiljev (77 pen, 84)

SLOVENIA v SERBIA 1-0 (1-0)

Stadion Ljudski vrt, Maribor 11.10.2011

Referee: Frank De Bleeckere (BEL) Attendance: 9,848

SLOVENIA: Samir Handanovič, Mišo Brečko (65 Branko Ilič), Marko Šuler, Boštjan Cesar, Zlatan Ljubijankič, Bojan Jokić, Andraž Kirm, Aleksandar Radosavljevič, Armin Bačinović (69 René Krhin), Dare Vršič (76 Valter Birsa), Tim Matavž. Trainer: Matjaž Kek

SERBIA: Bojan Jorgačević, Nemanja Vidić, Branislav Ivanović, Zoran Tošić, Dejan Stanković, Aleksandar Kolarov, Milan Jovanović (57 Miloš Krasić), Radoslav Petrović (51 Marko Pantelić), Miloš Ninković (72 Nenad Milijaš), Neven Subotić, Dragan Mrdja. Trainer: Vladimir Petrović

Goal: Dare Vršič (45+1)

ITALY v NORTHERN IRELAND 3-0 (1-0)

Adriatico, Pescara 11.10.2011

Referee: Antonio Mateu Lahoz (SPA) Attendance: 19,480

ITALY: Gianluigi Buffon (76 Morgan De Sanctis), Giorgio Chiellini, Daniele De Rossi, Antonio Cassano (56 Pablo Osvaldo), Federico Balzaretti, Alberto Aquilani (68 Antonio Nocerino), Andrea Barzagli, Mattian Cassani, Riccardo Montolivo, Sebastian Giovinco, Andrea Pirlo.
Trainer: Cesare Prandelli

NORTHERN IRELAND: Maik Taylor, Lee Hodson, Ryan McGivern, Gareth McAuley, Oliver Norwood (73 Connor McLaughlin), Chris Baird, Andrew Little, Steven Davis, David Healy (65 Warren Feeney), Corry Evans, Gorman (77 Niall McGinn). Trainer: Nigel Worthington

Goals: Antonio Cassano (21, 53), Gareth McAuley (74 own goal)

	P	W	D	L	F	A	Pts
Italy	10	8	2	0	20	2	26
Estonia	10	5	1	4	15	14	16
Serbia	10	4	3	3	13	12	15
Slovenia	10	4	2	4	11	7	14
North. Ireland	10	2	3	5	9	13	9
Faroe Islands	10	1	1	8	6	26	4

GROUP D

ROMANIA v ALBANIA 1-1 (0-0)

Ceahlăul, Piatra Neamţ 03.09.2010

Referee: Robert Schörgenhofer (AUS) Attendance: 13,400

ROMANIA: Bogdan Lobonţ, Cosmin Contra (56 Gabriel Mureşan), Gabriel Tamaş, Mirel Rădoi (Cap), Răzvan Raţ, Gabriel Torje, Răzvan Cociş (77 Ovidiu Herea), George Florescu, Ciprian Deac, Ciprian Marica, Daniel Niculae (64 Bogdan Stancu). Trainer: Răzvan Lucescu

ALBANIA: Arian Beqaj, Armend Dallku, Andi Lila, Debatik Curri, Kristi Vangjeli, Klodian Duro (82 Gjergj Muzaka), Lorik Cana, Ervin Bulku, Ansi Agolli, Ervin Skela (Cap) (79 Gilman Lika), Erjon Bogdani (57 Hamdi Salihi). Trainer: Josip Kuže

Goals: Bogdan Stancu (80), Gjergj Muzaka (87)

LUXEMBOURG v BOSNIA HERZEGOVINA 0-3 (0-3)

Josy Barthel, Luxembourg 03.09.2010

Referee: Veaceslav Banari (MOL) Attendance: 7,327

LUXEMBOURG: Jonathan Joubert, Kim Kintziger, Mathias Jänisch, Eric Hoffmann, Tom Schnell, René Peters, Stefano Bensi (46 Joël Kitenge), Gilles Bettmer (86 Tom Laterza), Dan Collette (76 Daniel Da Mota), Mario Mutsch, Lars Gerson.
Trainer: Michel Ney

BOSNIA HERZEGOVINA: Kenan Hasagić, Emir Spahić, Elvir Rahimić (68 Sanel Jahić), Miralem Pjanić (78 Ermin Zec), Zvjezdan Misimović, Edin Džeko, Safet Nadarević, Vedad Ibišević, Senad Lulić, Senijad Ibričić (73 Haris Medunjanin), Mensur Mujdža. Trainer: Safet Sušić

Goals: Senijad Ibričić (6), Miralem Pjanić (12), Edin Džeko (16)

FRANCE v BELARUS 0-1 (0-0)

Stade de France, Paris 03.09.2010

Referee: William Collum (SCO) Attendance: 76,395

FRANCE: Hugo Lloris, Bacary Sagna, Adil Rami, Philippe Mexès, Loïc Rémy (34 Mathieu Valbuena), Jérémy Ménez (69 Louis Saha, 80 Kevin Garneiro), Guillaume Hoarau, Florent Malouda, Yann M'Vila, Abou Diaby, Gaël Clichy.
Trainer: Laurent Blanc

BELARUS: Yuri Zhevnov, Aleksandr Kulchiy, Aleksandr Martynovich, Aleksandr Yurevich, Yan Tigorev, Sergei Omelyanchuk, Vyacheslav Hleb (89 Anton Putilo), Aleksandr Hleb, Vitali Rodionov (85 Sergei Kornilenko), Vitali Kutuzov (75 Sergei Kislyak), Igor Shitov. Trainer: Bernd Stange

Goal: Sergei Kislyak (86)

BELARUS v ROMANIA 0-0

Dinamo, Minsk 07.09.2010

Referee: Pavel Kralovec (CZE) Attendance: 26,354

BELARUS: Yuri Zhevnov, Igor Shitov, Sergei Omelyanchuk, Aleksandr Martynovich, Aleksandr Yurevich, Vyacheslav Hleb, Sergei Kornilenko (76 Vitali Rodionov), Aleksandr Kulchiy, Aleksandr Hleb (73 Anton Putilo), Vitali Kutuzov (87 Sergei Krivets), Sergei Kislyak. Trainer: Bernd Stange

ROMANIA: Costel Pantilimon, Vasile Maftei, Gabriel Tamaş, Cristian Chivu, Răzvan Raţ, Mirel Rădoi, George Florescu, Gabriel Torje (46 Răzvan Cociş), Bogdan Stancu (73 Daniel Niculae), Ciprian Deac (83 Ciprian Marica), Marius Bilaşco. Trainer: Răzvan Lucescu

LUXEMBOURG v BELARUS 0-0

Josy Barthel, Luxembourg 08.10.2010

Referee: Aleksandar Stavrev (MKD) Attendance: 1,857

LUXEMBOURG: Jonathan Joubert, Kim Kintziger, Guy Blaise, Eric Hoffmann, Tom Schnell, René Peters, Tom Laterza, Gilles Bettmer (62 Lars Gerson), Ben Payal (77 Michel Kettenmeyer), Charles Leweck, Aurélien Joachim (66 Daniel Da Mota). Trainer: Luc Holtz

BELARUS: Yuri Zhevnov, Aleksandr Kulchiy, Aleksandr Martynovich, Timofei Kalachev, Aleksandr Yurevich (87 Dmitri Molosh), Yan Tigorev (67 Anton Putilo), Sergei Omelyanchuk, Sergei Kornilenko, Vyacheslav Hleb (67 Vitali Rodionov), Sergei Kislyak, Igor Shitov.
Trainer: Bernd Stange

Sent off: Kornilenko (69)

ALBANIA v LUXEMBOURG 1-0 (1-0)

Stadiumi Kombëtar Qemal Stafa, Tirana 07.09.2010

Referee: Richard Trutz (SVK) Attendance: 10,000

ALBANIA: Arjan Beqaj, Armend Dallku, Lorik Cana, Debatik Curri, Ansi Agolli, Ervin Bulku, Klodian Duro (90+1 Andi Lila), Ervin Skela, Hamdi Salihi, Gjergj Muzaka (80 Jahmir Hyka), Erjon Bogdani. Trainer: Josip Kuže

LUXEMBOURG: Jonathan Joubert, Kim Kintziger, Guy Blaise, Eric Hoffmann, Tom Schnell, René Peters, Tom Laterza (81 Massimo Martino), Gilles Bettmer (90+1 Dan Collette), Daniel Da Mota, Ben Payal, Mario Mutsch.
Trainer: Luc Holtz

Goal: Hamdi Salihi (37)

ALBANIA v BOSNIA HERZEGOVINA 1-1 (1-1)

Stadiumi Kombëtar Qemal Stafa, Tirana 08.10.2010

Referee: Kristinn Jakobsson (ISL) Attendance: 14,220

ALBANIA: Arjan Beqaj, Andi Lila, Kristi Vangjeli, Armend Dallku, Lorik Cana, Ansi Agolli, Ervin Bulku, Klodian Duro, Hamdi Salihi (85 Jahmir Hyka), Gjergj Muzaka (65 Gilman Lika), Erjon Bogdani (46 Ervin Skela).
Trainer: Džemal Mustedanagić

BOSNIA HERZEGOVINA: Kenan Hasagić (46 Begović), Emir Spahić, Adnan Mravac (46 Pandža), Elvir Rahimić, Miralem Pjanić, Zvjezdan Misimović, Edin Džeko (89 Ibričić), Vedad Ibišević, Haris Medunjanin, Senad Lulić, Mensur Mujdža. Trainer: Safet Sušić

Goals: Vedad Ibišević (21), Klodian Duro (45+2)

BOSNIA HERZEGOVINA v FRANCE 0-2 (0-0)

Asim Ferhatović Hase Stadion, Sarajevo 07.09.2010

Referee: Felix Brych (GER) Attendance: 28,000

BOSNIA HERZEGOVINA: Kenan Hasagić, Emir Spahić, Elvir Rahimić (74 Ermin Zec), Miralem Pjanić, Zvjezdan Misimović, Edin Džeko, Safet Nadarević, Vedad Ibišević (74 Sanel Jahić), Senad Lulić, Senijad Ibričić, Mensur Mujdža.
Trainer: Safet Sušić

FRANCE: Hugo Lloris, Bacary Sagna, Adil Rami, Philippe Mexès, Karim Benzema, Florent Malouda (80 Blaise Matuidi), Yann M'Vila, Alou Diarra, Abou Diaby, Mathieu Valbuena, Gaël Clichy. Trainer: Laurent Blanc

Goals: Karim Benzema (72), Florent Malouda (78)

FRANCE v ROMANIA 2-0 (0-0)

Stade de France, Saint-Denis 09.10.2010

Referee: Pedro Proença (POR) Attendance: 72,299

FRANCE: Hugo Lloris, Anthony Réveillère, Adil Rami, Philippe Mexès, Gaël Clichy, Yann M'Vila, Alou Diarra, Damir Nasri (74 Yoann Gourcuff), Mathieu Valbuena (68 Loïc Rémy), Karim Benzema (86 Dimitri Payet), Florent Malouda.
Trainer: Laurent Blanc

ROMANIA: Costel Pantilimon, Cristian Săpunaru, Gabriel Tamaş, Cristian Chivu (Cap), Răzvan Raţ, Răzvan Cociş (87 Mihai Roman), Mirel Rădoi, George Florescu, Ianis Zicu (46 Ciprian Deac), Bogdan Stancu, Daniel Niculae (63 Ciprian Marica). Trainer: Răzvan Lucescu

Goals: Loïc Rémy (83), Yoann Gourcuff (93)

BELARUS v ALBANIA 2-0 (1-0)

Dinamo Stadion, Minsk 12.10.2010

Referee: Peter Rasmussen (DEN) Attendance: 7,000

BELARUS: Yuri Zhevnov, Aleksandr Kulchiy (75 Sergei Krivets), Aleksandr Martynovich, Timofei Kalachev, Yan Tigorev, Sergei Omelyanchuk, Anton Putilo (83 Vyacheslav Hleb), Sergei Kislyak, Igor Shitov, Vitali Rodionov, Dmitri Molosh (87 Aleksandr Yurevich). Trainer: Bernd Stange

ALBANIA: Arjan Beqaj, Andi Lila, Kristi Vangjeli, Armend Dallku, Ansi Agolli, Ervin Bulku (59 Gjergj Muzaka), Klodian Duro, Ervin Skela (81 Edmond Kapllani), Admir Teli, Gilman Lika (76 Elis Bakaj), Hamdi Salihi.
Trainer: Džemal Mustedanagić

Goals: Vitali Rodionov (10), Krivets (77)

BOSNIA-HERZEGOVINA v ROMANIA 2-1 (0-1)

Bilino Polje, Zenica. 26.03.2011

Referee: Fernando Teixeira Vitienes (SPA) Att: 13,000

BOSNIA HERZEGOVINA: Kenan Hasagić, Mensur Mujdža, Senad Lulić, Emir Spahić, Adnan Mravac, Haris Medunjanin (71 Darko Maletic), Miralem Pjanić, Elvir Rahimić, Zvjezdan Misimović (81 Senijad Ibričić), Vedad Ibišević (76 Zlatan Muslimović), Edin Džeko. Trainer: Safet Susić

ROMANIA: Costel Pantilimon, Cornel Râpă, Gabriel Tamaş, Dorin Goian, Răzvan Raţ, Gabriel Torje (71 Răzvan Cociş), George Florescu (76 Adrian Ropotan), Dan Alexa, Ciprian Deac (86 Ianis Zicu), Adrian Mutu, Ciprian Marica.
Trainer: Răzvan Lucescu

Goals: Ciprian Marica (29), Vedad Ibišević (63), Edin Džeko (83)

FRANCE v LUXEMBOURG 2-0 (1-0)

Stade Municipal Saint-Symphorien, Metz 12.10.2010

Referee: Matej Jug (SVN) Attendance: 24,710

FRANCE: Hugo Lloris, Anthony Réveillère, Adil Rami, Philippe Mexès, Yoann Gourcuff, Guillaume Hoarau (73 Loïc Rémy), Karim Benzema (63 Dimitri Payet), Florent Malouda (63 Samir Nasri), Alou Diarra, Abou Diaby, Gaël Clichy.
Trainer: Laurent Blanc

LUXEMBOURG: Jonathan Joubert, Guy Blaise, Eric Hoffmann, Tom Schnell, René Peters, Gilles Bettmer (84 Daniel Da Mota), Ben Payal, Charles Leweck, Aurélien Joachim (53 Joël Kitenge), Tom Laterza (69 Jeff Strasser), Mario Mutsch. Trainer: Luc Holtz

Sent off: Peters (54)

Goals: Karim Benzema (22), Yoann Gourcuff (76)

ALBANIA v BELARUS 1-0 (0-0)

Stadiumi Kombëtar Qemal Stafa, Tirana 26.03.2011

Referee: Markus Strömbergsson (SWE) Attendance: 13,826

ALBANIA: Samir Ujkani, Andi Lila, Kristi Vangjeli, Lorik Cana, Ansi Agolli, Ervin Bulku, Ervin Skela (81 Klodian Duro), Altin Lala, Admir Teli, Hamdi Salihi (90+3 Gjergj Muzaka), Erjon Bogdani (75 Elis Bakaj). Trainer: Josip Kuže

BELARUS: Sergei Veremko, Aleksandr Kulchiy (62 Aleksandr Bychenok), Aleksandr Martynovich, Igor Shitov, Dmitri Molosh, Yan Tigorev, Sergei Omelyanchuk, Vyacheslav Hleb, Sergei Krivets (46 Leonid Kovel), Anton Putilo (82 Pavel Sitko), Sergei Kislyak. Trainer: Bernd Stange

Goal: Hamdi Salihi (62)

LUXEMBOURG v FRANCE 0-2 (0-1)

Josy Barthel, Luxembourg 25.03.2011

Referee: Tom Harald Hagen (NOR) Attendance: 8,052

LUXEMBOURG: Jonathan Joubert, Guy Blaise, Eric Hoffmann, Tom Schnell, Charles Leweck (90 Jacques Plein), Gilles Bettmer, Ben Payal, Aurélien Joachim, Tom Laterza (54 Massimo Martino), Mario Mutsch, Lars Gerson (71 Daniel Da Mota). Trainer: Luc Holtz

FRANCE: Hugo Lloris, Bacary Sagna, Patrice Evra, Adil Rami, Philippe Mexès, Franck Ribéry, Yoann Gourcuff, Karim Benzema, Samir Nasri, Florent Malouda, Yann M'Vila.
Trainer: Laurent Blanc

Goals: Philippe Mexès (28), Yoann Gourcuff (72)

ROMANIA v LUXEMBOURG 3-1 (1-1)

Ceahlăul, Piatra-Neamţ 29.03.2011,

Referee: Hüseyin Göçek (TUR) Attendance: 13,500

ROMANIA: Ciprian Tătăruşanu, Cristian Săpunaru, Gabriel Tamaş (65 Dorin Goian), Florin Gardoş, Răzvan Raţ, Gabriel Mureşan, Adrian Ropotan, Bogdan Stancu (46 Gabriel Torje), Adrian Mutu (84 Marius Alexe), Ianis Zicu, Ciprian Marica.
Trainer: Răzvan Lucescu

LUXEMBOURG: Jonathan Joubert, Tom Schnell (90 Massimo Martino), Guy Blaise, Eric Hoffmann, Mario Mutsch, Ben Payal, Lars Gerson (60 Daniel Da Mota), René Peters, Gilles Bettmer (81 Tom Laterza), Aurélien Joachim, Charles Leweck. Trainer: Luc Holtz.

Goals: Lars Gerson (22), Adrian Mutu (24, 68), Ianis Zicu (78)

ROMANIA v BOSNIA HERZEGOVINA 3-0 (2-0)

Valentin Stănescu, Bucureşti 03.06.2011

Referee: Jonas Eriksson (SWE) Attendance: 8,200

ROMANIA: Ciprian Tătăruşanu, Cristian Săpunaru, Gabriel Tamaş, Paul Papp, Răzvan Raţ, Gabriel Torje, Gabriel Mureşan, Alexandru Bourceanu, Lucian Sânmărtean (63 Cristian Tănase), Adrian Mutu (83 Romeo Surdu), Ciprian Marica (87 Marius Alexe). Trainer: Răzvan Lucescu

BOSNIA HERZEGOVINA: Kenan Hasagić, Mensur Mensur Mujdža, Adnan Mravac, Emir Spahić, Senad Lulić, Elvir Rahimić, Haris Medunjanin (46 Vedad Ibišević), Miralem Pjanić, Zvjezdan Misimović, Senjad Ibričić (64 Semir Stilić), Edin Džeko (64 Zlatan Muslimović). Trainer: Safet Sušić

Goals: Adrian Mutu (37), Ciprian Marica (41, 55)

BOSNIA HERZEGOVINA v ALBANIA 2-0 (0-0)

Bilino Polje, Zenica 07.06.2011

Referee: Kevin Blom (HOL) Attendance: 9,000

BOSNIA HERZEGOVINA: Kenan Hasagić, Boris Pandža, Emir Spahić, Elvir Rahimić, Miralem Pjanić (77 Muhamed Bešić), Zvjezdan Misimović, Edin Džeko, Mensur Mujdža (73 Darko Maletić), Vedad Ibišević (61 Zlatan Muslimović), Senad Lulić, Haris Medunjanin. Trainer: Safet Sušić

ALBANIA: Samir Ujkani, Kristi Vangjeli, Armend Dallku, Lorik Cana, Debatik Curri, Ansi Agolli (60 Andi Lila), Ervin Bulku, Ervin Skela, Altin Lala (73 Gjergj Muzaka), Hamdi Salihi, Erjon Bogdani (46 Klodian Duro).
Trainer: Josip Kuže

Sent off: Lila (87)

Goals: Haris Medunjanin (67), Darko Maletić (90+1)

BELARUS v FRANCE 1-1 (1-1)

Dinamo Stadion, Minsk 03.06.2011

Referee: David Fernández Borbalán (SPA) Att: 26,500

BELARUS: Sergei Veremko, Aleksandr Martynovich, Timofei Kalachev (90 Vyacheslav Hleb), Vitali Trubilo, Yan Tigorev, Sergei Omelyanchuk, Andrei Voronkov, Anton Putilo (86 Sergei Kislyak), Maksim Bordachev, Dmitri Verkhovtsov, Igor Shitov. Trainer: Bernd Stange

FRANCE: Hugo Lloris, Bacary Sagna, Adil Rami, Franck Ribéry, Karim Benzema, Samir Nasri, Mamadou Sakho, Florent Malouda, Alou Diarra, Abou Diaby (73 Loïc Rémy), Éric Abidal. Trainer: Laurent Blanc

Goals: Éric Abidal (20 own goal), Florent Malouda (22)

BELARUS v BOSNIA HERZEGOVINA 0-2 (0-2)

Dinamo Stadion, Minsk 02.09.2011

Referee: Viktor Kassai (HUN) Attendance: 28,500

BELARUS: Yuri Zhevnov, Aleksandr Kulchiy, Aleksandr Martynovich, Timofei Kalachev, Vitali Trubilo, Sergei Kornilenko (63 Andrei Voronkov), Maksim Zhavnerchik (63 Pavel Sitko), Anton Putilo, Sergei Kislyak, Dmitri Verkhovtsov, Igor Shitov. Trainer: Bernd Stange

BOSNIA HERZEGOVINA: Kenan Hasagić, Boris Pandža, Saša Papac, Emir Spahić, Elvir Rahimić, Miralem Pjanić, Edin Džeko (80 Zvjezdan Misimović), Adnan Zahirović, Dejad Salihović (72 Darko Maletić), Senad Lulić, Haris Medunjanin (88 Zlatan Muslimović). Trainer: Safet Sušić

Goals: Sejad Salihović (22 pen), Medunjanin (24)

BELARUS v LUXEMBOURG 2-0 (0-0)

Dinamo Stadion, Minsk 07.06.2011

Referee: Anar Salmanov (AZE) Attendance: 9,500

BELARUS: Yuri Zhevnov, Aleksandr Kulchiy (87 Sergei Kislyak), Timofei Kalachev, Vitali Trubilo (62 Vyacheslav Hleb), Yan Tigorev, Sergei Omelyanchuk, Andrei Voronkov (46 Sergei Kornilenko), Anton Putilo, Maksim Bordachev, Dmitri Verkhovtsov, Igor Shitov. Trainer: Bernd Stange

LUXEMBOURG: Jonathan Joubert, Massimo Martino, Guy Blaise, Eric Hoffmann, Tom Schnell, René Peters, Charles Leweck (84 Dan Collette), Daniel Da Mota (77 Tom Laterza), Ben Payal, Kevin Malget (60 Joël Kitenge), Lars Gerson. Trainer: Luc Holtz

Goals: Sergei Kornilenko (48 pen), Anton Putilo (73)

LUXEMBOURG v ROMANIA 0-2 (0-2)

Josy Barthel, Luxembourg 02.09.2011

Referee: Serghei Karasev (RUS) Attendance: 2,812

LUXEMBOURG: Jonathan Joubert, Tom Schnell, Guy Blaise, Eric Hoffman (76 Ante Bukvici), Mario Mutsch, Aurélien Joachim (46 Joël Kitenge), Lars Gerson, Ben Payal, Gilles Bettmer, Charles Leweck, Daniel Da Mota (61 Mathias Janisch). Trainer: Luc Holtz.

ROMANIA: Ciprian Tătăruşanu, Alexandru Măţel, George Galamaz (62 Vlad Chiricheş), Dorin Goian, Răzvan Raţ, Răzvan Cociş, Costin Lazăr, Cristian Tănase, Gabriel Torje (76 Bănel Nicoliţă), Ciprian Marica (87 Bogdan Stancu), Gheorghe Bucur. Trainer: Victor Piţurcă

Goals: Gabriel Torje (34, 45)

ALBANIA v FRANCE 1-2 (0-2)

Stadiumi Kombëtar Qemal Stafa, Tirana 02.09.2011

Referee: Aleksei Nikolaev (RUS) Attendance: 15,600

ALBANIA: Samir Ujkani, Kristi Vangjeli, Armend Dallku, Lorik Cana, Debatik Curri (24 Altin Lala), Ansi Agolli, Ervin Bulku (70 Elis Bakaj), Ervin Skela (46 Jahmir Hyka), Admir Teli, Hamdi Salihi, Erjon Bogdani. Trainer: Josip Kuže

FRANCE: Hugo Lloris, Patrice Evra, Kaboul, Franck Ribéry, Karim Benzema, Samir Nasri, Anthony Réveillère, Florent Malouda (82 Marvin Martin), Yann M'Vila, Alou Diarra, Éric Abidal. Trainer: Laurent Blanc

Goals: Karim Benzema (11), Yann M'Vila (18), Erjon Bogdani (46)

ROMANIA v FRANCE 0-0

Național Arena, București 06.09.2011

Referee: Howard Webb (ENG) Attendance: 49,137

ROMANIA: Ciprian Tătărușanu, Srdian Luchin, Vlad Chiricheș, Dorin Goian, Răzvan Raț, Alexandru Bourceanu, Bănel Nicoliță, Răzvan Cociș, Costin Lazăr (43 Bogdan Stancu), Cristian Tănase, Ciprian Marica (90 Gheorghe Bucur). Trainer: Victor Pițurcă

FRANCE: Hugo Lloris, Bacary Sagna, Adil Rami, Éric Abidal, Patrice Evra, Yohan Cabaye (75 Samir Nasri), Yann M'Vila, Mathieu Mathieu Valbuena (71 Loic Rémy), Marvin Martin, Franck Ribéry, Karim Benzema. Trainer: Laurent Blanc

LUXEMBOURG v ALBANIA 2-1 (1-0)

Josy Barthel, Luxembourg 06.09.2011

Referee: Petteri Kari (FIN) Attendance: 2,132

LUXEMBOURG: Jonathan Joubert, Ante Bukvic, Guy Blaise, Tom Schnell, Charles Leweck (68 Aurélien Joachim), Gilles Bettmer, Daniel Da Mota (70 Stefano Bensi), Ben Payal (88 Joël Pedro), Mario Mutsch, Lars Gerson, Mathias Jänisch. Trainer: Luc Holtz

ALBANIA: Samir Ujkani, Franc Veliu (62 Ervin Bulku), Kristi Vangjeli, Ansi Agolli, Edmond Kapllani (46 Elis Bakaj), Klodian Duro (46 Gjergj Muzaka), Ervin Skela, Altin Lala, Admir Teli, Hamdi Salihi, Erjon Bogdani. Trainer: Josip Kuže

Sent off: Agolli (53), Bogdani (85)

Goals: Gilles Bettmer (27), Erjon Bogdani (64), Joachim (78)

BOSNIA HERZEGOVINA v LUXEMBOURG 5-0 (4-0)

Bilino Polje, Zenica 07.10.2011

Referee: Simon Lee Evans (WAL) Attendance: 12,000

BOSNIA HERZEGOVINA: Asmir Begović, Saša Papac, Emir Spahić, Elvir Rahimić (59 Adnan Zahirović), Miralem Pjanić, Zvjezdan Misimović, Edin Džeko, Mensur Mujdža, Vedad Ibišević, Senad Lulić (66 Darko Maletić), Haris Medunjanin (64 Senijad Ibričić). Trainer: Safet Sušić

LUXEMBOURG: Jonathan Joubert, Guy Blaise, Ante Bukvic, Tom Schnell, Charles Leweck, Gilles Bettmer, Daniel Da Mota (44 Aurélien Joachim), Ben Payal, Tom Laterza (83 Mathias Jänisch), Mario Mutsch, Lars Gerson. Trainer: Luc Holtz

Goals: Edin Džeko (12), Zvjezdan Misimović (15, 22 pen), Miralem Pjanić (36), Medunjanin (51)

BOSNIA HERZEGOVINA v BELARUS 1-0 (0-0)

Bilino Polje, Zenica 06.09.2011

Referee: Martin Atkinson (ENG) Attendance: 12,000

BOSNIA HERZEGOVINA: Asmir Begović, Boris Pandža (46 Zvjezdan Misimović), Saša Papac, Elvir Rahimić, Edin Džeko, Mensur Mujdža, Adnan Zahirović, Sejad Salihović (19 Semir Štilić), Senad Lulić, Senijad Ibričić (64 Ermin Zec), Haris Medunjanin. Trainer: Safet Sušić

BELARUS: Yuri Zhevnov, Aleksandr Kulchiy, Aleksandr Martynovich, Timofei Kalachev, Vitali Trubilo, Sergei Kornilenko (72 Stanislav Dragun), Anton Putilo, Sergei Kislyak, Pavel Sitko (77 Andrei Voronkov), Dmitri Verkhovtsov, Igor Shitov. Trainer: Bernd Stange

Sent off: Kalachev (34), Martynovich (85)

Goal: Zvjezdan Misimović (87)

ROMANIA v BELARUS 2-2 (1-1)

Arena Națională, București 07.10.2011

Referee: Alan Kelly (IRE) Attendance: 29,486

ROMANIA: Costel Pantilimon, Alexandru Mățel, Gabriel Tamaș, Cosmin Moți, Răzvan Raț (69 Răzvan Cociș), Costin Lazăr, Alexandru Bourceanu, Lucian Sânmărtean (29 Adrian Cristea), Gabriel Torje, Ciprian Marica (80 Bogdan Stancu), Adrian Mutu. Trainer: Victor Pițurcă

BELARUS: Yuri Zhevnov, Sergei Omelyanchuk, Yegor Filipenko (19 Pavel Plaskonny), Dmitri Verkhovtsov, Maksim Bordachev (89 Oleg Veretilo), Aleksandr Kulchiy, Stanislav Dragun, Sergei Krivets (60 Filipp Rudik), Sergei Kisliak, Pavel Nekhaychik, Sergei Kornilenko. Trainer: Bernd Stange

Goals: Adrian Mutu (19, 51 pen), Serghei Kornilenko (45), Stanislav Dragun (82)

FRANCE v ALBANIA 3-0 (2-0)

Stade de France, Paris 07.10.2011

Referee: Michael Koukoulakis (GRE) Attendance: 65,239

FRANCE: Hugo Lloris, Mathieu Debuchy, Patrice Evra (46 Anthony Réveillère), Adil Rami, Younés Kaboul, Yohan Cabaye (47 Marvin Martin), Bafétimi Gomis (80 Djibril Cissé), Samir Nasri, Florent Malouda, Yann M'Vila, Loïc Rémy.
Trainer: Laurent Blanc

ALBANIA: Samir Ujkani, Andi Lila, Kristi Vangjeli, Armend Dallku, Lorik Cana, Klodian Duro, Gilman Lika (81 Sabien Lilaj), Hamdi Salihi, Gjergj Muzaka (74 Ahmed Januzi), Jahmir Hyka (63 Elis Bakaj), Odise Roshi.
Trainer: Josip Kuže

Goals: Florent Malouda (11), Loïc Rémy (38), Anthony Réveillère (67)

	P	W	D	L	F	A	Pts
France	10	6	3	1	15	4	21
Bosnia Herzeg.	10	6	2	2	17	8	20
Romania	10	3	5	2	13	9	14
Belarus	10	3	4	3	8	7	13
Albania	10	2	3	5	7	14	9
Luxembourg	10	1	1	8	3	21	4

ALBANIA v ROMANIA 1-1 (1-0)

Qemal Stafa, Tirana. 11.10.2011

Referee: Gediminas Mažeika (LIT) Attendance: 3,000

ALBANIA: Samir Ujkani, Andi Lila, Lorik Cana, Admir Teli, Armend Dallku, Elis Bakaj (67 Jahmir Hyka), Hamdi Salihi, Altin Lala (Cap), Sabien Likaj, Odise Roshi (77 Gjergji Muzaka), Erjon Bogdani (46 Ahmed Januzi).
Trainer: Josip Kuže

ROMANIA: Silviu Lung, Srdjan Luchin, Gabriel Tamaş, Dorin Goian, Iasmin Latovlevici, Bănel Nicoliţă (63 Gabriel Torje), Alexandru Bourceanu, Costin Lazăr (87 Gheorghe Bucur), Răzvan Cociş, Ciprian Marica (46 Bogdan Stancu), Adrian Mutu. Trainer: Victor Piţurcă

Goals: Hamdi Salihi (24), Srdian Luchin (77)

FRANCE v BOSNIA HERZEGOVINA 1-1 (0-1)

Stade de France, Paris (FRA) 11.10.2011

Referee: Craig Thomson (SCO) Attendance: 78,467

FRANCE: Hugo Lloris, Patrice Evra, Adil Rami, Yohan Cabaye (61 Kevin Gameiro), Samir Nasri, Anthony Réveillère, Jérémy Ménez, Florent Malouda (61 Marvin Martin), Yann M'Vila, Loïc Rémy (82 Alou Diarra), Éric Abidal.
Trainer: Laurent Blanc

BOSNIA HERZEGOVINA: Kenan Hasagić (46 Asmir Begović), Saša Papac, Emir Spahić, Elvir Rahimić, Miralem Pjanić, Zvjezdan Misimović, Edin Džeko, Mensur Mujdža (61 Darko Maletić), Senad Lulić, Haris Medunjanin (71 Adnan Zahirović), Boris Pandža. Trainer: Safet Sušić

Goals: Edin Džeko (40), Samir Nasri (78 pen)

GROUP E

MOLDOVA v FINLAND 2-0 (0-0)

Zimbru, Chişinău 03.09.2010

Referee: Robert Malek (POL) Attendance: 10,300

MOLDOVA: Stanislav Namaşco, Alexei Savinov, Vadim Boreţ, Alexandru Epureanu, Igor Ţîgîrlaş (68 Igor Bugaev), Eugeniu Cebotaru, Viorel Frunza, Nicolae Josan (58 Alexandru Suvorov), Semion Bulgaru, Vitalie Bordian, Anatolie Doroş (75 Valeriu Andronic). Trainer: Gavril Balint

FINLAND: Otto Fredrikson, Petri Pasanen, Niklas Moisander, Sami Hyypiä, Roman Eremenko, Jari Litmanen (46 Kasper Hämäläinen), Tim Sparv, Jonathan Johansson, Roni Porokara (75 Mika Väyrynen), Aleksei Eremenko, Markus Heikkinen. Trainer: Stuart Baxter

Sent off: Hyypiä (36)

Goals: Alexandru Suvorov (69), Anatolie Doroş (74)

SWEDEN v HUNGARY 2-0 (0-0)

Råsundastadion, Solna 03.09.2010

Referee: Martin Atkinson (ENG) Attendance: 32,304

SWEDEN: Andreas Isaksson (46 Johan Wiland), Mikael Lustig, Olof Mellberg, Daniel Majstorovic, Behrang Safari, Ola Toivonen, Anders Svensson (33 Kim Källström), Zlatan Ibrahimović, Johan Elmander (49 Sebastian Larsson), Pontus Wernbloom, Emir Bajrami. Trainer: Erik Hamrén

HUNGARY: Gábor Király, Zoltán Lipták, Pál Lázár, Roland Juhász, Zsolt Laczkó, Krisztián Vadócz, Balász Dzsudzsák (46 Szabolcs Huszti), Gergely Rudolf (82 Tamás Hajnal), Vladimir Koman, Zoltán Gera, Ákos Elek (59 Tamás Priskin).
Trainer: Sándor Egervári

Goals: Pontus Wernbloom (51, 73)

SAN MARINO v HOLLAND 0-5 (0-2)

Olimpico Serravalle 03.09.2010

Referee: Samuel Lee Evans (WAL) Attendance: 4,127

SAN MARINO: Aldo Simoncini, Fabio Vitaioli, Damiano Vannucci, Maicol Berretti, Davide Simoncini (61 Simone Bacciocchi), Alessandro Della Valle, Carlo Valentini, Pier Filippo Mazza, Manuel Marani (76 Alex Gasperoni), Andy Selva, Matteo Vitaioli (82 Nicola Ciacci).
Trainer: Giampaolo Mazza

HOLLAND: Maarten Stekelenburg, Gregory van der Wiel, Hedwiges Maduro, Joris Mathijsen, Erik Pieters, Mark van Bommel, Dirk Kuyt (67 Ruud van Nistelrooy), Nigel de Jong (46 Rafael van der Vaart), Klaas-Jan Huntelaar, Wesley Sneijder, Eljero Elia (59 Ibrahim Afellay).
Trainer: Bert van Marwijk

Goals: Dirk Kuyt (16 pen), Klaas-Jan Huntelaar (38, 48, 66), Ruud van Nistelrooy (90)

SWEDEN v SAN MARINO 6-0 (3-0)

Malmö New Stadium, Malmö 07.09.2010

Referee: David Mckeon (IRL) Attendance: 21,083

SWEDEN: Johan Wiland, Mikael Lustig, Olof Mellberg, Daniel Majstorovic, Behrang Safari, Ola Toivonen (46 Andreas Granqvist), Sebastian Larsson, Kim Källström, Zlatan Ibrahimović (82 Marcus Berg), Pontus Wernbloom (69 Johan Elmander), Emir Bajrami. Trainer: Erik Hamrén

SAN MARINO: Aldo Simoncini, Fabio Vitaioli, Damiano Vannucci, Simone Bacciocchi (79 Carlo Valentini), Davide Simoncini, Alessandro Della Valle, Matteo Vitaioli, Pier Filippo Mazza, Manuel Marani (56 Maicol Berretti), Andy Selva, Nicola Chiaruzzi (72 Alex Gasperoni).
Trainer: Giampaolo Mazza

Sent off: Mellberg (33)

Goals: Zlatan Ibrahimović (7, 77), Davide Simoncini (11 own goal), Aldo Simoncini (26 own goal), Andreas Granqvist (51), Berg (90+2)

HOLLAND v FINLAND 2-1 (2-1)

Feijenoord Stadion, Rotterdam 07.09.2010

Referee: Aleksei Nikolaev (RUS) Attendance: 25,000

HOLLAND: Maarten Stekelenburg, Gregory van der Wiel, John Heitinga, Joris Mathijsen, Vurnon Anita, Mark van Bommel, Ibrahim Afellay (74 Jermain Lens), Nigel de Jong, Klaas-Jan Huntelaar (82 Ruud van Nistelrooy), Wesley Sneijder, Rafael van der Vaart (64 Eljero Elia).
Trainer: Bert van Marwijk

FINLAND: Otto Fredrikson, Petri Pasanen, Niklas Moisander, Veli Lampi, Mika Väyrynen, Roman Eremenko, Mikael Forssell (80 Eremenko), Tim Sparv, Daniel Sjölund (68 Jonatan Johansson), Kasper Hämäläinen (46 Roni Porokara), Markus Heikkinen. Trainer: Stuart Baxter

Goals: Klaas-Jan Huntelaar (7, 16 pen), Mikael Forssell (18)

HUNGARY v MOLDOVA 2-1 (0-0)

Ferenc Szusza Stadion, Budapest 07.09.2010

Referee: Libor Kovařík (CZE) Attendance: 9,209

HUNGARY: Gábor Király, Zoltán Lipták, Pál Lázár, Roland Juhász, Zsolt Laczkó, Péter Czvitkovics (46 Ádám Szalai), Balázs Dzsudzsák, Gergely Rudolf (64 Vilmos Vanczák), Vladimir Koman (88 Krisztián Vadócz), Zoltán Gera, Ákos Elek. Trainer: Sándor Egervári

MOLDOVA: Stanislav Namaşco, Alexandru Epureanu, Petru Racu, Igor Ţîgîrlaş, Eugeniu Cebotaru (71 Andrei Cojocari), Viorel Frunza (84 Igor Bugaev), Nicolae Josan (59 Anatolie Doroş), Semion Bulgaru, Vitalie Bordian, Alexandru Suvorov, Vadim Bolohan. Trainer: Gavril Balint

Goals: Gergely Rudolf (50), Vladimir Koman (66), Alexandru Suvorov (79)

HUNGARY v SAN MARINO 8-0 (4-0)

Ferenc Puskás, Budapest 08.10.2010

Referee: Hannes Kaasik (EST) Attendance: 10,596

HUNGARY: Gábor Király, Krisztián Vermes, Vilmos Vanczák, Roland Juhász, Zsolt Laczkó, Ákos Elek (64 Vadócz), Balázs Dzsudzsák, Gergely Rudolf, Ádám Szalai (64 Priskin), Zoltán Gera, Vladimir Koman (79 Péter Czvitkovics).
Trainer: Sándor Egervári

SAN MARINO: Aldo Simoncini, Carlo Valentini, Damiano Vannucci, Simone Bacciocchi (52 Nicola Albani), Alessandro Della Valle, Fabio Vitaioli, Maicol Berretti, Fabio Bollini (84 Michele Cervellini), Paolo Montagna, Manuel Marani, Matteo Vitaioli (77 Matteo Bugli). Trainer: Giampaolo Mazza

Sent off: Valentini (90+2)

Goals: Gergely Rudolf (11, 25), Ádám Szalai (18, 27, 48), Vladimir Koman (60), Balázs Dzsudzsák (89), Zoltán Gera (90+3 pen)

MOLDOVA v HOLLAND 0-1 (0-1)

Zimbru, Chişinău 08.10.2010

Referee: Florian Meyer (GER) Attendance: 10,500

MOLDOVA: Stanislav Namaşco, Victor Golovatenco, Alexandru Epureanu, Petru Racu, Eugeniu Cebotaru (69 Valeriu Andronic), Viorel Frunza (46 Igor Bugaev), Semion Bulgaru, Vitalie Bordian, Anatolie Doroş (78 Nicolae Josan), Alexandru Suvorov, Vadim Bolohan. Trainer: Gavril Balint

HOLLAND: Maarten Stekelenburg, Gregory van der Wiel, John Heitinga, Joris Mathijsen, Erik Pieters, Mark van Bommel, Dirk Kuyt, Rafael van der Vaart, Klaas-Jan Huntelaar, Wesley Sneijder, Ibrahim Afellay (90 Urby Emanuelson).
Trainer: Bert van Marwijk

Goal: Klaas-Jan Huntelaar (37)

FINLAND v HUNGARY 1-2 (0-0)

Olympic Stadium, Helsinki 12.10.2010

Referee: Alan Kelly (IRL) Attendance: 18,532

FINLAND: Jussi Jääskeläinen, Petri Pasanen, Niklas Moisander, Sami Hyypiä, Mika Väyrynen, Roman Eremenko, Mikael Forssell, Tim Sparv (72 Jari Litmanen), Daniel Sjölund (81 Shefki Kuqi), Roni Porokara (71 Aleksei Eremenko), Markus Heikkinen. Trainer: Stuart Baxter

HUNGARY: Gábor Király, Krisztián Vermes, Zoltán Lipták, Roland Juhász, Zsolt Laczkó (86 Vilmos Vanczák), Ákos Elek, Balázs Dzsudzsák, Gergely Rudolf (46 Vladimir Koman), Ádám Szalai, Zoltán Gera, Krisztián Vadócz (75 Ádám Pintér). Trainer: Sándor Egervári

Goals: Ádám Szalai (50), Mikael Forssell (86), Balázs Dzsudzsák (90+4)

FINLAND v SAN MARINO 8-0 (1-0)

Olympic Stadium, Helsinki 17.11.2010

Referee: Radek Matějek (CZE) Attendance: 8,192

FINLAND: Otto Fredrikson, Petri Pasanen, Niklas Moisander, Veli Lampi, Mika Väyrynen, Roman Eremenko (80 Shefki Kuqi), Mikael Forssell, Daniel Sjölund (46 Jari Litmanen), Aleksei Eremenko, Kasper Hämäläinen (70 Roni Porokara), Markus Heikkinen. Trainer: Olli Huttunen

SAN MARINO: Aldo Simoncini, Matteo Bugli, Michele Cervellini, Nicola Albani, Alessandro Della Valle, Fabio Vitaioli (72 Damiano Vannucci), Maicol Berretti (67 Alex Della Valle), Matteo Coppini, Matteo Vitaioli, Andy Selva, Paolo Montagna (79 Manuel Marani). Trainer: Giampaolo Mazza

Goals: Mika Väyrynen (39), Kasper Hämäläinen (49, 67), Mikael Forssell (51, 59), Jari Litmanen (71 pen), Roni Porokara (73), Mikael Forssell (78)

HOLLAND v SWEDEN 4-1 (2-0)

Amsterdam ArenA, Amsterdam 12.10.2010

Referee: Stéphane Lannoy (FRA) Attendance: 46,000

HOLLAND: Maarten Stekelenburg, Gregory van der Wiel, John Heitinga, Joris Mathijsen, Erik Pieters, Mark van Bommel (72 Wout Brama), Dirk Kuyt (29 Jermain Lens), Rafael van der Vaart, Klaas-Jan Huntelaar (84 Ruud Van Nistelrooy), Wesley Sneijder, Ibrahim Afellay. Trainer: Bert van Marwijk

SWEDEN: Andreas Isaksson, Mikael Lustig, Daniel Majstorovic, Behrang Safari (46 Oscar Wendt), Ola Toivonen (79 Marcus Berg), Sebastian Larsson, Anders Svensson, Zlatan Ibrahimović, Johan Elmander, Andreas Granqvist, Pontus Wernbloom (54 Kim Källström). Trainer: Erik Hamrén

Goals: Klaas-Jan Huntelaar (4, 55), Ibrahim Afellay (37, 59), Andreas Granqvist (69)

HUNGARY v HOLLAND 0-4 (0-2)

Ferenc Puskás, Budapest 25.03.2011

Referee: Carlos Velasco Carballo (SPA) Attendance: 23,817

HUNGARY: Gábor Király, Zoltán Lipták, Vilmos Vanczák, Roland Juhász, Zsolt Laczkó, Ákos Elek (79 Tamás Priskin), Balázs Dzsudzsák, Gergely Rudolf, József Varga (46 Krisztián Vadócz), Zoltán Gera, Vladimir Koman (46 Péter Czvitkovics). Trainer: Sándor Egervári

HOLLAND: Michel Vorm, Gregory van der Wiel, John Heitinga, Joris Mathijsen, Erik Pieters, Nigel de Jong, Dirk Kuyt (82 Ruud van Nistelrooy), Rafael van der Vaart (82 Kevin Strootman), Robin Van Persie, Wesley Sneijder, Ibrahim Afellay (63 Eljero Elia). Trainer: Bert van Marwijk

Goals: Rafael van der Vaart (8), Ibrahim Afellay (45), Dirk Kuyt (54), Robin Van Persie (62)

SAN MARINO v MOLDOVA 0-2 (0-1)

Stadio Olimpico, Serravalle 12.10.2010

Referee: Mark Courtney (NIR) Attendance: 714

SAN MARINO: Aldo Simoncini, Fabio Vitaioli, Damiano Vannucci, Pier Filippo Mazza, Davide Simoncini, Simone Bacciocchi, Michele Cervellini (60 Maicol Berretti), Fabio Bollini (67 Nicola Ciacci), Paolo Montagna (81 Matteo Coppini), Manuel Marani, Matteo Vitaioli. Trainer: Giampaolo Mazza

MOLDOVA: Stanislav Namaşco, Victor Golovatenco, Vadim Boreţ, Alexandru Epureanu, Andrei Cojocari (81 Alexei Savinov), Valeriu Andronic, Viorel Frunza, Nicolae Josan (69 Denis Zmeu), Vitalie Bordian, Alexandru Suvorov, Igor Bugaev (62 Anatolie Doroş). Trainer: Gavril Balint

Goals: Nicolae Josan (20), Anatolie Doroş (86 pen)

SWEDEN v MOLDOVA 2-1 (1-0)

Råsundastadion, Solna 29.03.2011

Referee: Knut Kircher (GER) Attendance: 25,544

SWEDEN: Andreas Isaksson, Mikael Lustig, Andreas Granqvist, Mikael Antonsson, Oscar Wendt, Pontus Wernbloom (65 Rasmus Elm), Sebastian Larsson, Emir Bajrami (Martin Olsson 73), Kim Källström, Zlatan Ibrahimović, Johan Elmander (89 Alexander Gerndt). Trainer: Erik Hamrén

MOLDOVA: Stanislav Namaşco, Igor Armaş, Victor Golovatenco, Vadim Bolohan, Vadim Boreţ, Petru Racu, Alexandru Gaţcan (83 Valeriu Andronic), Eugeniu Cebotaru, Viorel Frunza (46 Igor Bugaev), Anatolie Doroş (72 Anatoli Cheptine), Alexandru Suvorov. Trainer: Gavril Balint

Goals: Mikael Lustig (30), Sebastian Larsson (82), Alexandru Suvorov (90+2)

HOLLAND v HUNGARY 5-3 (1-0)

Amsterdam ArenA, Amsterdam 29.03.2011

Referee: Svein Oddvar Moen (NOR) Attendance: 51,700

HOLLAND: Michel Vorm, Gregory van der Wiel, John Heitinga, Joris Mathijsen, Erik Pieters (64 Urby Emanuelson), Nigel de Jong, Dirk Kuyt (90 Eljero Elia), Rafael van der Vaart, Robin Van Persie (46 Ruud van Nistelrooy), Wesley Sneijder, Ibrahim Afellay. Trainer: Bert van Marwijk

HUNGARY: Márton Fülöp, Pál Lázár, Vilmos Vanczák, Roland Juhász, Zsolt Laczkó, Krisztián Vadócz (90 Péter Czvitkovics), Balázs Dzsudzsák, Gergely Rudolf, Tamás Priskin (73 Attila Tököli), Zoltán Gera, Ádám Pintér (46 Vladimir Koman). Trainer: Sándor Egervári

Goals: Robin van Persie (13), Gergely Rudolf (46), Zoltán Gera (50, 75), Wesley Sneijder (61), Ruud van Nistelrooy (73), Dirk Kuyt (78, 81)

SWEDEN v FINLAND 5-0 (3-0)

Råsundastadion, Solna 07.06.2011

Referee: Antony Gautier (FRA) Attendance: 32,128

SWEDEN: Andreas Isaksson, Mikael Lustig, Olof Mellberg, Daniel Majstorovic, Emir Bajrami, Sebastian Larsson (89 Christian Wilhelmsson), Anders Svensson, Kim Källström, Johan Elmander (81 Pontus Wernbloom), Oscar Wendt, Ola Toivonen (25 Zlatan Ibrahimović). Trainer: Erik Hamrén

FINLAND: Anssi Jaakkola, Petri Pasanen, Niklas Moisander, Joona Toivio, Mika Väyrynen, Roman Eremenko, Perparim Hetemaj, Mikael Forssell, Markus Heikkinen (46 Markus Halsti), Aleksei Eremenko (80 Alexander Ring), Kasper Hämäläinen (46 Mika Ääritalo). Trainer: Mixu Paatelainen

Goals: Kim Källström (11), Zlatan Ibrahimović (31, 35, 53), Emir Bajrami (83)

SAN MARINO v FINLAND 0-1 (0-1)

Stadio Olimpico, Serravalle 03.06.2011

Referee: Andrejs Sipailo (LVA) Attendance: 1,218

SAN MARINO: Aldo Simoncini, Fabio Vitaioli (88 Simone Bacciocchi), Damiano Vannucci, Michele Cervellini, Davide Simoncini, Alessandro Della Valle, Fabio Bollini, Pier Filippo Mazza (77 Maicol Berretti), Manuel Marani, Andy Selva, Matteo Vitaioli (81 Paolo Montagna).
Trainer: Giampaolo Mazza

FINLAND: Lukas Hradecky, Petri Pasanen, Niklas Moisander, Veli Lampi, Mika Väyrynen, Perparim Hetemaj (84 Daniel Sjölund), Mikael Forssell (90 Berat Sadik), Markus Heikkinen, Aleksei Eremenko (68 Riku Riski), Kasper Hämäläinen, Jukka Raitala. Trainer: Mixu Paatelainen

Goal: Mikael Forssell (41)

SAN MARINO v HUNGARY 0-3 (0-1)

Stadio Olimpico, Serravalle 07.06.2011

Referee: Pavle Radovanović (MNE) Attendance: 1,915

SAN MARINO: Aldo Simoncini, Fabio Vitaioli (46 Alex Della Valle), Damiano Vannucci, Michele Cervellini, Giacomo Benedettini, Alessandro Della Valle, Matteo Vitaioli, Fabio Bollini (79 Simone Bacciocchi), Manuel Marani (64 Maicol Berretti), Andy Selva, Pier Filippo Mazza.
Trainer: Giampaolo Mazza

HUNGARY: Gábor Király, Zoltán Lipták (87 Ádám Pintér), Vilmos Vanczák, Roland Juhász, Zsolt Laczkó, Ákos Elek, Balázs Dzsudzsák, Imre Szabics (83 Tamás Koltai), Krisztián Németh, Tamás Hajnal (71 Péter Czvitkovics), Vladimir Koman. Trainer: Sándor Egervári

Goals: Zoltán Lipták (40), Szabics (49), Vladimir Koman (83)

MOLDOVA v SWEDEN 1-4 (0-2)

Zimbru, Chişinău 03.06.2011

Referee: Andre Marriner (ENG) Attendance: 10,500

MOLDOVA: Stanislav Namaşco, Igor Armaş, Victor Golovatenco, Vadim Bolohan, Alexandru Gaţcan (46 Igor Ţîgîrlaş), Petru Racu, Eugeniu Cebotaru (78 Artur Patraş), Igor Bugaev, Anatolie Doroş (63 Gheorghe Boghiu), Alexandru Suvorov, Stanislav Ivanov. Trainer: Gavril Balint

SWEDEN: Andreas Isaksson, Mikael Lustig, Olof Mellberg, Daniel Majstorovic, Sebastian Larsson, Anders Svensson, Kim Källström, Johan Elmander (76 Alexander Gerndt), Tobias Hysén (41 Emir Bajrami), Oscar Wendt, Ola Toivonen (69 Pontus Wernbloom). Trainer: Erik Hamrén

Goals: Ola Toivonen (11), Johan Elmander (30, 58), Igor Bugaev (61), Gerndt (88)

FINLAND v MOLDOVA 4-1 (2-0)

Olympic Stadium, Helsinki 02.09.2011

Referee: Anastassios Kakos (GRE) Attendance: 9,056

FINLAND: Lukas Hradecky, Niklas Moisander, Joona Toivio, Roman Eremenko, Perparim Hetemaj, Mikael Forssell, Kari Arkivuo, Daniel Sjölund (61 Teemu Pukki), Alexander Ring (72 Mika Väyrynen), Kasper Hämäläinen (77 Timo Furuholm), Jukka Raitala. Trainer: Mixu Paatelainen

MOLDOVA: Nicolae Calancea, Igor Armaş, Victor Golovatenco, Vadim Boreţ, Alexandru Epureanu, Eugeniu Cebotaru, Gheorghe Ovseannicov (69 Serghei Alexeev), Anatolie Doroş (55 Anatoli Cheptine), Alexandru Suvorov (55 Vitalie Bordian), Alexei Savinov, Denis Zmeu.
Trainer: Gavril Balint

Goals: Kasper Hämäläinen (11, 43), Mikael Forssell (52 pen), Armaş (70 own goal), Alexeev (85)

HUNGARY v SWEDEN 2-1 (1-0)

Ferenc Puskás, Budapest 02.09.2011

Referee: Damir Skomina (SVN) Attendance: 23,500

HUNGARY: Gábor Király, Zoltán Lipták (74 György Sándor), Zsolt Korcsmár, József Varga, Zsolt Laczkó, Ákos Elek, Ádám Pintér, Imre Szabics (80 Tamás Priskin), Gergely Rudolf, Tamás Hajnal (66 Zoltán Stieber), Vladimir Koman. Trainer: Sándor Egervári

SWEDEN: Andreas Isaksson, Mikael Lustig, Andreas Granqvist, Daniel Majstorovic, Sebastian Larsson (68 Ola Toivonen), Anders Svensson (53 Rasmus Elm), Kim Källström (88 Pontus Wernbloom), Zlatan Ibrahimović, Johan Elmander, Oscar Wendt, Christian Wilhelmsson. Trainer: Erik Hamrén

Goals: Imre Szabics (44), Christian Wilhelmsson (60), Gergely Rudolf (90)

MOLDOVA v HUNGARY 0-2 (0-1)

Zimbru, Chişinău 06.09.2011

Referee: Ivan Bebek (CRO) Attendance: 10,500

MOLDOVA: Artiom Gaiduchevici, Igor Armaş, Victor Golovatenco, Vadim Boreţ, Alexandru Epureanu, Eugeniu Cebotaru, Serghei Alexeev (73 Igor Ţîgîrlaş), Anatoli Cheptine (62 Anatolie Doroş), Alexandru Suvorov, Alexei Savinov, Denis Zmeu (46 Igor Bugaev). Trainer: Gavril Balint

HUNGARY: Gábor Király, Jóysef Varga, Vilmos Vanczák, Roland Juhász, Ysolt Korcsmár (69 Zsolt Laczkó), Ákos Elek, Ádám Pintér (64 György Sándor), Imre Szabics (82 Krisztián Vadócz), Gergelz Rudolf, Tamás Hajnal, Vladimir Koman. Trainer: Sándor Egervári

Goals: Vilmos Vanczák (7), Gergely Rudolf (83)

HOLLAND v SAN MARINO 11-0 (3-0)

PSV Stadion, Eindhoven 02.09.2011

Referee: Liran Liany (ISR) Attendance: 35,000

HOLLAND: Maarten Stekelenburg, Gregory van der Wiel, John Heitinga, Joris Mathijsen, Erik Pieters, Mark van Bommel (74 Hedwiges Maduro), Robin Van Persie, Kevin Strootman (86 Georginio Wijnaldum), Klaas-Jan Huntelaar, Wesley Sneijder, Dirk Kuyt (74 Eljero Elia). Trainer: Bert van Marwijk

SAN MARINO: Aldo Simoncini, Fabio Vitaioli, Damiano Vannucci, Fabio Bollini (68 Alex Gasperoni), Davide Simoncini (82 Simone Bacciocchi), Giacomo Benedettini, Matteo Andreini, Michele Cervellini, Pier Filippo Mazza (54 Matteo Coppini), Andy Selva, Matteo Vitaioli. Trainer: Giampaolo Mazza

Goals: Robin Van Persie (7, 65, 67, 79), Wesley Sneijder (12, 87), John Heitinga (17), Dirk Kuyt (49), Klaas-Jan Huntelaar (56, 77), Georginio Wijnaldum (90)

SAN MARINO v SWEDEN 0-5 (0-0)

Stadio Olimpico, Serravalle 06.09.2011

Referee: Steven McLean (SCO) Attendance: 2,946

SAN MARINO: Federico Valentini, Fabio Vitaioli, Damiano Vannucci, Fabio Bollini (84 Alex Gasperoni), Davide Simoncini, Simone Bacciocchi, Matteo Vitaioli, Michele Cervellini, Matteo Coppini (71 Matteo Andreini), Andy Selva, Manuel Marani (56 Giacomo Benedettini). Trainer: Giampaolo Mazza

SWEDEN: Andreas Isaksson, Mikael Lustig, Andreas Granqvist, Daniel Majstorovic, Kim Källström, Zlatan Ibrahimović, Johan Elmander (67 Tobias Hysén), Martin Olsson, Ola Toivonen (57 Sebastian Larsson), Christian Wilhelmsson, Rasmus Elm (65 Anders Svensson). Trainer: Erik Hamrén

Sent off: Simoncini (53)

Goals: Kim Källström (64), Christian Wilhelmsson (70, 90+3), Martin Olsson (81), Tobias Hysén (89)

FINLAND v HOLLAND 0-2 (0-1)

Olympic Stadium, Helsinki 06.09.2011

Referee: Manuel Gräfe (GER) Attendance: 21,580

FINLAND: Lukas Hradecky, Petri Pasanen (78 Jukka Raitala), Niklas Moisander, Joona Toivio, Roman Eremenko, Perparim Hetemaj, Mikael Forssell (86 Daniel Sjölund), Teemu Pukki (61 Mika Väyrynen), Kari Arkivuo, Alexander Ring, Kasper Hämäläinen. Trainer: Mixu Paatelainen

HOLLAND: Maarten Stekelenburg, Gregory van der Wiel, John Heitinga, Joris Mathijsen, Erik Pieters, Mark van Bommel, Robin van Persie (68 Eljero Elia), Kevin Strootman, Klaas-Jan Huntelaar (68 Luuk de Jong), Wesley Sneijder, Dirk Kuyt. Trainer: Bert van Marwijk

Sent off: Hetemaj (60)

Goals: Kevin Strootman (29), Luuk de Jong (90+3)

FINLAND v SWEDEN 1-2 (0-1)

Olympic Stadium, Helsinki 07.10.2011

Referee: Mark Clattenburg (ENG) Attendance: 23,257

FINLAND: Lukas Hradecky, Niklas Moisander, Joona Toivio, Mika Väyrynen (70 Timo Furuholm), Roman Eremenko, Teemu Pukki (60 Mikael Forssell), Kari Arkivuo, Tim Sparv, Alexander Ring, Kasper Hämäläinen, Jukka Raitala. Trainer: Mixu Paatelainen

SWEDEN: Andreas Isaksson, Mikael Lustig, Olof Mellberg, Daniel Majstorovic, Martin Olsson, Sebastian Larsson (68 Ola Toivonen), Kim Källström (87 Emir Bajrami), Zlatan Ibrahimović, Johan Elmander, Christian Wilhelmsson (54 Anders Svensson), Rasmus Elm. Trainer: Erik Hamrén

Goals: Sebastian Larsson (8), M. Olsson (52), Toivio (73)

HOLLAND v MOLDOVA 1-0 (1-0)

Feijenoord Stadion, Rotterdam 07.10.2011

Referee: Matej Jug (SVN) Attendance: 47,226

HOLLAND: Michel Vorm, Gregory van der Wiel, Jeffrey Bruma, Joris Mathijsen, Erik Pieters, Mark van Bommel, Robin van Persie, Kevin Strootman, Klaas-Jan Huntelaar, Rafael van der Vaart (78 Eljero Elia), Dirk Kuyt. Trainer: Bert van Marwijk

MOLDOVA: Stanislav Namaşco, Igor Armaş, Victor Golovatenco, Alexandru Epureanu, Petru Racu, Stanislav Ivanov, Eugeniu Cebotaru, Anatoli Cheptine (84 Gheorghe Ovseannicov), Serghei Alexeev (69 Igor Bugaev), Semion Bulgaru, Alexandru Suvorov (58 Denis Zmeu). Trainer: Gavril Balint

Goal: Klaas-Jan Huntelaar (40)

HUNGARY v FINLAND 0-0

Ferenc Puskás, Budapest 11.10.2011

Referee: Alberto Undiano Mallenco (SPA) Att: 25,169

HUNGARY: Gábor Király, József Varga, Vilmos Vanczák, Roland Juhász, Zsolt Korcsmár, Ákos Elek, György Sándor (59 Krisztián Vadócz), Imre Szabics, Tamás Priskin (59 Balázs Dzsudzsák), Tamás Hajnal (88 Zoltan Stieber), Vladimir Koman. Trainer: Sándor Egervári

FINLAND: Otto Fredrikson, Niklas Moisander, Joona Toivio, Mika Väyrynen, Roman Eremenko, Mikael Forssell (66 Timo Furuholm), Kari Arkivuo (55 Veli Lampi), Tim Sparv, Alexander Ring, Kasper Hämäläinen (85 Teemu Pukki), Jukka Raitala. Trainer: Mixu Paatelainen

MOLDOVA v SAN MARINO 4-0 (1-0)

Zimbru, Chişinău 11.10.2011

Referee: Petur Reinert (FRO) Attendance: 6,534

MOLDOVA: Artiom Gaiduchevici, Igor Armaş, Victor Golovatenco, Alexandru Epureanu, Petru Racu (70 Gheorghe Andronic), Eugeniu Cebotaru (78 Igor Ţîgîrlaş), Anatoli Cheptine, Serghei Alexeev (61 Igor Bugaev), Anatolie Doroş, Alexandru Suvorov, Denis Zmeu. Trainer: Gavril Balint

SAN MARINO: Aldo Simoncini, Giacomo Benedettini, Damiano Vannucci, Matteo Coppini, Alessandro Della Valle, Simone Bacciocchi (89 Nicola Albani), Maicol Berretti (67 Matteo Bugli), Michele Cervellini, Alex Gasperoni (76 Paolo Montagna), Andy Selva, Matteo Vitaioli. Trainer: Giampaolo Mazza

Sent off: Ţîgîrlaş (84)

Goals: Denis Zmeu (30), Simone Bacciocchi (62 own goal), Alexandru Suvorov (66), G. Andronic (87)

SWEDEN v HOLLAND 3-2 (1-1)

Råsundastadion, Solna 11.10.2011

Referee: Cüneyt Çakır (TUR) Attendance: 33,066

SWEDEN: Andreas Isaksson, Mikael Lustig, Olof Mellberg, Daniel Majstorovic, Martin Olsson, Sebastian Larsson, Anders Svensson, Kim Källström, Johan Elmander, Ola Toivonen (74 Pontus Wernbloom), Rasmus Elm. Trainer: Erik Hamrén

HOLLAND: Michel Vorm, Gregory van der Wiel, Jeffrey Bruma, Joris Mathijsen, Erik Pieters, Mark van Bommel, Robin van Persie, Kevin Strootman (81 Luuk de Jong), Klaas-Jan Huntelaar, Rafael van der Vaart, Dirk Kuyt (73 Eljero Elia). Trainer: Bert van Marwijk

Goals: Kim Källström (14), Klaas-Jan Huntelaar (23), Dirk Kuyt (50), Sebastian Larsson (52 pen), Ola Toivonen (53)

	P	W	D	L	F	A	Pts
Holland	10	9	0	1	37	8	27
Sweden	10	8	0	2	31	11	24
Hungary	10	6	1	3	22	14	19
Finland	10	3	1	6	16	16	10
Moldova	10	3	0	7	12	16	9
San Marino	10	0	0	10	0	53	0

GROUP F

ISRAEL v MALTA 3-1 (1-1)

Ramat-Gan stadium, Ramat-Gan 02.09.2010

Referee: Said Enjimi (FRA) Attendance: 17,365

ISRAEL: Dudu Awat, Tal Ben Haim I, Dani Bondarv, Beram Kayal (86 Eyal Golasa), Almog Cohen, Lior Refalov, Yossi Benayoun, Eran Zahavi (51 Gil Vermouth), Ben Sahar (73 Shlomi Arbeitman), Dedi Ben-Dayan, Tamir Cohen. Trainer: Luis Fernandez

MALTA: Andrew Hogg, Jonathan Caruana, Carlo Mamo, Gareth Sciberras, André Agius, Daniel Bogdanovic (57 Andrew Cohen), Roderick Briffa (82 Clayton Failla), Michael Mifsud, Shaun Bajada, Edward Herrera (80 Emmanuel Muscat), Jamie Pace. Trainer: John Buttigieg

Goals: Yossi Benayoun (7, 64 pen, 75), Jamie Pace (38)

LATVIA v CROATIA 0-3 (0-1)

Skonto Stadions, Riga 03.09.2010

Referee: Björn Kuipers (HOL) Attendance: 7,600

LATVIA: Andris Vaņins, Oskars Kļava, Juris Laizāns (87 Vitāljs Astafjevs), Deniss Ivanovs, Pāvels Mihadjuks, Aleksandrs Cauņa, Māris Verpakovskis, Andrejs Rubins (85 Jurijs Žigajevs), Girts Karlsons (63 Artjoms Rudņevs), Kaspars Gorkšs, Maksims Rafaļskis. Trainer: Aleksandrs Starkovs

CROATIA: Vedran Runje, Ivan Strinić, Josip Šimunić, Vedran Čorluka, Ivan Rakitić, Ognjen Vukojević (70 Danijel Pranjić), Eduardo (62 Nikica Jelavić), Darijo Srna, Ivica Olić, Niko Kranjčar, Mladen Petrić (84 Mario Mandžukić). Trainer: Slaven Bilić

Goals: Mladen Petrić (43), Ivica Olić (51), Darijo Srna (82)

MALTA v LATVIA 0-2 (0-1)

Ta' Qali National Stadium, Ta' Qali 07.09.2010

Referee: Tony Asumaa (FIN) Attendance: 6,255

MALTA: Andrew Hogg, Jonathan Caruana, Carlo Mamo (77 Ryan Fenech), Gareth Sciberras (77 Clayton Failla), André Agius, Shaun Bajada, Roderick Briffa, Michael Mifsud, Andrew Cohen, Emmanuel Muscat (59 Daniel Bogdanovic), Jamie Pace. Trainer: John Buttigieg

LATVIA: Andris Vaņins, Oskars Kļava, Juris Laizāns, Deniss Ivanovs, Pāvels Mihadjuks, Aleksandrs Cauņa, Māris Verpakovskis (90+2 Andrejs Perepļotkins), Andrejs Rubins, Kaspars Gorkšs, Maksims Rafaļskis (82 Vitālijs Astafjevs), Artjoms Rudņevs (70 Girts Karlsons). Trainer: Aleksandrs Starkovs

Goals: Gorkšs (43), Verpakovskis (85)

GREECE v GEORGIA 1-1 (0-1)

Georgios Karaiskakis, Piraeus 03.09.2010

Referee: Carlos Clos Gómez (SPA) Attendance: 14,794

GREECE: Michalis Sifakis, Giourkas Seitaridis (71 Kostas Mitroglou), Nikos Spyropoulos, Giórgos Samaras (59 Sotiris Ninis), Avraam Papadopoulos, Giórgos Karagounis, Dimítris Salpingidis, Vassilis Torossidis, Fanis Gekas, Sokratis Papastathopoulos, Kostas Katsouranis. Trainer: Fernando Santos

GEORGIA: Nukri Revishvili, Ucha Lobzhanidze, Malkhaz Asatiani, Kakha Kaladze, Aleksandr Amisulashvili, Zurab Khizanishvili, Gogita Gogua (87 Giorgi Merebashvili), David Kvirkvelia, Aleksandr Iashvili (54 Jano Ananidze), Levan Kobiashvili, Vladimir Dvalishvili (60 Nikoloz Gelashvili). Trainer: Temuri Ketsbaia

Goals: Aleksandr Iashvili (3), Nikos Spyropoulos (72)

CROATIA v GREECE 0-0

Stadion Maksimir, Zagreb 07.09.2010

Referee: Claus Bo Larsen (DEN) Attendance: 24,399

CROATIA: Vedran Runje, Ivan Strinić, Josip Šimunić, Vedran Čorluka, Danijel Pranjić, Ognjen Vukojević (57 Ivan Rakitić), Luka Modrić, Darijo Srna, Ivica Olić (73 Eduardo), Niko Kranjčar, Mladen Petrić (46 Nikica Jelavić). Trainer: Slaven Bilić

GREECE: Michalis Sifakis, Giórgos Tzavellas, Alexandros Tziolis, Giórgos Samaras, Avraam Papadopoulos, Giórgos Karagounis (70 Sotiris Ninis), Loukas Vyntra, Dimítris Salpingidis (59 Fanis Gekas), Vassilis Torossidis (90+2 Giourkas Seitaridis), Sokratis Papastathopoulos, Kostas Katsouranis. Trainer: Fernando Santos

GEORGIA v ISRAEL 0-0

Boris Paichadze National Stadium, Tbilisi 07.09.2011

Referee: Sascha Kever (SWI) Attendance: 45,000

GEORGIA: Nukri Revishvili, Ucha Lobzhanidze, Malkhaz Asatiani, Kakha Kaladze, Aleksandr Amisulashvili, Zurab Khizanishvili, Gogita Gogua (75 Tornike Aptsiauri), Jano Ananidze, Aleksandr Iashvili (46 David Siradze), Levan Kobiashvili, Vladimir Dvalishvili (63 Giorgi Merebashvili). Trainer: Temuri Ketsbaia

ISRAEL: Dudu Awat, Tal Ben Haim I, Dani Bondarv, Beram Kayal, Almog Cohen, Lior Refalov (75 Gil Vermouth), Dekel Keinan, Yossi Benayoun, Ben Sahar (53 Shlomi Arbeitman), Dedi Ben-Dayan, Tamir Cohen (61 Eran Zahavi). Trainer: Luis Fernandez

GEORGIA v MALTA 1-0 (0-0)

Boris Paichadze National Stadium, Tbilisi 08.10.2010

Referee: Alan Black (NIR) Attendance: 38,000

GEORGIA: Nukri Revishvili, Lasha Salukvadze, Malkhaz Asatiani, Kakha Kaladze, Aleksandr Amisulashvili, Zurab Khizanishvili, Gogita Gogua, Jano Ananidze (73 Murtaz Daushvili), Giorgi Merebashvili (46 Aleksandr Iashvili), Levan Kobiashvili, Vladimir Dvalishvili (46 David Siradze). Trainer: Temuri Ketsbaia

MALTA: Justin Haber, Jonathan Caruana, Carlo Mamo, Gareth Sciberras (69 Ryan Fenech), André Agius, Roderick Briffa, Michael Mifsud, Andrew Cohen (90 Massimo Grima), Shaun Bajada, André Schembri (80 Paul Fenech), Jamie Pace. Trainer: John Buttigieg

Goal: David Siradze (90+1)

GREECE v LATVIA 1-0 (0-0)

Georgios Karaiskakis Stadium, Piraeus 08.10.2010

Referee: Antonio Damato (ITA) Attendance: 13,520

GREECE: Michalis Sifakis, Giórgos Tzavellas, Alexandros Tziolis, Giórgos Samaras, Avraam Papadopoulos, Kostas Mitroglou (77 Dimítris Salpingidis), Giórgos Karagounis (90 Pantelis Kafes), Vassilis Torossidis, Sotiris Ninis (82 Giánnis Fetfatzidis), Sokratis Papastathopoulos, Kostas Katsouranis. Trainer: Fernando Santos

LATVIA: Andris Vaņins, Oskars Kļava, Vitālijs Astafjevs, Juris Laizāns (82 Andrejs Perepļotkins), Deniss Ivanovs, Aleksandrs Cauņa, Māris Verpakovskis, Andrejs Rubins (65 Jurijs Žigajevs), Kaspars Gorkšs, Dzintars Zirnis, Artjoms Rudņevs (73 Girts Karlsons). Trainer: Aleksandrs Starkovs

Goal: Vassilis Torossidis (58)

GREECE v ISRAEL 2-1 (1-0)

Georgios Karaiskakis Stadium, Piraeus 12.10.2010

Referee: Martin Hansson (SWE) Attendance: 16,935

GREECE: Michalis Sifakis, Nikos Spyropoulos, Giórgos Samaras (81 Kostas Mitroglou), Avraam Papadopoulos, Giórgos Karagounis, Loukas Vyntra, Dimítris Salpingidis (87 Giánnis Maniatis), Pantelis Kafes, Sotiris Ninis (15 Giánnis Fetfatzidis), Sokratis Papastathopoulos, Kostas Katsouranis. Trainer: Fernando Santos

ISRAEL: Dudu Awat, Dani Bondarv, Rami Gershon, Bebras Natcho (63 Gil Vermouth), Almog Cohen, Roberto Colautti (75 Elyaniv Barda), Etey Shechter, Dekel Keinan, Lior Refalov, Tamir Cohen (69 Elroy Cohen), Eyal Golasa. Trainer: Luis Fernandez

Goals: Dimítris Salpingidis (22), Nikos Spyropoulos (59 own goal), Giórgos Karagounis (63 pen)

ISRAEL v CROATIA 1-2 (0-2)

Ramat-Gan Stadium, Ramat Gan 09.10.2010

Referee: Wolfgang Stark (GER) Attendance: 33,421

ISRAEL: Dudu Awat, Tal Ben Haim I, Bebras Natcho, Gil Vermouth, Almog Cohen, Elyaniv Barda (56 Lior Refalov), Eley Shechter, Dekel Keinan, Yoav Ziv, Elroy Cohen (69 Eyal Golasa), Tamir Cohen (51 Roberto Colautti). Trainer: Luis Fernandez

CROATIA: Vedran Runje, Ivan Strinić, Josip Šimunić, Vedran Čorluka, Danijel Pranjić, Ivan Rakitić (77 Ognjen Vukojević), Eduardo (57 Mario Mandžukić), Luka Modrić, Gordon Schildenfeld, Ivica Olić (72 Mate Bilić), Niko Kranjčar. Trainer: Slaven Bilić

Goals: Niko Kranjčar (36 pen, 41), Shechter (81)

CROATIA v MALTA 3-0 (2-0)

Stadion Maksimir, Zagreb 17.11.2010

Referee: Duarte Gomes (POR) Attendance: 9,000

CROATIA: Vedran Runje, Vedran Čorluka, Danijel Pranjić, Ivan Rakitić (69 Ivo Iličević), Eduardo (78 Mario Mandžukić), Luka Modrić, Darijo Srna, Gordon Schildenfeld, Tomislav Dujmović, Niko Kranjčar, Mladen Petrić (61 Nikola Kalinić). Trainer: Slaven Bilić

MALTA: Andrew Hogg, Jonathan Caruana, Shaun Bajada, Gareth Sciberras (88 Paul Fenech), John Hutchinson, Massimo Grima, Roderick Briffa, Michael Mifsud, Daniel Bogdanovic (82 Kevin Sammut), André Schembri (70 Ryan Fenech), Jamie Pace. Trainer: John Buttigieg

Goals: Niko Kranjčar (18, 42), Kalinić (81)

LATVIA v GEORGIA 1-1 (0-0)

Skonto Stadions, Riga 12.10.2010

Referee: Manuel De Sousa (POR) Attendance: 4,330

LATVIA: Amdris Vaņins, Oskars Kļava, Vitālijs Astafjevs, Juris Laizāns (82 Kristaps Grebis), Deniss Ivanovs, Aleksandrs Cauņa, Andrejs Rubins, Kaspars Gorkšs, Dzintars Zirnis, Artjoms Rudņevs, Jurijs Žigajevs (86 Andrejs Perepļotkins). Trainer: Aleksandrs Starkovs

GEORGIA: Nukri Revishvili, Ucha Lobzhanidze, Malkhaz Asatiani, Kakha Kaladze, Aleksandr Amisulashvili, Murtaz Daushvili, Jano Ananidze (79 Lasha Salukvadze), David Kvirkvelia (69 Gogita Gogua), Aleksandr Iashvili (88 Alexandre Koshkadze), Levan Kobiashvili, David Siradze. Trainer: Temuri Ketsbaia

Goals: David Siradze (74), Cauņa (90+1)

GEORGIA v CROATIA 1-0 (0-0)

Boris Paichadze National Stadium, Tbilisi 26.03.2011

Referee: Paolo Tagliavento (ITA) Attendance: 55,000

GEORGIA: Nukri Revishvili, Lasha Salukvadze, Akaki Khubutia, Kakha Kaladze, Aleksandr Amisulashvili, Zurab Khizanishvili, Jaba Kankava, Murtaz Daushvili (73 Gogita Gogua), Aleksandr Iashvili (62 Otar Martsvaladze), Levan Kobiashvili, Vladimir Dvalishvili (46 David Siradze). Trainer: Temuri Ketsbaia

CROATIA: Vedran Runje, Ivan Strinić, Dejan Lovren, Vedran Čorluka, Ivan Rakitić (61 Ivan Perišić), Luka Modrić, Darijo Srna, Nikola Kalinić, Tomislav Dujmović, Niko Kranjčar (70 Nikica Jelavić), Mladen Petrić (84 Danijel Pranjić). Trainer: Slaven Bilić

Goal: Levan Kobiashvili (90)

ISRAEL v LATVIA 2-1 (1-0)

Bloomfield, Tel Aviv 26.03.2011

Referee: Milorad Mažić (SRB) Attendance: 10,801

ISRAEL: Dudu Awat, Tal Ben Haim I, Rami Gershon, Bebras Natcho, Beram Kayal, Lior Refalov (84 Gil Vermouth), Elyaniv Barda (69 Maor Buzaglo), Taleb Twatha, Yoav Ziv (66 Ben Sahar), Iyzhak Cohen, Omer Damari.
Trainer: Luis Fernandez

LATVIA: Andris Vaņins, Deniss Kačanovs, Ritus Krjauklis, Deniss Ivanovs, Māris Verpakovskis (73 Daniils Turkovs), Andrejs Rubins (57 Andrejs Pereplotkins), Ivans Lukjanovs, Kaspars Gorkšs, Maksims Rafaļskis (58 Jurijs Žigajevs), Artis Lazdiņš, Artjoms Rudņevs. Trainer: Aleksandrs Starkovs

Goals: Elyaniv Barda (16), Kaspars Gorkšs (62), Beram Kayal (81)

MALTA v GREECE 0-1 (0-0)

Ta' Qali National Stadium, Ta' Qali 26.03.2011

Referee: Michael Weiner (GER) Attendance: 10,605

MALTA: Justin Haber, Jonathan Caruana (46 Jamie Pace), Carlo Mamo, Gareth Sciberras, André Agius, John Hutchinson, Daniel Bogdanovic, Roderick Briffa, Michael Mifsud, Shaun Bajada (78 Ryan Fenech), André Schembri (90+1 Andrew Cohen). Trainer: John Buttigieg

GREECE: Alexandros Tzorvas, Giórgos Tzavellas, Giórgos Samaras, Avraam Papadopoulos, Giórgos Karagounis, Dimítris Salpingidis (61 Giánnis Fetfatzidis), Vassilis Torossidis, Sotiris Ninis (81 Panagiotis Kone), Sokratis Papastathopoulos, Kostas Katsouranis, Nikos Liberopoulos (70 Kostas Mitroglou).
Trainer: Fernando Santos

Sent off: Papastathopoulos (84)

Goal: Vassilis Torossidis (90+2)

ISRAEL v GEORGIA 1-0 (0-0)

Bloomfield, Tel Aviv 29.03.2011

Referee: Fredy Fautrel (FRA) Attendance: 13,716

ISRAEL: Dudu Awat, Dani Bondarv, Tal Ben Haim I, Rami Gershon, Bebras Natcho (52 Tal Ben Haim II), Beram Kayal, Almog Cohen, Lior Refalov (63 Gil Vermouth), Elyaniv Barda (71 Yossi Benayoun), Maor Buzaglo, Dekel Keinan.
Trainer: Luis Fernandez

GEORGIA: Nukri Revishvili, Lasha Salukvadze, Akaki Khubutia, Kakha Kaladze, Aleksandr Amisulashvili, Zurab Khizanishvili, Jaba Kankava, Murtaz Daushvili (46 David Kvirkvelia), Aleksandr Iashvili (63 Vladimir Dvalishvili), Levan Kobiashvili, Otar Martsvaladze (73 David Siradze).
Trainer: Temuri Ketsbaia

Goal: Tal Ben Haim II (59)

CROATIA v GEORGIA 2-1 (0-1)

Stadion Poljud, Split 03.06.2011

Referee: Stefan Johannesson (SWE) Attendance: 28,000

CROATIA: Vedran Runje, Josip Šimunić, Vedran Ćorluka, Danijel Pranjić, Ognjen Vukojević (71 Tomislav Dujmović), Eduardo, Luka Modrić, Darijo Srna, Mario Mandžukić, Ivan Perišić (71 Ivan Klasnić), Nikica Jelavić (46 Nikola Kalinić).
Trainer: Slaven Bilić

GEORGIA: Giorgi Loria, Lasha Salukvadze, Akaki Khubutia, Kakha Kaladze, Gia Grigalava, Guram Kashia (80 Jano Ananidze), Jaba Kankava, David Kvirkvelia, Aleksandr Iashvili (62 Murtaz Daushvili), Zurab Khizanishvili, David Siradze (56 Vladimir Dvalishvili). Trainer: Temuri Ketsbaia

Goals: Jaba Kankava (17), Mario Mandžukić (76), Nikola Kalinić (78)

LATVIA v ISRAEL 1-2 (0-2)

Skonto Stadions, Riga 04.06.2011

Referee: Alan Kelly (IRL) Attendance: 6,147

LATVIA: Andris Vaņins, Oskars Kļava, Ritus Krjauklis, Deniss Ivanovs, Artis Lazdiņš, Aleksandrs Cauņa, Maksims Rafaļskis (28 Jurijs Žigajevs), Aleksajs Višņakovs (71 Ritvars Rugins), Artjoms Rudņevs, Kaspars Gorkšs, Andrejs Pereplotkins (60 Edgars Gauračs).
Trainer: Aleksandrs Starkovs

ISRAEL: Dudu Awat, Yuval Shpungin, Tal Ben Haim I, Rami Gershon, Almog Cohen, Lior Refalov (79 Tal Ben Haim II), Tomer Hemed, Maor Buzaglo (69 Bebras Natcho), Dekel Keinan, Yossi Benayoun, Eran Zahavi (89 Eyal Golasa).
Trainer: Luis Fernandez

Goals: Yossi Benayoun (19), Tal Ben Haim I (43 pen), Cauņa (62 pen)

GREECE v MALTA 3-1 (2-0)

Georgios Karaiskakis Stadium, Piraeus 04.06.2011

Referee: Pawel Gil (POL) Attendance: 14,746

GREECE: Dimítris Konstantopoulos, Nikos Spyropoulos, Vangelis Moras, Alexandros Tziolis, Giórgos Karagounis (70 Pantelis Kafes), Dimítris Salpingidis (89 Kostas Mitroglou), Vassilis Torossidis, Sotiris Ninis (80 Lazaros Christodoulopoulos), Kostas Katsouranis, Kyriakos Papadopoulos, Giánnis Fetfatzidis.
Trainer: Fernando Santos

MALTA: Andrew Hogg, Jonathan Caruana, Gareth Sciberras, André Agius, Ryan Fenech, Daniel Bogdanovic (60 Andrew Cohen), Roderick Briffa, Michael Mifsud, John Hutchinson (87 Paul Fenech), André Schembri, Shaun Bajada (80 Clayton Failla). Trainer: John Buttigieg

Goals: Fetfatzidis (7, 63), Kyriakos Papadopoulos (26), Michael Mifsud (54)

ISRAEL v GREECE 0-1 (0-0)

Bloomfield, Tel Aviv 02.09.2011

Referee: Craig Thomson (SCO) Attendance: 13,100

ISRAEL: Dudu Awat, Yuval Shpungin, Tal Ben Haim I, Rami Gershon, Beram Kayal, Almog Cohen (61 Bebras Natcho), Lior Refalov, Etey Shechter (55 Omaer Damari), Yossi Benayoun, Eran Zahavi (55 Tomer Hemed), Omri Ben Harush. Trainer: Luis Fernandez

GREECE: Michalis Sifakis, Giánnis Zaradoukas, Giórgos Samaras, Avraam Papadopoulos, Giórgos Karagounis, Dimítris Salpingidis (84 Giánnis Maniatis), Vassilis Torossidis, Pantelis Kafes (42 Grigoris Makos), Sotiris Ninis (77 Giánnis Fetfatzidis), Kostas Katsouranis, Kyriakos Papadopoulos. Trainer: Fernando Santos

Goal: Sotiris Ninis (60)

CROATIA v ISRAEL 3-1 (0-1)

Stadion Maksimir, Zagreb 06.09.2011

Referee: Carlos Velasco Carballo (SPA) Attendance: 13,688

CROATIA: Stipe Pletikosa, Ivan Strinić, Josip Šimunić, Dejan Lovren, Vedran Čorluka (46 Eduardo), Ognjen Vukojević (46 Tomislav Dujmović), Nikica Jelavić (87 Nikola Kalinić), Luka Modrić, Darijo Srna, Mario Mandžukić, Niko Kranjčar. Trainer: Slaven Bilić

ISRAEL: Dudu Awat (46 Guy Haimov), Tal Ben Haim I, Rami Gershon, Beram Kayal, Taleb Twatha, Tomer Hemed, Yossi Benayoun, Eran Zahavi (68 Etey Shechter), Iyad Khutaba, Omri Ben Harush, Tamir Cohen (57 Eyal Golasa). Trainer: Luis Fernandez

Sent off: Tal Ben Haim I (51)

Goals: Tomer Hemed (44), Luka Modrić (47), Eduardo (55, 57)

MALTA v CROATIA 1-3 (1-2)

Ta' Qali National Stadium, Ta' Qali 02.09.2011

Referee: Tony Chapron (FRA) Attendance: 6,150

MALTA: Andrew Hogg, Emmanuel Muscat, Gareth Sciberras, André Agius, Ryan Fenech (88 Carlo Mamo), Clayton Failla, Roderick Briffa (74 Jamie Pace), Michael Mifsud (82 Ivan Woods), Andrew Cohen, John Hutchinson, André Schembri. Trainer: John Buttigieg

CROATIA: Stipe Pletikosa, Ivan Strinić, Dejan Lovren, Vedran Čorluka, Milan Badelj (82 Eduardo), Ognjen Vukojević, Darijo Srna, Mario Mandžukić, Ivan Klasnić (46 Nikola Kalinić), Ivan Perišić (68 Tomislav Dujmović), Šime Vrsaljko. Trainer: Slaven Bilić

Goals: Ognjen Vukojević (11), Milan Badelj (32), Michael Mifsud (38), Dejan Lovren (68)

LATVIA v GREECE 1-1 (1-0)

Skonto Stadions, Riga 06.09.2011

Referee: Stanislav Todorov (BUL) Attendance: 5,415

LATVIA: Andris Vaņins, Pāvels Mihadjuks, Oskars Kļava, Ritus Krjauklis, Aleksandrs Fertovs, Deniss Ivanovs, Olegs Laizāns, Aleksandrs Cauņa, Māris Verpakovskis (68 Artjoms Rudņevs), Aleksejs Višņakovs (83 Jurijs Žigajevs), Ivans Lukjanovs. Trainer: Aleksandrs Starkovs

GREECE: Michalis Sifakis, Giánnis Zaradoukas, Grigoris Makos (81 Giórgos Georgiadis), Giórgos Samaras, Nikos Liberopoulos, Giórgos Karagounis, Loukas Vyntra (72 Giánnis Maniatis), Dimítris Salpingidis, Sokratis Papastathopoulos, Kyriakos Papadopoulos, Giánnis Fetfatzidis (46 Alexandros Tziolis). Trainer: Fernando Santos

Goals: Aleksandrs Cauņa (19), Kyriakos Papadopoulos (84)

GEORGIA v LATVIA 0-1 (0-0)

Mikheil Meskhi, Tbilisi 02.09.2011

Referee: Leontios Trattou (CYP) Attendance: 15,422

GEORGIA: Giorgi Loria, Jaba Kankava, Guram Kashia, Kakha Kaladze, Aleksandr Amisulashvili (71 Vladimir Dvalishvili), Zurab Khizanishvili, Jano Ananidze (54 Shota Grigalashvili), Otar Martsvaladze, Aleksandr Iashvili (54 David Siradze), Levan Kobiashvili, David Targamadze. Trainer: Temuri Ketsbaia

LATVIA: Andris Vaņins, Oskars Kļava, Ritus Krjauklis, Aleksandrs Fertovs, Deniss Ivanovs, Artis Lazdiņš (88 Olegs Laizāns), Aleksandrs Cauņa, Māris Verpakovskis (77 Edgars Gauračs), Aleksejs Višņakovs, Ivans Lukjanovs, Kaspars Gorkšs. Trainer: Aleksandrs Starkovs

Goal: Aleksandrs Cauņa (64)

MALTA v GEORGIA 1-1 (1-1)

Ta' Qali National Stadium, Ta' Qali 06.09.2011

Referee: Pol van Boekel (HOL) Attendance: 5,000

MALTA: Andrew Hogg, Jonathan Caruana, Gareth Sciberras, André Agius, Ryan Fenech (60 Daniel Bogdanovic), Roderick Briffa, Michael Mifsud, Andrew Cohen (90+1 Ivan Woods), John Hutchinson, André Schembri (76 Jamie Pace), Clayton Failla. Trainer: John Buttigieg

GEORGIA: Nukri Revishvili, Jaba Kankava, Guram Kashia, Kakha Kaladze, Gia Grigalava, Zurab Khizanishvili, Jano Ananidze (77 Alexandre Kobakhidze), Otar Martsvaladze (66 Shota Grigalashvili), Aleksandr Iashvili (61 Vladimir Dvalishvili), Levan Kobiashvili, David Targamadze. Trainer: Temuri Ketsbaia

Goals: Kankava (15), Michael Mifsud (25)

LATVIA v MALTA 2-0 (1-0)

Skonto Stadions, Riga 07.10.2011

Referee: Richard Trutz (SVK) Attendance: 4,315

LATVIA: Andris Vaņins, Oskars Kļava, Pāvels Mihadjuks, Olegs Laizāns (76 Ritvars Rugins), Deniss Ivanovs, Aleksejs Višņakovs, Aleksandrs Cauņa, Māris Verpakovskis (90+1 Andrejs Rubins), Ivans Lukjanovs, Kaspars Gorkšs, Artjoms Rudņevs (88 Edgars Gauračs). Trainer: Aleksandrs Starkovs

MALTA: Andrew Hogg, Steve Borg, Gareth Sciberras (83 Paul Fenech), André Agius, Ryan Fenech (82 Carlo Mamo), Clayton Failla, Roderick Briffa, Andrew Cohen, John Hutchinson, André Schembri, Jamie Pace (70 Ivan Woods). Trainer: John Buttigieg

Goals: A. Višņakovs (33), Rudņevs (83)

GEORGIA v GREECE 1-2 (1-0)

Mikheil Meskhi, Tbilisi 11.10.2011

Referee: Daniele Orsato (ITA) Attendance: 7,824

GEORGIA: Nukri Revishvili, Shota Grigalashvili (51 Aleksandr Iashvili), Guram Kashia, Kakha Kaladze, Aleksandr Amisulashvili, Zurab Khizanishvili, Otar Martsvaladze, Jaba Kankava (42 Ucha Lobzhanidze), Levan Mchedlidze (65 Alexander Guruli), Levan Kobiashvili, David Targamadze. Trainer: Temuri Ketsbaia

GREECE: Alexandros Tzorvas, Nikos Spyropoulos, Alexandros Tziolis (56 Giórgos Fotakis), Aggelos Charisteas, Giórgos Karagounis, Loukas Vyntra, Dimítris Salpingidis (68 Stefanos Athanasiadis), Fanis Gekas (90+1 Panagiotis Kone), Sokratis Papastathopoulos, Kostas Katsouranis, Kyriakos Papadopoulos. Trainer: Fernando Santos

Goals: David Targamadze (19), Giórgos Fotakis (79), Aggelos Charisteas (85)

GREECE v CROATIA 2-0 (0-0)

Georgios Karaiskakis Stadium, Piraeus 07.10.2011

Referee: Howard Webb (ENG) Attendance: 27,200

GREECE: Alexandros Tzorvas, Giánnis Zaradoukas, Alexandros Tziolis (62 Giórgos Fotakis), Giórgos Samaras, Avraam Papadopoulos, Giórgos Karagounis (87 Grigoris Makos), Dimítris Salpingidis, Vassilis Torossidis (43 Loukas Vyntra), Fanis Gekas, Sokratis Papastathopoulos, Kostas Katsouranis. Trainer: Fernando Santos

CROATIA: Stipe Pletikosa, Ivan Strinić, Josip Šimunić, Dejan Lovren, Vedran Čorluka (75 Domagoj Vida), Ognjen Vukojević, Nikica Jelavić (61 Nikola Kalinić), Luka Modrić, Mario Mandžukić, Niko Kranjčar, Eduardo (52 Ivan Perišić). Trainer: Slaven Bilić

Goals: Giórgos Samaras (71), Fanis Gekas (79)

MALTA v ISRAEL 0-2 (0-1)

Ta' Qali National Stadium, Ta' Qali 11.10.2011

Referee: Bruno Paixão (POR) Attendance: 2,614

MALTA: Andrew Hogg, Jonathan Caruana (83 Steve Borg), Carlo Mamo, Gareth Sciberras, André Agius, Ryan Fenech, Roderick Briffa, Michael Mifsud, Paul Fenech (64 Edward Herrera), John Hutchinson, Ivan Woods (81 Christian Caruana). Trainer: John Buttigieg

ISRAEL: Dudu Awat, Dani Bondarv (57 Gil Vermouth), Rami Gershon, Bebras Natcho, Lior Refalov (49 Almog Cohen), Maor Buzaglo, Nir Biton, Taleb Twatha, Tomer Hemed, Ben Sahar (78 Tal Ben Haim II), Eyal Golasa. Trainer: Luis Fernandez

Goals: Lior Refalov (11), Gershon (90+3)

CROATIA v LATVIA 2-0 (0-0)

Kantrida, Rijeka 11.10.2010

Referee: Antony Gautier (FRA) Attendance: 8,370

CROATIA: Stipe Pletikosa, Ivan Strinić, Josip Šimunić, Dejan Lovren, Vedran Čorluka (34 Domagoj Vida), Ivan Rakitić, Luka Modrić, Darijo Srna, Mario Mandžukić (84 Nikica Jelavić), Niko Kranjčar (59 Ivan Perišić), Eduardo. Trainer: Slaven Bilić

LATVIA: Andris Vaņins, Oskars Kļava, Pāvels Mihadjuks, Deniss Ivanovs, Olegs Laizāns, Aleksandrs Cauņa, Aleksejs Višņakovs (88 Andrejs Rubins), Ritvars Rugins (81 Igors Tarasovs), Kaspars Gorkšs, Andrejs Perepļotkins (71 Edgars Gauračs), Artjoms Rudņevs. Trainer: Aleksandrs Starkovs

Goals: Eduardo (66), Mandžukić (72)

	P	W	D	L	F	A	Pts
Greece	10	7	3	0	14	5	24
Croatia	10	7	1	2	18	7	22
Israel	10	5	1	4	13	11	16
Latvia	10	3	2	5	9	12	11
Georgia	10	2	4	4	7	9	10
Malta	10	0	1	9	4	21	1

GROUP G

MONTENEGRO v WALES 1-0 (1-0)

Stadium Podgorica 03.09.2010

Referee: Anastassios Kakos (GRE) Attendance: 7,442

MONTENEGRO: Mladen Božović, Savo Pavičević, Marko Baša, Milan Jovanović, Simon Vukčević (87 Fatos Beqiraj), Mirko Vučinić, Radomir Djalović (83 Mitar Novaković), Branko Bošković (74 Vladimir Božović), Milorad Peković, Elsad Zverotić, Miodrag Džudović. Trainer: Zlatko Kranjčar

WALES: Wayne Hennessey, Sam Ricketts, Chris Gunter, David Edwards (68 Rob Earnshaw), James Collins (75 Craig Morgan), Ashley Williams, David Vaughan, Craig Bellamy, Steve Morison (78 Simon Church), Joe Ledley, Gareth Bale. Trainer: John Toshack

Goal: Mirko Vučinić (30)

ENGLAND v BULGARIA 4-0 (1-0)

Wembley Stadium, London 03.09.2010

Referee: Viktor Kassai (HUN) Attendance: 73,426

ENGLAND: Joe Hart, Glen Johnson, Ashley Cole, Steven Gerrard, Michael Dawson (57 Gary Cahill), Phil Jagielka, Theo Walcott (74 Adam Johnson), Gareth Barry, Jermain Defoe (87 Ashley Young), Wayne Rooney, James Milner. Trainer: Fabio Capello

BULGARIA: Nikolai Mihaylov, Stanislav Manolev (65 Veselin Minev), Ilian Stoyanov, Stanislav Angelov, Ivelin Popov (79 Georgi Peev), Chavdar Yankov, Valeri Bozhinov (63 Dimitar Rangelov), Ivan Ivanov, Zhivko Milanov, Martin Petrov, Stilyan Petrov. Trainer: Stanimir Stoilov

Goals: Jermain Defoe (3, 61, 86), Adam Johnson (83)

BULGARIA v MONTENEGRO 0-1 (0-1)

Vasil Levski, Sofia 07.09.2010

Referee: Vladislav Bezborodov (RUS) Attendance: 9,470

BULGARIA: Nikolai Mihaylov, Ilian Stoyanov, Veselin Minev, Stanislav Angelov, Ivelin Popov, Dimitar Rangelov (46 Valeri Bozhinov), Georgi Peev (66 Valeri Domovchiyski), Ivan Ivanov, Zhivko Milanov (46 Stanislav Genchev), Martin Petrov, Stilyan Petrov. Trainer: Stanimir Stoilov

MONTENEGRO: Mladen Božović, Savo Pavičević, Marko Baša, Milan Jovanović, Simon Vukčević, Mirko Vučinić, Radomir Djalović (77 Mladen Kašćelan), Branko Bošković (64 Vladimir Božović), Milorad Peković, Elsad Zverotić (68 Mitar Novaković), Miodrag Džudović. Trainer: Zlatko Kranjčar

Goal: Elsad Zverotić (36)

SWITZERLAND v ENGLAND 1-3 (0-1)

St. Jakob-Park, Basel 07.09.2010

Referee: Nicola Rizzoli (ITA) Attendance: 37,500

SWITZERLAND: Diego Benaglio, Stephan Lichtsteiner, Reto Ziegler, Steve von Bergen, Pirmin Schwegler (83 Moreno Costanzo), Gökhan Inler, Alexander Frei, Stéphane Grichting, David Degen (64 Marco Streller), Eren Derdiyok, Xavier Margairaz (46 Xherdan Shaqiri). Trainer: Ottmar Hitzfeld

ENGLAND: Joe Hart, Glen Johnson, Ashley Cole, Steven Gerrard, Joleon Lescott, Phil Jagielka, Theo Walcott (13 Adam Johnson), Gareth Barry, Jermain Defoe (71 Darren Bent), Wayne Rooney (79 Shaun Wright-Phillips), James Milner. Trainer: Fabio Capello

Sent off: Lichtsteiner (65)

Goals: Wayne Rooney (10), Adam Johnson (69), Xherdan Shaqiri (71), Bent (88)

WALES v BULGARIA 0-1 (0-0)

Cardiff City Stadium, Cardiff 08.10.2010

Referee: Jonas Eriksson (SWE) Attendance: 14,061

WALES: Wayne Hennessey, Chris Gunter, Danny Collins, Ashley Williams, James Collins, Sam Ricketts, David Edwards (69 Simon Church), David Vaughan, Steve Morison (82 Robson-Kanu), Joe Ledley (59 Andy King), Gareth Bale. Trainer: Brian Flynn

BULGARIA: Nikolai Mihaylov, Valentin Iliev (37 Pavel Vidanov), Petar Zanev, Blagoi Georgiev, Ivelin Popov, Dimitar Makriev (87 Chavdar Yankov), Georgi Peev (72 Dimitar Rangelov), Ivan Ivanov, Martin Petrov, Stilyan Petrov, Nikolai Bodurov. Trainer: Lothar Matthäus

Sent off: Gunter (90+3)

Goal: Ivelin Popov (48)

MONTENEGRO v SWITZERLAND 1-0 (0-0)

Stadion Podgorica, Podgorica 08.10.2010

Referee: Eduardo Iturralde González (SPA) Att: 10,750

MONTENEGRO: Mladen Božović, Marko Baša, Milan Jovanović, Simon Vukčević (84 Fatos Beqiraj), Mirko Vučinić, Radomir Djalović (90+2 Radoslav Batak), Branko Bošković (46 Mladen Kašćelan), Mitar Novaković, Elsad Zverotić, Miodrag Džudović, Stefan Savić. Trainer: Zlatko Kranjčar

SWITZERLAND: Marco Wölfli, Reto Ziegler, Steve von Bergen, Pirmin Schwegler, Gökhan Inler, Alexander Frei, Marco Streller (67 Eren Derdiyok), Stéphane Grichting, Valentin Stocker (76 Hakan Yakin), Scott Sutter, Xherdan Shaqiri (67 Tranquillo Barnetta). Trainer: Ottmar Hitzfeld

Goal: Mirko Vučinić (68)

SWITZERLAND v WALES 4-1 (2-1)

St. Jakob-Park, Basel 12.10.2010

Referee: Alain Hamer (LUX) Attendance: 26,000

SWITZERLAND: Diego Benaglio (8 Marco Wölfli), Stephan Lichtsteiner, Reto Ziegler, Steve von Bergen, Pirmin Schwegler (90+1 Gelson Fernandes), Tranquillo Barnetta, Gökhan Inler, Alexander Frei (79 Eren Derdiyok), Marco Streller, Stéphane Grichting, Valentin Stocker. Trainer: Ottmar Hitzfeld

WALES: Wayne Hennessey, Darcy Blake (54 Christian Ribeiro), Danny Collins, James Collins, Andrew Crofts, Ashley Williams, David Edwards (77 Steve Morison), Andy King, Simon Church, David Vaughan (89 Shaun MacDonald), Gareth Bale. Trainer: Brian Flynn

Goals: Valentin Stocker (8, 89), Gareth Bale (13), Marco Streller (21), Gökhan Inler (82 pen)

ENGLAND v MONTENEGRO 0-0

Wembley Stadium, London 12.10.2010

Referee: Manuel Gräfe (GER) Attendance: 73,451

ENGLAND: Joe Hart, Glen Johnson, Ashley Cole, Steven Gerrard, Rio Ferdinand, Joleon Lescott, Ashley Young (74 Shaun Wright-Phillips), Gareth Barry, Peter Crouch (70 Kevin Davies), Wayne Rooney, Adam Johnson.
Trainer: Fabio Capello

MONTENEGRO: Mladen Božović, Marko Baša, Milan Jovanović, Simon Vukčević, Radomir Djalović (77 Andrija Delibašić), Branko Bošković (83 Fatos Beqiraj), Mitar Novaković (62 Mladen Kašćelan), Milorad Peković, Elsad Zverotić, Miodrag Džudović, Stefan Savić.
Trainer: Zlatko Kranjčar

WALES v ENGLAND 0-2 (0-2)

Millennium, Cardiff 26.03.2011

Referee: Olegário Benquerença (POR) Attendance: 68,959

WALES: Wayne Hennessey, Chris Gunter, Danny Collins, Andrew Crofts, James Collins, Ashley Williams, Joe Ledley, Craig Bellamy, Steve Morison (65 Ched Evans), Aaron Ramsey, Andy King (65 David Vaughan). Trainer: Gary Speed

ENGLAND: Joe Hart, Glen Johnson, Ashley Cole, Scott Parker (89 Phil Jagielka), Michael Dawson, John Terry, Frank Lampard, Jack Wilshere (82 Stewart Downing), Darren Bent, Wayne Rooney (70 James Milner), Ashley Young.
Trainer: Fabio Capello

Goals: Frank Lampard (7 pen), Darren Bent (15)

BULGARIA v SWITZERLAND 0-0

Vasil Levski, Sofia 26.03.2011

Referee: William Collum (SCO) Attendance: 9,600

BULGARIA: Nikolai Mihaylov, Stanislav Manolev, Ivan Bandalovski, Petar Zanev, Blagoi Georgiev, Spas Delev (81 Zdravko Lazarov), Ivelin Popov (85 Stanislav Angelov), Dimitar Makriev (52 Tsvetan Genkov), Ivan Ivanov, Stilyan Petrov, Kostadin Stoyanov. Trainer: Lothar Matthäus

SWITZERLAND: Marco Wölfli, Stephan Lichtsteiner, Reto Ziegler, Steve von Bergen, Valon Behrami (17 Gelson Fernandes), Gökhan Inler, Alexander Frei, Marco Streller (77 Mario Gavranović), Stéphane Grichting, Valentin Stocker (67 Eren Derdiyok), Blarim Dzemaili. Trainer: Ottmar Hitzfeld

ENGLAND v SWITZERLAND 2-2 (1-2)

Wembley Stadium, London 04.06.2011

Referee: Damir Skomina (SVN) Attendance: 84,459

ENGLAND: Joe Hart, Glen Johnson, Ashley Cole (31 Leighton Baines), Scott Parker, Rio Ferdinand, John Terry, Theo Walcott (78 Stewart Downing), Frank Lampard (46 Ashley Young), Darren Bent, Jack Wilshere, James Milner.
Trainer: Fabio Capello

SWITZERLAND: Diego Benaglio, Stephan Lichtsteiner, Reto Ziegler, Philippe Senderos, Tranquillo Barnetta (90 Innocent Emeghara), Gökhan Inler, Eren Derdiyok (75 Admir Mehmedi), Valon Behrami (59 Blarim Dzemaili), Granit Xhaka, Johan Djourou, Xherdan Shaqiri.
Trainer: Ottmar Hitzfeld

Goals: Tranquillo Barnetta (32, 35), Frank Lampard (37 pen), Ashley Young (51)

MONTENEGRO v BULGARIA 1-1 (0-0)

Stadion Podgorica, Podgorica 04.06.2011

Referee: Alon Yefet (ISR) Attendance: 11,500

MONTENEGRO: Mladen Božović, Savo Pavičević (82 Mladen Kašćelan), Marko Baša, Mirko Vučinić, Radomir Djalović, Milorad Peković, Luka Pejović, Elsad Zverotić (72 Stevan Jovetić), Nikola Drinčić, Vladimir Božović (76 Ivan Fatić), Stefan Savić. Trainer: Zlatko Kranjčar

BULGARIA: Nikolai Mihaylov, Stanislav Manolev, Ivan Bandalovski, Petar Zanev, Nikolai Bodurov, Hristo Yanev (84 Tsvetan Genkov), Ivelin Popov, Ivan Ivanov, Marcos Marquinhos, Martin Petrov (88 Spas Delev), Stilyan Petrov (46 Chavdar Yankov). Trainer: Lothar Matthäus

Goals: Radomir Djalović (53), Ivelin Popov (66)

BULGARIA v ENGLAND 0-3 (0-3)

Vasil Levski, Sofia 02.09.2011

Referee: Frank De Bleeckere (BEL) Attendance: 27,230

BULGARIA: Nikolai Mihaylov, Petar Zanev, Nikolai Bodurov, Blagoi Georgiev, Ivelin Popov (81 Marcos Marquinhos), Ivan Bandalovski (46 Georgi Sarmov), Ivan Ivanov, Zhivko Milanov, Martin Petrov, Stilyan Petrov, Tsvetan Genkov (62 George Bozhilov). Trainer: Lothar Matthäus

ENGLAND: Joe Hart, Chris Smalling, Ashley Cole, Scott Parker, Gary Cahill, John Terry, Theo Walcott (83 Adam Johnson), Gareth Barry (80 Frank Lampard), Ashley Young (62 James Milner), Wayne Rooney, Stewart Downing. Trainer: Fabio Capello

Goals: Gary Cahill (13), Wayne Rooney (21, 45+1)

ENGLAND v WALES 1-0 (1-0)

Wembley Stadium, London 06.09.2011

Referee: Robert Schörgenhofer (AUS) Attendance: 77,128

ENGLAND: Joe Hart, Chris Smalling, Ashley Cole, Gareth Barry, Gary Cahill, John Terry, Stewart Downing (79 Adam Johnson), Frank Lampard (73 Scott Parker), Ashley Young, Wayne Rooney (89 Andy Carroll), James Milner. Trainer: Fabio Capello

WALES: Wayne Hennessey, Chris Gunter, Neil Taylor, Andrew Crofts, Darcy Blake, Ashley Williams, Joe Ledley, Jack Collison (85 Andy King), Steve Morison (68 Rob Earnshaw), Aaron Ramsey, Gareth Bale. Trainer: Gary Speed

Goal: Ashley Young (35)

WALES v MONTENEGRO 2-1 (1-0)

Cardiff City Stadium, Cardiff 02.09.2011

Referee: Luca Banti (ITA) Attendance: 8,194

WALES: Wayne Hennessey, Chris Gunter, Neil Taylor, David Vaughan, Darcy Blake, Ashley Williams, Joe Ledley, Craig Bellamy, Steve Morison (83 Hal Robson-Kanu), Aaron Ramsey (64 Andrew Crofts), Gareth Bale (90+4 Rob Earnshaw). Trainer: Gary Speed

MONTENEGRO: Mladen Božović, Saša Balić (83 Milan Jovanović), Radoslav Batak, Simon Vukčević, Stevan Jovetić, Mirko Vučinić (78 Andrija Delibašić), Radomir Djalović (57 Dejan Damjanović), Milorad Peković, Elsad Zverotić, Nikola Drinčić, Stefan Savić. Trainer: Zlatko Kranjčar

Goals: Steve Morison (29), Ramsey (50), Jovetić (71)

WALES v SWITZERLAND 2-0 (0-0)

Liberty Stadium, Swansea 07.10.2011

Referee: Björn Kuipers (HOL) Attendance: 12,317

WALES: Wayne Hennessey, Chris Gunter, Neil Taylor, Andrew Crofts (81 David Vaughan), Darcy Blake, Ashley Williams, Joe Allen, Craig Bellamy, Steve Morison (81 Simon Church), Aaron Ramsey, Gareth Bale. Trainer: Gary Speed

SWITZERLAND: Diego Benaglio, Stephan Lichtsteiner, Reto Ziegler, Steve von Bergen, Gökhan Inler, Eren Derdiyok, Valon Behrami, Granit Xhaka (81 Admir Mehmedi), Fabian Frei (71 Innocent Emeghara), Timm Klose, Xherdan Shaqiri (62 Ricardo Rodriguez). Trainer: Ottmar Hitzfeld

Sent off: Ziegler (55)

Goals: Aaron Ramsey (60 pen), Gareth Bale (71)

SWITZERLAND v BULGARIA 3-1 (1-1)

St. Jakob-Park, Basel 06.09.2011

Referee: Pavel Kralovec (CZE) Attendance: 16,880

SWITZERLAND: Diego Benaglio, Stephan Lichtsteiner, Reto Ziegler, Philippe Senderos, Gökhan Inler, Eren Derdiyok, Admir Mehmedi (83 Innocent Emeghara), Blarim Dzemaili, Granit Xhaka (88 Gelson Fernandes), Johan Djourou, Xherdan Shaqiri (90+1 Nassim Ben Khalifa). Trainer: Ottmar Hitzfeld

BULGARIA: Nikolai Mihaylov, Valentin Iliev, Petar Zanev, Blagoi Georgiev, Georgi Sarmov, Ivelin Popov, Ivan Ivanov, Zhivko Milanov, Martin Petrov (60 Vladimir Gadzhev), Stilyan Petrov, Tsvetan Genkov (70 Nikolai Bodurov). Trainer: Lothar Matthäus

Sent off: Milanov (65)

Goals: Ivan Ivanov (9), Xherdan Shaqiri (45+2, 62, 90)

MONTENEGRO v ENGLAND 2-2 (1-2)

Stadion Podgorica, Podgorica 07.10.2011

Referee: Wolfgang Stark (GER) Attendance: 11,340

MONTENEGRO: Mladen Božović, Mladen Kašćelan (46 Milan Jovanović), Simon Vukčević, Stevan Jovetić, Mirko Vučinić, Fatos Beqiraj (64 Dejan Damjanović), Milorad Peković, Elsad Zverotić, Vladimir Božović (80 Andrija Delibašić), Miodrag Džudović, Stefan Savić. Trainer: Zlatko Kranjčar

ENGLAND: Joe Hart, Phil Jones, Ashley Cole, Scott Parker, Gary Cahill, John Terry, Theo Walcott (76 Danny Welbeck), Gareth Barry, Darren Bent (65 Frank Lampard), Wayne Rooney, Ashley Young (60 Stewart Downing). Trainer: Fabio Capello

Sent off: Rooney (74)

Goals: Ashley Young (11), Darren Bent (31), Elsad Zverotić (45), Andrija Delibašić (90+1)

BULGARIA v WALES 0-1 (0-1)

Natsionalen Stadion Vasil Levski, Sofia 11.10.2011

Referee: Pawel Gil (POL) Attendance: 1,672

BULGARIA: Nikolai Mihaylov, Stanislav Manolev (51 Spas Delev), Georgi Terziev, Petar Zanev, Aleksandar Tonev, Ivelin Popov (70 Dimitar Rangelov), Iordan Miliev, Valeri Domovchiyski (61 Valeri Bozhinov), Ivan Ivanov, Vladimir Gadzhev, Stilyan Petrov. Trainer: Mihail Madanski

WALES: Wayne Hennessey, Chris Gunter, Neil Taylor, Andrew Crofts, Darcy Blake (41 Adam Matthews), Ashley Williams, Joe Allen, Craig Bellamy, Steve Morison (70 Simon Church), Aaron Ramsey, Gareth Bale. Trainer: Gary Speed

Goal: Gareth Bale (45)

SWITZERLAND v MONTENEGRO 2-0 (0-0)

St. Jakob-Park, Basel 11.10.2011

Referee: Olegário Benquerença (POR) Attendance: 19,997

SWITZERLAND: Diego Benaglio, Stephan Lichtsteiner, Steve von Bergen, Gökhan Inler, Eren Derdiyok (69 Innocent Emeghara), Valon Behrami, Ricardo Rodriguez, Granit Xhaka (85 Gelson Fernandes), Admir Mehmedi, Johan Djourou, Xherdan Shaqiri (79 David Degen). Trainer: Ottmar Hitzfeld

MONTENEGRO: Mladen Božović, Draško Božović, Radoslav Batak, Marko Ćetković, Radomir Djalović (66 Andrija Delibašić), Fatos Beqiraj, Dejan Damjanović, Luka Pejović (46 Vladimir Božović), Elsad Zverotić, Nikola Drinčić (72 Petar Grbić), Stefan Savić. Trainer: Branko Brnović

Goals: Eren Derdiyok (51), Stephan Lichtsteiner (65)

	P	W	D	L	F	A	Pts
England	8	5	3	0	17	5	18
Montenegro	8	3	3	2	7	7	12
Switzerland	8	3	2	3	12	10	11
Wales	8	3	0	5	6	10	9
Bulgaria	8	1	2	5	3	13	5

GROUP H

ICELAND v NORWAY 1-2 (1-0)

Laugardalsvöllur, Reykjavík 03.09.2010

Referee: Luca Banti (ITA) Attendance: 6,137

ICELAND: Gunnleifur Gunnleifsson, Sölvi Ottesen, Kristján Sigurdsson, Indridi Sigurdsson, Grétar Steinsson (76 Birkir Bjarnason), Jóhann Gudmundsson (87 Rúrik Gíslason), Veigar Gunnarsson (76 Arnór Adalsteinsson), Heidar Helguson, Egert Jónsson, Aron Gunnarsson, Gylfi Sigurdsson.
Trainer: Ólafur Jóhannesson

NORWAY: Jon Knudsen, Tom Høgli, Kjetil Wæhler, Brede Hangeland, John Arne Riise, Bjørn Helge Riise (57 Steffen Iversen), Henning Hauger, Mohammed Abdellaoue (88 Jan Gunnar Solli), Morten Gamst Pedersen, Christian Grindheim, Erik Huseklepp (76 Espen Ruud). Trainer: Egil Olsen

Goals: Heidar Helguson (38), Brede Hangeland (58), Mohammed Abdellaoue (75)

PORTUGAL v CYPRUS 4-4 (2-2)

Estádio D. Afonso Henriques, Guimaraes 03.09.2010

Referee: Mark Clattenburg (ENG) Attendance: 9,100

PORTUGAL: EDUARDO Carvalho, Bruno Alves, Ricardo Carvalho, Ricardo Quaresma, Miguel Angel Gomes "Danny" (61 LIEDSON Muniz), MIGUEL Monteiro, Manuel Fernandes (79 João Moutinho), Raul Meireles, Luis Cunha "Nani", Hugo Almeida (84 Yannick Djaló), Fábio Coentrão.
Trainer: Agostinho Oliveira

CYPRUS: Antonis Giorgallides, Elias Charalambous, Giórgos Merkis, Efstathios Aloneftis (56 Giánnis Okkas), Marios Ilia (66 Savvas Poursaitides), Konstantinos Charalambides (76 Marois Nikolaou), Michalis Konstantinou, Konstantinos Makridis, Marinos Satsias, Sinisa Dobrasinovic, Andreas Avraam. Trainer: Aggelos Anastasiadis

Goals: Efstathios Aloneftis (3), Hugo Almeida (8), Michalis Konstantinou (11), Raul Meireles (29), Miguel Angel Gomes "Danny" (50), Giánnis Okkas (57), Manuel Fernandes (60), Andreas Avraam (89)

DENMARK v ICELAND 1-0 (0-0)

Parken, København 07.09.2010

Referee: Douglas McDonald (SCO) Attendance: 18,908

DENMARK: Anders Lindegaard, Christian Poulsen, Simon Kjær, Daniel Agger, Leon Jessen, Lars Jacobsen, Christian Eriksen (56 Mads Junker), Thomas Kahlenberg, Nicklas Pedersen (71 Morten Skoubo), Dennis Rommedahl, Michael Krohn-Dehli (76 Martin Vingaard). Trainer: Morten Olsen

ICELAND: Gunnleifur Gunnleifsson, Sölvi Ottesen, Kristján Sigurdsson, Indridi Sigurdsson, Birkir Sævarsson, Jóhann Gudmundsson (90+2 Birkir Bjarnason), Heidar Helguson (77 Kolbeinn Sigthórsson), Eggert Jónsson, Aron Gunnarsson, Gylfi Sigurdsson, Rúrik Gíslason. Trainer: Ólaf Jóhannesson

Goal: Thomas Kahlenberg (90+1)

NORWAY v PORTUGAL 1-0 (1-0)

Ullevaal Stadion, Oslo 07.09.2010

Referee: Laurent Duhamel (FRA) Attendance: 24,535

NORWAY: Jon Knudsen, Tom Høgli, Kjaetil Wæhler (28 Vadim Demidov), Brede Hangeland, Bjørn Helge Riise, Henning Hauger, John Carew (38 Mohammed Abdellaoue), Morten Gamst Pedersen, Espen Ruud, Christian Grindheim (86 Ruben Yttergård Jenssen), Erik Huseklepp. Trainer: Egil Olsen

PORTUGAL: EDUARDO Carvalho, Bruno Alves, Sílvio Pereira, Ricardo Carvalho, Ricardo Quaresma (84 LIEDSON Muniz), Miguel Veloso, Manuel Fernandes, Raul Meireles, Luis Cunha "Nani", Hugo Almeida, TIAGO Mendes (72 Miguel Angel Gomes "Danny"). Trainer: Agostinho Oliveira

Goal: Erik Huseklepp (21)

CYPRUS v NORWAY 1-2 (0-2)

Antonis Papadopoulos, Larnaca 08.10.2010

Referee: Serge Gumienny (BEL) Attendance: 7,648

CYPRUS: Antonis Giorgallides, Elias Charalambous (86 George Efrem), Giórgos Merkis (81 Dimítris Christofi), Efstathios Aloneftis, Giánnis Okkas, Konstantinos Charalambides (46 Marinos Satsias), Michalis Konstantinou, Konstantinos Makridis, Sinisa Dobrasinovic, Andreas Avraam, Savvas Poursaitides. Trainer: Aggelos Anastasiadis

NORWAY: Jon Knudsen, Tom Høgli, Kjaetil Wæhler, Brede Hangeland, John Arne Riise, Bjørn Helge Riise (74 Petter Vaagan Moen), Henning Hauger, John Carew (83 Mohammed Abdellaoue), Morten Gamst Pedersen, Christian Grindheim, Erik Huseklepp (80 Espen Ruud). Trainer: Egil Olsen

Goals: John Arne Riise (2), John Carew (42), Giánnis Okkas (58)

PORTUGAL v DENMARK 3-1 (2-0)

Estádio do Dragão, Porto 08.10.2010

Referee: Eric Braamhaar (HOL) Attendance: 27,117

PORTUGAL: EDUARDO Carvalho, Képler Ferreira "Pepe", João Pereira, Fábio Coentrão, Ricardo Carvalho, Cristiano Ronaldo, João Moutinho, Raul Meireles, Luis Cunha "Nani" (88 Silvestre Varela), Hugo Almeida (69 Hélder Postiga), Carlos Martins (75 TIAGO Mendes). Trainer: Paulo Bento

DENMARK: Thomas Sørensen (32 Anders Lindegaard), Christian Poulsen, Simon Kjær, Per Krøldrup, Michael Silberbauer, Lars Jacobsen, Daniel Jensen (58 Christian Eriksen), William Kvist (72 Peter Løvenkrands), Nicklas Pedersen, Dennis Rommedahl, Martin Vingaard. Trainer: Morten Olsen

Goals: Luis Cunha "Nani" (29, 30), Ricardo Carvalho (79 own goal), Cristiano Ronaldo (85)

DENMARK v CYPRUS 2-0 (0-0)

Parken, København 12.10.2010

Referee: César Muñiz Fernández (SPA) Attendance: 15,544

DENMARK: Anders Lindegaard, Christian Poulsen, Simon Kjær, Daniel Agger (39 Per Krøldrup), Leon Jessen, Lars Jacobsen, Michael Krohn-Dehli (65 Christian Eriksen), Kasper Lorentzen, Nicklas Pedersen, Dennis Rommedahl, Mads Junker (46 Morten Rasmussen). Trainer: Morten Olsen

CYPRUS: Antonis Giorgallides, Elias Charalambous (28 Paraskevas Christou), Giórgos Merkis, Efstathios Aloneftis (55 Konstantinos Charalambides), Giánnis Okkas, Michalis Konstantinou, Konstantinos Makridis, Marinos Satsias, Sinisa Dobrasinovic, Andreas Avraam (63 Alexandros Garpozis), Savvas Poursaitides. Trainer: Aggelos Anastasiadis

Goals: M. Rasmussen (48), Lorentzen (81)

ICELAND v PORTUGAL 1-3 (1-2)

Laugardalsvöllur, Reykjavik 12.10.2010

Referee: Thomas Einwaller (AUS) Attendance: 9,767

ICELAND: Gunnleifur Gunnleifsson, Ragnar Sigurdsson, Birkir Sævarsson (85 Veigar Gunnarsson), Kristján Sigurdsson, Indridi Sigurdsson (85 Arnór Adalsteinsson), Grétar Steinsson, Ólafur Skúlason, Eidur Gudjohnsen, Heidar Helguson, Helgi Daníelsson, Theodor Bjarnason (68 Gunnar Heidar Thorvaldsson). Trainer: Ólafur Jóhannesson

PORTUGAL: EDUARDO Carvalho, Képler Ferreira "Pepe", João Pereira, Fábio Coentrão, Ricardo Carvalho, Cristiano Ronaldo, João Moutinho, Raul Meireles, Luis Cunha "Nani" (87 Miguel Angel Gomes "Danny"), Hugo Almeida (65 Hélder Postiga), Carlos Martins (77 TIAGO Mendes). Trainer: Paulo Bento

Goals: Cristiano Ronaldo (3), Heidar Helguson (17), Raul Meireles (27), Hélder Postiga (72)

CYPRUS v ICELAND 0-0

GSP Stadium, Nicosia 26.03.2011

Referee: Darko Čeferin (SVN) Attendance: 2,088

CYPRUS: Antonis Giorgallides, Valentinos Sielis (46 Jason Demetriou), Giórgos Merkis, Efstathios Aloneftis, Dimítris Christofi (73 Nektarios Alexandrou), Konstantinos Charalambides, Konstantinos Makridis, Chrysosthomos Michail, Sinisa Dobrasinovic, Andreas Avraam, Savvas Poursaitides (61 Marios Ilia).

ICELAND: Stefán Magnússon, Birkir Sævarsson, Kristján Sigurdsson, Indridi Sigurdsson, Gylfi Sigurdsson (90+1 Birkir Bjarnason), Hermann Hreidarsson, Rúrik Gíslason (63 Alfred Finnbogason), Jóhann Gudmundsson (59 Arnór Smárason), Heidar Helguson, Eggert Jónsson, Aron Gunnarsson. Trainer: Ólafur Jóhannesson

NORWAY v DENMARK 1-1 (0-1)

Ullevaal Stadion, Oslo 26.03.2011

Referee: Gianluca Rocchi (ITA) Attendance: 24,828

NORWAY: Rune Jarstein, Kjaetil Wæhler, Brede Hangeland, John Arne Riise, Bjørn Helge Riise, Henning Hauger, Mohammed Abdellaoue, Morten Gamst Pedersen, Espen Ruud (78 Daniel Braaten), Christian Grindheim, Erik Huseklepp (89 Steffen Iversen). Trainer: Egil Olsen

DENMARK: Thomas Sørensen, Christian Poulsen (70 Jakob Poulsen), Mathias Jørgensen, Daniel Agger, Michael Silberbauer, Lars Jacobsen, William Kvist, Christian Eriksen, Michael Krohn-Dehli (82 Thomas Enevoldsen), Dennis Rommedahl (90+3 Daniel Wass), Nicklas Bendtner. Trainer: Morten Olsen

Goals: Dennis Rommedahl (27), Erik Huseklepp (81)

ICELAND v DENMARK 0-2 (0-0)

Laugardalsvöllur, Reykjavík 04.06.2011

Referee: Fırat Aydınus (TUR) Attendance: 7,629

ICELAND: Stefán Magnússon, Birkir Sævarsson, Kristján Sigurdsson, Hermann Hreidarsson, Ólafur Skúlason (66 Alfred Finnbogason), Eidur Gudjohnsen, Gylfi Sigurdsson, Heidar Helguson (77 Jóhann Gudmundsson), Bjarni Eiríksson, Aron Gunnarsson, Kolbeinn Sigthórsson. Trainer: Ólafur Jóhannesson

DENMARK: Thomas Sørensen, Niki Zimling, Simon Kjær, Bo Svensson, Simon Poulsen, Lars Jacobsen, William Kvist (60 Christian Poulsen), Christian Eriksen, Michael Krohn-Dehli (46 Lasse Schøne), Dennis Rommedahl, Nicklas Bendtner. Trainer: Morten Olsen

Goals: Schøne (60), Christian Eriksen (75)

PORTUGAL v NORWAY 1-0 (0-0)

Estádio do Sport Lisboa e Benfica, Lisboa 04.06.2011

Referee: Cüneyt Çakır (TUR) Attendance: 47,829

PORTUGAL: EDUARDO Carvalho, Bruno Alves, Képler Ferreira "Pepe", Fábio Coentrão, Cristiano Ronaldo, João Moutinho, Raul Meireles, Luis Cunha "Nani" (86 Silvestre Varela), Carlos Martins (69 Rúben Micael), João Pereira (73 Sílvio Pereira), Hélder Postiga. Trainer: Paulo Bento

NORWAY: Rune Jarstein, Tom Høgli, Vadim Demidov, Brede Hangeland, John Arne Riise, Bjørn Helge Riise, Henning Hauger, John Carew (60 Mohammed Abdellaoue), Morten Gamst Pedersen, Christian Grindheim (83 Markus Henriksen), Erik Huseklepp (75 Daniel Braaten). Trainer: Egil Olsen

Goal: Hélder Postiga (53)

NORWAY v ICELAND 1-0 (0-0)

Ullevaal Stadion, Oslo 02.09.2011

Referee: Ovidiu Alin Haţegan (ROM) Attendance: 22,381

NORWAY: Rune Jarstein, Tom Høgli, Kjaetil Wæhler, Brede Hangeland, Henning Hauger, Mohammed Abdellaoue, Espen Ruud, Alexander Tettey, Christian Grindheim (80 John Carew), Erik Huseklepp (87 Simen Brenne), Jonathan Parr (68 Daniel Braaten). Trainer: Egil Olsen

ICELAND: Stefán Magnússon, Solvi Geir Jonsson, Birkir Sævarsson, Indridi Sigurdsson, Eggert Jónsson, Jóhann Gudmundsson (80 Steinthor Thorsteinsson), Helgi Daníelsson (90 Birkir Bjarnason), Eidur Gudjohnsen, Kolbeinn Sigthórsson (78 Veigar Gunnarsson), Hjörtur Valgardsson, Rúrik Gíslason. Trainer: Ólafur Jóhannesson

Goal: Mohammed Abdellaoue (88 pen)

CYPRUS v PORTUGAL 0-4 (0-1)

GSP Stadium, Nicosia 02.09.2011

Referee: Gianluca Rocchi (ITA) Attendance: 15,444

CYPRUS: Antonis Giorgallides, Paraskevas Christou, Giórgos Merkis, Giánnis Okkas, Konstantinos Charalambides (63 Nektarios Alexandrou), Konstantinos Makridis (38 Marios Nikolaou), Dimitris Christofi (80 George Efrem), Sinisa Dobrasinovic, Andreas Avraam, Savvas Poursaitides, Jason Demetriou. Trainer: Nikos Nioplias

PORTUGAL: Rui Patrício, Bruno Alves, Képler Ferreira "Pepe", Fábio Coentrão, Cristiano Ronaldo, João Moutinho, Rúben Micael (63 Miguel Veloso), Raul Meireles, Luis Cunha "Nani" (86 Miguel Angel Gomes "Danny"), João Pereira, Hélder Postiga (76 Hugo Almeida). Trainer: Paulo Bento

Sent off: Dobrasinovic (34)

Goals: Cristiano Ronaldo (35 pen, 82), Hugo Almeida (84), Miguel Angel Gomes "Danny" (90+2)

DENMARK v NORWAY 2-0 (2-0)

Parken, København 06.09.2011

Referee: Stéphane Lannoy (FRA) Attendance: 37,167

DENMARK: Thomas Sørensen, Niki Zimling, Simon Kjær, Daniel Agger, Nicolai Boilesen, Lars Jacobsen, William Kvist, Christian Eriksen, Michael Krohn-Dehli (70 Lasse Schøne), Dennis Rommedahl (65 Michael Silberbauer), Nicklas Bendtner (90 Nicklas Pedersen). Trainer: Morten Olsen

NORWAY: Rune Jarstein, Tom Høgli, Kjaetil Wæhler (46 Vadim Demidov), Brede Hangeland, John Arne Riise (61 Daniel Braaten), Mohammed Abdellaoue, Espen Ruud, Alexander Tettey, Christian Grindheim, Håvard Nordtveit, Erik Huseklepp (69 John Carew). Trainer: Egil Olsen

Goals: Bendtner (24, 44)

ICELAND v CYPRUS 1-0 (1-0)

Laugardalsvöllur, Reykjavik 06.09.2011

Referee: Boško Jovanetić (SRB) Attendance: 5,267

ICELAND: Hannes Halldórsson, Birkir Sævarsson, Kristján Sigurdsson, Eggert Jónsson, Jóhann Gudmundsson (88 Matthías Vilhjálmsson), Helgi Daníelsson, Eidur Gudjohnsen, Kolbeinn Sigthórsson (84 Alfred Finnbogason), Hjörtur Valgardsson, Birkir Bjarnason (84 Björn Sigurdarsson), Hallgrímur Jónasson. Trainer: Ólafur Jóhannesson

CYPRUS: Antonis Giorgallides, Paraskevas Christou, Giórgos Merkis, Giánnis Okkas (46 Konstantinos Makridis), Konstantinos Charalambides (83 Kyriakos Pavlou), Dimitris Christofi, Marinos Satsias, Nektarios Alexandrou (61 George Efrem), Andreas Avraam, Savvas Poursaitides, Jason Demetriou. Trainer: Nikos Nioplias

Goal: Kolbeinn Sigthórsson (5)

CYPRUS v DENMARK 1-4 (1-4)

GSP Stadium, Nicosia 07.10.2011

Referee: Marijo Strahonja (CRO) Attendance: 2,408

CYPRUS: Antonis Giorgallides, Giórgos Merkis, Giórgos Pelagia, Konstantinos Charalambides, Michalis Konstantinou (62 Dimitris Christofi), Sinisa Dobrasinovic, Nektarios Alexandrou, Andreas Avraam, Savvas Poursaitides (46 Athos Solomou), Jason Demetriou (71 Marinos Satsias), George Efrem. Trainer: Nikos Nioplias

DENMARK: Thomas Sørensen, Niki Zimling (68 Martin Jørgensen), Simon Kjær, Andreas Bjelland, Simon Poulsen, Lars Jacobsen (82 Michael Silberbauer), William Kvist, Christian Eriksen, Michael Krohn-Dehli, Dennis Rommedahl (71 Christian Poulsen), Nicklas Bendtner.
Trainer: Morten Olsen

Goals: Lars Jacobsen (7), Dennis Rommedahl (11, 22), Michael Krohn-Dehli (20), Andreas Avraam (45+1)

PORTUGAL v ICELAND 5-3 (3-0)

Estádio do Dragão, Porto 07.10.2011

Referee: Bas Nijhuis (HOL) Attendance: 35,715

PORTUGAL: Rui Patrício, Bruno Alves, João Pereira, Cristiano Ronaldo, João Moutinho, ROLANDO Fonseca, Raul Meireles (60 Miguel Veloso), Luis Cunha "Nani", ELISEU Pereira dos Santos, Carlos Martins (72 Rúben Micael), Hélder Postiga (88 Nuno Gomes). Trainer: Paulo Bento

ICELAND: Stefán Magnússon, Solvi Geir Jonsson, Birkir Sævarsson, Kristján Sigurdsson, Jóhann Gudmundsson (81 Kjartan Henry Finnbogason), Birkir Bjarnason, Gylfi Sigurdsson, Hjörtur Valgardsson, Aron Gunnarsson, Rúrik Gíslason (89 Arnór Smárason), Hallgrímur Jónasson (89 Matthías Vilhjálmsson). Trainer: Ólafur Jóhannesson

Goals: Luis Cunha "Nani" (13, 21), Hélder Postiga (44), Jónasson (48, 68), João Moutinho (81), ELISEU Pereira dos Santos (87), Gylfi Sigurdsson 90+4(pen)

DENMARK v PORTUGAL 2-1 (1-0)

Parken, København 11.10.2011

Referee: Nicola Rizzoli (ITA) Attendance: 37,012

DENMARK: Thomas Sørensen, Niki Zimling (70 Christian Poulsen), Simon Kjær, Andreas Bjelland, Michael Silberbauer (76 Simon Poulsen), Lars Jacobsen, William Kvist, Christian Eriksen, Michael Krohn-Dehli, Dennis Rommedahl (87 Jakob Poulsen), Nicklas Bendtner. Trainer: Morten Olsen

PORTUGAL: Rui Patrício, Bruno Alves, João Pereira, Cristiano Ronaldo, João Moutinho, ROLANDO Fonseca, Raul Meireles, Luis Cunha "Nani", ELISEU Pereira dos Santos (65 Ricardo Quaresma), Carlos Martins (65 Miguel Veloso), Hélder Postiga (78 Nuno Gomes). Trainer: Paulo Bento

Goals: Michael Krohn-Dehli (13), Nicklas Bendtner (63), Cristiano Ronaldo (90+2)

NORWAY v CYPRUS 3-1 (2-1)

Ullevaal Stadion, Oslo 11.10.2011

Referee: William Collum (SCO) Attendance: 13,490

NORWAY: Rune Jarstein, Tom Høgli, Kjaetil Wæhler, Vadim Demidov, John Arne Riise, John Carew, Morten Gamst Pedersen (46 Jonathan Parr), Espen Ruud (63 Simen Brenne), Alexander Tettey (82 Ruben Yttegård Jenssen), Christian Grindheim, Erik Huseklepp. Trainer: Egil Olsen

CYPRUS: Tasos Kissas, Elias Charalambous, Giórgos Merkis, Giórgos Pelagia (6 Stelios Parpas), Athos Solomou, Giánnis Okkas (82 Andreas Stavrou), Konstantinos Charalambides (62 Dimítris Christofi), Marinos Satsias, Sinisa Dobrasinovic, Andreas Avraam, Jason Demetriou. Trainer: Nikos Nioplias

Goals: Morten Gamst Pedersen (25), John Carew (34), Giánnis Okkas (42), Tom Høgli (65)

	P	W	D	L	F	A	Pts
Denmark	8	6	1	1	15	6	19
Portugal	8	5	1	2	21	12	16
Norway	8	5	1	2	10	7	16
Iceland	8	1	1	6	6	14	4
Cyprus	8	0	2	6	7	20	2

GROUP I

LITHUANIA v SCOTLAND 0-0

Dariaus ir Giréno, Kanas 03.09.2010

Referee: Cüneyt Çakir (TUR) Attendance: 5,248

LITHUANIA: Žydrūnas Karčemarskas, Deividas Šemberas, Ramūnas Radavičius, Tadas Kijanskas, Andrius Skerla, Mindaugas Panka, Edgaras Česnauskis, Tomas Danilevičius (90 Kestutis Ivaškevičius), Darvydas Šernas (80 Vytautas Lukša), Saulius Mikoliūnas (71 Robertas Poškus), Markus Stankevičius. Trainer: Raimondas Žutautas

SCOTLAND: Allan McGregor, Alan Hutton, Steven Whittaker (90 Christophe Berra), Stephen McManus, David Weir, Lee McCulloch, Darren Fletcher, Gareth Barry Robson (69 James McFadden), Kenny Miller, Scott Brown (76 James Morrison), Steven Naismith. Trainer: Craig Levein

LIECHTENSTEIN v SPAIN 0-4 (0-2)

Rheinpark, Vaduz 03.09.2010

Referee: Bülent Yıldırım (TUR) Attendance: 6,100

LIECHTENSTEIN: Peter Jehle, Lucas Eberle (45 Martin Rechsteiner), Michael Stocklasa, Yves Oehri (46 Franz-Josef Vogt), Martin Stocklasa, Mario Frick, Franz Burgmeier, David Hasler, Philippe Erne, Sandro Wieser (82 Ronny Büchel), Michele Polverino. Trainer: Hans-Peter Zaugg

SPAIN: Iker Casillas, Gerard Piqué, Carlos Marchena, Andrés Iniesta (65 Pedro Rodríguez), David Villa, Xavi Hernández (46 Cesc Fábregas), Fernando Torres (57 David Silva), Joan Capdevila, Xabi Alonso, Sergio Ramos, Sergio Busquets. Trainer: Vicente del Bosque

Goals: Fernando Torres (18, 54), David Villa (26), David Silva (62)

CZECH v REPUBLIC LITHUANIA 0-1 (0-1)

Andruv Stadión, Olomouc 07.09.2010

Referee: Alon Yefet (ISR) Attendance: 12,038

CZECH REPUBLIC: Petr Čech, Michal Kadlec, Roman Hubník, Jan Polák (69 Jiří Štajner), Martin Fenin (59 Tomáš Necid), Tomáš Rosický, Daniel Pudil (84 Roman Bednář), Zdeněk Pospěch, Jaroslav Plašil, Milan Baroš, Tomáš Hübschman. Trainer: Michal Bílek

LITHUANIA: Žydrūnas Karčemarskas, Deividas Šemberas, Ramūnas Radavičius, Tadas Kijanskas, Andrius Skerla, Mindaugas Panka, Edgaras Česnauskis, Tomas Danilevičius (90 Kęstutis Ivaškevičius), Darvydas Šernas (61 Robertas Poškus), Saulius Mikoliūnas (79 Vytautas Lukša), Marius Stankevičius. Trainer: Raimondas Žutautas

Goal: Darvydas Šernas (27)

SCOTLAND v LIECHTENSTEIN 2-1 (0-0)

Hampden Park, Glasgow 07.09.2010

Referee: Viktor Shvetsov (UKR) Attendance: 37,050

SCOTLAND: Allan McGregor, Alan Hutton, Lee Wallace (54 Barry Robson), Stephen McManus, David Weir, Lee McCulloch, Darren Fletcher, Scott Brown, Kenny Miller, Kris Boyd (66 Steven Naismith), James McFadden (46 James Morrison). Trainer: Craig Levein

LIECHTENSTEIN: Peter Jehle, Michael Stocklasa, Martin Rechsteiner, Yves Oehri, Martin Stocklasa, Frick (79 Fabio D'Elia), Franz Burgmeier, David Hasler (90+2 Nicolas Hasler), Philippe Erne, Wieser (71 Ronny Büchel), Michele Polverino. Trainer: Hans-Peter Zaugg

Goals: Mario Frick (47), Kenny Miller (63), Stephen McManus (90+7)

CZECH REPUBLIC v SCOTLAND 1-0 (0-0)

Eden, Praha 08.10.2010

Referee: Ivan Bebek (CRO) Attendance: 14,922

CZECH REPUBLIC: Petr Čech, Marek Suchý, Michal Kadlec, Roman Hubník, Tomáš Necid (84 Mario Holek), Jan Polák, Lukáš Magera (59 Roman Bednář), Tomáš Rosický, Zdeněk Pospěch, Jaroslav Plašil (90+4 Jan Rajnoch), Tomáš Hübschman. Trainer: Michal Bilek

SCOTLAND: Allan McGregor, Alan Hutton, Steven Whittaker, Stephen McManus, David Weir, Gary Caldwell (76 Kenny Miller), Darren Fletcher, Jamie Mackie (76 Chris Iwelumo), Steven Naismith, James Morrison (84 Barry Robson), Graham Dorrans. Trainer: Craig Levein

Goal: Roman Hubník (69)

SPAIN v LITHUANIA 3-1 (0-0)

Helmántico, Salamanca 08.10.2010

Referee: Gianluca Rocchi (ITA) Attendance: 16,800

SPAIN: Iker Casillas, Gerard Piqué, Carles Puyol, Andrés Iniesta, David Villa (76 Pablo Hernández), Joan Capdevila, Sergio Ramos (82 Álvaro Arbeloa), Sergio Busquets, Fernando Llorente (77 Aritz Aduriz), Santi Cazorla, David Silva. Trainer: Vicente del Boque

LITHUANIA: Žydrūnas Karčemarskas, Deividas Šemberas, Ramūnas Radavičius, Tadas Kijanskas, Andrius Skerla, Mindaugas Panka, Edgaras Česnauskis (85 Robertas Poškus), Tomas Danilevičius (82 Kęstutis Ivaškevičius), Darvydas Šernas, Saulius Mikoliūnas (59 Deividas Česnauskis), Marius Stankevičius. Trainer: Raimondas Žutautas

Goals: Fernando Llorente (47, 56), Darvydas Šernas (54), David Silva (79)

LIECHTENSTEIN v CZECH REPUBLIC 0-2 (0-2)

Rheinpark, Vaduz 12.10.2010

Referee: Stanislav Sukhina (RUS) Attendance: 2,555

LIECHTENSTEIN: Peter Jehle, Michael Stocklasa, Martin Rechsteiner, Yves Oehri, Martin Stocklasa, Thomas Beck (66 Nicolas Hasler), Mario Frick, Franz Burgmeier, Philippe Erne (78 Rony Hanselmann), Sandro Wieser (84 Ronny Büchel), Michele Polverino. Trainer: Hans-Peter Zaugg

CZECH REPUBLIC: Petr Čech, Marek Suchý, Michal Kadlec, Roman Hubník, Tomáš Necid (89 Milan Petržela), Jan Polák (59 Jiří Štajner), Tomáš Rosický, Zdeněk Pospěch, Jaroslav Plašil, Václav Kadlec (64 Roman Bednář), Tomáš Hübschman. Trainer: Michal Bílek

Goals: Tomáš Necid (12), Václav Kadlec (29)

SCOTLAND v SPAIN 2-3 (0-1)

Hampden Park, Glasgow 12.10.2010

Referee: Massimo Busacca (SWI) Attendance: 51,322

SCOTLAND: Allan McGregor, Phil Bardsley, Steven Whittaker, Stephen McManus, David Weir, Lee McCulloch (46 Charlie Adam), Darren Fletcher, James Morrison (88 Shaun Maloney), Kenny Miller, Steven Naismith, Graham Dorrans (80 Jamie Mackie). Trainer: Craig Levein

SPAIN: Iker Casillas, Gerard Piqué, Carles Puyol, Andrés Iniesta, David Villa, Joan Capdevila, Xabi Alonso, Sergio Ramos, Sergio Busquets (90 Carlos Marchena), Santi Cazorla (70 Pablo Hernández), David Silva (76 Fernando Llorente). Trainer: Vicente del Bosque

Sent off: Whittaker (89)

Goals: David Villa (44 pen), Andrés Iniesta (55), Steven Naismith (58), Gerard Piqué (66 own goal), Llorente (79)

SPAIN v CZECH REPUBLIC 2-1 (0-1)

Los Cármenes, Granada 25.03.2011

Referee: Viktor Kassai (HUN) Attendance: 16,301

SPAIN: Iker Casillas, Gerard Piqué, Andrés Iniesta, David Villa, Xavi Hernández, Joan Capdevila (58 Santi Cazorla), Xabi Alonso (46 Fernando Torres), Sergio Ramos, Sergio Busquets, Álvaro Arbeloa, Jesús Navas (86 Carlos Marchena). Trainer: Vicente del Bosque

CZECH REPUBLIC: Petr Čech, Michal Kadlec, Roman Hubník, Tomáš Sivok, Jan Rezek (84 Tomáš Necid), Tomáš Rosický, Daniel Pudil (78 Adam Hloušek), Zdeněk Pospěch, Jaroslav Plašil, Milan Baroš, Tomáš Hübschman. Trainer: Michal Bílek

Goals: Jaroslav Plašil (29), David Villa (69, 72 pen)

CZECH REPUBLIC v LIECHTENSTEIN 2-0 (1-0)

Strelecky Ostrov, Ceske Budejovice 29.03.2011

Referee: Ovidiu Alin Haţegan (ROM) Attendance: 6,600

CZECH REPUBLIC: Petr Čech, Michal Kadlec, Roman Hubník, Tomáš Sivok, Tomáš Rosický (84 Jan Polák), Zdeněk Pospěch, Jaroslav Plašil, Milan Baroš, Tomáš Hübschman, David Lafata (59 Tomáš Necid), Jan Morávek (56 Adam Hloušek). Trainer: Michal Bílek

LIECHTENSTEIN: Peter Jehle, Michael Stocklasa, Martin Rechsteiner, Martin Stocklasa, Thomas Beck, Mario Frick, Franz Burgmeier, Martin Büchel (10 Wolfgang Kieber, 81 Andreas Christen), David Hasler, Philippe Erne, Nicolas Hasler. Trainer: Hans-Peter Zaugg

Goals: Milan Baroš (3), Michal Kadlec (70)

LITHUANIA v SPAIN 1-3 (0-1)

Dariaus ir Girėno stadionas, Kaunas 29.03.2011

Referee: Laurent Duhamel (FRA) Attendance: 9,180

LITHUANIA: Žydrūnas Karčemarskas, Deividas Šemberas, Tadas Kijanskas, Andrius Skerla, Marius Žaliukas, Mindaugas Panka, Edgaras Česnauskis, Tomas Danilevičius (85 Dominykas Galkevičius), Darvydas Šernas (74 Tadas Labukas), Saulius Mikoliūnas (71 Ramūnas Radavičius), Marius Stankevičius. Trainer: Raimondas Žutautas

SPAIN: Iker Casillas, Raúl Albiol, Gerard Piqué (90 Sergio Ramos), Andoni Iraola, David Villa (54 David Silva), Xavi Hernández, Xabi Alonso, Álvaro Arbeloa, Javi Martínez, Fernando Llorente, Santi Cazorla (67 Juan Mata). Trainer: Vicente del Bosque

Goals: Xavi Hernández (19), Marius Stankevičius (57), Tadas Kijanskas (70 own goal), Juan Mata (83)

LIECHTENSTEIN v LITHUANIA 2-0 (2-0)

Rheinpark, Vaduz 03.06.2011

Referee: Artyom Kuchin (KAZ) Attendance: 1,886

LIECHTENSTEIN: Benjamin Büchel, Martin Stocklasa, Benjamin Fischer (72 Mathias Christen), Thomas Beck (84 Andreas Christen), Franz Burgmeier, Martin Büchel, Philippe Erne (87 Rony Hanselmann), Nicolas Hasler, Marco Ritzberger, Daniel Kaufmann, Michele Polverino. Trainer: Hans-Peter Zaugg

LITHUANIA: Ernestas Šetkus, Deividas Šemberas, Ramūnas Radavičius, Tadas Kijanskas, Andrius Skerla, Mindaugas Panka, Edgaras Česnauskis (68 Mantas Savenas), Tomas Danilevičius (46 Tadas Labukas), Darvydas Šernas, Saulius Mikoliūnas, Marius Stankevičius (46 Deividas Česnauskis). Trainer: Raimondas Žutautas

Goals: Philippe Erne (7), Michele Polverino (36)

LITHUANIA v LIECHTENSTEIN 0-0

Dariaus ir Girėno stadionas, Kaunas 02.09.2011

Referee: Ken Henry Johnsen (NOR) Attendance: 3,500

LITHUANIA: Žydrūnas Karčemarskas, Deividas Šemberas, Tadas Kijanskas, Marius Žaliukas, Mindaugas Panka (88 Mantas Savenas), Edgaras Česnauskis, Tomas Danilevičius, Saulius Mikoliūnas (64 Marius Papšys), Arūnas Klimavičius, Deividas Česnauskis, Arvydas Novikovas (46 Tadas Labukas). Trainer: Raimondas Žutautas

LIECHTENSTEIN: Peter Jehle, Michael Stocklasa, Martin Rechsteiner, Yves Oehri (52 Daniel Kaufmann), Martin Stocklasa, Mario Frick, Franz Burgmeier, Martin Büchel (90 Wolfgang Kieber), David Hasler, Sandro Wieser (46 Nicolas Hasler), Marco Ritzberger. Trainer: Hans-Peter Zaugg

Sent off: Česnauskis (75)

SPAIN v LIECHTENSTEIN 6-0 (3-0)

Las Gaunas, Logrono 06.09.2011

Referee: Harald Lechner (AUS) Attendance: 15,660

SPAIN: Iker Casillas, Raúl Albiol, Andrés Iniesta, David Villa, Xavi Hernández (46 Cesc Fábregas), Álvaro Negredo (61 Fernando Llorente), Juan Mata, Xabi Alonso, Sergio Ramos (54 Thiago Alcántara), Sergio Busquets, Álvaro Arbeloa. Trainer: Vicente del Bosque

LIECHTENSTEIN: Peter Jehle, Michael Stocklasa, Martin Rechsteiner, Martin Stocklasa, Thomas Beck (88 Rony Hanselmann), Mario Frick, Franz Burgmeier, Martin Büchel (81 Wolfgang Kieber), David Hasler, Sandro Wieser (71 Nicolas Hasler), Marco Ritzberger. Trainer: Hans-Peter Zaugg

Goals: Negredo (33, 37), Xavi Hernández (44), Sergio Ramos (52), David Villa (59, 79)

SCOTLAND v CZECH REPUBLIC 2-2 (1-0)

Hampden Park, Glasgow 03.09.2010

Referee: Kevin Blom (HOL) Attendance: 51,564

SCOTLAND: Allan McGregor, Alan Hutton, Phil Bardsley (76 Danny Wilson), Christophe Berra, Gary Caldwell, Charlie Adam (79 Don Cowie), Darren Fletcher, Scott Brown, Kenny Miller, Morrison, Steven Naismith (86 Barry Robson). Trainer: Craig Levein

CZECH REPUBLIC: Jan Laštuvka, Michal Kadlec, Jan Rajnoch, Roman Hubník, Tomáš Sivok, Milan Petržela (56 Jan Rezek), Tomáš Rosický, Jaroslav Plašil, Milan Baroš (90+2 Kamil Vacek), Tomáš Hübschman, Petr Jiráček (77 Tomáš Pekhart). Trainer: Michal Bílek

Goals: Kenny Miller (45), Jaroslav Plašil (78), Darren Fletcher (82), Michal Kadlec (90 pen)

CZECH REPUBLIC v SPAIN 0-2 (0-2)

Stadion Letná, Praha 07.10.2010

Referee: Paolo Tagliavento (ITA) Attendance: 17,873

CZECH REPUBLIC: Petr Čech, Theodor Gebre Selassie, Michal Kadlec, Roman Hubník, Tomáš Sivok, Tomáš Rosický, Daniel Pudil, Milan Baroš (62 Tomáš Pekhart), Tomáš Hübschman, Daniel Kolář (76 Kamil Vacek), Petr Jiráček. Trainer: Michal Bílek

SPAIN: Iker Casillas, Raúl Albiol, Gerard Piqué, Xavi Hernández, Fernando Torres (61 David Villa), Juan Mata, Xabi Alonso (70 Javi Martínez), Sergio Ramos (46 Carles Puyol), Sergio Busquets, Álvaro Arbeloa, David Silva. Trainer: Vicente del Bosque

Sent off: Hübschman (70)

Goals: Juan Mata (7), Xabi Alonso (23)

SCOTLAND v LITHUANIA 1-0 (0-0)

Hampden Park, Glasgow 06.09.2010

Referee: Kristinn Jakobsson (ISL) Attendance: 34,071

SCOTLAND: Allan McGregor, Steven Whittaker, Phil Bardsley (70 Stephen Crainey), Christophe Berra, Gary Caldwell, Don Cowie, Darren Fletcher, Barry Bannan (84 Robert Snodgrass), David Goodwillie, James Morrison (79 Graham Dorrans), Steven Naismith. Trainer: Craig Levein

LITHUANIA: Žydrūnas Karčemarskas, Deividas Šemberas, Ramūnas Radavičius, Tadas Kijanskas (61 Tomas Danilevičius), Marius Žaliukas, Darvydas Šernas, Saulius Mikoliūnas (77 Ričardas Beniušis), Linas Pilibaitis, Arūnas Klimavičius, Deividas Česnauskis, Tadas Labukas (46 Arvydas Novikovas). Trainer: Raimondas Žutautas

Goal: Steven Naismith (50)

LIECHTENSTEIN v SCOTLAND 0-1 (0-1)

Rheinpark, Vaduz 08.10.2011

Referee: Tom Harald Hagen (NOR) Attendance: 5,636

LIECHTENSTEIN: Peter Jehle, Martin Rechsteiner, Martin Stocklasa, Thomas Beck, Mario Frick, Martin Büchel (71 Wolfgang Kieber), Rony Hanselmann (75 Lucas Eberle), Nicolas Hasler, Marco Ritzberger, Daniel Kaufmann, Michele Polverino. Trainer: Hans-Peter Zaugg

SCOTLAND: Allan McGregor, Alan Hutton, Phil Bardsley, Christophe Berra, Gary Caldwell, Charlei Adam (76 Don Cowie), Darren Fletcher, Barry Bannan (73 James Forrest), Craig Mackail-Smith, James Morrison, Steven Naismith. Trainer: Craig Levein

Goal: Mackail-Smith (32)

LITHUANIA v CZECH REPUBLIC 1-4 (0-3)

Dariaus ir Girėno stadionas, Kaunas 11.10.2011

Referee: David Fernández Borbalán (SPA) Att: 4,000

LITHUANIA: Žydrūnas Karčemarskas, Ramūnas Radavičius, Gediminas Vicius, Andrius Skerla, Marius Žaliukas, Darvydas Šernas, Robertas Poškus (57 Mindaugas Panka), Saulius Mikoliūnas, Linas Pilibaitis (74 Ričardas Beniušis), Kęstutis Ivaškevičius (46 Arvydas Novikovas), Marius Stankevičius. Trainer: Raimondas Žutautas

CZECH REPUBLIC: Petr Čech, Theodor Gebre Selassie, Michal Kadlec, Roman Hubník, Tomáš Sivok, Jan Rezek (82 Zdeněk Pospěch), Jaroslav Plašil, Václav Pilař (70 Daniel Pudil), Milan Baroš (59 Tomáš Pekhart), Daniel Kolář, Petr Jiráček. Trainer: Michal Bílek

Sent off: Hubnik (67)

Goals: Michal Kadlec (2 pen, 85 pen), Rezek (16, 45), Darvydas Šernas (68 pen)

SPAIN v SCOTLAND 3-1 (2-0)

Rico Perez, Alicante 11.10.2011

Referee: Stefan Johannesson (SWE) Attendance: 27,559

SPAIN: Víctor Valdés, Gerard Piqué, Carles Puyol (46 Álvaro Arbeloa), Jordi Alba, David Villa, Xavi Hernández (62 Fernando Llorente), Sergio Ramos, Sergio Busquets, Pedro Rodríguez, Santi Cazorla, David Silva (55 Thiago Alcántara). Trainer: Vicente del Bosque

SCOTLAND: Allan McGregor, Alan Hutton, Phil Bardsley, Christophe Berra, Gary Caldwell, Charlie Adam (63 James Forrest), Darren Fletcher (85 Don Cowie), James Morrison, Craig Mackail-Smith, Barry Bannan (63 David Goodwillie), Steven Naismith. Trainer: Craig Levein

Goals: David Silva (6, 44), David Villa (54), David Goodwillie (66 pen)

	P	W	D	L	F	A	Pts
Spain	8	8	0	0	26	6	24
Czech Republic	8	4	1	3	12	8	13
Scotland	8	3	2	3	9	10	11
Lithuania	8	1	2	5	4	13	5
Liechtenstein	8	1	1	6	3	17	4

PLAY-OFFS

BOSNIA HERZEGOVINA v PORTUGAL 0-0

Bilino Polje, Zenica (BIH) 11.11.2011

Referee: Howard Webb (ENG) Attendance: 12,352

BOSNIA HERZEGOVINA: Asmir Begović, Emir Spahić, Elvir Rahimić, Miralem Pjanić, Zvjezdan Misimović (86 Senijad Ibričić), Edin Džeko, Sejad Salihović (68 Vedad Ibišević), Senad Lulić, Haris Medunjanin (67 Darko Maletić), Sanel Jahić, Adnan Zahirović. Trainer: Safet Sušić

PORTUGAL: Rui Patrício, Bruno Alves, Képler Ferreira "Pepe", Miguel Veloso, Fábio Coentrão, Cristiano Ronaldo, João Moutinho, João Pereira, Raul Meireles (81 Rúben Micael), Luis Cunha "Nani", Hélder Postiga (65 Hugo Almeida). Trainer: Paulo Bento

PORTUGAL v BOSNIA HERZEGOVINA 6-2 (2-1)

Estádio do Sport Lisboa e Benfica, Lisboa 15.11.2011

Referee: Wolfgang Stark (GER) Attendance: 47,728

PORTUGAL: Rui Patrício, Bruno Alves, Képler Ferreira "Pepe", Miguel Veloso, Fábio Coentrão, Cristiano Ronaldo, João Moutinho, João Pereira, Raul Meireles (63 Rúben Micael), Luis Cunha "Nani" (83 Ricardo Quaresma), Hélder Postiga (84 Carlos Martins). Trainer: Paulo Bento

BOSNIA HERZEGOVINA: Asmir Begović, Saša Papac, Emir Spahić, Elvir Rahimić (57 Darko Maletić), Miralem Pjanić (64 Muhamed Bešić), Zvjezdan Misimović, Edin Džeko, Sanel Jahić, Senad Lulić, Haris Medunjanin, Adnan Zahirović. Trainer: Safet Sušić

Sent off: Lulić (53)

Goals: Cristiano Ronaldo (8, 53), Luis Cunha "Nani" (24), Zvjezdan Misimović (41 pen), Emir Spahić (65), Hélder Postiga (72, 82), Miguel Veloso (80)

CZECH REPUBLIC v MONTENEGRO 2-0 (0-0)

Stadion Letná, Praha 11.11.2011

Referee: Martin Atkinson (ENG) Attendance: 14,560

CZECH REPUBLIC: Petr Čech, Theodor Gebre Selassie, Michal Kadlec, Tomáš Sivok, Tomáš Pekhart (90+3 David Lafata), Jan Rezek (81 Zdeněk Pospěch), Tomáš Rosický, Daniel Pudil, Jaroslav Plašil, Václav Pilař (90 Daniel Kolář), Petr Jiráček. Trainer: Michal Bílek

MONTENEGRO: Mladen Božović, Savo Pavičević, Milan Jovanović, Simon Vukčević (88 Andrija Delibašić), Stevan Jovetić, Mirko Vučinić, Dejan Damjanović (61 Vladimir Božović), Milorad Peković (80 Elsad Zverotić), Nikola Drinčić, Miodrag Džudović, Stefan Savić. Trainer: Branko Brnović

Goals: Václav Pilař (63), Tomáš Sivok (90+2)

MONTENEGRO v CZECH REPUBLIC 0-1 (0-0)

Stadion Podgorica 15.11.2011

Referee: Nicola Rizzoli (ITA) Attendance: 10,100

MONTENEGRO: Mladen Božović, Savo Pavičević, Stevan Jovetić, Mirko Vučinić, Fatos Beqiraj (57 Andrija Delibašić), Dejan Damjanović (76 Simon Vukčević), Elsad Zverotić, Nikola Drinčić, Vladimir Božović (79 Radomir Djalović), Miodrag Džudović, Stefan Savić. Trainer: Branko Brnović

CZECH REPUBLIC: Petr Čech, Theodor Gebre Selassie, Michal Kadlec, Roman Hubník, Tomáš Sivok, Tomáš Pekhart (84 Milan Baroš), Jan Rezek (60 Zdeněk Pospěch), Tomáš Rosický, Jaroslav Plašil, Václav Pilař (69 Daniel Kolář), Petr Jiráček. Trainer: Michal Bílek

Goal: Petr Jiráček (81)

TURKEY v CROATIA 0-3 (0-2)

Turk Telekom Arena, Istanbul 11.11.2011

Referee: Felix Brych (GER) Attendance: 42,863

TURKEY: Volkan Demirel, Hakan Balta, Egemen Korkmaz, Emre Belözoğlu, Hamit Altıntop, Gökhan Gönül (46 Gökhan Töre), Selçuk İnan (69 Mehmet Topal), Arda Turan, Burak Yılmaz (81 Umut Bulut), Giray Kaçar, Sabri Sarıoğlu. Trainer: Guus Hiddink

CROATIA: Stipe Pletikosa, Josip Šimunić, Vedran Čorluka, Ivan Rakitić (83 Danijel Pranjić), Luka Modrić, Darijo Srna, Gordon Schildenfeld, Tomislav Dujmović, Mario Mandžukić (90 Eduardo), Ivica Olić (85 Nikica Jelavić), Domagoj Vida. Trainer: Slaven Bilić

Goals: Ivica Olić (2), Mario Mandžukić (32), Vedran Čorluka (51)

CROATIA v TURKEY 0-0

Stadion Maksimir, Zagreb 15.11.2011

Referee: Pedro Proença (POR) Attendance: 26,371

CROATIA: Stipe Pletikosa, Josip Šimunić, Danijel Pranjić, Ivan Rakitić, Ognjen Vukojević (88 Eduardo), Luka Modrić, Darijo Srna, Gordon Schildenfeld, Mario Mandžukić (77 Nikica Jelavić), Ivica Olić (62 Ivan Perišić), Domagoj Vida. Trainer: Slaven Bilić

TURKEY: Sinan Bolat, Ömer Toprak, Egemen Korkmaz, Hamit Altıntop, Selçuk İnan, Umut Bulut (71 Halil Altıntop), Caner Erkin (36 Gökhan Töre), İsmail Köybaşı, Colin Kazım Kazım, Selçuk Şahin, Serkan Balcı. Trainer: Guus Hiddink

ESTONIA v REPUBLIC OF IRELAND 0-4 (0-1)

Lilleküla Stadium, Tallinn 11.11.2011

Referee: Viktor Kassai (HUN) Attendance: 9,692

ESTONIA: Sergei Pareiko, Raio Piiroja, Dmitri Kruglov, Aleksandr Dmitrijev, Tarmo Kink (67 Ats Purje), Martin Vunk (61 Joel Lindpere), Konstantin Vassiljev, Ragnar Klavan, Enar Jääger, Jarmo Ahjupera (55 Vladimir Voskoboinikov), Andrei Stepanov. Trainer: Tarmo Rüütli

IRELAND: Shay Given, Stephen Kelly, Stephen Ward, Sean St Ledger, Richard Dunne, Glenn Whelan (78 Keith Fahey), Aiden McGeady, Keith Andrews, Jon Walters (83 Simon Cox), Robbie Keane, Damien Duff (73 Stephen Hunt). Trainer: Giovanni Trapattoni

Sent off: Stepanov (35), Piiroja (76)

Goals: Keith Andrews (13), Jon Walters (67), Robbie Keane (71, 88 pen)

REPUBLIC OF IRELAND v ESTONIA 1-1 (1-0)

Dublin Arena, Dublin 15.11.2011

Referee: Björn Kuipers (HOL) Attendance: 51,151

IRELAND: Shay Given, Sean St Ledger, Stephen Ward, John O'Shea, Richard Dunne, Glenn Whelan, Stephen Hunt (59 Aiden McGeady), Keith Andrews, Kevin Doyle, Robbie Keane (67 Simon Cox), Damien Duff (79 Keith Fahey). Trainer: Giovanni Trapattoni

ESTONIA: Pavel Londak, Taavi Rähn, Dmitri Kruglov (18 Sander Puri), Vladimir Voskoboinikov (73 Ats Purje), Joel Lindpere (54 Tarmo Kink), Martin Vunk, Konstantin Vassiljev, Ragnar Klavan, Enar Jääger, Kaimar Saag, Taijo Teniste. Trainer: Tarmo Rüütli

Goals: Stephen Ward (32), Konstantin Vassiljev (57)

FINAL TOURNAMENT

GROUP A

POLAND v GREECE 1-1 (1-0)

National Stadium, Warszawa 08.06.2012

Referee: Carlos Velasco Carballo (SPA) Attendance: 56,070

GREECE: Kostas Chalkias, Vassilis Torossidis, Avraam Papadopoulos (37 Kyriakos Papadopoulos), Sokratis Papastathopoulos, José Holebas, Giánnis Maniatis, Kostas Katsouranis, Giórgos Karagounis, Sotiris Ninis (46 Dimítris Salpingidis), Fanis Gekas (68 Kostas Fortounis), Giórgos Samaras. Trainer: Fernando Santos

POLAND: Wojciech Szczesny, Łukasz Piszczek, Marcin Wasilewski, Damien Perquis, Sebastian Boenisch, Jakub Blaszczykowski, Eugen Polanski, Rafał Murawski, Maciej Rybus (70 Przemysław Tyton), Ludovic Obraniak, Robert Lewandowski. Trainer: Franciszek Smuda

Sent off: Szczesny (69), Papastathopoulos (44)

Goals: Robert Lewandowski (17), Dimítris Salpingidis (51)

RUSSIA v CZECH REPUBLIC 4-1 (2-0)

Municipal Stadium, Wroclaw 08.06.2012

Referee: Howard Webb (ENG) Attendance: 40,803

RUSSIA: Vyacheslav Malafeev, Alexander Anyukov, Alexei Berezutski, Sergei Ignashevich, Yuri Zhirkov, Roman Shirokov, Igor Denisov, Konstantin Zyryanov, Andrei Arshavin, Alexander Kerzhakov (73 Roman Pavlyuchenko), Alan Dzagoev (84 Aleksandr Kokorin). Trainer: Dick Advocaat

CZECH REPUBLIC: Petr Čech, Theodor Gebre Selassie, Tomáš Sivok, Roman Hubnik, Michal Kadlec, Jan Rezek (46 Tomáš Hübschman), Jaroslav Plašil, Tomáš Rosický, Petr Jiráček (75 Milan Petržela), Václav Pilař, Milan Baroš (85 David Lafata). Trainer: Michal Bílek

Goals: Alan Dzagoev (15, 79), Roman Shirokov (24), Václav Pilař (52), Roman Pavlyuchenko (82)

GREECE v CZECH REPUBLIC 1-2 (0-2)

Municipal Stadium, Wroclaw 12.06.2010

Referee: Stéphane Lannoy (FRA) Attendance: 41,105

GREECE: Kostas Chalkias (23 Michalis Sifakis), Vasilis Torosidis, Kyriakos Papadopoulos, Kostas Katsouranis, José Holebas, Giorgos Fotakis (46 Fanis Gekas), Giannis Maniatis, Giórgos Karagounis, Dimitris Salpingidis, Giórgos Samaras, Kostas Fortounis (71 Kostas Mitroglou).
Trainer: Fernando Santos

CZECH REPUBLIC: Petr Čech, Theodor Gebre Selassie, Michal Kadlec, Tomáš Sivok, David Limberský, Jaroslav Plašil, Tomáš Hübschman, Petr Jiráček, Tomáš Rosický (46 Daniel Kolář, 90 František Rajtoral), Václav Pilař, Milan Baroš (64 Tomáš Pekhart). Trainer: Michal Bílek

Goals: Petr Jiráček (3), Václav Pilař (6), Fanis Gekas (53)

POLAND v RUSSIA 1-1 (0-1)

National Stadiu, Warszawa 12.06.2012

Referee: Wolfgang Stark (GER) Attendance: 55,920

POLAND: Przemyslaw Tyton, Sebastian Boenisch, Damien Perquis, Łukasz Piszczek, Marcin Wasilewski, Jakub Blaszczykowski, Dariusz Dudka (73 Adrian Mierzejewski), Rafał Murawski, Ludovic Obraniak (90+3 Paweł Brozek), Eugen Polanski (85 Adam Małuszczyk), Robert Lewandowski.
Trainer: Franciszek Smuda

RUSSIA: Vyacheslav Malafeev, Aleksandr Anyukov, Aleksei Berezutski, Sergei Ignashevich, Yuri Zhirkov, Igor Denisov, Alan Dzagoev (79 Marat Izmailov), Roman Shirokov, Konstantin Zyryanov, Andrei Arshavin, Aleksandr Kerzhakov (70 Roman Pavlyuchenko). Trainer: Dick Advocaat

Goals: Alan Dzagoev (37), Jakub Blaszczykowski (57)

GREECE v RUSSIA 1-0 (1-0)

National Stadium, Warszawa 16.06.2010

Referee: Jonas Eriksson (SWE) Attendance: 55,614

RUSSIA: Vyacheslav Malafeev, Alexander Anyukov (81 Marat Izmailov), Alexei Berezutski, Sergei Ignashevich, Yuri Zhirkov, Roman Shirokov, Igor Denisov, Denis Glushakov (72 Pavel Pogrebnyak), Andrei Arshavin, Alexander Kerzhakov (46 Roman Pavlyuchenko), Alan Dzagoev.
Trainer: Dick Advocaat

GREECE: Michalis Sifakis, Giórgos Tzavellas, Sokratis Papastathopoulos, Kyriakos Papadopoulos, Vassilis Torossidis, Giánnis Maniatis, Kostas Katsouranis, Giórgos Samaras, Giórgos Karagounis (67 Grigoris Makos), Dimitris Salpingidis (83 Sotiris Ninis), Fanis Gekas (46 José Holebas).
Trainer: Fernando Santos

Goal: Giórgos Karagounis (45+2)

CZECH REPUBLIC v POLAND 1-0 (0-0)

Municipal Stadium, Wroclaw 16.06.2012

Referee: Craig Thomson (SCO) Attendance: 41,480

CZECH REPUBLIC: Petr Čech, Theodor Gebre Selassie, Michal Kadlec, Tomás Sivok, David Limberský, Petr Jiráček (84 František Rajtoral), Tomáš Hübschman, Jaroslav Plašil, Vaclav Pilař (88 Jan Rezek), Daniel Kolář, Milan Baroš (90+1 Tomáš Pekhart). Trainer: Michal Bílek

POLAND: Przemyslaw Tyton, Łukasz Piszczek, Marcin Wasilewski, Damien Perquis, Sebastian Boenisch, Jakub Blaszczykowski, Dariusz Dudka, Eugen Polanski (56 Kamil Grosicki), Ludovic Obraniak (73 Adrian Mierzejewski), Rafał Murawski (73 Paweł Brozek), Robert Lewandowski.
Trainer: Franciszek Smuda

Goal: Petr Jiráček (72)

	P	W	D	L	F	A	Pts
Czech Republic	3	2	0	1	4	5	6
Greece	3	1	1	1	3	3	4
Russia	3	1	1	1	5	3	4
Poland	3	0	2	1	2	3	2

GROUP B

HOLLAND v DENMARK 0-1 (0-1)

Metalist Stadium, Kharkiv 09.06.2012

Referee: Damir Skomina (SVN) Attendance: 35,923

HOLLAND: Maarten Stekelenburg, John Heitinga, Gregory van der Wiel (85 Dirk Kuyt), Ron Vlaar, Jetro Willems, Ibrahim Afellay (71 Klaas-Jan Huntelaar), Nigel de Jong (71 Rafael van der Vaart), Wesley Sneijder, Mark van Bommel, Arjen Robben, Robin van Persie. Trainer: Bert van Marwijk

DENMARK: Stephan Andersen, Daniel Agger, Lars Jacobsen, Simon Kjær, Simon Poulsen, Christian Eriksen (74 Lasse Schøne), Michael Krohn-Dehli, William Kvist, Niki Zimling, Nicklas Bendtner, Dennis Rommedahl (84 Tobias Mikkelsen). Trainer: Morten Olsen

Goal: Michael Krohn-Dehli (24)

GERMANY v PORTUGAL 1-0 (0-0)

Arena Lviv 09.06.2012

Referee: Stéphane Lannoy (FRA) Attendance: 32,990

GERMANY: Manuel Neuer, Jérôme Boateng, Mats Hummels, Holger Badstuber, Philipp Lahm, Sami Khedira, Bastian Schweinsteiger, Thomas Müller (90+4 Lars Bender), Mesut Özil (87 Toni Kroos), Lukas Podolski, Mario Gomez (80 Miroslav Klose). Trainer: Joachim Löw

PORTUGAL: Rui Patricio, João Pereira, Bruno Alves, Képler Ferreira "Pepe", Fábio Coentrão, João Moutinho, Miguel Veloso, Raul Meireles (80 Silvestre Varela), Cristiano Ronaldo, Hélder Postiga (70 Nélson Oliveira), Luis Cunha "Nani". Trainer: Paulo Bento

Goal: Mario Gomez (72)

DENMARK v PORTUGAL 2-3 (1-2)

Arena Lviv 13.06.2012

Referee: Craig Thomson (SCO) Attendance: 31,840

DENMARK: Stephan Andersen, Lars Jacobsen, Simon Kjær, Daniel Agger, Simon Poulsen, William Kvist, Niki Zimling (16 Jakob Poulsen), Dennis Rommedahl (60 Tobias Mikkelsen), Christian Eriksen, Michael Krohn-Dehli (90+2 Lasse Schøne), Nicklas Bendtner. Trainer: Morten Olsen

PORTUGAL: Rui Patricio, João Pereira, Bruno Alves, Képler Ferreira "Pepe", Fábio Coentrão, Raul Meireles (84 Silvestre Varela), Miguel Veloso, João Moutinho, Luis Cunha "Nani" (89 ROLANDO Fonseca), Hélder Postiga (64 Nélson Oliveira), Cristiano Ronaldo. Trainer: Paulo Bento

Goals: Képler Ferreira "Pepe" (24), Hélder Postiga (36), Nicklas Bendtner (41, 80), Varela (87)

HOLLAND v GERMANY 1-2 (0-2)

Metalist Stadium, Kharkiv 13.06.2010

Referee: Jonas Eriksson (SWE) Attendance: 37,750

HOLLAND: Maarten Stekelenburg, Gregory van der Wiel, John Heitinga, Joris Mathijsen, Jetro Willems, Nigel de Jong, Mark van Bommel (46 Rafael van der Vaart), Arjen Robben (83 Dirk Kuyt), Wesley Sneijder, Ibrahim Afellay (46 Klaas-Jan Huntelaar), Robin van Persie. Trainer: Bert van Marwijk

GERMANY: Manuel Neuer, Jérôme Boateng, Mats Hummels, Holger Badstuber, Philipp Lahm, Sami Khedira, Bastian Schweinsteiger, Thomas Müller (90 Lars Bender), Mesut Özil (81 Toni Kroos), Lukas Podolski, Mario Gomez (73 Miroslav Klose). Trainer: Joachim Löw

Goals: Mario Gomez (24, 38), Robin van Persie (73)

DENMARK v GERMANY 1-2 (1-1)

Arena Lviv 17.06.2012

Referee: Carlos Velasco Carballo (SPA) Attendance: 32,990

GERMANY: Manuel Neuer, Mats Hummels, Phillipp Lahm, Lars Bender, Holger Badstuber, Sami Khedira, Mesut Özil, Bastian Schweinsteiger, Lukas Podolski (64 André Schürrle), Thomas Müller (84 Toni Kroos), Mario Gomez (74 Miroslav Klose). Trainer: Joachim Löw

DENMARK: Stephan Andersen, Simon Kjær, Daniel Agger, Simon Poulsen, Lars Jacobsen, William Kvist, Christian Eriksen, Jakob Poulsen (82 Tobias Mikkelsen), Niki Zimling (78 Christian Poulsen), Michael Krohn-Dehli, Nicklas Bendtner. Trainer: Morten Olsen

Goals: Lukas Podolski (19), Michael Krohn-Dehli (24), Lars Bender (80)

PORTUGAL v HOLLAND 2-1 (1-1)

Metalist Stadium, Kharkiv 17.06.2012

Referee: Nicola Rizzoli (ITA) Attendance: 37,445

PORTUGAL: Rui Patricio, Bruno Alves, Fábio Coentrao, João Pereira, Képler Ferreira "Pepe", João Moutinho, Raul Meireles (72 CUSTÓDIO Castro), Luis Cunha "Nani" (87 ROLANDO Fonseca), Miguel Veloso, Hálder Postiga (64 Nélson Oliveira), Cristiano Ronaldo. Trainer: Paulo Bento

HOLLAND: Maarten Stekelenburg, Joris Mathijsen, Gregory Van der Wiel, Ron Vlaar, Jetro Willems (67 Ibrahim Afellay), Nigel de Jong, Wesley Sneijder, Rafael van der Vaart, Klaas-Jan Huntelaar, Arjen Robben, Robin van Persie. Trainer: Bert van Marwijk

Goals: Rafael Van der Vaart (11), Cristiano Ronaldo (28, 74)

	P	W	D	L	F	A	Pts
Germany	3	3	0	0	5	2	9
Portugal	3	2	0	1	5	4	6
Denmark	3	1	0	2	4	5	3
Holland	3	0	0	3	2	5	0

GROUP C

SPAIN v ITALY 1-1 (0-0)

Arena Gdansk 10.06.2012

Referee: Viktor Kassai (HUN) Attendance: 38,869

SPAIN: Iker Casillas, Álvaro Arbeloa, Sergio Ramos, Gerard Piqué, Jordi Alba, Sergio Busquets, Xabi Alonso, Xavi Hernández, Andres Iniesta, David Silva (64 Jesús Navas), Cesc Fábregas (74 Fernando Torres). Trainer: Vicente del Bosque

ITALY: Gianluigi Buffon, Leonardo Bonucci, Daniele De Rossi, Giorgio Chiellini, Christian Maggio, Claudio Marchisio, Andrea Pirlo, Thiago Motta (90 Antonio Nocerino), Emanuele Giaccherini, Antonio Cassano (65 Sebastian Giovinco), Mario Balotelli (56 Antonio Di Natale). Trainer: Cesare Prandelli

Goals: Antonio Di Natale (61), Cesc Fábregas (64)

REPUBLIC OF IRELAND v CROATIA 1-3 (1-2)

Municipal Stadium, Poznan 10.06.2012

Referee: Björn Kuipers (HOL) Attendance: 39550

IRELAND: Shay Given, John O'Shea, Sean St Ledger, Stephen Ward, Richard Dunne, Damien Duff, Keith Andrews, Glenn Whelan, Robbie Keane (75 Shane Long), Kevin Doyle (53 Jon Walters), Aiden McGeady (54 Simon Cox).
Trainer: Giovanni Trapattoni

CROATIA: Stipe Pletikosa, Gordon Schildenfeld, Vedran Ćorluka, Ivan Strinić, Darijo Srna, Ivan Rakitić (90+2 Tomislav Dujmović), Luka Modrić, Ognjen Vukojević, Nikica Jelavić (72 Niko Kranjčar), Mario Mandžukić, Ivan Perišić (89 Eduardo). Trainer: Slaven Bilić

Goals: Mario Mandžukić (3, 49), Sean St Ledger (19), Nikica Jelavić (43)

ITALY v CROATIA 1-1 (1-0)

Municipal Stadium, Poznan 14.06.2012

Referee: Howard Webb (ENG) Attendance: 37,096

ITALY: Gianluigi Buffon, Giorgio Chiellini, Daniele De Rossi, Leonardo Bonucci, Emanuele Giaccherini, Claudio Marchisio, Andrea Pirlo, Thiago Motta (62 Riccardo Montolivo), Christian Maggio, Antonio Cassano (83 Sebastian Giovinco), Mario Balotelli (69 Antonio Di Natale).
Trainer: Cesare Prandelli

CROATIA: Stipe Pletikosa, Darijo Srna, Vedran Čorluka, Gordon Schildenfeld, Ivan Strinić, Ivan Rakitić, Ognjen Vukojević, Luka Modrić, Ivan Perišić (68 Danijel Pranjić), Nikica Jelavić (83 Eduardo), Mario Mandžukić (90 Niko Kranjčar). Trainer: Slaven Bilić

Goals: Andrea Pirlo (39), Mario Mandžukić (72)

SPAIN v REPUBLIC OF IRELAND 4-0 (1-0)

Arena Gdansk 14.06.2012

Referee: Pedro Proença (POR) Attendance: 39,150

SPAIN: Iker Casillas, Sergio Ramos, Gerard Piqué, Jordi Alba, Álvaro Arbeloa, Sergio Busquets, Xabi Alonso (65 Javi Martinez), Xavi Hernández, Andrés Iniesta (80 Santi Cazorla), David Silva, Fernando Torres (74 Cesc Fábregas).
Trainer: Vicente del Bosque

IRELAND: Shay Given, John O'Shea, Richard Dunne, Sean St. Ledger, Stephen Ward, Damien Duff (76 James McClean) Keith Andrews, Glenn Whelan (80 Paul Green), Aiden McGeady, Simon Cox (46 Jon Walters), Robbie Keane.
Trainer: Giovanni Trapattoni

Goals: Fernando Torres (4, 70), David Silva (49), Cesc Fábregas (83)

ITALY v REPUBLIC OF IRELAND 2-0 (1-0)

Municipal Stadium. Poznan 18.06.2012

Referee: Cüneyt Çakır (TUR) Attendance: 38,794

ITALY: Gianluigi Buffon, Ignazio Abate, Andrea Barzagli, Giorgio Chiellini (57 Leonardo Bonucci), Federico Balzaretti, Andrea Pirlo, Claudio Marchisio, Thiago Motta, Daniele De Rossi, Antonio Di Natale (74 Mario Balotelli), Antonio Cassano (63 Alessandro Diamanti).
Trainer: Cesare Prandelli

IRELAND: Shay Given, John O'Shea, Richard Dunne, Sean St. Ledger, Stephen Ward, Aiden McGeady (65 Shane Long), Glenn Whelan, Keith Andrews, Damien Duff, Robbie Keane (86 Simon Cox), Kevin Doyle (76 Jon Walters).
Trainer: Giovanni Trapattoni

Sent off: Andrews (89)

Goals: Antonio Cassano (35), Mario Balotelli (90)

CROATIA v SPAIN 0-1 (0-0)

Arena Gdansk 18.06.2012

Referee: Wolfgang Stark (GER) Attendance: 39,076

CROATIA: Stipe Pletikosa, Ivan Strinić, Vedran Čorluka, Gordon Schildenfeld, Domagoj Vida (66 Nikica Jelavić), Danijel Pranjić (66 Ivan Perišić), Ivan Rakitić, Ognjen Vukojević (81 Eduardo), Luka Modrić, Darijo Srna, Mario Mandžukić. Trainer: Slaven Bilić

SPAIN: Iker Casillas, Sergio Ramos, Gerard Piqué, Jordi Alba, Álvaro Arbeloa, Sergio Busquets, Xabi Alonso, Xavi Hernández (89 Álvaro Negredo), Andrés Iniesta, David Silva (73 Cesc Fábregas), Fernando Torres (61 Jesús Navas). Trainer: Vicente del Bosque

Goals: Jesús Navas (88)

	P	W	D	L	F	A	Pts
Spain	3	2	1	0	6	1	7
Italy	3	1	2	0	4	2	5
Croatia	3	1	1	1	4	3	4
Eire	3	0	0	3	1	9	0

GROUP D

FRANCE v ENGLAND 1-1 (1-1)

Donbass Arena, Donetsk 11.06.2012

Referee: Nicola Rizzoli (ITA) Attendance: 47,400

FRANCE: Hugo Lloris, Mathieu Debuchy, Adil Rami, Philippe Mexès, Patrice Evra, Yohan Cabaye (84 Hatem Ben Afra), Alou Diarra, Florent Malouda (85 Marvin Martin), Samir Nasri, Karim Benzema, Franck Ribéry. Trainer: Laurent Blanc

ENGLAND: Joe Hart, Glen Johnson, John Terry, Joleon Lescott, Ashley Cole, James Milner, Steven Gerrard, Scott Parker (78 Jordan Henderson), Alex Oxlade-Chamberlain (77 Jermain Defoe), Ashley Young, Danny Welbeck (90 Theo Walcott). Trainer: Roy Hodgson

Goals: Joleon Lescott (30), Samir Nasri (39)

UKRAINE v SWEDEN 2-1 (0-0)

Olympic Stadium, Kyiv 11.06.2012

Referee: Cüneyt Çakır (TUR) Attendance: 64,290

UKRAINE: Andriy Pyatov, Oleh Gusev, Taras Mikhalik, Yevhen Khacheridi, Yevhen Selin, Andriy Yarmolenko, Anatoliy Tymoschuk, Yevhen Konoplianka (90+3 Marko Dević), Serhiy Nazarenko, Andriy Voronin (85 Ruslan Rotan), Andriy Shevchenko (81 Artem Milevskiy).
Trainer: Oleh Blokhin

SWEDEN: Andreas Isaksson, Mikael Lustig, Olof Mellberg, Andreas Granqvist, Martin Olsson, Rasmus Elm, Kim Kallstrom, Sebastian Larsson (68 Christian Wilhelmsson), Zlatan Ibrahimovic, Ola Toivonen (62 Anders Svensson), Markus Rosenberg (71 Johan Elmander).
Trainer: Erik Hamrén

Goals: Zlatan Ibrahimovic (52), Andriy Shevchenko (55, 62)

UKRAINE v FRANCE 0-2 (0-0)

Donbass Arena, Donetsk 15.06.2012

Referee: Björn Kuipers (HOL) Attendance: 48,000

UKRAINE: Andriy Pyatov, Oleh Gusev, Taras Mikhalik, Yevhen Khacheridi, Yevhen Selin, Anatoliy Tymoschuk, Andriy Voronin (46 Marko Dević), Andriy Yarmolenko (68 Olexandr Aliyev), Serhiy Nazarenko (59 Artem Milevskiy), Yevhen Konoplianka, Andriy Shevchenko. Trainer: Oleh Blokhin

FRANCE: Hugo Lloris, Mathieu Debuchy, Adil Rami, Philippe Mexès, Gaël Clichy, Samir Nasri, Alou Diarra, Yohan Cabaye (68 Yann M'Vila), Jérémy Ménez (73 Marvin Martin), Karim Benzema (76 Olivier Giroud), Franck Ribéry.
Trainer: Laurent Blanc

Goals: Jérémy Ménez (53), Yohan Cabaye (56)

SWEDEN v ENGLAND 2-3 (0-1)

Olympic Stadium, Kyiv 15.06.2012

Referee: Damir Skomina (SVN) Attendance: 64,640

SWEDEN: Andreas Isaksson, Andreas Granqvist (66 Mikael Lustig), Olof Mellberg, Jonas Olsson, Martin Olsson, Anders Svensson, Kim Källström, Sebastian Larsson, Zlatan Ibrahimovic, Rasmus Elm (81 Christian Wilhelmsson), Johan Elmander (79 Markus Rosenberg). Trainer: Erik Hamrén

ENGLAND: Joe Hart, Glen Johnson, John Terry, Joleon Lescott, Ashley Cole, James Milner (61 Theo Walcott), Steven Gerrard, Scott Parker, Ashley Young, Danny Welbeck (90 Alex Oxlade-Chamberlain), Andy Carroll. Trainer: Roy Hodgson

Goals: Andy Carroll (23), Glen Johnson (49 own goal), Olof Mellberg (59), Theo Walcott (64), Danny Welbeck (78)

SWEDEN v FRANCE 2-0 (0-0)

Olympic Stadium, Kyiv 19.06.2012

Referee: Pedro Proença (POR) Attendance: 63,010

SWEDEN: Andreas Isaksson, Andreas Granqvist, Olof Mellberg, Jonas Olsson, Martin Olsson, Anders Svensson (79 Samuel Holmén), Kim Källsträm, Sebastian Larsson, Zlatan Ibrahimovic, Emir Bajrami (46 Christian Wilhelmsson), Ola Toivonen (78 Pontus Wernbloom). Trainer: Erik Hamrén

FRANCE: Hugo Lloris, Mathieu Debuchy, Philippe Mexès, Adil Rami, Gaël Clichy, Hatem Ben Arfa (59 Florent Malouda), Samir Nasri (77 Jérémy Ménez), Alou Diarra, Yann M'Vila (83 Olivier Giroud), Franck Ribéry, Karim Benzema. Trainer: Laurent Blanc

Goals: Zlatan Ibrahimovic (54), Sebastian Larsson (90+1)

ENGLAND v UKRAINE 1-0 (0-0)

Donbass Arena, Donetsk 19.06.2012

Referee: Viktor Kassai (HUN) Attendance: 48,700

ENGLAND: Joe Hart, Ashley Cole, Glen Johnson, Joleon Lescott, John Terry, Steven Gerrard, James Milner (70 Theo Walcott), Scott Parker, Ashley Young, Wayne Rooney (86 Alex Oxlade-Chamberlain), Danny Welbeck (82 Andy Carroll). Trainer: Roy Hodgson

UKRAINE: Andriy Pyatov, Yevhen Khacheridi, Yaroslav Rakitskiy, Yevhen Selin, Denys Garmash (78 Serhiy Nazarenko), Oleh Gusev, Yevhen Konoplianka, Anatoliy Tymoschuk, Marko Dević (70 Andriy Shevchenko), Artem Milevskiy (77 Bohdan Butko), Andriy Yarmolenko. Trainer: Oleh Blokhin

Goal: Wayne Rooney (48)

	P	W	D	L	F	A	Pts
England	3	2	1	0	5	3	7
France	3	1	1	1	3	3	4
Ukraine	3	1	0	2	2	4	3
Sweden	3	1	0	2	5	5	3

QUARTER-FINALS

CZECH REPUBLIC v PORTUGAL 0-1 (0-0)

National Stadium, Warszawa 21.06.2012

Referee: Howard Webb (ENG) Attendance: 55,590

PORTUGAL: Rui Patricio, João Pereira, Képler Ferreira "Pepe", Bruno Alves, Fábio Coentrão, João Moutinho, Miguel Veloso, Raul Meireles (88 ROLANDO Fonseca), Luis Cunha "Nani" (84 CUSTÓDIO Castro), Hélder Postiga (40 Hugo Almeida), Cristiano Ronaldo. Trainer: Paulo Bento

CZECH REPUBLIC: Petr Čech, David Limberský, Theodor Gebre Selassie, Tomáš Sivok, Michal Kadlec, Jaroslav Plašil, Václav Pilař, Tomáš Hübschman (86 Tomáš Pekhart), Petr Jiráček, Vladimir Darida (61 Jan Rezek), Milan Baroš. Trainer: Michal Bílek

Goal: Cristiano Ronaldo (79)

GERMANY v GREECE 4-2 (1-0)

Arena Gdansk 22.06.2012

Referee: Damir Skomina (SVN) Attendance: 38,751

GERMANY: Manuel Neuer, Jérôme Boateng, Mats Hummels, Holger Badstuber, Phillipp Lahm, Sami Khedira, Bastian Schweinstiger, Mesut Özil, André Schürrle (67 Thomas Müller), Marco Reus (80 Mario Gomez), Miroslav Klose (80 Mario Götze). Trainer: Joachim Löw

GREECE: Michalis Sifakis, Giánnis Maniatis, Kyriakos Papadopoulos, Sokratis Papastathopoulos, Vasilis Torosidis, Giórgos Tzavellas (46 Giórgos Fotakis), Konstantinos Katsouranis, Grigoris Makos (72 Nikos Liberopoulos), Sotiris Ninis (46 Fanis Gekas), Dimitris Salpingidis, Giórgos Samaras. Trainer: Fernando Santos

Goals: Phillipp Lahm (39), Giórgos Samaras (55), Sami Khedira (61), Miroslav Klose (68), Marco Reus (74), Dimitris Salpingidis (89 pen)

SPAIN v FRANCE 2-0 (1-0)

Donbass Arena, Donetsk 23.06.2012

Referee: Nicola Rizzoli (ITA) Attendance: 46,145

SPAIN: Iker Casillas, Álvaro Arbeloa, Gerard Piqué, Sergio Ramos, Jordi Alba, Xavi Hernández, Sergio Busquets, Xabi Alonso, David Silva (65 Pedro Rodríguez), Andrés Iniesta (84 Santi Cazorla), Cesc Fabregas (67 Fernando Torres). Trainer: Vicente del Bosque

FRANCE: Hugo Lloris, Anthony Réveillère, Adil Rami, Laurent Koscielny, Gaël Clichy, Mathieu Debuchy (65 Jérémy Ménez), Yohan Cabaye, Yann M'Vila (79 Olivier Giroud), Florent Malouda (65 Samir Nasri), Franck Ribéry, Karim Benzema. Trainer: Laurent Blanc

Goals: Xabi Alonso (19, 90+1 pen)

ENGLAND v ITALY 0-0 (AET)

Olympic Stadium, Kyiv 24.06.2012

Referee: Pedro Proença (POR) Attendance: 64,340

ENGLAND: Joe Hart, Glen Johnson, Joleon Lescott, John Terry, Ashley Cole, James Milner (60 Theo Walcott), Steven Gerrard, Scott Parker (94 Jordan Henderson), Ashley Young, Wayne Rooney, Danny Welbeck (60 Andy Carroll). Trainer: Roy Hodgson

ITALY: Gianluigi Buffon, Ignazio Abate (90+1 Christian Maggio), Leonardo Bonucci, Andrea Barzagli, Federico Balzaretti, Daniele De Rossi (80 Antonio Nocerino), Riccardo Montolivo, Andrea Pirlo, Claudio Marchisio, Mario Balotelli, Antonio Cassano (78 Alessandro Diamanti). Trainer: Cesare Prandelli

Penalties: 0-1 Mario Balotelli, 1-1 Steven Gerrard, Riccardo Montolivo (miss), 2-1 Wayne Rooney, 2-2 Andrea Pirlo, Ashley Young (miss), 2-3 Antonio Nocerino, Ashley Cole (saved), 2-4 Alessandro Diamanti

SEMI-FINALS

SPAIN v PORTUGAL 0-0 (AET)

Donbass Arena, Donetsk 28.06.2012

Referee: Cüneyt Çakır (TUR) Attendance: 51,500

PORTUGAL: Rui Patricio, João Pereira, Képler Ferreira "Pepe", Bruno Alves, Fábio Coentrão, Raul Meireles (113 Silvestre Varela), Miguel Veloso (106 CUSTÓDIO Castro), João Moutinho, Luis Cunha "Nani", Hugo Almeida (81 Nélson Oliveira), Cristiano Ronaldo. Trainer: Paulo Bento

SPAIN: Iker Casillas, Álvaro Arbeloa, Gerard Piqué, Sergio Ramos, Jordi Alba, Xabi Alonso, Sergio Busquets, Xavi Hernández (87 Pedro Rodríguez), David Silva (61 Jesús Navas), Álvaro Negredo (54 Cesc Fabregas), Andrés Iniesta. Trainer: Vicente del Bosque

Penalties: 0-0 Xabi Alonso (saved), João Moutinho (miss), 1-0 Andrés Iniesta, 1-1 Képler Ferreira "Pepe", 2-1 Gerard Piqué, 2-2 Luis Cunha "Nani", 3-2 Sergio Ramos, Bruno Alves (miss), 4-2 Cesc Fabregas

GERMANY v ITALY 1-2 (0-2)

National Stadium Warszawa 28.06.2010

Referee: Stéphane Lannoy (FRA) Attendance: 55,540

GERMANY: Manuel Neuer, Holger Badstuber, Jérôme Boateng (71 Thomas Müller), Mats Hummels, Philipp Lahm, Sami Khedira, Toni Kroos, Mesut Özil, Bastian Schweinsteiger, Mario Gomez (46 Miroslav Klose), Lukas Podolski (46 Marco Reus). Trainer: Joachim Löw

ITALY: Gianluigi Buffon, Federico Balzaretti, Andrea Barzagli, Leonardo Bonucci, Giorgio Chiellini, Daniele De Rossi, Claudio Marchisio, Riccardo Montolivo (63 Thiago Motta), Andrea Pirlo, Mario Balotelli (70 Antonio Di Natale), Antonio Cassano (58 Alessandro Diamanti). Trainer: Cesare Prandelli

Goals: Mario Balotelli (20, 36), Mesut Özil (90+2 pen)

FINAL

SPAIN v ITALY 4-0 (2-0)

Olympic Stadium, Kyiv 01.07.2012

Referee: Pedro Proença (POR) Attendance: 63,170

SPAIN: Iker Casillas, Álvaro Arbeloa, Gerard Piqué, Sergio Ramos, Jordi Alba, Sergio Busquets, Xabi Alonso, Xavi Hernández, Andrés Iniesta (87 Juan Mata), David Silva (59 Pedro Rodríguez), Cesc Fábregas (75 Fernando Torres). Trainer: Vicente del Bosque

ITALY: Gianluigi Buffon, Ignazio Abate, Leonardo Bonucci, Andrea Barzagli, Giorgio Chiellini (21 Federico Balzaretti), Claudio Marchisio, Andrea Pirlo, Daniele De Rossi, Riccardo Montolivo (57 Thiago Motta), Antonio Cassano (46 Antonio Di Natale), Mario Balotelli. Trainer: Cesare Prandelli

Goals: David Silva (14), Jordi Alba (41), Torres (84), Juan Mata (88)